THE COLUMBIA HISTORY OF THE WORLD

A Cass Canfield BOOK
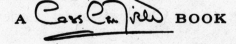

CONTRIBUTORS:

René Albrecht-Carrié Edward P. Lanning

Herman Ausubel William E. Leuchtenburg

A. Doak Barnett Maan Z. Madina

Jacques Barzun John A. Moore

Elias J. Bickerman Richard B. Morris

Hans H. A. Bielenstein John H. Mundy

Shepard B. Clough Ernest Nagel

Gerson D. Cohen Peter A. Pardue

Robert D. Cross Orest Ranum

Ainslie Embree Eugene F. Rice, Jr.

Rhodes W. Fairbridge Henry L. Roberts

John A. Garraty James P. Shenton

Nina Garsoïan J. W. Smit

Peter Gay Morton Smith

J. Mason Gentzler Fritz Stern

Henry F. Graff Alden T. Vaughan

Lewis Hanke Immanuel Wallerstein

Richard Hofstadter Herschel Webb

Graham W. Irwin R. K. Webb

Charles Issawi Lodewyk Woltjer

THE
COLUMBIA
HISTORY
OF THE
WORLD

EDITORS

JOHN A. GARRATY

PETER GAY

1817

HARPER & ROW, PUBLISHERS

NEW YORK, EVANSTON, SAN FRANCISCO, LONDON

The quotation on page 1007 is from "the first president to be loved by his" by E.E. Cummings in *Poems, 1923-1954,* published by Harcourt Brace Jovanovich, Inc. Used with permission.

Harper & Row, Publishers

Designed by Sidney Feinberg

Maps by Harry Scott

This edition published by Dorset Press, a division of Marboro Books Corp., by arrangement with Harper & Row, Publishers, Inc.

1981 Dorset Press
Second Dorset Press Printing, 1983
Manufactured in the United States of America

ISBN 0-88029-004-8
(Previously ISBN 06-011432-0)

LIBRARY OF CONGRESS CATALOG CARD NUMBER: 76-181621

Contents

PART III TOWARD MODERNITY

The Renaissance and Reformation in Europe

Building the Early Modern State

Toward One World

The Enlightenment

PART IV   THE AGE OF REVOLUTION

Europe: The Great Powers

Revolution in the Western World

Reaction and Rebellion

The Industrial Revolution

New Forces, New Ideas

PART V   THE MODERN WORLD

Toward Disintegration

The Great World War: 1914–1945

The Brooding Present

Maps

Foreword

It is difficult to imagine a more presumptuous title than *The Columbia History of the World*. Too much has happened to the structure of human knowledge and also to our own self-esteem in recent years to permit us any ease in presumption. Our intellectual capacities are measured by a truly remarkable faculty, but even we recognize that Columbia University is circumscribed by the incredible exponential growth of knowledge in this century. Man's efforts to understand the universe in which he finds himself, the processes by which he evolved, and the historical context of his being are now so formidable that no university can claim omniscience. Certainly we do not.

No other title, however, suffices to describe this work accurately. Professor Peter Gay of Yale University was a Columbia historian when the project was begun in 1965. Professor John A. Garraty continues to be an eminent member of our Department of History. Together they undertook to edit a large history of the world covering "everything" of historical importance from the birth of the universe down to the present day. Their idea was that this work, amounting to nearly half a million words, would be written entirely by Columbia professors, thus demonstrating that the sum of human knowledge of the past could be brought together in an authoritative way by the faculty of a single great university.

Now their work is done and while some of the contributors have moved to other responsibilities, the stamp of Columbia is found on every page. We find a balanced and judicious distillation of historical knowledge that is the characteristic mark of open minds. These are not ideologists seeking to convert naive readers to preordained views. We have here only wisdom and clarity, characteristics that have illuminated the various departments at Columbia University for more than a century.

The reader can peruse this volume, as I have, with the feeling that he is sitting in the midst of professional historians and other scholars as they talk to each other about their specialties. Each offers a capsule view for his colleagues without addressing the enormous wealth of evidence and detail which serve as a basis for the conceptions expressed. What emerges is an authoritative view of history as the members of a great faculty would present it to one another. It is Columbia's history of the world offered without affectation or presumption.

I confess to more than a little unbounded pride and enthusiasm for this extraordinary work. It displays a small portion of the competence of Columbia University in a way that anyone can appreciate. In the turmoil and struggle accompanying social change on campus, one is occasionally apt to forget the immense intellectual power which has been brought together with such great cost. I find it everywhere on campus and in the most unexpected places. Sometimes, as I walk by St. Paul's Chapel, I hear the choir rehearsing and am suddenly seized by the beauty of its music. Sometimes I will listen to a member of the faculty of the College lecturing on Dean's Day and find myself caught up by the art and clarity of his presentation. Recently I read a paper written by one of Columbia's University Professors and was struck by the lucidity of the mind that produced the manuscript. In this book, I am caught up in admiration of the scope and power of a truly competent Department of History at a great university.

Columbia continues to be a great center of comprehensive knowledge in the western world. One of our important roles is to act as an intermediary between the academic world and the larger community of intellectually curious readers. This book displays the talent of Columbia's scholars as disseminators as well as discoverers and organizers of knowledge.

WILLIAM J. MCGILL

Introduction

We live in the Age of World History, and as ages go, ours is relatively young. Until the fifteenth century, the many cultures of this earth developed in comparative isolation, their boundaries breached only by occasional traders, by border warfare, and by spectacular mass migrations, such as the "barbarian" invasion of the Roman Empire in the early centuries of the Christian Era. But after Columbus and Cortes had awakened the people of Western Europe to the possibilities, their appetite for converts, profits, and fame was thoroughly aroused and Western civilization was introduced, mainly by force, over nearly all the globe. Equipped with an unappeasable urge to expand and with superior weapons, conquerors made the rest of the world into an unwilling appendage of the great European powers; Africa, Asia, and the Americas became sources of raw materials, markets, objects of scientific curiosity, and places for the permanent settlement of Europeans. The peoples of these continents were, in short, the victims of a ruthless, unrelenting exploitation.

But then came the scientific and technological revolutions of modern times, which, in transforming the Western world, also transformed its non-Western dependencies. We are now witnessing two simultaneous, only apparently contradictory developments. World civilization is becoming more uniform, as the West imposes its techniques and its ideas. And the dependent nations are breaking away from the domination of the West, using these very Western techniques and ideas to establish their separate identities, and find their places in the councils of power. Isolation has become impossible; ancient empires like China and the newly self-conscious nations of Africa alike involve the whole world in their activities. Thus both the traditional division between Western and non-Western history and the patronizing assumption that non-Western is a kind of footnote to Western history have become obsolete. This, as we have said, is the Age of World History. It is therefore supremely the age *for* world history.

World history is hard to write, but this has not discouraged historians from writing it ever since the beginning of the craft among the ancient

Greeks. Medieval monks and Renaissance scholars tried their hands at it. Leopold von Ranke, the father of modern scientific history, rounded out his long and prolific career with an essay at world history, begun in 1886, when he was over eighty. When he died, ten years and several thousand pages later, he had only reached the fifteenth century. Of course, we should not read too much into Ranke's inability to finish his monumental task; he was, after all, a very old man when he began it. But we may take it as a symbol of the difficulties involved in such enterprises. Today, nearly a century after Ranke, writing the history of the world has become even more formidable a problem. We know more than Ranke did; our conception of history is larger, more inclusive, than his. But knowing more, we also realize how little we know. And one thing we know is that authoritative world history is beyond the grasp of any individual; life is too short, the subject-matter too diverse.

We say nothing here of cultural perspectives that limit vision: the obstacles that biases impose upon historians have been much exaggerated of late, most especially by those who insist that only blacks can properly describe the black "experience." That "it takes one to know one," is, when applied to the writing of history, we believe untrue. (If it were true, and if historians could be induced to believe it, they would have to confine their work to contemporary events in their own country, and among their own class, which would make nonsense of the whole historical enterprise.) It is, on the contrary, precisely the historian's function to transcend his inherited and acquired perspectives for the sake of a wider grasp and a higher objectivity. No: the difficulty in the way of writing world history is not parochialism but ignorance—not the poverty of the historian but the abundance of his materials.

Yet, hard as it is to write, and largely for that reason, world history is important, even essential, to us. We westerners need to know more about the world of which we are inextricably a part, just as the rest of the world needs to know more about us, and for the same reason. The obvious solution is a collaborative effort, one that brings together the special knowledge of many experts, and this is what we have attempted in the following pages.

Yet a history of the entire world written by (in this instance) forty authors presents another set of problems. Whatever its limitations, von Ranke's work is the product of a single mind; it has an intellectual and artistic unity; it is a whole, a thing in and of itself. A history written by many pens runs the risk of becoming a mere collection of essays or encyclopedia articles, held together only by the boards in which the parts are bound. Aware from the beginning of this danger, we sought to surmount it in several ways. First of all we decided to enlist our historians and other experts from a single university. Thus, our contributors knew one another personally; being in frequent, easy contact, we and they could repeatedly consult, debate, compare, and criticize in order to fuse our several efforts into one intellectual construct. This process went on at every stage of the book's development, over a period of more than five years.

Consider our first and most crucial problems: the preparation of an outline and the allocation of space to various regions and periods of time. How should the history of the early civilization of India be related to that of Egypt and China or, for that matter, of Mexico and Peru? How many chapters should the history of Africa occupy as compared with that of South America or Eastern Europe? As editors—one a historian of the United States, the other of Western Europe—we knew that any answer we could devise for such questions would be inadequate and surely distorted. We therefore asked our specialists to tell us how they proposed to organize their material and how much space they needed, bearing in mind the ultimate limitation imposed by our decision to produce a work that could be published in a single volume. Using draft outlines prepared by the contributors, and consulting with them at every stage, we eventually worked out the structure of our history. The result, as a reading of the table of contents will quickly reveal, is a global conceptualization of human history. What from our "Western" perspective are considered "exotic" areas have been allotted a fair share of our space and their histories are recounted not merely at those points where they impressed themselves on Western consciousness, but from their beginnings to the present day. This is a history of the world, not simply of "our" world.

The collaborative effort did not, however, end at this point. Whenever appropriate our authors consulted with one another in order to avoid repetition and omission, and they read and criticized their colleagues' manuscripts in all cases where they had special knowledge, and in many—out of friendship or curiosity—where they did not. Many of the following chapters bring together the writing of two and even three authorities, yet it is our belief that the parts of such chapters fit together as smoothly and as logically as those produced by a single mind.

Finally, our contributors have generously allowed us a remarkable latitude in organizing and editing their manuscripts. Given our common commitment to the production of an integrated synthesis of world history, all conceded that a more than ordinary editorial license was essential. Our object was to fuse the work of forty historians into one. Our method has been to try to impose a basic uniformity of approach, to supply connecting passages and cross-references, and to alter the individual prose styles of the authors (without too great artistic loss, we hope) in the interest of creating the illusion not that we two have written what follows, but that all of us have written it all. It goes without saying, however, that each author has remained the ultimate arbiter of the facts and opinions in his own sections. Each has carefully read and corrected our "final" version.*

This is *The Columbia History of the World*. As we have said, it was conceived and executed by Columbia professors. But over the years a number of our contributors, and one of us, have left Morningside Heights; ours is a peripatetic profession. We have nonetheless retained the name in our title because we believe that Columbia scholarship has long excelled in the approach to history that has governed the design and construction of this book, an approach broad-gauged both in its scope and in its purpose of communicating expert knowledge to a wide audience. The roster of past Columbians who have written such histories is long and distinguished. We need only mention Charles A. Beard, James Harvey Robinson, Carlton J. H. Hayes, Garrett Mattingly, and Allan Nevins to prove the point. It is our hope that collectively we have met the standard set by these and many other Columbia historians, and that our work will be as generously received by the public as was theirs.

Much of whatever merit this volume possesses it owes to Cass Canfield of Harper & Row. His faith in our idea encouraged us to work out the details, and his generosity enabled us to enlist the services of the many busy scholars whose brains and energies produced the book. He has guided and supported our efforts through countless drafts and around a hundred unforeseen difficulties. Beulah Hagen of Harper & Row has laboriously, patiently, and with a fine intelligence supervised the design of the book and seen our complicated manuscript through the press. Cass Canfield, Jr., Mel Arnold, and John Gordon, also of Harper & Row, have made important contributions to our project. We are deeply grateful. To thank individually all those who have helped our authors would be impractical in the space at our disposal; we leave that happy task to our colleagues. But we, as editors, wish to extend our loving thanks and appreciation to our wives, Gail Garraty and Ruth Gay, whose critical reading of the manuscript has been of great help and whose support at every stage has been truly invaluable.

JOHN A. GARRATY
PETER GAY

---

* For brief summaries of the professional background of the authors, see the Notes on Contributors, page 1167. These notes also indicate the particular chapters for which each is in whole or part responsible.

I

THE ANCIENT WORLD

Before History

The Ancient Near East

Asian Civilization

Classical Antiquity: Jews and Greeks

Classical Antiquity: Rome

Before History

1 The Earth and the Universe

Man, the great seeker, is as time is counted a newcomer to earth, yet his achievements, which we here relate, have been enormous. These achievements, whether for good or for evil, have been without exception the product of his chief distinctive quality, his power of thought.

As long as man has existed, his curiosity, one aspect of his ability to think, has driven him to search out his own origins. For centuries without number, while he has gradually subdued the earth and shaped it to his purposes, he has pondered about his past: the subject has probably occupied the minds of more of the best thinkers the species has produced than any other. The results have been impressive. Indeed, the knowledge that man has accumulated of the prehuman history of the earth, and of the universe of which the earth is a fragment, stands among his most magnificent accomplishments. Back through time and across distances he can measure but not really conceptualize, he has pursued his source. His quest has both inspired and appalled him; it has been relentless, compulsive, unending—and hopeless. We know much, and we know nothing. The origin of what is— man, the earth, the universe—is shrouded in a mystery we are no closer to solving than was the chronicler of Genesis.

Indeed, our best current knowledge, lacking the poetic magic of scripture, seems in a way less believable than the account in the Bible or in any of the ancient texts. All that we can say is that at the time of the beginning there was a large, dense mass of gas. This gas consisted of hydrogen,* the simplest of all the ninety-two chemical elements known to occur naturally. It was very hot, causing an intense light and much expanding motion.

Did this dense mass of gas originate in some prephysical state not open to further physical analysis? Some think it did. But others think that the

* Possibly matter was mixed with antimatter. If so some was hydrogen and some antihydrogen.

3

dense, hot matter was formed as the result of the contraction of a more tenuous phase of the universe and that it may thus be possible to learn something about earlier phases by detailed measurements and observations. In any case it appears probable that about 10 billion years ago the universe was in the hot and dense state just described and very different from what it is now.*

This original mass of gas underwent an evolution; gradually it was differentiated into galaxies, stars and planets. Two physical facts help explain how this happened. If we take a certain amount of a hot gas and let it expand, it will cool down; conversely, if a gas is compressed, it will become warmer, a phenomenon that may easily be demonstrated with an air compression pump. Second, in an extremely dense and hot gas, nuclear reactions can occur between the atoms of the gas. We know that the chemical elements are differentiated by the number of protons, neutrons and electrons in their atoms. Thus, a hydrogen atom consists of a heavy (electrically positive) proton and a light (electrically negative) electron. The next element, helium, consists of two protons, two neutrons, and two electrons. A neutron can be regarded as a combination of a proton and an electron, and so a helium atom can be formed from four hydrogen atoms. This is in fact what happens to hydrogen when its temperature is raised high enough.

At present there is a very large amount of helium in the universe. If we took 100 grams of "typical" matter, we would find about 70 grams of all the other elements combined. The fact that there is so much helium lends support to the theory of a very hot and dense phase early in the history of the universe. This evidence is not conclusive, however, because we also know that within stars like the sun, hydrogen is being transformed into helium even at the present time. But it is doubtful that the helium made within stars during the history of our universe could account for more than a small fraction of the total amount observed.

Because the gas was so hot, there was much light in the original universe. As the universe expanded, this light rapidly became dimmer; yet even now some of the primeval light is probably present. Its intensity and wavelength have been predicted to be such that it should now be best observable at radio wavelengths. Very recently it has been discovered that the earth is in fact irradiated from all sides by radio waves with the anticipated properties. This of course lends support to the picture of an early, very hot, phase of the universe, but other explanations for the radio radiation are perhaps possible.

After the original mass of gas had expanded and cooled, large clouds

* We should mention here that according to the "steady state theory" the universe has always presented about the same aspect. In this theory the apparent evidence for evolution is taken to be due to a local fluctuation.

separated themselves from the parent mass. In the mechanism responsible for this, gravity played an important role. Matter is subject to gravitational forces, but it is also their cause: every object on the surface of the earth experiences a downward gravitational force in proportion to its mass, but it is the matter of the earth that generates this force. If the earth were twice as massive (with the same volume) the force would be twice as large. The original mass of the gas in the universe can hardly have been completely uniform, and so some regions were slightly denser, and generated stronger gravitational fields than others. Since gravity tends to bring matter together, the denser regions tended to become even more compact. Thus the small variations present in the original mass evolved into denser clouds that gradually became separate from the expanding parent mass. From these clouds were later formed the galaxies as we see them today, each galaxy containing billions of stars and some gaseous matter.

At the conclusion of the first phase of the history of the universe, numbers of huge clouds composed of hydrogen and helium had become separate entities and so could start their own independent evolution. Again, these turbulent clouds contained variations, and, as before, the variations grew in importance as time went on; the clouds broke up into smaller and smaller subunits until ultimately "cloudlets" with masses like those of the sun and stars had become distinct. Gravity caused these cloudlets to contract and become denser. The increase of the pressure resulting from the contraction of the cloudlets caused the temperature to rise until they became luminous or, to put it simply, until they became stars.

The temperature inside stars is so high that nuclear reactions take place, transforming hydrogen into helium. It is the energy generated by these reactions which enables the sun and the stars to continue shining for very long times—about 10 billion years in the case of the sun. Some stars, however, are much more luminous than the sun and convert their hydrogen more rapidly. The analysis of the evolution of stars that have changed most of their hydrogen into helium shows that they will become dense and hot enough for more complicated nuclear reactions to occur, like those which change helium into carbon. A carbon atom consists of six protons, six neutrons, and six electrons, and so it can be built from three helium atoms. Other reactions make oxygen, and ultimately even elements like silicon and iron. In fact, it appears that nuclear processes within stars can lead to the formation of all the natural chemical elements.

In the evolution of our particular galaxy, the first massive stars that were formed from the gas evolved very quickly. After they had synthesized many of the heavier elements they reached the end of their lives and some exploded. (Such exploding stars are also seen today as supernovae, stars that suddenly flare up to tremendous brightness and then disappear.) The explosions ejected the elements that had been synthesized into the gas remaining in the galaxy. From this gas stars were again formed, among them our sun. This sequence of events explains why the sun does not consist only of hydrogen and helium, but contains also an admixture of other elements.

The mass of gas from which the sun formed slowly rotated, like most gaseous masses in the universe. A rotating body tends to be flattened. When the sun formed, some of the rotating matter remained behind in a flattened disk around the sun. At first the sun was not very hot, and so the material in the disk also remained cool. In this cold gas the various elements began to form molecules and other compounds. Some of these were rather sticky and coagulated first to form small dustlike particles, later, even larger units. Once a few larger units had been formed, gravity tended to bring in more matter until eventually bodies of planetary mass were formed. Meanwhile, the contraction of the sun triggered nuclear reactions. Its temperature increased so that it became luminous and began to heat the surrounding matter. This did not have much effect on the more massive planets far from the sun, like Jupiter and Saturn, but in the smaller planets closer to the sun the temperature rose enough for the volatile substances like hydrogen and helium to evaporate. Only the solids remained behind, and these compacted into the earth and surrounding planets as they exist today.

Most of the early material around the sun accumulated in the planets, where subsequent processes have changed it beyond recognition. Some of it, however, escaped the gravitational attraction of the planets and has remained relatively unchanged. It is almost certain that comets are made of this primitive material, and thus the study of them offers many exciting possibilities. Most comets remain far from the sun, but occasionally one ventures close to it. The sun's heat then causes the evaporation of some of the more volatile substances, giving rise to the spectacular comet tails.

In the neighborhood of the earth some other objects formed from the primitive material. One of these, the present moon, apparently was captured by the earth in a stable orbit. The surface of the moon is covered by craters, most of which must have been caused by the impact of pieces of solid celestial debris. These craters thus give visible evidence of the latest phases of the formation of the moon and planets by accumulation of partly solid material.

In the past the moon must have been very close to the earth. After the oceans had condensed on the surface of the earth the moon raised tides in the same way as at present, except that the tides were much higher because of the closeness of the moon. The tides correspond to a periodic rising and lowering of the water in the ocean. In shallow parts of the ocean strong tidal currents rush over the ocean floor which, in turn, resists them. Through these frictional forces the moon has a "grip" on the earth, and since the earth rotates faster than the moon revolves around the earth, the moon tends to lessen the rotation speed of the earth. In fact, it is probable that the original earth rotated about six times faster than at present, corresponding to a "day" of four (present) hours.

If one body experiences a force from another the converse must also be true. Thus, as the rotation of the earth slowed down, the moon's motion was also affected. The net effect has been an increase in the distance between the earth and the moon. As this distance increased, the tides became lower and the associated effects less significant. But even from observations made during historic times, in particular the observations of solar eclipses in antiquity, the lunar tidal effects can be demonstrated.

The matter from which the earth and the moon was formed was rather cold. But its compression during the formation of these bodies led to heating. Also, radioactive materials were present in the original material, giving the earth a rather hot interior. In earlier theories the internal heat of the earth was taken as evidence for the formation of the earth from hot material ripped out from the sun by some catastrophic event. It seems clear now, however, that this was not the case, because such hot material never could have condensed into planets. The hot gas would have expanded rapidly and become completely dispersed.

This, in rough outline, was the probable sequence of events that led to the formation of the earth from an original featureless mass of hydrogen. Not all steps in this sequence are yet completely certain, but it is unlikely that future observations will change our basic conclusion that the almost incredible diversity of galaxies, nebulae, stars, planets, and other objects present in our universe originated in a very simple state, and that the historical developments that led from this initial state to the complexities of the present universe were produced by phenomena that can be understood on the basis of modern physics.

Our galaxy is about 10 billion and our solar system about 5 billion years old. Having some knowledge about the past, we are tempted to speculate about the future. The sun will continue shining for another 5 billion years. After that it will brighten rapidly and also become very large, perhaps large enough to engulf the earth. Following a comparatively brief period of high luminosity, the sun will then dim and the solar system will become. dark and cold. It seems probable that the same fate will befall the other stars in our galaxy; all that will remain are large swarms of "dead" stars and planets.

Will new galaxies form again? The answer is unknown. Some believe that the present expansion of the universe will come to an end and that a period of contraction will follow. It is conceivable that as a result the universe will once again be brought into a dense hot state and that the evolutionary history of the present phase of the universe will be repeated.

For Further Reading

Abell, G., *Exploration of the Universe.*
Jastrow, R., *Red Giants and White Dwarfs.*
Motz, L., and Duveen, A., *Essentials of Astronomy.*
Struve, O., and Zebergs, V., *Astronomy of the Twentieth Century.*

2   The Geological Evolution of the Earth

When we look at the scenery of our planet there is much to delight the eye. A region of great natural beauty can be aesthetically enjoyed without asking: "How did it get that way?" Nevertheless, this question often comes to mind. It is particularly prompted by sights such as the Grand Canyon, the high Alps, the fjords of Norway, or the volcanoes of Japan.

The answer is generally to be found in looking at the land in *three dimensions.* If we stand on the rim of the Grand Canyon after crossing mile upon mile of nearly flat plain, we can see a slice cut into the crust of the earth right down to the oldest rocks. In our imagination we can cut a similar profile through any plain or mountain range and see the rocks in this third dimension. The golden rule of the bedding of sediments says that the rocks at the bottom are the oldest and those at the top are youngest. Even if the structures are tilted or folded by mountain building one can still follow the layers out to where a clear succession is discernible.

The third dimension is thus no great problem. It can be and is checked and confirmed repeatedly by geologists looking for oil or for water. But to recapture in our imaginations a picture of the ancient geography, we must also introduce a *fourth dimension:* time. We can strip away the younger rocks down to a certain level and visualize how that formation was originally deposited as sediments in the ocean. By collecting fossils and studying the type of rock, we can come up with a vivid picture of the ancient scene. Two fundamentally different kinds of rock exist—sedimentary, those laid down as particles of mud or sand in ancient oceans; and igneous, those erupted or intruded into the earth's crust in a molten state, as in volcanic lava. By plotting their distribution on paleogeographic maps for

Geochronology of the Planet Earth

ERA	PERIOD	EPOCH	TIME OF BEGINNING (millions of years ago)	GEOLOGICAL EVENTS
ARCHEOZOIC PROTEROZOIC	Precambrian (periods)	(many minor sub-divisions, but not of world-wide validity)	4,600	Origin of earth and solar system
			(?)4,000	Origin of life, in reducing atmosphere
			(?)2,500	Photosynthetic oxygen permitted first global oxidation of iron ores
			(?)1,500	First primitive animals
			700	Great "Eocambrian Ice Age"
PALEOZOIC	Cambrian		600	First shell-forming invertebrate animals (attributed to rising alkalinity of ocean)
	Ordovician		500	Ice Age in Africa
	Silurian		435	Caledonian mountain building
	Devonian		395	Acadian mountain building
	Carboniferous	Mississippian	345	Great Coal Age; reduction of CO_2 and rise in atmospheric oxygen
		Pennsylvanian (subsystems)	310	Hercynian-Appalachian mountain building
	Permian		280	Ice age in South America, Africa, Australia, India, and Antarctica; extinction of much Paleozoic life
MESOZOIC	Triassic		230	Beginning of major continental drifting. Age of Reptiles begins; world-wide red beds
	Jurassic		180	Age of Ammonites; mild world climate
	Cretaceous		135	Age of Chalk (planktonic foraminifera); extinction of much Mesozoic life
CENOZOIC	Tertiary	Paleocene	67	Alpine mountain building (world-wide, and continuing through Tertiary)
		Eocene	58	
		Oligocene	36	
		Miocene	25	Evolution of grasses and "modern" type mammals and birds
		Pliocene	7	Increasing mountain glaciation
	Quaternary	Pleistocene	2.0	"Great Ice Age," time of Stone Age Man; growth of major deserts
		Holocene	0.01	"Recent" development of agricultural, industrial, and literate man

each period of the geologic past we can reconstruct a pictorial record of our planetary history.

Every continent in the world possesses three basic types of structure. First, there is a very old nucleus of strong, hard crystalline "Precambrian" rocks (granites and related types), which are from 600 million up to several billion years old; this is called the shield. In North America it outcrops mainly in Canada; in Europe its equivalent extends from Scandinavia to Russia; in South America it lies in Brazil. Most of Africa is a shield, and so are India, Australia and Antarctica. Second, there are mountainous belts of folded sedimentary rocks of all ages, often with patches of volcanic formations and perhaps a core of granite; these are the fold belts. The shield actually consists of very ancient fold belts that have been worn down through erosion by rain and rivers. The younger folds, however, are still mountainous. The Appalachians of North America were folded between 400 million and 280 million years ago; folds of the same age occur in Europe and each of the other continents. The Rockies have a core of Precambrian shield rocks, but these were all dismembered by fracturing and are now overlapped or wrapped around by folds that are mostly dated about 100 million years. The Coast Ranges are younger, however, and it is evident that they are still growing, as is the entire border of the Pacific, with its constant earthquakes and lines of volcanoes—"the Girdle of Fire."

Third, there are the basins, which are plainland regions superimposed on the shield; they have slowly subsided at various times, and sediments have filled them up. Since the surface of any water body (lake or ocean) is horizontal, sediments can fill the basin to become a flat plain. Most of the great plains, the steppes and prairies of the world, were formed like this.

The shape of the land surface, i.e., its physical scenery, depends on its structural framework, its constituent rock types and the relative relief or degree of uplift, and also on the climatic history (its *inherited* features) and the soils that are produced by the climate and vegetation working together.

The history of each and every continent goes back to the early beginnings of the planet earth itself, about 4.5 billion years ago.

The ancestral earth did not possess an atmosphere such as we have today. Hot spots in the earth must have melted and volcanoes broke out on the surface, spreading lava on the land and liberating vast quantities of steam, but the steam condensed and from a few water droplets to start with, the great oceans have evolved. Rain falling on the rocks caused solution, thus furnishing salts. The once fresh ocean has gradually become salty so that today it contains 3.5 per cent of dissolved salts.

In reckoning time for million-year periods two systems are employed—"absolute" and "relative." Absolute time (in years) is worked out by analyzing a given radioactive element, such as uranium, which breaks down eventually to lead; the geochemist knows the rate of this breakdown, so he measures the ratio of uranium to lead in a certain rock and thus calculates its absolute age. All the different methods agree that the age of the earth is 4.5 billion years. Relative time measurement is a "common-sense" procedure based on the sequence of sediments laid down on the floor of the ocean. If we bore a hole in the ocean bed, the top samples obtained are the youngest; the bottom ones are the oldest. If we run absolute dating analyses of these samples, we get a double check on both methods. Fossils found in the older formations are more primitive than those found in the recent layers. Each epoch or age is characterized by a distinctive "assemblage" or "community" of fossils, so that anywhere in the world a correlation can be made. This extraordinary attribute was discovered by a modest English canal builder, William Smith, in the early nineteenth century—"Strata" Smith, founder of modern stratigraphy.

For many years geologists have been hunting to find the oldest rocks of the crust. Generally such rocks are covered over by younger sediments, so it is not an easy search. The oldest patches of crust found thus far are dated at more than 3 billion years.

From time to time during the geological history of the earth there have been periods of violent disturbance, marked by tremendous and repeated earthquakes, volcanic eruptions, and vast movements of the crust. In one belt the crust may have split apart and formed a new branch of the ocean. In another belt that formerly lay under the ocean, there was uplift of the land and mountains were formed. In these new mountain belts the layered and fossil-filled sediments of the ocean were folded, wrinkled, and buckled, but where rivers have carved deep valleys and canyons through them, geologists can now collect specimens of the fossils and work out the former sequence, which otherwise would be hidden beneath the sea. Through time, continents have grown in dimensions by successive addition of the new mountain belts, but the oceans too have grown in volume. The net result has been a planet of increasing complexity through time. While some "re-cycling" of materials goes on, the so-called steady-state principle, history does not repeat itself. New formations are added to old ones, so that earth history is cumulative and irreversible. This unending history of erosion on the one hand compensated by uplift on the other was first recognized in 1795 by James Hutton of Edinburgh as the great "geological cycle."

On the present-day coast we know how the tide rises and falls every day. In exceptional places, as in the Bay of Fundy in eastern Canada, the tide rises up to 50 feet. On a different scale, in geological time, over the course of millions of years, the ocean has periodically risen and fallen, flooding the land, only to retreat once more, leaving behind layers of fossil-filled sediments. This happened again and again throughout geological history. We are not sure just why it happens. Is it because of continental drift or changes in the polar positions? Changes in the speed of rotation of the earth? Changes in the actual size of the solid earth? Changes in the amount of water in the oceans? (During ice ages, water is removed and converted into ice.) All of these causes are probably involved, which makes it difficult to say which is most important.

The sequence of geologic time can now be measured, as mentioned above, in years; but numbers are difficult to remember, and in any case in the early days of geological science, the absolute method had not been invented, so it was convenient to pin name labels on rocks of the different ages. Thus the principal rock of New York City is called the Manhattan Schist, in northern Illinois we have the St. Peter Sandstone, around San Francisco there is the Franciscan Series. In England there is the London Clay, in Paris there is the Montmartre Gypsum. This naming is especially convenient since it is an insurance against any possible error in dating; the name will still identify the rocks regardless of date.

In geological names there is a hierarchy of labels for time divisions of decreasing importance or size, like a chain of command in the army. The top division in historical geology is the era, a time covering tens to hundreds of million years. Periods, epochs, ages, follow in descending order. The names are generally selected from either a descriptive feature or some state, mountain, or river where those particular rocks were first discovered. Some of the earliest names selected were also partly descriptive, suggesting the types of fossils or the character of the rock material.

Many of the basic geological principles were first worked out in Britain, and the oldest fossiliferous rocks there are found in north Wales; Cambria is the old Latin name for Wales, so these rocks were called Cambrian. The older shield rocks there are largely devoid of fossils, so were simply labeled Precambrian, and this name has stuck. All over the world, rocks more than 600 million years old are still called Precambrian.

In the younger rocks the fossils fall into characteristic groupings, and the parent rock eras were named accordingly—Paleozoic ("era of old life"), Mesozoic ("era of middle life"), and Cenozoic ("era of young life"). The number of divisions increases as we come closer to the present in geological time; with each younger era there is a slight change of scale, corresponding to greater and greater complexity. Thus the lengths of an era or period are not fixed, but divisions are simply drawn where they are appropriate.

The Precambrian Era. Because the oldest (Precambrian) parts of the earth's crust have been involved in a great deal of mountain building, melting, and general disturbance to the original sediments, they present great difficulties to the fossil hunter. Precambrian fossils have now been found in a number of places, but never fossils of highly advanced types. Generally they range from mere bacteria, to seaweeds, to primitive segmented animals like worms. These were soft-bodied organisms; if they had shells or some sort of hard parts it would be much easier to find them, but when soft-bodied creatures die, usually they are quickly destroyed by bacteria. It is only when an accidental event such as a quick burial by floods has interrupted decay that they have been preserved by fossilization.

The primitive algae (seaweeds) played an important role in the history of the earth. In early planetary evolution the atmosphere was poisonous to animal life, but bacteria and plants thrive on carbon dioxide, which is a gas given off with the clouds of steam by volcanoes. The plants, for their part, produce oxygen as a waste product. In the early history of the planet there was no oxygen, but gradually the plants produced enough of this by-product so that animals could evolve. Thus living organisms have given us our life-sustaining atmosphere.

How did life itself begin? According to one hypothesis, the early atmosphere may have been like that of Jupiter and other major planets today, condensed around the new planet during its formation. Another view suggests the emergence of the gases from the interior or by weathering of minerals. It may have contained hydrogen, ammonia, sulfur dioxide, methane, and some other inorganic hydrocarbons such as cyanide (HCN). Volcanic eruptions brought in steam that condensed to water and carbon dioxide. Clouds formed, rain fell, there were storms . . . lightning flashed. . . . Thinking about this problem, the Nobel prize-winning scientist, Harold Urey, mentioned to one of his students, Stanley L. Miller, that this mixture of materials could be duplicated in their chemistry laboratory. No sooner said than done: they set up a container with the right mixture of gases and subjected them to artificial electric sparks to simulate lightning. In a week a little red liquid started to form; analyzed, this was found to contain amino acids, the basic building blocks of organic life. From these sorts of compounds, by whatever method, it is generally believed that life began in shallow pools on the earth's surface, as a so-called organic soup.

A great age of biological experimentation was thus started in modern science, but it is evident that a still greater biological experiment had started on the earth's crust somewhere far back in Precambrian times. This first life may have appeared nearly 4 billion years ago. Evolution from these simple beginnings (organisms at the bacteria level) has probably been in the course of multiple experiments by nature; the most viable for any given time and place have triumphed. The secret is the infinite number of combinations for the carbon atom and its molecules that are possible over immense periods of time.

Geological studies of the fossil record of these last 4 billion years showed that evolution has continued without a breakup until today, recognizing a "principle of biologic continuity," which means that no science fiction collision with passing planets is permissible. Evolving life would have been wiped out. But the record is clear; there never has been a total write-off, followed by a restart. Geologists therefore recognize a "law of uniformity," which means that although there have been quite revolutionary "ups and downs" in earth history, conditions were *more or less* uniform through time. This principle goes hand in hand with another—the "law of actualism"—which states that the laws of physics and chemistry are timeless and we use present-day processes as our clues for interpreting the past. We reject the miraculous.

Only after a long period did the first plants start to evolve, and with them, through photosynthesis, free oxygen became available for the first time in the earth's atmosphere about 2.5 billion years ago. The tracks of wriggling worms preserved in the old sediments and the impressions of jellyfish and other primitive but oxygen-demanding animals thus appear only relatively late in Precambrian time. Extensive deposits of iron oxide ores were also formed at about this time in many parts of the globe. Older iron minerals are mainly the (oxygen-free) sulfides. Accordingly, by now there must have been abundant free oxygen in the atmosphere. The plants had done their work in creating a livable world for the eras of fantastic animal evolution which lay ahead.

Climatic conditions during the Precambrian were, for the most part, very similar to those of the present day, for the natural processes cannot operate except in the presence of water, which may not be either boiling or frozen. Nevertheless, several ice ages occurred during the Precambrian, and we believe these were related to periodic shifting of the continents with respect to the earth's rotational axis. This shifting is known as "continental drift," a still somewhat mysterious process whereby the earth's crust slowly migrates over a molten layer beneath.

The Paleozoic Era. With the end of the Precambrian 600 million years ago the foundations of the continents were well and truly laid. The Paleozoic Era began. The Paleozoic sea washed in over the continents again and again at intervals of millions of years, withdrawing from time to time only to transgress once more.

The records of these events are the sedimentary rocks. Very clear and richly fossiliferous sediments faithfully record the great transgressions across each continent. Certain less stable areas became basins and slowly subsided, so that today we can measure 5,000 to 10,000 feet of sedimentary thickness in them. Other "arches" or "domes" in the basement remained stubbornly resistant, and though the seas often washed over them, they did not subside and remained as islands.

Throughout the Paleozoic Era the equator lay across the United States, and the North Pole was situated somewhere beyond Hawaii with the South Pole in Africa. Rich fossil remains tell us of warm waters in America and Europe, and in the second half of the era land plants evolved to help cloak the earth and enrich the coastal swamps. Now developed the great flying insects, followed by the first amphibians (that evolved from the fish), and the earliest reptiles.

Six great subdivisions are recognized in the Paleozoic; in sequence they are the Cambrian period (as mentioned earlier); Ordovician (named for an ancient tribe of Wales); Silurian (named for a similar tribe in Wales); Devonian (named for the English county); Carboniferous (named for its coal formations; in the United States, two subperiods—Mississippian and Pennsylvanian—are often recognized); Permian (named for the district of Perm in the Urals of the U.S.S.R.). In time the era ranges from 570 million to 230 million years.

The Mesozoic Era. A great world-wide continental break-up in the late Paleozoic heralded the Mesozoic Era, which began about 230 million years ago. Fossils of the common Paleozoic forms of life disappeared almost completely, while a few vigorous survivors started to build up new genealogical lines. Life on land was dominated by the great reptiles, the dinosaurs, from which evolved also the flying reptiles. In the oceans and lakes there were swimming or wading reptiles, and the lowly forms of life: clams, corals, sea urchins. The ammonites (the coiled mollusks—the cephalopods, meaning "head in the foot") were the most remarkable of these lower animals because of the intricate convolutions of their shell patterns; careful study of these patterns makes it possible for geologists to place rock formations, containing ammonites, in their exact age order.

Three great subdivisions are recognized in the Mesozoic—the Triassic (named for a distinctive threefold division observed nearly two centuries ago in northern Europe), the Jurassic (after the fine outcrops in the Jura Mountains of Switzerland), and the Cretaceous (after the celebrated English chalk deposits, *Kreta* being Greek for limestone).

In North America the climate remained tropical, for the equator still lay across the country and the Triassic North Pole was situated somewhere near Japan. Accordingly, the soil of that time in America was red with iron oxides like the tropical soils of today. Extensive lakes, deltas, and swamps were the sites of "red beds" and were the homes of free-roaming dinosaurs that lived off the lush vegetation on the marshy shores. Generally the hinterland was dry; sand dunes built up in the deserts. In places lagoons were cut off from the sea and became the sites where salt and gypsum were deposited from the evaporating brine.

The Jurassic Period seems to have been a time of world-wide mild climatic conditions, marked by lush vegetation. No ice sheets covered the poles, both of which were situated in ocean areas (western Pacific and southern Indian Ocean) and thus equable currents prevented any extensive freeze-up. The equator of the time passed over what is now the southeastern United States, and so the climates were either warm and humid or else, in the more continental parts, hot and dry.

With the Triassic and Jurassic came the beginnings of one of the most extraordinary periods of geologic history—the pulling apart of the continents to form the Atlantic and Indian oceans. Where there had been low swampy plains and shallow basins of evaporating salts, there now appeared new branches of the deep ocean. Geologists are not quite sure how it came about. Was the earth's crust stretching—so that open splits became new ocean basins? Or was it merely thinning—resulting in the down-dropping of crustal hunks or segments the size of the Gulf of Mexico? Energetic exploration programs are attempting to bring light on these questions. Results indicate that both suggestions are right—in different places. The ocean floor in the mid-Atlantic is now known to be spreading apart at the rate of about two inches per year. Turning back the clock to the Triassic period shows that the site of the present Atlantic was then closed. Land animals could walk from North America to Europe and from South America to Africa, and even into Antarctica and Australia. It seems that there were just two giant continents: "Laurasia" in the north, "Gondwanaland" in the south. They were probably separated by a proto-Mediterranean, "Tethys," of variable width.

Deep fractures along the lines of the ancestral mountains initiated volcanic centers. Rotting vegetation in the sediments provided a trap for rising solutions that also came up these fractures, bringing in uranium, the great nuclear fuel potential of the future.

With the Cretaceous Period a new world-wide trend appeared, the appearance of microscopic marine plants and animals that formed shells of lime (calcium carbonate); the resultant formations are the white chalk, famous in England, but equally widespread in many parts of the world, from Texas to Australia. As in the Jurassic there were no glacial regions and the oceans were universally warm. The sea level was high and rose still higher during the period, so that the broad gulfs further invaded the continents, dividing the world into giant islands.

In many ways, the Cretaceous was a golden age for the creatures of the earth. Mild conditions were universal, but toward the end of the period new mountain-building upheavals disturbed the tranquillity. From the Alps to the Himalayas, from the Rockies to the Andes, new belts of volcanoes and folded mountain ranges emerged. The end of the Mesozoic era, like the end of the Paleozoic, was marked by widespread extinctions.

What mysterious blight wiped out so many organisms at the end of the Mesozoic? Some argue that it was due to polar shift and climate change, and the drier conditions did not favor the tropical vegetation that was their food. Others point to the widespread mountain building with its volcanoes and attendant dusts and poisonous gases. Yet others speak of excessive radiation fatally damaging the gene structures; such heavy doses of radiations are to be expected whenever the poles of the earth's magnetic field reverse, as they do periodically, or when novae explode somewhere in the universe. Another type of explanation stresses biological causes: universal epidemics or parasites or predatory mutual extinction or "race exhaustion."

It is an ecologic law that an area vacated by one group of organisms creates an environmental "vacuum" which rapidly tends to fill with another group of similar metabolic needs; in this case the dinosaur gap was filled by the mammals, which developed in great number and variety, with every sort of adaptation, from ocean and lake life (swimmers) to open range life (runners), to life in dense forests (fliers and climbers). Culminating the mammalian evolution came the ancestral apes and then man.

The Cenozoic Era. The latest era of geologic history is the time of modern-looking creatures. The Age of the Ape was at hand. The Cenozoic has two unequal subdivisions, the Tertiary (which began 67 million years ago) and the Quaternary (the last 2 million years). The origin of these terms is historical; two centuries ago, four divisions of geological time were recognized—the terms "Primary" and "Secondary" were used for Paleozoic and Mesozoic, but they were dropped after the Precambrian was discovered, and only the third and fourth labels survive.

Toward the end of the Cretaceous and in early Tertiary time, about 60 or 70 million years ago, there was a general revival of crustal uplift in many regions from the Alps to the Pacific, and considerable folding in the former marine troughs, so that thick deposits of eroded material were swept down by rivers and spread out over the adjacent plains and ocean floors. The paleogeographic maps of the Tertiary look very much like maps of today. Shallow gulfs gradually filled and dried out, leaving the present coastal plains. Around its entire seaboard the warm Atlantic Ocean continuously overlapped the continental borders, but today these are dry land and are the most densely populated.

Fossils of the Tertiary Period show close connections between the formations of eastern North America, the Mediterranean, and western Europe; these are familiar, modern-looking shells, mollusks, sea urchins, foraminifera, with traces of larger organisms like sharks and whales. The Pacific and Indian Ocean regions became more or less isolated from the Atlantic and developed similar but separate faunas.

The formations of the Tertiary were subdivided more than a century ago by Sir Charles Lyell, the guide and mentor of Darwin. Because of their "modern" types of fossil life he was able to do this on a whole basis of the ratio of living species represented. The international names eventually adopted were: Paleocene, Eocene, Oligocene, Miocene, and Pliocene. The fossils of the Paleocene had the least "modern" appearance; those of the Pliocene the most. All the more exotic forms had died out with the close of the Mesozoic; these included all the dinosaur-type reptiles, all the ammonites, the belemnites, several lines of brachiopods, and many echinoids (sea urchins).

One of the interesting groups of organisms that became very widespread during the Cretaceous but did not die out was the foraminifera, a class of simple, single-celled animals that build a delicate little shell of lime (often shaped like a minute snail); these had helped form the world-wide chalk formations of the Cretaceous. They have continued to flourish up until today. Many of them are planktonic, that is to say they float freely near the surface of the open sea, but certain lines began to build bigger and bigger shells; too heavy to float, they lay on the bottom or adhered to seaweeds. So fast was their evolution and so distinctive the small variations of the shell that they are now used almost all over the world for dating the marine formations. In the Eocene and mid-Tertiary these became larger, up to the size of half dollars, and in Europe they were called "nummulites," the coin shells. Some of the great pyramids of Egypt are built of nummulitic limestones consisting almost entirely of these organisms. By early Miocene some of the tropical forms reached the size of dinner plates, but they eventually became extinct.

The Quaternary Period, the time of the "Great Ice Age" and the last and shortest period in the geological record, began about 2 million years ago. It is subdivided into the Pleistocene and the Holocene or "Recent" epoch, the latter beginning only 10,000 years ago.

Ice ages seem to have recurred about once every 200 million years or so in the geological past. The "Quaternary Ice Age" is the latest, and it is actually still with us—as any Eskimo would agree. About 18 million square miles of the globe are still covered with ice. Through much of geological time, however, there have been no large ice sheets, for it is believed that ice ages are predictable "accidents" owing to a periodic coincidence of land and poles. When the poles coincide with water, there is no chance of building up big glaciers, and warm currents tend to melt the ice floes. During late Tertiary time the relative position of the continents to the earth's poles shifted from sites in eastern Siberia and in the southern Indian Ocean to their present positions. With the South Pole located in the great mountainous Antarctic continent, a series of important events began. First, precipitation in the mountains turned to snow and then ice; snowfields built up into glaciers and, growing larger, the glaciers spread out over the lowlands.

The freezing of Antarctica began about 3 or 4 million years ago and initiated a drop in the world's sea level, because water was not returned to the oceans by the normal melting in the summertime. The lowering in sea level caused all the land areas to become relatively higher and also wider. In this way the North American continent alone became enlarged by 2,200,000 square miles—an amount equal to approximately two-thirds the present size of the United States. At the same time renewed mountain building took place from Alaska to the Sierra Nevada, in the Andes, in the Alps, the Himalayas, and elsewhere, so that the high elevations became snow-capped and glacier-covered too. The Arctic Ocean became almost isolated by the lowering of sea level, and deprived of warm currents, ice floes formed over it. Mountain glaciers in northern Canada and Scandinavia spread out onto the lowland plains. Warm, moisture-laden air from the Atlantic continued to blow into these cold regions, but instead of rain, it fell as snow. At maximal stages glacier ice reached right across western Europe to Ireland and across North America from Illinois to New England. Cyclically the ice melted and there were warm "interglacial" episodes, though in the great mass of Antarctica the ice persisted.

The position of the planet earth in relation to the sun, which provides our warmth, is always changing a little bit. Neither the orbital ellipse nor the axis tilt is rigidly constant. In the geological past when there were usually no polar mountains, such small changes did not matter, but for a cooled earth, minor oscillations in the amount of solar heat received had profound effects. These astronomic cycles set up climatic changes of 20,000- to 90,000-year intervals, which grew progressively greater and greater, because less and less of the ice from the previous oscillation melted during the following mild swing. Since the complex mathematics of their prediction was worked out first by a Yugoslav scientist, Milankovitch, these climatic oscillations are often known as the Milankovitch cycles. It is against this background of tremendous climatic changes that man has evolved to his present state. It is tempting to suspect a cause-and-effect relationship.

In the early part of the Quaternary the ice in North America was limited to the mountains of Alaska, the Rockies, the Canadian Arctic, and Greenland. But, during the last million years, four oscillations brought continental glacier ice out across the prairies. The last advance reached to the present position of New York City and a line from Long Island out to Nantucket. Each of these "glaciations" has received a name from the particular state where its deposits were first mapped in detail and a similar sequence was mapped in the Alps (names given in parentheses)—in sequence, Nebraskan (Günz), Kansan (Mindel), Illinoian (Riss) and Wisconsin (Würm). In between each ice advance, which lasted in its extreme form only 10,000 to 20,000 years, there were long periods of mild or quite hot conditions, when the ice melted away more or less completely.

The long beginning phase of the Quaternary Ice Age has not been closely subdivided, but it has been given the general name Villafranchian in Europe or Blancan in North America, which probably covers deposits laid down even in the late Pliocene. During this early phase in many parts of the world gradual climatic changes in mountain areas played a most important role. Previously the mountains had been low in elevation and cloaked by subtropical forests; now with general uplift and a cooling climate, they became drier and the highest areas came above the tree line. With thinning vegetation, the former thick tropical soil became deeply eroded and the resultant debris filled the lower valleys with silt. Heavy siltation occurred along all the great rivers, and it is in these silt and gravel terraces that many of the fossils of that time are found, fossils ranging from ancestral horse to mammoth.

With the advance of ice across the plains two important changes took place. The usual climatic belts—tundra, prairie, conifer forest, broad-leaved forest, subtropical forest—shifted toward the equator. The tundra belt (with muskeg, mosses, and reindeer) was pushed down to the latitudes of Paris and Philadelphia. The tropical belt was extremely constricted, and the subtropics became broad deserts. In Africa, the Sahara extended southward and the Kalahari sands spread northward, to overlap in the now jungle-covered Congo. Hardly a tree in this modern rain forest does not have its roots in desert sands. Sand dunes left over from those stages in Europe and North America are also now mostly covered by trees and scrub, but the old sandy soil is still there.

Through the Quaternary, each time the continental ice fronts withdrew, the floods of meltwater scoured out much deeper valleys than existed before. Much of it went into the Mississippi and St. Lawrence, the Rhine and the Danube. With each successive glacial advance the colder oceans led to reduced evaporation and thus the drier conditions led to siltation of the rivers, which would otherwise have had sufficient energy to carry the sediment down to the ocean. At the beginning of each interglacial period there was a return of warm rainfall and renewed cutting down of the river channels. The result was that modern valleys are paralleled by numerous terraces of old flood plain deposits, now abandoned. Many of them have been washed away altogether. By the time each full interglacial was reached, vegetation had covered the landscape, and as a protective blanket it would cut down soil erosion so that sluggish "equilibrium" conditions returned. It is significant that man's twentieth-century role has been to cut down the trees and destroy the vegetation, setting up soil erosion that is quite comparable with ice age conditions. Man-made deserts of today thus re-create nature's desert of 20,000 years ago. Unfortunately, the process is not always reversible because the reserves of soil grow less and less.

In the interior basins in the Rocky Mountains, East Africa, central

Australia, and central Asia, after each glacial phase, the melting ice and the return of bountiful rains led to the build-up of immense numbers of fresh-water lakes. These "pluvial lakes" (partly owing to the lower oceanic evaporation of glacial times) were not able to persist through each glacial stage. With each succeeding interglacial condition they mostly dried up altogether or were reduced to salty brines as in the Great Salt Lake of Utah today. These pluvial lakes caused much confusion in the past, it being thought that they belonged to glacial stages. Actually they were short-lived and corresponded only to the transition stages from glacial to interglacial.

In the areas where the glacier ice had melted away, extensive belts of "till" were left behind. Till consists of the scooped-up soil and boulders that have been pushed and scraped off the land surface as the ice advanced. Much of it became frozen into the ice, and many boulders ("erratics") were carried distances of up to 1,000 miles from their source.

With the low sea level of the glacial stages the shallow Bering Straits offered a dry-land connection between North America and Siberia. North American horses strayed across and spread all over Asia and eventually reached Europe, while African and Eurasian animals like the wooly mammoth and mastodon (a giant elephant) reached North America. Bones, teeth, and tusks of these enormous animals are found right across the country in sediments dated up until only 5,000 years ago. They required large amounts of vegetation as foodstuffs, so they preferred to live near the coasts or swamplands. Since the last glacial stage the sea level has risen more than 300 feet, and coastal fishermen from Maine to Virginia are frequently hauling in these bones with their trawling nets.

The last general melting began about 17,000 years ago, slowly at first and hesitantly, with numbers of brief glacier readvances. Around the borders of the melting ice extensive lakes were formed, and every now and then these spilled over. In Europe the resultant rivers flowed out toward the North Sea and helped carve out the English Channel. In North America they flowed into the Mississippi, the Hudson, and the St. Lawrence with torrents of flood water that at times clouded half the North Atlantic with mud. At the same time the sea level rose faster than 10 feet in a century, so that by 6,000 years ago it stood near its present level. It seems to be no chance coincidence that in the folklore of most riparian peoples there are tales of the Great Flood. The Noachian deluge may also in part have been engendered by the marked increase in precipitation that occurred in early postglacial time in Anatolia and East Africa. Since 6,000 years ago that precipitation has been steadily decreasing.

By about 10,000 years ago approximately half the continental ice was gone and profound warming changes affected the world. Not least among the phenomena was the accelerated evolution of man, from his Stone Age existence to the stage when he first started building great temples along the Nile 5,000 or so years ago.

Postglacial time. This last 10,000 years is known as the Holocene Epoch, or informally as the "Recent" or "Postglacial" stage. Although marked by a general warm-up, there have been further brief climatic oscillations which produced "little ice ages" from time to time and changed the landscape somewhat. Apart from the polar regions, all the land ice was gone 6,000 years ago. That represented the warmest stage on earth for nearly 100,000 years. It is often called the "climatic optimum." Since that time the average annual mean temperature in the mid-latitudes has dropped about 5 degrees Fahrenheit, and we are now partway toward the next glacial phase (although it is not expected for several thousand years). From 1890 to 1940 there was an important warming phase again, but since 1940 it has had only minor fluctuations. Air pollution has had important effects on city climates, but the immediate trend of world climate is not known.

Several times since the climatic optimum, about 3,000 years ago, in early Roman times, and again in the Middle Ages (about A.D. 1350 to 1750), there have been "little ice ages" lasting a few decades, followed by another trend. In the arid Southwest of the United States early man had become an agriculturalist during the first millennium A.D., but after the 1200's the coming of cooler conditions in the north meant drier conditions in the south, and he was forced to abandon many of his riverside villages as the waters dried up; thus it was that when the Spanish arrived they found many of the Indians as nomadic hunters. Curiously enough, it was then that the horse, so useful to the Plains Indians, was reintroduced by the Spanish. The horse, which had evolved on these self-same plains, had become extinct during the last glacial stage (many were killed and eaten by the paleo-Indian), but was now brought back to his own.

Geological events consequent upon these planetary changes in climate are widely observed also in the Old World. The melting of ice from Scandinavia caused an unloading of the earth's crust, so that it has been steadily rising in the north, drying out harbors and creating new coastal lands. Parallel sinkings have occurred in the southern Baltic and North Sea (noticeable particularly in the Netherlands).

The warming trend that accompanied the fall of the Roman Empire in the Mediterranean lands was marked by desiccation, drought, and deforestation. Soil erosion resulted, and many of the Roman and Greek ruins are now buried under many feet of silt. The process was not local, for the same burial in silt can be seen as far away as Mohenjo-Daro in Pakistan or Angkor Wat in Cambodia. The same desiccating trends are reflected by the encroachment of deserts and the drying out of wells in the seventh to tenth centuries along the Great Silk Road across central Asia. The first Suez canal (a sweet-water canal built by Ramses II from Cairo to Suez) suffered the same fate. Small climatic oscillations are always modulating the major geological curves, and many events in human history seem to correlate very remarkably with environmental controls. In spite of suggestive writings by some explorers and historians such as Ellsworth Huntington and Arnold Toynbee, the field has never been researched by someone with scientific training and modern equipment.

The historical theory that ascribes many events in the human record to environmental causes thus receives powerful support from geology, but natural science teaches that single causes in open planetary systems are scarcely possible. The one theory does not explain everything. It never does. The 4.5-billion-year history of this planet points irresistibly to the conclusion that a living organism is created out of his environment, but it also shows that an organism modifies the total environment of his successors. This applies as equally to bacteria as to man.

For Further Reading

Adams, F. D., *The Birth and Development of the Geological Sciences.*
Albritton, C. C., Jr. (ed.), *The Fabric of Geology.*
Claiborne, R., *Climate, Man and History.*
Clark, T. H., and Stearn, C. W., *The Geological Evolution of North America.*
Darwin, C., *The Voyage of the Beagle.*
Dunbar, C. O., and Waage, K. M., *Historical Geology.*
Dury, G. H., *The Face of the Earth.*
Fairbridge, R. W. (ed.), *The Encyclopedia of Geomorphology.*
Harland, W. B., *The Earth: Rocks, Minerals and Fossils.*
Holmes, D. L., *Elements of Physical Geology.*
Hurley, P. M., *How Old Is the Earth?*
Investigating the Earth (Earth Science Curriculum Project, A.G.I.).
Mather, K. F., and Mason, S. L., *A Source Book in Geology.*
Rhodes, F. H. T. et al., *Fossils: A Guide to Prehistoric Life.*
Schwarzbach, M., *Climates of the Past.*
Shelton, J. S., *Geology Illustrated.*
Simpson, G. G., *Life of the Past.*
Stokes, W. L., and Judson, S., *Introduction to Geology, Physical and Historical.*
Takeuchi, H. et al., *Debate About the Earth.*

3   The Evolution of Life

Despite our knowledge of astronomy and geology, most men accept the earth as something enduring—timeless and endless. Today is yesterday; tomorrow will be another today. To be sure, many societies have their creation myths, but the events alluded to took place in the dim past. Yet there has always been evidence, literally at man's feet, suggesting that the earth of yesterday was indeed different from the earth of today.

Before man was able to develop a scientific view of the biological world and his place in it, he was forced to observe and speculate for millenniums about the nature and variety of living things, and about their origins and possible extinction. He observed peculiar formations in rocks—the fossils —and wondered about their cause and character. He observed erupting volcanoes, the eroding action of moving waters, the layering of rocks—and speculated about the antiquity of the earth and the changes it might have experienced with the passage of time. Leonardo da Vinci observed fossils of marine animals in the mountains of Italy and reasoned that at one time the region must have been covered by the ocean.

Before the nineteenth century, isolated observations and speculations of this sort were of little importance in intellectual history, since they were never related to a conceptual scheme of origin and change. There was, of course, an excellent reason why they should not be. The creation myth of Western man, as portrayed in Genesis, was for centuries the accepted view—accepted because it was divine scripture. The Genesis account of creation spread throughout the world, displacing earlier classical myths and, backed by the authority and presence of Western man, encountered only insignificant philosophical opposition. Yet gradually this view has been displaced in turn.

In the early years of the nineteenth century, an ever increasing volume of observation and speculation slowly led to the modern sciences of geology and biology. There is no aspect of geology or biology antedating 1800 that has not been replaced by better work done thereafter; the efforts of the earlier naturalists are now of interest almost exclusively to the historian of science. But, unlike us, the nineteenth-century investigators were not independent of the early naturalists. These founders of modern geology and biology were both led and misled by the observations and speculations of those who had gone before them.

The key ingredient in the change from nonscience to science was a

Biochronology of the Planet Earth

ERA	PERIOD	EPOCH	TIME OF BEGINNING (millions of years ago)	BIOLOGICAL EVENTS
ARCHEOZOIC PROTEROZOIC	Precambrian (periods)		4,600	Origin of the earth and solar system
			(?)4,000	Origin of life, leading to production of oxygen
			(?)1,500	First primitive soft-bodied animals; only a few fossils known; much evolution occurred, and main types of invertebrates and some aquatic plants existed
PALEOZOIC	Cambrian		600	Many aquatic plants; some plants invade land; trilobites, bracholopods, and many other invertebrates; shelly fossils begin to appear commonly
	Ordovician		500	Earliest known chordates; graptolites and corals widespread
	Silurian		435	Club mosses and other primitive land plants abundant; some arthropods may have invaded land
	Devonian		395	Fishes abundant; first amphibians; many land arthropods; horsetails, ferns, liverworts appear
	Carboniferous			Huge forests of primitive plants
		Mississippian	345	The Age of Amphibians
		Pennsylvanian	310	Reptiles appear
	Permian		280	Extinction of many Paleozoic organisms such as trilobites; amphibians decrease in importance
MESOZOIC	Triassic		230	Forests of conifers and cycads; first mammals; reptiles abundant and varied
	Jurassic		180	The Age of Ammonites; first birds
	Cretaceous		135	Extinction of dinosaurs and many other mesozoic organisms; flowering plants appear
CENOZOIC	Tertiary	Paleocene	67	Mammals abundant; first primates; flowering plants abundant
		Eocene	58	
		Oligocene	36	
		Miocene	25	
		Pliocene	7	
	Quaternary	Pleistocene	2.0	
		Holocene	0.01	

change in attitude. During the eighteenth and nineteenth centuries theory became less and less constrained by scripture and ancient authority and came to depend more and more on observation and experimentation.

If one were to have asked the question, "What has been the history of life?" at the middle of the eighteenth century, the answer might well have been, "Is there any reason to think that there has been a history of life other than the cycle of birth, maturation, and death? Have not things remained essentially the same since the time of creation, which Bishop Ussher tells us occurred in 4004 B.C.?" But in the nineteenth century, nature, and nature alone, became the guide to nature's secrets.

In retrospect, it is clear that there were two fundamentals to be established before men could recognize and study the problem of a history of life. One was a method, the other a discovery.

The method was that of the paleontologist. It slowly became apparent that the fossils which appeared so abundantly in some stratified rocks were the petrified remains of animals and plants that had lived in the past. The past, therefore, was not irretrievably lost. A paleontologist could study the fossils carefully and learn something of the structure and even the way of life of the extinct creatures—whether the organisms had lived in the ocean, in fresh water, or on land.

The discovery was that of the tremendous antiquity of the earth. As the geologists probed the earth's crust, they found that many of the rocks were layered or stratified. Careful study suggested that many of these beds of stratified rocks had been formed under water. One could imagine a river carrying debris to the ocean or an inland sea and depositing it in a delta. The earlier deposits would be successively covered by the later deposits. Slowly these sediments would change to stone with the oldest layer on the bottom and the youngest on top. The tremendous thickness of these layers suggested that they must have required a very long time for their formation. How long? Hundreds of thousands or even millions of years; therefore, the earth could not have been created in 4004 B.C. as Bishop Ussher had claimed.

Thus nature had been keeping a crude diary in the stratified rocks. Each layer of rock represented a capsule of time, and any fossils it contained represented the animals or plants of that time. By studying the fossils at successively higher levels one could learn if and how life had changed during that portion of the earth's history represented by these particular rocks.

The quarries of the Paris Basin provided some of the earliest evidence. Here there were layers of marl, sandstone, limestone, clay, sand, and gypsum. It became evident that the area, now dry land, had been at various times a lake or an arm of the sea. When French scientist Georges Cuvier

(1769–1832) studied the fossils in these formations he discovered something of great importance: the fossils of successively lower layers were more and more unfamiliar. Most of them in the lowest layers seemed to be entirely unknown: there were no living representatives on the coast of France or, for that matter, anywhere in the world.

The suggestion that some fossils represented species no longer living raised profound questions for the theologian, philosopher, and biologist. What of the commonly held belief that the earth had a fixed number of species which had existed from the moment of creation? Had there been a cycle of creation and extinction? Had there been organic change, or an evolution of life, as some of the Greek philosophers had suggested?

The work of Jean Baptiste Pierre Antoine de Monet, Chevalier de Lamarck (1744–1829), was one of the first attempts to provide a comprehensive answer. Lamarck rejected the belief that species were fixed either in number or in structure. The nature of a species at any one time—its structure, physiology, and way of life—depended on the demands of the environment, he reasoned. In the process of adapting to the environment, organisms changed. Those structures and processes that led to better adaptation would be used and, hence, further developed; those that did not would be employed less and degenerate. The use or disuse of structures would result in one kind of organism slowly changing into another. Lamarck subscribed to the prevailing view that such structures modified by use or disuse in one generation would be transmitted to the next generation by the hereditary process. Thus, the ancestors of today's life had been different animals and plants in the past.

Many of Lamarck's theories were validated by later workers, but history has not dealt kindly with him. He was right in his central thesis, the evolution of species, but today he is remembered mainly for proposing a mechanism of evolution that has not withstood the test of scientific analysis. There is no convincing evidence that the changes he assumed to come from the striving of the individual can be transmitted to its offspring.

The public and scientific acclaim for the "founder of modern evolutionary theory" goes to Lamarck's successor, Charles Robert Darwin (1809–1882). This is not entirely fair, since the judgment is based less on differences in the central ideas of the two men than on the way they stated their case. Lamarck presented skillful arguments to prove that evolution occurred, but failed to support his views adequately with data. He was more a philosopher than a scientist, but he lived in an age when scientists were highly suspicious of philosophical speculation because it had proved a poor means of understanding nature. Darwin's theory of evolution was also speculative, but he buttressed his hypotheses with what his contemporaries regarded as "overwhelming evidence."

Charles Darwin is probably the world's most widely known scientist. He was the effective promulgator not only of *the* most important idea in biological science but one that was to be felt personally by every educated individual associated with Western culture. Long before, Copernicus had demoted man's earthly abode from its place in the center of the universe to a remote corner of the cosmos. This was unsettling to men's sense of their own importance, but somewhat abstract: to the untutored eye the sun *seemed* to circle the earth in punctual obedience. Darwin's ideas, however, had an exceedingly personal impact: once men became aware of them, they found it increasingly hard to believe that their progenitors had emerged fully formed from the hand of the Creator. Darwin offered an Eden far less gratifying to the human ego: the gradual evolution of man from the apes, beasts that seemed totally devoid of virtue. Other animals might be loyal, strong, brave, useful, or beautiful, but the familiar apes and monkeys in the zoo were nervous, chattering sex deviates. If the biological facts had allowed Darwin to suggest that man had evolved from the noble race horse, the kingly lion, or even the faithful dog, it is probable that his theory would have encountered far less opposition—at least from the animal-loving British!

Since Darwin was the father of an important scientific theory with such personal implications, a theory which could be understood by nearly everyone, it is not surprising that his life and work should have been widely discussed, praised, abused, and analyzed. He was born on February 12, 1809, in Shrewsbury, England, on the same day that Abraham Lincoln was born in the backwoods of Kentucky. His father was a well-to-do physician, Dr. Robert Darwin, and his mother was Susannah Wedgwood, from the family of famous potters. The young Darwin was much interested in natural history. Lesser men delight in pointing out that he was an indifferent student, at both Edinburgh and Cambridge, where he attempted to prepare first for a career in medicine and then in the church. At the time the universities paid slight attention to biology or geology, in part because these sciences had so little to offer. Darwin was largely self-taught in science, and the most important part of this informal education took place between 1831 and 1836 when he sailed around the world on H.M.S. *Beagle*. The *Beagle* was dispatched by the British government on a mission of exploration and scientific discovery. Darwin spent much time ashore, especially in South America and Australia, where he collected and studied animals, plants, and fossils.

It was a decisive voyage. When Darwin set sail on the *Beagle*, he believed in the special creation of the species of animals and plants. It was the numerous observations that he made during the trip which stimulated him to seek alternative explanations for the origin of the variability of the living world.

After his return, Darwin married a Wedgwood cousin, and the two of them with their ten children were to spend most of their lives at Down, in the county of Kent. Ill health, possibly caused by a tropical disease contracted on his great voyage, forced Darwin to lead the life of a recluse. He rarely traveled and he received few visitors. His energies had to be carefully budgeted. But this semi-invalid managed to publish twenty major scientific books and numerous shorter articles. Most of these were outstanding contributions to science.

A naturalist in England soon comes to know many local kinds of animals and plants. There might seem to be an abundance of species there, but the magnitude of this variability pales into insignificance once that naturalist visits the wet tropics. Darwin was greatly impressed with the luxuriance of life and the great number of species of animals and plants he encountered in Amazonia. Of greater importance for the later development of his ideas, he observed that populations of what seemed to be the same species were subject to geographical variation. The individuals of one locality might be essentially identical, but they differed noticeably from the individuals of other localities. Were the distinctive populations of each locality created separately? Darwin also noted examples of fossil species that were obviously different from what seemed to be their living representatives. Were there cycles of creation and extinction? Observations of this sort suggested to Darwin that this variability of living varieties and species might be accounted for by evolution. Geographic variation might be explained by the evolutionary divergence of what had been originally a single homogeneous population. Similarly, might not the fossils be reminders of a population of animals that slowly evolved into the living types?

Hypotheses in science are of use only to the extent that they can be tested, but any direct test of the hypothesis of evolution seemed out of the question: evolution was assumed to occur slowly, so slowly that it could not be detected during the lifetime of the investigator. The species that were familiar to man were "fixed" in the sense that he had never observed them to change: embalmed animals from the tombs of ancient Egypt, for example, seemed to differ in no way from members of the same species that were still living.

There was nothing novel about a hypothesis of evolution. Lamarck had anticipated Darwin with such a notion, and Darwin's grandfather had anticipated Lamarck. Darwin's principal contribution to evolutionary theory was to explain its mechanism—how it might occur. The germ of his idea came from reading Thomas Malthus, who had suggested for man what Darwin had observed for wild species in many parts of the world: that rates of reproduction are so great that if all the offspring survived, any species could soon form a solid crust of life on the earth's surface. An oyster produces millions of young each year, an oak thousands of acorns. Yet the sea does not become a solid mass of oysters or the land an unbroken stand of oak trees. These events do not come to pass because the enormous rate of reproduction is balanced by an enormous rate of mortality, especially of the young.

Another ingredient in Darwin's emerging hypothesis was variability. He had observed this both in the geographic differences already referred to and in the lesser but distinct variations of individual members of a species in a single locality. One specimen might be slightly larger than another; one might have a heavy coat of hair, another a sparse coat; one might be more fleet of foot than another. Darwin assumed that much of this variability was inherited; that is, transmitted from generation to generation.

Darwin's explanatory hypothesis for the mechanism of evolution combined the notion of the huge rate of reproduction (and its corollary of a huge death rate) with the notion of variability. Might not there be a difference between the individuals that survived to maturity and those that died young—before the age of reproduction? In a cold climate, might not an animal with a warm coat of fur have a slightly better chance of surviving and leaving offspring than one with a sparse coat? If this was true, one could explain how evolution worked. In the population of animals in the cold locality there would be variability in the insulating effectiveness of the coats. Those with the thicker coats would have a better chance of surviving, especially in those years that were colder than average. Since the type of fur was assumed to be inherited, the offspring of the warmly clad animals would also be warmly clad. With the passage of generations, there would be a slow change in the population, brought about by differential mortality and the survival of the fittest.

Darwin called this process *natural selection,* the selection by nature of the individuals best able to survive and leave offspring. He suggested that nature had done for eons what man had done for generations. Man's artificial selection consisted of choosing for the parents of the next generation those domesticated animals and plants which had the characteristics best suited to his needs. From the variability present in wild horses, man had selected many breeds. Generation after generation, the fleetest mares and stallions became the parents in the lineage that was to produce the Arabian race horse. Other horses were selected for their strength. These became the war-horses of western Europe, capable of carrying a medieval knight, his lance and sword, and his cocoon of steel.

Darwin's hypothesis of the evolution of species need not have contradicted the idea of special creation. One could imagine the special creation of a million species, or whatever number there is on the earth, and the evolution of these with the passage of time—each species becoming better adapted to its environment. But Darwin suggested something very different, namely, a dawn of life with only a few very primitive creatures. As the ages passed, these progenitors of life had evolved into the diversity of later life, as illustrated by fossils as well as the species alive today.

In one of the greatest of all syntheses in science, *On the Origin of Species by Means of Natural Selection or the Preservation of the Favoured Races in the Struggle for Life* (1859), Darwin attempted to relate knowledge of the living world to his hypothesis of evolution. He and those who followed him found that what organisms were and did made sense in terms of evolution: the seemingly endless variety of species, the fact that they could be classified into natural groups, the peculiarities of embryonic development, the presence of useless vestigial organs, the fact of geographic distribution. These and many other observations fell neatly into place. Evolution ceased to be merely a hypothesis: it became a theory uniting a great variety of data into a meaningful whole.

Today biologists accept a modernized version of Darwin's hypothesis for the mechanism of evolution, namely the natural selection of randomly occurring variation. This was not always so. In Darwin's own lifetime he, and nearly all other biologists, fully believed that evolution had occurred. There was, however, increasing uncertainty about his explanation of how it occurs. Natural selection seemed probable enough, but Darwin and others of his time failed to understand both the origin of variability and how it might be transferred from generation to generation. Darwin's original belief in the random nature and spontaneous occurrence of hereditary differences was slowly abandoned for lack of evidence. Instead, he and others turned more and more to Lamarck's suggestion that the environment is directly responsible for the origin and type of hereditary differences. It was only in the years after 1900 that geneticists supplied the data showing that the Darwin of 1859 had been closer to the truth.

The history of life on the earth is read from the rocks that contain the evidence. Not surprisingly, the historian of life experiences one of the difficulties that besets the historian of civilized man—the earliest records are incomplete. The sedimentary rocks of the earth's crust contain a fair record of life during the past 600 million years, the span from the beginning of the Cambrian Period to the present. The sedimentary rocks older than the Cambrian have been much altered since they were formed and, on the whole, contain few fossils. Yet it is clear that life had a long history in Precambrian times. Complex animals were already in existence in that period: the Cambrian seas contained protozoans, sponges, corals, many types of shelled animals, echinoderms, arthropods, and various types of algae, fungi, and bacteria. Since these organisms undoubtedly evolved from simpler organisms, they must have done so in Precambrian times. Indeed, the only major group of animals that has not been discovered in the Cambrian is our own, the Chordata, which includes all the vertebrates and a few more primitive marine animals.

Thus the origin of life and its early evolution must have occurred during an immense span of time for which we have a meager record. The best that can be done is to speculate on what might have happened and, in the case of the origin of life, to see if the "what might have happened" can be duplicated in the laboratory.

Most scientists believe, though they have no proof, that life is a local product—that it did not originate elsewhere and then travel to the earth. They assume that before the appearance of life itself there must have been a period when organic molecules formed. The waters of the earth are thought to have gradually accumulated a variety of proteins, nucleic acids, and other molecules that today are produced only by other living creatures. Some of the chemical events that are assumed to have occurred can be duplicated in the laboratory by re-creating conditions that are believed to have existed on the earth when life first appeared.

Life must have first occurred when a complex molecule, or group of molecules, reached the stage where reproduction could take place: that is, raw material could be used to make more of itself. "Must have first occurred" because the ability to reproduce is the key element in any definition that distinguishes living from nonliving. The first living thing, or molecule, may have been similar to the nucleic acids, which throughout the history of life have been the basis of inheritance between generations and of the development of individuals within generations. Next there was probably a slow accretion of other molecules around the self-reproducing molecule, which thereby increased its efficiency of survival and reproduction. Thus Darwinian evolution very probably began at the molecular level.

The origin of life probably occurred about 4 billion years ago. The oldest known fossil organisms, which are believed to be about 3 billion years old, are representatives of two of the most primitive kinds of life still extant: the bacteria and blue-green algae. Before the Cambrian Period began, some 2.5 billion years later, many different kinds of aquatic bacteria, algae, and fungi had evolved. It was also in this dimly lighted period that the major group of animals appeared.

The seas of the Cambrian period teemed with a rich variety of life. There were many kinds of sponges, and in some parts of the Cambrian seas, these were so abundant that their skeletons formed huge reefs. There are impressions in Cambrian rocks of jellyfish, much like those still living. Mollusks and annelid worms flourished. Echinoderms were also common, but the Cambrian species were very different from those now living. Two of the most distinctive types of invertebrates that occurred in the Cambrian were the brachiopods and trilobites. The first are superficially like clams, but they are classified in their own major group, or phylum; only a few brachiopods are still living. The trilobites were primitive arthropods, the phylum that includes the insects, lobsters, centipedes, and spiders. They were complex animals with numerous legs and a broad shield-shaped head. Some were a foot and a half in length; all are extinct.

The fact that trilobites and other complex animals already existed in the Cambrian suggests that the evolutionary radiation of the main types of animals must have occurred during those immense Precambrian ages that have left such an incomplete fossil record. The evolutionary record from the Cambrian to the present is largely the story of an evolutionary waxing and waning within the different phyla. Groups appear, and evolve numerous species. Then some decline to extinction, while others continue to evolve and flourish.

One of the most momentous events that occurred in the Cambrian was the invasion of dry land by green plants. In the early Cambrian the most advanced plants were the algae, the group that includes the seaweeds of today. Late in the Cambrian some of the algae evolved into plants that could live on land. Little is known of these early plants—the fossil evidence is too incomplete. It was not until the Silurian, which began about 435 million years ago, that fossils of land plants became abundant. These are club mosses, representatives of which still exist. The diversity of land plants became greater in the following period, the Devonian, which began about 395 million years ago. Horsetails, ferns, and liverworts appeared. Representatives of all of these types are still living, but most of them are small. During the Devonian, however, these plants grew to great size, producing true forests, but this was nothing as compared to the luxuriance of plant life in the next major period, the Carboniferous, beginning 345 million years ago and ending 280 million years ago. The dead plants of the Carboniferous forests are of tremendous economic importance today, for they have become the deposits of coal that exist in such profusion in many regions of the earth.

These primitive land plants had passed their peak by the end of the Paleozoic era. Most have few living representatives, and their former position of prominence has been assumed by more advanced types. The conifers (spruce, pine, firs, and their relatives) are known from the Paleozoic, but they did not become prominent until the Mesozoic era, which began about 230 million years ago. Most of the familiar plants today are the flowering plants, which first appear in the fossil record near the end of the Mesozoic era, but during the Cenozoic era, which began about 67 million years ago, they began an evolutionary burst which was to result in their blanketing the earth with a coat of green.

Since, directly or indirectly, all animals depend on green plants for food, green plants had to invade dry land in advance of the animals. Once plants were established, many new evolutionary possibilities opened up. The first animals to take advantage of the new opportunities seem to have been the arthropods. It is possible that some scorpion-like land species existed in the Silurian. Thereafter a rapid evolutionary radiation of land-living arthropods occurred, and soon all the major types were present. These first animals to conquer dry land have never lost their numerical superiority; there are more species of arthropods today than there are species of all the other types.

The one phylum for which there is a reasonably complete fossil record is our own, the *Chordata*. The earliest known examples are the ostracoderms, which first occur in the Ordovician period. They belong to a group of fishes that is represented today by the lamprey and hagfish. The ostracoderms had no jaws, and in most aspects of their anatomy they were very primitive. Some of them soon evolved into other kinds of fishes, which flourished in the Devonian seas. These had jaws, and some had paired pectoral and pelvic fins. The paired fins were of special importance, since evolution was to mold them into the arms and legs of terrestrial vertebrates.

These fish evolved into the amphibians during the Devonian period. The first amphibians were quite unlike their present-day representatives, the frogs, toads, and salamanders. Many were huge and, in size and superficial form, resembled a thick-bodied alligator. Amphibians have never become completely at home on dry land. Even today the embryonic stages of nearly all must be passed in water or in a very moist situation. During the Carboniferous era one group of amphibians surmounted this limitation, evolving into reptiles. In comparison to the fishes, both the amphibians and the reptiles underwent many internal structural and physiological changes in their evolution from aquatic to terrestrial animals. Lungs replaced gills, legs replaced fins, and the circulatory, excretory, and reproductive systems showed many changes. The aquatic eggs of fish and amphibians evolved into a larger egg, containing much yolk, and surrounded by protective membranes and a shell that allowed the embryo to develop on dry land.

During the Mesozoic era the reptiles underwent a great burst of evolutionary diversification. Some took to the air, others to the seas; some became the huge dinosaurs. Two groups did something even more spectacular—they evolved into birds and mammals. Both of these events seem to have taken place at about the same time (late Triassic for mammals; Jurassic for birds), and they may be regarded as the latest major evolutionary experiments of the animal kingdom.

We are likely to look upon the mammalian way of life as obviously superior to the reptilian way. Yet natural selection did not render this verdict freely. The mammals remained inconspicuous during most of the

Mesozoic, when the reptiles were evolving such a spectacular array of species. At the end of the Mesozoic most of the reptiles became extinct, for reasons that are still wholly conjectural. It was only after this, during the Cenozoic, that the mammals began their main evolutionary developments.

For Further Reading

Appleman, Philip (ed.), *Darwin*.
Barlow, Nora, *The Autobiography of Charles Darwin, 1809–1882*.
Ghiselin, Michael T., *The Triumph of the Darwinian Method*.
Irvine, William, *Apes, Angels, and Victorians*.
Rhodes, F. H. T., *The Evolution of Life*.
Smith, John Maynard, *The Theory of Evolution*.

4   Human Evolution

The Cenozoic Era is appropriately known as the Age of Mammals. Beginning in the Paleocene, the little shrewlike mammals of the Mesozoic evolved into a vast number of different species. Including some that returned to the oceans, they occupied almost every conceivable environment. The adaptive radiations of the mammals were such that they became (with the exception of the insects) the most abundant and varied of all land animals. The Tertiary mammalian species are no longer with us, though some, such as the opossum, have changed little since then. All of the others have been replaced by newly evolved forms adapted to constantly changing environments and conditions of competition.

Man is one of the more recently evolved mammals. In zoological classification he is a primate—a relative of the apes, monkeys, lemurs, and tarsiers. The lemurs and tarsiers were the first primates; they evolved from simple insect-eaters of the Mesozoic. Their fossils, dating to the Paleocene and Eocene periods, are known throughout the northern temperate regions of the world. Early in the Cenozoic, probably during Eocene times, lemurs and tarsiers migrated southward to the tropics. In this new environment they soon evolved into three different strains: the New World monkeys, the Old World monkeys, and the great apes.

Within the order of the primates, man belongs to the same group as the great apes—the gorilla, chimpanzee, orang-utan, and gibbon. These apes closely resemble man in their skeletal structure, their teeth, and even their

CHRONOLOGY	B.C.	4,000,000	Earliest known hominids
		1,750,000	Definite stone tools
		600,000	*Pithecanthropus* evolves
		200,000	Possible *Homo sapiens;* use of fire
		95,000	*Homo sapiens* definitely evolved; burial of dead
		40,000	Modern man appears
		30,000	Earliest art
		9000	Beginnings of animal husbandry, probably also of agriculture

blood types. Their most important differences are their relatively small and simple brains, their inability to master complex languages, the lack of flexibility in their thumbs, the fact that they do not habitually walk upright, the ruggedness of their skulls and skeletons, their fangs and protruding muzzles, and the fact that they do not habitually make and use tools.

Man, however, is not descended from the apes as we know them today. Rather, both man and apes evolved from a varied group of large primates which lived in Europe, Africa, and southern Asia during the Oligocene, Miocene, and Pliocene periods. These creatures, the Dryopithecines, did not walk upright, make tools, or, as far as we know, talk. They were more apelike than manlike, but they had not yet developed all of the extreme characteristics of the modern apes. Some of the Dryopithecines lived in the trees, others probably on the ground. Most of their fossil remains are mere fragments, mainly teeth, which range from very apelike types to some that are rather similar to man's. The few whole or fragmentary skulls which have been recovered indicate that the very rugged bony superstructure of the modern apes had not yet been developed.

Almost all of the fossils that can be identified as human belong to the Quaternary period which, on present evidence, has lasted for about 2 million years. At least the latter half of this period has been abnormal in comparison with the Tertiary. It has been marked by repeated fluctuations in thermal levels, atmospheric circulation, and rainfall; advance and retreat of great continental glaciers; rise and fall of sea level; intensive mountain building; and rapid changes in faunas through extinction and the evolution of new species.

The Quaternary is divided into two epochs, and the earlier of these can be further subdivided in various ways. The major divisions that we will be

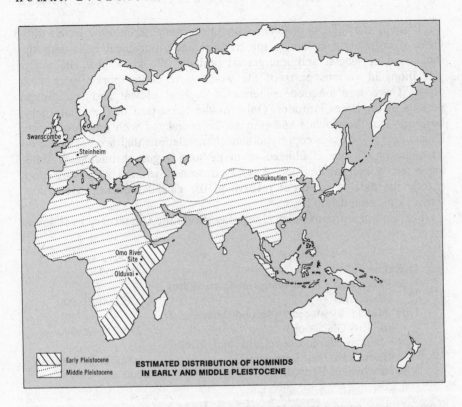

Swanscombe
Steinheim
Choukoutien
Omo River Site
Olduvai

Early Pleistocene
Middle Pleistocene

ESTIMATED DISTRIBUTION OF HOMINIDS
IN EARLY AND MIDDLE PLEISTOCENE

dealing with are the Villafranchian or Early Pleistocene (about 2,000,000 to 600,000 years ago), the Middle and Late Pleistocene (about 600,000 to 10,000 years ago), and the Holocene (the last 10,000 years).

The Quaternary begins with the appearance of fossils of the genera *Equus, Bos,* and *Elephas* (true horses, cattle, and elephants). Throughout the Villafranchian these and other new species coexisted with a number of older animals that had survived from the Pliocene and, in Africa, with primitive forms of man. There were climatic fluctuations and several periods of continental glaciation during Villafranchian times, but since little is known about them, the Villafranchian is usually treated as a single long epoch, without subdivisions.

During the Middle and Late Pleistocene there were four major periods of glaciation, separated by three long periods when the ice sheets retreated and possibly disappeared altogether. We are now in the early stages of a fourth interglacial period, which is distinguished geologically as the Holocene Epoch. The continental glaciers are still with us, though, for they continue to cover both Greenland and Antarctica.

Perhaps the biggest problem with Quaternary chronology is the difficulty of correlating events in the tropical and subtropical belts with the succession of glacial and interglacial periods. We know that the major glaciations in various parts of the world were contemporary with each other. There is also good evidence of cyclical pluvial and interpluvial periods in the lower latitudes. Only for the latest part of the Quaternary, however, can the glacials and pluvials be correlated with any confidence. Unless one wishes to accept hypothetical correlations that are not based on adequate proof, one is obliged to make such vague chronological statements as "Villafranchian" or "Late Pleistocene," without specifying more exactly the date of an event relative to the glacial sequence. Here, too, science still has much to learn.

For the sake of convenience, we may divide the Quaternary as follows:

Epoch	Years Ago
Holocene	10,000–0
Late Pleistocene (Third Interglacial and Würm Glaciation)	95,000–10,000
Late Middle Pleistocene (Second Interglacial and Riss Glaciation)	275,000–95,000
Early Middle Pleistocene (Günz and Mindel Glaciations, First Interglacial)	600,000–275,000
Villafranchian or Early Pleistocene	2,000,000–600,000

None of these dates except for those of the Holocene can be considered very exact. The further back in time one goes, the greater is the possibility of error. Some of the dates listed above may be in error by 200,000 or 300,000 years or more. Nevertheless, they seem to be the best possible estimates on the basis of the incomplete evidence with which we have to work.

When we talk about human evolution, we are dealing with two different kinds of processes: the evolution of the human body and the evolution of human behavior. The first of these, called *morphological evolution,* is a biological process which has been studied by physical anthropologists, geneticists, and human paleontologists. The second, *cultural evolution,* is a biosocial process that falls within the domain of archaeologists and cultural anthropologists. The two cannot, however, be fully separated. Each has exerted influence on the other, and both have obeyed the basic laws of evolution formulated by Darwin and his successors. Yet biological and cultural processes are different from each other, and the operation of natural selection is more easily seen in the biological than in the cultural sphere. It is nevertheless fruitful to view human behavior as adaptive, influenced by biological and environmental facts and shaping biological evolution. Behavior is not pure "culture."

As we peer back into the Pleistocene, it becomes progressively more difficult to be certain which fossils are those of men and which are those of apes. Eventually both blend in with the common Dryopithecine ancestors in such a way as to make impossible a decision on purely morphological grounds. Many fossils now recognized as clearly human were once the subject of intense debate. In order to avoid this problem, most anthropologists now use a behavioral, rather than a morphological, definition of man: *Man is the primate that habitually makes and uses tools.* With this definition, the classification of a fossil population as men or apes depends on the evidence (or lack of it) of associated tools, rather than on an assessment of the degree of physical similarity with one group or the other.

The earliest hominids are known collectively as Australopithecines, and comprise two major groups: *Australopithecus* and *Paranthropus*. All of the Australopithecines show a combination of manlike and apelike features. Their brains were small, near or within the range of brain size of the modern apes. They had well-developed muzzles, only slightly less protruding than those of a chimpanzee. On the other hand, they lacked the ape's fangs, and their dental structure was human (and modern) in almost every significant respect. *Australopithecus* walked erect, and *Paranthropus* probably did too. The principal differences between the two groups were in their size and ruggedness. *Australopithecus* was small, about the size of a modern chimpanzee, with a light body and a delicate skeleton. His skull showed only moderate development of apelike crests and ridges. *Paranthropus* was larger, perhaps the size of a gorilla, heavy-boned, with a very rugged bony superstructure on his skull.

All of the oldest hominid fossils—the only ones that can definitely be dated to the Late Pliocene or the Villafranchian—come from southern and eastern Africa. The oldest of them, from the Omo River in Ethiopia, are nearly 4 million years old and are the only known human fossils of Pliocene times. Still earlier fossils may be found some day, so we cannot say just how old "man" is. On the other hand, the concentration of early hominid finds in south and east Africa, and their absence from Pliocene and Villafranchian deposits elsewhere, makes it likely that it was precisely in that area that man evolved during Late Pliocene times.

No stone tools have yet been found in the early deposits of the Omo River. Nor have the numerous Australopithecine fossils from South Africa been found incontrovertibly associated with tools. In the latter case, there is reason to believe that the sites where their remains occur were not the places where they lived, but rather the dens of hyenas that had dragged in the bones of Australopithecines and other animals. Under such circumstances, one cannot expect to find men and tools in the same place!

Clearer evidence of the human character of at least some of the Australopithecines comes from Olduvai Gorge in Tanganyika. Here the skeletal remains of two different types of hominids have been found together in a level dated by the potassium-argon method at about 1,750,000 years ago, very early in the Villafranchian. The same level contains crude choppers roughly chipped from small cobbles. The classification of these remains has been the subject of considerable debate, some students claiming that they are Australopithecines and others that one of them represents a more advanced form of man. The weight of evidence, however, favors the interpretation that they are somewhat extreme forms of *Paranthropus* and *Australopithecus*. It might be assumed that, because *Australopithecus* is the more "modern" and "evolved" of the two, it was he who fashioned the tools. If so, *Paranthropus* may have furnished part of his diet. There is no direct evidence to substantiate such a conclusion, though, and it is possible that both groups made tools or even that they were made only by *Paranthropus*.

Once tools were regularly made and used, they became a factor in human evolution, setting limits to behavior and opening new possibilities in both the organic and the behavioral spheres. Primates that had not learned to use tools evolved through the normal processes of natural selection, those better adapted to their specific environments producing (on the average) more offspring and thus multiplying their adaptive characteristics in the population. With the advent of toolmaking, adaptation to the *behavioral* environment assumed an increased importance. The well-adapted Australopithecines, both as individuals and as communities, were those whose manual dexterity permitted them to make and use the cobble choppers, and whose upright posture left their hands free to employ them. Tools thus influenced the evolution of the flexible human thumb and gave meaning to the human posture—if, indeed, they were not responsible for the original evolution of that posture.

Australopithecus and *Paranthropus* coexisted throughout Villafranchian times, and *Paranthropus* may have survived into the early Middle Pleistocene. In a general sense, the ancestry of modern man can be found among the Australopithecines. If the two forms were capable of interbreeding, both may lie at the root of man's family tree. If not, *Australopithecus* almost certainly merits that honor.

Early in the Middle Pleistocene, the hominids spread out from tropical Africa, moving northward to North Africa and Europe and eastward across southern Asia as far as China. Most of the Middle Pleistocene fossils represent more evolved forms intermediate between the Australopithecines and modern man. The earlier fossils in this group belong to an evolutionary stage known as *Pithecanthropus* or *Homo erectus*. Representatives of this stage have been found in Java, China, and northern Africa. These individuals were larger than *Australopithecus,* smaller than *Paranthropus;* their brains were intermediate in size between those of the Australopithecines and of modern man; their muzzles and the bony superstructure of their skulls were more reduced than in the older forms, though the brow ridges and occipital crests were still very massive.

The largest group of *Pithecanthropus* fossils so far discovered was excavated in the 1930's at the famous Choukoutien caves in northern China. This site is important not only because of the skeletal material found there, but also because it yielded significant information about the behavior of its inhabitants. They were successful hunters, especially of deer; they used fire; and they engaged in that eminently human activity, cannibalism. *Pithecanthropus* bones were scattered through the deposit with the bones of the animals they hunted, and like the latter, the long bones had been split and the skull bases broken out for the extraction of marrow and brains. There is no indication that they practiced ritual cannibalism, like later and more evolved men, but it does seem that the Chinese *Pithecanthropus* ate their dead rather than bury them.

The stone tools discovered at Choukoutien were crudely made choppers and simple flakes, little different from the Villafranchian tools of Africa. It is likely that they were typical of *Pithecanthropus'* tools throughout most of the early Middle Pleistocene world. In North Africa the lithic assemblage includes some tools typical of the late Middle Pleistocene, but they are not well dated, so it is not clear whether they represent a late survival of *Pithecanthropus* or an early beginning of the new tool forms. In general, the early Middle Pleistocene is a time for which we know a good deal about human skeletal remains, but little about the stone tools that were being made and used.

Exactly the reverse is true for the late Middle Pleistocene. The world's museums are full of artifacts of this period. Numerous archaeological sites are known, and several different cultural traditions have been recognized and studied in detail. Yet with the probable exception of a few *Pithecanthropus* survivals in Java and North Africa, only two human fossils have been discovered which can be securely dated to late Middle Pleistocene times. These are the Steinheim skull from Germany and the Swanscombe skull from England. Little can be concluded from so small a sample, because we do not know how typical these two individuals were. Both had brains within the size range of modern man, and both show a combination of modern and primitive characteristics. The Swanscombe specimen consists of only the back and one side of the brain case; except for the great thickness of the bone, it is high-vaulted and modern in all significant respects and is often classified as *Homo sapiens*. However, the more complete Steinheim skull shows the same high vaulting and related features of the skull cap, but its massive face and heavily developed brow ridges are beyond the range of modern variation.

If these two skulls tell us little about late Middle Pleistocene man, his artifacts and habitation sites are much more informative. They are distributed throughout Africa, western and southern Europe (extending into Germany), southern Asia (the Arab countries, India, and China), and parts of Indonesia. There is some evidence that man had by then adapted to quite different environments. The African and Asian sites are concentrated in grasslands and river valleys, whereas the European sites are mostly found in zones that were covered by deciduous forest. Most of the late Middle Pleistocene sites consist of specimens redeposited in river gravels, but a few intact habitation sites have been found in Africa. The living floors of these sites, which were probably places where men paused during their seasonal food quest, give no evidence of the construction of shelters. They are all very small and could not have been occupied by more than a few families. As in the case of Choukoutien, they provide evidence of the hunting of many kinds of animals.

Three different late Middle Pleistocene tool traditions are generally recognized by archaeologists. The *Chopper/Chopping-tool tradition* of eastern Asia continued the Early Pleistocene tradition of crude choppers and simple flake tools. The *Flake tradition,* found in parts of western Europe and northern Africa, was not greatly different, but laid greater emphasis on small cutting and scraping tools rather than on heavy-duty chopping tools. The *Biface tradition* was by far the most important, widespread, and technologically sophisticated of the three. It spread throughout Africa, western and southern Europe, and southern Asia as far as India. The most typical tools, from which the tradition derives its name, were large pointed "hand axes" chipped on both faces. During the early Abbevillean phase of the Biface tradition, the hand axes were crudely made and accompanied only by simple flake tools, not really very different from those of the Flake and Chopper/Chopping-tool traditions. Chipping techniques were equally crude, and assemblages differed only in the shape of their heavy-duty tools and in the degree of their emphasis on flake tools. The later Acheulean phase, however, saw an increasing refinement of the hand axes and the successive addition of new tool forms and techniques. By the time of the Second Interglacial, the hand axes were being delicately shaped with wooden or bone batons. With them are found cleavers (straight-edged cutting tools) and flake tools made by the complex Levallois technique. The production of Acheulean tools involved not only functional considerations, but also an aesthetic element.

The coexistence of the sophisticated Acheulean industry with the simpler traditions raises a number of problems. Choppers and flake tools could have been made by a hand no more dexterous than that of an ape, while Acheulean technology required the fully opposable human thumb. But this need not mean that the different traditions were produced by fundamentally different kinds of men. The Swanscombe skull, with its many modern characteristics, was associated with Acheulean tools, but a slightly earlier phase of the Biface tradition was found with *Pithecanthropus* remains in Algeria. The Steinheim skull—far more modern than *Pithecanthropus*—was found with tools of the Flake tradition. Scant as the evidence is, it suggests that any of the major kinds of man was capable of producing any of the Middle Pleistocene tools.

Some authorities hold that variations in the late Middle Pleistocene tool kits reflect adaptations to different environments and ways of getting food. The Biface sites of Europe are concentrated in areas that were forested, while the Flake tradition sites are found beyond the limits of the Pleistocene forest, often near the sea. Men living in the temperate forests of Europe had resources quite different from those who lived along the shore, or on the African grasslands, or in the river valleys of eastern Asia. The exploitation of different food supplies would require different tools, and this fact is probably sufficient to explain most of the diversity of Middle Pleistocene stone tools.

This brings us to the beginning of the Late Pleistocene, some 95,000 years ago. By that time, as we have seen, the primitive Australopithecines had evolved into men with many of the characteristics of today's *Homo sapiens*. The upright posture, human dentition, and the human thumb had evolved by the beginning of the Villafranchian. Thereafter, evolution largely took the form of increasing brain size and complexity, reduction of the muzzle and the bony superstructure of the skull, and the gradual development of distinctly human behavior patterns. Stone tools are attested for the Villafranchian, controlled fire and cannibalism for the early Middle Pleistocene. The late Middle Pleistocene saw considerable refinement of lithic technology. The less tangible aspects of culture are not preserved among the material remains of the past, but it seems certain that other peculiarly human behavior patterns were also established during this time, if not earlier. One of these is language, without which the expanding cultural inventory could not have been passed on from generation to generation. Another is family organization, with its permanent association of males and females in small food-getting and child-rearing units. This reorganization of society also implies evolution from the narrowly restricted estrus cycle of the ape to the year-round sexual activity of the human female, because the permanent association of the family is based on the regular availability of the wife.

Outside of Africa, these early men occupied only a small part of the Old World, and they had not yet reached the Americas, Oceania, or Australia. Population was thin and irregularly distributed. The early men were hunters, using wooden spears and probably throwing sticks (as represented by the very few nonlithic artifacts found in Middle Pleistocene sites). Since they caught herd animals, they must have employed cooperative hunting techniques. They probably exploited a wide variety of plant foods, and their relative dependence on meat and plants undoubtedly varied according to the locally available resources. No more than a few households lived together, and they moved their camps frequently—probably seasonally—in order to take advantage of different food resources.

As we have seen, the Swanscombe and Steinheim skulls have many modern characteristics, including brains as large as those of many of today's men. They are unique specimens, however, and there is no way of knowing whether they are representative of whole late Middle Pleistocene populations. The Late Pleistocene, on the other hand, is represented by a large sample of human fossils, including many which undeniably belong to the species of modern man, *Homo sapiens*.

Fossil men are always the subjects of debate and divergent classifications. It is nearly impossible to get general agreement on the status of any given specimen or population. As a result, it would be very difficult to say when and where *Homo sapiens* first appeared. The principal difficulty is the "Neanderthal problem."

Neanderthal man proper, sometimes called "classic" Neanderthal, is represented by a group of fossils found in Europe, North Africa, and the Near East, all of them dating to the early part of the Würm glaciation. The Neanderthals were short men with extremely rugged skeletons and with a number of nonmodern specializations of the skull, teeth, and mandible, but with brains larger than the modern average. The name Neanderthal (sometimes "progressive" Neanderthal) is also usually applied to the Steinheim skull, to the European fossil population of the Third Interglacial, and to a number of non-"classic" European and Near Eastern fossils of early Würm times, all of which combine some Neanderthal features with others typical of more modern types. Still more distantly, one sometimes finds the more primitive Late Pleistocene men of Africa and eastern Asia identified as Neanderthals.

If there is no consensus in the definition of Neanderthal man, there is still less agreement as to his place in human evolution. For some anthropologists, Neanderthal man is a separate species, an extinct and sterile side branch of man's family tree. For others, he is a major stage in the evolution of humans from *Australopithecus* and *Pithecanthropus* to *Homo sapiens*.

Still others view him as no more than a racial variant of *Homo sapiens,* extinct as a population but contributing, along with other Late Pleistocene races, to the genetic make-up of today's populations. The last view seems most likely because it agrees best with the archaeological evidence and with modern evolutionary theory. If it is correct, all of the Late Pleistocene fossils were *Homo sapiens* and Steinheim and Swanscombe probably were too.

If the classificatory problems remain knotty, the archaeological facts are relatively clear. Most of the fossil remains of the Third Interglacial and of the first Würm stage are Neanderthals, Neanderthaloids, or other relatively rugged forms, primitive looking but with large brains and many modern characteristics. Two fragmentary skulls from Fontéchevade in France, associated with Flake tradition tools and dated to the Third Interglacial, seem modern in almost every significant respect.

Most of the Third Interglacial tool traditions represent continuations and modifications of the Biface and Flake traditions. In Europe and the Near East, however, a new lithic technology evolved, and many significant new kinds of behavior are evident in the archaeological record. Neanderthal man made tools characterized by Levallois and other special chipping techniques and by a number of small forms including points which could have been hafted to spears. Smooth-edged scrapers, common in Neanderthal sites, suggest the preparation of skins and hence probably the manufacture of clothing. We may assume that it was this invention that permitted Neanderthal man to penetrate into the cold country of central Asia as far as Uzbekistan. He often lived in caves and, for the first time in human history, buried his dead rather than eat them or leave them exposed to the elements. It has been argued that the practice of burial implies a conception of an afterlife. If this is true, then we find here the first evidence of religious beliefs and practices.

Some time between 30,000 and 40,000 years ago, completely modern men began to replace the Neanderthals and their relatives. The process of replacement has been more a subject of speculation than of serious study, but some general statements can be made about it. The modern types probably evolved over a fairly broad area rather than in some delimited locality. Apparently they flourished because they developed a more efficient food economy and consequently increased in number, rather than because of any innate physical superiority. They did not simply drive out or kill off the Neanderthals and other races; they also interbred with them. The earlier population patterns disappeared because they represented a minority contribution to the new gene pools. Taking the inhabited world as a whole, the replacement took place gradually, so that Neanderthal-like men may have lasted almost to the end of the Pleistocene in certain regions.

Throughout Europe, North Africa, and southern Asia, the new peoples carried with them a new kind of culture known as Upper Paleolithic. Their stone artifacts were made on the long, narrow, parallel-sided flakes known as blades, and they included many highly specialized tools and weapons. Bone and antler also became popular in the manufacture of artifacts. Spears were now definitely tipped with stone and bone points. Spear-throwers, harpoons, and traps made hunting more efficient. There is some evidence suggesting that a lunar calendar was used to keep track of the seasonal movements of game. It also seems that Upper Paleolithic men practiced encircling techniques, joining together to surround herds and drive them off cliffs. The efficiency of these new hunting techniques is eloquently attested by the enormous quantities of animal bones found in Upper Paleolithic archaeological sites.

The Upper Paleolithic also provides the earliest evidence of the construction of artificial shelters. House floors excavated in Czechoslovakia and southern Russia show that when Upper Paleolithic man was not living in caves he erected tents of considerable size. Perhaps the most significant aspect of these sites is that they show that several households lived together in a single encampment.

Another remarkable feature of Upper Paleolithic culture was its highly developed art. Aesthetic activities in earlier periods seem to have been limited to the refinement of the visual qualities of stone tools. In Upper Paleolithic Europe, however, we find the development of painting, sculpture, and personal ornament. The most famous artworks are the cave paintings of France and Spain. Bison, mammoths, horses, deer, and other game animals are the most common subjects, but there are also a few human portrayals (including one of a dancer wearing a deer-head mask) and some possibly symbolic geometric figures. Painting styles underwent a gradual evolution during Upper Paleolithic times, culminating in the beautiful realistic paintings of the Magdalenian culture at the very end of the Pleistocene. These cave paintings were long dismissed as of interest only to the archaeologist, but nowadays the Magdalenian paintings are generally recognized as being among the greatest works of art that man has produced.

Upper Paleolithic sculpture was generally executed in bone or ivory. The pieces are all quite small, and range from delicate engravings to three-dimensional figures. As with the paintings, the primary interest was in animal figures. It is the little female figurines, however, that have captured the attention of archaeologists and laymen alike. These carvings, the "Venuses," show women with greatly exaggerated breasts, bellies, and buttocks. The sculptors took so little interest in the face that the head is often no more than a featureless blob.

The cave paintings, engravings, and carvings of animals were apparently intended as hunting magic—"art for meat's sake," as the great anthropologist E. A. Hooton put it. Similarly, the Venus figures are considered to be the tangible reflections of household fertility cults, and the common practice of painting and ornamenting the dead before burial has been related to beliefs about an afterlife. There is, of course, no way of proving these hypotheses. In any case, his development of such sophisticated art and the special care he gave the dead indicate that Upper Paleolithic man enjoyed a much richer spiritual life than any of his predecessors.

The last great expansion of the human world took place during the Late Pleistocene. Man moved southeast into Australia and northward into Siberia. From Siberia he crossed the Bering Strait on the land bridge that existed during glacial times. Eastern Siberia and Alaska were free of glaciation and hence open to migration, and corridors southward through Canada opened up periodically when the glaciers retreated temporarily. We cannot yet date this first migration to the New World with any precision, but before the end of the Pleistocene man had occupied the unglaciated portions of Canada and the United States and had moved southward into large parts of South America.

With the end of the Pleistocene, about 10,000 years ago, the world's environments underwent many drastic changes. Thermal levels rose, the glaciers retreated, the seas rose rapidly, and many well-watered areas began to dry out. With the diminution of the great Pleistocene grasslands, the environments of the lower latitudes became more diversified. At the same time, many of the large game animals became extinct. Herds still roamed the remaining grasslands—zebra and antelope on the African savanna, bison on the North American plains, guanaco on the Argentine pampas—but elsewhere the remaining species of large mammals became comparatively scarce.

In adapting to the diversified and impoverished environments, men in different regions developed many new and different cultures. Compared with those of the Pleistocene, the Holocene cultures displayed far more regional differentiation and changed far more rapidly. Of the many innovations of the Postglacial epoch, two are particularly important because they have revolutionized the life of almost all humanity. These are plant cultivation and animal husbandry. These new techniques made possible sedentary year-round settlements and led to the growth of large, dense populations and of the urban, stratified, specialized, politically organized societies that we call civilizations.

Cultivation and animal husbandry developed separately in at least two broad areas: southern Asia from Mesopotamia to China, and America from Mexico to Peru. The principal cultivated plants in the nuclear area of the Old World were wheat, barley, and (in the Far East) rice; the first domesticated animals were cattle, sheep, goats, and pigs. In the New World the main plants were maize, beans, potatoes, and manioc. The latter two, as well as the domestic llama, alpaca, and guinea pig, were restricted to South America.

All available evidence points to the Near East as the area where these revolutionary developments first began. The natural habitats of the wild plants and animals were in the hills surrounding the Fertile Crescent on the north and east. The earliest known remains of domestic species, as well as the earliest large sedentary settlements based on agriculture, have been found in Israel, Syria, Turkey, Iraq, and Iran, with a very early extension westward to Greece. Sheep were domesticated in northern Iraq not long after 9000 B.C., wheat and barley in southwestern Iran by 7000 B.C. The cereals were probably cultivated still earlier in the western part of the area, for a substantial walled town was built at Jericho Oasis in the Jordan Valley about 7000 B.C., and it is almost impossible that so large a settlement could have existed in the Palestinian desert without an agricultural base.

In the New World the first centers of cultivation seem to have been in the highlands of Mexico, where squash was being grown before 5000 B.C. and maize, beans, and other plants by shortly after that date. Though these plants diffused southward to Peru at an early date, the South American staples (potatoes in the Andes and manioc in the tropical lowlands) and domestic animals are not known until after about 2000 B.C.

With the exception of manioc and perhaps rice (neither of which was among the earliest cultigens), the major cultivated plants and domestic animals of both the Old and New Worlds were derived from wild ancestors adapted to highlands environments. In both areas the earliest farmers were nomadic food gatherers in semiarid areas who relied on both wild grains and hunting, but who also exploited many other resources in order to survive. Within the nuclear highlands areas cultivation did not have any immediate profound effects on the way of life. The pattern of seasonal migration continued for a long time. The new crops served as no more than supplements to the diet of wild foods. It was when the cultigens were carried into new environments, especially lowlands areas, that they stimulated new experiments in agriculture, provided the economic base for rapid population growth, and spurred the development of towns and cities.

For Further Reading

Bordes, François, *The Old Stone Age.*
Clark, Grahame, *World Prehistory.*

The Ancient Near East

5   Mesopotamia

History begins in the Near East. As we have seen, the cradle of humanity lies probably elsewhere, but the historian's narrative cannot begin at the creation of the first Adam. The slow biological emergence of *Homo sapiens,* the sort of human being we are, precedes history, and the greater part of the existence of *Homo sapiens* also ran before the beginning of history. The essential difference between "prehistory" and "history" is mental. "History" means the conscious and intentional remembrance of things past, in a living tradition transmitted from one generation to another. For this there must be some continuous organization, be it the family of the chieftain in the beginning, or the school today, which has reason to care for the Past of the group and has the capacity for transmitting the historical tradition to future generations. History exists only in a persisting society which needs history to persist.

But a continuous and persisting society was late in coming. It came into being first in the Near East, and thus the historical tradition of Babylon and Egypt became the fountainhead of our historical memory. Many of our fairy tales may go back to the imagination of men who lived long before the foundation of Babylon or in the regions, such as north Europe, which remained outside the historical tradition that began in the Near East. But no living memory links us with the inventors of fire, with the masters who some 15,000 years ago painted walls of caves in France and in the Ural Mountains, or with the builders who, perhaps about 2000 B.C., began to erect the still-standing monoliths at Stonehenge in England. These men left signs, and they knew what those signs meant, but they left no written words, and their message cannot be clearly understood by us.

The pyramids, however, not only astonished every generation which succeeded their builders, but every new generation also learned that these gigantic edifices were royal tombs; Cheops, the name of the Pharaoh of the Great Pyramid, was known to the Greek historian Herodotus, who lived

CHRONOLOGY

B.C.		
	10,000	Wooden reaping knives set with flint blades used in Palestine
	9000	End of the Ice Age; domesticated sheep in the North Tigris valley
	7700–5700	Çatal Huyuk in Turkey; obsidian mined for tools; fertility cult indicates use of domesticated cattle
	7500	Extensive settlement at Jericho, weaving, fortification, remains of cultivated cereals
	7000	Pottery begins
	6500	Copper used in Turkey for trinkets; a dugout canoe used in Holland
	6000	Farming in Macedonia, pottery plentiful
	5000	Use of copper in Mesopotamia begins
	3300	Writing begins in Sumer; wheeled vehicles and wheel-made pottery, sailboats, and animal-drawn plows in Sumer; agriculture reaches Ireland
	3100	Invention of hieroglyphic writing in Egypt
	3000	Sumerian fashions prevalent in Ashur
	2800	Akkadian conquest of the Diyala region
	2700	Agriculture reaches China; royal inscriptions appear in Sumer; Sumerian script used in Akkad; Sumerian fashions prevalent in Mari
	2500	Writing in Mari (Sumerian script); keeping of daily accounts in Sumer; the pyramids completed
	2400	Writing in Assyria (Sumerian script)
	2350	Sargon I of Agade, first known empire
	2300	Copper common in Sumer; writing in the Indus Valley (local script)
	2250	Fall of the dynasty of Sargon
	2100–2000	Supremacy of Ur in lower Mesopotamia
	2100	The laws of Ur-Nammu of Ur, the earliest preserved lawbook
	1800	Assyrian temple built for a Sumerian god (Enlil)
	1750	Hammurabi of Babylon rules most of Mesopotamia; financial transactions in Sumer and Addad now commonly in silver
	1600	Fall of the dynasty of Hammurabi

midway between his time and our own. The ancient Egyptian language can still be heard daily in the Coptic churches, and the word "Coptic," through the Greek word *Aiguptos,* comes from the Egyptian name of Memphis, the first capital of the land on the Nile. "Babylon" has been a byword for four millennia, and some of the first pages of the Bible echo the voices of story tellers who instructed or amused their audiences on the banks of the Euphrates 5,000 years ago. For this reason, the archaeologists' discoveries of a forgotten kingdom or of an unknown language in the Near East fall within the scheme of our historical tradition. For the same reason, in the Near East, history imperceptibly leads back to prehistory. Therefore the historian has to go back to the beginning of the stable societies in the Near East where the idea of history was born.

As long as *Homo sapiens,* like his near-man ancestors and predecessors, was solely hunter, fisher, and collector of wild fruits and vegetables, there could be no persisting society. Like the other predatory beasts, man needed an enormous space for maintenance. English prehistorians believe that at this stage the total population of England and Wales amounted to no more than three or four thousand souls. This sparse population consisted of very small groups, a few families living together. To the present day the food-collecting bands in the Amazon basin comprise about twenty persons each, including children. Such groups were unstable biologically and socially. It appears from skeletal remains that two-thirds of the newborn died as babies, that at least a third of those who survived infancy died before the procreative age, and that almost all adults died before fifty. Like wild animals, men rarely lived beyond the age of fecundity.

This brevity of human life, together with a very high infant mortality (perhaps 75 per cent), casts doubt on the common explanation of the origin of agriculture as a result of the need of an increasing population. Perhaps food production should be connected with the domestication of animals, which must often have been attempted before it eventually succeeded. Dogs may have been tamed already by hunters in the food-gathering period. The domesticated sheep seems to have been known east of the upper Tigris about 9000. But the relation of the domestication of animals to that of cereals is enigmatic, and the latter remains a problem. Cultivation of cereals could originate only in a territory where these plants grew wild and man already reaped them. Why should he sweat to cultivate what he could get without any preparatory work?

Abel, the shepherd, was a child of nature. The farmer forces nature, and the history of our civilization begins with Cain, the first farmer. Agriculture, whatever its origins, made a stable society both possible and necessary. Husbandry not only provided more food and did it more reliably, but above all it furnished a sort of food, grain, which could be stored in pits for a long time to tide the society over those months when nothing else was available. Thus agriculture became and remained the foundation of civilized life.

The change to agriculture meant also a mental change. Man began to correct nature, and he did so with his eye on the future. Every *techne,* as Aristotle says, requires the idea of a result before the material realization of that result can be achieved. The men who learned to fell trees in the forests which began to cover the temperate regions of the Northern Hemisphere after the Ice Age, say after 9000, were no less ingenious than the first agriculturalists. In a modern experiment more than one hundred birch trees were felled with one polished stone ax, made and sharpened in Denmark about 4,000 years ago. However, the agriculturalist worked not for today, nor even for tomorrow, but for a distant and uncertain objective which was very remote when he planted a tree. The future had become for him a far-off yet foreseeable time. Symmetrically, the Past became valuable. Today was now a station on the long road from the Past to the Future.

The archaeological evidence, as well as the distribution of wild species of the earliest known domesticated plants and animals, points to the region from Iran to Palestine as the laboratory of the incipient agriculture and, thus, the birthplace of stable society and historical memory. It was a long process which probably began in the ninth millennium, of selection of seeds, of learning the elements of sowing, tending, and reaping cereals, of inventing and improving tools. For instance, the reaping knife set with flint blades was used in Palestine about 10,000, if only for cutting wild grass. The earliest known remains of cultivated cereals date from the eighth millennium: einkorn and emmer, two varieties of wheat which are no longer cultivated, and a type of barley. Our bread wheat is first attested somewhat later in Asia Minor. Goats and, probably, pigs were soon added to farm animals bred by man. At Çatal Huyuk in central Turkey, by the middle of the seventh millennium, people were worshiping a fertility goddess whom they represented in the act of giving birth to a man, a bull, and a ram.

We do not know why agriculture began in the Near East, rather than elsewhere, but it did so, and from here the art of farming spread to the four corners of the world, reaching Ireland by 3500 and China in the third millennium. For the civilized peoples of the Near East, nomads were now barbarians "who knew no grain."

The increased supply of food made the expansion of mankind possible. In the comparatively large and stable settlements of the new age—Çatal Huyuk was inhabited without interruption for at least 2,000 years until its destruction about 5700—men went on to discover new components of

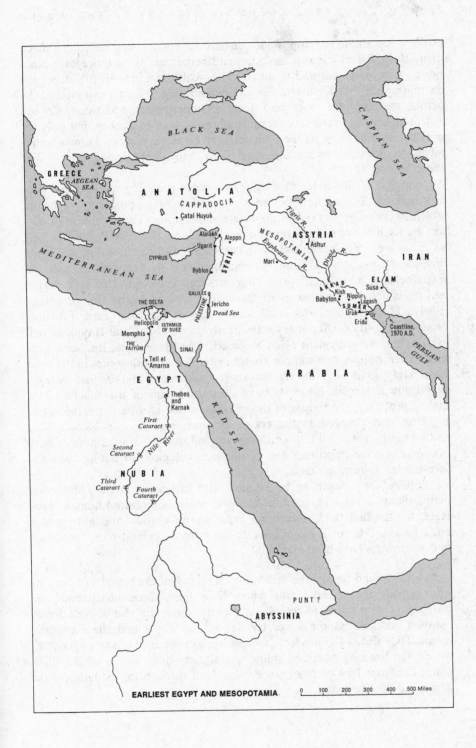

EARLIEST EGYPT AND MESOPOTAMIA

0   100   200   300   400   500 Miles

civilized life and to develop chance discoveries (which may have been made many times before) into techniques, and perpetuate them by regular practice as part of the cultural tradition. The wealth of Çatal Huyuk depended on mining the black obsidian in the neighboring volcanic mountains. As before, weapons and tools were made of stone, bones, and wood. Copper was used already in the seventh millennium, at least in Turkey, but only for trinkets. In Palestine we find the earliest known extensive human settlement—at Jericho, where the inhabitants had domesticated barley and sheep before 7000.

The first of the major new techniques were probably weaving and pottery making. The earliest known woven fabric was apparently of hemp, which began to be worked in the eighth millennium. The invention of pottery by itself is not so important; men could use stone vessels, baskets, and so on, as well. Yet, potter's clay—a combination of earth, water, and some ingredient (grit, straw) to prevent cracking—was the first artificial material manufactured by man. Its production required know-how. To make a pot and bake it hard required more know-how. Consequently, the art spread slowly. The invention was made somewhere in the Near East, probably around 7000. By 6000 pottery was already plentiful at Çatal Huyuk as well as at a farming settlement (Nea Nicomedia) in Macedonia. But some centuries later, pottery was still not known in Jericho and other sites in the Near East. Only gradually, during the sixth millennium, did its use become practically universal. Since styles of decoration and of manufacture (the make-up of clay, the shapes of the vessels) varied at different manufacturing sites and changed in the course of time, and since potsherds were neither easily destroyed nor worth carrying off, the remains of pottery have become the most important tool of the archaeologists for dating finds and ascertaining cultural contacts.

Pottery soon began to be painted with crescents, circles, and other motifs. Some designs imitated basketwork, others reproduced human faces. Here, for the first time, decoration expresses an abstract thought: though not a basket, this pot is *like* a basket. The purpose behind such decoration may sometimes have been magical.

In the second half of the fifth millennium, when the benefits of farming were already recognized in the whole Near East, some adventurous and imaginative men dared to colonize a country about the size of New Jersey between and around the lower courses of the Tigris and the Euphrates rivers. They did not come from the piedmont zone in the north (Assyria) which, fertilized by bountiful rains, was already tilled in the sixth millennium, but from Iran or from the Persian Gulf through the estuaries of the Tigris and the Euphrates.

We do not know who these pioneers were. Their neighbors in the north called them Sumerians; they called themselves "the dark-headed" and designated their country simply as "the land." Skeletal remains show that most inhabitants of Sumer were heavily boned, short men with long and narrow heads. Yet their sculptors represented them as round-headed. Their agglutinative language is not related to any other known tongue. Many geographical names in Sumer as well as many words relating to farming and other skills appear to have been borrowed by the Sumerians from some other language, perhaps that of a preceding wave of immigrants.

Sumer was a flat land of brown dust and mud, swept by stormy winds (the Babylonians believed that the sky had been forced apart from the earth by the wind) and devastated by unpredictable inundations of the twin rivers. In Mesopotamia the flood, which punishes sinful men, was first experience and then myth.

The first settlements of the colonists were huts in marshes alongside watercourses of the lower Euphrates. A Babylonian myth recalls how, in the primordial time, a god constructed a reed frame on the face of the waters and, pouring mud on it, made the floor of a hut. Had the Sumerians failed, they would have remained marsh dwellers like the present inhabitants of the same swamps, who still live in reed huts where the miry floor often oozes water at every step.

Through relentless toil guided by imagination, the Sumerians slowly transformed their perilous land into one of milk and grain, of date palms and sesame herbs. A Sumerian myth preserves a memory of the introduction of cereals from the eastern mountains. But in Sumer the poor wild barley became our barley which bears six rows. Dates, which are very nutritive, were the poor man's stock food in Mesopotamia. The exploitation of date palms demands knowledge of artificial pollination and also the gift of anticipatory patience. The farmer, who erected a mud wall around his trees, had to tend them five long years before they began to yield fruit.

The land had no stone and no metals. By firing clay at a temperature of 1,200 degrees the Sumerians fabricated clay blades which could be used as sickles. Happily, their alluvial plain required no water-raising devices.

The farmer, according to a Sumerian myth, was "a man of dikes and canals." He did not depend on rain, therefore he did not fear drought: as the modern experience of the Near East shows, he could feed ten times as many people as the farmer on an equal plot in the lands dependent on rain. The canals served as waterways and fishpounds; they watered palm groves and rich grasslands which furnished feed for sheep and cattle, and grain fields of fabulous fertility which could be reaped thrice a year. Herodotus heard that in Babylonia grain yielded two and three hundredfold. Barley production made possible feeding of sheep and cattle during the unbearably hot summer. The crop of cereals came in the spring and that of dates in the fall. With the products of their husbandry the Sumerians paid for the raw materials which were wanting in Sumer. In a Sumerian saga, a king of old gives grain to a ruler in Iran, but demands in return precious metals, gems, and building stone for the temple of his goddess.

Eridu, the southernmost city of Sumer, "situated on the shore of the sea" (the Persian Gulf), was also according to tradition the earliest; its foundation antedated the end of the fifth millennium. The first Sumerian cities were small mud settlements of 15 to 20 acres each. Soon house walls were made of mud bricks joined by bitumen. As the Book of Genesis says of Babylonia: "They had bricks for stone and slime had they for mortar." When the settlers became richer, they built shrines on platforms made waterproof with bitumen. Raised higher and higher, the terraced, multi-storied temple towers appear in the Bible as "the tower of Babel" challenging the heavens. As with medieval cathedrals, the Sumerian temples, now separated by enclosing walls, dominated the city and proclaimed its power and wealth.

In this age of the first cathedrals, probably around 3300, the Sumerians made their greatest contribution to the advance of civilization: the invention of writing. Many primitive peoples, such as the American Indians, have used pictures to convey messages, for instance a call to a raid. But the pictures necessarily referred to some concrete and particular fact. The Sumerian writing differed qualitatively from pictographs of primitive peoples. The schematic designs of objects (head, fish, and so on) here denoted species, and the signs, thus, were valid permanently. The Sumerians had different words for woman and her pudendum. But in writing, the design of the latter stood for the idea of woman. The picture of a foot also came to connote such different words as "to stand," "to go," and "to bring."

Using such pictorial symbols, a scribe could record "52 head of cattle." More complex ideas were expressed in the fashion of rebus: the combination of signs of "woman" and "mountain" denoted a female slave. (Slaves were bought from the mountain peoples around the valley.) The system was adequate for its original purpose: business accounting of temples.

Then the Sumerians (and, two centuries or so later, the Egyptians) made the decisive advance. They realized that the same syllabic sounds could appear in different words, so that the picture of fish, *ha* in Sumerian, could also indicate the syllable *ha* in other words. Since the Sumerian language consisted of unchangeable and variously combined monosyllables, a syllable became a writing unit and Sumerian writing came to consist chiefly of two sorts of signs—syllable signs and word signs. The Sumerians, having no cheap writing material but clay, wrote with a reed stylus on unbaked clay tablets. The end of a reed can easily be pressed into soft clay so as to make a wedge-shaped mark. Thus, the originally pictorial signs were reduced to mere wedges and combinations of wedges. Accordingly, we call this script "cuneiform," from the Latin word *cuneus,* meaning wedge. A sun-dried clay tablet is not likely to be destroyed, so an enormous quantity of records (close to half a million tablets) has come down to us in the ruins of ancient buildings.

The Sumerians and the Egyptians were not alone in the forefront of civilization about 3000. During the third millennium, other "irrigation" societies flourished also on the Indus and east and south of the Caspian Sea, and societies based on the use of metals prospered in Palestine and Asia Minor. Pictographic script was employed in the Indus Valley between about 2300 and 1700. Did the city of Susa in Elam, which also had a pictographic script in the third millennium, invent syllabic writing? We do not know.

The historian should not confuse facts and their recording. The earliest written reference to a boat comes from Sumer. However, a dugout canoe discovered in Holland was constructed about 6250, that is about 3,000 years before the invention of writing in Sumer. In this way archaeological discoveries supplement and correct written sources. Yet these discoveries are accidental. The earliest extant musical instruments come from royal graves in Ur. This surely does not mean that men did not play harp, lyre, and oboe before 2500. Above all, objects are mute; their sign language has to be interpreted with the help of written sources. The use of writing changed the mode of historical memory. Thereafter, until our age of audio-vision, eye, and not ear, counted. What had not been written down was lost forever. According to a later story, Enmekar, a legendary ruler of Uruk, had to drink foul water in the nether world because he had not left a written record of his victories for the instruction of future generations.

Our narrative must willy-nilly follow the course of written tradition which links us with the Sumerians, the Egyptians, and their heirs while neglecting peoples who were often no less gifted in other respects, but remained illiterate.

By 3300 B.C., when writing began, the Sumerians already used sail-boats, wheeled vehicles, and animal-drawn plows. They invented the first industrial machine providing continuous rotary motion: the potter's wheel which spins the clay as the craftsman shapes it. From Sumer this device invaded the whole Old World. In the third millennium technological and economic advances continued unabated. The walls of Uruk, built about 2700, were 18 feet thick and had a circumference of about 6 miles. The enclosed area provided refuge to men and cattle from the whole territory of the city. Metal tools became common: copper and bronze objects have been found in about 15 per cent of the graves in Ur dating about 2800, and in

80 per cent of the graves of three centuries later. By 2300 a Sumerian could buy a copper ax for the price of two sheep. A yoke was invented for harnessing draft animals, and shadoofs for raising water helped the gardener. Sumerians had the means for distilling barley beer; they also knew how to prepare medicinal drugs and cosmetics, and they could manufacture imitation precious stones.

The artisans' skills, taught orally and by imitation, were immediately usable for tanning hides or carving a statue. Reading and writing by themselves enabled the learner only to read and write. The essential problem of liberal education was and is: What to read? Nevertheless, the method of writing was so complex that merely to learn to read and write demanded a long and arduous training. This divided a small "white-collar" class of scribes from the mass of ignorant workers. School and apprenticeship, head and hand, now became separated. As a Sumerian text says, a son sent to a scribal school did not learn to plow his father's field. The function of the scribal school was rather to furnish secretaries, accountants, revenue officers, and other functionaries. This self-perpetuating bureaucracy produced an enormous quantity of written tablets. From about 2500 there were daily accounts, and monthly and yearly summaries of these accounts which carefully distinguished between food given to pigs and that given to piglets, and so on. Toward the end of the third millennium the standard unit of work—a "man-day"—appeared for calculating payments to unskilled workers. Such "paper work" was essential for keeping a complex economy going. Without a scribe counting every bunch of vegetables that left the temple stores there would soon be no food for daily rations of cattle and of dairymen.

Having learned to read, the scribes began to write. Soon book catalogs were required and compiled. Royal inscriptions began about 2700; the earliest yet known lawbook was promulgated by Ur-Nammu, a king of Ur, about 2100. Between these two dates the scribes created the first literature, ranging from epics to love songs.

These books reinforced the cultural unity of Sumer: the same books were read in Ur and in Nippur. However, in a civilization where reading and writing were so rare that some kings boasted of their mastery of these skills, the oral lore must have remained of great importance in shaping men's minds. The story of creation recited during the Babylonian New Year's feast ends with the appeal to the faithful to recite and impart to their sons the fifty names of the god Marduk which expressed his various powers. Yet the oral traditional has been lost and, except for the buildings and works of art, we see Sumer only as it appears in the writings of the Sumerian scribes.

Sumer consisted of a dozen small cities with their respective territories.

From Eridu one could see Ur. United by language, custom, and common gods, united also in contempt for the barbarians of the western desert and of the mountains to the east, these independent cities were in eternal conflict one with another for meadows and water rights. As a proverb put it: "You go and take the field of the enemy; the enemy comes and takes your field."

Although each city was ruled by an absolute monarch, absolutism did not mean despotism. As Athens was the city of Athena, the boundaries and fields of Lagash belonged to the god Ningirsu to whom Lagash had been assigned by the supreme, fate-determining deities. The ruler served as a bailiff of the gods, bidden by them to promote the weal of the city. He represented the community before the deity, but not the deity before the community. He had to observe the recognized rules of behavior and compel recalcitrants to do the same. Maintaining justice in the land, he saw to it that children supported their aged parents and he supervised weights and measures. The rights of private property, the only sure foundation of civil liberty, were sacred. The king himself had to pay for the land he wanted. A little man no less than a magnate had his rightful place in the city. Men were created to toil for the gods, and the professions were usually hereditary. There were no estates in the body politic. Accordingly, the rulers proclaimed that powerful men should not oppress widows and orphans, nor should a "man of one shekel" fall a prey to a man of many shekels. Slaves, mostly prisoners of war, were mainly used as household servants.

Royal despotism was also restrained by the economic power of the temples. Sacred land was inalienable; thus, with every generation, the temples became richer. In the twenty-fifth century, at Lagash, the ecclesiastical landed property amounted to perhaps a third of the territory of the city. A part of the sacred land was exploited directly by the temple; the rest was either given to temple personnel to supplement their food rations, or rented to sharecroppers. The temples had also their own craftsmen, from jewelers to carpenters, from fishers to merchants, and employed slaves in temple shops, particularly slave women in spinning. Since almost all our documentation comes from the temple archives, the role of secular property in Sumerian society must remain hazy for us. The rulers tried to obtain control of the sacred estates. They appointed themselves and members of their families high priests of the main temples. But the temples persisted while the rulers were mortal.

The king had to build temples and canals, but from the beginning he was also a war leader, at first represented as conquering enemies and killing lions single-handed. On one stele, the king of Lagash throws the god's net over the enemy. But by this time (the middle of the third millennium) victory had come to be conceived as a result of collective action.

On the same stele from Lagash the same king also leads his troops into battle. A stele from Ur pictures the king receiving the booty captured by his soldiers.

The army consisted of chariotry and infantry. The solid-wheeled chariots were drawn, it seems, by a now extinct species of asses. A warrior in each chariot hurled javelins into the enemy's ranks. The heavy infantry marched in several files; all soldiers wore the same uniform and carried the same weapons: short spears in Ur, heavy pikes and axes in Lagash. Were these disciplined battalions the king's retainers or the city militia? We do not know.

The battles pictured on Sumerian monuments and described in royal inscriptions were caused by squabbles between neighboring cities about irrigation, or by raids of barbarian tribes from the mountains of Persia in the east and of desert nomads from the west. But in the meantime, the populations to the north, from modern Baghdad up the two rivers, passed from barbarism to civilization. These men called their land *Akkad* and spoke a Semitic language, that is, a language of the great family to which Arabic, Hebrew, Phoenician, Egyptian, and most of the languages of the Near East belong. The Akkadians had long been in contact with the Sumerians: Akkadian Babylon was only 10 miles from Sumerian Kish. There was a steady infiltration of Akkadians into Sumer, and Akkadians soon became captivated by the Sumerian way of life. As far north as the city of Ashur, from about 3000, and as far northwest as Mari, on the middle Euphrates, from about 2700, men and gods lived in Sumerian fashion and were portrayed as if they were Sumerians.

The Sumerians never tried to extend their political power northward, and the Akkadians and their relatives to the north and west were busy protecting their cities from nomads and mountaineers, and colonizing the affluents of the twin rivers. For instance, by 2800 they occupied the Diyala region east of the Tigris. Meanwhile they eagerly took over the cultural achievements of the south. By 2700 they had adopted the Sumerian script for their own language. They probably did it first for some limited purpose, say accounting, but thus, unwittingly, they appropriated the secret of Sumerian power.

Toward the middle of the twenty-fourth century, Sargon I, from Agade, near Babylon, an Akkadian minister of the Sumerian king of Kish, subjugated Sumer and founded the first known empire, which extended from the Mediterranean to the Persian Gulf. His inscriptions were written in both Sumerian and Akkadian. Enlil, the supreme god of Sumer, made him without peer and gave him Elam, in the east. But in his western campaigns he knelt to the Semitic god Dagon, who gave him the "Upper Land." For later ages, Sargon became the prototype of the emperor. An Akkadian narrative about this "King of Battle" was still read a thousand years after his death.

His grandson Naramsin was the first ruler who proclaimed himself the lord of the world ("King of the four regions") and put the cuneiform sign of divinity before his name. On a relief, he, much taller than the other figures, is represented as fighting alone. His soldiers follow him in a loose formation. They have axes and spears, but the king shoots arrows. The use of bows in warfare and the breaking of the solid ranks of the Sumerian phalanx go together. The power of the Sargonid dynasty was based on the loyalty of its household troops: 5,400 men who ate bread daily before Sargon.

In a civilization where donkeys were the fastest means of overland transport, empires broke up and local powers survived. About 2250 the house of Sargon was swept away by barbarians from the east. At the end of the next century, the rulers of Ur, adopting the new title "Kings of Sumer and Akkad," reunited Mesopotamia from the Persian Sea to the Zagros Mountains. Some 18,000 records from local archives show centralization of government and economy under the new rule: 21,799 men were mobilized and paid for harvesting fields around Nippur.

The supremacy of Ur lasted 108 years. Then Ur was sacked by the Elamites and the other cities regained their independence until two centuries later, in the 1700's, Hammurabi of Babylon imposed his power on the land down the stream. Thereafter, Babylon was the hub of the world. Akkadian became the language of administration and business; the importance of Sumerian cities decreased and the Sumerian language died.

No natural frontier separated Sumer from the Semites, north and west. Semites probably joined the Sumerians in their colonization venture and continuously immigrated into Sumerian land. Akkadian words appear in the earliest Sumerian texts. Sumerian was intelligible only in Sumer while Akkadian, a Semitic dialect, was understood from Babylon to Egypt. The Sumerians, an exotic minority at the southern end of their universe, could preserve their separate nationality and impose their isolated language only so long as they enjoyed the monopoly of learning. Having taught everything they knew to the Akkadians, they were absorbed. The title "King of Sumer and Akkad" was still held by the Assyrian kings a thousand years after Hammurabi. But Hammurabi's fourth successor spoke of his subjects as "Akkadians and Amorites," the latter being Semitic invaders and immigrants from the western countries.

Yet the Babylonians won and kept their preeminence only by becoming Sumerians spiritually. They studied Sumerian without end, and in the scribal school a student whose mother tongue was Sumerian looked down on his Akkadian fellows. Only with the help of Sumerian grammars and lexicons compiled in Akkadian by the Babylonians is it possible for us to read Sumerian texts. (Akkadian texts were deciphered by analogy from the other Semitic languages.) Sumerian texts mostly come down to us in copies made by Babylonian scribes, just as we know Latin authors mainly through medieval manuscripts.

In fact, Babylonians and Assyrians identified themselves with the vanishing Sumerians. About 1800, an Assyrian king built a temple in an Assyrian city to his "Lord" Enlil, the supreme god of the Sumerians. Some decades later, Hammurabi called his subjects "the black-headed," the name which the Sumerians used for themselves. The Sumerians conquered their conquerors.

Our documentation for the period of Hammurabi's dynasty (eighteenth to sixteenth centuries) is abundant but again lopsided. Unlike Sumerian documents, which come from temples and palaces, it mainly concerns private persons. Hammurabi's laws help us to redress the balance. Still copied a millennium after his death, they constitute no systematic code. The 282 preserved articles of his collection, though many of them reproduce earlier enactments, deal with the legal questions which were acute in his time.

In pre-Hammurabi laws a bodily injury was compensated by the payment of damages; 60 shekels for a lost eye, and so on. In the laws of Hammurabi the system remained the same for a *mušhkenum,* a free man of lesser degree, but if a "gentleman" blinded an eye of another "gentleman" the principle of exact retaliation was applied: An eye for an eye, a tooth for a tooth. Hammurabi does not say anything about the bodily injury inflicted on a "gentleman" by a *mušhkenum,* but we can be sure it brought dire consequences. Hammurabi's point of view was pragmatic. The bodily integrity of a rich man was worth more than that of a poor man, and conversely a rich man could afford bigger medical expenses. Thus, the legal fee for an eye operation on a "gentleman" was twice as much as the fee to be paid by a *mušhkenum.*

The principle that social status determined one's rights and obligations also applied to slaves and women. The slave's function was to work for his owner. A citizen who blinded the eye of a slave paid a half of the latter's value to the owner. But except for his relation to his owner, a slave remained a person. He could own property, engage in litigation, and so on. He could marry a free woman, in which case their children were treated as free. Our term "slave" is actually a misnomer for him. He was rather a perpetual servant. The same Babylonian word that meant "slave" also meant a king's "minister."

The function of a wife was to provide her husband with legitimate sons.

Therefore, the adulterous wife and her paramour were both drowned. (But men could have secondary or temporary wives and slave concubines.) In all matters unrelated to their wifely functions, however, women were independent. They could own, buy, and sell property, lend and borrow money, and so on. A widow was free to remarry.

In the farming society of Mesopotamia, barley functioned as money and hired hands were generally paid in rations, men receiving twice as much as women. The sign meaning "price" and "buying" originally contained the picture of a grain measure. Silver, an imported material, mainly served to pay for other imports. All merchants, however, based their accounts on silver, and by the time of Hammurabi, virtually all business transactions were evaluated in silver (not, of course, in "money," for the silver was not coined). Artisans were paid in silver, shepherds in barley. The silver economy favored the capitalist. (The economic use of our word "capital," from the Latin *caput,* meaning "head," goes back to a Babylonian term which also meant "head" and had the same economic significance.) A bushel of seed yielded a harvest of some thirty bushels. Thus, in a normal year, a debt in barley could easily be repaid in kind at harvest time, although the customary interest amounted to 33⅓ per cent. But if a debt and its interest had to be paid in silver, the case was altered. The price of barley went down at harvest time, the usual term of a farmer's loan. Yet, to repay his silver debt, the farmer had to measure out barley "on the threshing floor" according to the current rate of exchange, as the loan contract stipulated. He was now at the mercy of the money market. A son who had borrowed 17 shekels to redeem his father from bondage had to sell himself because "he had no silver." A ruler of Uruk, in the nineteenth century, boasted that his reign was a time of such abundance that one shekel of silver bought three times as much barley as usual.

Hammurabi decreed that the "merchant"—that is, the professional moneylender—must accept payment from ordinary borrowers in grain and other commodities even for a silver loan, at a rate of exchange set forth by the royal ordinance. On the other hand, loans between merchants, even of commodities, had to be repaid in silver.

A century later, a successor of Hammurabi, proclaiming a general cancellation of debts, significantly excluded commercial loans. Thus, Babylonian documents illustrate the truth of the view of the Federalist Papers that the conflict between landed and moneyed interests "grows up of necessity in the civilized nations" and that the regulation of such conflicts forms "the principal task of the legislator."

The hegemony of Babylon was as short-lived as that of the Sumerian cities. Hammurabi dominated the Sumerian south and conquered Mari on the middle Euphrates only in the last ten years of his forty-two-year reign.

Thereafter, the Babylonian realm began to shrink, and Hammurabi's dynasty ended 125 years after his death when a Cassite chieftain from the Zagros Mountains seized Babylon. The Cassite dynasty allegedly reigned for 576 years, but Babylon was no longer a great power and the little land between the twin rivers lost its leadership.

Ancient Mesopotamia was rich only in cattle and agricultural produce. There were only two ways to acquire gold and silver: foreign war and foreign trade. A Babylonian story credits King Sargon with an expedition to protect merchants in Asia Minor. According to another text, Marduk, god of Babylon, spent twenty-four years in Asia Minor establishing caravan traffic between that country and Babylonia. In fact, Mesopotamia necessarily depended on waterways for transporting its bulky agricultural surplus, and the influence of Mesopotamian cities followed the course of the Euphrates. As early as about 2500 a king of Ur sent gifts to a king of Mari. Here, approximately at the latitude of Palmyra and Homs, the Euphrates begins to approach the Mediterranean. Farther north, east of Aleppo, the river flows only 100 miles from the Syrian coast. Though Babylonian agents in the eighteenth century penetrated as far as Hazor in Galilee, such cities as Mari and Aleppo effectively cut off the Mesopotamian cities from their own clients, and there is no reference to Egypt in Mesopotamian texts before the Egyptian conquest of Syria in the fifteenth century.

In the east, the Mesopotamians intermittently succeeded in extending their power as far as Susa, to which they sent wares via the Persian Gulf, but the Elamites in turn raided Mesopotamia.

Up the Tigris, the Assyrians protected Mesopotamia, but also isolated it, from the barbarian north. Whatever may have been the success of Sargon or of the god Marduk in Asia Minor, "Akkadian garments" were sold there by Assyrian intermediaries. In the nineteenth century Ashur established trading stations in the rich copper belt of Cappadocia. Donkey caravans carried tin, which was rare, expensive, and necessary for the production of bronze, a harder alloy of copper. They also carried standardized pieces of cloth and other commodities, and they took home gold and silver. Above all, one people after another appropriated the secret of Mesopotamian success: the art of writing. Rulers of Mari already used cuneiform writing about 2500, and the Assyrians followed a century later; Elamite was written in the same script about 2300. By 1800 Akkadian was a common language of chancelleries in Syria. In Asia Minor the Hittites used Akkadian in the seventeenth century, and soon adapted the cuneiform script to their own language. With the script went the knowledge recorded in writing. Students at Susa, about 1700, not only learned mathematics but solved problems "according to the Babylonian method."

Mesopotamian techniques of predicting the future were also used in

Susa, in Syria, and by the Hittites. The Sumerians had invented office equipment, a necessary tool of bureaucratic organization. They "filed" tablets in baskets by content and labeled each basket accordingly. In the eighteenth century, the kings of Mari used the same device for sorting their profuse correspondence. As a matter of fact, the exercise of statecraft was no longer possible in the Levant without the assistance of scribes. At Alalakh cuneiform tablets in Akkadian appeared toward the end of the eighteenth century when this little town of the kingdom of Aleppo became the seat of a semi-independent dynasty.

Simultaneously, the practical knowlege of Mesopotamian artisans was diffused through the adjacent lands. The spoked wheel, the plow with a seeding attachment, and sewers under street pavements entered into general use. Glazed earthenware was already being made at Alalakh by the sixteenth century.

While Mesopotamia became the southernmost province of the world united by the cuneiform script, it also became more and more remote from the mainstream of history. Copperwork was of great importance in the Mesopotamia of the third millennium; the ore came by the sea, probably from Oman. In the beginning of the second millennium extremely rich sources of this metal, which then was essential for civilized life, began to be exploited in Asia Minor and particularly in Cyprus. Our word "copper" comes from the name of this island. The new sources of wealth were Mediterranean and shifted the center of economic and manufacturing activity away from Mesopotamia.

It is symbolic that toward the middle of the seventeenth century a Hittite king raided Babylon. Soon afterward, the axis of history ran across the Mediterranean; from the Hittite capital, near the Black Sea, to the Egyptian Thebes, some 13 degrees west of Babylon. The Babylonians had become great as the first disciples of the Sumerians; now the peoples of the Mediterranean lands had learned from the Babylonians.

The scribal art diffused from Mesopotamia was a skill like that of a smith. Scribal schools prepared technicians for government, church, and business. Babylonian scribes boasted of their ability in calculating payrolls, delimiting fields, and so on. Just as smiths did not need to know the laws of natural science to perfect the fabrication of daggers, so a scribe learned merely from practice how to balance accounts, write down the meaning of an omen, or choose the appropriate clause of a contract from a convenient list of legal formulas. There were numerous reference works: vocabularies, mathematical tables, lists of animals, plants, stones, drugs and corresponding ailments, medical instructions arranged according to symptoms or parts of the body, collections of texts concerning the techniques of divination and worship, and so on.

Scribe, as well as smith, worked rationally. Babylonian physicians prescribed potions, ointments, and plasters mainly made of herbs, though the patient more often than not also sought the help of the exorcists and their spells. By 1900, Babylonian scribes handled mathematical operations which in our terms would be cubic equations with two unknowns. They already knew the result of the "Pythagorean" theorem, but no systematic and didactic book like Euclid's *Elements* has been found—no book, that is, which taught the science instead of teaching the problems. A typical Babylonian mathematical exercise would both state a problem—say the calculation for the construction of a dike—and demand its solution, specifying every step. Much later, probably in the fifth century, Babylonian scribes began to develop a very sophisticated theory of lunar phases which was necessary for calendar reckoning. Neither in astronomical texts nor elsewhere does there ever appear an idea of a general proof demonstrable by arguments. There is never any theoretical statement, and no divergent opinion is ever recorded. Yet there must have been some discussion before this or that hypothesis or process was accepted as authoritative. A Mari text of the nineteenth century mentions sending a physician to examine some healing herbs. But the tradition of the scribal school hid from the uninitiated the controversies and adventures of learning. As far as the written sources go, science in our, that is in the Greek, sense did not exist in Mesopotamia or generally in the ancient Near East.

Similarly, literature was produced for some practical purpose. A poem about the rage of the god Era was used as a charm against pestilence. There are love songs of which the first lines sound as though they were written for a hit parade: "I'm crazy with love for you." Their frankness leaves nothing to imagination, for they belonged to a fertility rite and were written for the sacred marriage between the ruler and the life-giving goddess of love.

The greater part of the literary texts has come down to us on school tablets. The students copied classics to learn spelling and style. The adventures of King Gilgamesh of Uruk were read at the Hittite court as well as in Megiddo in Palestine. On the Nile and in Susa in Iran scribes copied the myth of Adapa-Oannes, the wisest of men, who had ascended into the heavens yet failed to attain immortality.

The role of Sumer in this school tradition is evidenced by the fact that almost all gods, heroes, and men of Akkadian classical literature are Sumerians. But how can we explain that the Sumerian heroic sagas concerned Gilgamesh and other kings of the first dynasty of Uruk, who were supposed to have lived in the twenty-eighth century, according to our reckoning?

Since we do not know the authors, places, and times of composition of all these works, we are unable to understand them in their historical contexts. The modern reader discovers the quest of immortality, or the tones of wanton pride, in the epic of Gilgamesh, and compares him with Faust. Yet the earliest reference to Gilgamesh counts him among the gods. In a Sumerian myth, the goddess of love is a younger sister of her enemy, the goddess of death. Was there a streak of romanticism in the Sumerian soul? Does the juxtaposition of love and death express some eternal truth hidden in our unconscious?

The practical purpose of the scribal craft also explains why there was no writing of history in Mesopotamia. Rulers, dedicating objects to gods, referred to their deeds of piety, which included wars, as reasons for expecting divine blessing, but these ephemeral events were of no interest to posterity. When a king of Uruk, writing to the king of Babylon about 1800, mentioned the dispatch of Babylonian auxiliaries as something which had happened "two or three times" in the past, he did not quote the annals, but referred to conversations with his father and grandfather. What we have as Sumerian and Babylonian historiography are lists of kings which, in later compilations, briefly record some victories of old.

For Further Reading

Cambridge Ancient History, Vols. I–II.
Kramer, S., *History Begins at Sumer.*
Neugebauer, O., *The Exact Sciences in Antiquity.*
Mellaart, J., *Early Civilizations in the Near East.*
Hallo, W. W., and W. K. Simpson, *The Ancient Near East.*

6   Egypt

Egypt was, as the Greeks said, the gift of the Nile. Like a gigantic snake (720 miles from the first cataract to the sea), the Nile slithers through the desert which isolates its green valley. Eastward the desert continues to the Red Sea and, beyond it, into Arabia; westward it passes into the Sahara. When, about 2000, an Egyptian force marching to the Red Sea had to cross some 90 miles of the desert, donkeys carried spare sandals for the soldiers walking on the burning sand. Southward, the cataracts prevented any large invasion until about 730 B.C.

Nobody before Napoleon succeeded in conquering Egypt from the Mediterranean. In Mesopotamia mountaineers from the east and the nomads west of the Euphrates could enter the sown lowland at will. The enemy could invade Egypt only over the narrow isthmus of Suez; this happened in the eighteenth and in the seventh and later centuries B.C.

Dates before 2500 are approximate to the nearest century, thereafter to the nearest quarter-century.

B.C.		
	3000	Egypt unified under a single pharaoh; beginning of the Old Kingdom; appearance of writing
	2700	Copper in common use in Egypt; pictures used in graves as part of funerary arrangements
	2600	Egyptian conquest of Nubia; the pyramids begun (IV dynasty); the potter's wheel in common use
	2130	Beginning of the Middle Kingdom (XI–XIV dynasties)
	1825	Egyptian influence dominant in Byblos
	1750–1550	Hyksos in Egypt (XV and XVI dynasties)
	1550–1200	The New Kingdom (XVIII–XIX dynasties); wheeled vehicles become common, as does the use of bronze and labor-saving devices (bellows for blacksmiths, the shadoof for watering gardens); chickens introduced
	1375–1358	The Amarna Age; Ikhnaton's religious reforms

The Nile valley is so narrow that from the banks of the Nile one can sometimes see the desert sands on right and left. Thus, though Egypt is as large as Texas and New Mexico together (386,000 square miles), 99 per cent of the population crowds some 13,000 square miles of the "black land" (as the Egyptians called their country). The rest is the tan desert.

Villages clustered along the margins of the cultivated land and during the annual inundation stood out of the water like islands in the sea, as the Greeks used to say. The prevailing wind facilitated navigation upstream, and the current carried the vessels northward. An energetic ruler could easily dominate the whole valley. Territorial unity was normal in Egypt and exceptional in Mesopotamia.

Last but not least, the twin rivers of Mesopotamia ended in the Persian Gulf, the backwater of history. The Nile poured its waters into the Mediterranean world of the future.

Swollen by the rains in Abyssinia, the Nile begins its rise in the middle of August in Cairo and attains its maximum height in the beginning of October. Thus, the inundation comes after the harvest and moistens the earth parched by the summer heat that kills weeds and aerates the ground.

(In Mesopotamia, the inundation comes in the spring; summer evaporation makes the ground saline and thus, in the end, unproductive.)

The brown water of the flood leaves behind a deposit of silt rich in organic matters which renews the topsoil. After the inundation the Egyptian needed no more than a wooden hoe to till the muddy ground capable of yielding two and three crops in the year. Greek authors spoke with envy of the farmers who without effort collected the bounty of the Nile.

In fact, it was the backbreaking work of the fellah which sustained the agricultural civilization of Egypt through six millennia. The sand blown in from the desert encroached upon the cultivable land. Dikes and canals which regulated the flood and extended its benefits across a wider area had to be built, and reconstructed after each inundation. At the dawn of history, the Egyptians already marked the height of the successive rises of the river. Even the Nile could default, and the seven lean years which Joseph predicted to his pharaoh could become dire reality. As soon as man's effort slackened, the population dwindled. It totaled 8 million under the Romans in the first century A.D.; it was only 2 million at the beginning of the nineteenth century, under Turkish rule.

The crowding of population in the irrigated land determined the nature of the evidence available to us. Since the Egyptians wrote on sheets made out of stalks of papyrus (our word "paper" comes from this Egyptian plant name), humidity and time destroyed their archives. The mud-brick buildings also disappeared, since the Egyptians did not use baked bricks. But graves built at the desert's edge remained. In the delta, however, the distance made desert burial impracticable. Hence, almost no evidence comes from the northern country, and our reconstructions of the Egyptian past must be unbalanced and unreliable. Moreover, the Egypt that we know is mainly an Egypt of the dead. The pyramids are tombs. To understand life in the ancient Egypt we have first to know the world of the dead.

The Egyptian hereafter was unique. In the Mesopotamian Hades pale shades ate bitter bread and drank foul water. The mighty hero Gilgamesh could only become the shadowy ruler of the lower world. Man's sole hope was to bribe the powers of Hades by sacrifices and gifts. In Egypt death led into an afterlife where the gods assigned to the deceased the due portion of water for the cultivation of his Elysian field. As long as the corpse, or at least a material image of it, subsisted, life continued. Hence, the careful burial in dry sand which preserved the corpse. Mummification was already known at the beginning of the third millennium. The abundance of funerary imagery in burial chambers served the same purpose. Palaces and shrines were built of sun-dried mud bricks, and the first Egyptian building of limestone was the pyramidal grave of a pharaoh. For the Egyptian, as an Egyptian formula says, the grave was "the eternal home." And it is the "eternal home," its inscriptions, statues, reliefs, paintings, furniture, and so on, which tells us about the past of ancient Egypt.

Proverbial wisdom instructs us that only good words are to be said about the dead. The Egypt of the dead is peopled by well-fed men, and ladies who are young and good-looking. The pharaohs are benevolent, officials efficient, the lower classes busy and satisfied. Even the slave woman who grinds grain sometimes looks optimistic. The funerary texts give only isolated bits of evidence, and the historian must strive to elicit meaningful and correlated information from the eulogies.

The first agricultural settlements on high ground along the Nile and the Faiyûm, probably established in the fifth millennium, reveal no surprises. The villagers cultivated barley of the Mesopotamian type, emmer, and flax. They raised livestock and used pottery, flint tools, and some copper articles. Life of the same kind continued in Nubia as late as the third millennium, but in Egypt two new powers appeared around 3000 which for the next 3,000 years determined the style of Egyptian life: the pharaoh and hieroglyphs.

In predynastic times pictorial representations of hunt and battle show warriors who are equal. Then, suddenly, representations appear in which a giant bestrides his own men and his adversaries, single-handedly destroying the enemy or digging a canal. He is the pharaoh, and his name is written alongside the picture in hieroglyphs. For instance, the images of fish and of chisel, read in Egyptian as Nar-Mer, give the name of a pharaoh. Yet, the impression that the hieroglyphs and the pharaoh emerge together may be erroneous, since the texts of the same period written on papyrus have disappeared and the prehistory of the Egyptian writing remains unknown. The hieroglyphic signs were and remained pictorial: a man leaning on a walking stick meant old age. Various supplementary signs made hiero-glyphic writing capable of expressing any thought. Egyptian writing, like Hebrew and Arabic, did not indicate vowels, so we do not know exactly how the words were pronounced. Different scholars have had different theories and in accordance with these have inserted vowels in Egyptian names for the convenience of modern readers; thus it is not uncommon to find in different texts quite different spellings of the same name.

The first representations of the pharaohs show them wearing, now the white crown of the south, now the red crown of lower Egypt. It seems that the ruler of the south conquered the Delta. Thereafter there was in prin-ciple only one pharaoh. (This term comes to us through the Bible; it meant "palace" in Egyptian.) The history of Egypt became the story of the pharaohs. Its three millennia are divided among thirty dynasties, the last of which reigned between 378 and 342 B.C. The first two dynasties laid the foundation of the pharaonic civilization. The third settled in Memphis, near modern Cairo, immediately south of the delta, and here, about 2600, the kings erected the pyramids. For the whole period of the "Old Kingdom," from the unification of Egypt to the last pharaoh of Memphis (Eighth Dynasty), the Egyptian king lists counted 955 years.

During this millennium the pharaohs reclaimed brackish lagoons in the Delta and papyrus swamps in upper Egypt, where the rich hunted aquatic birds. About 2600 a royal officer founded twelve villages in the Delta. Storehouses where grain was laid up for the use in lean years covered the land. Barley or emmer bread and beer from barley remained the basic foods. ("Barley and beer" often meant any kind of salary.) Vegetables, particularly onions, supplemented the diet. Grapes and wine are first mentioned under the Second Dynasty (twenty-ninth to twenty-seventh centuries). Some 300 years later, under the Fourth Dynasty, there were five varieties of wine from the Delta, several sorts of beers, and some twenty bread products. A repast found in the grave of a noble lady of the Second Dynasty consisted of eight courses, from barley porridge to fresh fruits. Agricultural techniques remained simple. A wooden hoe was sufficient for the muddy ground and a small plot. From the Second Dynasty on, a light plow drawn by cattle aided the farmer. The houses were built of mud bricks, although those of the wealthy must have been quite comfortable. As early as the Second Dynasty, tombs were equipped with bathrooms for the next life of the owner.

Egypt abounded in excellent stone, from limestone, the building material of the pyramids, to porphyry and granite. In the first centuries of the third millennium the manufacture of heavy vessels made of hard stone was prodigious both in quantity and in workmanship. We still cannot understand how an Egyptian craftsman with his flint-pointed drill could hollow out rock crystal to make jars with sides as thin as paper. The use of stone for building was apparently more difficult. The tomb of the last pharaoh of the Second Dynasty was the first entirely lined with limestone. Stone vessels were for the wealthy, but the common use of the potter's wheel from about 2600 made pottery available to all. In the pit burials of the poor a clay cup for water and a dish for bread comforted the dead. The Egyptians imagined that the god Khnum fashioned men on a potter's wheel. Thus a technical device, invented within the historical period, could become the material for a myth.

The use of copper became more and more widespread during the third millennium. Toward the end of it the payments to workers, besides food and linen, often included copper utensils. From about 2750 copper tools, hardened by skillful hammering, facilitated large exploitation of quarries and the use of stone for building. Copper points for arrows were in use by 2100, and in a book written about 2000, the picture of a copper implement is a sign of an artisan.

However, flint tools and weapons, which could be easily and cheaply replaced, continued to be employed well into the second millennium. Flint was a native material; copper had to be brought from faraway lands. For the same reason, bronze, which required tin as well as copper, was not used for weapons and tools before the sixteenth century, a millennium later than in Mesopotamia, though the alloy is stronger and easier to cast than copper.

It seems that the pharaohs intentionally isolated the valley of the Nile and endeavored to make its economy self-contained. Cultural influence of Mesopotamia and Syria-Palestine was tangible in the predynastic times and under the first pharaohs, about 3000. The Sumerian motif of entwined monsters appears on Narmer's palette. But when Egypt became powerful, the pharaohs preferred tribute to trade. Under military protection, the Egyptians exploited malachite and turquoise veins and, perhaps, copper mines in Sinai. About 2600, the pharaohs conquered Nubia to the south of the first cataract; near the second cataract they established foundries for working Nubian copper.

As a matter of fact, Egypt, the richest agricultural country of the world, could well dispense with foreign trade, which mostly brought in objects of luxury. When an Egyptian author described a time of calamities, he mentioned the lack of cedar wood from Byblos usually used for expensive coffins. When, in the beginning of the fifteenth century, Queen Hatshepsut sent a trade expedition to the land of "Punt" (probably the Somali coast), an event commemorated in the reliefs of her funerary temple, the main product brought back by her five ships was incense for temple service. She sent her vessels in order to eliminate the middleman and to bring living incense trees which were planted as "a Punt" in her capital. Elizabeth of England could not have been more mercantilistic in the sixteenth century A.D. The economic isolation of Egypt, where seagoing ships were constructed in the manner of papyrus skiffs on the Nile, was also expressed in her exchange system. In Punt as well as in a bazaar in Egypt, goods were disposed of by barter; for instance, beads were exchanged for onions or cakes. Yet, to quote Aristotle, how can one find the number of sandals equivalent to a meal? Therefore, as the philosopher says, the invention of money, a universal standard of value, was a work of justice and equality. The Egyptians did not invent money, but they used copper, grain, silver, and gold as common denominators of value. Yet, as late as about 1170 a sarcophagus valued at about 5 pounds of copper was purchased for about 2½ pounds of copper, 1 hog, 2 she-goats, and 2 sycamore trees. By contrast with Mesopotamia, the self-contained economy of Egypt remained primitive.

The pyramids express the self-confidence of self-centered Egypt. The Great Pyramid, built in the middle of the twenty-sixth century, covers more than 13 acres and remains one of the largest buildings in the world. For almost 4,500 years it was also the tallest (over 480 feet). It was erected without machinery or scaffolding by the sweat of perhaps 100,000 workers and the ingenuity of Egyptian engineers who used levers and ropes. Men and cattle drew sledges up brick ramps to make a pile of some 2,300,000 limestone blocks weighing about two and a half tons each. The sides of the pyramid were oriented according to the four cardinal points, and the maximum error was about one-twelfth of a degree. Each side was to be 756 feet long at the base, and the maximum error was only a few inches.

Some 2,100 years later, Egyptian priests told Greek travelers that Cheops, the Pharaoh of the Great Pyramid, reduced the people to misery for his project. In fact, the annual working season for the building of the pyramids was presumably the late summer, when the Nile flooded and farming stopped. At that time the stones could be carried over water to the site of the pyramid. Since the mobilized peasants were paid in kind, the building of the pyramids was also a kind of relief work system. Modern man may ask whether the capital and labor extended in erecting the enormous funerary complex centered on the royal pyramid could not have been better devoted to low-cost housing. The same question, however, can be asked about Gothic cathedrals or the Temple of Jerusalem. The first need of any social system is to create incentives to make people do more work than that required by their immediate wants. As Adam Smith writes: "The desire of food is limited in every man by the narrow capacity of the stomach," but the desire for "conveniences and ornaments" is unlimited. When Smith wrote (1776), conspicuous consumption was, perhaps, the main lever of production. As he put it, with the greater part of the rich people the chief enjoyment of wealth consisted in the parade of riches. But Adam Smith wrote at the dawn of the Industrial Revolution. In earlier and poorer societies religion provided the incentive for works of economic supererogation; it raised common labor to the dignity of a ritual gesture. The Sumerian king is represented carrying on his head a basket with bricks for the foundation of a temple. When men of Lagash had to repair a canal, it was the canal of their god Ningirsu.

In Egypt, the pharaoh, a "great god" himself, linked mortal men to the eternal. He was represented on the temple walls worshiping the gods and associating with them, "the servants of the god" (priests, in our terms) were his delegates, and none of his subjects were ever pictured in association with a deity. The common people needed the pharaoh for eternal salvation, since the offerings without which the deceased could not exist were officially the pharaoh's gift: he alone had the key to the afterlife. His eternal life in the pyramid, thus, was directly related to the well-being of every Egyptian. Princes and courtiers were entombed around the royal pyramid, and images of their tenants and servants appeared on the walls of these tombs, so that their names, too, were "established forever." Through this living chain of hope the humblest worker on the Great Pyramid participated in the sacrament of pharaonic immortality just as men who raised the Gothic cathedrals labored in the hope of the eternal reward for their pains.

In due time the incarnate god became a corpse, and magic formulas were necessary to make the motionless body living in the hereafter: "This king Phiops dies not." Another set of charms was read by the mortuary priest in the tomb of a private man. A royal prince, in the twenty-fifth century, to ensure the continuance of oblations and liturgies after his death, endowed his tomb with twelve villages.

As early as the second quarter of the twenty-fourth century it became clear, however, that even a pharaoh could not be sure of perpetual repetitions of charms which had to be spoken daily to restore his body to life. The relevant texts began to be inscribed on the walls of his burial chamber so that, if necessary, the deceased himself would be able to speak the formulas of revivification.

In the middle of the twenty-third century these formulas began to be reproduced in the burial chambers of members of the royal family and of nobles who in this way usurped the unique privilege of the pharaoh. As one of the usurpers boasted: "I know every secret charm of the palace." By the end of the millennium anybody could copy this or that part of the royal liturgy in his tomb.

After his death, the pharaoh joined the immortal gods in the heavens. But since his subjects after their deaths continued to exist in the nether world, the deceased pharaoh became identified with Osiris, the king of the dead. Thus the same pharaoh, in the hereafter, was enthroned in heaven and was also "Osiris, Lord of the Lower World."

The pharaoh, being of divine essence, obtained eternal life as his right. His subjects had to prove that they deserved it. They needed the intercession of the pharaoh with the god Anubis, who led the dead into the other world. From about 2600, the titles and merits of the deceased were inscribed on the walls of his tomb. He did "what the pharaoh praised," whereas his "beloved wife" stated that she was held "in honor by her husband." In the course of time, these eulogies became more prolix. The deceased, for instance, said that he had taken swimming lessons with the royal children or had given bread to the hungry and clothing to the naked. The latter statement may to us sound like an expression of the idea of social justice. In fact, it only attests that the lord who speaks was wealthy and fulfilled his duty to his villagers, "so that I might become greater than the great ones."

It is more significant that, besides his own merits, the dead man needed the sympathy of the living to ensure his existence in the hereafter. As early as the middle of the twenty-fourth century, in the parts of the tomb where the text would be accessible to visitors, there appears the appeal to those "who love life and hate death" to make an offering or, at least, to wish that the deceased might be blessed with "a thousand of bread and beer." In making this appeal to the passerby, the dead man naturally stresses that he did "what men love and gods praise." He also promises to intercede for his helper with the powers of the other world. In fact, despite the belief in the nether world, the tomb remained the "eternal home" of the dead. From the days of the pharaohs to the age of the Caesars perennial graveside dialogue took place between the living and the dead. In the twenty-second century a son wanted to be buried in the tomb of his father so that he might see him every day. In the same period the Egyptians began to deposit letters to the dead in their tombs. For instance, a widow asked her dead husband to rescue her and their baby from servitude to his relatives. In the thirteenth century a widower, who obviously could not overcome his grief, wrote to his dead wife complaining that she prevented his heart from being happy.

But in the realm of the shadows neither one's merits nor the assistance of the living could be as potent as the arts of magic. As we have mentioned, ordinary man usurped the charms composed originally to help the pharaoh. From the beginning of the second millennium every dead man affluent enough to obtain the advantages of mummification was identified with the ruler of Hades as "the Osiris So-and-So." The wooden coffins were inscribed with spells to help the defunct overcome the hazards of the journey to the other world. The felicity of the Osirean realm was now accessible to the common man. "I live, I die, I am Osiris . . . I grow up as grain . . . the earth has concealed me. I live, I die, I am barley, I do not pass away. . . ." We remember Paul's argument for the bodily resurrection: "That which thou sowest does not sprout again except it die" (I Cor. 15:36). In Egypt, and only in Egypt, the living, the dead, and the gods were three species of the same substance. Again, only in Egypt, a king, victim of his evil brother, not only became god after death, but by his death assured the personal immortality of his devotees. The same egalitarian idea later marked the Jewish, Christian, and Muslim hopes of future life. On the other hand, in the Levant outside Egypt, and also for the Greeks, death ended life, and immortality was a miraculous gift of the heavens to an exceptional man: "And Enoch walked with God, and he was not, for God took him" (Gen. 5:24).

The evolution of Egyptian ideas about the hereafter paralleled the changes in this world. Pictorial representations began to appear in the graves about 2700 as a part of the funerary apparatus, and the deceased was represented as receiving the offerings due to him. At this time, the "great ones" were officers of the pharaoh, and the vizier was always a royal prince. By the middle of the third millennium, the vizier was a superbureaucrat heading several departments. By about 2300, local governors obtained the vizier's title so that they became equal to the chief of the central administration. Careers were opened to men of talent. One man who began as a "herdsman of cattle" and later served in 26 different offices died about 2350 as a director of royal works. Successful officials acquired wealth: about the middle of the twenty-sixth century one of them boasted that 2,500 asses were needed to carry away the sheaves of his fields. Rich and influential officials naturally desired to hand over their lucrative offices to their sons. Toward the end of the Old Kingdom a son regularly took the place of his father. Sometime later a governor boasted that he had been appointed to his office as an infant "of a cubit in height." The pharaoh was god; his high officials felt themselves demigods. By 2500 they were pictured in their tombs as masters of their estates, and on the walls of their graves they towered over the retainers and villagers. The noble whose ancestors had asked the favor of burial near the pharaoh and at the pharaoh's expense now built his tomb in his hereditary estate, "through love of the district where I was born." The noble now prided himself on furnishing water to his city and being beloved by "my entire city."

After Pepi II, who allegedly ruled ninety-four years and lived to be a hundred, a succession of short-lived pharaohs at Memphis lost control over the local viceroys. Of course, these kinglets soon became involved in wars one against another. At last, about 2130, the governor of Thebes prevailed over his rivals. His dynasty (the eleventh) and the two following reunified Egypt and kept law and order for some 400 years. We call this period the Middle Kingdom.

The task of the new pharaohs was not easy. Amenemhet I, the founder of the Twelfth Dynasty who about 2000 had overthrown the last king of the Eleventh Dynasty, was murdered, twenty-nine years later, in a palace conspiracy. The local governors continued to behave like monarchs. One of them in his tomb pictures his subjects, including priests and military, dragging his colossal statue (some 20 feet in height) to his mortuary temple. "Their hearts expanded when they saw the monuments of their lord."

The economy demanded more and more scribes, and the profession was open to talent. A man without a high-sounding title could send his son to the scribal school among the children of the "great ones." Toward the beginning of the second millennium, the scribes became a proud body. In tomb pictures of daily life of the Old Kingdom, the scribe is often represented as attending his lord, who is carried in a litter for inspection of his fields, but the paintings of the Middle Kingdom represent the scribes in the exercise of their service or as overseers of the workers in the field.

The founders of the Middle Kingdom preferred to be called not "mighty," but "benevolent" gods and, like simple mortals, chose names expressing personal piety. For instance the name Amenemhet put its bearer under the protection of Amun, the patron god of Thebes. The same pharaoh circulated propaganda tracts representing himself as the savior of Egypt predicted by a seer of old. The praise of Sesostris I was fittingly attributed to a political refugee who had foolishly run abroad at the accession of this benevolent ruler.

The officialdom of scribes was the mainstay of the unity of Two Lands. As in Mesopotamia, every governmental transaction was recorded in writing. Scribes accompanied marching soldiers, scribes counted crops, scribes recorded monthly inspections of sacred utensils in every temple and registered wicks made of old rags used for work inside royal tombs. The higher officials untiringly admonished the lower scribes to work with utmost zeal. Thus, in the third quarter of the fifteenth century an order was dispatched to an official with the stern warning: "You shall not slack, for I know that you are sluggish." The letter was found 3,200 years later, still unopened.

In the Old Kingdom, the scribe was often a son of a noble, even of a pharaoh, and received his education from the father and a tutor. Professional requirements compelled even a highborn youth to start at the bottom of the bureaucratic ladder. The aristocratic architect who built the pyramid of Pepi I (about 2300) began his career by carrying his "scribe's palette," helping with measuring rod, and so on, until he became Royal Builder. Consequently he knew how to deal with the workmen: "I never went to bed angry against anybody."

It is noteworthy that a man who was a master of propaganda for Sesostris I also wrote a book warning the students of writing schools that all manual occupations were demeaning. The scribe alone never lacked sustenance from the pharaoh; he alone was always an important official. "Nothing surpasses scrolls." No wonder that this scroll was copied without end in scribal schools. The new government appealed to the professional pride of the imperial bureaucracy. But this propaganda activity also attests a new understanding of the power of the pen. As a scribe of the twenty-second century wrote, "speech was mightier than any fighting." Sesostris I could, perhaps, believe he had been chosen as pharaoh by the sun-god when still unborn, but he knew and said that only the king whose name is remembered on account of his work does not die.

In the eyes of the scribe the social pyramid was a part of the world order. As soon as man comes from his mother's womb he runs to his master. The scribal idea was one of conformity to this natural principle. A good man listens to his superior; he is neither a talebearer against his colleagues nor deceitful toward the Palace. He must be a paragon whom everyone would wish to be like, yet not be overbearing. He makes "Egypt work with bowed head" for the pharaoh, but should not misuse his power. In this world view the washerman who refused to carry the laundry and the female slave who talked back to her mistress appear as symptoms of the revolution and become figures of the Egyptian apocalypse. Yet, when the officials in their funerary inscriptions stress their sinlessness: "I did not rob the poor," "I have not taken away a man's daughter, nor his land, either," they suggest that their colleagues were more rapacious. No independent evidence about the behavior of the officials of the Middle Kingdom has come to light as yet. But toward the end of the twelfth century, a scribe freed a tomb robber for a bribe. The gang repaid the loss to its unlucky member and continued its operations undisturbed.

Our perspective of the Middle Kingdom may, however, be distorted, since we lack material comparable to that of the Old Kingdom. Posterity regarded the language of the Middle Kingdom as classic. When it became fashionable to place scrolls in coffins as a kind of spiritual viaticum, classics accompanied the dead, and in this way, and also in school copies, some writings of the Middle Kingdom have come down to us. On the other hand, from Old Kingdom literature, the later scribes appreciated and copied only advice given to the budding bureaucrats. Thus, some views expressed by the authors of the Twelfth Dynasty may have been taken from older books now lost, and, therefore, may have been less startling to their contemporaries than they are to us.

It seems that the new feature of the Middle Kingdom was rather its emphatic style. The kings and their generals not only boasted of victories, but swore that their reports were true. A king erected his statue in the conquered Nubia to mark the new boundary. He says that the statue was made in order that "you might prosper because of it, and fight for it." The statues are often colossal, more than 50 feet in height, but the faces are grim and sad. We can even see the bags under the eyes. To please his patrons, the artist stressed the fatigue and worry of the pharaoh, worn down by his responsibilities. The sculptors of the Old Kingdom, no less masters of their craft, were more reserved. They, and their pharaohs, knew much more of kings and kingship than they chose to express.

Nothing succeeds like success. Toward the middle of the nineteenth century the pharaohs could suppress the "great chiefs," and the whole land was now administered direct from the palace. The pharaohs extended their power up to and beyond the second cataract. Egyptian influence was consolidated in southern Syria; in the last decades of the nineteenth century the rulers of Byblos used hieroglyphs and Egyptian titles.

The affluence of the river lands, in Egypt as in Mesopotamia, attracted the hungry dwellers of the deserts bordering the stream. A document of the nineteenth century mentions some Bedouin offering "to serve the pharaoh" since "the desert was dying of hunger." The Egyptian border post in Nubia turned them back. No unauthorized Nubian was permitted to go downstream; when Nubians came down for trade, they were sent back the next morning to the place whence they had come. A system of fortresses with ditches, ramparts, and the bastions, from which the archers could shoot arrows from three different directions, controlled the southern entrance to Egypt.

A more or less similar control was exercised at the Isthmus of Suez. But the bedouin from Palestine were not excluded from Egypt. When the famine was sore in his land, Abraham went down to sojourn in Egypt. Egyptian texts about 2000, and again in the thirteenth century, state that Asiatic herdsmen "as a favor" were permitted to enter Egypt, "to keep them and their cattle alive."

After the middle of the eighteenth century, the "wretched Asiatics" somehow succeeded in conquering lower Egypt. Following Egyptian tradition we call these invaders Hyksos, that is, "rulers of foreign land." In the same period, before or after the Hyksos, native princes seized control of the territories south of Elephantine. In upper Egypt power was seized by local magnates. At last, toward the middle of the sixteenth century, the princes of Thebes undertook a patriotic war against the Hyksos and their Egyptian allies who "had forsaken Egypt their mistress." The Hyksos were driven out, Nubia was reconquered, and Thebes again became the capital of a united Egypt. The "New Kingdom" began.

The New Kingdom (about 1550–1200) was a period of military expansion, that is, of enrichment. War was, until the Industrial Revolution, the fastest and the most direct way of capital accumulation. Booty and, afterward, the tribute of conquered lands stimulated the economy. The skill of captured and enslaved craftsmen sustained the economic growth. That the pharaohs extended the boundaries of Egypt in accordance with the command of gods was not surprising. The pharaoh Sesostris I, in the twentieth century, said of the sun-god of Heliopolis: He makes himself rich when he makes me conquer. The great hall of the Karnak temple, a forest of 144 stone shafts, each 50 feet high, cool on the hottest day, the two colossi of reddish sandstone, each 70 feet high, the treasury of the tomb of Tutankhamen, or the mighty obelisks of Thutmose III that now stand in Istanbul, Rome, London, and New York, thus fulfilling his hope that his name might endure forever and ever—all these wonders were paid for with the plunder of Nubia and Syria. The simplest soldiers profited from a successful campaign. They were "drunk and anointed with oil every day as at a feast in Egypt."

We do not know how much of the new wealth percolated to the nameless toilers of Egypt who had no means to erect tombs. But documents show that the bastinado and the shout of the taskmaster, "The rod is in my hand, be not idle!" were only a part of the real life. For instance an official reported about 1230 that three peasants of a royal domain ran away after having been beaten by the manager, and now there were none to till the royal land. The workmen at the royal tombs lived in pleasant two-room houses which were gaily decorated (dancing girls, protective spirits), and at least some of them read the perennial classics. They received decent salaries in kind, had a lunch break, three days of rest monthly, plus many days off on the occasions of festivals: they rejoiced until sunset at the accession of a new pharaoh. Disputes among them were settled by judges from their village. They even went on strike, "because of hunger and thirst" when rations were in arrears. And they had their own burial chambers in the mountain near their village. But they were a privileged, hereditary group.

Yet these glimpses of real life are rare. Equally rare is evidence about technical advances during the New Kingdom: the yoke resting on the necks of the cattle (it was previously lashed to the horns), wheeled cars, shadoofs for watering gardens, bellows for blacksmiths, the introduction of a new breed of rams and also of the chicken, "a bird that gives birth every day," and so on. Our sources, the eulogies of the dead and the self-praises of the pharaohs, speak to posterity and hence are not directly concerned with the routine of life.

For the same reason we know little about the meanings of changes which suddenly become visible. Experience taught the Egyptians that even pyramids cannot protect the corpse; therefore—many concluded—let us eat, drink, and be merry. But why did a scribe of the New Kingdom, like Horace and Horace's imitators in later ages, proclaim that literary works outlive the pyramids? In the sixteenth century Egyptian scribes began to visit ancient monuments as sightseers. One scribbled on a wall: "I have visited the pyramid of Zoser. It is beautiful." Why was he so much concerned about the present? Again, we can understand that affluence brings self-indulgence. Women in diaphanous dresses and unclad dancing girls people the decorations of the tombs in the fourteenth century. Yet in the no less affluent thirteenth century scantily clothed girls disappear from the walls—in one reused tomb such figures were repainted to show them decently dressed—and funerary subjects replaced the optimistic scenes of eternal happiness. The deceased now was not enjoying a festival in his garden, but praying prostrated under a palm.

How are we to understand the strangest figure of Egyptian history, the pharaoh Ikhnaton, who about 1370 undertook to reform the religion of

Egypt? After his death, some fifteen years later, his memory was damned, his residence city, which we call Amarna, about 160 miles south of modern Cairo, abandoned, and the old faith restored. The artificialities of Amarna art, which appeal to modern taste, and the anachronistic interpretation of Ikhnaton as a forerunner of Jesus, have made the name of this deformed and sullen pharaoh well known. He is described as the first monotheist. In fact, he proclaimed the solar disk as his own deity. Ikhnaton means: "Serviceable to the sun disk." He addresses the disk as, "Thou sole god, like to whom there is none other." In the language of polytheism this would mean that the god in question was the preferred one, but Ikhnaton worshiped no other god. The essential novelty of his theology was the doctrine that he alone knew the god and was its sole image on the earth. In private houses as well as in the tombs at Amarna sculptured icons expressed the new "Doctrine of Life": Ikhnaton and his family prayed to the sun. Its rays blessed them. His subjects prayed to him. The reform was not monotheistic but egocentric; only its intolerance was monotheistic. Throughout Egypt the names of the other gods were obliterated. According to Egyptian belief the destruction of the name destroyed the person. We need not wonder why Egypt did not revolt. The army remained faithful to the legitimate pharaoh.

The natural path of Egyptian expansion lay up the Nile. Between 1550 and 1450 the pharaohs of the New Kingdom, following in steps of their predecessors, colonized and Egyptianized the gold-producing land of Nubia, advancing the frontier to the fourth cataract. The savages to the south could not endanger the pharaonic forces. Despite some setbacks, Egypt held the greater part of Nubia securely almost to the end of the second millennium, and when the southern province finally became independent its rulers remained the devoted protégés of Amon-Re of Thebes.

For Further Reading

Cambridge Ancient History, Vols. I–II.
Černy, J., *Ancient Egyptian Religion.*
Emery, W., *Archaic Egypt.*
Erman, A., *The Ancient Egyptians: A Sourcebook of Their Writings.*
Gardiner, A., *Egypt of the Pharaohs.*
Hallo, W. W., W. K. Simpson, *The Ancient Near East.*

7   The New Levant

Syria and Palestine differed greatly from Egypt, although the Egyptian influence was here recognizable as early as 2700. Cities like Byblos and Ugarit were older than Memphis and on a level with Thebes as centers of civilization. Ugarit (modern Ras Shamra) on the Syrian coast opposite the easternmost cape of Cyprus controlled more than 80 towns and villages lying in a territory of about 40 square miles. The city could equip 150 seagoing ships for a trading expedition. Seven languages, from Cypriote to Sumerian, and five scripts occur in Ugaritic documents of the thirteenth century. In Egypt legal thinking was so undeveloped that the status of fellahs remains unclear to us, but the jurists of Ugarit distinguished between the service to be rendered to the king by an official owing to his rank, and his duties as a grantee of royal land. The Ugaritic language, akin to Hebrew, and the texts written in this language illustrate a civilization closely akin to that of Canaan (Palestine) on the eve of the Hebrew settlement. The mythological tales of Ugarit narrate deeds of Baal and other gods whom the Hebrews rejected. On the other hand, Ugaritic documents mention names and details that also appear in Biblical narratives, for instance, Abraham, or the adoption of a grandson by the grandfather, a legal act also performed by Jacob with regard to Ephraim and Manasseh (Gen. 48:5).

Thus, by contrast to Nubia, Syria remained to a considerable degree culturally independent of Egypt and rather indebted to Babylon. Even in the days of Egyptian supremacy the chieftains of Syria salaaming before the pharaoh ("Seven and seven times I fall at the feet of my lord") did so in the Babylonian language. During the New Kingdom, the worship of Syrian gods became popular in Egypt. The pharaoh Ramses II named his favorite daughter "Daughter of Anat" after the Semitic goddess of war also worshiped in Ugarit.

The pharaoh Thutmose I, about 1525, announced by anticipation that his empire extended from the third cataract of the Nile to the "inverted water" of the Euphrates, which unlike the Nile, runs from north to south. Afterward he actually reached the Euphrates. Two of his successors in the fifteenth century repeated the same feat. Well into the thirteenth century the pharaohs dreamed of the Euphrates frontier, and in the meantime tried to control as much of Syria as they could.

The conquest of Syria and her wealth began in earnest when the pharaohs mastered the instrument that made this task realizable: the horse.

Dates are approximate to the nearest decade

B.C.   1550   Hyksos expelled from Egypt; new model Egyptian
                army using chariotry and composite bows

        1525   Thutmose I claims Syria to the Euphrates; conse-
                quent war with Mitanni intermittent until 1410

        1500   Invention of alphabetic writing in Syria

        1400   The palaces of Crete destroyed; Mycenaean Greeks
                dominant in the eastern Mediterranean

1375–1350   The Amarna Age; Ikhnaton's religious reforms; Egypt
                paralyzed by internal problems; Hittite expansion
                destroys Mitanni

        1300   Egyptian revival; wars with the Hittites for Syria

        1270   Peace between Ramses II and the Hittites

        1230   Egypt invaded by the "sea peoples"; Troy destroyed
                by the Mycenaeans

        1200   Iron begins to come into common use; the palace of
                Pylos burned; beginning of the breakup of My-
                cenaean power

        1190   The Philistines (one of the "sea peoples") settle
                along the Palestinian coast

        1100   Egypt loses Nubia; camels in common use in north
                Arabia; use of lime plaster to make watertight
                cisterns opens dry areas for settlement

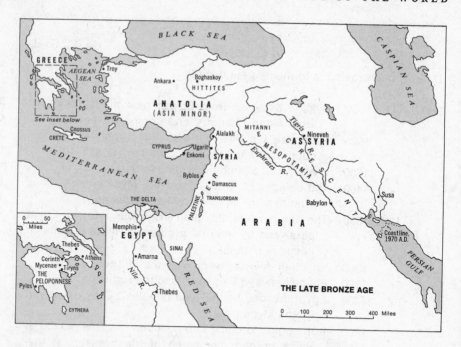

THE LATE BRONZE AGE

Horses were known in Mesopotamia as early as the twenty-first century: a Sumerian king proudly compared himself with a swift horse. In the eighteenth century, on the upper Euphrates and in Asia Minor, the horse was already harnessed to vehicles. But a longer time was needed for adapting the horse to the needs of warfare. The animal was really a pony, about 50 inches in height. Moreover, these horses were not gelded—a mare in heat let loose could stampede a whole camp. Hence until the thirteenth century horses were rarely used for riding. But two ponies harnessed to a light wooden chariot could transport a driver and a rider, who shot arrows from a composite bow that had an effective range of more than 600 feet. For the first time men possessed a highly mobile missile force which could destroy the enemy swiftly and definitively. The pharaohs now boasted of their knowledge of horseflesh and prowess in archery and other sports, while pictures in tombs represented the owners transported in horse-drawn vehicles to their estates.

The new weapon was very expensive. A horse cost as much as several slaves. Fine materials and perfect craftmanship were necessary for making chariots and composite bows. A pharaoh tried 300 bows before selecting his own (which nobody but he could bend, just as no other man could draw the bow of Odysseus). Thus, only rich and industrially advanced states could afford chariotry.

Unfortunately for the pharaohs of the New Kingdom, the sight of their chariots on the Euphrates was bound to provoke rich and mighty powers into making war against Egypt. Here again, to use Napoleon's maxim, geography explains history. An impassable desert separated Syria from Mesopotamia, except for the narrow green belt where the Euphrates approached the Mediterranean coast. This same northernmost part of Syria offered the best passage between Asia Minor and the lands to the south. The copper of Cyprus reached the continent through the ports in the same region. As long as the pharaohs remained roughly below the line Byblos-Damascus, they did not threaten the security of the powers outside Syria. The Egyptian control of the hub of communication lines in northern Syria hurt the cities of this region and the interests of such powers as the Mitanni beyond the upper Euphrates and the Hittites in Asia Minor. These potential adversaries also had chariots and archers. A poet of Ugarit described the invention of the composite bow and how the goddess of war killed the inventor in order to appropriate the weapon. At Ugarit not only the crew of a chariot but sometimes the horses were clad in mail. The Hittite kings used chariotry as early as about 1700, and their chariots in the fourteenth century held a crew of three. The pharaoh and his rivals in Syria fought with the same weapons, and no victory was ever final.

The struggle for Syria continued for almost the whole third quarter of the second millennium. Between the campaigns, the courts entertained amicable relations and the rulers on the Euphrates and in Asia Minor exchanged gifts and letters with the pharaohs. The king of Babylon, when he fell sick, expected to receive condolences from the pharaoh, and the statue of the goddess Ishtar traveled from Nineveh to Thebes to help an ailing pharaoh. The Asiatic kings sent their daughters with fitting retinues (for instance 317 girl servants) into the pharaoh's harem. But a king of Babylon was curtly rebuked for asking for an Egyptian princess in exchange. (He then begged the pharaoh to send him any good-looking Egyptian girl with a big dowry: who would dare to say she was not a princess?) Marriages were part of the bartering system, a form of international trade. And international trade, like domestic, was not above bazaar tricks and bargaining. A king of Mitanni discovered that statues of gold sent to him from Egypt were of gilded wood.

These transactions, the diplomatic correspondence, and the intermittent wars created the interdependence of the lands of the Levant. It was the first international age for the Near East. The courts from Susa to Thebes corresponded in the same Babylonian language, and from the Black Sea to Nubia chariotry dominated the military art. The use of this weapon required professional soldiers, and the new military technology changed the social structure. In Asia Minor and Syria the chariot warriors received fiefs in return for military service. In some Syrian cities they formed a kind of nobility, membership in which was conferred by the ruler. One of these feudal lords of Ugarit possessed 2,000 horses. Even in Egypt the military, enriched by the wars, came into the forefront of the society. The pharaohs now affected uniform. When the Eighteenth Dynasty became extinct, three generals in succession ascended the throne, and the last of them founded the Nineteenth Dynasty. One of these crowned generals stated that he equipped the temples of Egypt with priests chosen from the pick of the army. In other words, the military appropriated the choicest morsels of the Egyptian economy.

The other phenomenon of the new Levant was the emergence of a new great power. The troops fighting the Egyptian armies in the fourteenth century were directed from a faraway capital near the Black Sea, and when the peace came, it was inaugurated by the marriage between a pharaoh and a Hittite princess from Asia Minor.

The Hittite capital was Hattushash, modern Bogazköy, some 110 miles east of Ankara, the capital of Turkey. Thousands of clay tablets inscribed in cuneiform characters from the royal archives were found here. The grammatical structure of the Hittite language relates it to the Indo-European group, but the vocabulary is mainly that of the non-Indo-European indigenous peoples of Anatolia. The Indo-European invaders had completely forgotten their ancestral gods, and the civilization of the Hittites was essentially derived from Mesopotamia.

From their capital the Hittite kings with varying success extended their supremacy over a great part of Asia Minor. They preferred indirect domination: a conquered country or city became a vassal of the Hittites. About the middle of the fourteenth century, having destroyed the kingdom of Mitanni in northern Mesopotamia, they took over its Syrian dependencies and its role in the struggle with Egypt. About 1270 the struggle ended in stalemate. Ramses II made peace with the Hittites, who preserved their sphere of influence in northern Syria.

Ramses II was the last imperial ruler of Egypt. His fame reached Greek tradition and, through it, English poetry. He is the Ozymandias of Shelley. He fathered 162 children during his reign of 67 years, raised the most colossal of colossi (his statue at Abu Simbel is about 66 feet high), and covered the walls of his enormous temples with vainglorious pictures and inscriptions. "Look on my works, ye Mighty, and despair!" Today the tourists view his legless statue, 34 feet long, lying in the sand near Cairo, and stare at his mummy in the Cairo Museum. "Nothing beside remains."

Unknown to Ramses II and his Hittite rival, movements and inventions of little men were soon to end the might of the Hittites and to make the splendor of Egypt obsolete. About 1230, five years after Ramses' death, the "sea peoples" began to descend on Egypt. For some fifty years the pharaohs had to fight off the migratory waves by sea and by land. We do not know who these peoples were or whence they came. They swept away the Hittite empire and destroyed the cities of Syria and Palestine (which received this name from the Philistines, one of the "sea peoples" who settled there). Egypt survived but lost her empire in Asia.

Then, about 1100, the pharaohs lost Nubia, and for some four centuries Egypt, torn by internal dissensions, did not count in world politics. Blessed by the Nile, Egypt could afford to stand still while camel, lime plaster, iron, and alphabet changed the mentality of men and the equilibrium of political forces in Asia. By the end of the twelfth century men had trained camels to work for them, and camel caravans crossing the sand wastes changed the whole life of the countries around the Arabian desert. About the same time men learned to store rain water in cisterns lined with the new waterproof lime plaster. Much arid land now became habitable.

Iron, if fortified with carbon, is stronger than bronze, but its smelting demands special knowledge and it has to be shaped by hammer at red heat. The knowledge was probably first acquired about 2500 in Asia Minor, but for some unknown reason did not become common in the Levant before about 1200. By the tenth century, iron plow tips made tilling of heavy soil possible in Palestine. The main advantage of iron, however, was the universal distribution of iron ore, which is 500 times more common than copper in the earth. Even a small, low-grade iron deposit in the neighborhood was sufficient to free a city or a tribe from dependence on distant sources of copper, tin, and lead.

The creation of the alphabet was the most important advance in the transmission of knowledge between the invention of writing and the art of printing. After 1500, scribes in Syria, trying to invent a script fit for their Semitic dialects, hit on the device of a consonant alphabet. Hieroglyphs reproduced words; the cuneiform script was syllabic. But the inventors of the alphabet used signs to represent the ultimate particles, the "elements," as Augustine says, of writing, the single sounds on which syllables and words are built. In Ugarit an alphabet of 31 characters was already in use about 1400, and the scribes arranged the signs in essentially the same ABC order as the letters of our alphabet. About the same time there appeared the first predecessors of the Phoenician alphabet from which, via Greece and Rome, our alphabet has descended. The knowledge of hundreds of signs was necessary for both the hieroglyphic and the cuneiform script; this limited literacy to trained professionals. No great effort was needed to memorize two or three dozen alphabetic characters; now anyone could learn to read and write. The alphabet is democratic.

Our survey of the Bronze Age has centered on the Levant, particularly Egypt and Babylonia, two main sources of civilization. Now we must sketch the role of the Aegean region, the future Greek world, which in the Bronze Age was the outer province of the Levantine civilization.

Cyprus lies only 43 miles from Asia Minor and 76 from Syria. The north wind, as Homer says, carried a sailing ship from Crete to Egypt in five days, and chains of small islands linked Crete with Asia Minor and the mainland of Greece. As early as about 6000 the art of farming reached Cyprus and Greece; half a millennium later came pottery making. Corinth and Athens were settled before Babylon and Memphis. The Stone Age settlements in Greece and in the Aegean Islands lay mostly on or near the eastern coast, and Greece always turned eastward. Yet, for a long time, the Aegean peoples remained behind the advance in the Levant. Copper appeared in the Greek world only in the first, and bronze only in the last, centuries of the third millennium. But toward the end of the same millennium, the whole Aegean region became involved in the Levantine economy. Texts from Mari mention copper from Cyprus and imports from Crete. In the beginning of the sixteenth century, pupils in Egyptian scribal schools learned Cretan names. In the middle of the second millennium, inscribed cylinder seals from Babylonia reached Thebes in Greece. The architecture and the frescoes of Cretan palaces imitated the arts of the Levant.

These palace complexes appear in Crete about 2000 and some centuries later in Greece, where, until about 1400, the Cretan taste prevailed alike in feminine fashions and the form of shields. The unity of civilization in the future Greek region is striking in religion: there were no temples; the deities, foremost of whom was a great goddess, were worshiped in open-air places or in house chapels and caves. Yet, in several respects the "Minoans," as we name the inhabitants of Crete after their legendary king Minos, and the "Mycenaeans," as the inhabitants of Greece are called after Mycenae, the city of Homeric Agamemnon, were two different nations. The physical ideal of the Minoans was a lithe and slender person. The golden life-size masks of the Mycenaean rulers show large and bearded faces. The Cretan palaces were originally protected by bastions, but soon the fortifications disappeared, and the Cretan art shows society life, acrobats, and the beauty of nature, from bull to octopus. The Mycenaeans liked to represent battle scenes and hunting, and many of their palaces were built as parts of enormous fortifications which, like the acropolis of a Greek city, served as a refuge in time of war. Crowned by a relief of two heraldic lions protecting a column, a sign of the palace, the gate of the acropolis of Mycenae is the earliest historical relic of Europe: Agamemnon—if there was an Agamemnon—passed through this gate to make war on Troy. Cretan rulers were mummified in Egyptian manner, but built no pyramids. The enormous royal tombs of the Mycenaeans—the so-called Treasury of Atreus in Mycenae has a dome 43 feet high and 46 feet wide—were unknown in Crete.

A profusion of gold and silver objects found in these tombs, and the splendor of the palaces discovered in Crete and at Pylos, at the Bay of Navarino in the Peloponnese, evidence the wealth of the Aegean rulers in the second millennium. Some of this wealth percolated down to their subjects. Houses in the Cretan village were even furnished with clay pipes for sewage. But we do not know how this wealth was procured. Neither Greece nor Crete had natural riches. It seems that in the second millennium Greece and Crete formed a bridge for traffic between Europe and the Levant. The same neck rings were used from Syria to Scandinavia. Amber beads from the Baltic Sea reached Greece via the Adriatic. Fourteenth-century faïence beads, originally fabricated in Egypt, but probably imitated and certainly traded by the Mycenaeans, have been found as far afield as England and Georgia, in Transcaucasia. An Egyptian list compiled about 1400 mentions Knossus, Cythera, an island between Crete and the Peloponnese, and Nauplia, the ancient port for Mycenae. It is hardly by chance that Knossus, the greatest Cretan settlement, faced Greece.

The Aegean peoples were also craftsmen. An industrial city, Alasia, protected by a stone wall, flourished in copper-rich Cyprus (at modern Enkomi) in the second half of the second millennium. A ship wrecked off the southern coast of Turkey in the thirteenth century carried ingots and metal implements from Cyprus.

In the fifteenth century, the Mycenaeans, for unknown reasons, got the upper hand. In Egyptian texts the term referring to the Cretans disappeared. Between roughly 1400 and 1250 Mycenaean pottery was popular from Italy to the Turkish coast, and potters in Crete and Cyprus imitated the new mode. Passed from one tribe to another, Mycenaean objects reached England and southern Russia.

From this "all-Mycenaean" period we have texts which we can understand. Writing appeared in Crete as early as the beginning of the second millennium, and the earliest signs are already simplifications of pictograms. Neither this writing nor that used in Cyprus has been deciphered as yet. But Michael Ventris (1922–1956), an English amateur, decoded the syllabic script of some 90 signs which was used in Greece and in Crete (Knossus) in the fourteenth to thirteenth centuries. The deciphered language was pre-Homeric Greek. Except for some words incised on seals and vases we know this language only from inscribed clay tablets that were preserved because they became baked in conflagrations. The unbaked tablets as well as any texts written on perishable materials (papyrus, leather, wood?) have disappeared without a trace.

About two-thirds of the signs we read are proper names, among them the names of gods, which are Greek: Zeus, Poseidon, "the Mistress Athena," and so on. The rest of the words are mostly names of objects and crafts. We learn what we knew already or could surmise: the Mycenaeans had chariots and smiths. The interpretation of terms referring to social relations, for instance to landholding, remains tentative. Yet the tablets show the working of a bureaucratic apparatus similar to that of Sumer. Again tablets were "filed" and labeled according to the content, and the condition of every chariot wheel in the stores was recorded.

Clay tablets inscribed with signs similar to the earliest Sumerian script also have been found in Rumania. The use of clay tablets indicates a Mesopotamian model. Yet, the Creto-Mycenaean script owes nothing to the cuneiform. It does not fit the Greek language either, and for this reason the meaning of many words remains unknown or doubtful. The script was probably borrowed from some people of Asia Minor. The tablets show that in the second half of the second millennium the Mycenaeans spoke Greek. We cannot know, however, in absence of earlier texts, how old was the use of Greek in the Aegean world.

Empires and civilizations are short-lived. Prosperous and apparently secure about 1300, the Mycenaean world disintegrated before 1100. The palace of Pylos was burned about 1200, but the palace of Tiryns near Mycenae existed well into the twelfth century, and the citadel of Mycenae may have burned only toward the end of that century. The acropolis of Athens continued to be inhabited without interruption. Numerous sites were abandoned or lost their former importance, but other cities often rose in the neighborhood. Argos inherited Mycenae, Alasia (modern Enkomi) in Cyprus, a center of bronze industry, which declined in the eleventh century, perhaps because of the silting of her harbor. Her role was immediately taken over by the neighboring Salamis. When Salamis was destroyed by earthquakes in A.D. 332 and 342, it was rebuilt as Constantia, when Constantia was destroyed by the Arabs in A.D. 647, the city was succeeded by Arsinoë, the medieval and modern Famagusta, two miles off. It is true, however, that no palaces of the post-Mycenaean period, or other evidence of wealth, have yet been found in the Aegean region. For three or four centuries our evidence is essentially limited to pottery shards. When the "Dark Age" ends, in the eighth century, the Aegean region is Greek, and only the sagas of Agamemnon, of Nestor, and of the "Homeric" heroes preserve for the Greeks the memory of the proto-Greeks who built the palaces of Mycenae and Pylos.

For Further Reading

Chadwick, J., *The Decipherment of Linear B.*
Gurney, O., *The Hittites.*
Higgins, R., *Minoan and Mycenean Art.*
Platon, N., *Crete.*
Woolley, L., *A Forgotten Kingdom.*

8   Gods and Men

The preceding survey would have disappointed a Babylonian or an Egyptian scribe and, probably, a Mycenaean Greek. They would have said that it ignored the real causality of events: the gods. When the supreme god is angry with a land, says a late Egyptian sage, he exalts its humble people and humbles its mighty people. If the city of Ur was destroyed by barbarian invaders about 2000, it happened because Enlil, "the lord of all lands," sent the "evil storm" against the city. The gods sometimes acted arbitrarily, but generally they rewarded piety and punished evildoers. Men believed in the premise, without which no society can endure, that godly men prosper; and godliness was equated with piety. Therefore, an illness or a defeat was a punishment for sin. The loser had offended the gods. When the glorious dynasty of Sargon was overthrown by the barbarians the meaning of the catastrophe was obvious to Babylonian scribes: Enlil, the deity of Nippur, had punished the land because Naram-Sin, a king of Sargon's line, had sacked Nippur. Encircled by the enemy, Ramses II appealed to Amon, his divine father. "Has a father forgotten his son? Have I ever disobeyed your command? Have I not filled your temple with my booty? Can Amon care for the wretched Asiatics who do not know him. . . ." And Amon saved the pharaoh. "Worship your god daily . . . sacrifice prolongs life, and prayer expiates guilt."

This conception mirrors the reign of justice within any organized human society. The universe of Nature was confused and hostile. The alternation of seasons and the rhythm of stars were unrelated to man's deserts. Social life alone was orderly and, therefore, predictable. Man did not learn the idea of Law from Nature, but imposed it on the forces of Nature and the gods who governed these forces. Man was not yet interested in any causality that he was unable to influence. A weak link in the chain of beings, terrorized by lion and wolf, snake and scorpion, he regarded beasts as his peers and rivals. The rate of mortality was such that in the twenty-first century at Ur a tenth of the adults in a work gang died during one year, and a third of the children of a slave group died within a year. Man needed knowledge of the past to enable him to face the future with courage and intelligence. King Naram-Sin allegedly described one of his wars in order to teach future rulers not to become pusillanimous in the face of a barbarian invasion.

Happily for the godly man, the gods would indicate his future in dreams, but also by oracles, prophecies, and signs. Thus, in Babylonia, history was the servant of prognostication. From the twenty-fourth century on, the scribes collected and transmitted omens. For instance, the lungs of a victim sacrificed by King Ibbi-Sin of Ur, about 2000, exhibited a certain deformation. Afterward, the land rose against the king. A new occurrence of the same sign would foretell the same kind of trouble. There were also other kinds of omens which were derived from behavior of animals, from dreams, and so on. The idea that gods "write" their message on the liver and other organs of a sacrificed animal was an Akkadian concept which later, via scribal schools, reached Greece and Italy.

Enlil was the god of storm and Amon the sun-god. A god was a doer, who did this or that. As nature and mentality were essentially the same from the Indus to the Nile, the same functions were attributed to gods who bore different names according to the fantasies of their worshipers. The Hittites named the storm god Teshub, Arinna was their solar goddess, and so on. This does not mean that the pagans worshiped the phenomena of nature. Only the would-be reformers were so simple as to believe, as Ikhnaton did, that the sun disk itself was divine or, as Plato taught, that the stars were visible gods. The anthropomorphic personification, to use our own language, made the driver responsible for the good and evil that his car—the sun or storm—might do. By thus understanding the phenomena in anthropomorphic terms men tried to deal with what they could not control. From our point of view it is ridiculous to say that Amon saved Ramses II in the battle at Kadesh. But our historical explanations are too often no less metaphoric. For instance modern scholars say that after 1200, the "dynamic power" of Egyptian civilization was dead. The only advantage of such circumlocutions is that they mean nothing and for this reason do not prevent further search whereas the reference to Amon makes the explanation final.

A Greek philosopher as early as the sixth century B.C. observed that if cattle and horses could pray they would imagine their gods as cattle and horses respectively. And Aristotle noted that men imagined not only the forms of the gods but their ways of life to be like our own. The earthly cities of men became the models for the heavenly city of the gods, who were thought of as superkings. According to the Babylonian belief men were created to free the gods from work. Thus, the service of the gods was imposed on mankind. Like a king, a god lived in his palace, "the house of the god," which we inexactly call a "temple." Like the royal palace, the house of a god was not accessible to a common man. "The servants of the god," whom we call "priests," fed, clothed, amused, and otherwise took care of their masters. It was easy to understand the behavior of deities. A Hittite instruction for temple officials puts the doctrine neatly: "Are the minds of men and of the gods different? No. If a servant stands before his master he must be clean, and when the master has eaten and drunk, he is relaxed and kind. But if the servant is negligent, the master will punish him and his kin. Likewise, if a man angers of a god, the god will destroy him, his kin, his cattle and crops. Hence, be very reverent as to the words of a god. . . ." Accordingly, we can understand that when men became so numerous that the noise they made prevented the gods from sleeping, the gods sent a flood to destroy mankind. On the other hand, when Era, god of pestilence, ravaged the land, making no distinction between good and evil men, he was stopped at last by other gods, because, without their subjects, whence would the gods get their food offerings?

The anthropomorphic view of the divine world united the religious thought of the ancient Near East. Consequently its theological material exhibits one overall pattern.

Prayer is the link between the worshiper and the deity. Addressed to a superior being, the prayer praises the god in question and flatters him: he is the greatest of gods, nay, the only (true) god. Thus, he can and, therefore, must help the worshiper. The petitioner's claim may be supported by the reference to the state of the worshiper. "O Amon, give ear to one who is alone in the law court, who is poor. . . . May it be found that the poor man is vindicated. May the poor man surpass the rich," prays an Egyptian of the thirteenth century. About 1300, a Hittite queen prayed to the sun-goddess, the divine protector of her land: "Among men there is a saying: 'To a woman in travail the god yields her wish.' " Since the queen is (soon to be) in travail, the sun-goddess must grant life to her sick husband. Ramses IV petitioned the god Osiris to grant him high Nile floods so that he might make offerings to the gods and preserve his country: Osiris made the people and cannot abandon them. A god must help because he is father and king of his people; he cleanses sin, comforts the afflicted, and punishes evildoers. In short, he is both feared and loved. Thus, the workers on the royal tombs at Thebes prayed to Amon the "beloved god who listens to humble requests"; they knew that "though the servant was disposed to evil, yet the Lord [Amon] was disposed to be merciful."

Like a king, the god would punish men who offended him and would reward those who did what he wanted. Men placated him by sacrifices and gifts, but also by their righteousness. Although arbitrary and often immoral rulers, the gods, like earthly kings, insisted on the observance of law and order by their subjects. The rules of morality being virtually the same in the whole Levant, the list of sins was the same in all religions: taking the life or wife of another, false accusation, not giving water to one who asked for it, and so on. Except for the prohibition of the worship of other gods and the interdiction of idolatry, the Ten Commandments had been repeatedly prescribed in teaching—and broken in practice—ages before Moses. And several centuries before Jesus a Babylonian sage wrote down the rule: "Recompense with good the man who wrongs you."

The more the gods became a sort of interlocked directorate, the more an individual believer needed a personal and exclusive god to whom he paid constant devotion and from whom he expected personal attention. In twenty-first-century Lagash, children were named after the goddess Bau three times more often than after her august husband Ningirsu. The Babylonian often carried a seal showing him introduced to a high god by some lower deity, a kind of personal angel. King Adadnirari of Assyria (810–782) proclaimed: "Trust Nabu, do not trust another god."

In this way, what we call personal piety was born. The mother of Nabonidus, the last Babylonian king (556–539), was a devotee of Sin and three other gods of the city of Haran. From her childhood she sought after them. When Sin was angry with his city and went off to heaven, so that Haran was destroyed, she laid hold on the hem of his robe. Day and night she prayed for his return, she fasted, wore a torn dress, and praised Sin. After fifty-four years of desolation, Nabonidus, her son, restored the temple of Sin. Now, at the age of ninety-five, she prayed to Sin for her son: Let him not offend thee.

The essential unity of theological thinking made the unification of the pantheon possible and necessary. As early as about 2300, in Sumerian Lagash all local gods were considered members of the family or staff (musician, architect, and so on) of the principal god Ningirsu. Gods of different cities were similarly coordinated. In the age of the pyramids the theologians of Memphis declared that Atum, the principal god of Heliopolis, was heart and tongue, that is intellect and will, of their own Ptah. The same tendency operated on the international level. Arinna was not only "the mistress of the Hatti lands," but also "the queen of all the countries." "In the Hatti country thou bearest the name of the Sun-goddess Arinna, but in the land which thou madest the cedar land, thou bearest the name Hebat." At least the main deities became international. In the middle of the twelfth century, according to an Egyptian report, the prince of Byblos recognized that the Egyptian Amon provided for all lands. As early as about 2000, worshipers were called upon to proclaim the greatness of this or that god everywhere. When Ramses II appealed to Amon for help he exclaimed: "What will man say if even a little thing befall him who bends himself to your advice?" The gods had to pay a decent respect to the opinion of mankind.

For Further Reading

Frankfort, H., et al., *Before Philosophy.*

Asian Civilization

9   Early India

India has always been an immensely heterogeneous land of provincial fast-
nesses, linguistic and racial diversity, torn by conflict and invasions. Its
people have had little opportunity until recent times to develop a pervasive
sense of historical continuity or of national awareness, and much of ancient
Indian history is still shrouded in mystery. However, during the past century immense strides have been taken in archaeological research. The remains of large cities, monuments and inscriptions, and other artifacts of
great antiquity have been unearthed. Together with the earliest religious
literature they provide the basis for a relatively coherent reconstruction of
ancient Indian civilization despite the lack of conventional historical materials. What emerges before us is an extraordinarily rich panorama of
cultural achievements.

Paleolithic man roamed the Indian subcontinent, and there is scattered
evidence of prehistoric agricultural settlements in the northwest; but the
first great civilization to flourish there developed along the rich alluvial
banks of the Indus River and its tributaries in the third and second
millennia B.C. At Harappa and Mohenjo-Daro are the remains of two large
and expertly constructed cities which were the focal points of an archaic
culture extending for 1,000 miles along the Indus Valley. Thus far excavations have failed to reveal any surviving literature apart from brief unde-
cipherable inscriptions on emblematic seals. However, the uniformity of the
architecture and artifacts suggests the existence of a centralized state comparable to Egyptian and Mesopotamian civilization.

At Mohenjo-Daro the city was planned around a central citadel and
constructed mainly of good-quality burned brick. Spacious main streets
divided the municipal area into large blocks with smaller lanes serving the
residential sections. The houses varied in size from rows of small cottages
to larger dwellings of two and three stories with roomy interiors and bath-

CHRONOLOGY

Prehistoric Era

B.C. c. 3000–1500   Indus Valley civilization
      c. 1500–1200   Aryan invasions and earliest hymns of the Rig-
                     Veda

Vedic Era

B.C. c. 1200–900   Composition of the Rig-Veda
      c. 900–500   Later Vedas, Brahmanas, and early Upanishads

Rise of Jainism and Buddhism

B.C. c. 550   Birth of Mahavira and Gautama
      c. 322–185   Mauryan dynasty
      c. 273–237   Asoka
      c. 185–100   The Shunga and Kanva dynasties, the Laws of
                     Manu

Period of Invasions

B.C. c. 90   Earliest Saka invasions
A.D. c. 25   Kushan invasions
      c. 78–101   Kanishka
      c. 100–300   Rise of Mahayana Buddhism
      c. 300–800   Pallava rule in south India

Gupta Era

A.D. c. 320–335   Chandragupta I
      c. 335–376   Samudragupta
      c. 376–415   Chandragupta II
      c. 454–500   Hun invasions
      c. 540   End of Gupta dynasty

rooms. The elaborate municipal drainage system was without parallel in the ancient world until Roman times. While the architecture was relatively austere, there is ample evidence that the inhabitants generally enjoyed the comforts and facilities of a flourishing metropolis. The remains of fine jewelry, domestic articles of carved ivory, silver, copper, and bronze, and earthenware of good quality indicate that arts and crafts were highly developed. The larger temple-like structures—including pillared halls and a great bath 180 by 108 feet in size—suggest the presence of a well-established priesthood. Many of the engravings and artifacts reflected cultic practices common to all the great archaic civilizations—worship of the Mother Goddess, sacred animals, and related symbols. But the detailed features of the culture remain obscure. Equally enigmatic is its influence on later Indian civilization. Speculations abound, but reconstruction is substantially impossible at present, and it therefore remains one of the most challenging areas of Indian archaeological research.

The decline and demise of Harappa culture has been ascribed to a number of causes, such as the unusually massive inundations of the Indus and its tributaries which undermined the agricultural economy. The death blow probably came during the second millennium B.C. at the hands of the invading Aryan tribes from the northwest. The Aryans ("noble ones") were part of a larger Indo-European migration which left a common cultural heritage from Greece through Iran into India. The religious and social institutions of these invaders are reflected in the oldest stratum of the Veda (sacred "knowledge")—the most revered sector of traditional Hindu religious literature. The tribes were led by an aggressive warrior aristocracy mounted on horse-drawn chariots, and armed with copper and bronze weapons of good quality. Judging by the relatively inferior weapons discovered at Mohenjo-Daro, the defenders of the indigenous civilization were at a serious disadvantage. Furthermore, their food supply was dependent on a complex and vulnerable system of irrigation. By contrast the invaders were mobile. Their economy was based primarily on seminomadic techniques—cows and other animals that could move with the tribe—and they took what they needed from the lands they conquered.

Aryan tribal solidarity was based primarily on clan kinship standards, and there are indications of a functional stratification of warriors, priests, artisans, and slaves, which appears to be a structural precursor of the classical Indian "caste" system. The tribes were rigidly patriarchal and patrilinear, governed by an oligarchy of warriors or hereditary monarch, with tribal alliances formed chiefly for purposes of warfare and mutual protection.

Our knowledge of Aryan culture is derived primarily from the Samhita ("collection") of the Rig-Veda ("veda of hymns"). It was put into final form at a relatively late date, but reflects the core of a very archaic tradition. The hymns were preserved by priestly specialists, the Brahmans—a name derived from their principal function—to offer sacrificial prayer (Brahman) to the gods. They are strikingly varied—descriptive myths, invocations, and extended liturgies—but all present a coherent world view outlining the origin of the cosmos, the gods, man and society, and forming the center of a cult designed both to mediate between man and the gods and to cope with everyday needs.

The Aryans worshiped a well-defined pantheon of exalted and powerful deities, for the most part personifying natural phenomena—the sky and earth, rain, storm and lightning. The myths associated with the principal gods are sacred paradigms which in their ritual configurations provided the basis of tribal solidarity. They reveal the values, norms, and goals of the culture. The ideals of the warrior aristocracy are perhaps most forcefully outlined in the hymns associated with the storm god Indra. Equally important are Varuna—the god of justice—and Agni—the god of the sacrificial fire. All these hymns show that Vedic man took a positive view of the world around him; he was confident of his ability to grapple with his environment. His religious "anxiety" was outer-directed: there is very little evidence of the inward ascetic withdrawal and transcendental mysticism of later Indian civilization. The imagery is filled with an exuberant, this-worldly optimism. Life after death embodied the perfections of the phenomenal world.

The religious practices outlined in the second division of the Veda—the Brahmanas—represent a culmination of the worldly goals of the archaic cult. These great prose treatises are scholastic elaborations of the rituals necessary for proper performance of the sacrifice, and they evidence the emergence of a vast magical technocracy designed to manipulate both the external world and the gods themselves. In the hymns of the Rig-Veda, the high gods appear to be redolent with monumental dignity and active wills of their own, but in the Brahmanas the priest "compels" the gods to function as agents in a magical system over which he alone has control. The priests are "higher than the gods."

The growth of priestly power and status in Aryan society was an important element in the extension of Aryan political power. It is possible to trace, through geographical reference in the Veda, the slow but sure march of Aryan civilization from the Indus Valley down the western portion of the Ganges and its tributaries. One of the most striking examples of the religious means through which Aryan political power was advanced is to be seen in the greatest of all Vedic sacrifices—the ashvamedha ("horse sacrifice"). This rite was normally celebrated by a king who wished to dramatize important military conquests. One of its principal goals was to educate the populace in the values of Aryan society, in the new lines of authority, and the expectations of the elite. The sacrifice took a year to perform. It entailed the slaughter of hundreds of animals and the continual support of a large priestly staff. The king's retinue toured the countryside with the sacred horse designated for the final sacrifice. They marked out the boundaries of his territory, stilling local resistance and promulgating Aryan values by force and propaganda. The performance of this elaborate ritual presupposes a differentiated political and religious system with substantial economic resources derived not only from the expropriation of local produce and man power, but from settlement into fixed locations and systematic agriculture.

With the diffusion of Aryan culture during the ancient period came the development of caste as the basic principle of social stratification. The importance of the caste system in traditional Indian society can scarcely be exaggerated. It is difficult for Western observers to understand how a system of social organization so clearly in violation of their conceptions of "justice," "natural rights," and "fair play" could have become so fundamental a part of a great civilization. Social distinctions based on hereditary background, occupation, and economic status are, of course, nearly universal, but in India they reached a degree of institutionalization in law, custom, and religion unique in world history. The early Buddhist and Jain literature makes it clear that caste was a prevalent (if not the only) theory of society in northern India during the sixth century B.C., but its development is difficult to trace. It is probable that as the Aryan invaders battled their way down from the northwest through the Ganges Valley, they conquered and enslaved local peoples most of whom were darker and smaller than their Aryan foes. The most archaic word for slave is *dasa* (dark), and the classical word for caste is *varna* (color). This principle became the basis for a further development into four traditional *varnas,* but with the real point of distinction based on occupation: *brahman* (priest), the *kshatriya* (warrior), the *vaishya* (merchant), and the *shudra* (cultivator). However, specific hereditary status is more commonly represented by the word *jati* (birth) and related terms which signify membership in a particular local caste, clan, and family. In the past there have been as many as 3,000 castes (*jatis*) numbered.

Caste distinctions were hedged about with many barriers and taboos based on primitive notions of magical pollution which prohibited all but the most limited social contacts. In the classical form of the system only the three highest *varnas* were regarded as true Aryans and admitted to the full Vedic rites, initiation, and education. The *shudras* were for the most part excluded, but they remained an organic part of the society, tied to the land they cultivated or serving the higher castes. Beyond the pale of Aryan society were the debased "outcastes" and "untouchables," usually restricted to menial and ritually unclean tasks. Outcasting (permanent exclusion from Aryan society) was usually invoked for serious violations of caste taboos, and was used to reinforce the hereditary character of the system.

One of the most remarkable features of this system is that it did not impede extensive racial and cultural assimilation. Color distinctions as a real principle of discrimination were undercut, though they did not disappear completely. Much of the later orthodox literature is infused with cultic practices assimilated from the indigenous environment. Intermarriage became permissible, providing the woman married up (hypergamy) and within Aryan society. The caste system often transcended narrower tribal provincialisms and kinship ties, and created an environment in which a vastly diverse range of social forms could be brought under a relatively coherent system of mutual expectations and support.

Caste was diffused by the incorporation of many indigenous groups, with local leaders receiving suitable status and privileges. Part of the effectiveness of the system resulted from its self-regulating character. Each village and caste had its own council of elders who supervised and enforced the appropriate laws and customs. It was always an embarrassment for the community if caste violation became public knowledge, or if coercion from outside had to be invoked.

One of the most remarkable aspects of the system lies in the fact that it was a specifically religious institution. Conformity to caste was far more than an expedient mode of social organization and personal behavior. It was a religious obligation, and a form of personal piety. The specifically religious sanction appears first in the charismatic power of the Vedic sacrifice reinforcing Aryan solidarity and the hereditary rights of the priesthood and warrior elite; second, in the myths which elevate caste institutions to the status of essential sacred forms created by divine fiat. Later, as we shall see, the caste system was further reinforced by the theory of transmigration and ethical retribution. In all cases caste was held to be rooted in the eternal order of the universe; and it dealt with some of the most perplexing human enigmas—those with which Job was confronted: Why is there so much inequity, suffering, and misfortune in the world? It answered that all individuals are assigned their lot in life in accordance with a sacred order of fixed obligations and circumstances, and that each individual has at least the satisfaction of knowing his precise location in the universal order of things.

The caste system was immensely wasteful of human resources and seems repressive by modern standards. But given the sprawling social complexity of the Indian subcontinent and an economy of scarcity often approaching the famine level, the caste system long served as a relatively coherent solution to India's massive problems of social organization. However, caste did not go unprotested in the ancient period. It was only one of several theories of society.

In the latter half of the first millennium B.C. India seems to emerge abruptly into the light of history. The literature of the period contains much that is of historical value. Among other things, it reflects the struggle for control between the leaders of Aryan society and a new religious elite imbued with the teaching of the Buddha and of Mahavira—the founder of Jainism.

These developments in India were part of a larger pattern of social and cultural revolution throughout the civilized world from Greece to China. Provincial institutions and values were collapsing under the pressure of more complex forms of economic and political organization associated with new urban developments and imperial expansion, all driving toward wider social inclusiveness. In India during this period there was a rising urban economy with the earmarks of capitalistic affluence. But these advances were offset by massive power struggles between newly emerging states for control of territory and economic resources. The era was one of great brutality which involved the uprooting and extirpation of political minorities.

These hardships intensified earlier speculations about the great religious questions: the meaning of the self and the world, the origin and order of the universe. By the sixth century B.C., there were many new religious and philosophical schools which, despite doctrinal differences, sought new and more exalted spiritual answers to these perplexing issues. This is particularly clear in the last section of the Veda, the Upanishads, which presents a new religious theory in contrast with the older system of sacrificial and magical ritualism. The basic human problem in the Upanishads is one of personal salvation from bondage to the material world. The meaning of all external worldly forms is called sharply into question, and a new metaphysic asserts that the essential self, the soul (atman) of each individual, has its origin in a transcendent spiritual principle (Brahman); but it undergoes an endless cycle (samsara) of phenomenal rebirths, suffering, and death. It assumes a new physical form and status in each successive life depending on the ethical quality of actions (karma) in the preceding life. The law of karma means that for every thought and act there is an inevitable, retributive consequence—for better or for worse. Overt acts of hostility or aggression which harm other sentient creatures are particularly destructive, as are the inner impulses and ignorance which lead to these acts. Yet, the individual can ultimately attain spiritual release (moksha) from this cyclical round by practicing the yoga—an autonomous, inward self-discipline of mind and body designed to eliminate the sources of human error and evil. Ultimate salvation not only means final release, but the experience of eternal transcendence and bliss beyond all worldly finitude.

This new metaphysic was shared, in its rudiments, by most of the major religions which emerged during this formative period in India, but there were important differences between the Brahmanic version embodied in the Veda and those espoused by the non-Brahmanic schools—most important Buddhism and Jainism. From the Brahmanic perspective, the yoga and all other means of salvation were tied to priestly hereditary rights and authority. The Upanishads were part of the esoteric Vedic lore, dominantly restricted to the Aryan elite. The theory of karmic retribution was used to reinforce the caste system by making obedience to caste rules a precondition of salvation or at least improved birth status in the next life. By contrast, both Buddhism and Jainism rejected the religious authority of the Veda and the esoteric restrictions imposed on the new teaching. Their messages of salvation were preached openly without regard for caste. Personal conversion was the principal criterion for membership in monastic orders, and their communities included lay followers recruited from upwardly mobile urban commercial groups who held that religious and social standing should be based on proven abilities—not just on hereditary rights.

According to tradition both the Buddha and Mahavira, the founders of Buddhism and Jainism respectively, were from non-Aryan tribal clans. In their social teaching—particularly in Buddhism—anticaste criticism abounds:

> No Brahman is such by birth.
> No outcaste is such by birth.
> An outcaste is such by his deeds.
> A Brahman is such by his deeds.

Reconstruction of the Buddha's teachings as they were originally articulated in the sixth century B.C. entails difficult critical problems. However, the major forms of classical tradition represent him as teaching a theory of salvation that followed the so-called middle path—a mean between bodily self-mortification and self-indulgence. He emphasized a yoga at once exoteric and practical. The relative practicality of the doctrine is suggested by its basic axioms—the "four noble truths": 1. human existence is dukkha—an agonized bondage to the endless cycle of rebirths; 2. the cause of this agony is ignorance (avidja) of the illusory nature of phenomenal existence and also the desire (tanha) for it, which then inexorably and repeatedly forms the soul and chains it to the rebirth process; 3. the elimination of ignorance and desire will break the sequence and so precipitate final salvation—attainment of Nirvana; 4. the proper method is the "eightfold path," a combination of ethics (sila) and meditation (samadhi) which together lead to the attainment of wisdom (panna) and enlightenment (bodhi), and final salvation.

Mahavira promulgated a yoga which placed more emphasis on physical asceticism. Like the Buddha, he stressed the monastic ideal—the need to give up all worldly commitments for full-time concentration on the yoga. However, in both cases monastic requirements for the laity were considerably modified, and lay ethics stressed adherence to economically efficient virtues and contractual relationships relevant to the urban commercial environment.

Monastic asceticism was in no sense nihilistic. It sought new and more fruitful meaning in life by putting the finite and disrupted forms of the everyday world in perspective. It established a new and loftier framework of religious meaning, a more universal ethic, with remarkable potentials for social reconstruction.

The new political leaders of India during this period saw in Buddhism and Jainism valuable tools for support of the state. After provincial areas had been overwhelmed by force the universal ethics and pacifist teaching could help cement social solidarity. These potentialities were partially realized in the fourth and third centuries B.C. with the emergence of the Mauryan state—a centralized bureaucratic empire. The third Mauryan king —Asoka, whose rule began about 270 B.C.—was converted to Buddhism after his conquest of the subcontinent, and he promulgated a new ideology inscribed on stones and pillars throughout the empire. This ideology, through which Asoka hoped to unify his empire, was comprised of universal norms drawn chiefly from the Buddhist lay ethic—but also common to the other salvation religions. It tried to do away with persisting expensive and wasteful sacrifices. It bypassed caste criteria for social stratification, and it outlined economically efficient virtues which might also be expected to facilitate political integration.

However, Asoka's ideology appears to have been a thin veneer superimposed on the vastly confused and intractable Indian environment. After his death the empire was split into a number of parts. Both barbarians and Greeks invaded the northwest, and new dynasties dominated the Ganges Valley and the Deccan in the south.

It is at this point in Indian history that the Brahmanic core of early Indian culture begins to emerge as the dominant and finally the primary source of legitimate authority. In 185 B.C. the last Mauryan king was assassinated by his chief general, Pushyamitra, founder of the Shunga dynasty, who claimed Brahmanic descent. It is probable that the Shungas used the Laws of Manu (c. 200 B.C.)—the most authoritative of the ancient lawbooks—as the principal basis for social reorganization. In addition to the rules governing caste and other social institutions, the Laws of Manu offered a comprehensive theory of human action embodied in basic axioms central to orthodox Hinduism. The first axiom is represented by the "four goals": religious duty (dharma), wealth (artha), sensual satisfaction (kama), and final salvation (moksha). The second axiom is represented by the "four stages" which mark out the ideal development of individual human life from birth to death, centering particularly on the need to learn and uphold the law: the student, the householder, the ascetic, and the sage. These axioms represent an organic whole which endeavors to bring all phases of human existence under the discipline of Brahmanic values.

The dynastic and political confusions of this era obscure the growing Brahmanic solidarity. In the first century B.C. the Shungas were overwhelmed by the Satavahana empire; but the first Satavahana emperor celebrated the occasion with the horse sacrifice and depended on Brahmanic legitimation. The Satavahanas sponsored a richly diverse program in the arts and letters, as did their successors, the Pallavas. The Tamil states on the southern peninsula rose to a new power in the second century B.C. and later produced a magnificent literature of their own.

Though Buddhism slowly lost ground during this period in politics and social theory, many dynasties and feudatories retained Buddhist religious commitments. Buddhist art evolved into a highly refined expressive technique, reflected first in the ecclesiastical edifices (stupas and chaityas) at Bharhut, Sanchi, and Bodh-Gaya, and later in the sculpture of the Mathura and Gandhara schools. Of immense importance for the subsequent history of Buddhism in Asia was the doctrinal transformation of the early teaching which culminated in the development of Mahayana and later of Tantric Buddhism. The Mahayana ("great vehicle") emerges recognizably in the first century A.D. In the place of the older conservative ideal of the perfected monk practicing the yoga in isolation, it introduced the notion of the Bodhisattva ("being of enlightenment") who sacrifices his personal salvation in order to help other creatures by acts of love and compassion. Any person, not monks alone, might become a Bodhisattva, which accounts in part for the strong social grounding of Mahayana, and its missionary power. The Bodhisattva concept provided an important source for new forms of popular religion entailing the worship of heavenly Buddhas and Bodhisattvas. And at the same time Mahayana philosophy attracted many intellectuals to the Buddhist community.

The reinforcement of Buddhist tradition during this period was partly due to the influx of foreign invaders, first the Greeks—most notably under .

the Buddhist king Menander, and later the Sakas (Scythians), Pahlavas (Parthians), and Kushans. In the first and second centuries A.D. the Saka-Pahlava kings ruled an empire in the northwest which extended to the Deccan. A number of these kings converted to Buddhism, in part because they were at first regarded by the Brahmanic elite as barbarians—the equivalent of outcastes and worse. The greatest of these rulers was the Kushan king Kanishka I (c. A.D. 80), who apparently provided a favorable environment for the development of Mahayana theistic and philosophical literature.

These events in Buddhist religious life were accompanied by important developments in Hindu theism. While worship of the Vedic gods persisted, other deities of indigenous origin attracted followers. New names appeared in a bewildering variety and were incorporated in the later theistic literature as part of the Hindu pantheon. They were brought into the Brahmanic world view and placed under the authority of the Veda and its social values. The emergence of traditional Hinduism—with its profuse range of non-Vedic theistic symbolism and magical ritual—represents the adjustment of Aryan and early Brahmanic values to the archaic Indian environment. Nevertheless, the pristine authority of the Veda prevailed. The indigenous deities are usually represented as incarnations of the Vedic gods. These include the deities of other heterodox traditions—even the Buddha himself.

The fusion of Vedic and indigenous theologies in new settings can be seen in Hindu temple art—immensely rich in visual symbolism yet in one aesthetic framework. The most important cults during the early period were those devoted to the lesser Vedic gods Shiva and Vishnu. Both were popularized through extensive missionary activity, as is suggested by conversions to Shiva of rulers who must have found in Brahmanic values the means for strengthening their authority and stabilizing the social order.

One of the best examples of growing Brahmanic control over the immensely complex religious and social environment is to be found in the epic literature—the *Mahabharata* and *Ramayana*. These two massive encyclopedias of Hinduism inculcated orthodox values and institutions through the medium of epic drama. The most important text in the *Mahabharata* is the Bhagavad-Gita, written probably in the first century A.D. The Gita fuses into one superb whole many divergent strands of speculative philosophy, cultic theism, and worldly social theory. Its principal social message is that the supreme religious obligation of every man is to perform the duties of his own caste.

The power of the Sakas and Satavahanas was broken in the fourth century A.D. by the emergence of a new political power—the Gupta empire. This was an event of great importance for Indian civilization, one which probably more than any other consolidated Brahmanic orthodoxy and enriched Hindu culture. In A.D. 320 Chandragupta I ascended the throne. He undertook with all deliberateness to conquer the whole of the subcontinent —not only for personal dynastic aggrandizement, but to destroy barbarian power and to restore and bring to new fruition the sacred values of Aryan culture.

The social goals of the Guptas are reflected in epigraphs which speak of the struggle to "settle the castes and orders and to confine them to their duties." But this was not their only purpose. The arts and sciences reached new heights, and standards of courtly perfection were set which endured for centuries. The greatest of the Gupta rulers—Samudragupta (c. 335–376) was a man who could celebrate the pretentious horse sacrifice to dramatize his status as "Supreme King of Great Kings," yet also play the lute and compose poetry for the entertainment of his court. He surrounded himself with the finest artists, scholars, and scientists of his time. Allowing for exaggeration of the king's virtues by court chroniclers, it seems clear that Samudragupta and the Gupta leaders as a whole succeeded for a time in bringing political stability and new cultural unity to the troubled land.

At the height of its power, the Gupta empire dominated the subcontinent in a fashion not seen since the days of Asoka, and the search for cultural stability and social integration is reflected in a number of areas: the diverse (and hence unstable) philosophical environment of the earlier centuries was brought under the aegis of Brahmanic authority in the form of the six "orthodox" systems. Though each school was richly differentiated—ranging from ritualistic sacrificial theory to abstruse problems of logic—they all affirmed as a first epistemological principle the authority of Vedic tradition.

The drama, poetry, and musical theory of the era show a concern both for lyric beauty and for moral values. The poet and dramatist Kālidāsa (c. A.D. 400) glorified the ideal king "who punished only to maintain order and married only for the sake of progeny; and for whom material gain and pleasure were based on religious law." Even Vatsyayana, author of the *Kamasutra,* a treatise on the art of sensual love, insisted that his book was "in perfect accordance with the Holy Scriptures," and that in sexual matters one must "act in accordance with religious law . . . and not impulsively."

In general it is clear that all means—religious and philosophical—were enlisted to support the social order. So fortified, the Gupta empire probably could have survived indefinitely had it not been for the incursions of a new and ferocious foreign invader—already active in Europe and the Middle East—the Huns. By the end of the fifth century in India Hun suzerainty was spreading rapidly. Despite temporary revivals the empire was steadily torn apart. By the end of the sixth century the dynasty had been destroyed as a real political entity. Although some of its trappings were retained—Gupta coins were later imitated and the Gupta name adopted to lend dignity and legitimation to lesser kings—the achievements of the Gupta period, a culminating point in ancient Indian history, persisted at a deeper level, and remained a principal reservoir of India's cultural life into the medieval period and beyond.

For Further Reading

Bary, T. W., de (ed.), *Sources of India Tradition.*
Kosambi, D. C., *Indian Culture.*
Thapar, R., *Asoka and the Decline of the Maurya.*
Zimmer, H., *Philosophies of India.*

10   Early China

The Chinese are a historically minded people, and have assiduously collected and edited their documents for more than two millennia. In spite of this, the history of China is imperfectly known. While the general outline is clear enough, a careful analysis period by period has barely begun. This is partly because of the enormous amount of source materials, and partly because Chinese historiography poses peculiar problems which are only gradually being understood. Careful research will bring out new facts, and many generalizations will be in need of review. Chinese history is therefore in a state of flux, but for the same reason is one of the most exciting fields of modern historical research.

While the civilization of China evolved and survived throughout a longer span of time than that of any other nation in the world, it is not remarkable for its antiquity and does not unfold as early as the great cultures of the Middle East. It is only from the latter half of the second millennium B.C. that China started to take form as a social unit. These relatively late beginnings tempted some scholars in the past to seek the original home of the Chinese in Egypt or Babylon, in Central or Southeast Asia. They tried to derive the Chinese system of writing from cuneiform and even from the Hebrew alphabet. Discoveries since the 1920's have changed all this. It is clear now that the Chinese have inhabited their land since prehistoric times, and that, in spite of influences from abroad, their civilization has developed indigenously.

Primitive man lived in China as far back as the Early Pleistocene, but it

CHRONOLOGY

	B.C.	1523–1027	Shang dynasty (according to *Bamboo Annals*)
		1027–771	Western Chou dynasty
		770–256	Eastern Chou dynasty
		551–479	Traditional dates of Confucius
		c. 500	Beginning of Iron Age in China
		403–221	Age of the Warring States
		223	Ch'in annihilates Ch'u
		221–207	Ch'in dynasty

is not settled whether he was a direct ancestor of the modern Chinese. It is only in Neolithic times, whose beginning cannot yet be dated, that identifiable Chinese made their appearance in North China. The earlier part of the Neolithic is called the Yang-shao culture, after a village in western Honan, south of the Yellow River, where important discoveries were made in 1921. These and other excavations have shown that the Yang-shao culture was centered around the big knee of the Yellow River, including the lower Fen and Wei river valleys, a territory which has been called the "nuclear area of North China." The people had entered the food-producing stage, and lived in small and temporary villages. Primitive agricultural techniques, probably the slash-and-burn method, compelled them to move continually from one site to another after the soil had been exhausted. For reasons of defense, they preferred locations where rivers met or curved, and they liked to return to these favorite sites when the soil had recovered. Their most important crops were millet and wheat, and they kept domestic animals—dogs, pigs, sheep, and perhaps goats and cattle as well. But they also gathered food, hunted, and fished. They had learned how to make silk. Their pottery, painted in red and black, was rich in types and ornamentation, and may have received impulses from the Black Earth culture in southeastern Europe. Vessels, filled with food, were placed in graves, which indicates belief in an existence after death.

Gradually, this Yang-shao culture evolved into the Lung-shan culture, which has got its name from an archaeological site in Shantung. The Lung-shan age shows progress in all areas. Rice was added to the staple crops, and chickens and horses may have been domesticated. Hunting continued to furnish additional supplies. The villages were larger and inhabited for longer periods of time. People learned to dig wells and to build the first village walls. The pottery was predominantly gray and black and extremely

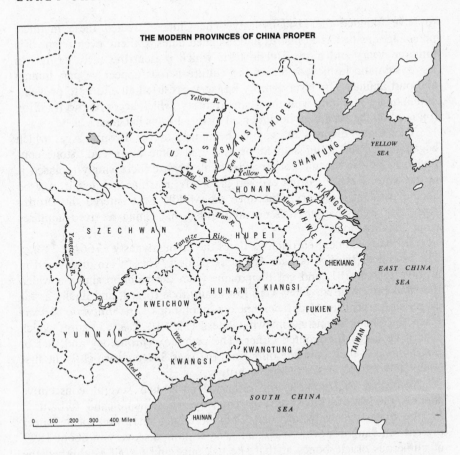

THE MODERN PROVINCES OF CHINA PROPER

varied in shape, including tripods with hollow legs and double boilers. Toward the end of the period, decorative geometric patterns became popular. Not only was the Lung-shan culture more advanced than the preceding Yang-shao, it also covered the much larger area of northern and southeastern China.

Traditionally, the Chinese have believed that civilization was created by wise rulers of remote antiquity. One of them introduced hunting, fishing, animal husbandry, and musical instruments, another agriculture and markets. A third added astronomical observations, chariots, and boats, while his wife taught the manufacture of silk, and a minister of his invented writing after having observed the tracks of birds in sand and clay. A few centuries later, three great sovereigns supposedly concentrated their efforts on devising a calendar, coping with floods, and constructing canals, dikes, and irrigation networks. The last of these sovereigns, Yü the Great, is said to have founded the Hsia dynasty. The Chinese treated these mythical personages as historical figures and assigned dates to them, even reigns of a hundred years and more. But in texts which present the early legends in less systematic fashion, some of the culture heroes appear as part human and part animal. The Hsia dynasty has so far resisted all efforts to prove its authenticity. It is only with the Shang dynasty, which according to tradition followed on the Hsia, that documented history begins in China.

The Shang dynasty marks the beginning of the Bronze Age, which began before the Lung-shan Stone Age had come to an end. Stone continued to be used in the countryside, while bronze increasingly replaced it in the cities. Bronze casting evolved gradually in China, so that it may be an independent discovery. But since the Middle East entered the Bronze Age 1,500 years earlier, it is not impossible that China received impulses from that direction.

Orthodox Chinese chronology dates the Shang dynasty 1766–1122 B.C. The so-called *Bamboo Annals* are more modest. These were discovered in a grave in A.D. 281, and got their name from the bamboo slips on which they had been written. They were lost again, then forged, and finally as far as possible reconstructed from ancient quotations. The *Bamboo Annals* place the Shang dynasty somewhat later, 1523–1027 B.C., figures which cannot be taken for granted either. The orthodox chronology and that of the *Bamboo Annals* coincide only from the year 841 B.C., which is the first completely reliable date in Chinese history.

According to tradition, the Shang dynasty had several consecutive capitals, the last of which was Yin. This city, whose name came to be used for the dynasty as a whole (i.e., Yin or Shang-yin), was located near present An-yang in northern Honan. The striking discovery in about 1899 of numerous oracle bones at that site has once and for all established the Shang as a historical dynasty. Divination by heating bones had been practiced as early as the Lung-shan period, and the Shang dynasty continued and refined this technique. The kings, assisted by diviners, put questions to their ancestors. Heat was then applied to bones, in the earlier period the shoulder blades of pigs, sheep, or cattle, later mainly tortoise shell. Cracks appeared, and from these the answers were deduced. The question, sometimes also the answer, was incised on the bone, and occasionally it was noted what actually happened. For example: "The diviner Ku asked: 'Should we hunt in Kuei, and would we have success with our traps?' That day, we caught 1 tiger, 40 deer, 164 wolves, 159 fawns, and some foxes which were rather small." More than 100,000 inscribed bones have been found, and on these appear not only the traditional names of most of the Shang kings, but also the names of some additional kings whose existence had not been known before. This makes it clear that the rulers of the Shang dynasty are historical persons.

A Shang king, also called the Son of Heaven, had administrative and religious duties. He was assisted by the nobility, which probably consisted largely of his own relatives and local chiefs. There seems to have been no strong, centralized bureaucracy. The cities, in particular the capitals, were surrounded by walls of stamped earth. The political and ceremonial center lay within the wall, while the craftsmen were settled outside, congregating in particular areas according to the specialties. Farther away, the farmers lived in villages, where their private dwellings mainly consisted of roofed pits. They grew wheat, millet, sorghum, and barley. Rice was known but perhaps not cultivated within the central region of the Shang state. The water buffalo had been tamed.

The king performed regular and complicated sacrifices to his ancestors and to various nature gods. The most common sacrificial animals were cattle, sheep, pigs, and dogs. The victims were usually burned or buried, often in sets such as two pigs plus three sheep plus five oxen. Other offerings consisted of precious objects or libations of fermented liquor. Functional and ornamental articles were also placed in the graves of the great to serve them in the hereafter. These included magnificent bronze vessels which are still acclaimed as supreme achievements of mankind. Human sacrifices were common, both at burials and at the consecration of buildings, and could involve more than a hundred victims at a single occasion. Male and female shamans acted as intermediaries between man and the spirits, but were at times sacrificed themselves if their efforts, for instance to produce rain, proved unsuccessful.

The exact size of the Shang state is unknown. It was not large, and centered on the Honan plain on both sides of the Yellow River. Its immediate neighbors were probably neither ethnically nor linguistically different, but the Shang people considered them "barbarians" as long as they did not recognize the Son of Heaven. These neighbors came increasingly under the influence of the more advanced Shang civilization, and learned among other things the technique of bronze casting. The Shang warriors maintained, however, their superiority in war. They protected themselves with helmets, body armor, and shields. Powerful composite bows of wood and horn as well as spears were used from a distance, dagger-axes with wooden handles in hand-to-hand combat. War chariots on two wheels and drawn by two horses took the place of cavalry. The horse was not yet ridden.

As shown by the oracle bones, writing was known in Shang times. The inscriptions make use of more than 2,000 different kinds of characters, which proves that the writing system was well advanced and that it must have rested on earlier stages. No remains of these earlier stages have so far been discovered. Further adaptations took place until the beginning of the Christian era, from which time onward the style of the script has stayed more or less the same.

Structurally, the Chinese writing system passed through four distinct stages. No alphabetic or syllabic scripts were developed, but each word came to be denoted by a different character. The earliest characters were pictographs for concrete words. A drawing of a woman meant a *woman,* or of a broom a *broom.* Such characters were in turn combined to form ideographs. A woman and a broom became a *wife,* three women together *treachery* or *villainy.* The third stage was reached with the phonetic loans, in which existing characters were borrowed for other words with the same pronunciation. The fourth stage was a refinement of the third: sense determinators, or radicals, were added to the phonetic loans in order to avoid confusion. Nine-tenths of the Chinese characters have been constructed by the phonetic method. Unfortunately, the phonetics were often borrowed for other than exact homophones. In such cases, the gaps have widened through the evolution of the language, until today characters may have utterly different pronunciations even though they share the same phonetic. The written language, despite its difficulties, has been an important unifying cultural and political link in China. Although many Chinese dialects are mutually unintelligible, the characters are comprehended through the eye, whatever their local pronunciation. One Chinese may not understand the other's speech, yet reads with ease his writing.

The Shang dynasty was overthrown by neighbors to the west, a people which called itself the Chou and was settled in the central Wei River valley. The Chou had been under the cultural influence of the Shang, so that their victory marked no major break in the growth of Chinese civilization. The orthodox chronology gives 1122 B.C. as the founding of the dynasty, whereas the *Bamboo Annals* place the event a hundred years later, in 1027.

The first Chou king chose the city of Hao, south of the Wei River, as his residence, and it remained the capital until 771 B.C. During this period, known as the Western Chou dynasty, China gradually emerged from the mists of antiquity. It is established that the kings granted fiefs to their relatives and allies, and conducted forceful campaigns against their neighbors. But the nobility grew in power, and the authority of the kings was correspondingly reduced. In 771 B.C. the last king of Western Chou was killed by a noble.

A year later, a son of the dead king was proclaimed successor, and Lo-yi became his capital. This city was situated east of the old capital, in Honan, some distance south of the Yellow River. During the Eastern Chou dynasty, unlike the preceding period, the royal domain was hemmed in on all sides by the fiefs of nobles, and the main functions of the kings were reduced to ceremonial and sacrificial matters. Significantly, Lo-yi was by no means the largest city of its time, measuring less than 2 by 2 miles.

While city walls up to a width of 13 yards were not uncommon, that of Lo-yi was only 5 to 6 yards wide, and clearly played little more than a symbolic role.

Although subsequent developments are not known in detail—not even the names of all the feudal states have been preserved—it is evident that power shifted outward, from the smaller centrally situated fiefs to the large states of the periphery. Of the latter, Ch'i comprised the Shantung peninsula and adjacent parts of the Great Plain, Chin had its point of gravity in southern Shansi, Ch'in gradually grew strong in the Wei River valley. To the south were two other and rather different peripheral states: Ch'u, occupying a vast territory in Central China, and Wu east of it on the coast. Both were only partially Sinified, and Ch'u in particular had a flourishing culture of its own. Its rulers even called themselves kings, a title which, from the Chinese point of view, should be reserved for the Son of Heaven alone. Beyond Wu, the dimly known Yüeh people lived along the entire coast from Chekiang to Indochina. A political system evolved in which one peripheral state after the other claimed leadership over the central states and defended them against its rivals. Aptly enough, the last period of the Chou dynasty, from 403 to 221 B.C., is known as the Age of the Warring States. After centuries of fighting, Ch'in finally gained the upper hand. The royal house of Chou ceased to be in 256. Ch'in annexed the weaker states, routed its greatest competitor, Ch'u, in 223, and two years later unified all of China under its rule.

The structure of the feudal system which took shape during the Chou dynasty has been obscured by later thinkers who looked on antiquity as a golden age and projected their utopia into it. Chou culture was not monolithic. There were pronounced regional variations in institutions, owing to local traditions and the degree of Sinification. People in the various states spoke different dialects and, as in the south, even different languages.

The Chou king was a busy man before and after his loss of political power. The formalistic observance of sacrificial and ceremonial matters demanded careful attention. He sacrificed to his ancestors, to Heaven, to the Gods of the Soil and the Crops, to the divinities of mountains and rivers, and to certain heavenly bodies; he inaugurated the seasons and supervised astronomical-astrological observations. Each ritual required particular robes, music, and dances. Then, there was the solemn investiture of feudal lords. The Son of Heaven took a lump of earth from the national altar to the Gods of the Soil and the Crops and gave it to the noble. The latter carried this to his fief and built his own altar over it. His religious duties were modeled on those of the king, but restricted to the local gods.

Traditionally, the highest aristocratic rank was that of duke, followed

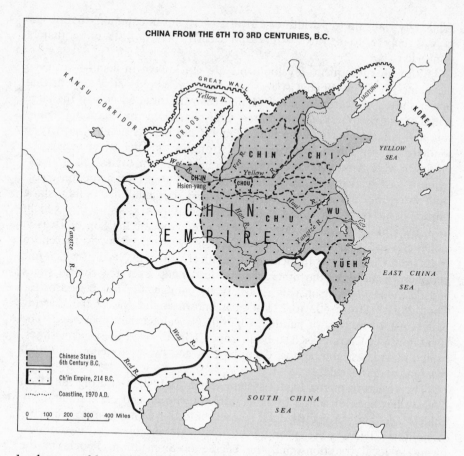

CHINA FROM THE 6TH TO 3RD CENTURIES, B.C.

by lesser nobles. This hierarchy broke down in the Age of the Warring States, when even in some of the old Chinese fiefs the rulers usurped the title of king. The nobles resided in their domains, where they created subfiefs for vassals of their own. The bonds between the feudal lords and the Son of Heaven were of a religious and frequently consanguineous nature, but these weakened in the course of time. Descent within the same lineage ceased to have significance, except for the injunction against intermarriage. For practical purposes, the important descent group became the clan. New clans were continuously forming through fission of the old, because the birth rate in the nobility was relatively high. As a result, in the last centuries of the Chou dynasty many nobles were reduced to straitened circumstances.

Much less is known about the daily life of the peasants, their economy, customs, and religion. China entered the Iron Age about 500 B.C., from which time onward a great variety of agricultural iron implements appear, including a primitive plow. But apart from idealized and untrustworthy accounts, there is no information on methods of land distribution and size of holdings. The peasants do not seem to have owned their land in the earlier period, but by the end of Chou had become proprietors through special reforms or simply through the passage of time. They rendered part of their produce as tax, performed corvée, and had to serve in war. Great winter hunts of the nobles, for which the peasants were called up, provided military training.

Scores of new cities were built in eastern Chou times, usually rectangular or square and on a north-south axis. They had double walls, and occasionally also a moat. The residences of the nobles and the administrative buildings were within the inner wall, while the craftsmen lived and worked between the inner and outer walls, clustering in particular quarters according to their enterprises. The shops of the merchants were also located there. Commerce was not yet looked down upon, and nobles themselves engaged in it without disgrace. Barter probably remained the common form of trade, but copper coins were gradually coming into use. Although slavery no doubt existed, there is no evidence that it was important for the economy.

The deterioration of the old order encouraged speculation about ways in which the imagined golden age of antiquity could be restored, about other and better forms of government, and about the purpose of existence. Some of the impoverished but educated nobles, who had come to form a class of officials, developed new ideas and tried to propagate them. Schools of thought evolved which for centuries fought and influenced each other. As long as none was victorious, this created an intellectual ferment which is singular in the history of China.

The most influential of all teachers, not in his lifetime but with increasing acclaim after his death, was Confucius. His traditional dates are 551–479. He came from the lower nobility and was a native of Lu, a small but renowned state at the foot of the sacred Mount T'ai. After pursuing studies in history, ritual, and music, after visiting the royal Chou archives in Lo-yi, and, perhaps, after a brief employment in his home state, Confucius spent the rest of his life as a teacher.

Confucius' views are known only through later works, and it is not easy to distinguish between his own teachings and the elaborations of his followers. Basically, he was concerned with the relation of man to man, and declined to engage in metaphysical speculation. As he saw the past, men had lived together in harmony under the sage rulers of the golden age. They had been truthful and wise, good and righteous, and had fulfilled their ceremonial obligations meticulously and with understanding of the moral content. Man had degenerated since then, but he is fundamentally good and can be salvaged through education. The key to this education is moral example, emanating from the top. If the ruler possesses the qualities of a Superior Man, his virtue will influence those around him. They, in turn, will be examples to others, until all mankind has been permeated. Such an ideal society requires the proper observance of the Five Relationships, in which each individual understands his particular relation to others: that between ruler and subjects, parent and child, elder and younger brother, husband and wife, and friend and friend. Confucius also emphasized the Rectification of Names, whereby he meant that reality and name should truly correspond to one another. Unless each thing lives up to its correct definition which is applicable to it alone, society cannot function. When Confucius lamented that a ruler no longer was a ruler, he wished to say that it is the essence of the ruler to rule well. The final goal is to harmonize the Way of Man and the Way of Heaven, with the king, or Son of Heaven, as intermediary between Heaven and Man.

Confucius was not an innovator. He neither proposed institutions which would break with tradition nor envisaged an end of the Chou dynasty. He wished to bring moral reform to the noble society in which he lived. His great successor Mencius went a step further. Mencius flourished in the latter half of the fourth century B.C., and is presumed to have died around 289. Traveling from court to court, he restated the views of Confucius and greatly contributed to the survival of Confucianism. But the political situation had deteriorated since the time of the master, and Mencius realized that the Chou dynasty was bound to fall. He argued therefore that a dynasty rules by the authority of the Mandate of Heaven, that this mandate is not perpetual, and that it depends on performance. Should a dynasty forfeit the mandate through lack of moral dedication to the welfare of the people, Heaven would take it back and grant it to a man worthy of founding a new dynasty. When the people reject their ruler, it proves that Heaven has withdrawn the mandate. This theory was later to have a great influence on Chinese historiography.

The adherents of the School of Law, or Legalists, aimed for a society very different from that advocated by the Confucianists. They did not bemoan the loss of a golden age, but attempted to devise new institutions suited to the new conditions. They believed that man is basically bad and that he must be curbed through stringent laws. The subjects, whose main function is to serve the state, should be made responsible for one another's conduct, and punishments should be meted out not only to the culprit but also to his relatives and neighbors. Efficiency of government should be the paramount consideration. Appointed officials, instead of hereditary nobles, should rule the state. The nation should always be prepared for war, and valor in battle should be rewarded. Some Legalists succeeded in having themselves appointed to high office in the state of Ch'in, and were there able to translate their theories into practice. This was an important factor in strengthening Ch'in, and in bringing about the unification of China.

Still other thinkers viewed matters solely in relation to their utility. The Moists, named after a certain Mo-tzu, or Master Mo, who flourished in the latter half of the fifth century B.C., opposed warfare, elaborate ceremonies, even music, and favored universal love. While the Confucianists argued that man's capacity for love is limited, and that it therefore should be dispensed from the family outward on a diminishing scale of intensity, the Moists claimed that anything less than universal love would be unprofitable and wasteful. The members of the school were tightly organized under dictatorial leaders and, for a while, achieved considerable political influence. Since they opposed war, they interfered in wars on the weaker side, seeking to restore balance and peace. This turned the Moists, paradoxically, into military experts.

The Naturalists, finally, represent a fairly late development in the thought of Chou times. They explained the universe in terms of Yin and Yang, forces which do not oppose but complement each other. The Yin principle is female, dark, and passive; the Yang principle is male, light, and active. Their interplay explains all functions of nature, such as the roles of man and woman, the alternation of day and night, and the succession of the seasons. The belief in Yin and Yang was later combined with the theory of the Five Elements. Listed in various sequences, among which the most popular was that of wood—fire—earth—metal—water, the elements were supposed to form a cycle which starts anew as soon as it is completed. The concepts of Yin and Yang and the Five Elements were taken over by Confucianism, and became influential from Han times onward. They were not only correlated with each other, but also with the directions of the compass, the seasons, colors, tastes, smells, organs, animals, grains, numbers, and so on. This pseudo-scientific scheme seemed to provide an answer to the coming and going of dynasties (each of which was believed to rule by virtue of a particular element), to illnesses and their cures, to the interpretation of portents, and to much else.

All these schools concerned themselves in various degree with man as a social and political animal. The only movement which categorically refused to do so was Taoism. Lao-tzu, who has been considered its founder, was, according to tradition, an older contemporary of Confucius and author of the text which became known as the *Tao te ching* or *Book of the Tao and Its Power*. Actually, this work belongs to a somewhat later period. It is exceedingly terse, aphoristic, and difficult, and has attracted an unusually great number of not always competent translators. One must turn to

Chuang-tzu, or Master Chuang, who lived in the latter half of the fourth and first years of the third centuries, to gain an understanding of early Taoism. The book which bears his name is not exclusively by him, but parts of it show the unmistakable marks of a highly original mind and a great literary talent.

The Taoists believed that in the material world everything is relative. Concepts exist only as contrasts. There can be no death without life, no goodness without evil. But behind the duality and illusions, there abides a unifying, primary principle, called the Tao. It cannot be defined, and it eludes intellectual pursuit. The Tao can only be intuitively understood in a mystical state reached through meditation. Some Taoists believed that this would be facilitated by certain breathing exercises and sexual techniques, which would also serve to prolong life. It is obvious that Taoism, in its pure form, was irreconcilable with any other school which attempted to define man's role in organized society. Only if man ceased the futile chase after illusions, and sought a state of naturalness, spontaneity, and disengagement, of passive simplicity, could he find fulfillment. This attitude is well exemplified by the following famous passage from the work of Chuang-tzu:

Chuang-tzu fished in the P'u River. The king of Ch'u sent two grandees to present themselves before him and say: "I wish to trouble you with the administration of my state." Chuang-tzu held the fishing rod, did not turn his head, and said: "I have heard that there is a sacred tortoise in Ch'u, and that she has been dead for three thousand years. The king keeps her, wrapped in cloth and placed in a box, in the ancestral temple. As regards this tortoise now, would she rather have died and because of that leave behind her bones and be held in honor? Or would she rather have stayed alive and trailed her tail in the mud?" The two grandees said: "She would rather have stayed alive and trailed her tail in the mud." Chuang-tzu said: "Go away. I will trail my tail in the mud."

Since Confucianism gradually became the Chinese state doctrine, its classical texts naturally gained an enormous prestige, and more than any other influenced the thought of later times. This is not to say that the Confucian classics—they date from Chou and early Han times—are all written in a Confucian spirit. Some works were simply adopted by the school and reinterpreted. Neither is it true that every classic deserves its fame. Among the more important is the *Book of Odes,* a collection of early poetry, whose date of compilation is disputed and has been given as somewhere between 800 and 600 B.C. It comprises 305 poems, ranging from folk songs to court compositions. The rhymes were standardized to satisfy the exacting taste of the royal court, and they were sung to musical accompaniments which have long been forgotten. Some of the odes seem undistinguished and pedestrian today. Others, such as this love poem in Burton Watson's translation, have a simple charm which has not lost its appeal:

> Blue, blue your collar,
>   Sad, sad my heart.
> Though I do not go to you,
>   Why don't you send word?
>
> Blue, blue your belt-stone,
>   Sad, sad my thoughts.
> Though I do not go to you,
>   Why don't you come?
>
> Restless, heedless,
>   I walk the gate tower.
> One day not seeing you
>   Is three months long.

Another early work is the *Book of Documents,* which in its present state has genuine as well as forged sections. It consists largely of speeches and statements attributed to legendary and historical personalities. These pronouncements are clearly not authentic but literary inventions of what people might or should have said. The genuine parts of the *Book of Documents,* like the entire *Book of Odes,* are written in archaic Chinese, and have great linguistic importance apart from their literary value.

The *Book of Changes* is one of the best known and most overestimated works in Chinese literature. It is fundamentally an early oracle handbook, whose interpretations are brief and obscure: "It is advantageous to cross the great river"; "In the 8th month, there will be misfortune." The Chinese, and not a few Westerners, have read a cosmological depth into this text which it does not possess.

Several of the classics are concerned with the ritual system of Chou times and, veering from the solemn to the trivial, discuss such matters as etiquette, ceremonies, music, education, and government. More important to the modern historian are the *Spring and Autumn Annals,* whose compilation is attributed to Confucius himself. They contain brief excerpts from the archives of Lu, arranged in chronological order, covering the years 722–481 B.C. That time span is therefore commonly referred to as the Spring and Autumn Period. In contrast to the *Book of Documents,* the *Spring and Autumn Annals* are not an idealization but a serious historical work. Together with the *Bamboo Annals* and the annals of the Ch'in state, they are the earliest surviving evidence of the awakening of historical perception in China. Since the *Spring and Autumn Annals* are extremely terse, another text has been appended to them, section by section, as an amplification. This is the *Tso chuan,* whose title is not fully understood, and whose narrative mixes the real and imagined past into a broad panorama. The *Spring and Autumn Annals* record, for instance, the death of a certain noble on a specific day in 507 B.C. with extreme brevity: "Ch'uan, the viscount of Chu, died." The *Tso chuan* says about the same event:

The viscount of Chu was in his gate tower and looked down on the court-yard. The doorkeeper sprinkled the courtyard with a water pitcher. When the viscount of Chu saw it, he became angry. The doorkeeper said: "Yi Yi-ku has urinated here." The viscount ordered him to be seized (Yi Yi-ku), but he could not be found. The viscount became even more excited and angry. Throwing him-self on a couch, he fell on a brazier with charcoal, was consumed by fire, and died. Before he was interred, they took five chariots and buried five persons with him. Chuang-kung (the posthumous name of the viscount), while being irascible and hasty, loved cleanliness. Therefore it came to this.

Later scholars found it difficult to reconcile the dry and uninspiring entries of the *Spring and Autumn Annals* with their belief that Confucius was the author. They convinced themselves that the work contained a hidden ap-praisal of historical figures, and tried to find the key by scrutinizing the wording of each passage. This approach was codified in two great com-mentaries which are counted among the Confucian classics. The belief that the *Spring and Autumn Annals* and later historical works contain hidden praise and blame became persistent not only in China but also in some Western circles. There are no grounds for it, and it has created much un-necessary confusion.

Esteemed and influential though these classics were, none was ven-erated as highly as the *Analects.* They were compiled some time after the death of Confucius, and are a fragmentary and unsystematic record of conversations and pronouncements attributed to him. The *Analects* were learned by heart not only by educated men in China but in all of East Asia, and their aphoristic sayings, a few of which are translated here, have been deeply admired precepts for two millennia:

The Master said: "To learn without thinking is in vain. To think without learning is dangerous."

The Master said: "If natural qualities exceed refinement, then one is uncouth. If refinement exceeds natural qualities, then one is like a clerk. If re-finement and natural qualities are equally combined, thereafter one is a Su-perior Man."

The Master said: "If someone is not full of eagerness, I do not instruct him. If he makes no effort, I do not enlighten him. If I lift up one corner, and he does not answer with the other three corners, then I do not repeat the lesson."

Tzu-kung asked: "Is there a single saying which one can act upon until the end of one's life?" The Master said: "Would it be reciprocity? What you do not wish done to yourself, do not do to others."

A text, which eventually ranked second only to the *Analects,* is the one ascribed to Mencius. It was probably written by his disciples. The work contains not only pronouncements of this great Confucian thinker, but also describes discussions between him and rulers of his time, portraying the skillful way in which he drove home his points. Whether these accounts have any historical trustworthiness is unclear. In any event, they idealize Mencius' confrontations with the feudal lords, as in this encounter:

Mencius said to king Hsüan of Ch'i: "If among the subjects of Your Majesty there were one who entrusted his wife and children to a friend and went on a trip to Ch'u, and if on his return the friend had let the wife and children freeze and starve, what should be done about it?" The king said: "He should cast him off." Mencius said: "If the Master of the Judges were unable to direct the judges, what should be done about it?" The king said: "One should dismiss him." Mencius said: "If within the state there is no good government, what should be done about it?" The king turned his head to the left and right and spoke of other things.

Further reading suggestions follow Chapter 11.

11   The Chinese Empire: The Formative Period

The unification of China had been made possible by a number of remarkable statesmen. They had introduced a series of reforms in the old Ch'in state which gradually had strengthened this feudal domain to the point where it could unify China under its rule. These reforms were inspired by the Legalist School: Laws were clearly promulgated and strictly enforced. The peasants were given ownership of their land and were permitted to buy and sell it. Irrigation projects were carried out to promote agriculture. Weights and measures were standardized. Appointed officials, instead of hereditary nobles, governed the people. The district (hsien) became the basic unit of provincial administration. The effectiveness of the army was increased through adoption of the powerful crossbow and through replacement of the clumsy war chariots by cavalry.

With the unification of 221 B.C., China for the first time in history became a single nation. The northern border enclosed the Liaotung Peninsula and southern Manchuria in the east, and the Ordos bend of the Yellow River in the west. It was defended by a Great Wall, which in major parts was based on earlier fortifications. Korea and the Kansu corridor did not belong to the empire. In the south, Hunan, parts of Kwangtung and Kwangsi, and perhaps also the Red River delta in Indochina were incorporated into the new state during 214. Kiangsi and Fukien in the southeast, and Kweichou and Yunnan in the southwest, were not yet Chinese. The seat of the central government was Hsien-yang, the capital of the former Ch'in state in the Wei River valley. The king of Ch'in became the Son of Heaven, but since the title of king had lost much of its prestige, he adopted a different and imposing designation: huang-ti. It means August Lord, but is usually translated as emperor. He was the First Emperor (Shih-huang-ti).

The institutions of the old Ch'in state were extended to all of the new Ch'in empire. The feudal system was abolished in favor of an appointed bureaucracy. In place of the former states, the country was divided into commanderies, consisting of varying numbers of districts. The laws, currencies, weights, measures, and even the distance between cart wheels were standardized. Carrying standardization to the extreme, a minister proposed in 213 B.C. that all books not sponsored by the Legalists should be burned, excepting only works on agriculture, medicine, pharmacy, and divination. The imperial library was designated to remain intact as a repository of knowledge. This policy was clearly intended to wipe out the intellectual opposition to Legalism and the centralized state.

If the Ch'in dynasty had lasted, the political effects of the Book Burning Edict would have been far-reaching. Legalism might have been permanently established as the state doctrine, and men of other persuasions excluded from government careers. The Confucianists have never tired of blaming the First Emperor for this attempt at intellectual restriction, conveniently overlooking the fact that they themselves suppressed their opponents as soon as they had the power to do so. But the consequences of the persecution were perhaps less harmful for literature than it might seem. Books in private possession cannot have been many, since they were bulky and expensive (copied by hand on wooden or bamboo slips, and tied together accordion fashion). In spite of threatened punishments, the edict could be evaded and books hidden.

An unanticipated catastrophe was the destruction of the entire imperial library in 206 B.C. during the civil war. But since the teachings of the schools were usually memorized and handed down orally from master to disciple, it was possible after 191 B.C., when the Book Burning Edict was belatedly rescinded by the Han dynasty, to reconstruct the texts from memory and from preserved manuscripts.

The First Emperor died on a tour of inspection in 210 B.C. Intrigues crippled the central government, and during the following year civil war broke out in the provinces. By the end of 207, the Ch'in dynasty had ceased to exist, a swift collapse traditionally blamed on the harshness of the Legalist state. But since the Legalists favored agriculture, and the peasants were the vast majority of the population, this view is not convincing. While the real reasons have not yet been explored, resurgence of regionalism must have been an important factor. As soon as the grip of the central government weakened, centrifugal forces asserted themselves. They were always strong under the surface, and continued to make themselves felt throughout Chinese history.

The victor in the civil war was a commoner, who became king of Han in 206, was proclaimed emperor in 202, and is known in history by his posthumous name as Emperor Kao. He retained Han as the name of his dynasty and dated it from 206, although it really began four years later.

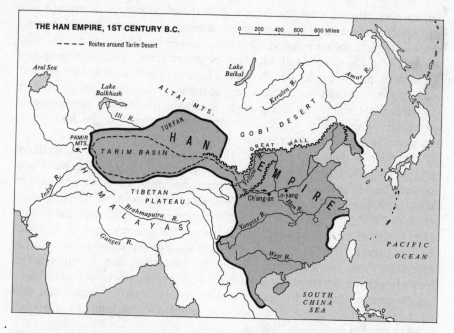

His descendants occupied the throne until A.D. 9. Then followed an interregnum, after which the Han dynasty was restored in 25 and remained in
power until 220. It is therefore customary to speak of the Former and
Later Han dynasties.

The empire was at first smaller than it had been in Ch'in times. The
northern Ordos Region had been taken by the nomads, and in the south a
Chinese adventurer had founded an independent state with the capital at
present-day Canton. Between 127 and 101 B.C. the energetic Emperor Wu
reconquered these lost territories, and further expanded the state by incorporating Kweichou, Yunnan, a large part of Korea, and the Kansu
corridor. Only Fukien on the southeast coast remained beyond the Chinese
border throughout both Han dynasties.

During the Han era, Confucianism adapted itself to the needs of the
empire and became the state doctrine. The Legalists had proved their
capacity for ruling, and if the Confucianists wished to outmaneuver them,
they were forced to accept some of their viewpoints and techniques. Without losing its moral zeal, Confucianism developed into a useful tool of
government, precisely because it was flexible and eclectic. It borrowed not
only from the Legalists, but also particularly from the Naturalists. Needless
to say, the more successful Confucianism became, and the more Confucius
was enshrined as universal sage, the more his followers departed from his
teaching.

The victory of Confucianism was therefore gradual. The first major success came in 141 B.C., when the Legalists were excluded from government careers. In 124 B.C., the Imperial Academy was established with a Confucian curriculum. To reconcile discrepancies in the transmission of the Confucian classics, and to establish standard texts, discussions were held in 51 B.C. and A.D. 79. The emperors participated on both occasions and acted as arbiters. In A.D. 175 the orthodox version of the classics was engraved on stone.

The Han government was modeled on that of Ch'in. This administrative system underwent many adaptations in the course of the centuries, but it was not basically altered. There was always more continuity than change in China's bureaucratic institutions, from the establishment of the empire in 221 B.C. until its fall in A.D. 1912.

The traditional nobility of Chou times had disappeared. Although Emperor Kao had taken the retrograde step of enfeoffing kings, they were gradually shorn of power. The royal dignity came to be conferred only on members of the imperial house, who after an abortive uprising in 154 B.C. lost all influence on the administration of their fiefs. The highest title in the nobility below the kings was that of marquis, followed by nineteen lesser ranks. Such titles were granted by the government as a reward for merit or as an act of favor and were frequently revoked. Whether they were kings or lesser nobles, the government kept a sharp eye on their conduct, and demoted them for real or imagined infringements of the law. Within a hundred years from the death of Emperor Kao in 195 B.C., for example, all of his marquisates had ceased to be.

The various departments of the central government were each under a minister, among whom the Chancellor was the most important. He was in charge of personnel, the state budget, expenditure, registers, and accounts, and acted also as a spokesman for the bureaucracy. The Grandee Secretary had supervisory duties similar to those of the Chancellor, while the Grand Commandant controlled the military. The Chancellor, Grandee Secretary, and Grand Commandant were jointly referred to as the Three Excellencies. Next in rank came the Nine Ministers, whose duties included management of ritual and education; direction of the imperial household; guarding of the palace; control of the imperial chariots, horses, and government pastures; administration of justice; supervision of the nobility, and contacts with the barbarians; registration of the imperial clan; collection of revenue and charge of the state granaries; and the processing of edicts and memorials. There was intentional overlapping of functions in order to provide checks and prevent fraud. Special officials had the duty to remonstrate with the emperor if his performance was poor, while others inspected the conduct of the bureaucracy. This was the origin of the later famous censorate.

The empire was divided into twelve provinces, which were merely groupings of territories for purpose of inspection. The large metropolitan area formed a thirteenth unit with Ch'ang-an as the capital in Former Han and Lo-yang during Later Han. Many of the following dynasties gave preference to the same two cities. For each province, one inspector was appointed who headed a sizable staff. He went on regular tours to scrutinize the performance of the officials and reported his findings to the central government. The provinces consisted of a varying number of commanderies, whose total grew from 36 in Ch'in times to 103 in A.D. 2. Each commandery was under an administrator, aided by departments. The commanderies were divided into districts, for which the central government appointed magistrates. The districts numbered 1,578 in A.D. 2, some 400 of which were abolished during Later Han for economic reasons. They consisted of still smaller administrative units, whose heads were not appointed by the central government but selected locally.

Civil servants were recruited by several methods. The upper echelons of the bureaucracy had the right to appoint their own subordinates. High officials enjoyed the special privilege to recommend sons or nephews, who were first given duties in the palace and then gradually absorbed into the bureaucracy. Unsolicited recommendations were a further possibility, but, as in all cases, the sponsor was held responsible for the conduct of his candidate. The emperor, at times, directly summoned men (who did not necessarily have to accept the invitation). Studies at the Imperial Academy could lead to official appointment. Finally, some offices were sold by the government as a source of revenue.

Historically more remarkable than these unsystematic forms of recruitment was the examination system, which, eventually, became the all-important entrée into officialdom. Its primitive beginnings were devised by the Han. The system began with edicts at irregular intervals—the first known case was in 196 B.C.—inviting specific officials to recommend morally upstanding men. From the middle of Former Han, it also became routine that each commandery annually recommended two men. A quota system was introduced in A.D. 102, based on the size of population and the location of each commandery. Written examinations were given but not required from every category of candidates.

The main cleavage in ancient China was between the educated and the uneducated, the literate gentry from which the officials were drawn and the illiterate peasants. The great gentry families had national importance. The small gentry had local influence and merged on the lower levels with the rich peasantry. The peasants, who constituted the bulk of the population, paid most of the taxes, had to perform corvée, and were called up for military service. The army consisted mainly of militia; professional soldiers were few. Merchants were discriminated against, a prejudice which became more pronounced in the course of history, but it was not yet strong enough in Han times to prevent the gentry from engaging in commerce.

The rigidity of Chinese society has been much exaggerated. The division into the educated and uneducated levels of society was not hard and fast. The line could be crossed, and the gentry readily absorbed newcomers. On the national level, few families remained influential for long. Each dynasty brought a new elite to the fore which rarely survived for long at the center of power. It would be overturned in the ruthless struggle of cliques, and others would move up to take its place. Social mobility seems to have been the rule, rather than the exception, in Chinese history.

While never codified in a constitution, power was shared by the emperor and the bureaucracy. Major policy decisions were discussed at the court, and the advice of high officials, if unanimous, was considered binding. The emperor did not interfere in the daily routine of the government departments. The appointment of high officials was a delicate matter in which the emperor's choice was frequently restricted; connections had to be considered at least as much as competence. The balance of power between the emperor and the bureaucracy was therefore subtle and shifting. At the one extreme, the emperor could content himself with a passive role. At the other, he could attempt personal rule by manipulating advice, by intimidating the officials, or by tripping them up on one or another of the many laws. Another device for concentrating power in the emperor's hands was the system of the Inner Court. The Inner Court consisted of such men as secretaries and the eunuchs of the imperial harem who had easy access to his person and could be dominated by him. Once the flow of documents to and from the throne had been channeled through the Inner Court, the influence of the high career officials, or the Outer Court, was automatically reduced.

If the emperor had not yet attained his majority, the empress dowager was entitled to govern in his place. Normally, empresses preferred to appoint one of their male relatives as regent. Nothing prevented an adult emperor, uninterested in government, from adopting the same course and formally or informally delegating his power. In such cases, the representative would usually head the Inner Court.

It follows that within the complex institutional structure many interests strove for influence: emperors, regents, the Inner and Outer Courts, sometimes ambitious empresses or empresses dowager, and always the ubiquitous cliques. But whoever succeeded in dominating the government never possessed unlimited power. Traditional China was not a despotism in any strict sense of the word.

The first regent was appointed in 87 B.C., and in the beginning the institution seems to have functioned well. It was only with Emperor Ch'eng's long reign (32–7 B.C.) that the situation changed. He took no interest in government and was willing to delegate authority to his mother's relatives. She belonged to the great Wang clan, and appointed, one after another, five members of that clan as regents. The last of these was Wang Mang, who gradually outmaneuvered all opposition, until in A.D. 9 he could declare the Han dynasty defunct and ascend the throne himself.

Wang Mang is one of the most discussed figures in Chinese history. The sources are biased against him, and his policies have been misunderstood. Many of his so-called reforms were in fact no reforms at all but merely continuations of Former Han practices. Where he departed from them, as in his attempt to redistribute land, he was guided by Confucian ideas and doubtless had the warm support of his Confucian advisers. There can have been no deep discontent with Wang Mang among the intelligentsia, since no gentry uprisings took place from A.D. 9 to 22. He fell because of events beyond his control, the cumulative effects of two major changes in the course of the Yellow River. Floods and famines set in motion large-scale migrations. Displaced and starving peasants banded together, the government armies were defeated, supporters of the Han house exploited the situation, and in 23 Wang Mang was killed by the rebels.

The nation was united again under a distant branch of the former imperial clan, officially in the year 25, although peace was not restored until 36. The new dynasty was called the Later Han. The regency was reintroduced in 89, whereupon the struggle between cliques became even more violent than it had been during Former Han. At times, even emperor and regent were pitted against each other. The eunuchs sided with the emperor, which increased their power in the Inner Court. The civil servants, from not unselfish motives, were hostile to the eunuchs, and continued to be so throughout Chinese history. In a great confrontation of 169, the eunuchs were victorious, only to be themselves annihilated in 189.

While the central government was being weakened through the conflict in the capital, rebellions broke out in the provinces. The most important one was that of the Yellow Turbans in 184. During decades of fighting, the leading generals maneuvered for personal power. When the last emperor of Later Han was finally forced to abdicate in 220, this was only the symbolic end of the dynasty. In practical political terms, it had ceased to exist long before.

Just as the virtue of the Son of Heaven was thought to permeate all of China, it was envisioned that it would spread in time beyond the borders.

Once the lesser people had been transformed through his moral guidance, they would willingly recognize him as the ruler of all men, expressing homage by the act of paying tribute. In short, the Chinese construed cultural superiority as moral supremacy.

It is true that during its formative period China had no contacts with other cultures of the same splendor. The Han Chinese were dimly aware of India and the Roman world, but these civilizations were too far away to shake their self-confidence. They could convince themselves of their own primacy. This attitude became instinctive in the course of time, although it required a certain capacity for self-deception. Tribute was a disguised form of trade, since the presents brought by foreign peoples were richly matched by Chinese gifts. It should have been obvious to intelligent observers that many missions reaching China from abroad were only attracted by the opportunity for profit.

It was even harder to ignore the fact that the nomads of the north could not be permanently curbed by either benevolence or force. At the same time that the Chinese empire was being founded, the Hsiung-nu in Central Asia had been organized into a tribal federation under a supreme ruler called the Shan-yü. Little is known about the ethnic background and linguistic affiliation of the Hsiung-nu. They raided China at will, and even came within sight of the capital. The Chinese bought peace by sending annual gifts and an occasional princess. In spite of his supposed place on the summit of a world hierarchy, the Son of Heaven in his letters addressed the Hsiung-nu ruler as an equal. This period of appeasement lasted until 133 B.C., when Emperor Wu took the offensive and the great Hsiung-nu wars began. Until the end of the second century B.C., Emperor Wu had the military initiative, which he used to expand the empire toward the northwest. A by-product was the conquest of the Western Region, a territory largely corresponding to the Tarim Basin and the Turfan Oasis. It was important for its famous trade routes, on which Chinese silk was carried to the West.

For the next half-century, Chinese and Hsiung-nu held each other in balance. This changed dramatically when dissension among the Hsiung-nu persuaded one of two rival Shan-yü to make peace with China, and to pay an unprecedented visit to the imperial capital in 51 B.C. The Chinese sources seriously misrepresent the event by depicting it as a subjugation of the Hsiung-nu. In reality, the Hsiung-nu had not been defeated. They simply offered peace, which meant to cease their raids, during a brief period of internal troubles. That China was the greater power of the two was acknowledged by the visit of the foreign ruler, but the visit was not an act of homage. Most Chinese officials misinterpreted it in typical Sinocentric fashion, and proposed that the Shan-yü, as a barbarian, should be ranked below the Chinese kings. The emperor had the good sense to refuse, and to treat the Shan-yü as an equal. Considered objectively, two independent nations had made peace. Whether it would last depended on the Hsiung-nu, not the Chinese. It lasted until the reign of Wang Mang, when a war party emerged among the Hsiung-nu. Wang Mang restrained it successfully by diplomatic and military means. At his death, the northern border was intact, and at least the northern silk route through the Tarim Basin remained in Chinese hands.

During the civil war after Wang Mang's fall, the Western Region was lost to China. The Hsiung-nu resumed their raids, and actively supported one of the Chinese pretenders to the throne. The founder of the Later Han dynasty reacted passively to the northern border problems, even to the point of evacuating a number of commanderies. The Hsiung-nu entered these territories and began to live in China proper.

In A.D. 46, a new dissension occurred among the Hsiung-nu, which in 49 led to a split between a southern and northern branch, each under a separate Shan-yü. The southern Shan-yü, in a weaker position than his predecessor a hundred years earlier, made peace with China and, at least symbolically, declared himself a subject. The Chinese government did not take this unexpected opportunity to defeat the northern Hsiung-nu and install the southern Shan-yü as an ally in the old grazing grounds north of the Gobi. Instead, the southern Hsiung-nu were permitted to remain in the Ordos Region and northern Shansi within the Chinese border. When the Chinese finally defeated the northern Hsiung-nu in a great offensive of 89, it was too late. Although the Western Region came under Chinese domination once again, other nomadic tribes filled the vacuum left by the northern Hsiung-nu in Central Asia. The southern Hsiung-nu stayed on Chinese soil, and formed a frequently hostile state within the state. China's grip on the northwest slackened, and the initiative shifted to the southern Hsiung-nu. In 308 the rupture took place, which in 316 led to the temporary loss of all of northern China.

The victory of the Hsiung-nu was facilitated by the depopulation of the northwest. Owing to the changes in the course of the Yellow River, and pressure from the Hsiung-nu and Tibetans in the northwest, a major migration from north to south took place in Later Han times. This led to the first great colonization of South China, through which in Hunan, Kiangsi, and Kwangtung alone the population quadrupled. The Chinese settled on the alluvial soil of the major river valleys, engulfing or absorbing the local aboriginals. Those who opposed Chinese rule were forced to withdraw into the lesser river valleys and the mountains. Because of the steep influx of colonists in Later Han, the more belligerent of the aboriginal tribes began to fight back. Whereas during the last two centuries B.C. the aboriginal uprisings (the Chinese called them rebellions) had been only three, their number increased to fifty-four during the first two centuries A.D.

It is clear, therefore, that the Han empire was not a Chinese island surrounded by barbarians. In the northwest, Hsiung-nu, Tibetans, and other tribesmen lived side by side with the Chinese and gradually proved the stronger. In the south, the aboriginals were step by step displaced by the Chinese and generally were the weaker. Only the Great Plain was inhabited solely by the Chinese.

By the end of Later Han times, the major characteristics of traditional China had taken form. In territory, the empire nearly corresponded to modern China proper. It had a highly centralized government under an emperor who reigned or ruled according to his preference. The main channels for the wielding of political power had been shaped. An efficient bureaucracy had been created, based on the principle of checks and balances. The examination system had been devised. Social rise was common. There were strong centrifugal forces under the surface, but rebels were rarely revolutionaries; they only strove for influence within the system. The script and literature were unifying forces. The bureaucracy engaged the energies of the ambitious. Confucianism offered a satisfactory explanation of man's role in society. Neo-Taoism and Buddhism appealed to those who sought greater spiritual depth. The achievements of China's civilization, coupled with its geographic isolation, had engendered a sense of superiority and a claim to moral and political supremacy among mankind.

The Han dynasty is a formative period not only of Chinese history but of its historiography as well. The work which created an entirely new genre and set a trend for two millennia is the *Historical Records,* compiled privately by Ssu-ma T'an and his son Ssu-ma Ch'ien, whose names rank with the greatest historians of all times. They conceived the idea of writing a complete history of China, from the legendary sovereigns to Emperor Wu. Ssu-ma Ch'ien finished this ambitious undertaking after 99 B.C. at great personal sacrifice. He was castrated on the order of Emperor Wu, who felt that he had been slighted in the work. During Later Han times, another remarkable family of historians continued on the same course. Pan Piao (d. A.D. 54) and his son Pan Ku (d. 92) compiled the *Documents of Han,* a history of Former Han. Similar histories were later written for all dynasties, sometimes lumping several minor ones together, but private efforts were supplanted by enterprises sponsored by the government and compiled by committees of scholars. It became standard practice for a new dynasty to publish an official history of its predecessor. In this way, their number has grown to twenty-four or twenty-five, depending on how they are counted.

The dynastic histories are not analytic studies in the Western sense. They are vast compilations of source materials, some copied verbatim, others abbreviated or paraphrased. The historian let the documents speak for themselves, and rarely expressed his own opinion, but since he made a selection, his role was more than that of a copyist. He had a viewpoint. His purpose was not to glorify each emperor or the ruling intelligentsia, nor to write handbooks for future generations of bureaucrats. He belongs, rather, to the common stage of early historiography, where history was thought to have been made by individuals alone. This is the reason why he concentrated on those who played important roles in their time: the emperors and empresses, officials, scholars and writers, eccentrics, the virtuous, and the rebels. Even the early historians of the Ssu-ma and Pan families were dimly aware of a further step in historical perception, since they also devoted sections to foreign tribes, and grouped materials under such headings as calendar, ceremonies, law, commerce, state sacrifices, portents and astrology, administrative geography, canals, and bibliography. But traditional Chinese historiography never came fully to realize or admit that impersonal forces also act as historical causes. The glory of Chinese historiography is therefore also its limitation. The format of the dynastic histories became standard, and provided the world with an unparalleled accumulation of source materials. At the same time, originality was stifled. There were independent historians of great talent who went their own way, but they stood outside the main tradition and had no lasting influence.

The reliability of the dynastic histories is uneven. Outright falsification of facts does occur, but is less common than distorted emphasis. Each dynasty wished to justify its own rise to power by discrediting the last ruler of the preceding one, and the dynastic historian was under pressure to select his sources accordingly. It is unlikely that he needed much persuasion. He was influenced by the Confucian philosophy of history, first clearly formulated by Mencius, which held that each dynasty ruled under the Mandate of Heaven. The historian simply chose or presented his documents in such a way that they seemed to prove why a dynasty founder had been worthy of the mandate and his predecessor not. In the same fashion, he gave short shrift to men who never received the mandate at all, describing them as bandits or usurpers for whom nothing good could be said. Documents which contradicted such interpretations were suppressed. For instance, if Wang Mang's attempt to found a dynasty had been successful, he would have appeared in historical writing with all the real and imagined attributes of a dynasty founder, basking in Heaven's approval. His overthrow and the restoration of Han made that impossible. Wang Mang shrunk into an incompetent schemer with delusions of grandeur.

* * *

With the collapse of Han, China fell apart into three territories: Wei in the north, Wu in the southeast, and Shu in the southwest. This period is usually called that of the Three Kingdoms, although Three States would be more accurate. The country was briefly reunited by the Western Chin dynasty (265–316), whose capital was Lo-yang. But the southern Hsiung-nu continued to live on Chinese soil as a hostile minority, and the long-delayed clash was about to take place. Their leader proclaimed himself emperor in 308, Lo-yang was taken in 311, and Ch'ang-an fell in 316.

From 317 to 589, China was divided. In the south, five Chinese dynasties followed on each other. All had their capital in the area of present Nanking. None was strong. They were not even in firm control of southern China, and at times dominated only the lower Yangtze valley and Chekiang. While a restoration of the empire was beyond the power of the southern dynasties, traditional Chinese culture was sponsored by their rulers, and flourished under their patronage.

In North China, the period was filled by a bewildering number of major and minor dynasties, most of them barbarian. Conquerors from the north and Tibet followed on the southern Hsiung-nu. All faced the same problem of how to superimpose their tribal aristocracies on China's social order, and how to adjust themselves to the Chinese system of government without losing their own identity. The longer a barbarian dynasty reigned, the more it succumbed to Sinification. This increased the discontent of conservative tribal elements, without lessening the tension between conquerors and conquered. Then, as later, no foreign dynasty was able to find a compromise. But before they were absorbed or swept away, the barbarians made lasting contributions to China's material and spiritual culture.

The centuries of division were an era of intense activity in philosophical and religious thought. The political disintegration had been a blow to Confucianism, identified as it had become with the orderly conditions of a unified empire. Thinkers looked afresh at man's role in society. Taoism went through several stages of adaptation and lost its earlier depth and serenity. Buddhism ceased to be a foreign religion, was assimilated into Chinese spiritual life, and proliferated into many sects.

The Neo-Taoists considered themselves followers of Lao-tzu and Chuang-tzu, but did not hesitate to reinterpret their sayings. They attempted to incorporate Confucius into Taoism by acknowledging him as the greatest of all sages, and by explaining his teaching in terms of Taoist metaphysics. They further asserted that man must be natural, as he cannot go against his nature. The Tao is nothingness, and therefore cannot guide him. Since the natural order of things cannot be changed, the Taoist does not need to reject society, provided that he stays mentally detached. A fashion developed among Neo-Taoist intellectuals and sympathizers to gather in some place of natural beauty and, spurning conventions, discuss metaphysical problems in a spontaneous and intuitive manner. Others took a less aesthetic and more hedonistic attitude, and advocated the unrestrained pursuit of pleasure.

The Taoists had early explored physical exercises for the prolongation of life, and had also turned to alchemy. In their stubborn search for the elixir of life, the alchemists were influenced by the theories of the Naturalists as well as popular medicine, and accidentally made a host of scientific discoveries. Some Neo-Taoists also developed a cult, according to which the human body is inhabited by vast numbers of gods whose cooperation is necessary for the achievement of immortality.

Taoism mingled more and more with popular religion. The legendary Yellow Lord (Huang-ti) and Lao-tzu fused into a single divinity, Huang-lao, and became for a time the supreme god in the Taoist pantheon. Influenced by Buddhism, the Taoists also established monasteries and convents. But religious Taoism broke into sects and never became a unified church.

Buddhism, in its Mahayana form, came to China half a millennium after the historical Buddha had lived in northern India. The first reliable reference to it dates from A.D. 65, and concerns the provincial court of an emperor's half-brother on the southern part of the Great Plain. Since Buddhism reached China through the Tarim Basin in Central Asia, this religion must have been known in the great cities of Ch'ang-an and Lo-yang earlier than 65. In any event, by the second century A.D. Buddhist monks were no longer unusual in China.

The first task of the Buddhist missionaries was to translate their favorite scriptures, a heroic undertaking. Some knew little or no Chinese, and had to depend on assistants and translation by stages. Furthermore, the Chinese language lacked counterparts to the Sanskrit and Pali terms of the original texts. In this dilemma, the early missionaries made use of Taoist terminology, which gave their primitive translations a Taoist flavor. The most famous of the pioneer translators was a Parthian, whose Chinese name is An Shih-kao. From 148 onward, he was active in Lo-yang for more than twenty years. Gradually the translations became more sophisticated, and reached a high level with Kumārajīva (d. 413), a Central Asian from Kucha, whose father was an Indian.

During the centuries of division, Buddhism was remarkably successful, and particularly appealed to the Chinese intelligentsia of the south and the barbarian rulers of the north. It was a time of sects. Hui-yüan (d. 416) introduced the cult of Amitābha, the Buddha of Measureless Light. This was the Pure Land Sect, which taught that believers could gain salvation through faith and would then be reborn in the Western Paradise or Pure Land. The T'ien-t'ai Sect received its name from a mountain in Chekiang. Its founder, Chih-yi (d. 597), attempted to synthesize the various Buddhist teachings. Each supposedly reflected one aspect of the truth, while the ultimate truth was revealed in the Lotus Sutra. Better known to Westerners is Ch'an (Japanese Zen) Buddhism, which, according to tradition, was brought to China by Bodhidharma. He seems to have lived in the fifth century, but the early history of Ch'an is very obscure. Soon after 675 it split into two schools, reunited, and then divided again into several branches. By the eleventh century, two major Ch'an sects remained: the Lin-chi (Japanese Rinzai) and the Ts'ao-tung (Japanese Sōtō). Ch'an reacted against scriptural Buddhism and religious practices. It claimed that Buddhahood is within man, not without, and that it is achieved through enlightenment. The disciple is prepared for enlightenment through physical hardship and intellectual frustration. What divided the Ch'an School was the question of whether enlightenment comes suddenly or gradually, the Lin-chi Sect taking the former view and the Ts'ao-tung Sect the latter. The Chen-yen or True Word Sect, finally, was transplanted from India to China in the eighth century by Amoghavajra. Influenced by Tantric Hinduism, this sect emphasized occult doctrine, magic formulas, masses for the dead, and cosmological drawings (mandalas).

As soon as Buddhism had put down roots in China, Chinese monks began to visit India. They went as pilgrims to the holy places, studied at the Buddhist centers, and collected Buddhist scriptures and relics. Some left accounts of their experiences. Fa-hsien went to India in 399 via the Tarim Basin and Pamir, returning by sea in 414. Hsüan-tsang departed from China in 629 and came back in 645, travelling both ways through Central Asia. Yi-ching left South China by ship in 671 and returned, again by sea, in 695, after a stopover of ten years in Sumatra. These were only the most famous of the many travellers who went to India driven by their faith.

Buddhism had entered China as a foreign religion, and its enemies continued to look upon it as alien. It was successful because it responded to spiritual needs adapted to Chinese conditions, compromising as Confucianism and Taoism had before it. The more Sinified Buddhism became, the less it had in common with the teaching of the Buddha, and eventually it degenerated. But before its spiritual and economic collapse, Buddhism lastingly influenced the thought and art of China.

For Further Reading

Creel, Herrlee G., *The Birth of China.*
Waley, Arthur, *Three Ways of Thought in Ancient China.*
Watson, Burton, *Early Chinese Literature.*
————, *Records of the Historian: Chapters from the Shih chi of Ssu-ma Ch'ien.*
————, *Ssu-ma Ch'ien: Grand Historian of China.*

Classical Antiquity: Jews and Greeks

12   The New Culture: 1200–200 B.C.

If the history of the ancient Western world were divided by content rather than convention we should recognize only two periods, the first from the appearance of writing to the invasions of 1200–900 B.C. which broke up the ancient Near East, the second from 1200 B.C. to the invasions of A.D. 400–700 which broke up the hellenized Roman and Persian empires. Of these periods the first, with the Neolithic which preceded it, saw the development of the physical and social techniques basic to human society—agriculture, pottery, metalworking, glassmaking, the domestication of animals, and the organization of men. The second saw an enormous increase of the civilized world in area, population, and equipment, important technical advances (glass blowing, concrete), and, more important, a profound change in the direction of human concern, from the mastery of the physical world to the discovery of the intellectual and spiritual life.

The great invasions which destroyed late Bronze Age civilization came from two directions. From the northwest a variety of tribes, called by the Egyptians the "sea peoples," began raiding the eastern coasts of the Mediterranean in the late thirteenth century. In 1200 the Hittite empire was destroyed and Cyprus raided. They then came down the coast of Syria, destroying the cities there, but were stopped at the entrance of Egypt. Some of them, the Peleshet, whom the Greeks were to call "Philistines," settled in Palestine, which gets its name from them. The rest dispersed, and traces of them are to be found in many regions around the Mediterranean. In Greece it was probably they who burned the Mycenaean palace at Pylos before 1200. During the next century new waves of barbarians, the Dorian Greeks and the "northwest" Greeks, overran the mainland (except Attica)

All dates are approximate, at best to decades.

B.C. 1250 Israelites beginning to invade Palestine
      1230 Destruction of Troy; "sea peoples" invade Egypt
      1200 Mycenaean palace of Pylos burned; the Hittite empire and
              Syrian coastal cities destroyed, perhaps by the "sea
              peoples"; beginning of the Iron Age
      1190 The Philistines settle on the Palestinian coast
      1130 Mycenae destroyed
      1100 Dorian invasion of Greece; Arameans using camels invade
              the Fertile Crescent
      1075 Collapse of Assyria
      1000 David rules most of Palestine and Transjordan
       925 Death of Solomon, separation of Israel from Judah
       900 Revival of Assyria, important artistic and military develop-
              ments (siege warfare, battering ram) through the follow-
              ing century; King Asa of Judah acts against the worship
              of gods other than Yahweh; development of heroic
              legend in Greece and among the Israelites; biography
              of David, Hebrew historiography

---

and the Peloponnese. Mycenae fell about 1130, and the Dorians pushed on through the southernmost islands as far as Crete and Rhodes, while the Greeks who had been displaced by these invasions themselves overran the central Aegean islands and, about 1000, the western coast of Asia Minor.

While these invasions from the northwest swept over Greece, Asia Minor, and the Mediterranean coasts, other hordes of invaders came from the southeast, from the fringes of the Arabian desert, where the semi-nomads, mostly Aramaic-speaking, began first to infiltrate and then to conquer the countries around the Fertile Crescent—Palestine, Syria, northern Mesopotamia, Assyria and Babylonia. The movement began early: the Israelites were already in Palestine before 1220. Farther north it seems to have become serious only after the fall of the Hittite empire in 1200. To the east it was delayed yet longer by the resistance of Assyria, which wore itself out in a generation of wars against the Arameans around 1100. But about this time the Arameans gained enormously in wealth, mobility, and striking power by their increased use of camels, hitherto rarely domesti-

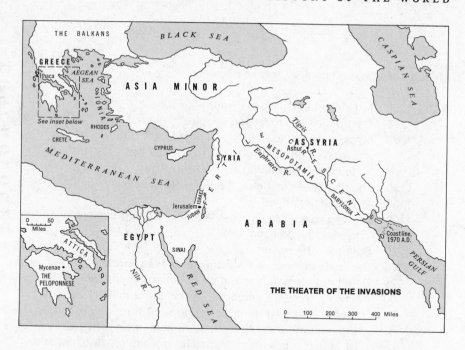

THE THEATER OF THE INVASIONS

cated in north Arabia. Therefore in the two centuries after 1100 they were able to drive the Assyrians back to the walls of Ashur itself, while in the south their kindred, the Chaldeans, infiltrated Babylonia about 900 and conquered it in the centuries following.

Nowhere through the arc of the Mediterranean coast from Greece to Egypt, or through the arc of the Fertile Crescent from Palestine to Babylonia, was the change uniform. Each little city and each little band of invaders was a law to itself. In this valley the city would hold out; in the next, it would be destroyed; in the third, invaders and city dwellers would live for a time side by side. In Palestine as in Greece, in Mesopotamia as along the coasts of Anatolia, what we find by the year 1000 is a patchwork. One city or tribe might temporarily conquer its neighbors and enjoy a few decades of more extensive rule, but such exceptions did not alter the over-all picture. Even in Egypt fragmentation prevailed. Occasionally the pharaonic tradition enabled a ruler to reunite the country; more often it enabled one to secure nominal recognition by local, really independent rulers; but most often the land was dismembered by mutually hostile princes, priests, and leaders of military clans. Assyria too, though it regained control of the neighboring territories in the late 900's and began a policy of expansion to secure the trade routes along the Tigris and across northern Mesopotamia, was in reality no exception to the particularism of the time. In a world of warring cities and tribes, the Assyrians were the most warlike. Consequently whenever they were at peace with themselves they could overrun their smaller neighbors, who could oppose them with only makeshift alliances. But the particularism which made possible Assyria's conquests prevented it from assimilating the cities and tribes it conquered. It could only collect booty, impose tribute, and appoint puppet rulers from and for the conquered peoples. As soon as the Assyrian armies were withdrawn the peoples were ready for revolt; the puppets had either to lead the revolts or be overthrown. Then the Assyrians would return. They used dreadful punishments to discourage revolts. But pillars of skulls erected in front of rebellious towns, captives impaled on stakes around the fortifications, prisoners burned alive and variously mutilated, failed to perpetuate submission. Thus the political history from 1150 to 750 remains essentially one of petty states, without major governmental developments. And even when the Assyrians developed a more coherent imperial organization after 750, the petty state remained the most stable form of ancient society. As a Greek poet said after the ultimate fall of Assyria, "A little city on a crag that lives in good order is stronger than the folly of Nineveh."

Culturally, however, these four centuries show both general advance and a number of important achievements by particular peoples. The general advance was the rebuilding of civilization after the barbarian invasions. In Greece and the Greek islands, in Asia Minor and coastal Syria (except for the Phoenician cities), in Palestine and many places along the Fertile Crescent, even the art of writing had been lost, almost all large buildings had been destroyed, houses had been replaced by huts. The pottery had steadily declined in technical skill without introduction of radically new forms—a change which suggests that the invaders had no forms of their own to introduce. There must have been an enormous destruction of tools and other artifacts, animals, men, and especially men with the skills to replace what had been destroyed. The replacement therefore required the slow civilization of the barbarians, which was the great achievement of these centuries. But the new civilization differed widely from the old.

The traditions of the new peoples perpetuated the ideals of their former barbarism; in literary terms, they were "heroic." They reflected, not the hierarchy of the Bronze Age imperial administrations, but the world of the invaders, in which a man's standing depended mostly on his own abilities. The pharaohs, high priests, and scribes of the former civilization were replaced by the warriors who stormed their cities, the sheiks who pastured their flocks along the edge of the Fertile Crescent, the prophets who led their tribes in desert wanderings and local wars. This primitive society admired especially stature and strength (Samson, Ajax), the physical

beauty of men (Absalom, Achilles), masculine friendship (David, Patro-
clus), skill in deception (Jacob, Odysseus), hospitality to strangers (Abraham, Menelaus), wisdom in dealing with men rather than book learning
(Nestor, the older stories of Solomon), and, above all, the friendship and
personal guidance of a god (Moses, Odysseus). With a reasonable share of
these good things a man could do well in life—acquire property, a wife,
and children, die at a ripe old age, and be given a magnificent funeral.
These were the legitimate goals of human endeavor.

During the years from 1100 to 750 this heroic ideal must have been
embodied in many poems and legends. Of these we have only two incomplete collections—the Homeric poems and the early material contained
(with many later additions) in the books of the Old Testament from
Genesis through II Kings. The histories of both these collections are
matters of such dispute about many points that it is difficult to determine
even "the common opinion." The following account, however, is defensible.

The Homeric poems—the *Iliad* and the *Odyssey*—were put into much
their present forms in Ionic territory during the eighth century. They incorporate earlier elements of various dates, but have not been much inter-
polated and therefore present us with a relatively uniform body of the
literature which was sung for entertainment in the courts of the petty kings
and the festivals of the little towns of the Ionian Greeks during the years
from 1150 to 750. Unfortunately, both poems deal chiefly with minor
elements of the story of Troy (destroyed about 1230) and therefore offer
little direct information about the later history of Greece.

The material collected in Genesis to II Kings did not reach its present
form until the end of the fifth century. Beside the legends, the collection
contains fragments of law codes, historical works, imaginative literary
compositions (notably the Joseph romance), borrowings early and late
from Mesopotamian mythology, and many minor elements. Most of these
have been worked over by three or four editors and cemented and
augmented by editorial inventions. The collection now begins with the
creation of the world, which it dates about 4000 B.C., and contains a
history of mankind from creation to the building of "the tower" of Babel, a
genealogy of the Semites from the flood to Abraham, and finally a history
of Abraham and his descendants down to 560 B.C. Of the elements which
here concern us, the legends, there are six main groups: those dealing with
the early history of mankind, the patriarchs, Moses, the "judges," Saul and
David, and the prophets. Almost no one now claims historical value for the
creation stories and their like. The "essential historicity" of the legends
about Abraham, Isaac, and Jacob is still defended by determined believers,
but a stronger case can be made for the view that these were legends about

the founders of Palestinian shrines whom the Israelites, after their conquest of Palestine, adopted as ancestors. Jacob's children had to be driven by famine into Egypt so that the Israelites, arriving from Egypt "470 years" later, could be represented as his descendants. (Similarly, the children of Hercules had to be banished from the Peloponnese so that they could lead the later Dorian invasion.) Once Jacob and his children have settled in Egypt the Old Testament knows practically nothing of their stay—a clear indication that there was no continuous tradition connecting the pretended "patriarchal period" of the 1700's with the exodus, which by Biblical chronology would have to be dated in the first half of the thirteenth century.

At this point a new cycle of legends begins. Its hero is Moses, a prophet of the god YHWH (probably "Yahweh")—a god unknown to the patriarchs (Exod. 6:3). From here on the tradition seems to be mainly Israelite in origin and, in outline, historical. The details, however, are fantastic; not only minor episodes but major ones like the covenant at Sinai may have been invented to provide Israelite origins for Canaanite ceremonies. (The covenant is to obey the law, said to be "the law of Yahweh"; but a desert deity is not a likely legislator, and the law now attached to the story is certainly descended, although remotely, from Canaanite material.) For "historical outline," thus, not much is left save that some Israelites escaped from Egypt under Moses, picked up adherents in the wilderness, fought off attacks by other tribes, were driven out of southern Palestine, and eventually conquered the western edge of Transjordan, where Moses died. The historical connection of Moses with Joshua is uncertain, and the legends of the Joshua cycle have suffered badly from later accretion and invention; they contradict both the archaeological evidence and each other.

But the Israelites did establish themselves in Palestine during the thirteenth century. For two centuries thereafter they fought with neighbors and rival invaders; legends from several tribes about the heroes of these local wars have been collected and elaborated in the book called Judges. Eventually central Palestine was subjugated briefly by the Philistines. A new cycle of legends told of the resistance to them, first under Saul and his son Jonathan, whom the Philistines eventually killed, then under David, who with his band of "mighty men" (at first fellow outlaws, later mercenaries) captured Jerusalem, made it his capital, and about the year 1000 created a sizable kingdom in Palestine and Transjordan. (Significantly, in his time heroic legend is displaced as the main element of the Biblical account by historical narrative, though popular imagination continued to produce heroic legends about both the kings and the wandering prophets of Yahweh, and later compilers made use of these.) Solomon, David's son, squeezed enough out of his father's kingdom to build in Jerusalem a palace for himself and a temple for Yahweh, to fortify some strategic cities, and to maintain a luxurious court. At his death, about 925, the northern Israelite tribes understandably revolted and set up a separate kingdom. Presently the subject peoples also revolted and the area returned to the pattern of petty tribal states characteristic of the age.

We have described the Israelite legends because of their importance for medieval and modern thought. From A.D. 391, when Christianity became the official religion of the Roman Empire, until 1859, when the credibility of the creation story was destroyed by Darwin, the Old Testament was the official authority for ancient history. Before the triumph of Christianity a similar, though less official, authority was enjoyed throughout the Greco-Roman world by the Homeric poems, which became the basic texts of elementary and secondary education. At first, however, both in Israel and in Greece, the legends were less important as accounts of past events than as portraits of ideal figures and adventures, which influenced the life of the new age.

The theater of this life was the city. As tribes settled down their territories broke up into city-states; only poor grazing lands remained tribal. Within the tiny area of the city-state, the city itself was infinitesimal, often no more than a couple of hundred yards from wall to wall. It was usually ruled by a hereditary king, who was the leader in war, the judge in peace, and the high priest at all times. This economy in administration was dictated by poverty as well as tribal tradition. Trade was negligible and confined to luxuries. The city lived on what it could grow in its fields, supplemented by fishing and hunting. Agriculture, however, was primitive; half the land was left fallow every year to prevent its exhaustion. The plants available for cultivation were little removed from their wild forms and yielded meager harvests. Consequently, given the small size of the city's territory, there was almost no surplus to support unproductive labor. Large priesthoods were out of the question. The new culture was at first spared their conservative economic, political, and cultural influence. Temples, too, were luxuries rarely possible. No large ones appear in Greece until the eighth century. In Israel, David's military success made possible Solomon's buildings, but their cost led to revolt.

Poverty also delayed the development of specialists. The ideal man, like the small farmer, could do everything for himself: the tradition pictured Odysseus, king of Ithaca, building his own house; Saul leaving his plow to lead an army. But some specialists there were. Divination, thought to result from possession by a spirit, was always a specialty of persons psychologically liable to such seizures. Another specialty was that of the metalworkers. Their secret craft was now more important because it included more feasible ways of working iron. Iron increased the productive capacity of the workers, and with better tools the craftsman became an object of more value and more political importance, especially since he was part of a small political unit, a city or a tribe, to which the gain or loss of a single skilled man was important. Concern for the individual is consequently one of the most important characteristics of the Homeric poems, the legends of the Old Testament, and the Western civilization which derives from them.

On the other hand, because the typical city-state was so small, everyone in it was aware of all the details of the life of his neighbors. The clearing house for gossip was the gate of the city. Here sat the old men of the city, the heads of the principal families, who were both the king's council and the local archives. To make a contract or record a sale, one "declared before those who sat in the gate." In such a small society, reputation became a matter of life and death. Acute concern for honor is characteristic of heroic legend. To revenge an insult, Achilles would imperil the whole Greek army; David, for the same reason, was ready to wipe out the household of Nabal, man, woman, and child (I Sam. 25:34). This concern for honor was an important motive for achievement—for bravery in warfare, but also for skill in speaking (the public assembly is, for Homer, "where men get honor"), and for skill in any kind of craft, even the humble arts of domestic service (Odyssey XV.320). Since the city needed the work of every man and woman, it praised or blamed each one according to the quality of his work. The slacker could not escape censure, nor the incompetent, worse than censure, ridicule.

Therefore, during the years from 1100 to 750 the cultural level of the newly occupied areas steadily rose. Poverty remained general, but when the political configuration changed momentarily, permitting a ruler to draw income from a larger area, sufficient wealth could be raised to finance monumental building and works of art. The greatest examples of these are the palaces of the Assyrian kings, which contained a new style of historical art—low reliefs of exquisite clarity narrating the rulers' triumphs. The figures of these reliefs are often masterpieces, combining stylized treatment with vivid, lifelike effect. The tradition thus established was continued to the end of the Assyrian empire in 612, and as the palace art of the greatest military power and wealthiest court of the age, it exerted a wide influence. The great reliefs were too costly to be directly imitated by lesser states, but their details and their vigorous treatment of animal figures were copied on minor works of art all around the Mediterranean.

In Greece and Phoenicia, hemmed in by mountains and warlike neighbors, the city-states turned to the sea to supplement their incomes. Here the arts were the handmaidens of commerce—in Greece, metalworking and pottery, in Phoenicia, ivory carving, silverwork, and the manufacture of colored glass and fine fabrics, especially admired for the "Tyrian purple" dye. Besides these luxury products, slaves (who could be kidnapped along the way), ores, and smelted metal in ingots came to be staples in this trade which gradually increased. Piracy and exploration went hand in hand with commerce. The Phoenicians sailed south to Egypt, thence west along the African coast, and finally through the Straits of Gibraltar to the Atlantic coasts of Africa and Spain. The Greeks in the west sailed along the Balkan coast, thence to Italy and Sicily; in the east they penetrated the Black Sea and discovered the Russian rivers. Neither Greeks nor Phoenicians kept out of each other's territories. Homer sings of Greek voyages to Egypt and of Phoenician traders in the Aegean. Several cities in Greece claimed Phoenician founders. Cyprus, where the copper mines were still important, kept its Mycenaean settlements and received new settlers from Phoenicia.

The Phoenician traders carried their alphabet wherever they ventured. To the traders the alphabet was merely a convenience for keeping records, but it was to become the shaping instrument of the literature, the learning, and the science of the Western world. Nor was it alone. Mesopotamian weights and measures and techniques of divination, the lunisolar calendar, and a host of decorative motifs and artistic and architectural techniques were taken over by the Greeks and contributed to the rapid growth of Greek civilization.

But this growth cannot be explained solely by Oriental influences or economic opportunities. A most important factor was the peculiar genius of the Greeks. As examples of this, let two characteristics of Greek culture suffice—the language and the love of beauty. Among the languages of the ancient world Greek is outstanding for its wealth of means to express *precisely* the relations between the subjects discussed. Where other languages simply string together clauses, at most with a few all-purpose conjunctions, Greek always makes possible, and often requires, a clear, detailed analysis of the whole complex of ideas which is to be expressed. A page written in some Semitic language, or in early Latin, is to a page of classical Greek as a brick pile is to an arch. And along with this amazing sense for linguistic and intellectual structure, the Greeks had an equally amazing sense for visible beauty, particularly that of the human body. If a sinner is a beautiful man, says Plutarch, the gods deal gently with him. When the Hebrews said that God, on viewing creation, saw that it was *good,* the Septuagint translators—though they tried to translate literally—felt compelled to say, "he saw that it was *beautiful.*" Little as they knew of Greek, they knew that "beautiful," not "good," was the common term of approval. The attitude lasted down to Christian times and spread, with Greek culture, throughout the Roman empire. Both Augustine and Gregory of Nyssa, consciously rejecting Greco-Roman values, argue that Jesus must have been ugly or the crowd would not have ill-treated him. No other literature of the ancient world even remotely approaches Greek in feeling for physical beauty and in intellectual structure. With these peculiar gifts, the Greeks set out on their course.

For Further Reading

Coulanges, N. Fustel de, *The Ancient City.*
Kirk, G. (ed.), *The Language and Background of Homer.*
Moscati, D., *The World of the Phoenicians.*
Vaux, R. de, *Ancient Israel.*
Rowley, H., *The Growth of the Old Testament.*

13   The Great Divide

The accumulation of men and belongings during the years from 1100 to 750 was neither uniform nor uninterrupted. The Assyrian conquests, in particular, had so gutted northern Syria that it remained unimportant during the next four hundred years. Everywhere, the rate of progress had been retarded by endemic wars between neighboring cities or tribes. These wars had their root in poverty and were primarily fought for control of land since, given the size of the cities' territories and their total dependence on local agriculture, even a small strip of land could make a large difference in diet. The wars left grudges, perpetuated the heroic ideal which led to war as a means to honor, and perpetuated poverty which led to war as a form of honorable theft.

But these wars were not very destructive—the Assyrian achievements were unique. Most buildings were of stone; fire only burned off the roofs. Killing, like everything else, had to be done by hand; therefore mortality was usually low. Nobody knew much about siege warfare (except, again, the Assyrians, who developed a good battering ram as early as the ninth century). The soldiers were farmers who had to get back to put their fields in shape for planting before the autumn rains fell, so victors had little time to do damage. Consequently, in spite of wars, the period from 1150 to 750 saw a great increase of population and wealth, and these brought with them diversification of culture.

Previously, small cities and tribal kingdoms were alike made up of

CHRONOLOGY

Dates ending in zero are approximate.

B.C.

780	Alphabetic writing begins in Greece (Phoenician alphabet)
776	Traditional date for the beginning of the Olympic games
760	First Greek colony on the Italian mainland (Cumae)
750	Large temples begin to be built in Greece; Amos' denunciation of the rich, Yahweh a god of justice
750–700	The *Iliad* and the *Odyssey* reach approximately their present forms
744	Accession of Tiglath-pileser III, reorganization of the Assyrian army and empire, beginning of the great century of Assyrian conquests, building, and historical art
740	Hosea's denunciation of the Israelites for their worship of gods other than Yahweh
722	Assyria destroys the kingdom of Israel
714	Sargon II of Assyria reduces Urartu
710	Sargon takes Babylon
700	Hesiod denounces the rich, Zeus a god of justice; development of hoplite tactics in Greece; monarchies in Greece giving way to oligarchies
690	Cimmerian invasion of Asia Minor
680	Scythian invasion of Armenia
672	Esarhaddon of Assyria controls western Media
671	Esarhaddon takes Egypt
663	Ashurbanipal of Assyria resubjugates Egypt
646	Ashurbanipal conquers Elam

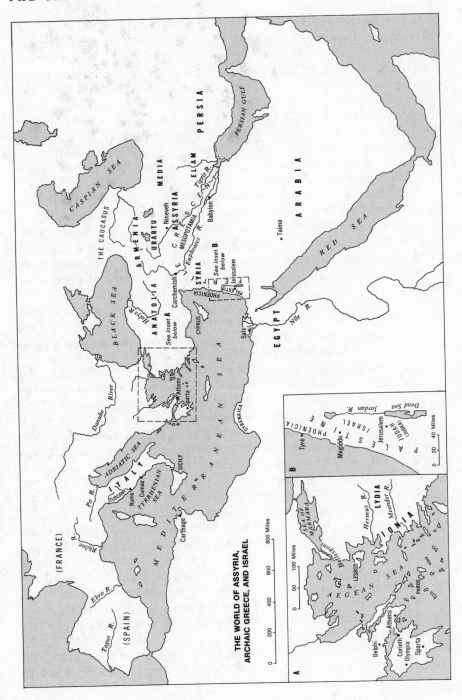

THE WORLD OF ASSYRIA,
ARCHAIC GREECE, AND ISRAEL

large families, not to say clans. The heads of these families were the king's influential advisers, whether or not they were called "the royal council." When quarrels arose, opponents could not easily be eliminated—they were too important to the state; nor could their power be broken and the victor's power greatly increased by economic reprisals—there was too little property to make much difference. With wealth came the possibility of decisive change. When the city had men enough, opponents could be exiled; when it had wealth enough, the victor could use their property to hire supporters and make his victory permanent. Therefore, both in the Near East and in Greece, the political patterns changed as one side or the other, the king or the council, gained the advantage.

The changes were uniform throughout large areas. In Greece the councils won; the kings were reduced to officials; the government became an oligarchy. In Anatolia outside the Greek cities, in Cyprus, Syria, Palestine, and the Fertile Crescent, the kings became absolute, the heads of the families lost their conciliar rank, and the royal council came to be made up of the king's great officers, appointed by him and often of no distinguished ancestry. No doubt the monarchic tradition of the Near East was influential in this development. It is dangerous to talk of ethnic tradition or character: the Greek cities of Cyprus became kingdoms on the Near Eastern model, as did the Phoenician coastal cities, but Carthage, equally Phoenician, became an oligarchy on Greek lines.

One important factor in the Greek development was the discovery of a new military technique, the use of a solid line of heavily armed spearmen (hoplites). The success of this technique in Greece, a rugged country ideal for light infantry armed with bows, is a mystery. But succeed it did; it saved Greece from Near Eastern domination and later enabled the Greeks to conquer the Near Eastern world and impose their culture on it. Greek art, literature, and philosophy could be produced, preserved, and propagated only because the Greeks made themselves individually the best soldiers and collectively the greatest military power of their age.

Their new technique, developing about 700, required men who could afford full armor and time for practice. So the wealthy men and their sons became the cities' crack regiments. No Greek city king could afford a hoplite force of his own; that required a large taxable area for its support. The fragmentation of Greece by rugged mountains, which made it difficult for a state to expand, was thus a factor in the triumph of the oligarchies. In the Near East, perhaps because the land was less fragmented, the kingdoms grew larger and the kings could afford mercenaries and so became absolute rulers.

This political differentiation accompanied a sharp cultural change. The Greek oligarchs were united in military cliques whose members had to hang together to preserve their military efficiency. Brought up on the heroic poems, they were intensely concerned about honor. So they had to govern by mutual consent; it became customary to pass the city offices around, by election, from one leading family to another. Hence in every city grew up both the custom of elections and a set of conventions as to what should and should not be done—an unwritten constitution. This is the background of later Greek constitutional law, almost unparalleled in the Near East.

Concern for honor and, even more, for wealth and mutual protection led the oligarchs to marry women from the ruling families of other cities. Consequently the ruling families became an international clique. The members of this clique gathered to see their in-laws and display their wealth at the festivals of the great religious centers. Most centers had cults of local heroes who were thought to protect the land and assure its fertility. The cult of these heroes commonly involved military and athletic contests; the Greeks were outstanding among the peoples of the ancient world for their love of athletics. In 776, we are told, the athletic and military games for the festival of Zeus at Olympia in the western Peloponnese were organized as a Panhellenic contest, recurrent every fourth year. Soon victory in these games became one of the highest honors of the Greek world. Other religious centers followed suit. Song and dancing were parts of the worship of the Greek gods. Contests in music and poetry were held at the shrine of Apollo in Delphi. Civic festivals with "games" were similarly developed, notably the festival of Athena at Athens. And all these contests were means of gaining honor.

Athletic and military concern alike focused attention on the male body. Since every citizen from twenty to forty-nine, if not a cripple, was liable to military duty and would have to stand in combat every few years, most cities prescribed athletic training as a form of military preparedness. A fine body was a means to honor and a source of pride. The Dorians, the most warlike of the Greeks, expressed their pride by exercising naked. Soon the gymnasium, "the place where men go naked," became throughout Greece the center in which upper-class citizens passed their leisure time. Male nudity became a major concern of Greek art. By putting a premium on exercise and consequent bathing, it made the Greeks the longest-lived people of their times. In the gymnasium, too, arose the discussions from which philosophy and political theory would grow, as well as the friendships which rapidly became homosexual love affairs. Homosexuality occurs all over the world; Greece was unusual in honoring it. Even in Greece, however, there were limits; homosexual intercourse commonly remained illegal. But the law was not enforced, and in many Greek cities the lover came to have a recognized part in the boy's education. He was the model and the guide who introduced the boy to the world of men. (Homosexuality between adults was thought ridiculous.) These developments did not occur in the Near East, where games were for children, singing and dancing were the work of professional entertainers, nudity was a disgrace, and homosexuality was a capital crime.

Homosexuality restricted population growth. This may have been one of the reasons for its popularity in Greece, where the tiny, infertile valleys were already overpopulated. But neither homosexuality nor the practice of abandoning unwanted babies could check population growth. Overcrowding led to emigration, both by individuals and in colonies, now possible because the cities had enough wealth to finance them. When a city chronically short of food wished to send out a colony, it would usually consult Apollo of Delphi. With his approval and prudently obscure advice, a leader and lawmaker would be appointed from one of the city's distinguished families, ships provided, and a body of colonists made up; sometimes even outsiders would be invited to participate. Choice of the location might be guided by the god—whose priests heard the reports of pilgrims from all parts of the world—and the advice of traders.

Before 750 there was a Greek colony at Cumae (north of Naples), and by 550 colonies were thick around south and southwest Italy, Sicily (except for the western, Phoenician tip), south France and east Spain, the north shore of the Aegean, the Hellespont, Sea of Marmora, and Black Sea, and the promontory of Cyrenaica on the north African coast. They vastly expanded the markets of Greece. They imported manufactured articles, wine, and olive oil; and they supplied raw materials—metals, grain, wood, tar, salt, fish, hides, and slaves. By relieving the population pressure and stimulating economic growth they made possible the glorious cultural achievements of Greece. Colonization also made the Greeks aware of the great world, with its infinite variety of peoples and customs—whence philosophic problems as to right and wrong. It confronted them with many different environments, it stimulated their adaptability, it developed their practical intelligence. The necessity of founding cities trained their founders in urban and in social planning. It made them legislators—and philosophers. Plato's *Republic* reflects the experience of colonization. The colonies were a frontier from which the Greeks derived an awareness of new possibilities, a willingness to experiment, and a "philosophic" detachment from established customs and ideas. These developments were not paralleled in the Near East.

Oligarchy, military tactics, athletics, homosexuality, colonization, and consequent intellectual attitude—Greece between 750 and 650 distinguished itself from the context of the eastern Mediterranean world. There, absolute monarchies reigned, supported by mercenary armies and ruling through councils composed not of men of wealth and stature but of royal appointees in charge of the branches of the government—the mercenaries, the corvée, the secretariat, the palace, and so on. With this return toward the ancient Near Eastern type of monarchy went related developments. The growth of royal power and income made possible a growth of professional clergy. In spite of the alphabet, the scribal class lived on as royal secretaries and administrators. As their efficiency (in tax collection) and the luxury of the courts increased, the small farmers were squeezed harder. Their reaction can be heard in the denunciations of the rich by the Israelite Amos, a prophet of Yahweh, convinced that his god was about to destroy the oppressors of the poor.

That Amos' prophecies have survived is surprising. For the most part we know of ancient history only from the upper classes—it was they who ordered the inscriptions and wrote the books. When, occasionally, we hear a lower-class comment it is thanks to quotation by a wealthy author or to a chance discovery of some poor man's papyri containing what the rich would not copy. But Amos owes his preservation to a different sort of accident.

The Israelites seem to have learned from Moses the worship of a god named Yahweh, a desert divinity, good in razzias, but no farmer. Consequently, in Palestine they began to worship the gods of the land, a family of fertility deities known from Ugarit—Father El and Mother Ashera, with their children Baal and Anath, Baal ("husband, master, owner") being the most popular. But this produced a reaction. Whether it came from the upper class of the invaders who may have wanted, for military purposes, to keep their followers separate from the Canaanites, or from the lower, who may have wanted to keep themselves distinct from the peasantry; whether it expressed the revulsion of the temperate desert people from the drunken Palestinian fertility rites, or the jealousy of the prophets of Yahweh at their new competitors, at all events, the claim was made that all Israelites were obligated to worship Yahweh and *only* Yahweh. They were his people, his "private property"; to worship any other god was an offense against him.

Just when this notion arose is uncertain because the later editors of the Old Testament have constantly written it into the early stories. Here our concern is not with its origin, but with its acceptance in the historical period. We first hear of royal action against the worshipers of gods other than Yahweh in the reign of Solomon's great-grandson Asa (913–873?). By the middle of the ninth century there was an active "Yahweh-alone" party of prophets led by Elijah and Elisha. The party is credited with having inspired a revolution in the northern Israelite kingdom about 840. Shortly thereafter the priest of the temple of Yahweh in Jerusalem organized a revolution there. But the movement was not able to impose its will on the country as a whole; indeed, it soon lost control even of the courts.

As a minority, it then turned to the discontented for support—hence its adoption of the works of Amos, who probably had not been part of it. Had he thought the worship of other gods important he would have given the practice a more prominent place in his list of the sins which Yahweh will punish. How party members felt on the subject can be seen in the tirades of Amos' successor, Hosea (about 740). For him, Israel was wedded to Yahweh; to worship other gods was to commit adultery. With Micah and Isaiah at the end of the eighth century, the themes of Amos and Hosea are fused and the principal traits in the party's picture of Yahweh are thenceforth fixed: he is a jealous god, who will not tolerate his peoples' worship of any other divinity, and he is a just god, who is particularly concerned to protect the poor.

The same concern for justice appears half a century later (c. 700) in Greek literature. As Yahweh called the shepherd Amos to prophesy, so the Muses told the shepherd Hesiod to sing of the things to come, and those that had been, and of the eternal gods. Hesiod's attempt to organize genealogically the Greek myths about deities gave classical status to a lot of material which wasted the time of Greek theologians to the end of paganism. At least the worshipers of Yahweh alone were spared this. Hating all other gods, they cut down mythology to stories of creation and of Yahweh's interventions on earth. But Hesoid and Amos agreed about the deity's present role in human society. Zeus, like Yahweh, was the ruler of the world and the god of justice; he punished the wicked, the unjust, and the oppressors of the poor. Amos was more concerned about justice *for the poor,* Hesiod, about justice. Amos expected the immediate destruction of Israel. Hesiod thought that men were going from bad to worse and would eventually be destroyed, but that meanwhile the righteous would be rewarded by peace and plentiful harvests, the wicked would be visited by plague, famine, and the disasters of war. The genuine prophecies of Amos were predictions of doom, but Hesiod offered practical advice: the wise man will be a careful farmer, so that he can afford to be just; the rules for farming follow. This explains why his work was preserved and why it gives us an invaluable picture of Greek village life. But his concern for justice places Hesiod's book beside the prophecies of Amos, not only in the intellectual and moral history of that time, but in the history of Western civilization.

These theological developments, and everything else in the Near East, were overshadowed by the revival of Assyria. Tiglath-pileser III, who seized the throne in 744, transformed the old kingdom into an empire. Instead of merely looting territories and leaving them under native rulers to rebel, he made frequent use of the practice, hitherto rare, of deporting part of a conquered people and replacing them with others, thereby splitting the territory politically. He cut territories into small provinces, usually under foreign governors. He built up a standing army to support these governors, no longer relying on a peasantry that would have to get back to their farms. Full-time professional troops drawn from many peoples formed a military machine able to survive the loss of Assyria itself. Thus, though the new Assyria was still unable to win over the peoples it conquered, it was able to split them up and to enlist some of their members in its service.

With this power Tiglath-pileser III resumed the Assyrian program of conquest—south to Babylon, north to Urartu, east to Media, and west to the Mediterranean. His successors pushed it farther than ever before. They destroyed the northern kingdom of Israel in 722, reduced Urartu to unimportance in 714, and recaptured Babylon in 710; Esarhaddon extended Assyrian control into Media before 672 and into Egypt in 671; Ashurbanipal resubjugated Egypt in 663, and pushed beyond Babylon to subdue Elam about 646.

With military expansion went an enormous expansion of wealth. The brilliant tradition of Assyrian art was resumed, with increasing naturalism, in pictures of military campaigns and court ceremonies. A library of 1,200 tablets of cuneiform texts, collected at Ashurbanipal's orders, preserved most of what we know about ancient Near Eastern literature—a dismal picture. The largest group of texts are interpretations of acts thought ominous; the next largest, dictionaries—so cumbersome was cuneiform writing; and the third, magic spells. The few literary texts are not Assyrian compositions, but copies of older ones. From royal correspondence, historical inscriptions, and treaties we see a different sort of mind—vigorous and matter-of-fact. But the aristocracy was a small group occupied by war, administration, and trade. Their educational tradition was dominated by the study of classical texts notable for their linguistic difficulty and their intellectual poverty. Hence, no doubt, the paradox of Assyrian civilization—the contrast between its magnificent achievements in art and architecture, military technique and organization, and its utter literary insignificance.

For Further Reading

Boardman, J., *The Greeks Overseas.*
————, *Pre-Classical.*
Smith, M., *Palestinian Parties and Politics That Shaped the Old Testament.*

14   The Century of the Minor Powers

To meet the threat of the new Assyrian empire, traditional enemies united
—for instance, the Israelites, the Phoenician cities, and the Aramean
kingdom of Damascus. Such local leagues were unsuccessful. Next came
what may be called national states among ethnic groups threatened by
Assyria, like Egypt, Babylonia, and Media. In Egypt the Assyrians helped
by killing off the local rulers except for one, Necho, whom they chose as
their agent. Thus Necho's son, Psammetichos I, could eventually unify the
country in the 650's. The Assyrians also cleared the way for union of the
Median tribes in the 650's and of southern Mesopotamia by the Chaldean
kingdom of Babylon about 625. Also the Assyrian defeat of the Cimmerians about 640 enabled the kingdom of Lydia to expand into central
Anatolia. These kingdoms allied against Assyria and fomented rebellions
among Assyria's subjects. Moreover, a new horde of nomads, the Scythians, had come through the Caucasus in the 680's and thereafter threatened
Assyria from the north. Nineveh, the greatest Assyrian city, fell to the
Medes and Babylonians in 612. The Assyrian army was broken up in 609.
The Scythians were eventually—in the 590's—driven back into Russia by
the Medes. By 585 the Near East was divided into four kingdoms, the
Lydians controlling western and central Anatolia to the Halys; the Medes,
everything from central Anatolia through the mountains around the Tigris
Valley to southern Persia; the Babylonians, Mesopotamia, Syria, and
Palestine. The fourth kingdom was Egypt.

All these kingdoms were absolute monarchies. The king's power rested
on his control of the army but also, now, on ethnic feeling. Of the Medes
we know almost nothing. The Lydian and eastern Greek cultures were
closely related, but not identical. To the Greeks the Lydians represented
Oriental luxury. Some important cultural innovations, notably coinage,
are said to have come from Lydia. In Egypt and Babylon ancient traditions were revived, ancient works of literature copied, and new works of
art created, following the fashions of ancient monuments, but displaying a
new technical skill and calculated simplicity. In particular, the Saite art of
Egypt (so called from the new capital, Sais, in the Delta) produced among
its many masterpieces a series of heads which show the first true portraiture since the Amarna Age.

The new Mediterranean states imitated the fashions of the Near East.
The lions, rosettes, and palmettes of Assyrian and Phoenician decoration

Dates ending in zero are approximate.

B.C. 650 Egypt united under Psammetichos I; Media united in reaction to Assyrian pressure; Archilochus of Paros, lyric poet

   646 Ashurbanipal's conquest of Elam; Lydians begin coinage

   640 Assyrian defeat of Cimmerians opens central Asia Minor for Lydian expansion

   625 Rise of the Chaldean kingdom of Babylon

   621 The Deuteronomic law code found in the Jerusalem temple; King Josiah's religious reforms; publication of the laws of Athens by Draco

   612 Nineveh falls to the Medes and Babylonians

   609 Necho II of Egypt conquers Palestine-Syria; Battle of Megiddo; death of Josiah

   605 Battle of Carchemish; Egyptians, defeated by Babylonians, retreat to Egypt

   600 Circumnavigation of Africa by Phoenicians; Sappho of Lesbos, first famous authoress; Corinthian pottery predominant in Greek trade; Greek monumental sculpture begins

   593 Solon's reforms in Athens

   590 Scythians driven out of Armenia by the Medes

   587 Destruction of Jerusalem by Nebuchadnezzar II of Babylon; the prophets Jeremiah and Ezekiel

   585 Battle between the Medes and the Lydians for control of central Asia Minor, the Halys fixed as boundary

   560 Pisistratus tyrant of Athens; Athenian black-figure pottery becomes the most popular Greek ware

   550 Cyrus of Persia gains control of Media

   540 "Second Isaiah," author of Isaiah 40–55, denies the existence of gods other than Yahweh

were perpetuated on the "Orientalizing" pottery of Corinth, popular all around the Mediterranean. Statues of Greek youths show Egyptian postures and wigs. The Etruscans, a mysterious people who gave their name to Tuscany (the region between Florence and Rome), incorporated so many Near Eastern elements in their art and religion that they were thought immigrants from Asia Minor, as perhaps their rulers were. The Etruscan kings grew rich from the copper and iron deposits of north Italy; their twelve cities ruled Tuscany, planted settlements in the Po Valley and controlled western Italy down to Cumae; their shipping gave its name to the Tyrrhenian Sea, and their trader-pirates were active even in the Aegean.

All these countries were much concerned with trade. Nebuchadnezzar II (604–562), the greatest of the kings of Babylon, besieged Tyre for thirteen years, hoping to control its far-reaching trade (described in Ezekiel 27). Nabonidus (555–539), the last of the Babylonian kings, established himself at Taima in the west Arabian desert to control the incense trade between south Arabia and the Mediterranean. (Incense, now fashionable as an offering to the gods, contributed enormously to the wealth of south Arabia, wealth which seems to have produced nothing worth mention.) The Saite pharaohs drew support from Greek mercenaries and merchants; a tyrant of Corinth named his son for Psammetichos. Necho II (609–594), Psammetichos' successor, tried to cut a canal from the Nile to the Red Sea, and sent a Phoenician fleet around Africa. The Lydians' invention of coinage is evidence of their economic interests; the wealth of the Lydian kings was fabulous—"as rich as Croesus." And the Greeks now rivaled the Phoenicians as the principal carriers of the Mediterranean.

Trade both required and produced both markets and goods. Markets were found in the growing colonies and the swelling populations of the old countries. Goods were supplied by increased agriculture, mining, and manufacturing. Corinth, with its florid pottery and metalwork, became a great city. Phoenician glass, dyed fabrics, and ivory, Arabian perfumes, Egyptian linens and faïence, amulets and papyrus scrolls, were money making luxuries. Slaves and metals remained major cargoes, though wine and oil perhaps took first place, and there was even shipping enough for trade in grain.

Profits from commerce and manufacturing produced a new rich class, distinct from the old, landed, oligarchic families, and jealous of the oligarchs' control of the government. But the increase of wealth also produced a new poor. Wealth could be lent. Money made lending easier, especially when, in sixth-century Greece, coins of small denominations were introduced. High rates of interest led to default, seizure of the debtor's land, and enslavement. Slavery meant competition for the artisan and the small farmer. As colonization fell off after 600, when the best places had been taken, the cities filled up with dispossessed and embittered men. A further cause for bitterness was injustice: the law, traditional and unwritten, could be shaped by the judges in favor of their fellow oligarchs. Therefore the late seventh century saw in Athens and Israel, and presumably elsewhere, the promulgation of written law codes.

Where law codes did not satisfy, the poor found leaders—men from the new rich or mavericks from the oligarchy—eager to overthrow the oligarchs and rule alone. Such a sole ruler the Greeks called a "tyrant." The word originally was not pejorative, but rapidly became so in the upper-class literature. Tyrants usually expropriated the property of their opponents, giving some to the poor, but more to their mercenaries and friends. They also used the money of the rich for public buildings (which provided employment) and for religious festivals and games. They were therefore popular. The oligarchs who escaped found support in the neighboring cities, normally hostile and glad to make trouble. Hence came attempts at counterrevolution which led to new murders, flights, and counterplots. Either counterrevolution or the initial threat of revolution might lead to an absolute ruler who represented the interests of the rich, but who would equally—qua absolute—be called a "tyrant." These developments, frequent in Greece, were not unparalleled elsewhere, for instance in the careers of Amasis of Egypt (568–526) and Nabonidus of Babylon (555–539).

Tyranny was the extreme example of the breakdown of standards, now everywhere evident. Here again the Greeks were the leaders and produced the most striking cases. Before 650, the poet Archilochus of Paros sang of his escape from battle at the cost of abandoning his shield—by traditional standards the ultimate disgrace. His poems set a fashion among poets, if not soldiers. The Greeks are the first people to produce individuals who are not afraid of going counter to common opinion not because of some supposed revelation, but just because they want to, *and* of celebrating the fact. This new, open defiance of laws and standards reflects the diffusion of authority in Greek society, where every city made its own laws and individuals could move freely from one to another. But the change was not limited to Greece. Everywhere trade and travel sophisticated the travelers and shocked the stay-at-homes; to every country came aliens with outlandish ways and opinions. These aliens were "impure"—since they did not observe the local purity laws—and might pollute others. So all around the Mediterranean we now find an increase of concern about "purity," a matter hitherto taken for granted. Apollo at Delphi was kept busy prescribing purifications, and Greece swarmed with less authoritative purifiers, many claiming to use the spells of the legendary Orpheus. Entire cities were "purified," among them Athens. In Babylonia, the Judeans, deported from Jerusalem in 597 and later, were exposed to all sorts of impure contacts. Therefore Ezekiel was a fanatic about impurity, to which he gave far more space than any previous prophet. The priestly lawmakers of his time were also more concerned with it than were the earlier legislators. But it is clear from Ezekiel's polemics and from the mixture of Judean and Babylonian names in later business documents that many Judeans were neglecting their purity rules, breaking away from their communities, and becoming unattached individuals.

In Greece this growth of individualism produced a new literature—personal lyric poetry. Lyrics, anonymous, and often intended for use in rituals, had hitherto been concerned with common experiences. Now, along the Ionian coast, appear poets who tell us their names and sing of themselves, their particular political contests and military adventures, their travels and homesickness, poverty and drinking parties, hates and loves. No earlier literature exists in which love plays so large a part. Significantly, the greatest of the new love poets, Sappho of Lesbos (c. 600) is the first woman to become famous as a writer. Love is the easiest adventure for the individualist, and for the respectable woman, in this period, it was the *one* adventure. She was shut up in her home; that was her realm—she would be angry if her husband stayed home and meddled in her business. Accordingly, Sappho's poems celebrated that love between women which was the obverse of Greek male relationships.

With such eroticism and, for men, the related interest in athletics, goes the development of Greek sculpture and drawing, which reflect a tactile awareness of the musculation of the male body. The first major works of sculpture—beginning before 600—are statues of naked youths, many of them memorials of individuals. The nudity probably comes from athletics, for women are shown clothed. These statues were painted, but the colors, and the Greek sense of color, are lost to us. Other factors in the new art were delight in elaborate linear patterns, seen in Ionian statues, and an equal delight in simplicity, seen in the Doric temples of the following age.

Of these many changes—increase in population and trade, extension of a monetary economy, breakdown of standards, and development of individualism and of the arts—the political concomitants differed somewhat in each city. Generally, trading cities had tyrants early and often—as did Corinth and the big cities of the Ionian coast and Sicily. Many small, out-of-the-way places never had them: their oligarchs stayed in power. For later history the peculiar developments in Sparta and Athens were of greatest importance.

In Sparta the Dorian invaders, much taller than the other Greeks, made the natives serfs (helots was the local word). They also conquered all the southern Peloponnese. With 600,000 acres of arable land, capable of supporting 30,000 warriors with their dependents and helots, they could afford to neglect colonization, keep their population at home, and become the greatest military power in Greece. Their worried neighbors backed a helot revolt in the mid-seventh century, which almost ruined the Spartans. Since they could not do without the helots, who did the agricultural work, they reorganized their state as a military camp. Helots were prohibited even from carrying their masters' weapons. (Aristotle remarked that those who carry the weapons decide the form of the government.) Citizens were forbidden to engage in agriculture or business; their lives were devoted to military duties. The most difficult but most important duty was the suppression of personality, for the decisive factor in battles now was the discipline of the hoplite line, in which every man must keep his assigned place and do exactly as ordered. To foster esprit de corps, boys were taken from home at twelve and brought up in troops, trained in military exercises, music (besides learning battle songs, they memorized and sang their laws), concern for what people thought of them, respect for elders, obedience, endurance, and silence. As youths they went into the secret police, to ferret out and murder potentially rebellious helots. As adults they went into the army. Luxuries were prohibited, domestic life reduced to a minimum; a soldier ate with his fellows in the mess hall. One visitor, after tasting the food, said, "Now I understand why the Spartans do not fear death." Rewards were honors which made life less comfortable: victors in the Olympic games were assigned to the front rank in battle. Sparta became a military machine devoted to perpetuating itself. The soldiers were buried in their red uniforms.

The rest of Greece admired Sparta, partly because of its military success, more because Spartan life was a training in "virtue" in the "good old-fashioned" sense, the sense inculcated in children by adults, who want of children respect, obedience, endurance ("Stop crying!"), and silence. Moreover, self-inflicted suffering satisfies deep psychological drives and is therefore usually prominent in primitive religions. Greek religion had little of it, and the growth of individualism and rationalism diminished what little there was. Repressed drives found prudential justification in the example of Sparta; what could not be excused as superstition was admired as wisdom. Sparta was therefore to inspire the Greek philosophical imagination: it showed what could be achieved by lawgiving—the imposition of a "rational" pattern on the life of an entire city. Lycurgus, the supposed "lawgiver" of Sparta, became the great legendary representative of a class whose first real members had been the lawgivers of colonies; the recognition of the importance of the "lawgiver" and the ideal of "the city with good laws" were probably derived from colonization. Sparta did not reciprocate the philosophers' admiration. It wanted unanimity, not speculation, and banished philosophers because they disagreed. But many philosophers (who would have liked to banish one another) were not deterred by this decision. Sparta became the chief historical source of the ascetic and authoritarian ideals which are at work in Plato's *Republic* and its philosophical followers.

Athens did not subject its neighbors; instead it gave them citizenship. By the end of the eighth century it had united Attica, a territory almost half the size of Long Island. Therefore it, too, at first had no need to colonize or trade. With economic change, the oligarchs gave way gradually. The law began to be published shortly before 621. Solon, in 593, abolished some debts, prohibited enslavement for debt, encouraged manufacture and trade, and reportedly so reformed courts and elections that the poorer citizens could restrain the oligarchy. Some thirty years later one Pisistratus came to power as tyrant, but followed the usual policy of tyrants with unusual moderation and success. He preserved the external forms of the government, improved the lot of the small farmers, won Athens a footing on the Hellespont, built up the city, and died peacefully in 527. The relative tranquillity of his reign went with its prosperity, to which an increase in Athenian trade also contributed. Important exports were olive oil and a new style of pottery, called "black figure" because of the elegant silhouettes of men and animals which cavort on its orange-red ground. This black-figure ware outsold Corinthian pottery all around the Mediterranean—a success deserved by the vigor and variety of its decoration.

Two sons of Pisistratus continued his rule in Athens until 514, when one of them was murdered. The survivor's reprisals increased and united his opponents. After he was driven out in 510, control was won by an alliance of oligarchic and democratic elements which established a new constitution, a compromise in which the *demos*—the majority of the citizens—had the ultimate say. The resultant democracy was a direct government by the citizen body, which itself formed the controlling assembly and decided even technical questions like the disposition of troops before a campaign. To assure that all the citizens had equal opportunity to hold office, officials came to be chosen by lot rather than elected. To assure the assembly's control over officials, their terms were limited to one year, at the end of which they were called to account before a court. But the citizen body which controlled this democracy was composed only of adult, free, native-born males—i.e., about one-sixteenth of the population; women, children, slaves, and aliens were excluded. To be granted citizenship was a rare honor. As always, however, the quality of the government depended less on its form than on the character of those in power. In Athens, the *demos* exhibited surprising moderation, the fruit of the oligarchic tradition of mutual forbearance, essential for the working of a democracy. Each side must be confident that the other will not push its victories too far; awareness of common interest must be stronger than mutual distrust. In Athens this awareness was intensified by the hostility of their neighbors and the threat of a return of Pisistratus' family. Another factor was the discovery of large deposits of silver, shortly after 490. Silver built a big navy, which produced employment, prosperity, and civic pride.

The political fortunes of the Near Eastern kingdoms from the fall of Assyria in 609 to the rise of Persia after 559 are of far less importance for world history than are the developments in Greece. But the history of the tiny kingdom of Judah ranks in importance with those of equally tiny Athens and Sparta.

All over the Near East "nationalistic" reactions against the Assyrians had been associated with the cults of "national" gods: Nebuchadnezzar II's enormous expenditure for the temple of Marduk in Babylon is a conspicuous example. So in Judea nationism saw a revival of the cult of Yahweh. Since Yahweh was now protector of the poor, this revival was associated with demands for legal reform. Sometime about 630, when Assyria was losing her grip, a lawyer in Jerusalem produced a new code as a program for future reforms, including the prohibition of the worship of gods other than Yahweh, and relief of the poor. He drew on older "Yahweh-alone" traditions, common usage, and ancient taboos, but his work was organized by his own thought, replete with his own invention, and cast in his own style. He represented it as "the law of Yahweh" and—probably—as the work of Moses, and he arranged to have it "found" by the high priest in the Jerusalem temple in 621. It was taken to King Josiah, authenticated by a prophetess, and accepted. Most of it is now preserved, with minor interpolations, in chapters 12–26 and 28 of Deuteronomy. King Josiah tried to enforce it, but he also tried at Megiddo to stop Necho II's invasion of Syria and so met his end in 609. His defeat seems to have been taken as proof of the error of his ways; the later prophecies of Jeremiah and Ezekiel show polytheism back in practice.

But the "Yahweh-alone" party held to the Deuteronomic code, and the code reshaped the party. Like the laws of Sparta, it was to be learned by heart, repeated morning and night, an ever-present monitor of its people. The central act of religion became the learning of the Law, and this it remains for most of Judaism. Moreover, the Deuteronomist inspired a school of followers, recognizable by their imitation of his style, who augmented his code with a "historical" framework eventually extended to include earlier collections of legends and court records. These they reworked to make one great "history," teaching that only when Israel worshiped Yahweh alone did it prosper, and whenever it worshiped other gods it was punished. Thus the "historical" half of the Old Testament began to take shape, while other writers of the school collected, edited, and improved the works of the "Yahweh-alone" prophets. To prevent worship of gods other than Yahweh, the Deuteronomist had proposed to limit sacrificial worship to Jerusalem. Consequently, when the Judeans were carried off to Babylonia, those who held to the code developed a nonsacrificial form of worship, which eventually became prevalent in Judaism and Protestant Christianity.

The party's position was strengthened by the fall of Jerusalem. Since Nebuchadnezzar's defeat of the Egyptians at Carchemish in 605 and subsequent takeover of the Syro-Palestinian coast, the city had been subject to Babylon. Popular, nationalist feeling encouraged revolt by the claim that Yahweh would certainly defend his city. The "Yahweh-alone" prophets, on the contrary, maintained that Yahweh was angered by the city's apostasy and would therefore prolong its servitude; accordingly they were pro-Babylonian. When Nebuchadnezzar, irritated by repeated conspiracies, plundered the city in 597 and destroyed it in 587, the party was able to say, "We told you so."

Moreover, among the exiles in Babylonia, whither Nebuchadnezzar deported most of the upper-class Judeans, the party had a strong position. Their nonsacrificial worship—prayer and praise (psalms), sometimes with reading and exposition of the Law—was inexpensive by comparison with sacrifice. It required no special clergy, equipment, temple, only a "meeting place" (Greek: *synagogue*). This became characteristic of Judaism. Another new characteristic was isolation. Observance of purity laws and the refusal to worship any god save Yahweh had been merely punctilious in Judea; in the diaspora—the "scattering" of Judean settlements outside Palestine—this behavior cut the observant off from the life of the world around and made them a peculiar people. This gave the party coherence, while the Law's great concern for the poor (a sign of its times) gave them the strength of mutual support, which must have won over many of their fellow exiles. Eventually they would return to Jerusalem and gain control of the restored temple. Deuteronomy would then become the basis for an official legal tradition. In yet remoter time its prohibition of the worship of any god other than Yahweh (an offense it would punish by death, Deut. 12–13) was to be an element in the hostility between the Jews and the Romans and was to be taken over from Judaism by Christianity and Islam —a tradition of intolerance from which the Western world has suffered much.

Not all the Judean exiles in Babylonia, however, were followers of the Deuteronomist. The prophet Ezekiel had a different style and vocabulary, and different legal opinions. Akin to him in these matters was a group of priestly collectors, editors, and inventors of ancient traditions, particularly of legal material, to whom we owe compositions so diverse as Leviticus and the superb creation story in Genesis 1. The notion of Yahweh as creator is also important in the greatest writer of the exile—and one of the greatest writers of all time—the so-called Second Isaiah, author of Isaiah 40–55, whose lyrical expressions of joy and hatred, release and revenge, are of unmatched power. But most powerful and magnificent of all is his concept of Yahweh, throned on the enormous circle of the heavens, declaring, "I am the first, and I am the last; and beside me there is no God." All gods of all other nations are mere idols which can neither hurt nor help. The religious conceptions of all other peoples are worthless. Such was the logical—or illogical?—conclusion of Yahwist thought.

For Further Reading

Andrewes, A., *The Greek Tyrants*.
Glotz, G., *Ancient Greece at Work*.
Noth, M., *A History of Israel*.
Rostovtzeff, M., *Greece*.
Smith, M., *The Ancient Greeks*.

15   Persia and Athens

Cyrus the Great began his career about 559 as a kinglet in southwestern Persia. He won over the Medes about 550, defeated Croesus of Lydia in 546, and then subjugated Asia Minor. Next he descended on Babylon. King Nabonidus, already at odds with the clergy of Marduk, the chief god, fell in 539. Cyrus then turned to northeastern Persia and was killed there about 530. His son, Cambyses, settled that frontier, then conquered Egypt in 525. On his death in 522 his successor, Darius, put down revolts all over the empire and set about organizing what Cyrus and Cambyses had hastily conquered.

The organization he created was the largest empire the world had seen. It initially included Asia Minor and adjacent islands, Armenia, Azerbaijan, Syria, Palestine, Egypt, northern Arabia, Mesopotamia, Persia, Afghanistan, Turkestan, Uzbekistan, the Tadzhik and part of the Kirgiz Soviet Republics, and western Pakistan. To these Darius himself added the rich Indus Valley and Thrace. Macedon and Cyrenaica submitted to him but

CHRONOLOGY

B.C.		
	c. 585	Thales of Miletus, beginning of natural philosophy (physics)
	560	Pisistratus becomes tyrant of Athens
	c. 550	Cyrus of Persia conquers Astyages of Media
	546	Cyrus conquers Croesus of Lydia
	c. 540	Xenophanes, philosophic monotheism; "Second Isaiah," nationalistic monotheism
	539	Cyrus conquers Nabonidus of Babylon
	525	Cambyses, Cyrus' successor, conquers Egypt
	c. 525	Pythagoras, the philosophic life; the Doric temples of southern Italy and Sicily
	522	Darius begins reorganization of the Persian empire
	510	Pisistratus' family expelled from Athens
	499	Ionian cities, aided by Athens, revolt from Persia
	c. 499	Athenian red-figure pottery
	490	Battle of Marathon, Persian expedition against Athens beaten off
	480	Xerxes, Darius' successor, invades Greece; Carthaginian invasion of Sicily defeated at Himera
	479	Battle of Plataea, Xerxes' army destroyed; Battle of Mount Mycale, Xerxes' Aegean fleet destroyed; Persia loses Macedon, Thrace, and Cyrenaica
	478	Athens creates the Delian League for liberation of Greek cities from Persia
	c. 475	Parmenides opposition of reality (changeless) to appearance (changing)
	458	Aeschylus' *Oresteia;* beginning of Pericles' predominance
	457	The "long walls" secure Athens from attack by land
	454	The treasury of the Delian League moved to Athens
	449	Athens makes peace with Persia
	447	Beginning of the Parthenon, work of Ictinus
	c. 447	The Sophists' study of argument and rhetoric; Pindar (lyric poetry), Sophocles (tragedy), Herodotus (history), Phidias (sculpture)
	431–404	The Peloponnesian War, ending with the destruction of the Athenian fleet, the long walls, and the Delian League; Socrates (moral philosophy), Hippocrates (rational medicine), Democritus (atomic theory), Aristophanes (comedy), Euripides (tragedy), Thucydides (history)
	c. 405	Egypt revolts from Persia

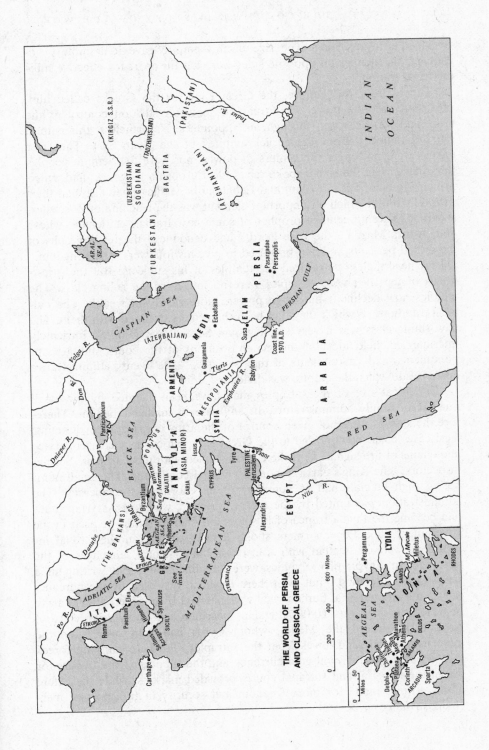

remained self-governing. The size of this empire gave it a military advantage: its enemies on opposite sides were too far apart for effective military cooperation.

The ruler of this empire, the Great King, as the Greeks called him, possessed absolute power. As usual, his power rested on control of the army and was exercised through his appointees. Nevertheless, this empire differed radically from the earlier empires of the Near East. The river valleys were no longer the centers of power, nor were the Semitic peoples the rulers. The Persians spoke an Indo-European language and ruled principally from Susa in Elam and Ecbatana in Media. They also had their own religion, in which an important element was the teaching of Zoroaster, a perhaps seventh-century prophet of some east Iranian cattlemen, whose god, Ahura Mazda, "the wise Lord," had denounced the fertility cults of the settled peasants and had promised to give his followers "the Kingdom." Darius nevertheless patronized the temples of his subjects. But the priesthoods of the river-valley temples were no longer of the ruling class. The temples now declined sharply in power, more slowly in wealth. The cultural traditions of which they had been the centers declined with them. The new ruling class was a very small group. Seven great families, intricately intermarried, held most of the major positions at the court, military appointments, and governments of the "satrapies," the twenty administrative districts into which the empire was divided.

The great size of the satrapies may have been dictated by the small number of family administrators. In any case, it invited rebellion. Therefore the satraps were not given control of the army corps in their domains; legal cases could be appealed to the Great King; an efficient courier service and chains of fire signals kept the court in touch with the satrapies. Special inspectors, "the King's ears," reported on local conditions. The small number of high officials had as complement an enormous bureaucracy. The administration was united by the use of Aramaic, which in Assyrian times had become the lingua franca of business and had begun to be used in the government. The Persian rulers spoke Persian to one another; royal inscriptions were in Persian with translations in the local languages of the satrapies. In Egypt, hieroglyphics were simplified for rapid writing in a script called "demotic," but even there Aramaic was used by the bureaucracy. This international bureaucracy was matched by an international army of which the core was 10,000 Persian spearmen and the Persian cavalry. After them ranked the Medes, whom Cyrus had won over, then the mercenary troops and levies from the satrapies. To these unifying forces should be added the royal gold currency and the support of the traders for whom the imperial and satrapal courts provided markets, while the extent of the empire made for more freedom and security in transport of merchandise than ever before.

These bonds held the empire of the Great King together for 200 years in spite of repeated crises. The death of each monarch touched off a contest for the throne and revolts in the provinces. Xerxes, Darius' successor, lost much of his fleet and army in his attempt to conquer Greece in 480–479. Macedon and Cyrenaica then broke away, and the Persians were driven out of Thrace and the coastal cities of western Asia Minor, but these latter they eventually regained. The Indus Valley was lost. Later on, satrapies became hereditary, the satraps built up private armies, and this led to revolts. Egypt broke away from 405 to 342. Cyprus was long fought over. But in spite of peripheral losses, harem intrigue, and bureaucratic inefficiency, the empire held together. The Persians never went beyond the Assyrians in the art of winning over the peoples they conquered. Like the Assyrians, they deported large groups and so created minorities dependent on them for protection. They also enlisted many in their army and bureaucracy and so won over a few. The prevalent attitudes of the subject peoples remained temporary subservience and latent hostility, but for the Persians, subservience sufficed.

The ruling class had a taste for magnificence. Artists from many subject peoples were employed to decorate palaces of which Susa, Pasargadae, and Persepolis have yielded sumptuous remains. Their sculpture shows the court on parade; the subject is stodgy, but the technique brilliant; Greeks and Lydians were the stonecutters. Many elegant vessels of gold and silver survive; the goldsmiths were Medes and Egyptians. And so on, for the other artifacts. When we ask what the Persians themselves did, the answer is: They ruled.

Their subjects were at least left free to follow their own traditions. In Egypt and Judea the concern for national tradition was compounded by wishful thinking. As the struggle against external domination became more difficult, men found consolation in fancy, retelling their "histories" with less concern for fact or spinning out legislation for imaginary states. Plato's *Republic* and *Laws* show the same reaction in Greece after the failure of Athens.

In Jerusalem, whither Cyrus had permitted the Judeans to return, cult and temple were reestablished and writers of the priestly and levitical schools gave the Genesis-Kings collection approximately its present form. The prophetic books also continued to grow, mostly by interpolation. But prophecy generally lost standing as men, despairing of immediate changes, turned wistfully either to the past or to the far-off future, to daydreams rather than prophecies. Stories of the good old days and collections of pious sayings and of lamentations were rivaled by accounts of the good time to come, when Yahweh would make Jerusalem the capital of all the earth.

Meanwhile the immediate concern of most men turned, as in Greece, to private life. Hence the Psalms, a collection of songs which has been, for 1,600 years, the daily devotional reading of pious Jews and Christians. Perhaps no other book has done so much to shape the Western mind. The collection contains a few songs from preexilic times, imploring Yahweh's blessings on the king (21, 46, etc.). A few retell the Mosaic legend in the spirit of postexilic times (105, 106, etc.). Yet more reflect the cult of the restored temple (134, 135, 136, etc.). But the main concern of the book is the private life of the righteous man—his determination to follow the law of Yahweh, his consciousness of his failings, his appeals for mercy, his fears of his enemies, and his hope in Yahweh. Like the Deuteronomic law, these poems were meant to be memorized. They make up a handbook of the spiritual life, constantly suggesting that the real world is a world of enemies from which the righteous man should turn to conversation with his god, i.e., to mild schizophrenia. The conversation repeatedly comes to the question: "Why do the righteous suffer?" To this the answer is only: "Trust in Yahweh and you will be saved."

For some, this assurance was not enough. The author of the poem in Job 3–26, perhaps the greatest intellect in the Hebrew tradition, stated the problem of evil with relentless clarity. What answer he came to, if any, will never be known. An editor has substituted a conclusion of pious resignation: God is incomparably great, therefore it is useless to question his doings.

In 546 the Persians subjugated the Greek cities along the west coast of Asia Minor. Intellectually, this had been the foremost area of the Greek world. Here the Homeric poems had taken shape; here the lyric poets had sung. Here, too, philosophy had begun about 585, with the speculations of Thales as to the possible origin of all things from some single element. This element, he thought, was water. That he was wrong is trivial. The important thing was his attempt to conceive nature as an intelligible order, a "cosmos." This intellectual daring was, in Ionia, fused with the new idea of individualism, that a man does well to disagree with common opinion. A philosopher says: "I have sought out for myself," a historian: "The stories told by the Greeks are many and ridiculous; I write what in my opinion is true." And Sappho writes: "Some say one thing is most beautiful, some another, but I say it is what you love."

From Ionia the spirit of inquiry spread abroad when the Persian conquest produced a wave of emigrants. South Italy and Sicily became briefly the centers of philosophic thought. Xenophanes, who emigrated about 545, argued that the primary substance must be single, eternal, unchanging, conscious, controlling all things—in a word, God. Thus physics led to metaphysics and theology. The contrast is striking between this monotheism and that of Second Isaiah, roughly contemporary. Second Isaiah's monotheism is a product of wishful polemic. Yahweh must be able to rescue the Israelites; therefore to control the world; therefore the other gods are mere idols. Yahweh remained a person and distinct from his creatures. Xenophanes' monotheism attempted to secure acceptance for the idea of an omnipresent, primary substance to which he had been led by philosophy —to make this substance acceptable he called it "God." Both lines of thought led to attacks on idolatry and on popular notions of the gods.

Xenophanes' thought was carried on by a school at Elea where Parmenides (c. 475) demonstrated the contradictions between the notions of being and of change—in other words, between metaphysics and common sense. Maintaining that we should not trust the senses, but judge by reason, he chose metaphysics and conceived of reality as changeless being. Back in Ionia, Heraclitus took the other horn of the dilemma and insisted that reality is constant change, like a fire, of which all things are but brief configurations. Meanwhile, Pythagoras, a Samian aristocrat who had emigrated to south Italy about 530, had turned in a new direction. He conceived of philosophy as a way of life to be realized in a private society. Men who rejected the standards of the world need not resign themselves, like the Psalmists, to converse only with God. He founded a brotherhood to practice the spiritual life and reform the rest of society. Within a century revolutions destroyed his brotherhood, but in the new world, with its growth of private life, its political exiles and *déracinés,* his idea lived on. It inspired Plato and a line of later imitators, through monasticism, to the present day.

Intellectual and political ferment in south Italy and Sicily accompanied economic and artistic development. The Doric temples of Selinus, Paestum, and Acragas (Agrigentum)—wonderfully calm, simple buildings—stand as monuments to the genius of their architects and the wealth of their cities. "The men of Acragas," said one visitor, "dine as if they expected to die tomorrow, and build as if they expected to live forever."

The whole Greek world was attacked by Persia and Carthage early in the fifth century. Darius sent spies to the western Mediterranean and two exploratory expeditions to Greece; the first was shipwrecked in 492, the second beaten off by the Athenians at Marathon in 490. The main attacks, Persian and Carthaginian together, came under Xerxes in 480. They failed. Xerxes lost much of his fleet at Salamis, while the Carthaginians were annihilated at Himera. The next year the rest of Xerxes' fleet was destroyed at Mount Mycale, and the land army he had left in Greece was destroyed at Plataea. The Greeks had solid body armor, longer spears, and better athletic training. To the Persians these defeats, though serious, were peripheral; they did not damage the main structure of the empire. But to the Greeks, victory was all-important. Even Marathon was a cause of enormous pride to Athens; it was the first time, we are told, that Greeks had ever stood up to Persian troops. When the new Athenian fleet played the leading part in the victory of Salamis, Athens could claim to have been the savior of Greece, and the claim was a major factor in the building of her later empire. Another factor was the instability of Sparta, where the upper class were opposed to foreign campaigns because they increased the powers of the kings. Accordingly Sparta left the liberation of the Greek cities around the Aegean to the Athenians.

For this task the Athenians were well equipped. The cities were almost all seaport towns, and the coast was deeply denticulated; thus a naval force had a tactical advantage. Many of the cities were Ionian, and so were the Athenians. They were familiar with the Aegean because of their trade, while both trade and democratic government had given them businessmen-politicians skilled in negotiation, aware of economic interests, and able to draw an advantageous contract.

Such a contract created in 478 the Delian League, so called because it met and stored its money on Delos, the Ionian island shrine of Apollo. (Sanctuaries were always chosen for treasuries, the god being guard.) The contract bound the signatories to follow a common foreign policy and to contribute ships or money, as assessed by Athens. Athens contributed the most ships and commanded the entire fleet. League members paid, in assessments, enough to maintain about 100 ships. These ships Athens provided, gaining military experience while the allies learned how to pay taxes. Beside these, Athens contributed about 100 ships of her own and the large allies, taken together, about the same number; in all, 300 ships and 60,000 men. This force freed the Greek cities around the Aegean; the liberated cities joined the league. Others were forced to come in. Athens also conquered islands held by non-Greek peoples, sold the inhabitants as slaves, and settled their lands with Athenian colonists. When members tried to withdraw from the league, they were conquered and forced to remain. Thus the Delian League in fact became an Athenian empire. Athens intervened in her allies' domestic policies by supporting democratic parties and setting up governments similar to her own. These parties and governments were usually loyal to Athens, but the people of the allied cities never thought themselves Athenians. As in other Near Eastern empires, one political group dominated its neighbors, but was unable to assimilate them. Like the Persians, Athens enlisted individuals from subject states in her military forces and so secured the loyalty of some. She went beyond the Persians in securing the support of a party in each subject city by political affiliation—"political ideology" now appears as an important factor in alliances. But she remained, in relation to her subjects, an alien ruling power.

Athens' acquisition of an empire abroad and her development of democracy at home were complementary. The empire paid directly for half of the city's ships; indirectly, as a preferential trading area, it paid more. This money paid the citizens who participated in Athens' assemblies and the jurors who served in her courts. Without pay the poor could not have attended to these offices. Above all the navy had to have oarsmen, and oarsmen had to be paid.* The wages of the oarsmen—36,000 for 200 ships—came from the empire. Since the oarsmen were the poor, the poor favored imperialism. Since the poor—as always—were the majority, democracy perpetuated imperialism. Leadership came from the newly rich traders who profited from the empire, as opposed to the landed aristocracy. It was the latter who furnished the best troops of the army, but in the 460's there were only 300 cavalry and about 10,000 hoplites. Further, in 457 a pair of "long walls," connecting Athens with its harbor, was completed. The Greeks were still inexperienced in siege warfare; they could do nothing against a fortified city save try to starve it out. With these walls Athens could not be conquered, for she controlled the sea and could not be starved. The navy could now dispense with the army.

The democrats, however, had got involved in central Greece and needed the army to hold it down. Also they were backing an Egyptian revolt against the Persians and that took a large force. It was no time to alienate fighting men. Pericles, the new leader of the democratic party, therefore moved slowly. But a series of defeats abroad forced him to make peace with Persia in 449 and with the powers of mainland Greece in 446. Thus the army's role and the aristocracy's importance were minimized, but the navy remained essential to control the overseas league. Military employment was replaced by a building program, of which the Parthenon is the masterpiece, financed by the league's treasury. This was supplemented by economic measures: the coinage of most league members was replaced by Athenian issues. Law cases were made transferable to Athens, assuring a steady flow of visitors, business, and bribes. Resultant rebellions by league members were profitably suppressed. Colonization was pushed and an expedition sent to the Black Sea, whence Athens got much of its grain and salt fish, and where it sold much of its wine and oil. Cheap food was a mainstay of democracy; it helped the poor in the city and cut down the income of the landed aristocracy. These measures kept Athens relatively prosperous, but ruined the other cities of the league. The eclipse of the Ionian coast, begun by Persian conquest, was finished by Athenian liberation.

Moreover, Athens' prosperity frightened her enemies. Thebes, the main

---

*Sailing boats were for trade. Ships fought by ramming each other; in such a fight a sail boat had no chance against a more maneuverable oared ship.

city of central Greece, remembered Athens' attempt to dominate the district. Megara's trade was ruined by Athenian rivalry. Corinth also felt the loss of trade, and she was angered by Athenian interference with her colonies. And Sparta felt that her position as the leader of Greece was threatened. The resultant "Peloponnesian" war broke out in 431, two years before Pericles' death. It was interrupted by a truce from 421 to 414, and ended in 404. The upshot was the ruin of Athens, which had lost between a half and two-thirds of her citizens; her territory had been plundered annually for twenty years; about 500 warships had been lost; her people were starving. She surrendered to the Spartans; the long walls were pulled down, the fleet and the overseas territories were given up, and the Delian League was dissolved.

The Athenian "empire" was the shortest-lived of all the Near Eastern empires and also the smallest; at its greatest extent it encompassed only Attica, most of the Aegean islands and the coastlands on the north and east, a sprinkling of strongholds around Greece, southern Asia Minor, and the Black Sea, and one colony in Italy. But the cultural development of Athens, in this brief period, transformed Western history.

Novelty in human institutions is always a matter of degree. There had previously been big cities and influential bourgeoisies. But about 50,000 Athenian citizens governed an empire. Of these, perhaps 15,000 were well-to-do. They constituted a new kind of market and power. The art created for them is radically different from that created for the rulers of Egypt, Assyria, and Persia, because, by comparison with those rulers, even the wealthiest Athenians were almost indigent. Alcibiades, one of the richest men in the city, had an estate of less than 75 acres. The high officials of the state and its honored guests dined at the public table; the *pièce de résistance* was a barley loaf with goat's milk and cheese. On festival days there was meat, the loaf was wheat, and there might even be a sesame cake. Such austerity transformed art and aesthetics; limited means necessitated simplicity. To simplicity, already characteristic of Greek elegance, Athenian art added a delicacy of feeling, a lighter touch, and an interest in sentiment. This more economical and appealing art, for these reasons, became "classic."

This new bourgeois restraint also affected Athenian architecture. Where former empires produced palaces, Athens produced public buildings: colonnaded marketplaces, gymnasia, monumental law courts and assembly places, theaters, music halls to seat thousands—all unknown to pre-Greek building. Even temples were designed less for the service of gods than for the delight of citizens. Religious services remained simple. The priesthoods were elective offices, sought as public honors. The temple was, in its ground plan, a hut with a porch in front, a storage room behind, and a surrounding colonnade. But the structure was now of marble and the proportions a wonder to the world. Even in the temples restraint of decoration and delicacy of feeling prevailed. In place of the squat, bulldog strength of earlier temples, the new Doric style was higher and lighter; even more so the Ionic, now adopted. The figures of sculpture, too, became lighter. Bourgeois mentality appeared in the naturalism, present even in figures of the gods; bourgeois morality, in the restraint of this naturalism by reverence and by the common-sense notion that art "should" represent beautiful things.

The intellectual interests of this Athenian bourgeoisie were also practical. First came rhetoric. To speak well was prerequisite for power in the assembly. In a law court it might be a matter of life or death. One had to speak for oneself, and the jury might number several hundred. Therefore in the first half of the century there appeared traveling teachers known as sophists ("men who make you wise"), who taught, besides rhetoric, "how to do well in life." They specialized in devising plausible arguments for almost any claim—hence the term "sophistry." This technique contributed both to the breakdown of moral standards and to the danger of lawsuits. The man who could not afford to be trained by a sophist needed a professional speechwriter. Such writers also wrote sample speeches to demonstrate their powers. Some had admirers who carried around and repeated their masterpieces. Henceforth speeches were an important form of the new prose literature of entertainment. Since these professional writers often demonstrated their skill by arguing against common opinion, their work also contributed to the breakdown of traditional standards and consequent development of moral philosophy.

The Athenians had little tolerance for philosophic teaching which had no practical application. Therefore the major developments in speculative physics were still made in Ionia, where Democritus (c. 430) actually anticipated nineteenth-century physics by adding, to Heraclitus' continual change, the specification that what is changing is a congeries of atoms. Scientific medicine also began in Ionia with Hippocrates, who argued that to understand an illness one must take into account the whole patient and his environment and must base one's treatment on experience of similar cases.

Nevertheless, Athens became the center of the philosophical thought of the Western world. Socrates, an idle stonemason, made it so. He drifted around the city with a circle of rich or beautiful young men, entangling respectable citizens in arguments about "justice," "bravery," "piety," and the like. Since he was highly skilled in argument, he made them look foolish. In 399 various victims accused him of corrupting the youth and introducing the worship of new deities. He was found guilty and executed.

We can only guess at his teachings from the unreliable reports of his pupils, but some results of his work are certain. He changed the main concern of philosophy from physics to ethics. He developed the question-and-answer method of treating problems and so contributed to the discovery of logic. He created the private "philosophic life" devoted to intellectual investigation and indifferent to the surrounding society. Finally, he formed a circle of disciples who would propagate his teachings. His death made many of these disciples enemies of democracy. Since democracy was to prevail in Athens through the next four centuries, Western philosophy inherited from the Athenian schools a tradition of separation from government and an affectation of superiority to public officials.

The condemnation of Socrates was in striking contrast to the freedom allowed Athenian dramatists. Oligarchic Greece had honored the gods with contests in athletics and lyric poetry, chiefly at rural shrines where the rich and their followers were the principal audience. Democratic Athens made these contests part of its civic festival of Athena and added to them, for its festivals of Dionysus, contests between dramatic poets and teams of performers. Elsewhere the older style of lyric continued to flourish; Pindar, its greatest master in the fifth century, died in 438. But for the bourgeois taste of Athens, drama added to the lyric more naturalistic presentation, the portrayal of human problems and passions, philosophic argumentation, cross-questioning, the confrontation of conflicting personalities—in a word, the life of the city. And, as in the life of the city, almost anything might be called in question, particularly in comedy which had behind it a tradition of ritual abuse in the Dionysiac festivals. During the Peloponnesian War, Aristophanes produced plays attacking the all-powerful demagogues of the war party, lamenting the losses, and advocating peace. He was equally free in ridiculing at least some of the gods, and even in tragedy critical discussion of generally accepted standards was common. Any radical idea attributed to Socrates can be matched in the great tragedies of Aeschylus, Sophocles, and Euripides. Perhaps the difference lay in the fact that the dramas always ended with virtue vindicated. This dubious virtue should not distract us from their great historical importance as the first examples of a new form of entertainment, a form more popular, more thought-provoking, lyrically beautiful, and profoundly moving than any the world had heretofore seen.

Even more important than the drama, in the long run, was the development of a prose literature read for pleasure. Speeches have already been mentioned. The greatest works, however, were the histories, of which Herodotus' and Thucydides' are preserved. Herodotus' history is an account of the eastern Mediterranean world from the beginning of the last Lydian dynasty (c. 672) until the complete ruin of Xerxes' expedition in

479. Thucydides' is a history of the Peloponnesian War. History had been written before (brilliantly, for instance, by the author of the life of David in I and II Samuel); it appeared independently in different civilizations and with different values. The specific value of Greek historiography is to ask questions. The authors did not begin from knowledge but from inquiry. They set out to discover something. Herodotus asked the cause of the Persian war and found it, not in any particular fact, but in the whole panorama of Greek relations with the Near East.

The great thing about Herodotus' history is the scope. A Greek from Asia Minor, won over by Athens, he reflects the trading tradition behind Ionian thought and its interest in geography. He is the Greek traveler, curious about all the sights, customs, and legends of the lands he visits. Why do they do this? How do they explain that? A weary Egyptian priest once said, "The Greeks are always children." In Herodotus we glimpse the delight of these grown-up children in the extent and variety of the world. But, like a traveler, he is always an outsider; he has never seen a great government from the inside and has no good notion of how one works.

Thucydides, on the other hand, when he set out to discover just why the Peloponnesian War had gone as it did, had a good notion of the likely reasons. He had been a member of the board of generals which controlled Athens. The great contribution of his work, therefore, is the conception of history as a concatenation of specific causes with specific results. He is remarkable, too, for his capacity to rise above facts and view a long series of them as a single process, or reduce a complex of events to a single pattern. In these respects, and with his sardonic picture of human behavior, he has been the teacher of rulers and has shaped history by shaping the beliefs of those who studied him. His own beliefs, and those of Herodotus, had been shaped by Homer. Both thought of war as the proper subject of history. But each strayed from the Homeric theme to indulge his own interests, Herodotus in foreign lands, Thucydides in Athenian politics.

In this respect Thucydides represents the interests of the Athenian bourgeoisie, Herodotus of the uprooted. For the man who stayed in his own city, politics, business, and agriculture were the major concerns, and it was now settled, at least in Athens, that business and agriculture were beneath the dignity of literature. The political achievement of Athens, therefore, is the most serious and specific record of its culture. That record is double.

On the one hand Athens is the classic example of successful democratic government of a large territory. In Athens itself the attachment to democracy was strong enough to survive the debacle of 404, throw off a tyranny, and maintain itself, in spite of interruptions by outside powers, down to Roman times. Moreover, democracy was not merely a political peculiarity;

it was linked with the ideals of freedom in private life, equality in opportunity to hold public office, and an education which sought to produce adaptability rather than to perpetuate a pattern. For democracy thus conceived as a way of life, the great speech written for Pericles by Thucydides (II.35 ff.) is evidence, exposition, and apology.

On the other hand, Athens was also the classic example of the failure of democracy. Her rule had ended in tyranny abroad and demagoguery at home. Abroad she subjugated her allies, looted them, and imposed on them, in the name of democracy, rulers from the lower classes who could hold their positions only with her help and would therefore be her spaniels. At home the courts were a farce enlivened by capital punishment, while the assembly repeatedly refused to recognize unwelcome facts, make necessary sacrifices, and reward and punish justly. When the Spartans took the city, survivors and exiles joined in pulling down the long walls to the sound of flutes, "believing that day was the beginning of freedom for Greece."

For Further Reading

Boardman, J., *Greek Art.*
Bowra, C., *Ancient Greek Literature.*
Ehrenberg, V., *The Greek State.*
Frye, R., *The Heritage of Persia.*
Jaeger, W., *The Theology of the Early Greek Philosophers.*
Porada, E., *The Art of Ancient Iran.*
Zimmern, A., *The Greek Commonwealth.*

16   The Fourth Century to the Death of Alexander

From the fall of Athens to the fall of Persia the military and political history of Greece is complicated but trivial. Sparta declared the Greek cities on the mainland and in the Aegean "free"; those in Asia Minor were given to Persia in return for help in the war. Presently they revolted with the connivance of the Persian viceroy in Asia Minor, Cyrus, who was preparing an attack on his elder brother, the Great King, Artaxerxes II, and wanted Greek support. When Cyrus was killed in the attack (401), the satraps in Asia Minor tried to reconquer the cities; the cities appealed to Sparta for help and got it. This angered Persia, so she financed the rebuilding of the long walls of Athens and instigated an Athenian and Theban attack on Sparta. The Spartans were forced to withdraw from Asia Minor

B.C. 404–371 Spartan hegemony in Greece
      404 Greek cities of Asia Minor given back to Persia
400–394 Spartan intervention in Asia Minor
      399 Trial and execution of Socrates
      395 Persia finances Greek attacks on Sparta
      394 Rebuilding of the long walls of Athens begun with
           Persian help
      378 Formation of the Second Athenian League
      371 Battle of Leuctra, Sparta decisively defeated by Thebes
371–362 Theban hegemony in Greece; Spartan control of the
           Peloponnese ended; establishment of the Arcadian
           League; the legal and historical books of the Old
           Testament reach approximately their present form;
           Plato teaching in Athens; Praxiteles; Isocrates
      359 Philip II becomes king of the Macedonians
      341 Persia reconquers Egypt
      338 Battle of Chaironea, Philip II defeats Athens and
           Thebes and subjugates Greece; Aristotle, Diogenes,
           Demosthenes
      336 Philip II assassinated; Alexander succeeds
      334 Alexander invades the Persian Empire
      333 Defeat of Darius III at Issus
      332 Capture of Tyre
      331 Foundation of "Alexandria by Egypt"; defeat of Darius
           III at Gaugamela; capture of Babylon, Susa, and
           Persepolis
      330 Capture of Ecbatana; death of Darius III
      329 Conquest of Bactria
      328 Conquest of Sogdiana
      327 Invasion of Pakistan
      326 Conquest of the Indus Valley
      325 Return across south Persia
      323 Death of Alexander in Babylon

CHRONOLOGY

in 394. Their withdrawal was followed by a half-century of intermittent warfare in Greece. First Sparta was cock of the walk for twenty years. Then Thebes developed a new military technique, that of massing troops in one area to break through the opponent's line, which could then be attacked from its unarmed flank. This technique made Thebes briefly (371–362) the strongest power in Greece. She set up an "Arcadian League" in the center and southwest of the Peloponnese to keep Sparta down. But while she and Sparta were at war, Athens had organized a new league including many of her former island allies and a few on the mainlands. When Thebes collapsed, she emerged as the strongest power in southern Greece. By that time, however, Greek politics was soon to be overshadowed by the growth of Macedon, whose king, Philip II, would appropriate and develop the Theban technique and back it up with cavalry.

The growth of Macedon was the most important example of a phenomenon now going on all around the Mediterranean—the development of large "Hellenized barbarian" states in which the culture of the ruling class was mostly Greek, but the population mostly non-Greek—or Greek of such a savage sort that the Greeks would scarcely recognize it. Beside Macedon and Epirus in northern Greece, the old Milesian colony of Panticapaeum in south Russia became the center of such a kingdom. So did the Carians, a people of southwest Asia Minor who now became practically independent of Persia. Although the rulers of the new kingdom of Egypt (from 404 on) continued Saite traditionalism in their elegant art and official inscriptions, they became dependent on Greek mercenaries, the land was full of Greek traders, and traces of Greek culture were everywhere visible. Egypt's reconquest by Persia in 341 was a blow to Greek economy. Similarly in Carthage, while Punic continued to be used, the form of government, the intellectual life, and the bric-a-brac were alike Hellenized. In Sicily Dionysius I, tyrant of Syracuse, built up a kingdom which contained most of Sicily, the toe and heel of Italy, and points along the Adriatic; his court was a center of Greek culture, but his subjects were largely non-Greek and he relied on the non-Greeks to support him against the Greeks. In Etruria the Etruscans, long imitators of the Greeks, were almost ruined by invasions of the Celts in the 380's, but the admiration of Greek culture was implanted in the area, and when Rome grew up it would show deep Greek influence.

These new Hellenized states were the results of a long radiation of Greek culture—a new civilizing of the barbarians—which had gone on unnoticed around the Greek colonies. The northeastern and central Mediterranean had been transformed from a world of Greek cities and scattered tribes of barbarians to one of Greek cities and settled states of considerable size with civilized rulers. This change made the Greek cities second-rate powers. It also ruined their trade. The new countries produced much of their own wine and olive oil and even local imitations of Greek manufactured wares. At the same time the revolts in the western Persian satrapies, the wars between Persia and Egypt and between the Greeks and Carthaginians in Sicily, the civil wars of the tyrants in Sicily and south Italy, and the Celtic invasions in north Italy, all destroyed rich markets. But in Greece the necessity of buying food abroad continued unchanged. The consequent economic crisis led to revolutions and counterrevolutions. These were made worse by the wars, which disrupted trade, ruined farms, and filled the cities with refugees and exiles whose poverty complicated the social problem.

Consequently men fled the country. Greeks were already, because of their armor and training, the foremost mercenaries of the Near Eastern states. Now their numbers abroad redoubled and Greece itself filled up with mercenaries. Nevertheless, the century saw major cultural achievements, mostly in Athens and mostly the results of specialization. Specialization in speechwriting and speaking now produced its greatest masters, the writer Isocrates and the orator Demosthenes. Similar specialization appears in sculpture: Praxiteles, the most imitated artist in history, produced the statue sufficient to itself, unrelated to architectural setting, probably devoid of content, a sheer expression of delight in the plastic and tactile qualities of human beauty and in the dazzling technical proficiency of the artist. His statues of female nudes were set up in temples as goddesses. The same development of technique and neglect of consequences appeared in finance, in which banking now became a specialty, newly important because mercenaries had to be paid. And in civic administration the experts on finance were at loggerheads with the newly professional generals, neither group willing to recognize the other's needs. Even the gods specialized: the shrines of Asclepius, a specialist in healing, spread to every part of the Greek world. But the two fields in which specialization yielded its most significant results were war and philosophy.

Socrates had created the philosophic life, but he was not a professional philosopher. A number of his pupils became "professionals" in that they made philosophy the thing they "did." The greatest of these was Plato, who left Athens in disgust after Socrates' execution in 399, but returned after 387, settled in a suburb called Academia, and established a private society, nominally for the worship of the Muses, which endured until A.D. 529 when the emperor Justinian closed it in the interest of Christian truth. It was the first example in Europe of an endowed institution for humane studies.

Just what Plato taught orally is not known, but his published works have influenced all subsequent Western philosophic and theological thought. His perfection of Socrates' question-and-answer technique led toward the discovery of formal logic and the rationalistic criticism of common beliefs (important in Hellenistic thought and in Christian polemics against paganism). He gave classic expression to dualism, beginning with the duality in all objects between the form, which can be known and must therefore be permanent, and the material, which is always changing and therefore unknowable. Hence there are two worlds—the world of forms, being, knowledge, light, beauty, truth, the mind, reason, and the philosopher; the world of matter, change, ignorance, darkness, error, falsity, the body, sensation, and the workman. Hence the good life is an escape from the world of the body; asceticism is the handmaid of philosophy. Finally, Plato was a superb artist; his style and his literary form—the dialogue—became models; his myths of creation, the soul, and the afterlife, his imaginative pictures of the ideal state and the idealized Socrates, have been perennial sources of inspiration.

In the long run, even Plato's influence was overshadowed by that of his pupil Aristotle, the completely professional philosopher. His dry treatises deal with the problem posed by the development of specialization: What is the structure of the whole of knowledge wherein each of the specialists' subjects has its place? In other words, how are these subjects related? This problem is basic to systematic philosophy and also to the practical task of organizing the many branches of knowledge for cooperation, as in a university or an academy of sciences. But Aristotle's importance was not at once apparent because he could not fully answer the problem. He laid the bases for an answer by his studies of logic, his classification of the ways in which objects differ (the categories of knowledge), his detailed accounts of a number of fields of knowledge (logic, metaphysics, physics, zoology, psychology, ethics, political theory, rhetoric), and his creation of much scientific terminology. These were to be the tools of the mind, and eventually the mind would win, but its time was not yet.

At the moment, the Greek world was filled with the consequences of specialization in war. These became fully apparent only when worked out by a brilliant soldier who was also an absolute ruler of a large people: Philip II of Macedon. None of his smaller or less warlike neighbors could stand against him. Striking first on one side, then on the other, making peace with one enemy as a prelude to attacking the next, between 359 and 339 he extended Macedonian control south to central Greece and east to the Sea of Marmara. Goaded by Demosthenes, the Athenians tried several times to stop him. Finally, when they sent their forces to protect Byzantium (Istanbul), Philip suddenly marched into Greece, defeated them and their allies at Chaironea in 338, subjugated the Peloponnese, established Macedonian garrisons at key points, organized the Greek cities in a league under his control, proclaimed a general peace, and began preparations for an attack on Persia. In the midst of these he was assassinated in 336.

His son, Alexander, carried on his policy. After liquidating other claimants to the throne and smashing opponents in the Balkans and Greece, he was able in 334 to invade Asia Minor. In that year he took the cities of the west coast and the center of the country; in 333 he entered Syria, defeated the Great King (Darius III) at Issus, and proceeded down the coast to Tyre, probably intending to cut off the bases of the Persian fleet and prevent its making trouble in Greece. The siege of Tyre—until then an island, he made it a promontory—held him up until August of 332; thereafter he took Egypt. Returning from Egypt in 331 he set out for Persia, where Darius had raised another army. Alexander smashed it at Gaugamela in October. Babylon, Susa, and Persepolis, with immense treasures, next fell, and Persepolis was destroyed. Thence he turned north to Media, taking Ecbatana in 330, thence east in pursuit of Darius. But Darius was murdered by one of his own satraps. Alexander thereupon declared himself Darius' successor and pressed on to reconquer "his" kingdom. This led him through six years of fighting in Afghanistan, Uzbekistan, Khazakstan, and Pakistan, down the Indus Valley and back across southern Persia to Babylon, where (after a year of reorganization and another expedition to Media) he died on June 10, 323, in the palace of Nebuchadnezzar II. He was thirty-two years old.

For Further Reading

Ehrenberg, V., *The People of Aristophanes.*
Friedlander, P., *Plato.*
Griffith, G. (ed.), *Alexander the Great.*
Jaeger, W., *Demosthenes.*
Ross, W., *Aristotle.*
Sinclair, T., *A History of Greek Political Thought.*
Wilcken, U., *Alexander the Great.*

17   The Hellenistic World

Alexander's generals carved his conquests into kingdoms. When, by 276, their wars of succession stopped, three great powers, ruled by three great families, had emerged: Macedon of the Antigonids; Egypt, with Palestine, Cyrenaica, and Cyprus, of the Ptolemies; and Asia, from Anatolia to Afghanistan, of the Seleucids. In the meantime a fourth great power had appeared in the west. By 268 Rome had won control of all Italy south of the Po Valley. But the courts of Macedonia, Syria, and Egypt paid hardly

B.C. 323–276   Wars of Alexander's successors, emergence of the three major Hellenistic kingdoms: Antigonid Macedon, Ptolemaic Egypt (with Cyrenaica, Cyprus, and Palestine), and the Seleucid empire (southern Asia Minor, Syria, Mesopotamia, Media, Iran, Afghanistan); Menander and the "new comedy" (of manners), Epicurus, Zeno (founder of Stoicism), Theophrastus

c. 290   The colossus of Rhodes

279   Galatians devastate Thrace, Macedonia, and north Greece, some then cross to central Asia Minor

275–215   Zenith of Alexandria as center of the new "Hellenistic" culture; Aristarchus, Archimedes, Euclid, Eratosthenes, Theocritus, Apollonius Rhodius, Manetho and Berossus; development of alchemy and astrology; translation of the Pentateuch into Greek (the Septuagint)

268   Rome in control of all Italy south of the Po Valley

215   Serious native revolts in Egypt begin

c. 175   The great altar of Pergamum

---

any attention to the events in Italy, a land as far away from the Greek world as America was from Europe in the nineteenth century.

The Greek powers sparred with one another, but established peace within most of their territories. At the same time economic changes diminished the bellicocity of the Greek cities. Alexander had coined the Persian treasures to pay his troops, and many came home with their gains. Money thus became available to pay for new ships and rebuild ruined farms. Even more important, the opening of the Near East gave jobs to the unemployed and homes to the homeless of Greece. The colonists lived better than before. They now could eat white bread; barley was for slaves. They could also afford the products of the old country, their native wines, olive oil, and pottery. Pottery now began to imitate silverware, it was no longer a luxury; the standard of wealth had risen. Goldsmiths copied and developed Persian styles with great delicacy and magnificence.

This prosperity was the economic basis of a new cultural flowering in Greece. The center of concern was the everyday life of the well-to-do. Even the manufacture of terra-cotta statuettes was raised to a fine art. Sculptors

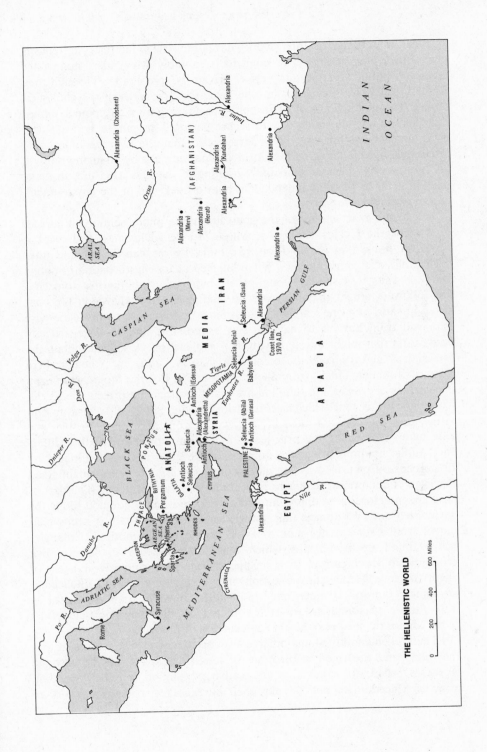

THE HELLENISTIC WORLD

0   200   400   600 Miles

extended the range of their work, developing new interests in realism, portraiture, and pathos. The comedians, notably Menander, abandoned farce and politics for the intrigues of private bourgeois life. Through their Roman imitators they became the ancestors of modern psychological drama. The new schools of philosophy, disagreeing on many points, agreed that the aim of philosophy was to secure personal happiness, conceived as psychological equilibrium. They agreed also that the average man could attain this, not by changing the world around him, but by changing himself. So "philosophy" became essentially training to live the good life, to make oneself as far as possible independent both of luck and of the environment, of approval and disapproval.

As to the exact nature of the good life, three major schools disagreed. First came the Cynics ("Dogs"), whose founder, Diogenes, had made a name for himself in the mid-fourth century by his caustic wit and utter neglect of social conventions. (When laughed at for masturbating in public Diogenes said he wished he could satisfy hunger by rubbing his stomach.) His followers taught that man was an animal and that the good life consisted in satisfying one's animal needs. Since needs cause trouble, the wise man will train himself to have as few as possible and to disregard any convention that might interfere with their satisfaction. A second school, the Stoics, was named from the colonnade (Greek, *stoa*) in Athens, where Zeno, its founder, taught from about 300 to 270. For the Stoics, man is an incarnation of reason, the thinking fire that produces and directs the world. The good life is that which accords with reason; this is also wisdom and virtue, and the consciousness of his own wisdom and virtue enables the wise man—trained by the practice of asceticism—to regard with indifference public opinion, private misfortune, and even death itself. Finally the Epicureans—Epicurus was an older contemporary of Zeno—maintained that man is a temporary congeries of atoms, dissolved at death. The part of wisdom, therefore, is to enjoy life while we have it, and the good life is the untroubled one. Wisdom is that knowledge and training which keeps men out of trouble. It teaches men to avoid political and emotional entanglements, build up friendships which make them secure in society, live economically, take care of their health, tolerate pain, and have no fear of death. In sum, Hellenistic philosophy taught indifference and intellectual arrogance. It inspired much later rationalism, but Christian asceticism as well. Strong personalities are still attracted by the central article of its faith: Man is the master of his fate and captain of his soul.

The Hellenistic kingdoms differed widely. Macedon was unique in that the rulers and the ruled were, more or less, one people. In the east the Seleucids relied, for control of the native population, on their standing army of Macedonians and Greeks, their bureaucracy, and the network of

Greek cities across their domains. Alexander left a string of Alexandrias from Egypt to central Asia as military centers, to protect his conquests and his lines of communication. The Seleucids and other Hellenistic rulers followed his example; cities named for various members of their dynasties (Seleucia, Antioch, etc.) were founded everywhere to control the lands around them.

In Egypt the Ptolemies became Greek pharaohs. They founded very few cities, since they did not want their power limited by the right of self-government which went with a Greek city. Instead, both the native Egyptians and the Greek settlers in Egypt, often military colonists, were governed by royal officials. Legally the immigrants and their descendants remained foreigners employed in the royal service. All economic activity was supervised by the king. The government decided which fields were to be planted and with what; where the crops were to be sold and for how much. It regulated transportation, processing, manufacturing, trade, and banking. Nothing escaped taxation. Even abandoned babies were collected and sold—the proceeds going to the privy purse. Since the government rightly distrusted both taxpayers and tax collectors, this system required endless bookkeeping and an immense bureaucracy which, always oppressive, became ruinously expensive, and so contributed to a series of native revolts beginning in 216. But from about 275–215 the system made the Ptolemies the richest Hellenistic rulers. Inspired by Greek analytic thought and organization—they set up a separate department for each branch of economic activity—theirs was perhaps the greatest technical achievement of the age. And it brought out men of the new managerial psychology who found their calling in the service of the kings. We have most of the business records of one of them, yet we do not know whether he had a family.

The wealth thus accumulated was lavished upon Alexandria, the greatest city in the world. Legally it was not "in" Egypt, but was a Greek city "by" Egypt. Here Hellenistic culture reached its acme. The court attracted brilliant writers. New literary forms—the epigram, the pastoral of Theocritus, the literary epic of Apollonius Rhodius—came to the fore. The Ptolemies turned their genius for organization to the patronage of science and scholarship. A royal institute was founded, legally for the cult of the Muses, whence its name, the Museum. Royal funds provided for buildings, support of members, and accumulation of an enormous library. Alexandria became the greatest center of historical and scientific studies in the Greek world. But this brilliance was paid for by denial of Greek city life to the rest of the country; the Hellenization of the Egyptians lagged far behind that of the Syrians.

Beside the major kingdoms a number of minor Hellenistic states grew up, for instance, Pontus and Bythinia in northern Asia Minor. Their most important action during this age was to protect themselves against the Seleucids by inviting into Asia Minor the barbaric Celts (Galatians) who had devastated Greece in 279–278 and now, established in central Anatolia, terrorized the cities along the coast, breaking up Seleucid rule. On the coast the dynasts of Pergamum, with Ptolemaic help, stood off both Seleucids and Galatians and built up an autocratic court supported by a suppressed countryside. The Pergamene sculptors produced the greatest work of the age, a dramatic frieze of gods battling giants, to commemorate the Galatian wars. The Pergamene library was second only to the Alexandrian, and the technique perfected there of preparing skins for writing ("parchment" comes from the Latin *pergamena,* "pergamene") was to save, in the Middle Ages, many ancient texts which would have disappeared had they been written on more fragile material. By contrast to Pergamum, Rhodes carried on the tradition of the Greek city-states. The shift of trade to the eastern Mediterranean made it a great shipping and banking center. It beat off the Antigonids with the help of the Ptolemies and vice versa. Its fleet restrained piracy; its sea law started an international tradition; the security and freedom of the city made it the home of eminent philosophers and artists. Its colossal statue of the sun god Helios was one of the wonders of the world.

All these different states shared a single culture, usually called Hellenistic. This culture was consciously Greek and international, rooted in the common feeling of the Greeks abroad, where differences between Spartan and Athenian paled beside those between Greek and native. A curious consequence of this was that anyone, whether native or Greek, came to be called a Greek if he possessed the culture. And this culture was not linked to any political power or even, necessarily, to any religion. Superficially it was a matter of costume, language, and technology; profoundly, of the analytic way of thought. Thus, later, native rulers like the Maccabees promoted Hellenization as necessary for power and independence. By assimilation of this culture the most ambitious natives rose to power in Greek society, while the Greeks, by accepting the Hellenized natives, half-consciously deprived the native masses of leaders. The language of this culture was a new dialect called "common" Greek, an international tongue which was eventually to disseminate Greek philosophies and Near Eastern religions (including Judaism and Christianity).

The Greek elements of Hellenistic culture should not conceal its profound difference from the culture of classical Greece. Classical Greece had been a world of tiny city-states with conciliar governments. In the Hellenistic world many such cities survived, more were created, and some succeeded in preserving their independence. They were the centers from which Hellenistic culture radiated, but they did not dominate their culture, nor was their civic life its main characteristic. Hellenistic culture was dominated by the big monarchies and characterized by the life of their capitals. These cosmopolitan cities were new sociological phenomena, far different from classical Athens, not to mention Sparta. In classical Greece the land had been held chiefly by private citizens in small estates; in the Hellenistic world the most important holdings were the vast domains of the kings, temples, and great officials. In classical Greece the cults of the city gods had been the center both of petition and of patriotism; in the Hellenistic world patriotism was expressed in the cults of the deified kings, and petitions were more often addressed to deities without political affiliations, like Asclepius, the god of healing. In the classical world, of small economic and political units, private citizens had been of considerable importance, politics had been a major concern of the average man, and the arts and philosophy had been politically oriented. In the larger Hellenistic world, private persons were usually of no importance—to be heard, they had to riot. In big cities like Alexandria, street mobs were the counterpart of the royal bureaucracy. Therefore private persons concerned themselves with their private affairs and "lived unnoticed," as Epicurus advised them, and so did philosophy and art (except when motivated by political patronage). Finally, and for the same reason, in small cities, both of classical Greece and of the Hellenistic age, the civil administration and army (if any) were run by amateurs: the same man was in turn farmer, officer, judge, and so on. Therefore politics was full of factional conflicts. In the Hellenistic monarchies administration and army were run by professionals, and the history was one of bureaucratic intrigues and palace revolutions.

This increase in professionalism was characteristic of all fields of activity in the Hellenistic world. Its consequences were increased technical proficiency, the collection and systematization of previous knowledge, and the standardization of products, which improved in quality, but lost their individuality and originality. In geography Eratosthenes calculated the circumference of the earth with an error of less than 1 per cent; in astronomy Aristarchus of Samos propounded the heliocentric theory of the solar system. This was the age of the botanist Theophrastus, the mathematicians Euclid and Archimedes. On the other hand, pseudoscience invaded medicine, producing an increase in the practice of bleeding, which persisted to the middle of the nineteenth century and probably killed more patients than any diseases except the great plagues. Alchemy was another "discovery" of this age; astrology flourished. But in spite of such aberrations the collection and systematization of knowledge in all fields was the greatest achievement of the Hellenistic age. The structures of Hellenistic learning were to be the foundations of the Renaissance.

A second characteristic of the age was the innumerable technological advances, from the appearance of the bill of exchange in banking, the water-lifting screw and the threshing drag in agriculture, the sternpost rudder in shipping, the copying machine in sculpture, down to the five-drachma-in-the-slot machine for dispensing holy water in Ptolemiac temples. Collectively the new technology much increased human power and efficiency. Indeed, the Hellenistic age may be symbolized by one of the most famous of these advances, the first known lighthouse, at the port of Alexandria; its fire is said to have been visible for 35 miles.

Finally, the new Hellenistic culture penetrated and changed the Near East, one of the greatest revolutions in ancient history. But it was a slow process. Greek styles in sculpture led the invasion, carried by coinage, terracotta and metal statuettes, and decorations on household objects. These were recommended by their lifelikeness—a virtue often most admired when least mastered. This penetration had already begun in the fifth and fourth centuries. With Alexander came the Greek language, Greek business practices and technology, and the experimental, inventive attitude which, for instance, revolutionized the agriculture of Egypt: better breeds of cattle and sheep, new crops, and better seeds for the old ones were introduced; iron at long last replaced bronze for common tools; irrigation was reorganized and greatly extended; more nutritious wheat flour replaced the ancient emmer—at least in the diet of the middle and upper classes. Under Ptolemy II daily rations of wheat or wheat bread were given to government officials and employees, including slaves.

Much slower was the spread of Greek civic life, both legal and cultural. When a city was founded for Greek settlers the citizens had to be given the rights customary in Greek cities—election of magistrates, their own assembly and courts, government by majority rule, a modicum of freedom of speech, freedom from enslavement for debt and from bodily punishment before conviction, the right to public trial, and so on. They also required the normal amenities of Greek life—a theater (which might double as an assembly place), an open market (colonnaded if possible), courts and gymnasia.* These rights and pleasures of Greek life were long limited to the few "citizens" of the new cities—Greeks without citizenship, natives, and slaves were carefully excluded. But the pattern gradually spread by extension to native Near Eastern cities. And even those natives who perpetuated their ancestral political forms were deeply influenced by Greek culture. The conventional image of Buddha is a creation of the Greek artistic tradition. The influence of the Greek cities of Syria and northern

---

* The gymnasium now changed from a social center for the adult to a secondary school. To athletic and military training were attached music, poetry, and rhetoric, the beginnings of "higher education." These became necessary because the children's Greek was corrupted by the native servants. Even girls had to be sent to school.

Mesopotamia made the later Aramaic (Syriac) culture of those areas the main instrument for the Hellenization of Islamic thought. And the Hellenization of Palestine by Greek cities shaped both Judaism and Christianity.

Slowest of all was the penetration of Greek literature and philosophy. The Greeks soon found educated natives to explain to them, in Greek, the contents of native traditions. The histories of Egypt and Babylon were even recast in something approaching Greek historical form for the Ptolemies and Seleucids by the third-century Egyptian priest Manetho and Babylonian priest Berossus; the Jewish law was translated into Greek, reportedly at the behest of Ptolemy II, who had many Jews to govern. Natives who had learned Greek even tried their hands at original literary compositions in Greek styles on native subjects—we have anti-Greek pamphlets written in Greek by Egyptians, and fragments of a Greek tragedy on the Exodus. Doubtless it was the prestige of Greek which worked against translation and imitation of Greek literature in native tongues. Anyone who aspired to write a literary work of a Greek sort aspired also to write it in Greek. Consequently the native literatures lived on through the Hellenistic and early Roman periods primarily by imitation of earlier native forms.

For Further Reading

Forbes, R., and Dijksterhuis, E., *A History of Science and Technology—1.*
Grube, G., *The Greek and Roman Critics.*
Marrou, H., *A History of Education in Antiquity.*
Neugebauer, O., *The Exact Sciences in Antiquity.*
Sambursky, S., *The Physical World of the Greeks.*
Tarn, W., *Antigonos Gonatas.*
Tarn, W., and Griffith, G., *Hellenistic Civilization.*

Classical Antiquity: Rome

18 The Roman Republic

In the summer of 204 Ptolemy IV of Egypt died, leaving a five-year-old son. Philip V of Macedon and the Seleucid Antiochus III promptly moved to seize Ptolemaic territories. Antiochus occupied Palestine in 201; after some fighting the Seleucids held the country for half a century. Philip tried to take territories controlling the Hellespont. This frightened Athens, Rhodes, and Pergamum, and they appealed to Rome. Rome defeated Philip in 197 and stripped him of his domains outside Macedon. Though she left the Greek cities independent, the war gave her de facto control of Greece, and the Greeks turned to Antiochus for help. Rome then defeated him at Magnesia in 190.

The defeats of Philip and Antiochus began a new era in the political history of the eastern Mediterranean—the eight hundred and thirty years of Roman supremacy, from 190 B.C. to A.D. 640 (the Moslem capture of Alexandria). The stability of this power can be matched in Western history only by that of Egypt. Moreover, Rome in 200 B.C. had already existed for half a millennium and the Roman government lived on after 640 in the Byzantine empire for another eight hundred years. Roman political and legal thought has shaped every subsequent state of Europe and also those of European inspiration. Therefore the spotlight of Western history, hitherto focused on the Near East and Greece, now shifts to the Roman world.

The legends about the origins of Rome, as of the Greek cities and Israelite tribes, may to some degree reflect what actually happened, but the degree is certainly small and not precisely calculable. Whatever the origins, there were some settlements on the Roman hills in the eighth century B.C. and the city was there by the end of the seventh. Its early history was distinguished by two most important characteristics—its willingness to

B.C.   387 Rome destroyed by the Celts
338 Rome in control of Latium
268 Rome controls Italy south of the Po Valley
264–241 First Punic war; most of Sicily made a province (the first)
238 Sardinia and Corsica taken from Carthage
218–202 Second Punic war (218–216 Hannibal's victories); plays of Plautus, earliest major works preserved from Latin literature
204 Death of Ptolemy IV of Egypt
201–198 Antiochus III takes Palestine
200–197 Rome defeats Philip V of Macedon
195–179,
154–133 Roman subjugation of Spain
184 Censorship of Cato; 1,000 talents spent on sewers
181 Foundation of Aquileia; completion of the conquest of Italy south of the Alps
167 Roman citizens freed of direct taxation
149–146 Takeover of Macedonia and most of Greece; Corinth razed; third Punic war; destruction of Carthage, its territory annexed as the province of "Africa"; Punic works on agriculture translated into Latin by order of the senate
144 First high-level aqueduct in Rome; introduction of hydraulic cement
135 Big slave revolts begin (in Sicily)
133 Tiberius Gracchus murdered
129–102 Continued annexations: 129 the province of "Asia" (ex Pergamum), 122 the Balearics, 121 Narbonnese "Gaul," 105 Tripolitania, 102 Cilicia
121 Gaius Gracchus murdered
114 Marius enlists landless men for the army
91–89 Revolt of the Italian allies (critical period)
87–83 Sulla's subjugation of Greece and Asia (Athens ruined, Mithridates VI of Pontus defeated)
81–79 Sulla's dictatorship (death, 78)
67 Pompey suppresses piracy
66–62 Pompey's defeat of Mithridates VI and Tigranes of Ar-

---

grant citizenship to aliens and its ability to unite other cities to itself. These gave it the manpower which overwhelmed the Hellenistic kingdoms and the political stability which carried it from the fifth century to the first without a revolution. By contrast the Greek cities, poor and democratic, could not afford to grant citizenship, which carried a share in the government and a claim on the food supply. In Rome, where the populace voted by blocks, an additional citizen meant only a very small fraction of a block's vote, and food, in fertile Italy, was not a critical problem. When a slave was enfranchised in a Greek city he became a resident alien and had no loyalty to the city. He might support a tyrant or an enemy. When a slave was enfranchised in Rome he became a Roman citizen, albeit of the lowest class, and his children would be of higher station. Rome, when it defeated a rival, could afford to take the citizens as well as the land. The manpower would be an advantage in its next war, and the new citizens would find some consolation for their former defeat in their profits from the following victory. Similar considerations cemented alliances. Many of Rome's "allies" were acquired by force, like Athens', but, unlike Athens', once in the gang they shared in the loot. Moreover, Rome, itself an oligarchy, supported the local aristocrats, made them dependent on its support, and allied them to its own ruling class through intermarriage. And revolts brought terrible punishments.

In 387–386 a Celtic invasion destroyed both the city and its records. Records can hardly have been plentiful in any case, for although writing was known in the area from the seventh century on, literacy did not become common until late in the third. For the period prior to the Celtic raid, therefore, we have only legends. After the Celtic raid we can trace with more confidence the areas Rome assimilated or allied to itself. First came the Latin towns south of the Tiber (by 338), then the Samnites of central Italy (by 290), then the Etruscans to the north and the Greek cities of the southern coasts. By 268 it controlled the entire peninsula south of the Po Valley and the northwestern Apennines, and had united its territories by a network of colonies.

By this time Rome's unite-and-share-the-plunder policy had made it the keeper of a military man-eater which none of its neighbors could defeat, but which had to be fed with plunder if it was not to turn on its keeper. Sicily was the richest country at hand. Since much of Sicily was occupied by the Carthaginians (in Latin, *Poeni*), intervention there led to a struggle with Carthage in two long "Punic" wars, 264–241 and 218–202. Rome's victory in both was due to her superiority in manpower and her ability to hold her allies. In the first war she lost 700 ships (manned by 140,000 men) to the Carthaginians' 500, but nonetheless forced Carthage to sue for peace. In the second war, when the Carthaginian general Hannibal invaded Italy with 26,000 men, Rome had available for service 273,000 Roman citizens and 379,000 allies. Therefore, although Hannibal smashed three Roman armies in succession at Trevia (218), Trasimene (217), and Cannae (216), and although these victories won him support from the Celts of the Po Valley and the Greek cities of south Italy, his invasion finally failed because the bulk of the allies remained loyal to Rome. He never won over enough troops to attack the city. Rome was able to keep one army on his trail and send other armies to conquer Carthaginian Spain, suppress a revolt in Sicily, keep Macedon busy in Greece, reconquer the Po Valley, reconquer south Italy, and finally invade North Africa. And the war with Carthage was so far from exhausting her that she was able to defeat Macedon in 197 and Antiochus in 190.

But now the common interest of Rome and its allies in plunder changed the Roman system. Big enough to defeat anything in sight, it no longer wanted more members. The more members, the less plunder per member. Therefore, beginning with Sicily in the first Punic war, conquered cities were no longer customarily made allies, nor were conquered lands customarily used for the foundation of new colonies in which allies as well as Romans received grants. Instead, the newly acquired territories were now organized as provinces. Allies generally contributed military service but were self-governing in domestic affairs, had certain rights guaranteed by treaties in relation to Rome, and were free of tribute; provincials were usually free of military service, but subject to Roman governors, devoid of civic rights, and obligated to pay tribute. The change from alliance and colonization to the creation of provinces was not uniform—almost nothing in the administrative history of the Roman republic was—but it was frequent from 250 on, and after 175 it was general.

This change cut off the largest item in the allies' benefit from the wars—the distribution of land to colonies in which they participated. It greatly increased Rome's profit. Not only was the tribute of the provinces paid to Rome, but Rome farmed to private companies the task of collecting the tribute. These companies raised the necessary capital by selling stock, then recovered their outlay by seizing as "tribute" all they could get. Their rapacity yielded high returns. It also led to innumerable suits between Romans and provincials. Of these, and of most other civil cases in the province, the Roman governor was the final judge. Governors served without salary (Rome, like most ancient cities, thought public offices honors for which the recipients should pay). But they had a generous allowance for expenses: the parsimonious but honest Cicero saved the equivalent of $540,000 from his allowance as governor of a minor province for two years. And this was nothing to what a dishonest man could make from bribes. Besides the profits of administration, Rome and her generals got the lion's share of the booty and the cash payments extracted from the defeated, payments which, from the Punic Wars on, were greatly increased. Finally, the accumulation of capital in Rome made the Romans the principal partners in companies which supplied the needs of the Roman army and navy. In these, and in the tax-collecting companies, the wealthy families of the allies also participated; under Roman protection the Italian allies, particularly the Greeks, took over most of the trade of Greece and Asia Minor, and many of their poor relations were employed as agents of the tax-collecting companies. But most of the poorer citizens of the allied towns were burdened with the fighting and rewarded only with the soldier's miserable pay and trivial booty.

Along with the allies, many Roman citizens were alienated from their government. Rome had long ago gone through the customary evolution from a kingship to an oligarchy of "patrician" families. During the fifth and fourth centuries popular leaders had opened the civic offices and priesthoods to nonpatrician candidates. But here the movement toward democracy had stopped. The final authorities in the state were several assemblies of citizens who voted not by individuals but by companies or tribes. The rulers so gerrymandered these voting units that most could be swung by the few rich voters. Moreover, the wide geographic distribution of the citizens made assemblies difficult to attend and easy to control. And their powers were strictly limited. Bills had to be accepted or rejected without amendment. The presiding magistrate sat, the assembly stood. Control even of general policy by the assemblies was therefore out of the question. But the principal offices of the state were annual, and most could not be held twice. Therefore the officers could not long control policy either. Thus control fell into the hands of the senate, nominally an advisory council composed of the former holders of the four highest offices. Almost all senators came from wealthy landowning families. Their vast profits as generals and governors were invested almost entirely in land, and the price of land skyrocketed.

Small landowners formed the bulk of the army. Throughout the ancient world it was customary to admit to a city's army only men with a minimal landholding. The men had to provide their own weapons, property was a guarantee of patriotism, and only responsible citizens could be permitted in the military organization which controlled the state. During Hannibal's invasion many farms had been ruined by pillage or neglect. The wars threw vast numbers of slaves on the market, and the exploitation of Sicily provided cheap grain. The soldier returning to his ruined farm found himself facing ruinous competition. (Roman methods of slave management were remarkable for inhuman economy; on big estates slaves were kept in prisons, treated as animals, and worked, not until they dropped, but until their efficiency dropped. Then they were sold, usually to the state mines, where conditions were harder and the mortality rate necessitated the purchase of the very cheapest slaves—the supply of condemned criminals did not suffice.) Given such competition, many small landowners sold out (for the excellent prices their senatorial neighbors offered), went up to Rome, and, when their money was gone, swelled the mass of the unemployed.

Between the small landowners and the senators were the bourgeois families of means. They were not very numerous—in 225, about 23,000 out of 273,000 citizens (adult males). Nor were most of them very rich; anyone who had more than $100,000 capital was included in the class. But some of the bourgeois made huge fortunes in trade and as war contractors, and most of them bought shares in the tax-collecting companies. Consequently they were happy to have the tax-collecting companies loot the provincials. On the other hand the senatorial families extended to the provinces the policy of protecting the local aristocracies. And some senators, as governors of provinces, were sufficiently honest to provide the protection for which the provincials paid them. Accordingly, as tax-collecting companies were sued for extortion or governors for taking bribes, conflict after conflict arose between the senators and the bourgeois. The class feeling of each group was sharpened, and the senatorial families (the *nobiles*—well known) used their influence to prevent outsiders from securing high government offices. This embittered the capable bourgeois, who made fortunes of senatorial size but were excluded from political power and social prestige.

Thus the economic consequences of Rome's success made the allies discontented and envious, ruined the small farmers, and created among the ruling classes a sharp rift between business on the one hand, government and landowning on the other. The ruined farmers became a huge city mob, ready for any violence. At the same time, the wars created an enormous population of desperate slaves, both in the cities and in the countryside, and the victories surrounded Italy with a ring of provinces in which all Italians were hated, but Romans most.

This situation developed slowly, and while it developed, Rome's policy of plunder steadily extended the area of its control. The Punic Wars had brought in Sicily, Sardinia, Corsica, and Carthaginian Spain. This last was a great economic prize because of its rich silver and lead mines; holdings there were consolidated and extended by continuous wars against the natives down to 179 and again from 154 to 133. The Po Valley was conquered between the Punic Wars and reconquered after the second; then Roman territories were pushed north to the head of the Adriatic, where Aquileia was founded in 181. In 149 anti-Roman revolts brought the annexation of Macedon and in 146 of the rest of Greece; Corinth, which had led the resistance, was destroyed, and only a few favored cities (Athens, Sparta, Delphi) remained allies. At the same time, Carthage was forced into war and destroyed and its territory annexed as the province of "Africa" (146). In 133 the last ruler of Pergamum left his state to Rome on the condition that she protect its independence; after a revolt in 129 it was made the province of "Asia." The Balearic Islands were taken in 122, the district around Narbonne in 121, Tripolitania in 105, Cilicia in 102.

By this time, however, the friction between the parts of the Roman machine had become so great that the whole was about to burst into flame. A series of slave revolts—the first in Sicily from 135 to 132—were inconveniences rather than dangers, for not even the provincials would commonly join with slaves. Indeed, a big slave revolt in a province made the provincials sensible of their dependence on Rome for protection. More serious was the revolt of the Italian allies in 91. Rome defeated this by granting most of the demands which had occasioned it, notably for Roman citizenship. She began by rewarding those who remained loyal, then won over by generous terms the less resolute of the rebels, finally made examples of the most determined. Divide and conquer had always been her policy. The crisis was past by 89; the fighting went on for a while thereafter.

Rome ceded more easily to the demand for citizenship because her supply of citizen soldiers had continued to dwindle, and her mob of citizens without property, to grow. Of the attempts to reverse these changes the most famous were those of the Gracchi brothers in 133 and 123. Relying on bourgeois support, they advocated extension of citizenship to the allies, resettlement of small farmers on public land (hitherto rented to senators at minimal rates) resumption of colonization, and provision of grain at less than market rates to feed the Roman poor, pending their resettlement. The longest-lived of these measures was the last: most of the Roman mob preferred poverty and indolence in Rome to the hard work of a small farmer, and when one party began to bribe them with public money, the other could not offer less, so cheap grain gradually became free grain, and other "relief" measures went on increasing through the centuries until the imperial government broke down.

After the introduction of poor relief, the Gracchi's most important achievement was to get themselves murdered by their senatorial opponents. This produced an enduring feud between the majority of the senators and a Gracchan minority supported by the bulk of the bourgeoisie. The majority also had their bourgeois supporters, and both sides, with varying success, bid for the mob. There was no clear-cut class struggle. But the security of senatorial rule gave way to bitter party battles in which anything could happen.

What did happen was that a popular and capable bourgeois general named Marius found a way to raise plenty of troops and good ones—he simply enrolled any men he could get, asking no questions about property and preferring those who looked like good fighters. Such men, largely from the rural proletariat, had little financial interest in the Roman state and less concern for it. They were not a citizen militia, but a body of professional soldiers, fighting not for Rome, but for money. Their pay was minimal, and the senate, with tight-fisted, Roman stupidity, would do nothing significant to increase it. The state was chronically short of money because the senate would not consent to tax Romans—they had abolished direct taxation of citizens in 167. Nor would they permit the soldier to rise from the ranks—officers must be of bourgeois fortune or better. So pay was fixed. Beyond pay came booty, which depended on victory, which depended on the general. Finally, the soldiers might hope for some special reward provided their general won his war and had sufficient political influence to persuade the senate to grant his soldiers land. Therefore the soldiers were loyal to their generals, not to the senate.

Other generals followed Marius' example. They and their armies were soon fighting for control of the state. Each general, when in power, declared his chief opponents public enemies and put prices on their heads.

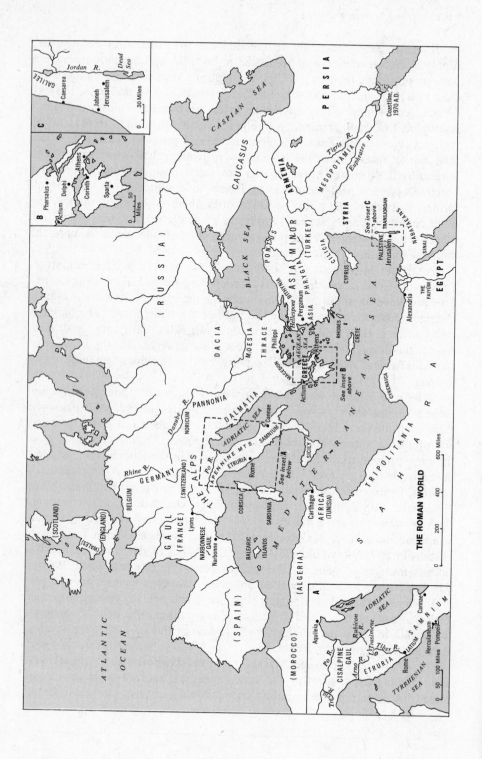

THE ROMAN WORLD

Coastline, 1970 A.D.

0   200   400   600 Miles

Inset A (lower right)

Po R.
CISALPINE
Arno R.
GAUL
Rubicon R.
ADRIATIC
SEA
The R.
Aquileia
ETRURIA
L. Trasimene
Tiber R.
Rome
LATIUM
SAMNIUM
Cannae
Herculaneum
Pompeii
TYRRHENIAN
SEA
0   50   100 Miles

Inset B (upper left)

Pharsalus
Actium
Delphi
Athens
Corinth
Sparta
0   50 Miles

Inset C (upper left)

GALILEE
Jordan R.
Dead Sea
Caesarea
Jabneh
Jerusalem
0   30 Miles

PERSIA
CASPIAN SEA
CAUCASUS
(RUSSIA)
ARMENIA
MESOPOTAMIA
Tigris R.
Euphrates R.
BLACK SEA
PONTUS
ASIA MINOR (TURKEY)
BITHYNIA
Hellespont
Pergamum
ASIA
PHRYGIA
CILICIA
SYRIA
See inset C above
TRANSJORDAN
PALESTINE
Jerusalem
NABATAEANS
SINAI
CYPRUS
EGYPT
THE FAIYÛM
Alexandria
DACIA
MOESIA
THRACE
MACEDON
Philippi
GREECE
See inset B above
Actium
Athens
AEGEAN SEA
RHODES
CRETE
CYRENAICA
MEDITERRANEAN SEA
Danube R.
PANNONIA
NORICUM
DALMATIA
ADRIATIC SEA
Cannae
SAMNIUM
APENNINE MTS.
Po R.
ETRURIA
Rome
See inset A below
SICILY
CORSICA
SARDINIA
Carthage
AFRICA (TUNISIA)
TRIPOLITANIA
SAHARA
THE ALPS
(SWITZERLAND)
GERMANY
BELGIUM
Rhine R.
GAUL (FRANCE)
Lyons
NARBONNESE GAUL
Narbonne
BALEARIC ISLANDS
(SPAIN)
(MOROCCO)
(ALGERIA)
ATLANTIC OCEAN
(SCOTLAND)
(ENGLAND)
(WALES)

Fortunately for the senate, the ultimate victor was one of their party, Sulla, who had trained a devoted army in the east. There he had ruined Athens, suppressed a revolt in Asia (the provincials murdered some 80,000 Italian residents), and forced Mithridates VI of Pontus, who had inspired the revolt, back to his own dominions. After returning to Italy in 83, and defeating his opponents and capturing Rome in 82, Sulla liquidated his enemies, restored control to the senate, retired to private life in 79, and died the following year without having done anything to alter the basic conditions which produced the conflicts. These, therefore, were soon resumed. This time, after considerable jockeying, the two generals who emerged as leaders were Pompey and Julius Caesar.

Pompey had crushed a Spanish revolt in 72, put down piracy, a pan-Mediterranean plague in 67, finished off Mithridates of Pontus and Tigranes of Armenia in 66, and in 63 constituted, from conquered territory, the provinces Bithynia and Pontus, and Syria. He brought back his army to Italy in 62 and, after some political haggling, was able to settle it on grants of public land (59).

Caesar, at that time a political ally of Pompey's, was rewarded for his alliance with the governorship of the Gallic (Celtic) provinces in the Po Valley and France. Thence he conquered the rest of France, Belgium, and bits of Holland, Germany, and Switzerland. He then broke with Pompey and, at the end of 50, was poised in the Po Valley, ready to descend on Rome. Pompey's army, meanwhile, already old in 62, had grown twelve years older and was nine years out of training. And Pompey had done nothing even to reassemble it. When Caesar crossed the Rubicon and invaded Italy, Pompey and the senators fled to Greece. Here they organized an impromptu army which was defeated by Caesar's veterans at Pharsalus in 48. Pompey fled to Egypt and was there murdered. Caesar followed him to Egypt and met Cleopatra VII. She was twenty-two at the time, he, fifty-four. He restored her to the throne; she named the baby Ptolemy Caesar. Caesar meanwhile returned to Rome in 47. In 46 he defeated the senatorial forces in Africa, in 45 the Pompeian forces in Spain. On March 15, 44, he was murdered.

Caesar had not wished to break entirely with the old order and had therefore, on his return to Rome, reconstituted a rump senate consisting of all but his most determined opponents. To this senate the rule of the state reverted after his assassination, but not for long. Caesar's army was on hand, waiting to be paid and anxious to avenge him. The senate, desperately anxious to effect a balance of power, allowed his murderers to take over the governorships of the eastern provinces, where they raised armies. Meanwhile, Caesar's officers, Mark Antony and Lepidus, put themselves at the head of armies in western Gaul and Spain; his nephew Octavius, whom he had adopted in his will (hence the change of his name to Caesar Octavian), won the support of his veterans in Italy. By the end of 43 Octavian, Antony, and Lepidus had allied and forced the senate to give them sweeping powers for constitutional reform. The first things swept away were their senatorial opponents, who were proscribed as public enemies and mostly murdered. The eastern armies were defeated at Philippi in 42. Thereafter the alliance degenerated into a rivalry between Octavian, who controlled the west, and Antony, who controlled the eastern provinces and Egypt—he married Cleopatra in 37. (Lepidus retired to the priesthood and to drink.) The resultant war was settled by the battle of Actium on September 2, 31. Antony and Cleopatra committed suicide in 30, and Octavian reached Alexandria. Cleopatra had prepared a fleet to take Ptolemy Caesar, now sixteen, to India, but Octavian persuaded the boy to return and had him murdered.

Octavian did not annex Egypt to the territories of Rome, but subjected it to himself. He also took over the remains of Antony's army. Now there was no military force in the Mediterranean world capable of standing against that of which he was the commander (*imperator,* whence the title "emperor"). Legally he was an official of the Roman republic, but in fact the republic had ended.

Paradoxically, our intellectual debt to republican Rome is far greater than its intellectual achievement. The early Romans had little respect for literature, art, and science; these were not the proper concerns of a Roman gentleman. When they did become fashionable, it was largely through the influence of Greek house slaves, following the conquest of south Italy. Therefore it was the Greek forms which became fashionable; old Roman work was almost wholly lost. The new imitations of Greek works were at first in Greek; Latin was a peasant language with few words for abstract thought: "sincerity," for instance, is properly a quality of honey unmixed with wax; the word *felix* which came to mean "fortunate" originally meant "fertile." But in the theater, to reach a popular audience, Latin had to be used. So the earliest considerable pieces preserved from Latin literature are the plays of Plautus, from about the end of the second Punic war, and these are all imitations or adaptations of Greek comedies. So are those of Terence, a half-century later, who follows Plautus, like a dancing master following a drunken sailor.

Since so little is preserved of Hellenistic comedy the works of Plautus and Terence are among the chief sources for our knowledge of the later Greek theater and were the models which inspired the revival of classical comedy in the Renaissance. Similarly in philosophy our most extensive connected exposition of Epicureanism comes from the Latin poem of Lucretius (a contemporary of Pompey), while the philosophical works of

Cicero (murdered in 43 on the orders of Octavian and Antony) are one of the best sources for our knowledge of second- and first-century Stoicism. Catullus, of the same generation, shows what Greek erotic poetry must have been for passion and directness. Sallust, one of Caesar's henchmen, gives a fair imitation of Greek historical techniques, and Cicero's speeches are products of Greek rhetoric. This is not to say these authors had no virtues of their own—the peasant vigor of Plautus, the romanticism which breaks through Lucretius' rationalism, the surprising tenderness of Catullus, the urbanity and worldly wisdom of Cicero are peculiar to these authors, but the major elements in their works are Greek. Their chief contribution to intellectual and artistic history is this transmission of Greek elements to the Latin West, the Middle Ages, the Renaissance, and the schoolboys of modern times. Perhaps the most original things we have from the period are Cato's work on agriculture, an unrivaled expression of Latin peasant mentality, and Caesar's report of his Gallic wars, an adaptation of historical form to the needs of political propaganda, written in the terse Latin of a Roman aristocrat and electric with the charge of a great analytical mind. But if we look for originality beyond such personal characteristics, we find little. Cicero does show us a new stage in the history of philosophy—the return of philosophy from the professional philosopher to the man of the world; its practice as part of the life of a distinguished barrister and politician. Here the force of Cicero's example, especially in wedding philosophy to legal rhetoric, was of great importance. So was his development of Latin prose style and vocabulary for the expression of philosophic ideas—whose ideas they were does not matter. Once Cicero had created the language, Augustine could think in it.

In the fine arts the one great achievement of the republican period was ruthless portraiture. One look at the stony faces of their funerary statues explains the terrible realism of their foreign policy and slave economy. But in the applied arts few peoples have so distinguished achievements. Their roads, bridges, and aqueducts, some of which are still in use, are masterpieces of functional form and original thought. The arch had been known for millennia, but the Romans were the first to realize its possibilities, both for beauty and for utility, for bridges, monumental entrances, and the creation of vast, open interiors. It was function that the Romans themselves admired. Aqueducts, said Pliny, are more valuable than useless pyramids. But like the pyramids, these great public works were enormously costly: only the vast capital accumulation and cheap labor supply of Rome made their construction possible. The standard road, for instance, was 15 feet wide and, with its foundations, 4 feet deep; each foot of length, therefore, required 60 cubic feet of construction: first a layer of flagstones, then a bed of rubble, then a layer of concrete, and on top a surface of concrete, squared stone, or pounded gravel. Moreover, the roads did not follow previous tracks, but were laid out to run as straight as possible and with minimal gradients; this required much cutting, filling, terracing, and bridge building. In the Hellenistic world there had been almost no paved roads. The Roman network was built for military movements and official messengers, but, once built, facilitated a great increase of trade.

Cities, too, bear the marks of the Roman practical genius. Roman architects loved balance and grandeur; with the money and labor at their disposal they were able to cut and terrace and fill and produce great squares and vistas with monumental buildings on either side, in a fashion far beyond the means of their Hellenistic predecessors. The repertory of Hellenistic forms—porticoes, temples, and so on—was taken over, the units immensely enlarged, and new forms developed, especially for public entertainment, a major concern of the big cities. The Roman formula for management of the mob was "bread and circuses." The circus, primarily a track for chariot races, was a new architectural form. The enlarged theater was no longer a hollowed-out hillside, but a free-standing building in which an artificial hillside of seats confronted a many-tiered stage, loaded with architectural decorations, though still shallow by modern standards. At the end of the republic appeared the amphitheater, used especially for gladiatorial games. (The practice of making men fight animals or each other for public amusement was developed by the Romans on a scale unparalleled. Large numbers of trained gladiators were kept by Rome and other cities and by private individuals. Prisoners of war and condemned criminals were used without special training. These shows were the most popular form of public entertainment from the second century B.C. to the third A.D. The tradition survives in bullfighting.) Perhaps the most important creation of Roman public architecture, however, was the sewer. Underground sewage had hitherto been rare. The development was forced on the Romans first by the location of their city in valleys between a number of sharp hills, then by its great size. Underground sewage, in turn, made possible the maintenance of larger cities, which otherwise would have been decimated by disease. With sewage, in importance, went water supply. Aqueducts made possible, and tolerable, the expansion of city populations far beyond their previous numbers.

In private architecture, as in public, the Romans excelled in functional buildings—huge warehouses and towering blocks of one- and two-room tenements, easier to admire than to live in. Standard blocks of such tenements appear as part of the city planning of Roman colonies in the third century B.C. The increase of city population in such housing led to a new distribution of services. Instead of separate markets and residential districts, there were small shops lining the ground floor fronts of the tenements, to supply the residents' everyday needs. We know little of the houses of the rich, save that they steadily increased in magnificence—and therefore rapidly became obsolete and were rebuilt. A house which in 78 B.C. was thought the finest in Rome was merely an average house thirty-five years later. Cicero spent about $700,000 for his town house and said that one could not live as a gentleman on less than $120,000 a year. Even more magnificent were the country places which, at the end of the republic, began to be surrounded with elaborate gardens. Some of them, like Cicero's eight, were merely businessmen's pleasure places of a couple of hundred acres, but others were vast estates, centers of manufacturing as well as farming, dependent on the outside world only for luxuries.

Roman building was made possible by the discovery of cement which would harden under water and was therefore far superior to the previous lime mortar. It was perhaps the most important of Roman technological discoveries, though rivaled by glass blowing and the introduction of water mills and windmills and also of rotary mills which made possible the use of animals to grind grain. The senate was concerned about agricultural techniques and in 146 ordered the translation into Latin of a 28-volume Punic work on agriculture. Here both Romans and Carthaginians were indebted to Greek achievements. A debt to Egypt was the solar calendar of 365 days, introduced (and corrected with an additional day every fourth year) by Caesar to replace the Roman lunar calendar with its wild irregularities.

Warfare, however, the Romans themselves revolutionized. For the thrusting spear of the Greek soldier they substituted the throwing spear. After their shower of spears had broken the enemy's ranks they finished the fight at close quarters with a short sword, edged and pointed for both cut and thrust. Both spear throwing and swordplay required space, so they abandoned the Greek phalanx and developed an open formation of small groups of men. This had several advantages: Fresh fighters could move up to replace the weary and wounded; forces could easily be shifted sideways; adaptation to irregular terrain was easier.

The most important of Roman technical advances, however, was the development of jurisprudence, the technique of legal interpretation which enabled its practitioners to decide whether and with what effect a general law would apply in a given case. Such questions had always faced judges and juries wherever actions were judged and disputes settled in accordance with fixed laws. In Rome, however, their settlement became the province of a special group of private individuals called jurisconsults, at first members of senatorial families, who were recognized experts on the meanings of the laws. Their opinions gradually acquired almost the force of law because a judge was limited in practice to choice between the opinions submitted to him by jurisconsults. Furthermore, judges themselves, as well as contesting parties, frequently solicited opinions from jurisconsults. The chief judicial officer of Rome (the "urban praetor") annually, on entering his office, issued an edict indicating the rules he would apply in court; these rules soon became traditional, and many were based on, or shaped by, the opinions of jurisconsults. The origins of this development were two: First was the extreme brevity and consequent obscurity of the early Roman laws, which necessitated expert interpretation. Second was the prestige of the great Roman families, which made the small man seek support by soliciting from one of their members a favorable opinion on his case. But when each party to a case came prepared with an opinion of a noble supporter, the opinion which prevailed would be that of the supporter recognized as an authority on the law. Thus the prestige of learning was distinguished from that of position; it came also to be independent of politics.

The content of this learning was primarily tradition. Laws were to be interpreted as they had been in the past. To learn the tradition one had to frequent the house of a jurist, watch him in action, and talk with him. When Greek philosophy became popular in Rome, particularly in the age of Cicero (who was not a jurist, but a barrister), the jurists applied philosophical methods—exact definition, classification, logical inference—to the topics of Roman law and thus transformed the isolated traditions of their predecessors into a legal system. But they shunned pure theory and legal philosophy. They did not question the validity of institutions or established rules. Their concern was to determine how the rules would apply in particular cases. By such determination in many exemplary cases they made the meaning of the law predictable and the same for all. This rivals the political union of the Mediterranean world as the greatest achievement of the Roman republic.

For Further Reading

Frank, T., *Life and Literature in the Roman Republic.*
Gelzer, M., *Caesar.*
Lewis, N., and Reinhold, M., *Roman Civilization: Vol. I: The Republic.*
Scullard, H., *From the Gracchi to Nero.*
Syme, R., *The Roman Revolution.*
Taylor, L., *Party Politics in the Age of Caesar.*

19   The Augustan Empire

During the thirteen years of war between Octavian's appearance as Caesar's heir and his final defeat of Antony (44–31) his soldiers had repeatedly taken advantage of his difficulties to drive hard bargains. His major concern, therefore, once he got rid of Antony, was to free himself from dependence on the army, without losing its loyalty.

The first step was to reduce its size. After taking over Antony's forces he had about 500,000 men under arms. Of these, he tells us, "I settled in colonies or sent back to their own cities a little more than 300,000, and to all of these I allotted lands or granted money as rewards for military service." The lands and money came mostly from the expropriation of his opponents' properties. Since most of the soldiers were Italians and were settled in Italy, their presence now guaranteed his security. By the time of his death the army had been reduced to 175,000 men, mostly distributed along a frontier of some 7,000 miles. Pay and pensions, both good, came from him; the commanding officers were his appointees and were shifted frequently so they could not build personal followings among the soldiers.

Along with reduction of the army Octavian had to strengthen his position in other ways. The first was to make his power legal—a matter of great importance to Roman opinion. He therefore had himself voted by the senate such powers as he needed, being careful to have them covered by republican titles. The "republican" government went on much as before, only the officials were his nominees and did what he told them. Thus the façade of legality was preserved.

He was equally aware of the importance of practical interests and appealed to those of the Roman mob, the bourgeoisie, the senate, and the provincials.

The mob was venal by tradition, so he could, and did, proceed by direct donatives from his spoils to each citizen. Moreover, he reorganized the grain supply, using the grain of Egypt, on a lavish scale. The water supply, too, was vastly improved by new aqueducts. He provided games and other public entertainments and spectacles of unprecedented magnificence. An enormous building program beautified the city and made work for those who wanted it. But Octavian was not one to trust to gratitude. His benefactions were backed up by a quadruple set of guards to keep one another, as well as the citizens, in check. There were two bodies of his own "praetorian" guards as well as guards of the city, and police and fire brigades—the first such forces Rome ever had. Finally, to prevent trouble,

CHRONOLOGY

B.C.	31	Battle of Actium, Octavian victorious
	31–A.D. 68	The Julio-Claudian dynasty (Augustus, his stepson Tiberius Claudius, and members of Tiberius' family); the classical age of Latin literature: Vergil, Horace, Livy, Ovid, Seneca, Petronius; Philo of Alexandria reconciles Judaism with Greek philosophy
	28	Purge of the senate. Octavian *princeps*
	27	Crisis officially over, governorships of unarmed provinces restored to the senate, Octavian voted the title "Augustus"
A.D.	6	Judea taken over by the Romans, revolutionary "messianic" movements development
	c. 30	Jesus crucified
	43–85	Conquest of Britain
	60	Paul sent to Rome for trial
	64	The great fire in Rome; Nero's persecution of the Christians
	66	Jewish revolt in Palestine
	69–96	Flavian dynasty (Titus Flavius Vespasianus, and his sons Titus and Domitian)
	70	Destruction of the temple of Jerusalem, end of the sacrificial cult prescribed by the Old Testament, end of the priestly aristocracy; ben Zakkai's court in Jabneh becomes the center of Pharisaic law and piety

-----

popular assemblies and elections of officers were reduced to formalities and the choice of candidates was controlled.

The bourgeois were easy to win over. Caesar had been popular with them; Octavian succeeded to his popularity and did much to deserve it. Of Italian bourgeois background himself, he gave many bourgeois, mostly from Italian cities, places in the senate. For many more he created places as financial inspectors or even governors of minor provinces. And for the most successful there were the important "prefectures"—praetorian prefect, prefect of the grain supply, or prefect of Egypt (which was always governed by a man of bourgeois rank; no senator was permitted to set foot in it without permission of Octavian).

75–100	The four Gospels written
79	Eruption of Vesuvius, destruction of Pompeii
96–180	"The five good emperors" (Nerva, Trajan, Hadrian, Antoninus Pius, Marcus Aurelius); cooperation of senate and *princeps;* the principate passed on by adoption of competent men; Latin satire and history: Martial, Juvenal, Tacitus, Suetonius; Greek historians and philosophers: Epictetus, Arrian, Plutarch, Appian; Romance and parody: Apuleius and Lucian
101–106	Trajan's conquest of Dacia
105–106	Annexation of "Arabia" (the Nabataean kingdom)
113–117	Trajan's conquest of Armenia and Mesopotamia
115–117	Revolt and destruction of the Jews in Cyrenaica, Egypt, and Cyprus
118	Hadrian, Trajan's successor, abandons most of Mesopotamia and Armenia
131–135	Revolt of bar Kosiba, Judaism in south Palestine wiped out
180–192	Commodus, son of Marcus Aurelius; accord between senate and *princeps* breaks down
193–235	Severan dynasty (Septimius Severus, his two sons and two grand-nephews); Augustan order gradually disintegrates
c. 200	Codification of Jewish law in the Mishnah by Rabbi Judah the Prince

---

The senate, in fact, was the most difficult problem. Many senators resented their loss of real power. Many resented Octavian as an upstart, from bourgeois and Italian, not Roman, stock. Yet if the façade of legality was to be maintained, if his rule was not to degenerate into a tyranny (and, consequently, remain dependent on the army), the cooperation of the senate had to be secured. Votes were no problem. The senate could be— and was—packed with subservient appointees. But the surviving "genuine" senators were men of widely influential families and vast wealth. They could not be ignored. They had to be either conciliated or exterminated.

Since the senators were anxious not to be exterminated, Octavian's policy of conciliation succeeded. He purged the senate in 28 of its "unworthy" members, but at the same time made himself its leader (*princeps*, whence "prince") and made clear that he expected to govern with it. Here pride and the maintenance of appearances were of great importance. Octavian was careful to treat the senators with the greatest politeness and to maintain every detail of the traditional *decorum*—a Roman word and a major Roman concern. He scrupulously consulted the senate about unimportant questions.

Of important questions the most difficult was control of the provinces, since the governors of the provinces commanded the armies there. Provincial governorships had been the most valuable rewards of a public career; the senate would never relinquish them; nor would Octavian relinquish control of the army. The solution was reached in 27 B.C. Octavian retained command of all those provinces in which considerable forces had to be stationed, but governed them by delegates whom he appointed from the senate. The remaining governors were appointed by the senate. In gratitude the senate voted him the title *Augustus*—"the revered."

This was not quite deification. Octavian had had Caesar deified by the senate in 42 and had since been officially "the son of the god"—by adoption. The new title brought him a step nearer deity. He refused official deification—it would have offended the senators, who would have had to participate in the official worship—but he made himself, even for the senate, an object of religious awe. Provincials were permitted to worship him.

For the senate, however, the most important object of religious awe was Rome itself. Augustus therefore made himself the protector of the Roman tradition and above all of religion. Roman religion had always been somewhat impersonal. A superstitious reverence for "the proper way of doing things" was the strongest religious experience of the average Roman. Republican government had been largely a structure of rituals. As a successful revolutionary, Augustus hoped to revive the respect for such rituals —in others. He saw in reverence for the established order a bulwark for his regime. He therefore made himself patron of the old Roman family life (laws encouraging marriage and childbearing, penalizing celibacy and adultery), traditional class distinctions (laws limiting manumission of slaves, prohibiting intermarriage of freedmen with senatorial families), and ancient religious ceremonies (82 temples rebuilt, old priesthoods revived, cult associations encouraged, domestic worship restored by law). Horace and Vergil were set to writing verses glorifying Augustus, the origins of Rome, the simple, rural, Roman life, the pleasures of patriotism, and the propriety of dying for one's country. Livy retold Roman history in cineramic style. With imperial favor these works became the classics of secondary instruction. It is difficult to estimate their influence on the Western mind; they are so much part of us that we take their values for granted and their epigrams for truisms. For Augustus' purpose they expressed the Roman tradition in the Roman language and provided a Roman literature to distract the upper classes from Greek free thought and rally them to the ancient Roman order as represented by his regime.

In the provinces the cult of Rome spread widely, hand in hand with that of Augustus. Nor was it all flattery. In Greek *romé* means "strength," and to the ancient mind the rise and rule of Rome might well seem the work of a supernatural power which had become, through Augustus, the protectress of the world. The provincials had been almost ruined by the civil wars and therefore saw the maintenance of peace as the greatest of virtues. Augustus was sincerely hailed as "the savior of the world." Moreover, he was interested in the prosperity of the provinces—they were his domain. His bourgeois financial inspectors checked with expert eyes on tax collectors and governors alike. His control of the senate and of elections enabled him to prevent the appointment of unsuitable governors even for the senatorial provinces, while the provinces under his direct control were governed by his own appointees ("legates") whom he held strictly to account. In general his reign marked the beginning of tranquil and comparatively just government for the provinces. The wealthy provincial families had most to gain from social stability at home and international peace. The one protected their land ownership and their loans; the other improved conditions for trade. Many already had ties with Roman aristocrats. They backed Augustus. The poor hated the tax collectors and the foreign officials, and dreamed of a time when they would again be free. But meanwhile they acquiesced.

Thus Augustus had escaped the army's control. The army had been cut down and split up, and other supports had been found for his regime in the settlements of his veterans, the Roman mob, the Italian bourgeoisie, the remodeled senate, and the wealthy families of the provinces. But the army still existed. Professional training and tactical knowledge made it far superior to any citizen force that could be mustered against it. It remained the ultimate basis of the emperor's power, but also a constant threat to it. For should the newly established concord break down, the emperor would be forced to fall back on the army and in so doing would fall again into its control. After Augustus' death this happened from time to time, but the pattern he had created survived as the "formal cause" of the empire at least to the fall of the Severan dynasty in 235. Until then political history was one of adjustments as various elements of the complex increased or diminished in power.

These adjustments we need not follow in detail. In outline there were three periods. From Augustus' death until A.D. 96 relations between the emperors and the senate were more or less strained; consequently much administration came to be done by the emperor's secretaries. The senate, denied power, turned to conspiracies, Stoic philosophizing about the natural liberty of man, and vicious gossip about the emperors. This led to executions for treason; many senatorial families were extinguished, the richer bourgeoisie were decimated, and the imperial estates were vastly increased by confiscations. This policy increased the emperors' dependence on the troops stationed in Rome, especially the praetorian guard, which took advantage of the situation to extort privileges and money. Jealousy of the praetorians and knowledge of the weakness of the emperor's position tempted the frontier armies to revolt. Revolts under Nero in A.D. 68 ended the so-called Julio-Claudian dynasty (of Augustus' wife's family) and installed the "Flavians"—Vespasian, a popular general, succeeded by his sons Titus and Domitian. Under Domitian the government again degenerated to a terror.

With the assassination of Domitian in 96, however, the senate succeeded in installing a candidate of its own, Nerva, who promptly secured his position by adopting as successor a successful frontier general, Trajan. Trajan further strengthened the imperial office by commanding his troops in person. The conquests of Dacia (western Rumania) and "Arabia" (roughly, east and south Transjordan and Sinai) yielded enormous loot which financed gifts to the troops and the Roman mob, games, and a building program, especially of roads. The senate, by intermarriage and imperial appointment, gradually came to be more representative of the wealthy families of all the western provinces; provincial interest strengthened its support for the emperor. The Stoics discovered that true freedom was not political, but moral, and that the emperor was the servant of divine reason to maintain order on earth. The resultant concord lasted through the reigns of Trajan's three successors—Hadrian (117–138), Antoninus Pius (138–161), and Marcus Aurelius Antoninus (161–180)—and might have lasted longer had not Marcus' son, Commodus, been an egomaniac.

Commodus' accession was the beginning of a period of almost constant conflict between the emperors and the senate, and his murder in 192 led to a repetition of the crisis of 68. This time the successful general, Septimius Severus, was unable to reestablish good relations with the senate—many senators with provincial connections had backed his opponents and suffered accordingly. Further, he was of bourgeois family and his wife was a Syrian. He replied by packing the senate with appointees from the eastern provinces, hitherto usually excluded; by giving many positions, formerly reserved for senators, to bourgeois, especially easterners; by further welfare measures for the Roman mob; by extension of citizenship or colonial status to many provincial cities, and by showering favors on the frontier armies.

The old praetorians were cashiered, and a new and larger praetorian guard was formed from frontier troops. Under his son, Caracalla, the government became openly a military dictatorship. The army's loyalty to the family enabled a couple of juvenile second cousins to succeed Caracalla; then, in 235, an officer risen from the ranks wiped out the family and proceeded to govern with almost no regard for the senate or the traditional civilian order. The Augustan balance of powers was at an end.

From 27 B.C. to A.D. 235, however, the Augustan political structure had controlled England, Wales, and southern Scotland, all Europe south of the Rhine-Danube frontier, all Africa north of the Sahara, Egypt, Palestine, Syria, Turkey, Armenia, and districts in the Caucasus and south Russia. Save for the brief civil wars of 68–69 and 193–197, these had been years of peace; rebellions were rare. The provincial aristocracy's loyalty to the emperors made garrisons in the provinces unnecessary. One legion with auxiliaries (about 10,000 men) sufficed for Algeria, Tunisia, and Morocco. There were no Roman troops in the territory of modern France save for the personal guard of the governor at Lyons, 500 men. The army, though its strength gradually rose to about 300,000 as barbarian pressure on the northern frontier increased, was less than 1 per cent of the adult population.

This freed the national income for extension of cultivated land and improvement of the standard of living. The characteristic forms of Roman civilization appeared everywhere—roads (over 60,000 miles), bridges, aqueducts, and above all, cities. Before the great plague of 166 the inhabitants of the empire probably numbered between 75 million and 100 million. Increase of population produced increase of equipment—houses, tools, domesticated animals, orchards, vineyards, seed—which transformed the economic situation of occidental man. Knowledge also (the most important form of equipment) was increased and disseminated; the greatest wealth of the empire was its population of skilled farmers and artisans whose labor supported the whole structure. Selective breeding improved the quality of herds and crops. Vines resistant to cold and humidity were developed. After the French language, French wines are the most important Roman remains north of the Alps. In Africa, Palestine, Jordan, and Syria, Roman methods of irrigation supported cities in areas which even now are desert.

The characteristic form of this civilization was the small city of approximately 50,000 inhabitants, a mile or two in diameter. Only in the frontier provinces were the new cities walled. Life was secure even in the countryside, where the rich built magnificent villas on their estates. The money and labor which formerly went into city walls now went into paving, sewers, aqueducts, arcades along the main streets, and public buildings of which the largest were usually those for the pleasure of the citizens: the circus, the amphitheater, at least one theater, invariably several baths. The Greeks had commonly bathed in cold water; from Augustus' time on, the Romans made the hot bath the center of a free man's afternoon, and architecturally developed public baths into vast complexes—a large cold bath, smaller warm baths, a hot room, dressing rooms, and often colonnades, gymnasiums, lecture rooms, and so on. In Rome the baths of Caracalla covered 45 acres. Even a village might have two or three public baths. Cleanliness, hitherto a luxury of the rich, became common.

After these buildings for public relaxation, the next largest were the temples of the gods and the buildings for public business; forums (open squares, usually arcaded), law courts, and markets. Administrative structures, the equivalents of "city hall" and "federal building," were absent— city administration was by locally elected, annual officers serving without salary, and imperial administration in the provinces was limited to the governors and their staffs; when the breakdown came in 235 there were only about 200 civilian officials with direct imperial appointments in the whole empire.

Of the city's industrial establishments, grain mills with four or five large grindstones, turned by donkeys, were often the largest. Shops were small affairs, most manufacture was by artisan-shopkeepers with a few slaves working under their direction, and most agricultural processing was done in the countryside. As for housing, a few of the bigger places had blocks of tenements, six or eight stories high, honeycombs of one-room residences without even kitchens—the inhabitants ate in taverns. Occasionally there were more luxurious "apartment houses." In most towns, however, private buildings were low, only one or two stories. The poor lived in blocks cut up into two- or three-room cubbyholes. The middle-class house would have a central courtyard giving light and air to the small rooms opening onto it. The rich multiplied courtyards and added cloisters and mosaic pavements and fountains and even private baths. In Africa houses were sometimes constructed underground as refuges from the heat; in the northern provinces there were houses with central heating. Even lower-class buildings, in many cities, had running water somewhere, piped in from the municipal aqueduct which also supplied public fountains. By the middle of the third century even the public buildings in a small Egyptian town had glass windows.

The city population was composed of landowners, shopkeepers, artisans, and servants. Food came from the surrounding countryside; supply and variety varied from season to season. Manufacturing was by handicrafts and mostly for local consumption. Trade was a minor factor in the total economy because transportation was slow and costly. (Italy lost its pottery trade to the western provinces because it was cheaper to move the Italian potters than to ship the pots.) Apparent exceptions—for instance, the shipment of Egyptian grain to Rome or the import of perfumes, jewels, and silk from the east—had little influence on the economy of the average city, which remained one of local subsistence.

So was its intellectual life. At the gymnasium the classics—Greek in the east, Latin in the west—were drilled into the boys. Adults encountered them chiefly on the stage, where traveling companies of actors kept them alive. There were all sorts of itinerant entertainers, from philosophers or rhetoricians (difficult to distinguish) down to sleight-of-hand artists and men with dancing bears. But the main entertainments were indicated by the main buildings: the baths, the circus for chariot races, the amphitheater for gladiatorial shows. (The use of torture for public amusement increased through the second century.) Usually there was no bookstore, but larger cities did have public libraries, and rich families had libraries in their villas.

The main religious concern of the city was the cult of the local gods. These had usually been identified with the Roman Jupiter, Juno, and Minerva, or with Mars-Apollo and Venus-Aphrodite, the patrons of the Caesarian house. Their priests were usually elected annually. Rich men contested for these honors; there was no priestly class. The priesthoods of the imperial cult were similarly sought after. Augustus and later emperors had been deified after death by the senate; their cults were now everywhere established and the common expression of loyalty. They were the chief alien element in the religious life of the small city, which otherwise turned to its local gods for its daily needs.

The government of the city was principally local; usually it consisted of an assembly, elected magistrates, and a system of courts. These the empire was usually glad to recognize, since it was reluctant to multiply, and pay, officials, and therefore had no staff for local government. So it everywhere encouraged urbanization and left the cities to themselves, provided they paid their taxes and their debts and maintained order. This limited local independence fostered local patriotism. Wealthy men competed for civic offices, although these carried no salaries and often obligated the incumbent to provide, at his own expense, municipal services or entertainments. And everywhere cities were enriched with public buildings and lands as monuments of private munificence.

The great achievement of the Augustan political settlement was to provide the framework for two hundred and fifty years of this peaceful, provincial life of the small cities which made up the bulk of the enormous empire. It was a life of considerable comfort and elegance. An epigram of the time says that six hours of the day are for work, the rest, for life. A single Greco-Roman artistic style became common, producing innumerable artifacts—metalwork, pottery, carving—which still command admiration. The great public monuments—bridges, aqueducts, theaters, temples—continued the tradition of the republic and survived to be the wonders of the medieval world.

These practical achievements were matched by a practical philosophy, directed, as in the Hellenistic world, to the achievement of "the good life." The upper class turned to Stoicism—desperately during the civil wars and reigns of terror, optimistically when good relations between the senate and the emperors were reestablished. Lower-class thought was permeated by the teaching of the Cynics, a school of vagrant preachers who made "philosophy" an excuse for the rejection of ordinary social decencies. Preaching, indeed, was characteristic of all this "philosophy"; even the greatest Stoics of this time, Seneca, Epictetus, the emperor Marcus Aurelius, were mainly concerned to drive home familiar principles. The same is true of Plutarch, the outstanding Platonist, and Philo, an eclectic who sought to justify Judaism. "Philosophy" retained its Hellenistic meaning: "the practice of a peculiar discipline in daily life." Jews, Egyptian priests, and self-styled Indian sages all passed as "philosophers."

Homiletic Stoicism runs through all the literature of the period. The rhetoricians have little else to say. The most remarkable product of Stoicism in poetry was satire, in epigrams and versified diatribes, which enabled writers to combine morality with popular appeal; in attacking vice they could describe it with revolting and readable details. Martial and Juvenal used this technique to the full and are therefore famous. Petronius is more famous for his satirical picaresque novel, of verse and prose alternately, which has equally readable details, but none of the revolting morality; he was a favorite of Nero's, and Stoicism appears in his works only in parody. Much the same tradition was continued, with wide individual variations, by Apuleius and Lucian.

Stoic influence was stronger in the historians, of whom Tacitus was the greatest. A master of innuendo and understatement, Tacitus saw history as political intrigue and was determined to defend the senatorial party. The brilliance of his work, in spite of these limitations, makes the later Suetonius seem a scandalmonger and men like Appian, Arrian, and Dio Cassius, mere compilers. But their works are often more reliable, in total effect, than Tacitus' special pleading. As artistic achievements, however—polished presentations of his sardonic view of the world—Tacitus' histories are unrivaled save by Thucydides.

From this peak literary history plunges into a sea of collectors and commentators, industrious men with mediocre minds. Nor is the history of the fine arts more rewarding. The early years of the empire saw some brilliant fresco painting and mosaics. Pompeii and Herculaneum preserve examples prior to 79. But this was decoration rather than fine art. Much sculpture was throttled by the dead hand of classicism, though Roman realism survived in vigorous portraits, and a new artistic form—the narrative frieze with a historical subject—became prominent. The great Roman architectural tradition lived on, and increased means made possible larger and larger buildings. All in all, however, the artistic output of the imperial age, like the literary and the philosophical, was mediocre. This holds, too, for scientific and technological thought. There was much collection of accepted results, and some application of known principles; but little was new.

In spite of this prevailing conservatism and the social stability it both reflected and produced, some major changes came about in the two centuries and more from the death of Augustus to the death of Severus Alexander. Some have already been mentioned: the increase of population and of wealth, especially in equipment, the spread of agriculture and of cities, the extension of membership in the senate to rich families from all parts of the empire,* the establishment everywhere of cults of the deified emperors, the spread of Stoicism and the permeation of all classes by its basic suppositions.

Connected with this last point was a far-reaching change in the privileges accorded persons of inferior social status. Stoicism had long preached the brotherhood of man, and contrasted natural rights with social privileges. By the Severan period, married women had attained an independence unparalleled in antiquity, and thenceforth the liberty and large legal rights of women would be characteristic of the Western world. Children and slaves, too, had been protected from arbitrary exercise of paternal authority. The position of slaves had improved for economic as well as legal and humanitarian reasons. The suppression of piracy sharply cut down the supply of new slaves; the end of civil wars and conquests reduced it yet further; the common practice of manumission diminished the supply of existing slaves. It became more economical to work estates with free tenant farmers. One consequence of this, however, was a decline in legal respect for the free man as such. The law now began to distinguish between freemen of upper and lower class—*honestiores* and *humiliores*. The former were exempt from humiliating procedures and punishments to which the latter were subject.

At least equally important was the change in religion during the first two centuries. Cults of Near Eastern deities spread widely in the west: Isis

* At the end of the first century 80 per cent of the senators were Italian, at the end of the second, only 40 per cent.

of Egypt and her son, Harpocrates; Yahweh of Jerusalem and Jesus, his son; Mithras, the Persian; Cybele of Phrygia, "the great Mother of the Gods," and her consort, Attis. All these deities had, attached to their regular cults, special ceremonies which promised the participants blessing in this life and well-being in the life to come. Life after death now occupied much of the common worshiper's concern. These special ceremonies were commonly secret initiations called "mysteries"; they admitted one not only to future bliss, but also to the circle of fellow initiates who could be helpful connections. In a humdrum world the appeal of secret societies and occult knowledge was understandable. There had always been a large element of superstition in Roman culture, and it increased in late Antonine and Severan times. The spread of the Oriental cults, and of magic and astrology, was a symptom of this general increase. Among these cults two, Judaism and Christianity, became the major religions of the Western world.

The Judaism of the Greco-Roman world is a riddle. In the first place, where did the Jews come from? The Greek (and thence the Roman) term "Jew" looks like a geographical term and should mean "Judean," i.e., resident of, or emigrant from, the tiny district around Jerusalem. But this poor hill country could never have supported a large population. Yet in 1 B.C. there were large "Jewish" populations not only in Palestine and Transjordan, but also in Egypt, Cyrenaica, Cyprus, western Asia Minor, Syria, the Greek islands, Rome, south Italy, Tunisia, Arabia, Mesopotamia, Persia, and Armenia, perhaps a total of 3 million. That all these were descendants of the perhaps 50,000 inhabitants of Judea in 600 B.C. is unlikely.

Many certainly were converts or descendants of converts; probably more had been first called "Jews" by their neighbors because they worshiped the god whom the Jews worshiped. The syncretistic Judean worshipers of Yahweh—the majority during the monarchy—doubtless carried his cult with them into exile and taught it to their neighbors. This would explain the syncretistic worship of Yahweh in fifth-century Egypt and Mesopotamia, and the prominence of Yahweh in the polytheistic magical papyri. With the rise of a Judean state in the second and first centuries B.C. many of these worshipers of Yahweh, including the descendants of the north Israelite exiles, probably came to be called by the name of the most prominent community of their god's adherents, and adopted Judean ways.

This rise of a Judean state began when quarrels between rival candidates for the Jerusalem priesthood and attempts to Hellenize the cult led, in 168 B.C., to revolts against the city government and the Seleucid kingdom. A military leader, Judas "Maccabeus," turned the revolts into a guerrilla war. His brothers and their children, who eventually won the war,

took over the high priesthood of Jerusalem (in violation of the Pentateuchal law), conquered most of Palestine and parts of Transjordan in the
late second and early first century, and forcibly converted large bodies of
the population to their brand of Judaism. But they quarreled among themselves, and were ousted in 37 by a Jewish politician named Herod who had
been recognized as king by the Roman senate. Herod, like the Maccabees,
made himself the patron of "Jews" all over the empire. He lavishly rebuilt
Jerusalem, especially the temple, which he made one of the most famous
buildings of the Greco-Roman world. In his reign ancient Judaism reached
the apogee of its power and prestige.

But what was it? A great variety of beliefs and practices which can best
be called "the cult of Yahweh," since they were all regarded as obedience
or worship of "the Lord," the god not to be named, whose greatest temple
was that in Jerusalem. The official authority as to the religion there was the
high priest of the Jerusalem temple, an appointee of Herod, for whom
many Jews had little respect. There was a rival temple-in-exile in Egypt,
staffed by descendants of the legitimate high-priestly line, but they, too,
seem to have had little influence with the majority of the Jews. There were
in Palestine three unofficial schools of legal interpretation—and consequently of religious practice—organized as sects: the Pharisees, in one
dubious passage said to number 6,000, the Essenes, said on better authority to number 4,000, and the Sadducees, an even smaller group. These
sects were sharply opposed to one another. The mass of the people belonged to none but followed their own traditional practices. They were also
ready to listen to holy men whose teachings were often peculiar.

One of these holy men, named John, came to be called the Baptist
because he introduced a new rite of immersion ("baptism") which, he
claimed, would take away sin as well as impurity. Great crowds went out to
him for baptism, and he preached to them against the vices of the rulers
and prophesied the imminent end of the world. His preaching was so
successful that one of the rulers, a son of Herod, had him executed about
A.D. 30. His disciples persisted as a sect for some time after his death; some
of them are said to have believed he was the Messiah—the "anointed"
king whom "the Lord" was expected to send to save his people.

Another holy man was Jesus, who began his career by going to John
for baptism. When baptized, he had a vision in which he saw a holy spirit
coming down on him and heard a voice from heaven, presumably the
Lord's, declaring him "my son." The spirit then drove him into the desert,
whence he returned to Galilee, began "to cast out demons" (that is, to
quiet maniacs), and was believed to perform other miracles. He also
preached on moral questions, and was criticized by the Pharisees for
neglect of their religious law. From the large following thus attracted, he

chose twelve assistants. To them he revealed that he was the Messiah and that the end of the world would come in their lifetime. With them he went up to Jerusalem for the Passover, and there, in a private meal, he gave them bread and wine which he said were his body and blood. Later that night he was seized by the temple authorities. The next day they handed him over to the Romans as a would-be revolutionary, and the Romans had him crucified.

On the third day thereafter his disciples began to see him risen from the dead. Later they had a vision of his ascent to heaven, themselves received the holy spirit, and began to preach a baptism "in his name" which not only took away the sins of the penitent, but also conferred the holy spirit and assured salvation in the judgment to come at the end of the world. This preaching led to their persecution by the temple authorities, who did not wish to be blamed for Jesus' death, and also by the Pharisees, probably because the members of the new sect were no more observant of the Law than their teacher had been. Many therefore fled the city. Thus the new cult was carried to the neighboring territories and eventually to Antioch, where the adherents first called themselves "Christians," that is, adherents of the new "Christ" (Messiah). Meanwhile a Pharisee named in Hebrew Saul (in Greek, Paul), who had played a prominent part in the Jerusalem persecution, was converted by a vision of Jesus and, after adventures in Palestine and Syria, began a series of missionary journeys through Cyprus, Asia Minor, and Greece, leaving groups of converts in most of the cities he visited. He also occasionally returned to Jerusalem. There in the middle fifties he was involved in a riot in the temple, seized by the Roman authorities, sent to the procurator in Caesarea and eventually to Rome for trial, and—here the story, as told in the Acts of the Apostles, breaks off. Later tradition says that he was executed in Rome, probably in the early sixties.

For this account of the work of Jesus, his immediate disciples, and Paul, the sources are the four Gospels, written in the last quarter of the first century; the Acts of the Apostles, originally a sequel to the Gospel According to Luke; and the letters of Paul, dating mainly from the fifties. These sources disagree with one another, and sometimes with themselves, in many points—for instance, their stories of the resurrection. Further, they all represent Christian tradition as it was after one or two generations of reflection, controversy, exaggeration, and invention. Finally, they are full of incredible stories of which some—those of the resurrection will again serve as instances—may be of historical value as reflections of subjective experiences. Consequently, no more than the main outlines of the history can be ascertained with certainty. Of the events described above, Jesus' choice of the twelve and their role, his arguments with the Pharisees, and his teaching about himself are matters of particular dispute. The history given by Acts is full of riddles, and we know nothing of the history in areas Acts neglected, for instance, Alexandria and Rome.

Hence the early history of Christianity cannot be followed in detail. We can see that there were in the beginning many conflicting interpretations of Jesus' teaching and career, and that gradually a consensus—a rudimentary church—began to be built up. An important part of this development was eventual agreement as to a list of books accepted as authoritative—the present Old and New Testaments. Even more important was the development of a standard organization for individual churches: an overseer ("bishop") supported in questions of policy by a board of elders ("presbyters," eventually "priests"), and in matters of administration by several assistants ("deacons"). The bishop was the authority on the legal as well as the devotional tradition of the church. He held a court to which believers were expected to bring their claims against each other. But the most important element in the growth of his power was his control of the church's charitable funds and organizations and of its cemetery. Christianity spread largely as a mutual protective association of people of small means.

Another factor in the development of Christianity was its separation from Judaism. Paul's practice in coming to a new city was to preach first in the synagogue. Usually he won over some of the Jews and more of the pagans who reverenced the Lord but were not prepared to observe the more painful requirements of Pentateuchal law—circumcision, for instance. Presumably other missionaries did likewise. The resultant disputes between converts to the new sect and the majority of the synagogue members led to the common antithesis between "the Christians" and "the Jews." The Christians claimed—and still claim—to be "the true Israel," but in practice they came to be mostly of pagan background and soon ceased to think of themselves as Jews or to be recognized as such by other Jews. Thus by gradual fission Christianity changed from a Jewish sect to a "new" religion.

Since this religion worshiped a man who had been crucified by the Romans for attempted rebellion and since the quarrels between its adherents and the Jews were frequent occasions of civil disorder, its members were often in trouble with civil authorities. When a great fire destroyed much of Rome in 64, Nero's officials put the blame on them. Since the scrupulous members would not participate in the worship of gods other than Jesus and the Lord, popular opinion stigmatized them, along with Jews and philosophers, as "atheists," and popular imagination (aided by the practices of some libertines and the ritual words of the communion meal) turned their secret meetings into orgies of copulation and cannibalism. Consequently, local persecutions became more frequent. Nevertheless, by the end of the Severan period there were Christians in every part of the empire and in every class of society. Though there was no empire-wide organization, most bishops were in approximate agreement on questions of doctrine and discipline, and this agreement had produced a sort of orthodoxy, "the catholic"—the universal—"church."

During this same period the other forms of Judaism changed no less than Christianity. Jewish resentment of Roman rule in Palestine led to a major revolt in 66. This led in 70 to the capture of Jerusalem by Titus and the destruction of the temple, which put an end to the official sacrificial religion. (Titus was the most efficient reformer of ancient Judaism.) At the same time the temple in Egypt was closed to prevent disturbances. In this revolt the Sadducees, mostly wealthy, pro-Roman, and concentrated in Jerusalem, were killed off by the rebels. The Essenes and other parties who supported the revolt were liquidated by the Romans. But a leading Pharisee, Yohanan ben Zakkai, managed to escape from Jerusalem, make his peace with the Romans, and get their permission to establish a court at Jabneh. With Roman approval his court became the chief authority in Palestine for the settlement of questions of religious law, numerous and important because of the destruction of the temple. It laid down the main lines for the reorganization of Judaism around the already existent synagogue worship, with almsgiving, penitence, and prayer replacing sacrifice. It also settled the question as to which books should be considered sacred. (The list decided on, different from the Christian list, was taken over in the Reformation by the Protestants.) From ben Zakkai, leadership passed to a descendant of the great teacher Hillel of Herodian times, whose family had traditionally headed one wing of the Pharisaic party. Next the diasporic Judaism of Cyrenaica, Egypt, and Cyprus rose in revolt against the Romans in 115–117. The cause and course of the revolt are obscure, but its end was the annihilation of Judaism in these provinces. Finally, the control of Palestinian Judaism temporarily passed from the house of Hillel to anti-Roman rabbis of whom the greatest, Akiba, backed a Messianic pretender named bar Kosiba* in a revolt from 131–135 which ended with the wiping out of Judaism in southern Palestine.

For a short period the Roman government seems to have considered stamping out Judaism altogether—circumcision and teaching of the Law were prohibited. But this did not last. Presently the Hillelite court was re-established—now in Galilee and supported by Roman soldiers. A Roman commission investigated the Jewish law and suggested changes to diminish conflicts between Jews and gentiles. This was followed by codification of the law and publication of the code under Rabbi Judah the Prince in the late second and early third centuries. His code, the Mishnah, became the

* Commonly called "bar Kokeba." The correct form of his name has only recently been determined.

basis of study in both Palestine and Mesopotamia, the commentaries on it being eventually collected in the Palestinian and Babylonian Talmuds. The Mishnaic type of Judaism spread gradually through the Greco-Roman diaspora, becoming dominant, it seems, only in the fifth and sixth centuries, but thereafter remaining the characteristic form of the religion.

For Further Reading

Carcopino, J., *Daily Life in Ancient Rome.*
Dill, S., *Roman Society from Nero to Marcus Aurelius.*
Gibbon, E., *The History of the Decline and Fall of the Roman Empire,* chs. 1–6.
Lewis, N., and Reinhold, M., *Roman Civilization:* Vol. II, *The Empire.*
Lietzmann, H., *History of the Early Church.*
Moore, G., *Judaism,* Vol. I.
Neill, S., *The Interpretation of the New Testament, 1861–1961.*
Nock, A., *St. Paul.*
Rostovtzeff, M., *Rome.*
Schweitzer, A., *The Quest of the Historical Jesus.*
Stenico, A., *Roman and Etruscan Painting.*
Wheeler, M., *Roman Art and Architecture.*
————, *Rome Beyond the Imperial Frontiers.*

20   The Later Roman Empire

The fifty years from the murder of Severus Alexander in 235 to Diocletian's defeat of Carinus in 285 were a period of anarchy. Diocletian, during his twenty-year reign, reestablished order and reorganized the empire, but his retirement in 305 was followed by another outbreak of civil war, and it remained for Constantine, after reuniting the empire in 324, to continue and extend the earlier changes. He developed a polity strong enough to prevent serious revolts, defend the frontiers, and secure regular succession to the throne.

The primary factor in the anarchy had been military insubordination. Again and again, all around the empire, frontier troops mutinied and set up their commanders as emperors. The consequent internal chaos left the frontiers open to the barbarians. All the countries along the Rhine-Danube frontier were ravaged. From the Black Sea, Gothic pirates sailing through the Hellespont plundered the Aegean cities. In the east the new Sassanid Persian empire undertook the reconquest of northern Mesopotamia and the annexation of Armenia. Even Egypt and Africa were raided by savage

---

tribes who had grown numerous along the fringes of Roman cultivation. These raids destroyed much property and many lives; not only was the open countryside laid waste, but numerous cities were captured. Moreover, the raids occasioned further insubordination in the army. Most divisions had strong local ties and were concerned to defend their own districts, and many refused to be transferred to areas where they were more needed.

A.D.
391	Theodosius I prohibits pagan worship
406–407	Gaul overrun by Alans, Sueves, and Vandals
410	Rome sacked by the Visigoths; Britain abandoned
435–453	Attila, king of the Huns, raids the Danube provinces
439	Carthage taken by the Vandals
454	Ostrogoths settle in Pannonia
459–487	Ostrogoths loot the Balkans; Isaurians in Asia Minor and Syria imperial succession in the West comes to an end
493	The Bulgar invasions of Thrace begin
533	Beginning of Justinian's attempt to reconquer the west
540	War with Persia
568	Lombard invasion of Italy; Avars dominant along the Danube
572	Visigoths reconquer Spain
602	The emperor Maurice overthrown by the army; Phocas installed
610	Phocas overthrown by Heraclius
610–626	The Avars at the gates of Constantinople; the Persians overrun Asia Minor, Syria, and Egypt; the empire reorganized as a set of military administrative districts
626	The Avars destroyed outside Constantinople; Serbs and Croats settle in the Balkans
627	Battle of Nineveh, the Persians decisively defeated and forced to withdraw from the empire
636	Battle of the Yarmuk; Syria lost to the Arabs
641	Death of Heraclius; loss of Egypt to the Arabs

They set up their commanders as local rulers and organized their own local defense. Finally, the movements of Roman armies to repel the raiders or fight civil wars were almost as hard on the countryside as the raids themselves.

All these military operations had to be financed, and money had to be raised to buy off barbarians who could not be driven off. As the ruin of the countryside and the breakup of trade cut down income from taxes, the money had to be coined. There was plenty of copper for it, but silver was lacking, so the silver content of nominally silver coins was cut to a minimum, then, at the worst period, replaced by a thin silver plating. Prices soared. Eventually even the government could not live on its own money—the principal taxes had to be paid in kind.

Recovery began as the breakdown had begun, with the army. First the Goths were crushed in the Balkans in 268–269, then the emperor Aurelian in 271 pulled Roman forces and settlers back from Dacia (western Rumania) to the Danube. This greatly shortened the frontier and made it more defensible. The settlers strengthened the provinces south of the river, which had been depopulated by Gothic raids, while the evacuated territory gave the remaining Goths room to settle and reduced their pressure on the frontier. Aurelian could then withdraw troops from the Balkans to resubjugate the east and Egypt in 271–273 and Gaul in 274. This enabled the empire to survive another attack of military insubordination which ended with the triumph of Diocletian.

In territory the new empire was almost identical with the old; only southern Scotland, the Rhine-Danube salient, and Dacia had been lost. Its primary concern, however, was one which had hitherto been minor: security from attack. All cities were now fortified. Rome itself began to build new walls in 271. Moreover, walls and ditches, or strings of towers, and supporting military roads, were constructed around the entire frontier, even across the deserts of north Africa.

Concern for defense implies the primacy of the army. Under Diocletian its strength was raised to about 400,000. To make it efficient yet keep the units loyal was the fundamental problem for Diocletian and Constantine.

The background of many third-century revolts, especially in the western provinces, had been the local loyalties of the frontier troops, hitherto stationed for their whole tour of duty, usually twenty years, in their native province. Consequently the army was now divided into first- and second-class troops, and only the latter were left in their own provinces, mostly as border guards. Further, to check ambitious generals, the civil government was almost everywhere separated from the military, and the provinces—all of them now governed by imperial appointees—were so fragmented that few could offer any considerable basis for revolt. At the same time the army units were fragmented, and command of the units was given mostly to men who had risen from the ranks and had no experience of civil government or ties with the civilian population. Finally, the first-class troops were commonly concentrated in cities somewhat back from the frontier, as mobile forces capable of striking an invasion at any point. For this purpose they were given special training and strengthened by enlarged cavalry units. Since all units, foot and cavalry alike, were of relatively small size, and the force in any city was made up of many units of different backgrounds, the chance of revolt by first-class troops was small, and these first-class troops kept the provincial forces along the frontiers in awe.

The chance of revolt by first-class troops was further diminished by the fact that many of them were foreigners. Because of the government's insistence that all cultivable land be taxed, many landowners obligated to provide recruits preferred to give money rather than a man. With the money the government hired barbarians individually, to serve in the regular army. Since these barbarians were picked for their fighting ability while the men sent by landowners were generally the worst who could pass muster, the levies from the provinces went largely into the second-class frontier guards and the first-class troops got a large proportion of barbarians who, as isolated aliens, were not likely to revolt. The employ of whole tribes of barbarians as units under their own leaders was a different matter. This led to serious revolts by these tribes, but not by the regular army.

Both the loyalty and the efficiency of the army were directly dependent on its proper upkeep. This proved the most difficult problem Diocletian and Constantine had to face. Although agricultural production had improved since Augustan times—the use of wind and water mills was extended, and the silo, the cold cellar, and hay were discovered—yet deforestation, erosion, and exhaustion of the soil and of mines and quarries had impoverished the empire. Yet worse was the widespread destruction of property, especially farm buildings and livestock, orchards and vineyards. The rural population had no financial reserves, so a raid which carried off livestock or destroyed vineyards put the affected area out of production for a long time. Consequently the financial burden, which for the Antonine empire had been considerable, was worse for the Constantinian empire.

Most of this burden had to be borne by the peasantry, for the great majority of the empire's production was agricultural. But the peasants had already been paying almost all they could. A little more could be squeezed out of them, and traders and artisans and even senators could be made to pay something—and were. But this did not suffice. People gave up keeping accounts for fear of taxation. Therefore the government cut salaries by debasing the currency and then supplementing money salaries with payments in kind which sufficed only for subsistence. Moreover, it squeezed the well-to-do families of the small cities until many of them were reduced to poverty.

The earlier empire had made the city councils responsible for collection of taxes from the city territories. Similarly, it had held them responsible for the maintenance of roads, bridges, and post stations in their territories, and had also imposed on them occasional levies in kind to meet extraordinary needs. With anarchy and inflation the taxes had mostly become nominal, but levies in kind had become routine. Diocletian, unable to stabilize the currency, resorted to an annual tax in kind assessed on land. The city councilmen were made personally responsible for the total assessed on their city's territories. From them the produce went to the provincial governors for transport to officials specified by the paymaster general. By these officials it was paid out as rations to all government employees, military and civil alike.

This tax remained the chief source of imperial income down to the fifth century. It entailed considerable social changes. Land had to continue to be cultivated in order to yield its assigned quota. Therefore the farm laborers had to stay on it to cultivate it. Similarly the municipal councilmen had to remain in office to collect or make up for their quotas, and the officials of the provincial governor to transport the produce, and so on. Consequently a series of laws fixed these and more classes of the population, and their descendants, in their places and professions. Moreover, this system required a large secretarial staff to draw up the census, estimate the needs, make the allotments, certify the collection, check the transfers, investigate delinquencies, try the offenders, and so on. This was doubtless a major reason for the fragmentation of the provinces. Provincial governors had now so much supervision and adjudication on their hands that one was needed (with his staff, of course) for every small district. Besides the trebling of the provincial administrations, the bureaucracy of the central government proliferated fantastic titles, and with every title went not only a state salary but the opportunity—which soon becomes a legally recognized right—of demanding fees from the public for performance of the prescribed service. Thus the taxpayer had to support both the army and the bureaucracy. The bureaucracy came to number thirty or forty thousand. This was only a tenth the size of the army, but bureaucrats were more expensive than soldiers. Besides their salaries and their fees were their bribes. And worst of all, the empire could not afford enough of them to do the paper work the system required—especially since every copy of every document had to be written individually. Without efficient filing systems the accumulation of documents became unmanageable and there were innumerable opportunities for evasion of the laws. Finally, with the proliferation of the bureaucrats, edicts proliferated defining their functions, revising the definitions, creating exceptions and then exceptions to the exceptions. Since the regular recourse from bureaucratic injustice was through the law, the multiplication of lawsuits and lawyers and courts immediately complemented the multiplication of the bureaucracy and still further increased the size and importance of the nonproductive population.

These luxuries ruined many city councilmen who had to make up the deficits of their districts. In the countryside the financial pressure fell hardest on the small landowners. The rich were able, through bribery and influence, to have the assessments on their holdings minimized and to avoid paying even the minimum. Therefore this period, especially in the West, saw a growth of great estates. The rich had already used the opportunities of the civil wars and invasions to buy up or appropriate the ruined or deserted farms of their neighbors. Now increased taxation led many of the peasants to make over their properties to the rich landlord of the neighborhood in exchange for protection from the city council's tax collectors and a guarantee of the right to live on and work the land. Thus the peasants were gradually transformed to serfs. Eventually law ratified the change; the great proprietors were given criminal jurisdiction over the territories of their estates. At the same time the law further developed its long-standing distinction between the upper and lower classes. Normally upper-class individuals might not be tortured to secure evidence, or subjected to humiliating punishments, or compelled to labor on public works, or required to provide animals, housing, or other services for public officials. None of these exemptions held for the lower classes.

Most prominent among the rich landowners who profited from these developments were the senators. Hostility between the senate and the army had been one of the main causes of the fall of the Severan dynasty in 235. Through the following period of anarchy and invasions the army necessarily gained in power and senators were eventually excluded from military commands. But no military leader had the time or the forces to suppress the senate thoroughly; it would have required a major civil war. When Diocletian and Constantine fixed their capitals in the east, the senate, remaining in Rome, was reduced to a city council. But the city was Rome; its prestige was still of great importance. Moreover, the senate was made up of the empire's richest landowners, protected by legal privileges and family connections. It escaped annihilation through subservience and serious taxation through bribery and influence. So senatorial wealth increased. Senators' villas now became villages, centers both of subsistence economy and of local government and defense, important links in the transmission of classical farming techniques to the Middle Ages.

On the other hand, in the imperial government the senate became merely an audience to which decisions might be announced for acclamation. All laws and important appointments were made by the emperor. All decisions on policy were made in the imperial council (or bedchamber). The imperial council was composed of the most important military commanders (below whom were the regional commanders, *duces* and *comites,* whence came the dukes and counts of the Middle Ages), the commander of the imperial guards, the head of the provincial administration (who was also chief justice and paymaster general), the head of the imperial estates (the emperor owned almost a fifth of the arable land), the treasurer (who controlled coinage, receipts, and expenses in precious metals, and imperial monopolies, such as mines and arsenals), the secretary for legal affairs, and the head of the records office (who was also in charge of appoint-

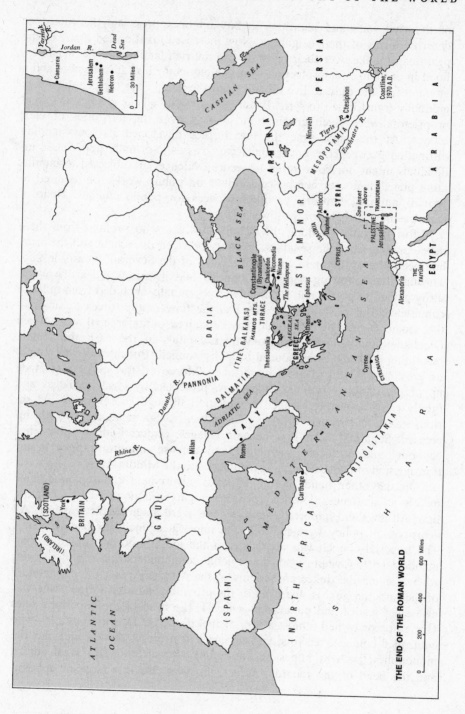

THE END OF THE ROMAN WORLD

ments, couriers, and intelligence). Not a member of the council, because he was a eunuch, the grand chamberlain of the imperial palace had great influence because of his access to and knowledge of the emperor, not to mention the empress.

The government thus reverted to the Oriental pattern—a despotism resting on control of an army and acting through a royal council composed of executives arbitrarily appointed by the king. The Greek experiment was abandoned. Even in law, trial by jury died out. All that survived was a literary tradition from which subsequent ages would draw inspiration.

The nature of the new government was reflected in the new titles, trappings, and rituals of the court. These, like the government, had their beginnings in earlier periods, but only now were developed consistently. Everything that had to do with the emperor became "sacred"; he no longer wore the old Roman toga, but a purple triumphal robe, embroidered with gold and jewels, and a diadem, symbol of Hellenistic kingship, studded with pearls or with the rays of the sun-god; he was surrounded always by a military escort; his ministers and officials customarily wore military uniform; he was hailed as "King" and "Autocrat." As the court was predominantly military, and the army predominantly from the Latin provinces, so the language of the upper administration, even in the East, now became Latin, and remained so for more than a century.

The new monarch needed a new capital. Rome called up too many memories, and worse, the senate was there. Moreover, the concern for defense demanded a capital nearer the dangerous frontiers. And since the court and central administration fed on taxes paid in kind, and transport was expensive by sea but even more expensive by land, the court was best located at a seaport in the richest part of the empire—the east. Constantine's choice was Byzantium, which he renamed Constantinople. The situation was superb economically—controlling the crossroads between Europe and Asia, the Black Sea and the Aegean—and also strategically—a spacious, well-watered, easily fortified peninsula within striking distance of the lower Danube, where barbarian pressure was greatest, and with good communications to Antioch, the base for defense against the Persians.

One advantage of the new capital, in Constantine's eyes, was its lack of the religious establishment of ancient Rome. Fifty years of anarchy had made many converts to Christianity. Some turned to its promises for future life, or of immediate grace for refuge from the present world. More found companionship and financial security in its communities and their charities, on which the disasters of the civil society made many dependent. The resultant combination of the growth of Christianity and the ruin of the state made the imperial policy toward the new religion an acute question. Both Christians and pagans believed that the gods would punish men who did not worship them properly.

While Christianity had been uncommon and the empire prosperous, the Christians' refusal to worship the pagans' gods had been generally ignored. But now Christians were everywhere, and the disasters of the empire proved that the gods were angry, presumably at the Christians' "atheism."

In 249 the emperor Decius decided to stamp out Christianity. But next year he was killed trying to stop an invasion of the Goths. This ended the persecution and probably persuaded many that the Christians were right— "the deaths of the persecutors" became a favorite theme of their propaganda. The next two reigns were equally brief and disastrous. Then Valerian renewed the persecution in 257 and was captured, with much of his army, by the Persians in 259. His son Gallienus called off the persecution and officially permitted the practice of Christianity.

So matters stood until the end of Diocletian's reign, when in 303 Gallienus' edict was rescinded and persecution renewed. By this time Christians were so numerous that the decision to persecute involved a great economic sacrifice and administrative effort. This probably influenced Constantine, when he seized power in the west in 306, to let persecution there lapse. His mother Helena's devotion to Christianity, his own belief that he was under the protection of the Christians' god, and the strength of Christianity in Italy and the east, which he hoped to conquer, also shaped his decision. After his conquest of Italy in 312 he arranged with his eastern co-emperor for toleration of all religions, but immediately began in his own domains to patronize Christianity. After eliminating his co-emperor in 324 he seized the treasures and estates of most pagan temples—the treasures he particularly needed to restore the supply of gold and silver currency—but he gave vast sums to the Christians, especially for building. Bishops all over the east were authorized to draw on imperial funds for repairs of damages from the persecutions. Magnificent churches were built at Rome and in many cities of Italy, as well as Nicomedia, Antioch, Jerusalem, Bethlehem, and Hebron, while Constantinople received a whole choir. All these churches were lavishly endowed. Others throughout the empire received from the state annual subsidies of food for distribution to the poor. The Christian clergy were exempted from service as city councilmen, a privilege which led to an epidemic of vocations among the well-to-do of the cities and cut down sharply the resources on which the cities could draw to meet their expenses; finally Constantine had to prohibit ordination of councilmen. The bishops' powers were increased by the increase of the funds they controlled. Civil and criminal law was also revised in the Christian interest and more or less according to Christian standards. Sunday was made a holiday as "the day of the sun," so pagans as well as Christians would observe it. Celibates were permitted to inherit property. Divorce was made more difficult, concubinage and pederasty outlawed, illegitimacy penalized. Gladiatorial games were prohibited—though they continued in the west until the beginning of the fifth century. Beside the expropriation of the lands and treasures of pagan temples, animal sacrifice was prohibited, but this prohibition, too, remained a dead letter. A few temples were destroyed. Obstacles were put in the way of conversion to Judaism. Finally Christians were favored in appointments, benefactions, petitions, and appeals. The upper administration became largely Christian.

Christianity was not merely the cult of a new god (or gods—the Christians were not quite clear on this point). It was an *organized* cult, as none of the pagan cults had been. It was also an *intolerant* cult, not only intolerant of those who worshiped other gods without the state's permission (this paganism had often been), but intolerant, by inheritance from Deuteronomy, of anyone who worshiped any other god at all, and thence, by theological extension, of anyone who practiced Christianity "incorrectly." These two characteristics were complementary: the intolerance had done much to build up the organization; the organization made the intolerance effective.

In Constantine's time the organization was still loose. The bishops of large districts met as occasion required under the presidency of the bishop of the chief city of the district. There was no empire-wide church government. The bishop of Rome claimed a vague preeminence, but even in the west important bishops sometimes contradicted him. However, the members of the church thought of it as a unity, corresponded with one another, were concerned about the treatment of their fellow members in other parts of the empire, and were in approximate agreement on teaching and discipline. A man expelled from the organization in Alexandria or Antioch would usually find its doors closed to him in Rome or Carthage, and vice versa. Moreover, this organization had a tradition of independence from the civil government, indeed, of hostility to it.

Now, for the first time, there were two great powers within the empire —the state and the church. No longer were priests merely civil officials in charge of religious affairs, as they had been hitherto in Greco-Roman tradition. They now belonged to an organization essentially different from the civil government, one claiming a different (and higher) authorization. The bishops were happy to accept Constantine's patronage and willing, in return, to follow his directives. They would also use their influence in the service of the state—with the fourth century begins their condemnation of Christians who refuse to perform military service. But they did not become members of the imperial council, nor did they normally invite imperial officers to participate in their councils. From now on, these two organizations, civil and ecclesiastical, were to live side by side, through alternating conflicts and alliances.

The alliance initiated by Constantine immediately involved him in difficulties. The Church was anxious to use him to implement its intolerance. The consequent treatment of pagans and Jews has already been mentioned. "Heretics," that is, minor Christian parties, were more energetically persecuted. And competing groups within the main organization now battled for government patronage, the victors using the power of the state to suppress their opponents. This policy backfired in Africa, where the growth of great Roman estates had produced a large class of landless agricultural migrants who hated the Roman government and became violent supporters of the party the government decided to oppose (the "Donatists"). Constantine eventually gave up the struggle; persecution was a luxury he could ill afford.

In the east a dispute broke out between Alexander, Bishop of Alexandria, and one of his presbyters named Arius, over the relation between the "Word" or "Son" of "God" which had been incarnate in Jesus, and "God" himself, now called "the Father"—his name, Yahweh, having been generally forgotten. Practically all Christians now worshiped "Jesus, the Son of God" as a god, and would not consider giving up this practice. Were there then two gods? Or were the Son and the Father somehow one? Arius took the first position, making the Son an inferior god created by the Father. Alexander excommunicated him, but many neighboring bishops supported him. Constantine's ecclesiastical advisers at first backed Alexander, and Constantine summoned all the bishops of the church to a council in 325 at Nicaea. Some three hundred showed up and adopted a creed to which all "orthodox" Christians were thenceforth required by the state to assent; it asserted belief in God the Father, and in Jesus Christ the Son of God "of the same substance as the Father." All bishops were willing to sign this, except two who were deposed and banished, as was Arius. Later on, however, Constantine came under the influence of pro-Arian advisers and called other councils which readmitted Arius to communion and condemned his leading opponent, Athanasius, who had succeeded Alexander as bishop of Alexandria.

The situation in Egypt began to look like that in Africa. In Egypt, though, the opposition to the government was centered in a new class of social institutions, the monasteries. Withdrawal from society had taken a variety of physical and psychological forms in the ancient world. Most conspicuous had been that of the Cynics. But in the late third century Cynicism withered away. As anarchy and consequent poverty spread, there was less to spare for wandering preachers; a man who rejected society now had to find some place where he could support himself, otherwise society would reject him, too. Hence the Christian hermit. Diocletian's policies augmented the movement, not only by persecuting the Christians in the cities, but also by increasing and regularizing the tax on cultivated land. Land which would not yield enough to pay both the tax and the cost of cultivation was now, if possible, disowned, since if ownership were admitted the government would tax it anyhow. Much of this disowned land was good enough for subsistence farming. On it the hermits settled.

By the time of Diocletian's retirement (305) hermits were so thick near the Faiyûm that one of them, the legendary Antony, formed a loose organization of solitaries, mainly for mutual protection and common worship. About 320 in upper Egypt an ex-soldier named Pachomius founded a monastery—a community with a definite head, common residence, common discipline, common daily worship, and division of labor, under the direction of the superior, to meet the needs of the community. By the time of his death in 346 he had established nine monasteries for men and one for women, with some three thousand inmates. By this time, too, there were many ascetics and possibly some beginnings of organization (whether native or imported from Egypt is uncertain) in Palestine, Syria, and Asia Minor.

The first monks were mostly social misfits, and many were of peasant stock. They usually hated cities and tax collectors, and had no appreciation for the higher aspects of classical culture: they perpetuated, along with other elements of Cynicism, its contempt for learning and its identification of asceticism with virtue. The few more educated were often men from city families who had been ruined by taxation and had no love for the government. The first monasteries accordingly paid no taxes. Located in desert areas, they governed themselves. Politically their growth provided bases for heretics and a consequent drain on the military forces of the government; economically they aggravated the shortage of labor both directly and by extension of celibacy, cut down income from taxes, and, in this first period, contributed no important products or services to the surrounding society.

Thus Constantine's empire was from the beginning a structure of mutually repellent elements. The monasteries were antisocial; the alliance with the organized Church entailed the hostility of discontented parties within the organization, as well as those expelled (the heretics) and rival religions. The "New Rome" (Constantinople) was in obvious rivalry to the old; its location in the eastern half of the empire would necessitate the creation of a practically independent center of command for the German frontier. The new imperial council and the old Roman senate (still the richest body in the empire) were barely on speaking terms. The government was composed of two separate structures, the army and the civil government. The army was held in control by balancing the first-class troops against the frontier guards, and the first-class troops themselves were a mosaic of forces of different types from different backgrounds.

Similarly, the civil government was composed of half a dozen great departments, each used to spying on the other.

The burden of this complex structure fell on the officials of the cities and the peasants from whom they had to squeeze the produce. The system reduced many officials to bankruptcy and many peasants to serfdom, and it further exacerbated the age-old hostility between city and countryside which had been a weakness of all Greco-Roman civilization. In Syria and Egypt, where the countryside still spoke Aramaic (Syriac) and Egyptian (Coptic) while the cities spoke Greek, this hostility was particularly serious. Finally, the whole structure was now surrounded on north, east, and south by enemies, ready at the first sign of weakness to invade and plunder. Nevertheless, the Constantinian structure survived for three hundred years.

Its survival was largely due to the fragmentation of the army and the solidity of the bureaucracy. Generals, whose men might revolt if they were removed, were always counterbalanced by other generals. The great bureaucrats had no militant following; beneath each was a line of lesser bureaucrats, every one anxious first to keep his own place, next, to advance. From 324 to 602 no emperor in the east was overthrown by a usurper. In the west, however, where the balance of elements in the military forces was not preserved, the emperors, falling more and more under the power of their generals, became mere puppets; at last (shortly before 500) the office disappeared.

The failure in the west to control the army was partly the result of geographical factors, partly of personality and chance. Until 375 the emperors were military men who kept strong holds on their armies; then the throne passed to Gratian, a bookish adolescent. The resultant revolts and civil wars produced a series of juvenile and incompetent emperors under whom the central control rapidly disintegrated. They also stripped the northern frontiers of their best troops and left them open to the barbarians. The Rhine frontier was overrun in 406–407 by the Alans, Sueves, and Vandals; Rome was sacked by the Visigoths in 410; Italy, Gaul, Spain, and finally North Africa were successively looted; Carthage fell in 439. Such fragments of the empire as could be patched up in the wake of the barbarians were necessarily dominated by the military. Since the military was now predominantly barbarian "allies," its leaders could not, themselves, take over the imperial office. The last emperor to reign in Rome was merely deposed; he was not important enough to be killed.

The survival of the empire in the east, like its fall in the west, was due to a combination of geographic factors, personalities, and chance. Geographically its dangerous frontier was shorter and more easily defensible, roughly 800 miles as against 1,300. Of these 800 dangerous miles, about

250 were on the eastern frontier bounded by Persia. The Persians normally observed treaties, and they had no intention of leaving their homes and moving en masse into the Roman territories, as the barbarians did. The major barbarian powers had to be faced only along the lower Danube, which was large enough to make a good boundary. South of the Danube a defensible mountain barrier ran across Thrace; south of that the straits separating Asia Minor from Europe were impassable to barbarians who had no fleets. Consequently the rulers in the east were less dependent on their armies. Further, when the succession of strong emperors in the east was first broken, in 395, adroit ministers managed—after a few uneasy years—to secure a generation of comparative peace during which dangerous commanders were eliminated and the tradition of civilian administration was firmly established.

The army, now about 350,000 men in the east alone, had been split by the Constantinian tradition into some 250,000 second-class troops along the frontiers and about 100,000 first-class troops. These latter were now split into two classes and five armies, each with its own commander in chief, kept in check by his rivals. At the same time the landward fortifications of Constantinople were strengthened. Thus when barbarian pressure again became acute the government, secure in its capital, could bargain with the barbarians, if necessary fight them, if defeated let them loot the northern provinces until the exhaustion of those forced them to move to the west. In such bargaining the eastern government could draw on money accumulated from the Greek islands, Asia Minor, Syria, Cyprus, Palestine, Egypt, and Cyrenaica which, though often disturbed by riots or border raids, were in the main secure. The same resources paid its troops and kept them quiet.

In spite of these advantages the history of the eastern empire was far from tranquil. The northern provinces were invaded in the early 400's by the Visigoths, in the 430's by the Huns, in the later 400's by the Ostrogoths, in the early 500's by the Bulgars, in the later 500's by the Avars, not to mention lesser peoples. But Constantinople stood off all attacks, the straits barred progress to the south, and the waves of invaders spent their force, often in fighting each other. Wars with Persia ended disastrously in 363, but the Persians were content with the settlement they then extorted and there was little more fighting until the early sixth century. During the fifth century the government was repeatedly in danger of falling into the power of its Gothic "allies," forces which had been employed as units under their own leaders. To balance these the emperors depended chiefly on troops from Isauria (the southeastern nub of Asia Minor), mountaineers who took advantage of this dependence to raid their neighbors, striking as far as Palestine. Eventually, in 488, the Goths went west to the greener pastures of Italy and the government shortly thereafter crushed the Isaurians.

Internal security, thus restored, was the basis for Justinian's attempt to reconquer the west, beginning in 533. His generals retook most of the north African coast, the southern coast of Spain, the western Mediterranean islands, Italy, and Dalmatia. This expansion frightened Persia, which began war in 540. Pressure on the northern front continued, too. Nevertheless Justinian held his conquests. His successors even survived another war with Persia, though it prevented them from doing much to stem the Lombard invasion of Italy or the Visigothic reconquest of Spain. What finally brought down the structure was not foreign defeat, but, as in the third century, loss of control of the army. Economies ordered by the emperor Maurice in 602 occasioned a revolt of the northern army, which killed him and installed one of its officers, Phocas, who proved a tyrant. The eastern army revolted. The Persians took the opportunity to overrun Syria and Asia Minor. In 610 Heraclius, son of the exarch (governor general) of Africa overthrew Phocas. Now the Persians advanced into Egypt and the northern barbarians (this time, the Avars) to the walls of Constantinople. But the city held out, the Avars were defeated, and after another year's fighting the Persians were forced to withdraw. The Roman and Persian empires, however, had both been exhausted by the effort and neither could now stop the Arabian tribes organized by Muhammad and his followers. Syria was lost in the 630's, Egypt, Cyrenaica, and Tripolitania in the 640's, and the Roman Empire was reduced to its Byzantine form.

For Further Reading

Bury, J., *History of the Later Roman Empire from the Death of Theodosius I to the Death of Justinian.*
Chadwick, H., *The Early Church.*
Gibbon, E., *The History of the Decline and Fall of the Roman Empire,* chs. 7–47.
Lot, F., *The End of the Ancient World and the Beginning of the Middle Ages.*
Nock, A., *Conversion.*
Ure, P., *Justinian and His Age.*

21 Late Roman Society and Culture

Throughout the three hundred years from Constantine's death in 337 to the reign of Heraclius in the 600's the political structure of the Constantinian empire was preserved with only peripheral changes of its form, though its extent was altered by loss of the west in the fifth century, and its economic, social, and cultural character was altered by continued development.

Economically the most conspicuous characteristic of the period was the transfer of property. The cities and their temples, the well-to-do, land-owning families of the cities, and the merchants and shopkeepers, as well as the small landowners of the countryside, were stripped of their holdings. The barbarians, the emperor's estates, the great landowners (especially the Roman senators), the bureaucrats, the churches, and the monasteries acquired some of this wealth, but much was destroyed in war and perhaps 20 per cent of the cultivated land was abandoned because high taxation made it unprofitable to farm marginal tracts.

The most important factors in the transfer of property were conquests and raids, imperial confiscations, taxes, bureaucratic extortion, and private donations. Most of the western empire changed hands by conquest in the fifth century and much of it again in the sixth. In the east no territory was officially lost, but repeated barbarian raids led to the abandonment of much land in the northern provinces and also in Egypt and Cyrenaica. The Vandals, after their conquest of North Africa in the 430's, reintroduced large-scale piracy to the western Mediterranean and raided the coasts for a century.

Within the empire Constantine's confiscation took the properties of the cities and temples; eventually the cities were allowed a third of the incomes from their former lands for maintenance of their buildings. Confiscations, following occasional revolts and frequent trials for treason, sorcery, or heresy, brought a steady flow of lands to the imperial estates. The impoverishment of the middle class and the peasants by taxation led to the transfer of their lands to the estates of larger landowners and of the emperors, the largest of all.

What the emperors took with one hand they gave with the other, but not to the same people. Taxes went primarily to support the army, the court, and the bureaucracy; these were the largest regular items in the budget. Extraordinary imperial grants vastly enriched the churches and later the monasteries, as well as the great officials of the court and their

CHRONOLOGY

A.D. c. 250 Plotinus, beginning of Neoplatonism
       330 Constantinople becomes the imperial residence
       331 Constantine's expropriation of the temple's properties; Constantine's endowments of Christian churches; Eusebius' fusion of classical and Biblical historiographic traditions
       351 Apollo expelled from Daphne by the relics of St. Babylas
       381 The Council of Constantinople, the doctrine of the Trinity completed
       391 Theodosius I prohibits all pagan worship
       400 The Senate of Constantinople, mainly bureaucrats, has 2,000 members; tax collectors commonly need military escorts
       410 Sack of Rome by Visigoths, followed by Christian apologetics, notably Augustine's *City of God*
       431 The Council of Ephesus, Nestorius condemned, half of Syria alienated from the imperial Church
       439 Capture of Carthage by the Vandals, the West completely overrun by barbarians, piracy rife in the western Mediterranean; the imperial administration in the East begins to use Greek
       451 The Council of Chalcedon, the Patriarch of Alexandria condemned, Egypt alienated; the system of patriarchal jurisdictions completed
       496 Conversion of the Franks to Christianity
       500 Many big landlords have private military forces and prisons
       529 The Platonic Academy in Athens closed; all pagans ordered to become Christians; revolt of the Samaritans
       534 Completion of Justinian's law code
       560 Samaritans and Jews join in revolt
       641 Death of Heraclius; loss of Egypt to the Arabs; the Gospels have been translated into ten languages, Christian missionaries are working in China

families and favorites; thus political power was consolidated as economic power.

Private giving, which had formerly gone to the towns for games, baths, gymnasiums, theaters, and the like, now went largely to the churches for buildings, decoration and upkeep, the salaries of the clergy, and the support of the monks, but also for alms to the poor, hospitals, orphanages, maintenance of widows and unmarried girls (in ecclesiastical terminology, "virgins"), and other charities. In the pagan world charity had been almost exclusively a concern of the rich and a means to civic honors; Christianity made it also a duty for the poor and a means to eternal salvation. The churches' income from donations was therefore more widely based than that of the cities had been. Ecclesiastical wealth made religious offices attractive, the more so because celibacy was not yet required. Both simony and the sale of offices in the bureaucracy increased during the fifth century. By that time, too, the monastic movement has been taken over by polite society. Most monasteries lived on their endowments and paid taxes; manual labor by monks was exceptional in the east and unknown in the west. The clergy, the monks, and the bureaucrats were three new, or newly enlarged, groups whose labor, if any, was at best nonproductive, and whose care and feeding were an additional burden on the peasantry. It is worth noting, finally, that neither trade nor industry figured among the most important forms of exchange of property in these three centuries. Far more capital changed hands through conquest and robbery, taxation and governmental expenditures, official corruption and private charity.

Important changes in the social structure accompanied these movements of capital. The Orientalization of the imperial court and of the great households imitating the court increased the number and influence of eunuchs. Below the court circle, the higher bureaucrats, especially in the east, began to constitute a new hereditary aristocracy, as son followed father into the administration, perpetuating family power and augmenting family fortunes. By the end of the fourth century the senate of Constantinople, largely composed of such families, had 2,000 members.

Great ecclesiastical families also began to spring up in the east, in spite of the rule that bishops, priests, and deacons might not marry after ordination. But in the west, the bishops of Rome, from the end of the fourth century, decreed that married men, if ordained, should thereafter abstain from intercourse. (The efficacy of this decree is difficult to estimate.) Since orthodox monasticism also required celibacy, church officials had to be replenished continuously from other classes.

While these privileged classes expanded, those which had to bear the burden of taxation steadily diminished in spite of repeated laws fixing their members in their callings. The well-to-do of the cities escaped into the bureaucracy and the church. Lesser provincial administrators, underpaid and overburdened, also found the priesthood attractive. Lawyers, too, found the church congenial; they contributed not a little to the disputes about heresy. As the bourgeoisie thus shrank, tax revenues declined. Hence the economies, finally fatal, in the upkeep of the army. Already in the fifth century the inferior frontier troops had begun to be assigned plots of land to cultivate in lieu of salaries; their training and effectiveness suffered.

Finally the peasants, who bore the bulk of the burden, fled wherever they could. Many went into the monasteries, some became migratory agricultural laborers, some got into the army, some into the church, some into the cities. Everywhere the shortage of farm labor became more and more serious. In consequence the legal condition of tenant farmers, whom the Constantinian polity had bound to the land as serfs, was gradually reduced almost to slavery. They had to pay taxes as well as their rent to the landlord; they could not sue him (except for overcharging in rent). They were forbidden to alienate property, be ordained, or enter a monastery without their landlord's consent. Since they were exempted from military service, even conscription could not set them free.

Inevitably the peasants came to hate both the government and the rich. Their hatred manifested itself in many ways. Sometimes, seizing upon ecclesiastical quarrels, they supported whichever faction opposed the government. In Africa, Spain, and Gaul peasants repeatedly supported political revolts. In Africa and Egypt many peasants joined the marauding tribes along the fringes of the cultivated land; these tribes became so populous that considerable military forces failed to contain them. Everywhere men took to the mountains, woods, and deserts to live as bandits. The world became full of robbers.

Even when they remained on the land, the peasants violently resisted the tax collectors; the collectors, in turn, made ever more use of torture. By the end of the fourth century collectors commonly had to be backed up by military force. Much of the army was tied down to garrison duty, preventing revolts and helping to collect taxes. This lowered its efficiency and raised the number of troops needed. Military expenditures rose, and taxes with them. By the end of the fifth century landlords commonly had their own illegal bands of armed retainers—and private prisons. This situation made effective resistance to the barbarians impossible. Large landowners and city authorities did not dare give arms and military training to the peasantry. They preferred to risk an invasion by a few barbarians rather than a general peasant revolt. When the barbarians did break in, the peasants either took the opportunity to revolt and plunder for themselves or joined the invaders; they rarely did anything to resist them. Not that they were unable to resist. For instance, the barbarians had no difficulty overrunning Spain, but the forces sent to drive them from the country had less trouble with them than with peasant revolts. Moreover, when the Goths finally established themselves, their violation of local martyr's shrine led to a popular rising in which they were defeated. Had there been any such popular support for the Roman government, it is inconceivable that the barbarian tribes, which normally numbered about 20,000 fighting men, should have overrun Italy, France, Spain, and North Africa and dominated a population of about 10 million. The Roman Empire in the west fell only because most of its subjects would not fight to preserve it.

While the empire was going to pieces the church was extending and consolidating its conquests. Conversions in northern Mesopotamia had begun as early as the second, perhaps even the first, century; during the third and fourth they were extended to Persia and beyond. The official adoption of Christianity in the Roman Empire made it a suspect religion in the Persian; the church there had many martyrs. Armenia was converted before the time of Constantine, and became a base for further conversion in the Caucasus. The fourth century saw the conversion of the Irish to "orthodox" (Nicaean) Christianity and of the Goths and Vandals to Arianism. Conversion of the Germanic peoples continued through the fifth century and thereafter; the great prize was the conversion of Clovis and consequently of his Franks in 496. In the fourth century the conversion of Ethiopia was begun; the Nubians adopted Christianity in the time of Justinian.

The consolidation of Christianity within the empire was a complex process of which the three chief aspects were its acquisition of adherents and property, the organization of church government, administration, and discipline, and the determination of doctrine. In all of these the church relied on help from the state. Except for the brief restoration of paganism by Julian in 361–363, imperial patronage continued; this sufficed to convert the prudent. From the end of the fourth century pagan worship, whether public or private, was prohibited under severe penalties. All temples were closed; many were granted to individuals for destruction or to Christian communities for use as churches; more were destroyed by Christian vandalism which went unpunished. The Christians' fanatical hatred of worship of other gods was in striking contrast to the tolerance of many pagans, who were willing to accept Jesus as a new deity. Fanaticism proved an advantage; tolerance facilitated conversions and fanaticism made them profitable. In the fifth century pagans were gradually barred from the civil service and the army, then from legal practice, finally, under Justinian, from teaching. In 529 Justinian closed the Platonic Academy in Athens and ordered all pagans to become Christians. Those who refused were exiled, their property confiscated. Agents were sent out to destroy temples and forcibly convert the peasantry in districts still pagan. Monasticism had already been important in conversion of country districts; it would continue to be so beyond the imperial frontiers. Much had also been done by great Christian landowners who converted their tenants. These methods reduced paganism to unimportance, though in remote country districts all around the Mediterranean it survived the empire.

However, Christianity had competitors within the empire—its two half sisters, Judaism and Samaritanism, and the strange religion founded by Mani, a Mesopotamian prophet, reportedly of Persian family, who during the middle of the third century had represented himself as the final revelator of whom the Buddha, Zoroaster, and Jesus had been forerunners. With adherents scattered from the Atlantic coast to China, Manicheism was an international religion; as such it was relentlessly persecuted by both Rome and Persia, the one intent on using Christianity, the other Zoroastrianism, to consolidate their realms.

Judaism and Samaritanism were dealt with more gingerly, since they were protected through most of the fourth century by the tradition of Roman law, which authorized their practices. Here Christian vandalism took the lead; destruction of synagogues followed close on destruction of temples. Early in the fifth century the erection of new synagogues was prohibited, and thereafter Jews and Samaritans, like pagans, were expelled step by step from the civil service and the army, from all public dignities, and from the practice of law. These measures were followed in the sixth century by others yet more severe. Many synagogues of the Samaritans, in particular, were destroyed. They revolted in 529 and 560, in the latter revolt being joined by the Jews. Both Jews and Samaritans welcomed the Persian and Arab invasions of Palestine and took these opportunities to square accounts by destroying churches and massacring the Christians.

The church's growth complicated the problems of disciplining its members, administering its property, and governing its organization. Since the great persecutions, when many of the baptized had sinned by apostasy, postbaptismal sins had been deemed forgivable—the few who denied this became heretics. Practice required that those who had sinned after baptism should confess to their bishop or his deputy and should be assigned penance, usually severe, after the performance of which they would be readmitted to communion. During the fourth century the increase of infant baptism and the flood of time-serving converts lowered the standard of Christian behavior and made penance both more common and easier. Finally a scandal in Constantinople in the late fourth century led to the abolition of the confessor's office and penance was left to the individual's conscience. The east thus temporarily gave up the task of disciplining the laity save for open scandal or heresy, for which the penalty was excommunication, but in the west the penitential discipline was preserved and with it the power of the church as an agency of forgiveness. Discipline of the clergy was always in the hands of the bishop, who could order his clerics about as he chose. The monks vowed to obey the superior of the monastery, and Justinian put all monasteries under the jurisdiction of the bishops. Finally the bishop controlled the administration and disposition of church property.

Thus the enormous growth of church property and personnel caused a corresponding growth in the power of the bishops. By Justinian's time the personal income of the bishop of a rich see was as great as that of the highest government officials, and the patriarchs were in a class with the senators. In a good-sized see the cathedral alone would have fifty to a hundred clergy; in a patriarchal see it would have three or four hundred— mostly in the minor orders—to say nothing of monks and nuns. Bishops accordingly lived in great style, and episcopal elections were often violently contested; one in Rome left 137 dead in a day's fighting. Therefore the rules were more sharply defined and the approval of the presiding bishop of the regional council, now called "the metropolitan," was made prerequisite. Further organization and consolidation soon followed. Finally in 451 the Council of Chalcedon completed the process by which most imperial territories were subjected to five great sees—Egypt and Cyrenaica to Alexandria, Palestine to Jerusalem, Syria to Antioch, most of Asia Minor, Thrace, and Greece to Constantinople, and the west to Rome. The incumbents of these five sees came to be known as "patriarchs," by distinction from the mere metropolitans, their subordinates.

This consolidation, however, made conflicts between the sees even sharper. Rome and Alexandria were jealous of the growth of Constantinople and tried to break up its power by attacking the orthodoxy of its bishops. The fourth century offered little opportunity for this tactic. Constantine's successor in the east, Constantius, was Arian and his successor, Julian, pagan; subsequent emperors until Theodosius generally avoided religious controversies, and when Theodosius organized the Council of Constantinople in 381, to restore the Nicaean position, the opposition had disintegrated. (The council declared the Holy Ghost of the same substance as the Father and the Son and so completed the official trinity, "one God in three persons.")

In the fifth century, however, a controversy broke out over "Christology"—the relation of God the Son to Jesus the Christ, in whom the Son was incarnate. Since the physical Jesus had been born, suffered, and died, he had to be human. But since the church worshiped "Jesus Christ the Son of God," Jesus had to be united with the Son. This much was at first admitted. But was the union merely one of agreement and cooperation, as partners are united in a company, or was it some sort of mixture or fusion?

Something like the former point of view was energetically defended by Nestorius, Patriarch of Constantinople, who was so indiscreet as to attack, in consequence, the popular use of the term "Mother of God" as a description of Mary, whose cult was rapidly growing. This gave the Patriarch of Alexandria, Cyril, his chance. He allied with Rome and secured Nestorius' condemnation in the Council of Ephesus, 431. Constantinople was discredited and Antioch, where Nestorius had been very popular, was deeply divided.*

At Rome, however, the triumph of Alexandria produced deep uneasiness. In the next generation the Roman patriarch Leo allied with Constantinople, and the Council of Chalcedon in 451 condemned the Alexandrians for heresy because they taught that the two natures in Jesus Christ had been fused into one, the human lost in the divine as a wine drop in the sea. Leo declared that the union was perfect, but the natures remained perfectly distinct; this contradiction in terms became the orthodox position. The monks and peasants of Egypt and the populace of Alexandria solidly supported their patriarch; when orthodox patriarchs were sent out thereafter they needed military guards. The "monophysite" (one-nature) position also won much support in Syria, Asia Minor, and Armenia; indeed, the Armenian, Coptic, Ethiopic, and "Jacobite" Syrian churches still hold to various modifications of it.

The imperial government supported the decisions of the councils, expelled the heretical bishops and clergy, and made over their church properties to orthodox appointees. But the heresies became matters of intense popular dispute, and the adherents of the heretics fought vigorously to defend their clergy and churches. As a result, these doctrinal squabbles not only damaged the authority of the eastern patriarchates, but also caused widespread violence, tied down large numbers of troops, and destroyed much property.

The triumph of the church was thus a Pyrrhic victory, but it was a victory. All over the empire churches were erected from the stones of former temples and a Christian culture from the elements of the former pagan world. The chief elements lost were the pagan cults and the amenities of the small cities—the games, the gymnasiums, the police and fire brigades, the libraries, and so on. But these were not entirely lost. Athletic and gladiatorial games were replaced by chariot races as the great popular amusement. Shows in which wild animals were killed continued

---

* Many of Nestorius' followers later emigrated to Mesopotamia, where the Nestorian church eventually became the principal form of Christianity within the Persian empire and carried its missionary work as far as China.

popular. The baths remained, in spite of Christian anathemas, the major centers of relaxation. The larger towns still employed professors and doctors. Monastic and church libraries began to accumulate.

The techniques of classical culture were also continued with little change, though some things were taken over from the barbarians. (By 325 the wardrobe of a high Roman official in Egypt included breeches.) On the farms the peasants perpetuated from generation to generation their traditional skills. The knowledge of engineering for irrigation and the like was still available when there were funds to employ it. Military techniques had been extended by the increased use of cavalry and missile weapons, although the old Roman training for infantry maneuvers and camp fortification was no more. In the fine arts the chaos of the third century had produced a shortage of skilled craftsmen in the provinces and a consequent breakdown of traditions, particularly in sculpture. Of the resultant untrained work some was brilliant, some merely gauche. The early fourth century saw a vigorous revival of the older skills; thereafter stylization set in and became, by the time of Justinian, grotesque. Some arts, however, particularly those *de grande luxe,* throve on stylization; for patterned silks, cloisonné enamels on gold, carved porphyry, and gold coinage the late empire is unrivaled. In the great villas and imperial churches mosaic decoration glittered as never before. The churches were at first basilicas—elongated barns—but deforestation (to which their erection and the heating of the baths alike contributed) led to increased use of stone vaulting and eventually to the creation of the great domed churches of which Constantinople's St. Sophia (Holy Wisdom), built for Justinian, is the supreme example—the most skillful, daring, breathtaking, magnificent achievement of all ancient architecture.

Classical medicine was perpetuated with an ever increasing dosage of fantastic pharmacopoeia. The elements of classical law were now collected and codified, the codification carried through under Justinian becoming the basis of most modern European legal codes. The pagan tradition of historical writing was continued by many writers and produced in Ammianus Marcellinus the second greatest historian in Latin literature. Of his account of the empire from Nerva to the death of Valens we have only the concluding books beginning with the later years of Constantius, but these tell us what his subject was. They deal with that section of the history in which he himself participated as a high military official and of which his penetrating vision saw the tragedy.

In philosophy the age saw a final revival of pagan scholarship and speculation, on the one hand a great series of commentaries on the works of Plato and Aristotle, on the other, Neoplatonism, a heroic effort to reconcile the classics of pagan literature which everyone officially admired, the ultimate monotheism of Greek philosophy which everyone officially accepted, and the world of demons, magic, and astrology in which everyone actually believed. Plotinus, about 250, the earliest representative of Neoplatonism, was primarily concerned with philosophical thought as a means of ascent from the world to mystical union with "the One." His successors, however, took over his way of salvation and made it a religion. Magical rites and pagan ceremonies served them for sacraments; the Greek classics were their sacred literature, which they rendered innocuous by allegorical exegesis, as the Christians did the Bible. The things they lacked, for competition with Christianity, were a simple story and a simple style capable of appealing to the common man.

Stylistically they were bound by the tradition of classical rhetoric, the principal subject taught in the secondary schools. This rhetoric attempted to teach the students to write in styles elaborated from those of Greek orators seven centuries dead. The resultant compositions were almost incomprehensible to anyone who had not gone through the training. Neoplatonism therefore never stood a chance against the superior rhetoric of the Gospels. But the classical rhetoricians had a firm hold on the professorships in the principal cities; training under them was the first step of a barrister's career. This was a public misfortune, for such training was likely to produce men incapable not only of leadership but even of clear, simple thought and expression. Moreover, it inculcated the ancient beliefs that practical questions, manual labor, manufacturing, and trade are all vulgar, and that dialectic, not experiment, is the way to knowledge. One reason for the decline of the empire was classical education.

All these elements of classical culture—medicine, law, history, philosophy, rhetoric, and education—not only survived into Christian times, but were appropriated by Christianity, thanks, largely, to the conversion of the city councilmen and lower government servants. But the appropriation was superficial. Greek was now almost lost in the west; Latin survived in the east only for those who were going into the upper levels of government or legal interpretation, as distinct from pleading: its use by the central administration ended about 440. In the west there was considerable translation of Greek works into Latin. The Greeks generally did not think Latin works worth translating.

As Christians with classical training increased in number, so did Christian works on classical models. Neoplatonic ontology had its counterpart in the theological speculations as to the Trinity, creation, and incarnation. Commentaries on the philosophic writers and the Homeric poems were matched by commentaries on the Bible using the same methods and reaching much the same conclusions. The rhetorical effusions of the pagans were more than matched by rhetorical Christian sermons. The pagan tradition of historiography was continued by Christian authors like Procopius, who in Justinian's time almost equaled the classical historians—as a scandalmonger. Eusebius of Caesarea wrote the earliest preserved church history and made it, perhaps by laziness, a new type of history, the annotated source book with specification and purportedly exact quotation of the sources. (Classical authors had preferred to rewrite sources in their own style and generally without acknowledgments.) Another element in Eusebius' books, this derived from the Bible, is the intent to demonstrate that human history is the working out of a divine plan. This concern was sharpened after 410 when Christian writers had to answer the pagan argument that Rome had prospered while it worshiped the pagan gods, and fallen when it started to worship Christ. The most successful answer, Augustine's *City of God,* was an elaboration (in twenty-two books) of the position: Who cares about Rome? All that matters is the Church.

Not only did Christianity perpetuate the forms of classical culture, it also extended them to the lower classes within the empire and the barbarians without. By the end of the sixth century the Gospels had been translated into Coptic, Nubian, Ethiopic, Syriac, Sogdian, Armenian, Georgian, Gothic, Thracian, and Latin. In all of these languages except Sogdian, Latin, and perhaps Thracian, the translation was the first written literature; in almost all it was soon followed by translation of other Christian works of classical forms. From these beginnings a considerable number of these languages developed native literatures of at least some classical coloration. Both inside the empire and beyond it, the monasteries not only converted the rustics but educated some of them.

While culture was thus extended to the lower classes, lower-class elements became prominent in the culture. Many of the emperors were men of military training and little cultivation. They surrounded themselves with men of their own type, not only in the high military offices, but also in the legal ones. It is probably in part from the influence of this circle that the law became appallingly brutal. Savage penalties like burning men alive became frequent, tortures atrocious beyond description were commonly used on all but persons of the highest classes, and sometimes even on them. But these changes were too widespread to be explained solely by the influence of the uppermost court circle. Much was probably due to the cumulative effect of the prominence of torture through the centuries in popular entertainment, more to the gradual brutalization of the people by poverty, taxation, and barbarian inroads. To poverty and the pressure of taxation must certainly be attributed much of the vast corruption and oppression at all levels of government.

With these changes are to be associated the fantastic growth of superstition and credulity in all classes. Origen in 250 recognized that the eclipse reported by Matthew as occurring at the time of the crucifixion (the day before a full moon) could not have happened; he concluded that the statement in Matthew was an interpolation. Augustine, 150 years later, said the impossibility of an eclipse proved the occurrence of a miracle. The increase of poverty and economic and governmental pressure led to a decline of mental as well as physical health. This was reflected not only in the terrible tortures, but in the fanaticism and violence of the religious conflicts about incomprehensible formulas, and in the universal atmosphere of suspicion which makes this age seem an example of mass paranoia. Outright insanity seems also to have become more frequent, and many forms of it were commonly understood as the results of demonic possession. Demons were everywhere; every church had a large staff of exorcists, and they were kept busy; rabbis were no less famous than saints for their abilities to command spirits; all philosophers believed in the efficacy of magic, and many considered it the most important branch of philosophy. Reasoning, but reasoning from fantastic premises, increased, while the rationalistic attitude (the most precious legacy of classical Greece), which is largely a matter of common sense in the choice of premises, survived only in books. Medicine was overrun with recipes for amulets.

Even more efficacious than amulets were the relics of holy men, especially martyrs, whose cult had grown up everywhere since the persecutions of the fourth century. Such relics were sovereign against demons; the expulsion of Apollo from Daphne (a suburb of Antioch) by the relics of St. Babylas was world-famous. Beside the relics of martyrs were those of Biblical worthies; these were constantly being "discovered"; the most famous such discovery was that attributed to Helena, Constantine's mother, of "the true cross." Special churches, built to house the most effective relics, became centers of pilgrimage and famous for their miraculous cures. In the pagan world the sick had gone to shrines of Asclepius and Sarapis for similar cures, but now the going, the pilgrimage, became a religious exercise; healthy pilgrims outnumbered the sick, and centers of pilgrimage, especially Jerusalem, were thronged. Holy men, most often monks, were honored no less than martyrs, and this in their lifetimes. Everywhere saints took over the old gods' functions: they sent rain, averted storms and blight, drove away pestilence and enemies, and so on. An oceanic literature recounted their lives and miracles. And most important was the cult of Mary, the all-holy Mother of God.

Even this cloud of protectors was not sufficient to keep away sin. The wide extension of the consciousness of sin was one of the major results of the triumph of Christianity. This consciousness was less an awareness of individual transgressions than a perception of the necessary imperfection of life in the physical and particularly in the social world. "The world [meaning lay society], the flesh, and the devil" were almost three aspects of man's fallen condition, from which Christianity was primarily a means of escape. Escape was salvation. A life lived "in the world" could hardly lead to salvation, and the further a man was involved in the world, the worse his chances. Because of these common assumptions the church was not primarily concerned to provide guidance for government, nor even for life in the world; its concern was to get men out. Men who did live "in the world" accepted the prevailing conception of this world as a vestibule to an eternal life. The quality of that life, whether bliss or torment, would be determined by a man's relation to the church and its all-sufficient sacraments. But for a Christian who survived the sacraments they were only the beginning. Beyond them lay the wilderness of the spiritual life. Even those who physically fled from the world had still the flesh and the devil to cope with. Introspection, hitherto the luxury of a few philosophers, became now a major concern of millions of baptized Christians. And the officially approved orientation of Western man was shifted from the world without to the world within.

Official approval did not, of course, entail universal practice. The peasants continued to be concerned primarily with getting food from the soil. Had they not, the whole society would have collapsed and the religious would have had no leisure for introspection. The hundreds of thousands in the army, the tens of thousands in the civil government, the unnumberable laity who accepted Christianity because it was the best way to get on, all continued their customary mundane concerns. But the new orientation was now represented by an organization even larger than the civil government, and the government officially recognized and supported that organization's claims. From now on, Western history would be one of continuous adjustments between the demands and representatives of the new orientation and of the old. The ancient world was a thing of the past; the Middle Ages had begun.

For Further Reading

Dill, S., *Roman Society in the Last Century of the Western Empire.*
Rand, E., *Founders of the Middle Ages.*
Richmond, I., *Roman Britain.*
Taylor, H., *The Emergence of Christian Culture in the West.*

II

THE WORLD: 500-1500

The Arabs

Asia and Africa

Medieval Europe

Byzantium

The Arabs

22   The Arabs and the Rise of Islam

Beyond the fact that they originated in the Arabian Peninsula, the earliest history of the Arabs is not well established. Indigenous sources exist in the form of legends, although aside from a few inscriptions, nothing in writing has been found. However, the Arabs are mentioned in ancient chronicles of the Persians, Romans, Greeks, Hebrews, and other peoples of the pre-Christian and early Christian era, and important ruins and small artifacts which are still being discovered confirm these early contacts. But it was only with Muhammad's coming and the foundation of Islam in the seventh century A.D. that the history of the Arabs began to be recorded.

The Arabs of pre-Islamic times represented two ethnic groups: those of the south and those of the north. The difference between the two groups reflects the duality of pre-Islamic history and culture as well as geography, for the vast desert of central Arabia created a natural boundary between them. The northerners were primarily nomads; the southerners possessed a more settled, urban civilization.

Whatever their exact geographic origin, the Arabs of the south possessed, by the end of the second millennium B.C., an advanced culture similar to that of Egypt and Mesopotamia. They had a tradition of urban living, a highly developed social organization, a unique system of irrigation, and a relatively advanced technology.

During the 1,700-odd years before the advent of Islam, several kingdoms flourished in this region. The most important of these was the Minaean-Sabean-Himyarite succession of states.

Sometimes one state was dominant; at other times several kingdoms coexisted. The remains of their dams, fortified cities, temples, and castles —some of which still exist—indicate the sophistication and advanced level of their civilization. This civilization was based primarily on agriculture and trade, but much of its wealth came from the production of frank-

CHRONOLOGY

B.C.	853	First reference to the Arabs in an inscription of the Assyrian Shalmaneser III
	900?–A.D. 530	The Minaean-Sabean-Himyarite succession of states in south Arabia
	24	Expedition of Aelius Gallus to south Arabia
A.D.	105–106	Fall of the Nabataean kingdom
	273	Zenobia, Queen of Palmyra, captured by the Emperor Aurelian
	530	Christian Abyssinia's invasion of south Arabia
	570?	Birth of Muhammad in Mecca
	575	Persian occupation of south Arabia
	602	Fall of the Lakhmids, Arab vassals of Sassanid Persia
	608	Building of the Kaaba in Mecca as the main shrine in pagan Arabia
	622	Hijra (migration) of Muhammad from Mecca to Medina—beginning of the Islamic era
	624	Muslims defeat the Meccans at the Battle of Badr
	630	Mecca is conquered by Muhammad and becomes the spiritual center of Islam
	632	Death of Muhammad; succession of Abu Bakr as the first caliph
	633–637	Arabs conquer Syria and Iraq
	634	Death of Abu Bakr; succession of Umar
	639–642	Arabs conquer Egypt
	640–643	Arabs conquer Persia
	644	Murder of Umar; succession of Uthman
	656	Murder of U'hman; succession of Ali, first civil war in Islam
	657–659	Battle of Siffin; arbitration between Ali and Mu'awiya; the Kharijites
	661	Murder of Ali; succession of Mu'awiya; accession of the Umayyads with Damascus as the capital

incense and myrrh. In the ancient world these substances were as precious as gold and could be compared in importance to oil in the economy of the Middle East today. Both are gum resins extracted from trees that grow only in southern Arabia and Somalia. A complex organization was developed for producing and distributing these commodities, which not only enriched the Arabs but also brought them into contact with the peoples living in the lands bordering the Mediterranean Sea and the Indian Ocean.

From what we can learn from surviving inscriptions, intellectual life did not match commercial and agricultural and artistic achievements. It seems to have concentrated almost exclusively on formulating a legal code for the regulation of property relationships.

One of the south Arabian tribes, the Minaeans (who flourished in fertile northern Yemen between the eighth and third centuries B.C.), had camel caravans that traveled as far north as Memphis in Egypt and as far west as the Atlantic coastline of Africa. They also engaged in trade with Delos, in Greece.

The Sabeans eventually absorbed the Minaeans and other principalities and created a kingdom based on a feudal system of aristocratic families that prevented the rise of any strong, centralized system of government. In Western culture the Sabeans are commonly regarded as the symbol of ancient Arab civilization. The Old Testament narrative of Bilkis, the Queen of Sheba (Sabea), and her journey from Marib—the capital of Sabea—to visit Solomon, is one of the best-known stories of the Bible and an oft-repeated theme in Western art.

The Sabeans in turn were gradually taken over by the neighboring Himyarites. During the Hellenistic era, the Himyarites lost their chief source of prosperity when part of the Indian trade was diverted to Egypt, but in 24 B.C. they still had the strength to escape Roman domination by repulsing Aelius Gallus, the general sent by Augustus Caesar to conquer the area.

In the first few centuries A.D., Christianity came to Arabia. Judaism already had a foothold, and by A.D. 525, Judaism had gained such an influence in the Himyarite kingdom that the rulers themselves were converted and began to persecute the Christian population. This persecution, together with prodding from Byzantium—which wanted to strike a blow at its ancient adversary, Persia—led to Christian Abyssinia's invasion of south Arabia in A.D. 530. The Abyssinian governor, Abraha, conquered south Arabia, then tried to move northward, but he failed to advance beyond Mecca. Forty years later (575), his son and second successor lost south Arabia to Chosroes I, a Persian king of the Sassanid dynasty, and south Arabia remained a Persian province until the invasion of the Muslims.

Because of their pivotal geographic location between the Far East and India on the one hand, and the Mediterranean and western Europe on the other, the Himyarites had been able to control important trade routes over which passed the fabled frankincense and myrrh as well as rare woods from south Arabia and exotic products from India and China on their way to the West.

One route from southwestern Arabia toward Syria ran through the Hijaz, with stops at Mecca and Medina, to Transjordan and Palestine. A western branch led to the Mediterranean, an eastern one to Damascus, Homs, Hama, and Aleppo. Another, chiefly concerned with Indian trade, went through the Persian Gulf, up the Euphrates, then westward through Syria to the Mediterranean.

These two main routes were instrumental in shaping the character of two Arab states in the north: the Nabataean kingdom at Petra ("the rose-red city, half as old as time") lay on the former route, the kingdom of Palmyra on the latter. These states, unlike the isolated kingdoms of the South, gravitated into the Hellenistic and Roman orbits. Although their peoples were unmistakably of Arab origin, their culture was strongly in-

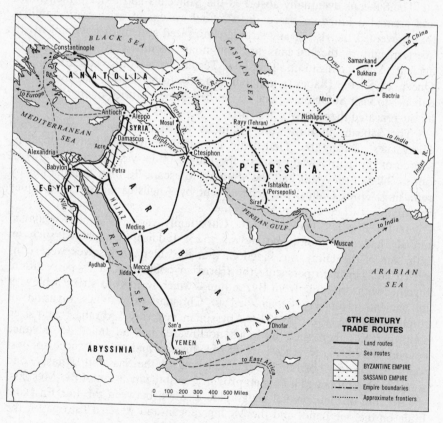

fluenced by the Aramaic and Hellenistic civilizations, a fact confirmed by the impressive architectural ruins at Palmyra and Petra, by inscriptions on artifacts and coins, and by a study of their cults, which are of classical origin.

The Nabataean kingdom flourished from the fifth century B.C. and controlled an area extending from the Gulf of Aqaba to the Dead Sea, including a part of northern Hijaz. It lost its independence in the first century B.C. when it became a vassal of Rome, and it was absorbed into the Roman Empire in A.D. 105 when Trajan created *Provincia Arabia* with its capital at Petra.

The history of the kingdom of Palmyra, equally Aramaicized and Hellenized, and its relations with the Roman Empire is more dramatic. Situated in a fertile oasis, Palmyra controlled the caravan routes between the Euphrates and Syria. Its principal economic activities revolved around commerce and banking, but the archers of Palmyra became famous mercenaries. In the long duel between Rome and the Parthians, Palmyra sided with Rome and prospered accordingly. A pseudo-Roman city of temples and forums whose ruins still rise dramatically out of the desert was the result. In 260 Odenathus founded a ruling dynasty and asserted his independence from Rome. His widow Zenobia ruled after his death as regent for their son, but in 273 the Roman emperor reconquered Palmyra and destroyed the queen's glorious dreams of continued independence. Zenobia was captured, bound in chains of gold, and taken to Rome. She ended her days at a villa in Tivoli while her distant city abruptly fell, like Petra, into decline.

Poetry is the principal source of information on the material and spiritual life of the Bedouins and other Arabs. As they put it, their poetry was "the archive of their triumphs, the depository of their memories." Pre-Islamic poetry is an authentic and vivid product of this pagan era, of the nomadic, seminomadic, and sedentary Arabs of the north and central peninsula. The tribal prince-poet Imrul-Kais (d. 540) was a central figure among the Bedouin poets; he attracted many other poets to his circle and helped establish the classical Arabic tongue. The *Seven Odes,* an early collection of poems, gives a vivid if romanticized picture of desert life and sets the pattern for the ode form in Arabic literature.

Between the third and sixth centuries of the Christian era, the power of Rome waned in the north, as did the prosperity of the urbanized Yemenite states in the south. During this period the relations between these sedentary settlements of the Arab world and its nomads underwent a profound change. The civilized settlements of the south fell into decay, and the pastoral nomad once more replaced the peasant and the townsman.

The reasons for the resurgence of the nomads are cloudy, but they swallowed up whole settled communities and spread out not only over the entire peninsula but even beyond it to the borders of Byzantium.

The life of the desert can be reconstructed from Arabic sources. Although these are of a much later date, they reflect a reality which has remained unaltered for centuries—silhouetted against an unchanging, inscrutable landscape. Although there were a few stable settlements in the interior of the peninsula, such as Mecca and Medina, and some Jewish agricultural colonies in the northern Hijaz, they were tiny islands in a sea of steppe, rock, and shifting sand, and the majority of the people were Bedouins roaming over the desert in a monotonous seasonal pattern in search of pasturage. The Bedouin, with his camels, his tents, and his fierce tribal independence, was of ancient Semitic stock. He worshiped spirits dwelling in trees, streams, and stones. Social organization pivoted around the tribe. The foundation of Bedouin life was unswerving tribal loyalty which was based on collective responsibility, the protection of the individual and the guest against outside threats, and enforced when necessary with implacable vengeance.

The sheik, or sayyid, was the elected head of the tribe, chosen by the elders. His authority and prestige were mainly of a moral character. He was first among equals—*primus inter pares*. Usually he led the tribe in battle, acted as conciliator when peace was restored, and mediated tribal blood feuds. Leaving the tribe without assurance of alternative allegiance was to invite death, for to survive in the desert alone was impossible. Nevertheless the Bedouin turned away from every social organization that went beyond the orbit of his own tribal group.

The raid was a recognized outlet for aggressions and material gain and an almost everyday occurrence in the relations between tribes. The long, bloody, seemingly endless wars of pre-Islamic pagan Arabia sprang out of either raids or personal blood feuds which, because of the code of tribal solidarity and collective responsibility, involved whole tribes. Occasional truces were declared for religious holidays and fairs.

Both Byzantium and Persia tried to protect themselves against the barbaric tide by supporting new Arab buffer states on their frontiers. On the Byzantine border there were the seminomadic Ghassanids, vassals of Byzantium, while the Lakhmids served as satellites of the Persian Sassanids. These buffer states represent the transition from the civilized, settled life of Syria and Mesopotamia to the pure nomadism of the Syro-Arab desert and of central Arabia. Through them, foreign customs and ideas filtered into the world of the nomads, breaking up its monotony and softening its austerity.

The Ghassanids and the Lakhmids were enemies and, like their patrons, constantly hoped to exterminate each other. Their wars and the personalities and careers of their rulers live on in the colorful songs of the Bedouin poets.

Muhammad, the man destined to be the Prophet of a new world religion as well as the spiritual and temporal leader of his peoples, was born in Mecca between A.D. 570 and 580. (Information about his early life and religious training is sparse and unreliable.) He came from a respectable but minor branch of the powerful Quraysh tribe. His father Abdallah died before his birth, his mother when he was only six. The orphan was raised first by his grandfather, Abd al-Muttalib, and then by his uncle, Abu Talib. During this period the family lived in humble circumstances, but Muhammad achieved wealth and position at the age of twenty-five by an advantageous marriage to the wealthy widow, Khadija, who was fifteen years his senior. Her money provided him with the ease and independence needed to investigate and appraise the religious situation in Arabia.

The strong monotheism, the theory of revelation, and the Biblical element in the Koran all suggest that Muhammad was exposed to both Christian and Jewish influences. However, his versions of Biblical stories indicate that they were indirectly acquired—most likely from Jewish and Christian traders and travelers whose religious knowledge was sketchy and apocryphal. That he was influenced by the *hanīfs,* native holy men dissatisfied with Arabian paganism, is also possible.

What compelled Muhammad to undertake his world-shaking career will always remain shrouded in mystery. What is clear is that he was disturbed and disgusted by the idolatry of his contemporaries and their lack of devotion to Allah, the true God. He was painfully aware that the disciplined religious life of the Jews and Christians about him contrasted sharply with the materialistic paganism of his compatriots. Time and again he withdrew to a cave under Mount Hira, near Mecca, for meditation and prayer. Here many insights came to him "like the breaking of the dawn."

According to tradition, Muhammad's Call, the legendary revelation of Allah, came suddenly and dramatically in 611, when he was about forty years old. Descriptions in the Koran, as well as a number of traditional stories, suggest that the Call was a flash of divine insight delivered by the angel Gabriel. Muhammad had no idea then of founding a new religion. His ambitions were of a more modest kind; he hoped to bring to his people a unified Arab revelation similar to that of the Christians and Jews. The early chapters of the Koran are brief and evangelistic, dealing mainly with the unity of God, the wickedness of idolatry and materialism, and the imminence of divine judgment.

At first, few answered the Call, and those who did were of humble position. Muhammad's few influential supporters, in addition to his wife, were his powerful friends Abu Bakr and Umar, and his sons-in-law Uthman and Ali, who succeeded him as the four "rightly guided" caliphs. Apart from this intimate circle, few were interested in his message of reform. However, as Muhammad became more confident in the importance of his mission he openly attacked the prevailing paganism and its leaders. Naturally this antagonized the powerful merchants who controlled Meccan society; they feared that his reforms would deprive Mecca of its unique and profitable position as a center of both pilgrimage and trade. Their opposition gradually turned to persecution, and some of his followers fled to Coptic Christian Abyssinia where they found asylum under the ruling Negus. The support of his powerful relatives enabled Muhammad to maintain a foothold in Mecca, but he experienced one setback after another. First his wife died; then the sympathetic patriarch of his clan, whose successor was hostile to him. Muhammad's lack of success in Mecca, coupled with his abortive attempt to spread his message in Ta'if, led him to search for a new, more promising horizon. He found it at Yathrib (or Medina), a city 250 miles northeast of Mecca that had originally been settled by Jewish tribes.

Medina was a sophisticated city; it attracted many pagan Arabs who eventually outnumbered its Jewish founders. It had no stable government but was constantly torn by feuds between the rival Arab tribes of the Aus and Khazraj, with the Jews often controlling the balance of power. After prolonged negotiations Muhammad finally agreed to his famous *Hijra* (migration) to Medina in 622, a date which marks the beginning of the Islamic calendar. The Medinese saw in him a man of power, discipline, and spirit who could serve as an arbitrator and conciliator rather than a religious leader. Unlike the Meccans, they had few strong religious convictions. Muhammad had some followers in Mecca, but the majority played a waiting game. They would accept the religious aspect of Islam provided it satisfied their political and economic needs.

This move of Muhammad and his followers to Medina proved to be a pivotal one for the whole development of Islam. Once in Medina, Muhammad's revelations changed in character; they became less prophetic and religious and more regulatory and secular. Islam, the religion and church, became a community and a state, with Muhammad as the lawgiver, the supreme judge, the commander in chief, and the ruler.

Once Islamic power was thus centralized, Muhammad concentrated on the conquest of his native city, Mecca. Here, his abilities as a leader came to the fore. His forces brilliantly defeated the Meccans in the Battle of Badr (624), and gained control of the vital caravan routes to the north. Badr was Islam's first ordeal by battle, and its cause was greatly strength-

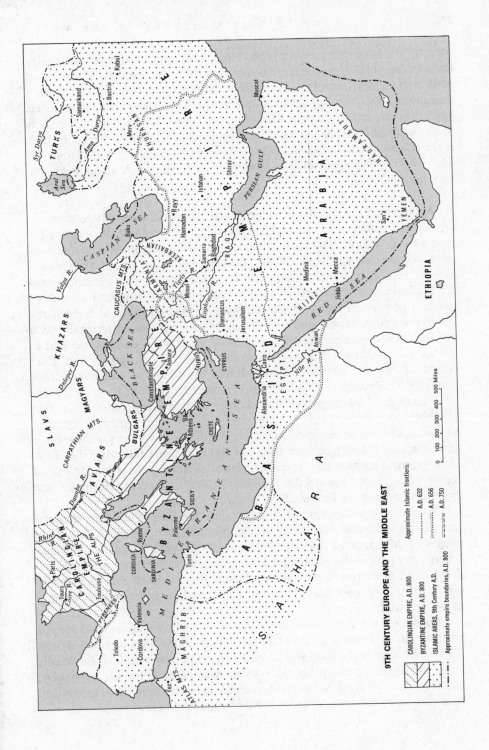

9TH CENTURY EUROPE AND THE MIDDLE EAST

CAROLINGIAN EMPIRE, A.D. 800

BYZANTINE EMPIRE, A.D. 800

ISLAMIC AREAS, 9th Century A.D.

Approximate empire boundaries, A.D. 800

Approximate Islamic frontiers:

A.D. 632

A.D. 656

A.D. 750

0   100 200 300 400 500 Miles

ened by the overwhelming triumph. The victory was considered prophetic; the Meccan infidels had been defeated by Allah himself in the person of Muhammad and his followers. In 630, Muhammad entered Mecca as a conqueror—the victory achieved more through negotiation than force. Thus Muhammad's success was complete. The Kaaba and other holy places were now in Islamic hands and purified of paganism. Religious faith replaced old tribal blood ties. Opposition was practically wiped out. By 632, when Muhammad died, almost the whole of the Arabian Peninsula had embraced Islam.

Muhammad's sudden death threatened the dissolution of the community he had struggled to create. First there was the problem of selecting his successor, or caliph. This task threatened to disrupt political and religious unity and precipitated some of the bloodiest battles in Islam. Muhammad had left no heir or clearly designated successor; in fact he had undermined the traditional tribal system of government by taking temporal as well as spiritual power into his own hands. Since he had proclaimed himself the last of the Prophets and said that his unique mission would terminate with his death, there was no need for a spiritual successor, but someone had to fill his role as head of state, commander in chief, lawgiver, and chief justice. During the confusion that followed his death, several rival parties arose, each claiming priority in the appointment of a caliph.

The original Meccan converts, those who had emigrated with him to Medina, based their claim on belonging to the Prophet's tribe of Quraysh and being the first to embrace Islam. His Medinese supporters, on the other hand, claimed priority because they had supported him following the Hijra. Both groups, comprising the most influential among the Companions of the Prophet, leaned toward the traditional tribal method of selecting a new chief from among the best qualified of their number.

A third group, the legitimists, advocating the idea of a divine designation as opposed to the traditional elective principle, supported Ali, a paternal cousin of Muhammad and the husband of his only surviving daughter. Lastly, there were the influential Umayyads; the aristocrats of Mecca although the most recent converts to Islam, they claimed that their traditional position of leadership, based on power and position, entitled them to name the caliph.

An open breach between these diverse elements was avoided by the swift action of a small group of senior Companions who nominated Abu Bakr as Muhammad's successor. Abu Bakr, an unprepossessing, but kindly man, slightly stooped by his sixty years, was revered for his gentleness, humility, and piety. His selection seemed most appropriate, for he had been chosen by the dying Prophet to lead the faithful in prayer.

Muhammad's death created other problems. It acted as a signal for revolt to many of the outlying tribes in central and eastern Arabia whose conversion to Islam had been at best lukewarm. The disciplined yoke of Islam threatened their nomadic independence, and they were grateful for the opportunity to throw it off.

Abu Bakr's awesome task was not only to be an effective religious leader, but also to solidify the shaky unity of the Islamic community. He was remarkably successful. In his short reign of two years, this meek man consolidated the diverse components of Islam and launched the Arabs on their path of conquest. Before his death in 634, Syria, Iraq, the southern provinces of Persia, and the Byzantine empire had all fallen to the Arab conquerors.

To avoid difficulties, Abu Bakr had wisely appointed Umar to succeed him, and the nomination was unanimously accepted. The reign of Umar (634–644) saw the further expansion of the Arab empire. What began as typical Arab raids for booty into Iraq and Syria developed into campaigns of permanent conquest. The small Arab detachments, really mere raiding parties, were led by able commanders (Khalid ibn al-Walid being one of the best known) and struck with lightning swiftness deep into the surrounding countries. They met little effective resistance. One battle after another was won by the seemingly unconquerable Arab armies, brilliantly using the desert as their ally. In the north the Arabs entered Damascus in 635. Then after the decisive battle of Yarmuk (636) the Byzantine emperor Heraclius abandoned Syria. Jerusalem fell in 637. In the east the Arabs won even more spectacular victories against the Persian empire. After the battle of Qadisiya (637), they conquered the whole of Iraq. The battles at Nihawand (641) and Isfahan (643) finally broke Persian power, and the empire fell into Arab hands. In Egypt the pattern was the same: an Arab army under Amr ibn al-Ass struck in 639. By 642 all of Egypt was under Arab domination.

Thus in a single decade a host of highly organized, sophisticated, and settled societies found themselves conquered by migratory Arab tribesmen. The Persian empire which had existed for centuries was no more, and mighty Byzantium was forced back to the Taurus Mountains in Asia Minor.

What contributed to these spectacular Arab conquests? The inspiration of Islam was of primary importance: it provided the Arabs, for the first time, with a cohesive centralizing force and the dramatic reality of a new and vital religion. The Muslims believed that divine intercession enabled them to scatter the armies of the infidels. The wars of conquests, moreover, provided opportunities for heroism and booty which the Arabs traditionally relished, and which they now pursued in the name of Islam, with missionary zeal. What had begun as a triumph of force soon became a religious and spiritual crusade—a holy war (jihad). Everywhere the Islamic conquerors gained converts as well as territory.

For the conquered peoples, the task of shifting from old to new rulers was not difficult. Most of them had long been alienated by cruel and corrupt Persian and Byzantine bureaucratic administrations. Moreover, in Egypt and Syria the Christian population was strongly opposed to the centralizing and Hellenizing tendencies of the Byzantine bureaucracy and the Orthodox Church. Umar's organizational abilities also contributed greatly to the Arabs' success. He regularized the legal position of the millions of non-Muslim subjects in his domain and set up an efficient administrative system for the empire. Muhammad had established the precedent of "tolerance" for the "People of the Book," the Jewish and Christian communities in the northern Hijaz. Umar left these communities undisturbed except for the payment of an annual tribute in the form of poll tax (jizya); indeed, he extended the principle of toleration to cover not only all Christians and Jews in the empire, but also the Zoroastrians of Persia. Non-Muslim groups formed their own self-administered communities, lived under their own civil codes, and were governed by their own religious leaders. This system prevailed throughout Islam until the end of the Ottoman period and still exists in a restricted way in parts of the Middle East that have not yet been thoroughly secularized. European Christians claimed that the Muslims gave unbelievers, mainly Christian and Jews, the choice of conversion to Islam or death by the sword, but this was not the case. From a practical point of view, mass conversions to Islam would have meant abandoning the jizya, a considerable source of revenue.

The Muslim conquerors, however, sought to maintain their identity as a separate ruling class. Overall authority in the conquered provinces was established by the appointment of military commanders as governors. Arab garrisons maintained order throughout the empire. Individual Arabs in the newly won territories were forbidden to acquire land outside Arabia proper and were discouraged from mixing with the local populace. Yet while the Arabs held the ultimate power, they wisely left civil control in the hands of their non-Muslim subjects—the Hellenized Christians and Persians experienced in local government.

Umar, whose piety, sense of justice, and puritanical simplicity are proverbial, was responsible for laying the foundations of the empire. In 644 he was assassinated by a discontented Persian slave as he was praying in a mosque in Medina. Uthman, a son-in-law of Muhammad, and a member of the influential Umayyad family of the Meccan tribe of Quraysh, was then elected caliph. Although noted for his mild manner, piety, and closeness to the Prophet, Uthman turned out to be a somewhat irresolute ruler and was accused of appointing his kinsmen to leading positions in the empire. Some, however, were able generals and governors who carried the banner of Islam north into Asia Minor and Byzantium, and on the eastern front, into Bactria, Kabul, and Ghazni.

The problem of Islamic society at this time was the impact of the Empire upon it. The earliest Muslims were now wealthy notables. A second urban generation was in the making, raised amid the amusements and the luxuries of Alexandria, Damascus, Ctesiphon, and the camp cities of Basra and Kufa. Also, politics, power, and prestige had become ends in themselves, and Uthman was too weak to halt the trend. The legitimists in Kufa, being pietists and theocrats, raised the banner of revolt first. Then in 656, a party of regicides from the army in Egypt came to Medina to present Uthman with grievances concerning his misrule. Uthman, though conciliatory on the surface, was basically adamant. A long siege of his quarters ensued, in which attempts to persuade him to abdicate were made. Upon discovering that Uthman was stalling only to allow the Syrian troops he had secretly sought from Mu'awiya, the Umayyad governor of Syria, to arrive in Medina to defend him, the regicides stormed his palace. They murdered him as he sat, resigned to his fate, reading the Koran. The first blow was dealt by Abdallah, son of Abu Bakr, the first caliph. This murder of a caliph by a fellow Muslim was the first direct challenge to the moral and religious authority of the caliphate as a bond of unity in Islam.

Ali was immediately elected as Uthman's successor. An esteemed and pious Muslim, a tragic-noble hero, Ali, the cousin and son-in-law of Muhammad and his male next of kin, had many virtues as warrior, counselor, and friend. But he lacked the talents necessary to govern a divided and restive state, being both indecisive and inflexible, as well as lacking in energy and foresight.

Opposition to Ali began in Mecca headed by Aisha, the widow of the Prophet, who hated him, and by Talha and Zubair, who had been the Prophet's Companions, and who had their own eyes on the caliphate. They had previously been enemies of Uthman and had formed the real centers of opposition to him in Medina even prior to the advent of the Egyptian regicides. Now, with complete disregard of their previous role in the events leading to the murder, they defiantly withdrew to Mecca, withheld their recognition of Ali, and demanded the punishment of the guilty. Ali bore no direct responsibility for the crime, but the opposition insisted that by failing to use his prestige and standing more effectively to protect Uthman, and by failing to punish the regicides after his accession, he had implicated himself in the murder. Soon afterward, a pro-Uthman party developed around the opposition, crying for war and vengeance. After gathering their forces in Mecca, Aisha, Talha, and Zubair moved to Basra in search of local support.

In October, 656, Ali moved against them and left Medina at the head of his army—never to return there again. And from that day to the present, Medina ceased to be the capital of the Islamic empire. The encounter which followed became known as the "Battle of the Camel" after the camel Aisha rode as she urged her supporters to fight on. This first battle of Muslim against Muslim ended in victory for Ali, but not before many illustrious Companions including Talha and Zubair had lost their lives. Aisha, "the Mother of the Faithful," was captured but was permitted to return to Medina, where she lived in obscurity the rest of her life.

Ali, realizing his unpopularity in Basra, made nearby Kufa his capital. His position as caliph appeared secure, but in reality his authority was constantly being challenged, both by tribal insubordination and by conflicting councils of pietists and theocrats in his own camp.

As for the rest of the empire, Ali was generally recognized as the new caliph. The new governors he had appointed were accepted everywhere but in Syria, where Mu'awiya, the able Umayyad governor, forcibly refused to resign. Mu'awiya withheld his fealty and accused Ali of condoning the regicides. Ali led an army and met the Syrian forces at Siffin by the Euphrates in 657. When the battle went against them, the Syrians dramatically raised copies of the Koran on the point of their lances and appealed for arbitration. The arbitration which followed in 659 was unsuccessful, for it ended in a stalemate—Mu'awiya refusing to recognize Ali as caliph, and Ali neither abdicating nor accepting Mu'awiya as governor of Syria. But the arbitration was, in effect, a moral victory for Mu'awiya, reducing Ali's status as sole caliph to that of a pretender. Moreover, the arbitration brought forth other difficulties for Ali. After the "Battle of the Camel," where many Meccan and Medinese supporters had perished, Ali was left at the mercy of his soldiers—the anarchic and undisciplined nomadic Arabs. An important group among them, known as the Kharijites (seceders), revolted in protest against his willingness to arbitrate. The Kharijites, the oldest religious sect of Islam, were subdued by Ali in 659, but they continued to reappear as puritanical, militant movements throughout the later history of Islam.

Ali, weakened by the Kharijite revolt and declining morale among his supporters, was assassinated in 661 in Kufa by a Kharijite. Hasan, his eldest son, was proclaimed caliph in Kufa while Mu'awiya was recognized in Damascus. A few months later, Hasan reached an agreement with Mu'awiya. He retired on a royal pension to the pleasures of his harem in Medina, and Mu'awiya was then proclaimed the sole caliph of the empire at Jerusalem in 661, with Damascus as his capital. As the center of state shifted from Medina, to Kufa, to Damascus, and the leadership of the community changed from the Companions of the Prophet to the Umayyads, a new era was born.

For Further Reading

Andrae, Tor, *Mohammed, the Man and His Faith.*
Arberry, A. J., *The Koran Interpreted.*
Gibb, H. A. R., *Mohammedanism.*
Hitti, P. K., *History of the Arabs.*
Lewis, Bernard, *The Arabs in History.*
Watt, W. M., *Muhammed: Prophet and Statesman.*

23   The Disruption and Decline of the Arab Empire

Mu'awiya's problem during his nineteen-year reign was to reunite the demoralized and decentralized empire in order to ensure its continuity and cohesion. His answer was not to rejuvenate the ideal Islamic theocracy of Medina, but to create a centralized Arab kingdom, based on Arab dominance in the empire. In Syria, Mu'awiya ruled as an Arab sheik, the first among equals, his authority as caliph being more on a moral than a religious basis, depending on the consent and loyalty of the dominant Arab element in the empire. Arab participation in government was made effective through two loosely organized consultative bodies of notables, the *shūrā,* the council of sheiks with important executive powers, and the *wufūd,* representing the tribes. Mu'awiya rarely resorted to force; skillfully managing the empire on a purely personal basis, he relied on his power of persuasion to "make friends and influence people."

Elsewhere Mu'awiya ruled through energetic, capable, and forceful provincial governors such as Ziyad, the governor of Iraq, who maintained strong discipline over that turbulent and rebellious province. But while Mu'awiya himself ruled as an Arab sheik, his successors became increasingly autocratic, relying on the Syrian army to control the empire. Mu'awiya also established a tradition of excellence in administration, more Byzantine than Arab in character. The governing procedures of the East Roman Empire current in Syria were followed, and the old administrative system, together with its local Christian personnel, was employed. The troublesome problem of the succession, which had been decided in the past either by controversial election or by civil war, was regulated by Mu'awiya five years before his death. Simple hereditary succession was too alien to the Arab mind to be readily acceptable unmodified, so Mu'awiya, with

680	Death of Mu'awiya; succession of his son, Yazid; massacre of Husayn and Alids at Karbala
685–687	Shi'ite revolt in Iraq; beginning of Shi'ite extremism
710–711	Muslims invade Spain and the Indus Valley
717	Initiation of internal reforms by Umar II
732	Muslim forces halted near Poitiers by Charles Martel
750	Abbas defeats Marwan II; fall of the Umayyads; accession of the Abbasids
754	Death of Abbas; succession of Mansur
756	The Umayyad Abd al-Rahman founds the independent Emirate of Cordova
762–763	Mansur founds Baghdad as the new capital
786	Accession of Harun al-Rashid; Abbasid courtly life at its best
788	Morocco becomes independent under the Idrisid dynasty
799–800	Independent Aghlabid dynasty in Tunisia
803	Harun deposes the Barmecids, the family of Abbasid viziers
809–813	Civil war between Amin and Ma'mun
813–833	Reign of Ma'mun
825	Aghlabids start conquest of Sicily
833–842	Reign of Mu'tasim; beginning of domination by Turkish bodyguards
865–905	The Tulunid dynasty in Egypt and Syria
871	Rise of the Saffarids in Persia
892	Baghdad again becomes the capital
890–906	Appearance of the Carmathians in Iraq and Syria
910	Establishment of the Shi'ite Fatimid caliphate in North Africa
929	Abd al-Rahman III, emir of Cordova, adopts title of caliph
932	Shi'ite Buwaihid dynasty founded in Persia
935–969	Ikhshidis rule Egypt
945	The Buwaihids occupy Baghdad and control the Abbasid caliph

969	Fatimids conquer Egypt and build Cairo, as the capital
970	Seljuk Turks enter Persia
1030	Breakup of the Umayyad caliphate of Spain into small kingdoms
1055	Seljuks seize control of Baghdad
1061	Normans initiate their conquest of Sicily
1070–1080	Seljuks capture Syria and Palestine
1071	Battle of Manzikert; Seljuks capture Asia Minor from the Byzantines
1085	Christians seize Toledo and begin reconquest of Spain
1096	Crusaders arrive at Constantinople and advance in the Near East
1099	Crusaders capture Jerusalem
1127	Zangi, a Seljuk officer, captures Mosul; beginning of Muslim reaction against Crusaders
1171	Saladin overthrows Fatimids, reestablishes orthodoxy, and founds Ayyubid dynasty in Syria and Egypt
1187	Saladin defeats Crusaders at Hittin and captures Jerusalem
1221	Mongols ravage Persia
1236	Christians take Cordova
1250–1260	Rise of the Mamluk sultanate in Egypt and Syria
1258	Mongols under Hulagu Khan capture Baghdad, ending the Abbasid caliphate
1260	Mamluks stop the Mongols in Palestine
1379–1401	Tamerlane ravages Persia, Iraq, and Syria
1453	The Ottoman Turks capture Constantinople from the Byzantines
1492	Christians capture Granada; Ferdinand and Isabella expel Muslims and Jews
1498	Vasco da Gama discovers the route to India around the Cape of Good Hope
1517	Ottomans destroy the Mamluks and conquer Syria and Egypt
1639	Ottomans seize Iraq from Persia

characteristic diplomacy, found a compromise. He made succession hereditary but subject to the consent of the tribal parliamentary system he had
previously devised. Together with the *shūrā* of Damascus he nominated
Yazid, his son, and the nomination was confirmed by the *wufūd* speaking
for the various tribes. The compromise, though declared a heretical innovation by the Muslim aristocracy in Medina, tended to make the position
of caliph hereditary, and overtly established the Umayyad empire which
lasted until 750.

The Umayyads produced able rulers who departed from the path set up
by their pious predecessors. They emphasized the political and economic
aspects of government and ruled more like kings than religious leaders.
Historians writing during the succeeding dynasties depicted them as plea-
sure-loving, worldly usurpers who, except for Umar II (717–720), were
not fit to be called caliphs. It is true that most of the Umayyads relegated
religion to a secondary place and in their private lives enjoyed the material
benefits of their empire. Nevertheless, despite their worldliness, they always
posed as the true champions of Islam. Military expansion was energetically
resumed and conquests were carried forward into new lands. Within a
hundred years the Islamic empire reached its geographic limits. In the East,
they conquered Transoxania, Baluchistan, and Sind; and Muslim rule became permanent along the Indus. In the West, they swept over North
Africa, and crossed the Straits of Gibraltar into Spain, where an Arab-
Berber (Moorish) culture developed over eight centuries, leaving a lasting
mark on both Spain and Islam. The wave of conquest in the West carried
into the lands of the Franks, but was checked by Charles Martel, at the
Battle of Tours (732), only a hundred miles from Paris. In Asia Minor
Arab armies conducted repeated campaigns against the Byzantine empire.
In one assault, Arab soldiers reached Chalcedon, across the Bosphorous
from Constantinople. In another, during the reign of Suleiman (715–717),
Arab armies laid siege to the city for fourteen months. But the fortifications of the capital proved impenetrable. Only seven centuries later, with
the aid of gunpowder, were the Muslims under the Ottoman Turks able to
capture the city.

While vastly increasing the territory of the empire, this second era of
expansion caused acute economic and fiscal problems. The treasury depended on the state's share of the booty, the poll tax and a land tax
(*kharaj*). The Arabs were in a more advantageous position. They paid no
taxes (except for a small religious tax, *zakāt*, to support the needy), and
were in fact enrolled in the imperial registry (*dīwān*), each receiving a
regular payment from the state treasury. Umayyad fiscal difficulties started
when their subjects adopted Islam in increasing numbers and stopped paying taxes. To treat all the faithful equally, Umar II (717–720) freed all

Muslims, irrespective of origin, from the poll and land tax. This, together with the loss of booty from conquests, upset the fiscal system. The disastrous effects on the treasury forced the caliph Hisham (724–743) to stress that: "Although poll taxes fell off upon conversion to Islam, land taxes did not." This measure later became the model for taxation policy in Islam. It was opposed by non-Arabs, who considered it unfair to non-Muslim landowners. Discontent with the land tax led to widespread alienation, even active opposition.

As rulers and subjects coalesced to form a civilization, four social classes emerged. At the top were the ruling Arabs, who lived in garrison cities. Beneath them were the non-Arab Muslims, whose conversion to Islam was so rapid that by the eighth century they far outnumbered their rulers. Although better educated, they were rarely accepted socially and had to attach themselves to an Arab family or tribe as clients (*mawālī*). In the West, the *mawālī* became Arabicized. But in the East the Arabs were ultimately absorbed by their subjects, and while Islam remained the dominant religion, Iranian, Turkish, Berber, and Indian characteristics prevailed. The non-Muslim subjects, "the People of the Book" (*dhimmīs*) —Christians, Jews, and later, Zoroastrians, pagan Berbers, Hindus, and others—were classified as second-class subjects. They enjoyed freedom of worship and lived according to their own laws, with limited rights in civil matters. At the bottom of the social ladder were the slaves, Greeks, Turks, Armenians, Kurds, Spaniards, Berbers, and Negroes. Islam, while declaring "manumission as pleasing in the sight of God," accepted slavery. This institution left its mark on Islamic society more than in the West—economically, through the profitable slave trade, socially through the institution of concubinage and the harem, and politically as individual slaves gained power as favorites, bodyguards, and rulers.

The Umayyads were responsible for the Arabization of the state and the development of a distinctive Arab culture. Trained Arab government personnel were lacking in the early period, so the Umayyads relied on local talent. These kept records in Greek or Persian. As the Islamic state attained maturity, significant reforms were carried out to nationalize it. As qualified Arabs became available, they replaced the former Greek and Persian officials. By the end of the Umayyad period, government records were being kept in Arabic, and Arabic had become the official language of the empire. When the Umayyads rose to power, Byzantine and Sassanid currency were in wide circulation. The Umayyads adopted this currency as media of exchange, sometimes after stamping the old coins with a Koranic inscription. But Abd al-Malik (685–705) introduced Arab Muslim coins with the same value as the old.

Anxious to maintain their dominance in the empire, and to preserve their ancient heritage, the Arabs remained proud of their past, their language and lineage. But during the Umayyad period, they became exposed to the influences of more sophisticated civilizations. And despite the political instability of mid- and late-Umayyad times, the beginning of a great intellectual awakening, which came into full bloom in the Abbasid period, was in the making.

Internal weakness and dissension, sharpened by the economic and social injustices perpetrated under their rule, finally led to the downfall of the Umayyads. Large groups among the *mawālī* and Arabs, disenchanted with Umayyad policies and jealous of Umayyad dominance, joined anti-Umayyad parties, such as the puritanical, militant Kharijites, who flourished in Iraq, Iran, and Khurasan, and the Shi'ites, formerly the legitimists, who condemned the Umayyads as usurpers and considered Ali and his descendants as the only legitimate heirs to the caliphate.

The Shi'ite opposition to the Umayyads started when Ali was murdered and his younger son, Husayn, became the head of the Alid house. While Mu'awiya reigned, Husayn made no claims to the caliphate. But when Mu'awiya died (680), he set out for Kufa at the head of a small band of supporters, primarily from the families of Companions, in expectation of local support for his bid to the caliphate. On the way, he was surrounded at Karbala by troops of Mu'awiya's son Yazid, who had been proclaimed caliph in Damascus. When Husayn refused to return to Medina, he was massacred together with his followers and his head sent to Yazid in Damascus. Although the slaying of the Prophet's grandson passed unnoticed at the time, it gained significance later as the Shi'ite movement crystallized and Muslims became divided along religious and theological lines into two major camps, Sunnites (orthodox) and Shi'ites. To Shi'ites, the massacre symbolized the sufferings and maltreatment they endured at the hands of the orthodox majority. As a result, Karbala has become to them a most holy place, and the date of Husayn's death a day of mourning. Husayn's martyrdom and Umayyad suppression of his support in Kufa, Medina, and Mecca weakened Alid opposition. But the resentment harbored against the Umayyads remained.

Another factor contributing to the downfall of the Umayyads was the tribal wars among the nomadic Arabs, whose spirit of independence and resentment of any form of centralizing authority had not diminished. But while in pre-Islamic times they fought among themselves in small isolated units, under the Umayyads they organized into two large feuding factions. One main division, the South Arabian party, had moved northward from Yemen about two centuries before Islam after the breaking of the Ma'rib dam and the ensuing disintegration of economic and political life in southern Arabia. They had settled in the area east of the Jordan River and the Dead Sea, claiming ancestry from Qahtan (Joktan of the Book of Genesis). The rival North Arabian party, which moved northward from the central and northern parts of the Arabian Peninsula, claiming ancestry from Adnan (Ishmael), was much more nomadic in character. Rivalry between the two parties persisted throughout Islamic history, reaching its height under the Umayyads, when it affected every aspect of political life, especially in Syria.

Finally, in 750, the rule of the Umayyads was supplanted by that of the Abbasids. The center of the empire shifted eastward from Syria to Iraq, from Damascus to Baghdad. To their restive contemporaries, the Abbasids must have represented a new revolutionary force. Claiming descent from Abbas, an uncle of the Prophet, and posing as the true champions of Islam in the tradition of the "rightly guided" caliphs, the Abbasids had conducted an intensive propaganda campaign against the Umayyads, their monopolization of power, their haughty manner, and their worldly extravagances. The fact that the campaign focused on turbulent Iraq and Persia was no mere accident. Persia, especially, because of its remoteness, its strong Shi'ite sentiment, and the awareness, rather certitude, of its populace of their cultural superiority over the conquering Arabs became an easy target for Abbasid propaganda. The black Abbasid banner of revolt that became the emblem of the new dynasty was raised in 747. In 749, Abbas, the founder of the new dynasty, was proclaimed caliph. Marwan II, the last of the Umayyads, still reigned in Syria, but the following year, his army was routed. The systematic liquidation of the Umayyad clan followed.

The movement which had brought the Abbasids to power was based on a widespread revulsion against the impiety of the Umayyads. This impiety affected the whole organization of society, material and moral. The new dynasty radically changed the existing state of things. First came the destruction of the political unity of the Islamic state under one caliph. The one important Umayyad who escaped the wrath of the Abbasids, Abd al-Rahman, fled to Spain and founded a new Islamic state. He and his successors challenged the authority of the Abbasids for three centuries, claiming for themselves the title of caliph. This caliphal dualism, which became a salient feature of Islamic political history, was a departure from the pattern previously established. It was the beginning of a long and dangerous process of political and territorial fragmentation. By the tenth century, as Abbasid control of the state waned, the established pattern lost ground to such an extent that even illustrious political theorists, such as Mawardi (d. 1058), were unable to bridge the gap between theory and practice. It was not until much later, long after the fall of the Abbasids and the shifting and division of the ruling power, that Islamic political thinking came to grips with the facts. Ibn Taymiyya (d. 1328), was realistic enough to recognize that the traditional caliphate was gone, once and for all. By insisting that any state in the empire administered by and in accordance with the Divine Law was Islamic, regardless of whether or not it was ruled by a caliph, he legitimized the political and territorial disunity which had become the dominant rule in practice.

Other aspects of caliphal unity were also changed fundamentally. The immediate caliphal family, whose composition reflected the social and political tolerance prevalent at the time, underwent a gradual evolution. The Abbasids, like the Umayyads, regarded the caliphal family as superior to all others, but with a difference—they had no scruples against marrying non-Arabs. In fact nearly all the Abbasids were the sons of non-Arab slaves. Ethnic purity counted for little and had no relevance in the strict Arab or Umayyad sense. This caused another basic change: the caliph no longer depended on the support of the Arab ruling caste. He became a personal autocrat, surrounded by pomp, imposing his will through a skilled bureaucracy and a professional army, very much in the Byzantine and Sassanid style.

Moreover, the problem that the *mawālī* posed for the previous regime dissipated as they were allowed to assimilate. In the name of equality, the new converts aspired to a position corresponding to the growing effective influence they exercised. The outspoken element among them was the Persians. As the principal supporters of the new regime, they were the chief beneficiaries of the change, but other groups also won equal status with the Arabs. By the eighth century the term *mawālī* had ceased to exist. This did not mean that regional antagonism had come to an end, but rather that regionalism was acquiring a new shape. An exclusive Arab society was evolving into an international society wherein all Muslims were equal, irrespective of national or racial origin. Hostility toward the Arabs continued, but in a modified fashion. For now it stemmed from a sense of equality, a healthy competitive spirit, in a society open for all. It expressed national pride, the superiority of the Persians, for instance, over the Arabs.

There was a certain amount of Persian influence in the capital early in the Abbasid period, and it became considerable by the beginning of the ninth century. Soon afterward, Abbasid control in Persia began to disintegrate. Ex-caliphal officials, generals, and scions of local noble families founded their own petty dynasties in different parts of Persia and Central Asia. Some of these little states either coexisted with or were supplanted by the more considerable states of the Samanids (874–999) of eastern Persia and Turkestan and the Buwaihids (932–1035) of western Persia. Abbasid control over the empire was further undermined when, in 945, a branch of the Buwaihid dynasty captured most of Iraq, moved into the capital city of Baghdad, and deprived the caliph of all but his prestige. The caliph's power was eroded not only in the Persian East but also in the West. In Syria, Arabia, Egypt, even in Iraq itself, a succession of short-lived, virtually independent dynasties emerged, such as the Hamdanids (929–1003) of

Aleppo, and the Marwanids (990–1096). In Egypt and most of Syria, where Abbasid control had never been popular, caliphal officials asserted their power and established two independent dynasties—the Tulunids (865–905) and the Ikhshidis (935–969). They were succeeded by the Fatimids, who moved into Egypt from Tunisia in 969 and founded Cairo, which became the capital of a powerful and prosperous state noted for cultural and artistic achievements and for extensive trade relations with Europe. Even in remote Arabia, the caliph's authority was undermined. The most serious challenge was posed by Carmathian sectarians, a heretical Shi'ite sect that controlled Mecca, until the Fatimids destroyed it and brought the Hijaz with the holy cities of Mecca and Medina under their control.

Abbasid power was further weakened by the rise of a succession of theocratic city-dynasties, such as the Sharifs of Mecca, and the heretical Shi'ite Ibadis in Oman. Before the rise of the Fatimids, the Aghlabids (801–909) had succeeded in establishing themselves in North Africa, as well as in gaining a firm foothold in Sicily and parts of southern Italy. Farther west, Morocco, another independent Shi'ite dynasty, the Idrisids, came to power. In Spain, the westernmost portion of the empire, the process of disintegration set in much earlier when in 756 the Umayyad Abd al-Rahman, after escaping the persecution of the Abbasids, was recognized as ruler by both Arab and Berber. His Umayyad successors went a step further by having themselves recognized as independent caliphs. After the collapse of Umayyad power in Spain, although the Islamic element was strengthened by the advent from North Africa of the puritanical Almoravids and Almohads in the eleventh and twelfth centuries, the country remained politically independent. During this isolation from the rest of the Islamic world, a period of eight centuries, a remarkable Spanish-Muslim culture evolved that left a lasting imprint on the arts and sciences of both medieval Islam and Christian Europe.

By the end of the tenth century, the great Arab empire of the Abbasids had thus become politically fragmented among several states of varying strength, size, durability, and independence. Both the capital, the wealthy and cultured city of Baghdad, and the caliphate fell under the control of secular, non-Arab rulers. The caliph legitimized the usurpation of his power by a new princely ruler by investing him with the right to rule, in his name, but that was a mere formality designed to close the gap between the ideal caliphate and political practice. He had lost all but his spiritual prerogatives as the head of the Islamic community. However, the rise and fall of these now forgotten medieval Islamic states constitutes an important chapter in the development of Islamic civilization. In spite of their precarious existence, subject to the constant challenge from within and without of new and jealous aspirants, these states, for several centuries, provided large sectors of the empire with governments that were generally formal and orderly with a strong devotion to Islam and a remarkable appreciation of learning, culture, and the arts.

With the caliphate thus dismembered and weakened, and orthodox Islam challenged by varying interpretations and even heterodoxies, the time was ripe for change. This was provided by the Seljuk Turks, who had entered Persia at the beginning of the eleventh century and wrested control of the whole country from the Ghaznavids of Afghanistan and north India, and from the existing local dynasties.

The Seljuks belong to a linguistically interconnected group of peoples, generally known as Turks, who emerged from the steppes of central Asia as nomadic tribes in the early Middle Ages, over several centuries moved into Persia and western Asia in successive waves, and became converted to Islam. Turks, no doubt, existed in the empire earlier as slaves and body-guards, but it was with the rise of the Seljuks to power that the Turkish element in the empire gained ascendancy. In 1055, after establishing his control in Persia, the Seljuk Tughril Beg (d. 1063) entered Baghdad, deposed the last Shi'ite Buwaihid, and reestablished Sunnite orthodoxy under the titular leadership of the caliph.

The Seljuk empire stretched over Persia, Kurdistan, and Iraq and lasted until the mid-twelfth century, but it was always loosely united and, in the twelfth century, was split up among smaller but related dynasties ruled by Seljuk princes. Simultaneously, but lasting until the mid-thirteenth century, another succession of Turkish dynasties, founded by former slaves and officers of Seljuk princes, arose in Iraq, Kurdistan, and Persia. Despite the violence characterizing their reign, the Seljuk Turks provided the territories they occupied with relative stability, an orthodox Islamic government, and some able rulers, such as Alp Arslan (1063–1072) and Malik Shah (1072–1092). However, their epoch represents the superiority of Persian over Turkish culture. The Seljuks in almost all fields appreciated the administrative and artistic genius of their Persian subjects and utilized Persian talent and experience in the administration of their empire. The first three Seljuk sultans relied on Persian viziers, such as the able Nizam al-Mulk, and on Persian bureaucracy. Their restoration of Sunnite orthodoxy and their posing as the protectors of the caliphate and as patrons of orthodox Islamic learning and scholarship were welcome changes in those troubled times. But the orthodoxy they reestablished, because of the Shi'ite and Murtazilite challenge, had become reactionary and restrictive. It had an adverse effect on future progressive thought and development in Islam. Seljuk rule also gave impetus to the large-scale westward influx and settlement of other warlike nomadic Turkish tribes from central Asia, whose language and character thus became permanently impressed on large areas of the Middle East, especially Azerbaijan, Kurdistan, and Anatolia.

Nowhere was the impact of the Seljuks more decisive than in Anatolia. The border which had separated Islam and Byzantium for more than four centuries was permanently breached, and the Islamic-Byzantine balance of power was altered for all time in favor of Islam. As early as 1050, Tughril Beg had invaded Asia Minor. After defeating the Byzantine forces and capturing the emperor in the decisive battle of Manzikert (1071), the Turks penetrated central and western Asia Minor and established the Seljuk Sultanate of Rum with Nicaea (Iznik), not far from Constantinople, as the capital. Other nomadic Turkish tribes, recently converted to Islam, poured into the area, thus beginning the permanent "Turkification" of Asia Minor.

Meanwhile, two parallel developments appeared. One was the rise of the Ayyubid dynasty in Egypt and Syria as the defender of Sunnite orthodoxy in Islam; the other was the Crusades. The Crusades, with all their noble and not so noble episodes, meant more to the West than to the East. Their effect on contemporary Arab-Muslim society was minimal; except for the ruins of Crusaders' fortifications along the Syrian coast and the memory, still lingering in the Arab-Muslim mind, of Saladin's achievement as the champion of Islam against Christian aggression, nothing remains. Even as a medium for the transmission of Arab-Islamic culture to the West, the Crusades played no more than a secondary role. The main areas of East-West communication were in Sicily and Spain.

Saladin, a Kurdish-born officer of the Zangid dynasty of Syria, rose to power in Egypt in 1169 after two centuries of Shi'ite Fatimid rule. Before him, the main military opposition to the First Crusade (1097–1100) and the Second Crusade (1147–1149) came from the Zangids of Syria. But it was his personal achievement to unite the Islamic opposition under his powerful leadership and effectively check the Crusaders. In 1187 the Latin Kingdom of Jerusalem, set up by the first Crusaders in 1099, was reconquered. Saladin died in 1193, but his dynasty, the Ayyubids, continued in Egypt, Syria, and western Arabia until 1250.

At this date an invasion far more devastating and disruptive than the Seljuk incursion of two centuries earlier was in the making—that of the Mongols, who fell upon the empire in successive waves spreading unprecedented havoc and destruction everywhere. One of the last Abbasid caliphs, Nasir (1180–1225) had made an unsuccessful attempt to restore the original powers of his office by instigating one of the shahs of Khawarizm against Seljuk domination in Iraq and Kurdistan. By the early part of the thirteenth century, the shahs of Khawarizm were in control of most of Persia, and in a battle in 1194 they defeated the Seljuks and replaced them as masters of Iraq.

The ascendancy of the Khawarizm shahs, however, was short-lived.

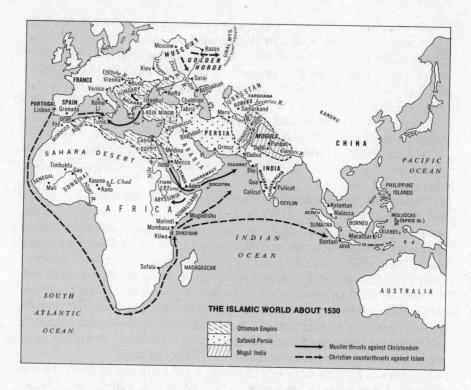

THE ISLAMIC WORLD ABOUT 1530

Ottoman Empire
Safavid Persia
Mogul India

→ Muslim thrusts against Christendom
--→ Christian counterthrusts against Islam

Earlier in the twelfth century, pagan Mongolian tribes moved into central Asia and established an extensive empire under the leadership of the redoubtable Chinggis Khan. By the time he died (1227) Chinggis Khan and his hordes had shaken to their foundations many a state from China to eastern Europe. Parts of Russia and Khawarizm were left in ruins. Transcaucasia and Azerbaijan were likewise overrun, although Baghdad, situated farther south, was spared for the moment. This vast empire lasted for three centuries. Its administration was a curious combination, partly centralized and partly a mélange of federated vassal states united under the supreme ruler, the Great Khan, who resided in remote China.

In 1253 the Mongols rode westward again, this time under the leadership of Hulagu, a grandson of Chinggis Khan, who succeeded to a substantial portion of the empire. Hulagu and his Mongolian hordes swept over Persia, reaching Alamut in the north Persian mountains in 1256, where they put an end to the dreaded and heretical order of the Assassins, whose grand master had conducted a campaign of terrorism in the Middle East. The Mongols then poured into Iraq and, as they drove toward Baghdad, plundered or destroyed everything in their path, including the elaborate canal system on which much of the agriculture of the land depended. In 1258, after a brief siege, the wealthy and cultured capital of the Abbasids fell to the pagan hordes. Many of the populace were slaughtered and the city was sacked and given over to flames. The sickly Abbasid caliph Musta'in, along with hundreds of his officials, was also slain, and with the passing of the last reigning Abbasid, the caliphate came to an end, except for an insignificant claimant whom the court in Cairo retained on pension for political ends. Hulagu then advanced against the Seljuks and the Atabegs in Asia Minor, and after destroying their power moved on to Syria. Here, for the first time, he was checked. For in Syria, the Mongols came face to face with a new and rising force: the Mamluks, a new dynasty of Turkish and Circassian ex-slaves, bodyguards, and fief-holding officers under the Ayyubids, who had risen to power in Egypt and Syria and seized control in 1250.

But Hulagu had changed the political map of the Middle East. Before his death in 1265, he was the undisputed ruler of an empire that stretched from India to Syria with only formal feudal homage paid to the Great Khan. After his death, Iraq and Persia passed on to his successors, the Il-Khans, who made Tabriz their capital. The Il-Khanid's rule (1265–1335), at first alien and undistinguished, gradually improved as the pagan Mongols embraced Islam and learned to appreciate and put to use Persian administrative and artistic genius. They were succeeded by a series of lesser dynasties, most of which were overrun by the armies of Tamerlane at the close of the fourteenth century.

Tamerlane, a descendant of Chinggis Khan, began his destructive conquests from his base in central Asia. After overrunning Persia and Iraq and sacking Baghdad in 1393, he moved on into Asia Minor and Syria. His extensive empire collapsed shortly after his death in 1405, but two Timurid dynasties arose as successors, one line in Persia lasting for almost a century, and the other in India becoming the Mogul empire.

At the time of Tamerlane's invasion, Asia Minor was under the domination of the Ottoman Turks while Syria and Egypt were under the Mamluks. Mamluk rule, with its two successive dynasties, the Bahri (1250–1390) and the Burji (1382–1517), provided Egypt and most of Syria with an effective government. In 1517, after a reign of over 250 years, Mamluk rule gave way to that of the Ottoman Turks.

For Further Reading

Brockelmann, Carl, *History of the Islamic Peoples.*
Hitti, P. K., *History of the Arabs.*
Lewis, Bernard, *The Arabs in History.*

24   Islamic Civilization

To attempt a summary appraisal of a major civilization that evolved over a period of several centuries in a large and heterogeneous part of the world is no simple task. Although the civilization that flourished during the period of greatness of the Arab and Islamic empires had a relatively uniform character, it was complex and variegated, a product of the interaction of many peoples with widely diverse religious and cultural traditions. The unsophisticated Arab invaders were able to impose not only themselves but also their language and their religion on the more populous and more civilized conquered territories. Naturally, the culture which developed was neither purely Arab nor purely Islamic; it drew heavily upon local sources. But the new culture was not just a mixture; it was a new and original creation whose various elements were fused together into a recognizable system. Nevertheless, in its unique assimilative power, its comparative tolerance, its consciousness of its own superiority and self-sufficiency, and its atomistic view of life and the universe, it was genuinely Arab-Islamic, and Arabic was the chief instrument of culture, Islam the unifying and dominating factor in the system.

The Arab-Muslim conquerors were, like their pre-Islamic predecessors, a primitive people with a nomadic, scarcely transplantable culture, particularly deficient in the material and artistic fields. But they had special gifts and qualities of their own which served them well initially: racial and religious solidarity, devotion to a triumphant faith, expectations of reward —worldly and otherworldly, and an openness to knowledge and development in all areas. But above all, they had a language and a religion to offer to the world.

Arabic, the youngest Semitic tongue, had, in those early times, a highly developed oral, but virtually no written, tradition. Its most sophisticated expression was in the form of poetry vividly depicting the life of the proud, defiant, intractable Bedouin. In a concrete and highly individualistic manner, it described the passions of the Bedouin, his tribulations and joys, the merciless desert environment, the futility of life. But from occasional, amazingly perceptive hints there emerges a vague hope of better things to come. This poetry, because of the purity of its diction and form, its excellent treatment of limited themes, and its elaborate and intricate meter and rhyme, became the poetic model for later Islamic poets.

Since Arabic was the language of the Prophet and the Koran, it became

A.D.   500–622 Pre-Islamic poetry flourishes in Arabia
          650 Official version of the Koran established in the
               reign of Uthman
          670 Building of the Great Mosque of Qayrawan in
               Tunisia
          691 Building of the Dome of the Rock in Jerusalem
               by Abd al-Malik
          696 Arab coinage is introduced by Abd al-Malik;
               Arabic becomes the official administrative
               language of the empire
          751 Arabs learn papermaking from captured Chinese
               prisoners; use of paper spreads westward in
               the empire
          765 A school of medicine founded in Baghdad
          767 Death of Abu Hanifa, founder of Hanafite School
               of Law
          785 Building of the Great Mosque of Cordova by
               Abd al-Rahman
          795 Death of Anas ibn Malik, founder of the Malikite
               School of Law
      813–833 Reign of Ma'mun; translation movement; Arabic
               science and learning flourishes; espousal of
               Mu'tazilism as the official theology
          815 Death of Abu Nuwas, celebrated poet of Abbasid
               court
          820 Death of Shafi'i, founder of the Shafi'ite School
               of Law
          850 Death of Kindi, first Arab philosopher
          855 Death of Ahmad ibn Hanbal, founder of the Han-
               balite School of Law
          869 Death of Jahiz, literary figure
          870 Death of Bukhari, famed for his compendium of
               Tradition
          875 Death of Muslim, famed for his compendium of
               Tradition
          876 Building of Ibn Tulun mosque in Cairo
          877 Death of Hunayn ibn Ishaq, most prominent
               translator of Greek works

CHRONOLOGY

922   Execution of Hallaj, Sufi mystic, for heresy

925   Death of Razi (Rhazes), physician and scientist

950   Death of Farabi (Pharabius), philosopher

965   Death of Mutanabbi, neoclassical poet

970   Mosque-university of al-Azhar built in Cairo by the Fatimids

1010   Firdawsi, Persian poet, completes his *Epic of Kings*

1030   Death of Biruni, physician, physicist, astronomer, mathematician, geographer, and historian

1037   Death of Ibn Sina (Avicenna), physician and philosopher

1067   Nizamiyya Madrasa (academy) established by the Seljuk vizier Nizam al-Mulk in Baghdad; Ash'arism established as the orthodox theology

1111   Death of Ghazali, mystic and theologian

1123   Death of Omar Khayyam, poet and astronomer

1198   Death of Ibn Rushd (Averroes), Aristotelian philosopher

1229   Death of Yaqut, geographer

1273   Death of Jalal al-Din al-Rumi, Persian mystic and poet

1325   Ibn Battuta begins his travels

1353   Completion of Alhambra in Granada

1390   Death of Hafiz, Persian lyric poet

1406   Death of Ibn Khaldun, Arab historian

the sole and divine key to knowledge and doctrine. With the Arabization of the empire and the flowering of learning and scholarship, Arabic became the chief instrument of everyday speech, as well as of culture, replacing Aramaic, Coptic, Greek, and Latin. Arabic also exerted an enormous influence on other Muslim languages like Persian and Turkish; these adopted not only the Arabic script and much Arabic vocabulary but also Arab literary tastes and traditions.

Besides their language, the Arabs contributed Islam to the civilization of the Middle East. The religion as it evolved in the Koran and the Traditions of the Prophet had a universal appeal, despite its distinctively Arab orientation and coloring. Islam is a monotheistic faith whose essential core of belief is the unity of Allah, the wholly transcendent God. According to Islam, Muhammad, the Messenger of Allah and the last and the greatest of an ascending series of prophets, is wholly human, having no claim to divinity. While offering attractive concessions and promises to the believer, Islam rigidly stresses a set of fundamental dogmas and practices. It requires on the one hand belief in the uniqueness of God, the truthfulness of the Prophet's Mission, the divine origin of the Koran, a hierarchy of angels, and the Last Day of Judgment. It prescribes, on the other hand, the obligation to profess the faith, perform the five daily prayers, give alms (*zakāt*), fast during the month of Ramadan, and—if possible—make a holy pilgrimage (*hajj*) to Mecca once in a lifetime. To this foundation of dogmas and duties, prohibitions were added against drinking wine, eating pork, usury, gambling, and image representations. Believers were also enjoined by Islam to holy war (jihad). The new faith also accepted the pre-Islamic institutions of slavery and polygamy, but required greater restraint and more humane treatment. From this simple set of basic dogmas and regulations that claimed universal application and validity, Islam in time developed into an elaborate political, social, intellectual and legal system, with the *Sharī'a,* the divinely revealed law, as its all-pervasive code.

The Arab-Muslim civilization represents one of the great creative achievements of human history. From the ninth century onward, after the initial period of borrowing and absorption, a remarkable and distinct civilization flourished, not only in and around the capital city of Baghdad, but throughout the Middle East, Persia, Central Asia, India, North Africa, Sicily, and Spain. The efflorescence of the civilization was facilitated by the pressure of certain favorable conditions—a rich and diversified cultural heritage, ample wealth and leisure, a common language, a common religion, and the support by Muslim princes and their courts of the arts, learning, and literature.

The artistic contribution of the civilization was immense. In architecture, gracious and orderly cities were built and adorned with mosques, palaces, gardens, fountains, libraries, bridges, and public baths. The structural beauty and meticulous decoration of surviving Islamic monuments display not only the sophistication and versatility of Islamic art and architecture, but also both the eclecticism and the originality of the civilization that produced them. So do Islamic decorative and industrial arts, such as pottery, tilework, metalwork, woodwork, glassware, jewelry, textiles, brocades, carpets, leatherwork, papermaking, bookbinding, and illumination. After a period of imitation Islamic craftsmen evolved new techniques and styles producing exquisite artistic creations in all these forms.

The literary achievement of the civilization was as abundant as it was diversified, reflecting Arab, Persian, Hellenistic, and other cultural and religious backgrounds. It made rich contributions to many fields of science and learning—in literature, religion and law, in music, history, geography, philosophy, medicine, mathematics, and astronomy. The earliest contribution was in prose and poetry. The rhymed prose of the Koran, the first major literary document in Arabic, influenced the early development of the style. Arabic prose excelled in belles-lettres and the essay, and achieved sophistication and grace at the hands of noted men of letters, some of whom were non-Arabs, such as Jahiz (d. 869). Poetry, the most esteemed literary genre among the Arabs, also developed along new lines. Pre-Islamic poetry, which had been transmitted orally, was standardized and written down under the Umayyads, but a new kind of poetry, with new forms and themes, evolved during the Abbasid period as a result of Persian influences, the ease and luxury of life in a metropolis, and the patronage of caliphal or princely courts. The new poetry, however, was short-lived and was superseded by a neoclassical poetry, as seen in the work of the popular Mutanabbi (d. 965).

The intellectual awakening that began under the Umayyads as the Arabs became exposed to more advanced civilizations came into full bloom in the Abbasid period. In Mecca and Medina, certain theologians and pietists rejected Umayyad worldliness. They isolated themselves in these two holy cities to devote themselves to religious study and scholarship. Interest in Islamic religious and legal sciences and learning spread to other important centers in the empire, where religious scholars formed circles in time identified as distinct "legal" and theological schools of thought. Religious, legal, and theological studies were in principle based upon the two main sources of all Islamic knowledge, the Koran and Tradition, a collection of reports of the acts and sayings of the Prophet and his Companions. The Koran, which had been compiled and standardized during the reign of Uthman, was universally accepted as the basic source. But the need to interpret its symbolism and ambiguities and to explain and apply its prescriptions to new situations gave rise to the development of grammar, lexicography, exegesis, jurisprudence, and scholastic theology. As for the body of Tradition, it was in a state of flux during the first two centuries of the empire. Thus it became necessary to compile and standardize it. This gave rise to another distinctively Islamic science, which ultimately produced six standard compilations of Tradition, the most universally recognized of which are those of Bukhari (d. 870) and Muslim (d. 875).

Jurisprudence was also cultivated. It gave Islam its religio-legal system of the *Sharī'a*. The *Sharī'a* governed all aspects of life, including belief, ritual, and civil, criminal, constitutional, and international law. It was both a code of law and a pattern of conduct—a political and social ideal with the double purpose of ensuring man's happiness in this world and in the world to come. It defined man's relation both to Allah, and to the community and its Prophet, and (later) to the empire and the reigning caliph. This comprehensive code developed and systematized by the Islamic jurists in accordance with the Koran and Tradition was from the beginning an ideal system. The legal material in the Koran and Tradition was limited. While adequate for the early Muslims of Mecca and Medina, it could not meet the increasing needs of a community expanding both geographically and culturally. As a result lawyers and judges took local custom and legal practices prevalent in the conquered territories, Islamicized them, and incorporated them into the *Sharī'a* system. Further, the use of principles such as analogy and the consensus of scholars enabled jurists to expand the prescriptions in the Koran and Tradition to deal with unprecedented cases. The importance which prominent jurists attached to these principles and to Tradition as sources of law gave rise to different schools of legal thought. These finally crystallized around four orthodox rites, the Malikite (after Anas ibn Malik, d. 795), the Hanafite (after Abu Hanifa, d. 767), the Shafi'ite (after Shafi'i, d. 820), and the Hanbalite (after Ahmad ibn Hanbal, d. 855). As the *Sharī'a* system achieved its maximum development in the ninth century, the forces of conservatism gradually set in, preventing further innovations. The *Sharī'a* became a closed system. The ascendancy of a conservative and restrictive attitude toward the development of the *Sharī'a* was in part a reassertion of Islam's original claim that the law emanated from God, the true and only Lawgiver. Even before the *Sharī'a* ceased to be in tune with political and social realities, a secular law was being developed alongside it, based on executive decrees and the decisions of secular courts. In modern times the *Sharī'a,* as a code of law, has been superseded by secular codes of law patterned on Western ones. This is true of all branches of the law except the limited area of personal status—marriage, divorce, and inheritance.

Important contributions were also made in history, biography, geography, and the social sciences. Under the Umayyads, the writing of history acquired a new importance—that of preserving the distinctly Arab character of the empire from the inroads of the conquered civilizations. It began with biographical literature about the Prophet, but soon developed to include monumental works covering a wide area including universal and local histories, and histories of tribes, dynasties, and institutions. Major advances were also made in the methods of writing history which culminated in the development of the more narrative and interpretative types of histories, best exemplified in the work of Ibn Khaldun (1332–1406), the greatest Arab philosopher of history. Similarly, the study of geography received much attention in Islam. The extent of Islamic conquests, the institution of the holy pilgrimage, and the penetration of Muslim traders into distant lands encouraged the study of geography and resulted in encyclopedic works, such as that of Yaqut (1179–1229).

Islamic religious literature drew heavily on Christian and Jewish sources. Both the Koran and Tradition contain a great deal of material that indicates a strong Talmudic and Apocalyptic influence. The indebtedness of the legal system itself to these sources, along with the Roman-Byzantine legal system, is also obvious. However, Islamic theological literature, which was only initially influenced by Syriac Christianity, together with Islamic philosophy and the sciences, including medicine, mathematics, chemistry, physics, and astronomy, also bear the direct impress of Greek thought. The intellectual awakening which began under the Umayyads and bore fruits under the Abbasids came partly from the translation into Arabic of Greek (as well as Persian, Sanskrit, and Syriac) books and treaties. The translation movement started under the Umayyads. The translators were mainly Syrians, Nestorians, Christians, and Jews. Greek manuscripts were translated either directly from the original or indirectly from Syriac versions. Under the Abbasids, the movement became well organized, reaching its height under the reign of Ma'mun (813–833), who founded a library-academy and sent scholars as far as Constantinople in search of material. The most prominent translator was Hunayn ibn Ishaq (809–877), a Nestorian Christian physician and superintendent of Ma'mun's academy. He and other academicians translated many works, including those of Galen and Hippocrates in medicine and Dioscorides in botany, as well as Plato's *Republic* and Aristotle's *Categories* and *Physics*. Other Syrians, the "pseudo-Sabians" of Harran, were also active in the translation movement. Thabit ibn Qurrah (836–911), the leading translator of this school, and his disciples are credited with the translation of Greek mathematical and astronomical works, including those of Archimedes and Euclid.

The translation movement, which lasted until the end of the ninth century, was followed by a period of original contributions. In theology, jurisprudence, philology, linguistics, and literature, creativity came earlier than in philosophy and the sciences. Muslim scholars, mostly of Persian origin, adapted their borrowings to their needs and built up their own scientific and philosophical systems. One of the most original thinkers and physicians of medieval times was Razi (Rhazes, 865–925), whose encyclopedic work on medicine was translated into Latin in Sicily as early as 1279 and widely used in Europe as a textbook. Ibn Sina (Avicenna, 980–1037), best known as a philosopher-physician, codified Greco-Arab medical thought. His work was translated into Latin in Spain and soon superseded other medical textbooks. But the Arab interest in medicine was primarily clinical and surgical, rather than theoretical. They also made important contributions in alchemy and botany, which were closely allied to medicine, and in astronomy. Technical terms of Arabic origin in these disciplines abound in Western languages—for example, azimuth, nadir, and zenith in astronomy; alchemy, alcohol, alembic, alkali, antimony, and tutty in chemistry; julep, soda, and syrup in medicine—indications of the permanent mark of Arab culture and its penetration of Europe. The Arabic numerals, together with the vital zero (*ṣifr,* cypher), were transmitted to Europe via Spain. Modern trigonometry as well as algebra and geometry are in considerable measure Arab creations.

In its initial stage of development, philosophical thought in Islam was controlled and conditioned by religion, and was mainly the product of theological speculation. The introduction of Greek philosophy and logic in the ninth century, however, gave rise to a distinct Islamic philosophy (*falsafa*) which had a far-reaching impact on the rationalistic and theological outlook of Islam. The earliest representative of this new school was the philosopher Kindi (d. 850), who strove, like all the other Islamic thinkers, to harmonize Greek philosophy with Islam. Farabi (Pharabius, d. 950) and Ibn Sina continued Kindi's work. Farabi built a philosophical and political system inspired by Greek and Islamic ideas. The greatest Aristotelian philosopher in Islam was the Spanish Arab Ibn Rushd (Averroes, d. 1198), whose commentaries on the Arabic translation of Aristotle's works were rendered into Hebrew and Latin, giving rise to Avervoism, an important school of philosophical thought in medieval Europe.

With the passage of time Islam itself, as a religion and way of life, underwent profound changes affecting its unity. As the empire expanded, Islam became increasingly exposed to Hellenic, Jewish, Christian, Zoroastrian, and animistic influences. Some of these elements were assimilated and became incorporated in the system; others, too alien to Islamicize, were generally rejected, but gave rise at times to certain heretical sects. The major schisms in Islam, however, arose earlier, before alien beliefs and ideas had a noticeable effect on belief and ritual. On the one hand, purely Arab and purely political arguments, such as the right of succession to the caliphate, led to differing religious interpretations that split the Islamic community into two major branches—the Sunnites and the Shi'ites, including such extreme subdivisions as Isma'ilism with its Assassins, Carmathians, Nusayris, Duruzes, and other heterodoxies. The extremism of the latter movements represents the dissatisfaction of certain oppressed elements among the less privileged classes with the existing political, social, and religious order and their attempt to force a change. On the other hand, contact with Greek Christianity in Syria early in the Umayyad period stimulated critical thinking regarding certain established beliefs and doctrines. This gave rise to new religio-philosophical schools of thought, one of the earliest of which was the Qadarite, which preached a doctrine of free will as against the strict predestinarianism of traditional Islam, and its emphasis on the Transcendence and Almightiness of God. The Qadarite doctrine and Islam's initial acceptance of Greek philosophy and Greek logic led to the development of a more rationalistic theology by the Mu'tazilites based on the Unity and Justice of the God-head. For a brief period, during the reign of Ma'mun (813–833), when the rationalist and scientific spirit in Islam was prevalent, the Mu'tazilite doctrine was espoused by the state and made the official theology. The dominance of the Mu'tazilites, however, did not long endure. Their extremism and intolerance triggered a violent reaction among traditionalists which led ultimately to the acceptance in Islam of Ash'arism (after Ash'ari, d. 935). This was a deterministic and authoritarian system of theology, based on the rejection of all causality and the strict adherence to the literal meaning of the Koran. The triumph of this static, formalist theology was a major factor in the decline and the ultimate disappearance of independent speculation and inquiry in Islam.

Finally, Islam witnessed the rise and spread of Sufism, the Islamic counterpart of mysticism, which had far-reaching effects upon Islamic society and its faith. As a reaction against both the intellectualism of the Mu'tazilites and the philosophers and the formalism of traditional orthodoxy, Sufism grew rapidly among both Sunnites and Shi'ites, not as a separate religious sect, but rather as a more meaningful, more personal, approach to piety. From rudimentary beginnings exemplifying the best in Islamic piety, it became increasingly ascetic as it absorbed Christian, Gnostic, Neoplatonic, and Buddhist elements. In the process, it developed a variety of forms, including pantheistic Sufism. The excesses of certain devotees and their pantheistic tendencies, such as the Persian Hallaj (d. 922), who was executed for heresy, resulted in the condemnation of Sufism by orthodoxy. But the yearning for a more personal religion made the mystic way irresistible to many devout Muslims, including Ghazali (d. 1111), the greatest of Muslim theologians. By reconciling the new scholasticism with the intuitive, mystical religion of the Sufis, Ghazali assured for Sufism a permanent position in Islam. By the twelfth century, as Sufism attracted more and more people from all strata of Islamic society, numerous Sufi orders each with its own monasteries, ritual, and doctrine were organized and spread from one end of the empire to the other.

For Further Reading

Arberry, A. J., *Aspects of Islam*.
Gibb, H. A. R., *Arabic Literature*.
————, *Studies in the Civilization of Islam*.
Von Grunebaum, G. E., *Medieval Islam*.
Nicholson, R. A., *A Literary History of the Arabs*.

25 The Jews in the Arab World

The renowned toleration that the Jews enjoyed under Muslim rule was not the product of native Muslim liberality. No less than Christians, the peoples of Islam claimed exclusive possession of the truth and exhibited unconcealed contempt for other religions. Muslim theologians and demagogues produced an anti-Jewish literature that was informed by a hatred of the Jews and Judaism that in no way falls short of its Christian counterpart.

The Jewish experience under Islam began with massacre and expulsion from the northern half of the Arabian Peninsula. The "Pact of Umar," although historically questionable, nevertheless reflected the prevailing attitude of Muslim rulers and jurists: infidels (*dhimmis*) deserved protection only at the price of displaying marked subservience to Muslims and their faith. The persecution and humiliation endured by the Jews of Almohade North Africa (1147–1276) and Zaydi Yemen (c. 1165 and after) were unmatched in their brutality by any Christian state prior to the anti-Semitic excesses of nineteenth-century czarist Russia.

Nevertheless, it remains true that in Babylonia, Spain, North Africa, Egypt, and Ottoman Turkey, Jews enjoyed centuries of uninterrupted tranquillity. In these countries, where felicitous conditions deprived them of much of a political or economic history, the story of the Jews is truly the

A.D.	500–550	Compilation of Babylonian Talmud
	c. 650	Beginning of Babylonian Gaonate
	760–763	Gaonate of Yehudai
	c. 760	Anan, religious leader
	c. 800	Beginning of Karaite sect
	882–942	Saadiah Gaon
	c. 950	Hasdai ibn Shaprut of Cordova, physician and scholar
	968–1038	Gaonate of Sherira and Hai
	992–1055	Samuel ibn Nagrela of Granada
	c. 1000–1148	Golden Age of Spanish Hebrew literature
	c. 1075–1141	Judah ha-Levi, poet
	1135–1204	Moses Maimonides
	1147–1148	Almohade conquest of Spain

record of Jewish activity within the framework of their own autonomy, of their internal tensions and adjustments to new political cultural contexts. Men of distinction reflect an individuality, and frequently an originality, that are all but unknown in the Jewish communities of Christian Europe.

The crucial factor favoring the Jews was that in every land conquered by the Muslims the Jews were but one of several non-Arab groups. In states where political alignments often corresponded to ethnic loyalties, the presence of the Jew was not as obvious, and certainly not as keenly felt, as in areas peopled predominantly by one ethnic stock. Second, in many areas the Muslims found the Jews concentrated in considerable numbers and possessed of a tradition of communal organization. In such cases, it was far less costly, and often quite advantageous, to mobilize the services of cooperative Jewish leaders whose interests in maintaining a quiescent and disciplined community coincided with those of the alien conquerors.

When the armies of Umar ibn al-Khattab overran Mesopotamia and Iran (636–640), they found a sizable population of Jews living alongside several other Aramaic-speaking peoples. Eager for a swift return to normality, the Muslims confirmed the relationship that had prevailed under the Persian empire between the central government and subject peoples, and they appointed native personnel to administer the internal affairs of the various groups. As a tolerated "people of Scripture," the Jews of Babylonia, like their Christian neighbors, were classified as a protected minority to be governed directly by an exilarch from their own ranks. Besides keeping the peace in the Jewish community, this prince was to be accountable for the regular collection of the poll tax and other special tributes imposed by the Muslims on all conquered peoples.

The great majority of the million-odd Jews in the new Arab empire were concentrated in one area. Many farmed their own lands and others worked as artisans or merchants in towns frequently peopled overwhelmingly by Jews. All aspects of their civil and religious life were administered by Jewish officials in accordance with their own law codified in the Babylonian Talmud (c. 500) and by institutions financed by taxes collected from all Jews living in the territories taken from Persia and Byzantium. The powers of legislation and adjudication reposed with rabbinic academies, or high courts, patterned largely after those of the Palestinian rabbinate and headed by presidents known as Geonim. Highly developed communal machinery run with a tight discipline by an officialdom largely recruited from a limited circle of leading Jewish families made the Jewish settlement in Mesopotamia a kind of oligarchic state-within-a-state.

By 725 the burdensome taxation and the heavy hand of the oligarchy aroused the same kind of organized opposition among disaffected Jews that the Umayyads had generated among Persian and Arab Muslims. Particularly in the outlying areas of Persia, political and economic resentment erupted in armed revolts coupled with programs of legal and religious reform. Vestiges of long-suppressed sectarian faith and usage found small but willing audiences, who responded to the appeals of charismatic chieftains to establish independent Jewish societies. Although the revolts were quickly crushed, discontent continued to smolder in many quarters. The most impressive coup of these missionaries was the conversion (c. 750) of the ruling families of the bellicose Khazar tribes north of the Caucasus to a syncretist form of Judaism. However, this Jewish kingdom, which survived until about 1000, remained isolated from Jewish society at large, although it became a byword for Jews dreaming of the resurgence of Jewish political power. In the Near East itself, the sects quickly receded into obscurity and failed to present any sustained challenge to rabbinic control.

The internal policies of the Abbasids, following their seizure of power in 750, provided further opportunities for the extension of exilarchic-rabbinic influence. Bent on consolidating the vast Muslim empire into a cohesive unit directed from Baghdad, the Abbasids supported any activity that would draw minority groups further into the orbit of their own lieutenants, who, in the case of the Jews, were the exilarch and his rabbinic associates. Seizing the new opportunity, the exilarch in 760 appointed to the Gaonate of the senior academy of Sura a sage consumed by the vision of a religiously uniform Jewry. Although afflicted with blindness, Yehudai Gaon managed in the three years of his presidency to launch a program that was to leave a permanent stamp on all Jewish culture. Outlawing any deviation from Babylonian religious usage, Yehudai's campaign raised the Babylonian Talmud to quasi-Scriptural status and drove the Palestinian corpus into an obscurity from which it never quite emerged. Even in Palestine, the Babylonian Talmud became the supreme source of Jewish law and from there made its way to the Palestine-oriented Jewish communities of Byzantium and Italy. Hence, even when communication between Jews of Muslim and Christian countries had been virtually severed, medieval Jewish religion and community structure retained a basic uniformity.

The Gaonic program of suppressing local differences stimulated powerful reaction on the part of those disaffected with the ruling class. Far from being antinomian, the anti-Talmudic heresiarch Anan (c. 760) and the Karaite, or "Scripturally oriented," sect that emerged from his activity around 800 combined elements of ultrapietism with a reaffirmation of the centrality of Palestine to Jewish faith, a tendency which the Babylonian leadership had been laboring to attenuate. Astutely renouncing messianic activism, the new sect won official Abbasid toleration and succeeded in stimulating many to migrate and live a life of mourning and deprivation in the Holy Land. There the Karaites soon matured into a synagogal organization in which wealth, scholarship, and formal community structure—led by a Davidic prince—played stabilizing roles. Their missionary vigor also enabled them to establish sizable communities throughout the world from Egypt and Byzantium to the African Maghreb and Christian Spain.

The great social changes that overtook Arab society in the wake of the Abbasid economic and cultural programs in the eighth and ninth centuries inevitably had profound effects on Jewish society. The increased premium placed on ability rather than on ethnic or even religious origins opened new avenues to Jews. By 900 some had gained employment as civil servants and the right to practice medicine, and in 908 a few were empowered to function as state bankers. Thanks to their connections with the court, the new Jewish rich played an ever increasing role in the affairs of their community and especially in the choice of communal officers. The social metamorphosis was discernible even in the highest echelons with the admission of foreigners of talent and of scholarly members of the banking families to positions of influence in the academies.

However, by far the most pervasive effect of the new atmosphere in Baghdad was in the cultural and religious changes that could be discerned in all quarters of Arab society. The adoption of Arabic as the language of the empire, coupled with the Abbasid sponsorship of a huge program of translation of works in many subjects from Greek, Syriac, and Persian, converted Baghdad into the cultural emporium that Alexandria had been in Hellenistic times. Muslims, Christians, and Jews exchanged ideas freely. Philosophical circles abounded, and with them skepticism and religious deviation of every sort. The air of middle-class individualism evoked new expressions of freedom from the yoke of authoritarian discipline. An aggressive anti-Gaonic literature poured forth steadily in the ninth century from orthodox Karaites, Marcion-like gnostics, and, to cap them all, from the resurgent rabbinic academies of Palestine that had begun to reclaim old prerogatives. In Iran some Jewish communities had refused to pay their assessments to the exilarch and had to be brought into line by force. Even the two Babylonian academies were at each other's throats over the solicitation of funds in new Jewish territories in North Africa and Spain. By 900 the efficient exilarchic machine of the seventh and eighth centuries had become a memory.

In a daring move, doubtless inspired by Abbasid techniques, a strong-willed exilarch appointed to the presidency of Sura in 928 Saadiah b. Joseph al-Fayyumi, an Egyptian scholar who had distinguished himself as a protagonist of Babylonian rabbinism. While the unbridled ambitions of the exilarch and the Gaon soon brought them into open conflict, and drove the rabbinic institutions into even worse straits than before, Saadiah's short term as Gaon provided him with the opportunity to circulate throughout the world a series of works that were to signalize the advent of a new era in Jewish culture. For if Baghdad had replaced Alexandria, Saadiah became its Philo. Writing voluminously and incessantly, he translated the Scriptures into Arabic, composed codes and commentaries in the vernacular, and, as a crowning achievement, issued a philosophical defense of Judaism that remains a classic specimen of Arabic Kalam. Frustrated in his political ambitions, he had consciously and deliberately provided the models for a synthesis of Jewish and Arabic cultures, the fruit of which would become manifest only later in another corner of the Arabic world.

The splintering of the Abbasid empire by the Fatimids of North Africa and Umayyads of Spain in the tenth century enabled the Jewish communities of Ifriqiya, Egypt, Palestine, and Spain to end their umbilical dependence on Babylonian religious institutions. The desperate efforts of two of the greatest Geonim, Sherira (968–1006) and his son Hai (1004–1038), to retain the loyalties of outlying Jewish communities generated a correspondence which has delighted historians but which did not halt the centrifugal shift to new poles. Although the secessionist Muslim rulers permitted contacts between the Jewries of east and west to continue, they preferred to see local capital invested at home. Accordingly, they fanned the pride of their own Jewries by encouraging them to develop native communal institutions and in time even permitted local heads to assume princely Hebrew titles like Nagid or Nasi.

Of these new communities by far the most scintillating emerged in Andalusian Spain. As friendly *dhimmis* in an area where many—but by no means all—Christians were openly hostile, the Jews were accorded the full measure of Muslim toleration and, on occasion, employment as petty officials. Active in commerce, in vine and silk cultivation, in textile manufacture, and in the state-supported slave trade, many amassed considerable wealth and culture. While Jewish educational facilities existed there by 800, until about 1000 Spain represented a major benefactor of the Babylonian academies. The first Jewish prayer book was compiled by a Gaon of Sura (c. 860) in response to a request by a Spanish community, perhaps Barcelona.

The decisive turn came in the wake of the campaign of Abd al-Rahman III (912–961) and al-Hakam II (961–976) to make Cordova the Baghdad of the west. After achieving military and naval mastery over their neighbors, these Umayyads launched an extensive building program and attracted men of science and letters to their capital. Libraries and universities sprang up alongside royal palaces and gardens, gaining for the capital renown as "the jewel of the Maghreb."

The temper of the age inspired the head of the Jewish community to undertake a similar program for his own group, of course on a smaller scale. Hasdai ibn Shaprut, a physician who had served the court with distinction in several diplomatic missions, lavished considerable sums to draw men of Jewish law and letters to Cordova and to provide them with libraries. Obviously obsessed with the idea of Jewish rebirth politically as well as culturally, he spared no efforts to make contact with the Jewish king of the Khazars and to inquire whether the latter had any information on the date of the messianic era. It was a fantasy, to be sure, but one which shaped the mentality of more than one of his circle.

Although civil wars in the beginning of the eleventh century dismembered the Umayyad kingdom into a congeries of petty states, and thereby put an end to the integrity of the Andalusian Jewish community, the period of "the petty kings" (1020–1086) and of their Aloravide successors (1086–1148) became "the golden age" of Spanish Jewish culture. Since each petty monarch fancied his own bailiwick as a new Cordova, the new courts welcomed talent and support from any quarter. In this Babel of ethnic groups struggling for social and political mastery, the Jews were among the few who were above suspicion of conspiring to traduce their rulers to Umayyads, Christians, or "Slavs." Jews of wealth and culture everywhere soared to positions of influence. What was particularly attractive about them, according to contemporaries, was their elegance in Arabic speech and manners, qualities esteemed above all others by the *reyes de taifas* as marks of ability. In such a climate, Saadiah's synthesis and Ibn Shaprut's example became models for the Jewish courtiers, who vied with one another in endowing poets and grammarians, philosophers and rabbinic jurists.

If Jews required any vindication for this new style of life they found it in the spectacular career of Samuel ibn Nagrela. An alumnus of the academy of Cordova and of Ibn Shaprut's circle, he possessed a rare combination of gifts: he was a skillful Hebrew poet, a superb Talmudist, a master stylist in Arabic, an astute military strategist and political administrator. His meteoric rise to the vizierate of Granada (c. 1030–1056) became a byword to Jew and Muslim alike. The resentment of the Muslim mob, cleverly aroused by demagogues, erupted in 1067 in a massacre which took the life of his son and successor along with those of hundreds of Jews of Granada. While no Jew ever again attained such heights of power in medieval society, the Jewish courtier tradition, epitomized by the Ibn Nagrelas, remained at the heart of Sephardic culture for centuries.

The courtier tradition prized as its outspoken goal the creation of a type who integrated and synthesized the wisdom of Greece—in Arabic garb—with the legacy of Israel. Sporting the Hebrew title of Nagid simultaneously with that of Vizier, the Ibn Nagrelas lavished support on their favorites—rabbis, poets, exegetes, philosophers, mathematicians, astronomers—and aggressively claimed the equality of the Spanish rabbinate with that of Babylonia. Entranced by Arabic verse, they strove to revive the vitality of the Hebrew language—which they set to verse in Arabic meter!—so that the bards of Jacob might vie with the poets of Ishmael. Thus the glorious poetry of Solomon ibn Gabirol, Moses ibn Ezra, and Judah ha-Levi; the philosophic treatises of Ibn Gabirol (Avicebron), Ibn Daud (Avendauth) and Ibn Zaddik; the scientific treatises of Abraham bar Hiyya and Abraham ibn Ezra—all these were the works of genuine intellects sensitive to every ripple of Arabic culture and, accordingly, seized by its love of beauty and knowledge.

In much smaller measure, and with a more traditionally rabbinic orientation, native Jewish culture flowered simultaneously in Qairawan, Egypt, and Palestine. But for a brief period of persecution (1009–1021) under the insane Fatimid al-Hakim, the Jews prospered as merchants, artisans, and civil servants. Karaites and Rabbanites lived side by side, often cooperating with each other in civic affairs and cultivating separately new methods of study of Scripture and rabbinic literature.

The Almohade avalanche that swept across North Africa and Andalus (1146–1148) put an abrupt end to *dhimmi* life in the lands of western Islam. While many Jews perished—along with Christians and Muslims—the majority either fled to Egypt and Christian Spain or persisted for more than half a century in adhering to Judaism secretly. While their efforts to reconstitute their Andalusian pattern of life in Aragon, Castile, and Provence were only partially successful, they brought to Latin Europe a rich legacy that influenced the course of European scholarship and philosophy as a whole and of northern Jewish culture in particular.

Ironically, the summa of Andalusian Judaism appeared at the time that Almohade control was at its highest. The works of Moses Maimonides (1135–1204), issued in Egypt, but prepared during decades of wandering and furtive life under fanatical rulers of the Maghreb, remain to this day the only systematic codification of all of Jewish law and the most incisive synthesis of Jewish faith with Aristotelian philosophy. However, all of his monumental works betray the underlying despair of reflective men of Arab society—epitomized in sociological terms some two centuries later by Ibn Khaldun—of achieving lasting satisfaction in public service. To be sure, Maimonides was not the first philosopher to suggest that freedom could be attained only through contemplative withdrawal in a society rigorously controlled by law and reason. However, he was the first to lay out a detailed Jewish blueprint for such a pattern of life, and to show the exiles of Andalus how they might find solace and certainty in a strange world. In Ayyubid Egypt, where he found political freedom and financial security, he established a dynasty of communal heads which persisted until the end of the fourteenth century. However, the society envisioned by the Jewish philosopher-king was never to become a reality. Long-entrenched Jewish patterns of life, coupled with the upheavals in the Middle East beginning with the thirteenth century, left the work of Maimonides a solitary epitaph to a glorious culture.

Jewish community life in the lands of Islam persisted down to modern times. However, the decay that weakened Arab society and culture affected the Levantine Jew as well. The renaissance that Ottoman Jewry enjoyed in the sixteenth and seventeenth centuries was basically a resurgence of Sephardic culture that had become totally Hispanicized and, in any case, never an integral part of Ottoman society and culture. It remained for Jews enflamed by the European Enlightenment to rediscover the glories of Babylonia and Andalus and to recapture the treasures of the Judeo-Arabic experience.

For Further Reading

Abraham ibn Daud, *The Book of Tradition.*
Finkelstein, Louis (ed.), *The Jews, Their History.*
Goitein, S., *Jews and Arabs.*
———, *A Mediterranean Society,* Vol. I.
Guttmann, J., *Philosophies of Judaism.*
Husik, I., *A History of Medieval Jewish Philosophy.*

Asia and Africa

26   Sub-Saharan Africa

Although southern Africa was the birthplace of man as we know him, two thousand years ago Africa south of the Sahara was still a sparsely occupied land. In the center and south lived small groups of Bushmen, nomadic hunters and gatherers still in the Stone Age. The east was inhabited, though thinly, by Kushitic peoples who herded cattle and grew cereal crops but had not yet learned the use of iron. Only the Sudanic belt stretching across the continent from the Atlantic Ocean to the edge of the Ethiopian plateau supported a relatively large population. This region had known settled agriculture since about 3000 B.C., and its inhabitants, of mixed racial composition but basically Negro, were technologically in advance of their neighbors to the south. Whereas most Africans at that time were food collectors, the Sudanic Negro was a food producer. In the area of the Niger Bend in West Africa he had succeeded in domesticating his own cereals, such as sorghum and an African type of rice, crops he had found were better suited to his environment than the wheat and barley of western Asia.

About the fourth or fifth century B.C. the art of iron smelting was imported into the Sudan from Egypt by way of Nubia, with the result that the Sudan's Negro inhabitants gained a powerful advantage in the struggle for survival against nature on the one hand and against other Africans, living still farther south, on the other. Whether as hunter or warrior, farmer or fisherman, the possessor of iron weapons, tools, and implements could outfight and outproduce Stone Age man. Moreover, since there was no Bronze Age in sub-Saharan Africa, the coming of iron had an even more decisive impact there than elsewhere in the ancient world. Iron technology, added to larger numbers, better agricultural methods, and, possibly, greater social cohesion, enabled the Negroes to expand throughout the African continent. They did so at the expense of the indigenous inhabitants of the area, whom they conquered, absorbed, or displaced.

CHRONOLOGY

A.D.		
	c. 3rd–4th cents.	Rise of empire of Ghana
	4th cent.	Rise of Christian kingdom of Axum (Ethiopia)
	c. 800	Founding of the kingdom of Kanem
	c. 1040	Mission of Abdallah to the Goddala
	c. 1076	Almoravid conquest of Ghana
	c. 1090	Conversion to Islam of *mai* of Kanem
	11th–14th cents.	Building of "Great Zimbabwe" complex
	c. 1100	Earliest evidence of stone mosques on East African coast; founding of Timbuktu
	12th–16th cents.	Rule of Zagwe dynasty in Ethiopia
	c. 1200	Rise of sultanate of Kilwa
	1203	Sack of Ghana by Sumanguru of Susu
	1230	Accession of Sun Dyata of Mali
	1235	Battle of Kirina
	1324–1325	Pilgrimage to Mecca of Musa I, *mansa* of Mali
	c. 1464	Accession of *sonni* Ali Ber of Songhai
	1482	Building of Elmina Castle (São Jorge da Mina)
	1488	Doubling of Cape of Good Hope by Bartholomeu Dias
	1493	Accession of *askiya* Muhammad the Great of Songhai
	1498	Arrival of Portuguese on East African coast
	1590–1591	Moroccan invasion of the western Sudan

To begin with, the Negroes (or Bantu, as they are known in the east and south) had to confine themselves to the drier regions where the cereals they took with them on their migrations, or found already in cultivation, could grow. But after the introduction into Africa of Southeast Asian "wet-zone" crops like the yam and the banana (brought to Madagascar by Indonesian colonists during the first five centuries A.D.), they found it possible to move into the humid forests, low-lying river valleys, and coastal plains as well. This gradual occupation of almost the whole of the arable soil of Africa by the Negroes of the west and by the Bantu of the east and south—the fundamental fact of African history—took approximately 1,500 years. It was almost complete when, at the end of the fifteenth century, the Portuguese rounded the Cape of Good Hope on their way to India and met black-skinned men living close to the southern tip of the continent in the area now called Natal.

During the millennium and a half of the Negro-Bantu migrations sub-Saharan Africa was largely cut off from the rest of the world; indeed, most of the interior remained unknown to outsiders until well into the nineteenth century. Geography dictated this isolation. In the first place, the Sahara Desert, while never a total barrier to intercourse between north and south, at least strongly discouraged it. The trans-Saharan trade routes, too, connected the Mediterranean and Middle East with the Sudan, not with sub-Saharan Africa as a whole. Second, almost all the great rivers of Africa descend to the sea via rapids and waterfalls, and thus fail to provide an easy means of communication (such as all other continents possess) from the coast to the interior. Nor can the coast itself be said to welcome the overseas mariner; much of Africa is fringed by mangrove swamp and sand bar, there are few natural harbors along its shores, and on the Atlantic side the surf is heavy. Third, wide areas of the African savanna are infested with tsetse fly, the carrier of the debilitating disease known as sleeping sickness, which affects both man and beast. In such areas draft animals cannot be used. Thus, until the coming of mechanical transport in modern times, the only way to cross most of the continent was to walk, carrying one's belongings on one's head.

The earliest states in sub-Saharan Africa therefore grew up enjoying little or no direct contact with the outside world. They arose along two main axes: one running east and west across the broad belt of the Sudan; the other north and south along the highland spine which stretches from Nubia and Ethiopia at one end to Kipling's "great, grey, green, greasy" Limpopo River at the other. Typically, the rulers of these states were divine kings upon whose continued personal well-being the prosperity of their kingdoms depended. When a king became senile or impotent, he was ceremonially killed, and a new, healthy monarch installed in his place.

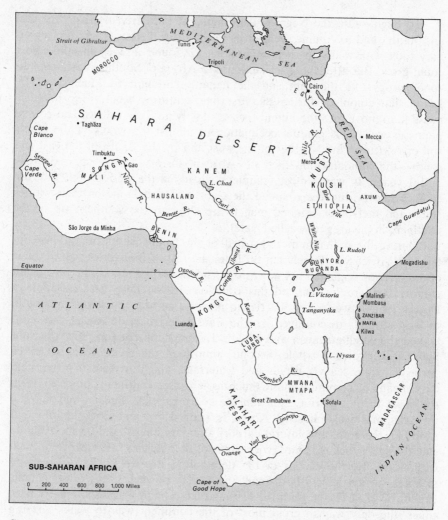

SUB-SAHARAN AFRICA

0   200   400   600   800   1,000 Miles

Such a ruler was in theory despotic, as befitted a near-divinity, but in practice his freedom of action was circumscribed by custom and by his council of advisers. The early African kingdoms were not feudal monarchies, but somewhat loosely organized groupings of tribes and peoples, held together by bureaucrats whose loyalty was to the king alone. By contrast, local chiefs governed their own domains and owed to their paramount ruler not detailed obedience but periodic tribute, and men and supplies in time of war.

The reason states grew up in some areas rather than in others seems in most cases to have been connected with the demands of long-distance trade. Of this a clear example is provided by the empire of Ghana. Extending at the height of its power from the upper reaches of the Senegal River to the northern curve of the Niger Bend, Ghana arose about the third or fourth century A.D., began to decline at the end of the eleventh century, and finally disappeared from history during the fifteenth. To the Arabs it was known as "the land of gold." Its ruler, the *kayamaga* ("king of gold"), was reputed to be the richest and most powerful monarch in all the Bilad as-Sudan ("land of the blacks"). Yet Ghana had few natural resources of its own. Its wealth derived from the levies it was able to impose on the trade across the Sahara, by means of which the gold, slaves, and kola nuts of West Africa were exchanged for North African manufactures, horses, foodstuffs, and salt.

Another sub-Saharan kingdom well known to the ancient world was the state of Kush in Nubia. Like Ghana, Kush owed its prosperity to trade. Its ivory, ebony, gum, hides, ostrich plumes, and slaves were carried down the Nile to Egypt and across the Red Sea to Arabia and Mesopotamia. For long Kush was a dependency of Egypt, culturally as well as politically, but about 1000 B.C. its rulers broke away from the suzerainty of the pharaohs and, especially after the transfer of the capital from Napata to Meroë about 540 B.C., developed their own distinctively African civilization and culture. Meroë was eventually conquered in the fourth century A.D. by Axum, a state of northeastern Ethiopia. Under the influence of missionaries from Syria the rulers of Axum adopted the Monophysite Christian faith, thus laying the foundation of the kingdom which was ultimately to develop into modern Ethiopia. The scriptures used by the Ethiopian Church today were translated from Greek into Ge'ez, the language spoken in Axum, as long ago as the sixth century.

The main rival of Christianity in Africa, Islam, began to penetrate south of the Sahara soon after the Arab conquest of Egypt in 641. In the western and central Sudan Arab and Berber merchants from North Africa proved effective proselytizers, and for the most part the new faith spread easily and peacefully. The commercial advantages that conversion brought with it—the art of writing, a settled law, access to an expanding and profitable market—were highly attractive to those who depended on trade with Muslim North Africa for their wealth and power. By the eleventh century Islam had become the religion of most of the desert nomads and of many of the rulers of the caravan termini on the southern side of the Sahara. In some cases, however, these conversions were nominal, and paganism continued to flourish even in supposedly Islamized areas. The chief of one desert tribe, while on pilgrimage to Mecca, was shocked to discover that he and his people had scant knowledge of the true Faith. He returned home determined to effect a thorough religious reformation and, to assist in this task, recruited in North Africa a famous teacher and divine, Abdallah ibn Yasin. Arriving in the Sudan, Abdallah tried to reform his patron's tribe by preaching and persuasion. But peaceful methods failed, and he formed a fighting corps of young zealots, the Almoravids, launching them in holy war against all who refused to heed the call to orthodox Islam. An obvious target for attack was pagan Ghana, already weakened by drought and famine and by a century or more of warfare with desert tribes. In 1076 the Almoravids overwhelmed Ghana and sacked its capital.

No large state succeeded Ghana as the dominant power in the western Sudan until the thirteenth century. By this time the chief contenders for supremacy were Sumanguru, king of Susu, and Sun Dyata, chief of the small but militarily powerful kingdom of Nyani. When at the decisive battle of Kirina (1235) Sun Dyata's forces defeated Sumanguru's, the way was cleared for the creation of Mali, the second great empire of the western Sudan.

The years of Mali's dominance were from the mid-thirteenth to the mid-fourteenth century. Its territory extended from the lower reaches of the Gambia and Senegal rivers to a line running from the Asben oasis in the Sahara to the Niger-Benue confluence in what is now Nigeria, and its rulers made their influence felt as far north as the borders of Morocco and Tunis. Stronger and richer than Ghana had ever been, Mali was also better known to the outside world. In 1324–1325 one of its *mansas,* or emperors, Musa I, made the pilgrimage to Mecca. He took with him a huge train of courtiers, servants, and slaves, and a treasure in gold dust weighing, by modern calculation, 3,800 kilograms. According to contemporary accounts, the largesse he distributed in Egypt and the Holy Places plus the liberal spending of his entourage depressed the price of gold on the Cairo exchanges for a generation. The unheralded appearance of so wealthy a king from the "Land of the Blacks" made a deep impression, and from the reign of the *mansa* Musa onward, Mali, or "Malel," began to appear regularly, in an approximately correct position, on the maps of the Middle East and Europe. Before long, indeed, the reputation of West Africa as a source of gold was to arouse the cupidity of both the Muslims of North Africa and the Christians of western Europe.

Between the eastern confines of Mali and the region of Lake Chad lay Hausaland, where already in the time of Ghana the seven Hausa city-states were being formed: Kano and Rano, Daura and Biram, Katsina, Gobir, and Zazzau. As a people the Hausa never joined together under one rule, but competed fiercely among themselves for trade and political power. Protected by strong city walls, they developed a highly urbanized society, excelling as manufacturers and long-distance merchants. The rulers and magnates of the towns tended to be Muslims, of greater or lesser orthodoxy, but most rural Hausa remained pagan until the nineteenth century and beyond.

East of Lake Chad the kingdom of Kanem was founded by Zaghawa nomads about A.D. 800. In the eleventh century the ruling dynasty of this kingdom accepted Islam, and under the *mai* (king) Dunama I (1097–1150) the frontiers of the state were extended north across the desert to the Fezzan and westward into Hausaland. Dunama is said to have had 30,000 horsemen under his command. Over the centuries the center of gravity of Kanem gradually moved from the eastern to the western side of Lake Chad, and the state changed its name to Bornu. Among the kingdoms of the Sudan, Bornu had the reputation of being more rigorous in its religious observances than most of its neighbors. It had cultural as well as commercial links with the Middle East, maintained a rest house at Cairo for pilgrims going to Mecca, and in the seventeenth century imported Turks to instruct its soldiers in musketry. It survived as an independent kingdom until the age of European imperialism.

In the Niger Bend region, meanwhile, a new power had arisen to challenge the might of Mali. About 1464 a warrior king, the *sonni* Ali, came to the throne of the riverine state of Gao in the middle Niger. By his death in 1492 he had created the Songhai empire and had extended his rule over the whole of the western Sudan. The military supremacy of Songhai rested on cavalry, on levies of foot soldiers, and on flotillas of war canoes which patrolled the thousand miles of the "navigable Niger." The dynasty of rulers who succeeded Ali, known as the *askiyas,* maintained his conquests and systematized the imperial government he had created. A bureaucracy, manned mainly by slaves, levied dues on trade and collected taxes, and a conscript army kept the peace and ensured that the trade routes remained open. The government was run by a council of ministers with clearly defined duties and responsibilities. In the great days of Songhai the mosques of Timbuktu and Jenne were famous throughout northern Africa for their piety and scholarship; students came from many parts of the Muslim world to study in them. Until the death of the *askiya* Da'ud in 1582, Songhai was a prosperous, powerful, and outwardly stable empire. But within a decade it had disintegrated, struck down by invaders from the north.

Relations between Songhai and the sultanate of Morocco had long been less than cordial. The basic cause of hostility was competition for the trans-Saharan trade and the valuable salt mine of Taghaza in the northern desert. Without the salt of Taghaza Songhai could not live, but Morocco claimed the territory in which the mine lay. The Moroccan sultan, too, had an army which urgently needed employing lest its commanders seek to satisfy their ambitions at home and at their master's expense. Spurred on by hopes of rich booty in the Land of the Blacks and using as an excuse an insulting message received from the reigning *askiya,* the sultan, in 1590, dispatched an army of 3,000 men due south across the desert.

Initially the Moroccans were everywhere victorious. The much larger armies of Songhai, consisting of cavalry with spears and lances and foot soldiers armed with bows and arrows, were easily mastered by Moroccan cannon and muskets. The capital, Gao, and the main towns along the Niger fell to the invaders in rapid succession. But in the south, where the terrain favored guerrilla tactics rather than open warfare and where the Moroccan superiority in fire power could not be brought to bear, the Songhai more than held their own. The central government had been destroyed and the caravan termini occupied, but the war went on. The invaders obtained less loot than expected, and after replacing the field commander more than once and dispatching several columns of reinforcements without improving the situation, the Sultan of Morocco lost interest. His soldiers were abandoned in their distant outposts beyond the Sahara and, in course of time, were absorbed in the indigenous population.

The Moroccan invasions brought down the Songhai empire, but left no enduring monument in the western Sudan. More than ten years of warfare devastated the countryside. Learning, culture, and prosperity were destroyed, the trans-Saharan trade declined, and the petty states which replaced Songhai maintained no imperial tradition. Timbuktu the Golden, revered by its chronicler as "that exquisite city, pure, delicious and illustrious, dearer than any in the world," became what it is today, a mud-built town of a few thousand inhabitants at the edge of the barren Sahara.

From about the second century B.C. Greek traders based on ports in the Red Sea began sailing south around Cape Guardafui to "Azania," as the coast of East Africa was then called. Azania produced palm oil, ivory, tortoise shell, rhinoceros horn, and slaves. All were valuable commodities, and thus Azania naturally provoked the interest of the ancient Mediterranean world. Some of the reports on East Africa gleaned from itinerant Greek traders and ships' supercargoes were surprisingly accurate. Ptolemy's *Geography,* compiled between the second and fifth centuries, described a "great snow mountain" in the East African interior, and claimed that the River Nile had its source in inland lakes. Both pieces of information were true—the snow mountain is clearly Mount Kilimanjaro—though both were vehemently denied for the next 1,500 years by geographers less well informed than Ptolemy.

Merchants from south Arabia, the Persian Gulf, and northwestern India had also long traded with the East African coast, and continued to do so after the rise of Islam cut the Christian traders of the Mediterranean off from the commerce of the Indian Ocean. In course of time some of these Asian merchants settled in East Africa permanently. They were joined by religious refugees from Oman and Shiraz on the Persian Gulf, by men who sought a sanctuary where they could practice in peace beliefs regarded as heretical in their homelands. The total number of immigrants was probably quite small, but their impact on the East African coast was considerable. They were responsible for beginning the process whereby a chain of independent settlements grew up all along the coast from Mogadiscio in the north to Sofala in the south. These settlements existed on, and for, trade; modern historians have characterized them as the "city-states" of medieval East Africa.

By the mid-thirteenth century there were between thirty and forty of these states, many located for ease of defense on islands. None appears to have willingly recognized the supremacy of any other, but for a century or more one of them, Kilwa, attained preeminence. The rulers of Kilwa built mosques, palaces, and bathhouses of coral and stone, minted their own coins, and were wealthy enough to import porcelain from China. The ruling dynasties of all the city-states were Muslim, the populations they controlled were a mixture of immigrant Arabo-Persians and indigenous Bantu. The resulting amalgam of foreign and local languages, customs, and racial stocks produced in course of time the distinctive East African culture known as Swahili.

The East African city-states possessed far-ranging economic influence, but their political control did not extend more than a few miles inland from the coast. The interior peoples themselves brought the wealth of East and Central Africa to the shores of the Indian Ocean. Columns of slaves balancing elephants' tusks on their heads plodded for hundreds of miles along bush tracks as they were driven to the markets of Kilwa, Mafia, Mombasa, or Malindi. On arrival burdens and bearers alike were sold to traders who shipped them to Arabia and Persia and India. Gold from the Limpopo Basin and copper from Katanga were similarly transported over long distances to Indian Ocean ports.

In Central Africa at this period the leading interior state was governed by a monarch known as the Mwana Mtapa, the "Monomotapa" of later Portuguese accounts. The Mwana Mtapas ruled a 700-mile stretch of the Zambezi Valley between the Kariba Gorge and the sea. They were heirs to an even older dynasty which had been responsible for building the fortress-shrine of Great Zimbabwe in Mashonaland (Rhodesia). The tall stone ruins of Zimbabwe stand today as a mute reminder of the existence of large-scale political organization in the depths of Central Africa long before the first Europeans set foot on the coast.

Throughout the savannas and forests of sub-Saharan Africa the processes of state formation threw up many rulers like the Mwana Mtapas. In the region of the southern Congo arose the Lunda-Luba empire of the Mwata Yamvo. In the Great Lakes country of interior East Africa the cattle-herding Cwezi kings held dominion until their overthrow about the beginning of the sixteenth century by Lwo invaders from the north, who established in their turn the states that grew into Bunyoro and Buganda. A century or more before this the *manikongo* (king of Congo) had maintained such state that the first Portuguese who arrived at his capital were amazed at its opulence. The king of Portugal made haste to form an alliance with this prince of tropical Africa, since his kingdom was obviously too powerful to be conquered. The first European visitors to the state of Benin in the Niger Delta were equally impressed. They traded eagerly with its inhabitants for cloth, pepper, and gold, and found the local people courteous, shrewd, and, in the words of one sixteenth-century English account, "verrie gentle and loveing."

Before the coming of the European, Africa south of the Sahara was in the preindustrial stage of economic development, but in many areas its people had created highly organized networks of long-distance trade. Large states and polities had been established, in some cases consisting of territories and populations greater in size than those which existed at the time in Europe. Of the outside world, however, Africans in general remained profoundly ignorant. It was perhaps mainly for this reason that they were about to be overwhelmed by the greatest tragedy in the history of their own or any other continent, the 400-year-long maritime slave trade.

For Further Reading

Davidson, Basil, *The African Past.*
————, *The Lost Cities of Africa.*
Fage, J. D., *A History of West Africa: An Introductory Survey.*
Oliver, Roland, and Fage, J. D., *A Short History of Africa.*

27   The Chinese Empire: The Great Era

By 577, the long period of political disunity in China was nearing its end. Two major dynasties divided the nation between themselves, a Chinese one in the south and a barbarian one in the north. The most influential statesman in the latter was a Chinese, Yang Chien, who in 581 dismissed the last

A.D.		
	581–618	Sui dynasty
	605–610	Grand Canal built
	612–614	Korean campaigns
	618–907	T'ang dynasty
	627–649	Reign of T'ai-tsung
	630	Defeat of Eastern Turks
	656	Defeat of Western Turks
	690–705	Reign of Empress Wu
	713–755	Reign of Hsüan-tsung
	751	Battle of Talas River
	755	Rebellion of An Lu-shan
	780	Tax reform
	821	Peace between China and Tibet
	840	Uighur empire destroyed
	841–845	Religious persecutions
	879	Looting of Canton
	907–960	China divided
	960–1126	Northern Sung dynasty
	1004	Peace between China and Liao
	1024	World's first paper currency
	1044	Peace between China and Hsi-hsia
	1069–1076	Wang An-shih in power
	1125	Liao empire destroyed
	1127–1279	Southern Sung dynasty
	1130–1200	Chu Hsi
	1135	Lin-an capital of Southern Sung
	1141	Peace between China and Chin

boy emperor, ascended the throne himself, and founded the Sui dynasty. His posthumous name is Emperor Wen. He defeated the south in 589, and thereby reunited China. Emperor Wen's rise to power was very similar to that of Wang Mang, with the difference that he was successful. The dynastic historians treat him therefore not condescendingly as a usurper, but respectfully as the man who received the Mandate of Heaven.

The Sui dynasty consisted of only two rulers. Emperor Wen died in 604, and was succeeded by his son, possibly his murderer, Emperor Yang. But in spite of its short reign, the Sui was a period of great activity. A centralized bureaucracy was restored and staffed. Ch'ang-an became the capital, with Lo-yang as a subsidiary one. Agricultural and fiscal reforms were attempted. Since the Yangtze delta was emerging as the key economic area, and the capitals depended on it for grain and other supplies, the first Grand Canal was built between 605 and 610. It made use of earlier canals, and connected the area of present Hang-chou with the Yellow River, a distance of more than 500 miles. The Great Wall was reconstructed as a defensive barrier at the northern border.

The Sui dynasty did less well in the field of foreign policy. The empire had shrunk since Han times. The Ordos Region had been lost, as well as all possessions in present-day Manchuria and Korea. The Tarim Basin in Central Asia was no longer under Chinese control, except briefly between 609 and 611. In Yunnan and Kweichou, a Thai-speaking tribe was in the process of founding the state of Nan-chao, which remained independent until 1252. Fukien, on the other hand, had become an integral part of the nation. It had been assimilated through a gradual, peaceful immigration of Chinese colonists, which had begun in the last decades of Later Han. In addition, the Sui dynasty managed to regain possession of the Red River delta in Indochina.

Emperor Yang made the mistake of imitating the Han dynasties in his relations with Korea. He wished, at all costs, to reestablish Chinese rule, which embroiled him in an expensive and inconclusive war. In 612 he attacked the North Korean state of Koguryŏ, but only conquered southern Manchuria to the Liao River. A campaign in 613 had to be discontinued. While Chinese troops reached Pyŏngyang in 614, they were unable to take it.

This military debacle was aggravated by pressure from the Turks, who had become the dominant tribe in Central Asia since the middle of the sixth century and had brought vast territories under their rule. In 582 their nation split into the Eastern and Western Turks, both of whom were a threat to China. A great raid in 615 caught Emperor Yang unawares. He was almost captured, and after his escape withdrew to the lower Yangtze region. Thereafter, the Sui state crumbled with amazing swiftness. Rebellion broke out all over the country, and in 618 Emperor Yang was murdered. Perhaps the two rulers of the dynasty had tried to achieve too much too soon. Certainly the centrifugal forces, strengthened through the long period of division, could not be quickly curbed, and asserted themselves again when the new central government showed signs of weakness.

The victors of the civil war were the Li, a noble Chinese family from the northwest, who may have had some barbarian ancestors. An important factor in their success was a temporary alliance with the Eastern Turks. In 618, Li Yüan, then in his early fifties, was enthroned as the first emperor of the T'ang dynasty, with Ch'ang-an as his capital. His rivals were defeated in a number of brief campaigns, lasting until 623. Meanwhile, the alliance with the Eastern Turks faltered, and the Turks invaded China in 622 and 624.

The first emperor of T'ang had named the eldest of his three sons heir apparent. This provoked the middle son, Li Shih-min, to ambush and kill his brothers on July 2, 626. He then forced his father to abdicate, and took the throne himself. Emperor T'ai-tsung, as he is known in history, represents a typical historiographical problem. While not the first emperor of T'ang, he is depicted as the actual founder of the dynasty, the man who received the Mandate. The dynastic historians focus on him from the beginning of the rebellion and play down the roles of his father and brothers. T'ai-tsung's murder of his brothers and dethronement of his father were justified by distorting history and by portraying him as the only talented member of his family, a superior military genius and leader of men. This is not to say that T'ai-tsung was a bad ruler. He was forceful and intelligent, and had the ability to select competent assistants. He also adopted a policy of religious tolerance, which remained generally characteristic for the T'ang until the ninth century. When T'ai-tsung died in 649 and left a stable empire to his son Kao-tsung, the only danger to his house came from a woman.

One of T'ai-tsung's harem ladies, named Wu, became a concubine of the new emperor in 650, and managed to have herself appointed empress five years later. Through intrigue, strength of will, and, where necessary, murder, the Empress Wu made herself the dominating figure at the court. When Kao-tsung died at the end of 683, a grown son of hers succeeded to the throne. But, because he showed signs of independence, she demoted him within two months and replaced him with her youngest son. This worthy did not interfere in matters of state, and in 690 officially abdicated in favor of his mother. She ascended the throne in her own right, and proclaimed the Chou dynasty. Since the dynastic historians were biased against the Empress Wu, there is the usual difficulty of obtaining a balanced view. So much is certain, that, while vindictive, cruel, and power-

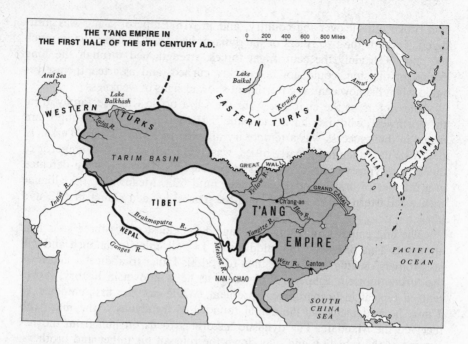

THE T'ANG EMPIRE IN
THE FIRST HALF OF THE 8TH CENTURY A.D.

hungry, she also was a great monarch. Her reign came to an end in early 705, when, aged eighty and feeble, she was overthrown and her eldest son reinstated. She died before the end of that year. With her grandson Hsüan-tsung, who reigned from 713 to 755, the T'ang dynasty reached its cultural zenith, and also began its steep political decline.

The first half of the T'ang dynasty was a period of vigorous foreign involvement. T'ai-tsung had resumed the campaigns against Koguryŏ, and his son finally destroyed this state in 668. But within a decade the Chinese were expelled, and Korea was united under the Silla dynasty, which remained in power until 935. Beyond Korea, the Chinese had been aware of the Japanese islands and their inhabitants at least since Former Han times, and the first official Japanese embassy had reached China in A.D. 57. During T'ang, Japan received profound cultural impulses from China, both directly by sea from the Yangtze delta and by diffusion via Korea.

Whereas China had achieved little in the Korean wars, it was triumphant in Central Asia. After a new raid of the Eastern Turks, the Chinese took the offensive, captured the Turkish ruler in 630, and reduced his nation, comprising the area of present Inner and Outer Mongolia, to vassal status. The Eastern Turks rallied at the end of the seventh century, but peace was restored in 725. Two decades later, in 744, the Eastern Turkish empire was broken up by the Uighurs, another Turkish-speaking people, who had become allies of China. The power of the Uighurs lasted until 840, when they were defeated by still another Turkish tribe, the Kirghiz.

The Western Turkish empire, mainly comprising West Turkestan, Dzungaria, and the Tarim Basin, posed a more distant threat. China contested the Tarim Basin, and regained it in campaigns lasting from 640 to 648. On the insistence of the energetic Empress Wu, Chinese armies then invaded West Turkestan in 656, the Turkish ruler was taken prisoner, and his empire ceased to exist. West Turkestan became what amounted to a Chinese protectorate.

This was the peak of Chinese expansion in Central Asia, but soon the situation was dramatically changed with the appearance of the Arabs. Muhammad's death in 632 had not halted the Muslim conquests. Ctesiphon, the residence of the Sassanid kings on the Tigris, was conquered in 637; a Sassanid prince reached Ch'ang-an as a refugee in 674. From 705 onward, the Arab warrior Khotaiba ibn Muslim gradually gained possession of West Turkestan. After his death in 715, although China regained a foothold through diplomatic means, this did not prevent the Arabs from garrisoning Bukhara and Samarkand. If the Chinese wished to maintain their presence in West Turkestan, a military clash was unavoidable. It came in 751 at the Talas River, not far from present Tashkent. The Arabs won with the help of the Karluks, a Turkish-speaking tribe, who during the battle made a surprise attack on the Chinese from the rear. With this defeat, China lost its position in West Turkestan forever. Among the Chinese prisoners taken by the Arabs at the Talas River were men who knew how to make paper—an art discovered in China at least 650 years earlier. As an unexpected by-product of the battle, paper manufacture spread to Samarkand and Baghdad, was from there carried to Damascus, Cairo, and Morocco, and entered Europe through Italy and Spain.

Tibet was unified early in the seventh century, and its king Srong-bcan-sgam-po sent an embassy to China in 641 to ask for a Chinese princess in marriage. This was arranged, and according to Chinese tradition the princess did much to civilize the uncouth Tibetans. Actually, Tibet's advance was due less to a princess' influence than to the general diffusion of the Indian and Chinese cultures. Although the Tibetans were converted to Buddhism at this time, their warlike spirits were not yet dampened. From 670 to 821, they repeatedly fought the Chinese and asserted themselves in the western Tarim Basin. They even temporarily took and looted Ch'ang-an in 763. The Arabs also suffered under the Tibetans, so that the caliph Harun al-Rashid in 798 offered China military cooperation. But the threat receded, no joint action took place, and the Tibetans made peace with China in 821. During the following centuries, their nation mellowed into a theocracy and lost its belligerence.

In their heyday of foreign involvement, the Chinese also intervened in northern India. An ambassador spent two years at King Harṣa's court during the early 640's. Returning on a second mission in 647, he found that Harṣa had just died without an heir, and that a certain Aryuna had made himself the ruler. On Aryuna's order, the Chinese delegation was massacred. The ambassador succeeded in escaping, raised troops in Nepal, arrested Aryuna, and brought him as a prisoner to Ch'ang-an. One hundred years later, in 747, Chinese troops crossed the Pamir Mountains and made a brief appearance in northern India.

In the south, China occupied the Red River delta in Indochina throughout T'ang times. Only toward the southwest, in Yunnan and Kweichou, the Chinese met with utter failure. The independent state of Nan-chao continued to flourish in that region and repelled with ease all Chinese invasions.

Meanwhile, Chinese and foreigners met peacefully in the great port of Canton and in other places on the southeast coast. Shipping was primarily in the hands of Arabs and Persians. Jews are known to have been among the traders in Canton. Arab sources report that in the ninth century a voyage from Persia to China took 130 to 140 days. The foreign merchants were provided with special quarters in Canton, and had considerable freedom in governing themselves. A temporary setback for overseas trade came in 879, when Canton was taken and looted by a rebel, and many foreigners lost their lives. The Arabs used this interval for developing a trade route to Japan and Korea.

The vigor of early T'ang times sprang not only from the ambitions of energetic rulers, but also from the smooth functioning of the bureaucratic institutions, which followed the traditional pattern. Three offices formed the chief organs of the central government: the Imperial Secretariat in charge of making policy, the Imperial Chancellery which reviewed it, and the Secretariat of State Affairs which implemented it. The Six Ministries were concerned with personnel, revenue, rites, war, justice, and public works; the Nine Offices had similar administrative duties. The Board of Censors scrutinized the performance of the civil servants and, in bursts of courage, even of the emperor himself. The provincial administration was very similar to that of Sui and Han times.

The examination system had been reintroduced by Sui and was improved by T'ang. A candidate for office prepared himself by studying with a tutor, in the public school of his local district, or at the Imperial Academy in the capital. He then enrolled for an examination in his chosen field, such as literature, law, or mathematics. If he was successful, he received a title which corresponded to the type of his examination. The most respected among these titles was that of Presented Scholar, and all who received it were, as implied by the wording, introduced to the emperor. Theirs was a literary degree, since knowledge of the Confucian classics was valued more highly than specialism in practical subjects. T'ang is therefore, after the Han, the second great period of Confucian exegesis, and the approved version of the classics was finally engraved on stone tablets in 839. To receive an official post, however, the degree was not enough. The candidate had to pass a further placement test. Once he was in office, advancement depended on additional examinations and merit ratings. The emperor's relatives, holders of noble and honorific titles, and sons of high officials did not need to earn the scholarly degrees, and could directly take the placement tests. While tensions existed between the degree holders and this privileged group, the majority of the career officials had entered the bureaucracy through the examination system. The Empress Wu contributed much to that development, since, from political motives, she favored degree holders.

In agriculture, the so-called equal field system, whose origins go back to earlier times, was tried and failed. It was designed to grant 100 *mou* (about 13.7 acres) of land to each male at the age of twenty-one. Unless he died earlier, 80 *mou* reverted to the state when he reached sixty. The remainder became his permanent property. Smaller lots were given to widows, invalids, and similar distressed categories. Officials received considerably larger units, known as service portions, as long as they were employed by the government. In theory, complete equity was possible through the routine and continuous redistribution of land; in fact, supply and demand were out of step. Although the population total did not grow during at least the first half of the T'ang dynasty, regional proportions kept changing through a great migration from north to central and southern China. In areas of dense or, through the influx of migrants, sharply increasing population, a continuous public redistribution of land was technically infeasible. In spite of this, the poll tax remained geared to the ideal, though largely fictitious, system of equal land allotment. The increasing disorder in tax collection reached the point where a reform became necessary. In 780, the Double Tax was introduced, which was levied twice each year in the sixth and eleventh months. It was a land tax, proportionate to the area held by each owner. Henceforth, the government lost interest in the size of holdings. Since large estates paid large taxes, there was no longer any good fiscal reason to oppose their formation. This may have contributed to the growth of landlordism in China.

As in earlier periods, the merchants were discriminated against, and the government sought to monopolize the production and sale of important commodities, particularly salt, iron, liquor, and tea. Tea became a truly national Chinese drink only in T'ang times. It was characteristic of the government's attitude toward commerce that it tried to gain control of the tea trade as soon as this promised to become a major source of income.

T'ang civilization reached its height in the reign of the art-loving

Emperor Hsüan-tsung (713–755), who was a great patron of poetry and painting, of literature, theater, and scholarship. But he was unprepared for the political convulsion which cost him his throne. A development had taken place in the military field, whereby professional troops had gradually supplanted the militia of earlier times. Border territories were placed under Regional Commanders, who controlled both the military defense and the civilian administration, and therefore possessed exceptional power. One of these men, An Lu-shan, revolted in 755 at the northeastern frontier, conquered Lo-yang and Ch'ang-an, and proclaimed himself emperor. Hsüan-tsung fled and abdicated in favor of his son. The rebellion continued for several years, and was not fully suppressed until 763. Of crucial importance for the T'ang government was the assistance of the Uighurs, who exacted their reward, including a daughter of the emperor.

It is sometimes asserted, owing to a misunderstanding of the Chinese statistics, that the bloodletting of the civil war reduced China's population by two-thirds or more, but that was not the case. The population hovered around the 50 million level from Han to T'ang, without massive changes. A major factor preventing population growth was probably infanticide. Sons were preferred and daughters an economic liability. The abandoning of newborn girls served therefore as a check. It is only from the end of T'ang that China's steady population increase began.

While the T'ang nominally survived until 907, power shifted from the central government to hereditary Regional Commanders, most of whom had no national ambitions. The dynasty finally collapsed in another civil war, which increased in violence from 874, and in which the last two emperors were murdered.

The empire of China's powerful and demanding allies, the Uighurs, had crumbled sixty-seven years earlier, and that event had brought important religious repercussions. Previously, the T'ang dynasty had been a period of relative religious tolerance. Buddhism had flourished, and other religions had benefited also. The first Zoroastrian temple was built in Ch'ang-an in 621, and the first Nestorian Christian missionary had reached that city in 635. Manicheism came to China in 694, and received preferential treatment for good tactical reasons: the Uighurs converted to it, and it was important not to affront these allies. The defeat of the Uighurs by the Kirghiz in 840 changed that situation. Manicheism immediately came under attack in China, and religious persecutions began. They lasted from 841 to 845, and were through Taoist influence extended to other foreign religions. Manicheism, Nestorianism, and Zoroastrianism were wiped out. Buddhism, which had met with earlier setbacks in 446 and 574, survived, but suffered enormous economic losses. The great wealth of its temples and monasteries was confiscated, shrines were closed, and monks and nuns were secularized. Buddhism never fully recovered, and degenerated spiritually during the following centuries. Islam, which still had few followers in China, was apparently unaffected by the persecution. It was only later that Islam became a great religious force in the western border regions.

Half a century was to pass before the empire was unified once more. Five successive dynasties ruled the north. Ten other states appeared in the rest of China, excluding Nan-chao in the southwest. The dynastic historians, obsessed with the Mandate of Heaven, considered the northern dynasties as legitimate, and this brief period of Chinese history is therefore known as that of the Five Dynasties. It was another time of turmoil, yet it was also an era of great cultural activity, in which, among other achievements, printing came of age. The technique of block printing seems to have been developed by the Buddhists and Taoists, but much of its early history remains obscure. The oldest printed texts discovered so far are Buddhist sutras. During the Five Dynasties, the Confucian classics were printed for the first time, and the technique became respectable. Movable type was invented soon thereafter, but block printing was cheaper and continued to be the common method.

The empire was reunited by the Chinese general Chao K'uang-yin (d. 976), who established the Northern Sung dynasty (960–1126), and chose K'ai-feng on the Grand Canal as his capital. His dynasty did not have the military vigor of a T'ang or Han, and was early forced to make territorial concessions. Toward the end of T'ang, the Mongolian-speaking Khitan had founded a large Central Asian state, comprising Manchuria, Inner Mongolia, and the greater part of Outer Mongolia. Its rulers called themselves emperors from 907, and adopted the name of Liao for their dynasty in 947. A decade earlier, in 938, the Khitan had gained possession of northern Hopei and northern Shansi, and they retained these areas as long as their empire lasted. The Sung were not only unable to reconquer the lost territories, but even had to pay annual tribute to Liao from 1004. Korea, since 935 under the Koryŏ dynasty, was similarly reduced to a tributary of the Liao.

In the northwest, China was also retreating. The Tibetan Hsi-hsia dynasty made itself master of the Kansu corridor and the Ordos Region, threw off Chinese rule, and defeated the Sung armies. China agreed in a peace treaty of 1044 to pay tribute to Hsi-hsia as well. In the south, Sung had lost the Red River delta, where Annam emerged as an independent state from the tenth century onward. In the southwest, the border against Nan-chao remained unchanged.

Although Sung China was smaller than the T'ang state, its population was much larger, perhaps around 100 million by the early twelfth century.

One factor favoring population growth was the introduction in the eleventh century of early-ripening rice from Indochina. This made two rice harvests possible each year, feeding larger numbers of people and thereby reducing the need for infanticide.

The central government was reorganized in a form differing slightly from the T'ang. A Council of State became the important policy-making and executive body under the emperor, assisted by a bureau of scholars and a number of agencies including the censorate. Below the Council of State were the Secretariat-Chancellery in charge of personnel and law, the Finance Commission, and the Bureau of Military Affairs. In the local administration, the provinces were no longer divided into commanderies, but into prefectures and subprefectures, each consisting of a varying number of districts.

The examination system was still evolving, and candidates now had to pass three consecutive levels of tests. The first hurdle was an examination given by either the local prefectures, the government schools in the provinces, or the Imperial Academy in K'ai-feng. Successful candidates proceeded to a more advanced examination in the capital. The third stage was an examination conducted by the palace. Among the final degrees, that of Presented Scholar remained the most respected. The better an examinee had done, the more important the office he received. Sons of high officials continued to be a privileged group, and could be directly nominated for office. Sale of office persisted, but on a limited scale and offering little hope for advancement.

In the military field, the founder of Sung had decided against reviving the militia. He relied on a professional standing army, but made sure that the provincial detachments were not large enough to endanger the dynasty. K'ai-feng was protected by special units. Cavalry was neglected.

Northern Sung witnessed an unprecedented expansion in industry and commerce, which led to a coin shortage and the world's first paper currency. Experiments with so-called Flying Cash had been made as early as 811, in T'ang times. The government had then issued money drafts which could be used in transactions and eventually exchanged for cash. During Sung, both the government and private banks emitted drafts and certificates. This trade was monopolized by the government in 1024, and the various notes were converted into paper currency.

Because of growing demands particularly by agriculture, the government arsenals, and shipbuilding, the output of pig iron increased greatly during Northern Sung, which in turn increased the demand for fuel used in iron smelting. Since charcoal was not available in sufficient quantities, mineral coal became more and more a substitute. Mineral coal had been used on a limited scale from at least the fourth century A.D.; with the eleventh century, it became the most important fuel in China. Commerce also expanded; porcelain manufacture flourished; the tea trade increased; cotton came into general use. Yet, although the merchants organized themselves in trade associations and guilds, they remained a functionally weak middle class. They suffered under the government's confiscatory policy of monopolizing large profitable enterprises through a licensing system, as it did with the trade in tea, salt, and agricultural implements. Moreover, merchants were held in low esteem by the Confucian state. The Chinese ideal remained the well-bred official, not the successful businessman, and the highest ambition of even the merchants themselves was to see their descendants absorbed into the scholar-gentry.

Among the many new fashions developing in Sung China, only two will be mentioned here: chairs were adopted, and foot-binding became popular.

The latter has been interpreted as marking a decline in the status of women, but that is probably a misconception. Foot-binding was a vogue, to which the women did not object.

Gradually, the economic position of the government worsened, owing to increasing expenses for the civil bureaucracy and military defense. A reform party appeared among the officials, led by Wang An-shih (d. 1086), who was a slovenly but brilliant man, unorthodox in behavior and thought. His program was not all of his own design and included ideas which had been tried before in Chinese history. He was opposed by a conservative party, led by a number of famous and respected statesmen. In 1069, Wang An-shih became chief minister, and set out to rationalize government and finance. He abolished superfluous posts in the bureaucracy and modernized the examination curriculum. He changed the basis of the land tax, so that it was assessed not only on the size of each holding but also on the productivity of the soil. He commuted corvée into a money payment. He established government pawnshops which offered the peasants loans at the relatively low rate of 20 per cent. To stabilize the market, he had the government buy basic commodities when prices were low and sell them when prices were high, a method which had been tried as early as Han times. He also once more replaced professional soldiers with a militia, and attempted to set up a cavalry.

It is difficult to know how successful the reforms were, and how much they met with passive resistance and bureaucratic inertia. Wang An-shih retired himself in 1076, but his party remained in power until 1086. The conservatives dominated the government from 1086 to 1094. For most of the time between 1094 and 1126, the reformers were again in control, but they were no longer led by a man of Wang An-shih's caliber, and in the violent reaction to the military disaster of 1126, they were swept away.

A menacing new power had appeared in the north. The Jurchen, Tungusic-speaking tribes in Central Manchuria who were ancestors of the Manchus, had risen against their erstwhile Khitan masters in 1114, had proclaimed the Chin dynasty in the following year, and, aided by Sung armies, had destroyed the Liao empire in 1125. The victors immediately fell out with each other, and the Sung discovered that their new neighbors were infinitely more belligerent than the Khitan had been. In 1126 the Jurchen took the Sung capital, K'ai-feng, looted it, and carried off the emperor and his father. Neither ever saw China again.

Pursued by the Jurchen, the Sung forces withdrew southward, and the following period is therefore known as the Southern Sung dynasty (1127–1279). Lin-an, the present-day Hang-chou, became the capital in 1135. It was situated in Chekiang, in the midst of China's richest agricultural region, and grew into what was then the most splendid city in the world. It

CHINA AROUND A.D. 1140

.... Coastline, A.D.1970
ᴖᴖᴖᴖ Great Wall

Chin Empire
Southern Sung Empire

Lake Baikal

Amur River

Sungari R.

SEA OF JAPAN

Liao R.

CHIN EMPIRE

KORYŌ

HSI HSIA

YELLOW SEA

Wei R.   Yellow River   GRAND CANAL

K'ai-feng

TSINLING MTS.   Han R.   Huai R.

TIBET

Brahmaputra R.

Lin-an

EAST CHINA SEA

Yangtze River

SOUTHERN SUNG EMPIRE

NAN-CHAO

West R.

Red R.

ANNAM

SOUTH CHINA SEA

0   250   500 Miles

had a population of about a million and a half, and Marco Polo described it later as the world's largest and most beautiful city. The war dragged on inconclusively until 1141, when the border between Chin and Southern Sung was drawn along the Tsinling Mountains and the Huai River. Sung also agreed to pay an annual tribute. Except for the Hsi-hsia state in the northwest, the Chin empire controlled all of northern China and Manchuria. Mongolia did not belong to the Chin, and soon was to bring forth new and even more formidable conquerors.

The defeat by the Jurchen was a great blow to Chinese pride, but it was not an economic disaster. While the promising industrial development was brought to a halt, the most productive agricultural area was in the lower Yangtze Valley. In every field, save brute military strength, Southern Sung was superior to Chin, so that the loss of northern China meant little to the average southerner.

It was a time of booming maritime trade, and this was no longer in the hands of foreigners. The Chinese had learned to build superior ships, which called at ports as far away as India's west coast. The magnetic compass may have been discovered in China during the Han dynasty, and the floating compass needle had been known since at least the fourth century A.D. The instrument had not been needed in the predominantly coastal and inland shipping of the earlier period, but with the maritime expansion of Sung times it seems to have become standard equipment on seagoing vessels. In the West, there is no record of the magnetic compass until 1190, so that the invention may well have spread from China via the Middle East to Europe. This possibility is strengthened by the fact that Arabs during the thirteenth century used a floating compass needle shaped like a fish, just as the Chinese did before them.

The Sung scholars interested themselves in many other fields of knowledge, such as archaeology, history, agriculture, mathematics, geometry, geography, cartography, astronomy, and forensic medicine. The Chinese mathematicians of this time may have been the most advanced in the world. Sung was also a period when the experience of the past was collected, categorized, and preserved in great encyclopedic works.

In the field of Confucian thought, there were the same attempts to systematize and codify. During the Han dynasty, Confucianism had adapted itself to become a practical tool of government. After a period of decline, it had asserted itself again in T'ang times, and had been reinforced by the exegetic studies of the classical commentators. Sung was the last great period of adjustment. The Neo-Confucian thinkers, influenced by Taoism and Buddhism, attempted to harmonize the Confucian classics into a homogeneous whole, and to provide Confucianism with a metaphysical superstructure which so far had been lacking. To do so, they had to reinterpret the classics, to read much into them which was not there, and to explain away all contradictions.

Neo-Confucianism split into two major branches, the Rationalistic and the Idealistic schools. The first of these received its final form through Chu Hsi (1130–1200). He distinguished between principle and matter. All matter, whether animate or inanimate, has its own principle without which it cannot exist. The invention of a boat is no more than the material expression of the already existing principle. All principles are part of an eternal oneness, which is the Supreme Ultimate. The Supreme Ultimate is totally present in each material object, but only the principle pertaining to that particular object is able to manifest itself. The rest is kept out by the impurity of matter. This concept made it possible to reconcile earlier doubts about the nature of man. Goodness and evil depend on each individual's degree of purity. The purpose of education is to reduce impurity. Self-cultivation and a proper understanding of the classics must therefore be more conducive to this goal than technical specialization. All men together form society which has its own principle called the Way. Good government means to conform to the Way.

The most famous exponent of the Idealistic School, Wang Yang-ming, who lived much later (1472–1529), maintained that principle and matter are a single entity, and that sagehood is achieved through intuitive knowledge. But it was Chu Hsi's interpretation which became orthodox and unshakable in the field of education. His and his school's understanding of the classics came to form the basic curriculum hammered into the heads of all candidates for office. This was expected to foster the high moral character needed for governing and guiding the people, yet it also encouraged conformity and penalized independence of mind.

For Further Reading

Gernet, Jacques, *Daily Life in China on the Eve of the Mongol Invasion, 1250–1276.*
Waley, Arthur, *The Life and Times of Po Chü-i.*
———— (trans.), *Monkey.*
Watson, Burton, *Chinese Lyricism.*

28 The Chinese Empire: Foreign Rulers and National Restoration

One of the greatest conquerors the world has known was born about 1167 as the son of a minor Mongolian chief and given the name Temüjin. His tribe was dominated by the powerful Tatars, who had their grazing grounds in what now is eastern Mongolia. Tatar, in the West corrupted to Tartar, was only gradually replaced by Mongol as a general term for all people belonging to that particular language group. The change in appellation was entirely due to the fact that Temüjin was a Mongol. During years of tribal fighting, he subdued the Tatars, Kereits, Oirats, and Naimans, and became the master of the Mongolian-speaking people. His supremacy was confirmed in 1206, when the Mongolian diet recognized him as Chinggis Khan, which may mean Universal Ruler.

CHRONOLOGY

A.D.	c. 1167–1227	Chinggis Khan
	1217	Mongols conquer Tarim Basin
	1221	Mongols conquer West Turkestan and Afghanistan
	1222	Chinggis Khan raids India
	1227	Mongols conquer Hsi-hsia
	1229–1241	Ögödei Great Khan
	1234	Mongols conquer Chin empire
	1238	Mongols take Moscow
	1240	Mongols take Kiev
	1241	Mongol victories at Liegnitz (Silesia) and Mohi (Hungary)
	1251–1259	Möngke Great Khan
	1252	Mongols conquer Nan-chao and eastern Tibet
	1258	Mongols take Baghdad, conquer Korea
	1260–1294	Khubilai Great Khan
	1274	Mongols raid Kyūshū
	1275–1292	Marco Polo in China
	1279	Mongols conquer Southern Sung
	1280–1367	Yüan dynasty
	1281	Unsuccessful Mongol invasion of Kyūshū
	1293	Unsuccessful Mongol invasion of Java
	1368–1644	Ming dynasty
	1336–1405	Timur (Tamerlane)
	1424	Death of Yung-lo Emperor
	1405–1433	Voyages of Cheng Ho
	1419	Death of Tsong-kha-pa
	1421	Peking capital of China
	1428	Annam independent
	1449	Oirats raid China
	1514	Coming of the Westerners
	1522	Tax reform
	1550	Tatars raid China
	1557	Portuguese gain possession of Macao
	1607	Peace between China and Japan
	1618	Outbreak of fighting between Manchus and China
	1644	Suicide of last Ming emperor; Manchus enter Peking

Chinggis Khan continued his intensive campaigns to establish a great Mongolian empire. Hsi-hsia submitted in 1209. Chin was invaded in 1211, but the Mongols suspended this attack and shifted their attention westward. They conquered the Tarim Basin and half of Turkestan in 1217. By 1221, the remainder of West Turkestan, Afghanistan, and part of Persia were in their hands. The next year, Chinggis Khan personally conducted a raid into northern India. Other forces invaded Russia in 1223. An uprising of Hsi-hsia in 1224 persuaded Chinggis Khan to return from West Asia, but he died in 1227, shortly before the final defeat of that state. His son Ögödei became Great Khan in 1229, and made Karakorum the capital of the Mongolian empire.

The Mongols began their final attack on Chin in 1232 and, with ill-advised support from the Southern Sung, completed it in 1234. Then they struck again toward the west, took Moscow in 1238 and Kiev in 1240. There followed the famous two-pronged raid into Europe, with the stunning victories at Liegnitz in Silesia and at Mohi in Hungary, both in April, 1241. Mongolian cavalry penetrated to Vienna and the Adriatic, whereupon the armies withdrew as suddenly as they had come. One reason may have been that no territorial conquests had been intended, another that the struggle over the succession after Great Khan Ögödei's death in December, 1241, required the presence of the high nobles in Karakorum. The political situation remained fluid for a decade, in the course of which the Mongols avoided major military involvement.

The enthronement of Möngke, son of Ögödei's younger brother, in 1251 signaled a renewal of vigorous expansion. In 1252, the Mongols subjugated the state of Nan-chao in southwest China, and thereafter took eastern Tibet. The final conquest of Persia came in the following year. In 1258, the Mongols destroyed the Abassid Caliphate of Baghdad, and during the same year brought Korea to heel.

When Great Khan Möngke suddenly died in 1259, two of his brothers competed for the throne. Khubilai won and was recognized as Great Khan from 1264. He shifted his capital from Karakorum to Khanbaligh (City of the Khan), the future Peking. Although Khubilai does not seem to have known Chinese, he chose in 1271 the Chinese name of Yüan for his dynasty. His forces launched an attack on Southern Sung, took its capital in 1276, and then swiftly overpowered the rest of China. A remnant of the Sung navy, with the last child emperor on board one of the ships, was sunk in 1279.

During the Chinese wars, a variety of new weapons was brought into action, including firearms. Gunpowder had been used for military purposes in China since the tenth century, and may have been discovered much earlier. The Sung forces employed fire arrows and explosive grenades, and

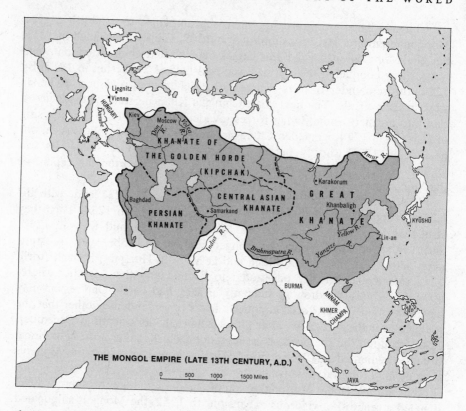

THE MONGOL EMPIRE (LATE 13TH CENTURY, A.D.)

they experimented with land mines, poison gas projectiles, and smoke screens, all of which utilized gunpowder in various ways. Cannons began to replace catapults in the thirteenth century. Knowledge of gunpowder spread to the Jurchen and Mongols, who soon were hurling projectiles at their inventors and each other. Whether the appearance of gunpowder in Europe during the fourteenth century is due to independent discovery or diffusion from China remains an open question.

The Yüan, officially dated 1280–1367 in China, was the first foreign dynasty to govern the entire nation. But Khubilai was not only emperor of China; he was also Great Khan of a huge empire, in which China merely formed a part. This Mongolian empire was divided into khanates, each ruled by a descendant of Chinggis Khan. The Great Khanate comprised Mongolia, Manchuria, Korea, China, and the major part of Tibet. The Central Asian Khanate, later divided among two dynasties, consisted of the Tarim Basin, Dzungaria, West Turkestan east of the Amu Darya, and eastern Afghanistan. The Persian Khanate included Persia, Mesopotamia, West Turkestan west of the Amu Darya, and western Afghanistan. The

Khanate of the Golden Horde, also called the Khanate of Kipchak, possessed southern Russia and Kazakstan. It divided in 1255 into the Golden Horde of southern Russia, and the White Horde of Kazakstan, but was reunited in 1378.

The Mongolian dynasties of the various khanates went their separate ways, adjusting to local civilizations, and ruling their domains independently. Yet despite developing tensions, they remained in touch with one another, and loosely recognized the Great Khan as their sovereign. Messengers and merchants, technicians and craftsmen, office seekers and adventurers, moved freely through the vast empire. European powers sent envoys, and many Westerners served in the Mongolian armies through coercion or choice. It was a time of unprecedented cultural cross-fertilization.

At first, the Mongols had simply exploited their Chinese possessions, but Yeh-lü Ch'u-ts'ai (1189–1243), a Khitan descending from the founder of the Liao dynasty, succeeded in moderating that policy. He had become an adviser of Chinggis Khan in 1218, and retained influence over Ögödei until 1239. Owing to his efforts, the Chinese civil service was partially revived, and taxes were collected in an orderly fashion. It was only after West and Central Asian merchants offered the Mongols a larger income through tax farming that Yeh-lü Ch'u-ts'ai lost the confidence of his ruler. When Khubilai had become Great Khan and conquered all of China, he recognized that this big and populous country could not be ruled without the cooperation of its inhabitants. Early in his reign, he reintroduced the Chinese bureaucracy, and one of his successors restored the examination system in 1315. Nevertheless, it was not easy for the Chinese intelligentsia to be appointed to the higher posts. Southerners were discriminated against, because they had surrendered last. While northerners were treated better, they had to compete not only with their Mongolian masters but also with other foreigners. Khubilai did not hesitate to employ officials from the far reaches of the world if they were useful to him. This cosmopolitan policy not only excluded Chinese from coveted posts, it also insulted their Sinocentric sensibilities.

Commerce flourished, although the Mongols attempted to monopolize the production and sale of valuable staples in accord with Chinese practice. Foreign trade was mainly in the hands of Central Asian Muslims, who entered into partnership with Mongols. A national paper currency was introduced. To supply Khanbaligh with grain and other commodities from the key economic area at the lower Yangtze, the Mongols constructed a new Grand Canal system, and also experimented with coastal shipping.

The careful attention which Khubilai gave to the administration of his empire did not keep him from further, though unsuccessful, military ventures. On the Asian continent, campaigns against Burma, Annam, and Annam's southern neighbor Champa led to no permanent conquests. Neither did a Mongolian embassy to the Khmer kingdom, shortly after Khubilai's death in 1294, leave any lasting results except for an invaluable account by a Chinese participant. He vividly described Angkor Thom and Angkor Wat, which today are towering ruins, but then teemed with life. Khubilai's maritime expeditions fared even worse. When the Japanese completely ignored the Great Khan, Kyūshū was raided by an armada in 1274, and formally invaded in 1281. These engagements were failures and not repeated. A naval attack on Java also came to nothing. Troops were actually landed in 1293, but they could not exploit their early victories and had to be reembarked.

The Mongols showed considerable tolerance in religious matters, and the Buddhist monasteries went through a period of economic recovery. Khubilai favored Buddhism, and was personally inclined toward Tibetan Lamaism. Nestorianism enjoyed its final flourishing. While it had disappeared from China after the persecutions of 841–845, it had been kept alive among some of the Central Asian tribes. Several members of Chinggis Khan's house were Nestorian Christians, such as Ögödei's principal wife, and Khubilai's mother. With the victory of the Mongols, Nestorianism reentered China. The church became so strong that a chain of archbishoprics and bishoprics stretched from Samarkand to Khanbaligh, and that it could insist on rebaptizing Christian prisoners of war before admitting them to services.

Diplomatic contacts between West and East were lively. The European envoys were almost exclusively Franciscan friars, eager to proselytize for the Roman Catholic Church. Some of them left important accounts. In 1245, Pope Innocent IV dispatched the Italian Franciscan John of Plano Carpini, accompanied by the Polish friar Benedict, to call on the Great Khan. Four years later, King Louis IX of France joined with the papal legate in sending the French Dominican André de Longjumeau to Karakorum. The king also supported the Flemish Franciscan William of Rubruck, an astute observer, who visited in Karakorum from 1253 to 1254 and later described the international life in the Mongolian capital. In contrast to these envoys, the Italian Franciscan John of Monte Corvino was more missionary than diplomat. He was sent out by Pope Nicholas IV in 1289, reached Khanbaligh in the middle of the 1290's after stops in Persia and India, and remained there until his death sometime between 1328 and 1332. He claims in his letters to have been well received, to have made thousands of converts, and to have translated the New Testament into Mongolian. The Pope made him an archbishop in 1307. Another Italian Franciscan, Odoric of Pordenone, was also active in Khanbaligh for three years during the late 1320's. His countryman, the Franciscan John of Marignolli, was sent by Pope Benedict XII from Avignon in 1338, arrived in Khanbaligh in 1342, presented a large western horse, and then stayed as a missionary until 1345. The horse created a deep impression at the court. Poems were written in its honor, such as the "Ode to the Heavenly Horse," and a court painter depicted the Great Khan riding on its back.

The achievements of these and other missionaries were short-lived. With the fall of the Yüan dynasty, Nestorianism was expelled from China forever. The Roman Catholic Church lost its foothold, and was able to return only at the end of the sixteenth century. Apart from Buddhism and Taoism, this left only one major religion, Islam, which was slowly gaining strength in Kansu and Yunnan.

While many clerics were able writers, Western merchants did not feel the need to relate their experiences. Their names and travels have mostly been forgotten—with one magnificent exception, the Venetian Marco Polo. He tells in his *Description of the World* how his father Niccolo and uncle Maffeo traveled to Bukhara in 1260. They joined a Mongolian embassy to the court of Great Khan Khubilai, who asked that they should fetch him one hundred learned Christians, and oil from the lamp of Jesus' grave in Jerusalem. The Polo brothers were back in Europe in 1269, and were detained there until 1271. They set out again with letters from Pope Gregory X and the requested oil, but not the learned Christians. This time, the teen-aged Marco accompanied them. Traveling through Central Asia, they arrived at Khubilai's court in 1275. Marco Polo gives a fascinating account of conditions in China. He claims to have entered the service of the Great Khan, and to have been governor of Yang-chou, north of the lower Yangtze, for three years. The Polos left China in 1292, after a stay of seventeen years. They went by sea to Persia in the bridal escort of one of Khubilai's daughters, and reached Venice in 1295. Soon thereafter, in 1298, Marco Polo was imprisoned by Genoa, and then dictated his account to a fellow prisoner. Marco Polo's contemporaries found it difficult to believe that he was truthful, and all doubts have not yet been stilled. While systematic and detailed, the work contains questionable statements and some peculiar omissions.

Many other foreigners flocked to the Great Khan's court. There were blond and blue-eyed men, perhaps Scandinavians, who told that their country had constant daylight, Hungarians, physicians from Greece, and at least one goldsmith from Paris. Others came from the Caucasus, Asia Minor, Arabia, even North Africa. Among the Muslims, the most famous traveler was Ibn Batuta (1304–1377/78) who visited China in the 1340's. Naturally, the traffic was not all from West to East. The Mongols sent envoys in the opposite direction, but little is known about their journeys. One who did leave an account is the Nestorian monk Rabban Sauma, who was born in Khanbaligh about 1225. In 1287 and 1288, he visited Byzantium, Rome, Paris, and Gascony, and saw the kings of France and England.

It is not clear when civil war again broke out in China. The beginnings of uprisings can never be clearly dated in Chinese history. They had to reach a level of more than local impact before they began to worry the government and to provoke countermeasures on a national scale. That stage was reached in Mongolian-ruled China toward the middle of the fourteenth century. Assessing the reasons for the uprisings is also a problem, and the various steps leading to the expulsion of the Mongols have not yet been fully explored. Local conditions, including floods and famine, must have been important factors. With increasing power, the ambitions of the rebels grew. Some of the movements, such as the White Lotus Society, had religious overtones. Chu Yüan-chang, the eventual victor, was a peasant who briefly had been a Buddhist monk. He became a rebel leader, cooperated with the White Lotus Society, and may have belonged to it. By 1367, he controlled the lower Yangtze Valley and southeast China. In early 1368, he proclaimed himself emperor of the Ming dynasty. Khanbaligh fell that year. The northwest was conquered in 1369, Szechwan in 1371, and Yunnan in 1382. As of 1382, all of China proper was again ruled by a Chinese dynasty. But while the Mongols had been defeated, they had not been annihilated. They retreated to their homeland, from which, once more, they threatened the Chinese border.

Ming was the last Chinese dynasty before the Manchus and the fall of the empire, a period of maturity but also of declining vigor. The founder, customarily called the Hung-wu Emperor,* was a suspicious, harsh, but capable monarch, who dominated the government until his death in 1398. The only successor of comparable caliber was his fourth son, who in 1402 dethroned a nephew and became the Yung-lo Emperor (d. 1424). He transferred the capital in 1421 from Nanking to Peking, the former Khanbaligh. The later rulers were generally mediocre.

The Ming dynasty continued China's traditional bureaucratic institutions, with the ancient system of checks, balances, and overlapping duties. During the first years of the dynasty, the civil service was headed by the Imperial Secretariat, below which were the Six Ministries for personnel, revenue, rites, war, justice, and public works. Noted scholars performed literary tasks for the government. The important Office of Transmission channeled all correspondence to and from the central government. There

---

* Each Ming and Manchu emperor used a single era name, by which the years of his reign were dated. It has become practice to refer to the rulers by these names. The Hung-wu Emperor is consequently the emperor of the Hung-wu era.

were directorates for astronomy-astrology and imperial parks. The Imperial Academy supervised all schools, and was at the same time an institution of learning. This system was changed in 1380, when the Hung-wu Emperor took the important step of abolishing the Imperial Secretariat. He thereby crippled the career bureaucracy, or Outer Court, which lost its chief spokesmen and coordinators. As a substitute, the emperor created the Grand Secretariat, staffed by an irregular number of never more than six Grand Secretaries, who usually did not belong to the career bureaucracy. The Grand Secretariat was a device for concentrating power in the hands of the emperor, and therefore formed part of the Inner Court.

From 1428, the empire was divided into thirteen provinces, plus the two metropolitan areas of Peking and Nanking. Each province had its regular staff of officials which was supervised by sporadically dispatched governors from the capital. Occasionally, some provinces were combined under a viceroy. The provinces were divided into circuits, and these into prefectures, subprefectures, and districts. The districts numbered between 1,100 and 1,200. As in earlier times, district magistrates were the lowest officials appointed by the central government. The common people had considerable latitude in administrating their own affairs. Influenced by a Sung system, an attempt was made to combine households into units of 110, led by the ten most prominent households. Within each unit, all households were collectively responsible for taxes and labor service.

The censorate was a separate branch of the bureaucracy, but it did not offer a separate career. Officials might pass through posts in both the civil service and the censorate. The function of the censorate was twofold, to impeach delinquent officials and, more dangerously, to remonstrate with unjust or negligent emperors. It was headed by the Chief Surveillance Office in the capital. Regional Inspectors were attached to the provinces and frontier zones. Offices of Scrutiny in the capital and the provinces, though independent from the censorate, had similar duties. In the appointment of censors, younger men were generally preferred, since it was thought that they would fulfill their obligations more diligently if their advancement depended on that performance. However, careers could also be ruined by too forthright criticism of the emperor or powerful officials. The censorate had an honorable tradition of integrity and courage, but the temptation always existed to impeach only the less influential culprits.

The military consisted of a small professional army, in which the positions of soldiers and lower-ranking officers were largely hereditary. Tests in military skills were also used for the recruitment of officers. The troops were stationed at the capital, in the provinces, and on the frontier. Auxiliaries were enrolled for border defense, and the Great Wall was reconstructed during the fifteenth and sixteenth centuries.

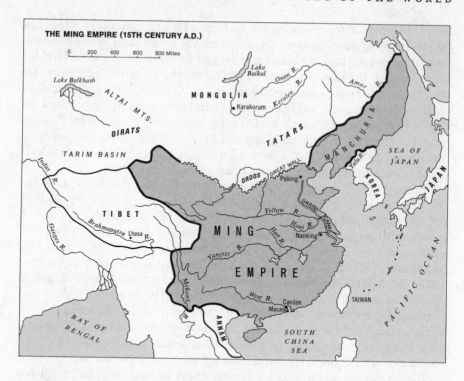

THE MING EMPIRE (15TH CENTURY A.D.)

While the sons of high officials could still receive direct appointments and while sale of offices continued, the majority of the officials entered the bureaucracy through the examination system. Candidates studied with private tutors, in the local schools, or at academies endowed by philanthropists. They then started the strenuous climb through progressively harder triannual examinations. First came the prefectural examinations, which led to the degree of Flourishing Talent, or Bachelor. The second step was an examination in the provincial capital. Those who passed received the degree of Recommended Man, or Licentiate. The last step was an examination in Peking. If successful, the candidate became a Presented Scholar, or Doctor. Study at the Imperial Academy was not a prerequisite, and, at least in the latter half of the dynasty, the majority of degree holders had not attended it. Licentiates might be appointed to office, but only Doctors could expect satisfactory careers.

The examinations were conducted with elaborate safeguards. Each candidate was isolated in an individual cell. A number was used instead of his name, and a scribe copied his paper to prevent recognition of handwriting. The weakness of the system lay not in its operation but in its subject matter. Neo-Confucianism was the state orthodoxy, from which no departure was permitted. The official version of the classics was published in 1417. From 1487 onward, the further restraint was placed on the examinees that they had to express themselves in a set form of specified length, called the Eight-legged Essay. At the very time when China was approaching its confrontation with the West, the examination system ceased to reward independence and initiative. Yet, in spite of its faults, the system did recognize talent, and thereby contributed to social mobility. Few families remained influential for long, although certain provinces, as for instance Fukien, were intellectually dominant. To prevent regional injustice, a quota system was introduced.

The Ming dynasty continued the routine of collecting the land tax twice each year, graded according to size and productivity of the holdings. It imposed many other levies, as well as corvée for males aged sixteen to sixty. Since taxation had become overly complicated, and increasingly unfair, a reform was gradually carried out during the course of a century, beginning with 1522. The application of the reform varied, depending on local conditions, but in essence it simplified the procedure by combining the various taxes, and substituting silver for payments in kind. As this reform indicates, Ming was a period of expanding money economy. Paper currency was abolished early in the dynasty. Copper remained the standard for lower denominations, while silver increasingly came into use for the higher ones. This benefited commerce, although the government maintained the traditional hostile attitude to merchants. It tried to monopolize the production and sale of such items as salt, iron, and tea. It also set up state factories, generally staffed with hereditary artisans, and attempted to manufacture goods, from arms to porcelain. None of this prevented the growth of private business, which was aided by excellent communications. China's canal system was improved during Ming, and the Grand Canal was enlarged.

In the field of foreign relations, the Ming dynasty sought to fit other nations into its tribute system. In order to benefit from trade, even some distant states were willing to acquiesce in the Chinese view of the world, according to which all people had their appropriate and subordinate relationship to the Son of Heaven. But despite this ideal, China continued to suffer much grief from some of its neighbors.

At the very time when the Ming dynasty was founded, a threat had arisen from the West. The two parts of the Central Asian Khanate had been reunited after 1369 by Timur (1336–1405), known in Europe as Tamerlane. He claimed descent from Chinggis Khan, and set out to restore the Mongolian empire. In 1381, he conquered Persia, where the khanate had lapsed, and in 1395 he subjugated the Khanate of Kipchak. Three years later, he raided India and looted Delhi. Between 1400 and 1402, he subdued Mesopotamia and Syria, and captured the sultan of Turkey. Timur then planned an attack on China, but died before he was ready to launch it. His state dissolved swiftly. All that was left of the once great Mongolian empire was Mongolia and the successor principalities of Kipchak.

The Hung-wu Emperor had taken the offensive against the Central Asian Mongols. In 1372, Chinese troops entered Karakorum. New victories followed in 1388 and 1390. The Yung-lo Emperor personally led five campaigns against the Mongols, and died on the last one in 1424. Although these efforts temporarily extended Chinese influence beyond the northern border, the Ming armies were unable to destroy the enemy or to take possession of the Ordos Region and the Tarim Basin. They had to fall back on the Great Wall. Fortunately for China, Mongolia was no longer united, but divided between the Oirats and Tatars. The former invaded China under Khan Esen in 1449 and captured the emperor himself. He was released in the following year, much to the displeasure of his brother who had succeeded him. A century later, the Tatar Khan Altan raided China for two decades from 1550 onward, and made peace only after considerable Chinese concessions.

The Jurchen of Manchuria, whose ancestors had founded the Chin dynasty (1115–1234), were fairly well controlled by the Chinese until the 1580's. In Korea, the Koryŏ dynasty, which had survived the period of Mongolian overlordship, was replaced in 1392 by the Yi dynasty. It deeply admired Confucianism and acknowledged tributary relationship to China.

Tibet, evolving further into a theocracy, also maintained tributary ties with China. A Buddhist reformer, Tsong-kha-pa (d. 1419), founded the Yellow Church, which gradually gained ascendancy over the Red Church. The successive Dalai Lamas, residing in Lhasa, managed through adroit politics to extend their temporal power over Tibet, whereas the Tashi or Panchen Lamas of the Tashi-lhunpo monastery at Shigatse gained greater influence in religious matters. Both dignitaries were claimed to be reincarnated divinities. From the 1570's onward, the Mongols were converted to the Yellow Church.

On its southern border, the Ming dynasty attempted the reconquest of Annam. Army upon army was dispatched, but only by 1414 was that state under Chinese control. Four years later, the Annamese rose again, and after a decade achieved independence under the Le dynasty (1428–1788). Henceforth, Ming China was content to keep tribute-trade relations with all its southern neighbors.

On the oceans, early Ming was a period of expansion, culminating in the seven voyages of the eunuch admiral Cheng Ho. Between 1405 and 1433, his fleets of up to sixty-two ships ranged as far away as Arabia and

East Africa. One purpose was to assert Chinese power. The rulers of Palembang on Sumatra, and of Ceylon, for example, were taken prisoner and brought to China. Another purpose may have been to satisfy the court's demand for exotic items. Cheng Ho brought back from Africa a minor zoo, including giraffes, ostriches, and zebras. But with Cheng Ho's death, Chinese naval displays on the high seas came to an end. Private Chinese merchants continued to go abroad, and in the sixteenth century were trading in Thailand, on the Malayan peninsula, Java, and the Philippines. Their numbers were not yet great, and those who stayed were undoubtedly absorbed into the local populations. Large-scale emigration from southeastern China, leading to permanent settlements abroad, started only with the Ch'ing dynasty.

China's relations with Japan veered between acrimony and amity. From the early fifteenth century until the middle of the sixteenth, Japan engaged in trade with China, masked as tribute. Japanese pirates, whose forces included Chinese, raided and traded simultaneously along the coast of southeast China. Although these pirates were derisively called Wo-k'ou, or Dwarf Bandits, the Ming government was unable to cope with them. In 1590, Hideyoshi became master of Japan, and two years later attacked Korea. Chinese troops were sent to the peninsula, but made a poor showing against the Japanese. Peace was finally restored in 1607 between China and the recently established Tokugawa shogunate.

The most important, though at that time least understood, event of the Ming was the coming of the Westerners. These were no longer the individual clerics, adventurers, and war prisoners of Mongol times, but a vanguard of the technologically superior Western civilization. The scene was being set for a fateful political and cultural clash three centuries later. Only thirteen years after Vasco da Gama had circumnavigated Africa, the Portuguese took Malacca in 1511. In 1514, they appeared off the coast of Canton, and an official squadron reached that city in 1517. The conduct of the Portuguese was such that they were expelled from China and remained excluded for decades, but in 1557 they managed to gain possession of Macao, and soon established a virtual monopoly on the China trade.

Meanwhile, a Portuguese navigator in the service of Spain, Fernão de Magalhães (Magellan) had reached the Philippines in 1521. Although he was killed in a local war, Spain took possession of the islands. The Dutch occupied the Indonesian archipelago from 1596. These nations strove to break the Portuguese trade monopoly of China. The Dutch tried to take Macao in 1622, while the British, relative latecomers in the Far East, attempted to force entrance to Canton in 1637. Both were repulsed by the Portuguese. As an alternative, the Dutch in 1624 established the fortress of Zeelandia on Taiwan, which island was not yet Chinese. The Spaniards also founded a settlement on Taiwan two years later. They were expelled by the Dutch in 1649, and the Dutch were driven off by a Chinese soldier of fortune in 1662.

Macao, the Portuguese commercial base, also became a stepping stone for the second missionary effort of the Roman Catholic Church. In contrast to the Franciscans of the Mongolian era, the highly educated Jesuits who came this time met the Chinese intelligentsia as equals. They were experts in mathematics, astronomy, physics, and geography. One of them, the great Matteo Ricci (1552–1610), was summoned to Peking in 1601 and stayed there until his death. Ricci translated Euclid into Chinese, wrote on contemporary European mathematics, and drew a world map. Among his successors, the versatile German Johann Adam Schall von Bell (1591–1666) composed a treatise on the telescope, was officially appointed to reform the Chinese calendar, and later cast cannons for the Chinese government. Another was the Fleming Ferdinand Verbiest (1623–1688) among whose many achievements was another map of the world and a series of astronomical instruments for the Peking observatory. Furthermore, the Jesuits were not only willing to accept positions in the Chinese bureaucracy and to adjust themselves to the Chinese world view, but also to explain Christianity in Chinese terms. They emphasized the similarities between Christianity and Confucianism, equating the Christian God with the Chinese Heaven, and raising no objection to ancestor worship. This explains why the Jesuits made converts in some circles, but also why they left no lasting mark. Europe, on the other hand, was greatly affected by the activities of the Jesuits in China. Through their writings, Western intellectuals received their first comprehensive knowledge of the country's history and customs.

The last hundred years of the Ming was a period of gradual political decline. In particular the willfulness of the Wan-li Emperor (1573–1620) created an administrative problem. He refused to give a single audience for twenty-five years, and withdrew to those parts of the palace where regular officials had no access. This produced a vacuum which compelled the eunuchs to play a political role. They came to dominate the Inner Court, since only they could see the emperor and act as his real or assumed spokesmen. That it pleased them cannot be doubted. How competent they were is another question. The fact remains that, given a balance of power in favor of the Inner Court, the absence of imperial initiative, and no clear delegation of authority, the eunuchs could not have acted otherwise. The traditional accusation that they were compulsive schemers and usurpers of power misses the point. Tensions increased during the last decades of the dynasty, until all branches of the bureaucracy, and even the Inner Court, were involved in an accelerating struggle between factions. Meanwhile, other menaces arose from two directions, from the Jurchen without and rebellion within.

The Jurchen had taken possession of Manchuria, and in 1616 proclaimed an imperial dynasty. Open fighting with China began two years later, and increased in violence after 1629. From 1635, the Jurchen called themselves Manchus, a term of unknown origin and meaning, and in 1636 they adopted the name of Ch'ing for their dynasty. In China, two rebel leaders were at this time emerging as major threats to the Ming, of whom Li Tzu-ch'eng was the more competent and dangerous. The government armies, badly led and fighting a war on several fronts, went from defeat to defeat. On April 25, 1644, Li Tzu-ch'eng took Peking, and the last Ming emperor hanged himself on a hill overlooking his palace. The Chinese general Wu San-kuei might have saved him, but he failed to arrive in time, and on May 27 went over to the Manchus with his entire army. These joint forces routed Li Tzu-ch'eng, who, after defiantly having declared himself emperor, evacuated Peking on June 4. He then disappears from history. On June 6, the Manchus entered the city and announced a period of mourning for the last Ming ruler. From October 30, 1644, a Manchu emperor sat on the throne of China.

For Further Reading

Hucker, Charles O., *China: A Critical Bibliography.*
de Rachewiltz, Igor, *Papal Envoys to the Great Khans.*
Moule, A. C., and Pelliot, Paul, *Marco Polo: The Description of the World.*

29 Early Japan

Proximity to China was the most important outside influence in shaping Japan's civilization, but native conditions produced certain features in its political and social life that were unique. The most striking of these was the tradition of political decentralization. China's great size alone necessitated political complexities that Japan did not need. Moreover, Japan's rainfall is plentiful, and her rivers are short; therefore, what public works were necessary for water conservation and flood control were small in scale and local in range. China's long, dangerous land frontier in inner Asia meant that the most urgent need for political and military control was at precisely the point farthest from the center of the country. Japan, however, after the

A.D.

552	Traditional and approximate date for the introduction of Buddhism from Korea
710	First permanent capital at Nara
794	Capital at Heian-kyō (Kyoto)
1185	Minamoto clan victorious in struggle with Taira
1192	Minamoto Yoritomo receives title of Shogun
1274, 1281	Abortive attempts by Mongols under Khubilai Khan to invade Japan
1333	Overthrow of Kamakura shogunate
1338	Establishment of new shogunate dynasty, the Ashikaga

aborigines had been conquered or absorbed about the ninth century, enjoyed maritime frontiers that were practically immune from foreign invasion. Military threats to the stability of the central regime remained, but they were internal.

Such basic facts of geography determined the most striking difference between the political needs of China and Japan. Chinese unity depended on a strong, bureaucratic, rationally organized central administration, exerting authority uniformly over its great territory by means of local units that, though powerful, were closely controlled by the central government. Japan could make do with a far looser kind of organization, permitting relatively great independence even in the provinces that were near the capital, and almost total autonomy in frontier areas. This pattern of political organization endured through most of Japanese history. When the nation tried in the seventh and eighth centuries to adopt something closer to the Chinese model, the attempt failed.

A second characteristic of Japan and its people that successfully resisted Chinese inroads until modern times was the tendency for political and military offices to be regarded as inheritable family possessions. The system of civil service examinations and the meritocracy of literati that China developed as a response to her bureaucratic needs was scarcely tried at all. The Japanese, in other words, resisted outside influences when they did not suit national needs. This capacity to resist has been no less characteristic of their civilization than the remarkable willingness to adopt as their own whatever foreign traits seemed desirable to them—first from Korea and China, and more recently from the Western world.

Archaeological evidence indicates a succession of primitive cultures in the Japanese islands. There was a Paleolithic culture of uncertain age, then two Neolithic cultures lasting from about 8000 B.C. to the early years of the Christian era, then a Bronze Age society that was in contact with the civilization of mainland Asia. Physical similarities between the Japanese people and the races of northeast Asia, together with the probable linguistic kinship between Japanese and Korean, are further evidence of early migrations of continental peoples to the Japanese islands, though it seems likely that the modern Japanese have other racial strains, from Southeast Asia, the islands of the Western Pacific, and from the Caucasoid peoples of northern Siberia.

The earliest Japanese society of which there is historical knowledge existed in the fifth or early sixth century of the Christian era. The characteristic unit of political organization was an extended family of provincial aristocracy known as *uji,* each with a more or less well defined territorial base. One such *uji* (which we know as "imperial") had its base in the province of Yamato, the modern Nara area. This clan had exercised some kind of religious and cultural leadership over the others for some time before there could be said to be much political unity of the Japanese people. A native myth, first written down in the seventh century and no doubt colored in its literary form by Chinese ideas, described the origins of the imperial *uji.* Jimmu, the legendary first "emperor" and ancestor of all later ones, is said to have established a centralized state in 660 B.C. The date was probably a fabrication based on Chinese portent theories, and even the belief in political centralization may have been a rationalization by later Japanese in order to convince themselves that the ancient and "normal" condition of their country was similar to that of big, civilized, bureaucratic China.

The primitive Japanese religion, Shinto, was animistic, seeing godhead in all the forces of nature and society. The "emperor" (how inappropriate are Western and Chinese words to describe early Japanese conditions!) was chief priest. As he was very holy, it was thought that practical affairs were best carried out by subordinates. These were characteristically heads of *uji* attached to the imperial clan and permitted by hereditary right to perform certain functions or to hold certain offices of state.

The introduction of Chinese Buddhism from Korea about the middle of the sixth century has great symbolic significance for Japan. Before that time material progress and the development of national cultural identity had been gradual, aided by stimulation from continental Asia that was no more than intermittent and casual. After that time, both material and nonmaterial change became much more rapid, and took the form of conscious imitation by the Japanese of virtually every aspect of contemporary

Chinese civilization. With the Buddhist religion came the associated fine and useful arts: painting, sculpture, architecture, music, work in bronze and other metals, textile making, and pharmaceutical and medical arts. The classic Chinese language became and remained for several centuries the medium for Japanese written communication in religion, public affairs, and scholarship. Of more lasting importance, the Chinese characters soon came to be adopted—in a complex system mixing ideographic and phonetic elements—for writing the Japanese language.

Chinese social and economic institutions were harder to imitate. Native institutions held out longer against them, and in some instances reemerged after the first intoxication with Chinese culture had receded. Some impor-tant Chinese institutions were never successfully copied at all. The elaborate continental systems of military conscription and corvée were attempted, but soon abandoned. The Chinese civil service examination system was scarcely attempted. In this crucial instance the native tradition, strongly hereditary and aristocratic, proved too powerful.

Such acculturation in the social and economic spheres, as was more or less successful, operated principally in the direction of the centralization of the state, the strengthening within the central government of the imperial institution, and the development, at Nara (710) and Kyoto (794), of urban centers from which flowed the influence of the new continental culture.

The Nara period (710–794) was the classic age of Chinese civilization in Japan, when at least the upper classes imitated Chinese ways with considerable success. The removal of the capital to Kyoto in 794 by the Emperor Kammu signalized a general reaction against too great a surrender of native ways. In particular there was a reaction against the Buddhist church, which had become so powerful under the patronage of the Nara court that it had at one point threatened to substitute a theocratic government for the native imperial system. Buddhism remained the principal religion of aristocratic Japan, and in the early part of the Heian period (794–1185) took on new significance as a religion of the common people, but it was never again to occupy so high a position in the political life of the country.

Kammu probably had more personal power than any other emperor of Japan. Within a generation after his death the emperor's purely political role in the central government had declined sharply, although his ritual or symbolic role continued. As usual in aristocratic Japan the change took the form of a rise to power of another family claiming hereditary justification for its authority. The Fujiwara clan had a history of long service to the throne. Its remote ancestors had been hereditary functionaries of the Shinto religion, and more recent Fujiwara nobles had helped the imperial line in its contest with the Nara theocracy. In the late ninth and tenth centuries heads of the clan established a hereditary dictatorship, reducing the emperors to puppets.

As the emperors' strength in the central government waned, so did the central government's control of the provinces. In part this was the result of an old practice of granting immunity from central taxation to the lands of certain ecclesiastical institutions and noble houses. For example, the Fujiwara family derived its political power from an economic base of extensive tax-free lands in the provinces. Such "private" holdings grew by a process similar to the "commendation" of European feudalism: local cultivators gave up their land titles to tax-free neighbors in exchange for protection that the central authority was no longer able to provide.

The fine arts of the Heian period, particularly its literature, immortalize the patricians of the capital city and their haunted concern with earthly evanescence. Another concern with refinement and taste in every aspect of life is equally conspicuous in these works. *The Tale of Genji* (c. 1000), by the court lady Murasaki Shikibu, is the classic masterpiece of Japanese prose and Japan's oldest true novel.

A new military aristocracy arose during the early Heian period to suppress rebellions and to subjugate the aborigines. This class was separate from the civil aristocrats of the capital, though not at first independent of central governmental command. Two such families, the Taira and the Minamoto, contended for power in the twelfth century. After a brief period in which the victorious Taira dominated the central government, the Minamoto made a comeback. Minamoto Yoritomo vanquished the Taira in 1185 and added their vast "private" holdings to those of his own, thus creating an enormous complex of domains outside imperial control. Yoritomo set up headquarters in Kamakura, not far from modern Tokyo. He further strengthened his control over the provinces in 1192 when he obtained from the Emperor the office of Shogun, meaning "general in chief," and implying military command in the name of the central government in areas too distant for its influence to reach.

The government and land systems of the Kamakura period (1185–1333) reached a degree of complexity never attained in Japan before or since. The territory of the country was fragmented into many administrative units, most of them quite tiny. A few of these were still subject to the fiscal powers of the imperial government, but most were private, and especially in the east, subject to the Kamakura shogunate. The shogunate acted as general peacekeeper for the whole country through appointees, known as constables, stationed in all of the provinces. The imperial government continued to exist in Kyoto, and even exerted a measure of legal authority (including the right to legitimize the Kamakura government), but its effectiveness diminished continuously.

The Kamakura shogunate faced its most severe test in 1274 and 1281, when Khubilai Khan's Mongol troops invaded the northern shore of Kyushu. The prowess of arms of the western warriors, and lucky typhoons that destroyed both invading fleets (the *kamikaze* of later legend), preserved Japanese independence. However, the invasion was ultimately destructive to Kamakura power, for the government was forced to permit the local lords of Kyūshū a degree of independence that forecast the end of Kamakura's precarious control over them. When an alliance of provincial forces overthrew the shogunate in 1333, the decentralizing tendencies in Japanese society proved once again stronger than the forces for unity.

Another family of soldiers, the Ashikaga, held the title of shogun from 1338 to 1573. From the start their rule was threatened by dissidence from provincial soldiery, complicated until 1392 by a dynastic schism in the imperial family. Even at their strongest, about the beginning of the fifteenth century, the Ashikaga failed to exercise firm unified control, and after that time the country declined further toward feudal fragmentation and disorder.

The Ashikaga shoguns revived interest in commercial relations with China that had declined since the early part of the Heian period. Simultaneously, Japanese pirates pillaged the mainland coast, establishing a reputation for Japanese ferocity in East Asia, but also, in some instances, building a foundation for more peaceful relations.

This was the age of greatest social disruption in Japanese history, but it was also an age of relatively broad social mobility. Skill at arms, rather than family pedigree, was the best means for a man to win land, wealth, and power. In the process most of the old aristocratic families lost out to new ones. The extreme fragmentation of the individual units of land tenure was somewhat simplified as successful soldiers established rule over relatively large territories. Such local rulers were known as daimyos (feudal lords), their subordinate soldiery as samurai (a word that originally meant "attendant").

Between the late Heian and Ashikaga periods, Buddhism finally became a truly popular religion. Nichiren Buddhism, the only native variety, founded in the thirteenth century, was highly nationalistic and intolerant of other faiths, but the most significant new religious teachings of the middle and late Heian period emphasized the worship of the Bodhisattva Amida. Pessimistic about man's moral capacity to achieve enlightenment by himself, the Amida cult put forth the promise that everyone—including women—would be saved by accepting the grace freely given by Amida.

Also of great significance was the Zen sect, introduced from China about 1200. Zen Buddhists protested against the ritualism and intellectualism of earlier sects, and asserted that a disciplined program of introspection and meditation was the proper path to enlightenment. The great monasteries of Kyoto played a major role in the economic and cultural life

of the Ashikaga period, being centers of private foreign trade and trans-
mitters of a renewed wave of influence from Chinese learning and arts. Zen
priests and Zen institutions were instrumental in the development or perfection of monochrome painting, the cult of the tea ceremony, landscape
gardening, and even military arts like fencing and judo. A Zen-inspired
aesthetic helped shape the classic drama (No). Even the Neo-Confucian
philosophy of the Sung, of gigantic import for later Japanese education and
thought, was first brought to Japan by teachers of the great Zen monasteries.

For Further Reading

Keene, Donald (ed.), *Anthology of Japanese Literature From the Earliest
     Era to the Mid-Nineteenth Century.*
Reischauer, Edwin O., and John K. Fairbank, *East Asia: The Great Tradition.*
Sansom, G. B., *Japan: A Short Cultural History.*
Tsunoda, Ryusaku, William Theodore de Bary, and Donald Keene, *Sources of
     Japanese Tradition.*
Warner, Langdon, *The Enduring Art of Japan.*

30   India

A striking passage in the Vishnu Purana, a Hindu religious text of the
seventh or eighth century, mocks the endless succession of kings of India
who had boasted, "This earth is mine, it is my son's, it belongs to my
dynasty," not knowing that "they themselves are but foam upon the wave."
That this statement reflects historical experience as well as the conventional hyperbole of religious pessimism is suggested by the historical
records of India for the centuries between the breakdown of the Gupta
empire in the sixth century and the establishment of the hegemony of the
Turks in the twelfth century. While some dynasties lasted as identifiable
ruling families for centuries, virtually nothing is known of the personalities
or the achievements of most of the hundreds of rulers whose names are
preserved in archaeological and numismatic evidence. Nor is there evidence of any great movements that altered the social structure, or of events
whose influence was felt throughout society during this period. Here, perhaps, is an essential point of contrast between the Western, or European,
historical experience and that of India: at no time does Indian history have

CHRONOLOGY

A.D.	
500	Pandyas ruling at Madurai
c. 540	End of Gupta dynasty
c. 540	Rise of Chalukyas at Vatapi
c. 606–646	Harsha of Kanauj
700–800	Spread of Buddhism to Nepal and Tibet
711	Arab invasion of Sind
c. 750	Rise of imperial Pratiharas; rise of Rashtrakutas
760	Palas in Bengal
c. 846	Rise of Cholas and defeat of Pallavis
c. 970	Reemergence of Chalukyan power and defeat of Rashtrakutas
1001	Beginning of raids by Turks under Mahmud of Ghazni
1024	Destruction of Somnath by Mahmud
1175	First Indian expedition by Muhammad Ghuri
1192	Defeat at Tarain of Prithvi Raja by the Turks
1206–1290	Slave Dynasty (beginning of Delhi Sultanate)
1290–1320	Khalji Sultans
1320–1413	Tughluq Sultans
1336	Founding of Vijayanagar
1347	Founding of Bahmani Sultanate
1398	Invasion of Timur
1414–1451	Sayyid Sultans
1451–1526	Lodi Sultans
1498	Arrival of Vasco da Gama

real analogues to monumental events like the invention of printing or the steam engine, the Reformation or the Enlightenment.

The history of India in the period after 600, therefore, depends less on events and movements than on the defining characteristics of politics and society. One of these was the essentially unstable multistate system that was the normal political arrangement everywhere on the subcontinent. According to Hsüan Tsang, the Chinese Buddhist pilgrim who visited India in the middle of the seventh century, India was divided into seventy kingdoms. The figure may not be accurate, but it indicates the nature of political life: the existence of numerous small states. This political situation is often spoken of as fragmentation or disunity, as if in contrast to a more normal state of political unity, but in fact, control of large areas of the subcontinent by a single ruler was always exceptional. The numerous small kingdoms constituted a web of conflicting sovereignties, each of which regarded conquest as the means of legitimizing claims to kingship. Such conquest did not involve outright destruction of other rulers, but only the acknowledgment of defeat by the payment of tribute. When the opportunity came, the tribute would cease to be paid, and the defeated ruler would resume his independence.

War was the business of kings, and this meant that frontiers were never precisely defined or acknowledged by other rulers. Within his own territories, control by the ruler did not penetrate very deeply into the fabric of social life; aside from making war, the principal function of the royal government was to collect taxes. Indian political thinkers continued to insist that the king's right to tax was balanced by his duty to protect the people: "He who receives taxes and still fails to slay thieves incurs a double blame, namely in this world the dissatisfaction of his subjects and in the next the loss of heaven."

Other defining characteristics of the period relate to its social and cultural institutions. Religious beliefs and practices, while still based on the ancient Vedic scripture and cultus, expressed themselves through the two great sectarian divisions of Hinduism, Vaishnavism, the worship of Vishnu, and Shaivism, the worship of Shiva. Almost all the complexities of Indian religious experience, metaphysical speculation, mythology, and cultic practices were subsumed in these fluid but enduring syntheses of Hindu devotion. A corollary was the erosion of the two great heterodoxies, Buddhism and Jainism. Closely linked with these changes in the religious structure was a tendency for what may be termed "Sanskrit culture" to become the common property of the dominant religious and intellectual groups everywhere in India. But, at the same time, the speech of the ordinary people was diverging more and more from that of the Sanskrit of the intellectual classes.

A fourth general characteristic of the period is the social organization commonly, but not very accurately, known as the caste system. No single unified system existed then or later, but, allowing for regional variations, it is possible to make generalizations that are valid for social organization in all parts of India. Caste groups in some form were everywhere and at all levels of culture accepted as the normal pattern of society. That this implied no unusual degree of fragmentation either in theory or in practice is evidenced by its acceptance in both the sacred and secular literature of the period as the normative pattern for a just and orderly society.

The overarching feature of the system was the ascription of social status on the basis of ritual purity. No agreed hierarchial ranking existed for all groups, even within a small region, with one vital exception: Brahmans everywhere claimed, and were recognized as possessing, a degree of ritual purity that elevated them above all other castes. This higher status was defined only in terms of the ritual practices of Hinduism, and implied no superiority in either economic or political position. In practice, however, most positions of trust and responsibility in the various kingdoms were filled by Brahmans. The religious literature of the period completes the tendency, observable from early times, of exalting Brahmanic claims and emphasizing the degradation of the most ritually impure. For the first time a few texts declare that some groups are so ritually defiling that even the sight of them is polluting.

Remarkably little is known of the economy that supported these political and cultural institutions, but during this period there seem to have been no innovations either in agricultural technique or in items of production. The most impressive feature of the economy was its ability to meet the demands for revenue imposed by the various rulers and to adjust to the vagaries of the monsoon climate while maintaining a very large population over a long period of time. This does not mean, as has been sometimes suggested, that India in the seventh and eighth centuries enjoyed a high standard of living; as the modern world knows, large populations may be an index of poverty. It does suggest, however, that optimum use was being made of resources within the limits of technical achievements, and that these were well adjusted to the political and social systems.

According to the best estimates, the population of India from the first century of the Christian era until the nineteenth century was about 100 million. This population was overwhelmingly agrarian, although there were many cities of great antiquity and fame. Most of these, such as Benares, Ujjain, and Kanchipuram, were centers of religious pilgrimages. Other cities grew up around great forts, such as Ajmer in the north and Devagiri in the south, or around a ruler's court. Such cities naturally attracted trade and commerce. Some industries, largely textile production and metal handicrafts, were also located in the cities, but village craftsmen must always have been more numerous and more important for the economy. The staple crops were wheat, rice, and in the less-fertile areas varieties of millets. Cotton textiles and spices remained, as they had been for centuries, the main items in India's export trade. Horses from Western and Central Asia were perhaps the most sought-after import. Much of the sea trade between India and other countries had passed into the hands of Arabs, although in earlier centuries Indians themselves had traveled widely throughout the eastern seas.

It is against the background of this mature civilization, with its well-developed mechanisms of social control, that the seeming political fragmentation of the Indian subcontinent must be seen. The outlines of the political history of the period are confusing because dynasties, not geographic regions, are the focus of attention. Boundaries were seldom permanent even for a generation. Furthermore, a small tributary state might rise to prominence in one area, fade into insignificance, and then in a few generations emerge again as a considerable power. Given these complexities, all that can be done is to identify the centers of political power in the main geographic regions and, when relevant, to note their cultural roles.

In south India, two important dynasties emerged at the end of the sixth century, the Pandyas and the Pallavas. The Pandyas, with their capital at Madurai, and the Pallavas, whose capital was Kanchipuram, controlled between them the rich coastal areas south of Madras. Both dynasties retained importance until the beginning of the tenth century. The Cheras ruled the adjoining lands along the western coast in what is now Kerala, but their history is very obscure, although their ports were centers for trade with both Western Asia, Southeast Asia, and China. Evidence of another kind of link with the world beyond is found in the career of Shankaracharya (c. 788–820), the most influential of Hindu theologians, who was a native of Kerala. The centers of study and worship that he, or at least his immediate disciples, established at Badrinath in the Himalayas, Puri in Orissa, and Dwarka in Gujerat indicate both communications between distant places and the pervasiveness of Hindu doctrine.

In the Pandya and Pallava kingdoms religious and cultural changes of great importance were taking place. Buddhism and Jainism had both been strong, but in the seventh century they were weakened by a great resurgence of devotional Hinduism, and within two centuries they had virtually disappeared. The devotional, or bhakti, cults were divided into two main groups, centered on either Shiva or Vishnu, but both shared an intense and passionate emotionalism. Little is known of the historical origins of bhakti. It probably represents a fusion of Dravidian elements with the Vedic, or Aryan, religion that had penetrated the south centuries before. Both the Shaivite and Vaishnavite cults produced a vast devotional literature in Tamil that colored the lives of the people and gave the area an identity and self-awareness that it has never lost. The Hindu resurgence found architectural expression at Mamallapuram and Kanchipuram in rock carvings and temples that are among the glories of Indian art.

The successors to the Pallavas and the Pandyas were the Cholas of Tanjore (c. 846–1279), among the best known of Indian dynasties. Under Rajaraja (985–1012) and Rajendra I (1012–1044), Chola armies raided the north as far as the delta of the Ganges, naval expeditions were sent against the kingdom of Srivijaya in Sumatra, and Ceylon was conquered. This successful expansion was matched by brilliant cultural achievements. Numerous temples were built throughout the Chola dominions, the largest and most splendid being erected about A.D. 1000 at Tanjore, the capital. Tamil religious literature continued to flourish, and in the twelfth century Kamban, one of the greatest of Tamil poets, wrote a version of the Sanskrit epic, the *Ramayana*. The Cholas when north India passed under Muslim rule in the thirteenth century also patronized Sanskrit learning; it was to a very considerable extent in southern temples and monasteries that Sanskrit culture was preserved.

The history of the Deccan Plateau (roughly the area above the southern coastal littoral and south of the Narmada River) is distinct from that of the southern dynasties, although inextricably linked through cultural and political contacts. The Chalukya dynasty, with its capital at Badami, controlled this region from the sixth century to the middle of the eighth. Geography led the Chalukyas into frequent wars with rulers of both south and north India, but their overthrow came in about 752 from one of their own tributary states, the Rashtrakutas. By the end of the century the Rashtrakutas were masters of all of the Deccan, and had begun to expand toward the north. Under Govinda III (793–814) their power extended from the Gangetic plain to Cape Comorin, although control over this vast area was never very firm. The Rashtrakutas were great builders, their most memorable achievement being the great temple of Ellora, carved from solid rock. They were also patrons of literature, in both Sanskrit and Kannada, the language of the area where their political power was based.

The Rashtrakutas were replaced as the dominant political power in the Deccan at the end of the tenth century by a tributary chieftain who claimed descent from the Chalukya kings. This new Chalukya confronted the Cholas in a long series of wars throughout the next two centuries. The dynasty was less involved in the political life of the north than were its predecessors, thus sharpening the division between north and south. It is of great political and cultural significance that after the Rashtrakuta expansion no power based in the south exercised political control in the north until the eighteenth century.

There were no dynasties in north India in the seventh and eighth centuries of the importance of those in the south. Following the breakdown of the Gupta empire, in the sixth century the invading Huns established short-lived kingdoms under Toramana and Mihirkula. It is probably the reign of these kings that the *Puranas* and other Hindu texts describe with horror as the time when "kings of churlish spirit, violent temper, and ever addicted to falsehood" inflicted "death on women, children, and cows," and seized the property of their subjects. Early in the seventh century, Harsha (c. 606–646), the ruler of a principality north of Delhi, created an empire that included much of the Gangetic plain up to Bengal. Harsha is better known than any other king of ancient India with the exception of Asoka, but his fame is somewhat accidental, since his court chronicler, Bana, was a writer of genius and the Chinese pilgrim Hsüan Tsang left a memorable record of a visit to Harsha's court at Kanauj. His empire of loosely controlled tributary states did not survive his death.

Toward the end of the eighth century two new dynasties, the Palas of Bengal and the Pratiharas of Rajasthan, began a struggle for the control of north India. Possession of Kanauj, the old capital of Harsha, was the symbol of hegemony. The Palas were originally based in eastern Bengal, but they had added most of Bengal and Bihar to their kingdom. Under Dharmapala (c. 770–810), they advanced far into the Punjab, bringing Kanauj and many of the smaller states of western India under their suzerainty. They were patrons of Buddhism, and their gifts to the great monastic center of learning at Nalanda as well as to temples throughout their dominions kept the old religion alive at a time when it was disappearing elsewhere in India. Tantric Buddhism, with its emphasis on magic rituals and the worship of deities, had become dominant in Bengal, and this form of Buddhism passed during the Pala period to Tibet. Contacts were also made by the Palas with the Sailendras, the Buddhist rulers of Sumatra and Java.

Pala influence in north India was challenged and finally overcome by the Pratiharas, a dynasty which had its origins in Rajasthan, and which had conquered most of central India. By 835 it was in control of Kanauj and the Gangetic plain. For the rest of the century the Pratiharas were the greatest power in north India. Their administrative system followed the familiar Indian pattern: central territories ruled directly by the king, outlying areas in the hands of tributary chieftains. The ruins of numerous temples show the Pratiharas to have been great builders who carried on the styles and techniques pioneered during the Gupta period. Shiva was the most popular deity, but temples were also erected to Vishnu, and the Jains were also patronized by the rulers.

The Pratihara power weakened early in the tenth century, although the dynasty ruled at Kanauj until 1019. Continual wars with the Palas on their eastern frontiers and with the Rashtrakutas from the south were probably important in this decline, but, as with other Indian empires, the existence of strong tributary states within the administrative structure made the failure of central control inevitable. Political power throughout north India passed to local chieftains, most of whom belonged to what had become known as Rajput clans. For the next two centuries the political history of the north is complicated by the rivalries and struggles of the principal clans. The origin of these clans can probably be traced to the Huns and other invaders who had established their power in Rajasthan in the sixth and seventh centuries.

The political system of the Rajputs has often been described as a kind of feudalism, but the term is misleading. The central feature of Rajput polity was not a contractual relationship between lord and vassal but blood relationships within a clan. The clan leader made grants of lands and in return was assisted in war by the levies of the grantees, but both in fact and in theory such service was considered a duty owed to the clan as a whole, not just to a political leader.

Almost all of the Rajput courts were centers of Sanskrit learning, with the rulers patronizing dramatists, poets, and theologians. Much of the literature produced during this period was mannered and artificial, but an interesting exception was the bardic chronicles which glorified the deeds of royal patrons. These chronicles emphasized a chivalric code that saw death in battle as the natural end of the hero, with acts of individual heroism being exalted without reference to their effects. Temple architecture, too, displayed artistic creativity. At Khajuraho in central India the Chandella kings built a great temple complex that is unique in India both for the placing of numerous structures in a unified pattern and for the sculptured representation of erotic pleasures. Another great temple complex was begun at Bhuvaneshwar in Orissa about the same time. Both of these probably reflect the strong contemporary influence of Tantric cults of Shaivism. The wealth of the Jains, largely derived from trade, is shown by the splendor of the temples they erected on Mount Abu in southern Rajasthan.

Rajput hegemony in north India came to an end when Prithvi Raja, the Chauhan ruler who had established his power in the region around Delhi, was defeated in 1192 while leading an alliance of Rajput kings against an invading army under the Turkish ruler Muhammad Ghuri. The Rajput clans did not by any means disappear as territorial powers. Some of them fought the invaders throughout the following centuries of Muslim rule. But

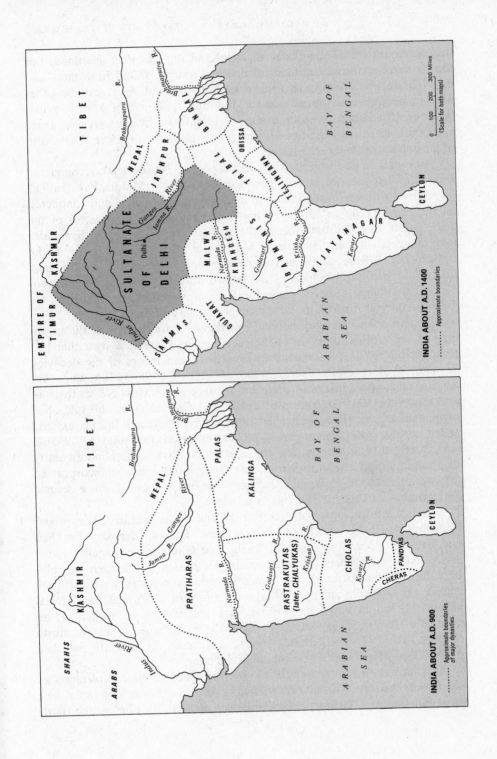

INDIA ABOUT A.D. 1400

········ Approximate boundaries

0   100   200   300 Miles
(Scale for both maps)

EMPIRE OF TIMUR

TIBET

KASHMIR

NEPAL

JAUNPUR

BENGAL

ORISSA

TRIBAL

TELINGANA

SULTANATE OF DELHI

Delhi

MALWA

KHANDESH

SIND

BAHMANI

VIJAYANAGAR

GUJARAT

SAMMAS

Indus River

Ganges River

Jamna R.

Brahmaputra R.

Narmada R.

Godavari R.

Krishna R.

Kavari R.

ARABIAN SEA

BAY OF BENGAL

CEYLON

INDIA ABOUT A.D. 900

········ Approximate boundaries of major dynasties

TIBET

SHAHIS

ARABS

KASHMIR

NEPAL

PRATIHARAS

PALAS

KALINGA

RASTRAKUTAS (later, CHALYUKAS)

CHOLAS

CHERAS

PANDYAS

Indus River

Ganges River

Jamna R.

Brahmaputra R.

Brahmaputra R.

Narmada R.

Godavari R.

Krishna R.

Kavari R.

ARABIAN SEA

BAY OF BENGAL

CEYLON

they never recovered their hold on Delhi and the Gangetic heartland. For the next five centuries the focus of political history shifted from them and their Hindu predecessors to the Turks from Central Asia and the other Muslim peoples who gained control of India. It should be kept in mind, however, that Hindu civilization remained dominant in most areas of India and that even at the height of Muslim power probably no more than a fifth of the population embraced Islam.

Although in the end it was Central Asian Muslims who conquered India, the first push of Islamic power came from the Middle East. In 711 an Arab expedition invaded Sind, in the lower Indus Valley, and conquered all the territory up to Multan. This region fell under the control of the Caliphate of Baghdad until the middle of the ninth century, and then under two independent Muslim rulers. Meanwhile, the marchlands of India, Baluchistan, Seistan, and much of what is now Afghanistan, traditionally under Indian cultural influence, had passed into the hands of Islamic peoples. This Islamicization of the borderlands was of great consequence, for it provided bases through the centuries for attacks on India.

The great advance into the vital heartlands of India came at the beginning of the tenth century from the Kingdom of Ghazni, a state that had been established in Afghanistan by Turkish commanders of the decaying Samanid dynasty of Persia. Mahmud of Ghazni (998–1030) made numerous raids into India, and while his primary aim was to collect treasure and slaves for his vast empire in Persia and Central Asia, the raids had permanent effects. They destroyed the already weakened Pratiharas, and added considerable Indian territory to the Ghaznavid empire. All of Sind acknowledged his authority, and the land of the Shahis, the Hindu dynasty that had long controlled the district west of the Indus, was also incorporated into the empire along with other territory east of the Indus. Lahore became the capital of the Ghaznavids' Indian province.

Further Muslim expansion came at the end of the twelfth century under Muhammad Ghuri, the leader of the new Turkish dynasty that had established itself at Ghur, north of Kabul. The Ghuris moved against India, partly like their Ghaznavid predecessors, in search of plunder, but also with the intention of establishing themselves as a territorial power. They defeated the Muslim rulers of Sind and Lahore in 1186, and then moved against the Rajput kingdoms. Prithvi Raja, the ruler of Delhi, heading an alliance of Rajput kings, was defeated at the great battle of Tarain, north of Delhi, in 1192. The Ghurids pushed on eastward. By 1201 they had reached Bengal and sacked the capital of the ruler.

It is important not to overstress either the speed or the completeness of the Turkish victory. Muslim powers had been on the borders of India since the eighth century; Turkish raids had begun two centuries before the Battle of Tarain and another 130 years would pass before the Muslim armies penetrated to the extreme south. Nevertheless, the power of the Rajputs was broken at Tarain. The Turkish victory has often been explained as proof of their devotion to a common fanatical creed and the equality of all their soldiers in contrast with the divisiveness of the caste system and the lack of social concern engendered by the Hindu religion. Actually, the courage of the Hindu armies impressed even their adversaries; thousands died bravely on the field of battle. Nor were the armies of the Ghurids any more homogeneous than those of the Indians: many of the soldiers were undoubtedly Indian slaves or conscripts. The Turks' chief advantages were in military organization, tactics, and equipment. They depended essentially on horsemen armed with light bows, a force far swifter and more mobile than the cumbersome Indian armies, with their elephants and vast numbers of infantrymen.

After the death of Muhammad Ghuri in 1206, India ceased to be part of the Ghurid empire. During the thirteenth century the Delhi Sultans added little new territory to the original conquest of the Ghurids. However, under Balban (1266–1287) authority was centralized and the power of local chieftains broken, since the Turkish view of the functions of state inherited from the Persians was far different from the Indian. This move toward centralization remained characteristic of Muslim polity in India, even though it was seldom fully realized in practice. Another feature of the political system established in this period was the tacit realization that the Hindus could not be forced to accept the religion of Islam, and that to govern the country compromises would have to be made. This meant recognizing the Hindus as *dhimmis,* a status originally intended for Christians and Jews, but not for idolators. There were certainly many instances of religious persecution, including the destruction of Hindu temples, and sometimes (during wars) forced conversions, but in general expediency required limited toleration. There was little change in either the methods or the personnel of local government, so that Hindus remained in charge of revenue collection. Many Hindu chieftains maintained their status in their old territories by agreeing to pay tribute to the new government.

The Islamic overlords of India never solved the problem of arranging for an orderly succession; the death of a ruler always signaled a factional struggle. The victors after the death of Balban were the Khalji family. Under Ala-ud-din (1296–1316), the most energetic member of the new dynasty, the Delhi Sultanate expanded greatly. After taking the great Rajput strongholds at Chitor and Ranthambor in Rajasthan, Ala-ud-din's armies moved south. By this time the empires of the Cholas and the Chalukyas had given way to four main successor states: the Yadavas at Devagiri, the Kakatiyas at Warangal, the Hoysalas at Dorasumdura, and a revived branch of the ancient Pandya family at Madurai. All of these kingdoms were invaded, their capitals plundered, and the rulers forced to acknowledge suzerainty.

After Ala-ud-din's death a new dynasty, the Tughluqs, seized power in Delhi, and under Muhammad Tughluq (1325–1351), the Sultanate reached its greatest territorial extent. The southern kingdoms, whose allegiance to the Sultanate after Ala-ud-din's initial victories had been minimal, were once more subjugated. With all India except Kashmir, Orissa, and remote areas in Rajasthan within the Sultanate, no ruler since Asoka had included so much of India within his empire. At the same time that he was building up this vast empire, Muhammad Tughluq endeavored to exercise close control over the economy, fixing prices, replacing gold and silver money with copper and brass tokens, and regulating exports and imports. However, he lacked the administrative machinery to enforce such sweeping reforms, and his great empire began to dissolve. By the time of his death in 1351, most of the territory seized during the previous fifty years had been lost. The invasion of north India by Timur, who sacked Delhi in 1398, speeded the decline. None of the Muslim rulers of Delhi could reverse the process of decay until the establishment of the Mughal power in the sixteenth century.

The realignment of political power that began in the middle of the fourteenth century demonstrated many of the features characteristic of the breakup of previous Indian empires: the emergence of nuclear geographic regions as political units; the reassertion of independence by old dynasties and lineages that had paid tribute to the central power; the tendency of provincial governors and military commanders to seize power in areas under their control. While political unification provides the focus for Indian history, the movement toward regionalism was no less creative and dynamic. Neither in a cultural nor in a political sense was this movement anarchic or even particularly confused; many of the great achievements of both Hindu and Muslim civilization are associated with the regional kingdoms. Nor is there any reason to suppose that the lives of the people were any harder under the regional kingdoms than under the great empires. The collection of the land revenue, the major function of Indian governments, went on in more or less the same way under large or small political units.

Of the Muslim kingdoms that emerged in the fourteenth century, the Bahmani Sultanate was the most important. Its capital was first at Gulbarga and then at Bidar. Originating in a revolt by the military commanders of the Sultanate's southern possession, it controlled all of the Deccan Plateau north of the Krishna River for 150 years beginning in 1345. Then it, too, fell apart. Provincial governors established their independence and set up five Sultanates: Berar (1490–1568), Ahmadnagar

(1490–1633), Bidar (1487–1609), Bijapur (1490–1686) and Golkunda (1512–1687).

Bengal became an independent Muslim kingdom in 1338, and following Timur's invasion at the end of the century, Muslim succession states were formed in the territories more directly under Delhi's control—Malwa, Gujerat, and Khandesh. In all these states, the majority of the population was Hindu, but the courts were centers of Islamic learning and culture.

Hindu power revived in two important areas, Rajasthan and south India beyond the Krishna River. A number of Rajput clans had fled before the invading armies of the Sultanate and taken refuge in the deserts and hills, and with the decay of the power of Delhi two principalities, Mewar and Marwar (modern Udaipur and Jodhpur), gained control of much of Rajasthan.

In south India, a powerful Hindu kingdom that took its name from its capital, Vijayanagar, city of victory, was founded about 1336 by the descendants of the Yadava dynasty, deposed by the Sultans. Even more than the Sultanate of Delhi, Vijayanagar appears to have been a military state. A Portuguese traveler in the early years of the sixteenth century estimated that it regularly maintained a million men under arms, although, given the resources of the area, this must be an exaggeration. In any case, Vijayanagar was frequently at war especially against the Sultanates to the north, and the use of cannon as well as cavalry indicates that the rulers had adopted the new techniques introduced by the Muslims.

Reflections of the power and wealth of the kings of Vijayanagar can still be seen throughout south India, for many of the great gateways and pillared halls on the temples were built by them. The capital itself was thought by contemporary European travelers to be larger than Rome, and the great waterworks, the splendor of the temples, and the elaborate ritual of the court impressed every visitor.

Vijayanagar flourished for more than 200 years, but in the middle of the sixteenth century it was undermined by the growing independence of its tributary chieftains and by pressures from the Sultanates to the north. In 1564 the Sultanates formed an alliance that defeated the Vijayanagar army and destroyed the great capital city. Although the dynasty maintained itself in an attenuated form, it never recovered its power. Some of the empire fell to the Sultans, but most of it was divided up among their former chieftains at Madurai, Tanjore, and Ginji. But again, these small kingdoms continued the religious and cultural traditions of Hindu civilization.

Nor did the decay of the central authority of the Sultanate cause much diminution of Islamic influence in India. Despite its loss of power, Delhi remained a center of Islamic culture and influence to which scholars, artists, and theologians came in great numbers. All of the independent

Muslim kingdoms that arose in the fourteenth century, especially the great Bahmani Sultanate, duplicated the role of Delhi as patrons of Islamic culture. In India as elsewhere Muslim rulers were great builders of cities, forts, mosques, and tombs, and such activity continued throughout the Sultanate period. The Turks had been deeply influenced by Persian culture before they entered India, and Persian literature and art set the standards of taste and provided models for the Indian writers and artists that the rulers and nobility patronized.

The permanent existence of a large Muslim minority was undoubtedly the most significant result of the Islamic invasion. Political control by the Turkish intruders would pass, as had the rule of other foreigners, but for the first time an invader had come with cultural and religious institutions of a kind that resisted assimilation to the Indian cultural patterns. But just as the Muslims were not absorbed into Hinduism, neither was India overwhelmed by the culture of Islam as was the case with many of the civilizations conquered by the Muslims. What was visible in India in 1500, after three centuries of Muslim political presence, is still visible: two cultures and two religions living within the confines of their institutional forms. There were, of course, areas of contact and mutual assimilation. Many low-caste Hindus became Muslims, but they took with them styles of life—as, for example, marriage customs—that were not substantially modified by the change of religion. The Hindu upper classes who were employed in the Muslim courts and armies learned Persian and adopted Persian manners and dress. But at the profoundest level of theological and philosophical thought there are no signs that either civilization deeply affected the other. It is significant that the followers of poet-saints like Kabir (d. 1518) and Nanak (c. 1469–1538), who show influences from both Hinduism and Islam, either founded a new community, as with Nanak and the Sikhs, or a new sect within Hinduism that appealed mainly to the lower castes, as with Kabir.

For Further Reading

Basham, A. L., *The Wonder That Was India.*
Brown, W. N., *Man in the Universe: Some Cultural Continuities in India.*
de Bary, William T., et. al. (eds.), *Sources of Indian Tradition,* Vol. I.
Thapar, Romila, *A History of India,* Vol. I.

31 Southeast Asia

About two and a half thousand years ago the ancestors of the peoples who today occupy Southeast Asia began leaving their homelands in China and Tibet, driven by motives that are lost to history. Traveling south, down fertile valleys and across rich alluvial plains toward the sea, their migrations continued for many centuries. Although they had to push aside or absorb the small groups of aborigines they found in their way, for the most part the passage was peaceful. Some settled in mainland Southeast Asia, becoming the Chams and Khmers of Vietnam and Cambodia, the Pyus and Mons of Burma and western Thailand, and the Malays of the Peninsula. Others took to the sea and, spreading through the Indonesian archipelago, became the ancestors of interior peoples like the Bataks of Sumatra and the Dyaks of Borneo, and also of the coastal and riverine groups of the islands, who are known collectively as Malayo-Indonesians. The most venturesome of all sailed their frail outrigger canoes to distant Polynesia and Oceania, but New Guinea marked the limit of their expansion southward.

In prehistoric times the peoples of Southeast Asia developed a distinctive and complex agricultural civilization. Their main cereal crop, then as now, was rice. In growing it they employed both the *ladang* or dry cultivation method and the *sawah* or permanent irrigation system, bringing the latter to near perfection, especially in Java. They were among the first men to domesticate tubers and legumes, and some of their crops, notably the yam, they exported to the rest of the world. Their work animals were the ox and the water buffalo. They worshiped their ancestors and spirits which they believed to be immanent in fields and streams. Their descent and inheritance systems were matrilineal. Over the centuries they devised a corpus of social custom and tradition (*adat* in Malaysia and Indonesia) which survives still and, functionally, is the equivalent of Western common law.

Culturally the strongest external influence on early Southeast Asia was exercised by India. Hinduism and Buddhism spread widely in the area, bringing with them the art of writing, along with new deities, epics, and mythologies. From India came the idea of a despotic God-King who must be supported by his subjects as their necessary link with the supernatural forces that control the world. Brahman priests were employed by ambitious Southeast Asian rulers hoping to expand their dominions and, through consecration as divine kings, to legitimize their conquests. Imported Indian

C H R O N O L O G Y

A.D.		
	c. 657–681	Reign of Jayavarman I (Khmer)
	671	Visit to Srivijaya of the pilgrim I-tsing
	732	Accession of Sanjaya (Java)
	929	Accesson of Sindok (Java)
	1002–1050	Reign of Suryavarman I (Khmer)
	1044	Founding of Empire of Pagan (Burma)
	c. 1222	Founding of Singosari (Java)
	1268	Accession of Kertanagara (Java)
	1287	Mongol conquest of Pagan (Burma)
	1292	Visit of Marco Polo to Perlak (Sumatra)
	1293	Mongol invasion of Java; founding of Empire of Majapahit
	1330–1364	Rule of Gaja Mada, *mapatih* of Majapahit
	1350	Founding of T'ai kingdom of Ayut'ia (Siam)
	c. 1402	Founding of Malacca
	1431	Fall of Angkor (Khmer)
	1448–1488	Reign of Trailok (Siam)
	1450	Promulgation of the "Palace Law" of Siam
	1511	Portuguese conquest of Malacca

----

ideas on ritual, ceremony, and court procedure and, especially, on what a king was entitled to demand from his subjects had a powerful impact on state formation throughout Southeast Asia.

The earliest state of which clear evidence survives was Funan, founded in the Mekong Delta not later than the first century A.D. by Kaundinya, the "King of the Mountain." Funan was a maritime state, and maintained commercial relations with India, Persia, and China. Its greatest king was Jayavarman (d. 514), who lived in a palace with a tiered roof, rode on an elephant, and governed walled cities whose inhabitants prized gold, silver, pearls, and engraved ornaments, and who delighted in cockfighting and pigfighting. Funan survived until the seventh century, when it was subjugated by one of its own feudatories, the state of Chenla.

North of Funan and Chenla lay the kingdom of Nam-Viet, which ruled the lands now known as Tongking and Annam in northern and central Vietnam. Nam-Viet had been under Chinese domination since its annexation by the Han emperor Wu Ti in the first century B.C. It remained part of China for the next thousand years, regaining its independence only with the fall of the T'ang dynasty in the tenth century. A millennium of Chinese rule left a strong imprint. Both Tongking and Annam and the subsequent Annamite empire which ruled both regions followed the Confucian political ethic, at least in theory, and government was administered through a scholar-official mandarinate. But, despite heavy attacks by the Mongols in the fourteenth and fifteenth centuries, the Annamites succeeded in avoiding full assimilation, and were able to keep their own language and customs. By the end of the fifteenth century they had absorbed the kingdom of Champa which lay on their southern border.

West of Annam and Champa arose in the ninth century the Khmer empire of Cambodia. It was the Khmers who elevated the principle of the *deva-raja,* or God-King, to the highest peak it attained in Southeast Asia. During the reign of Suryavarman II (1113–c.1150) the building of the mighty temple complex of Angkor Wat began. The main sanctuary at Angkor Wat is 130 feet high, and stands on a stone-encased platform which is itself 40 feet high and 750 feet square. Nearby a later ruler constructed Angkor Thom, whose central feature, the Bayon, is a massive pyramidal temple surmounted by a golden tower resting on four gigantic carved heads. Artistically, the temples of Angkor were a supreme achievement, but build-

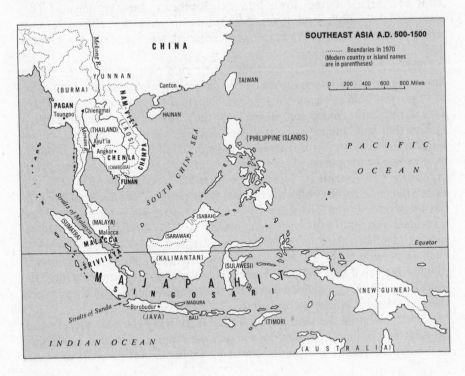

MAP 28,

ing them placed a heavy economic strain on the Khmer empire. An army of craftsmen worked for many decades to erect and decorate the temples, hundreds of priests, dancers, musicians, and officials served in them, and the labor of tens of thousands of villages was needed to pay for their upkeep. At the height of the empire's prosperity 12.5 million acres of rice fields lay under permanent cultivation, watered by a network of canals and reservoirs stretching for hundreds of miles. In the end the Khmers rebelled against their God-Kings. They turned to the type of Buddhism preached by missionaries of the Mahavihara sect, who preferred poverty and austerity to ornate temples and ceremonies. By the early fifteenth century Angkor had been abandoned. The Cambodian kingdom survived, though much reduced in size and power and under constant threat from its neighbor to the west, the T'ai state of Ayut'ia.

The T'ai, or Shan, peoples originated in Yunnan. During the eighth century they had formed a kingdom there, Nan-chao, which acted as a buffer between Tibet and China. The Chinese emperors wished to swallow up Yunnan, and the T'ais fought a losing battle for their independence; eventually the Nan-chao kingdom was obliterated by the Mongols in the thirteenth century. For many hundreds of years before this, however, the T'ais had been filtering down into the Southeast Asian peninsula. They occupied the middle and lower Menam basin, and the T'ai state from which modern Siam, or Thailand, is descended was founded at Ayut'ia in 1350.

From Ayut'ia the T'ais expanded their rule over much of the Malay Peninsula and into lower Burma. They defeated Cambodia in a long series of wars, and held in check the strong Chiengmai kingdom of Laos. As they carved out living space for themselves, they developed an administrative system that was unique in Southeast Asia. Elsewhere the struggles of one kingdom or dynasty against another were of small concern to the ordinary man unless he happened to get in the way of the fighting or was plagued by especially heavy taxation. The mass of Southeast Asians lived in self-sufficient villages, cut off as effectively from their political superiors as from the outside world. In the T'ai state, by contrast, a centralized bureaucracy and a codified system of law, both inaugurated by King Trailok (1448–1488), welded together rulers and ruled in a hierarchical social structure in which each man understood his own duties and privileges. The government was divided into civil and military branches and run on departmental lines by ministers with clearly defined roles. By the standards of the time and place, the T'ai state was efficiently organized.

To the west of the land of the T'ais lay Burma. Here by the eleventh century the dominant political power was the empire of Pagan, established at the expense of the indigenous Mons by an immigrant people from inner

Asia known to history as the Burmans. When Mongol invaders destroyed Pagan at the end of the thirteenth century, a long period of near-anarchy set in. On the one hand the hostility of the tribesmen of the Shan hills to the north prevented the Mongols from profiting by their conquest; on the other these same tribesmen proved unable to create a state of their own stable enough to replace Pagan. It was not until the sixteenth century, with the rise of the dynasty of Toungoo under King Tabinshwehti (1531–1550) that modern Burma began to emerge.

In mainland Southeast Asia the major states were land powers. Essentially, their economic strength derived less from trade than from their own agricultural productivity supplemented by the profits of a certain amount of interregional exchange. But in the Indonesian archipelago the reverse was true: the key to political dominance lay in sea power, in the ability to make sudden raids on the ports and coastlines of one's rivals, and in the possession of sufficient naval strength to dictate one's own conditions of trade. Not only the seaborne commerce of the archipelago was at stake. Vessels plying between the Middle East, India, and China had to sail past Indonesia's front door. They could pass either through the Straits of Malacca between the Malay Peninsula and Sumatra or through the Straits of Sunda between Sumatra and Java; these were the only practicable seaways connecting western and eastern Asia. A power strong enough to control both straits, therefore, could place a stranglehold on what, as early as the fifteenth century, was one of the most important maritime trade routes in the world.

The state that profited from this situation was the empire of Srivijaya, which had its capital at Palembang on the southeast coast of Sumatra. From the seventh to the tenth centuries the rulers of Srivijaya, the unchallenged overlords of the straits of both Sunda and Malacca, intercepted and taxed long-distance commerce in these waters. In addition to ruling most of Sumatra, Srivijaya exercised authority over the coastlines of the Malay Peninsula and western Java. It was not until the eleventh century that its commercial hegemony began to be challenged. Chaotic conditions along the south coast of China following the collapse of the T'ang dynasty reduced the volume of long-distance trade, and as traffic passing through the straits declined, so did Srivijaya's revenues. The Cholas of southern India, too, resenting what they regarded as extortionate demands by Srivijaya, attacked the empire in 1025, devastating many coastal settlements on both sides of Malacca Straits. Srivijaya survived this catastrophe, but with its strength diminished. By adopting in desperation ever more arbitrary and piratical tactics it incurred the enmity of a widening circle of neighbors, and by the fourteenth century it had ceased to exist.

The chief competitors and immediate heirs of Srivijaya were the Javanese. By the eighth century Java was being ruled by the Buddhist kings of the Sailendra dynasty. Little is known in detail about the Sailendras, but their memory has been spectacularly preserved by their numerous stupas and chandis (monumental tombs) which still stand in the central Javanese plain. Of these the monument known as the Borobudur is, to the modern eye, the most impressive. At Borobudur eight interconnected stone terraces rise in pyramidal form to cap a natural hill. The five lower terraces are square-cornered, the top three circular. The inner walls of each terrace are covered with thousands of friezes sculptured in bas-relief and illustrating the texts of Mahayana Buddhism. From base to summit the structure rises to a height of more than 100 feet. A pilgrim visiting the Borobudur had to walk for nearly three miles along its terraces and pass more than four hundred images of the Buddha before he reached the summit, where, presumably, enlightenment through meditation on the lessons he had absorbed during his ascent awaited him.

In the mid-eighth century the Sailendra kings were replaced by the Sanjayas, who adopted Shaivist Hinduism as their court religion in preference to Buddhism and, like their predecessors, left many monuments in stone to testify to their beliefs. By this time, however, the political and economic center of gravity in Java was moving east. Better use of agricultural land, leading to an increase in population, and success in capturing the trade formerly controlled by Srivijaya, gradually brought east Java to the forefront. In the Brantas River valley a succession of kingdoms rose and fell over the next three centuries. The story of the founding of the last of these, Singosari, is told in the Old Javanese epic, the *Pararaton,* or Book of Kings. It was Singosari, under King Kertanagara (1268–1292), that faced the formidable challenge of a Mongol armada sent south by Kubilai Khan.

Most states in Southeast Asia maintained diplomatic relations with China, and some, as far back as Sui and T'ang times, had paid tribute in exchange for Chinese recognition and protection. But the Mongols sought more than tribute or a merely formal recognition of their superiority. They required actual submission, and were prepared to go to war to secure it, as the history of Vietnam and Burma had already borne witness. King Kertanagara of Singosari, however, resolved to defy the Mongol empire. When the Great Khan's envoys arrived in east Java in 1289, he detained them for a time in prison, and then sent them back to their master empty-handed. The Khan collected a large army and fleet and launched them against "the impudent southern barbarians" of Java in 1293.

Mongol aggression, however, was soon defeated by Javanese duplicity. Kertanagara, spurring his people on to resist the invader, had used so heavy a hand that the populace rose against him, capturing his capital city and putting him to death. Kertanagara's son-in-law and heir, Vijaya, welcomed the Mongol commander and accepted his aid in defeating the rebels. But once Vijaya had regained the capital he turned on his allies and attacked them while they were split into small groups engaged in pacifying —on his behalf, as they supposed—the surrounding countryside. The remnants of the Mongol force fought their way to the coast, thankfully boarded their ships, and sailed back to China, never to return. The victorious Javanese king celebrated his triumph by building a new capital for his state at Majapahit.

During the fourteenth and early fifteenth centuries the empire of Majapahit ruled eastern Java and the islands of Madura and Bali, and maintained economic and diplomatic links with lesser states in the Indonesian archipelago and the Southeast Asian peninsula. It was the last, and greatest, of the Indo-Javanese kingdoms. More is known about it than any of its predecessors, chiefly because of the wealth of surviving written records, including the long epic poem known as the *Nagarakertagama*. Composed in 1365 by a Buddhist priest, the *Nagarakertagama* is a paean of praise to Gaja Mada, *mapatih* or chief minister of Majapahit from 1330 to 1364.

Gaja Mada appears on the Javanese historical scene as the commander of a royal bodyguard charged with suppressing a rebellion against the king of Majapahit in 1328. This task completed, the king repaid the devotion of his servant by stealing the latter's wife. Shortly afterward Gaja Mada prevailed on a surgeon who was operating on their royal master to allow the knife to "slip." Since the heir to the throne was a woman, he was able to seize supreme power and hold it for the next quarter of a century.

The *Nagarakertagama* portrays Gaja Mada as a master administrator. He reformed agriculture, the judiciary, the police force, and the taxation and forced labor systems. He organized a land survey and a census, and arranged for the repair of roads, bridges, and irrigation channels. He supervised the army and navy and gave instructions to diplomatic missions going to foreign lands. He even found time to issue regulations governing the terms on which pious foundations might accept gifts. There was apparently no branch of government that Gaja Mada did not personally supervise and control, and when he died in 1364 four ministers were appointed to take over his duties.

The empire of Majapahit, whose court religion was a mixture of Hinduism and Buddhism but whose people remained for the most part animists, had been founded in 1293. It was in the same decade that a new religion, Islam, gained its first foothold in Southeast Asia at Perlak on the northern coast of Sumatra. During the following two centuries Islam spread gradually through the islands and into the Malay Peninsula. The readiest converts to the new faith proved to be the rulers of port cities and coastal principalities who derived their wealth from trade. They found that their economic interests were better served if they were of the same religion as the merchants who came to buy from them, and by this time Muslim Arabs, Persians, and Gujeratis from northern India were coming to Southeast Asia in ever increasing numbers. With wealth derived from trade the new men of Islam challenged and overthrew older interior states like Majapahit, whose revenues came chiefly from agriculture and whose world view did not extend beyond Southeast Asia. The richest and strongest of the new Muslim powers was Malacca, on the west coast of the Malay Peninsula, founded in the early fifteenth century by a refugee prince from Sumatra.

Malacca rapidly became the chief commercial emporium in Southeast Asia. Like Srivijaya before it, it lay at the junction of the Indian, China, and Java seas. To its harbor came traders from all over Asia, eager to exchange cottons, silks, and foodstuffs for the pepper, cloves, nutmegs, mace, camphor, sandalwood, pearls, aloes, benzoin, and musk that another new class, the merchant adventurers of Western Europe, were even then beginning to covet. The more the Europeans learned about Southeast Asia, the more desirable its riches seemed. When the Portuguese navigator Vasco da Gama pioneered the sea route from Europe to the Indies at the end of the fifteenth century, the Europeans prepared to make Southeast Asian trade their own.

For Further Reading

Coedès, George, *The Indianized States of Southeast Asia.*
———, *The Making of Southeast Asia.*
Hall, D. G. E., *A History of South-East Asia.*
Heine-Geldern, Robert, *Conceptions of State and Kingship in Southeast Asia.*

Medieval Europe

32 The Early Middle Ages

The Middle Ages began with the decline of Rome. As early as the third century, Rome's population was dropping and her economy beginning to break down or decentralize. Her cities—focal points of culture, commerce and communication—slowly withered. The dominance of Greco-Roman civilization weakened as new forms of once-submerged local cultures began to rise. Provincial separatism threatened political unity. Men increasingly sought to secede from the coercive and unprofitable unity of the empire into what they hoped would be the wealth of independence and autarchy.

All was not disintegration, however. Rome's decline was marked by inventive periods of renascent centralism and rebuilding. One such age, that of Diocletian and Constantine (A.D. 284–337), laid the institutional foundations of the Middle Ages. Society was divided into functional orders, ranging from farmers and artisans to the honorable professions and the military and administrative elites. Each service had its rewards, its type of law—some had their own courts. Brought to defend the frontiers, foreign allies lived by their own laws under imperial protection. The medieval idea of social functional orders each having its own law was already a reality in late Roman times. Furthermore, the distinction between slave and freeman weakened. On the one hand, imperial law invaded private right, thus easing slavery; on the other, as state service was required of all, service invaded freedom. By public law, the peasant was bound to his land and the soldier to his arms. In short, although long retarded during the invasions following Rome's fall when enslaved captives again abounded, slavery and freedom both weakened. The ministerial or functionally servile character of medieval society was being born.

The relationship of Christianity to the empire also set the tone for the Middle Ages. After Constantine, church and state were allied. Christian monotheism canonized imperial unity, and in return, the state provided the

CHRONOLOGY

Roman and Byzantine Emperors

A.D.	284–305	Diocletian
	306–337	Constantine
	527–565	Justinian I
	717–741	Leo I the Isaurian

Frankish Kings and Western Emperors (Since 800)

416–751	Merovingian house
741–928	Carolingian house
768–814	Charlemagne
813–840	Louis the Pious
876–888	Charles III the Fat

German Kings and Emperors

919–1024	Saxon or Ottonian house
919–936	Henry I the Fowler
936–972	Otto I
983–1002	Otto III
1024–1137	Salian house

French Kings

888/987 ff.	Capetian house

Roman Pontiffs

492–496	Gelasius I
590–604	Gregory I
858–867	Nicholas I
1073–1085	Gregory VII
1088–1099	Urban II
1130–1143	Innocent II

Ecclesiastical Intellectuals

260–340	Lactantius
c. 340–420	Jerome
354–430	Augustine
816–840	Agobard, archbishop of Lyons
c. 810–c. 877	Johannes Scotus Erigena
847–882	Hincmar, archbishop of Reims

model for church organization and law. As we shall later see, imperial Christianity was a kind of Neoplatonic naturalism, one in which the cult of the emperor and the patriotism of *Romanitas* seemed to harmonize with the faith, enabling apologists to say that the successive ages of a presumably eternal empire were similar to those of an unfolding Christian vision. On the other hand, Christianity had sprung up partly in reaction against the dominant Greco-Roman culture, as a way of setting its various subject peoples free. It is therefore not surprising that, at the very moment this religion became the premier state cult, a new form of secession, that of hermits and monks, spread throughout the Mediterranean basin. Indeed, no sooner had the church become the lesser partner of the state than it began to suffer grave divisions. In the form of the Arian heresy, an imperialist party made its appearance in 337. The Goths and the other Germans in the imperial military service soon adopted this heretical belief to set them apart from the ordinary Christians of the empire they were being called in to police. Defiance of the state church emerged in such groups as the North African Donatists (c. 311), and other regional secession early found expression in dogmatic variations. The upwelling of heresies was the religious counterpart of the civil wars that disrupted the political and economic unity of the empire.

Great though its effort had been, late Rome began to fall as separatism and withdrawal recurred with renewed vigor. What pushed the empire over the brink, however, were the cataclysmic Hunnic raids that transformed the gradual filtering of the Germans into imperial service into mass movements by whole peoples. These movements precipitated a series of invasions whose cycles lasted well into the tenth century. During the first of these cycles or waves, the Western empire ceased to exist (476), and was replaced by a group of quasi-national German kingdoms. Justinian's (527–565) great counterattack followed, its effects soon erased by the renewed German movement of the Lombards into Italy, by the Slavic irruption into the Balkans, and by the loss to Islam of Syria, Egypt, and, in the early eighth century, Spain. The rise of the Carolingian Franks in the West (750–800) and of the Isaurian emperors in Byzantium restored stability for a time. Combined with renewed Muslim incursions and new Magyar slave raids from the East, the assaults of the Scandinavians during the ninth and tenth centuries again spread destruction everywhere. On the whole, however, this later cycle was less significant than those of earlier times, and resulted in serious settlement only in the British Isles and Normandy. Thereafter, although Slavic and even Asiatic attack occasionally flicked the West's frontiers, the age of the invasions was really over. Indeed, the last of the invasions had built relatively stable states over a wide arc reaching from Scandinavia to Kiev in Russia, and had thereby eradicated the barbarism of nomadic and tribal folk from most of Europe.

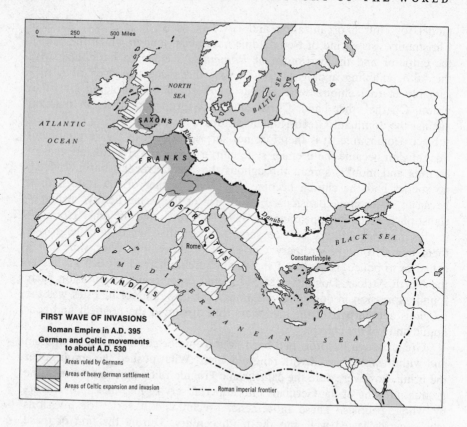

FIRST WAVE OF INVASIONS
Roman Empire in A.D. 395
German and Celtic movements
to about A.D. 530

Areas ruled by Germans
Areas of heavy German settlement
Areas of Celtic expansion and invasion   ·—·—· Roman imperial frontier

During this age, a cultural, institutional, and economic scission destroyed Mediterranean unity. The loss of the Balkans to the Slavs broke the
bridge between the Greeks and the Latins, and, by the tenth century,
Islam's domination of the western Mediterranean lessened their maritime
contacts. The Greek and Latin churches also gradually drew apart. Byzantium's attempts to placate the Christians of Egypt and Syria and its later
submission to Anatolic iconoclasm harmed relations with Rome. More, her
inability to defend Italy against the Lombards together with the obvious
advantage for missions of working with the German kingdoms inspired
Rome's pontiffs to turn their attention westward. By 781 Rome ceased to
date documents by the eastern emperor's regnal year and by 800 reinsti-
tuted the western empire by crowning the Frank, Charlemagne.

Scission was illustrated in other ways also. Each successive reconstruction of the western empire was smaller than its predecessor. Rome ruled
from Britain to Syria, Charlemagne (768–814) only northwest continental
Europe, much of Italy, and a sliver of Spain. Around 1000 the German
empire embraced Germany and most of Italy, but, save its eastern reaches,

all of France escaped its power. Although often reversed by spasmodic rebuilding, moreover, political scission was accompanied by economic decentralization, by a partial decline in urban centers, and by a loss of knowledge and culture. Decay, in short, continued until well into the Middle Ages.

If, however, the nations and empires of the age of the invasions are examined more closely, decay is seen to be an inadequate term. Based between the Rhine and the Loire, Carolingian power ruled extensive regions in Germany well beyond Rome's ancient frontiers, and the later German empire was centered still farther eastward. By Carolingian times, although still partly found in Italy, the generative centers of Latin culture had shifted from the Mediterranean to northwest Europe, and by the end of the last wave of invasions in the tenth century relatively stable Christian monarchies had put an end to the primitive tribalism of Scandinavia and of the Slavic and Magyar peoples to the east. Also, along with Christian missions, a measure of the urban civilization of the Mediterranean had spread into these hitherto untouched areas. The age of the invasions, therefore, was not only one of decline; it was also one in which a weakened version of a once high Latin civilization spread beyond its earlier confines to eradicate Europe's ancient barbarism.

As in both Islam and Byzantium, moreover, a new culture was being created in western Europe. By Carolingian times, the Latin church provided a new sense of identity with its language, law, and theology, and had begun to unite the West's nations and peoples. In late Rome, Christianity was almost coterminous with *Romanitas,* barbarians being excluded. By 800, the main distinction was between the Christian and the non-Christian, the erstwhile barbarians having become members of the New Rome's ampler society, the Latin church. Along with this went the spread of urbanism, once limited to Rome's territories. In spite of setbacks during actual invasions, the revival of towns within the empire's frontiers and, more, the implantation of preurban nuclei beyond these bounds marked both the Carolingian and the later German empires, not to speak of Anglo-Saxon England. Nor did the men of this time merely ape antiquity. Art and architecture were self-consciously classical in style until well into the ninth century, but the basic elements of the Romanesque that flowered in the eleventh century were already being limned. Again, although much Carolingian thought merely echoed earlier Augustinian and Neoplatonic modes, the court and church of this empire produced lively theological rebels, good political minds, and the first of the medieval philosophical system builders, Johannes Scotus Erigena (c. 810–c. 877). The Carolingians, then, had all but reversed the decline begun in Rome.

The implanting of civilization required government, and the Germanic

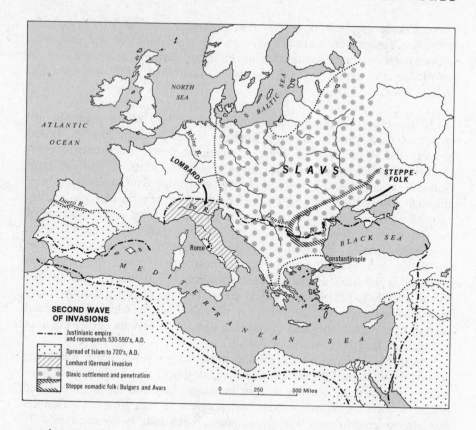

SECOND WAVE OF INVASIONS

Justinianic empire and reconquests 530-550's, A.D.

Spread of Islam to 720's, A.D.

Lombard (German) invasion

Slavic settlement and penetration

Steppe nomadic folk: Bulgars and Avars

0   250   500 Miles

peoples contributed much to its building. Their primitive law, involving trial by combat or ordeals and a firm sense of tribal or national identity, suited the circumstance of the age of the invasions. At first, their sense of identity was sharpened by their contact with the Romans. Their national laws were codified in the fifth and sixth centuries, and both Roman law and religious practices initially set them apart from the conquered provincials. In time, however, national identity weakened as the peoples fused together. Then Roman law and institutions no longer served only the provincials, but were also extended to the conquerors themselves. Early in the conquest, the military office of the late Roman count of the city was adopted by the successor states and thence slowly spread well beyond the frontiers of the old empire to become the basic unit of medieval local administration. The medieval manorial structure had its antecedents in Rome's latifundia. Another step in this process of adoption was the absorption of the idea of the empire by the German states. Although the high point of this capacity to transcend tribal or national units was the establishment of the western empire under Charlemagne, the idea also informed both earlier and later attempts to unify individual nations. A Visigothic king was a kind of emperor; tenth-century kings of Wessex called themselves "emperors of England"; eleventh-century Castilian princes claimed to be emperors of Spain.

Monarchy was the typical form of government of the early Middle Ages. Derived from German institutions and Roman imperial traditions, early medieval monarchy tended toward dynastic transmission and, when it was successful, toward single succession. Such was the strength of localism, however, that the invasion age was over before it was possible to eradicate the impediment caused by the regular subdivision of inheritances among a prince's successors. Besides, the growth of the dynastic tradition was slowed by the existence among both the Germans and the Romans of the idea that a senate, or better, that the army or the people in arms, had the power to elect its prince. Although elements of this electoral idea persisted everywhere, triumphed in Spain's Visigothic state, and were revived among the later Carolingians to become the standard pattern for the medieval German empire, dynastic succession slowly gained ground, principally because of the need for a political office that transcended any particular social, regional, tribal, or national group. In a time of invasions and severe cultural shock, when new political units were being constituted and when hitherto strange and often hostile peoples were thrown together, a dynastic prince was required to arbitrate or still conflicts.

It was a mark of the early medieval state that its princes, although sprung from particular peoples (*nationes*), soon transcended national limitations. The Carolingians were Franks, and the rise of their empire may be fairly described as the conquest of much of Western Europe by that people, but the peak of Carolingian power saw not only the reintroduction of the imperial idea, but also the employment of Englishmen, Spaniards, Italians, and other Germans in imperial service. As a result, although not completely, because it did not include all of Latin Europe, this empire set normative patterns for the whole of medieval governmental, legal, and social institutions.

The whole structure of law had begun to change. Before the invasions, the Germans maintained peace within their tribes or nations by means of the solidarity of extended family groups. Matters were settled between them by compensation and only rarely, as in wartime, by princes or priests acting for the nation as a whole. During the invasions and subsequent settlement, however, when families were uprooted and broken up, and when peoples with their own laws were mixed together, a new law to police their relationships was called for. This law was naturally administered by the new prince. Following Roman legal tradition, the prince's law was a common law, one that transcended tribal, national, and family groups alike by accenting the responsibility of the individual and reducing the protection given him by his nation's law or by his family.

The new princes and kings everywhere sought to create hierarchies of officers loyal to themselves. All society was to be divided into groups performing duties ranging from the farmer's drudgery to the counsel offered a prince by a high officer. Originating in late Rome's functional orders, the ancient articulation of society into many social groups gradually simplified during the early Middle Ages to the point where it seemed useful to classify complex reality under three grand headings, the economic (*laboratores*), the administrative or martial (*bellatores*), and the ecclesiastical (*oratores*). With this, moreover, went a full measure of the idea of the ministry or duty (*ministerium*) of those who served prince and society, a conception that evoked a service ethos which marked all of Europe's aristocracies and even peoples throughout the Middle Ages. In this period, however, service to a prince or to his officers was the main way of climbing into the aristocracy. Obversely, when a new service cadre was being built, old local aristocracies were often absorbed or obliterated. Among these were the ancient German and Nordic sacral nobilities and the Roman provincial senatorial aristocracies.

Peculiar to the service personnel of this age, and, to some degree, to their successors throughout the Middle Ages, was the degree to which personal allegiance bound them together. This partly derived from the near-synonymity of public and private institutions among the primitive Germans, but it also reflected the tendency to confuse these areas evidenced in Rome long before it fell. The officer's oath to the emperor, the expansion of the client-to-patron relationship in the late empire, and the growth within and without the Roman army of armed clienteles bound to commanders or great families—groups analogous to the retinues of Germanic and later Nordic war leaders—are evidences of this tendency. In addition, the German and Roman system of clientage had, in both origin and growth, elements of servility and freedom, the first accenting duties and service, and the second, right and privilege. So efficacious for maintaining peace and social solidarity was this system of binding *iuniores* to *seniores* or men to masters that the Carolingians and many much later princely houses sought to extend it to all their subjects in spite of strong opposition both aristocratic and plebeian.

Although real, the triumph of the service ethos and of social hierarchy under a prince was mitigated by both political principles and firmly rooted interests. Enshrined, for example, in a Frankish edict of 609, the principle that judges or counts were to be chosen from the areas in which they were to exercise office derived from Roman practice and canon law. That officers should have tenure and not lose the fruits of service at the whim of princes was known to the Romans, Visigoths, and Franks. Furthermore, the idea that officers exercising a *ministerium* were judged upon performance had also long been applied to princes and even to dynasties. A pope used this argument to justify the Carolingian replacement of the Merovingian house in 752, and in 833 the magnates and bishops used it to depose Charlemagne's successor, Louis the Pious. Closely related to this principle was the right of magnates to elect their prince, a practice, as noted on page 369, used by the Visigoths, and others thereafter. Lastly, derived from Roman and German antecedents, magnates and prelates often exercised their authority in councils where, as was stated in an assembly at Pitres in 864, law or judgment was promulgated by a prince with the consent of the magnates and the people.

The service elites included churchmen, members of an institution that had grown apace during the collapse of Rome and later invasions. Shielding the conquered provincials and serving as a refuge for Rome's fading aristocracies, the church absorbed the traditions of Rome's government. In

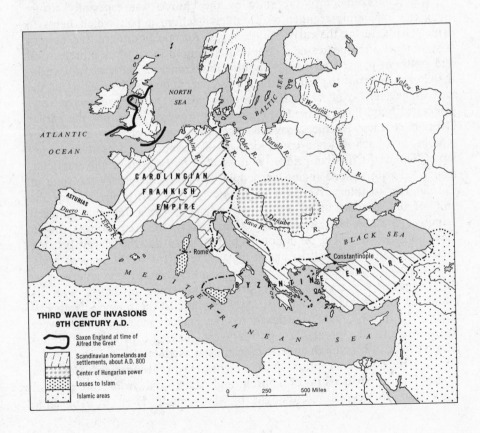

**THIRD WAVE OF INVASIONS
9TH CENTURY A.D.**

Saxon England at time of
Alfred the Great

Scandinavian homelands and
settlements, about A.D. 800

Center of Hungarian power

Losses to Islam

Islamic areas

0   250   500 Miles

spite of the enduring vigor of the classical idea of lay education, the initial illiteracy of the Germans and the frequent disruptive invasions gradually gave the church a near-monopoly of literacy and of learning in law and government. As a result, the church helped to equip Europe's new states with their constitutions and legal systems, serving, indeed, as a model for them. If princes tried to build nonhereditary service cadres, the church did better with its celibate bishops. Where direct contact with Rome was weak, as in England, or nonexistent, as in Scandinavia, forms of salary and tenure used by the church for its clergy provided models for secular offices. The idea of the *ministerium* described above was also reinforced by a church whose notion of office was firmly based upon the fitness of an individual, and not of a family. Lastly, while princes invaded the jurisdictional community of the extended family or of national and tribal groups by insisting upon the individual's responsibility for certain crimes, the church had long since gone further by holding each man penitentially accountable for all his actions.

The reinforcement of the state by the church was especially strong along the expanding frontier of Latin civilization, a fact which helps to explain why, during the early Middle Ages, Europe's northern and eastern governments often possessed a cohesion lacking in those of its more central and southern parts. Heir to the cultural intolerance of the classical world, the church rejected the tribalism, family conceptions, and religions of the barbarians and, to effect their conversion, aided emerging emperors and princes to build their states. Each successive wave of invasions, the earlier German or later Nordic, provoked the appearance of new empires or nations, and each saw the conversion of the invaders and of their homelands. The new Christian princes were exalted by being in a universal cult, associated with no one region or people. Suitably enough, in the time of Carolingian greatness, Agobard of Lyons (c. 779–840) pleaded for the unity of all Christians under one prince and one law in a tract that attacked primitive German law. Augmenting their power, the new princes fought local nobilities or tribal or national chieftains; so did the clergy because these were initially bound to pagan cults. The defeat of the ancient gods, therefore, was equally profitable to prince and church. First regularized by the Visigoths, the revival of the priest's unctioning of kings, with its baptismal and ordinative qualities, aptly symbolized the religious authentication of princely might. Furthermore, the ancient idea that kings were themselves priestly spread through the West, making a prince the administrative head of his church and director of its apostolate.

This religious conception of the highest lay office derived from the Constantinian partnership of church and state, and from the parallel absorption of Neoplatonic thought by the church. Even in Augustine

(354–430), this was partly a naturalist philosophy. It stressed the excellence of God's creations, and the consequent material absence of evil in nature. As part of nature, man was capable of goodness, his passion designed to people heaven with saints, his reason to make him harmonize with God's and nature's good. In social terms, this good was order, peace on earth wherein man could be educated to Christ. The maintenance of this peace gilded all of man's institutions, including his monarchies and even his swords, with reflected divine light. From Lactantius (260–340) of Constantine's time to the so-called Norman Anomymous of the late eleventh century, men of this persuasion believed the spheres of heaven and earth to be so closely intertwined that the notion of surrendering a man's body to the keeping of his government while giving over his soul to his church seemed absurd. Although to such men the spiritual was superior to the material since it was the end to which all effort tended, the two spheres were not separable—nor were the institutions that advanced their causes.

This alliance of church and state, however, was marked by ambivalence. Princes, for example, were at least vestigially secular or tolerant about religion. Jews were citizens under Rome and remained so under the German princes. Save in seventh-century Spain, where a rising tide of Semitized urbanism announced Islam's forthcoming invasion, Jews were protected, often indeed privileged, and clerical complaints made little impression on princes who needed their useful mercantile and administrative services. Even later, during Castile's revival of the imperial dream, the conqueror of Toledo in 1085 styled himself emperor of the two religions when writing to Muslims, and an eleventh-century count of Barcelona promised fair justice to Christian, Muslim, Jew, and heretic alike. This measure of tolerance displeased the clergy and their followers. Not that they wished to convert others by force. That was rare, if only because it made the church's advance so clearly depend upon the secular sword. Instead, from late Rome on, ecclesiastical liberty was defined as the monopoly of the right to convert and to prevent the loss of believers into heresy or another religion.

There was also a deeper source of the Christian's rejection of the naturalist philosophy or attitude described above. Because his cult was in its origin partly a way of resisting a chauvinistic Greco-Roman culture with its accent upon civic pride and duty and upon bodily and mental education, many an early Christian saw little good in health, learning, or service to society, asserting that he had seceded not only from the state, but also from the people. Later on, the monks of the Constantinian age continued some of this tradition. They left the world and gave up its pleasures, but they also made sure that they were relieved of their duties to family or to civil or military service. This withdrawal from life paralleled an intellectual urge to extol heaven and deprecate the world. Although some still asserted man's innate capacity to attain a part of the divine good, the greater Latin fathers, Augustine and Jerome (c. 340–420), insisted upon man's natural inadequacy, and his need for God's grace. As the agency of grace, the church, to such men, was clearly superior to the state. Although according to Gelasius I (492–496), the priest and the prince divided the world's government, this pope did not doubt that the former judged the latter. On the other hand, the disruptive strength of these ideas could not yet be fully exploited. In an age of invasions and mass defections to Islam, the church needed the civil sword. Again, until most of Europe had become Christian, the church gained much by its alliance with the state. Long ago, Augustine had set its tone, first by regretfully permitting and then by demanding the exercise of religious coercion by the state against the Donatist heretics.

Albeit reluctantly, then, the partnership of state and church and the presidency of the former was generally admitted in the West during the invasion age. All the same, the cultural identity of the West was largely supplied by the church. By the early ninth century, Arabic, Greek, and Latin demarcated not only three separate cultures but also differences in the relationship of the church to the state in the three areas. Under Islam the two were nearly indistinguishable. Among the Greeks, especially under the iconoclast emperors, the church was subordinate to the prince. Although in the West, Visigothic kings were the apostles of their nation's church, and Frankish and later German emperors headed their clergy, the Latin mind was convinced that the church was wholly autonomous spiritually, and Charlemagne's own court clergy attacked the meddling of Greek emperors in theological matters. This restive independence was earlier observable in Gregory I (590–604), who, as a Roman, dealt carefully with the Eastern emperor, but did not hesitate to threaten Western princes with losing their offices were they to contravene church law. Perhaps, also, the Roman's rage at having been conquered by barbarians was expressed by the hostility of his church toward German culture. Whereas unconquered Greek welcomed into its liturgy the languages of the peoples its preachers converted, Latin not only monopolized the cult, but also, after the Carolingian reform, vigorously suppressed German vernacular literature, first in Germany itself, and then, far later, in England and Scandinavia.

The day of the church, however, had yet to come. Still sometimes looking to Byzantium for aid and inspiration, the Roman see did not yet really head the Latin communion. Local churches were often almost independent bodies, and frequently superior to Rome in doctrinal culture and learning. They were also usually dominated by their princes, who appointed the higher clergy and called their councils. Nor was the notion of citizenship in Christ yet sufficiently strong to subordinate older secular ideas. That, for example, Christendom was not coterminous with citizenship is amply shown by the privileged status of Jews under the Carolingian and later German emperors. The persistent strength of secular ecumenical ideas, such as that of the empire, still competed with the churchman's Christendom. Although a pope claimed the right to grant the empire, the idea of universal monarchy was still attractive quite apart from its religious attachments.

Thus constituted, the empires and greater kingdoms along Europe's frontiers were characteristic of the age of the invasions. Almost all, however, eventually collapsed. The greatest was the Carolingian, and its history is an example, though a not quite typical one, of the fate of the others. In the ninth century, Nordic, Magyar, and Muslim invaders ravaged its land, but not everything can be blamed on them. The earlier Carolingian imperialism of the Franks had taught them much. In Scandinavia, the Carolingian state and church provided a model for the new kingship and its centralizing agencies that expropriated quasi-sacral kinglets and tribal nobilities. It was these who emigrated, hoping to return home to their "rightful" place, but often destined to fail or to find empire abroad. Furthermore, the invasions did not always disrupt large states. True, in regions like France and the Low Countries, where dukes and counts made bastions of their small realms, the best defense was local. Elsewhere, however, as in Germany, barbarian raids provoked the building of a new empire during the tenth century. In short, although terrible, the invasions were not a prime cause of Carolingian disintegration.

More significant was a repetition of the process of scission whose origins have been seen in Roman times. Dormant while the Carolingians were successful, this divisive urge had not been eradicated. Charlemagne's house had inherited the usual problem of the relationship of the head of state to his service cadre: the servitor sought to amplify his rights, while the prince emphasized his service. From Rome onward, the danger here was that tenure in office, imitating that of the monarch himself, could become hereditary. This tendency had been arrested when the Carolingians gained power. A massive expropriation of church property had enabled them to build an army whose triumphs had provided advancement abroad for the scions of established families and for new recruits, thus exalting service and depressing right. Expansion necessarily slowed down, however, partly because the empire's threatened neighbors learned to resist by imitating its institutions, and partly because, by its victories, the empire soon reached the limit imposed by the technological level of the time upon transport and communication. In this circumstance, privilege began to prevail over service among the imperial officers and soldiery. In 877, for example, in order to mount an expedition to Italy and to settle the succession upon his son, the emperor Charles the Fat was obliged to allow his officers the right to be succeeded by their sons. By 900, this right had become customary in most of France's duchies and counties. When higher officers exacted hereditary succession, the prince attempted to win the loyalty of their subordinates by granting them the same right. Subvassals eventually came to enjoy hereditary succession to office and salary, but with little advantage for the prince, whose call for loyalty was rarely heard at their level in time to restore his power.

This fact shows that the drive toward establishing hereditary right to office reflected general social aspirations and economic patterns more than the magnates' desire to usurp their posts. Although the spread of civilization and consequent economic growth had inspired centralization in the primitive lands beyond Rome's ancient frontiers and had even provoked significant renewals in areas within those bounds, the general movement of society still continued to be toward political decentralization and economic autarchy. This being the case, at a time when monarchy by dynastic succession was the normal form of government, the claim to a peculiar and innate liberty by families of traditional leadership seemed to be the firmest guarantee of local society's freedom from outside demands. On a higher level, from Roman times on, this freedom had been partly won by the division of a realm among a ruler's successors, a practice that led, in the Carolingian age, to the emergence of effectively independent subkingdoms and, in eleventh-century France, to the devolution of royal power to dukes, counts and even seigniors.

The dissolution of central power was also more than an expression of local separatism. If all the arts of civil sedition had been explored before the Carolingians lost out in France and Germany between 887 and 987, the constitutional and other principles adduced above convinced magnates and churchmen that they were working not only for their own good but also for the rights of others. An example may be seen in the clergy's search for freedom. From Charlemagne's day on, churchmen sought to "reform" the church. Royal councils must not determine doctrine. Princes must neither appoint nor judge prelates, and the lesser clergy should be free from control by local notables. Monks should abjure the world, and secularly minded clergy should be purged. Churchmen also actively intervened in deposing Louis the Pious in 833, and, in the mid-ninth century, Nicholas I (858–867) asserted papal authority with astonishing vigor. Profiting from civil war, Nicholas anathematized a king of Lotharingia, attacked the customary independence of the local churches, and denounced lay domination of the church, urging bishops to wield effectively the two swords, spiritual and material. When the mutual anathemas launched by Rome and Constantinople over the Balkans are added, the revolutionary tone of the later Gregorian age seems not too far away.

This ecclesiastical attempt at freedom had unanticipated results. Churchmen could neither foresee the new invasions nor perceive that their efforts would encourage political decentralization. No sooner had they spoken out than they began to suffer from the anarchy of the times and from subordination to local lay authority. They therefore slowly reversed their stand and tried to rebuild an authority they had irreparably weakened. Plagued by Muslim raids and civil war, Nicholas I's successors turned now to fading Frankland, now to Byzantium, in a vain attempt to police and protect central Italy. In Frankland, Hincmar of Reims' (847–882) mid-ninth-century aerial act, balancing his affirmation of ecclesiastical liberty against his defense of the Carolingian state, was no more successful.

Elsewhere, however, particularly along Europe's frontiers, the old way soon reasserted itself. The German church succeeded where Hincmar had failed precisely because it subordinated itself in order to rebuild the empire. From the council of Hohenaltheim in 918 through the Ottonian and early Salian houses, this church became the firm support of a renewed empire. Its monasteries served as academies for an imperial prelatry, and its bishops were appointed by the court, frequently from the blood royal. Secular administration, first of towns and then of whole counties, was entrusted to the imperial bishops of Germany and Lombardy, who had no progeny to inherit their offices, and a large part of the army was normally raised from ecclesiastical benefices.

A new empire had been fashioned, one whose achievement was not limited to bringing the local church to heel. Its chiefs also built a new service cadre, which, early seen in Henry the Fowler's (919–936) frontier militia, flowered into the servile or nonhereditary *ministeriales* of the Salian period. Of course, these institutions were not unique to Germany. Other princes, even the weak Capetians (beginning 987) of France, controlled their local churches and were served by a dependent soldiery and official-dom. But the empire's controls were greater, and its reach wider than those of any other state. In fact, after the late-tenth-century reconquest of Italy, the Roman church bowed to German power for the first time. The Donation of Constantine, that papal claim to supremacy over western secular author-ity, had been received silently by the Carolingians, but was called a fraud by Otto III. If a Carolingian had judged the fitness of a pope for his office, the later Germans treated Rome much like an ordinary imperial see. From 966 onward, they appointed foreigners to Rome and even deposed three rival Italians at Sutri in 1046. Rome was also penetrated by northern doctrine at this time. Widely accepted in the northern churches from Carolingian days, the *filioque* clause—an attempt of the Latins to claim an orthodoxy superior to that of the Greeks—was finally admitted into the Roman creed just a few years before a Lorrainer cardinal deposited the bull that broke Rome's link to Constantinople in 1054.

Although great, the empire suffered from fatal weaknesses. Even in Germany, imperial power was not broadly enough based. It relied too much upon the church. Furthermore, its *ministeriales* were thought servile largely because the older service groups were already so free, constituting an aristocracy capable of resisting the emperors and of imitating them by building its own ministerial cadres. The empire was also too small. West of the Rhine and the Rhone, its hold was weak and most of France escaped its sway. Italy had fallen to the empire in the late tenth century largely because of the natives' desire to rid themselves of the Burgundians, but French pressure was resumed early in the next century by the Normans in southern Italy. Since the larger part of western Europe lay outside the empire, moreover, German domination of the universal Roman church was both anomalous and unforgivable. This fact explains why the churchmen of the later Gregorian age were able to go beyond the balanced views of the past and state their position of the relationship of the spiritual to the temporal power in extreme terms.

Even before that revolutionary age, churchmen had begun to grasp their opportunity. Illustrative of the often inadvertent way in which they acted was the Cluniac monastic movement founded in 910. Rising when the church was ruled by secular princes, Cluny modeled itself upon contemporary institutions, holding in lordship its churches and monasteries and unhesitatingly invading episcopal rights if it was in its interest. Nor, so long as its ends were served, did Cluny oppose secular might. Indeed, because its monks owed the empire much, Cluny even stood aside during the later revolutionary days of the Gregorians. Basically, however, these Benedictines pointed in a new direction. In France and elsewhere, for example, Cluny's partners were often new local princely or seignorial families. To these Cluny applied the traditions of royal dynastic burials and commemoratory services, thereby corroborating the rise to power of these local lines. It also restored church unity, partly by its own monarchical structure of government and Europe-wide unity and partly by its direct affiliation to St. Peter's at Rome rather than to the local bishops. Linking local princelings or seignorial lines to the ecumenical church, Cluny had bypassed the premier governmental institutions of the age of the invasions: the empire, the nation, and their dependent local churches.

What Cluny began, the papacy completed. The century beginning about 1050 experienced a revolution in which the papacy replaced imperial and national princes as the leader of Europe, thereby creating the Christian

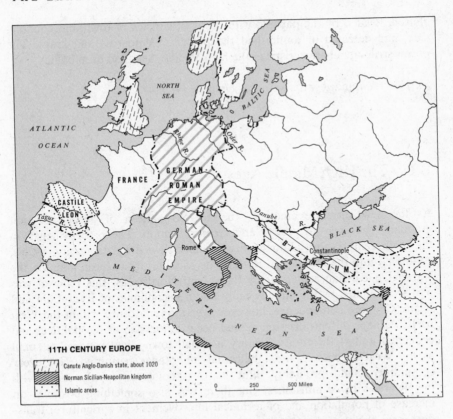

11TH CENTURY EUROPE

Canute Anglo-Danish state, about 1020
Norman Sicilian-Neapolitan kingdom
Islamic areas

0   250   500 Miles

republic dimly envisaged in earlier times. First came preparatory steps: the break with Byzantium, papal sanction for holy wars, the loss of imperial control of papal elections, and rigorist attacks upon old ecclesiastical customs, such as clerical marriage, venality of office, and secular appointment. The struggle reached revolutionary proportions under Gregory VII (1073–1085) and Urban II (1088–1099). In the name of ecclesiastical freedom, "reformers" battled the old state churches and, when resisted, incited laymen to reject their sacraments and to expel their clergy. Anathemas released service cadres from their obedience to princes, thus encouraging the devolution of political power described above. The ensuing civil war rent Europe, leading to a reaction in which the church's tiller was returned to the moderate hands of men like Bernard, abbot of Clairvaux (1115–1153) and Innocent II (1130–1143). By this time, however, although much of the old church remained, clerical freedom had triumphed, all of Europe's nations had been severely shaken, and the German empire had begun its slow descent. An alliance of the ecumenical elements in the church, headed by the papacy, with the aristocracies of town and country-side, had defeated or diminished the power of emperors and kings. The power structure characteristic of the high Middle Ages had been built.

Further reading suggestions follow chapter 34.

33   The High Middle Ages

As the new structure emerged, the age-old pattern of decentralization gradually gave way to growth and recentralization. The process began in the tenth century and, although occasionally slowed by depression cycles, continued into the fourteenth. Both in the Mediterranean basin and, via the Varangian Russian route, in the Baltic and North seas, this renewal was partly stimulated by the initially more mature economies of Byzantium and Islam. Of more consequence, however, was the renascence within the West itself. Perhaps decentralization ceased because the size of the political and economic unity—the rural seigniory or small town—had become as small as the West's technical and intellectual inheritance permitted. Not every community could profitably mint its own coins or supply itself with metalware, salt, or millstones. But there was also something positive: an increase of population and of technical improvement in agriculture, transport, and the use of natural power. To implant and promote these improvements, however, social agencies were required. In part, the old royal or imperial states of the invasion age performed this function. In wide areas, however, these were replaced by the newer regional principalities: Flanders, Normandy, Catalonia. More general than either and more intense in its capacity to mobilize society was the petty rural seigniory and small town. But these, we may be sure, would have created little but anarchy had they not been allied to a grander body, the ecumenical church.

Churchmen intervened in many ways. Bishops often played the role of princes or seigniors. More inventive were the monks. Since the foundation of Cluny in 910, they were arrayed in groups and orders that reached beyond the frontiers of the dioceses, often extending through the whole of the Latin West, thus enabling them to mobilize resources on a grand scale. Until the mid-twelfth century, the main source of land credit was mortgage loans supplied by monasteries. In partnership with new princes and seigniors, Cluny revived the older centers of Western settlement. Around 1100, a host of new orders, Cistercians, Templars, Premonstratensians,

Roman Pontiffs

A.D. 1198–1216 Innocent III
      1294–1303 Boniface VIII
      1316–1334 John XXII

German Emperors

1138–1268 Hohenstaufen house
1212–1250 Frederick II
      1268 Death of Conradin
1314–1347 Louis of Bavaria, Wittelsbach

English and French Princes

      1154 ff. England's Angevine house
     987–1328 France's Capetians
    1285–1314 Philip IV the Fair
1266/1268 ff. Anjou cadet line in Sicily-Naples

Orders of the Church

        910 Cluny (reformed Benedictine)
       1098 Cistercian order
1118/1128 Templars (military order)
       1120 Premonstratensians (canons-regular)
       1201 Humiliati (quasi-mendicant)
       1209 Franciscans (mendicant)
       1215 Dominicans (mendicant)

Churchmen and Intellectuals

1079–1142 Peter Abelard
1090–1153 Bernard of Clairvaux
1126–1198 Averroes
c. 1130–1202 Joachim of Fiore
1225–1274 Thomas Aquinas

Church Councils

1179 III Lateran
1215 IV Lateran
1245 I Lyon
1274 II Lyon
1311 Viennne

carried the expansion into a second and greater stage, moving capital and personnel from old communities and enterprises to new ones throughout Europe. The religious, in short, supplemented the intense local mobilization of seigniory and town with an ecumenical capitalization.

Assembled in councils, moreover, the churchmen who invented the ideal of the *pax Dei* during the late tenth and early eleventh centuries showed that their church was also capable of policing them by substituting for the failing empires or monarchies of the invasion age. The *pax* flourished precisely where central government was weak, and where the jealous particularism of seigniory and town might have made life impossible. Before splitting into its component parts, the law of the peace touched everything, protecting merchants and farmers, regulating debts, just price, and sound coinage, and accenting the social duty of the knight or soldier. More, since peace within is wedded to war without, the *pax* stimulated aggression. In towns around 1100, it unified the community, brigading it to seek freedom from its rulers, serving sometimes to precipitate revolution, sometimes to repair revolution's wounds. Again, in 1095, a council busy with peace legislation saw Urban II launch the first crusade to "recover" Jerusalem, the end of a century-long evolution of the *pax dei* into the *bellum romanum*. In brief, the Latin church lifted a localist society out of itself and sent it forward into the world about it. And, as a consequence, Rome, the papal see, became Europe's capital.

In replacing emperors and kings, the popes were aided by the rural seigniory or small town. The devolving of state power, first upon kinglets, then upon counts or dukes, and finally, as in twelfth-century France, upon local families, had made these latter the chiefs of minuscule states. No mere landlord, a seignior did not simply exploit private lands; he governed something public, a whole community. In return, he profited from the village church, courts, common economic facilities, and labor and taxes for common causes. Seigniors sought to reduce all inhabitants to being equal members of a community, equal in service. Deprived of access to courts beyond the seigniory's frontiers, freemen became villeins, inhabitants of the jurisdictional area of the *villa*. At the same time, the Roman private slave disappeared, ascending into villeinage. Other institutions, such as the German extended family and the national laws known since antiquity, weakened or disappeared.

This description is necessarily oversimplified. Even in France, north and central Italy, and some adjacent areas in Germany and Spain, where the rural seigniory was early developed, differing degrees of servitude long remained and real slavery continued on Europe's frontiers from Scandinavia to the borders with Islam. Nor did community unity ever wholly include the clergy, the martial or governing elite, or others under special law, such as merchants and Jews. Finally, although seignorial taxes and controls on marriage, inheritances, and residence were also known there, towns differed from rural seigniories. Being larger than villages, their history was more lively, and, because larger numbers of knights or merchants resided there, seigniory in town earlier had a collective or political cast. Dissimilarities aside, however, whenever rural seigniory or town unity created a community, a common law or custom appeared, one that implicitly set bounds to seignorial authority. At first in the town but finally also in the village, this stage was followed by one in which the inhabitants sought to participate in the exercise of judicial and political power. It is noteworthy, however, that where the authority of a unitary state remained vigorous, as in Germany's central reaches or in England, the evolution of this sense of community was slowed and town and village liberties did not grow so rapidly. But these were not the regions celebrated for cultural or other innovation during the high Middle Ages.

Beginning around 1000 and continuing almost to 1350, then, two powers, one ecumenical and the other local, led Europe's rise. This rise cost foreigners dearly. By 1250, Islam had lost all of Spain save Granada. By 1300, as they rose to dominate Baltic and North Sea trade, the Germans had pushed beyond the Elbe, seizing the Baltic littoral and settling in both Poland and Hungary. More dramatic were the major crusades that swept the Muslim from the central and eastern Mediterranean and established Latin beachheads from Syria to Tripoli. Admittedly, the Latins lost much to counterattacks, including Jerusalem, but when the assault was resumed shortly before 1200, Byzantium with the Aegean and Black seas fell to them, and Islam slowly ceded the western Mediterranean, including the Balearics. Aided by the Mongol irruption, Latin merchants and missions also penetrated the Near East and even Asia.

Though less spectacular, Europe's internal growth was far more significant. Drainage pushed the northern oceans back, and, by 1300, all the major river valleys, from the Po to the Garonne and eastward to the Elbe, had been cleared. The incomparably rich northern plain stretching from England into Germany was gradually shorn of its primeval forest. In spite of the already clear superiority of northern over southern productivity, however, the potentiality of this region was not yet fully realized, except in north France and Flanders. Although cheaper than in antiquity, overland transport remained expensive, and the easy shipping of the Mediterranean still enabled her naturally poorer areas, especially favored Italy, to support a relatively larger population.

This expansion was accompanied by the growth of towns. From before 1000, urban renewal was evident everywhere, although inland towns seemed to forge ahead at first. Cologne, for example, was, until about

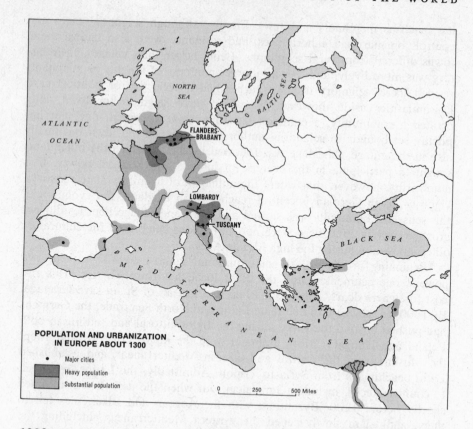

POPULATION AND URBANIZATION
IN EUROPE ABOUT 1300

- Major cities
  Heavy population
  Substantial population

0   250   500 Miles

1200, the largest city in northern Europe. The towns of France's central highlands early created an infectious vocabulary that spread the words "bourg" and "bourgeois" everywhere. By 1300, however, areas favored by geography had moved ahead. The towns of Flanders and Brabant had outstripped their rivals on the Rhine and Meuse and, with their export woolens, had become the largest industrial complex in northern Europe. Italy's advance was equally dramatic: Milan, Venice, Florence, and Genoa had populations approaching 100,000, and, as in Flanders, each was surrounded by so many smaller towns that Lombardy and north central Italy were dominated by urban life in an almost modern manner. Yet, lacking really unified or national states, medieval society possessed nothing analogous to the *megalopoloi* of antiquity or to early modern national capitals. Indeed, the large village or small town was typical of urban life in this age: a market, a church, and a jurisdictional area were the usual constituent elements of both town and village. Although large cities were interested in sanitation, housing, public building, and aesthetic unity, overall planning was usually restricted to new settlements, necessarily of modest size. These, starting about 1100 and reaching from Spain to trans-Elbian Germany, introduced the right-angle grid form, a layout often extended to the fields outside town and village walls.

Town and village were close not only in physical structure but also in their interests. During this age of economic expansion, towns often showed neighboring villages the way to freedom and sometimes helped them to gain it. Often, as in eastern Germany, urbanization forwarded immigration and the settlement of the land. But town and village were also far apart. If townsmen often farmed and villagers mined and manufactured, specialization separated the two, one being more industrial and the other more agricultural. Besides, the town was a better focus of communications, hence of government and of all sorts of techniques. It was also either initially larger or growing more rapidly, and hence more powerful. A result was that, as each tried to increase the profit derived from its specialties, combat between town and countryside became an essential ingredient of medieval life, one often illustrated by townsmen's attempts to extend their rule over nearby villages under the guise of freeing them from their lords. Similar combats also took place between areas of high urbanization and those providing raw materials. Aquitaine and England supplied the cloth towns of Flanders, and since the sovereign of Flanders was the French king, the French and English houses were forever embroiled. Similarly, Sicily and Apulia provided much of the grain and other commodities needed by north Italy's burgeoning cities, a fact that led to wars between the two parts of the peninsula. Involving popes, emperors, and other nations, these struggles were stilled only by the reduction of the south and the smashing of her unity shortly before 1300.

A striking aspect of the Latin age of expansion was the role played by the French and Italians. In the eleventh century, the French invaded Germanic areas in England, the Low Countries, and Lorraine, and even settled as far east as Hungary. Until about 1200, Spain's defeat of Islam depended on French immigration. Frenchmen were also Europe's foremost Crusaders, and their law and institutions took root in the Near East from the Holy Land to Greece. By the mid-thirteenth century, French was spoken from Jerusalem to Dublin, and Spanish, German, English, and even Italian literature and architecture were modeled on France's Gothic styles. As for the Italians, although French culture produced the age's first great ecclesiastical academies at Paris and Oxford, they founded the first two secular professions, law and medicine, which then spread slowly throughout Europe. Individually small, the Italian urban republics, allies of the papacy in its struggles against German dominance, created governments whose tightness and complexity far surpassed the loose structure of

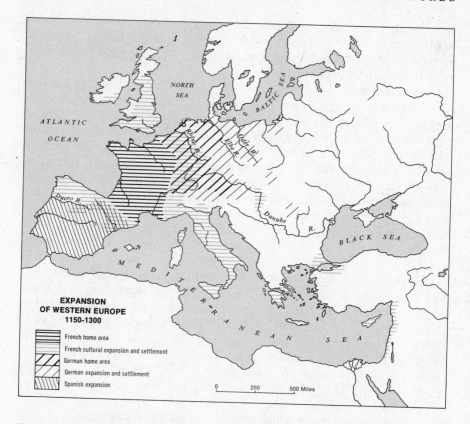

EXPANSION
OF WESTERN EUROPE
1150-1300

French home area
French cultural expansion and settlement
German home area
German expansion and settlement
Spanish expansion

0   250   500 Miles

Europe's monarchies. Italian sea power swept Islam and Byzantium from the Mediterranean and Black seas. By 1300, Lombard merchant-bankers had penetrated the Near East, North Africa, and much of Europe, from England to the Rhine and Danube and on to Constantinople.

Not that all was bliss in Italy and France. The former lacked the strength to free herself from her neighbors. In the eleventh and twelfth centuries, the Norman French helped drive out the Greeks and Muslims, and in the thirteenth, the French house of Anjou finally crushed the German Hohenstaufen. Although thirteenth-century France was a relatively peaceful land, constant minor warfare between the Capetians and their greater vassals, especially the Angevins, marred the twelfth century, and the early thirteenth saw the conquest of southern France by the north. Again, the Germans played a diminishing role in Italy, France, and the Crusades largely because they were busy settling their own north and east. As this slow change in the movements of peoples shows, the age of invasions was finally over. Although a preliminary and brief reversal of the invasion pattern had taken place in Carolingian times, the Germans had generally moved toward France and Italy until about 1000. Thereafter, a great reversal sent them and their neighbors toward Europe's peripheries, incidentally setting the stage for French and Italian success. The result was that, until about 1300, the two regions where the jealous localism of seignorial power and the independent town was most fully realized set the pace for the economic, cultural, and religious life of Western Europe and spearheaded its warlike expansion.

While two peoples led Europe's growth during the high Middle Ages, the church seemed to rule her. No longer content or able to be second after the Gregorian age, the clergy undertook to command. The church had its war, the crusade or *bellum romanum*. When combined with the ecclesiastical control of marriage and divorce, the crusade gave the popes a controlling hand in European diplomacy. The church's objective was to unify the *respublica christiana,* an ideal that had become a reality in the Gregorian age. Partly replacing the older monarchies, the church moved to regulate society and thereby to create a domestic peace in which the Christian citizen could be educated to future bliss. The military elite and soldiery were policed by the idea and the law of just war. In economic life, the practical mechanism of the just price and the condemnation of usury were employed to achieve a similar end. Furthermore, although often attacked, the same purpose was served by the "realist" position adopted by contemporary philosophers and theologians. The priest's miracle of the mass enhanced the presidency of the clerical order, and reinforced the sense of a direct link between God's eternal ordinance and the institutions of this earth. Indeed, circumstances justified clerical hope. At a time of expanding populations, newly cleared fields, new towns, and growing personal freedom, nature herself seemed beneficent. Headed by a church of divine foundation, man's institutions seemed capable of enabling him to achieve happiness.

Nor did the hierarchy and secular clergy lead these movements alone. The monastic militia was quite as active. The clearing of forest and marsh by the Cistercians and other orders is well known. The military orders provided Europe's best soldiers, and, until the rise of Lombardy's merchant-bankers in the thirteenth century, the Templars specialized in papal and state finance. New orders or foundations everywhere appeared to house the aged, the sick, the destitute, and the fallen. The growth of social service was financed by a variety of religious institutions, some, such as the indulgence, originally related to the Crusades, others to the pressures exerted on the well-to-do by the growth of the penitential system. The thirteenth century also saw the fulfillment of earlier efforts in education: the formalization of the university system and preuniversity schooling for the laity in the larger towns.

In this time of successful leadership, ecclesiastical thinkers increasingly turned to examine the reality of this world. One aspect of this was the West's new receptiveness to Arabic or Aristotelian scientism. Another was the churchmen's heightened interest in both ideal and practical forms of ecclesiastical and secular government. Of still greater significance was a gradual change in the monastic ethos. Although spiritual withdrawal still attracted many, physical withdrawal faded before the attractions of active engagement in the world's life, in helping the sick or the poor or, as with the Mendicants, in animating the church's mission by preaching and stimulating penance at the world's crossroads.

As in most human affairs, a measure both of failure and of excess marked this effort. Of the latter, an instance was the deprecation of the soldier and businessman whose careers, according to clerical rigorists, could not be followed without sin. Bernard of Clairvaux even denied the possibility of a just war among Christians, and the oft-repeated blanket condemnation of usury attacked an essential economic function in the name of a utopian conception of brotherhood. Luckily, the effects of this rigor were tempered by circumstances. Bernard really wrote to promote the Crusade. The climax of the onslaught on usury coincided with the rapid rise of social corporations, the craft and trade guilds, in the thirteenth century. It also inadvertently encouraged the creation of new forms of partnerships and investment contracts that helped improve economic institutions and state finance. Palliation aside, however, excessive rigorism illustrates the clergy's own brand of moral tyranny, its own spiritual usury. In this period, also, the intellectuals' idea of the relationship of nature and man to God seemed to many unsatisfactory or imperfect. The attempt to use the Aristotelian system here not only contradicted several Christian doctrines but also failed to resolve basic philosophical and moral problems: freedom, determinism, individual responsibility. As a result, the relationship of clerical intellectuals to Aristotelian or other naturalist thought was always ambivalent. The probing attack on the Latin Averroists— naturalist Aristotelians named after the Muslim philosopher and commentator Averroes (1126–1198)—and even on the moderate Thomas Aquinas (1225–1274) in the 1270's is a celebrated example of this uncertainty.

In solving problems, the church was often torn by internal conflict. Although bishops and popes were generally supreme, there were other authorities and other sources of inspiration. Among the former were the *magistri,* the teachers in the schools and universities, a largely autonomous group. So sanguine was this age that the *magistri* were able to "canonize" ancient and non-Christian philosophies on the grounds that they were bound to support the Christian vision. They also repeated Peter Abelard's (1079–1142) dubious dictum that truth is engendered by questioning and fathered by disputation. As to inspiration, a principal source was the monastic tradition. Enthusiasts of the Gregorian age had spread everywhere the monks' conception of a wholly spiritual church, whose members lived in apostolic poverty, freed from the stains of the flesh and of material possessions. Useful for the assault on the old state churches, this utopian separation of the spiritual and material had to be modified when the church had come to rule the West. But the dream haunted the Latin mind partly because such utopias are seductive and partly because they enable enthusiasts to condemn those in power for failing to attain impossible ideals. Many also condemned others because of their own frustrations and failings. Although often beloved and appealed to, for example, the only too visible papacy was a prime target for this escapism, being blamed for its exercise of practical political power and for their own failures by both local churchmen and utopian dogmatists. More extreme minds, furthermore, went beyond this to assert that any part of the church at peace with the moral equivocation or ambiguity of this world should be cut off root and branch. Theirs was a vision of heaven on earth.

Among these critics, some turned toward heresy, a term meaning not so much divergent thought as the building of secessionist sects. The ideas of these groups had been both spread and even encouraged in the battles with the old state churches during the Gregorian epoch. The repudiation of revolutionary enthusiasm by the bulk of the church, however, drove many to found their own sects, all of which shared, in greater or lesser degree, several characteristics. They were elitist, expressing this either in terms of the priesthood of all "true believers" or in the creation of a "heretical" hierarchy. They attacked the "orthodox" clergy, often relying on ancient canons invalidating the sacraments of those they considered morally vitiated. All rigoristically separated spirit and matter, although only one sect, the Cathars, partly moved by Eastern ideology, emerged as really dualist or Manichean.

These sects also flourished especially in north Italy and in south France, thence up the Rhone to the valleys of the Meuse and Rhine. Heresy, then, grew best in regions marked by rapid economic or cultural growth. Since, however, such areas were also most inventive of "orthodox" thought and institutions, particularly monastic, commercial and cultural expansion are not enough to explain the spread of heresy. As significant is another fact, namely that the regions in which political fragmentation was most apparent boasted unusually lively heretical movements. Both orthodoxy and heresy may therefore be said to have flourished least in those areas where the older medieval unitary states, together with their state churches, were most strongly retained.

Indeed, where, as in twelfth-century England, churches were still partly state agencies, princes were quick to undertake the repression of heresy. Fearing to rely on the secular sword and vainly hoping to persuade, the church was slower to act. But repeated missionary failures eventually forced its hand. By 1209 a crusade had to be launched against the heretics in Languedoc, and in the 1230's the new papal inquisition was instituted there and in Lombardy, whence it slowly spread through much of Europe. But force was not enough; heresy or secession was really undermined by Rome's readiness to accept new religious enthusiasms. Yielding to the pleas of the secular hierarchy and the older orders, Rome had resisted the creation of new orders or devotions until about 1200. Around that time, however, the admission of the Lombard *Humiliati* and other groups signaled a change of heart that resulted in the recognition by Rome of the Franciscans (1209), the Dominicans (1215), and the other mendicant orders together with the lay devotional groups associated with these friars. These saved the day by opening the door to enthusiasm and by renewing the parish, the pulpit, education, and charity.

That there were difficulties is undoubted. Mendicant preachers were the bane of the secular clergy, and the professors of Paris fought the friars' invasion of the university's halls. More serious was the exaggeration of old monastic ideals. The Franciscan imitation of apostolic poverty both deprecated the glory of the rest of the church and, because impossible here on earth, led to shifty deception and serious conflict within the order. Furthermore, wild enthusiasm so strengthened old ideas of spiritual progress, recently expressed by Joachim of Fiore (c. 1130–1202), that some preached the imminent coming of an age of spiritualized monasticism in which the old church and its sacraments would have little or no place.

None of these were more than threats, however, until another triumph of this happy age had borne its fruit, the emergence of the lay spirit. This was a compound of two elements: the growth of literacy among laymen and the emergence of a lay ideology. The beginnings of the first coincided with the Gregorian troubles when many clergy were expelled from the church by the radical "reformers." Before that time, apart from the Jews, some Italians, and a very few others, literacy and hence most technical knowledge had been limited to churchmen. Afterward, things changed, partly because a mature society requires greater specialization of function and partly because of the trouble within the clerical order itself. At first in Italy, the secular professions of medicine and law, together with their schools, such as Salerno and Bologna, appeared. Similarly, with the French leading the way, a secular literature emerged that both echoed and

THE HIGH MIDDLE AGES

caricatured its churchly antecedents. Around 1300, however, the triumph of the lay spirit was as yet incomplete. In much of Europe, the clergy still controlled education and offered scribal service, and local or national churches still either provided the reward or served as a recruiting ground for officers of state. Only Italy and adjacent areas or occasional towns elsewhere seem almost modern with their partly lay schools and their secular professions, political, legal, medical, and artistic. But the basic step toward creating literate lay professions had been taken. Busy seeking their freedom, however, the clergy did not at first feel the loss of their power. After all, the duties from which they withdrew were those that placed them under secular authority in case of fault or failure. The creation of lay literacy was therefore as much the work of the clergy as of the laity. Their withdrawal provided the need, and they were themselves the first teachers and perhaps the first recruits for the new lay professions.

To literacy must be added the lay spirit—the emulation and rivalry of the clergy by the laity. This spirit had never been absent in the West, but it had usually been expressed in terms of the conflict of the church (*sacerdotium*) and the state (*imperium*) or the old competition between the nonliterate order of the *bellatores* and the literate one of the *oratores,* a combat always limited by the fact that neither could do without the other. With the victories of the church in the Gregorian age and the resulting sharper separation of the clergy from the laity ("the two peoples," as the jurists called them), the issue became more broadly social. The appearance of professional jurists, for example, not only eliminated the clergy's monopoly of literacy, but also weakened their claim to be the sole judges of moral life here on earth. Jurists loved to repeat those Roman texts that likened judges to priests. Admittedly, the legal profession did not always reinforce lay solidarity. Its members endlessly rehearsed the ancient argument that the robe was as necessary for the republic as the sword, if not more so. A combat between ordinary citizens and professionals over who was to administer justice, promulgate law, and elect judges gradually spread from Italy through the West. On the other hand, legal professionalism weakened ecclesiastical solidarity as well. If canon lawyers argued that just judges were of greater value to the church than the secluded religious, intellectuals and monks complained from the twelfth century that the church was no longer governed by its ancient canons but instead by Justinian's worldly code.

The lay spirit was expressed in ways largely borrowed from the ecclesiastical order or transmitted by it. The clerks' pejorative view of laymen, for example, was soon imitated by jurists. Churchmen believed that the source of true nobility was not blood or family tradition, but virtue, a notion naturally dear to careerists. This idea was quickly seized upon by jurists, and their emphasis upon an individual's attainments as against lineage (an idea only dumbly shared by the sword's servitors) permeated the literate professions. All the same, much of the lay spirit seemed opposed to that of the church. Although essentially religious, for example, the lay idea of romantic love was decidedly earth-centered. Against the clerk's salvation stood the layman's earthly fame. The revival of these great themes certainly reflects the turn toward the world that was reversing the spiritual withdrawal of late antiquity on which the church had been built. In spite of this, it is also clear that some of these ideas moved clerks as well as laymen. Since the clergy sought to remake the world into a school for pilgrims on their way toward heaven, earthly glory could without blasphemy be paralleled to sanctity. That there was conflict between clergy and laity here is evident, however, especially when the spread of the monastic ethos is examined. As the growth of monastic orders under the Gregorians and the later movement of the mendicant orders of the thirteenth century show, the penetration of the church by a revived sense of the monk's spiritual vocation had again and again revitalized the priesthood. At the same time, however, the penetration of the layman's world by this same strong sense of vocation had reinforced an old belief that if, while dutifully performing his earthly calling, a layman withdrew in spirit from terrestrial corruptions, he could pronounce upon religion quite as competently as a priest or a monk. Empowered by literacy, this conviction constituted the cutting edge of laicism.

The state is the natural repository of the lay spirit, but it was typical of the high middle ages that this entity was not as majestic as in antiquity or modern times. Other than the relatively decentralized economy of the time, a reason for this was the triumph of the church in the Gregorian age. Men felt themselves to be citizens not merely of a nation, but also of a *respublica christiana* equipped with its peace, the *pax dei,* and its war, the crusade or *bellum romanum*. Nevertheless, the secular state was still to be reckoned with. Large towns and even rural seigniories created tight little communities that soon revived the ancient notion of citizenship in a *patria*. Nor had the old nations ever entirely disappeared. Although sometimes transmuted into mere racial or regional pride, folk traditions often served to cement national or quasi-national institutions, especially on the frontiers of Latin Europe, as in Spain, England, and Hungary. Lastly, the growth and consequent recentralization of the economy naturally fostered political centralization.

This helps explain a basic reversal in the evolution of the Western state. In the past, political power had devolved upon ever lesser figures, from emperors, as it were, to simple seigniors, a process accompanied by geographical decentralization or political separatism. In some measure, the passage downward of political power continued until into the fourteenth century, as is shown by the movement toward democracy in the Italian urban republics and the growth of aristocratic limitations upon the freedom of Europe's monarchs. On the other hand, political recentralization was everywhere apparent as early as the twelfth century, expressing itself in such varied ways as Milan's conquest of much of Lombardy and the attempt of England's aristocracy to run the central government for its own benefit, rather than to dismember it.

In this circumstance, although deprived of independent moral sanction by the church, the idea of the state began to grow again. To the men of the time, the republic became a fictional but eternal body whose changing needs often required new taxes and laws. Obviously, political decentralization gave more weight to local law or custom than it has today. In divided Italy, for example, town statutes took precedence over the *ius commune* of the Roman law taught in the schools. Yet, this medieval adaptation of ancient law spread, not because it was linked to any state, but because its exponents derived from it legal norms that served to link together independent political entities by providing common models. As the study of law grew, so also did the study of politics. Past tradition, although rich in ideas of elective monarchy, conciliar participation in government, concepts of political contract, and hatred of tyranny, had mainly dealt with one form of organization, monarchy, and had centered on the relationship of princes to the church. The increased complexity of both civil and ecclesiastical society now produced true political philosophy, a somewhat autonomous science derived from Islam and the ancients. By 1300, thinkers were avidly debating the merits of government by a prince as against that of the aristocratic few or the popular many, investigating the implanting in particular regions of these various forms in divine and profane history, and even trying to tie their use to national character or to geographical or astral factors.

The idea of the state was most developed in Italy, partly because, in and after the Gregorian age, the erosion of the empire's power combined with rapid urban growth to create really independent republics. To the jurists of Italy, the witching hour was the Peace of Constance in 1183 when Lombard cities ceased recognizing any "superiors on earth." At about the same time, these cities also began to elect their *potestates* or heads of state. Of course, Italy was not unique. The republican form, men thought, was suited to the city, whereas a village was too small for independence, and a kingdom was too large for the easy accommodation of regional differences. Towns everywhere won some autonomy, especially those lying along the frontiers of princely states, as in the Low Countries, Rhenish and south Germany, and the French Midi. Actually, urban independence endured for long only in Italy and a few adjacent regions, a fact that created a distinction between northern and southern urbanism. In the north, town freedom was usually limited by princely authority. Hence, as they grew, northern towns often split, part of the area or administration falling to the commune and part being retained by the lord. Such splitting was further echoed in the relationship of town to countryside. Although northern towns always expanded their jurisdictions beyond their gates, only southern cities subdued whole provinces. When that happened, indigenous aristocracies either fell into clientage or found profit in leaving princely service to lead an urban republic. Thus southern gentlefolk became increasingly urban while the reverse obtained in the north. There, where princes still could divide in order to rule, the never easy relation between burgher and rural gentleman was consciously and intentionally exacerbated.

The republican form suited the town, but what groups controlled the republic was the touchy question. In the tenth and eleventh centuries, when towns began their rise, they usually contained elements ranging from the martial aristocracy to simple artisans and peasants. Thereafter, the need for community solidarity when fighting a prince or lord normally stimulated ideas of common citizenship and equality before the law. Besides, liberty often meant revolt, an effervescence that accelerated the ascent of lower social groups. In general, however, the twelfth and early thirteenth centuries saw most towns led to victory by relatively aristocratic elements. Where princely power was weak and urban growth rapid, the old martial and administrative cadres mixed with rising business elites to provide leadership in the republic and fostered and profited from its economic enterprises. Where princely power was strong or urban growth slow, however, the martial cadre tended to split, part becoming the new and somewhat rural nobility of the prince and part assimilating to the burghers, or, as they were often termed, the merchants. Nevertheless, even where this latter pattern held sway, a patrician group inevitably appeared in the course of time, one imitating the manners and lineages of the gentlefolk. Here again the distinction between urban society in northern and southern Europe can be stated only in relative terms. Evidence of family pride, towers often graced patrician town houses, but they were less numerous and humbler in the north than in the "skyscraper" cities of Italy.

Aristocratic dominance was rarely complete. Although rebellion often forced their unwilling hands, ruling groups were usually open to new wealth. First in Italy but also soon beyond the Alps, increased social maturity required training in government, law, and the arts. Patricians resisted this trend, partly because paid service let lesser folk hold office and partly because it meant higher taxes, thus exciting rate payers against oligarchies. Being used to paid service in seignorial or princely retinues, however, gentlemen speedily entered the other professions, legal and literate. In Italy at least, salaried political command (the office of the *potestas*) automatically went to those with experience of war. Well before 1300, therefore, the old nonliterate tradition of the martial aristocracy had been weakened by the conviction that, to be a gentleman, one had to be competent in both arms and letters. Still, there was social tension here. Lawyers, we have seen, claimed to be more useful to the republic than soldiers, thus gilding their doctor's tassels with more carats than they allowed the knight's spurs or belts. Lineage accents blood right, but expertise makes career the path to nobility.

Far more important a threat to aristocratic government, however, was the rise of "the many" to participation in politics in the thirteenth century, an ascent made possible by the guilds, organizations modeled either on earlier spontaneous associations, such as early town communes and merchant guilds, or on old state-regulated colleges providing community services. The first great surge of guild corporatism waited until shortly before 1200, when increased economic specialization forced small businessmen and artisans to combine against those who controlled their raw materials and sales. Because law regulated economy, in later years the guilds pushed slowly into government. Naturally, their success varied. Where princes were strong, guilds were encouraged in order to check patrician exponents of town independence. In such cases, while corporatism made progress, freedom declined. Where towns were free, however, the growth of guilds was initially slower, but long before 1300 it was clear that they would win out, and that the simple people would have a greater share of community wealth and political power than in the past. At the same time, larger entrepreneurs reacted by building or reinforcing their associations, merchant, banking, or industrial. In Italy, the professions of law and medicine organized to raise standards and hoist fees. As a result, guild equalitarianism never really triumphed; indeed, it helped to rend the social fabric of the community. Law and literature came to distinguish the bourgeois from those who worked with their hands. Where gentlefolk lived in town, as in Italy, vehement, if unsuccessful, attempts were made to expel them from business and government. Unhappy prophecy of future social war though this was, the relative success of the democratic urge of corporatism indicates that it completed the process of the passing down or devolution of political power started so many centuries before.

Small towns and villages evolved in a manner similar to great cities. They often leagued together to attain or defend their freedom. Much as in town, immigrant villagers were protected from seizure by their old lords. Countryfolk issued constitutions and law codes, sometimes using standard models, such as those of Lorris in France or Flemish law in north Germany, and sometimes adapting the customs of a nearby city. A measure of judicial or executive power often fell to villagers, who entrusted it to elected officers, consuls in the south and *jurati* or mayors in the north. The complex differentiations of city society spread to the country. By 1300, the difference between rural bourgeois and peasant was apparent in the French Midi. In general, then, the distinction between the great and the small medieval nucleus was one of degree. The village attained less independence and less self-government than did the town. Contemporary political thinkers explained this by asserting that a village was too small for freedom because it could not provide itself with sufficient specialized services for a good or rounded life. It needed specialists to represent it in foreign courts, to direct defense and bring outside aid, military, and economic. By its clientage, therefore, the village paid lordly houses, ecclesiastical institutions, or nearby cities for this special personnel. In consequence, although many elements of self-government were embedded in it, the basic form of village government was the petty monarchy of the seigniory.

The church was Europe's greatest government. Although the papacy directly ruled only the small principality around Rome and, from time to time, had a vague suzerainty recognized by secular powers like England, Sicily, or the Holy Land, its ecumenical authority and Europe's power structure described above enabled the church to wield more political power than any other Western government. Like Europe's other large "states," its constitution was monarchical. Free of imperial might from the latter eleventh century, the church's prince was chosen by the cardinals, Rome's local clergy, themselves appointed by the reigning pope. Although the pope legislated only in council, his grants or privileges and his rights to install or appoint bishops and other clergy and to tax churches and monasteries were ample indeed by the 1250's. Equally significant were his and his court's judicial decisions that created legal and constitutional precedents to regulate the "moral" jurisdiction of the clergy over the laity and to settle disputes within the church.

Not that the church was wholly monarchical. The regular clergy even moved toward democracy. Improving on Cluny, Cistercian houses elected their abbots, who, in turn, assembled in all-powerful annual conclaves, a system extended by papal order to the Benedictines in 1215. Most democratic were the Dominican friars, all of whose officers, save the general, were elected for brief terms. Equally consequential was the ancient conciliar idea. An aspect of this was the cardinals' assertion of their right to be consulted by the pope in grave matters. Starting in 1122 and culminating in 1215, general papal councils served as the church's principal legislative body, and their success, together with the Hohenstaufen crisis, inspired a stronger conciliar movement from 1245 to 1312. General councils then met about once every twenty years, and by the end of that time, raucous voices were heard advancing conciliar to the detriment of papal authority and demanding regular meetings. When papal encouragement of provincial councils and the jurists' emphasis upon a college's rights as against its head are added, it is evident that although monarchy ruled the church, by 1300 it was limited, even threatened, by a lively conciliar impulse.

Between the ecumenical church and the rural seigniories and towns were Europe's secular monarchies and principalities. The older medieval type of state still flourished into the eleventh century. Canute's Anglo-Scandinavian thalassocracy, Castile's revived Hispanic empire, and the German empire with its dependent church and ministerial service cadre illustrate the continuity of these older, quasi-Carolingian forms. During and after the Gregorian age, however, these states declined, as the local clergy and aristocracies were gradually freed from princely control. To this basic cause may be added the rise of Italy and France. Italian towns helped break imperial power south of the Alps, and emigrants from France aided clerical "reform" in weakening the unity of Spain's Castilian Empire. From the mid-eleventh century, a hundred years of successive waves of French settlement submerged the Anglo-Saxons, and the restive independence of the French seigniors threatened England's ancient unity. In short, although many elements of the older state were everywhere retained, especially in frontier areas like Spain, England, Scandinavia, and Hungary, old governments everywhere suffered partial disintegration in the Gregorian age and after.

Curiously, the same period also witnessed the slow reversal of political decentralization and the laying of new foundations on which to build future regional or national states. Although prompted by many things, such as Hispanic and English resistance to France's military or cultural pressure, the renewed centralization everywhere paralleled the contemporary expansion of the economy and the concomitant growth of towns and commerce. In some regions, of course, circumstances prevented the building of centralized states. The Hohenstaufen attempt to revitalize the empire during the thirteenth century by shifting the base of their power to southern Italy failed before the opposition of the popes, the Lombard cities, and the French invasion of Italy. After the death of the greatest of the Hohenstaufens, Frederick II, in 1250, the historian of the state should turn his attention from the institutions of the empire itself to those of its successors, the Italian republics and German regional principalities. Other regions were more advantaged. In England, from the mid-twelfth century, the institutions of an original national unity were updated by the French dynasty of the Angevins using Continental models, especially Italian Roman law, to mold the most unified of Europe's prenational states. Even in France, the very model of "feudal" decentralization, steps toward unification were taken in the thirteenth century when her once puny monarchy absorbed all the greater feudatories save Guienne and Brittany.

Because governments needed to mobilize their citizens, centralization was accompanied by a rise of regional or national parliaments and courts. Frequent rebellions show, however, than an equally impelling motive was the desire of communities and seigniors to control princely authority. Rebels often found external allies. German emperors undercut their restive princelings by demanding that the notables in each particular local area be consulted about important matters. The popes also usually asserted that such consultation was a prince's duty lest he be condemned as a tyrant. As a result, the aristocracies of small districts and those with strong unitarian traditions no longer attempted to decentralize state power but instead to control or restrain the central government itself. Exemplified in England, Aquileia, Aragon's Sicily, parts of Spain and Hungary, this pattern was not to be found everywhere. In France, a much larger country, regionalism resulted in much provincial autonomy and in somewhat decentralized royal courts and assemblies. Still, by around 1300, these centralist agencies were appearing nearly everywhere. What was new about them was not theory. Princes of the past had usually issued law and levied war and taxes with the consent of notables, but these new assemblies were larger, their meetings more regular, and their representation of regions and social orders more formal. Unlike those of contemporary city republics, however, these assemblages rarely seized legislative initiative from their princes, and scarcely distinguished between their judicial and legislative functions.

As these new foci of men's loyalty emerged around 1300, the appeal of Rome began to wane. This could not have been foreseen by contemporaries. Rome had led the West to great success, her alliance with Italy and France had placed her on the side of the most powerful forces in Latin culture, and Europe's border powers had needed papal aid. Rome had financed and directed the Crusades and supported the crusader-states spread from Jerusalem to Byzantium in the Near East. From England to Sicily and from Hungary to Portugal, frontier states had called upon the popes either to diminish pressures from within Europe or to support their own outward expansions. The Iberian Muslims were defeated by holy wars, but Portugal and Aragon emerged from under Castilian hegemony as papal fiefs. Rome gave Ireland to England in the twelfth century, but aided England against the French Capetians in the early thirteenth. Throughout the thirteenth century, from Innocent III to Boniface VIII, the pope was Europe's arbiter, his city her real capital. In 1268 the execution of Conradin, the last scion of the Hohenstaufen line, seemed to confirm the victory of the *sacerdotium* over the *imperium,* of the Roman church over secular power.

This victory, however, was bought too dearly. In the latter stages of the conflict between empire and papacy, the popes isolated the emperors from other secular princes by stating that each king was emperor in his own realm. Finally, in the decisive moments of the mid-thirteenth century when her alliance with Lombardy's cities and dissident German princelings was not enough to defeat the Sicilian Hohenstaufen, Rome called upon France for help. Although they were successful against the Hohenstaufen, the dangers of this alignment became clear the moment the French had established themselves in Provence and Italy. It not merely reinforced the French belief that France was another Holy Land, the peculiar agent of providence, but the French party in the Roman curia also grew in might. Rome's inability to disentangle itself from French power was a major reason for the defeat of Boniface VIII at the hands of Philip IV of France, a defeat aptly symbolized by the momentary seizure of that pontiff by French allies at Anagni in 1303. Similarly, the conflict between the Germans under the emperor Louis of Bavaria and Pope John XXII (1316–1334) resulted from the removal of the papal seat to Avignon in 1309 and its subservience to French interests.

In the earlier battle, Boniface had summoned a council to excoriate royal tyranny, and Philip had proposed a similar assembly to judge the pope's heresy. This was no mere repetition of Gregorian patterns. What gave it force was the new lay spirit embodied in the nation or state. A miniature Jerusalem to its citizens, an Italian republic taxed its clergy and demanded their loyalty. French kings thought to revive the Crusade by "reforming" the church and unifying Europe under their aegis. Whole social orders shared these princely convictions. Mimicking Hohenstaufen propaganda, French gentlefolk called themselves sons of Charlemagne, whose sword had "won the world" for Christ, and pledged themselves to restore the church to pristine purity by stripping her of wealth and worldly cares. Nor was the church able to repulse these aggressions, at once both lay and utopian. She was herself a house divided. Her own utopian dream of freedom from worldly concerns exploded ruinously in the civil war between the rigorist and laxist parties within the Franciscan order. To defeat the Hohenstaufen, also, Rome had called upon the local churches whose prelates met in councils from 1245 on. Not unpredictably, the hostility of the bishops to Rome's privileged Mendicants led to the repression of new religious orders and devotions by 1311, thereby stilling hopes of Christian progress. The Franciscans of all shades then seceded temporarily from Rome to side with Louis of Bavaria. At the same time, the local churches resisted papal centralism and generated a conciliar idea that threatened

Rome's monarchy. Still immature, however, lay power did not yet win the victory. That was still two centuries or more in the future. It is nonetheless apparent that the new states, national or regional, were beginning to replace the ecumenical church and the particularistic rural seigniory and town as the focus of Western man's loyalty.

Further reading suggestions follow chapter 34.

34   The Late Middle Ages

These great struggles between church and state occurred during the apogee of the Middle Ages, a time when it still seemed possible that all dreams, however contradictory, might come true, but also a time in which the constituents of the crisis that erupted around 1350 were already discernible. One element was the increased resistance to Latin expansion. Islam's early counterattack has already been mentioned, as has its disruption by the Mongol assault. A second wave began in the late thirteenth century. The Muslims repulsed Latin raids on North Africa and continued to hold Granada until 1492, by which time Ottoman power had slowly spread from Anatolia to the Danube. Even shattered Byzantium long preserved a tenuous independence between the Latin and Islamic blocs. Obviously, the men of 1300 could not predict these events and continued to whistle in the dark. Some placed their hope of resuming the Crusades by building utopian plans for Latin unity. Others condemned war and vaunted missions instead. By the mid-fourteenth century, however, even the once lively missionary movement was everywhere failing. By 1300, moreover, Latin aggression had turned upon itself. On a scale unequaled since Gregorian days, the holy war or crusade had come to be employed in European internal conflicts, especially in the wars against the Hohenstaufen. Europe's central regions, France and Italy, quailed before the rise of peripheral powers. The English invasion and defeat of France in the fourteenth century and the halting of England's conquest of Ireland and Scotland illustrate this volte-face. Only in Germany did the older pattern of outward expansion still obtain for a time, although there too the later 1300's saw the first serious counterattacks by Nordic and Slavic peoples.

Of equal consequence was the sharpening of social tensions within Europe. The rise of the *respublica christiana* in the Gregorian or Crusade age, for example, had decisively weakened the Roman idea of secular

Princes and Dynasties

A.D.   1273/1314/1438 ff.   Hapsburg emperors
                   1328   French Capetians replaced by Valois
                   1485   English Angevins replaced by Tudors

Soldiers, Magistrates, Artists, and Business-men

c. 1267–1337   Giotto, son of Bondone, of Florence
  1313–1354   Cola, son of Rienzi
       1394   Death of John Hawkwood
c. 1395–1456   Jacques Coeur
c. 1394–1476   John Fortescue

Intellectuals

  1221–1274   Bonaventure
       1282   Death of Siger of Brabant
c. 1214–1292   Roger Bacon
  1274–1308   John Duns Scotus
c. 1250–1312   Peter Dubois
c. 1240–1313   Arnold of Villanova
c. 1235–1315   Raymond Lull
  1265–1321   Dante Alighieri
       1328   Death of John of Jandun
c. 1275–1342   Marsiglio of Padua
c. 1300–1349   William of Ockham
  1304–1374   Francis Petrarch
c. 1329–1384   John Wycliffe
c. 1369–1415   John Hus
  1483–1546   Martin Luther

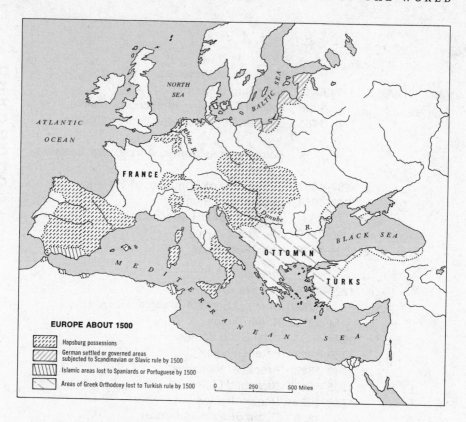

ATLANTIC
OCEAN

NORTH
SEA

BALTIC SEA

FRANCE

Rhine R.

Danube R.

BLACK SEA

OTTOMAN

TURKS

M E D I T E R R A N E A N   S E A

EUROPE ABOUT 1500

Hapsburg possessions

German settled or governed areas
subjected to Scandinavian or Slavic rule by 1500

Islamic areas lost to Spaniards or Portuguese by 1500

Areas of Greek Orthodoxy lost to Turkish rule by 1500

0   250   500 Miles

citizenship. By 1215, the church had introduced legislation severely restricting Jews and Muslims in Christendom. But law was only part of the
picture. Another part derived from the devolution of political and social
power. Anti-Jewish outbreaks often accompanied the attempts around 1100
of urban mercantile and ministerial groups to break the power of their
princes. Two hundred years later, the rising of the plebs against the ruling
aristocracies of Western towns and villages evoked more profound waves
of anti-Jewish and, in Spain, of anti-Muslim fervor. The growth of central
government also played a part. England's precocity in inventing anti-Jewish
propaganda paralleled the rapid growth of the Crown, its initial incapacity
to tax the aristocracy, and the consequent squeezing of its Jews. Increasingly hated and impoverished, England's Jews were expelled in 1295.
Everywhere in the later Middle Ages, the Jews were reduced to marginal
economic functions, pushed back toward Islam's frontiers, or forced to flee
toward Europe's eastern reaches, there to play for a time their past role as
merchants and favored capitalizers. That these attacks were as much social

as ideological is clearly shown by the failure of Latin missions. By 1300 in both Italy and Spain, the appearance of the category of the "new" or "quasi"-Christian suggests that Latin society could find little place even for the Jew or Muslim who had converted.

Similar social divisions developed among Christians. The growth of personal liberty during the high Middle Ages had paradoxical results. The freeing of ministerial elites from their princes left those remaining behind, as the once-favored Jews, in "cameral servitude." In the countryside, not all villagers attained the same measure of freedom. By 1300, these disparities invited classification, an effort that led to the defining of old duties as new servitudes. Being sometimes a method of pressuring farmers to surrender land in exchange for liberty, however, this did not always spread serfdom. Only when or where labor was in short supply, as during the plagues or in eastern Germany in the fifteenth century, were farmers again bound to the land. These pressures naturally led to rural social conflicts that, beginning in France as early as the 1280's, gradually became nearly endemic. The urban parallel was more political. Guilds or corporations had attained political power, and as we have seen, this democratization was accompanied by a growing social rigidity, separating nobles or patricians from the commoners, the bourgeois from the hand worker. In Italy, republican government soon reached stagnation as those still excluded from real power were reduced to a minority. Naturally, given the Italians' past experience of ever broader political participation, the excluded did not easily resign their hopes. The result was that revolts such as that of Florence's Ciompi in 1378 punctuated late medieval town life, and elections became mere preludes to revolutionary upheavals.

This social conflict was part of a general malady whose grander manifestations were a general decline of population in most regions, repetitive waves of sickness, and a faltering of economic growth. Nature has been blamed for these cataclysms. That the weather worsened is possible. Certainly, also, sickness was everywhere, although demographic decline seems to have started before the plague of 1347. But the crisis was probably precipitated by overpopulation that, after 1300, had weakened Western living standards by forcing farmers almost everywhere to cultivate marginal soils. Yet this does not explain why men were not able to use available resources more inventively. With few exceptions, the inventions men of this age were able to make were principally social, and hence could not increase the quantity of production so much as they could speed distribution and concentrate means for producing export commodities. These inventions required heavy investment and intense mobilization of labor and resources, and there is no doubt that, in view of these needs, Europe's institutional structure around 1300 left much to be desired. The investment in the church, charitable services, and education was heavy, perhaps excessive. In the towns, guild corporatism maximized profits and multiplied monopolistic restrictions. In the countryside, the subdivision of inheritances emphasized maintaining status rather than capitalizing production. Commerce was similarly inhibited by the persistence of provincial, seignorial, or urban autonomy and particularism.

During the harsh fourteenth and fifteenth centuries, Europe pulled itself together. Nature helped as plagues pruned man's excessive numbers. Man helped too, and his inventions show where he was going. Four-wheeled wagons and square-rigged ships both moved and supplied ever larger concentrations of mankind. The cost of cannon and of the fortifications to withstand them outran the finances and defenses of the independent town and seigniory. Printing gave teaching or command a uniformity essential for summoning unheard-of numbers for peace or war.

More consequential than these largely fifteenth-century inventions were the earlier institutional innovations that made their reception possible. All weakened past particularisms—urban, seignorial, or provincial. Everywhere, even in divided Italy and Germany, the unit of political concentration became larger. Along with grander size came a more intense economic mobilization. Already dimly outlined in Italy before 1300, the whole panoply of state-regulated banking and monetary policy, bullion-measured trade balances, and state-chartered companies slowly spread to the rest of Europe. Paralleling the multiplication of social orders, the economy was increasingly brigaded into guilds, naturally hostile to change, but forced by state-owned enterprise and by the prince to admit innovation. Because corporate interests often conflicted and because the guilds never organized the whole of industry or trade, other groups had roles to play in the interstices of the economy. Among these were Jews and Lombards resident in foreign lands who were privileged to lend money at usury. More prestigious were the princes' favorite financial wizards such as Jacques Coeur (c. 1395–1456), part entrepreneur, part state officer, part black marketeer. Highest of all was the prince himself, who, when these others had evoked enough popular hatred, emptied their gold-laden purses into his treasury.

The prince was the chief symbol or agent of human mobilization. Medieval political theory had rightly argued that because it transcended particular parties, the institution of monarchy was suited for large areas with diverse and conflicting regional interests; within society, also, the prince was called to play a similar part. Himself a member of no one social order, he policed to his own profit the endemic conflicts of late-medieval social groups. In towns, for example, the poor fought against the medieval equivalent of sales taxes while the rich battled graduated real property or income taxes. When a prince was invited to intervene to pacify strife, he usually collected both taxes. Because war is often an external projection of inner social conflict or, as in France during the Hundred Years' War, a desperate invitation to foreigners to settle insoluble civil wars, the prince found his natural empire in warfare and foreign affairs. His regime also policed the intense pugnacity of the age by repressing the militias, both aristocratic and plebeian, with their self-defeating local and class conflicts. He domesticated the armed hosts of men deracinated by civil war and economic woe. Permanent military units, regularity of payment, and career predictability had their start in Italy's condottieri and France's royal companies of the early fifteenth century. In the meantime, each social group or region produced a new military arm to express its combativeness. The gentry and yeomanry created cavalry; the towns, artillery; while from hill and mountain came a real infantry, an arm capable of attacking in the open field. As in economic life, this brigading produced its heroes, the great captains, deputies of their princes and forerunners of the generals who replaced the plainsong of medieval war with the differing rhythms of different arms in the polyphony of the modern battlefield.

How to endow a prince with the requisite powers was the political conundrum of late-medieval man. In much of Europe, as in France or England, where religious and social protections and powers had long been attached to kings and their houses, the matter seemed simple. There traditions merely had to be amplified to produce the divine-right monarch of modern times. Elsewhere, however, majesty had to be created. In Germany, power had fallen to local princes in the fourteenth century, but sovereignty itself for long remained associated with the emperor alone. Furthermore, Turkish and French pressures forced the building of eastern and western marches, a veritable carapace for Germany, that led to a Hapsburg imperial revival. By the eve of the Reformation, German local princes were obliged to seek a new solvent of empire and thus assert their sovereign powers.

Progress was also slow in Italy. Although foreign influence was important there, the basic step was to conjure forth the prince and his authority from republican institutions. To expand the limited jurisdictions and tenures of short-term offices into grants of unrestricted free will (*liberum arbitrium*) in perpetuity took time. In fact, few principates grew out of those offices, such as that of the *potestas,* that had arisen when towns were winning freedom from the empire. Such offices had been fettered by aristocratic fear of tyranny or monarchy. Most principates instead derived from the police and tribunician power of later democratic offices, such as the people's captaincy. Appropriately enough, just as she had earlier led the way to republicanism, Milan showed others the way to the principate. In spite of success, however, the victory of the princes was never complete. From Holland to Italy, republics survived in the interstices between the expanding regional states and nations. True, most were no longer popular governments, but aristocratic. The great republic of Venice had come to symbolize patrician stability in the eyes of Europe's aristocracy by the early fifteenth century.

Nor did the princes triumph totally within their states. To perform their centralizing functions, they needed general assemblies and new courts, institutions that also voiced the reluctance of local interests and aristocracies to bow to princely authority. Royal judicial and administrative offices often fell to gentlefolk or wealthy bourgeois. Rural aristocracies and urban oligarchies everywhere sought to retain the independence of their urban or seignorial jurisdictions, and to maintain their own armed retinues or troops. Admittedly, aggressive localism sometimes served to advance later centralization. In France, the Burgundian and other appanages as well as the stubborn independence of such areas as Foix and Brittany mobilized local society in new ways, creating professional armies, central courts, and even new assemblies or parliaments, thus constituting cohesive blocks for the eventual building of the French nation. But in the later Middle Ages the role of these provinces or groups of provinces and their heads—the dukes of Burgundy, Brittany, and others—was initially divisive and had much to do with the interminable civil strife that rent France during the Hundred Years' War (1338–1453). It is also likely that the shattering of the precocious or somewhat premature unity that had been built in France during the thirteenth century had its origins in the aristocratic and provincial reaction against the centralizing monarchy around 1328, when the Capetians were replaced by the Valois.

The type of resistance and its success varied, and the contrast between England and France, the two powers nearest modern nationhood, shows the dimension of this difference. Inhabiting a smaller area, traditionally more centralized and less beset by foreign invasions, England's aristocracy did better than its French counterpart. Although by the accession of the Tudors in 1485 a powerful monarchy had been established, England had deposed and slain two kings in the late Middle Ages, and came into modern times with a parliament able to limit the crown's fiscal prerogatives, and a judicature ostensibly enforcing the Crown's common law, but really speaking the piece of the aristocracy from which it was recruited. This was partially true in France, but there restraints upon the royal prerogative were local, expressed in the rights of provincial assemblies and courts. Again, in spite of the prince's effort to push a *ius commune* based on Roman antecedents, the basic law was still the regional or provincial customs. On the other hand, frequent invasions imposed on France a need for a standing army and thus enabled her kings to reduce the national estates or assemblies to powerlessness. Although the French legal profession was learned and mighty, the judges of the royal courts or *parlements* rarely dared to refuse a royal ordinance, the normative legislation of the land. Curiously, in spite of their impotence, the French estates' conception of conciliar and electoral government and the French judges' theory of natural rights were more developed than they were on the other side of the Channel. Not as busy as were the English with the exercise of real power, French gentlemen and jurists apparently had more time to ruminate about what they lacked.

Whatever form it took, resistance was everywhere aristocratic, and it is therefore necessary to turn back to trace the history of those of gentle birth. Except for the clergy, those holding governmental and military office or possessing substantial wealth were the first elements to become free, that is, to possess property by hereditary right, to marry freely, and to limit service owed. Even before 1300, however, liberty was not enough. A burgher patriciate ruled the great towns, equaling rural gentlemen in wealth and leisure. More disheartening was the fact that a real measure of freedom had been gained by all townsmen and also by substantial numbers of country-folk. In this circumstance, what was needed was not liberty, but instead privilege. With the emergence of this conception, the basic social tone of the nobility and bourgeois notables of early modern Europe was already being limned. Nobility meant privileged exemption from taxes and other ignoble service. The bourgeois was one whose nails were not blue with labor's stains. Rural gentlefolk and town patricians, all—to use the phrase of the time—"lived nobly."

To live nobly was not always to live happily. The frictions and agonies of the late Middle Ages afflicted the rich as much as the poor. Gentle lineages were everywhere destroyed. Town patriciates were attacked by the plebs. Outrun by the princely state, aristocratic martial power was severely weakened. By 1500, only the Venetian urban oligarchy could maintain an artillery equal to that of a major prince. Given the state's capacity to mobilize large numbers of soldiers, gentlefolk were no longer numerous enough to constitute a force that could really dominate the field of battle.

A second threat came from the prince. Princes had always elevated their servants into knighthood, thus building new service cadres. Beginning late in the twelfth century, the new centralizing states slowly monopolized the right to grant knighthood and were consequently tempted to view nobility simply as a revocable reward for "virtue," that is, for service. But princes did not have it all their own way. Their need to make their rewards attractive combined with aristocratic ideas defending the hereditary transmission of wealth, of position, and of government office to impede the rational conception of service. As early as the late twelfth century, even modest gentlemen insisted that, dubbed or not, the sons and grandsons of knights were as noble as their progenitors. The function of knighthood was therefore giving way to nobility's function-free privilege. In the later Middle Ages, men of high bourgeois and gentle birth successfully held more than their share of education in the liberal arts and of the cadetships that led to high civil and military office. If gentlemen no longer ruled the battlefield as knights, they made sure that they commanded most of the troops deployed upon it. This faculty of the aristocracy, bourgeois and gentlefolk alike, explains why the republican or conciliar tradition of medieval town government had come by 1500 to have little appeal for the humble people, whose livelier sons bought their way up in society by means of service to a prince. At the same time, it also tells us why the privileged orders of the early modern Western state became the repository of that tradition. It is not surprising, then, that in modern times, the stronger the aristocracy, the sooner the fall of the monarchy.

As centralizing states and nations arose, the ecumenical church began to sink. As late as about 1350, this prospect could scarcely have been imagined. When Louis of Bavaria died in 1347, the threatened secession of the Franciscans collapsed, and the conciliar idea that had flourished around 1300 seemed dormant. At no time was papal taxation and the right to appoint to benefices so developed as under the popes at Avignon, and churches such as that of divided Germany were subject to much papal interference. The papal victory, however, was more apparent than real. In spite of nagging, the Crusades—save in Prussia—had petered out. The Templars were abolished in 1312, the first monastic order to succumb to lay attack. Resurgent Islam repulsed the missionaries. Aided by the Inquisitor's ubiquitous eye, the bishops assembled in Vienne in 1312 had stifled the creation of new popular devotions and dampened the hope of spiritual progress within the Latin communion. Unable to expand, the regular clergy, as the cathedral chapters before them, were captured by the scions of burgher and noble elites. Hospitals and other charitable agencies suffered the same fate. If, except during the plagues and wars, the secular clergy were better trained and better behaved than before, they and their bishops more and more came under state control. In France, Italy, England, and Aragon, republics and princes limited papal rights of appointment, claiming to discover special virtues in their native sons. However quietly, the secular states were winning the battle, and the purses of their citizens showed where their hearts had gone. State budgets increased far more rapidly than Rome's in the fourteenth and fifteenth centuries.

In 1378, matters came to a head in the Great Schism. The conflict between the Avignonese and Roman papal lines reflected the divided regional and national interests of Latin society. The split obliged the rival popes to have recourse to every expedient to raise money and support for their causes and, therefore, to surrender control of local clergy to local powers. What had been rare before became normal; what had been permissible in success became oppressive in defeat. Unable to refuse the peremptory commands of the growing state, ecclesiastical critics escaped into angry denunciations of the rival pontiffs. They likened papal taxes upon those assuming ecclesiastical office to simony. Justifiable when devoted to happy peace at home and successful crusade abroad, indulgences and penitential campaigns appeared to be as immoral as they were unsuccessful when sunk in the popes' efforts to reconquer or hold their place in Italy. Everywhere, local churchmen objected to papal or curial regulation, and the lesser clergy frequently tried to impose upon their prelates standards of behavior which they themselves rarely attained. Voices were heard—John Wycliffe (c. 1329–1384) in England, John Hus in Bohemia (c.1369–1415)—urging laymen to "reform" the church if the clergy would not, and threatening secession from its communion were this not undertaken. Finally, a mounting desire to obliterate this extremist dissent, to reestablish church unity, and, at the same time, to "reform" the church "in head and members" led to a revival of conciliar ideas. At Pisa in 1409, again at Constance in 1414, and lastly at Basel in 1431, the clergy assembled in great councils to preserve their church.

Although the church was unified at the councils, the conciliar movement itself largely failed. Rigoristic reformism pushed to the point of heresy helped to defeat it. Hus was burned at Constance in 1415, but the conciliar fathers could not suppress his movement, a national secession of the Bohemians that was never to be wholly eradicated. Conciliar "democracy" also threatened prelatry. Although bishops happily "reformed" Rome or diminished curial prerogatives, they did not enjoy being "reformed" by their own subordinates, who took over the direction of the councils toward the end. And if princes gained much from the conflict between pope and council, they were soon reminded both by alert popes and by experience with their own estates or parliaments that secular and ecclesiastical monarchy had much in common. By the end of the last council at Basel, princes and popes had combined to defeat conciliarism. Arrayed in ecumenical orders, the still vigorous Mendicants as well as the decrepit monks found little voice at the councils, bodies dominated by the local secular clergy. They therefore seceded and gave the fathers little help. Besides, tradition threw its weight to Rome. Negotiating for church unity, the representatives of the Greek Orthodox communion disappointed the conciliar fathers by turning from them to the papacy. Lastly, after their initial enthusiastic support of the conciliar idea, the local clergy began to have second thoughts about overthrowing the popes and entrusting themselves wholly to the citizens and princes of their fatherland. That a contract between a nation and its church such as the French Pragmatic of Bourges of 1438 wherein were enshrined Gallican liberties and ecclesiastical freedom should in fact so profit the prince and so little advance "reform" or freedom was enough teaching on this point. The clergy were gradually becoming aware that they were replacing an ecclesiastical with a secular master, one whose capital was much nearer to their parishes than Rome. What had begun with high hopes at Pisa and Constance petered out in despair during the interminable council at Basel that closed in 1449.

Although Rome seemed to have won the day, nothing could have been further from the truth. After the councils had failed, a combat with the cardinals of the Sacred College, the senate of the church, rent Rome until the Protestant revolution. Even the conciliar idea was not wholly moribund; it was revived by the kings of France to force concessions from the papacy. Furthermore, the nations were clearly winning. The national organization of the clergy had been recognized at both Pisa and Constance, and had been partly confirmed by papal concordats with the traditional national churches in 1417. After the councils, the Italian nation also won its case. It was not long before the pontifical office and the Roman curia became Italian monopolies. This did not much hurt France, Spain, or the Hapsburgs in southern Germany. These close neighbors, always prompt to intervene in Italian affairs, could exact substantial advantages from reluctant Rome. For governments farther away, however, such as England or the German princely states, things were not so easy. To the old but now increasingly feverish complaints about money flowing to Rome were added fears that Rome's concessions to the Hapsburgs or to France prejudiced northern interests. In this circumstance, a new "reformism," one that could no longer take the conciliar way, was about to be born.

These changes in institutions were accompanied by a gradual transformation of the ways intellectuals dealt with the world. The implicit naturalism of the age when Aristotle was received in the Western schools had always elicited opposition, even when expressed by such a prestigious figure as Thomas Aquinas. The assertion that man's natural reason enabled him to comprehend a substantial part of God's mystery and to attune himself to nature, God's creation, is strong stuff in any age. Nor was this opposition merely an echo of Bernard of Clairvaux's earlier doubt that human reason could explain the mysteries of revealed religion or the real quandaries of man's life. This doubt provided one set of questions, of course, but there were others derived from the "realism" of an age that had sought to link God, nature, and man, and that had therefore somewhat "divinized" man and his institutions. Otherwise conflicting schools of thought, the extremist naturalists called the Parisian Averroists and Bonaventure's (1221–1274) antinaturalist Augustinians, agreed on one thing, namely that the teachings of natural philosophy simply could not be accorded with the experience of the faith or the needs of man's hope. Indeed, according to John Duns Scotus (c. 1264–1308) and his followers, the desire to link God with the world risked binding the divine spirit, the very principle of freedom, to the necessary sequences of mundane experience. To these grave criticisms of the thirteenth century, circumstances added several new ones during the later Middle Ages. One of these was the fact that the Aristotelian-Thomistic position was closely linked to the institutions that flowered in the thirteenth century, which were precisely those institutions that were being cast down later on. Another and more consequential debility was that a naturalist philosophy is unsatisfactory in an age when men seem best to express themselves in civil war and when nature itself seems determined to be as unlovable as possible.

Around 1300, men first tried to save the naturalist and "realist" philosophies of the past, sometimes by attacking the competence of earlier spokesmen and sometimes by extending the system into a kind of totalitarianism. Roger Bacon (c. 1214–1292) and Raymond Lull (c. 1235–1315) endeavored to unify all knowledge by means of the certitudes of mathematics. These intellectual schemes, moreover, were often wedded to a dream in which Christian progress would create a perfect society, headed by pope or prince, designed both to conquer nature for man and to unify the world for Christ. Some were also apocalyptic. Bacon, for example, thought to mobilize Christendom to defeat the coming Antichrist, cruel precursor of a happy age to come. Others dreamed of reanimating the crusade or of converting Muslims, Jews, pagans, indeed, the world. The failure of these hopes, however, led to a recession of this kind of utopian and progressive thought after 1350.

On the other hand, now stripped of quasi-scientific Aristotelianism, the "realist's" sense that the only true reality in the world and its institutions was the divine essence flourished as never before. This was sometimes expressed in mystic experience. To the mystics, orthodox or not, who pullulated in the later Middle Ages, the individual's relationship to, or unity with, the divine became far more important than his institutional affiliation. Those less mystic, as Wycliffe or even Hus, were convinced that the only reality serving to justify human institutions was immediate conformity to the divine design. While often encouraging quietism or personal withdrawal, such views also led either to an anarchic individualism that left the church no serious role to play in salvation's plan or, as in Wycliffe's teaching, to outright rejection of the practical institutional structures of this world, ecclesiastical and secular.

Another way of handling the problem of naturalism and "realism" and, incidentally, of avoiding their hazards, was to admit that man's reason and experience of nature provided only insufficient analogies to enable him to understand the truths of faith and revelation. Although this idea was far from new, the greater richness of the Latin philosophical tradition enabled men to propound the autonomy of the various sciences, theological and natural, even before 1300. In theology or the faith could be discovered a reality of psychic certainty or conviction that could not be found in the probabilistic world of nature and philosophical reason. As developed by Duns Scotus and William of Ockham (c. 1300–c. 1349) and their followers, this "terminism" or philosophical discretion freed the deity from being bound by definitions applicable only to his creations in nature—something distinctly to his advantage in an age of plagues, famines, and civil wars. The distinction between what is heavenly and what earthly enabled thinkers of this persuasion to view the actual institutions of this world less censoriously than enthusiasts of the "realist" commitment. It was his dislike of their distinctions that made Wycliffe anathema to Parisian theologians, and that in turn made them exaggerate Hus's views and have him burned at the Council of Constance. In brief, the men of the Ockhamist *via moderna* were often profoundly conservative. Their separation of heaven from earth often enabled them to live without too great a straining of conscience among fallible men and confessedly imperfect institutions.

To cut heaven from earth, however, does not always bring peace. The danger of separating philosophy from theology, as did the Parisian Averroist John of Jandun (d. 1328), was that, to preserve theology from earth's contamination, philosophy had to be given a nearly complete autonomy to fulfill man's earthly life in terms of natural moral ends. John's companion, Marsiglio of Padua (c. 1275–1342), applied this standard to government and the church, contrasting the freedom of divine precept with the coerciveness of human law and legislation. As a result, although retaining an educational function, the earthly church became a creation of man's history, subordinate to his will, and deprived of an innate capacity to force obedience. Although intending only to "reform" it, these men of the 1300's had begun to strip the sacred garniture from the church militant, a decisive step in the direction of modern secularism.

Naturally, the schoolmen of the *via moderna* did not go so far. Ockham and his followers rarely doubted that God had clearly and directly defined the earthly church. Inadvertently, however, their inquiry as to how He had done this practically reduced the sources of indisputable authority to the sparse and vague recommendations of the New Testament. What had been built since then, the real church of history with its theoretical superiority over lay power, could be judged only in terms of relative probabilities deduced from history or from the varying weights of conflicting authorities. Although not revolutionary, then, the *via moderna* was terribly ambivalent, and transformed psychic conviction into mere intellectual probability. As Luther (1483–1546) was to show, revolution could come from this source. Its emphasis upon the New Testament as the sole source of authority reinforced a desire to bring the church back to the pristine simplicity it supposedly once possessed. Resigned to the necessary imperfection of man and his institutions, moreover, its adherent could avoid Hus's fate, and seek friends and alliances which although imperfect or even corrupt could help "reform" the church.

Paralleling these intellectual changes was the continuance of the secularization of learning. As early as around 1300, lay intellectuals, although rarely equal to the clerical schoolmen of their day, invaded fields hitherto reserved to the clergy. A jurist, Peter Dubois (c. 1250–1312), proposed to "reform" the church, to abolish its military orders, and drastically to cut back monasticism. Dante Alighieri (1265–1321) rehearsed theological and philosophical arguments to prove that, in the world, secular authority was equal to ecclesiastical. The noble missionary Raymond Lull and the pope's doctor, Arnold of Villanova (c. 1240–1313), won reputations or notoriety for theological speculation.

The increasing awareness of the distinction between theology and natural and moral philosophy, moreover, gave added meaning to the slow recuperation of classical texts and traditions. Roger Bacon early claimed that, although lacking the Christian dispensation, Cicero's or Seneca's moral teaching was as good as or better than any available in Christian writings. And if Petrarch (1304–1374) still lamented "his" Cicero's polytheism, others had long since excused him by claiming that pagan pundits mentioned the cults of their day not out of admiration, but only to discipline the plebs—a sentiment not unknown to the later theologians of the *via moderna,* who blushed at the practices in the popular church of their day. Indeed, the attempt of Averroists like Siger of Brabant (d. 1282) and John of Jandun to discuss free will, immortality, or the aim of man's terrestrial life in terms of what Aristotle and other philosophers had said shows that although they had no intention of destroying the faith, the Christian vision had already become only one of several dealing with the great questions of religion and man's fate.

To add to this, the church lost a large part of its ancient ideal of progress. In its age of growth, the church moved with a sense of advancement, producing ever new orders, ever new devotions, ever unfolding new teachings to aid man in his ascent toward heaven. At its apogee, a moment so full of friction, this sense had evoked from enthusiasts, especially Franciscan extremists, a rigid and revolutionary conception of progress defined by a historically timed sequence of ages of spiritual ascent. The failure of these utopian fancies as well as the repression of their exponents had induced churchmen and other intellectuals to turn away from this idea. From Bonaventure to Petrarch, this was partly replaced by accenting the progress toward God of each individual during his life upon earth, and by rejecting the notion of the future improvement of the church itself in history.

Although efficacious in amplifying a strong man's sense of purpose, this was a real defeat for the church as an institution, for it took away its "religion" of history by making it surrender to secular man and his institutions the deceptive but ever appealing hope of moral progress in history. By the time of Cola di Rienzi, tribune of the people and proto-tyrant of Rome in 1347 and 1354, the secularization of the idea of progress, with its whole apparatus of successive and ever better ages, of prophetic men who come before their time, and with its consolations of inevitable future joys, was well under way.

As the luster of the medieval church dimmed, Europe's secular institutions began to shine ever more brightly. Rome's ancient myths and those of the early medieval sacral monarchies were applied anew to decorate the new principates and states. Nations, thinking of their citizens as sons of Aeneas, superior to others by virtue of race and innate genius, began to view themselves as God's repositories of freedom. By-products of Aristotelian thought reinforced this particularism. The idea became common that geography, climate, or even astral determination selected those frontiers within which men were naturally endowed with a will to be free, to govern themselves, or to dominate others. Each people found in its character or institutions perfect embodiments of these flattering myths. Thirteenth-century German publicists praised their people's ability to rule others, and saw in their elected monarchy a proof of the peculiar freedom of the German spirit. The idea of the natural *franchise* of all things French and of all Frenchmen was equally popular on the other side of the Rhine. John Fortescue's (c. 1394–1476) praise of England's free law and glorious constitution is too close to today's versions of these tales to be described here. None of these ideas was altogether new, but all flourished and multiplied in the later Middle Ages because the unity of Christendom was disintegrating. That a new and unifying idea of Europe, an intrinsically secular one, was being born is beyond doubt, but its effects were not yet felt and were anyway always to be subordinated to the particularism of Europe's parts.

As regional states or nations-to-be were being raised up, so were the individuals who led them. This age of crisis discovered an astonishing cast of princes, soldiers, merchants, and artists. Possessed by an exaggerated desire for career or advancement, they suited the monarchies or principates in which they flourished, for they combated established aristocracies and old interest groups. Many among them were those whose virtue or service to a prince enabled them to rise from humble origins. They were schooled and they served in a time of almost unimaginable coerciveness. Although this contributed to the general psychic malaise of the age, the constant threat of force drove a few to shine with unprecedented brilliance. Greatness also had ready models and fitting rewards. Princes were given full power (*arbitraria potestas*) to lift up those who served them or to crush those who stood in their way. In lesser measure, their captains, intellectuals, men of money, and artists were granted the same gratification. Like the estate royal in its relationship to the estates or orders of its subjects, the greatest men were of no one single order. Giotto of Florence (c. 1267–1337), John Hawkwood (d. 1394), and Jacques Coeur were practitioners of no one craft or business. Nevertheless, theirs was not a wholly arbitrary world. The corporate organization of society and enterprise built a stable standard for judging an individual or a group. This structure told even the greatest man that he had a game to play and that it had rules.

There was another dimension here too. Churchmen had rarely denied that all who lived well and faithfully were as good in God's eyes as the religious. This idea had begun to put on social garb when the church ruled the West, when even clerks were tempted to believe that a just judge was more valuable to Christendom than a monk. As the church declined, this principle began to obviate the need for the religious as a special social group. At the Council of Constance, the fathers expressly repudiated the claim that a *religio*—or membership in an order—lent a man a special claim to God's love. The day had begun when the good man, whatever his earthly vocation, could be a monk in his inner calling. In the new world being created in the later Middle Ages, one did not have to be a monk, a priest, or a prophet to have justification. It was enough to be a great artist or captain, indeed, to be a great or a good man at anything.

It is perhaps this unification of the practical and spiritual in the soul of each man, itself the very essence of later secularism, that is the greatest legacy of the later Middle Ages. That it had "advantages," there is no doubt. Without the spiritual liberation of the professions of learning, knowledge would still be impeded by external and ecclesiastical restraints. Without the loosing of the soldier's profession from ecclesiastical inhibitions, Europe's culture would not have conquered the world. On the other hand, born of combat between men and of an almost superhuman effort to comprehend everything within the heart of each and every man, this legacy also imposed upon Western man a grave psychic strain that has only now begun to destroy modern Europe's secular religions and philosophies.

For Further Reading

GENERAL HISTORIES

Brooke, Christopher, *Europe in the Central Middle Ages.*
Hay, Denys, *Europe in the Fourteenth and Fifteenth Centuries.*
Jones, A. H. M., *The Decline of the Ancient World.*

INSTITUTIONAL STUDIES

Bloch, Marc, *Feudal Society.*
Cochrane, Charles N., *Christianity and Classical Culture.*
Kantorowicz, Ernst H., *The King's Two Bodies: A Study in Mediaeval Political Theology.*
Leff, Gordon, *Medieval Thought: Saint Augustine to Ockham.*
Mundy, J. H., and Reisenberg, Peter, *The Medieval Town.*
Pirenne, Henri, *Economic and Social History of Medieval Europe.*
Rosenstock-Huessy, Eugen, *The Driving Power of Western Civilization: The Christian Revolution of the Middle Ages.*
Schnurer, Gustav, *Church and Culture in the Middle Ages.*

35   The Jews in Medieval Europe

In 425, Gamaliel VI, patriarch of the Jews of the Roman Empire, died without a male heir, and Theodosius II abolished the Jewish patriarchate permanently. Although the Jews of the world probably still numbered well over three million, there was a solid basis for the Christian hope that Judaism would soon be unknown. Palestine had become so depopulated of Jews and the Jews at large so sapped of energy for concentrated activity—they had even failed to bring to fruition the grant of Julian to rebuild their temple in Jerusalem (361)—that no protest was heard when the last symbol of centralized Jewish autonomy had been withdrawn. Moreover, the Jews had sustained several legal blows at the hands of virtually every Christian emperor. Forbidden in the fourth century to proselytize, build new synagogues, own Christian slaves, or hold political office, they had patently lost some of the basic privileges formerly conceded them as a *religio licita* and perhaps, since 212, as full Roman citizens. Finally, although there was still a vast Jewish population in Persia living under an exilarch and with an

A.D.   c. 359   Jewish calendar committed to writing by Hillel II

            425   End of Jewish patriarchate

    425–475   Compilation of Palestinian Talmud

    613–711   Visigothic persecutions of the Jews in Spain

    813–840   Reign of Louis the Pious; earliest known diplomas of privileges to Jews

 1040–1105   Rashi (Solomon ben Isaac of Troyes), commentator on Bible and Babylonian Talmud

       1144   Death of William of Norwich; beginning of medieval blood accusation

       1215   Fourth Lateran Council; yellow badge

       1290   Expulsion of Jews from England

       1306   Expulsion of Jews from France

       1348   Black Death persecutions; beginning of ghettoization in Germany

       1391   Pogroms in Spain; beginning of Marranism

       1481   Inquistion proceedings begin in Spain

       1492   Expulsion of Jews from Spain

       1516   Establishment of ghetto in Venice

 1648–1658   Chmielnicki uprisings and massacres in Ukraine and Poland

       1666   Sabbetai Zevi's abortive messianic movement collapses

CHRONOLOGY

effective network of Jewish courts and communal services, in view of the sealed borders between Rome and Persia, the Jews of the empire were largely cut off from their Babylonian brethren.

However, the Jews had not lost all their vigor, certainly not their tenacity to their faith, ritual, and communal separation, nor even their readiness to win new adherents. Socially and economically no worse off than their gentile neighbors, in most cases they found the new deprivations more humiliating than troublesome. Few Jews had ever owned slaves, and even fewer had ever nourished hopes of attaining political office. Even when old synagogues became unusable, services could be conducted wherever a "quorum" (*minyan*) of Jews and a Torah scroll could be mustered. As for missionary activity, not all Jews had approved such efforts even when they had been licit. While aggressive proselytizers of necessity had to become circumspect, conversion to Judaism was never totally renounced or stopped.

Second, the upheavals that traumatized the empire during the barbarian invasions affected the Jews *as a group* considerably less than they did many another people of Europe. Heirs to a diaspora mentality for more than nine centuries, the mobility forced by the successive incursions of Goths, Vandals, and Lombards was probably less unsettling for Jews than for others. Engaging in a variety of handicrafts as well as in agriculture and sailing, they were especially well represented among the itinerant merchants known as "Syrian traders." Not that the Jews were the Bedouin of Europe. Outside of Palestine and Parthia they were largely concentrated in the great cities—Antioch, Alexandria, Constantinople, Rome. On the other hand, what Strabo had observed of them in the days of Octavian Augustus was even more true in the days of Romulus Augustulus: "Hardly a city of the civilized world has failed to absorb them." Hence, when forced to take to the road, they readily found comrades at the next stop.

Finally, while the machinery for centralized religious direction had been removed and the great rabbinic academies of Palestine had either closed down or dwindled to insignificance, the Jews of the Diaspora had long since overcome total dependence on them. The procedures for the regulation of the Jewish calendar, the backbone of Jewish observance and for centuries the guarded privilege of the patriarchate, had been reduced to theoretical principles and committed to writing and publicized by a Palestinian patriarch, Hillel II (c. 359). The basic principles of Jewish law had been compiled and issued as the Palestinian Talmud (c. 425–475), and this was followed in the sixth century by several compilations of rabbinic homily, known as midrash, which provided the rationale for Jewish faith. The conditions favorable to the preservation of a basically uniform Jewish culture without recourse to Palestine thus lay at hand. No testimony to the wide currency of these works is as revealing as Justinian's proscription of Jewish "deuterosis" (rabbinic law and exegesis).

While Justinian's measure was not totally effective, the increased tempo and violence of anti-Jewish preaching and activity did have effects. Repeated expulsions, occasionally accompanied by massacre (Alexandria, 411; Antioch, 592; Jerusalem, 630), decrees of compulsory baptism (Spain, 613; Byzantium, 632; Gaul, 633; perhaps also in northern Italy, 661), popular riots, interminable denunciations in Church councils along with prohibitions of normal social intercourse between Jews and Christians, and civil disabilities everywhere made the sixth and especially the seventh centuries a dark age for European Jewry. Many converted to Christianity. Others feigned Christianity or fled to outlying areas. But a long tradition of faith and rationalization of adverse circumstances, along with several external factors, enabled a sufficient number to weather the storm.

Paradoxically, the very same Rome that was now bent on crushing the Jews was largely responsible for their survival. However Christian the empire may have become, it never quite eradicated many of the legacies of its Latin past. Paramount among these was the Roman reverence for law and precedent, which dictated the right of the Jews to live as Jews with their own judges, teachers, and institutions. The extreme decrees of proscription were never totally enforced, and in the original heart of the empire Gregory the Great reaffirmed the principle that became normative for Christian prelates and monarchs: "Even as the Jews ought not be permitted to do . . . more than is legally permitted them, so ought they not suffer the curtailment of those [rights] which have been conceded them." The Jews were thus classified as tolerated infidels rather than as heretics who could expect no quarter.

Nor were the Jews unique in their resistance to orthodox Christendom. The Church never quite overcame heresy and schism; neither it nor the state was ever totally free to concentrate solely on the Jews. And by the middle of the eighth century an entirely new set of factors had actually tipped the scales in the Jews' favor.

The rise of the Carolingian monarchy simultaneously with the great conquests of Islam facilitated open Jewish community life in most areas of the Western world. Indeed, the methods of government of Latin Christians as well as of Muslims actually made it advantageous in many respects to remain Jewish. Having to rule over vast territories in which they represented minority elements, Franks as well as Arabs gladly exploited Jewish talents. Abolishing the later Roman institution of personal citizenship, the new Christian rulers dealt with the Jews by defining their rights contractually. Most commonly the king, local count, or archbishop granted a group of Jews a charter guaranteeing their rights to engage in business and live as a self-governing community in return for special imposts to be collected by the Jews themselves. The rulers were thus assured a steady income from a group in whose interests it lay to develop the commercial vitality of their area. Since they had conceded them special benefits, the rulers could be confident of Jewish loyalty.

Jews were quick to respond to these opportunities, and many settled in cathedral towns or county seats under the supervision of men of means and learning of their own faith. Spires, Worms, Mayence, Troyes, Paris, Narbonne—these were but a few of the centers where a rapidly growing Jewish population engaged mainly in commerce. By 1020 the Jews of the Holy Roman Empire had become a sizable and conspicuous group and had begun to take their cultural destiny into their own hands.

Academies of higher learning sprang up in the great urban centers, generating a flurry of literary creativity (in Italy as early as the tenth century and in France and Germany in the eleventh century and after). Although the Jewish culture of these countries rested on the same scriptural and Talmudic foundations as that of Jews of Muslim lands, it quickly developed into a separate cultural branch popularly known as Ashkenazic (from the medieval Hebrew name for Germany) that reflected the atmosphere of the dominant milieu. The new literature consisted principally of commentaries on Scripture and rabbinic literature, anthologies of law, exempla, liturgical poetry, religious history, and, later on, mystical treatises. While ingenuously claiming to preserve a tradition that was impervious to outside pressures, the commentaries of Rashi, the itinerant Abraham ibn Ezra, and the Kimhis of the Provence dovetailed neatly with the needs of a subculture living in an age and area predicated on faith in scriptural revelation and ultimate retribution in the final judgment. Hence, while the Jew lived in a world committed to excoriating and converting him, he found that the premises and more than a few of the forms of his own civilization had been appropriated by his overlords. The endless dispute between Judaism and Christianity was conducted in a context of shared premises.

For more than three and a half centuries Jewish society in Europe flourished. Even in Byzantium the caesaropapist rulers saw the advantage of letting the Jews practice their faith, and traditionally rabbinic and sectarian Karaite communities lived side by side. While wealthier Jews functioned principally as merchants, with interests as far as Egypt and India, the occupational distribution of pre-Crusade Jewry ran a gamut of pursuits—from farming and handicrafts to medicine and slave trading. Conflicts with Christians were rare and quickly settled. No one could foresee the calamity that struck the Jews in 1096 and the subsequent steady decline in their position in all of Europe north of the Pyrenees.

The first rumors of the intention of the Crusaders to purge Europe of its "Christ killers" were dismissed as pure hysteria; as a result whole communities of German Jews paid with their wealth, lives, or forced baptism.* The denunciation of such riots by the papacy and by Bernard of Clairvaux, coupled with effective measures by the emperor, prevented a recurrence of the catastrophe in the Second Crusade (1147). However, the onslaughts proved to be more than an ephemeral outburst. Deep-seated hostilities, nourished by a steady stream of clerical fulminations, had surfaced. Guild and merchant burghers exploited Christian theory for their economic interests and demanded the isolation of the Jews. Although the papacy adhered to its position of opposing violence, it, too, revived the old conciliar provisions for their humiliation, social sequestration, and relegation to occupational misery. Usury, a pursuit originally as hateful to the Jew as to the heirs to his Biblical ethos, now became his principal outlet, one with which he lived in cynical and bitter resignation. Aaron of York, the archetype of Shylock, learned to live by his cash and wits, and, if need be, to pack bag and baggage and start anew elsewhere.

A formidable coalition of mob, church, and state drove the Jews to the periphery, and ultimately quite out, of medieval society. Excluded from trade, handicrafts, and the professions, deprived of the right to bear arms, the Jew by the thirteenth century was treated as a necessary evil whose only claim to toleration lay in his monetary usefulness as a "servant of the royal treasury." Ecclesiastical campaigns against usury soon resulted in the frequent cancellation of Jewish claims, confiscation of Jewish estates, and the refusal of civil authorities to enforce notes. The wars against the Catharist and Albigensian heresies were followed by a concerted drive to convert the Jews. The Fourth Lateran Council (1215) enjoined temporal rulers to compel Jews and Muslims to wear a badge distinguishing them from Christians, to curtail Jewish traffic in money, and to confine Jewish worship to forms that would not give offense to Christian sensibilities. Subsequently, the new Dominican order was empowered to preach to the Jews in their own synagogues. These decrees were capped by sporadic mob attacks and mass arrests for ritual murder and desecration of the host, "proved," on occasion, by torture. The intensification of popular piety and the growing resentment against Jewish usury culminated in a series of expulsions: from England in 1290, Normandy in 1296, France in 1306 and again in 1394— to mention but the most notorious of them. In Germany, where the emperor depended on the good will of local dukes and margraves, the Jews led a precarious and checkered existence, characterized by local contracts permitting them to reside in limited numbers, often for a specified number of years. Inevitably a growing number gravitated to eastern Europe where

---

* The Holy Roman Emperor, Henry IV, distracted by more immediate threats to his power, did what little he could to quiet the atmosphere and permitted the forcibly baptized to revert to their faith.

Jews were welcome and accorded special privileges reminiscent of the days of the Carolingians. Others continued to live in the Papal States, where the popes (often governed in their own area more by interests of state than by Christian theory) permitted them to live as their wards. But by far the largest and most prosperous Jewish population in the fourteenth century was the one in Spain, where well-organized communities enjoyed the special protection of the rulers of Aragon and Castile.

Thanks to favorable conditions, Sephardic Judaism, as the Spanish branch is called, continued to encompass the most diverse social and religious types. Never as monolithically orthodox as its Ashkenazic sister, Spanish Jewry included a long line of courtiers—diplomats, tax collectors, physicians, astronomers, and translators who made their careers in the royal service—and of intellectuals—from outright Averroists and Bible critics to sophisticated mystics, professional poets, simple fundamentalists, and a few who gained distinction as translators of works of Arabic philosophy and science, thereby gaining for the Jews the title of "cultural middlemen of Europe."

However, even in Spain upheaval and dissolution began in the fourteenth century. The growing restiveness of the Third Estate in Spain bestirred the Jewish masses to demand a greater voice in communal affairs and more equitable conditions for themselves. Social cleavages, open and often intense, frequently resulted in conflicts between the old Jewish aristocracy and the rapidly increasing *nouveaux riches* that could be resolved only by royal intervention. The miasma of Christian fanaticism traversed the Pyrenees steadily. Dominican preaching, ritual accusations, factional intrigues against Jewish courtiers, together with the ravages of the Black Death combined to unsettle the Jewish communities.

The first blow came swiftly and terribly during the interregnum of 1391. Fanned long and hard by a fanatical archdeacon of Seville, the riots spread quickly. While thousands of Jews died as martyrs, several hundred thousand saved their skins by accepting baptism. Since by Christian theory such baptism was binding, open "relapse" to Judaism was prosecuted as heresy. Accordingly, while some fled to safer shores, the overwhelming majority remained at least formally Christian. Of these, many thousands adhered privately to the faith of their fathers (thereby earning the Spanish epithet of Marrano, or "swine"). Moreover, since as "New Christians" they could exercise their diplomatic and commercial talents without restraint, and simultaneously pursue the traditional Jewish course of supporting a strong central monarchy, they soon found the hatred once reserved for all Jews directed principally at them. A wave of despair in the ranks of the Jews themselves swelled the ranks of the New Christians in 1413–1415 and, in turn, intensified the hostility of the lower classes of Old

Christians against the Marranos. A wave of anti-Marrano pogroms was followed by a flood of vitriolic pamphlets and an undisguised campaign of social ostracism all over Spain. In desperation, many New Christians lent sympathetic ears to Jews and Judaizing Marranos, and Marrano communities mushroomed, with their own churches, synagogues, cemeteries, and guilds. Others, particularly the highly placed, demanded an official inquisition that would extirpate the backsliders and clear the remainder once and for all. The Spanish Inquisition, which began its proceedings in 1481, initiated a series of revelations and a wave of terror that shook Spain to its foundations. Finally yielding to the claims of the Grand Inquisitor, Tomás de Torquemada, that the presence of Jews in Spain was the chief source of New Christian backsliding, the Catholic monarchs issued their decree of expulsion in the summer of 1492. Four years later, Portugal followed suit, thereby completing the task of purging the peninsula of open Jewish adherence.

While the Reformation and Counter Reformation brought new miseries to the remnants of Occidental Jewry—most notably in Italy, where walled ghettos were established in all major cities—the migration of some 200,-000 Jews swelled the established Jewish settlements in Italy, eastern Europe, and the Ottoman Empire, and generated new ones in Holland, England, and France. Sephardic culture enjoyed a revival in Italy, Holland, and the Ottoman Empire only to suffer a major setback in the Near East following the collapse in 1666 of the messianic movement led by Sabbetai Zevi.

In eastern Europe, however, Jewish life attained a new autonomy and richness that persisted despite increased violence and persecutions after 1648. But these communities were largely isolated from the mainstream of European society. For them, now the majority of European Jewry, the Middle Ages did not actually end until 1917. However, echoes of a new age had long since permeated their "pale of settlement," stimulating the bearers of the oldest living culture of Europe to seek new horizons.

For Further Reading

Abrahams, Israel, *Jewish Life in the Middle Ages.*
Baron, Salo W., *A Social and Religious History of the Jews,* Vols. II–XIV.
Finkelstein, Louis (ed.), *The Jews, Their History.*
Katz, J., *Exclusiveness and Tolerance.*
———, *Tradition and Crisis.*
Marcus, J. R., *The Jew in the Medieval World: A Source Book 315–1791.*
Parkes, J. G., *The Conflict of the Church and the Synagogue.*
Schwarz, L. W. (ed.), *Great Ages and Ideas of the Jewish People.*

Byzantium

36 Early Byzantium

No contemporary of medieval Constantinople, or rather New Rome, would ever have doubted that it was the center of the civilized Christian world, the one and incomparable city. "We knew not whether we were in heaven or on earth," a wonder-stricken ambassador of the prince of Kiev reported late in the tenth century to his master. "For on earth there is no such splendor or such beauty, and we are at a loss how to describe it." Nearly two centuries later, this awe still found an echo in a leader of the Latin army preparing to capture the city for the first time:

. . . those who had never seen Constantinople marvelled greatly at it, for they could not conceive that the world held so mighty a city, when they saw the height of the walls, the great towers enclosing it all around, the splendid palaces, the lofty churches (the number of which was so great that none could believe it who had not seen it with his own eyes), and the length and breadth of the city that lorded it over all others. And know ye that there was no man so bold that his flesh did not creep thereat, and this was no wonder. . . .

Nevertheless, the epithet "Byzantine" has acquired a connotation of intrigue, degeneracy, and treachery, inherited from Edward Gibbon, whose masterpiece has blinded its readers to the fact that the *Decline and Fall* of his Roman Empire required some eleven centuries, a span as yet unequaled by the healthiest body politic.

Even for the medieval specialist, Byzantine history often proves bewildering, for it refuses to conform to the accepted criteria of what is normally regarded as the Middle Ages. All the characteristic aspects and institutions of this period in western Europe—a decentralized, deurbanized world supported by an agricultural economy, held together by the complicated human bonds of feudal loyalties, and focused on the church as its central institution—seem to disappear east of the Elbe, south of the Danube, and in the lands of the eastern Mediterranean during most of the

millennium separating the dedication of Constantinople by Constantine I in A.D. 330 and the loss of the city to Islam in 1453.

The state which developed on the shores of the Bosphorus and which dominated the imagination and often the reality of the contemporary world until the twelfth century responded to other traditions and loyalties. It has been characterized as a combination of Greek culture, Roman institutions, and Christianity, but it may be identified equally satisfactorily by the three objects of its ascending allegiance: the City, the Emperor, the Faith.

The city of New Rome, on which loyalties focused increasingly with the gradually shrinking boundaries of the Empire until it came to be almost conterminous with the State, represented for its citizens far more than the great geopolitical center admired by later generations. It was founded as the heir of the Old Rome with all the privileges and prerogatives of the former capital of the classical world, but cleansed of its pagan associations. The presence within its walls of the Church of the Holy Wisdom (Hagia Sophia) in which the emperors were crowned made of it simultaneously an image of the Heavenly Jerusalem, and supernatural guardians watched over its safety. So enormous was the prestige of Constantinople that even its Muslim foes believed that its capture would be the ultimate heroic deed heralding the trumpets of the Last Judgment and the coming of the Messiah. The safety of the city guaranteed the survival of the empire and of Christianity itself.

The emperor was likewise heir to the rights and powers of the Roman *autocrator,* but he, too, far transcended their limitations. As "Friend" and even more as "Imitator" of Christ, he left behind all human glories to become the image of the Heavenly King. From the days of Constantine I, official theory maintained that "as there is one God . . . so there is one king. . . . Crowned in the image of heavenly kingship he steers and guides men on earth according to the pattern of his prototype," and eight centuries later a Byzantine official still admonished his son to serve the ruler ". . . as if he were God." The emperor was Christ's vicar on earth and His co-ruler, his true state symbolized by the great purple and gold double throne, half of it empty to mortal eyes, on which he transacted all official affairs.

Opposition to the emperor "crowned by God" was blasphemy and sacrilege, yet beyond his omnipotence loomed the orthodoxy of the faith. Throughout the history of Byzantium the problem of orthodoxy dominated all others. The highly trained logical minds of the theologians and intellectuals and the passionate devotion of the people demanded clear-cut, if subtle, formulas and a wholehearted adherence to them. The empire could exist only if the purity and uniformity of its faith mirrored that of the Heavenly Kingdom. The only possible challenge to the imperial authority was in defense of the faith, through the demonstration that, far from being the image of Christ, the emperor was the image of the Antichrist. Behind the agitated and often bloody history of the Byzantine state, characterized like its Russian successor, as "autocracy tempered by assassination," stands the unshakable conviction of the people that the empire was the direct reflection of God's will, and their ultimate allegiance, transcending all earthly loyalties, to their conception of the Christian faith.

The dominance of the emperor and the centralization of the state give a curiously classical aspect to the Byzantine empire while simultaneously seeming to prefigure the absolutism of early modern times, but they awaken no reminiscence of the hierarchical feudal monarchy of the medieval West. Similarly the urban structure, commercial economy, elaborate bureaucracy, and literate society which characterize most of Byzantine history seem atypical to students of the European Middle Ages, whose tendency has consequently been to isolate Byzantium from the contemporary world or to ignore it altogether. This conscious or tacit estrangement of the two halves of the Mediterranean is not of recent date—some of it was quasi-inherent and could be traced back to Antiquity—but the first overt manifestations of antagonism do not seem to antedate the seventh century.

Not even the difficult period following Justinian's death in 565 was sufficient to bring about a total restructure of the society which preceded it. When Heraclius I, the son of the governor of Carthage, arrived at Constantinople in 610 at the head of a victorious fleet to found a new imperial dynasty, the Mediterranean was still the central link in the empire. In spite of the Lombard invasion of Italy and the presence of native barbarian dynasties in Gaul and Spain, most of the rulers in the West formally acknowledged their inferiority to the imperial majesty. Far from stressing his independence, King Childebert of the Franks addressed his letters to "the glorious, pious, eternal, renowned, and triumphant Lord, ever Augustus, my father, the Emperor Maurice." Even Pope Gregory the Great recognized the authority of the emperor and awaited the imperial confirmation of his election before assuming the responsibilities of the Roman see. The social and economic transformation of the empire from the Late Roman pattern of vast estates cultivated by tenants bound to their land to one of free peasant communities composed of small farms granted by the state in return for military service was incomplete and gradual. Nevertheless, the presence of deep-rooted dissimilarities beneath the seemingly smooth surface of cultural uniformity and continuity provided a constant and fundamental source of misunderstandings and alienation ever ready for exploitation.

At the height of Roman unification distinctions had survived between the Greek-speaking East and the Latin West, between the richer, intellectual, and urbanized Orient, where cities such as Alexandria, Antioch, and Athens traced their cultural and political pedigrees far beyond Roman pretensions, and the poorer, predominantly rural, and recently civilized Occident, which owed most of its institutions to the Latin conquerors. By the end of the sixth century, these distinctions were intensifying. The Roman veneer was wearing thin in the western Mediterranean, in spite of Justinian's partial reconquest, whereas the eastern provinces, preserved from the horrors of barbarian invasions, continued to flourish, their institutions, schools, and economy unimpaired, their classical tradition unaltered.

The unifying effect of the Christian faith, which had replaced to some degree that of Roman political centralization, was similarly undermined by the divergent Latin and Greek traditions in the choice of scriptural authorities. From the earliest Christianization of the empire, the West distinguished more clearly between "the things which are Caesar's" and "the things that are God's" than the East, which preferred St. Paul's injunction that "the powers that be are ordained of God." Even more fundamentally, Greek theologians saw the Christian promise of salvation fulfilled by the Resurrection and stressed that the Kingdom of God might already be accessible to the believer—"we all with open face beholding as in a glass the glory of the Lord, are changed into the same image from glory to glory"—while their Western counterparts, still awaiting the ultimate perfection of Christ's second coming, preferred the less ecstatic formulation of St. Paul's words, "For now we see through a glass darkly; but then face to face." In the more narrowly ecclesiastical sphere, the Greeks never altered their belief, supported by numerous passages from the Acts of the Apostles, that the final authority in doctrinal matters lay in the church assembled in council, whereas Rome soon moved to the claim that this authority had been vested solely in the successors of St. Peter. These divergent interpretations had a profound effect on the political thinking of their societies and on the complicated relations of the church and the state. Papal infallibility was unacceptable to Eastern theologians. On the other hand, if the heavenly kingdom was truly at hand, and Christ already ruling as king, the emperor might understandably be acknowledged as his colleague and image. If this event was still essentially in the future, such a belief became untenable, and Western fathers would ultimately always reach the position that the ruler was a sinful mortal subject to ecclesiastical strictures.

This latent antagonism between the two halves of the Christian empire was intensified by a number of circumstances even before the accession of Heraclius. At the human level, a linguistic wedge was driven between the two ends of the Mediterranean. The common language of the East had always been Greek, as that of the West was Latin, but from the second century B.C. the educated classes and all officialdom had been completely bilingual. Justinian's *Code* was still promulgated in Latin in the mid-sixth century, even though Greek was preferred for current legislation. By the end of the century, however, Pope Gregory I admitted that he knew no Greek, and within a generation the two halves of the former empire were incapable of understanding each other. Greek intellectuals sneered at the "barbarian" speech of the West, and even where contempt did not inject additional obstacles, all relations perforce passed through the distorting mirror of translation.

On purely physical grounds, communications were also impaired by the continuous migration of Slavic tribes into imperial territory. The ultimate source of difficulties lay in distant Central Asia, where the internecine struggle of various Turco-Mongol tribes hurled a number of them in successive waves toward the West during the first millennium of the Christian era, but the absence of a hermetic geographical barrier in the East left Europe open to these nomad invasions ranging unchecked across Transcaspia and the steppes of southern Russia all the way to the Hungarian plain. Thus, events occurring far beyond the ken of "European" powers repeatedly upset their political calculations. The advance of the Huns in the fourth century, driving the Goths across the Danube, heralded the barbarization of the West and simultaneously helped their Iranian allies, the Alans and Sarmatians, to overrun the Slavic tribes scattered between the Elbe and the Dnieper. In the sixth century, the Avars crossed the lower Volga, smashed the Turkic empire of the Bulgars east of the Sea of Azov, briefly threatened Constantinople together with the Persians, and finally settled at the end of the traditional invasion route in Hungary, until Charlemagne annihilated them in 796. Although their siege of the capital proved ineffectual, the Avar invasion was critical for the empire because of its intensification of the southern movement of the Slavs. Crossing the Danube as early as 517, the Slavs reached the Peloponnese by 578. Instead of keeping to the hit-and-run pattern of their nomad predecessors, they began to settle in the lands which they had overrun. The emperor Maurice temporarily checked their advance, but they profited from the neglect of the Danube frontier when war broke out with Persia after Maurice's murder in 602. Hence, at the beginning of the seventh century, the Balkans and much of Greece were all but completely Slavicized, and the great imperial highway through the Balkans, the Via Egnatia linking Thessalonike with the region of Venice, became to all purposes inaccessible.

The loose tribal pattern of the Slavic confederations was insufficiently advanced to form a homogeneous state, but cohesion was provided by the next Turkic group, the Bulgars. Unable to withstand the pressure of the

Khazars advancing westward toward the northern Caucasus and the Crimea, the Bulgar khan, Asperuch, reached the Danube by 679. His successors exploited the difficulties attending the downfall of the Heraclid dynasty to entrench themselves in their new home, where they fused the Slavic tribes, whose language and customs they appropriated, into a unified state consitituting a permanent threat on the northwest frontier of the empire. For some two centuries thereafter, the great classical and early Christian centers of the Balkans, Athens, Corinth, Thebes, Salona, lost all contact with the world of which they had been an integral part. Illyricum, as the area was then called, had been politically tied to the East while simultaneously recognizing the ecclesiastical jurisdiction of Rome. As such it had provided a meeting point for Greek and Latin traditions. Now, reduced to a vacuum and a no-man's-land, it eventually emerged no longer a bridge between the two imperial cultures but a bone of contention destined to envenom negotiations between Constantinople and Rome.

The necessity of defending both the Euphrates against the Persians and the Danube against the Avars, Slavs, and Bulgars probably accelerated the transformation of the outwardly civilian pattern of the classical Roman Empire into an openly military administration. The origin of the new provincial system based on *themes,* or military districts, governed by generals with civilian as well as military authority and defended by locally recruited troops, is still disputed. Some of its aspects may well go back to the extraordinary commands created by Justinian and Maurice in the sixth century, but the earliest identifiable *themes* seemingly date from the period of the Heraclian dynasty, and as such must in some way be associated with the imperial crisis of the seventh century.

The most serious element of this crisis was undoubtedly the unforeseen and overwhelming expansion of the Arabs, which swamped the Persian realm and wiped imperial rule from Africa, Palestine, Syria, and Armenia. The Arabs had long been familiar to the empire as minor border nuisances, or as allies against Persia, but no portent had heralded the explosion of their power in the decades following the death of the prophet Muhammad in 632. To be sure, some of the seeds of the disaster may have been planted much earlier. Native resentment against the dominant Greek culture which had overshadowed their older traditions had burst forth periodically in the East since the days of Alexander the Great. The Roman Empire, and subsequently official Christianity represented by the same emperor, fell heir to this smoldering hatred. For all of the hypothetical "exhaustion" of Byzantium and Persia, or the "fanaticism" of the Arabs, it remains difficult to explain the Muslim blitzkrieg, and particularly the rapid capitulation of such formidable fortress-cities as Alexandria, Damascus, or Ctesiphon to small, poorly equiped Arab detachments, untrained in siege

warfare, and facing sophisticated fortifications and highly skilled professional armies, unless we postulate some degree of fifth-column activity on
the part of disaffected native religious minorities, such as the Jews, and
particularly the Monophysites, whom Justinian's legislation had reduced to
second-class citizenship. Whatever their causes, however, the Arab victories revolutionized the history of Europe probably to a greater degree
than the earlier Germanic invasions.

Although the Byzantine fleets armed from the middle of the seventh
century with the "secret weapon" of Greek fire, which induced uncontrollable panic among the enemy, kept the mastery over the sea until the
beginning of the ninth century, the empire found itself perpetually on the
defensive in the East. Indeed, until the emperor Leo III lifted the siege of
Constantinople in 717, Byzantium fought for its very life. Its richest
provinces, its sources of food and manpower, its commercial and industrial
centers, spared by earlier disasters, were now lost beyond recall. Consequently, the militarization of the state grew apace, the imperial economy
had to be refocused on Asia Minor and the capital, and the empire, with no
resources to spare, turned its attention resolutely away from the West. All
the appeals of Rome and northern Italy, threatened by the Lombard advance, all Western objection to the dogmatic concessions by which the
Heraclian dynasty attempted to pacify the Monophysite provinces lying in
the Arab path, fell on deaf or helpless ears. As a result, Rome, its protests
and needs disregarded, gradually saw less and less reason to keep faith with
a distant and neglectful master and sought new protectors among the
nearby Frankish rulers.

Within the ecclesiastical community, the new situation heralded a
serious alteration in the existing balance of power. The Muslim domination
of Alexandria, Antioch, and Jerusalem left the Patriarch of Constantinople
sole head of the Eastern church in much the same way as the pope in
Rome had always been the supreme authority in the West. This new status
could not fail to increase his pretensions, and the patriarch reaffirmed his
"Ecumenical" title, first assumed in 587. Whatever the true implications of
this ambiguous term, it unquestionably scandalized and offended the
papacy, and embittered the relations between the two sees. The rejection
by Rome of the decrees of the Constantinopolitan Council of 692, which
dealt primarily with matters of discipline and custom, underscored the fact
that the divergences between the two churches were reaching down to the
minutiae of everyday practices. In the capital itself, however, the new
solitary status of the patriarch left him bereft of all effective support
against the overwhelming power of the emperor.

The growth of imperial authority in this period is one of its most
interesting aspects. There is no doubt that this power had long existed; in a

sense the emperor was still the Roman autocrat who had merely transferred his divinity from his person to his office. Still functioning to all intents as *Pontifex Maximus,* the ruler had appointed bishops, summoned and presided over church councils, and promulgated their decisions as imperial decrees. Constantine I's burial in the Church of the Holy Apostles, surrounded by the effigies of his twelve colleagues, left little doubt as to his own estimate of his position. Yet the apostles had been ordinary mortals, and imperial supervision of church affairs, however extensive, did not permit the emperor to interfere in matters of doctrine. With the opening years of the seventh century, the empire began to take an increasingly religious aspect, and the new imperial title of *Basileus,* or king, replacing the earlier Latin terminology, had unmistakably supernatural connotations. The ship which bore Heraclius to the throne in 610 was protected by an icon of the Virgin. His great campaigns to avenge the theft of the True Cross from Jerusalem by the Persians took on the aspects of a crusade: the church melted down its treasures to equip the imperial army, Heraclius hailed his fallen soldiers as martyrs, the Persian shrine at Ganzak in Azerbaijan was destroyed in retaliation for the sack of Jerusalem, and the emperor personally carried the relics of Christianity back to the holy city. Imperial art lingered significantly over the haloed figure of the young David, "the Lord's anointed," and the cross and bust of Christ replaced classic victories on the imperial coins, whose legends proclaimed the piety and orthodoxy of the rulers.

Far more seriously, Heraclius and his descendants bypassed canonical channels in their attempts to find dogmatic formulas acceptable to both orthodox and schismatic. Instead of awaiting a conciliar decision, as the Eastern tradition demanded, the emperors often promulgated new doctrines on their own initiative and in their own name. Since these formulas defined the operation of Christ's will or energy, they concerned directly the doctrine of His nature. Thus the emperors overstepped the bounds of mere supervision and intruded into the realm of dogma. Many of these innovations, including the assumption of the new imperial title, antedate the rise of Islam and cannot, therefore, be attributed to its influence. Yet the presence over the border of a major power in which church and state were indistinguishable, and whose caliph wielded authority as the direct successor of God's prophet rather than as an earthly ruler, cannot have been entirely without effect. In his desperate struggle to save Christendom from the might of Islam, the emperor was forced to match every one of its aspects, and as such, to take on some of the spiritual traits of the "Commander of the Faithful." The result was to make Byzantium a middle ground between Muslim theocracy and the increasing separation of church and state which was to characterize the West.

From the earliest manifestation of the danger to the empire in the East, its most urgent concern was to save the capital from the repeated attacks of the Arabs, and to salvage whatever territory might still be held in Asia Minor. The successors of Heraclius bent all their energies to this task, and his last descendant, Justinian II (685–695, 707–711), even sought the alliance of the barbarian khan of the Khazars, whose strategic position in southeastern Russia permitted him to attack the Arabs from the rear. Despite their efforts and compromises, the emperors found themselves repeatedly at bay, facing at once foreign onslaught and internal discontent. So desperate was the situation in 661 that Heraclius' grandson, Constans II, even fled Constantinople to seek shelter in Italy, incidentally demonstrating that the imperial abandonment of the West was still more a matter of necessity than deliberate policy.

The task of bringing some stability out of the disaster was left to the first Oriental dynasty on the imperial throne, the Isaurians, natives of the distant mountains of southeastern Anatolia. The first Isaurians, Leo III and Constantine V, were remarkable generals with an exalted concept of their duties. To Leo III belongs the glory of hurling the Arab armies back from the walls of Constantinople in 717, thus marking the first definitive check of Muslim power some fifteen years before Charles Martel's victory at Poitiers set the high-water mark for Arab expansion in the West. Constantine V, benefiting from the internal troubles of the caliphate attendant upon the overthrow of the Umayyad dynasty in 750 and the removal of the Muslim capital from Damascus to more distant Baghdad, reestablished imperial control over most of the crucial economic and recruiting territory of Asia Minor. At the same time he halted the advance of the Bulgars at Anchialus in 763 and consolidated the Balkan frontier with a system of fortifications and with transported Syrian and Armenian settlers.

In the civilian realm, the Isaurians likewise concerned themselves with the welfare of their subjects. Following the pattern of their predecessors, they associated their sons to the throne to avoid the danger of civil war in cases of disputed successions. The pattern of the *themes* was extended throughout the empire, the fiscal system overhauled, the heads of the bureaucracy linked more closely with the imperial palace. Great functionaries such as the Praetorian Prefects or the Masters of the Army of the late Roman period, whose power might overshadow that of the emperor, disappeared together with their Latin titles from the imperial rosters, and were replaced by men with more circumscribed jurisdictions. A briefer legal code, the *Ecloga,* replaced for many practical purposes the unwieldy bulk of Justinian's great *Corpus.* Abandoning the ecumenical scope and classical tradition of the Justinianic legislation, the *Ecloga* also marked a new stage in the evolution of a new Christian society. The paramount

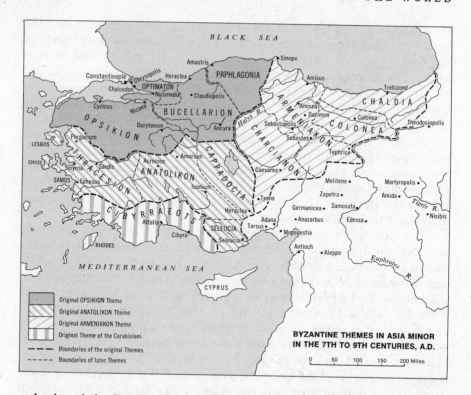

BYZANTINE THEMES IN ASIA MINOR
IN THE 7TH TO 9TH CENTURIES, A.D.

authority of the Roman paterfamilias was sharply limited by the recognition of numerous rights to women and children. Marriage ceased to be a dissolvable human contract and became an irrevocable sacrament. In the criminal sphere, numerous mutilations, of which the favorite was blinding, gave an Oriental cast to the new Code, though in many cases these provisions, so distasteful to modern sensibilities, reflected the concern of Christian legislators, since they replaced the death penalty, thus giving to the criminal an opportunity to repent his misdeeds.

The all-inclusive powers assumed by Leo and Constantine provoked the violent confrontation between the state and the church known as the Iconoclastic Controversy, which embittered the whole Isaurian period as well as much of the next century. In the preface to the *Ecloga* Leo III had summed up his duties in terms of a divine mandate:

Since God has put in our hands the imperial authority, according to His good pleasure . . . —bidding us after the manner of Peter, the head and chief of the Apostles, to feed his most faithful flock—we believe that there is nothing higher or greater that we can do in return than to govern in judgment and justice those who are committed by Him to our care.

The emperor may even have gone so far as to claim that he was both "king and priest." Such claims might rise logically from the growing spiritualization of the imperial authority, and they were not incompatible with the concept of the emperor as the equal of the apostles, but they could not pass unchallenged in the deeply religious society of the eighth century. Obviously unacceptable to St. Peter's other successor in Rome, they likewise drove the usually docile Eastern Church into rebellion.

The immediate subject of the dispute concerned the reverence due to religious images, or icons, but the ultimate implications reached to the very bases of theology and political theory. Earlier scholars often traced Leo III's aversion to icons to his Oriental background and to Islamic influences, a thesis reinforced by the accusations of ecclesiastical writers. More recently, however, it has been observed that the opposition to images originated within the church rather than with the emperor, and that archaeological discoveries, in the Umayyad desert palaces in particular, show that Muslim iconoclasm primarily characterized the puritanical Abbasid dynasty coming to power some twenty years after Leo's first iconoclastic decree. Whatever the immediate circumstances, an iconoclastic tradition was also deeply ingrained in the Christian heritage; the second commandment against the making of graven images was difficult to disregard.

In their defense of icons, their Iconodule partisans argued that the Decalogue had been intended for the Jews and that its precepts had been radically affected by the coming of Christ. The most distinguished theologian of the party, St. John of Damascus, went on to formulate the basic argument that the rejection of Christ's icons was in essence a rejection of the very core of Christianity, the doctrine of his incarnation: "If you do not worship the image neither do you cherish the Son of God who is the living image of the invisible God . . . I worship the image of Christ as God incarnate," a position reaffirmed a century later by the patriarch Photius: "He who denies that Christ can be painted, denies Him to have been born a man, and he who does not adore His image, clearly does not adore Him either." On both sides the arguments, far from dealing with reason or superstition, rested on fundamental points of doctrine. Under the circumstances, imperial decrees forbidding the worship of icons became religious rather than political pronouncements directly affecting the daily lives of all men, and projected the controversy far beyond the closed circle of intellectual disputations into smoldering or open civil war.

The century-long struggle, which outlived the Isaurian dynasty, may at first seem inconclusive for all of its repercussions. The initial period of Iconoclasm inaugurated by Leo III came to an end in the third generation during the reign of the empress Irene, who did not hesitate to have her son Constantine VI blinded to maintain herself in power. At the Second Council of Nicaea (787) presided over by her appointee, the patriarch Tarasius, the Iconoclastic doctrine was condemned. Irene's shocking coup d'état soon provoked a violent reaction which drove her from the throne and ended the dynasty, but the second period of Iconoclasm sponsored by the emperors Leo V, Michael II, and his son Theophilus ended in the ultimate victory of the Iconodules at the Council of Orthodoxy in 843. Nevertheless, the internal upheavals of the empire seriously compromised its international position, and the achievements of the early Isaurians were partly undone. The armies of the great Abbasid caliph Harun al-Rashid once again reached the neighborhood of Constantinople early in the ninth century, and civil war convulsed the eastern provinces after the murder of Leo V in 820. In the Balkans, the initial victories of Irene's successor, Nicephorus I, against the Slavs in Greece were more than offset by the disaster of 811, in which the emperor himself fell in battle before the reconstituted power of the Bulgars. Only the seemingly providential death of their khan, Krum, before the walls of Constantinople saved the besieged capital two years later.

The alienation of Italy grew apace. One of the by-products of the Arab conquest of Egypt and Palestine had been a massive flight of the orthodox Christian population toward southern Italy, which was largely re-Hellenized in the course of the seventh century. Early in the next century, Iconodule refugees, seeking asylum in Rome, pushed Pope Gregory III to condemn Leo III's innovations and his meddling in doctrinal affairs. The emperor's retaliatory transfer of Illyricum from the papal jurisdiction to that of the patriarch of Constantinople envenomed relations still further, and Rome drew closer to the Franks. Half a century later, the usurpation of Irene provided both the papacy and Charlemagne with an excuse for the coronation of a new emperor at Rome on Christmas day 800.

The international position of the emperor had been temporarily compromised by these developments, but within the empire, the Council of Orthodoxy proved but a Pyrrhic victory for the church. One of the crucial aspects of the controversy had been the *Basileus'* tampering with the faith. As St. John of Damascus had firmly stressed:

It appertains not to kings to make laws for the Church. Kings have not preached the word to you, but apostles and prophets. . . . Political welfare is the concern of kings: the ecclesiastical system is a matter for pastors and doctors; and this, brethren, is an act of brigandage.

Yet throughout the controversy, religious doctrine had invariably reflected the imperial will: inaugurated by Leo III and Constantine V, Iconoclasm had later been reestablished by Leo V and his successors, its first check was due to Irene's personal devotion to the cause of images, and the final victory of Orthodoxy was brought about by the empress-regent Theodora II. In their challenge of ecclesiastical authority, the emperors had emerged victorious. Thereafter, powerful patriarchs might occasionally exploit moments of imperial weakness, but by the middle of the ninth century the imperial apotheosis had been achieved. Post-Iconoclastic art presenting the haloed figures of the imperial consorts crowned by Christ and sharing with him a spaceless-timeless eternity underscored the victory. This confirmation of the newly achieved imperial status had far-reaching consequences. It blocked the possibility of Byzantine compromises with the upstart Germanic emperors and spread among the soon-to-be-converted Slavs the concept of the supreme rights of the imperial autocrat as head of the Orthodox church.

Even the seriousness of the international crisis may have been overstressed by later historians eager to blacken the reputation of Theophilus' son Michael III in order to justify his murder in 867 by the usurper Basil I, the Macedonian. The most serious reversals of the ninth century occurred at sea, where the neglect of the imperial navy, implicated in earlier seditions, led to the seizure of Sicily and Crete by Arab expeditionary forces from North Africa. The control of the sea lanes slipped temporarily from Byzantine hands. Far to the north, the spreading activity of the Vikings stretched constantly outward. In successive years, their expeditions struck Constantinople both from the Mediterranean and across the Black Sea from the new Scandinavian bases in Russia. Nevertheless, the empire successfully weathered these storms. Both Scandinavian attacks against the city were repulsed, and the imperial fleet, though unable to retake the lost islands from the Arabs, conducted successful raids on the Egyptian coast and reappeared in Dalmatia. On land, the Muslim capture of Amorium, the homeland of the reigning dynasty, in 838, was balanced by the renewal of the Khazar alliance and the great imperial victory of Poson in 863 which reestablished Byzantine domination over most of Asia Minor.

The vitality of the empire gradually emerging from the Muslim and Iconoclastic crises is perhaps best illustrated by its intellectual effervescence. The fostering of culture and the support of education had always been an imperial concern. The University of Constantinople had first been reorganized by Theodosius II in 425, but had fallen on hard times in the seventh century and perhaps even been closed in 726. Re-created by Michael III's uncle, the Caesar Bardas, and fostered by Bardas' rival, Theoctistus, the empress' favorite adviser, it soon became once more a brilliant cultural center closely linked with the imperial court. Far from being a theological school of the type later found in the West, the imperial university was a training school for the civil service. It had faculties of law and medicine as well as philosophy, mathematics, astronomy, and rhetoric.

The fame of its first director, Leo the Mathematician, was so widespread that the caliph vainly sought to entice him to Baghdad, and Muslim as well as Christian students flocked to his lectures. Equally distinguished was his colleague Photius, soon to be head of the imperial chancellery and patriarch, whose surviving notes are one of our best sources of information on lost classical works.

One of the most far-reaching triumphs of the young university intellectuals was the spread of the imperial culture and faith beyond the limits of the state. When the Russian attack of 860 made the renewal of the Khazar alliance imperative, the man chosen for this delicate mission was the most distinguished linguist among Photius' students, Cyril of Thessalonike, better known as Constantine. The activity of Cyril and his older brother Methodius bore even greater fruit in the West. Traveling in 863 to the court of the new Slavic principality of Great Moravia, the brothers brought with them not only the requested Christian Scriptures, but also a translation of the liturgy into the Slavic language, for which Cyril's linguistic talent had devised an alphabet. The following year, the ruler of the Bulgars likewise entered the Christian community, receiving baptism from a Greek bishop and changing his pagan name from Boris to Michael in honor of his imperial godfather. The work of Cyril and Methodius eventually proved transitory in Moravia, and even the Byzantine aspect of Bulgarian Christianity was temporarily compromised, but the foundation had been laid for the permanent cultural protectorate of the empire over Slavic eastern Europe.

One of the most dramatic aspects of the imperial revival in the ninth century was a violent clash with Rome: the Photian schism. In Constantinople the accession of the moderate and learned Photius to the patriarchal throne in 857, and the abdication of his intransigent predecessor Ignatius was an episode in the aftermath of Iconoclasm. In the ecclesiastical sphere, the problem raised was that of conciliar competence in the deposition of a patriarch. To the Eastern church, the conciliar decision was sufficient and final, but Pope Nicholas I maintained that only he had final jurisdiction in a matter of such importance. Engaged as he was in asserting his supreme authority over Western rulers and ecclesiastical dignitaries, Nicholas could not accept the designation of a patriarch, which for all of its traditional precedents was patently uncanonical, while the emperor could tolerate no interference with his prerogatives. The Isaurian adjudication of Illyricum to Constantinople still rankled at Rome, and the entire problem was reopened by the conversion of Bulgaria. The quarrel dragged on for some twenty years, beyond the life spans of both emperor and pope. Photius was excommunicated, deposed, and rehabilitated; Boris-Michael, making the most of the ambiguous status of Illyricum, equivocated, intrigued, and blackmailed to achieve the autonomy of the Bulgarian church. But, in the long run, the victory lay with the empire. Nicholas I's successor, John VIII, recognized the legitimacy of Photius' position, tacitly overlooking his uncanonical appointment, and subsequent popes, embroiled in the Roman crises of the ninth and tenth centuries, were in no position to challenge imperial prerogatives. Bulgaria remained within the spiritual and cultural sphere of Constantinople.

The schism itself, though boding ill for the future, reflects the survival of considerable Christian unity in this period. For all the acrimony of their messages, ambassadors and papal legates hastened unimpeded back and forth across the Mediterranean; diplomatic relations were maintained; the controversy ended in reconciliation and the renewal of communion between the two churches. Even in the midst of the difficulties, Cyril and Methodius' mission to Moravia, sponsored by Photius, received the blessing of Nicholas I. The breach between the East and the West was far from complete.

37   Later Byzantium

The imperial recovery initiated by the Amorians came to full flower with the reconstitution of the ecumenical empire by their successors the Macedonian emperors, who maintained themselves on the throne from 867 to 1056. The most immediate achievement of the new dynasty lay in the rapid expansion of the imperial frontiers. In the East, following the earlier victory of Poson, the Byzantine armies passed to the offensive, making the most of the fragmentation of the declining Abbasid caliphate. Recapturing the strategic pass of the Cilician gates controlling the access to Syria as early as 876, and crossing the Euphrates near Malatya in 931, the emperors pushed the attack along the entire border. The Syrian cities of Edessa, Aleppo, Antioch, Tiberias, Nazareth, and Damascus fell one by one, and in 975 the armies of the co-emperor John I Tzimisces reached the suburbs of Baghdad and possibly the vicinity of Jerusalem. The Transcaucasian campaigns of Basil II after 1000 rounded out the northeastern frontier with Armenian and Georgian territories. In the Balkans, the initial success of the Bulgars at the beginning of the tenth century, when their czar Symeon, following the example of his predecessor Krum, had besieged Constantinople, soon met with reverses. Symeon's son, Czar Peter, settled for a sonorous title and a secondhand imperial bride. But the final solution

was to come with Basil II, remembered by posterity under the ominous title Killer of the Bulgars. Abandoning the compromise peace of the preceding centuries, Basil attacked in the West as well as in the East, provoked by the belligerent attitude of the new Bulgarian czar Samuel. The final annihilation of the Bulgarian army in 1014 and the death of Samuel from shock at the sight of the blinded remnants of his troops sent back by Basil II marked the end of the First Bulgarian Empire. Its lands reverted to the empire in the form of ordinary *themes,* its autonomous ecclesiastical organization was reabsorbed into the fabric of the patriarchate of Constantinople. Farther afield, the Byzantine navy finally swept the Arabs from Cyprus and Crete by 965. The strategic port of Bari, throwing off its Carolingian allegiance, had long since opened its gates to an imperial army which went on to reconquer much of southern Italy. Once again the empire stretched from Palestine to the Adriatic, which was controlled on its Dalmatian as well as its Italian side through the overlordship of Venice. The imperial territory was now closer to that of Justinian's heyday than to the shrunken possession of the Heraclians and Isaurians.

Force of arms always proved the decisive factor in the imperial reconquest, but military victory was invariably prepared by the intricate workings of the highly sophisticated imperial diplomacy. In his book *On the Administration of the Empire,* destined for the edification of his heir, Basil I's grandson Constantine VII Porphyrogenitus expounded the arcana of imperial policy. The enemy was to be neutralized through alliances with his opponents, pacified with gifts, drawn into the imperial sphere of influence, and finally annihilated. This blueprint was systematically put into effect. The Bulgars were first immobilized by an imperial alliance with their neighbors the Croats. Next, Czar Peter received the title of *Basileus* and became the emperor's son-in-law. Then came the ruthless final settlement of the "Bulgarian question" by Basil II. In similar fashion, Constantinople recognized Ashot I of Armenia as king and addressed him as "son," before swallowing most of the territory of Armenia in the eleventh century. Negotiations with the Petchenegs of the Ukrainian steppes neutralized the danger of Russian raids, since the Petchenegs could lie in wait for returning raiders at the vulnerable portage of the Dnieper rapids. The death of the Kievan prince Sviatoslav, killed in ambush in 972 at the very point designated by Constantine VII, testifies to the effectiveness of the imperial military intelligence. The second stage of imperial policy was reached with the Christianization of Russia under Vladimir I in 989, which drew the country still closer to the orbit of Constantinople. Elaborate diplomatic relations were also maintained with the caliphate, as the presence of a mosque and an official styled "Consul of the Arabs" at the imperial court reveal.

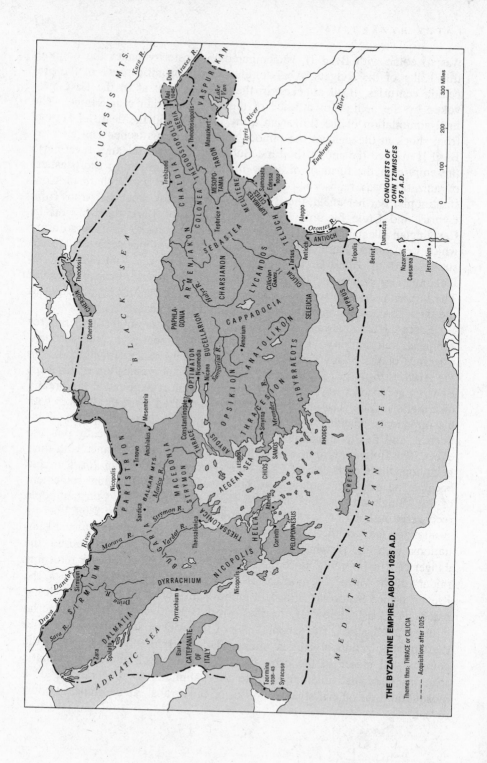

THE BYZANTINE EMPIRE, ABOUT 1025 A.D.

Themes thus: THRACE or CILICIA
—·—·— Acquisitions after 1025

CONQUESTS OF
JOHN TZIMISCES
975 A.D.

CAUCASUS MTS.

Kura R.

Araxes R.

Ani 1045

Dvin

VASPURAKAN

Lake Van

Tigris River

Iberia

Theodosiopolis

Manazkert

Euphrates River

Theodossiopolis

CHALDIA

COLONEA

ARMENIAKON

Trebizond

MESOPO-TAMIA

TARON

Samosata

Edessa 1032

TELUCH

Sebastea

MELITENE

Melitene

Germanicia

Euphrates River

PAPHLA-GONIA

CHARSIANON

LYKANDOS

Aleppo

Orontes R.

ANTIOCH

BUCELLARION

Tephrice

Halys R.

CAPPADOCIA

Cilician Gates

CILICIA

Antioch

Tripoli

Damascus

BLACK SEA

OPTIMATON

Nicomedia

Nicaea

Sangarius R.

Amorium

ANATOLIKON

Tarsus

SELEUCIA

Beirut

Nazareth

Caesarea

Jerusalem

CHERSON

Theodosia

Cherson

Constantinople

THRACE

OPSIKION

THRACESION

Meander R.

Smyrna

CIBYRAEOTS

CYPRUS

Mesembria

Anchialus

Tenovo

Sardica

BALKAN MTS.

PARISTRION

MACEDONIA

Maritsa R.

STRYMON

ABIDUS

AEGEAN SEA

SAMOS

LESBOS

CHIOS

RHODES

Nicopolis

Morava R.

Strymon R.

BULGARIA

Vardar R.

THESSALONICA

Thessalonica

HELLAS

Athens

Corinth

NICOPOLIS

PELOPONNESUS

CRETE

Danube River

Drava R.

Sava R.

SIRMIUM

Sirmium

Drin R.

DALMATIA

Zara

Spalato

Dyrrachium

DYRRACHIUM

Nicopolis

ADRIATIC SEA

Bari

CATEPANATE OF ITALY

Taormina 1038-43

Syracuse

MEDITERRANEAN SEA

0   100   200   300 Miles

The eminent success of the Macedonian emperors resulted in a large measure from the stability of the dynasty, which made possible a long-term and consistent policy. A remarkable allegiance developed between the people and the legitimate imperial line, and the Macedonian emperors adopted the shrewd tactic of associated outstanding military figures to the throne as co-emperors or tutor-emperors. By enlisting such distinguished personalities as the admiral Romanus Lecapenus and the great generals Nicephorus II Phocas and John I Tzimisces, the legitimate rulers offset their own shortcomings while preventing these able men from undertaking seditious enterprises. At the same time the Macedonians came close to achieving a true dynastic principle while remaining ostensibly within the Roman constitutional framework which made of the emperor an elected magistrate. The legal fiction was maintained as before: the successive emperors were formally acclaimed and crowned, but the belief that the only true emperor was a *porphyrogenitus,* a son of the reigning monarch born in the *porphyra,* or purple chamber of the palace, entrenched itself in the popular mind. Neither the youth nor the illegitimate birth of the sickly Constantine VII Porphyrogenitus, nor the minority of Basil II and his brother Constantine VIII, nor even the ludicrous vagaries of the foolish old women who closed the Macedonian line, could break the passionate allegiance of the people to the dynasty. The sons of Romanus Lecapenus, the great magnates of Basil II's early reign, and the adopted son of the elderly empress Zoë all learned at their expense the popular belief that God himself watched over the Macedonian house. The succession was not effectively challenged so long as a single member of the family could be found.

Both the legitimate members of the dynasty and their coopted colleagues maintained high ideals of public service. Despite the growth of the bureaucracy necessitated by the expansion of the empire, no aspect of the life of his subjects lay beyond the attentive supervision of the ruler. The scholarly Constantine VII informs us of every minutia of imperial ceremonies and of the functioning of the *theme* system; the new general codification of the *Basilics* matched in size and inclusiveness the *Code* of Justinian. Our best mirror for the paternal if close regimentation of daily life is found in the manual of city administration called the *Book of the Prefect.* Not the church but the state maintained hospitals, orphanages, and asylums; imperial monopolies determined the types, standards, and prices for every type of silk and brocades; even in the other sectors of the guided economy, wages, prices, and workmanship were closely supervised. Legislation protected native artisans and merchants from foreign competition, but also took measures against unfair domestic practices, profiteering middlemen, price fixing, and the dumping of goods. Taxes were constantly watched and abuses severely punished. With unexpected realism for the

Middle Ages, the law acknowledged that interest on loans was usury and a sin in the eyes of the church, but that the welfare of the citizens was best served by the recognition of the practice and the regulation of its rates. The activities of foreign merchants were strictly overseen: they were restricted to specific residential quarters outside the walls, forbidden to settle permanently even there, allowed to enter into the city only in small unarmed groups watched over by an imperial official, forced to sell at fixed prices, and forbidden to export certain items. The balance of international trade solidly favored the empire, and Constantinople was its center.

Within the city walls, urban planning preserved the seemly appearance of the capital from individual fantasies:

. . . we decree that no one may erect [protruding balconies or solaria] unless they be separated by a distance of ten feet from that of the neighbors. Similarly if anyone wishing to alter the roof of his house should cover it with marble slabs, he shall not be allowed to carry out this alteration until he remove to the above mentioned ten foot interval from the neighboring buildings.

Nor did the countryside escape the all-seeing eye of the emperor. To prevent extortion or collusion with local magnates, governors of *themes* were forbidden to own land within their jurisdiction or receive gifts during their term of office; neither they nor any member of their family might marry within the district. Imperial legislation repeatedly protected the rights of soldier-farmers to their land as long as they performed their military duties. The free farmer communities were sedulously guarded against the pressure of wealthy or powerful neighbors: land within the community had to be offered for sale first to relatives or co-owners, then to immediate neighbors, then to other members of the community, and only failing all these to outsiders. Men might not buy land from persons outside their social class; specifically the *dunatoi,* or mighty, could not acquire the lands of the poor. A soldier's land alienated for whatever reason, especially debt, was subject to a thirty-year moratorium; if illegally acquired, it reverted to the original owner with all its improvements, and the buyer was not indemnified. Finally the community was jointly responsible for the taxes of its members. These regulations clearly left little margin for private initiative, but they testify to the constant responsibility of the state toward its citizens.

The wealth of the empire, drawn from commerce and conquest, manifested itself in the splendor of its buildings, which dazzled foreign visitors in the capital and in the whole of the imperial territory. In Constantinople, the *Book of Ceremonies* celebrated the magnificence of imperial protocol, and the monarchs repaired the damaged dome of Hagia Sophia, restoring it to its former splendor, extended the palace, and built new churches. From the Euphrates to Italy, great buildings and collections of illuminated manuscripts still reflect the extent of the "Macedonian renaissance" whose influence may even have reached Muslim Spain.

Culture was indispensable for any successful career. Except for the bluff Basil II, the emperors personally led the way and continued to favor intellectuals. Leo VI the Wise, the student of the learned Photius, was an excellent rhetorician; his son Constantine VII turned the imperial palace into a meeting place for scholars and literati. University graduates continued to fill the upper reaches of the civil service, and even middle-class women, such as the mother of the scholar-diplomat Michael Psellus, were sufficiently literate to supervise the homework of their sons. The only recognized aristocracy was one of administrative office and court dignity, not birth or wealth, and uneducated boors, whatever their social background, were subjects for derision and contempt.

So much brilliance attracted the admiration, envious and ill-willed though it might be, of contemporaries. Macedonian Constantinople, with a population approaching the million mark, ten times that of most contemporary Western capitals, was the cynosure of all eyes. Muslims, Jews, and Christians, Syrians, Armenians, Greeks, Russians, Bulgars, Italians, Germans, Normans, and Anglo-Saxons rubbed shoulders in the capital, vying for advancement and favors. Russian tribesmen, whose first focus had been the caliphate, now shifted their sights toward Tsargrad, the imperial city, first as raiders and pirates, later as treaty merchants, spiritual sons, and members of the famed imperial Varangian guard. Bulgar and Russian princes, and even the Western emperor Otto I intrigued to obtain imperial brides and to associate themselves with the ruling dynasty. The manifest antagonism of Otto's ambassador, Bishop Liutprand of Cremona, cannot disguise his grudging admiration. Liutprand's entire report of his unsuccessful mission was a willful distortion and reads like a parody of the complaints of latter-day tourists: the food was garlicky and bad, the natives rude, buildings drafty, drinking water almost unobtainable, and customs officials unreasonable. But not even he could remain unmoved at the sight of the emperor seated on the great throne flanked by bronze lions and gilt trees filled with birds. At the ambassador's approach the lions roared, the birds sang, and the throne was raised aloft by invisible means. With unconscious candor Liutprand admits that ". . . when the lions roared and the birds sang each according to its own species at my entrance, I experienced no terror and felt no admiration because I had been thoroughly warned about these things by those who knew them well." The unwarned Russian ambassadors thought themselves in heaven.

In the eyes of the world, and most of all in its own, Byzantium seemed at its zenith, and its greatest danger probably stemmed from the complacency and arrogance with which the imperial authorities viewed their exalted state. The ultimate purpose of Constantine VII's advice to his son was "that the nations may bring thee their gifts and thou mayest be adored of them that dwell upon the earth." The emperor insisted that no foreigner was worthy of entering the imperial house and stressed the fact that the princess Maria Lecapena granted to Peter of Bulgaria was not a *porphyrogenita*. The same would be said of Otto II's bride, Theophano. The full imperial princess Anna was granted to a Russian bridegroom only under the double stress of civil war and threatened invasion.

Similarly, the Byzantine chancellery recognized the existence of other imperial titles only in moments of direst crisis. The ambassadors of Michael I might greet Charlemagne as *Basileus* at the moment when the Bulgars were at the gates of Constantinople, and Michael II write to Louis I as "my imperial brother" in 824 while civil war was raging in the East, but hardly had Byzantine armies retaken Bari in 876 than Basil I accused his Carolingian counterpart of usurping the imperial title. Liutprand of Cremona was curtly reminded that the only emperor of the Romans resided in Constantinople and that his master, "the King of the Germans," had best remember that fact. Saving face even in times of trouble, the chancellery never failed to underscore the gulf separating barbarian *basilei* from the one and only true *"Basileus* and *Autocrator* of the Romans." Such an attitude is easily understandable and perhaps excusable in its chronological context. In the East, the disintegrating Baghdad caliphate was the plaything of barbarian generals, acting as kingmakers among the pathetic descendants of the Abbasid house. In the West, the imperial dream, fallen into chaos after the disappearance of the Carolingians, was barely emerging from the destruction wrought by the new Viking and Magyar invaders. The pope himself, unable to keep mastery even over his own city of Rome, was in no position to maintain the haughty tone of Nicholas I. The Macedonian *Basileus* would indeed have had to be superhuman to overlook his military and cultural preeminence.

For all its justifications, the self-involvement of Byzantium with its achievements and its great past was a potential threat to its future. The antiquarian qualities of its intellectual and artistic "renaissance," enchanted with archaism and anachronism, the scorn of barbarian learning and the refusal to learn from foreigners, the inability to understand the language of fellow Christians—all these were ominous harbingers. In size, military prowess, careful legislation, wealth, and culture the Macedonian empire might seem a reincarnation of Justinian's, but it added few innovations or improvements to the past it so jealously guarded.

Internally, serious cracks threatened the brilliant surface of society. The necessity constantly to repromulgate the legislation against the encroachments of great landowners did not augur well for its effectiveness, and most of its provisions had to be repealed during the course of the eleventh century. A powerful landed aristocracy grew steadily outside court circles, threatening the imperial authority and disrupting the economy. Attached to their lands and concerned with the safeguarding of the frontiers, these provincial magnates viewed with contempt and antagonism the civilian bureaucracy, largely risen from the middle class, which crowded around the court and reciprocated their hatred with interest. The Church, which had mastered the techniques of arousing popular support during the period of Iconoclasm, often sided with the military against the emperor. When the extinction of the Macedonian line freed the various factions to play kingmakers, military and civilian emperors alternated on the throne in an increasingly acrimonious struggle.

Meanwhile new threats grew unnoticed both in the East and in Italy. The difficulties in the West were largely nonmilitary, although a band of Norman adventurers profited from the disaffection of local Byzantine generals to conquer most of southern Italy. As in the case of the earlier Photian schism, the Great Schism of 1054 had both Roman and Constantinopolitan aspects. At Rome, the activity of the Saxon emperors brought new Germanic pressures to bear on the papacy, while the growing influence of the reforming party within the Church revived the ideas of papal supremacy and independence from secular interference once formulated by Nicholas I. The election of reforming popes by the middle of the century, and their alliance with the new Norman state, whose conquests made it the natural enemy of Byzantium, understandably stiffened the attitude of Rome toward the East. In Constantinople, the ambitious patriarch Michael Cerularius, making the most of the prestige of his see among the Slavs and of the weakness of the last Macedonian heiresses, attempted to reassert the authority of the Church against the Crown. Refusing all compromises, he thwarted imperial policy, plotted with the army, and fomented popular uprisings. The East-West controversy, which centered ostensibly on theological questions, ended in a deadlock, but was not immediately irreparable. The emperor-consort, Constantine IX Monomachus, worried by the Italian crisis, was ready to make concessions. The main violence of the quarrel came from the intractable personality of Michael Cerularius and the equally intransigent papal legate, cardinal Humbert of Silva-Candida. Even after Michael's riots had blocked all negotiations and Humbert had theatrically laid his bull of excommunication on the high altar of Hagia Sophia on July 16, 1054, the breach might have been healed. The legates were legally powerless, since the pope's death in April had canceled their mandate. The mutual excommunication of the patriarch and the legates did not necessarily involve the ultimate protagonists: the pope and the emperor. No one could guess at the time that this schism would be more permanent than the many which had preceded it, and, in fact, all cooperation between Rome and Constantinople was not ended, as the Crusades later demonstrated. But the schism manifested once again the fundamental differences separating the two halves of Christendom. The Latins kept a memory of Byzantine double-dealing from the conflicting policies of the emperor and the patriarch; the Greeks did not forget the scandal of rude and unorthodox foreigners profaning the holiest shrine of their sacred city. Mutual antagonism was strengthened, and the lesson of the ease with which popular risings could be instigated in defense of the faith was not lost on posterity.

The threat in the East was more immediately evident. The imperial system of balance of power in this area had been destroyed by the Petcheneg replacement of the Khazars and the neutralization of help from Christianized Russia, gradually cut off from the Black Sea. The buffer kingdoms of Bulgaria and Armenia had been obliterated by the annexations of Basil II. The new military frontier society which had grown in central Anatolia out of the perpetual state of war with the Muslims had little in common with the population of the capital. Such were the inauspicious conditions under which the empire had to face the unforeseen attack of the Seljuk Turks.

The primary interest of the Seljuks was not the West, but rather the control of Baghdad and the rich lands of northern Syria as well as the destruction of the Fatimid caliphate in Egypt, whose power threatened the Abbasids and whose heterodox Shi'ite beliefs were an abomination to the rigidly orthodox Turks. The imperial defeat at Manazkert in 1071 by the Seljuk sultan Alp Arslan was not the final catastrophe that it is often depicted as being, but the loss of Anatolia by the empire was a gradual and indirect result of the Turkish invasions. Preoccupied with the task of consolidating their power farther to the east, the Seljuks used Asia Minor as a dumping ground for their restless Turcoman contingents, whose normal pattern of nomadism and pillage presented a constant threat to any stable society. Moreover, the Seljuks had neither sufficient personnel nor the administrative experience to handle the vast territories they had overrun. Anarchy resulted, and Asia Minor was fragmented among local tribal chieftains. The warlike and pastoral Turcomans, who required large expanses of grassland for their flocks, obliterated cities, deforested the land, destroyed its agriculture, and permanently altered its climate and economy. Anatolia became a land of steppes, marshes, and dust bowls. The untamed Byzantine border soldiers, the *akritai,* found much in common with the fanatical Turcoman warriors, the *gazi,* and many conversions to Islam altered the sociological picture as well. The entire fabric of urban, sedentary, Christian Asia Minor was transformed. With the coming of the Seljuks the last main source of imperial resources and manpower was irretrievably lost.

The collapse of the Byzantine state under the stress of these losses and of internal strife was averted for a time by the accession in 1081 of Alexis I Comnenus, the representative of one of the great Anatolian families. But the victory of the Comneni also marked the domination of the state by the military aristocracy, which gradually resulted in the obliteration of the civilian bureaucratic pattern Byzantium had inherited from the Roman past. Since it was out of the question for Alexis I to renew the Macedonian legislation curbing the great landowners, of whom he was one, the government relied more and more for its defense on mercenaries and the good will of provincial magnates, to whom it granted large estates, or *pronoia,* in exchange for their services. In theory the recipients of these territories, the *pronoiars,* were imperial officials, and their lands never became hereditary. But the military character of the grants, the fiscal and legal immunities which were soon associated with them, and the gradual binding of the peasants to these lands assimilated them far more to Western feudal holdings than to the centralized bureaucratic system of the earlier empire.

Alexis Comnenus and his successors, John II and Manuel I, were brilliant commanders. At the head of their armies or maneuvering skillfully among their divided enemies, the Comneni regained much of the lost territory. It was the empire's Indian summer. The Balkans were successfully defended against Norman inroads from Italy, the Petchenegs and Serbs defeated, the coast, if not the interior, of Anatolia reconquered. Marriage alliances were negotiated with Hungary and Germany. By the middle of the twelfth century imperial armies made victorious reappearances in Syria and Italy. Manuel Comnenus' entrance into Antioch in 1159, adorned with the full imperial regalia and surrounded by the glittering Varangian guard, followed at a distance by the unarmed king of Jerusalem, and preceded by the bareheaded and barefooted prince of Antioch leading the emperor's horse by the bridle, spelled out all too clearly to a population enchanted by visible symbols who was the master of the Crusader states.

However, these remarkable achievements proved transitory. The decentralization of the government forced the emperor to rely heavily on expensive mercenary contingents, and the catastrophic defeat of Myriokephalon in 1176 completed the disaster of Manazkert one century earlier. The *pronoia* multiplied, limiting imperial jurisdiction. Central European alliances proved inconclusive, and the powerful Hohenstaufen empire stood in the way of Western reconquests. The economic stability of the empire was deeply compromised, and the imperial currency had to be devalued. The concession of extensive trade privileges and customs im-

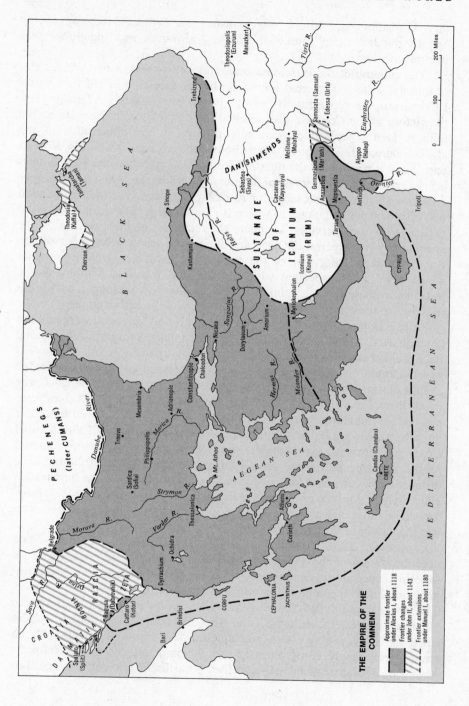

THE EMPIRE OF THE
COMNENI

Approximate frontier
under Alexius I, about 1118

Frontier changes
under John II, about 1143

Frontier extensions
under Manuel I, about 1180

munities to Venice in 1082, soon followed by similar grants to the other Italian maritime cities, showed the seriousness of the crisis. For the first time, the balance and initiative of trade turned against Constantinople, and the imperial fleets gradually atrophied as foreign merchants took over. The long nautical and commercial tradition tracing its origin back to ancient Greece was coming to an end.

Most serious of all, the breach with the West deepened beyond recall during the period of the Crusades. The growing antagonism between the Latins and the Greeks was not a systematic or constant phenomenon. The break in ecclesiastical ties that followed the Schism of 1054 did not preclude further contacts. The bride of John II Comnenus was a Hungarian princess; his son Manuel married the sister-in-law of the Holy Roman Emperor Conrad of Franconia. On their way to the Holy Land in 1097, the Crusaders stopped in Constantinople, and with the exception of the count of Toulouse, all of the leaders acknowledged the overlordship of the emperor Alexis I by doing him homage and swearing the full feudal oath. Despite misgivings caused by the presence among the Crusaders of his bitter Norman enemies, the emperor gave them supplies and his armies guided them as far as Antioch.

Circumstances seemed even more favorable during the reign of Manuel I. The emperor, twice married to Latin princesses, seems to have possessed a singularly winning personality and to have been enamored of Western ways. Latin chroniclers speak of him as a perfect knight, invincible in tournaments, and praise his munificence and generosity. Manuel encouraged concessions and amiable discussions in matters of religion, and his troops campaigned side by side with the Latin armies in Egypt. The very transformation of Byzantine society in this period brought it closer to that of the contemporary West. The vast *pronoia,* worked by serfs and all but free of imperial supervision, the turbulent military aristocracy, the gradual deurbanization of the land, and the reliance on a rural economy provided an atmosphere familiar to the Latin feudal nobles. On the basis of these outward similarities the two societies momentarily fraternized, and the fate of future relations hung in the balance.

Disastrously for Byzantium, the forces of disruption were, however, to gain the day. Imperial diplomacy and good intentions could not dispel the atmosphere of mutual distrust and dislike present from the first confrontation. The disasters of the late eleventh century had abated none of the emperor's pretensions; like the later Bourbons, "they had learned nothing and forgotten nothing." Alexis' daughter the princess Anna Comnena sneered at the boorishness and deceit of the Latin "barbarians," while the demands of Byzantine court ceremonial shocked the touchy pride of Western barons. The imperial authorities in Constantinople, alarmed from the

first by the arrival of the Normans, saw their fears justified by the Crusaders' refusal to return Antioch to them, although the oath sworn by their
leaders included the retrocession of all reconquered imperial territory. On
their side, the Crusaders claimed that the withdrawal of the imperial army
before Antioch had been a betrayal which freed them from their commitment. This version, envenomed by Norman propaganda, gained currency in
the West, particularly at Rome, where the pope, faced by the formidable
threat of the German empire, was in no position to dispense with the
support of his Norman allies. Increasingly in Latin eyes, therefore, the
Greeks became traitors as well as heretics unfit to consort with true Christians. In 1147, the leaders of the Second Crusade had seriously discussed the
seizure of Constantinople on the way to Palestine, and blamed imperial
treachery for their failures. The marriage in 1186 of the future emperor
Henry VI and the Norman heiress Constance made the Holy Roman
Empire the heir of Norman enmity toward Byzantium. By the Third Crusade relations had deteriorated to the point where Latin leaders preferred
to avoid imperial territory, and both Frederic Barbarossa in the Balkans
and Richard Lionheart in Cyprus comported themselves as though on
enemy soil. The death of Manuel Comnenus brought matters to the explosion point. A coalition of imperial officials, outraged by the favors show-
ered by the emperor on the Latins, of the Greek clergy, still unreconciled
with Rome, and of the city population of Constantinople, ruined by the
commercial concessions granted to Italian merchants, backed Manuel's
cousin Andronicus Comnenus. A formidable uprising in 1182 resulted in
the murder of the Latin empress dowager, the overthrow of her young son
Alexis II, and the massacre of all the Latins in the capital. Within twenty
years Western retaliation brought about the sack of Constantinople by the
Fourth Crusade. The irrevocable had now taken place.

The enigmatic figure of Andronicus Comnenus, enlightened reformer
and brutal oppressor, brilliant general and sensual voluptuary, soon disappeared in the whirlwind which he had raised, leaving a defenseless empire stripped of its last bulwark against the aroused fury of the West: the
military aristocracy decimated by the imperial reign of terror. In spite of
the paradoxes of his character, Andronicus had at least shared his family's
devotion to duty; his successors, the Angeli, seem to have raised their
sights no higher than family feuds and personal enrichment, while the
empire spiraled downward into chaos. The Normans renewed their attacks,
seizing the strategic ports of Dyrrachium and Thessalonike. Native Balkan
rulers reasserted their independence: the brothers Peter and Asen in
Bulgaria and the Grand Župan Stephen Nemanja in Serbia laid the foundations of new states on former imperial territory. Far to the east, a
secondary Comnenian line entrenched itself in Trebizond under the pro-

tection of the powerful queen Tamar of Georgia and refused to recognize the Angeli, while other Comnenian territories in Asia Minor were swallowed by the minor Seljuk successor states. Under these conditions it is little wonder that an effective opposition could not be made by the fragmented empire when the armies of the Fourth Crusade appeared under the walls of Constantinople in June, 1203.

Unfortunately for the future of Eastern Christendom, the Latins furnished no better answers for the crisis than had been found by the Greeks. The greatest damage to the new Latin empire created by the Crusaders was probably the bitter hatred instilled in the native population by the brutal sack of the capital and by the attempt to force Latin practices and jurisdiction on the Greek Church. The leaders of the Crusade were themselves aware of the harm of their actions; the chronicler Geoffroi de Villehardouin sadly confessed that because of the sins of the looters, "Our Lord began to love them less," and Pope Innocent III wrote with profound indignation:

How can the Church of the Greeks be expected to return to devotion to the Apostolic See when it has seen the Latins setting an example of evil and doing the devil's work so that already, and with good reason, the Greeks hate them worse than dogs.

Ominously the Greek historian in exile, Nicetas Choniates, recorded the native point of view:

The accursed Latins . . . lust after our possessions and would like to destroy our race . . . between them and us there is a wide gulf of hatred. . . . Even the Saracens are merciful and kind [in comparison with these creatures] who bear the cross of Christ on their shoulders.

Only in the Morea, as the Peloponnese came to be called, did the Latins wisely invite the cooperation of their Greek subjects; elsewhere the insulted *pronoiars* and the population in general rallied sullenly around their implacable clergy.

Even on its own terms, however, the new empire was not viable. Factions had appeared among the leaders of the Crusade even before the siege of Constantinople, and the entire expedition had been excommunicated by Pope Innocent III. The Venetians were the only gainers from the events. They obtained control of the new Latin patriarchate of Constantinople together with the church of Hagia Sophia, and made their doge "lord of a quarter and a half of the Roman Empire"; all the bases necessary for an absolute control of communications and trade were in their hands. The new emperor, Baldwin of Flanders, was in a far more precarious position. Elected with the help of the Venetians, who feared the greater prestige of

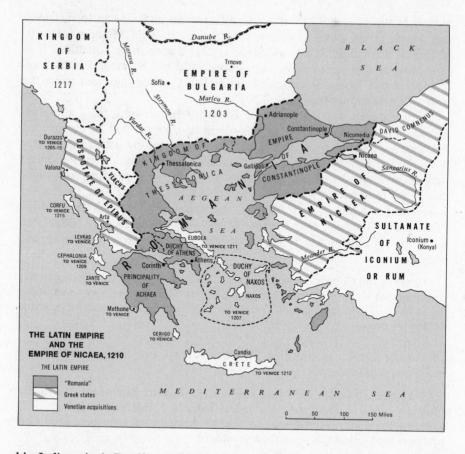

THE LATIN EMPIRE
AND THE
EMPIRE OF NICAEA, 1210

THE LATIN EMPIRE

"Romania"

Greek states

Venetian acquisitions

his Italian rival, Boniface of Montferrat, Baldwin was at best a compromise choice. From the first, the characteristic weakness of the Latin empire, as of the Crusader kingdom of Jerusalem, was the inability of the ruler to assert his superiority. Chosen by his equals, with an inadequate territorial base and a sacked capital, hampered by the multiple regulations of feudal customs, the emperor was entirely dependent on the good will of vassals whose primary interest was the consolidation of their own domains. The Greek empire in exile at Nicaea proved too strong to be driven out of Asia Minor, and in Epirus another Greek dynasty defied the intruders. The papacy remained antagonistic to a patriarchate created without its permission. Rashly the Crusaders spurned the overtures of the third and ablest of the Asen brothers, Kalojan, or Johannitza, whom Innocent III had crowned king of Bulgaria almost immediately after the capture of Constantinople. Reviving the bitter memory of Basil II, Kalojan styled himself "killer of the

Romans," whom he routed near Andrinople in April, 1205. Less than a year after his coronation, Baldwin of Flanders vanished on the battlefield, and two years later Boniface of Montferrat, king of Thessalonike, fell in the Bulgar war. Despite the accession of Baldwin's abler brother, Henry of Hainault, the empire was soon at bay:

> The land of Constantinpole was as if deprived of all protection. The lord emperor . . . was a pauper. All the paid knights departed. The ships of the Venetians, Pisans, Anconitans, and other nations were ready to leave, and some indeed had already left. When we saw that the land was abandoned we feared danger because it was surrounded by enemies. Asen, king of the Vlachs, menaced it from the north, Vatatzes [of Nicaea] from the east and south, and Manuel [of Epirus] from the west. Therefore we proposed to negotiate. . . .

Only the division of the enemy permitted survival for a time. On July 25, 1261, almost without opposition, and probably with the collusion of the city population, a Greek army reentered triumphantly into Constantinople.

The victory of 1261 belonged to the emperor of Nicaea, although his empire, hemmed in between Latin and Seljuk principalities and unrecognized by Trebizond or Epirus, had had an inauspicious beginning. The first emperor in exile, Theodore I Lascaris, was not of outstandingly noble family, and his coronation outside Constantinople, albeit by the patriarch, was of dubious legitimacy. The policy of the Lascarid emperors to return to earlier Macedonian traditions of social legislation, a guided economy, and centralization around a learned court produced at best a pale shadow of former splendor. The main trump of the Nicaean house was its unquestionable diplomatic skill, which made it the true heir of its more powerful predecessors. Intriguing with the Western emperor to exploit Hohenstaufen opposition to the papacy, which now rallied to the Latin empire; allied with Kalojan's great successor, John II Asen; continually fomenting dissentions among its enemies, Nicaea outstayed all its rivals. First the ruler of Epirus, who also claimed the imperial title, fell before the Bulgars at the Battle of Klokotnica in 1230. A decade later, after the death of Czar John II Asen, who styled himself "In Christ our God Czar and Autocrator of the Bulgars," and proved the equal of Nicaea in duplicity and talent, the Second Bulgarian Empire, sacked by the Mongols, began to disintegrate. The last Latin emperor, Baldwin II, ascended the throne in 1228 as a child of eleven, adding the troubles of a long regency to an already impossible situation. The capture of most of the lords of the Morea in 1259 at the Battle of Pelagonia allowed the new Nicaean emperor, Michael VIII Paleologus, to blackmail them out of most of their lands. His alliance with Genoa in 1261, neutralizing the Venetian navy, sealed the doom of Constantinople. On August 15, the Feast of the Assumption of the Virgin, preceded by the icon symbolizing her return to her favorite city cleansed of heretical pollution, Michael VIII entered Constantinople in a solemn procession. At the church of Hagia Sophia, the emperor and empress were recrowned to underscore the reestablishment of legitimacy and tradition.

The remarkable talent of Michael VIII had won back the imperial prize, but even though he successfully walked the tightrope of international intrigue for the rest of his days and bested all the coalitions raised against him, his accession proved the beginning of a two-century agony for the empire. The catastrophic results of the Fourth Crusade could not be undone: the empire regained by Michael was only a fragment. In northern Greece and the Morea, Frankish principalities survived. Venice kept the control of the sea lanes and of the islands of the archipelago. Trebizond remained out of reach, and the loyalty of Epirus and the Morea was at best doubtful. Most of Asia Minor was in enemy hands, and in the Balkans the Serbian empire of the Nemanjids grew constantly more threatening. Not even the national, Greek cohesion of the new empire, stripped of its Slavic and Oriental lands, could offset the fact that little more than a narrow band of territory on either side of the capital was an inadequate base for the survival of the state. No longer the master of its own destiny, the empire lingered at the sufferance of external forces.

The internal situation accelerated the process of disintegration. The Paleologues had neither the prestige nor the power to maintain the Nicaean attempt at social legislation against the *pronoiars,* whose centrifugal tendencies obliterated the last vestiges of centralization. Unchecked grants of fiscal immunity perilously reduced the shrunken finances of the state. The abandonment not only of trade but of the remaining customs revenues to the Italian republics left Constantinople at their mercy. From the middle of the fourteenth century, Byzantium, bereft of its navy, became a minor land power, flooded by cheap goods from the West, its gold reserves drained out by the unfavorable balance of trade enforced by Italian warships. In 1348 the revenue of Constantinople was a paltry 30,000 gold pieces as against the 200,000 of Genoese Pera across the Golden Horn. The imperial crown jewels went to secure indispensable loans, and in 1355 the strategic island of Tenedos commanding the entrance to the Straits had to be sold for 30,000 ducats. The ultimate humiliation was reached in 1369 when the emperor John V was arrested for debt in Venice, while seeking financial assistance in the West.

The poverty of the empire also intensified internal disorders. In 1304 unpaid Catalan mercenary companies ravaged Asia Minor, stormed across the Straits, wrested Athens from its Frankish dynasty, and installed themselves for sixty years in central Greece under the distant overlordship of the king of Aragon. In 1342 the wealthy city of Thessalonike was seized by a popular party, which proclaimed a program of social welfare and religious puritanism, massacred the upper classes, and established a commune which maintained itself until 1350, thus isolating the city from the rest of the empire. The development of local separatist tendencies, also visible in aristocratic circles, exploited quarrels within the imperial family resulting from the absence of a clear order of succession. Both the opposition of the young Andronicus III to his grandfather Andronicus II and the usurpation of John VI Cantacuzenus against the legitimate heir John V Paleologus found regional support which weakened still further the cohesion of the empire.

The continuous state of civil war in the mid-fourteenth century also aided foreign powers. At various points in his career, John Cantacuzenus owed his survival to the support of the Serbian czar or the Ottoman sultan. The danger in Serbia was the first to manifest itself. Nemanja's second son, Stephen the First-Crowned, had been recognized as king as early as 1217, and two years later his brother St. Sava had been consecrated archbishop by the patriarch of Nicaea. Checked at first by internal difficulties and the rise of the Asen dynasty in Bulgaria, the Nemanjids began to regain their superiority with the accession of Stephen-Uroš II Milutin in 1282. By 1299 the Serbian czar successfully coerced Andronicus II into giving him his daughter the princess Simonis in a marriage which reflected all too well the new fallen state of Byzantium. Not only was Simonis, a *porphyrogenita,* given to a barbarian whose court had horrified the imperial envoys, but there was little hope that the five-year-old princess would have much influence over a man old enough to be her grandfather. The final crushing of the Bulgars in the next generation at the Battle of Velbužd in 1330 laid the basis for the Serbian expansion under its greatest czar, Stephen-Uroš IV Dušan (1331–1355). Overrunning the whole of Macedonia, and profiting from the war raging around John VI Cantacuzenus, Dušan had himself crowned at Skoplje in 1346 with a new and threatening title: "In Christ our God pious *Basileus* and *Autocrator* of the Serbians and the Romans." The subsequent conquest of Albania, Epirus, and Thessaly bolstered Dušan's claim that he was "Lord of almost the whole of the Roman Empire." Constantinople could only thank providence for the czar's premature death and the rapid disintegration of his realm, which preserved the city from Serbian domination.

Where the Serbs had failed, the Turks would be successful. The origins of the Ottoman state are lost in legend, but two factors seem to have provided for its greatness. Its exposed position close to Constantinople meant either early annihilation by the empire or the forging of a powerful nucleus under the stress of constant war. The remoteness of the Ottoman principality from the East did not imply a lack of communications, for the great east-west highway across Anatolia kept it in economic and, more importantly, ideological contact with the centers of Islam. Perpetual de-

BYZANTINE LANDS
UNDER MANUEL II

BYZANTINE TERRITORY

about 1340
about 1350
in 1403

0   50   100   150 Miles

fenders of Islam, placed in the first line of battle, the Ottomans revived the ideal of the *gazi* warrior for the faith, and consequently rallied Muslim loyalties against the infidel. Byzantine internal dissensions furthered their undertakings. Despite its expansion in western Asia Minor, the Ottoman state was still a minor power when its support of John Cantacuzenus made possible its expansion into the Balkans. The victories of Sultan Murad I, master of Andrinople in 1365, of Macedonia and southern Serbia at the Battle of the Marica in 1371, lord of the Balkans on the tragic field of Kossovo in 1389, which cost the life of the victor, isolated Constantinople from the West. Only the ill-fated campaign of Murad's son Bayezid I Ilderim against a new Mongol invasion led by Tamerlane, culminating in the Turkish disaster at Ankara in 1402, gave another fifty years' grace to the empire.

Faced with mortal threats in the east and the west, and a hopeless situation at home, the only conceivable salvation for Byzantium lay in help from the Latins. Realizing the common danger, some Westerners rallied against the Turks, but both the latter-day crusades of Nicopolis (1396) and Varna (1444), insufficiently planned and supported, ended in disaster. In the main, the West, concerned with its own problems—the Babylonian Captivity of the Church and the Hundred Years' War—had little attention to spare for distant Eastern woes. Even when the Latins were willing to help Byzantium, the price they invariably demanded was the recognition of the Roman ecclesiastical superiority which they had failed to impose during their own domination. Again and again—in 1274 at Lyons, in the name of the shrewd Michael VIII, who may have thought that Constantinople was "well worth a mass"; nearly a century later, by the emperor John V in person, during his journey for help to Rome; finally, in desperation, at the Council of Florence in 1438–1439—Byzantine rulers accepted the union with Rome. But, though they might do this in their own name, they soon found that they could not force the union on their subjects. Fanning the memory of Latin hatred, appealing to the people to save their faith from heresy, the Orthodox clergy made it impossible to implement the imperial policy, and the repeated failure of the union after solemn oaths only instilled further in Western minds the long-held beliefs about Byzantine duplicity.

The last blow to the empire was the disaffection of the intellectuals, the traditional supporters of the court. The migration of scholars which enriched Italian culture was a drain on the empire; insufficient talent remained, and for the first time mental stagnation and anti-intellectualism manifested themselves at Constantinople. The artistic tradition proved strong enough to produce another renaissance and such masterpieces as the Church of the Chora, later renamed Karije Djami, but the intellectual milieu was permeated with the archaising traits already visible in a lesser degree under the Macedonians. Authors seemed to seek refuge from the grimness of the present in the more glorious past in an atmosphere of unreality which offered no solutions. Despite the translation of Western works into Greek and the continuation of active interchanges, Aristotelian logic failed to win over most Greek scholars from their traditional attachment to Platonic idealism. The new methods and concepts attending the revival of learning in the West found no echoes in Eastern antiquarianism. The enormous popularity of the Hesychast doctrine with its total concentration on the mystical vision of a reunion with God out of time and space bears witness to the contemporary Byzantine rejection of the nascent humanism of the West. The traditional loyalty to the City, the Emperor, the Faith gave way to the acrimony of religious controversies; the intellectuals departed, while religious leaders, rejecting the "heretical" emperor and his obedient tool, the patriarch, sought guidance away from the capital in the intransigent and otherworldly monastic community on Mount

Athos. The empire was finally turning away from its millennial tradition of intellectual inquiry, from its past loyalties, from the realities of the present.

Bereft of external support and of its own inner core, Byzantium could only await passively the recovery of Ottoman power. On May 29, 1453, the army of Sultan Muhammad II breached the land walls of Constantinople after having dragged its entire fleet overland into the Golden Horn to isolate the city from the sea. Faithful to his trust, the emperor Constantine XI died in the ruins of his capital. Belatedly, the West was shocked by the long-expected news, but the Orthodox world could only solace itself with legends that the church of Hagia Sophia had miraculously and secretly been preserved from desecration.

The political importance of the empire had ended long before the fall of the city, but its intangible influence had always transcended its physical boundaries. Imperial dreams had always been tied in some degree to a vision of Constantinople: Carolingian and Saxon emperors, Norman kings, the distant Queen Tamar of Georgia, and the Slavic rulers of the Balkans had all aped the formulas of Byzantine protocol and chosen to be represented adorned with the imperial regalia. Italian painters working for Renaissance patrons instinctively turned to Byzantine models when they sought to represent the true Christian ruler: Piero della Francesca's *Constantine the Great* at Arezzo, and Benozzo Gozzoli's *Magi* in the Medici chapel in Florence are unmistakable portraits of the emperor John VIII Paleologus. In tangible terms, both the Greek refugee scholars and the manuscripts they had brought with them preserved the imperial intellectual tradition. The mixed religious, linguistic, and artistic tradition of the present-day Balkans still reflects the ambiguous status of medieval Illyricum and the extent of imperial prestige among the western and southern Slavs.

Far to the north, in distant Moscow, emerging in the fifteenth century from the Mongol domination which had cut it off from the rest of Christendom, the ecclesiastical advisers of the prince sought to preserve the imperial institutions and claims, and to exploit the memory of Byzantine glory to their own advantage:

> Because the Old Rome has collapsed on account of heresy . . . and because the Second Rome which is Constantinople is now in the possession of the godless Turks, thy kingdom O pious Tsar, is the Third Rome. It surpasses in devotion every other, and all Christian kingdoms are now merged in thy realm. Thou art the only Christian sovereign in the world, the Master of all faithful Christians. . . .
>
> All Christian empires are fallen and in their stead stands alone the Empire of our ruler in accordance with the prophetical books. Two Romes have fallen, but the Third stands, and a Fourth there will not be.

For Further Reading

Cambridge Medieval History, Vol. IV.
Diehl, C., *Byzantium: Greatness and Decline.*
Grabar, A., *The Art of Byzantium.*
Hussey, J. M., *The Byzantine World.*
Ostrogorsky, G., *History of the Byzantine State.*
Runciman, S., *Byzantine Civilization.*
————, *A History of the Crusades.*
Vasiliev, A. A., *History of the Byzantine Empire.*
Vryonis, S., *Byzantium and Europe.*

38 The Slavs and Early Russia

The Slavs, who in the fifteenth and sixteenth centuries saw themselves as the true heirs of the Roman tradition, began their historical career in obscurity, controversy, and confusion. Almost every step of their early development—the original homeland, the migrations, tribal names, and foreign contacts—has been attended by fierce disagreement. Although random references may occur as early as Herodotus, precise information concerning the Slavic peoples does not go back before the sixth century A.D. and their effective political role begins only in the ninth.

Recent scholarship suggests that the Slavic homeland was far more extensive than the Pripet marshes to which historians had formerly confined them; most of the broad agricultural lands stretching north of the Carpathians from the Elbe to the Vistula and perhaps even to the upper Dnieper should be considered. From this indefinite area, probably centered on the Oder and the Vistula, the Slavic tribes fanned out in three directions.

The eastward migration toward the Ukraine must have begun even before the spread of the Irano-Scythian nomads to this area around 500 B.C., but the Iranian element remained dominant for centuries in southern Russia as Sarmatians and Alans succeeded their Scythian kinsmen in the steppes linking Asia and Europe around 200 B.C. Whether or not the Antes, who survived the passage of Goths and Huns and moved westward from the basin of the Don to rule the lower Dniester and Danube until they were annihilated by the Asiatic Avars in the first years of the seventh century, were Sarmatians or Slavs is still hotly debated. Byzantine sources assure us that they spoke a Slavic language in the sixth century. But what-

SOUTHERN SLAVS	WESTERN SLAVS	EASTERN SLAVS (Russia)
c. 517 Slavic tribes begin to cross the Danube into the Balkans		
c. 679 Bulgars cross Danube	c. 628–658 Principality of Samo in Moravia	7th cent. Scandinavian infiltration of Russia begins
c. 680–1018 First Bulgarian Empire		
813 First Bulgar siege of Constantinople		
	846–870 Reign of Rastislav in Great Moravia	c. 860 Riurik in Novgorod; first Russian raid on Constantinople
864 Baptism of Boris-Michael of Bulgaria	863–864 Cyrillo-Methodian mission to Moravia	c. 880–912 Rise of Kiev under Oleg
	906 Magyars sack Great Moravia	
	10th cent. Premyszlid dynasty in Bohemia; Piast dynasty in Poland	c. 968 End of Khazar empire
	992–1025 Reign of Boleslav the Brave in Poland	989 Baptism of Vladimir of Kiev
		1035–1054 Zenith of Kiev under Laroslav the Wise; Metropolitan of Kiev created
	1102–1138 Boleslav III of Poland	1113–1125 Reign of Vladimir Monomakh at Kiev
	1140–1173 Vladimir II hereditary king of Poland	1157–1174 Reign of Andrei Bogolubskii at Suzdal
1168–1196 Stephen Nemanja founds the Serbian Empire		1169 Suzdal sacks Kiev
		1176–1212 Vsevolod "Big Net" prince of Suzdal
1197–1207 John Asen (Kalojan) founds the Second Bulgarian Empire		1198–1205 Zenith of Galici under Roman of Smolensk
1217 Coronation of Stephen I as Czar of Serbia		
1218–1241 Zenith of the Second Bulgarian Empire under John II Asen		1223 Mongol defeat of the Russian princes at Kalka
1241 Mongol sack of the Second Bulgarian Empire	1241 Mongol sack of Poland	1242 Alexander Nevski's victory over the Teutonic Knights at Lake Peipus; Golden Horde settles in southern Russia
	1253–1258 Zenith of Bohemia under Ottokar the Great	
		1282 Mongols sack Galicia

SOUTHERN SLAVS	WESTERN SLAVS	EASTERN SLAVS (Russia)
	1300 Wenceslas II of Bohemia king of Poland	
	1301 Wenceslas III of Bohemia crowned king of Hungary	
	1306 Accession of Luxemburg dynasty in Bohemia	1325–1341 Ivan I Kalita founds the Muscovite state
1336–1355 Zenith of Serbia under Stephen IV Dusan		1328 Metropolitan see moves from Kiev to Moscow
	1333 Restoration of Poland under Casimir III	
	1347 Emperor Charles IV king of Bohemia	
1371 Ottoman victory over Serbia on the Marica		1380 Dimitri Donskoi's victory over the Mongols at Kulikovo
1389 Ottoman victory at the first Battle of Kossovo	1386 Marriage of Jadwiga of Poland to Jagiello of Lithuania	1387 Galicia absorbed by Poland
	1410 Polish defeat of the Teutonic Knights at Tannenberg	
1448 Ottoman victory at the second Battle of Kossovo; Ottoman domination of the Balkans	1447 Union of Poland and Lithuania	
	1466 Second Peace of Thorn	1480 Ivan III proclaimed Czar and Autocrat of Russia
	1526 Ottoman victory at Mohács	1533–1584 Reign of Ivan IV the Terrible
	1547 Hapsburgs become hereditary kings of Bohemia	1552–1556 Russians take Kazan and Astrakhan
	1572 End of Jagiellonian dynasty in Poland	1598–1605 Boris Godunov Czar of Russia
		1604–1613 "Time of Troubles"; Polish intervention in Russia
		1613 Accession of Michael I Romanov in Russia
	1620 Battle of White Mountain; end of Bohemian independence.	

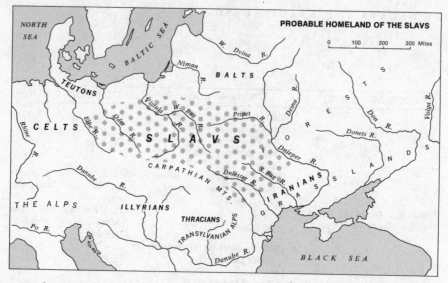

ever the origin of the Antes, Iranian influences dominated their political institutions, and the Iranian world reached across the Russian Slavic tribes deep into central Europe as Sarmatian groups, such as the Croats and the Serbs, fled from the Huns to settle northwest of the Carpathians.

With the beginning of the Christian era, other Slavic tribes began to filter southward through the passes of the Carpathians and the plain of Hungary toward the Danube, which they crossed at the beginning of the sixth century, moving in the direction of Greece and Dalmatia. Like their eastern cousins, the southern Slavs weathered the overlordship of Goths, Huns, and Avars before most of them became part of the Balkan Bulgar empire toward the end of the seventh century. Finally, the vacuum left in central Europe by the westward migration of the Germanic tribes was gradually filled by Slavs, who began to cross the Elbe in large numbers into modern Bohemia and Moravia as well as in a considerable section of Germany by the third century A.D. By the seventh century, when all but the northernmost Slavic tribes were subject to the Avar empire, the migrations had all but ended, and only the future Polish tribes remained in the original heartland of the lower Oder and Vistula.

As tribe after tribe shook off Avar dominion, future national groups began to emerge from the amorphous Slavic mass, although we have no evidence for major differentiation even in language before the end of the first millennium. A fleeting state under the semilegendary leader Samo (c. 623–658) freed the Slavs of Moravia and Bohemia. The First Bulgarian Empire provided a framework for the Slavic tribes in the Balkans. The Croats and Serbs, pressed by Frankish expansion, moved southward to settle west of the Bulgars in the Dalmatian hinterland at the invitation of the emperor Heraclius. Far to the east, the Slavs, settled along the Dnieper, benefited from the establishment of the Turkic Khazar Empire which replaced the Avars and Bulgars in southern Russia, spreading its more benevolent overlordship over the neighboring tribesmen, and bringing them into the orbit of a more civilized world through its role as middleman in the active trade linking the brilliant civilization of the Baghdad caliphate and the more primitive world to the north.

Until their Christianization in the ninth and tenth centuries, the Slavs generally lacked the political and military organization needed to create cohesive independent states. Probably because of their contact with the Khazars and with the Bulgar state on the middle Volga, the Russian tribes may have developed trading cities along the great waterways linking the Baltic with the south. But Slavic society was primarily agricultural rather than truly nomad. Their tribal institutions centered on the authority of the family and the community of property. Their primitive military system forced them to accept, sometimes even to welcome, the protection of superior powers. Traditional accounts repeatedly point, rightly or wrongly, to foreign leaders uniting the scattered Slavs: Samo, the "Frankish merchant" from the West, Riurik, the Viking chieftain in Russia, more than two centuries later. Modern historians likewise see foreign elements as the catalyst bringing about the creation of Slavic states: Sarmatians, Avars, and Bulgars in central Europe and the Balkans, Iranians, Khazars, and eventually Scandinavians in Russia. And yet, in all cases, it was not the outsiders who left their imprint on the new states, but the Slavic substratum. Whether the Antes were Sarmatians or Slavs, whether the name *Rus* should properly designate Vikings or Slavs, the Antes of the sixth century and the Rus of the ninth spoke Slavic languages and were regarded as part of the Slavic world by their contemporaries. The Bulgars of the ninth century still addressed their chieftains as "khan" and wore the trousers and turbans of Asiatic nomads, but soon thereafter the Christian Bulgar ruler forgot his Turkish ways and language to become a Slavic "czar." Sooner or later everywhere, persistent and pervasive Slavic customs overcame the foreign pattern imposed upon them and broke through to the surface.

Among the Slavic groups, the southern branch was the first to attain real political power. Direct Slavic control of Greece had been broken by the crushing defeat inflicted on them at Patras in 805 by the emperor Nicephorus I, but the strategic position of the Bulgarian empire in the Balkans made for the creation of a powerful state poised between the Byzantine and Latin worlds. The conversion of Czar Boris-Michael in 864 and the perpetual Bulgar threat to Constantinople forced concessions from the Eastern empire. By the tenth century, Czar Peter, brother-in-law of the Byzantine emperor, boasted his own autonomous patriarch and church, and was ceremoniously styled *Basileus,* an honor rarely conceded to foreigners. Thereafter, Byzantine control of the Balkans was never secure, and the initiative passed repeatedly to the Slavic states. To be sure, the internal weakness of Bulgaria interfered with the development of the first empire. The traditional clan structure had not been obliterated, and the chieftains, or boyars, opposing the centralizing efforts of the Crown, exploited dynastic quarrels, while Byzantium watched for the opportunity to reconquer its lost territories. By 1018, under the savage attacks of the emperor Basil II, the First Bulgarian Empire collapsed.

But the reestablishment of imperial power in the Balkans soon proved ephemeral. The Second Bulgarian Empire emerged by the end of the twelfth century during the chaos attending the fall of the Comnenian dynasty and the sack of Constantinople by the soldiers of the Fourth Crusade. Repeating the pattern of its predecessors, the Asen dynasty oscillated between East and West, receiving the crown from Pope Innocent III, yet dealing fatal blows to the Latin empire of Constantinople and intriguing simultaneously with and against the rival Greek empire of Nicaea.

When the Bulgars gave way after 1241 to the great Mongol invasion sweeping into Europe, the leadership of the Balkans remained in the hands of Slavs but moved farther west to the Serbs who had gradually emancipated themselves from Carolingian, Hungarian, or Byzantine domination. The Serbian empire of the Nemanjids came nearest to toppling Byzantium under the great czar Stephen-Uroš IV Dušan, who extended his rule over imperial lands from the Adriatic to the Aegean Sea and had himself crowned *Basileus* of the Serbians and the Romans. Dušan's dream was to create an empire on the model of Constantinople, but the position of his realm athwart the Balkans also made of it a meeting place and channel of transmission for both Western and Eastern influences—a remarkable Byzantine-Latin culture based on Slavic foundations. Dušan's court was reorganized on a Byzantine model, though some Slavic titles were preserved; the Serbian parafeudal system followed the Byzantine pattern; the new emperor flaunted his Orthodoxy and severely persecuted the "Latin heresy." Yet he simultaneously carried on active negotiations with the papacy and Venice, and Serbia grew rich on its transit commerce, even if the talent of Dušan's grandfather at counterfeiting Venetian currency won him a place in Dante's *Inferno*. The hybrid character of medieval Serbia is perhaps best exemplified by the great royal monastery of Dečani, where Franciscan architects from the Dalmatian coast raised a Byzantine dome over a striped façade of white and purple marble directly reminiscent of Italian counterparts at Siena or Orvieto, while on the interior walls the Nemanjid rulers are portrayed in the full imperial regalia of the Constantinopolitan court.

In spite of all of their aggressiveness and achievements, however, the early promise of the southern Slavs never reached total fulfillment, nor did their state survive the Middle Ages. Decentralized and quarreling among themselves, the Balkan states went down like a house of cards before the Ottoman onslaught. Except for isolated resistance in the mountains of Albania and some surviving vassal princes, the entire Balkan peninsula was Turkish by 1463. Its Slavic population would have four more centuries to wait before making its next bid for an independent political role.

To the western Slavs must belong the honor of creating the first national state devoid of foreign superstructure, and of providing the basis for later Slavic cultures. Great Moravia in the mid-ninth century sprang from the same territory as Samo's earlier state. The support of Constantinople allowed Prince Rastislav (846–870) to withstand the double threat of the Carolingians and the Bulgars, and to reunite the tribes of Bohemia and Moravia for a time while extending his dominions toward the Elbe and the Vistula. The new principality did not long survive him. The Magyar invaders from the East, urged on by the Germans, wiped out even the trace of the capital of Velehrad in 906 and drove a permanent wedge between the southern, western, and eastern branches of the Slavs. However, the contribution of Great Moravia was not exclusively political. As part of Rastislav's negotiations with Byzantium, the famous mission of Saints Cyril and Methodius in 863 brought both Greek Christianity and literacy to the area. The antagonism of German missionaries who won the ear of Rastislav's successor drove their Greek rivals from Moravia, and Bohemia came to acknowledge the ecclesiastical jurisdiction of the see of Regensburg, but Methodius' disciples found refuge in Bulgarian lands. The school they founded at Ohrid in Macedonia became a great religious and cultural center, while the alphabet that Cyril had given to the Slavs survived temporary political vicissitudes to be adopted by their southern and eastern branches. No longer illiterate, endowed with their individual religious liturgy, the Slavs now developed the literary traditions which ensured their cultural survival even in moments of political eclipse.

The native dynasties of the Premyszlids of Bohemia and the Piasts of Poland claimed in later times to be the heirs of Moravia. But in rejecting the Greek ties of Methodian Christianity and turning to the Latins, the western Slavs broke fundamentally with their southern and eastern cousins, who remained in the orbit of Byzantium. The Czech dukes, later kings of Bohemia, successfully imposed their authority over the population and preserved the autonomy of their territory against the Magyars and Poles, as well as against the imperialist pressure of the Germans. For a brief moment the Premyszlids seemed about to dominate central Europe: in 1300 Wenceslas II of Bohemia was crowned king of Poland and raised his young son,

Wenceslas III, to the Hungarian throne in the following year. From the beginning, however, Bohemia had accepted the ecclesiastical authority of the Latins, and it remained within their orbit even after the creation of native Czech bishoprics. The Premyszlid dynasty had likewise acknowledged itself the vassal of the Holy Roman Empire. This position brought power and honor to Bohemia—its de facto interference in German affairs was given a legal basis in the thirteenth century when the Bohemian king became one of the seven imperial electors—and the identity of the nation was maintained, but the Germanization of the area grew steadily. By 1306, after the murder of Wenceslas III placed a Luxemburger on the Czech throne, Bohemia became inextricably meshed in the nexus of the Western empire.

The remoteness of the Polish tribes left in the Slavic homeland delayed their evolution and unification until the end of the tenth century, and Poland never became as fully identified with the West as Bohemia. Fearful of the German eastward push across the Elbe, Duke Mieszko I (c. 960–992) upon his conversion took the fateful step of placing his realm under the direct suzerainty of the papacy, thus following Bohemia's path away from the other Slavs and toward the Latins. Yet his great successor, Boleslav I the Brave (992–1025), the true creator of the Polish state, obtained an independent archbishop for his realm, and his conquests led him as much to the East as to the West. He took Pomerania in 992–994, Prague in 1003, and Kiev in 1018. The ambivalence of Poland reflected in Boleslav's campaigns was as much a danger as a source of strength. These far-flung conquests could not be maintained, and the centralization of the kingdom was compromised. King Boleslav III (1102–1138) divided his realm into five principalities, thus bringing the centrifugal tendencies into the open, and the Mongol invasion of 1241 weakened the kingdom still further. In the north, the establishment of the order of Teutonic Knights in Pomerania intensified the German pressure and cut Poland from the Baltic at the very time when the Bohemian rulers were laying claim to the Polish crown.

The native reaction under the last of the Piasts, Casimir III the Great (1333–1377), restored Polish fortunes, and the University of Cracow, founded in 1364, soon proved a match for its great rival at Prague as a center of learning. The political revival culminated after Casimir's death, when, in 1386, the daughter of his Anjevin successor, Queen Jadwiga, married the powerful duke of still-pagan Lithuania, Jagiello. The union of Poland and Lithuania in 1447 gave additional luster to the joint kingdoms. The great victory of Tannenberg in 1410 stopped the eastward advance of the Teutonic Knights. The Second Peace of Thorn in 1466 restored Poland's access to the sea, albeit sowing in the process the seeds of future

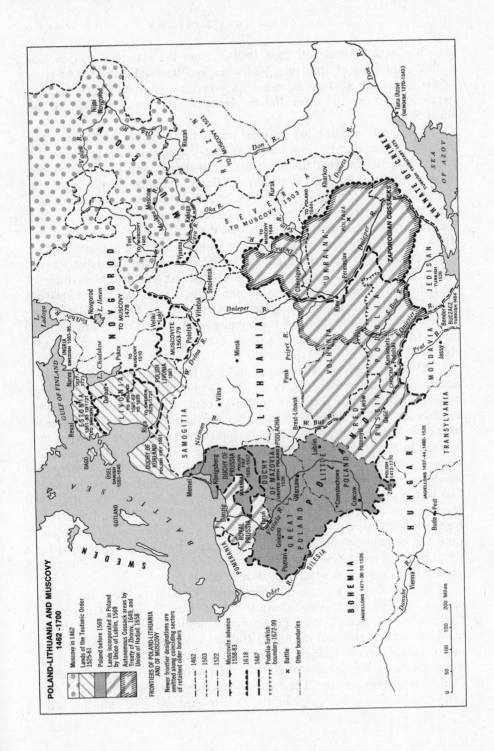

POLAND-LITHUANIA AND MUSCOVY 1462-1700

Muscovy in 1462

Lands of the Teutonic Order 1525-61

Poland before 1569

Lands incorporated in Poland by Union of Lublin, 1569

Autonomous Cossack areas by Treaty of Zborov, 1649, and Union of Hadjac 1658

FRONTIERS OF POLAND-LITHUANIA AND OF MUSCOVY

Newer frontier designations are omitted along coinciding sectors of retained older borders

1462

1503

1522

Muscovite advance 1558-83

1618

1667

Podolia-Turkish boundary 1672-99

× Battle

Other boundaries

0   50   100   150   200 Miles

catastrophes by cutting off East Prussia from the rest of Germany. Jagiello's acquisition of Moldavia, Wallachia, and Bessarabia in the last years of the fourteenth century extended his power over an enormous corridor stretching between the Oder and the Dnieper and from the Baltic to the Black Sea.

Poland had reached her apogee, but if the kingdom had more than doubled its size and the German thrust been stopped, the danger from the East, where the growing Russian state faced the western Slavs across the upper Dnieper, had not been allayed. The continuing allegiance of the Poles to Western Christianity, Catholic or Protestant, and territorial rivalry alienated them from their eastern kinsmen. Ottoman advances in the Balkans and the Ukraine soon syallowed the Jagiellonian conquests in the south. After the dynasty came to an end with the death of Sigismund II in 1572, Poland was still strong enough to interfere in the affairs of Russia during the "Time of Troubles" of the seventeenth century. Nevertheless, the failure to align itself clearly with either the East or the West deprived Poland of effective supporters at the moment when the pressure of divisive interests affirming the rights of the nobility against the Crown strained the fabric of the state. The stage was all but set for the partitions of the eighteenth century.

Although relatively latecomers on the European political and religious stage, the eastern Slavs in Russia ultimately became the most powerful group of all. The Slavs must have reached the area of the Dnieper as early as the first millennium B.C., but considerable controversy persists over their early history. A recurrent disagreement rages over the role of the Vikings in the formation of the early Russian state in the ninth century. Some Soviet scholars continue to play down the coming of the Vikings as incidental and purely ancillary, while most other specialists accept the thesis that in the ethnic, if not necessarily the geographical sense, the *Rhos* or *Rus* were originally Scandinavians who provided the unifying framework for the still-scattered Slavic tribes. In any case, the majority of the agricultural and commercial population of the Dnieper basin was Slavic, and the tribes had developed beyond a primitive level of culture under the influence of the Khazar empire to which they were tributary.

The Scandinavians were not newcomers to Russia. From the eighth century on, they had traveled down the great rivers from the Baltic to the Caspian and the Sea of Azov, drawn by the profitable trade with Baghdad in which the Khazars and the Volga Bulgars were middlemen. Whether or not a "Scandinavian khanate" was actually established in the region of Tmutorakan on the isthmus of Kertch, the presence of Vikings is attested by the early ninth century. The routes favored by the northern traders first carried them along the Volga or the Don toward the East. Muslim coins vastly outnumber Byzantine ones in the Viking hoards of Sweden and Gottland. Gradually, however, the fame of Constantinople, the fabulous Mikligarðr of northern legends and Tsargrad of the Russians, brought the Scandinavians by way of the Dvina-Dnieper system, which became the classic "Way from the Varangians to the Greeks," into the Black Sea. The Rus first attacked the Byzantine capital in 860.

The earliest Viking center, according to Russian tradition, was in the region of the northern city of Novgorod, to which the semilegendary Riurik had come together with his brothers and retainers. Before the end of the ninth century, however, his kinsman, Helgi or Oleg, had moved southward to the strategic city of Kiev, commanding the Dnieper route on the westernmost limit of the Khazar sphere, and laid there the foundation of the new state. From Kiev the Rus attacked the neighboring Slavic tribes and continued their attempts against Constantinople. Progress was slow, the conquest of the Slavs took generations, and the extensive commercial advantages conceded by Byzantium were occasionally offset by disasters such as the death of Prince Sviatoslav, ambushed in 972 by the nomad Petchenegs at the instigation of the empire. Nor was the process of Christianization smooth. An early bishopric seemingly established in the 860's was swamped in a pagan reaction. The baptism of the princess-regent Olga some one hundred years later likewise failed to anchor the new faith. It was only around 989 that Sviatoslav's bastard son, Vladimir I the Saint, was converted together with his people, accepting the ecclesiastical jurisdiction of Constantinople in exchange for an imperial bride.

Under Oleg and his successors, especially after the Magyar move to central Europe and Sviatoslav's sack of the Khazar capital of Itil in 968, Kiev became the chief city of Russia until the latter part of the twelfth century. At no time, however, was it the capital of a centralized state, but rather the senior in an agglomeration of military and commercial city-states, most of them ruled by members of a single dynasty claiming descent from Riurik. Of variable importance at different times, these included Chernigov and Pereiaslav near Kiev; Novgorod and Smolensk in the north; Polotsk and Halicz (Galicia) in the west; Tmutorakan far to the south; and Rostov the great, Riazan, Suzdal, and Vladimir in the East. Hence a centrifugal tendency was an intrinsic part of the early Russian political structure. The death of Vladimir I in 1015 unleashed dissensions among his sons. The murder of two of them, Boris and Gleb, gave Russia its first national saints and earned for their older brother the epithet Sviatopolk the Accursed. The surviving brothers, Iaroslav at Kiev and Mstislav at Tmutorakan, divided the Russian lands along the Dnieper, and only after Mstislav's death without heirs in 1035 did Iaroslav reunite the power into his own hands for some twenty years.

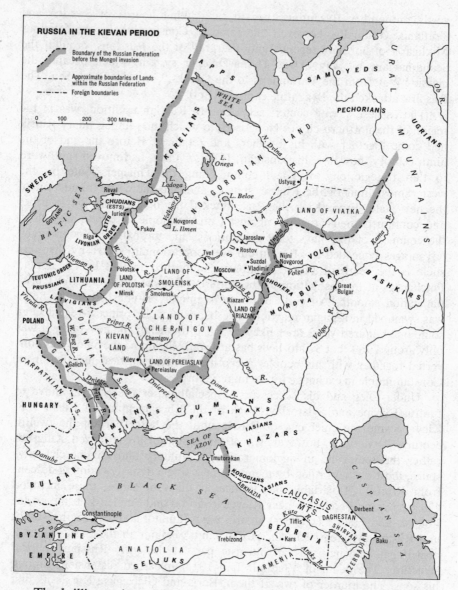

RUSSIA IN THE KIEVAN PERIOD

Boundary of the Russian Federation before the Mongol invasion

Approximate boundaries of Lands within the Russian Federation

Foreign boundaries

0   100   200   300 Miles

The brilliant reign of Iaroslav the Wise marked the apogee of Kievan Russia and stamped the later culture with many of its characteristics. The authority of the "Great Prince" of Kiev was temporarily unchallenged by the subordinate cities, and his bishop was raised in 1037 to the dignity of a metropolitan, although a brief attempt to substitute a Russian for the traditional Greek incumbent proved premature. Iaroslav expanded the Russian frontiers into the southern steppes and in the direction of Lithuania and Poland. His far-flung political and family connections throw light both on the international aspect of the mid-eleventh-century European world and on Russia's position within it. The old ties of the Riurikids with Scandinavia were still maintained as Northmen came to support Iaroslav against his brother Sviatopolk. The prince's children married in the West as well as in the East: Vsevolod to a Byzantine princess, Anna to King Henry I of France, and Iziaslav to the daughter of Harold Hardrada of England. Most significantly for the future, neither the quarrels with Constantinople over the metropolitan of Kiev nor even a brief war in 1041–1043 could stop the pervasive Byzantine influence on Russian culture. The first systematization of Russian customs, the *Russkaia Pravda,* begun under Iaroslav, bears the stamp of imperial legislation. The Slavonic scriptures of the Cyrillic school had been adopted by the Russians, but the metropolitan remained a Greek under the jurisdiction of the patriarch of Constantinople, and Byzantine canon law governed the Russian Church. The great intellectual and religious center, the Monastery of the Caves, was modeled on the Byzantine community of the Studites. The architecture, mosaic decoration, and the very name of the magnificent new cathedral of Kiev, St. Sophia, underscored its indebtedness to the imperial tradition.

Kievan society, reflected in the compilations of traditional customs, charters, and literary works, was largely urban and aristocratic, but specialists still dispute the relative importance of commerce and agriculture in its economy. In each city, the prince—part war leader, part chief capitalist, through his vast estates and commercial interests—ruled with the help of his retainers or *druzhina,* the advice of the noble council (duma), and of the city assembly (*veche*). The countryside paid a tribute which the prince collected at first in person on periodic tours but later received through his local representatives. The old equalitarian clan society of the Slavic tribes had long since given way to a complicated class structure. The *druzhina* and the local nobles eventually coalesced into a single noble class, the boyars, and the city militia with its elected commander was distinct from the prince's foreign followers. Trade guilds and peasant communities represented common interests. The peasants or *smerdy* were personally free and generally unbound to the land, but slaves, half-free indentured servants, and various ecclesiastical classes were also part of the social structure. Considerable variation existed even in this typical pattern, especially in the relations of the prince and the city. Thus in Novgorod, which never received a ruling dynasty, ultimate power rested in the *veche,* and the prince was more an administrator than a ruler. Even in Kiev, the *veche* asserted itself on occasion, meeting without being summoned in 1113 to invite to the city the ruler of its choice.

The death of Iaroslav the Wise in 1054 proved a turning point in

Kievan history. His defeat of the Pechenegs brought a new and fiercer Asiatic group, the Polovtsy, called Cumans by the West, into the southern Russian steppes. The newcomers cut off the northern lands politically and commercially, if not culturally, from Byzantium, thus progressively strangling the profitable Kievan trade. The Great Schism of 1054 between Rome and Constantinople eventually forced Russia to choose sides in the religious quarrel. Geographically isolated from the southern Slavs in the Balkans by the Polovtsy, religiously alienated from its western kinsmen in Poland who had thrown in their lot with Rome, Russia gradually withdrew into a separate sphere. Simultaneously, Iaroslav's political testament unwittingly strengthened the latent decentralization of his realm.

My sons [he admonished], I am about to quit this world. Love one another, since ye are brothers by one father and mother. If ye dwell in amity with one another, God will dwell among you, and will subject your enemies to you, and ye will dwell in peace. But if ye dwell in envy and dissension, quarreling with one another, then ye will perish yourselves and bring to ruin the land of your ancestors, which they won at great effort. Wherefore, remain rather at peace, brother heeding brother. The throne of Kiev I bequeath to my eldest son, your brother Iziaslav. Heed him as ye heeded me, that he may take my place among you. To Svyatoslav I give Chernigov, to Vsevolod Pereyaslav, to Igor the city of Vladimir, and to Vyacheslav Smolensk.

It was evidently not Iaroslav's intention to splinter the state and he had reaffirmed the seniority of the "Great Prince" of Kiev, but he proved most accurate in his prophecy of destruction. According to this system of appanages, the princes of the various cities were not to remain in them perpetually but to rotate according to a pattern of seniority, with the eldest member holding Kiev. Unfortunately, the continuous game of musical chairs proved faulty from the start. Some cities, such as Novgorod, remained autonomous and were not included in the system. In others, the ruling family either entrenched itself or sought to wrest more attractive domains from its kinsmen. Twice driven from Kiev, Prince Iziaslav sought the help of the Poles and even attempted to offer his principality to the pope. In 1097, at the Conference of Liubech, the rival princes attempted to resolve the difficulties by halting the carrousel and making the principalities hereditary. Between 1113 and 1125 Vladimir II Monomakh succeeded in reestablishing the preeminence of Kiev. A sense of unity based on a common language and culture, common religious institutions, and interrelated dynasties lingered on. The narrator of the famous *Lay of Igor's Campaign* bitterly denounced in 1185 the quarrels of the princes. But the centrifugal process could not be reversed.

Sacked in 1169 and impoverished by the disappearance of its trade,

Kiev sank slowly into obscurity while rival centers grew on its periphery. Novgorod in the north maintained and expanded the tradition of the merchant republic and kept its ties with the West through its membership in the Hansa. Volynia and Halicz (Galicia) in the southwest were united under Prince Roman of Smolensk (1198–1205) in opposition to Polish and Lithuanian expansionist tendencies. In the northeast, the principality of Vladimir-Suzdal under Prince Andreĭ Bogolubskiĭ (d. 1174) and his brother Vsevolod "Big Nest" (1176–1212) preserved the tradition of Byzantine absolutism and the old link with the Caucasus and the East through the Volga trade and the marriage of Bogolubskiĭ's son with Queen Tamar of Georgia.

The Mongol invasion of the thirteenth century dealt the final blow to Kievan culture. The first defeat at the Battle of Kalka in 1223 merely crushed a confederation of Russian princes allied now to the Cumans, but the great raid of Batu's Golden Horde between 1236 and 1241 overwhelmed the Volga Bulgars, took Riazan and Vladimir, sacked Kiev, and swept through Galicia-Volynia. By 1242 Batu settled in southern Russia, establishing his capital at Sarai on the lower Volga. For two centuries and a half thereafter, the Golden Horde dominated the Russian principalities. Cultural unity was shattered as well. The White Russian lands in the west were gradually absorbed by Lithuania. The Ukrainian territories of Galicia-Volynia, only remotely affected at first, gradually moved into the Latin orbit. The Great Russians of the center and the eastern principality of Vladimir-Suzdal bore the brunt of the "Tartar Yoke."

Except in the initial devastation and during subsequent punitive expeditions, the Mongol control of Russia was normally exercised at a distance. The khans of the Golden Horde did not attempt to penetrate the forest belt of the north which was unsuited to Mongol cavalry. They merely imposed a heavy poll tax to be collected by the local princes on all their Russian subjects except for the clergy. The princes themselves were forced to obtain their charters or *iarlyks* from the khans, to travel constantly to distant Sarai in order to obtain privileges or to justify their conduct. The coveted title of "Great Prince" and chief tax collector was usually auctioned off to the highest bidder. Much of the central Russian territory of Kiev, Chernigov, and Pereiaslav was turned into pasture land for the nomads as the agricultural population fled northward. Depopulation, economic and cultural regression, and isolation undoubtedly followed, although the final assessment of the Mongol impact on Russian history cannot yet be made.

Of the main surviving principalities, Galicia-Volynia failed to preserve its identity past the fourteenth century as an independent unit. Flourishing at first under Daniel (1235–1265), the son of Roman of Smolensk, who accepted the royal crown of Galicia from Pope Innocent IV in 1253, the new capital at Lwow became a worthy cultural and commercial successor to Kiev. Then, abandoning its western alignment, sapped internally by the divisive activity of its powerful boyars, and sacked once more by the Mongols in 1282, the principality rapidly disintegrated. Volynia was absorbed by Lithuania, while Galicia fused with Poland in 1387. The Latinization of the boyar ruling class deepened the separation of the area from the Slavic lands to the east.

To Novgorod and its "younger brother" Pskov, protected by their remoteness from direct Mongol interference, fell the task of containing the eastward advance of the Teutonic Knights. In contrast to aristocratic Galicia, the northern cities developed to the maximum their commercial character and attendant republican institutions. The Novgorod *veche* was all-powerful, and the rights of the prince were sharply limited by the treaty inviting him in to rule. The distance from the Mongols made for considerable freedom of action, while the enormous wealth of a trading empire extending deep into Siberia increased Novgorod's power. Under the leadership of Alexander "Nevski," a junior member of the house of Vladimir, the city won its epoch-making victory on the ice of Lake Peipus over the Teutonic Knights in 1242. The danger from the west was over, and Novgorod continued to flourish, although its autonomy was somewhat compromised by Nevski's scrupulous loyalty to the Mongols, while the absence of a central authority gradually helped sap its strength.

The main focus of later history lay in the northeastern Great Russian lands of Vladimir-Suzdal which were directly subject to the Mongols. Repeatedly the princes of the Vladimir family obtained the all-important *iarlyk* of "Great Prince," making them the official representatives of the conquerors. Even though the principality itself was fragmented into appanages according to the old Kievan custom, and the title of prince of Vladimir was more titular than real, the *iarlyk* usually remained within the family. Finally, it came to rest in the very junior branch of Moscow, where Daniel, the youngest son of Alexander Nevski, established in the second half of the thirteenth century a dynasty which successfully freed itself from the Mongols and extended its dominion over the other Russian principalities.

The leadership of Vladimir and especially of Moscow, with its obscure early history, in throwing off the "Tartar Yoke" is an enigma for which many solutions have been proposed: the geographical isolation of the northeast, where the Mongol armies seldom penetrated and to which the population of other regions had fled for refuge; the frontier character of the area, which meant that the authority of the prince would presumably not be hampered by entrenched boyars or *veches;* the development of a feudal hierarchy based on an agricultural-serf economy: the old trade connections

THE RISE OF MUSCOVY 1300-1533

KEY TO CITIES SOUTH OF MOSCOW

A = Aleksin   PR = Pereiaslav Riazan
Ka = Kaluga   R = Rostislavl'
Ko = Kolomna   S = Serpuchov
O = Obolensk   T = Tarusa

Muscovy, 1300
Muscovy, 1462
Muscovy, 1533
Teutonic Order

Muscovy frontier, 1462
Frontiers of Lithuania and Novgorod in 1462
Muscovy frontier, 1503
× Battle

of Vladimir with the south and the east, extended to Asia by the *Pax Mongolica;* the tradition of Byzantine autocracy fostered at Suzdal by Andrei Bogolubskiï and later revived for the benefit of Moscow; the talent of the titular prince of Vladimir in obtaining the *iarlyk* of tax collector and the adoption of Mongol bureaucratic practices; all have been adduced and rejected as possible explanations. It now seems reasonably clear that no single explanation will suffice to explain the complexity of the process, even where the causes have been correctly diagnosed. In the case of Moscow, additional factors should be considered as well: the dynastic continuity which allowed the patient accumulation of small domains without arousing disastrous antagonisms, begun by Daniel's son Ivan I Kalita (Moneybag, 1325–1341) and continued in successive generations; the dying out in the fourteenth century of democratic institutions such as the *veche,* and the deliberate revival of Byzantine autocratic principles under the sponsorship of the clergy; the support of the Church, which transferred the Russian metropolitanate to Moscow in 1328, asserted its independence by repudiating the Byzantine compromise with Rome at the Council of Florence, and turned its allegiance inward to support the claims of the new champion of Orthodoxy. Finally, the prudent loyalty to the Mongol overlords, maintained until the moment when the disintegration of the Golden Horde made possible the victory of Ivan I's grandson Dimitri Donskoĭ at the battle of Kulikovo in 1380, enormously enhanced the prestige of Moscow and bolstered its pretensions of sovereignty.

With the reign of Ivan III the Great (1462–1505) and his son Vasili III (1505–1533) the task of Moscow was all but accomplished. Formal submission to the Mongols was repudiated by 1480. Moscow's last Russian rivals, Tver and Novgorod, bowed to its overlordship. Step by step, Lithuania was pushed back from her eastern conquests. Crowned Czar and Autocrator in 1480 after his marriage to the Byzantine heiress Sophia-Zoë Paleologue, Ivan III had made good his claim to be "Lord of all the Russias." Under Ivan IV the Terrible (1533–1584), Moscow finally turned to outward expansion: in the west, in Livonia; in the east and south, against the splintered remains of the Golden Horde—Kazan in 1552 and Astrakhan on the Caspian in 1556. The power of the boyars remained to be crushed, ecclesiastical divisions to be resolved, and the challenge of Poland to be met in the "Time of Troubles" which marked the end of the Riurikid dynasty and the reign of Boris Godunov (1598–1605). But the half-Byzantine half-Oriental czar, supported by a bureaucracy trained in Mongol financial and diplomatic techniques, and by a clergy which developed for his benefit the mythology of the Third Rome, needed only the Western methods imported by Peter the Great to make his autocracy complete.

For Further Reading

Cherniavsky, M., *Tsar and People.*
Cross, S. (ed.), *The Russian Primary Chronicle.*
Dvornik, F., *The Slavs in European History and Civilization.*
———, *The Slavs: Their Early History and Civilization.*
Grabar, A., *Medieval Art in Eastern Europe.*
Vernadsky, G., *A History of Russia.*

III

TOWARD MODERNITY

The Renaissance and Reformation in Europe

Building the Early Modern State

Toward One World

The Enlightenment

The Renaissance and Reformation in Europe

39 The State System of the Italian Renaissance

No historical period has a name at once so plausible and so contested as the Renaissance. Fifteenth- and sixteenth-century intellectuals coined the term to assert the superiority of their own age over the "middle," or "dark," ages. (They coined those terms too.) So from the beginning "Renaissance" was a polemical word, even a bullying one. By calling the age between their own day and antiquity "dark," they stamped it for centuries as an age of cultural squalor. By giving their own period a name pregnant with images and metaphors of light, awakening, spring, youth, vigor, and innovation, they demanded that everyone admire it.

Consider how a fifteenth-century Florentine scholar sketched the history of poetry from the Augustan age to his own time: poetry, he wrote, flourished in Rome until Claudian, a contemporary of St. Augustine:

After Claudian, who was well nigh the last of the poets whom ancient times brought forth, almost all poetry decayed, because of the weakness and avarice of the emperors, and also perhaps because art was no longer prized, since the Catholic faith began to abhor the figments of poetic imagination as pernicious and a vain thing. Poetry, therefore, lying prostrate without honor or dignity, that great man Petrarch recalled it as from an abyss of shadows into the light, and giving it his hand, set the fallen art upon its feet.

In the sixteenth century, Giorgio Vasari, the author of the great series of lives of the Renaissance painters, gave a similar picture of the history of painting, sculpture, and architecture. Art, he insisted, had reached perfection in the classical world. But after Constantine, like poetry, it began to decline, first slowly, then rapidly under the pressure of the barbarian invasions and the iconoclastic zeal of the Christians. Vasari's dismal picture of medieval art shaped European taste for centuries and underlies the use of the word "Gothic" as a term of stylistic abuse by fifteenth-century men

CHRONOLOGY

A.D.

1250	Death of Frederick II and beginning of the imperial interregnum
1308	Removal of the papacy from Rome to Avignon
1321	Death of Dante
c. 1325	Beginning of regular sea traffic between Italy and northern Europe via the open Atlantic
1327	Earliest mention of an artillery piece in the documents
1342	Petrarch's *Italia mia*
1347	Outbreak of the Black Death
1378	Beginning of the Great Schism
1385–1402	Reign of Gian Galeazzo Visconti, Duke of Milan
1404–1414	Reign of Ladislas of Durazzo, King of Naples
1414	Opening of the Council of Constance
1434	Accession to power in Florence of Cosimo de' Medici
1450	Francesco Sforza becomes Duke of Milan
1457	Publication of the first surviving dated printed book
1469	Succession to power in Florence of Lorenzo the Magnificent
1494	First French invasion of Italy; fall of the Medici and reestablishment of the Florentine Republic
1497	Vasco da Gama reaches India by sea
1502	The Spanish conquer Naples
1513	Machiavelli's *Prince*
1530	Fall of the last Florentine Republic; return of the Medici
1535	Charles V occupies Milan as an imperial fief

of letters. At last appeared Cimabue and Giotto, artists "able to distinguish the good from the bad." They abandoned the old style and "began to copy the ancients with all ardor and industry," thus initiating what Raphael and Michelangelo consummated—the expression is Vasari's own—a renaissance of the arts.

Fifteenth-century intellectuals imposed a similar periodization on the history of religion, for they complemented their admiration for pagan antiquity with a corresponding veneration for Christian antiquity. They studied St. Jerome as well as Cicero, the Greek fathers as well as Greek philosophers, believing that true religion and literature had flourished together during the early centuries of the Roman Empire. Both had been gradually barbarized after the fifth century, and true gospel piety had been almost extinguished during the middle age by the barren subtleties, logic chopping, and arid and arrogant elaboration of scholastic theologians. And just as now, in their own age, good letters were being raised as from the grave, painting and sculpture and music reborn, so also religion was sharing in the same *renovatio* or renewal, the same *reformatio* or reformation (a usage that was to form one link between the revival of letters and the Protestant Reformation), as a reviving knowledge of the early church showed how Christianity could be stripped of the vain accretions of centuries and restored to its ancient purity and simplicity.

There are sound reasons for not withholding our admiration from the cultural achievements of the Renaissance. The cities of Italy and the museums and libraries of the world preserve an inheritance of unparalleled richness and variety: paintings and frescoes by Masaccio, Botticelli, Raphael, and Titian; statues by Donatello and Michelangelo; churches and palaces by Brunelleschi, Bramante, and Palladio; masses, operas, madrigals, and instrumental music by Palestrina, Gabrielli, and Monteverdi; love poems, epics, and tales by Petrarch, Boccaccio, and Ariosto; moral and educational treatises; influential works of history (like Machiavelli's *History of Florence* or Guicciardini's *History of Italy*), of philosophy (like Marsilio Ficino's *Platonic Theology* and Pietro Pomponazzi's *On the Immortality of the Soul*), of political theory, scholarship, and science. For centuries Italy was the school of Europe as Athens had been the school of Hellas.

So we can give our admiration legitimately enough. The difficulty with "Renaissance" lies elsewhere: in a tendency to accept the vernal metaphors contemporary intellectuals built into the word as adequate descriptions of the period itself. No one need take the idea of rebirth literally, of course, and argue that fifteenth-century Italy was Roman Italy reborn. On the other hand a great many people, influenced as much by images of youth and spring as by the reading of texts and documents, believe that innova-

RENAISSANCE ITALY, 15TH CENTURY

0   50   100 Miles

tion, prosperity, and modernity were as central to the period as cultural brilliance. To what extent is this true?

Certainly the hundred years before and after 1450 were enormously fertile in innovation. But the great discoveries and historical mutations of the age were not confined to Italy; while even in Italy continuity and tradition mark the age as deeply as change and innovation. The history of discovery and novelty must be balanced by the equally interesting and important story of the survival and adaptation of traditional institutions, social distinctions, professional disciplines, and modes of thought.

The fact that innovation during the fourteenth and fifteenth centuries was a European-wide phenomenon is well illustrated by the history of technology. The most remarkable technological innovations of the Renaissance were printing with movable metal type, the use of gunpowder to propel cannonballs and bullets, and important advances in shipbuilding and navigation. In none of these was the contribution of Italy indisputably central. The complex prehistory of printing involved China and every region of Western Europe. Johann Gutenberg perfected the process in the little ecclesiastical city of Mainz, and in 1457 his son-in-law, Johann Fust, printed the first surviving dated book, an edition of the Psalms in Latin. The first mention of gunpowder in the sources is by the English Franciscan scientist and theologian Roger Bacon in the late thirteenth century. The first mention of a gun occurs in 1327 in the records of the Florentine republic, and the first illustration in an English manuscript of the same year, a crude fire pot designed to shoot arrows. Innovation in navigation and shipbuilding was similarly international. Regular traffic between northern and southern Europe via the open Atlantic began about 1325. In the next century and a half bigger ships, improvements in steering and propulsion like the stern rudder and new kinds of sails and rigging, the use of the compass and astrolabe to estimate course and position more reliably—all of these steps to the great discoveries and to the "Atlantic Revolution" of early modern times—were taken by Europeans of every nation. By the early fifteenth century Portuguese and Spaniards, rather than Italians, were in the vanguard of exploration and discovery of new trade routes and new worlds.

Just as northern Europe shared the originality and creativity too often carelessly assigned only to Italy, so also Italy shared in full measure the continuity and traditionalism too often carelessly attributed only to the north. This is clearly evident even in Italian thought and culture, fields in which the word Renaissance was first used and to which it is still applied with particular appropriateness.

Much importance, for example, has been attached to fourteenth- and fifteenth-century men's morbid preoccupation with death. It is well to remember that the first great representation of the dance of death—that in the Campo Santo in Pisa—comes from fourteenth-century Italy. We are accustomed to think of allegory as a medieval device, a peculiarly well-adapted response to the need of medieval Christians to understand works of classical literature in an acceptably Christian context. But the same use of allegory to Christianize pagan works, whose assumptions are often profoundly secular and hostile to Christian values, continued in the Renaissance, both in Italy and in northern Europe. Medieval scholars had allegorized Ovid; in the fifteenth century a professor of the humanities at the University of Florence still considered it useful to allegorize Vergil's *Aeneid:* Aeneas was the human soul, Dido represented the trammels of the flesh, Latium the promised land where at last the soul gratefully arrives. The survival and adaptation of the scholastic method is especially instructive. One of the great intellectual creations of the twelfth and thirteenth centuries, this method of analysis, organization, and debate remained a powerful and developing intellectual tool throughout the fifteenth and sixteenth centuries, and particularly in Italy. Indeed, the liveliest centers of scholastic philosophy in all Europe were the Universities of Padua and Bologna, and a line of brilliant commentators on Aristotle's *Physics* forms an unbroken bridge between the scientific and philosophical achievements of Oxford and Paris in the fourteenth century and the revolutionary discoveries of Galileo at the end of the sixteenth.

The implications of the word "Renaissance" or the complacent view Italian fifteenth-century intellectuals had of themselves are equally deceptive if they lead us to assume that the period was necessarily one of economic expansion. The conditions that nourish periods of cultural brilliance are various and complex. The experience of the Italian Renaissance suggests that a generalized prosperity is not always one of them.

The most striking evidence is demographic. In 1347 a merchant ship sailed from Tana in the Crimea to Messina in Sicily. On board were rats infected with the plague. Although the work of a single bacillus, the disease took several forms. Bubonic plague, so called from the buboes or swellings on the bodies of the victims and carried to humans by fleas from the sick rats, attacked the lymphatic gland system. Pneumonic plague, much more devastating, attacked the lungs. It was highly communicable and almost always fatal. From Sicily the Black Death swept the western Mediterranean littoral in 1347, raged in Italy, Spain, and France in 1348, reached Switzerland, Austria, Germany, the Low Countries, and England in 1349, and Scandinavia and Poland in 1350. Plague hammered Europeans again and again in the fourteenth and fifteenth centuries and continued its ravages, though with diminished intensity, in the sixteenth and seventeenth centuries. Reliable estimates of the loss of human life vary from 12 to 70 per cent, depending on the region, with a global loss for the years between 1348 and 1377 of no less than 40 per cent. For example, the population of the rural countryside around the Tuscan city of Pistoia had been about 31,000 in the mid-thirteenth century. In 1401 it was less than 9,000. The number of inhabitants of the city itself fell from 11,000 in 1244 to 6,000 in 1351 and to 3,900 in 1415. "No one wept for the dead," wrote a Sienese chronicler, "because everyone expected death himself."

The shock halted more than two centuries of European demographic and economic growth. Until far into the fifteenth century population variously declined, partially recovered, then fell again, or stagnated at a level well below that of 1347. Long-term economic development followed a similar pattern, a decline of industrial and agricultural production and volume of trade reflecting the shrinking markets and smaller labor force of the later fourteenth and fifteenth centuries. Italy was not exempt from the European-wide contraction. Indeed, it has become fashionable to speak of the "depression of the Italian Renaissance." The customs records of Genoa and Venice chart a decline in the volume of goods exchanged. The output of woolen cloth, Italy's most important manufacture, was smaller in the fifteenth century than at the end of the thirteenth. Florence, which had once produced as many as 100,000 bolts of cloth a year, was manufacturing only 30,000 in 1500. The cultural renaissance was not, as historians have long assumed, grounded on an expanding commercial and industrial activity, rising prosperity, and increasing wealth.

The material condition of Renaissance Italy, however, was less grim and much more complex than words like "depression" might suggest. Even in the later fourteenth and fifteenth centuries the consequences of demographic contraction were not entirely negative. Fewer workers meant higher wages; fewer mouths to feed meant lower prices for grain and a larger share of what the land produced for the survivors. There is evidence too that lower grain prices encouraged landowners and peasants to diversify their crops and give part of their time and labor to more expensive and profitable foods like wine, oil, cheese, butter, and vegetables. Abandoning marginal land, they devoted greater effort to improving the more fertile soils. South of Milan more than 90 kilometers of navigable canals and a host of smaller irrigation works were constructed between 1439 and 1476. Important drainage operations were undertaken in southern Tuscany and the Roman Campagna. Ordinary Italians in the fifteenth century probably ate more and had a more balanced diet than their more numerous thirteenth-century ancestors.

Italians faced more serious challenges than declining numbers: fiercer competition from foreign merchants and manufacturers and the loss of the monopolistic position on which their economic supremacy had for so long been based. They responded to these challenges too with skill and energy. To compensate for the decline in the export woolen industry, they concentrated on manufacturing silk, one symptom of a larger adaptation of the Italian economy to foreign competition: the concentration by Italian craftsmen on quality rather than quantity, on beauty rather than utility. In the fifteenth and sixteenth centuries Italy came increasingly to specialize in the manufacture and export of luxuries for the rich: artistic metalwork, decorative armor, elaborate furniture, bronzes, glass, ceramics, embroidery, fine leather goods, cloth of silver and gold. England clothed German burghers with serviceable woolens; Italy dressed German princes in silk brocades.

Ottoman expansion in the eastern Mediterranean, the competition of foreign merchants at Alexandria and Beirut, in the Bosphorus and Black Sea, and the establishment of a direct sea link with India by Vasco da Gama shattered Italy's monopoly of the spice trade. The foundation of successful banking houses in Castile, France, Germany, and the Netherlands in the fifteenth century broke its monopoly of international banking. Italian merchant-bankers adapted resiliently to changing economic circumstances. Not only did Italy continue to trade profitably in the eastern Mediterranean; in the later sixteenth century more pepper reached Venice via the Levant than 100 years earlier. Bankers rationalized the organization of their firms, generalized novel accounting techniques like double-entry bookkeeping, and developed more sophisticated instruments of credit and exchange. The Medici Bank was smaller than the great Florentine banks of the early fourteenth century; but in the days of its greatness it was better managed and more efficient.

The long downward trend given such impetus by the Black Death was reversed in the last decade of the fifteenth century. Demographic recovery, plainly discernible by the 1470's and 1480's, reached boom proportions in the sixteenth century, when many Italian cities doubled in size. Indeed, the sixteenth century was an age of economic expansion all over Europe. Every index, whether of industrial and agricultural production or volume of commercial and financial exchange, swung sharply upward. Italy shared in this expansive prosperity—as it shared in the earlier contraction. The Renaissance was an age both of catastrophe and of promise.

The word "Renaissance" has for many years suggested modernity as well as innovation and prosperity. In this perspective the Renaissance appears less as the rebirth or revival of a distant and glorious antiquity than as the origin and beginning of the modern world, the prototype of modern European civilization.

If we search fifteenth- and sixteenth-century Italy for the seeds of modernity, we will find them in abundance. Italians were the first to regularize and formalize diplomatic relations between states. They invented the resident ambassador, the permanent representative of one sovereign formally accredited to another, looking out for the interests of his home government and sending regular reports back to it on the situation and capabilities of the foreign state. The idea and practice of balance of power, the conscious manipulation and balancing of one power against another, of one coalition against another, so characteristic of the relations among European powers in the modern world, emerged for the first time in Italy toward the end of the fifteenth century. Realpolitik, political behavior divorced from religious and ethical norms, is universally practiced in the modern world. The most celebrated manual of realpolitik was written by an Italian in 1513: *The Prince* of Niccolò Machiavelli.

Ideas and institutions of an apparently prophetic modernism were common in other areas of life. The Medici Bank anticipated the modern holding company. A German sociologist has found the earliest clear expressions of bourgeois values in fifteenth-century Florence: the maxim that time is money; and the notion, so difficult for the aristocrat to grasp, that expenditures should not exceed one's income. Art historians point out that sixteenth-century Italian artists invented modern landscape painting and the still life and that the public buildings of Washington go back directly to architectural practices first made fashionable by Filippo Brunelleschi. Italian humanists founded modern historical scholarship, created the idea and practice of liberal education, established new scholarly disciplines like numismatics and epigraphy. An earlier generation used to call Petrarch the first modern man.

None of these statements is untrue. But their cumulative effect should make us uneasy—for two reasons. First, because it is also easy to cite personalities, ideas, or institutions that make the fifteenth century look like the end of an era rather than the beginning of a new one: the ascetic and visionary piety of the Dominican monk Savonarola, for example; or the taste of cultivated Italian aristocrats for medieval romances of chivalry; or the dependence of men of every condition on astrology and magic. Second, because the idea of the modern is itself problematical and ambiguous. We will reach a juster view of the Renaissance—and of our period too—by abandoning undue emphasis on modernity and by trying to understand it instead as a period of rapid and fundamental change, of transition from one firmly contoured civilization to another. Periods of transition—our own, the Renaissance, the two and a half centuries between Diocletian and Clovis, between antiquity and the Middle Ages—can be interpreted with equal plausibility as ages of new beginnings or of crises in traditional values and patterns of life. To the Roman historian the proliferation of the villa, for example, the great landed estates of the late empire, is evidence of fragmentation and decline, of the disintegration of the essentially urban city-state civilization of the ancient world. But to the medievalist a history of the villa is the prehistory of the manor and of manorialism, and it speaks to him of vigor and a creative adaptation to changing circumstance. Or take the spread of Christianity: a death blow to the secular assumptions of classical thought, but also the foundation of the new Christian civilization of the future. The identical situation exists in the Renaissance: on the one hand, a crisis of medieval institutions and values, strikingly apparent in the great ecumenical institutions of papacy and empire, in feudal government, in the very foundations of thought and feeling; but in a reversed optic an age of germination and novelty. It is therefore not surprising to learn that books with the apparently contradictory titles of *The Autumn of the Middle Ages* and *The Dawn of a New Era* are about the same period.

The new era, however, was not the modern one, if we use the word modern with the meaning it has, for example, in the phrase "modern art." For the assumptions of modern art—the revolutionary movement that began when Picasso painted his *Demoiselles d'Avignon* in 1907—are most hostile to those of Renaissance art, while modern taste and sensibility have been formed and satisfied not by Praxiteles and Raphael but by Greek archaic and Romanesque sculpture, the art of the steppes, Japanese prints, and African masks. Nor can we argue, to take one more example, that modern science began in the Renaissance. The Renaissance did indeed lay the foundations of Newtonian science; but in science as in art the period begun by the Renaissance ended in the late nineteenth and early twentieth centuries, notably with the physics of Planck and Einstein.

The present position of Western Europe in the world suggests a similar periodization. Until the fifteenth century Europe had been the docile pupil of Greco-Roman antiquity and of the more sophisticated cultures of the Far and Near East. After 1500 not only was Europe a cultural and technological creditor; by the last decades of the nineteenth century the whole globe was the political and economic hinterland of the tiny western peninsula of the Eurasian land mass. In our own century this European domination of the world has disintegrated with incredible swiftness. Because our own period too is one of rapid transition, its characteristically "modern" features point forward to an unknown future, not back to the Renaissance; whereas the seeds of modernity we discover in the Renaissance are today the withered blossoms of a vanishing traditional past.

It is important to keep another fact in mind when we discuss the problem of the modern. Between us and the Renaissance lie the industrialization of the West and the French and Russian revolutions. The gulf is enormous, and it requires a very considerable imaginative leap to cross it. The jump will be easier if we remember that in the fifteenth and sixteenth centuries men still gave their political loyalty to persons rather than states. "Fatherland," "patrie," and "patria" normally meant the region or town where they were born, not the whole territory ruled by their prince. Wars were dynastic and personal and rarely involved national, to say nothing of economic, interests. When men revolted, their hope was to return to the "good old days" and the "good old law," not to create a new society. The economy was overwhelmingly agrarian, even in the most urbanized areas of the continent like north and central Italy. Society was landed and aristocratic. The political, economic, and social structure of Renaissance Europe was closer to that of the Roman Empire, Ming China, and feudal Japan than to contemporary Europe or America.

Let us therefore use the word Renaissance in a perfectly neutral sense to denote a particular period of time, roughly the years from the Black Death in the middle of the fourteenth century to the early seventeenth century, and not only in Italy but in all of Europe. We can (depending on the kind of material we are studying and our perspective on it) understand much of this period as the crisis time of medieval civilization; we can also see it as a period of creativity and new beginnings. Better still we should understand it as both: as a period of transition between one distinctive civilization and another. Looked at in this last perspective, the Renaissance was the beginning of early modern Europe, that is, of preindustrial modern Europe. And provided we keep firmly in mind that during the Renaissance Europe was an "underdeveloped" society, we can go further and say that Renaissance men built the foundations for the Europe which endured until the second half of the nineteenth century. (Since the two world wars it has been building a new sort of civilization whose contours are still only dimly discernible.)

In the transition from medieval to early modern Europe two developments are of particular interest and importance: the emergence of a vigorous lay culture in fifteenth-century Italy and the Lutheran revolution in Germany.

During most of the fifteen centuries between the fall of the Roman Empire in the fifth century and the Risorgimento, the national movement of the nineteenth century, foreigners ruled a disunited Italy. In the Middle Ages Italy was divided into three spheres of power: northern Italy and part of central Italy (notably Tuscany) belonged to the Holy Roman Empire of the German kings and was known as the *Regnum Italicum;* Rome and the rest of central Italy were under the sovereignty of the popes; southern Italy and Sicily formed a separate kingdom.

With the virtual withdrawal from Italy between 1250 and the early years of the fourteenth century of the ecumenical powers of empire and papacy, this division of power and the political order based on it collapsed. Effective imperial power in Italy broke down during the imperial inter-regnum of 1250–1275 and was never again restored. By 1300 the city states of Lombardy and Tuscany were in practice free and independent of their nominal feudal overlord. The removal of the papacy from Rome to Avignon in the early fourteenth century bestowed a similar de facto inde-pendence on the rest of central Italy; and when the popes sought to make effective their sovereign rights within the papal states after the return of the curia to Rome at the end of the century, they did so less as universal spiritual monarchs than as rulers of a particular Italian state. This relative freedom of action lasted for 200 years, until the French invasion of 1494 and the struggle of France and Spain during the first half of the sixteenth century to dominate the peninsula. Spain was the victor, and from about 1530 to the establishment of the national Italian kingdom in the nineteenth century, the house of Hapsburg, first the Spanish branch, then the Austrian branch, ruled in Italy. A notable characteristic then of the period we call the Renaissance is that it was the only period in the history of Italy be-tween antiquity and the nineteenth century when Italians controlled their own political destiny.

Since antiquity northern and central Italy had been exceptionally dense with towns. Nowhere else in Europe was urban life more dynamic and sophisticated; nowhere was resistance to the claims of presumptuous over-lords more tenacious. Wherever medieval cities flourished—in south Ger-many, the Netherlands, Catalonia, and Provence, as well as in Italy—resistance to political unification in the larger framework of a territorial state was particularly marked. In Italy civic particularism grew with the cities' ability to defend it. By the end of the thirteenth century their wealth and power had made them virtually immune to the interference of pope or emperor. The collapse of imperial authority and the withdrawal of the papacy to Avignon made permanent the de facto independence won in earlier struggles. The result was the atomization of the peninsula. Renais-sance Italy, in its liveliest areas, was, like classical Greece, a congeries of fiercely independent, competing, warring city-states.

A sense of national identity was not entirely absent, for geography made it easy to visualize Italy as an intelligible unit, its frontiers drawn by Nature herself: on three sides the sea, to the north the barrier of the Alps. Dante had expressed the linguistic kinship of all Italians, and his *Divine Comedy* worked to make that kinship an effective linguistic unity. The recognized intellectual and artistic primacy of Italy in the Renaissance aroused pride in all Italians. That non-Italians were barbarians was as self-evident to them as the parallel conviction had been to the Greeks. In a famous canzone entitled *Italia mia* (1341–1342) Petrarch described Italy as "the loveliest country of the earth" and called on Italians to revive the ancient Roman virtues. By the fifteenth century it was a commonplace of humanist rhetoric that Italy was sacred soil where no barbarian had any right to be. The poignancy of the famous last chapter of Machiavelli's *Prince* flows from this conviction. Writing after Italy had become the battle ground of foreigner invaders, he quoted *Italia mia* and called for a virtuous ruler to arise and liberate Italy from the "barbarous domination that stinks in the nostrils of everyone."

Machiavelli believed passionately in liberty, but in a liberty that made unity impossible. To lament the failure of the independent city-states of Italy to unite is to read back the aspirations of the nineteenth century into an earlier and very different age. For the Renaissance idea of liberty no more implied unity than it implied democracy. In internal politics it meant freedom from the rule of one man or of one family; in international affairs it meant independence from foreign domination (and to the Florentine every non-Florentine was a foreigner). Statesmen often distinguished the interests of particular states from the interest of Italy as a whole, but they never doubted for a moment that there was a necessary connection between the independence of the individual state and that of Italy as a whole. The idea of unity would have destroyed the very bases of their rule; the practice of unity would have destroyed liberty itself, as they understood it. An Italian state did not exist. No one seriously imagined that it would be desirable to have one.

Yet though Italians did not achieve unity, a structure of order gradually emerged from the apparent chaos of the early fourteenth century. The process was bloody, for its mainspring was the desire of every statesman to aggrandize his territory, of every city to colonize as large a hinterland as possible. In 1395 the emperor Wenceslas raised the Milanese territories of the Visconti to the dignity of a duchy, giving its ruler, Gian Galeazzo (1385–1402), a factitious legitimacy. From the fastness of a fortress from which he rarely emerged, he directed his captains east against Verona, Padua, and Mantua; then south against Pisa, Florence, and Perugia. Although his successors rapidly lost his more distant conquests, he laid the permanent territorial foundations of a Milanese state in the Lombard plain. A decade later Ladislas of Durazzo, king of Naples, launched a campaign of aggressive expansion from the south. Marching north from Naples, he annexed part of the Papal States. In March, 1414, he took Rome, sacked the city, then entered the basilica of St. John Lateran on horseback to venerate the relics of the apostles. He moved on toward Florence; but he too died before he could reach the city, contemporaries said of poison administered by a Perugian courtesan in the pay of the Florentines. Although for centuries Venice had been an exclusively maritime power, she too expanded rapidly on the Italian mainland in the fifteenth century. A desire to secure the vital trade route from Venice to the Brenner Pass and the need to protect her food supply in the lower Po Valley and to buffer herself from the predatory attacks of the Milanese sharpened her aggressiveness. By the middle of the century she had built a compact territorial state which included Padua, Vicenza, and Verona, extended to the Brenner in the north and to the Lake of Como and the river Adda, her frontier with the duchy of Milan, in the west.

The gradual expansion of the strong and the loss of independence by the weak rationalized the political map of Italy. Five principal states emerged: the pontifical State, the Kingdom of Naples, the Duchy of Milan, the Republic of Venice, and the Republic of Florence. In the interstices were the military principalities. The lords of cities like Mantua and Ferrara, Rimini and Urbino, were professional warlords. Their territories were generally poor and mountainous. They recruited from the petty nobility and impoverished peasantry and maintained their independence and solvency by hiring themselves and their soldier subjects out to the five major powers as mercenaries. The tone of their courts was seigneurial and military; feudal and chivalric ideals lingered longer here than anywhere else in Italy. It is not surprising that the loveliest courtly romance of the sixteenth century, Lodovico Ariosto's *Orlando Furioso,* and the most elegant expression of the Renaissance idea of the gentleman, Baldassare Castiglione's *Courtier,* come from the aristocratic ambiance of these military courts.

The governments of the five large states combined the principles of aristocracy and monarchy in a rich variety of constitutional structures. The Papal States were an ecclesiastical principality composed of many small seigneuries and cities very imperfectly obedient to their elected sovereign; Naples was a feudal monarchy whose king shared political power with a factious and tumultuous baronage; Milan was a ducal despotism; Venice a republic ruled by a closed hereditary aristocracy; Florence a republic in flux. Everywhere but in Venice the pattern of change was from the rule of a few to the rule of one man or one family. Florence is typical. In the middle of the fourteenth century the city was a republic; 200 years later she was a grand duchy, ruled in hereditary succession by the Medici, who, having begun as merchant-bankers no cleverer or richer than a hundred others, rose in the fifteenth century by skillfully manipulating the levers of patronage and intimidation to become the respected political bosses of the city. By the sixteenth century they were princes and popes, allied by marriage to the greatest kings in Europe.

The social structure of the Italian states was rigidly inegalitarian. The Republic of Florence is again representative. In 1500 its population was approximately 70,000. Contemporaries distinguished three principal social groups. They called the members of the highest group *ricchi,* because they were the richest men in the city; *principali, grandi,* the "first citizens," because they monopolized political power and rotated the principal offices in the state among themselves; wise men, *uomini savi,* because they were men accustomed to the exercise of power, of wide experience of the world, traveled, and well educated; "members of the great houses" or, collectively, *le case,* because the visible signs of their wealth, power, wisdom, and magnificence were their houses, those enormous piles which dwarfed, then as now, all the other houses and shops around them: the Palazzo Pazzi built by Brunelleschi; Alberti's Palazzo Rucellai; Michelozzi's Palazzo Medici; and most impressive of all, the great Strozzi Palace of Cronaca. These men were not only rich and politically influential, they also enjoyed the highest social position in the city. Their families were old and famous in the history of the republic. They were *nobili* and exhibited noble virtues. Above all they were men, as the great historian Francesco Guicciardini memorably put it, with an appetite for fame and greatness, *uno appetito di grandezza.*

Below the patricians were the *mezzani* or *populari,* the commoners, the men of moderate means. To distinguish them sharply from the *grandi* some contemporaries called them the *populo minuto* (a confusing term because by the end of the eighteenth century the phrase had shifted its meaning and come to denote a proletariat rather than a middle class). They were shopkeepers, bakers, butchers, winesellers, druggists; painters and sculptors; carpenters and stonemasons, lawyers, notaries, permanent civil servants, and schoolmasters: men like Lucca Landucci, who owned a pharmacy opposite the Palazzo Strozzi and passed his life in the political, economic, and social shadow of that grim and serene façade; or like Niccolò Machiavelli, head of the second chancery, a salaried civil servant, dependent on the patronage of *grandi* like the Soderini, Ruccelai, or Medici, a man, as he described himself in the preface to *The Prince,* "of humble and obscure condition."

In terms of the guild structure of the city, the *grandi* matriculated almost exclusively in one or more of the seven major guilds—the *arti maggiori;* the *mezzani* comprised the fourteen lower guilds, the *arti minori.* In fact the guild affiliations of the two groups were even narrower than this suggests. Many members of the *arti maggiori* were "men of moderate means." This was especially the case in the guilds of druggists, notaries, and retail merchants. The *grandi,* on the other hand, monopolized the four great guilds of crucial importance and power: those of the cloth merchants (the *Calimala*), the wool manufacturers (*Arte della Lana*), silk manufacturers (*Arte della Seta*), and the bankers (the *Cambio*). The mentality and cultural horizon of the *mezzani* were therefore typically those of the shopkeeper and the craft guild which controlled their economic activities and gave them a limited participation in the city's government. They were men of property, but of property on a small scale. Their world was bounded by the shop over which they lived, the guild hall, and the parish church. They could read and write the vernacular; they had enough arithmetic to do their accounts. But their intellectual interests were narrow, traditional, and conformist.

Economic cleavage fed social discrimination and resentment. The patriciate looked down on the *popolo minuto*. They were, said Guicciardini, "poor and ignorant and men of little capacity." The *mezzani* feared, envied, emulated, and angrily resisted the domination of the patricians. What they wanted is made vivid for us by Machiavelli, for the most articulate spokesman of the Florentine *mezzani* was also the greatest political theorist of the age. His bias was antiaristocratic, and he thought that the best government for Florence would be a *governo populare,* a regime in which the people, that is, the *popolo minuto,* would participate fully in political life: for, as he wrote in the *Discourses on Livy:*

One should always confide any deposit to those who have least desire of violating it; and doubtless, if we consider the objects of the nobles and of the people, we must see that the first have a great desire to dominate, while the latter have only the wish not to be dominated, and consequently a greater desire to live in the enjoyment of liberty; so that when the people are entrusted with the care of any privilege or liberty, being less disposed to encroach upon it, they will of necessity take better care of it; and being unable to take it away themselves, will prevent others from doing so.

This divergence of interest colored every aspect of life, not only in Florence but in every Italian city.

Below the *grandi* and *mezzani* were the masses, by far the largest social group in every Renaissance city. Contemporaries called them the poor (*poveri*), the pleb, the dregs (*infima plebe*); or the mob, the crowd, the vulgar, the multitude. About one-third of this group (or one-quarter of the city's people) was made up of the *sottoposti* of the guild of cloth manufacturers: that is, the wool carders, spinners, weavers, cutters, fullers, and so on who supplied the labor force of the wool industry, the backbone of Florentine economic life. The remainder was the varied mass of domestic servants (a very large group which included a substantial number of slaves—Tatars, Russians, Alans, Rumanians, even Greek Christians—imported from the East by the Venetians and Genoese); the apprentices and journeymen of the multitude of trades whose masters comprised the lesser guilds; the workers in the building trades. Men of this class were socially invisible and excluded totally from participation in the political life of the city. Guild regulation and municipal ordinance wove a tight network of oppression. Their lot was misery and want. Strictly controlled, totally dependent on their employers, they concentrated in the slums of S. Spirito and S. Croce. Our main evidence about them comes from court records: a stream of tales of violence and degradation, illiteracy, open and universally condoned exploitation, and a latent hatred which on rare occasions burst out in open revolt. A contemporary wrote about them: "If the lowest orders of society earn enough food to keep them going from day to day, then they have enough." The vast majority of Florentine political writers hardly mention them: Machiavelli's sympathy for the *popolo minuto* did not include the pleb. He wrote always—this indeed was his unquestioned assumption—as though the *grandi* and *mezzani* made up the totality of the population of the city.

Not only the pleb were excluded from political life; so also were the populations of the towns and countryside which the larger city-states subjected as they expanded. Venice ruled terra firma—as did Florence the steadily growing part of the old county of Tuscany she was coming to dominate—like a miniature colonial empire, with aristocratic governors appointed by the Senate or elected by the Grand Council. Venice was not a territorial state in the strict sense; it was a city-state linked to its dependent possessions on the mainland only as ruler and ruled. Her mainland subjects were not Venetian citizens. No representative institutions developed through which their desires and legitimate interests might influence Venetian policy. They felt no sense of community with Venetian ambitions, no sense of belonging to a larger unit that could command their loyalty and devotion. On the contrary, Venice treated them as colonials economically as well, by trying to make herself the entrepôt of every commercial transaction, forcing mainland merchants to buy and sell from and to Venetian citizens only, forcing Ravenna, for example, to give up importing goods directly from overseas and even from other parts of northern Italy. This is one reason city-states hired condottieri. The ruling class could not trust the loyalty of their own subjects.

For Further Reading

Brucker, Gene A., *Renaissance Florence.*
Burckhardt, Jacob, *The Civilization of the Renaissance in Italy.*
de Roover, Raymond, *The Rise and Decline of the Medici Bank, 1397–1494.*
Gilbert, Felix, *Machiavelli and Guicciardini: Politics and History in Sixteenth-Century Florence.*
Hay, Denys, *The Italian Renaissance.*

40   Humanism and Society

The *grandi* of the Italian cities are no longer important to us because they were an exclusive and effective ruling class. They interest us because it was their needs, their interests, their tastes and manners which, overwhelmingly, shaped Renaissance art and culture. In order to understand Renaissance civilization we must probe again the nerve of wealth and power. Let us begin by looking at two concrete examples of the Renaissance elite, one a Venetian aristocrat, the other a Florentine patrician family.

Andrea Barbarigo (1400–1450) was a typical Venetian aristocrat of the fifteenth century. Since the main economic activity of Venetian nobles was maritime commerce, he spent his youth learning this trade under the quasi-official patronage of the Venetian state. As part of the pattern of perpetuating a ruling class, Venice maintained several services for educating and launching young members of the aristocracy. They received a legal apprenticeship in one of the city's busy commercial courts. Here they learned the rudiments of commercial law and studied arithmetic and accounting. They were allowed to sail on the state's armed galleys (which made yearly or twice-yearly voyages to England and Flanders, Constantinople and the Black Sea, or to Beirut and Alexandria) as "bowman of the quarter-deck." As a bowman Barbarigo ate in the captain's mess with the officers and established merchants, learning from their experience the fundamentals of his trade; and most important of all he was allowed to load a small cargo of his own without paying freight. These voyages were his apprenticeship to the sea. They gave him experience at first hand of trade and of commercial conditions abroad and, because he was able and lucky, allowed him to increase the small capital sum of 200 ducats that was all his widowed mother could give him to begin on.

Barbarigo prospered. By the time he was thirty he was active in the main areas and departments of foreign trade, importing cloth from England, cotton from Syria, wool from Spain. In 1430, for example, the Senate sent five galleys to Flanders. On one of these Barbarigo loaded six bales of pepper. The galley on which he had rented space went directly to Bruges. Here an agent sold the pepper and with the money bought English goods: 23 barrels of tinware and pewter and 23 bolts of woolen cloth. The money involved had been transferred from Venice to Bruges to London by bills of exchange. In the winter of 1430 Barbarigo disposed of his English imports in Venice itself. He sold most of the cloth through his godfather's shop on

A.D.   1341   Petrarch crowned poet laureate on the Capitoline in Rome.

1353   Boccaccio's *Decameron*

1375   Coluccio Salutati appointed chancellor of the Florentine Republic

1404   Pier Paolo Vergerio's *Concerning Liberal Studies*, the first humanist treatise on education

1414   Poggio Bracciolini discovers Quintilian's *De institutione oratoria* in the library of the monastery of St. Gallen in Switzerland

1429   Leonardo Bruni finishes his *History of Florence*

1440   Lorenzo Valla's *On the True Good* (or *On Pleasure*)

1450   Pope Nicholas V founds the Vatican Library

1456   Giannozzo Manetti enters the service of King Alfonso of Naples

1462   Establishment of the Platonic Academy in Florence

c. 1469   Marsilio Ficino finishes translating into Latin the dialogues of Plato, the first complete translation into any Western language

1469   Birth of Erasmus

1486   Pico della Mirandola, *Oration on the Dignity of Man*

1505   Erasmus publishes Valla's *Annotations on the New Testament*

1516   Pietro Pomponazzi's *On the Immortality of the Soul*

the Rialto, to which customers came from all over northern Italy; he sold the pewter in Apulia, Ferrara, and Verona. With the proceeds he prepared shipments to send in the spring of 1431 with the Venetian fleets going to the Levant. Again his plans were conditioned by the transportation facilities arranged by the Venetian Senate, which that year had decided to send one fleet of unarmed cogs to Syria and the usual three fleets of armed merchant galleys: one to Alexandria, one to Beirut, and one to Constantinople and the Black Sea ports. Barbarigo shipped to Beirut a varied consignment: Florentine cloth he had bought from the Venetian branch of the Medici; the remainder of his English cloth; sheepskins bought in Apulia after he had sold part of his English pewter there; canvas, used in the East to pack raw cotton in; and two bags of *grossi* (silver coins minted in Venice for export to the East). For the return trip to Venice his agent in Beirut bought spices and raw cotton at Acre in Palestine and 250 ducats' worth of gold thread from Constantinople which Barbarigo later shipped overland to London.

This is an abbreviated picture of Barbarigo's business activities in 1430 and 1431, but typical of his activity throughout his life, although in his later years (especially after his marriage in 1439 to a girl who brought him a dowry of 4,000 ducats, a substantial increase in his capital) his scope widened. He invested everything in trade, so much so indeed that once in 1442, at a time when he had about 10,000 ducats' worth of goods going and coming between England and Egypt, he had to pawn a ring to borrow 10 ducats. He was a true merchant of Venice.

The Strozzi family of Florence, after the Medici the greatest Florentine family of the Renaissance, were the same manner of men as Andrea Barbarigo. One branch of that extraordinary family is of particular interest, the one whose greatest member was Filippo di Mateo di Simone degli Strozzi, that is, Filippo, son of Mateo, son of Simone of the clan of Strozzi.

Simone, founder of the line, matriculated in the wool guild in 1397. With his father and a brother he was a partner in a wool manufactory. The firm's total capital was between 4,000 and 5,000 florins and the average return was 14 per cent, about 200 florins a year and the major part of his income. Simone also sold insurance on commercial shipments from western Mediterranean ports to Italy. The fee was between 2 and 5 per cent. Such private insurance transactions were a handsome supplementary income for men who had the financial security to make good the occasional losses. He also had money invested in land and urban real estate: a town house, a tavern, and four small farms. At the end of his life these properties and his household goods were valued at 4,500 florins. Finally, he invested in government bonds. In 1345 the commune had consolidated its obligations into a funded debt, paying 5 per cent annually. This communal debt was called the *monte*. Simone had 1,400 florins invested in *monte* bonds.

When Simone died in 1424, his sole heir was his son Matteo. Matteo's business activities and investments were much the same as his father's. In a census made in 1427 for purposes of taxation his name appears among those of 247 heads of family with more than 4,000 florins of taxable property, placing him in the upper 2½ per cent of the population, though well below the eighty-six patricians with fortunes of over 10,000 florins. Politics was his undoing. In the ruthless factional fighting of the ruling class, predatory taxation, confiscation, and banishment were favorite weapons. When Palla Strozzi, a distant cousin and Cosimo de' Medici's archenemy, fell in 1434, Matteo was involved in his ruin. Cosimo exiled him and forbade him to liquidate his real estate in Florence. A year later he was dead, leaving a wife and small children. By 1459 Alessandra, his widow, had sold most of the family property except for the ten-room house in town and one very small farm in the country; and as her three sons grew to manhood they took the path of exile in their turn, virtually penniless, their sole resource their more affluent relatives.

Filippo di Matteo degli Strozzi (1428–1491) left Florence in 1441. He went to work for some Strozzi cousins who had built up a commercial and banking firm in Naples. He worked his way up in the firm and ultimately took it over. So sensitive was his handling of risky ventures of international scope that he built up one of the greatest fortunes of his day and restored the splendor and reputation of his family. When the ban against him was lifted in 1466 he returned to Florence. In 1471 his fortune, almost entirely invested at that time in the firm (known in Florence, like the Medici bank, as a *bancho grosso*), amounted to 31,649 florins; by 1483 it had risen to 112,281; and in 1491–1492 it stood at the colossal sum of 116,000 distributed as follows: real estate, 17,000; personal and household possessions, including jewels, 12,000; cash 52,000; and business investments 35,000. His children married into the core of the Medicean oligarchy. In 1489 he began the Palazzo Strozzi. He was as splendidly housed in death as in life. His three sons buried him in Santa Maria Novella, in a family chapel decorated by Filippo Lippi and in a tomb by Benedetto da Maiano.

The Barbarigo and Strozzi were members of a tiny elite. The Venetian nobles numbered some 1,500 in a population of about 100,000. In Florence the 600 names on the tax lists of 1403 and 1427 included every man in Florence who could effectively manipulate the levers of political and entrepreneurial command. We shall not be far wrong if we imagine a ruling group in every Italian city of about 2½ per cent of the population. To the poor everyone in this group seemed rich; but of course some were much richer than others, and solvency varied from immense wealth at one extreme to near ruin at the other. When they lost their money, or if prince or despot confiscated their property, if their rivals banished them, if their line died out, families dropped out of the patriciate. At the same time there was a steady influx of new men into the top rank of the business and political community. An able ambitious man moved into the city from the countryside; he made money by trade and moneylending; he founded a merchant-banking company of international reach and made a great deal more money; he matriculated in a major guild, acquired citizenship, and bolstered a shaky social position by advantageous marriages; by spinning the necessary web of influential friendships and dependent clients he got himself elected or appointed to public office; if he remained fertile and lucky, he founded a dynasty. Older families might call him a parvenu; by the third generation, though, the family was unquestionably patrician.

The organization of economic life gave patricians an ample leisure. Their firms required careful and alert supervision; but slowness of communication allowed them to space out the crucial decisions of buying cheap and selling dear. Their wool or silk manufactory was run by a manager who shared the profits; the senior partner had only to see that it was run well. They normally leased their farms to tenants on a profit-sharing basis, called in Tuscany *mezzadria*. The farm rarely brought in more than 5 per cent; but the arrangement left the landlord free. Most patricians devoted their leisure to politics: to seeing that the rich also ruled. Simone degli Strozzi was prior in 1421 and for some months treasurer of Arezzo. His son Matteo went on diplomatic missions and held a variety of magistracies. The Venetian aristocracy sitting in the Grand Council elected all officers of state, served on commissions and as ambassadors, took their turn as military commanders and provincial governors. A typical Venetian noble interrupted his commerce in pepper, sugar, nuts, tin, copper, skins, wax, and pearls to govern Treviso on the mainland or to command the Venetian galleys at the defense of Candia against the Turks.

Men of this sort had the self-confidence of the rich, powerful, and successful. They were proud of their capacity to get to the top of the social heap and stay there, to staff the offices of state and church; to advise the prince on the government of the commonwealth. Shaped by their business and political activities, they were competitive and self-reliant, individualistic, calculating and daring. They were men of wide experience and international perspective, and at the same time passionately devoted to their city and to the grandeur of their families. They were in short a new kind of lay aristocracy, different in its needs and interests from the feudal nobility of earlier centuries. The chivalric code of that old nobility and the scholastic learning of the clerical university answered their needs very imperfectly. The ideal men of the past, the monk and the knight, were no longer useful models. It is therefore not surprising that they became the enthusiastic patrons of a "new learning," of humanism, an educational and cultural program that offered them an ideal of man more in harmony with what they were and what they aspired to become.

Humanitas, from which both "humanist" and "humanism" derive, is a classical word and a classical idea. Cicero used it to translate the Greek *paedeia,* education or culture. The second-century grammarian Aulus Gellius defined it as "knowledge and instruction in the good arts." Fourteenth- and fifteenth-century humanists revived the word. "To each species of creature," wrote one, "has been allotted a peculiar and instructive gift. Galloping comes naturally to horses, flying to birds. To man only is given the desire to learn. Hence what the Greeks called *paedeia* we call *studia humanitatis.* For learning and training in virtue are peculiar to man; therefore our forefathers called them *humanitas,* the pursuit of activities proper to mankind." Humanists were men who taught and studied the *studia humanitatis,* the humanities, the good, humane, or liberal arts (*bonae artes, humanae artes, artes liberales*). Their intellectual interests were primarily literary, rhetorical, historical, and ethical; they typically wrote poems, orations, letters, plays, histories, works of scholarship, and a very wide range of moral treatises. Their literary language was normally Latin, and their admired models were classical. Some of them, indeed, were almost literally persuaded that everything it was really important for mankind to know was contained in the literatures of classical Greece and Rome, that is, in the works of ancient pagans like Plato, Cicero, and Livy and of ancient Christians like St. Augustine and St. Jerome. We mean by humanism, then, an educational and cultural program based on the study of the classics and colored by the notion of human dignity implicit in the word *humanitas.*

Humanist intellectuals occupied an honored place in society and exercised educational, professional, and cultural functions rather different from medieval intellectuals. Medieval intellectuals were almost always clerics; the cultural institutions in which they worked were the monastery and the university; it was their function to train priests and to study, organize, explain, and pass on to their successors the traditional substance of the Christian faith. Italian humanists were more frequently laymen; they worked in secondary schools, printing offices, and informal academies; they were teachers, civil servants, and independent men of letters, very closely tied to the rich and powerful. The sons of *grandi* were their pupils; indeed, many princes, merchants, bankers, lawyers, and rentiers patronized humanistic studies and were themselves enlightened amateurs, while humanists were often men of remarkable political and social importance, moving as equals among the great. Petrarch was the friend of princes and nobles. A line of distinguished humanists—Coluccio Salutati, Leonardo Bruni, Poggio Bracciolini—were chancellors of Florence. They drafted the official correspondence of the republic; wrote, registered, collected, and published the acts of the citizens directly invested with power, and generally supervised the lower echelons of the civil service. By the criteria of education, office, property, and income, the social rank of their friends, and the respectability of their children's marriages they were virtually indistinguishable from patricians. Whereas medieval intellectuals had educated priests, therefore, it became the function of humanists to educate the ruling class of the Italian city-states and principalities and to provide them with a philosophy of man in harmony with their needs and aspirations.

At the heart of the Renaissance philosophy of man is an assertion of human dignity. "What a piece of work is a man! how noble in reason! how infinite in faculty! in form and moving how express and admirable! in action how like an angel! in apprehension how like a god! the beauty of the world! the paragon of animals!" Hamlet's words combine pagan and Christian themes of great antiquity, some from classical philosophy and literature like the celebrated chorus in praise of man in Sophocles' *Antigone,* others from the Bible, the Greek church fathers and the medieval mystics: God created man in his own image; he is God's special care; for his sake God made all things and himself became man; he rules the world, and all other created things in it are subservient to him; he joins in himself the mortal and immortal and bears in his own nature the image of the whole creation (for this reason man is called a microcosm or little world); no science, art, or doctrine escapes the penetration of his mind. Italian humanists and philosophers of the Renaissance attached great importance to these themes and discussed them in a series of treatises entitled *De hominis dignitate,* on the dignity of man. The most moving of them is Giovanni Pico della Mirandola's *Oration on the Dignity of Man.*

In Pico's view man's greatest claim to nobility is that he has no fixed position in the hierarchical chain of being which philosophers considered the fundamental principle of order in the universe. The traditional structure was a simple one: inanimate matter, plants, animals, men, angels, and God. Rocks exist, plants live. Animals, men, angels, and God not only exist and live, they also know, each in a manner appropriate to him. Sensible knowledge is proper to animals; rational knowledge is proper to men; intellectual or intuitive knowledge is proper to angels. God's mode of knowing is far above even intellectual knowledge and almost inconceivable to the limited capacities of human beings. Man's median position between animals and angels is reflected in the diversity of his cognitive faculties and the complexity of his mental operations. For though his appropriate faculty is reason, he shares sense and imagination with brutes and intellect with angels. He can therefore know in three different ways: through his senses, by reason, and by intuition (helped in this very often by God's grace). Pico took one important and novel step beyond this scheme. Emphasizing both man's capacity to know in different ways and his moral freedom and responsibility, he argued eloquently that man contains in his own nature the possibility of the most varied development, that he can freely choose to become akin to any being, become like a rock or plant or beast if he turns toward evil, like the angels if he turns toward good. Man, that is, defines his own place in the hierarchy of being, rising or falling in it according to the nobility or baseness of what he chooses to know and love. Man is potentially capable of becoming all things—he can be a human bear or lion, dominated by cruelty, lust, and greed; or he can keep his head among the stars, his eyes fixed on heavenly things, and become a human angel or even, in certain ecstatic states, his mind rapt in contemplation and separated from the body, a kind of mortal god.

The notion that each man should freely and harmoniously develop all sides of his nature is the root of Renaissance individualism and of some of the most characteristic emphases of Renaissance thought: the greater stress laid on moral philosophy than on logic and metaphysics; the importance attached by many thinkers to the freedom of the will; the rehabilitation of the active life and the conviction that human personality develops most fully in the context of family and civic responsibility; a more generously secular conception of happiness which broadens its conditions to include wealth, pleasure, health, and beauty as well as piety and virtue. Such shifts of emphasis and value implied no direct repudiation of traditional ideals. They were rather an effort to resolve some of the antitheses of the immediate medieval past by understanding them not as alternatives but as necessarily complementary. The ideal man, it was suggested, should be both rich and virtuous, excel in both arms and letters, not only contemplate divine things but also act prudently in the world to benefit his family, friends, and city. He will then be a true individual, not only because the soul of every human being is immortal and unique, individually created by God and equally precious to him, but also because he has activated all of his own unique potentialities. The type of the *uomo universale* expressed this ideal individualism in practice. The great humanist architect Leon Battista Alberti (1404–1472) was a Florentine patrician, playwright, poet, moralist, man of letters; mathematician, architect, archaeologist, and art critic; an accomplished singer and organist; in his youth a skillful runner, wrestler, and mountain climber; handsome and affable, admired by his contemporaries as the phoenix of the age, a new Socrates.

The positive value assigned to wealth by many Italian intellectuals of the Renaissance is a good example of this more inclusive view of human nature and the world. Medieval men, at least in theory, had admired poverty more than wealth and considered riches a hindrance to salvation, attitudes shaped by the ideals of a monastic culture and derived from the Biblical bias against wealth and from the teaching of ancient Stoic philosophers that happiness comes from virtue only and that neither misfortune nor lack of temporal goods can trouble the tranquillity of the true sage. Petrarch modified the ascetic ideal of poverty by suggesting the virtue of the golden mean, Horace's *aurea mediocritas,* and by pointing out that Cicero had not protested against wealth as such but only against the abuse of wealth. After 1400 what Petrarch had advanced reluctantly, Florentine and Venetian humanists systematically defended. Seeing the problems of getting and spending with the eyes of citizens who claimed proudly that their self-acquired wealth was the foundation of their city's greatness, they praised international commerce and banking and encouraged the rational quest for property and profit. They maintained that wealth is a necessary condition of happiness and helps to develop the moral life. Thus Alberti, in a fascinating book on the family, argued that whatever increases a man's power to benefit his family and city is a good. Riches certainly do this. They foster a dignified, honorable family life; they are indispensable if the city is to be adequately defended and appropriately embellished with statues, fountains, and public buildings. They free men to exercise virtues like benevolence and charity more effectively. They promote happiness. For it is just as absurd to imagine that we can be satisfactorily happy if we are ill or ugly or lonely as it is to think we can be happy if we are poor. Riches bring a noble spirit inner freedom and cheer. Therefore the wish to be rich and to be good are not incompatible. True happiness consists in the possession of both capital and virtue.

A parallel shift of emphasis gave positive value to the body. The nude, much neglected by painters and sculptors since the fall of Rome, regained much of the importance it had enjoyed in antiquity. During the High Renaissance the idealized human form was the central subject of art. In humanist educational theory and practice physical training began to receive a novel attention as an integral part of a liberal education. In 1440 the humanist Lorenzo Valla published one of the most famous books of the Renaissance, his *De voluptate* (On the True Good). The Epicurean interlocutor in the dialogue defends nature, pleasure, and the human body. Nature is good; following natural impulses is pleasurable. To follow nature is the path to virtue. Therefore, those who condemn pleasure condemn nature herself. All pleasure is good, *omnis voluptas bona est;* so we should not suffocate the spontaneous inclinations which bring us joy. Valla himself did not share these opinions. The Christian interlocutor criticizes the Epicurean for speaking of "nature" rather than God and opposes a Christian pleasure of the soul, foretaste on earth of the beatific vision yet to come, to physical *voluptas.* But other thinkers soon combined the arguments of

Valla's two interlocutors to form an influential and attractive Christian Epicureanism, best flavored perhaps in Sir Thomas More's praise of pleasure in the *Utopia*. The result was a gradual rehabilitation of the natural, an emphasis on the dignity of the whole man, body and soul, and a healthy respect for pleasure, defined by Valla as a "joyful movement of the soul" combined with "a suave well-being of the body."

For many centuries thinkers had distinguished the active from the contemplative life, preferred contemplation to action, and found the model of the contemplative life in the monastery. Renaissance intellectuals redefined contemplation, passionately defended action, and asserted that the best lives combine the two, just as they combine wealth and virtue, physical and intellectual pleasure. Petrarch began the change. He wrote a book in praise of contemplation called *On the Solitary Life*. The contemplative withdrawal he praised, though, was not monkish but scholarly, a retired and studious leisure devoted to literature and philosophy. Other scholars developed his argument. Truth, they said, is more important than action. Cicero's political activity benefited one city for a limited time, but his writings on how to live well and virtuously have benefited all ages. For actions die with the men who made them, but thought, triumphing over the centuries, endures forever. The man who acts judiciously is admirable; but the man who has been able, as Vergil says, to know the causes of things is a god among men. Let men give themselves to the active life insofar as their human nature, family affection, and love of homeland demand. But let them remember that they were born to contemplate celestial things and seek the highest good—knowledge of the truth.

The argument assumes already that the active life has legitimate claims. These claims were put with increasing vigor by men committed to civic life. Their major premise was an assumption about the relative powers of the two principal faculties of the soul, reason and will. The will is free and in our power, whereas our knowledge, as one humanist put it, is no more than rational doubt. The object of the will is to be good; that of the intellect is truth. It is therefore safer and better to will the good than to strain reason in abstract speculation. The first is never without merit; the latter can often be polluted with crime and then admits no excuse. From the superiority of will to intellect they deduced the superiority of the active life to speculation and a program of civic humanism which condemned intellectual pursuits divorced from political and social commitment. Wise men should actively occupy themselves with the affairs of their commonwealth. Man is a political animal whose overriding duty is to his family, friends, and country. Civic duties do not distract men from higher things; they perfect men. So the active life, which prudently manipulates human beings, is to be preferred to the speculative life which contemplates the divine. "To tell the truth," says Salutati in a striking passage, "I will boldly affirm and openly confess that I will happily give up to you and to those who lift their speculation to the sky, all other truths, if only the truth and reason of things human are left to me." Solitary speculation, the lonely search for truth and the unshared joy of its discovery, these are lesser goods. It is nobler to be always active in the service of one's country by increasing its wealth and occupying its offices. Man, said Alberti, is born to be useful to man; and every citizen is obligated, after God, to his country. Noblest of all, however, is the man who combines speculation and action, who joins wisdom and learning in fulfilling family obligation, military service, and civic responsibility. When Alfonso, king of Naples, asked the humanist Giannozzo Manetti, then in his service, what was the proper duty of man, Manetti answered: *agere et intelligere,* to act and to know; and Alberti defined man as a mortal but happy god because he combined capacity for virtuous action with rational understanding. Both men were echoing wonderful lines from Cicero's *De finibus:* "Just as the horse is born to run, the ox to plow, the dog to scent a trail, so man, as Aristotle says, is born to two things, to know and to act, and in this he is almost a mortal god."

Complementing the Renaissance philosophy of man was a profound and distinctive piety. The point is worth emphasizing, for the myth of the wicked Renaissance, that beguiling mixture of artistic splendor with poison, perversion, and paganism, is still with us. Murder was indeed too often the instrument of policy. Evidence of unusual sexual practice is readily available—the more so because Renaissance Italy ranks with eighteenth-century France and several periods in the art and literature of India and Japan as one of the major sources of erotica of classic merit. On the other hand there is no evidence that anyone was an atheist or passed from an admiration of classical literature to a worship of the pagan gods. Renaissance Italy was a Christian society where the temperature of piety was high. This does not mean that styles of piety remained the same. On the contrary, important changes were under way.

One such change was a growing hostility to scholastic theology. Fifteenth-century men attacked the great summas of the thirteenth and fourteenth centuries on several grounds. Their style was barbarous and therefore incapable of persuading men to love God and their neighbors. They were too complicated, hiding simple religious truths under a mass of riddles, enigmas, and syllogisms. Theological reformers regularly compared themselves to Hercules fighting the hydra (the entangling syllogisms of scholastic theology) or to Alexander cutting the Gordian knot. Scholastic theology was disputatious and promoted contention rather than peace and concord. When the theologians raised knotty difficulties, opposed authorities *sic et non,* probed *quaestiones* in disputations and reconciled them by a subtle logic, they were rather pandering to their own dialectical pride than serving the faith. Finally, their effort to make theology a science, that is, to establish a systematically ordered body of true and certain knowledge derived from the certain but undemonstrable principles of revelation, was misguided, arrogant, and dangerous, for it produced only sophistry, arid intellectualism, emotional poverty, and lack of charity.

To this discredited theology Renaissance intellectuals opposed a piety which they claimed to be simpler, more pure, more personal and emotional, more eloquent, more humbly and accurately dependent on the divine text, directed less toward the presumptuous and inevitably disputatious goal of trying to *know* God in his fullness than toward the more human and possible aim of ardently loving him, more scholarly, more intimately and persuasively concerned with moral teaching. It was a learned piety; it was Biblical and patristic in inspiration; its orientation was ethical.

It was Petrarch who gave the phrase *docta pietas,* learned piety, its currency. Piety is knowledge, love and worship of God. Since piety is true wisdom also and since the philosopher is a lover of wisdom, the true philosopher is a man who loves God and true philosophy is necessarily a Christian philosophy, a *philosophia Christiana.* Petrarch knew, of course, that many ignorant, uncultivated men had achieved a noble sanctity. But a learned piety is nobler still. By learning he meant knowledge of classical literature. For piety and wisdom come from two sources—from the Christian God and from the ideas and examples of the greatest pagan ancients. Did not Cicero describe "one single god as the governor and maker of all things, not in a merely philosophical but in an almost Catholic manner of phrasing it, so that sometimes you would think you were hearing not a pagan philosopher but an apostle"? The idea of *docta pietas,* by assuming the harmony of Christianity and classical culture, defined for Renaissance men the proper relation between their enthusiasm for the antique and their firm commitment to Christian values.

The idea had other implications. True theology should be eloquent, a "union of piety and wisdom with eloquence." Its study should require historical sense, critical method, and knowledge of languages, notably Greek and Hebrew. True theology, in sum, should be Biblical; not a science but a positive wisdom, a holy learning derived from the holy page of Scripture. Examples of such a theology were conveniently at hand—the works of the Greek and Latin fathers. The simple Biblical piety Renaissance thinkers attributed to them justified their own aversion to scholastic method, their insistence on a return to the sources in their original languages, the normally exegetical form of their own theological work and the end they sought—an eloquent and vibrant personal piety joined to moral probity. Above all, the Biblical work of the fathers became a model for their critical study and correction of the Biblical text itself. Valla applied his passion for linguistic precision, his scrupulous flair for the way words gradually change their meanings, the philological techniques acquired in studying classical texts, to a critical probing of the text of the New Testament. Erasmus published Valla's *Annotations on the New Testament* in 1505, and the book influenced his own vastly more important Biblical and patristic studies.

Yet for Renaissance Christians learning and scholarship were always at the service of an ethical impulse. The end of humanist education was to teach men to live well and happily. From the many possible options offered by traditional Christian theology, Renaissance thinkers chose for special emphasis the freedom of the will and Christ's ethical teaching. From reading philosophy, they thought, man will learn to know himself, to recognize his own human dignity. This will encourage him to learn to live well and to flee all vices like the worst pest. The Bible, church fathers, and mystics teach the same lesson. From them the wise man will learn to hate vice and love the good, gradually learn, with God now helping his cooperative will, to live well and happily, and to die well, in the tranquil assurance of salvation.

For Further Reading

Garin, Eugenio, *Italian Humanism: Philosophy and Civic Life in the Renaissance.*
Goldthwaite, Richard, *Private Wealth in Renaissance Florence: A Study of Four Families.*
Holmes, George, *The Florentine Enlightenment 1400–1450.*
Kristeller, Paul Oskar, *Renaissance Thought: The Classic, Scholastic, and Humanist Strains.*
Martines, Lauro, *The Social World of the Florentine Humanists.*

41 Renaissance Art

The works of Renaissance artists, beautiful and civilizing in themselves, luminously supplement the evidence of texts and documents. "The good painter," wrote Leonardo da Vinci, "must paint principally two things: man and the ideas in man's mind." Because Leonardo and his contemporaries did indeed choose these as their subject, few sources make so attrac-

A.D.   c. 1255–1319   Duccio di Buoninsegna
      c. 1276–1337   Giotto
          1377–1446   Filippo Brunelleschi
      c. 1386–1466   Donatello
          1387–1455   Fra Angelico
          1401–1428   Masaccio
          1404–1472   Leon Battista Alberti
      c. 1426–1492   Piero della Francesca
      c. 1430–1516   Giovanni Bellini
          1431–1506   Andrea Mantegna
          1444–1510   Botticelli
          1444–1514   Bramante
          1452–1519   Leonardo da Vinci
          1471–1528   Albrecht Dürer
          1475–1564   Michelangelo
          1477–1576   Titian
      c. 1478–1510   Giorgione
          1483–1520   Raphael
          1494–1534   Correggio
          1511–1574   Giorgio Vasari
          1518–1590   Andrea Palladio
          1518–1594   Tintoretto
          1528–1588   Paolo Veronese

tively explicit the humanist philosophy of man as do Renaissance paintings, sculptures, and buildings.

The most distinctive artistic invention of the Renaissance was perspective. It distinguishes Renaissance painting from medieval painting. But not only that. Exact geometrical perspective is uniquely found in Western art between the early fifteenth and the early twentieth centuries. Wall paintings and mosaics from Pompeii suggest that an approximation of it was known to Hellenistic and Roman artists. Many Chinese and Japanese landscape painters were able, by empirical means, to achieve breathtaking illusions of distance. However, exact perspective construction—and more important the wish itself to depict objects in a unified space—was invented in Florence about 1420, remained perhaps the most important single characteristic of Western art until the Post-Impressionists, was unknown to any previous culture, and is absent from the art of all non-Western civilizations.

The invention of perspective threw open a window on the world. "I describe a rectangle of whatever size I please," wrote Alberti, "and I imagine it to be an open window through which I view whatever is to be depicted there." In the Renaissance the painting surface lost its opacity and became a clear pane through which we look into a world of rationally related solids, where the objects represented seem to have the same sizes, shapes, and positions relative to each other that the actual objects located in actual space would have if seen from a single viewpoint. Using a geometry of converging visual rays, perspective projects the illusion of a unified, continuous, and infinite three-dimensional space upon a two-dimensional plane. Probably invented by the architect Brunelleschi, with the sculptor Donatello and the painter Masaccio one of the seminal trio who founded the Renaissance style in Florence, and in Italy, and first described by Alberti, its principles and methods were fully worked out during the fifteenth and early sixteenth centuries by painter-theorists like Piero della Francesca, Leonardo, and Albrecht Dürer. The earliest surviving work of art that uses the new technique is Masaccio's fresco of the Trinity in the church of Santa Maria Novella in Florence, painted about 1427.

There is a suggestive parallel between the discovery of perspective in art and the renewed sense of historical distance which enabled Renaissance scholars and artists to understand antiquity more exactly and objectively. Medieval men had very little perspective on antiquity because no chronological line divided it from their own age. They knew only two great periods, one of light and one of darkness, before Christ and after Christ. They believed that the second great period of world history had begun with the simultaneous founding of the Roman Empire and the birth of Christ and that they themselves were living near the end of that same period.

Renaissance historians drew two sharp chronological lines instead of one. They invented the tripartite division of European history into ancient, medieval, and modern which even today remains the basis of our chronology. This new periodization of history modified profoundly men's sense of the past. Because the medieval historian believed that his own historical epoch had begun with the reign of Augustus, he was unconscious of the intellectual and imaginative gulf that had to be crossed in order to understand the ancient world. Apart from the inescapable fact that it was pagan, it could have for him no special character or style. The Romans were his contemporaries. The familiarity imposed on him by a theological periodization weakened his ability to see Rome as a culture complete in itself, quite different and separate from his contemporary world. By sharply dividing medieval from ancient history and their own age from the recent past, Renaissance historians ended this deforming familiarity. Their new periodization created the historical perspective on which the modern sense of history depends. They came to realize that a thousand years separated them from classical Rome. They realized too that this past was dead, that it formed a distinct historical period, remote, complete in itself, over. Disciplined by the insight that the arts and literature of antiquity were the historical expressions of a particular period and a unique society detached from their own, they gradually built up through the critical and historical study of ancient texts an image of ancient thought and institutions more nearly approximating ancient reality than any achieved before.

Nowhere is this imaginative reappropriation of the antique more striking than in the visual arts. A whole vocabulary of classical forms reentered Western art. Brunelleschi not only invented perspective. He went to Rome, studied the ancient ruins, and then subtly joined together columns and pilasters, arches and pediments in original buildings of incomparable harmony and grace. Painters and sculptors copied antique sarcophagi and collected coins and inscriptions. Inspired by the "excellent works of the Greeks and Romans," they covered the walls and ceilings of the peninsula with classical quotations: swags and garlands, Nereids and Tritons, fauns and nymphs; Roman armor, standards and trophies; the gods and goddesses of Olympus.

At the same time Renaissance representations of classical antiquity show a grasp and understanding of the ancient past qualitatively different from the medieval. Medieval artists had illustrated classical themes like the story of Dido and Aeneas. They had also reproduced classical motifs and forms, imitating from a coin the profile of a Roman emperor, or from a bas-relief the gracefully draped figure of a Roman matron. What is curious, though, in medieval art is the invariable disjunction of classical theme and classical motif. The Dido and Aeneas illustrating a manuscript of Vergil appear anachronistically as a medieval noble and his lady playing chess. Conversely, the Roman matrons who greet each other at Reims cathedral are the Virgin Mary and St. Elizabeth, for the scene is a Visitation. In the Renaissance, on the other hand, for the first time in more than 700 years, artists found for the substance of ancient literary texts historically and artistically appropriate forms. They reintegrated classical theme and classical motif. The classical deities shed their clothes and regained their ancient grace and attributes. A renewed consciousness of anachronism put Dido and Aeneas in classical dress. Ancient representations of Hercules were no longer used to represent David. A sharpening archaeological expertise re-created scenes from ancient history of enormous splendor and plausibility. This plausible rendering of classical themes is a fundamental criterion for defining the Renaissance in art. It is also tangible, and beautiful, evidence that new windows had been opened on the classical past.

The generalization of perspective and artists' enthusiastic admiration of the "excellent work of the Greeks and Romans" posed the central problems of Renaissance aesthetics, those of realism, harmony, and imitation. Perspective made it possible to represent the external world more realistically. It was, in a sense, a return to nature; and it gave new weight to the notion that the best painting is that which imitates nature successfully, a conviction the more solidly held because the injunction "follow nature" had been bandied about by moral philosophers for centuries. It is the function of the painter, wrote Alberti, "to render with lines and colors, on a given panel or wall, the visible surface of any body, so that at a certain distance and from a certain position it appears in relief and just like the body itself." Does this mean that it is the function of the painter to start us salivating before a bowl of fuzzed and bursting peaches? Certainly Renaissance artists and their audiences enormously enjoyed and valued representational virtuosity, the convincing rendering of transparent draperies, the sheen of pearls, subtle effects of cloud, storm, and light, the minute imitation of plants, animals, and fruits. Leonardo went so far as to call Narcissus the first painter because he saw his likeness reflected in a pool and to say that the "true painting" is a reflection in a mirror.

But the realistic imitation of nature was not the only function Renaissance painters thought their art should have. Representations of nature should be beautiful as well as accurate; and by beauty they typically meant the harmonious ordering of ideal forms, forms at once recognizably natural, but more beautiful than any actually observable in nature. A ravishing example is Raphael's *Galatea,* commissioned about 1510 by Agostino Chigi, a Sienese who made his fortune as a papal banker. The central figure of Raphael's fresco is the milk-white sea nymph Galatea, the beloved of Acis. Raphael learned her history and attributes from verses by

Theocritus and Ovid and from the contemporary Italian poets Angelo
Poliziano and Pietro Bembo. Against a background of sky and sea veined
like an antique marble, Nereids and Tritons, hippocamps and cupids,
celebrate her triumph. The scene is a vision of antiquity consciously disciplined by archaeological expertise: the figures come directly from a
Nereid sarcophagus. Raphael's successful effort to make the figure of
Galatea an image of ideal beauty represents a conscious revival of the
similar effort of ancient art. "To paint a beautiful woman," he wrote about
the *Galatea* to his friend and patron Baldassare Castiglione, "I need to see
many beautiful women. . . . But since there is a dearth both of good
judges of what is beautiful and of beautiful women, I use as my guide a
certain idea of the beautiful that I carry in my mind." This idea of the
beautiful he derived in practice from the canons of classical art and from
the example of ancient sculpture. The same idealizing impulse controls the
tight geometry of the composition. Like every Renaissance artist, Raphael
intended to imitate nature; but he regarded nature as ordered, harmonized
by geometry, just as Copernicus and Kepler were certain they would find
ideal geometrical patterns behind the confusing particularity of observed
experience. Thus Galatea's head is at the apex of a triangle. The horizon
divides the picture space into two equal parts, locked together in a musical
harmony by intersecting circles: the three flying *amors* outline the circumference of the upper circle; the figures around Galatea mark the lower
circumference of the other. In the center of rational nature is a beautiful
human being.

Clearly, Renaissance art was a humanistic art, and not only because,
like literary humanists, Renaissance artists admired and imitated antique
models. Artistic activity in the high Middle Ages had normally been an
anonymous communal enterprise controlled by the clergy and directed by
ecclesiastical authority to orthodox religious ends. By the sixteenth century, humanists had replaced clerics as the typical "inventors" of the subject matter of works of art. It is not surprising, therefore, that Renaissance
art is a learned art. Renaissance paintings must be read, for they were
consciously designed to tell stories, teach lessons, and inculcate humanist
ideals of knowledge, conduct, and piety. They are humanist also in style;
for the harmonies of their composition derived from the harmony of the
human body, "because from the human body," in the words of an Italian
mathematician who also wrote an early treatise on double-entry bookkeeping, "derive all measures and their denominations and in it is to be
found all and every ratio and proportion by which God reveals the inner-
most secrets of nature." Admiration of the harmony of his body and of the
world arouses man's admiration and love of God; by imitating nature in his
art man imitates the creativity of God and becomes himself a creator in the

realm of art. Ideas such as these are one source of the romantic idea of artistic genius. When the great romantic historian Jules Michelet took one short step more and defined the Renaissance as the discovery of the world and of man, he peopled the whole peninsula with geniuses and created the image of the age which has ever since provoked admiration and contention.

For Further Reading

Benesch, Otto, *The Art of the Renaissance in Northern Europe.*
Berenson, Bernard, *The Italian Painters of the Renaissance.*
Panofsky, Erwin, *Renaissance and Renascences in Western Art.*
Shearman, John, *Mannerism.*
Wittkower, Rudolf, *Architectural Principles in the Age of Humanism.*

42   The Reformation: Doctrine

When in October, 1517, an almost unknown Augustinian friar named Martin Luther posted ninety-five theses against indulgences on the door of the castle church of Wittenberg, a small university town in the territories of Frederick the Wise, elector of Saxony, the Roman church had been for many centuries the most powerful ecumenical institution in Europe. From Cracow to Lisbon, from Edinburgh to Palermo, its teachings defined every man's faith. The spirituality of its saints shaped his devotions. Its priests baptized him when he entered the world and buried him when he died. Its authority and blessing touched rich and poor, priest and layman, noble and commoner, king and subject. The church united Western European society in one common corps of Christendom, made it one body whose head was Christ.

The organization of this universal church was monarchical, sacerdotal, and sacramental. Punishing blows had weakened its worldly power: the humiliation of Pope Boniface VIII by the king of France and the exile early in the fourteenth century of the papacy from Rome to Avignon; the Great Schism later in the same century, when the shocking spectacle of two and even three rival popes excommunicating each other provoked the calling of a series of councils to reform the church in head and members; the increasingly successful efforts of kings and princes to subject the personnel and property of the church in their dominions to their control. As

A.D. 1505 Martin Luther joins the Augustinian Order
      1512 Luther appointed professor of Holy Sciptures at the University of Wittenberg
      1516 First edition of the New Testament in Greek
      1517 Luther's theses against indulgences
      1518 Zwingli called to be minister at Zurich
      1520 Luther's *Open Letter to the Christian Nobility of the German Nation, The Babylonian Captivity of the Church,* and *On Christian Liberty;* Luther's excommunication
      1521 Diet of Worms
      1524 Erasmus defends the freedom of the will against Luther
      1525 Conrad Grebel baptizes Georg Blaurock: the beginning of Anabaptism; the Reformation established in Zurich
      1527 The Schleitheim Confession, first Anabaptist doctrinal statement
      1529 Colloquy of Marburg
      1531 Death of Zwingli at the Battle of Kappel
      1534 First complete edition of Luther's translation of the Bible
      1546 Death of Martin Luther
      1564 Death of John Calvin

---

early as 1420 a pope wryly observed: "Not the pope but the king of England governs the church in his dominions." On the other hand, in the area of faith and morals Roman claims had become more comprehensive, in the area of church government more sharply monarchical. Curial lawyers identified the universal church with the Roman church and the Roman church with its supreme head, the pope. Just as the universal church cannot err in matters of faith and morals, so the pope cannot err—one assumption behind the doctrine of papal infallibility. Lawyers also identified the church with the ecclesiastical hierarchy. In this perspective the church was an "empire" ruled by the laws, ordinances, and will of its sovereign, who inherited the powers and prerogatives attributed to the sovereign prince in Roman law: *Quicquid principi placuit legis habet vigorem* (The will of the prince has the force of law).

The ecclesiastical hierarchy monopolized the right to interpret Scripture and administer the sacraments, the objective exclusive channels of

God's saving grace: baptism, confirmation, penance, the Eucharist, marriage, ordination, and extreme unction. The clergy was the first order in society and a class apart, separated from the laity by the indelible mark of ordination. The basis of the priest's authority was his miraculous and unique power to change the Eucharistic elements into the very body and blood of Christ. The doctrine of transubstantiation was the only medieval contribution to dogma in the strict sense, as the Mass was the heart of medieval sacerdotalism. When the priest said, "This is my body," he transformed the sacramental bread and wine into the body and blood of Christ, while their accidents, everything about the elements perceivable to the senses, remained those of bread and wine. He reenacted on the altar the incarnation and crucifixion. God again became flesh, Christ again died sacrificially for man's salvation. By eating the body of Christ the communicant shared his death and resurrection; for, as St. Ignatius had written in the apostolic age, the sacramental meal is "the medicine of immortality." Only through the priest as mediator could this grace reach the laity. Clerical power and the preeminent position of the church in society rested on this monopoly.

Between 1517 and the death of John Calvin in Geneva in 1564 revolutionary changes shook this hierarchical, sacerdotal, sacramental church to its foundations. A handful of religious geniuses denied the authority of Rome, abolished the Mass, broke the priesthood's control of access to salvation, created original systems of Christian doctrine, and founded new churches and sects. In less than forty years they shattered the millennial unity of Western Christendom.

The first half of the sixteenth century was a tragic and heroic age, humanized for us by paradox and irony. Not the least of its ironies is that this revolution in the church has come to be called a "reformation."

Reformers believe that the institution they want to improve is fundamentally healthy and good. Martin Luther was not a reformer. He did not want to purify monasteries by enforcing their rules more strictly or by raising the spiritual and intellectual level of monks and friars; he wished to get rid of monasteries entirely. Like many of his contemporaries, he deplored abuses in the papacy; but he was as radically hostile to worthy popes as he was to unworthy ones, for he believed that the pope was Antichrist. His mature purpose was not to correct abuses in, for example, the sacrament of penance; he wanted to abolish the sacrament because it had no scriptural foundation. In spite of its name, the Protestant Reformation was not in any fundamental way an effort to reform the church in head and members; it was a passionate debate on the proper conditions of salvation. Its serious concern was not with abuses but with the very foundations of faith and doctrine. Protestants reproached the clergy not for ignorance or for keeping concubines but for teaching false and dangerous things. They did not attack the corruption of institutions; they attacked what they considered to be the corruption of faith itself. Luther intended to restore Biblical Christianity, but he made a revolution. Like Jesus, he brought not peace but a sword. He came not to reform but to destroy—and then restore.

Luther's beginnings were conventional enough. The son of a prosperous miner of peasant stock, he received a sound elementary and secondary school education, and at eighteen matriculated in the University of Erfurt. There he followed the usual course of study in the faculty of arts: logic, some literature and mathematics, ethics, physics, and metaphysics, taught, wherever possible, from Aristotelian texts interpreted by members of the Nominalist school descended from the great fourteenth-century philosopher William of Ockham. He received the B.A. in 1502 and the M.A. in 1505. Obeying his father's wishes, he next enrolled in the faculty of law, the normal road to high office in church or state. He had just become a law student when, returning to Erfurt after a visit to his parents, he was caught in a thunderstorm and thrown to the ground by a bolt of lightning. In a moment of terror, fearful of death and possible damnation, he cried out: "St. Anne, help me, I will become a monk." Within a month, over the angry protests of his father, he joined the mendicant order of St. Augustine.

The next years were for Luther a period of the most intense torment, anguish, and doubt. He was, apparently, in every way a model monk: he was obedient, chaste, and studious; he obeyed the rule of his house and order; he ignored no discipline, penance, or religious exercise. But no peace came. His monkish good works brought no inner security. The more humbly he meditated on the majesty and justice of God, the more intense became his own feeling of sinful unworthiness. In the last year of his life, in the preface to a collected edition of his works he described the root of his despair: "Though I lived as a monk without reproach, I felt that I was a sinner before God with an extremely disturbed conscience. I could not believe that He was placated by my satisfaction. I did not love, yes, I hated the righteous God who punishes sinners, and secretely, if not blasphemously, . . . I was angry with God." God is just, a righteous God. Luther suffocated with the overwhelming sense that he was weak and impure, and that every effort he made to satisfy God's justice and righteousness, to merit salvation, was a failure. While he was saying his first Mass in 1507, he was so terrified by the disparity between his own sinfulness and God's justice, so appalled that a man as base as he should presume to transform the wafer and wine into the body and blood of Christ, that he almost collapsed.

In 1511 Luther's superiors transferred him from Erfurt to Wittenberg, and in 1512 he became professor of Holy Scriptures at the town's new university. He read voraciously: St. Augustine, the mystics, scholastic theology, humanist commentaries and editions of the Bible. He lectured on Genesis, the Psalms, and finally Paul's Epistle to the Romans. He found his solace and solution in St. Paul:

At last, by the mercy of God, meditating day and night, I gave heed to the context of the words, namely, "In it the righteousness of God is revealed, as it is written, 'He who through faith is righteous shall live.'" (Romans 1:17) There I began to understand that the righteousness of God is that by which the righteous lives by a gift of God, namely faith. And this is the meaning: the righteousness of God is revealed by the Gospel, namely, the passive righteousness with which merciful God justifies us by faith, as it is written, "He who through faith is righteous shall live." Here I felt that I was altogether born again and had entered paradise itself through open gates.

By the end of 1516 Luther had won his private battle. His terror before an angry God subsided and a tranquil assurance of God's mercy calmed and fortified him. His struggle to *earn* salvation gave way to a total passivity and trust and faith in Christ. Holding firm to Paul's belief that man is justified by faith alone without the works of the law, he came to believe that God's justice is a free acquittal of the guilty. He knew he was no less sinful now than he had been before, but he was totally convinced that God, in his purely gratuitous and mysterious mercy, had chosen him for salvation.

Between 1517 and 1520—haphazardly, without premeditation, under the pressure of events—Luther drew the consequences of his hard-won understanding that man is justified by faith alone. In the spring of 1517 a Dominican friar arrived near Wittenberg to sell indulgences, part of a campaign arranged by Pope Leo X, the archbishop of Mainz, and the Augsburg banking house of Fugger to raise money for rebuilding St. Peter's in Rome. In the early sixteenth century an indulgence was the transfer by the pope of superfluous merit accumulated by Christ, the Virgin Mary, and the saints to an individual sinner in order to remit all or some of the temporal penalties for sin later to be suffered in purgatory. Papal doctrine held that such transfers of divine credit could benefit not only the living but the dead as well. The Dominican salesmen even promised that as soon as a coin dropped into the collector's box a soul would fly up out of purgatory to heaven. Luther was horrified at this caricature of what he conceived to be the true economy of salvation. Because he believed that man was justified by faith alone, he argued that the pope could remit only those penalties he had imposed himself. He denied that saints had superfluous credits or that merit could be stored up for subsequent use by others. He branded indulgences as positively harmful, for actually imperiling salvation by giving simple people the dangerous impression that they could buy their way into heaven.

Luther's theses were the work of a reformer. He was attacking abuses and superstitions that had grown up around the sacrament of penance. But during the controversy aroused by his attack—which Pope Leo X momentarily brushed aside as a "monk's quarrel"—Luther drew more radical consequences from his unshakable conviction that salvation comes not from ourselves but through faith in Christ the Redeemer. Faith in Christ implies, he felt, the unique authority of the word of God revealed in Scripture; the Bible is the *only* source of religious truth because it is the concrete locus of the Word of God, the written record of the revelation of God in Christ, the channel through which God reaches those to whom he has granted the grace of faith. Looking one day for new Biblical arguments with which to buttress his criticisms of indulgences, he compared the Latin and the Greek texts of the verse traditionally cited as the scriptural authority for the sacrament of penance. The Vulgate, the Latin translation of St. Jerome, reads, "Do penance"; he found in the Greek, conveniently available to him in the recently published edition of the Greek New Testament by the great humanist Erasmus of Rotterdam, the rather different injunction, "Be patient." With a logic devastating for traditional belief and practice, he decided that the sacrament had no scriptural foundation and must consequently be abolished. Astonished, but undismayed, Luther found himself the leader of a revolutionary attack on the Roman Church.

Three celebrated tracts of 1520—*An Open Letter to the Christian Nobility of the German Nation, The Babylonian Captivity of the Church,* and *On Christian Liberty*—sum up the work of demolition. In them Luther attacked every fundamental assumption on which the medieval church had rested. Since only Scripture is infallible, popes and councils can, and have, erred. Not only was the pope's claim to preeminence in Christendom a usurpation; the pope was Antichrist: "O pope, not most holy, but most sinful. O that God from heaven would soon destroy thy throne and sink it in the abyss of hell." He called most Christian the opinions of Hus and Wycliffe, long branded by the church as notoriously heretical. To the rejected sacrament of penance he added the sacraments of confirmation, marriage, holy orders, and extreme unction. By rejecting holy orders he erased the distinction between a spiritual estate (pope, bishops, the secular and monastic clergy) and a temporal estate (kings, princes, nobles, merchants, craftsmen, and peasants), the distinction between priest and laymen, thus ending, as he put it, "the detestable tyranny of the clergy over the laity." In its place Luther put his conception of a priesthood of all believers. Because all Christians share one baptism, one gospel, one faith, and one church, he argued, they are equal in the realm of the spirit, all alike members of a single spiritual estate, all priests. He struck at the heart of sacerdotalism by redefining the sacrament of the Eucharist. He denied that the Mass was a repetition of Christ's sacrifice on the cross. He denied the doctrine of transubstantiation. He denied that the sacrament worked, as medieval theologians had taught, by its own innate virtue and power. On the contrary, since men are justified only by faith, the sacrament must be a function of the faith of the recipient. Here is the root of Lutheran individualism. The faith which makes the sacrament effective is one's own, given by God freely and gratuitously to each individual to whom he chooses to be merciful. The individual soul stands alone before its savior and creator.

Arguments like these were not the commonplaces of a "monk's quarrel." In October, 1520, a papal bull of excommunication reached Wittenberg. Luther burned it publicly. The next year the emperor summoned him to appear before the Diet, meeting at Worms. On the evening of April 18, 1521, Luther stood before his king and the representatives of the German nation. He was asked to recant his books. He replied in German:

Unless I am convinced by the testimony of the Scriptures or by clear reason (for I do not trust either in the pope or in councils, since it is well known that they have often erred and contradicted themselves), I am bound by the Scriptures I have quoted and my conscience is captive to the Word of God. I cannot and I will not retract anything, since it is neither safe nor right to go against conscience. May God help me! Amen.

The next day, April 19, Charles V answered in French, a reminder that the German king was a foreigner in Germany. His statement is as moving, as true to the characters and vision of the man who spoke it, as was Luther's:

It is certain that a single friar errs in his opinion which is against all of Christendom and according to which all of Christianity will be and will always have been in error both in the past thousand years and even more in the present. For that reason I am absolutely determined to stake on this cause my kingdoms and seigniories, my friends, my body and blood, my life and soul. For it would be a great shame to me and to you, who are by privilege and preeminent standing singularly called to be defenders and protectors of the Catholic faith, if in our time not only heresy but even suspicion of heresy or decrease of the Christian religion should through our negligence dwell after us in the hearts of men and our successors to our perpetual dishonor.

The emperor condemned Luther as an obstinate heretic and put him under the ban of the empire.

Luther summed up his teaching in two lapidary formulas: *sola fide* ("by faith alone") and *sola scriptura* ("by Scripture alone"). They answer the fundamental religious question, "What is the proper relation between man and God?" by attributing as much as possible to God and as little as possible to man. Man's principal faculties are his intellect, by which he distinguishes truth from falsehood, and his will, by which he distinguishes good and evil and orders his moral life. Luther's estimate of human nature was uncompromisingly pessimistic. Human reason is deformed and blind, incapable of saving truth. The human will is in bondage, free only to choose among different degrees of sin. All goodness, truth, and virtue come from God: all weakness, falsehood, and sin come from nature, especially human nature. Apart from God's grace, the human condition is hopeless. "It is not only the privation of a property of the will," wrote Luther in his commentary on the Epistle of St. Paul to the Romans, "nor only the privation of light in the intellect, of virtue in the memory; but the absolute privation of all righteousness and of the power of all strengths, of body and soul, of the whole man interior and exterior. Further, there is in man a positive inclination to evil, a disgust for the good, a hatred of light and wisdom, a delight in error and darkness, a flight from and abomination of good works, a race toward evil."

This assessment of man, so different from that of the Italian humanists, may seem hard and cruel; but for Luther and for thousands of his contemporaries it was demonstrably full of peace and sweetness, because, as Luther put it in this same commentary on Romans, "it teaches us to seek all assistance and all salvation, not from ourselves, but from without, through faith in Christ." For the doctrine of *sola fide* emphasizes both man's nullity and God's merciful concern for his salvation. Man is saved by faith without the works of the law. His own deeds, his own merit, count for nothing. He has no merit. Man cannot cooperate in his own salvation. Nothing he can do by his own effort brings him closer to God. If God were merely just, he would surely damn him. But God is also merciful; and so, mysteriously, gratuitously, he chooses to save some men, freely acquitting them of their guilt. Although they have been, are still, and will remain sinful, he gives them faith and considers them just. They, in turn, though fully conscious of their unworthiness, become joyfully confident, exactly as Luther had himself, of God's mercy and believe firmly that Christ has shed his blood for their salvation. Justification by faith alone, delicately balancing pessimism about man against optimism about God, is the cornerstone of classical Protestant theology.

Sola scriptura is a special case of *sola fide*. Because fallen man is morally and spiritually helpless, he cannot reestablish contact with God. God must reestablish contact with man. He does so through the incarnation of his Son. He justifies man by mercifully granting him faith in his son, who is also his Word, as in the memorable opening of the Gospel of John, that Word who is also named Wisdom, Christ, Redeemer, Second Person of the

Trinity, and the canonical Scriptures. For man receives the gift of faith by hearing and reading the Bible. Since Christ is the author of the written Word, the Eternal Word can be known from the written Word. This is why the sermon, that is, the explication of a portion of God's Word, dominates the Protestant church service and why Luther saw the Bible as the only infallible source of religious truth.

Locating the sole source of religious truth in Scripture was not an ideal way of ensuring Christian unity, for Biblical texts can be and have been interpreted in a bewildering number of different ways. Catholic and Protestant alike believed that true understanding of Scripture was a gift of the Holy Spirit. They agreed too that individuals should not interpret Scripture as they pleased; that could only mean that everyone was free to go to hell in his own way. But while Catholics institutionalized the Spirit's guidance in tradition, in the pope, and in the church, Protestants either claimed that the Spirit gave them individual guidance, or argued, in the face of all evidence to the contrary, that the Bible is simple, clear, and easy to understand. The difficulties inherent in such claims became obvious as soon as other reformers, guided, as they firmly believed, by the Holy Spirit, began to interpret Scripture as personally as Luther had done. Each considered his own interpretation normative; each attributed other interpretations to the inspiration of the devil. From these divergent readings of Scripture sprang new varieties of Protestantism. In the sixteenth century the most important were Zwinglianism, Calvinism, and Anabaptism.

Huldreich Zwingli (1484–1531), the reformer of German Switzerland, was, after Luther, the most creative theologian of the century. In 1519 he began to preach the gospel in the Grossmünster in Zurich. Luther influenced him profoundly. By the end of 1520 he had made the two fundamental Lutheran principles the heart of his theology: justification by faith alone and the sole authority of Scripture. He drew many of the same consequences from these principles that Luther did; he attacked monasticism, relics and the veneration of saints, and purgatory. He preached predestination and the bondage of the will and the reduction of the sacraments from seven to two.

Zwingli's originality was to spell out the consequences of *sola fide* for liturgical and sacramental simplification more consistently and radically. In liturgy and decor Zwingli was the first Puritan. Offended by corporeal representations of divine things and by the sensuousness of the traditional service, he banished from his church the "trills" of music and the "luxuriously and sleekly" painted images of saints. He broke up the organ in the Grossmünster and knocked out its stained glass windows, for he wished his congregation to have ears only for the Word of God and eyes only for

Scripture. The Gesù in Rome has become the symbol of a Catholic interior: blazing with gilt, stucco, and marble, smoky with incense, its theatrical perspectives reverberating with the serpentine polyphony of Palestrina and the massed bronzes of Gabrieli. Zwingli created in Zurich the representative Protestant interior: whitewashed walls, plain benches for the congregation, a wooden table and a simple wooden cup for the celebration of the Supper.

Zwingli's "sacramentarianism," the denial of the Real Presence of Christ in the sacramental elements of the Eucharist, came from his passionate concern to reduce religion to its essentials. Like Luther, Zwingli rejected the Catholic Mass; in 1525 he persuaded the town council to abolish it in Zurich. Both Luther and Zwingli rejected the doctrine of transubstantiation as unscriptural, implausible, and a scholastic sophistry. But Luther remained convinced that Christ was present in the sacrament, arguing both that his real body and blood coexisted in and with the substances of bread and wine and that the efficacy of the sacrament depended on the faith of the believer. Zwingli went further. If man is justified by faith alone, if God grants us this faith through hearing his Word, if the virtue of the sacrament depends on the believer's faith, then it must follow that the sacrament of the altar is not a channel of grace and that the Eucharistic Christ is not objectively present in it. The Lord's Supper or communion service is therefore not a physical partaking of the body and blood of Christ, but a spiritual eating, a commemorative service celebrated in memory of the redemptive death of Christ.

The differences between Lutheran and Zwinglian teachings about the sacrament of the altar reflect different interpretations of Biblical texts. In October, 1529, Luther and Zwingli met at Marburg in Hesse, hoping to heal the breach between them and present a united front to the Catholics. Their dialogue posed vividly the problem of authority lurking in the idea of *sola scriptura*. Luther began the debate by chalking on the tabletop Christ's words of institution: *Hoc est corpus meum* ("This is my body"—Matt. 26:26). Johannes Oecolampadius, the reformer of Basel, replied for the Zwinglians, saying that in this sentence the word *est* or "is" meant *significat*, "represents" or "stands for." And to prove that the word ought to be understood symbolically, he cited the sixth chapter of John, where Jesus promises eternal life to whoever eats his flesh and drinks his blood, but lest his disciples take him literally, explains: "It is the spirit that quickeneth; the flesh profiteth nothing" (John 6:63). Oecolampadius concluded that Jesus meant us to eat his body symbolically and spiritually, not literally and physically. But Luther with his customary massive certainty stood by his own reading of the text: "I won't argue about whether *est* means *significat*. I rest content with what Christ says, and He says: *This is my body.* Not even the devil can change that. Therefore believe in the pure word of God and glorify Him." A rapid exchange between Luther and Zwingli ended the debate:

Zwingli: We urge you too to give up your preconceived opinion and glorify God. I do not give up my text either, and you will have to sing another song.
Luther: You are speaking in hatred.
Zwingli: Then let John 6 cure your ignorance.
Luther: You are trying to overwork it.
Zwingli: No! No! This text will break your neck.
Luther: Don't brag. Our necks don't break so fast. You are in Hesse now, not in Switzerland.

Clearly Luther and Zwingli had different spirits. Each thought his spirit holy; each accused the other of spiritual witchcraft and insinuated that he was inspired by the devil.

Although *sola scriptura* means that scripture is normative both in faith and in morals, Luther and Zwingli relied on the Bible primarily to guide them in matters of faith and doctrine. The interest and importance of the Anabaptists is that they understood *sola scriptura* to mean a minute and literal ordering of human life according to the commandments of the Sermon on the Mount, and used the Bible primarily as a model of behavior.

Anabaptism arose during the early stages of the Reformation in Zurich among members of Zwingli's circle who protested his gradualism and demanded an immediate break with all antiscriptural ceremonies and doctrines. It crystallized as a distinct variety of Protestantism on January 21, 1525, when Conrad Grebel, a layman and the son of a wealthy Zurich merchant, rebaptized a former priest named Georg Blaurock, who in turn rebaptized the other men and women present in his house. They called themselves Brethren. (Their enemies named them Anabaptists, or "rebaptists," in order to bring them within the jurisdiction of an ancient law of the Justinian code carrying the death penalty for rebaptism.) The Swiss Brethren produced their first important doctrinal statement, the Schleitheim Confession, at a synod which met in February, 1527. After twenty years of persecution, sporadic excess, and near extinction, the sect received its permanent doctrine, organization, and name from Menno Simons (1496–1561). The Brethren were first called Mennonites in the 1540's.

Anabaptists ordered their lives according to three fundamental principles: adult baptism, separation from the world, and the literal observance of Christ's commandments.

Biblical literalism is picturesque, touching, and morally formidable. A few Anabaptists babbled like infants because Jesus commanded them to become like little children; or persuaded credulous virgins that it was impossible for them to be saved without sacrificing their virtue, for, they argued, the Lord said that only he who is willing to part with what he holds most dear to him can enter the Kingdom of Heaven. All Anabaptists refused to swear oaths because Jesus said, "Swear not at all"; and because Paul advised the Corinthians not to go to law, they spurned lawyers and never went to court. Reading that the earliest Christians held their property in common, they broke the locks on their cellar doors, shared their goods with one another, and lovingly practiced evangelical communism. Christ said, "Resist not evil" and ordered Peter to sheath his sword. Anabaptists were normally pacifists and nonresistant in the face of persecution.

They rightly believed that a life so different from the lives of ordinary men could be led only apart from the world. Anabaptists were separatists who preferred to live in segregated communities as far removed from "civilization" as possible. They were, in a sense, Protestant monks, though their ascetic withdrawal embraced men, women, and children. As citizens only of heaven, they rejected the state, civil government, civil coercion, and even the idea of a Christian magistracy. They refused to bear arms, to hold civil office, or to serve the state in any capacity. All creatures, they believed, were either good or bad, believers or unbelievers, in the world or out of the world, Belial or Christ. The good must have no truck with the wicked.

The sign of their separation, of their repentance and rebirth in Christ, of their membership in a society of believers who had consciously chosen Christ, was adult or believers' baptism. Baptism is the sociological sacrament; it links the individual to society. Infant baptism presupposes a church; adult baptism creates a sect. Luther, Zwingli, and later John Calvin retained and defended the ecumenical conception of the church inherited from the Middle Ages. To Anabaptists who argued that membership must be restricted to true believers, to those with faith, they answered that since no reliable criteria existed to distinguish the elect from the hypocritical majority, the Word of God, purely preached, must be available to everyone. Since the ecclesiastical community must therefore include everyone, every child must be initiated into it by infant baptism, just as circumcision initiated male infants into the holy community of Israel. Anabaptists, on the other hand, consciously chose Christ as adults. They formed a voluntary association of true believers, a gathered society of the regenerate; thus they considered infant baptism meaningless. Their ecclesiastical organization was the voluntary congregation, the conventicle, and they founded the first sixteenth-century sect, a type of religious association that was to flourish in the modern West, especially in Britain and the United States.

By 1530 Western Europe was seething with theological debate and controversy. The most creative phase of the religious revolution was over. Every conceivable doctrinal and ecclesiological position had apparently been formulated, adopted, and defended. It remained to organize and order, to make the classical statement of what Protestantism had become. This was the achievement of John Calvin (1509–1564).

Calvin was born in Noyon, a small town in northern France, a quarter of a century after Luther and Zwingli. His father was a prosperous notary, his background solidly middle class. He received an admirable education. He studied scholastic philosophy and theology at the University of Paris and law at the Universities of Orléans and Bourges. He mastered patristic and contemporary theology, and practiced the humanist's historical and philological techniques of textual criticism. His first book was a humanistic commentary on the *De clementia,* an ethical treatise by Seneca. Between the publication of this commentary in 1532 and the end of 1533, he had what he later laconically described as a "sudden conversion." He fled from France and settled in Basel, where, in 1536, he published the first edition of the *Institutes of the Christian Religion.* He was barely twenty-six.

Calvin's *Institutes* is the summa of classical Protestantism. Reworked and expanded constantly over the next twenty years, beautifully written, keenly and subtly argued, it organized the theological insights of the first generation of reformers into a clear, comprehensive, and effective statement. Calvin restated the fundamental Lutheran and Protestant doctrines: the unique authority of the evangelical standard and justification by faith alone. Zwingli and the Strasbourg reformer Martin Bucer shaped his view of the sacraments and bequeathed to him their puritanical passion for whitewashed simplicity and decorum. And although Calvin, like Lutherans, Zwinglians, Anglicans, and Catholics, feared, hated and persecuted the Anabaptists, one important tendency of Anabaptism penetrated his Protestantism: its concentrated drive to maintain the moral purity of the community of the faithful by an elaborate discipline. The idea of an ecclesiastical discipline enforced by the ban (and the character and emphasis Calvin gave to the idea of predestination) are the two most characteristic details of this majestic book.

The purpose of Calvinist discipline was to keep the Lord's Supper from profanation by making sure that everyone's life and manners were exemplary and that the beliefs of every member of the community conformed to the teaching of the *Institutes,* which the city council of Geneva declared in 1552 to be "well and saintly made, and its teaching the holy doctrine of

God." To ensure that all adult members of the church attend the Lord's Supper unspotted by heresy, blasphemy, or wickedness, a Consistory of elders sought minutely to regulate their thought and action. During the long period of Calvin's ascendancy in Geneva (1541–1564) they prosecuted fornication, fighting, and swearing, laughing or sleeping in church, promiscuous bathing, card playing, and dancing. They forbade theatrical performances and tried to close the taverns and replace them with community eating houses furnished with Bibles. If wrongdoers refused to mend their ways, they were excommunicated, banned from the society of their fellows and from the Supper. If they laughed at excommunication, they were handed over to the secular authorities for punishment. The "fraternal correction" of the Consistory touched high and low, and disciplined a commonwealth whose holiness astonished Europe. Geneva, wrote the Scottish reformer John Knox in 1556, "is the maist perfyt schoole of Chryst that ever was in the erth since the dayis of the Apostillis. In other places, I confess Chryst to be trewlie preachit; but maneris and religioun so sinceirlie reformat, I have not yit sene in any uther place."

Calvin emphasized predestination in order to reinforce the central truth of justification by faith alone, in order to make forever clear the greatness of God and the nullity of that "teeming horde of infamies," man. He wished to make inescapably plain that the Holy Spirit and God's grace were sovereignly independent of man's will and works. By his eternal and immutable counsel God ordains some to salvation and eternal life, others to eternal damnation. The salvation of the elect is an act of God's free mercy, taken with no regard whatever for human merit. The condemnation of the reprobate is an act of God's justice. Why, we painfully ask, does God take pity on some but not on others? There is, says Calvin, no other answer but that it pleased him to do so. God chooses some few and rejects the rest "for no other reason than that he wills to exclude them." His judgment is just and irreprehensible, although man's puny reason cannot grasp it. The reprobate, then, are incomprehensibly but rightly condemned. But this is not all. Because the reprobate are justly condemned, they are condemned by their own fault. "Accordingly, man falls as God's providence ordains, but he falls by his own fault." Calvin himself confessed the doctrine a horrible one: *Decretum quidem horribile fateor*.

For Further Reading

Bainton, Roland, *The Reformation of the Sixteenth Century*.
Erikson, Erik H., *Young Man Luther: A Study in Psychoanalysis and History*.
Monter, William, *Calvin's Geneva*.
Wendel, François, *Calvin: The Origins and Development of His Religious Thought*.

43   The Reformation: Society

From Wittenberg and Zurich, Strasbourg and Geneva, in printed books, popular pamphlets, and broadsides, by preaching, through personal contacts between monks and priests, commercial travelers and students, the sweetly cruel good news of revolutionary Protestantism penetrated to peasant and aristocrat, to craftsmen and merchants, in virtually every territorial and city-state of Europe. For the first time in centuries, religious doctrines were in open competition, and for a few years individuals had the freedom to choose among them. Why did some men remain Catholics? Why did others become Lutherans or Zwinglians or Calvinists? Why did still others become Anabaptists?

Protestant penetration of the peasantry offers an initial perspective on the dialogue of ideas and interests in the Reformation era, the more interesting because the first phase of the Lutheran religious revolution coincided with a violent peasant revolt (1524–1525), the last and most desperate of a series of uprisings that had begun in the fourteenth century. The clearest statement of peasant grievances, the so-called Twelve Articles of the Peasants in Swabia (January–February, 1525), began by demanding for every congregation the right to choose its own pastor to "preach to us the Holy Gospel purely and clearly, without any human addition, doctrine or commandment." The most important article was against serfdom: "It is the custom hitherto for men to hold us as their own property; and this is pitiable, seeing that Christ has redeemed and bought us all with the precious shedding of His blood, the lowly as well as the great, excepting no one. Therefore, it agrees with Scripture that we be free, and we will to be so."

The relation between peasant grievances and evangelical Lutheranism in these demands is not a simple one. The grievances themselves were not new: for at least two centuries peasants had protested against serfdom, tithes, restrictions on their right to use the common fields, woods, streams, and meadows, and against their landlords' efforts to raise rents and increase labor services. Very frequently too in the past peasants had drawn on the spiritual egalitarianism of the New Testament to buttress radical claims for social and economic reform. Even the election of priests by the congregation was common in medieval Germany. On the other hand, the Lutheran bias of the articles is plain enough. While Luther no more caused the Peasant Revolt than Voltaire caused the French Revolution,

A.D.
1509–1547	Reign of Henry VIII of England
1515–1547	Reign of Francis I of France
1516	Concordat of Bologna
1519	Election of Charles V as emperor
1521	Diet of Worms; beginning of Hapsburg-Valois wars
1524–1525	Peasant Revolt in Germany
1525	Battle of Pavia; Francis I taken prisoner
1526	Defeat of Hungarians by the Turks at the Battle of Mohács
1527	Sack of Rome by an imperial army
1528	Basel and Berne accept Reformation
1530	Diet of Augsburg; German Protestant princes declare faith in the Augsburg Confession
1534	Day of Placards; Act of Supremacy
1538	Geneva accepts the Reformation
1540	Society of Jesus approved by the pope
1542	Roman Inquisition established
1545	Opening of the Council of Trent
1546	Death of Martin Luther
1547	Battle of Mühlberg: Charles V defeats the Protestant Schmalkaldic League
1547–1553	Reign of Edward VI of England
1547–1559	Reign of Henry II of France
1553–1558	Reign of Mary of England
1555	Religious Peace of Augsburg on the principle of *cuius regio, eius religio*
1556	Abdication of Charles V in Spain and Empire; accession of Philip II of Spain
1559	Peace of Cateau-Cambrésis: end of Hapsburg-Valois wars

some of his doctrines were used to sanction it. (To pillage a monastic landlord was easier when it could be believed that monasticism was a perversion.) One of Luther's most famous books was named *On Christian Liberty*. An idea like the priesthood of all believers suggested more secular equalities. Above all, Luther embodied for the peasants the promise of the gospel itself and the hope that on new foundations of Biblical Christianity would soon arise a new and more just society.

Luther himself answered the peasants in his *Admonition to Peace: A Reply to the Twelve Articles of the Peasants in Swabia* (April, 1525). About the article condemning serfdom he said:

This is making Christian liberty an utterly carnal thing. Did not Abraham and other patriarchs and prophets have slaves? . . . Therefore this article is dead against the Gospel. It is a piece of robbery by which every man takes from his lord the body, which has become his lord's property. For a slave can be a Christian, and have Christian liberty, in the same way that a prisoner or a sick man is a Christian, and yet not free. This article would make all men equal, and turn the spiritual kingdom of Christ into a worldly external kingdom.

Luther wrote another tract about the peasants a month later, *Against the Robbing and Murdering Hordes of Peasants,* in which he urged princes and nobles to unite, smite, slay, and stab, "remembering that nothing can be more poisonous, hurtful, or devilish than a rebel." Luther only encouraged landlords to do what they were doing already; and he had no illusions about the German nobles; he called *them* "furious, raving, senseless tyrants." But it was the peasants who died. "Should someone wish to erect a victory monument because he has defeated the rebellious peasants," wrote the greatest German artist of the period, Albrecht Dürer, "let him use this design." The projected monument is a column. Around the base are cattle, sheep, and pigs; farther up are baskets of bread, cheese, eggs, and fruit; from the shaft hang a milk churn, agricultural implements, a cage of chickens; on the top sits a peasant with a sword plunged between his shoulder blades.

Until the end of his life peasants formed the majority of the large audiences that gathered to hear Luther preach in Wittenberg. Clearly Luther could and did find converts among the peasantry. Yet the alliance of Lutheran church and secular prince, forged in the crisis of 1525, and the ecumenical repression of the revolt by lords secular and ecclesiastical, Catholic and Protestant, made most peasants apathetic conformists. When they had freedom of choice they preferred to join a sect, apart from the state church; otherwise, they adopted docilely the religion of their prince.

The response of the urban population offers a different perspective on the spread of Protestantism. The free imperial city of Augsburg is a representative example. During Luther's and Zwingli's lifetimes the city, which almost a century before had provoked an admiring Italian to remark that the burghers of Augsburg were better housed than the kings of Scotland, was at the zenith of its prosperity, famous for the manufacture of textiles, clothes, shoes, and books and home of some of the largest and richest trading and banking firms in Europe. The profits of the house of Fugger from trade, royal moneylending (the Fuggers were the principal bankers of the Hapsburgs), and mining concessions in the Tyrol (silver), Hungary (copper), and Spain (mercury) averaged more than 50 per cent each year between 1511 and 1527. Anton Welser-Conrad Vöhlin and Company traded with Venice and Antwerp and helped finance the first Portuguese voyages to India. The Hochstetters manipulated the market with unprecedented bravura and became the most hated monopolists of their day. Herwarts and Grossembrots, Paumgartners and Rems, were other merchant bankers of the same stamp. Below these international tycoons was a middle class of guild masters, shopkeepers, local merchants and manufacturers, the master printers and the owners of small manufactories producing fustian and linen. At the bottom were the journeymen, the *armen Weber* (poor weavers), the workers in the building trades, and domestic servants.

The religious choices of the inhabitants of Augsburg corresponded to their positions in the social hierarchy. The merchant-bankers remained Catholic, while in the early 1520's Lutheranism attracted a majority of the independent masters and many workers. During the peasant war, Anabaptist missionaries held secret meetings in cellars and gardens and, according to local chroniclers, converted some 800 people, mostly poor weavers. The arrival of Zwinglian preachers in 1526 complicated the religious life of the city even more. By 1530 Catholicism was in full retreat except among the very rich; the Council had broken the Anabaptist hold on the workers by executions and expulsions; Luther retained many adherents among the middle class of citizens; and the sympathies of the government were Zwinglian. In one German city, then, during one decade, 1520–1530, when its inhabitants had relative freedom of religious choice, financial capitalists remained loyal to the traditional faith, petty manufacturers and shopkeepers became Lutherans, and workers turned to Anabaptism.

It is a hopeless enterprise to try to explain a pattern of religious choice of this sort by supposed affinities between particular systems of theological doctrine and the interests and aspirations of particular social classes. There is no innate harmony between Lutheranism and the psychological and ethical needs of petty manufacturers. Luther's social and economic teachings were exceptionally primitive, rooted in the traditional world of the peasant rather than in that of the nascent capitalist. At other times and places his doctrines captured kings, princes, knights, urban patricians, and peasants. Anabaptism, to be sure, found its converts principally among the disinherited—a doctrine so uncompromisingly hostile to established society it could hardly do otherwise—but Conrad Grebel was a Zurich patrician and several leaders of the sect were aristocrats. And it would be absurd to argue that Fuggers, Welsers, and Hochstetters remained Catholics because sixteenth-century Catholicism justified the acquisitiveness of monopolists and moneylenders. They remained faithful to Rome because they had loaned vast sums to their Catholic emperor, Charles V; they were fettered to him with hoops of gold. Every interest which held them to the Haps-burgs held them to the traditional faith as well.

It is not surprising then that Augsburg's pattern of religious choice was not the only one. Paris offers instructive variations. Between 1520 and 1530 the relatively small numbers of Protestant converts came from two main groups: intellectuals, mostly clerics connected with the university, and the urban working class. By the 1530's the social composition of Parisian Protestantism was more varied. During the night of October 17–18, 1534, Protestants papered the walls of the city with scurrilous placards attacking the Mass. Even the king found one on the door of his bedroom at the château of Amboise. The government reacted by burning as many of the culprits as it could catch. The surviving lists of men and women caught or condemned in absentia record their ranks and occupations. Most of the individuals listed were members of the working, lower-middle, and middle classes. One group consisted of journeymen dyers, weavers, masons, cooks, and carpenters; another of substantial entrepreneurs, goldsmiths, printers, and minor civil servants. A larger group was made up of modest artisans and retail traders: bookbinders, engravers, hatters, cobblers, illuminators, cabinetmakers, bakers, grocers, and four singers from the royal chapel choir. The lists also record a scattering of quite different types: a theologian and four Augustinian monks, the poet Clément Marot, several aristocrats and their wives, and a handful of rich merchants. In later decades Calvinism made enormous progress among the aristocracy and gained many adherents among the more substantial burghers. Conversely, petty artisans, shopkeepers, and workers, the masses of the capital, turned into some of the most fanatical Catholics in Europe.

Sixteenth-century European towns had roughly similar social structures, and similar tensions and bitterness everywhere separated class from class. The financial power of the merchant-bankers threatened the independence of guild masters, who, in turn, were transforming their journeymen into workers and themselves into small capitalist entrepreneurs. Each cordially hated the other. Sixteenth-century religions were to a large extent socially and economically neutral. They could and did appeal to any urban social group, just as they found adherents also among peasants and nobles. Local conditions determined the pattern of choice. What makes local diversity intelligible during the years when townsmen had reasonable freedom of choice among competing churches and sects is the tendency of members of different social groups to choose different religious affiliations. One result was almost invariably the same: the religion of the poor was different from the religion of the rich. By 1540 the wealthier citizens were Catholic in some towns, Lutheran in others, Zwinglian or Calvinist in still others. And in each town a religion different from that of the wealthy polarized the sentiment and piety of petty artisans, journeymen, and workers. Religions were becoming ideologies.

Only among princes have we enough evidence to examine the sociology of conversion at the level of the individual.

The economic and political advantages of a Lutheran conversion seem so obvious that the difficulty is rather to account for the fact that throughout Luther's lifetime the princely majority in the German Diet was Catholic. The aim of the German princes was the same as that of the more powerful and successful monarchs of Western Europe: to make themselves the untrammeled masters of a sovereign state. Becoming a Protestant gave a prince a new and widely admired reason for resisting his nominal overlord, the Catholic emperor. It fulfilled that very old ambition of secular rulers to be "pope, archbishop, bishop, archdeacon, and deacon" in their own territories. For the Protestant ruler automatically became *summus episcopus* ("head bishop," though some preferred the more classical Pontifex Maximus) of an autonomous territorial church: he controlled ecclesiastical patronage and appointments; he reformed abuses and supervised morals; he enforced uniformity of faith and liturgy on his subjects; in practice he even defined doctrine. Breaking with Rome also made him richer; he could dissolve monasteries and confiscate their land. He could not keep everything for himself. Too many vested interests were involved. But Margrave Philip of Hesse, one of the most important Protestant princes, managed to keep a typical 40 per cent.

Yes not even these advantages could tempt a majority of the princes into the Protestant camp. In the first place, conversion was a revolutionary act, risky and dangerous. From 1520 until his death in 1546 Luther was an excommunicated heretic under the ban of the empire. Charles V was determined to repress heresy. In 1547 he invaded the electorate of Saxony with Spanish troops and defeated the Protestant Saxons at Mühlberg. The elector was captured and imprisoned. Refusing to abjure his faith, he lost his electoral title and much of his territory. In the second place, a Catholic prince could win by persuasion and blackmail almost as much added power and wealth as the Protestant gained from a dangerous conversion. His tactic was to extract concessions from Rome in exchange for each move he made to suppress heresy: an expansion of the jurisdiction of his courts over the clergy; permission to tax the clergy regularly; a bull empowering him to visit monasteries and reform abuses; complete control of ecclesiastical appointments. The result for Catholic as for Protestant was a territorial church under princely control.

Clearly no simple formula will explain the religious choices of the German princes. One elector of Brandenburg was a zealous Catholic; his son, whose political and economic interests were no different from his father's, became a Lutheran. For Albert of Hohenzollern, cynical grand master of the Order of Teutonic Knights, reform appears to have been indistinguishable from secularization. In 1525, on Luther's advice, he renounced his clerical calling, secularized the order's lands, and made himself the first duke of Prussia. Others embraced the new faith because they believed that what Luther said was true. Princes remained Catholics for reasons equally varied. Some, like the prince-bishops, felt their own power and legitimacy to be inextricably intertwined with that of Rome. Some feared that religious revolution would turn into social revolution. "Do not fail to realize," wrote Duke William of Bavaria to his brother in 1527, "that a creed which allows each man to interpret his faith according to his taste and will must breed civil disobedience and ultimately rebellion and bloodshed." Others were as certain as Charles V that "a single friar errs in his opinion which is against all of Christendom," and would have as willingly renounced their states as their religion.

Princely conversion is important because the choices of princes determined the religious geography of Germany. Freedom of religious choice for most burghers, peasants, and knights—for everyone except princes and the ruling oligarchies of independent city-states—a freedom always relative at best, lasted barely twenty years. By the 1540's repression and persecution had radically curtailed it. As the coercive governments of city-states and principalities enforced religious uniformity within their territories, the religious preferences of magistrates and princes overwhelmed those of citizens and subjects. By mid-century the *ius reformandi,* the right to order the religious affairs of a territory, had become an attribute of princely sovereignty. The subject enjoyed only the *ius emigrandi,* the right of emigrating to a state whose prince's religion was the same as his. Just as the personal decisions of sovereigns determined war and peace in this dynastic age, so their personal theological convictions determined the fate of the Reformation in their states. The religious Peace of Augsburg (1555) made this novel sovereignty of the prince's conscience part of the public law of the empire. It allowed electors, princes, and imperial cities to choose between Catholicism and Lutheranism, and it made the religious choices of rulers binding on their subjects.

"He who rules a territory determines its religion." This is the phrase in which lawyers of a later generation defined the German religious settlement in 1555. The same principle increasingly shaped the religious choice of individuals everywhere in Europe. In 1542 an invigorated and militant papacy established a Roman Inquisition to discover, try, and judge heretics. It successfully rooted out almost every trace of Protestantism in Italy. The personal devotion of Charles V, the crusading tradition of the Spanish monarchy, and a popular piety kept hot and sharp by attacks on the large Jewish and Muslim minorities assured the Catholicity of the Spanish kings. Systematic persecution effectively suppressed dissent among their subjects. The government expelled Jews and Muslims. Inquisitors suspicious enough to jail the founder of the Jesuit order and the archbishop of Toledo, primate of all Spain, made the country equally uncongenial to Protestants. Powerful inducements also bound the Valois kings of France, Francis I (reigned 1515–1547) and Henry II (1547–1559), to the Catholic church. They needed papal support both in their struggle against the Hapsburgs and to accomplish their dynastic ambitions in Italy; while even before Luther's attack on indulgences an agreement with the papacy—the Concordat of Bologna (1516)—had consolidated their hold on the French church. They too, after a few years of comparative laxity, moved vigorously against heresy. At the death of Henry II in 1559 the vast majority of Frenchmen were Catholics.

The case of England is especially instructive, the more so because the English Reformation began as a constitutional rather than a religious crisis. No properly religious motive complicated Henry VIII's ecclesiastical policy. In theology Henry was a good Catholic all of his life. He had even attacked Luther in print, and a grateful pope had conferred on him the title *Defensor fidei* (defender of the faith). Nor did he break with Rome in order to strengthen his control of the English church and clergy. His powers were already as great as those the king of France acquired under the Concordat. He disposed freely of all important ecclesiastical benefices. He taxed the clergy. The laws known as praemunire restricted appeals to the papal court and protected royal courts from clerical interference.

Henry's motives were personal and dynastic: he wanted a male heir and his wife, Catherine of Aragon, had given him only daughters. Besides, he was in love with the charming Anne Boleyn. Since scripture forbids a man to marry his brother's wife, and Catherine was the widow of Henry's older brother, Arthur, only a papal dispensation had made it possible for Henry to marry her. Now he wished the pope to annul the marriage his predecessor had sanctioned. In ordinary circumstances he would have had no difficulty. Reconciling canon law and the exigencies of royal coupling had for centuries been a major subject of negotiation between popes and princes. But the circumstances were not ordinary, and the pope refused.

Henry's wife was Charles V's aunt; and Charles, whose army had sacked Rome in 1527, had too much power to be resisted.

Henry therefore took by force what he could not get by negotiation. To create a legitimate authority in England to annul his marriage, he forced the clergy to recognize him as head of the church in England "as far as the law of Christ allows" (1531). As the Archbishop of Canterbury put it: *Ira principis mors est* (The anger of the prince is death). Then, pushed by the king and his great minister, Thomas Cromwell, Parliament, kept in session from November, 1529, to April, 1531, legislated the independence of the English church. The Act of Appeals (February, 1533) cut every judicial link with Rome and made the Archbishop of Canterbury's court the highest and only legitimate ecclesiastical tribunal for English cases. The archiepiscopal court promptly annulled Henry's marriage to Catherine, and in the autumn Anne Boleyn gave birth to the future Queen Elizabeth. (An Act of Succession confirmed the child's legitimacy.) Finally, the Act of Supremacy (November, 1534) made Henry without qualification the "only supreme head in earth of the church of England called *Anglicana Ecclesia.*"

Like the German princes, Henry was now *summus episcopus,* lay bishop of his church and kingdom. It followed that the religion of his people must be the religion of the church's head. Doctrinal deviation was at once heretical and treasonable: Henry established the Anglican *via media* (middle way) by burning heretics in pairs, papists on one side and Anabaptists or "Lutherans" on the other. During the last years of his reign, and again in the reign of his Catholic daughter Mary, some Protestants expediently exercised the *ius emigrandi,* going into exile in Switzerland and Germany. The more elastic consciences of the majority created the sixteenth-century paradigm of *cuius regio, eius religio.* Nimbly following the doctrinal preferences of their sovereigns, Englishmen were Roman Catholics in 1529, Henrican Catholics from 1534 to 1547, moderate, then extreme Protestants under Edward VI (1547–1553), Roman Catholics once more under Mary (1553–1558), and again moderate Protestants under Elizabeth I.

In the Middle Ages the Western church had been a European corporation. During the first half of the sixteenth century it broke apart into a large number of local territorial churches—national churches, princely churches, provincial churches, even churches confined to the populations of a single city or, as in Poland, of a single aristocratic estate. Secular rulers exercised a predominant control over these churches: whether a church was Protestant or Catholic in doctrine, appointments to its offices, taxation of its members, jurisdiction, administration, and discipline were in their hands. In this perspective the Reformation appears as an aspect of the emergence of the sovereign state and the culmination of the long medieval struggle between secular and clerical authority. In the sixteenth century the balance of power swung decisively and finally from church to state and from priest to layman.

These results were unintended, for it had been the dream of the great reformers to give all glory to Christ and to restore the one, true universal church to its pristine splendor. Nor were the results achieved without resistance. The triumph of the territorial church and the coercive claims of Europe's secular rulers to be the religious arbiters of their dominions sucked religion into the fundamental political struggle of the age: that between royal and princely efforts to unify the state and centralize its administration and the defense of local and corporate privilege, the "liberties" of nobles and clergy, monasteries and universities, provinces and cities. For some Protestants and Catholics refused to emigrate because their religion differed from their king's; these resisted bitterly when he tried to convert them. If their king was Protestant, as in England, aristocratic reaction fought him under the banner of Catholicism. Where he was a Catholic—and most European monarchs ultimately became the allies of a reformed and reinvigorated Catholicism—Protestantism secured its political base at the level of the principality, province, or city, and the slogans of groups resisting the encroachments of centralizing monarchs were evangelical. The competing religions were as neutral politically as they were economically and socially. But just as religious choice reflected social cleavages, so too did political divisions take on a religious coloration. Once the struggle between centralizing "absolutism" and the defense of local "liberties" fused with the struggle between Catholicism and Protestantism, Europe stood on the threshold of a century of civil and religious war.

From this fortuitous sixteenth-century alliance of Protestantism with the defense of traditional "liberties" has sprung an irony as odd as the Reformation's name: the popular association of Protestantism with liberalism and democracy. Sixteenth-century Protestants were neither liberal nor democratic. On the contrary, most of them were elitist persecutors, like almost everybody else. Apart from their theology, their most valuable legacy to the future was precisely their failure to reunite Europe in a Protestant faith. The continent was to remain religiously fragmented. The broken shell of uniformity encouraged intellectual and religious diversity. It made possible, in time, a tolerance and liberal temper inconceivable in the age of the Reformation.

For Further Reading

Cohn, Norman, *The Pursuit of the Millennium.*
Dickens, A. G., *Reformation and Society in Sixteenth-Century Europe.*

Hillerbrand, Hans J., *The Reformation: A Narrative History Related by Contemporary Observers and Participants.*

Olin, John C., *The Catholic Reformation: Savonarola to Ignatius Loyola: Reform in the Church 1495–1540.*

44 The Counter Reformation

Not all the religious reformers of the sixteenth century were Protestants. Even before Luther's time there had been some monastic reform in Italy, and humanists in the papal services had reproached the Church's leaders in Rome for their lack of spirituality and their vices. Quite independently of Rome's influence, reform of the Church had also begun in Spain under Ferdinand and Isabella. But these beginnings of change, important as they were, scarcely deserve to be called a Catholic Reformation; they were inspired either by persistent medieval spiritualism or by new humanistic theories of the contemplative life. They differed greatly from those which would be carried out after 1536 partly as a response to Protestantism. Reformers like Gasparo Contarini, Reginald Pole of England, and Francisco Jiménez of Spain held similar, quite aristocratic conceptions of the devout life; thus their programs, both monastic and educational, lacked the repressive, regimental character of later reforms inspired by the ominous Cardinal Caraffa and St. Ignatius of Loyola. Indeed, the early generation found their influence insignificant in Rome, and were swept aside by Caraffa, who as Pope Paul IV instituted harsh changes reinforced by an Inquisition.

In any discussion of Catholic reform, therefore, the principal focus must be on Rome and the papacy, not on monastic or regional changes. In Rome complacency about spiritual matters, combined with a myopic concern for Italian affairs, made the popes of the sixteenth century overconfident. The Church had never been without critics of Luther's sort; thus Pope Leo X and his cardinals saw no cause for alarm when the monk posted his ninety-five theses on the door of the castle church of Wittenberg.

This complacency explains the papacy's failure to respond to Luther's charges of corruption. Time after time Rome had triumphed over reform movements, and Leo X saw no reason for abandoning time-tested weapons for controlling men of Luther's stamp. The last great reform movement, Conciliarism, had strongly threatened papal sovereignty but at the Council of Constance (1414–1417) the papacy had emerged victorious. The principal north European reformer, John Hus, had been burned at the stake as

A.D.

1528 Founding of the Capuchin order

1536 Commission of Cardinals established by Pope Paul III to reform the papal court

1540 Founding of the Society of Jesus

1542 Roman Inquisition established by the papal bull *Licot ab initio*

1545–1547 First session of the Council of Trent

1548 Publication of the *Spiritual Exercises* by St. Ignatius of Loyola

1549 Death of Pope Paul III

1551–1552 Second session of the Council of Trent

1555 The Peace of Augsburg, religious-political settlement of Germany; Gian Caraffa elected as Pope Paul IV

1558 Diego Laynez elected general of the Society of Jesus

1559 Death of Pope Paul IV

1560 Carlo Borromeo launches Catholic "model" reform as archbishop of Milan

1562 Neo-Scholasticism stimulated by publication of the *Loci Theologici* of Melchor Cano

1562–1563 Third and final session of the Council of Trent

1564 Revised *Index of Prohibited Books* promulgated by Pope Pius IV

1568 St. John of the Cross founds the discalced Carmelites

1572 St. Bartholomew's Day Massacre in France

1573 Veronese called before the Inquisition to defend the orthodoxy of his painting

1575 St. Philip Neri reforms and extends the Oratory

1582 Death of St. Theresa of Avila

1584 Publication of the Jesuit educational program, the *Ratio Studiorum*

1586 Robert Bellarmine publishes Volume I of *Disputation Against the Heretics of Our Times*

1609 St. Francis of Sales publishes the *Introduction to the Devout Life*

1629 Edict of Restitution restores much land to the Roman Church in Germany

1648 Peace of Westphalia

a heretic immediately after the council, thus demonstrating that papal control over church doctrine could be transformed into brutal political action. This example overawed later centuries. Several times Luther and his supporters feared that like Hus his life might end at the stake.

So long as papal control over doctrine remained secure—and this control was strengthened in the period between Constance and Luther—Rome did not fear reformers. Moreover, the Conciliarist challenge taught the popes that reformers could threaten their authority only if some king or prince supported their cause. The French monarchy had used the Conciliarists to gain concessions on church taxes and offices. Conflicts over money and church offices had to be kept separate from theology; thus the papacy strove to make its peace with secular rulers. Both kings and popes actually wanted to keep the Church as it was, a source of revenue for nephews and favorites, and the bargains they struck led to a decline of papal influence in northern Europe, and to a progressive nationalization of the French, English, and Spanish churches. But in Germany, a patchwork of territories where bishops often exercised great secular power, no settlement had been reached with the princes. Papal influence, and therefore papal revenues, remained high, which encouraged the princes to support "reform." Therefore, while Leo X considered the possibility of another alliance between secular princes and otherworldly reformers remote, that is just what developed under Luther.

By late 1520 Rome had lost control of the Church in Germany. Its initial responses had been based on the pope's power to define church doctrine. In the fifteenth century Pope Pius II had decreed that an attack on his power or even an appeal to a church council was heretical. But few German princes took these decrees seriously. If Luther was to be burned, it must first be proved that not merely his conduct but also his preaching and theology were heretical. Recognizing this necessity, Leo X sent his best theologians to debate Luther, but he underestimated how much his spiritual authority had been undermined. Indeed, the worldliness of Rome had its counterpart among several German princes.

In several places in Europe the popes could cancel the right of priests to preach or administer the sacraments, order their books burned, and possibly have them imprisoned, tried, and burned as heretics. But in Germany this was not so. Papal power to enforce edicts and excommunications depended on local Church officials; if they joined the rebel princes supporting Luther, Rome's control was lost. Careful diplomacy with the princes and victory in the theological war with Luther were, between 1520 and 1536, the papacy's only recourse. These weapons proved ineffectual because the papal diplomats could not gain the cooperation of the secular rulers. Lutheranism spread across northern Germany, and other reformers rebelled in Switzerland, France, England, and even in Italy itself.

Appeals for a church council had been made in Germany almost from the start, to the papacy's horror. But only the pope could call such a council, and no pope would do so unless he was sure that he could control its proceedings. Charles V, Holy Roman Emperor, who had his own grievances against the papacy as well as against the Lutherans, wanted a council, but his principal enemy, Francis I, king of France, opposed him because the Lutherans curtailed Charles's military power. Indeed, the Catholic Francis even allied himself with the heretic Germans in the long Hapsburg-Valois wars of the sixteenth century.

As questions of church reform and doctrine sank into the abyss of court politics and war after 1520, Europe's rulers failed to grasp what effect Luther's call to action would have on their subjects. Princes and popes accustomed to ignoring public opinion scarcely noticed the hot anger against corrupt and lazy clergymen which began to sweep across northern Europe. Since the opinions of the bourgeois, peasants, and minor nobles were of little consequence to the court politician, the Reformation became a social revolution without the rulers of Europe recognizing it.

Negotiations, theological debates, and war continued, with the Protestants holding the initiative until 1536. In that year Pope Paul III, whose motives for reform were of the most pragmatic sort, acted to curtail financial abuses and sexual license in Rome. At first improvements were sporadic, since the self-perpetuating clique of Italian families controlling the papacy was slow to awake to the Protestant threat in Italy and to the need for reform. Paul III even came to believe a church council necessary, though he dreaded the prospect and delayed calling it until he believed that the papal nuncios could control its proceedings. Finally, after a tricky agreement with Charles V, and after numerous delays, the Council of Trent began work in 1546. Papal power had become stronger by then, especially under Cardinal Caraffa's influence; the Vatican once again took an interest in the Church beyond the Italian frontiers. As cardinal and as Pope Paul IV after 1555, Caraffa combated abuses and immorality, while remaining rigidly conservative on matters of doctrine. Caraffa's program became the Counter Reformation.

Before 1542 investigations of heresy had been a local affair; Caraffa's "Holy Office" made them a papal matter. Soon no one was above suspicion. Even some cardinals were questioned as the atmosphere in Rome became tense. The extremely devout Bernardino Ochino, head of the newly founded Capuchin order and a prominent reformer who had chosen to remain loyal to Rome, fled to Protestant Geneva when "invited to Rome," afraid that the Holy Office intended to charge him with heresy.

Ochino was not the only reformer confronted with the terrible choice between flight and conforming to Caraffa's orthodoxy. The "Erasmians" and those who placed moral and Biblical teachings above existing practice were silenced, as courts which could imprison or burn persons for heresy imposed a generally Thomistic, thirteenth-century conception of the faith and the Church.

Thus, by 1546, papal power over the Church had been restored. Charges of immorality lost significance as a result of Caraffa's proceedings in Rome. Consequently, when papal officials at the Council of Trent proposed that doctrine be the first subject on the agenda, the majority of prelates agreed. Considering the size of the Church and the thousands who had the right to attend, the number present—only about fifty voting members—was small. After the council's initial decision, neither Charles V, the Protestants, nor "Erasmian" reformers could have much influence. Papal nuncios, Dominican theologians, and the Italian clergy joined to prevent any diminution of papal power or compromise with the Protestants. Having at last perceived the dangers of Protestantism, the papacy was now ready to maneuver and, if need be, to send armies to destroy its enemies. Papal diplomats controlled the council in almost every proceeding. Hopes for church unity were doomed from the beginning, for in the first, year-long session, Luther's teachings on justification, grace, free will, and the Mass were pronounced anathema.

In rejecting Lutheranism, the council extended the papal foundations of the Counter Reformation to the Church as a whole. It acted very cautiously on doctrinal questions, for there was considerable danger that in rejecting one heresy it might create others. Trent's formulation of church doctrine, although grounded on an old-fashioned Thomistic world view and refined by two hundred years of scholasticism, would stand firm for centuries.

Within the Church itself, on the other hand, the revitalization of thirteenth-century conceptions of knowledge, nature, and the universe would lead to the harassment of some of the boldest speculators and greatest scientists of the era, like Leonardo Bruni and Galileo. Moreover, Trent's declaration that the Latin Vulgate of St. Jerome was the sole canonical text of the Bible blighted historical scholarship on the early Church and the life of Jesus. The work of preparing critical editions of church fathers continued among Catholic scholars, especially since the Council of Trent had upheld church tradition as a source of faith and doctrine, but historical investigation as such declined after 1560, and subsequent heavy censorship by the Church made the scholar's life precariously dependent on the Inquisition in many parts of Europe.

At later sessions the council decreed the suppression of the office of "indulgence seller" and the strengthening of the powers of the bishops. The latter proposal would have reduced royal power in most dioceses far more than papal power, and for this reason the decrees were not accepted in strong states like France. In recognition of the need for better education of priests, new or revived religious orders, like the Oratory, were designed to complement the decisions at Trent. The council lasted, with three long intermissions, until 1563; then Pope Pius IV's bull *Benedictus Deus* confirmed its decrees, reasserted papal authority, and made it clear that further discussion was unnecessary. In the same year Pius issued strict rules for religious art and a revised *Index of Prohibited Books*. An ascetic quality unknown for centuries settled over Roman life.

Departing from its policy of ignoring spiritual concerns in favor of Italian politics, the papacy again adopted a global view of the Church as a God-sanctioned spiritual authority. Kings and princes would, of course, count for more in the opinions of papal diplomats than ordinary souls, but the need to minister to the millions of faithful had once again been recognized. Much remained to be done to regain control of the spiritual forces in Europe, even in states which had remained Catholic. But the bold statements about stamping out heresy once again took on meaning under Paul IV and his successors. The papacy inspired many devout young persons to follow its commands. Ignatius Loyola, founder of the Society of Jesus, made obedience to the "Hierarchical Church" the first rule in his *Spiritual Exercises,* the most influential devotional tract of the era. Loyola and the Jesuits followed Caraffa's lead, blindly accepted papal dogma, and then grew spiritually militant through traditional devotions. Between 1540 and 1555 the Society of Jesus grew rapidly, becoming a dominant force in the Counter Reformation. Through the Jesuits, who took on the task of educating princes and aristocrats, the Church prepared a new Catholic elite.

Free now of charges of license and corruption, the papacy once again assumed diplomatic leadership in Europe, claiming to be a force for peace, but, at the same time, a force for the suppression of Protestant nations. It assumed the burden of winning back heretics throughout Europe. Germany, then France and England, and finally the Netherlands became battle grounds where Jesuits, priests, and papal-supported troops converted and combated heretics. The papacy's overambitious ally in Spain, Philip II, made the Counter Reformation more political than ever as he sought to extend Catholic-Spanish power. By 1572 the Counter Reformation had developed into its final militant stage, subordinating its peacemaking role and helping to provoke war and violence until 1648.

For Further Reading

Chadwick, O., *The Reformation.*
Evenett, H. O., *The Spirit of the Counter-Reformation.*
Jedin, H., *History of the Council of Trent.*

Building the Early Modern State

45   The Golden Age of Spain

The history of sixteenth- and seventeenth-century Spain is full of extraordinary contrast, of victories and failures, of wealth and poverty, of supreme cultural achievements and also of degradation, drudgery, and despair. For most of this period Spain expended its resources and manpower on war in northern Europe. For decade after decade, Spanish troops, and mercenaries paid with Spanish money, marched and countermarched across the Alps, the Netherlands, and Germany, fighting people who seemed as alien to them as the Indians of America.

This preoccupation with northern Europe was new to Spanish history and is all the more striking when set against Spanish disunity and poverty at home. The culture of Spain was Mediterranean, and throughout the Middle Ages contacts with the north of Europe had been insignificant. But all this changed as a result of the dynastic accidents of the Hapsburg family, marriages, births, and deaths which ultimately united the Spanish crown with the great possessions of that family in Germany and the Netherlands. This Hapsburg unity, if anything, remained the long-term cause for Spanish involvement in northern Europe. Charles V, who ruled Spain from 1516 to 1556, was also the Holy Roman Emperor, sovereign duke over the provinces in the Low Countries, Burgundy, Austria, Styria, and almost innumerable other, lesser territories in addition to being king of Bohemia and Hungary, and Duke of Milan, Naples, and Sicily. As part of this great Hapsburg Empire, Spain was called upon to play a very special role in European affairs. The course of Spanish history was determined by this Hapsburg link in one of the most politically and socially disruptive periods of modern times, beginning with the Reformation and ending with the Peace of Westphalia in 1648.

Charles V, and then his son Philip II (1556–1598), also made northern Europe the center of Spanish interest because of mercantilist

A.D. 1545 Opening of Potosi mines, Bolivia
      1556 Abdication of Charles V; his son, Philip II, becomes king
            of Spain
      1557 Bankruptcy of Spanish Crown
      1568 Outbreak of revolt in Netherlands
      1571 Victory of Lepanto, against Turks; repression of revolt of
            the Moriscos
      1575 El Greco arrives in Spain
      1579 Disgrace and arrest of principal minister, Antonio Pérez
      1584 Direct Spanish intevention into French civil wars
      1587 Sir Francis Drake destroys Spanish fleet at Cádiz
      1588 Defeat of the Spanish Armada
      1591 Revolt of Aragon
      1597 Bankruptcy of Spanish Crown
      1598 Death of Philip II: Philip III, his son, becomes king; Lope
            de Vega presents *Arcadia*
      1605 Cervantes publishes Part I of *Don Quixote*
      1609 Expulsion of the Meriscos
      1612 Suárez publishes *De Legibus ac Deo Legislatore*
      1616 Spanish forced to leave Japan
      1621 Rise to power of Count Duke Olivares
      1628 Zurbarán, the painting *St. Serapion*
      1630 Velázquez completes painting *Vulcan's Forge*
      1640 Revolt of Catalans and Portuguese
      1643 Defeat of Spanish army by French at Rocroi

notions. With New World treasure and Netherlands trade the Hapsburg Empire seemed to form the basis for a very powerful state. To keep these lands and interests together in a period of revolt, Charles V and Philip II raised taxes until they provoked rebellion in Spain itself, and permanently dislocated and damaged the Spanish economy.

For Spain, Hapsburg rule meant subordination of national interests to those of the whole empire. Charles V believed that God had given him power to keep peace among all his diverse subjects, and to protect them from all enemies, be they Turks or French. To accomplish this purpose, Charles claimed, he had the right to call for military and financial aid in any part of his vast domain. Charles's Spanish subjects accepted this traditional, feudal principle of kingship, despite the alien origins of their ruler and his interests. Their submission brought them decades of fighting against France, against Lutheran rebels, against Turks, and, finally, against Calvinists.

But for these wars, Hapsburg rule would have had little impact on Spain. Charles V did not wish to impose common laws or a centralized government on all his possessions. He exploited Spain's resources but otherwise was prepared to leave the country to its own devices. For the Spanish people, Hapsburg rule was all giving and no receiving.

Spain's traditional enemies threatened her trade and security. The Spanish conquest of Granada in 1492 had cleared the peninsula of Muslim rule but had not eliminated Muslim-Turkish power in the western Mediterranean, or freed the Spanish mind of centuries-old fears and suspicions of foreigners. Turkish fleets harried the seas between Spain's east coast and her possessions in southern Italy. Would this Turkish presence cause Spanish Muslims to rise against the Christians? North African pirates, though not a serious military threat like the Turks, persistently raided and pillaged merchant vessels and coastal towns, forcing Spain to maintain a large fleet of galleys. How long would this expensive nuisance endure? The Spanish had hoped that the potent Hapsburgs would bring help from the north against these traditional enemies, but aside from a minor campaign in North Africa, Charles did nothing for them.

Under Philip II, Hapsburg imperial concerns continued to determine Spanish policy. Since Philip himself was not Holy Roman Emperor, keeping the peace in Germany was left to Philip's uncle and later to his cousins. But for all that, Spanish involvement in northern Europe did not decrease: Philip himself, after all, ruled the Netherlands. Though the Spaniards could hope for little territorial gain, Philip's involvement there, and in Burgundy, made France and Spain mortal enemies throughout the sixteenth and seventeenth centuries. Furthermore, dynastic ambition had led Philip to marry Henry VIII's daughter, Mary Tudor, heir to the English throne. This

EUROPE 1559-1600

Spanish Hapsburgs
Austrian Hapsburgs
Venetian possessions
Holy Roman Empire boundary
× Battle

again embroiled Spain in dangers from which little gain could be expected. Would the Spanish also have to pay for armies to suppress rebellions in England? Only the defeat of the Armada in 1588 by the English navy prevented this from happening.

To encourage the Spanish people to fight and to make economic sacrifices, Charles and his descendants exhorted the Spanish aristocracy and clergy to accept as a divine mission the task of preserving political order and religious orthodoxy in Europe. Had they not defeated the Muslims with God's help? This refrain pervaded Spanish politics and culture throughout her "golden age." Now the Hapsburgs wanted the Spanish, as the strongest, most orthodox, and "purest" people in Europe, to police Germany and the Netherlands, control France, and invade England, this last after that kingdom had fallen to a heretic queen, Elizabeth. This incredible program actually appealed to Spanish noblemen; not all the responsibility for Spain's later decline lies on Hapsburg shoulders. The Spanish nobility, overstocked with younger sons and short on money, was attracted by military commands, booty, and land in northern Europe. Since both Charles V and Philip II were very devout themselves, and since the Spanish nobles made at least a semblance of being so too, belief in Spain's divine mission was not difficult either to rouse or to sustain.

The "holy wars," as they were described to the taxpayers, began under Charles V in the 1520's, against Turks, Lutherans, and their allies, the French. Then in 1568, a rebellion broke out in the Netherlands which required large armies, notably those commanded by the great Duke of Alba, to repress Calvinists and rebels in provinces which had already become economically crucial to the survival of the Spanish empire in Latin America, and to Spain herself. Later, in 1618 during the reign of Philip III (1598–1621), after a twelve-year truce, Spain attempted to reconquer the Netherlands, and in doing so became involved in the general European war. Decline seemed inevitable after the failure of the Armada, but the Spanish struggled on. Neither of Philip II's successors, Philip III and Philip IV, nor able minister-favorites like Olivares, were able to break the mold which had shaped Spanish policy since the 1520's. Thus a crusading spirit, sustained by a tarnished chivalric code and by fanatical preaching against foreigners and heretics, gave coherence to what were in actuality mere dynastic claims. Various wily ambassadors who understood *raison d'état* attempted to base policy on real Spanish interests, but they failed.

Spain's huge American profits, especially the gold and silver from Mexico and Peru, were thus squandered. Many royal ministers were painfully aware of this waste and of the disastrous economic and commercial effects of borrowing and inflation. But policies did not change; reason was never allowed to penetrate the shield of prayers and hopes which held Spain together—even after the destruction of the great Armada. Spanish agriculture was also sacrificed to these wars; the *mesta* (large-scale sheep raising) meant higher revenues for the state than grain or cattle. Consequently crop failures brought starvation for Spaniards already living on a subsistence level. Taxes on commercial transactions, and policies favoring merchants dealing in war materials and colonial products, led to the decline of traditional Spanish industries. After decades of docility and support for their kings, peasant and aristocratic rebellions became more frequent as conditions worsened. Since strong regional identities persisted, entire provinces, not merely aggrieved classes, rose against the Hapsburgs.

The unity of Aragon, Catalonia, Castile, and other Spanish provinces (and Portugal for a time) was never very solid. The ties had originally been little more than dynastic, and the Hapsburgs failed to make them more substantial. Neither centuries of crusading, nor the Muslim enemy, nor even common economic interests had brought unity to the Spaniards. They had no common political institutions, for even the Church was controlled by nobles with regional interests. Spain never got what it most needed in the sixteenth century: quiet and isolation from Europe's turmoil. The colonization of the New World was essentially a Castilian effort, not a Spanish one, and so were the wars in northern Europe. Since Charles and Philip gave offices to those who served Hapsburg interests most zealously, the Castilians came to dominate not only foreign affairs but also internal administration. The Hapsburgs seem to have sincerely intended to uphold provincial laws, but their Castilian officials became increasingly hostile to regional political interests.

Despite his close attention to the endless reports and letters which he received when he was abroad, Charles was an absentee ruler for twenty-three of his nearly forty years on the Spanish throne. And though Philip II and his successors rarely left Spain, their government became increasingly remote from the country. Philip II picked Madrid as his capital and stayed there because it was the geographic center of the peninsula. He and his descendants virtually ceased to travel outside Madrid; the royal presence nearly always meant the king's Castilian officials. Fewer and fewer Cortes (consultative assemblies) were held, and Castilian practice became the model for the entire peninsula.

The extension of Castilian influence, no matter how offensive in other provinces, was inevitable, for Castilians paid proportionately more taxes and served the royal administration more faithfully and longer than the others. The consequences of this subtle Castilianization of the monarchy in the long run were to be disastrous. Provincial Spaniards began to look upon the monarchy itself as foreign; gradually Hapsburg officials, and finally Hapsburg policies, came under attack. The Revolt of Aragon in 1591 should have been a warning to Philip II, but he was too obsessed with the Dutch rebels to look into its causes. Instead he merely crushed the uprising.

But if Spain underwent enormous difficulties, these in no way impeded an extraordinary spiritual and cultural flowering. Along with the hardships came the exhilaration of conquering an empire of gold in America, and of playing the leading role in the salvation of all peoples from heresy. To many Spaniards it seemed that God had chosen them once again to play a special role in the world, and had given them the gold and armies to do it. This attitude helps explain the enormous spiritual vitality of the art and literature of Spain during the Golden Age.

Spiritual fervor, rigid orthodoxy, and firm convictions about man's place in the universe, and the social hierarchy graded from popes, kings, dukes, merchants, on down to peasants, pervaded the Spanish cultural and political achievement under the Hapsburgs. The *Spiritual Exercises* of St. Ignatius of Loyola (1491–1556) quickly became an extremely influential devotional work. It had enormous political and literary consequences as well, accompanied as it was by a monastic way of life to which its readers might adhere, and strict obedience to the pope. St. Theresa of Avila's (1515–1582) *Way of Perfection* contributed to the general Spanish religious and political dominance of Europe by appealing to women to reform the Carmelite order, and to found new monastic houses.

Spanish sculpture and architecture during the Golden Age had less impact on the rest of Europe, chiefly because the great Italians, notably Michelangelo and Bernini, continued to make Rome the capital of Europe in those arts. In painting, however, the unique spiritual intensity found in Loyola's thought manifested itself in a long and impressive list of primarily religious painters. Though Greek by birth and trained in Italy, El Greco (1547–1614) captured Spain's spiritual mood during his productive years in that country. The ascetic quality of El Greco's Spanish style jars with its modernity; only the asceticism survived in the works of Zurbarán (1598–1664) and Murillo (1617–1682). Sure in their faith, almost deintellectualized, the Spanish religious painters reflected the mood of a people with a divine mission in the world, and also, as in Murillo's paintings of commoners, the popular, more humane aspect of religion. Unafraid as they were of either sentimentality or harshness, Spanish religious artists stressed the themes of love in the Holy Family, the sufferings and miracles of the saints, and the miracles of the sacraments.

Secular painting reached its apogee in the court portraits of Velázquez (1599–1660). Whether in the face, dress, or hair of a little princess, or the massive body of Philip IV, Velázquez created a glow in his portraits which suggest that those he painted, be they kings or dwarfs, were set apart from the world.

By contrast, the political and religious idealism of Spain also inspired pathos and satire. The revived courtly poetry and manners of the sixteenth century could be ridiculed in plays and novels. Cervantes (1547–1616) accomplished the almost impossible task of satirizing chivalry without making *Don Quixote* unbelievable in the eyes of his contemporaries. His great novel, an incomparable picture of all aspects of Spanish society in his day, portrays sympathetically the contrasts between Spanish idealism and the harsh social and economic realities of Spanish life.

The last years of the sixteenth century proved crucial for Spain's future. Forced by exhaustion and defeat to curtail his imperial ambitions, Philip II had a splendid opportunity to examine critically the aims of the Spanish crown in Europe. But he was surrounded by partisans of the old northern-oriented policy whose only "solutions" to local dissent were military repression and the Inquisition. These same men continued to govern under Philip III and, in spirit, even under Philip IV. The government of Spain had become monolithic, racist, rigidly Catholic, and unable to conceive of any way of obtaining its ends except by force.

Sacrifices and hardships still seemed worthwhile to Hapsburg ministers, clergymen, and the Castilian nobility, but by 1600 the rest of Spain had come to resent paying taxes and furnishing troops without obtaining anything in exchange. Yet dissidents scarcely dared attack imperial policy, not only because they feared reprisals against their persons but because they still believed that kings had the right to manage foreign affairs any way they pleased. Defense of provincial liberties, therefore, became the rallying cry of non-Castilians. Despite further signs of breakdown and violence in the 1630's and 1640's, the monarchy refused to change its policy or to remove objectionable officials. The provincials protested, refused to cooperate with hated officials, and then took up arms. Too late, Olivares, Philip IV's great minister, attempted halfway reforms but without curtailing the northern war against the Dutch rebels and France. He failed to placate the provinces. Rebellions broke out in Catalonia and Portugal in the 1640's, the rebels joining with the French against their own government.

Spanish dominance in Europe had been based on unity and orthodoxy at home as much as on American silver and on military might. The Catalan revolt undermined unity, and Spanish power slowly declined. The war ended in 1659, but for the rest of the seventeenth century and into the eighteenth the Hapsburg legacy stifled the intellectual and economic life of the country. Wars and the crusading ideology had welded together an orthodox and snobbish aristocracy and clergy which held all the reins of power in the state. Intellectual life had been crippled by censorship and the Inquisition, which had been used against anyone protesting against either official theology or state policy. At last, even the combination of despair and hope that had sustained the last generation of great poets and artists— Lope de Vega, Murillo, and Velázquez—gave out. What remained was only fear: of foreigners and of the unknown. Spain's greatness was no more. The culture of the *Sieclo d'Oro* remained, but politically much had been lost, most obviously (and most disastrously) the northern lands that were to become the Dutch Republic.

For Further Reading

Elliott, J. H., *Imperial Spain 1469–1716.*
Lynch, J., *Spain under the Hapsburgs,* Vol. I.
Mattingly, G., *The Defeat of the Spanish Armada.*

46   The Rise of the Dutch Republic

Although the dramatic rise of the Dutch Republic to the status of a major power in the seventeenth century could not have occurred if it had not had a healthy and efficient political organization, the republic had few of the characteristics of a modern state. It was a loose confederation of provincial estates, themselves nothing more than confederations of towns and privileged groups, and continually in conflict over hopelessly complicated problems of sovereignty. In addition, each province had a stadtholder, usually a prince from the House of Orange, who sometimes acted as an executive but remained constitutionally an officer of the sovereign provincial estates. In a way the republic was a curious medieval relic, an improbable institutional platypus, rather than a prototype of a national political organization of modern times.

Since it was undeniably a success, the Dutch Republic raises some interesting questions: Was monarchy, absolute or constitutional, the only viable answer to the organizational problems posed by the sixteenth- and seventeenth-century transformations in Europe? That question aside, what special circumstances made the Dutch success possible?

On the eve of the revolt against the Hapsburgs, the Netherlands constituted even less of a national unity than the other countries of western Europe. As late as the fifteenth century the Dukes of Burgundy had acquired a number of independent territories in the Low Countries, and during the first half of the sixteenth century their Hapsburg successors had added still others. The result was essentially a personal union. Culturally Flanders and Brabant were united with the north by the common Dutch language. But the court, as well as the southern Walloon provinces, spoke French. Economically, the Netherlanders were a heterogeneous lot. Rural, sometimes backward provinces were thrown together with the most advanced and most urbanized regions in Europe: Flanders, Brabant, and Holland. Politically, in spite of princely efforts, the provinces guarded their independence, cooperating, as it were, only in order to thwart efforts to make them cooperate. The Estates General did not represent the nation; it was a mere congress of provincial embassies. Centralist ideas existed only among the professional jurists of the prince's councils. The high nobility, although participating in these councils, were too self-centered to be concerned with centralizing reforms.

However, after Emperor Charles V had abdicated (1556) and Philip

A.D.   1556   Abdication of Charles V of Hapsburg as Lord of the Netherlands; succession of Philip II of Spain

            1559   Philip II leaves Netherlands and returns to Spain, which becomes center of his government; beginning of opposition of higher nobility against government of king's confidants in the Netherlands

 1566–1567   First outbreaks of large-scale revolts as well as iconoclastic movements against the Church; Philip II sends the Duke of Alva to suppress the uprising; William of Orange flees the country

            1572   Successful attack of William of Orange, who occupies provinces of Holland and Zeeland

            1576   Other provinces join the rebellion (Pacification of Ghent

            1579   Walloon nobility defects from the rebellion (Treaty of Arras); Alexander of Parma commander of the Spanish troops

            1581   Revolutionary Estates General depose Philip II as Lord of the Netherlands

            1584   Assassination of William of Orange

            1585   Parma takes Antwerp; rebels withdraw behind the great rivers

 1588–1609   Dutch drive the Spanish out of the northern Netherlands: attempts at liberation of the south fail

 1609–1621   Truce between Republic of the United Netherlands and Spain

 1625–1648   The Republic joins the anti-Spanish coalition

            1648   Peace of Westphalia: de jure recognition of independence of the Republic

II had transferred the center of government to Spain (1559), this high nobility, having lost the prominent position it had held under Charles V, became the first rallying force in the revolt against Spanish rule. The nobles formed a league under William, Prince of Orange, to protect their interests, but their actions provided a catalyst for widespread popular discontent. Population pressure, inflation, and lagging wages had a particular impact on the Netherlands with its highly advanced and vulnerable economy. Earlier, the discontented groups had not been very homogeneous, a fact which helps to explain why Charles V had succeeded in maintaining an uneasy political balance. Now they came together, helped by the widespread demand for religious toleration, the ideological bond between the otherwise dissident groups.

Since the late 1550's the Calvinists had been strengthening their organization, and by the early sixties they were alarming the authorities by forcibly freeing jailed preachers and smashing religious images. Such outbreaks occurred mainly in the socially disturbed southern industrial regions, where a temporary economic crisis attracted discontented burghers as well as workers to the Calvinists. Their organization, like that of the Huguenots in France, had a military as well as a religious function. After the collapse of a movement among the higher nobility, the lower nobility took recourse in 1566 to what was supposed to be a nonviolent action. This triggered a revolt in the cities, marked by wild, iconoclastic acts against the Church, symbol of law, order, and the establishment. Against such an improbable coalition of nobility, bourgeoisie, and industrial workers, the government of Philip II was isolated and powerless.

The same disharmony which had caused the revolt, however, was also responsible for its failure. The violent behavior of the lower classes reminded many members of the nobility and higher bourgeoisie of the interests they shared with the government, and in the spring of 1567 the movement collapsed.

At this point peace might have been restored had Philip II not instituted a reign of terror and revenge. Too many people, compromised in the early rebellion, had fled the country; their only hope of return lay in a revolution under William of Orange. Orange himself went through a remarkable change in exile; he realized that narrow class interests had ruined the revolt and that his only hope was to unite nobility and bourgeoisie. A political genius of the first order (crafty as the serpent and innocent as the dove of Scripture), William of Orange prepared the ground patiently, stressing in his propaganda a program of constitutionalism and toleration.

In 1572 William invaded the Netherlands from the east and the south. His attack failed, but a separate invasion by the so-called Seabeggars, pirates supported by a leavening of freedom fighters, provided him with a foothold in the coastal provinces of Holland and Zeeland. In spite of furious Spanish assaults he managed to consolidate his position. It was of incalculable importance that William's first government was organized in the province of Holland, where the nobility was far less important than in the southern provinces, and where the guilds lacked the strong influence on town government of their counterparts in Flanders and Brabant. Power lay in the hands of a merchant clique that was willing to support William, provided the ultimate authority resided in their provincial estates. Although not much inclined to Calvinism, most of the merchants were not very enthusiastic Catholics either, and they were willing to adopt the faith of William's comrades for political reasons. Moreover, Catholic Church properties were a convenient source of revenue essential to finance the war.

The situation became more complicated in 1576 when the other provinces rejoined the revolt against Spain. The Flemish and Brabant towns had a long history of class war, with the guilds, now the driving revolutionary force, opposing the patriciate and the nobility. The Walloon provinces were the strongholds of the nobility, who joined the revolt out of disappointment with Philip II's policy, but who still cherished the idea of an aristocratic government under the king. The southern grandees did not want to accept William of Orange, an equal, as their leader, but William cleverly staged a number of democratic coups in Brussels, Ghent, and other southern cities. Thus the savior of oligarchy in Holland had become the hero of guild democracy in the south.

William tried desperately to reconcile the clashing social groups behind a national program to be carried out by the Estates General, which now assumed legislative power. However, the southern nobility now found good reason to seek reconciliation with the Spanish king. Their battle cry was defense of Catholicism against Calvinist extremism. Wherever they came to power the Calvinists unleashed a reign of terror. William tried hard to make them accept a Peace of Religion, a real charter of toleration. The extremists were not interested in peace, however, and often only super-ficially in religion. The Flemish cities and the nobility were old enemies, and this was a life-or-death struggle. The Walloon provinces, strongholds of the nobility and Catholicism, finally signed a treaty with the king (1579) and ended their rebellion; the revolutionary hardliners in the Estates General pushed through the deposition of Philip (1581), declaring solemnly that a tyrant who broke his contract with his people could law-fully be removed from power. The process of polarization was completed. Military power was going to decide the outcome of the conflict. Philip II's new governor general, Parma, skillfully blending mercy, moderation, and military force, had conquered the whole of the south and northeast, including Antwerp, by 1588, at which time he was preparing for the final invasion of Holland and Zeeland. The rebels were weakened by the assassination of William of Orange (1584) and by the nearly lethal assistance of unreliable or inept governors like Anjou, the youngest of Catherine de Médicis' dismal brood, and by Leicester, Queen Elizabeth's "sweet robin." They managed to hold out, however, and then the defeat of the Spanish Armada and the Spanish involvement in the French civil war enabled them to drive the Spanish from the north and to negotiate the Twelve Years' Truce (1609). In spite of some weak Dutch attempts after 1621 to reconquer Flanders and Brabant, the boundaries of the military stalemate of 1609 persisted, and were formalized in the final peace treaty of 1648.

Dutch historians have oft deplored the separation of the Low Countries, which they interpret as a defeat for the Netherlands' national community. However that may be, this rupture was a decisive factor in the success of the Dutch Republic. The struggle between nobility and guild-democracy in the south, resulting in the failure of William of Orange's attempts at a Greater Netherlands Confederation, suggests that social and political conflicts would have ripped this construction apart if all the provinces would have been liberated. Moreover, in such a larger political construction, encompassing the present-day Low Countries, the presence of three equally strong provinces in the Estates General, Flanders, Brabant, and Holland, would have precluded any harmonious development of central government; but the province of Holland could easily dominate the northern rump state. The rapid economic expansion of the Dutch in the seventeenth century could not have occurred without their merciless blockade of Antwerp: southern capital, skills, and manpower flowed to the north, so that instead of competing with the north, the south contributed to its blooming.

Strong leadership was also an ingredient in Holland's expansion; the merchant patriciate knew how to tend its interests better than monarchs generally did. And above all, the enigma of the rise of the Dutch Republic can be explained by the fact that it was small enough to be run as a mercantile city-state, but large enough to defend itself against princely conquerors. When England and France overcame their lack of social cohesion and other weaknesses, the republic would be in danger. But that did not happen until late in the seventeenth century.

Nevertheless, the first half of the century was a period of continuous political and religious crisis and threatening social revolt. The troubles began immediately after the conclusion of the Twelve Years' Truce with Spain. The oligarchy had forced the truce upon an unwilling war party because its regular European trade was suffering severely from the war and the financial situation was appalling. The war party was led by Prince

Maurice of Orange, commander of the army, and by orthodox Calvinists, who considered any agreement with the "Spanish Papist-beast" an offense against God. The colonial lobby also joined the war party to protect their interests in the Spanish and Portuguese overseas possessions which brought the powerful city of Amsterdam to the side of Prince Maurice. This war party would not have succeeded had not the lower classes and lesser provinces, jealous of Holland's leadership, endorsed its coup d'état in 1618. The prestige of die-hard Calvinism among the lower classes gave this alliance much of its dynamism.

It was characteristic of the times that the whole conflict had been built around the purely theological clash between liberal Arminians and ortho- dox Predestinarians. The Holland politicians supported the Arminians, partly out of conviction, partly because the Arminians accepted the power of the state over the church. Prince Maurice chose the orthodox party without understanding much about the theological subtleties. He won, but it was again characteristic for the purely political significance of this theological conflict that after the coup d'état the prince did not give his orthodox allies the power and influence they had demanded. On the other hand, most members of the Holland patriciate conformed nominally to the Calvinist rigorists and remained in or soon returned to power. After 1625 Frederick Henry of Orange, Maurice's successor, made use of the same coalition to impose his war policy and his alliance with the France of Richelieu (1635), but he could not prevent the Holland oligarchy, rein- forced since the late 1620's by the return of Amsterdam to its side, from regaining power and imposing the Peace of Westphalia (1648) upon an unwilling war party.

This pattern of power alternating between the Orangists and the mercantile patrician factions has remained a distinctive feature of the Dutch Republic. Each shift involved a coup d'état, but these were dull, bloodless affairs compared to the political upheavals in England and France. The Orangist coup d'état of 1618 cost only one life, that of the Grand Pensionary of Holland, Oldenbarneveldt. Other Orangist coups occurred in 1650 and 1672, the former totally without violence and the latter proving fatal only for the leaders of the republican faction, the brothers De Witt.

The return to power of the republican faction in 1650 and again in 1702 indicates that the oligarchic government and the hegemony of the province of Holland were deeply rooted in the social and political struc- ture. Popular commotions were never strong enough to bring about a suc- cessful revolt. At the same time the influence of the Orangist war faction throws light on the ambiguous position of the republic: the economic nature of the state seemed to justify the peaceful city-state mentality of the patrician faction; on the other hand it became increasingly clear that the republic was not a city-state but rather a small and vulnerable nation with the wealth and duties of a great power. The alternation between mercantile and expansionist regimes offered a pragmatic solution to the problems posed by an impossible situation. It was precisely the illogical and antiquated character of the Dutch constitution that maintained an efficient bourgeois economic policy and provided military protection in time of danger.

For Further Reading

Geyl, P., *The Netherlands in the Seventeenth Century*.
————, *The Revolt of the Netherlands*.
Wilson, C., *The Dutch Republic*.

47 The Collapse of France

In the sixteenth century the only state that seemed capable of curbing Hapsburg power, notably the might of the Spanish armies, was France. Under Francis I (1515–1547) the French monarchy seemed to shrewd observers, including no less an authority than Niccolò Machiavelli, the very model of a large kingdom—politically stable, efficiently centralized and administered, and possessed of a magnificent court and a powerful army. Francis was admired and envied by kings and ministers all over Europe, chiefly because he seemed to wield enormous powers over his subjects, in assessing taxes. The claims to absolute power and the magnificence of the châteaus on the Loire River were indeed impressive.

A closer look, however, reveals weaknesses. French kings did not have to convoke the Estates General to levy taxes, to be sure, but large numbers of powerful, wealthy, and privileged subjects could not be taxed at all. To raise money from the church and from members of the third estate, they had to negotiate with bishops, town councils, and other assemblies. The French government resembled those of other European states more than some foreign observers realized.

On the other hand, Francis and his descendants held almost absolute control over the church, especially after the Concordat of Bologna (1516), which assured the king the right to select the abbots and bishops of the realm, who controlled enormous wealth. This patronage gave Francis great

power and large revenues. Moreover, royal control of the intellectual and cultural life of the kingdom was nearly complete. Francis I had the reputation of being one of the leading patrons of the arts and learning, his greatest coup being the attraction of Leonardo da Vinci to France.

When Lutheran teachings began to spread in France they therefore caused little stir. A few humanists, to say nothing of Francis' own sister, found the new religion attractive, but once its heretical character was recognized powerful institutions of suppression swung into action. The Sorbonne, the high court of the Parliament of Paris, and the Assembly of Bishops all condemned Luther's position, and France remained overwhelmingly Catholic throughout the first storm of religious reform.

Not for long; the ideas of John Calvin were not so easy to suppress as those of Luther. Perhaps because he had been born and educated in France, Calvin's doctrines proved congenial to many Frenchmen. And his conception of church government admirably suited tastes of French dissident social groups. Francis I had established his absolutist regime over the opposition of many provincial nobles and town oligarchs. Both groups resented his centralized government bitterly. Thus after about 1555 Calvin's ideas caught on in many sections. Under Francis' successor, Henry II, it seemed that tiny sects were springing up everywhere, holding Bible-reading sessions and prayer meetings at homes and gathering clandestinely to hear newly arrived preachers from Calvin's headquarters in Geneva. First artisans and merchants, then important local leaders, then royal officials and even noblemen began to be found in these secret meetings. From town to town the proselytizers moved, organizing gatherings and making converts.

Calvinism hit France at a particularly unpropitious moment for the Crown. The eroding Hapsburg-Valois wars had exhausted and bankrupted the country. Popular rebellions similar to the peasants' wars in Germany flared in rural districts, while in towns unemployment and general misery left artisans and the *menu peuple* ripe for riots and civil war. Population increases combined with currency devaluation continued to send prices soaring. However, these problems alone do not explain the popularity of Calvinism in France; the strongest support of the "new religion" came from groups who opposed royal absolutism without regard for the economic troubles of the times. Francis I and Henry II had allowed two families, the Guises and the Montmorencys, to accumulate an inordinant amount of power, rousing many jealousies. By 1555 they controlled most important government posts along with many rich places in the religious hierarchy; in some provinces they ruled almost like kings with their own armies. Francis had the strength and wit to hold the Guises and Montmorencys in check, but Henry could not control them. They soon clashed

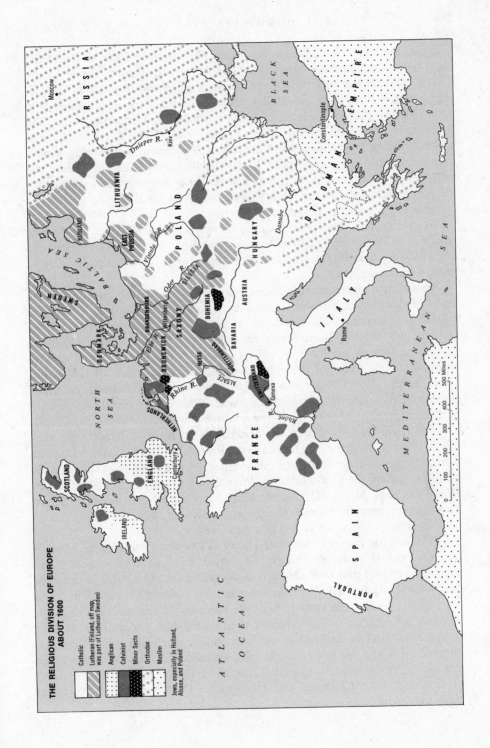

THE RELIGIOUS DIVISION OF EUROPE
ABOUT 1600

Catholic

Lutheran (Finland, off map, was part of Lutheran Sweden)

Anglican

Calvinist

Minor Sects

Orthodox

Muslim

Jews, especially in Holland, Alsace, and Poland

RUSSIA

Moscow

Dnieper R.

Kiev

LITHUANIA

KURLAND

EAST PRUSSIA

POLAND

Vistula R.

Oder R.

SILESIA

BOHEMIA

HUNGARY

AUSTRIA

BAVARIA

WÜRTTEMBERG

SAXONY

Wittenberg

BRANDENBURG

Elbe R.

BRUNSWICK

HESSE

ALSACE

SWITZERLAND

Geneva

Rhine R.

Rhône R.

FRANCE

NETHERLANDS

Canterbury

ENGLAND

SCOTLAND

IRELAND

NORTH SEA

BALTIC SEA

SWEDEN

DENMARK

ATLANTIC OCEAN

SPAIN

PORTUGAL

ITALY

Rome

MEDITERRANEAN SEA

Danube R.

OTTOMAN EMPIRE

Constantinople

BLACK SEA

0   100   200   300   400   500 Miles

with one another in an effort to dominate him. Both had married into the royal family, which meant that their rivalries posed a grave threat to the Crown. Thus at the very time that Calvinism was spreading across France, Henry found his power crumbling because of the rivalries of these two great families. Perhaps because of his very weakness, Henry persecuted the Protestants far more severely than Francis had. They were condemned without trial or inquisition; mere hearsay was sufficient for burning a man at the stake. Both royal and petty local officials were pressed to prove their orthodoxy by zealously rooting out heretics in a desperate effort to terrify his people into submission. Henry even had Ann du Bourg, a prominent member of Parliament, immolated for heresy.

Suspicion, fear, and false accusations spread across France. Few knew who was a Protestant and who was not—indeed, many royal officials did not know what a Protestant was. For some, mere ownership of a Bible made a man a heretic.

Under such circumstances social upheaval was probably inevitable, but when Henry was accidentally killed in a jousting accident in 1559, the Calvinists interpreted his death as a sign of God's favor. Abandoning secrecy and stealth, they began to hold their services openly. Within months of Henry's demise they held a general synod in Paris itself almost within a stone's throw of the chief civil and religious courts of the realm. Great nobles like Condé and Coligny followed by hundreds of other prominent men openly espoused the cause. With royal officialdom heavily infiltrated, all hope of crushing the new faith collapsed.

The royal line itself was in jeopardy after Henry's death. His successor, Francis II, lived less than a year. Francis' brother, Charles IX, was a mere youth and dominated by his mother, Henry's widow, Catherine de Médicis, and by the Guise faction. When Charles died in 1574 the third of Henry II's sons, Henry III, became king, but while he was more intelligent than his brothers he lacked energy and will—he was no more than a courtier trying to wear the crown of a great nation.

In effect, for two decades after Henry II's death, Catherine de Médicis was the virtual ruler of France. She tried hard to restore order and domestic serenity and over strong Guise opposition she sought a compromise with the Calvinists. "Le couteau vaut peu contre l'Esprit" (The knife is worthless against the spirit), her able minister, Michel de l'Hôpital, announced hopefully. Catherine forced rival theologians and princes to meet together to seek a resolution of their differences. She possessed real political gifts, and her policy might have succeeded if the issue had seemed less crucial to the contesting parties, but she failed to appreciate the depth of feeling of both Catholics and Protestants. Thus her reasonable policy came to naught.

Guises and Montmorencys, Protestants and Catholics, subverted her efforts at every turn. Amid confusion and unrest the Protestants swiftly increased their strength. By 1562 there were more than 2,000 congregations in France, really different sects which quarreled among themselves almost as bitterly as they resisted the Catholics. In that year war broke out between the Guises and Montmorencys. Catherine became a virtual prisoner of the Guises, who unleashed a religious terror, burning and jailing Protestants wherever they could apprehend them. Rival armies clashed in Paris and other cities, then scourged the countryside killing and looting. For thirty years this war raged sporadically, interspersed with occasional truces but never producing a clear-cut victory for either side.

Then on August 24, 1572, came the St. Bartholomew's Day Massacre. With Catherine's knowledge, the Guises prepared to assassinate all the Protestants in France. In the capital fanatics smashed down doors, stabbed the heretics in their beds. In a matter of days as many as 30,000 Calvinists including Coligny, admiral of France, were brutally murdered. Even this dreadful slaughter did not destroy the new faith, however. The conflict went on, each side gradually improving its organization. On the Catholic side, an unofficial holy league sprang into existence to help the Guises crush out the heretics wherever they could be found. Help came to the Calvinists from Protestant groups in Holland, England, and Germany, while the fanatically religious Philip II of Spain dispatched men and money to the Catholic cause.

The long conflict finally came to a head in 1588. Acting in conjunction with Philip II, who launched his great armada against Protestant England at this time, the Guises seized power in Paris. In this crisis Henry III decided that the political threat of the Guises was greater than the religious threat of the Protestants. He arranged to have the Duke of Guise murdered in his very presence during a royal council. Still the chaotic struggle went on, and a few months later Henry III was himself assassinated. Before his death he had named the Protestant leader, Henry of Navarre, as his heir, but French Catholics would not accept a Protestant king. For ten years more the fighting raged on. Finally Navarre, abjuring Protestantism, came to terms with Rome. In 1598 peace was finally restored to France.

To make sure that it would endure, Henry IV declared a general amnesty and issued the Edict of Nantes, granting religious and political freedom to all his subjects. The Protestants, called Huguenots, formed a kind of state within a state. Henry did not find this congenial, but he realized that he had no choice. Accepting this limitation on his authority, he worked feverishly to expand the commerce of France, and he rebuilt her devastated cities. But in 1610, despite all his efforts to persuade his countrymen to forget the past, he was himself assassinated. Civil and religious war again erupted, not to end until 1624 when Cardinal Richelieu took over the reins of government.

For Further Reading

Elliott, J. H., *Europe Divided, 1559–1598.*
Kingden, R. M., *Geneva and the French Protestant Movement 1564–1572.*
Neale, J. E., *The Age of Catherine de Medici.*
Roelker, N., *Queen of Navarre, Jeanne d'Albret, 1528–1572.*

48   Elizabethans and Puritans

Among the great powers to arise on the Atlantic, England came last, shortly after Spain and France. In the hundred years between the mid-fourteenth and mid-fifteenth centuries, Englishmen had to cope with a drastic reduction of population by the Black Death, a prolonged economic stagnation, and the sporadic outbursts of the Hundred Years' War against France. They suffered too the consequences of feudalism in dissolution—a disputed crown, the collapse of effective national and local administration, the corruption of justice, and private wars among noble chieftains at the head of bands of mercenaries. The picture was not entirely black, for these same years saw the virtually complete disappearance of servile status, some prosperity among those of the lower orders lucky enough to survive, and a flourishing university life; nor was there any diminution of the nation's artistic impulse, whose greatest legacy in this century was the perpendicular style, the last and perhaps loveliest expression of Gothic architecture. But the gradual working out of a new stability after the middle of the fifteenth century was welcome, great malefactors aside, to the whole country.

The Tudors, ultimately victorious in the dynastic struggle, were heirs to this gratitude. They carried further the stabilization begun under the last Yorkist kings and brought the country safely through Reformation, Counter Reformation, and the threat of a Spanish invasion. Though it was absolutist in principle and often harsh and corrupt in execution, Tudor policy in its main intentions coincided with the deepest aspirations of Englishmen until nearly the end of the sixteenth century.

The brilliantly engineered despotism of Henry VII (1485–1509)—a wily, grasping, pacific, and extremely able monarch—was based on refurbished machinery of the royal household. He left the monarchy firmly

A.D.	1485	Battle of Bosworth; accession of Henry VII
	1509	Death of Henry VII; accession of Henry VIII
	1529	Fall of Cardinal Wolsey
	1529–1536	Reformation Parliament
	1536–1540	Dissolution of the monasteries
	1540	Execution of Thomas Cromwell
	1547	Death of Henry VIII; accession of Edward VI
	1553	Death of Edward VI; accession of Mary I
	1558	Death of Mary I; accession of Elizabeth I
	1563	Thirty-Nine Articles; Statute of Apprentices
	1570	Elizabeth I excommunicated by Pope Pius V
	1587	Execution of Mary, Queen of Scots
	1588	Defeat of the Spanish Armada
	1600	East India Company chartered
	1603	Death of Elizabeth I; accession of James I
	1611	Authorized Version (King James Version) of the Bible
	1618	Beginning of the Thirty Years' War
	1625	Death of James I; accession of Charles I
	1628	Petition of Right adopted; assassination of the Duke of Buckingham
	1629–1640	Period of personal rule: the "Eleven Years' Tyranny"
	1640	Short Parliament (April–May); Long Parliament convenes in November
	1641	Execution of the Earl of Strafford; Irish Rebellion begins
	1643	Death of John Pym
	1642–1646	First Civil War
	1645	Execution of William Laud, Archbishop of Canterbury
	1648	Second Civil War; Pride's Purge
	1649	Execution of Charles I
	1653–1658	Protectorate under Oliver Cromwell
	1658	Death of Oliver Cromwell, succeeded as Lord Protector by his son Richard
	1660	Restoration of Charles II
	1662	Beginning of the "Bartholomew Ejections" following Act of Uniformity; expulsion of ministers creates English Nonconformity

----

established, financially solvent, and of no mean account in European affairs. Much of this legacy was wasted by his son, Henry VIII (1509–1547), an intelligent, cruel, self-indulgent Renaissance prince. Henry fancied himself a warrior and could seldom be bothered with the hard business of day-to-day governing; the inherited machinery was worked, therefore, by his chancellor Cardinal Wolsey, who gathered power and wealth into his own hands with a magnificence of style that far outdistanced his efficiency. The forms did not long survive Wolsey's fall in 1529. To deal with the administrative problems posed by the Reformation, new ad hoc institutions were created, still cast, however, in the medieval mold of government by essentially judicial bodies. Some, like the Court of Augmentations and the Court of First Fruits and Tenths, which dealt with the main financial consequences of the Reformation, had only a brief existence. Others were permanent, or were intended to be so. The main precedent was the Court of Star Chamber, which had evolved in the fifteenth century to deal with public order, a field in which the common law was notoriously defective. In the sixteenth century were added the Court of Requests, to deal with poor men's causes; the Councils of the West and the North, to govern those remote and rebellious regions; and, in Elizabeth's reign, the Court of High Commission, with a broad mandate over ecclesiastical affairs. Providing swift, cheap justice in contrast to the convoluted, hardened, and costly procedures of the regular common law courts, these Tudor creations formed a parallel and at least potentially competitive system of justice. But the rivalry remained latent, and the courts were, on the whole, popular.

A more fundamental change in the Tudor constitution grew from two further instances of the medieval process known as "going out of court," whereby one after another institution of the royal household (the origin of all medieval government) had separated itself from the household to become an established, bureaucratic department of state, still subject to the ultimate power of the king but free from his day-to-day interference. Under Thomas Cromwell, Henry VIII's chief minister in the 1530's, the key office of secretary of state—the king's closest confidential servant who had acquired a special importance in foreign affairs—made this transition and began its evolution, by division, into the principal ministries of modern central government. So too the king's council, hitherto an informal body of royal advisers, emerged as the Privy Council, a more regularized committee of ministers who decided and implemented policy. Not many aspects of English life escaped the scrutiny of "conciliar government" in the century between the Reformation and the Civil War. To finance, defense, diplomacy, and religion were added the supervision of foreign trade and the new efforts at colonization, the regulation of the quality and consumption of goods, the organization of apprenticeship, and efforts to solve the chronic problem of poverty, culminating in the Poor Law of 1601, which guaranteed state aid to the destitute, probably the most important piece of social legislation before the nineteenth century. But such measures were a far cry from modern welfare legislation. The intention behind them was profoundly conservative—to keep the country quiet and men in their places; the machinery was not that of enlightened humanitarianism but of social police.

The reach of Tudor policy far exceeded its grasp. Unlike modern governments, Tudor ministers had neither an army, nor police, nor corps of salaried, responsible civil servants to implement their policies. In the localities they had to depend on the justices of the peace, unpaid officials drawn from the ranks of nobility and gentry. Created in the fourteenth century to help keep the peace, the J.P.'s had by the sixteenth century become administrative officers as well as judges. Locally, their often selfish and tyrannical rule worked because English society was hierarchical and deferential. In the sixteenth century they were more or less effective instruments of national policy as well: a degree of cooperation was assured because they held their posts at the pleasure of the Crown and because in general they supported the dynasty and its intentions. But individuals among them could ignore legislation they did not like—against enclosures, for example, or against Catholics or Puritans. Tudor government depended on mutual accommodation between the Crown and the landed classes, a system that could not survive an estrangement.

In the Middle Ages, it has been said, Parliament was an occasion rather than an institution—a periodic meeting of the king's council reinforced by the summoning of feudal magnates and, at times, representatives of the freemen of the counties and towns. As it grew into an institution, Parliament divided into two parts. The representatives of the lesser nobility (the knights) came together with representatives of the towns to form the House of Commons, merging two potentially powerful segments of society that in other countries were likely to remain separate. The greater nobles and the bishops were thus left to evolve formally by the early sixteenth century into a House of Lords.

At the opening of that century, the future of Parliament was not bright. It was cumbersome and inconvenient, and kings would gladly have dispensed with it, had it not been necessary to them for two reasons. The highest form of declared law, the statute, required parliamentary assent. This power never degenerated into a formal and occasional exercise in registration, nor was it supplanted (though it was supplemented) by the royal prerogative of legislating by proclamation. When Henry VIII said that he at no time stood so high in his estate royal as when he was in his parliament, he was speaking more than flattery: ultimate sovereignty rested in the king in parliament. The use of statutes to accomplish the Reformation confirmed this function of Parliament, feeding a tradition of necessary association that could not easily be undone. Still more important was the requirement that Parliament consent to taxation. Had Henry VII succeeded in his intention of endowing the Crown through careful financial management, this power might have lost much of its significance. But the extravagance of Henry VIII, the inefficiency of the tax system, and above all, the drastic rise in prices wrecked such hopes. Still, Tudor monarchs summoned parliaments as seldom as possible, and when one was summoned, they and their ministers made certain that it was carefully managed.

After the reign of Queen Mary and her marriage to Philip II of Spain, anti-Catholicism became a major factor in English life, in the ensuing century inextricably linked to hatred of Spain, the foremost Catholic power as well as a colonial giant to be felled. Queen Elizabeth I (1558–1603) rode the crest of this wave of religious and secular patriotism. The queen could be perverse, mean, and petulant; she could procrastinate almost endlessly; her appetite for flattery was unceasing; and her involvements with favorites like the Earls of Leicester and Essex were embarrassing or even dangerous. She was at times the despair of her ministers. Yet she was intelligent and tough-minded, courageous, and (perhaps even in her apparent follies) capable of playing a role brilliantly. She was a consummate politician, able to manage her ministers and to dominate an increasingly rebellious Parliament, now by scolding them like an outraged governess in a nursery, now by giving in graciously to their complaints. In her hands the Tudor constitution reached the pinnacle of its success, though by the end of her reign more and more signs of trouble were appearing.

The defeat of the Spanish Armada in 1588 and the country's growing awareness of its good fortune fed a swell of creative energy bursting out in all directions—in exploration, in economic life, in intellect—that is almost without historical parallel. Broad-windowed country houses proclaimed the end of strife that had subjected architecture to the needs of defense; their style, adapting medieval forms, owed little to the classicism so rapidly advancing on the Continent. This independence of Continental models was paralleled in other fields. In music, the English reached a level of accomplishment they were never to attain again. A school of English historians and antiquaries laid the intellectual foundations for the struggles of the next century. The new learning, imported early in the century and of such importance in the reworking of English government and religion, had been assimilated; so had the Calvinist infusion of mid-century. Now theologians built a distinctive Anglican theology, led in Elizabeth's reign by the great transmitter of medieval tradition, Richard Hooker. In literature the age was preeminent, adding to a cluster of poets and dramatists of whom any nation might be proud three transcendent geniuses in Edmund Spenser, Ben Jonson, and William Shakespeare.

The finest works of the Elizabethan renaissance actually appeared in the reign of James I (1603–1625). But the Elizabethan constitution did not survive the change in dynasty so well as did Elizabethan culture. For all his abilities, James I did not have the art of the Tudors. But even had he had it, his lot would have been little easier: he was heir to Elizabeth's troubles too.

James I of England was also James VI of Scotland. He had come to the Scottish throne as an infant, following the forced abdication of his mother, Mary, Queen of Scots, who after twenty years as a prisoner and center of innumerable Catholic plots was executed by her cousin Elizabeth. His claim to the English throne lay through his great-grandmother, whose father, Henry VII, had married her to the then king of Scotland. The prospect of England promised James liberation in three directions—from the tutelage of the Scottish nobles who had made a mockery of his philosophical commitment to royal absolutism and the divine right of kings; from the leaders of the Scottish Church, the most radical of Calvinist establishments outside Geneva; and from the chronic poverty of his native country. On all three counts he was destined to disappointment.

From the 1570's opposition had been growing in the House of Commons. By clever management and by occasionally yielding, Elizabeth and her ministers had managed to keep it within bounds, but in James's reign it reappeared with new virulence, a vocal minority able from time to time to draw active or tacit support from less committed but increasingly discontented members. In 1604, some of the Commons presumed to lecture the king, in an *Apology*, about their interpretation of the constitution and their privileges; James, no mean scholar and fond of pontificating, lectured back. The issue was thus joined in a way that helped to defeat every effort of the king's essentially conciliatory policy.

James faced similar opposition in religion. The Elizabethan church had aimed at comprehension—absorbing into the national church the widest possible range of religious views, omitting only those Catholics who threatened the security of the country. But agreeing to differ on points of theology was far from satisfying to the more ardent spirits inspired by a Calvinism much more corrosive than the mild Calvinist infusion that had gone into the Thirty-Nine Articles. "Puritans" were dedicated to purifying the church of all remnants of popish superstition. Some of them wanted, moreover, to replace the bishops by a presbyterian form of church government, like that in Scotland; others, more radical, wanted to dispense with all centralized ecclesiastical rule in favor of congregational autonomy, or Independency. To a king whose convictions were put succinctly in his famous aphorism "No bishop, no king," the Puritan program was anathema. Again James was willing to compromise or at least to hear the objectors out, but the Puritans came to the Hampton Court Conference in 1604 determined not to yield an inch and drove the king to uphold a similarly rigid position. The one positive result was a decision to retranslate the Bible: the "King James" or Authorized Version appeared in 1611.

Opposition in church and state was sporadic; financial difficulties pressed continually. James had expensive tastes, a family, and an unfortunate weakness for favorites. But as his costs rose, his income did not. Much of the capital of the Crown—the royal lands—had been sold to help pay for the war against Spain. The rigid tax system produced nothing like a fair return on values, and the general rise in prices caught not only the

Crown in an inflationary squeeze but landowners and businessmen as well, making them the more reluctant to consent to new taxes.

The leaders of the opposition and much of its residual strength were to be found among the gentry, that range of middling landowners who had been the major beneficiaries of the sale of monastic lands by a needy Crown. The depression of the 1590's and the steady rise in prices severely hurt men whose standard of living had been rising. Not all of them were willing to keep down expenditure or to run their estates (or to have them run) in a business-like fashion, the more necessary as capitalistic methods spread in agriculture. The luckiest were those whose estates held timber or mineral resources, or on whose lands a growing town encroached. Some were able to enlarge their fortunes by the profits of office. But wealth, whether rising or declining, is an insufficient explanation of growing hostility among the gentry to interference by the central government. They were accustomed to rule in their localities; the state's very reliance on them increased their natural pride and their pretensions. More and more of them were educated in the "public schools" like Eton and Winchester, originally founded to train boys for the priesthood, in Oxford and Cambridge, or in the Inns of Court, England's "university" of the common law. Not that these young gentlemen were well educated or that they turned scholars or professional men; but they got a certain finish that increased their sense of superiority as a privileged order to be defended against encroachments. Whatever the precise balance of economic and social factors, there is no doubt that the gentry were outgrowing the Tudors' leading strings.

To a remarkable degree the ambitions of the gentry had come to center on Parliament: as natural leaders of their communities, they felt they belonged there; it sat at Westminster, where the fashionable world also assembled, and good behavior there might earn favorable notice and open possibilities of office. Peers, the titled aristocrats, sat in the House of Lords as a matter of right. But their sons, who were commoners at law (unlike Continental aristocracies), and the heads of prominent gentry families sought election to the Commons. They gradually took over the representation of England's towns, which counted far more seats than the counties for which sons of peers or leading gentry might naturally stand. The townsmen, with their limited vision, were happy enough to get out from under the burden of parliamentary attendance, to avoid paying wages to their representatives when gentlemen were willing to serve for nothing, and perhaps to bargain for favors in return for choosing one eager gentleman rather than another. The Crown was under constant pressure to increase the number of seats, and from 298 members in the first Parliament of Henry VIII the membership rose to 467 in the first Parliament of James I.

Neither king nor parliamentary opposition wanted to abolish the other or to bring about a revolution, let alone modern limited monarchy. Both Parliament and the king looked backward, James and his advisers to royal powers under the Tudor constitution, the members of Parliament to their own interpretation of that constitution and their place in it, and further to the idea of an unbreakable "fundamental law." Although this law invariably covered the privileges of each of its interpreters, it was no mere selfish rationalization: the notion itself has a certain moral impressiveness, and to the more articulate of its believers, it represented actual historical truth as a creative if mistaken generation of scholars had disinterred it. Both sides set to searching out precedents and, of course, found them. Historians today agree that the best precedents were nearly all on the king's side: the royal prerogative had been an inexhaustible storehouse of power to deal with new situations as they arose, and privileges, historically, flowed from royal grace. But the prerogative had never been defined; the early seventeenth-century conflict lay between increasingly discordant efforts to define the extent of royal powers. As their claims grew more irreconcilable, both sides were forced into extreme actions that no one would have predicted or wanted.

In James's reign, the principal disputes concerned money and foreign affairs. The king and his ministers tried to escape from the pinch of inflation on one side and grudging and inflexible parliamentary supply on the other by a series of expedients—a prerogative upward revision of customs, a statesman-like proposal to commute feudal dues in exchange for a regular parliamentary grant, devising ingenious monopolies to increase particular trades, placate the powerful, and fill the royal coffers. All the expedients failed. In foreign policy, James's intentions were admirable. A peaceable man, he started his reign by ending the war with Spain, but to those who remembered the Armada and feared the pope, this was compromising with the devil. The situation worsened when the Thirty Years' War broke out in 1618. The Protestant champion in the first stage of the war, the Elector Palatine of the Rhine, was the husband of James's daughter. But while public and parliamentary opinion was strong for intervention, it was equally unwilling to pay for a land war. James's opponents were, however, free with advice, whereas the king held that foreign policy was for his determination and that Parliament had no right to meddle.

The opposition in the Commons had created a number of procedures—the committee of the whole house, not subject to the usual rules, was one—to increase its chance to discuss or obstruct royal policy, and certainly James and his ministers managed Parliament less well than their predecessors: the House of Commons, in the famous phrase of one historian, had won the initiative. James added to his difficulties in 1616 by dismissing the chief justice of the Court of King's Bench, Sir Edward Coke, so providing the parliamentary opposition with its first leader of genius. As a minister under Elizabeth, Coke had yielded to no one in violent pursuit of suspected traitors, but in the courts he emerged as an equally fanatical defender of the common law. The king contended, quite correctly, that the judges, holding office at his pleasure, were his servants, "lions under the throne," as Sir Francis Bacon called them. But Coke, holding to his passionate belief in the supremacy of the law, precipitated his dismissal by refusing to consult in advance about decisions. When he entered the Commons in 1621, he brought his formidable learning to bear against the king. Under his guidance, the old medieval process of impeachment was revived —a procedure in which the Commons prosecute and the Lords try—and turned against corrupt ministers and monopolists, against Coke's archrival, the Lord Chancellor Sir Francis Bacon, and Lionel Cranfield, Earl of Middlesex, the London merchant who had become James's principal minister in the twenties. Impeachment remained a formidable if cumbersome weapon for dealing with dangerous or beaten opponents into the next century.

When James's reign ended in 1625, no final conflict was in prospect; within five years his son Charles I (1625–1649) had made it inevitable. As Prince of Wales, Charles and the Duke of Buckingham, his favorite as he had been his father's, had gone off to Madrid to arrange a Spanish marriage, much valued by James, highly unpopular among his subjects. The suit was rebuffed, the rejection rankled, and after his accession Charles and Buckingham decided on war against Spain, a brief, inglorious episode that, like an equally disastrous quarrel with France in 1626–1627, brought no advantages and considerably worsened the financial situation. The House of Commons had refused the king the customary life grant of customs revenues known as tunnage and poundage; Charles proceeded to collect them without authorization and resorted to forced loans as well, victimizing those who refused on principle to pay. Coke's reply to the king's desperate and unwise moves was the resounding if ineffectual Petition of Right in 1628, declaring it illegal to collect money without parliamentary consent, to quarter troops in private households, to imprison without showing cause, or to apply martial law to civilians—to all of which Charles had resorted to get his way. Meanwhile the ascendancy of the foolish and irresponsible Buckingham had alienated both Lords and Commons; foiled in an attempt at impeachment in 1626 by the king's dissolving Parliament, and again in 1628 by a prorogation, they were at last cheated of their victim by an assassin in 1628. By that time, many of the moderate opposition leaders had withdrawn, either to support the king or to the sidelines, leaving the zealots in control, above all the noisy demagogue Sir John Eliot. When the stormy parliamentary session of 1629 was ended by a dissolution, the Commons ordered the Speaker held in his chair while they passed three hysterical resolutions condemning as enemies of England anyone who paid the unauthorized tunnage and poundage, advised its collection, or introduced innovation in religion. Charles determined to rule without calling another parliament.

As an exercise in government, the "Eleven Years' Tyranny" was not unimpressive. The financial problem was dealt with by a careful husbanding of resources, a ruthless and unpopular enforcement of often forgotten feudal rights, and many other expedients, the most famous of which was a decision to extend the collection of ship money—for the outfitting of warships—from the port towns, which had traditionally paid, to inland towns. When an opposition leader, Sir John Hampden, refused to pay, the judges upheld the king's right, with only one dissent, a decision no doubt correct in law, but one that brought the judiciary into still further contempt, as other arbitrary acts of government were helping to discredit the once popular conciliar courts like Star Chamber. The government also made a last attempt at effective enforcement of old social legislation—commercial regulations, for example, and limitation of enclosures—and at firm central administration of the poor law. These actions further alienated many among the gentry and the merchants who disliked central interference with what they deemed their own proper concerns. Such opponents were primarily motivated, no doubt, by selfish and narrowly defensive considerations, but dubious motives merged with or were transmuted into a principled protest against the uncertainties and unfairness of arbitrary government and in the end were not untinged with nobility.

Two men came increasingly to determine government policy in the 1630's and to dominate the dark imaginings of the opposition. One was Thomas Wentworth (later Earl of Strafford), who had stood out against Buckingham in 1627 and had been imprisoned for refusing the forced loan. The next year, however, appalled by the excesses of some of his colleagues, he emerged as a king's man, a step true to his anti-Puritanism and his essentially loyal, authoritarian nature, but one that labeled him a turncoat in the eyes of a resurgent opposition. Wentworth was first put in charge in the north of England and then, after 1633, in Ireland, where he ruled effectively and despotically, careless of the dangerous resentments he was creating; in 1639, he was called back from Ireland to deal with the mounting crisis. The other man was William Laud, Archbishop of Canterbury after 1633, narrow, dedicated, and determined to put the internal government of the church in order. His emphasis on ritual and discipline offended the lively anti-Catholicism of the country, already alarmed by the intense and open Catholicism of Charles's queen, Henrietta Maria of France, and by the teachings (perhaps unnecessarily provocative) of a new school of theologians who, turning against the Calvinist heritage in Anglicanism, inaugurated what has come to be known as the "high church" tradition. Wentworth and Laud spoke of their policy of "Thorough," a resolute determination to rule justly and efficiently, as they saw it, against all obstacles, an impolitic course that ultimately brought both of them and their king to the scaffold.

The precipitating blunder was a decision to impose the Anglican prayer book on Presbyterian Scotland. The resulting Scottish rebellion had to be suppressed, and the shortage of funds made resort to Parliament a necessity. The Short Parliament in 1640 ended in deadlock, but the new parliament, reluctantly summoned at the end of that year and famous as the Long Parliament, met determined first on a reckoning with Strafford, who was believed ready to turn his Irish army against England. When it became clear that the attempt at impeachment would fail in the Lords, the Commons substituted a bill of attainder, declaring Strafford guilty of treason, and forced it on the unwilling Lords and the grief-stricken king by mob action and the threat of worse to come. He was beheaded in 1641. Laud too was imprisoned, but not put to death until 1645. Once Strafford's execution had removed the prime villain, Parliament turned to pass a series of reforming statutes. It provided that it could not be dissolved without its own consent, required that a parliament be called every three years, declared ship money illegal, and demolished much of the machinery that had been brought into disrepute, including the conciliar courts. Charles had little choice but to consent.

In January, 1642, having already turned London against himself, Charles made the fatal blunder of invading the House of Commons to arrest five leaders who, forewarned, had fled; the king then left his capital. He was still willing to make some concessions, even to the extent of agreeing to the exclusion of bishops from the House of Lords. But he found the sticking point in a demand that Parliament be given control of the armed forces, now vital to the suppression of a rebellion that had broken out in Ireland. In June, in the Nineteen Propositions, Parliament demanded control of the executive power as well. Charles raised his standard at Nottingham in August, and the Civil War began.

In November, 1641, in a vote on a manifesto called the Grand Remonstrance, nearly half of the Commons had swung to support the king. On this, and on the sympathy of most of the nobility and of much of the country, the king was able to rely. Still, the pattern of loyalties in the Civil War was extremely complex, reflecting personal and regional rivalries, ambitions and resentments, mixtures of interests and beliefs that varied from individual to individual, perhaps a clash of generations as well—at any rate the royalist members of the Long Parliament were younger, on an average, than the supporters of the parliamentary cause. The usual geographical generalization is that north and west were more likely to be royalist, the wealthier south and east parliamentary, but exceptions abound.

Without a king and without many of its members, Parliament ruled by ordinance, negotiating an alliance with the Scots, reconstructing the army, and launching England on the road to presbyterian church government. The most remarkable innovation was in the field of finance, where the invention of the excise and a prototype of the later land tax for the first time broke through the inflexibility of medieval taxation. The genius behind this parliamentary program was John Pym, a brilliant manipulator who had served in the parliaments of the twenties, established his ascendancy in the Short Parliament, and managed Strafford's trial and attainder; Pym was able to get his way by a consummate playing off of conservatives and extremists in the House. But after his death in 1643, Parliament did not recover its effectiveness, and the initiative passed to the army. While the bulk of the officers had gone over to the king, the "New Model" Army created for Parliament threw up its own leaders under the command and inspiration of an obscure country gentleman named Oliver Cromwell. Victories began to fall to him in 1644, and in 1646 the king fled to the Scots and surrendered.

Parliament and army fell out. Immediate issues like disbanding and arrears in pay were superficial reflections of deeper divisions. A victorious army, thirsting for further reform, resented its technical subordination to a self-satisfied and ineffective assembly. Parliament feared the growing radicalism of the army. This clash had its religious dimension in that Parliament was committed to a curious blend of presbyterian organization and civil supremacy, abhorrent both to true theocratic Presbyterians like the Scots and to the religious enthusiasts in the army who have been lumped together under the catch-all term "Independents." In normal times such profound questioning of the organization and purpose of civil society would have been kept in obscurity by the restraints of the traditional forms of social hierarchy. But those restraints had disappeared in the Civil War, and the army became a seedbed of radicalisms, the most famous of them the doctrines preached by the Levellers, who have been claimed, with some if not entire justice, as ancestors of modern democratic thought. Cromwell's enormous authority helped him to control his enthusiastic subordinates, but he found the necessary political ballast in his son-in-law, Lieutenant General Henry Ireton, a profound, conservative political thinker who was the author of the succession of draft constitutions that punctuate the negotiations of the late 1640's; Ireton's death in 1651 was a perhaps fatal blow to the prospects of stability of a Cromwellian regime.

Cromwell and his associates negotiated seriously with the king to preserve the monarchy and the changes that had been accomplished. Charles invariably eluded them, reaching a peak of deviousness when he agreed to accept a presbyterian church and so launched the Scots against the English in the second Civil War in 1648. Cromwell, a profoundly religious man, was likely to conclude, once he had been convinced of a course of action, that God had spoken to him; he finally came to believe that it was necessary to get rid of Charles Stuart, "that man of blood." Parliament was purged of its reluctant members, and Charles was seized and brought to trial before a specially created tribunal whose lawfulness he refused to recognize. He was convicted on the charge of high treason against the state and executed on January 30, 1649.

By 1651 Cromwell had suppressed the bitter resistance in Ireland and Scotland. Meanwhile England had been ruled as a republic by the remnant left after Colonel Pride's purge, the Rump, a rule increasingly inept and corrupt. In 1653 Cromwell went down to the House with troops and drove the members out. He then tried the experiment of a parliament elected by Independent congregations, an assembly of considerable respectability and much radicalism that was so occupied with talk and projects that it in turn was dissolved. Finally, under the first written constitution, the Instrument of Government, Cromwell undertook to rule as Lord Protector, a monarch in all but name, with a powerful Council of State, a submissive single-chamber legislature, and indispensable support from the army. The nature of Cromwell's military rule was emphasized in 1655 when the country was divided into districts, each in charge of a major general, its monarchical nature reinforced in 1656 when a second chamber was added to Parliament.

Although much was done, most of the wide-ranging reforms canvassed in the 1640's and in the short-lived "Barebones Parliament" of 1653 remained unenacted. Cromwell found himself, moreover, forced by the realities of power into policies and attitudes that would have shocked him when he had sat as a back-bench member of Parliament. Despite his genuine commitment to religious toleration, he had to deal harshly with troublemakers among the fanatics, including the Levellers and the Fifth Monarchy Men under whose influence he had passed at certain stages in his career. Even his neutered parliament caused him trouble, forcing him to dissolve it as soon as possible. His war with Spain (which won England Jamaica) was a policy Elizabethan enough for any Puritan taste, but Puritan England also fought the Dutch, who were Protestants, in the interests of trade. What Cromwell and his major generals set out to do, above all, was to make England into a godly commonwealth, by reforming the church and universities and by enforcing a moral revolution. These policies were not calculated to endear him to ordinary men; still, for those whose Puritan motivation was deep, these were magnificent years. The memory of this attempt at a new society survived among men of a Puritan persuasion for a century and a half and made its contribution to a new reforming impulse in the nineteenth century. The intensity of the Puritan vision survives in its two greatest literary monuments: John Bunyan's *Pilgrim's Progress,* and *Paradise Lost,* the greatest English epic poem, the last superb embodiment of a prescientific religious universe, by Cromwell's Latin secretary, John Milton.

Cromwell had steadily resisted advice to make himself king, though his institutions and his style edged more and more toward monarchy. After he died in 1658, he was succeeded by his ineffectual son Richard. But it was only a matter of time before the Stuarts were restored. In 1660 General George Monk, the commanding general in Scotland, came down to England with Presbyterian support, and recalled the remaining members of England's last legitimate Parliament—the Long Parliament—which dissolved itself. The new Parliament, encouraged by the conciliatory Declaration of Breda issued by Charles II from his Continental exile, recalled him as king in May, 1660.

In law, the whole period since 1642 was a blank, yet much was changed in the restored state and church. The statutes of 1641 still stood, and the machinery of conciliar government was not reerected; Charles's principal minister in the first years of Restoration was the Earl of Clarendon, one of the reformers of 1641 who had gone over to the royal cause. The financial inventions of the 1640's were carried over, and feudal dues were finally abandoned in exchange for a parliamentary grant. The Navigation Act that had been passed in 1651 was reenacted and expanded into a code of regulations that governed England's trade with her colonies and foreign countries for more than a century and a half. The church came more fully under royal (or ministerial) control after 1664, when an agreement that the clergy would no longer tax themselves removed the major reason for maintaining a more than nominal existence for Convocation, the Church's legislative body. The greatest change in the church, however, grew from the fierce loyalty to Anglicanism evident in the Parliament elected in 1660. Accommodation with the Puritans was rejected, even with the Presbyterians who had done so much to bring about the Restoration; a series of statutes—the so-called (and probably miscalled) Clarendon Code—deprived a fifth of the parish clergy who refused to subscribe to the Thirty-Nine Articles and to use the Book of Common Prayer and visited a number of civil disabilities on laymen who refused to conform to the Anglican Church. Thus the early 1660's saw the creation of a body of Dissenters or Nonconformists; the old Anglican ideal of comprehension had been abandoned, with far-reaching consequences in the religious, social, and political life of England.

Charles II could rely on the loyalty to both church and king of a Parliament and most of a country determined that the experiments of the 1640's and 1650's would not be repeated. He was himself extremely skillful; he had a standing army, as his father had not; as his reign advanced, more and more effective use was made of "the influence of the Crown"— the distribution of pensions, offices, and honors to gain political ends. With all these advantages he was able to dispense with Parliament for the last four years of his reign. But the finances continued in a bad way, despite the improvements made, and the notorious subsidies he got from Louis XIV of France were smaller in fact than in fame. What he won was won by politic yielding and clever management. Even so, opposition developed, based on the "country" as opposed to the court, and able to play on a residual Puritanism among the proscribed and sometimes persecuted Dissenters. At the end of the 1670's, in the midst of anti-Catholic hysteria provoked by baseless rumors of a "popish plot," the proposal was made to exclude Charles's brother, James, from the succession to the throne because of his open Catholicism. On this issue, men of country and court persuasions condensed into parties, nicknamed Whigs and Tories. In their pursuit of James, the Whigs overreached themselves in 1680–1681. Parliament was not called again in the reign, the town corporations were systematically remodeled to secure their loyalty, and the Whig leader Shaftesbury fled the country in 1682. With these developments to reinforce the monarchical loyalities of most of the country, James II succeeded to the throne in 1685 with broad support and even some enthusiasm.

Stupid and bigoted, James threw away all his advantages by a resolute attempt to restore Catholicism—not only by suspending laws against Catholics (and incidentally Dissenters) but, in the end, by trying to insinuate Catholics into positions of authority in the church, the universities, and the army. Any hope that this policy might disappear with James's death collapsed when his long-barren second wife, Mary of Modena, bore him a son in 1688. The threat to the church cracked the loyalty that had been expressed in doctrines of divine right and passive obedience. Although there was no national uprising, a coalition of Whig and Tory leaders issued an invitation to William of Orange, stadtholder of the Netherlands, to come to England, an invitation fully welcome to him, since gaining the English throne would mean bringing England firmly into the coalition against Louis XIV, of which William was the leader. His claim to England was more, however, than his being the Protestant champion of Europe: his mother was a daughter of Charles I, and his wife was Mary, the elder daughter of James II by his first, Protestant wife, Clarendon's daughter. When William landed in England and started his long march toward London, James's support gradually evaporated, and he fled to France. In violation of all constitutional logic, a Convention Parliament declared the throne vacant and offered it jointly to William and Mary.

Known since as the Glorious Revolution, this change of rulers was celebrated in the eighteenth century as yet another deliverance—by a curious coincidence it came exactly a century after the defeat of the Armada—and consecrated by the superb rationale of John Locke's second treatise on government, it became the basic political legend of a hundred and fifty years. The reality, as always, was more complex. The apparent harmony of the Revolution no more than interrupted fifty years of political violence, to which indeed the change of rulers added a new dimension. At no time in English history was party feeling so strong as under William and Mary or under Mary's sister Anne (1702–1714); it was grounded in differences about the exclusive claims of the church against the Dissenters, about the role of the king (the return of the Stuart pretenders from France remained a possibility down to 1715), and above all about who was to be in office. In an interesting transition, it was the post-Revolution Tories who took over the political footing and the ideology of the country orientation that had underlain pre-Revolution Whiggism; and, appropriately, some leaders of this new Toryism overreached themselves in 1714, as the Whigs had done thirty years before, by intriguing for a restoration of the Jacobite pretender. This and the unpopularity of the Peace of Utrecht, which Anne's Tory ministers had negotiated to end the War of the Spanish Succession in 1713 destroyed Toryism as a political force, however loyal obscure country gentlemen remained to Tory principles. When Queen Anne died childless in 1714, the crown passed uncontested, under terms of the Act of Settlement of 1701, to the elector of Hanover, who became King George I; he was descended from the marriage of the daughter of James I to the Elector Palatine of the Rhine.

The "Revolution Settlement" is the name given to a series of statutes passed in a dozen years or so after 1689, guaranteeing that parliament would meet annually and that the life of a parliament would be limited to three years; that the king would be Protestant; that judges would hold office during good behavior instead of at the king's pleasure, so ensuring their independence; that Dissenters could practice their religion openly, though they were not relieved of the civil disabilities visited on them by the Clarendon Code. The Bill of Rights of 1689, with the Habeas Corpus Act of 1679, provided a set of broad guarantees of the liberty of the subject. To these statutory provisions must be added as further insurance of the permanence of the settlement the act of union in 1707 that merged England and Scotland into the United Kingdom of Great Britain, and the new, firm basis given to government finance by the founding of the Bank of England in 1694 and the regular organization of the national debt in the following year.

In the Revolution, Parliament had secured its existence and its rights as an indispensable partner in the governing process. But it was by no means the dominant, and was far from an equal, partner. Although the king was limited in some ways that he was not before 1688, he was still the active head of government: ministers were responsible to him, not Parliament; he was in, not above, politics. But the party disputes, like the religious disputes that had so fully engaged men's attention in the seventeenth century, wore themselves out in sterility. Thanks to the astute political management of Sir Robert Walpole, the leading minister (he rejected the then pejorative term "prime minister") from 1721 to 1742, and to his perfection of the use of royal "influence," thanks too to the desire of Englishmen to be left alone to get on, to make money, and to live quietly, England had by the 1720's entered a period of political stability. She was no longer an example of violence to be abhorred, but an example of liberty—real, if partial—to be admired and imitated by eighteenth-century reformers elsewhere.

For Further Reading

Ashley, Maurice, *England in the Seventeenth Century.*
————, *The Greatness of Oliver Cromwell.*
Bindoff, S. T., *Tudor England.*
Elton, G. R., *England under the Tudors.*
Kenyon, J. P. (ed.), *The Stuart Constitution.*
Neale, Sir John, *Elizabeth I and Her Parliaments.*
————, *The Elizabethan House of Commons.*
————, *Queen Elizabeth.*
Ogg, David, *England in the Reign of Charles II.*
Plumb, J. H., *The Origins of Political Stability in England, 1675–1725.*
Stone, Lawrence, *The Crisis of the Aristocracy, 1558–1641.*
Trevelyan, G. M., *The English Revolution, 1688–1689.*

49   The Thirty Years' War

Historians are fond of stressing the importance of the Scientific Revolution of the seventeenth century, and of the opening up of vast economic opportunities in Asia, the Americas, and Africa for Europeans. But they often fail to mention how insignificant or even irrelevant these developments appeared to the overwhelming majority of Europeans who lived and fought in that age. The discoveries of Brahe, Galileo, and Harvey in physics and physiology went unnoticed by Europe's ruling elites. The founding of trading companies in America by Sir Walter Raleigh, for example, did not much influence the prevailing modes of social and political life for decades. Turning their backs on these pioneering efforts and enormous opportunities, Europeans squandered most of their energies in a massive war.

The violence broke out first in 1618 and soon extended all across the continent. It was much more brutal and destructive than either the earlier feudal conflicts or the more modern wars which began during the reign of Louis XIV in the late seventeenth century. Not until the twentieth century would the Western world again know the wanton pillaging, raping, and killing of a semiguerrilla force which no government could command. As the last great war of the condottiere generals, those men who hired themselves out to governments, then raised armies which preyed on the peasants and townsmen, the Thirty Years' War stands unique—a series of bloody campaigns in which civilians often suffered more grievously than soldiers.

Actually war had geen raging sporadically in Europe since the 1520's. In Germany the assassination of Henry IV in 1610 only delayed a resumption of the struggles between France and the Hapsburgs, a struggle reminiscent of the wars of Charles V and Francis I a century earlier. In the Netherlands the Dutch readied themselves for another clash with the Catholic power of Spain. In Italy the French and Spanish prepared to resume their contest for control of the passes across the Alps.

It would have been understandable, if not necessarily sensible, had the powers clashed over control of foreign empires, of trade routes and rich farmlands, or if social conflicts had triggered the fighting. Instead, they spilled their blood and treasure over relatively minor religious differences and spilled more for pure dynastic aggrandizement. Europe's elite—the kings, diplomats, scholars, and churchmen—took little interest in science or far-off lands.

Why they indulged in such madness so soon after such disasters as the

A.D.   1612   Ferdinand II becomes king of Hungary and Bohemia
       1618   Defenestration of Prague
       1620   Battle of White Mountain
       1621   End of the Spanish-Dutch truce
       1623   Maximilian of Bavaria receives electoral vote held previously by Palatinate
       1624   Richelieu enters and soon dominates royal council; French-Dutch treaty
       1626   Defeat of Danish troops in Brunswick by Count Tilly
       1629   Edict of Restitution
       1630   Electoral Assembly of Regensburg insists on Wallenstein's resignation; Gustavus Adolphus lands in northern Germany, is subsidized by France
       1631   Capture and massacre of Magdeburg
       1632   Battle of Lützen, Hapsburg defeat; death of Gustavus Adolphus
       1634   Assassination of Wallenstein
       1635   Treaty of Prague; French declaration of war against Spain
       1636   Capture of Corbie by the Spanish
       1639   Revolt of the Nu-Pieds in France
       1640   Revolts of the Catalans and the Portuguese
       1643   Defeat of the Spanish by the French at the Battle of Rocroi; war between Denmark and Sweden
       1646   Invasion of Bavaria by Swedish and French troops
       1648   Peace of Westphalia

Armada and the bloody religious wars in France attracted the attention of some of the best minds of Europe during this thirty years of war: men like the statesman Sully, the philosopher Thomas Hobbes, and the lawyer Hugo Grotius. Such men agreed that no single ruler, but rather the awful reality of European power politics, explained the wasteful conflict. Hobbes put it clearly when he said that violence was the natural result when nations either sought to conquer other nations or feared being themselves overrun. In the early seventeenth century every country of Europe fell into one or another of these categories, if not into both.

The exhausted and bankrupt powers of the Holy Roman Empire had seen the Treaty of Augsburg (1555) as no more than a truce, not as a permanent solution of the religious question. Gradually treasuries were replenished and the new generation of nobles grew to fighting age. The German Jesuits injected a revived religious zeal among Catholics, and Calvinist preachers preyed with equal force on their followers in Augsburg and the Palatinate. (No account of the Calvinists had been taken at Augsburg except perhaps a tacit agreement to burn them as heretics, but by 1600 this faith had made important inroads among the nobility and bourgeoisie of the Netherlands, France, Scotland, and England.)

In 1585 the city of Cologne, which had been under Lutheran control, reverted to Rome. This heralded a Catholic revival in northern Germany, a Lutheran stronghold. Jacques Callot's great engravings vividly depict the inquisitions, hangings, burnings, and general misery that plagued the region in the following years. The balance of power swung back and forth erratically until in 1618 a rebellion in Bohemia triggered a general war which, shifting from district to district, endured for thirty years.

Once the balance of forces had been destroyed, state after state struggled brutally for dominance in the Holy Roman Empire. (The playwright Bertolt Brecht, writing with the equal carnage of World War I in mind, recapitulated the horror of the era graphically in *Mother Courage.*) The many tiny principalities of the empire formed Protestant and Catholic leagues. Religious differences were magnets attracting the ambitions of the great Catholic families, the Hapsburgs and the Wittelsbachs, who formed foreign alliances with the pope and with Spain, thus enmeshing Germany in the larger struggles of the Counter Reformation. Similarly, German Protestants allied themselves with French Huguenots and with the English and the Dutch.

With the continent thus divided, the youthful Hapsburg king of Bohemia, Ferdinand, sought to restore the imperial policies of Charles V. In alliance with his Spanish cousins he launched a reckless campaign to exterminate Protestantism from the empire. In his own Bohemia he levied heavy taxes on Protestants and closed their churches. Powerful Protestant

THE THIRTY YEARS' WAR 1619-1648

0 50 100 Miles	▦ Hapsburg possessions
✕ Battle	▬ Holy Roman Empire boundary
	◄--► Spanish supply route

nobles would not tolerate such treatment. Bohemia being an elective monarchy, they deposed Ferdinand, choosing the Protestant prince Frederick of the Palatinate as king. Frederick knew, of course, that this meant war, but he counted on aid, especially from James I of England, his father-in-law. James, however, unlike most kings of the epoch, disliked fighting. Besides, he had no money for foreign campaigns. He did nothing. Since Frederick could offer them little to fight war but a good cause, the Lutheran princes of Germany also refused to help. Ferdinand, on the other hand, swiftly obtained a powerful army led by an excellent general, Count Tilly, appointed by Maximilian of Bavaria, whose Catholic zeal was reinforced by the desire to snatch the electoral hat from his relative Frederick's head along with the Bohemian land. Spain also provided Ferdinand with money and troops. Thus between Spanish forces striking from the Rhine and Bavarians from Bohemia, Frederick's army was smashed at the Battle of White Mountain outside Prague in 1620.

At this point the Bohemian conflict seemed a mere incident. Actually it was the prelude to a continent-wide disaster, for which Ferdinand was chiefly responsible. Interpreting the reasonable refusal of the Protestant states to support Frederick's hopeless cause as a sign of weakness, he unleashed the terrible Counter Reformation throughout his domains. Hapsburg officials invaded every principality, imposing harsh taxes and wiping out the cherished rights of nobles and businessmen. All the German princes found the freedom they had won from Charles V in the sixteenth century now in grave danger. The fate of Frederick of Bohemia heightened their alarm; Ferdinand treated him as a renegade, deposed him, and gave his land and his electoral authority to Maximilian.

Although no united resistance emerged, warfare now became general. The king of Denmark, unwilling to stand by idly while Ferdinand's Spanish allies controlled the Palatinate, attacked the Rhineland with an allied force only to be defeated badly. Ferdinand's brilliant General Wallenstein then wrecked havoc on the Lutherans of northern Germany. Now the war took on a life of its own. Most of the fighting had been done, according to the custom of the time, by mercenaries. When after years of costly campaigning the rulers ran out of money, the mercenaries extracted their wages in the form of plunder, rape, and senseless destruction. Troops of armed men roamed the countryside in search of peaceful towns to loot. They blackmailed entire communities, pillaged churches and monasteries. No nationality or religious faith was safe from attack; no noble too prestigious, no peasant too poor, to escape their hunger for booty. Ragged hordes of camp followers followed each armed band, scavengers feeding on the wreckage. For months and for years armies of from 10,000 to 40,000 men subjected Germany to senseless slaughter and pillage, all in the name of religion. Only the generals profited, attacking whom they pleased without consulting the princes whose standards they carried, setting themselves up practically as sovereigns in captured territory. Wallenstein even became the acknowledged ruler of the Protestant duchy of Mecklenburg.

Military success led Ferdinand in 1629 to issue the Edict of Restitution ordering the return to Rome of all church lands seized in the Protestant principalities since 1552. This was a direct blow at the north German Lutheran and Calvinist princes and also, of course, a revocation, at least of the spirit, of the Peace of Augsburg. At the apogee of his power, Ferdinand summoned the German princes to meet with him at Regensburg and called upon them to join him in a war against the Dutch. He considered this as a fair exchange with his Spanish cousins for the help they had given him in Bohemia, but the German princes saw the situation differently—they refused; what is more, they forced Ferdinand to discharge the unpopular General Wallenstein.

Ferdinand was still the strong man of central Europe, but foreign powers alarmed by the imbalance of forces he had created were beginning to intervene. French envoys moved unobtrusively among the princes at Regensburg. The French, guided since 1624 by the astute Cardinal Richelieu, allied themselves with the Dutch and began to challenge the Hapsburgs in Mantua and other parts of Italy. More significant, a new force, King Gustavus Adolphus of Sweden, now threw his weight into the conflict. Seeking to restore his Mecklenburg relatives to their lands, he marched a well-organized army, sustained by Protestant zeal and French money, into Germany. Combining political and military skills astutely, he formed an alliance with Protestant Brandenberg and Saxony, and in 1631, at the Battle of Breitenfeld, defeated an imperial army. Thereafter he swept over the Rhine and in a series of successful battles advanced clear to Munich. While his troops pillaged Bavaria, his Saxon allies captured Prague.

In desperation Ferdinand restored Wallenstein to command of his army. Wallenstein then marched into Saxony, leaving a trail of wreckage in his wake. But after months of maneuvering and destruction he was finally defeated by Gustavus on the field of Lützen, although Gustavus was killed in the battle. For a time Wallenstein seemed more of a threat to Ferdinand than to his enemies. Ferdinand, however, undermined the general among his own junior officers and then discharged him; soon thereafter he was murdered. Ferdinand then pressed the war against the Swedes, gaining slowly. Sweden's Brandenburg and Saxon allies, tired of the war and fearful of Swedish designs on Pomerania, were soon ready to abandon the contest. After winning an important victory at Nördlingen in 1634, Ferdinand was able to negotiate a peace under his own harsh terms at Prague in 1635. He was now free to help the Spanish in the Netherlands.

That war had gone badly for Spain, but Ferdinand might well turn the tide. To prevent this, France declared war on Spain and increased its subsidies to the Swedes and to another of Ferdinand's foes, Bernard of Weimar. This was a desperate gamble for Richelieu, for Spain was the greatest power in Europe and his own resources were limited. The French army was small and ineptly led and the royal treasury was almost empty. But the cardinal was convinced that the Hapsburgs posed a threat to all

Europe; the risk had to be taken. With Spain also almost exhausted by the long and costly struggle, the outcome seemed to depend upon which side first collapsed rather than which could win a military victory.

The tide went first one way, then the other. French prospects looked bleak in 1639 when a popular uprising occurred in Normandy, but Richelieu successfully suppressed these rebels. Then in the early 1640's French troops took both Alsace and the vital Alpine passes. Rebellions in Spanish Catalonia and in Portugal forced the chief Spanish minister Olivares to pull troops back from the Netherlands to restore order. Finally, in 1643, French forces won a decisive victory over the finest units of the Spanish army in the Battle of Rocroi.

Such was the chaos of the times, however, that each victory caused counterbalancing shifts among the contesting forces. After Rocroi the Dutch began to fear the French more than the Spanish. Similar realignments occurred in northern Europe. The Hapsburgs gave up their dream of reclaiming Protestant church lands, and after four years of negotiations, constantly complicated by the shifting fortunes of war and the outbreak of civil disturbances in various districts, the exhausted rivals signed the Peace of Westphalia in 1648. A bewildering exchange of territory and money took place among the German states. Sweden was given a place in the German diet. France got control of Metz, Verdun, and Toul, along with part of Alsace. The Dutch and Swiss achieved their independence. And as for the original cause of the war, religion, the delegates agreed merely to reestablish the principle laid down at the Peace of Augsburg in the previous century: each prince would determine the religion of his people now, even if he was a Calvinist. As a result the Hapsburgs drove all Protestants from their land, and many of the Lutherans and Calvinist princes compelled their Catholic subjects to choose between conversion and emigration.

After thirty years of war much of Germany lay in ruins, the fields untilled, the forests untended, the towns devastated, their crafts and industries destroyed. One-third of the population had died either in battle or from plague, malnutrition, or similar war-related catastrophes. Recovery would take decades if not whole centuries. Such were the terrible consequences of this enormous and bloody conflict for Germany and most of the rest of Europe.

But at Westphalia no one really expected, despite these terrible losses, that a long or a just peace had been achieved. The war between France and Spain continued unabated until 1659. Elsewhere the settlement had been made by exhausted powers but powers perfectly willing to consider resuming the struggle once their strength had been recovered. Indeed, one of the reasons why Sweden had conceded peace at last had been her growing concern over the other Baltic powers. At best a precarious balance had been reached. The nations returned to more regional interests. But at least for the moment peace had returned to Germany.

For Further Reading

Clark, G. N., *The Seventeenth Century.*
Holborn, H., *A History of Modern Germany.*
Wedgwood, C. V., *The Thirty Years' War.*

50   The Rise of Modern Political Thought

The fundamental changes that transformed Europe in the sixteenth and seventeenth centuries produced corresponding changes in the ways men thought about politics. Within roughly 200 years, beginning with Niccolò Machiavelli and ending with John Locke, political philosophers recognized and responded to these changes—the slow emergence of secular politics and the irremediable splintering of religious unity—by devising a theory for the modern state.

The essential ideas underlying political thinking in the Christian Middle Ages had been fairly simple: fallen man required controls; repressive political institutions are the kind of check that sinful humanity had invited after Adam. On the positive side, kings and judges also had the task of aiding men to lead a Christian life in this world by giving them their rightful place in the hierarchy of society and enabling them to respect the men and institutions that existed for the protection and propagation of the True Faith. Of course, while it was easy to agree on these propositions, priests and statesmen, theologians and philosophers, interminably, often bitterly, debated over what they meant in practice: How was authority to be divided between pope and emperor? Who was to appoint the higher functionaries of the Roman Catholic Church—the secular or the religious arm? Over these intensely practical issues, supporters of one side or the other had wrangled for centuries, and which side prevailed depended more on the fortunes of diplomacy and arms than on the logical merits of the case. When Machiavelli, early in the sixteenth century, founded modern political thinking, he did nothing to settle these disputes, but much to suggest that they were becoming irrelevant.

It is significant that Machiavelli was a product of Renaissance Florence —a diverse, sophisticated urban culture and small though potent city-state

CHRONOLOGY

A.D.

1494	Invasion of Italy by French troops
1513–1521	Niccolò Machiavelli writes *The Prince* and *The Discourses on the First Ten Books of Livy*
1517	Martin Luther posts 95 theses on church door at Wittenberg; Reformation usually dated from this moment
1525	Sack of Rome
1562–1594	Series of religious wars in France
1572	St. Bartholomew's Day Massacre in Paris, slaughter of the Huguenots
1576	Jean Bodin publishes *Six Books of the Republic*
1594	Henry IV takes Paris
1610	Henry IV is assassinated
1618–1648	Thirty Years' War
1642	Civil war begins in England
1649	Charles I of England beheaded
1651	Thomas Hobbes publishes *Leviathan*
1656	James Harrington publishes *The Commonwealth of Oceana*
1658	Oliver Cromwell dies
1660	Restoration of the monarchy in England; Charles II (1660–1685)
1661	Louis XIV of France assumes sole rule after death of Mazarin
1670	Baruch (Benedict de) Spinoza publishes, anonymously, *Tractatus Theologico-Politicus*
1685–1688	Reign of James II in England
1688–1689	Glorious Revolution; James II dethroned; William and Mary
1690	John Locke publishes *Two Treatises of Civil Government,* written ten years before

struggling for expansion and survival amid a ruthlessly competing group of similar states fighting for similar stakes. An experienced public servant and a keen observer, Machiavelli witnessed this spectacle without any illusions; a classicist and a pagan, he was not surprised to find that the princes of the Church behaved quite as viciously as their secular enemies. In 1512, when the shifts of political fortunes compelled Machiavelli to retire, he used his involuntary leisure to put down his reflections on politics in orderly form, and wrote two books that were to become classics in political theory: the *Discourses on the First Ten Books of Livy,* a set of aphorisms and short essays on ancient and modern politics, and *The Prince,* a disenchanted little book that would shock readers for centuries.

Freed as he was from religious convictions or superstitions, Machiavelli saw politics as a purely secular affair. It was, quite simply, the combat of men in search of power. Since men are all alike—all brutal, all selfish, all cowardly more or less—politics must follow universal rules, rules as applicable to Machiavelli's day as they had been to ancient Rome. The successful ruler therefore is the man who has studied his fellow man, both by reading history and by observing his contemporaries, and is willing to exploit their weaknesses. This cool prescription arose not from some supposed lack of moral sense, which many of his readers professed to detect in Machiavelli, but from his deeply pessimistic appraisal of human nature. The prince (so runs his most notorious maxim) must be both lion and fox: he must both terrorize and deceive his subjects. While Machiavelli did not have a taste for despotisms—in fact he greatly preferred sturdy, self-reliant republics—his own time, he thought, was too corrupt to permit any alternative to the kind of ruthless Renaissance despot that he saw all around him.

Machiavelli was a master stylist, pungent and vigorous, and from his own day on he found apologists eager to clear him from the widespread charge that he gloried in evil; he was, his supporters insisted, a scientist of politics who saw the world more clearly than others and reported what he saw with his own peculiar lucidity. This is an inadequate, or at least incomplete, view of the man: he was, first of all, a product of his time, in which the techniques he appraised so clinically were widely practiced; what was to shock other countries and later ages did not shock his compatriots and contemporaries. In addition, he was a man of passion: he was passionately committed to the active life; he was passionately hostile to the papacy for inviting foreign invaders to Italian soil for its own political profit. But while his supposed "scientific attitude" was not all he represented, it was his particular contribution to political theorizing: Machiavelli successfully detached politics from ethics and from theology, and presented it as a secular activity to be practiced and studied for its own sake. It was a fateful legacy.

Machiavelli was so intent upon establishing the autonomy of politics that he had little to say about religion apart from his comments on papal diplomacy. Yet, in the very decade in which he wrote his masterpieces, Martin Luther was to place religious questions squarely into the center of political speculation. For the Protestant reformers—for John Calvin and the others quite as much as for Luther—politics was something of an embarrassment. As good and in many respects perfectly traditional Christians, they were provoking and leading a great rebellion while, at the same time, they preached submission. They agreed with Catholic theologians at least in this: one of the primary duties of a Christian man was to obey constituted authority, no matter how wicked it might be. The evil king was a scourge sent by God, to be endured rather than resisted. As we have seen, Luther denounced the German peasantry in the most brutal terms for rising up against its princes; while he found many of their demands reasonable, he could not accept their defiance of those whom the Lord had set above them. Again, in 1559 Calvin counseled the French Huguenots to remain peaceful subjects of their Catholic rulers; while he could not help sympathizing with the sufferings of his coreligionists, the sin of rebellion seemed to him inexcusable. But in a Europe irrevocably split apart, with Catholics and Protestants equally unwilling to surrender to the other and equally insistent that their own faith was the only true one, and with regions, cities, even families divided in their religious allegiances, such inculcation of passivity could not remain a tenable policy for long. By the 1570's, therefore, two distinct theories had emerged to deal with the new situation: one, most exhaustively stated in Jean Bodin's *Six Books of the Republic,* devalued religion in behalf of a revived antique idea—sovereignty; the other, best represented by the anonymous pamphlet *Vindiciae contra tyrannos,* developed into a full-fledged system the rudimentary medieval notion that it might be lawful to resist the tyrant. These theories pointed in opposite directions while they tried to deal with the same issue: the first, stressing the right of the ruler over all subjects within his jurisdiction, moved toward the idea of modern absolutism; the second, by concentrating on the right of the subject against the impious tyrant, moved toward the idea of modern constitutionalism. Hobbes and Locke, the two greatest political theorists of the seventeenth century, while they agreed on much, became the supreme representatives of these two strands.

Thomas Hobbes was born in 1588, the year, as he himself liked to point out, of the Spanish Armada. And all his long life was spent in a time of turmoil, a virulent combination of religious, political, economic upheaval that England had not seen for more than a century and a half, a civil conflict culminating with the killing of Charles I and the establishment of a commonwealth under Cromwell. These events, combined with

Hobbes's philosophical materialism, shaped his political thinking: the *Leviathan,* one of the great books in the literature of political theory, appeared in 1651, two years after the execution of the king. The greatest evil in the world, Hobbes insists, is civil war; the central task of the political thinker, therefore, is to find the way to civil peace. In pursuit of this task, Hobbes developed a rigorously consistent system of rule and obedience, securely founded on his view of human nature. Man's most distinctive quality, Hobbes argued, is egotism—the pursuit of pleasure and the avoidance of pain at the expense of others. It is no peaceful pursuit; goods are scarce, and men always want more than they have: "I put for a general inclination of all mankind, a perpetual and restless desire for power after power, that ceaseth only in death." Employing that favorite metaphor of seventeenth-century political theorists, the state of nature in which men exist without the dubious benefit of political institutions, Hobbes argued that given human nature, such a state must be a "war of every man against every man," an orgy of mutual suspicion inevitably issuing in mutual murder, a life without morality or comfort or civility—"solitary, poor, nasty, brutish, and short."

But Hobbes saw man as equipped with reason as well as with the desire for pleasure and power, and man's enlightened search for self-preservation would therefore lead him to abandon the disastrous state of nature for a system of political order secure enough to forestall civil war and strong enough at the same time to protect all subjects. It is precisely because men are so egotistical that the state must engross all possible power. "Covenants, without the sword, are but words, and of no strength to secure a man at all." It follows that men must, figuratively and literally, give up their swords to the sovereign—"that great Leviathan . . . that mortal God"—whose control is absolute.

The theory sounds terrifying, but its logic is impeccable, and its bearing, be it noted, is wholly secular and wholly utilitarian. There is only one justification for the state: its capacity to keep order. The old sources of authority—legitimacy, tradition, religious foundations—were of no interest to Hobbes at all. While Hobbes refuses to allow the subject any right to resist the sovereign, the task of the sovereign is to protect the subject, and rebellion against him only proves the sovereign unfit to rule. Hobbes's utilitarian theory thus poses an interesting paradox: revolutions are illegal, but successful revolutions make the new regime legitimate, through their very success; Hobbes was interested not in tyranny—he was an individualist, and his theory was, after all, not hostile to any form of government, even republics—but in the logic of politics.

Great works of the mind rise above, and last beyond, the occasion that brought them forth, but they will always bear the marks of their origins.

Hobbes wrote during and against civil strife; thirty years after him, when the republican interlude was over and the Stuart monarchy had been restored, Locke would write during and against a different menace: the possibility of a Catholic succession in a Protestant, or at least Anglican, country. The brother and heir to Charles II was a declared and determined Roman Catholic, and even before his accession in 1685 as James II it was clear that his reign would mortally offend the vast majority of Englishmen. Locke's political writings came out of this atmosphere; they are a notable attempt to formulate the right to resistance while, at the same time, guaranteeing the state enough power to rule effectively. Locke wrote his *Two Treatises of Government* before the Glorious Revolution of 1688 which expelled James II and brought in the Protestants William and Mary, but he published them after that revolution, in 1690. Intended as the justification for future action, they came to be read as the justification of a triumphant revolution.

Like Hobbes, Locke used the device of a prepolitical state of nature, but to different effect. In their original condition, Locke argued, men enjoyed the right to "life, liberty, and estate," and it was obvious that they would contract to found a political society only because in such a society these rights would be better protected than they would be without a state. The civil power thus established had the right to make laws, and reserved enough authority to make them stick, but it existed quite clearly only for the sake of the public good. A government was thus distinct from, and the servant of, society. It followed, as Locke did not fail to point out, that there were certain conditions when societies might legitimately refuse their obedience to their government, especially when the government had betrayed its trust, when it invaded the inviolable rights of all men, when, in a word, it degenerated from a government of laws into a despotism.

Locke took good care to define the reasonable powers of the state widely enough to make legitimate rebellion a rarity. Still, he enunciated a significant set of principles which would acquire a certain explosive verve in the eighteenth century, in France and in Britain's American colonies: government is a sacred trust; men have imprescriptible rights; revolution is a last but always a possible resort. Much like Hobbes in this as well, Locke founded this trust and these rights not on theological or historical arguments, but on the philosophical theory of human nature. Thus, while Locke was scarcely a secularist himself, and while his theory was hedged around with conservative caution, he pushed political thinking into modernity.

For Further Reading

Aaron, R. I., *John Locke.*
Allen, J. W., *Political Thought in the Sixteenth Century.*

Chabod, Federico, *Machiavelli and the Renaissance.*

Dickens, A. G., *Martin Luther and the Reformation.*

Dunn, John, *The Political Thought of John Locke.*

Franklin, Julian H., *Jean Bodin and the Sixteenth-Century Revolution in the Methodology of Law and History.*

Gerbrandy, Pieter S., *National and International Stability: Althusius, Grotius, van Vollenhoven.*

Gilbert, Felix, *Machiavelli and Guicciardini.*

Goldsmith, Maurice M., *Hobbes's Science of Politics.*

Gough, J. W., *John Locke's Political Philosophy.*

Krieger, Leonard, *The Politics of Discretion: Pufendorf and the Acceptance of Natural Law.*

McShea, Robert J., *The Political Philosophy of Spinoza.*

Monter, Edward W., *Calvin's Geneva.*

Pelikan, Jaroslav, *Spirit vs. Structure: Luther and the Institutions of the Church.*

Plamenatz, John, *Man and Society, Vol. I.*

Raab, Felix, *The English Face of Machiavelli.*

Reynolds, Beatrice, *Proponents of Limited Monarchy in Sixteenth-Century France: Francis Hotman and Jean Bodin.*

Ridolfi, Roberto, *The Life of Niccolò Machiavelli.*

Sabine, George H., *A History of Political Theory.*

Smith, Russell, *Harrington and His "Oceana."*

Strauss, Leo, *The Political Theory of Hobbes.*

Vreeland, Hamilton, *Hugo Grotius, the Father of the Modern Science of International Law.*

Wendel, François, *Calvin.*

Toward One World

51   The Commercial Powers

The spectacular discoveries of the fifteenth-century European navigators opened a new chapter in the history of mankind. Portuguese exploration of the African coasts and islands and Columbus' discovery of a totally new world began a quest which brought most of the earth into the scope of European man. All over the world Europeans forced themselves into the ken of people who had been living in relative isolation and self-sufficiency. This dramatic and painful process, which lasted until the end of the eighteenth century, began a gradual movement toward one world and a system of international relations affecting the daily lives of people in every corner of the earth. After a brief halt in the nineteenth century, a new wave of exploration and colonization created the reality of today, with all its problems and tensions: this is the heritage of European expansion.

The age of discovery was filled with tumultuous events as small bands of adventurers penetrated into strange new worlds in pursuit of profit and dreams, and as their discoveries were consolidated into vast empires by following generations, the excitement and drama continued. It is paradoxical that the sixteenth-century colonial conquests were made by Spain and Portugal, two countries that did not play very large roles in the European commercial life of the time. The chief commercial powers were not especially interested in colonial expansion, nor were they worried by the Treaty of Tordesillas (1494) by which Spain and Portugal had confidently divided up the overseas world between themselves.

From the strictly commercial point of view the discoveries had come too early, before the European economy had been integrated into a single market, an integration that was necessary before the intensive colonial exploitation of the seventeenth and eighteenth centuries could take place. At the beginning of the sixteenth century Europe still consisted of a number of small regional economic systems. Although interregional trade was profitable and important, the economy was still predominantly agrarian.

A.D.   1494   Treaty of Tordesillas divides overseas world be-
              tween Spain and Portugal

     1570's   First raids by English and Dutch on Spanish empire
              in South America; breakdown of Portuguese mo-
              nopoly in the Indian Ocean

       1600   Foundation of English East India Company

       1602   Foundation of Dutch East India Company

       1609   Foundation of Bank of Amsterdam

       1619   Foundation of Bank of Hamburg

       1621   Foundation of Dutch West India Company

       1624   Dutch drive English out of spice trade of the East
              Indies

       1629   Dutch obtain rights to trade at Arkhangelsk

       1635   Foundation of Compagnie française des îles
              d'Amerique

       1639   English establish themselves in Madras

       1651   Navigation Acts in England, directed against Dutch
              trade

  1652–1674   Period of Anglo-Dutch wars; peace of 1674 results
              in division of colonial spheres of influence be-
              tween England and Holland, in which East Indies
              go to the latter and America to England

  1689–1713   Period of Anglo-Dutch coalition wars against France
              of Louis XIV

       1713   Peace of Utrecht gives England trading rights in
              Spanish American empire; decline of the Dutch

The Mediterranean was the most important of these regional economies. It was centered in Venice, which, besides dominating the Mediterranean trade, was the almost exclusive channel through which luxury goods
from Asia reached the rest of Europe. The northern European economy
was dominated by the Hanseatic League, while the Netherlands and England dominated that of western Europe.

These commercial powers profited far more from colonial exploitation
than did Spain and Portugal, which could not absorb all the exports of their
colonies or market them effectively elsewhere on the continent. Spain was
drained of her American silver by foreign merchants, and in spite of direct
access to Asian producers, the Portuguese could not force Venice out of
the spice market. When more diversified colonial products, such as sugar,
tobacco, coffee, tea, Brazilian wood, and textiles were produced in the
seventeenth century, the Iberian nations proved even less capable of controlling their distribution.

However, in the sixteenth century it was not easy to predict which of
the commercial powers would dominate the growing European market.
Regional trade was expanding, creating markets to absorb the products of
colonial exploitation. The emphasis was, however, shifting from luxury
goods to grains and manufactured products like cheap textiles. In the first
half of the sixteenth century Antwerp seemed to get the lead, profiting from
its crucial location, as well as its thriving local industry and strong home
market. Annual imports into the Netherlands amounted to seven guilders
per capita around the middle of the century; comparable figures were one
and a half guilders for both England and France. Nevertheless, Antwerp's
trade was still too exclusively dependent upon luxury goods and its money
market. The final shift of the European staple market toward the Netherlands came with the rapid increase of bulky seaborne trade, and for
various reasons, among which the course of the Netherlands' revolt looms
very large, Amsterdam, not Antwerp, became the center of this commerce.

One more step in the integration of the European economy was necessary to bring this about. The relative autarky of the regional economic
systems was based upon their agricultural self-sufficiency. The Netherlands
were the one exception: a highly urbanized area which imported a part of
its food supply, mainly grains, from the Baltic. Amsterdam specialized in
this trade. By around 1500 the Dutch Baltic fleet already equaled that of
the Hanseatic League, and Dutch ships dominated traffic through the
Danish Sound. In the second half of the sixteenth century population pressure began to cause grain shortages in the Mediterranean area, some of
catastrophic magnitude. Although the Hanseatic League tried to exploit
this situation, the Dutch, already specializing in the grain and other bulk
trades, easily won this valuable market. They had developed a new type of

cheap, efficient freighter, the "flute" or "flyboat," which was too much competition for the old-fashioned Hanseatic carriers. Philip II of Spain confiscated whole Dutch fleets in his harbors during their rebellion against his authority, but it became clear even to his slow-working mind that Spain needed the services of the Dutch. Economic considerations prevailed over political and religious ones. After his troops had occupied Antwerp (1585), the trade and financial activity of that city shifted to Amsterdam, and this business, grafted upon the existing northern shipping and trade, produced Amsterdam's remarkable rise. In the seventeenth century, it was the financial and trade center of the Western world.

Thus, by the beginning of the seventeenth century, the struggle to control the European market had been decided. Venice declined to the status of a secondary regional market and soon could not even defend its monopoly of the Levant trade in the Mediterranean financial market against Genoese, English, and Dutch rivals. The Hanseatic League's cumbersome political structure made it impossible to carry out an efficacious economic policy. Its strength was increasingly undermined by the rivalries of its members; Hamburg, for example, prospered at the expense of the other towns. Late in the sixteenth century the League lost the last remnants of the English cloth trade with Germany. South German cities like Augsburg and Nürnberg suffered from the decline of their overland trade with Venice, which the Dutch absorbed.

The powerful kingdoms of France and England failed to profit from the shifts in European trade patterns. France was too much weakened by civil war to play an active role, while England's trade was too little diversified to challenge the Dutch. Moreover, in the expansion of strictly commercial capitalism, mercantile expertise and the availability of credit were crucial, and governments could do little to create such facilities. Even under Colbert, when France had an infinitely more powerful government than at the beginning of the seventeenth century, French expansionist commercial policy was largely a failure: a convincing illustration of the prevalence of efficiency and competitiveness over government protectionism. In the Netherlands both expertise and credit were abundantly available. The Dutch also profited from inertia. In a time of slow communications, once-established trade patterns were not easily changed, which helps to explain why the English failed to market their own cloth or find outlets other than the Dutch ones.

Still another element entered into the Dutch success. Successful commercial operations were best carried out by small, specialized, mercantile communities. All the great commercial centers began as independent city-states, or urban leagues like the Hansa, in which government policy was geared to commercial needs. At the end of the sixteenth century it had become increasingly clear, however, that commerce had to be supported by some state power to prosper. Such power did not have the overwhelming impact upon trade movements that the more efficiently organized nation-states of the eighteenth and nineteenth centuries had, but it was substantial. The smaller, defenseless commercial centers succumbed. The Netherlands Republic was large enough for the time being to defend its trade against the larger but poorly organized monarchies.

Yet the intricate trade system upon which the Dutch prosperity rested was precariously balanced. Of the various branches which came together in Amsterdam, Dutch observers considered Baltic grain the "mother trade." Baltic products had to be exchanged for other goods, and herring figured large in these transactions. But herring were caught along the coasts of England and Scotland. The fishing industry also needed salt, which was imported from Spain, France, and (later) the West Indies. Trade with Spain and France brought in wine and silver. Silver helped pay for Baltic commodities and for imports from the East Indies. Further revenue came from shipping and from financial operations. Essentially, the Dutch had only services to offer; they could survive only as long as their seaborne trade went on uninterruptedly in all of its interdependent branches. As an envious English observer puts it, the Dutch were like "a fair bird suited with good borrowed plumes; but if every Fowl should take his feather, this bird would rest near naked." To defend their host of unarmed freighters, a large naval force was vital, but the Dutch also relied upon that typical, and usually fragile, device of the weak: the appeal to international law, in which they became experts, from the time of Hugo Grotius (1583–1645) onward.

During the course of the seventeenth century it became clear that England was the only power that could challenge the Dutch. In colonial enterprises it had preceded the Dutch by many decades; as early as the 1570's the English had made effective inroads into the Spanish-American empire. The Dutch had a strictly commercial conception of colonization, and lacked the surplus population to provide their American enterprises with sufficient settlers. Consequently they contented themselves with the control of the trading ports in the Antilles, vital for their smuggling trade with Spanish America and the slave trade. They accepted the loss of New Amsterdam to England in the 1660's without much regret, and in much the same spirit they abandoned their holdings in Brazil to Portugal (1630–1657).

Economic competition between England and the Netherlands became much more bitter after 1650. English commercial interests pushed a hesitant Cromwell to pass the Navigation Acts and launch the first of a series of Anglo-Dutch wars (1652–1654), an example followed less hesitantly by Charles II in 1665. The situation became even more perilous for the Dutch when the French defender of mercantilism, Colbert, brought France into the economic war against Holland. This Anglo-French coalition almost finished off the Dutch in 1672. Dutch trade, however, showed a remarkable resilience. To a great extent the maxims of the late sixteenth century still held true. Navigation acts were hard to enforce against cheap Dutch shipping. Colbert's prohibitive tariffs hurt France as much as the Netherlands. His trading companies lost money. Yet, despite the fact that as late as the 1690's the Dutch merchant fleet, totaling 568,000 tons, was still more than three times as large as that of the English, England's was increasing.

The Dutch Republic finally succumbed under the financial burden of protecting itself during the coalition wars against Louis XIV. Bearing the lion's share of the cost of the Anglo-Dutch army (1689–1713) it had to abandon naval superiority to the English. After the Peace of Utrecht (1713), the English reaped the profits of the opening up of Spanish America and the Dutch sank to the level of a second-rate power.

Other than purely military and financial causes account for the Dutch decline. American products, in which the Dutch never had shown much interest, became much more important for the European market. A different type of colonial exploitation came to the fore, as the powers sought to market industrial products in their growing overseas settlements. With the increasing importance of industry, an exclusively mercantile economy was bound to decline. An even heavier blow was the gradual disappearance of the staple-market type of European trade, made obsolete by improved communications in the eighteenth century. The Netherlands remained an extraordinarily strong financial center, but its commodity market and its political power declined.

The eighteenth-century emergence of France and England as commercial, colonial, and increasingly industrial powers, based upon large populations and great natural resources, produced a different, world-wide economic contest, demanding a much more intensive mobilization of national resources, and a different conception of imperialist economic policy. In this new configuration, small, strictly commercial powers could play only a minor role.

For Further Reading

Barbour, V., *Capitalism in Amsterdam in the Seventeenth Century.*
Penrose, B., *Travel and Discovery in the Renaissance, 1420–1620.*
Rich, E. E., and Wilson, C. H. (eds.), *The Economy of Expanding Europe in the Sixteenth and Seventeenth Centuries* (Vol. IV of *The Cambridge Economic History of Europe*).
Wilson, C., *Profit and Power.*

52   The Ottoman Empire

In the second half of the thirteenth century the shattered lands of Anatolia seemed a singularly unsuitable locale for the rise of a new world empire. Devastated for some two centuries by the conflicts of local dynasts whom the Seljuks were increasingly incapable of controlling, Asia Minor sank into chaos after the crushing victory of the Mongols at Köse-dagh in 1243 swept from it the last vestiges of centralized authority. The history of the origin of the new Turkish principality which arose in the extreme northwest of the peninsula under the leadership of Osman I (1290?–1326) is obscured by legends created at a later date, but the new state emerging clearly into history with Orkhan I (1326–1359), the second sultan of Ottoman tradition, was based on a combination of military and religious forces which gave it both its initial impetus and its remarkable staying powers.

The conquest of Anatolia in the eleventh century had been largely the work of warrior groups known as *gazis* whose common tie was their devotion to the jihad, the holy war spreading the faith of Islam by force of arms. At first of mixed origin, then increasingly Turkicized in the twelfth and thirteenth centuries through new migrations, the *gazis* formed a separate frontier society which spearheaded the Muslim advance toward the West, and it is among them that we should seek the roots of the Ottoman state with its fundamental marcher characteristics. Far removed from the centers of Seljuk power, in an exposed position bearing the brunt of Byzantine counterattacks, the Ottomans depended only on their stubborn dedication to the Muslim cause and on their military prowess for their survival. The traditional suspicion of frontiersmen for effete sedentary cultures increasingly opposed the *gazis* to the weakening Seljuk rule and freed them from the onus of its collapse. Even their militant Islamic faith differed from the learned and strictly orthodox beliefs of the Seljuk court. Undisturbed by theological speculations, devoted to popular practices and mystical beliefs of dubious orthodoxy brought to them by wandering dervishes, the Ottoman *gazis,* to their great advantage, could paradoxically both share the superstitions of the local non-Muslim population and rally the allegiance of other Muslim groups as the true sword-bearers of Islam against the Infidel.

Leaving behind them the East, where Muslim chieftains opposed them as unorthodox upstarts and barbarians, the Ottomans turned first to the West, where they could exploit the enthusiasm they aroused for the holy

A.D.	1326–1359	Reign of Orkhan I
	1359–1389	Reign of Murad I
	1365	Ottoman capital shifted to Andrinople in Thrace
	1371	Ottoman defeat of the Serbs on the Marica
	1389	First Battle of Kossovo
	1402	Defeat of Bajazet I Yilderim by Tamerlane
	1444	Ottoman defeat of the Christian "Crusade" at Varna
	1448	Second Battle of Kossovo
	1451–1481	Reign of Muhammad II the Conqueror
	1453	Ottoman capture of Constantinople by Muhammad II the Conqueror
	1514	Ottoman defeat of the Safavids at Caldiran
	1517	Ottoman capture of Cairo; surrender of Mecca
	1520–1566	Reign of Suleiman I the Magnificent (*Kanuni*)
	1521	Ottoman capture of Belgrade
	1522	Ottoman capture of Rhodes
	1526	Ottoman defeat of the Hungarians at Mohács
	1529	First Ottoman siege of Vienna; Ottomans acquire Algerian bases
	1534	Ottoman capture of Tabriz and Iraq
	1536	Ottoman alliance with Francis I of France
	1547	Larger part of Hungary ceded to the Ottomans
	1555	Ottoman-Safavid peace
	1571	Battle of Lepanto
	1606	Peace of Sitvatorok
	1630	*Memorandum* of Koça Bey
	1641–1687	Reign of Muhammad IV; abolition of the *devşirme*
	1656–1676	Ottoman revival under Köprülü viziers
	1683	Second Ottoman siege of Vienna
	1696	Capture of Azov by Peter the Great
	1697	Eugene of Savoy's defeat of the Ottomans at Zenta
	1699	Peace of Karlowitz
	1703–1730	Cultural revival under Ahmed III
	1718	Peace of Passarowitz
	1724–1730	Victories of Nadir Shah in Transcaucasia
	1726–1742	Opening and closing of the first Turkish press
	1757–1774	Reign of Mustafa III; Ayans granted official status
	1774	Treaty of Kuçuk Kaynarca
	1783	Russian annexation of the Crimea

war and the quarrels of Byzantine and Balkan rulers. Little more than a quarter-century after Orkhan had made Brusa (Bursa) his capital, his son Murad I (1359–1389) moved to Andrinople (Edirne) in Thrace. Thereafter, the Ottomans always considered "Rumeli" (the land of the Romans) as against "Anadolu" the core of their empire.

Until they crossed into Europe, the Ottomans were hardly distinguishable from a number of other Anatolian successor states, but the great victories of Murad at the Marica (1371) and in the first Battle of Kossovo (1389) gave him mastery of the Balkans at the same time as he asserted his domination over the Anatolian princes. At his death on the battlefield of Kossovo, the Muslim dynasts of the East, the Christian princes of Serbia and Bulgaria, and the Byzantine emperor himself were tributary to the Ottoman sultan. The Christian failure to take advantage of Tamerlane's rout of Murad's successor, Bajazet I Yilderim, at Ankara in 1402, and of the subsequent decade of wars between Bajazet's sons sealed the fate of Constantinople. Muhammad I (1413–1421) pursued a cautious policy of consolidation, but his son Murad II (1421–1451) and his more famous grandson Muhammad II the Conqueror (1451–1481) turned back to an all-out military policy of conquest and annexation. The Anatolian beys were again reduced to obedience, the Hungarians and Balkan princes defeated at Varna (1444) and the second Battle of Kossovo (1448). Finally, in 1453, Constantinople fell after a four months' siege. The city's position necessarily made of it the capital of the new empire, which was as much European as Anatolian.

This triumph of Muhammad II after eight centuries of Muslim assaults ensured his fame, but Turkish expansion had not yet reached its high-water mark. Christian bridgeheads were swept from the Balkans, Rhodes was captured, Italy seriously threatened, while at the other end of his empire Muhammad II defeated the new Turkoman state of the Akkoyunlu (White Sheep) created in northeastern Asia Minor and Iran by Uzun Hasan. The Conqueror's son Bajazet II adopted a more cautious policy, but the crowning conquests were added by his son and grandson, Selim I the Grim (1512–1520), and Suleiman I the Magnificent (1520–1566). The establishment of Ottoman sovereignty in the Crimea and south Russia in the days of the Conqueror had given the Turks control of the Black Sea. (In 1569 plans were even made for a Volga-Don canal which would give them access to the Caspian and Central Asia.) At Caldiran in 1514 Selim routed the new Persian dynasty of the Safavids, who had succeeded Uzun Hasan, and whose militant Shi'ite creed had rallied many of the heterodox elements among the Turkoman tribes; Suleiman went on to take Tabriz, their capital, and to conquer Iraq. In the south, Selim's armies swept across Syria into Egypt, and forced the Muslim Holy Cities of Mecca and Medina to acknowledge his suzerainty. In the West, making the most of the Emperor Charles V's difficulties with Francis I of France and the Protestant princess of the Schmalkaldic League, Suleiman extended his control over the Mediterranean. Aided by Algerian corsairs who accepted his overlordship and provided him with a fleet, he defeated Venice and her allies of the Holy League at Prevsna in 1548. On land, the sultan crushed the Hungarians at Mohács in 1526; by 1547 he had forced the Hapsburg empire to recognize his control of much of Hungary and to pay a yearly tribute. Hampered by overextended lines of communications, the Ottomans failed to capture the imperial city of Vienna which they attacked in 1529, but by the middle of the sixteenth century most of Eastern Europe, Western Asia, and North Africa, together with the Mediterranean and Black seas, were in their hands.

The spectacular victories of the Turks owed much to the remarkable leadership of the first ten sultans and to the support they commanded as the champions of Islam. But the crucial element seems to have been their absolute yet flexible military ideology—the raison d'être of the *gazi* state. Unencumbered by the elaborate traditions of earlier Islamic civilizations in Arabia and Iran, the Ottomans bent all circumstances to their advantage with the shrewd adaptability of frontiersmen. Both fanaticism and tolerance they profitably exploited, and they learned many useful techniques from their enemies. The Ottoman fleet that came into being in the sixteenth century copied Venetian models; European renegades contributed knowledge of firearms and helped to make Ottoman siege and field artillery invincible. Long before the creation of the world empire, the system of recruitment known as the *devşirme* (child tribute) replenished the ranks of the Turkish army by conscripting able-bodied Orthodox Christian boys and forcibly converting them to Islam. Yet until the sixteenth century Christian contingents continued to serve among the Ottoman forces and were even rewarded with fiefs. All means were acceptable if they served the ends of the holy war.

As late as the victory of Muhammad II over Byzantium, the Ottoman realm was still largely in an embryonic state, retaining many features of the original marcher principality, but in the century which culminated in the reign of Suleiman I, to whom Ottoman tradition gives the significant title of *Kanuni* (the Lawgiver), it was transformed into a full-fledged Muslim world empire, albeit one exhibiting a number of idiosyncratic features.

The basic form and institutions of the Ottoman state followed the classic Muslim pattern, since the sultan was the eternal defender of the faith. By the sixteenth century, faced with the growing threat of the Shi'ite Safavid empire in Iran, Turkish Sunnite orthodoxy increased in rigidity. The unalterable law of Islam, the *Shariat,* embracing both religious and

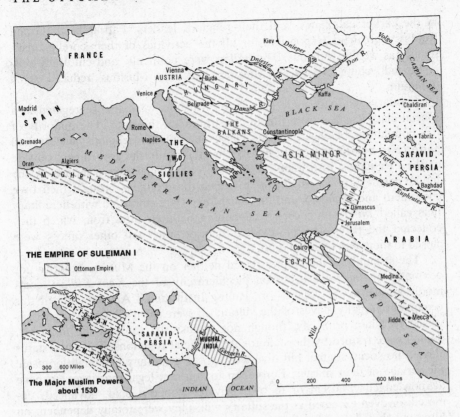

THE EMPIRE OF SULEIMAN I

Ottoman Empire

The Major Muslim Powers about 1530

secular spheres, was the law of the empire, and in fact received more direct application and support from the Ottomans than from any other Muslim ruler.

In spite of its orthodoxy, however, Ottoman society was rigidly compartmentalized in a thoroughly atypical pattern. The Muslim subjects of the sultan were barred from a significant role in the government. The imposition of second-class status on non-Muslim *zimmîs,* who paid the poll tax and were excluded from office, was not surprising, nor was the tolerance which permitted and (up to a point) protected their existence. Earlier caliphs had acted in the same manner. The division along religious rather than ethnic or even cultural lines of the non-Muslim communities or *millets* created by Muhammad II for the Orthodox, Armenians, and Jews was not unusual, since this too fitted the theocratic Muslim tradition. The remarkable feature of the *millets* was their exclusive and hermetic nature. Their members could not move from their community except through conversion to Islam; they were segregated from the rest of society as they had not been in the earlier caliphates, and their religious leaders, Patriarchs or Grand Rabbis, were held responsible for all the activities of their coreligionists, secular as well as religious. The *millets* were politically and culturally self-contained, contact between Muslims and non-Muslims reduced to a minimum.

Similarly, and still more amazingly, Muslims were also segregated in a special class isolated from the administration of the state. The majority of the population belonged in this class, and all the religious leaders had perforce to be drawn from it, but its contribution to the government outside of the "Religious Institution" took only one official form: service in the feudal cavalry known as *sipâhîs,* to which those eligible brought their own equipment and retainers, and for which they were rewarded with hereditary fiefs called *timars* or *zi'āmets,* depending on their size, from which they collected the taxes which provided their revenue. All other offices were closed to them and their children.

The strength of the empire rested neither on the Muslim majority nor obviously on the *millets,* but on the hierarchy of the *Kapi Kullari,* commonly known as the "Slave" or "Ruling Institution." All members of this group were legally slaves of the sultan; all were born Christians and converted to Islam primarily, though not exclusively, through the *devşirme;* and all were trained by the state for their official functions. The slave status carried no social stigma, but divested the *kullars* of any personality outside the service of their master. Forbidden to contract legal marriages, to have acknowledged children, or to own private property, paid, advanced, demoted, or even executed at the sultan's will, they were totally dependent on him, and their honors and possessions reverted to him at their death. The most famous component of the *Kapi Kullars* was the crack regiments of the Janissaries, who formed the backbone of the Ottoman army, but all officials, from the palace cooks and gardeners to provincial governors and the Grand Vizier himself, were drawn from the Slave Institution. By this remarkable, if precariously balanced, tour de force, the Ottoman empire obtained a superlative group of administrators, entirely devoted to their duties (since they were isolated from the interests of the rest of the population), undistracted by personal allegiances and preoccupations, and dependent for their careers and their very lives on the demonstration of their efficiency and loyalty. Simultaneously, their nonhereditary status precluded the formation of a powerful ruling elite which might threaten the authority of the sultan.

The hierarchy of the Ruling Institution provided a formidable instrument for the centralized absolutism which characterized the Ottoman state. A number of similar structures focused on the capital likewise promoted the cohesion of the empire and the all-inclusive might of its ruler. Islamic theology still admitted of no clerical body in a spiritual or sacramental sense, but in practice the learned *Ulemas* represented the Religious Institution. Now for the first time they were grouped under a hitherto nonexistent religious head of the state, the *Sheyh-ül-Islam.* In the same way, the local interpreters of the *Shariat,* the *kadis* or judges, were answerable not to the provincial governors, but to the two *Kadiaskers* residing in the capital. Finally, after 1530, the granting of feudal *timars,* once the prerogative of local dignitaries, was removed to the jurisdiction of the sultan. Hence, no external or internal element was in a position to interfere with the absolutism of the central government controlling the separate compartments of state which were too isolated from one another to present any serious threat. Even the danger of family rivalries, perpetually present in a polygamous society without a clear law of succession and consequently vulnerable to harem intrigues, was allayed by the decree of the Conqueror that all male relatives of the reigning sultan were to be executed at his accession: ". . . to whomsoever of my sons the Sultanate shall pass, it is fitting that for the order of the world he shall kill his brothers. Most of the *Ulema* allow it. So let them act on this."

Under the reign of Suleiman the Magnificent, the cresting wave of *gazi* enthusiasm, the elaborate if rather inhuman *kullar* system; the technological superiority in war; the supervision of the state in all matters; the continuing tolerance which gave asylum to the Jews fleeing from Spanish persecution and benefited from their skills; the wealth derived from the east-west trade which made of Brusa a major Mediterranean mart where the spices and cottons of India were exchanged for the woolens of Florence, the silks of Gilan, or local brocades—all these things made possible for a time a continuation in the pattern of conquests, a superlative bureaucracy, and a government far superior to that of most of its contemporaries. The Ottoman Empire dominated not only the Muslim world but much of the Mediterranean as well.

In 1571, five years after Suleiman's death, the Christian world rejoiced immoderately at the victory of Lepanto, where at long last an Ottoman fleet had been defeated by the ships of a new Holy League. Lepanto, however, was a minor triumph, another century at least would have to pass before any serious alteration in the political balance took place. But Ottoman strength slowly began to weaken in the seventeenth century. The most immediate manifestation of change was an ending of further Muslim conquests. Occasional fragments of territory were still added, but after more than two centuries of almost unbroken victories, the Ottoman armies now began to falter. They could not break through the opposition of the Hapsburgs in Europe, of Russia in the Ukraine, or of the Safavids in Iran. The walls of Vienna from which Suleiman had retreated in 1529 remained unbreached. Control of the Mediterranean passed out of Ottoman hands, while far to the east, Muslim fleets failed to sweep the Portuguese newcomers from the Indian Ocean. Russian expansion gradually blocked the alternate overland routes to Central Asia and its wealth. At Sitvatorok in 1606, the sultan Ahmed I agreed for the first time to a negotiated peace with the Infidel. Within twenty years the great Safavid ruler Shah Abbas I (1587–1629) wrested away Baghdad and the Armenian border provinces from the Turks. By 1699, after the failure of the second siege of Vienna (1683), the victories of Peter the Great at Azov (1696), and of Prince Eugene of Savoy at Zenta (1697), the Ottomans, as the defeated party, surrendered Hungary (except for the Banat of Temesvár), Transylvania, Croatia, the Morea, and most of Dalmatia to the westerners at the Peace of Karlowitz (1699). Three years later, Russia's presence on the Black Sea was conceded by the temporary abandonment of Azov. The high-water mark of Ottoman might was a thing of the past.

Western travelers noted the parlous state of the Turkish empire torn by violent rebellions and economic crises. Ottoman intellectuals such as Koça Bey, in his famous *Memorandum* presented to the sultan Murad IV in 1630, and Haci Halife in 1653 tried to suggest remedies for the military and economic disasters. But a combination of internal failures and external circumstances seemingly beyond control were turning the tide against the Ottoman Empire in which the vital *gazi* tradition had finally died, leaving only a monumental but cumbersomely expensive and increasingly hidebound structure.

Internally, the state could not maintain the precarious balance of its superhuman machinery. The absolute centralization and efficiency of the administrative structure, which had been the source of its strength, depended ultimately on the perfection of the rulers at its apex. The early sultans had fulfilled the onerous demands of their office with remarkable dedication, but the system of selecting the ruler militated against the continuation of this pattern. The merciless decree of the Conqueror was abandoned by the end of the sixteenth century, but its substitute was if anything more disastrous. All princes, except the sons of the sultan, were herded from childhood into separate palace apartments where they were confined for life in total isolation from the world, deprived of normal human experiences, and all but uneducated. A decree of 1617 granting the succession to the oldest member of the ruling house rather than to the sultan's sons ensured the accession of one of these "Caged Princes," necessarily unprepared for his duties, if not altogether unfit, and as such the puppet of one of the rival factions.

The growing strain of wars requiring larger and better armies gradually made obsolete the feudal *sipâhî* cavalry, which was no match for the technological advances of seventeenth-century warfare. More and more reliance was placed on the paid Janissary contingents. Not only did the expense of their upkeep strain the finances of the state, but their indispensability predisposed them more and more to violence and blackmail. Demanding higher pay and greater benefits, among these the right to pass their status on to their sons, thereby destroying the fundamental character of the Slave Institution, they became a hereditary Muslim privileged class, especially after the abolition of the *devşirme* by Muhammad IV (1641–1687). The Janissaries exploited the growing weakness of the sultans in order to crush any opposition to themselves, push their commanders into the Grand Vizierate, and play kingmakers. Between 1590 and 1634 they were to all purposes masters of the capital, while dissident *Celâlî* bands roved the countryside, terrorizing the villagers. The Ruling Institution was beginning to crumble.

External circumstances aggravated the crisis. By the seventeenth century, the discovery of new sea routes to the East left the great Ottoman markets, which had depended on overland trade, stranded in a backwater. The mass of cheap silver imported from the New World swamped the Turkish economy, cutting the value of the standard Ottoman coin, the silver *akçe,* almost in half as early as 1584 and precipitating an uncontrollable inflation. Ottoman currency was driven from international markets as the balance of trade turned against the empire and brought widespread poverty and discontent in its wake. Western technology surpassed Turkish traditional methods, frozen by the Muslim guild system.

Caught in an inescapable spiral of difficulties, forced to support an enormous bureaucracy on a still primitive economy increasingly inadequate to the task, the Ottoman Empire began to give way in all sectors. The frontiers cracked, the *sipâhîs* became obsolete at the very moment when the state could no longer afford a paid army. The system of land tenure and taxation tied to the military conquests, which provided new lands for fiefs granted to the *timariots* who in turn served as tax collectors, broke down, and in the absence of adequate fiscal machinery or revenue, the state was forced to farm out and increase the taxes, intensifying both the poverty and the anger of the population. Ruined by inflation, the *timariots* and peasants swelled the ranks of the malcontents, while the underpaid bureaucracy grew incompetent, venal, and restive.

Perhaps the crucial element blocking any alleviation of the difficulties was the arrogant assumption of Muslim superiority which the Ottomans had inherited from their predecessors and which had been reinforced by their own sweeping victories. The first sultans had been willing to acquire valuable techniques from their foes, and their tolerance had won the loyalty of the majority of their subjects. Muhammad the Conqueror still read

Greek books, encouraged humanists, and had his portrait painted by Gentile Bellini, but in the more rigid orthodox Muslim empire of Suleiman I, the Ottomans came to believe that nothing of conceivable worth could be learned from the barbarous infidels. Non-Muslim subjects, who controlled most of the empire's trade and finances, came under increasing oppression and were prevented from contributing their talents to the state. Religious opposition blocked the printing of works in Turkish until the eighteenth century, even though the Jewish, Armenian, and Greek communities had maintained presses for centuries. The enormous technological and intellectual advances which thrust Western Europe into the modern era were contemptuously ignored by the Ottomans.

Some officials were aware of the danger and sought to avert it. Between 1656 and 1676 the Köprülü Grand Viziers achieved a real revival. The Janissaries were temporarily crushed, finances were improved through confiscations and a tax reform, non-Muslims were shielded, and an artistic renaissance was encouraged. The capture of Crete from the Venetians increased the prestige of the empire. But the reformers provided no real solutions. The goal proposed for the state was merely a return to the institutions of Suleiman Kanuni and a reassertion of the fundamental Muslim tradition. By the end of the century the failure of the second siege of Vienna and the disastrous Peace of Karlowitz demonstrated the ineffectiveness of the reform.

With the loss of its power and prestige, extenal pressures on the Ottoman empire increased. As far back as the sixteenth century, Francis I of France had been granted a monopoly of trade with the Ottomans and the protectorate over the Christian shrines in Palestine. By the eighteenth century these concessions had turned into the famous "Capitulations" which gave Westerners quasi-control of Ottoman trade and all but extraterritorial status in the empire. Because of their contact with the Christian subjects of the sultan, who acted as middlemen, Westerners first extended to them some of their own privileges and immunities, then began to see themselves as the perpetual guardians of their interests. The French were acting as protector of Catholics from the eighteenth century, the Russians of the Orthodox a little more than a century later. Ultimately, Protestant missionaries from England and America played a similar role. Under these circumstances, the Christians came to look outside the empire for help in moments of difficulty and to render the state only a divided allegiance. This trend was intensified by the importation of nationalist ideas from the West in the course of the nineteenth century. The Ottomans on their part began to suspect indiscriminately the loyalty of all their non-Muslim subjects. The components of the empire increasingly pulled asunder.

Simultaneous with the alienation of minority groups, the vacuum left by the steady disappearance of the *timariots* was filled by the powerful tax farmers, who developed into a hereditary privileged class. These *ayans,* absentee landlords of great estates, exploited the declining economy and interposed themselves between the government and the peasantry to the detriment of both. Supported by armed bands of the dispossessed, usurping the power of the local governors, given official status by a decree of Sultan Mustafa III (1757–1774), some of the *ayans* succeeded in forming local dynasties in Rumelia and Anatolia which successfully defied the central authorities. Signs of separatism began to show in distant border areas.

By the beginning of the eighteenth century, the recognition of Western military superiority and the example of Russia's transformation under Peter the Great were leading some Ottomans to consider Westernization. But progress was slow. The first reaction to the crisis under Sultan Ahmed III (1703–1730) was to retreat into epicureanism, mysticism, and prodigality, which enhanced Ottoman culture but only deepened the gulf between the wealthy ruling class and the mass of the people. Humiliating defeats continued to accumulate: all Hungary, north Serbia, and part of Wallachia were lost at the Peace of Passarowitz (1718). Nadir Shah of Iran harassed the eastern front. Finally Ahmed III was toppled from the throne and some reforms were introduced with Western help into the obsolete Ottoman army. Through most of the century, however, these attempts produced few significant reforms. The main alterations were still purely technological in nature. The Turkish printing press finally authorized in 1726 was shut down in 1742 after producing fewer then twenty books.

The factor most operative in pushing the Ottomans onto a resolute path of Westernization was probably the constant increase of Russian power. The shock of the Treaty of Kuçuk Kaynarca (1774), which recognized Russia's control of the entire northern coast of the Black Sea, extended to her the system of Capitulations, and acknowledged the czar's protectorate over subjects of the sultan, was deepened in 1783 by Catherine the Great's annexation of the Khanate of Crimea, the first major loss of a primarily Muslim territory. Almost simultaneously, Napoleon's expedition threatened the safety of Egypt, and Russia annexed the semi-independent Christian kingdom of Georgia in 1801, thus threatening Transcaucasia and the eastern provinces of Turkey. The problem now facing the empire was clearly one of life and death.

Formidable obstacles still confronted the reformers. The *ulemas,* fearing for the purity of the faith, the Janissaries, worrying about losing privileges, and the *ayan* beys bent on thwarting any move toward centralization, joined together to oppose change. The government, furthermore, no longer controlled its finances. The proclamation by Selim III (1789–1807) of a "New Order" reorganizing the army, ending many abuses, reforming tax-

THE OTTOMAN EMPIRE, 1792 AND 1878

Ottoman Empire (1792—main map; 1878—inset map)

Ottoman boundary, 1792 (— · — · — approximate limits)

North African states under Ottoman suzerainty, 1792

Areas under autonomous and tribal rulers

Vassal states, 1878

(YEAR) Areas lost (1774-1792, main map; 1792-1878, inset map)

TRIB. = Tributary　IND. = Independence won　BR. PROT. = British Protectorate

The Balkan Peninsula, 1878

ation, and establishing permanent Turkish embassies in European capitals provoked a coalition of the *ayans* of Rumelia and the Janissaries which ended in the deposition and murder of Selim and the massacre of most of the leaders of the reform party. Nearly twenty years were needed by Selim's successor, Mahmud II (1808–1839), to undercut the power of the *ayans* of Anatolia, the so-called *Derebeys* or "Valley Lords," and to win over the religious authorities. Then he challenged the Janissaries, who were finally slaughtered in 1826.

The annihilation of the Janissaries opened the way for the period of reforms known as the Tanzimat. The first major decree, the Hatt-i Sherif of Gulhane, proclaimed in 1839 in the presence of representatives of foreign powers, guaranteed the basic rights of life, liberty, and property, and promised military and fiscal reforms. This statement of principles was implemented by a series of centralizing measures: the final revocation of all *timars;* the control of religious foundations or *vakfs* and the diversion of their revenues to the state; the creation of ministries, administrative committees, and provincial assemblies of notables; the promulgation of a new penal code; the opening of technical schools. Since Christians had not been given sufficient reassurances or representation in the provincial councils, and to justify in Western eyes the Ottoman's claim to be a European power, the Hatt-i Humayun of 1856 complemented the earlier decree by abolishing the system of *millets* which had segregated non-Muslims, and ending the secular powers of their various religious heads. Liberty of conscience was guaranteed to all, as were security and property; Christians became eligible for civilian offices. Finally, in 1876, under the leadership of Mihrdat Pasha, a constitution was announced and a constitutional assembly elected.

Yet these extensive reforms failed to achieve their objectives in the face of lukewarm support and heavy traditionalist opposition. A radical transformation of the government was theoretically possible through the assimilation of the new regulations to governmental *kanuns* or decrees authorized by Muslim tradition, but as long as the sacred *Shariat* remained the law of the land, two mutually hostile systems were forced into uneasy coexistence. Western institutions were at best skin deep, and no machinery existed for their implementation. The spread of nationalist ideas, first among the minorities but eventually in the Turkish ruling class, was incompatible with the concept of a Muslim empire based on a community of faith and not on national or cultural origins. Moreover, the new ideas exacerbated the antagonism between the state and the minorities, which exploded into violence. Separatist tendencies first manifested themselves in the Serbian risings of 1804 and 1815 and the Greek war of independence of 1822–1830. But the insurrections were not restricted to Christian areas: rebellions in Bosnia and Albania, the establishment of a quasi-independent Egypt under Muhammad Ali by 1840, and the rise of Arab nationalism were all indices of the general disintegration of the empire. The economic situation continued to deteriorate. Large-scale high-interest loans from the West only made matters worse, and in 1875 the Turkish government was forced to repudiate its obligations. In 1883 a Public Debt Control created to protect the debtors' interests infringed on Ottoman sovereignty by giving foreign powers some supervision of the revenues and financial administration of the state.

The main underlying purpose of the reforms—the safeguard of the imperial territory and the solace of national pride—was also lost in the

THE OTTOMAN EMPIRE, 1908-1913

Ottoman Empire (1908—main map; 1913—inset map)

Ottoman boundary, 1908 (— - — approximate limits)

Dependent states

British-occupied or protected areas

(YEAR) Areas lost (1792-1908—main map; 1908-1913—inset map)

IND. = Independence won   BR. PROT. = British Protectorate

The Balkan Peninsula, 1913

accumulation of failures during a century of almost continuous war. Serbian autonomy was won at the Treaty of Andrinople in 1829, Greece became independent the following year, Egypt was autonomous by 1840. Support for the rebels came from England, France, and Russia, who had jointly destroyed the Ottoman fleet at Navarino in 1826. Russia advanced in both Thrace and Transcaucasia. Fear of Russia's expansion in Central Asia, which threatened British interests in Iran and India, and of her control of the Dardanelles, briefly extorted in 1833 through the secret clauses of the Treaty of Unkiar-Skelessi, alarmed the Western powers and led to the Crimean War of 1853–1856, which gave a breathing spell, but no more, to the Ottoman government. In the famous phrase of Czar Nicholas I, "the Sick Man of Europe," unable to function under his own power, lived only at the mercy of outside forces and to serve their interests. In 1878 the Congress of Berlin, under the "honest brokerage" of Bismarck, partitioned Bulgaria, gave Bosnia-Herzegovina to Austria, proclaimed the independence of Serbia, Rumania, and Montenegro, granted Russia the city of Batum with part of Transcaucasia, and established the French in Tunis and the British on Cyprus, while demanding still further reforms.

Westernization like all other methods seems to have failed. A violent traditionalist reaction under the new sultan Abdul-Hamid II turned once more to political and religious fanaticism. The promised constitution died stillborn in 1877; a policy of repression and terror was launched against the minorities. As new pieces of territory were wrenched from the empire and the violence of nationalism grew apace, as plan after plan, frustrated by the dead hand of traditionalism failed to function, the thoughts of intellectuals veered from reform to revolution.

For Further Reading

Coles, P., *The Ottoman Impact on Europe.*
Davison, R., *Turkey.*
Lewis, B., *The Emergence of Modern Turkey.*
Lybyer, A. H., *The Government of the Ottoman Empire in the Time of Suleiman the Magnificent.*
Saunders, J. J., *The Muslim World on the Eve of Europe's Expansion.*
Vaughan, D., *Europe and the Turk: A Pattern of Alliances 1350–1700.*
Wittek, P., *The Rise of the Ottoman Empire.*

53   European Voyages of Exploration

In the early fifteenth century Christian Europeans knew less of the world beyond their borders than had the ancient Greeks or Romans. To the south and east of Europe lay a crescent of Islamic states, whose rulers willingly allowed trade with infidels but opposed penetration by Europeans into their territories. Journeys to China, like those of the Polos a hundred and more years before, were impracticable, since Muslims barred the path. West of Europe lay the Atlantic Ocean, the "Green Sea of Darkness," considered impassable by Christian and Muslim alike. Indeed, in 1400 Europeans lagged far behind Asians, particularly the Arabs and the Chinese, in the ability to sail for long distances over open water.

A.D.		
	1415	Portuguese capture of Ceuta
	1433	Cape Bojador rounded by Gil Eannes
	1482	Building of Elmina Castle (São Jorge da Mina)
	1484	Discovery of Congo estuary by Diogo Cão
	1488	Doubling of Cape of Good Hope by Bartolomeu Dias
	1492	Discovery of America (Bahama Islands) by Christopher Columbus
	1494	Treaty of Tordesillas
	1497	Voyage to North America by John Cabot
	1497–1498	Voyage to Calicut (India) by Vasco da Gama
	1500	Discovery of Brazil by Pedro Cabral
	1510	Portuguese capture of Goa
	1513	First sighting of the Pacific by Núñez de Balboa
	1519–1521	Conquest of Mexico by Hernán Cortés
	1519–1522	Circumnavigation of the world (begun by Ferdinand Magellan, completed by Sebastián del Cano)
	1529	Treaty of Zaragoza
	1531–1538	Conquest of Peru by Francisco Pizarro
	1534–1535	Exploration of Gulf of St. Lawrence by Jacques Cartier
	1553	Voyage to Archangel by Richard Chancellor
	1576–1578	Search for the Northwest Passage by Martin Frobisher
	1585	Planting of first English colony in North America (Roanoke Island, North Carolina)
	1596	Voyage of Willem Barents to Novaya Zemlya
	1600	Founding of the English East India Company
	1602	Founding of the Netherlands East India Company
	1606	Discovery of Australia by Willem Janszoon
	1642	Discovery of Tasmania and New Zealand by Abel Tasman

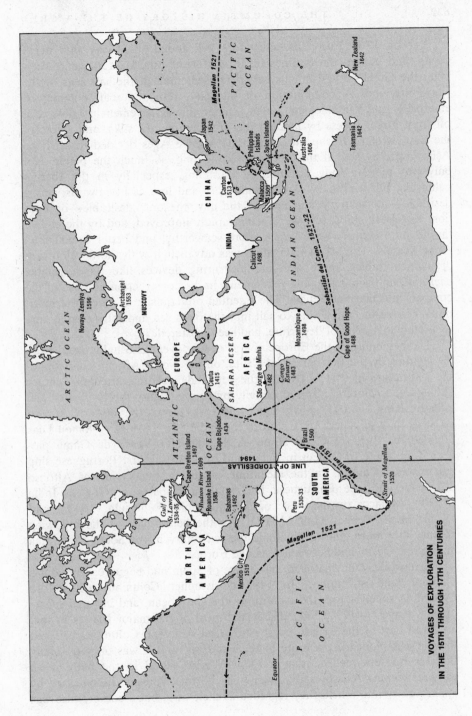

**VOYAGES OF EXPLORATION
IN THE 15TH THROUGH 17TH CENTURIES**

MAP 52

Yet by 1700 European navigators had found their way into every ocean, had plotted the outlines of all continents but Australia, and knew what the Greeks and Romans never guessed, that all the salt seas of the world are one. A combination of audacity, religious zeal, commercial enterprise, and technological advance made this achievement possible. Cut off from direct access by land to the precious metals, silks, and spices of the East, western Europeans of the late Middle Ages decided to seek the Asian trade by sea. If this necessitated fighting, so much the better. Not only was there a long tradition of crusading, especially in the Iberian peninsula, but a military career, with glory and loot as its rewards, was a desirable—for many young men of the day, the only desirable—occupation. European ships, too, were being rapidly improved, and by the end of the fifteenth century were larger, more seaworthy, and better armed than Asian vessels. The art of navigation was advancing, with the development of nautical tables, more accurate measuring devices like the astrolabe, backstaff, and ship's log, and refinements in the construction and use of the compass and mariner's chart. The essential prerequisite of successful maritime exploration, the ability to sail into the open sea and return safely and accurately to a point of departure, had been mastered.

The beginning of the European Age of Discovery is usually dated from the capture by the Portuguese of Ceuta, on the North African coast opposite Gibraltar, in 1415. During the remainder of the fifteenth century Portuguese explorers, inspired initially by Prince Henry the Navigator and later by King John II, slowly made their way down the western African coast as they searched for a path to the Indies. In 1488 Bartolomeu Dias doubled the Cape of Good Hope. A decade later Vasco da Gama pioneered the route to Calicut in India, and by 1513 the first Portuguese ship had reached Canton. In the meantime, under the leadership of Alfonso d'Alboquerque, the Portuguese had established bases at Goa in India (1510), Malacca on the west coast of the Malay Peninsula (1511), and Ormuz in the Persian Gulf (1515). For the better part of the following century they were able to dominate the sea routes in the South China Sea and Indian Ocean and between Asia and Europe.

Meanwhile, a navigator in the service of Spain had begun carving out a different kind of empire. In 1492 Christopher Columbus (Cristoforo Colombo) sailed across the Atlantic to the Caribbean, and in three subsequent voyages (1493–1504) discovered most of the major islands in that area and part of the eastern coast of Central America. Columbus believed that he was pioneering a route to the Far East, and it was only gradually that his masters realized that a "New World" stood in the path of an explorer seeking Asia by sailing west. The Portuguese were disconcerted by Spain's entry into a field they regarded as their own, but a compromise was engineered. By the Treaty of Tordesillas (1494), the two powers "divided" the world by running an imaginary line north and south 370 leagues west of the Cape Verde Islands on the west coast of Africa. All new lands to the west of this meridian were to belong to Spain; everything to the east of it was to be Portuguese.

The empire the Portuguese created was mercantile, and consisted of a chain of bases on the African and Asian coasts linked and protected by sea power. The Portuguese were never strong on land in Africa or Asia, and never tried to be; to have created a territorial empire against the wishes of the local rulers would have been beyond their strength. In the New World, on the other hand, there were no states capable of withstanding the Spaniards. In about 1520, by which time most of the Atlantic coasts of Central and South America had been plotted and it had become clear that there was no way through the Americas into the Pacific (first sighted by Núñez de Balboa in 1513), the age of the conquistadors began. Possessing horses and firearms, neither of which had been seen before in the New World, the Spaniards were able to conquer huge stretches of territory with very small numbers of men. Mexico fell to Hernán Cortés in 1519–1521 and Peru to Francisco Pizarro in 1531–1538. Other conquistadors established Spanish rule in the intervening areas. Thus the whole of Central and South America (with the exception of Brazil, which became Portuguese because it lay east of the demarcation line of 1494 and because it had been discovered by a Portuguese, Pedro Cabral, in 1500) was gradually turned into a Spanish colonial empire.

The Americas soon began to yield gold and silver in abundance and provided land suitable for European colonization, but the Spaniards still hoped to find their own trade route to the East. In 1520 Ferdinand Magellan (Fernão de Magalhães), a Portuguese in Spanish employ, discovered the straits that bear his name, passed through them, and crossed the Pacific Ocean to the Philippines. There he was killed, but his lieutenant, Sebastián del Cano, brought one of Magellan's ships home to Spain around the Cape of Good Hope, thus completing the first circumnavigation of the world.

The wealth obtained by the Portuguese and Spaniards from their overseas possessions encouraged other Europeans to imitate them. During the reign of Henry VIII of England a ship from Bristol, commanded by a Venetian, John Cabot (Giovanni Caboto), made the first trans-Atlantic journey—the first at any rate since the voyages of the Vikings in the eleventh century—to North America, touching at Cape Breton Island and Newfoundland in 1497. Jacques Cartier, in the service of Francis I of France, explored the St. Lawrence River and estuary in a series of voyages between 1534 and 1541. These discoveries, however, did not lead to colonization, or even to occupation. The English and French and, later, the Dutch had the same aim as the Portuguese and Spaniards; they wanted their own sea route to Asia. Since the Iberian powers discouraged competitors in the South Atlantic, other Europeans were obliged to seek their fortunes to the north. In the end neither the Northwest Passage (to the north of Canada) nor the Northeast Passage (north of Norway and Russia) proved practicable, but in the process of searching for them men like the Englishmen Hugh Willoughby and Richard Chancellor (1553), Martin Frobisher (1576–1578), Davis (1585–1586), and Henry Hudson (1609–1610), and the Dutchman Willem Barents (1594–1596) greatly increased Europe's geographical knowledge.

In the seventeenth century the pattern of European discovery and expansion changed. The revolt of the Dutch against Spain roughly coincided with the period (1580–1640) during which the Spanish and Portuguese crowns were united. As a result, the Dutch were able to harm Spain effectively by attacking Portugal overseas. They soon drove the Portuguese from the west coast of Africa (though only temporarily from Angola), and from Ceylon, the Spice Islands, and Malacca. The English, too, after the founding of the East India Company in 1600, appeared in Asian waters in ever increasing strength, and took commercial supremacy away from the Portuguese in India, and later in China. Whereas the Spanish and Portuguese navigators and explorers had been in the service of their sovereigns, the Dutch and English sailed the oceans of the world as agents for commercial concerns, the great East India Companies. For these companies the profit motive was preeminent; they did not encourage exploration for its own sake or for reasons of glory or religion. The discovery of the northeastern coast of Australia by Willem Janszoon in 1606 was not the result of a planned reconnaissance but of an error in navigation. Abel Tasman sailed to Tasmania and New Zealand in 1642, but his employers, the Netherlands East India Company, made no attempt to profit from what he found. It was not until the late eighteenth century, with the coming of the age of scientific exploration, that the last remaining major geographical puzzle, the location and extent of Terra Australis, was solved, and not until the nineteenth that the penetration of the interior of the non-European continents as opposed to the charting of their coastlines was seriously undertaken.

A direct result of Europe's Age of Discovery was the Atlantic slave trade. A traffic in black Africans arose almost as soon as the Portuguese made their first probes down the West African coast in the fifteenth century. Not, however, until the development of the sugar, cotton, and tobacco plantations in the New World from the seventeenth century onward did the trade reach substantial proportions. Africans were transported across the

Atlantic to provide a labor force when it was found that neither the indigenous Amerindians nor imported white indentured servants were able or willing to work the plantations and mines. Initially handled by the Portuguese on their own account or as agents of the Spanish government, the trade was progressively taken over by the British, Dutch, and French. It lasted for approximately 450 years, only coming to a gradual end during the latter half of the nineteenth century. In all, somewhere in the region of 10 million slaves were carried to the New World. The total population loss to Africa, however, was much greater. To the number of slaves landed in the Americas must be added the men, women, and children who died during the infamous "Middle Passage" across the Atlantic, to say nothing of those who died on the African coast while awaiting transshipment, or while in transit from the interior to the coast, or in the wars between African states that were directly attributable to the slave trade.

The effects on tropical Africa of four and a half centuries of continuous and systematic plundering of its human resources were profound. The slave trade inhibited political, economic, and social development, culled out the young and healthy from a population already debilitated by endemic disease, and created or exacerbated intertribal and interstate hostilities. For hundreds of years Africans fought and enslaved one another to meet an insatiable overseas demand for black labor.

The Age of Discovery and the ensuing first phase of European expansion thus produced very different results in different parts of the world. In Asia, trade was the primary European object, and the great chartered companies vied with one another and with competing Asian traders for the profits of an increasingly valuable commerce. Before the end of the eighteenth century few thought in terms of permanent European territorial dominion or ownership. In the Americas, by contrast, land-grabbing and colonization were the accepted objectives from the beginning. The local inhabitants were everywhere conquered, and then destroyed, incorporated into European empires or colonies, or driven farther and farther into the interior, defeated by the white man's diseases as well as by his guns. In Africa, except in the far south, the only significant European interest was a traffic in human beings. No colonization took place, no agricultural crops were produced for export, and no industry developed.

For Further Reading

Albion, Robert G. (ed.), *Exploration and Discovery.*
Curtin, Philip D., *The Atlantic Slave Trade.*
Nowell, Charles E., *The Great Discoveries and the First Colonial Empires.*
Parry, J. H., *The Age of Reconnaissance.*

54 India: 1500–1750

The unification of the whole Indian subcontinent under a single political authority had been the aim of many ambitious rulers, but only two dynasties, the Mauryas in the third century B.C. and the Tughluqs in the fourteenth century, had achieved this goal, and they only briefly. A new, and quite self-conscious, movement toward political domination of the whole region began in the sixteenth century under the Mughal dynasty and reached fruition at the end of the seventeenth century. The Mughal empire began to dissolve almost at the moment of its greatest territorial expansion, thus seeming to repeat the history of its predecessors, but the transference of many of its institutions, as well as the memory of imperial control, to the new political hegemony established by the British at the end of the eighteenth century gives it a special dimension in the history of India.

While contemporaries did not regard the arrival in 1526 of a new group of Turks under Babur as particularly significant, the subsequent history of his dynasty marks 1526 as the beginning of the modern era in India. The search for methods of political integration that characterized the reigns of Akbar (1556–1605) and Aurangzeb (1658–1707), the establishment of important commercial relationships with the European powers, and the growth within the empire of new and dynamic regional forces represented by the Marathas, all linked the empire of the Mughals with modern India.

Babur, the founder of the empire, was a Turkish chieftain who had established a small kingdom at Kabul after having been driven out of his principality in Central Asia by other Turkish tribes. This new Turkish intrusion is one more reminder that India was never isolated, despite the many unique features of its culture, but was continually being affected by events on its borders from Central Asia and China to the Near East. Babur's empire, stretching from Kabul through the Punjab and the Gangetic plain to Bengal, was temporarily lost under his son Humayunto Sher Shah, one of the Afghan chieftains who had gained power in the last years of the Delhi Sultanate, but was regained by his grandson Akbar.

Territorial expansion and political centralization were the dominant themes of Akbar's long reign. Agra was the Mughal capital, and from this strategic position control was maintained over the Punjab, the Gangetic heartlands of the old sultanate, and, somewhat tenuously, Afghanistan. Akbar began expanding toward the south and east, conquering the Mus-

A.D.	1510	Portuguese capture Goa
	1526	Defeat of the Lodi Sultan by Babur
	1526–1530	Reign of Babur
	1530–1538	Reign of Humayun
	1538	Death of Guru Nanak
	1538–1555	Interregnum under Sur dynasty
	1555–1556	Humayun restores Mughal authority
	1556–1605	Reign of Akbar
	1565	Fall of Vijayanagar
	1600	British East India Company receives charter
	1605–1627	Reign of Jahangir
	1628–1658	Reign of Shah Jahan
	1634	English begin trading in Bengal
	1639	Founding of Fort St. George, Madras
	1658–1707	Reign of Aurangzeb
	1674	Shivaji crowned king of Marathas; French found Pondicherry
	1690	Founding of Calcutta
	1708	Death of Guru Govind Singh
	1739	Nadir Shah raids Delhi
	1742	Marathas raid Bengal
	1744–1748	War between French and British in India

lim kingdoms of Gujerat, Malwa, and Bengal, which had been independent
for more than a century. The ruthlessness of this expansion, especially in
areas where there was strong resistance, is typified in the account of
the conquest of Gujerat by one of Akbar's generals: "We burnt and
destroyed the towns of Kari and Kataria. . . . We realized an enormous
booty, and after plundering and destroying nearly three hundred villages
in the course of three days, we re-crossed the Rann. After crossing, we
destroyed the districts of Malia and Morbi."

Since to control an empire in India was always more difficult than to
acquire one, Akbar's administrative and political arrangements are of
particular interest. Previous Muslim rulers had drawn their main support
from their Turkish military commanders, but these officers were not inclined to strengthen the sultan's power at the expense of their own. Akbar,
however, forged an alliance with the Rajput chieftains, who were Hindus,
thus creating a counterweight to the powerful Turkish commanders. The
Rajput princes had become independent during the last century of the rule
of the Delhi sultans, and the conquest of their strongholds was necessary
before Akbar could expand southward. But in contrast to his treatment of
the independent Muslim rulers whom he deposed and whose territories he
incorporated into the empire, Akbar allowed the Rajput rulers who submitted to retain their lands. The allegiance of the Rajput chieftains to the
Mughal empire was cemented by marriage alliances between Akbar and
princesses of the leading Rajput families; thus for the next 150 years,
groups that had traditionally been most resistant to Muslim rule provided
security to the Mughal dynasty.

A concomitant of the Rajput compromise was Akbar's general policy
of religious accommodation. This was not analogous to the toleration of
the modern Western world but to the latitudinarianism of early Hanoverian
England. The fundamental religious dilemma posed for Muslim rulers in
India was the fact that the vast majority of Hindus could not be brought
into the Islamic fold. The problem had long been "solved" by a practical, if
uneasy, acceptance of the continuance of Hindu rights along with an
emphasis on the priority of Islamic practices. By giving virtual religious
equality to Hinduism, Akbar obtained a more positive basis of support for
his dynasty, and at the same time freed himself from deference to the
opinions of the *ulemas,* or Muslim theologians, who intransigently demanded that the rulers seek the spread of Islam and the destruction of
idolatry. Akbar's abolition of jizya, the special tax imposed on non-Muslims, and his granting the Hindus permission to build temples were regarded by orthodox Muslims as proof of his apostasy.

Akbar also strengthened royal power by rationalizing the procedures
for assessing and collecting land revenue. The central portions of the em-

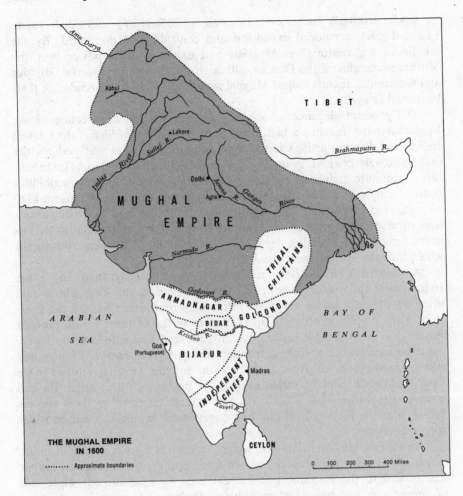

THE MUGHAL EMPIRE
IN 1600
········· Approximate boundaries

pire were surveyed, and fixed assessments replaced the arbitrary demands
of the tax collectors. The empire was divided for administrative purposes
into provinces, and these were then divided into districts and subdistricts.
Officials were paid in cash rather than in land, an attempt to solve one of
the most persistent problems of earlier Indian rulers. Granting of land, or
jagirs, had been common among both Muslim and Hindu rulers, but this
deprived the central treasury of income and provided officials with territorial bases for building up their own authority. Akbar did not succeed in
regaining all the land that had been alienated in the past or in paying all
salaries in cash, but he moved the empire in the direction of centralization
and away from the old political pluralism.

Under Akbar's successors, Jahangir (1605–1627) and Shah Jahan (1628–1658), territorial expansion and centralization continued. By the middle of the century the Mughals had extended their power over the Muslim sultanates of the Deccan, although the two most powerful, Bijapur and Golkunda, acknowledged Mughal suzerainty without surrendering their territorial integrity.

The graceful elegance associated with the art and architecture of the Mughal dynasty reached a high point during the reign of Shah Jahan, when Indian and Persian artistic forms were combined in what was perhaps the only genuinely creative synthesis of elements from Islamic and Hindu culture. Miniature paintings reflecting both Persian and Indian sensibilities portray a style of courtly life that, while light and delicate, had also a kind of mannered formalism. The architectural forms favored in Shah Jahan's time survive in the great palace complex in the Red Fort at Delhi as well as in the famous Taj Mahal at Agra, the most splendid of the numerous tombs with which the Mughals memorialized their fame.

Aurangzeb (1658–1707) realized more completely than any other Indian ruler the ancient dream of the chakravartin, the king who would bring all of India under his sway. Fifty years of warfare pushed the frontiers of the empire almost to Cape Comorin in the extreme south, brought Assam for the first time under Muslim rule, and maintained control over the tribesmen on the northwest frontier. Yet this great empire disintegrated within thirty years of Aurangzeb's death, for the internal stresses were working against its preservation even at the beginning of his reign. He had come to the throne after a fierce struggle against his three brothers and his father, and the factionalism this had engendered expressed itself in widespread uprisings.

As with all Muslim rulers who sought to control a great empire in India, Aurangzeb's principal problem was to find support for his regime. Akbar had turned to the Rajputs, but the alliances he had formed, while still of importance, had been weakened during the wars of succession. Personal religious convictions and his understanding of the political situation led Aurangzeb to emphasize the Islamic nature of the empire. He gave prominence in the administration to Muslim commanders, tried to set standards of manners and morals that conformed to the Islamic ideal, and supported Islamic "truth" against Hindu "falsehood." He replaced Hindu officials with Muslims, discouraged Hindu religious practices offensive to Islam, and beat a general retreat from the easy pluralism of Akbar's regime. There was no widespread persecution, but Hindu temples, notably at such places of peculiar sanctity as Benares and Mathura, were destroyed. And while Muslims could not replace the numerous minor Hindu tax officials, fewer Rajputs received high appointments in the army.

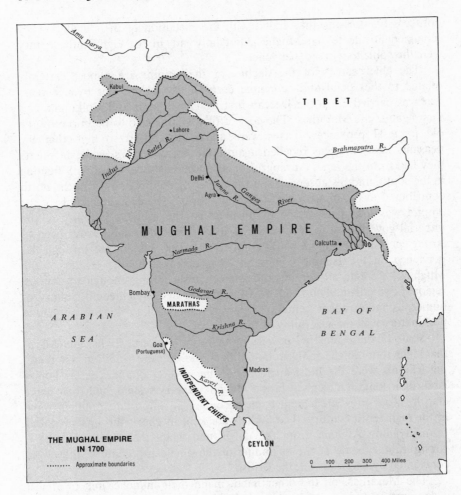

THE MUGHAL EMPIRE
IN 1700

········ Approximate boundaries

Aurangzeb's religious policies naturally roused resentment, but they were not an important factor in the weakening of the imperial structure. Public opinion, as representing the feelings of the Hindu masses, can scarcely have existed as a political force. The Rajputs of Marwar, one of the largest of the Rajput states, rebelled in the second half of the reign, but this resulted from Aurangzeb's attempt to annex their territories, not from religious zeal. The Rajput rebellions were contained with a fair measure of success, not only by Aurangzeb but also by his weak successors, and the Rajputs maintained their alliance with the Mughals well into the eighteenth century. In the Punjab, the Sikhs' militant desire for political independence, not their response to Aurangzeb's religious policy, led to a violent but unsuccessful uprising that ended with the execution of their leader. They remained hostile to the Mughals, but only late in the eighteenth century were they able to win independence.

The chief causes of the decline of the empire are almost certainly related to the social and economic costs of expansion. For twenty years war was carried on in the Deccan first against Bijapur and Golkunda, and then against the Marathas. The cost of this fighting had to be borne by the old imperial provinces. Taxes were apparently raised so high that the peasants in some areas rebelled against the tax collectors, while in others they fled from the land. Aurangzeb was continuously occupied with fighting in the south, and his absence from the center of political power in the north contributed to the breakdown of local authority. The economic crisis of the empire was thus part of the political crisis: the growing inability of the imperial government to control the regional forces that had always been so strong in India. Aurangzeb's attempt to shore up his empire through dependence on the Islamic community was defeated by the failure of the Mughals to create an administrative mechanism strong enough to counter regional dynamism. The result was the growth in the eighteenth century of numerous independent centers of power, which acknowledged only in a perfunctory way the suzerainty of the emperor.

Some of these regional powers, notably the Rajputs, Sikhs, and Marathas, had roots in the indigenous political and cultural tradition. Of these, the Rajputs were the most ancient, but the poverty of their desert homeland, their long involvement in the Mughal military system, and their fierce clan loyalties prevented them from becoming an important political force in the eighteenth century. The Sikhs were kept in check through pressures from invading Afghans from the north, and when they finally created a strong military state at the beginning of the nineteenth century, they were confronted by a new power, the British.

The Marathas, on the other hand, made their influence felt in almost every part of India, and in the middle of the eighteenth century seemed likely to become the successors to the Mughals. From fortresses in the hilly country south of Bombay, they had carried on guerrilla warfare against Aurangzeb for twenty years. Their leader, Shivaji (1627–1680), who was crowned king in 1674, claimed a special role for the Marathas as defenders of Hinduism and enemies of the Muslim invaders. Early in the eighteenth century his chief minister, the Peshwa, seized power and under his leadership the Marathas expanded rapidly, bringing most of central India and large areas of the Deccan under their control. At the same time the kingdom lost its unitary constitution and became a confederacy of military commanders who carved out territories for themselves. The Marathas captured Delhi and controlled the emperor at times, but they never substituted a Maratha for a Mughal as emperor. Like all the other Indian rulers of the time, whether Muslim or Hindu, they sought formal legitimization of their power through recognition as officials of the empire.

The Marathas reached the height of their power in 1761, but they were then defeated at Panipat, the historic battlefield north of Delhi, by a combination of Afghan and Mughal forces. The individual Maratha chieftains, however, particularly the rulers of Indore and Gwalior, remained formidable powers, and it was they, not the Mughals, who challenged the British in the late eighteenth and early nineteenth centuries.

Other centers of independent power were formed out of provinces of the empire by the Mughal governors, but not through rebellion or by explicitly defying imperial authority. Gradually the empire lost control over revenue and appointments, including that of successors to the governors. In the Deccan, the viceroy established his independence from Delhi in the 1720's, as the Nizam of Hyderabad. (This dynasty remained the most important Muslim ruling house in India up to 1948.) The governors of Oudh, the province in the fertile central plains north of the Ganges, became independent a little later, and vied with the rulers of Hyderabad for control of the imperial court.

Bengal, the third of the great provinces to become independent, had not been in the mainstream of the political and cultural life of India during the Mughal period, but assumed a new status in the eighteenth century. Trade, which had formerly moved inward toward the great imperial cities, now responded to the demands of European, Armenian, and Arab merchants for such products of Bengal as textiles, sugar, and indigo. This trade was never of great importance to the Indian economy as a whole, which remained overwhelmingly dependent upon local agricultural production, but high profits made it especially attractive to foreign merchants. By the middle of the eighteenth century the French and the English were engaged in a bitter struggle in India to dominate this commerce. The defeat of the French by the British was an aspect of the world-wide struggle of the two great powers, but it was hastened by the superior trading position of the East India Company in Bengal. The French in India were dependent upon the political and financial support of Paris, but the English used the profits of the Bengal trade to maintain a high degree of autonomy from home control.

Once the French were defeated, the East India Company's economic power brought it in conflict with the Nawab of Bengal, who by this time was aware of the threat that the foreign powers posed to the integrity of his government. In 1756 the new Nawab, Siraj-ud-daulah, sought to prevent any further encroachments on his sovereignty by driving the English out of their settlement at Calcutta. The English, along with a group of powerful

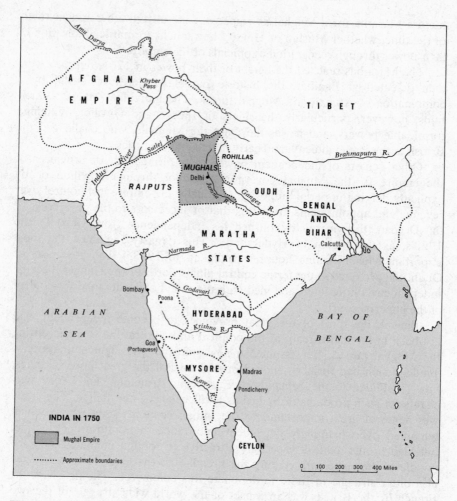

Hindu merchants, responded by supporting a rival claimant to the throne, and overthrew Siraj-ud-daulah in 1757 at the Battle of Plassey. The next eight years were marked by a series of quarrels between East India Company officials and the new Nawab, and in 1765 a decisive change in the political history of India took place. The Company forced the Mughal emperor to recognize its right to collect the revenue of Bengal. Within twenty years the East India Company was the actual ruler of Bengal.

The establishment of British power in India was thus not the result of military invasion but of participation, in a manner familiar to Indian political history, in a dynastic struggle. The expansion of British territorial control beyond Bengal in the next fifty years also conformed to a recognizable Indian pattern, the new power using the resources of the Gangetic heartland to conquer the rest of India. Mughal administrative institutions, although decayed and ramshackle, still existed in many areas, and everywhere local rulers acknowledged the suzerainty of the emperor, even though he had long since ceased to exercise authority beyond the walls of Delhi. The East India Company itself issued its coins in the emperor's name until 1835.

But emphasis on continuities in styles and patterns of political experience should not mask the changes resulting from the British conquest. The government established in Bengal at the end of the eighteenth century sought to maintain the old legal and judiciary system; that it was unable to do so was an indication that the new state carried with it values and presuppositions that made necessary different forms of administration. Technological advances in communications, particularly the telegraph and railway, combined with the nineteenth-century understanding of the role of the nation-state to permit a degree of political control and an integration of government and society unique in Indian history.

For Further Reading

Ahmad Aziz, *Islamic Culture in the Indian Environment.*
Habib, Irfan, *The Agrarian System of Mughal India.*
Ikram, S. M., *Muslim Civilization in India.*
Spear, Percival, *A History of India,* Vol. II.

55   Japan and China

Japanese historians refer to the late fifteenth and early sixteenth centuries as the "warring states period," the time when the country came closest in all of its history to complete disunity. Shoguns of the Ashikaga family continued to reign in Kyoto, but were powerless outside their own small domain. The imperial court, impotent as before, lacked the means even to keep up its ceremonial role in the style of previous times. The only true effective political units were the domains of virtually autonomous provincial daimyos. Though the total number of these at any one time might run into the hundreds, there were never more than twenty or thirty with large domains, and these ruled at most a few provinces. Warfare among them was so frequent that there was practically no time when the entire country was at peace.

Three military men accomplished reunification between 1568 and

1615. The first of these, Oda Nobunaga, puppetized, then removed from office, the last Ashikaga shogun. By the time of his assassination in 1582 he had conquered a formidable block of territory in the central provinces. His lieutenant Toyotomi Hideyoshi, a man of peasant stock, completed the military victories over the central daimyos, and the pacifying alliances with the more distant of them, that restored an effective national government for the first time in nearly 200 years. Hideyoshi's palace at Momoyama gave its name to a brief period of brilliant, if gaudy, virtuosity in the visual arts. The age, in fact, was one of vigor and dash in all aspects of society. Overseas commerce flourished, and attempts to conquer Korea in 1592 and 1597, while abortive, seemed to forecast a national policy of overseas expansion.

The third reunifier was Tokugawa Ieyasu, a member of a minor daimyo family who had risen to national prominence as Nobunaga's vassal and later Hideyoshi's ally. In 1600, two years after Hideyoshi's death, he won the battle (at Sekigahara) that established him as the successor to Hideyoshi's power, though he did not finally destroy Hideyoshi's family until 1615, a year before his own death. Ieyasu's greatest achievement was to give legitimacy and continuity to the new national government, a feat he accomplished by having the emperor confer on him the hereditary title of shogun.

Japan's first contact with Europeans had occurred in 1542, when Portuguese merchants visited its shores. They were followed in the next few years by traders and missionaries from other Catholic countries. The Europeans in Japan had dealings with numerous local rulers, as well as with the principal figures in the central government. The Japanese learned from the West the use of firearms and certain other military techniques that aided reunification. Tobacco was another Western import. However, the most important aspect of Western culture introduced was surely the Christian religion. By late in the sixteenth century the number of Japanese Christians may have been as high as 150,000. Whole domains of western Japan were converted when their daimyos became Christians. Nobunaga was friendly to the Christians, in part because he saw the Buddhist church as an impediment to political unification. From the time of Hideyoshi, however, a reaction set in. Japanese rulers came to mistrust Christianity, then reject it. They began to suspect that European missionary activity might be a prelude to political conquest by the Spanish king (as they knew it had been in the Philippines). Furthermore, the zealous devotion of Japanese Christians convinced the authorities that fidelity to their religion took priority with them over the obligations of Japanese subjects.

The persecution of Christians began under Hideyoshi, in 1597. Ieyasu's attitude was intermittently intolerant (because he was a pious

Buddhist) and tolerant (because he wished to encourage foreign trade). The appearance in 1600 of Dutch and English merchants, the first northern Europeans in Japan, increased Japanese fear of Roman Catholicism by acquainting them with the religious warfare of post-Reformation Europe. Moreover, it gave them the idea that trade was possible without Christianity, for the Protestants in the Far East were not interested in proselytizing.

Rebellion by the Catholic community of Shimabara, in Kyushu, in 1638 spelled the doom of Christianity in Japan, and with it of unrestricted commerce with European countries. The government, which itself used Dutch technical advice and material to win its bloody victory over the rebels, feared the disruption that might result in the future if foreign Christians were to make league with Japanese dissidents. The result was a radical policy of seclusion (prohibiting Japanese from traveling abroad) and exclusion (prohibiting foreigners from visiting Japan) that lasted from 1640 to 1853. The only exception to the rule was to permit a handful of Chinese and Dutch merchants to trade under strict shogunal surveillance in the West Kyushu city of Nagasaki. In the meantime the practice of Christianity by the Japanese was stamped out with utter ruthlessness.

The Tokugawa political and social system lasted for more than two centuries. Its architects' aims had been to ensure peace and the perpetuation of Tokugawa family power, and in this they were remarkably successful. Politically, the keystone of the system was a balance between central and peripheral authorities, a characteristic historians call "centralized feudalism." Socially, it was the sharp differentiation of the military from the working classes, and the hereditary privileges of the former.

At the apex of the Tokugawa state was the shogun, a hereditary monarch whose title was military, but who came more and more to resemble a civilian-bureaucrat king. The shogun through his government (bakufu, or shogunate) performed two functions. He controlled directly his own extensive lands. These comprised about one-quarter of the agricultural land of the country situated mostly in the central provinces of Honshu from the Kanto Plain to the Kyoto-Osaka region, but also including outlying commercial, strategic, and mining centers. The remaining territory of the country was divided into approximately 260 han, or feudal domains. The shogun's jurisdiction over these lands and their rulers, the daimyos, did not extend to internal governance or taxation, but he strictly regulated their external relations by preventing alliances or warfare among them or with the outside world. He required certain dues from them, such as road building and aid in castle construction. Most important, from the middle years of the seventeenth century he required each daimyo to perform "alternate attendance" (sankin kōtai), that is to reside at his capital,

Edo (now Tokyo), on a regular basis one year out of every two. Thus he kept the daimyos under observation and forced them to divert to double residences of a suitable level of grandeur income that might otherwise have been spent on defense.

The daimyos were ranked by size of domain and further grouped into three classes according to the closeness of their feudal relationship to the shogun. The inmost group, the *shimpan* daimyos (cadet lords), were heads of side branches of the Tokugawa family. In addition to governing their domains, which tended to be large and strategically located, the cadet lords were regularly consulted about shogunal policy. However, they were rarely permitted to assume regular administrative offices in the shogunal bureaucracy. Shogunal heirs were chosen from this group when the direct line failed. The second group were the *fudai* daimyos, or hereditary vassals. The family founders had been vassals of the Tokugawa from the 1580's, the band of warriors from Ieyasu's native province of Mikawa with whose support he won the empire. Newly raised to the rank of daimyo after the Battle of Sekigahara, they governed the 140-some domains (typically small and centrally placed) that Ieyasu had carved out for them from the territory he had conquered. The *fudai* daimyos filled the chief administrative positions of the shogunal government.

The third group were the *tozama* daimyos, or "outside lords." Their ancestors had been domain lords coequal with the Tokugawa before 1600. Some had been allies of Ieyasu at Sekigahara, some neutrals in the fight. Only a few of the late-fifteenth-century daimyos who survived into the Tokugawa period had been enemies in 1600. Notably these were the lords of Satsuma (in southern Kyushu), Hizen (in northern Kyushu), and Chō-shū (in western Honshu), three territories too remote and powerful to be easily destroyed. The Tokugawa made peace with them, and they accorded the shogun grudging obeisance as a price for their survival. They, and the *tozama* group as a whole, were "outsiders" in several senses. Their domains tended to be in the remote peripheral provinces. They were on the average larger than other domains and had a larger measure of freedom in internal affairs. Throughout the period the shogunate continued to claim as a right of suzerainty the power to confiscate or relocate any *han*. With *shimpan* and *fudai* domains this was a real power, but after the first few years the shogunate lacked the will or the practical means to dispossess the larger *tozama han*. The penalty which the *tozama* lords paid for their relative autonomy and security was that they had virtually no voice in national affairs, which were under the jurisdiction of the shogunal government.

The shogun, daimyos, and samurai formed a governing class set off by strict marks of behavior and treatment from commoners. Samurai men wore swords as caste marks, but with the coming of peace the purely military character of the caste changed. They remained a pensioned and privileged aristocracy, and they continued to perform administrative and judicial functions. Since they were always the most highly educated group in society (along with the Buddhist clergy), they manned the learned professions—medicine, teaching, and scholarship.

The majority of the population were peasants, and the land tax which they paid to feudal rulers was the chief form of public revenue. Beyond collecting taxes and overseeing the administration of justice, the military classes left village government in the hands of a self-perpetuating local elite. Rural economy was always somewhat restricted by technical backwardness, and sometimes especially so because of plagues, floods, or other natural disasters. Yet, there was a gradual increase in the Tokugawa period both in the quantity of farm products and in the part retained by peasants for their own consumption.

A growing merchant class created numerous commercial centers throughout the country, in most of the "castle towns" as well as in the major cities of the shogunal domain: Edo, Osaka, Kyoto, and Nagasaki. The traditional Japanese attitude toward merchants was ambiguous. In accordance with a Confucian prejudice against commerce, their theoretical and legal status was near the bottom of society. Yet, samurai and daimyos needed the economic services of merchants and rewarded them with a considerable degree of favor. An important theme in the economic and social history of the period is the growing indebtedness of the government and the samurai to the merchant class.

To complete the picture of the political and social system in the Tokugawa period one must mention the emperor and his court in Kyoto, totally isolated from politics and from political affairs of every kind. Though the imperial institution reemerged into politics at the close of the period, its importance until then was wholly as a vestigial center of the indigenous national religion and as a symbol of the unity of the country and the legitimacy of the government.

Peace and prosperity produced a cultural renaissance that reached its greatest brilliance in the Genroku calendrical era (1688–1704). The haiku (17-syllable poems) of Basho, the puppet plays of Chikamatsu, the novels of Saikaku, and the woodblock prints of Moronobu bespeak an urban civilization of considerable refinement.

Education broadened under Tokugawa rule. In the seventeenth century the samurai class progressed from rough, spartan soldiery to a cultural elite, largely through domain-sponsored academies of the Neo-Confucian persuasion. Education then trickled down to the commoner classes, mostly to city-dwelling males, but increasingly by the nineteenth century even to peasants and to women. By the end of the period Japan may have ranked as high in point of literacy as the most advanced countries of western Europe.

Japanese history of the mid-seventeenth to mid-nineteenth centuries is devoid of dramatic institutional developments. Warfare was stilled; rulers of varying ability succeeded one another in orderly fashion; change was slow. Cities grew, but the population of the country remained remarkably stable (at about 30 million) from 1720 to 1850. The outside domains grew more independent, the central government more bureaucratic. There were evidences of sluggishness in the shogunate's rule and even of a relative enfeeblement in contrast with certain of its feudatories. Yet Tokugawa power was far from collapse when the West intruded. The collapse as it actually happened was the direct result of the shogunate's failure to solve with its traditional means an unprecedented problem—the threat to national security occasioned by the forced end of seclusion by the United States in 1853.

It was fortuitous that Americans should have been the people to open Japan. Before long others more powerful or with longer-established interests in the Far East would certainly have acted, and within months after the initial overtures Japan faced a concert of powers (including Great Britain, France, and Russia) demanding diplomatic and trade relations. The unequal treaties with all the powers granting extraterritoriality for their nationals in Japan were accepted at gunpoint between 1854 and 1867.

Acquiescence in this national humiliation stirred up fierce internal opposition. The leading protesters were outside domains traditionally aloof or hostile, such as Satsuma and Chōshū. Some critics could be found far closer, among the cadet lords and in cliques of shogunate officials out of power. Until 1860 the quarrel raged at the daimyo and upper samurai level, but then it spread to the lower samurai and the commoners. At first critics attacked specific shogunal policies, but increasingly in the 1860's their aim was more radical—to supplant the Tokugawa with a new and more effective ruling group.

From the beginning the antishogunal movement appealed to the name of the emperor, as the superior legal and moral authority from which the shogunate claimed its legitimacy. Some imperial courtiers joined the ranks of the dissidents, and the Kyoto court itself furnished a base from which they attacked the shogunate. The victory over the shogunate in armed confrontation from 1866 to 1868 was called an imperial victory, though the true heirs to the Tokugawa were a coalition of activists from samurai and courtier ranks who fought with the armed and fiscal backing of the great western *tozama* domains, Satsuma, Chōshū, Hizen, and Tosa.

China, too, in this era was dominated by a powerful regime; indeed, the rulers of the Ch'ing, or Manchu, dynasty were the most successful foreign conquerors in Chinese history. The story of how the Manchu* people succeeded in conquering and ruling China from 1644 to 1911 begins in the far northeast several decades before the end of the Ming. The Ming government maintained control over the regions north of the Great Wall by delegating authority to the chiefs of local tribes, which it attempted to keep divided and weak. However, in the first decades of the seventeenth century, while the Ming court was absorbed in enervating factional quarrels, the chieftain of one Jurchen tribe, Nurhachi, unified the area now known as Manchuria through a combination of military campaigns and marriage alliances. He organized the Jurchen warriors into companies of 300 men, grouped first under four, and later eight, divisions called Banners, each identified by its own flag. Tribal leadership had been hereditary, but the eight Banners were placed under the command of seven of his sons and one nephew, and Banner officers were appointed by Nurhachi. The companies and Banners were not autonomous combat units, but pools from which troops were mustered when needed. In time, Chinese and Mongol Banners were also organized.

It was this form of military organization that enabled Nurhachi's successors to conquer China. In 1616 Nurhachi proclaimed himself emperor of the Later Chin dynasty, and in 1625 established his capital in present-day Mukden. This was a momentous move, for Mukden was in an agricultural area, settled and cultivated by Chinese. To rule a sedentary population required methods and institutions far different from those suited for nomadic tribes, and Nurhachi met the challenge by choosing the only model available to him, the Chinese system of civil administration.

Nurhachi died in 1626, but the trend toward adoption of Chinese institutions continued under his successors. The Six Ministries and Censorate were established in Mukden in 1631. Chinese scholar-officials, some of whom had previously served the Ming, were appointed to the highest positions in the civil administration as well as in the armies. As bureaucracy supplanted the looser forms of tribal organization, the power of the ruling clan over the tribes and of Nurhachi's sons within the clan increased. Equally important, the Chinese system of government enabled the Manchus to win the allegiance of the Chinese gentry, and to administer territories conquered by Manchu armies.

The proclamation of the Ch'ing (Clear) dynasty at Mukden in 1636 set the stage for the conquest of China. Rebellions had broken out in north China in the 1630's, and in 1644 the rebel army of Li Tzu-ch'eng captured

---

* The name Manchu, the origin of which is obscure, was not adopted until 1635; it is used here for the sake of convenience.

Peking. When the Ming general Wu San-kuei called on the Manchus for aid, Banner troops streamed into north China and rapidly dispersed the rebels. The Manchus then occupied Peking themselves and proclaimed it the capital of the Ch'ing dynasty.

Remnants of the Ming armies withdrew to the south, where they set up satrapies, which were tolerated by the Manchus for several decades. But this anomalous situation could not be permitted to continue, and as soon as the Manchus felt secure in the north, south China and Taiwan were subjugated (1675–1683).

Military conquest was an impressive feat, but the major task facing the Manchus was ruling the vast and populous empire. The Manchu people comprised perhaps 2 per cent of the population of China. How were they to maintain internal cohesion and political supremacy?

In order to safeguard Manchu racial and cultural identity, the traditional clan system was preserved, marriage with Chinese was forbidden, and Manchuria was blocked off to Chinese emigration. Some of these barriers eventually broke down, and the Manchus came to adopt many Chinese customs, but until the twentieth century they did not become assimilated.

Superior military power had enabled the Manchus to conquer China, and steps were taken to ensure the preservation of military supremacy. Banner units were stationed at strategic locations throughout the empire. Small units, overlapping commands, the periodic transfers were among the measures designed to prevent any commander from becoming dangerously independent. Efforts were made to encourage the continuance of military prowess in the peacetime garrisons, and Manchus were forbidden to engage in manual labor or commerce. By the late eighteenth century inactivity and financial corruption led to the deterioration of the Banner forces, but by that time the Ch'ing had consolidated power through other means.

The Manchus realized that to govern China, the cooperation of the Chinese, above all, of the gentry class, was necessary. The house therefore ruled in much the same fashion as a native dynasty. This was the key to their success, and their greatest achievement. As a visible symbol of submission, Chinese were required to braid their hair in the Manchu queue, but in general, they were allowed to retain their own customs. Attempts to abolish Chinese women's practice of binding their feet and to encourage Chinese scholars to learn the Manchu language failed and were soon abandoned. Only minor alterations were made in the political organization inherited from the Ming. The civil service examination system continued to be the principal method of recruiting officials and of fostering ideological indoctrination and intellectual conformity. The hierarchy of examinations was complex, but basically unchanged from the three stages—district, provincial, and metropolitan—of Ming times. Examination requirements for Manchus were less rigorous, but of course the overwhelming majority of the more than a million degree holders at any given time were Chinese. Only a small percentage of the 40,000 or so officials were Manchu. Most of these held key posts in the central government or the military, while the day-to-day administration of the empire was conducted by Chinese.

China proper was divided into eighteen provinces, most of which were grouped into pairs to form larger units; as under the Ming, the governors of provinces and the viceroys of paired provinces were jointly responsible for the areas under their jurisdiction. Until the nineteenth century, the majority of viceroys were Manchus, while most governors were Chinese. The lowest level of direct administration was the district, of which there were some 1,400 to 1,500 with an average population of about 200,000, each under the supervision of a Chinese district magistrate. On the local level, the system of dividing the populace into units of 100 and 10 households was also retained.

In the capital, the Six Ministries and the Grand Secretariat headed the bureaucracy. Each ministry had two presidents, one Manchu and one Chinese, and four vice-presidents, two Manchu and two Chinese. There were equal numbers of Chinese and Manchus in the Grand Secretariat and in the Censorate as well. A new body, the Grand Council, created in 1729, eventually replaced the Grand Secretariat at the top of the government apparatus. It concentrated on urgent matters, while the Grand Secretariat handled more routine affairs. This innovation eased the task of the emperor, but ultimate authority and responsibility remained in his hands, and the system worked smoothly only when an emperor exercised this authority.

The ruling house was fortunate enough to produce two outstanding emperors during the first 150 years of the dynasty, whose combined reigns amount to almost one-half of the entire Ch'ing period. The K'ang-hsi Emperor (1661–1722) was an energetic and conscientious administrator and an able military leader. In addition to subjugating south China, he conquered Mongolia. Through holding special examinations and sponsoring important scholarly projects, such as the compilation of the *History of the Ming* and the *Complete Poems of the T'ang Dynasty,* he demonstrated his desire to rule as a Confucian monarch, and attracted a large number of the most eminent Chinese scholars to the service of the dynasty. Although at first many Chinese had naturally been hostile to the alien conquerors, by the end of the reign of the K'ang-hsi Emperor it is probable that the vast majority of the population, including the gentry guardians of the Chinese tradition, looked on the Manchu monarch as the legitimate possessor of the Mandate of Heaven.

Under the K'ang-hsi Emperor's grandson, the capable Ch'ien-lung Emperor (1736–1796), the Ch'ing reached its zenith. Tibet, after several revolts against Ch'ing influence, was made a protectorate. Ili and Turkestan were conquered, adding more than 6 million square miles of territory. By the late eighteenth century, the largest area in the history of China was under the administrative supervision of the imperial government. The record of the reign was marred by corruption during the last two decades, owing largely to eunuch influence. In 1796 the Ch'ien-lung Emperor retired, not desiring to appear unfilial by remaining on the throne longer than his illustrious grandfather. A son succeeded him, but the old emperor, still vigorous, retained real power until his death in 1799, making his rule the longest in Chinese history.

In retrospect we can see that the mid-Ch'ing was the twilight of traditional Chinese civilization. Within the eighteen provinces, peace reigned, commerce prospered, and the gentry devoted themselves to the finer things in life. Exquisite lacquer and porcelain wares were produced in unprecedented quantities, for export to appreciative connoisseurs in Europe as well as for domestic consumption. Scholars delved more deeply and more thoroughly into the classical past than ever before, even challenging the authenticity of parts of the accepted Confucian canon. Poets debated whether technique, moral content, feeling, or inspiration was the essence of great poetry. In *The Dream of the Red Chamber,* China's greatest novel, Ts'ao Hsueh-ch'in portrayed the decline of an aristocratic family and suggested that escape from this world was the only solution to the sorrow and futility of human love.

On the lower levels of society there were fewer pleasures and simpler worries. The long period of peace, combined with the widespread use of crops introduced from abroad which could be grown on previously uncultivated soil, such as the sweet potato, the peanut (used for cooking oil), and maize, caused a population explosion. By the end of the eighteenth century the population of China may well have reached the 300 million mark. Pressure on the land was intense, and when in 1796 a rebellion inspired by a combination of religious fervor of the Buddhistic White Lotus sect and animosity toward the Manchus broke out in north China, it spread rapidly among the discontented peasantry. The rebels were not well organized, but the Banner forces were ineffectual. The years spanning the turn of the century were spent in the slow and costly suppression of the rebellion.

The White Lotus Rebellion was quashed and the crisis seemed to have passed. No one could have foreseen that the barbarian emissary, the Englishman Lord Macartney, who had come in 1793 to petition for trade privileges and who had graciously been granted an audience in spite of his perverse refusal to kowtow before the Son of Heaven, was the herald of a new order, which within a few generations would humiliate and ravage the glorious empire of the Ch'ing.

For Further Reading

JAPAN

Ernst, Earle, *The Kabuki Theatre.*

Hibbett, Howard S., *The Floating World in Japanese Fiction.*

Keene, Donald (ed.), *Anthology of Japanese Literature from the Earliest Era to the Mid-Nineteenth Century.*

Reischauer, Edwin O., and Fairbank, John K., *East Asia: The Great Tradition.*

Tsunoda, Ryusaku, William Theodore de Bary, and Donald Keene, *Sources of Japanese Tradition.*

CHINA

Ch'ü, T'ung-tsu, *Local Government in China under the Ch'ing.*

Ho, Ping-ti, *The Ladder of Success in Imperial China.*

Ts'ao Hsueh-ch'in, *The Dream of the Red Chamber.*

56 Aztec and Inca Civilizations

Once the Spanish monarchs Ferdinand and Isabella had been convinced that Columbus had discovered an extensive archipelago of hitherto unknown islands, they began to build an empire in this New World with astonishing speed. Their conquistadors became leaders in that explosive geographical expansion whereby Europeans discovered more territory in seventy-five years than in the previous thousand. In this brief period, these remarkable men, variously impelled by curiosity, thirst for gold, and missionary zeal, found the Pacific Ocean and traversed its enormous expanse; explored great rivers (the Amazon, the Magdelena, the Mississippi, the Orinoco, the Plata); conquered a region larger than forty Spains; and sailed their tiny ships around the world. The men, hitherto unknown, who accomplished these extraordinary feats did so with little aid from the Crown, which shrewdly gave only formal authorization to act in the name of Spain. The bold conquistadors invested their own blood and fortunes, driven in the hope of winning honor and riches.

When the Spanish reached mainland America they encountered three different civilizations: those of the Aztecs, the Mayas, and the Incas. They

B.C.	5000	Beginnings of agriculture in Mexico
	2000	First Peruvian ceremonial centers
	900	Chavín unification of Peru
	800	Olmec unification of Mesoamerica
A.D.	300–600	Teotihuacan empire
	600–800	Huari and Tiahuanaco empires
	900	Fall of classic Maya civilization
	1400–1519	Aztec empire
	1438–1538	Inca empire

were greatly impressed not only by the gold to be looted, but also by the sophisticated, metropolitan character of these peoples of Mexico and Peru. In Mexico they found cities to rival and perhaps surpass those of Europe; in Peru, an empire of heroic magnitude. They marveled at these civilizations set in the midst of Indian country, and, happily for historians, they wrote about what impressed them: the ferocity of the Aztecs; the talented craftsmen of Cholula and Cuzco; the intellectual and scientific achievements of the Mayas; the efficiency of the Inca administration and its social security system; the immense pyramids and temples that studded the cities and towns of two continents.

The first step toward civilization, the cultivation of maize, beans, squash, and other plants, had been taken in the Mexican highlands about 5000 B.C. or perhaps still earlier. Knowledge of cultivation spread rapidly from this center, reaching as far south as Peru during the fourth millennium B.C. In area after area, farming stimulated experiments with local plants, and some of these (especially potatoes and manioc) became staples more important than those originally diffused from Mexico. The effects of cultivation on population and society differed, however, from area to area. In Mexico, Central America, and the northern and central Andes, where environmental and historical circumstances favored genuinely productive agriculture, and where reliable sources of protein (such as fish, wild game, or domestic meat animals) were abundant, cultivation led to a rapid expansion of population.

Within this broad territory, civilization developed only in Mesoamerica (Mexico and northern Central America) and the central Andes (Peru and Bolivia). These areas possessed two advantages which were largely responsible for the growth of their civilizations: a concentration of population in relatively restricted zones, and an integrated yet ecologically diversified environment with multiple centers of innovation and diffusion. Dense populations in restricted regions provided the background for urbanism and the personnel to fill the many roles required by a highly specialized society. The interchange between centers in different situations guaranteed the flow of stimuli across the whole area and gave rise to the expansive tendencies that led to the formation of states and empires.

These ancient American societies had in common features essential to all civilizations: intensive agricultural economies; large concentrated populations; intensive social stratification; a high degree of occupational specialization; governmental authority that cross-cut kinship and locality; statewide organization of food production; efficient distributive systems covering large areas; standing armies; diversified patterns of settlement; monumental architecture; and the concentration of major public functions in a limited number of centers (usually, but not always, cities). In addition they had features that some of their Old World counterparts of the sixteenth century lacked. Church and state were so closely linked as to be practically the same institution. Clans, lineages, and other kinship units were institutionalized within the political structure. Land was owned either by the kinship groups or by the state itself, not by individuals or families. On the other hand, none of the American civilizations had iron technology, draft or riding animals, the plow, wheeled vehicles, firearms, or true seagoing ships.

Since they had developed in different environments and under different historical conditions, these people evolved, in spite of their similarities, into different kinds of societies, with different goals and organized on different principles. Throughout most of their history the Mesoamericans and the inhabitants of the central Andes were isolated from each other. Certain basic innovations, such as the cultivation of maize, pottery making, and metallurgy, spread from one area to the other, or outward from the intervening territory. At no time, however, was there the sort of direct contact between Mesoamerica and Peru that was so common in the history of the nations of the Old World.

The earliest Mesoamerican civilization, that of the Olmecs, evolved along the Gulf of Mexico some time before 1000 B.C. After about 800 B.C., it exerted influence on the social and religious organization of an area extending from the Valley of Mexico to modern El Salvador. We do not know just how this expansion took place, but it seems to have spurred the development of civilization all over Mesoamerica.

To the north, especially in the Valley of Mexico, large cities soon grew up. During the Christian era the competing imperialistic designs of the major cities colored the whole history of the Mexican highlands. City after city—Teotihuacán, Tula, Azcapotzalco, and many others—rose to power and was then destroyed. Teotihuacán, founded about the time of Christ, became the largest city ever built in preconquest Mesoamerica. Its people established the largest of the ancient Mexican empires, extending from the Valley of Mexico to the highlands of Guatemala and lasting from about A.D. 300 to 600.

By the early sixteenth century the Aztecs of Tenochtitlán, along with their uneasy allies Texcoco and Tlacopán, dominated Mexico, holding sway over much of the southern part of the country. The Aztecs were an incredibly bloodthirsty people, and their empire was more a military machine than a political state. They left conquered governments intact, sending out armies on a regular schedule to collect tribute. They were more concerned with taking prisoners to be sacrificed by tens of thousands to Huitzilopochtli and other gods than with the peaceful administration of conquered territory. In a sense, the Aztec dominion was not an empire at all, but an immense battle ground on which their conquest was ever being refought. The only real integrating element was provided by the merchants, a special class of state-controlled capitalists who traded widely through Mexico while serving also as ambassadors, spies, and at times soldiers.

In the tropical country to the south, especially in the Petén area of Guatemala, the Maya civilization developed. This was a nonurban society; a dispersed and essentially rural population was organized around cere-monial centers which were the seats of government, commerce, and reli-gion, but which largely lacked the residential districts that would have made them into cities. The Olmecs had discovered the rudiments of writing and the calendar, and the Mayas improved these—as well as the science of astronomy—into complex, sophisticated intellectual systems. The classic Maya civilization of the Petén was based on tropical slash-and-burn farm-ing, rather than on intensive agriculture. Eventually (about A.D. 900) the ceremonial centers disintegrated when the constantly increasing population outstripped a diminishing food supply. Outlying Maya areas, especially in Yucatán, continued to flourish but were repeatedly conquered by the great cities of Mexico. What the Spaniards found in Maya country were the decimated, "Mexicanized" remnants of a once great civilization, its cere-monial centers abandoned and in ruins, the remaining noble families locked in a bitter civil war.

Peruvian civilization had its beginnings on the desert coast, where the first ceremonial centers were built about 2000 B.C. Small states, organized very much like those of the classic Mayas, extended over parts of the coast and highlands. About 900 B.C. one of these, the Chavín civilization, under-went an expansion very much like that of the Olmecs, spreading through-out the northern half of Peru. For a millennium and a half thereafter, the

PRE-COLUMBIAN EMPIRES

0   500   1,000 Miles

people of this area were organized around ceremonial centers similar to those in the land of the classic Maya.

Meanwhile cities were growing up in southern Peru, outside the area of Chavín influence. About A.D. 600 two of these, Huari and Tiahuanaco, carved out empires that, between them, included all of Peru and Bolivia and part of northern Chile. However, these empires, and the cities that founded them, survived only two or three centuries. Thereafter southern Peru and Bolivia reverted to a purely rural world of little tribal groups living in villages. These tribes engaged in incessant feuds. The Huari conquerors, however, had carried urban life and imperialism to northern Peru. Cities soon replaced the old ceremonial centers there, and one of them, Chan Chan, conquered much of the Peruvian coast.

Surprisingly, the final and greatest round of empire building originated in the rural south, not in the urban north. First the Incas, combining military ingenuity with diplomatic finesse, subjugated many of the little tribes of the southern Peruvian highlands. Then, their armies expanded by units from the new provinces, they conquered all of the Andean coast and highlands, from northern Ecuador to the Maule River in central Chile. They brought all of this territory under a single administrative system, establishing the rule of Cuzco in every province. This system was both complex and efficient. Inca governors subdivided the entire population of the empire into groups of ten persons, and were thus able to control the activities of every farmer and craftsman. Men paid taxes in the form of labor. An up-to-date census was kept in the capital and a thoroughgoing social security system neutralized the effects of localized droughts and other natural disasters. Almost all of the population of the Inca empire—including the people of Cuzco, the capital "city"—lived in little villages. The few real cities allowed to survive were those that posed no threat to the integrity of the empire.

The Spanish conquest of these large, far-flung, culturally advanced, and warlike civilizations was swift. Mexico was crushed in three years, Peru in six. How did a handful of European adventurers manage to overrun such vast stretches of territory with such seeming ease? The Spanish enjoyed the advantages of cannons, horses, superior personal armor, and fleets of almost impregnable sailing ships. They were also constantly reinforced by new arrivals from Spain. These advantages, however, cannot explain the victory of so few over so many, especially since the Indians were fighting on their own terrain; the answer lies in the weaknesses inherent in the Indian societies.

For one thing, the Indians were completely immobilized when deprived of their emperors. The Spaniards kidnapped both the Aztec and the Inca emperors; until each was killed his absence paralyzed resistance because the pyramidal political systems depended on decisions being made by the semidivine individual at the top. Still more important in the case of Mexico was the burning hatred of the provincial peoples toward their Aztec overlords. The army that conquered Tenochtitlán was really an Indian army captained by a few Spaniards. Similarly, the permanent civil war in the Maya country played no small part in the fall of Yucatán. The Maya groups would not unite against the invaders and could therefore be crushed one by one. The same situation existed in Peru, where the Incas had the added disadvantage of being overextended. Their empire was so large, and communications so difficult across the mountains and desert, that a second capital had been established at Quito. The Spanish arrived in Peru near the end of a disastrous civil war between two royal brothers, one based in Cuzco and the other in Quito. By adroit diplomacy the Spanish succeeded in prolonging the civil war, sometimes intervening on one side and sometimes on the other. While the Inca armies destroyed each other, the Spanish gradually took over the territories that the Indians were too busy to administer, until, after six years, they owned the whole empire.

For Further Reading

Coe, Michael D., *The Maya.*
———, *Mexico.*
Lanning, Edward P., *Peru Before the Incas.*

57 Spain and Portugal in America

The Spaniards did much more than explore, intrigue, and pillage in the New World; they worked to implant a Christian, European civilization in a domain that eventually stretched from California to Patagonia. Their empire included the viceregal capitals at Mexico City and Lima; mining camps such as Guanajuato in Mexico and Potosí in upper Peru; Asunción in the middle of South America a thousand miles from Buenos Aires, Santiago de Chile, Quito, Bogotá, Caracas, Havana, Guatemala City, and, far across the Pacific, Manila in the Philippines. By the seventeenth century some of these towns competed in size and significance with European cities and easily outshone the largest English, French, and Portuguese settlements overseas.

Even before the heroic age ended, Spain began to devise an administrative system to control its empire. The first voyage of Columbus was a somewhat haphazard affair, but arrangements for the second were carefully supervised, and thereafter all colonial affairs were regulated, from the time a would-be emigrant applied for a permit to leave Spain through the disposal of his estate after his death in America. The House of Trade was established in 1503, the Laws of Burgos governing Spanish-Indian relations were drawn up in 1512, the Council of the Indies was organized in 1524. Indeed every action was so minutely prescribed by law that one needed a license to hunt for wild pigs on a Caribbean island. So many thousands of ordinances were passed that only with great difficulty were they codified and published as the massive, four-volume *Recopilación de Leyes de los Reynos de las Indias* (1680). The forest of laws continued to grow so rapidly that later attempts to issue an up-to-date compilation always failed. From the Supreme Council of the Indies in Spain, presided over by the king himself on important occasions, down through the viceroys and judges to lesser officials, a host of functionaries struggled to maintain the economic and political interests of the Crown. Regional

A.D. 1492 Columbus reaches the New World

1500 Cabral lays basis for Portugal's claim by landing in Brazil on his way to India

1519 Cortés begins the conquest of New Spain (Mexico)

1524 Council of the Indies established by Spain

1535 Antonio de Mendoza, first viceroy in Spanish America, begins rule in Mexico; Lima, Peru, is founded by Pizarro

1549 Permanent settlement of Brazil begun by Governor Thomé de Souza, and the Jesuits begin missionary labors

1550 Bartolomé de Las Casas and Juan Ginés de Sepúlveda debate at Valladolid whether the Indians are natural slaves according to Aristotle's doctrine

1551 University charters granted for universities in Mexico and Peru

1580 Philip II annexes Portugal and her empire, a "captivity" lasting until 1640

1624 Dutch begin their 30-year rule in Pernambuco, Brazil

1680 Publication of the Spanish colonial code: *Recopilación de Leyes de las Indias*

1759 Jesuits expelled from Brazil

1767 Jesuits expelled from Spanish America

1780 Unsuccessful rebellion by Tupac Amaru against Spanish rule in Peru

variations of laws and institutions developed, but this ponderous, complicated bureaucracy managed to hold the empire together for more than three centuries.

The Spanish sovereigns also had great authority and responsibility in ecclesiastical matters, owing to papal concessions in establishing the system of church-state relationship known as the Patronato Real. The Crown agreed to maintain the church in the Indies, but in return exercised pontifical powers except in purely spiritual matters. No church, monastery, or hospital could be built without the king's permission; no priest or friar might go to America without his express license. In the administrative, economic, and juridical affairs of the church in the New World he was dominant.

The Portuguese sovereigns obtained similar powers in Brazil, but in other respects Brazil differed significantly from Spanish America, for it was only one part—and for long not the most important part—of a sprawling aggregation of territories ruled from Lisbon. Portugal's colonial administration was loose and weak; she had so many other cares that she could not protect Brazil from foreign interlopers. Throughout a part of the sixteenth century, France powerfully rivaled Portugal in Brazil. Philip II of Spain annexed Portugal and all her overseas possessions in 1580, and until 1640 Brazil was an unwilling part of the Spanish empire. The Dutch established themselves in Pernambuco in 1624 and were expelled only thirty years later.

Brazil was poor, too, compared to Spanish America. The Indians that the Portuguese encountered were largely nomadic, and thus were no easily harnessed labor force to be exploited the way the sedentary and organized Aztecs, Incas, and Mayas were exploited by the Spaniards. Ecclesiastics sought to protect the Indians in the Spanish empire, but no widespread battle was fought to protect the Brazilian Indians, despite the notable labors of the Jesuit António de Vieira in the seventeenth century. Brazil had to import Negro slaves, an expensive operation, and though she became the world's leading exporter of sugar for a time, it was only late in the seventeenth century that gold was found in Minas Gerais. Brazil's combined agricultural and mineral production never sufficed to support a population as large as that of Spanish America: some 3 million people inhabited Brazil in 1800, mostly along the coast, while 18 million were found widely dispersed in the Spanish possessions.

The rhythm of history was different too. The sixteenth century was the exciting, dynamic period in Spanish America when Hernán Cortés, Francisco Pizarro, and other epic heroes made the great conquests and society was established: the "forgotten" seventeenth century was a quiet time with few significant events. In Brazil, on the other hand, only in the seventeenth century did the bandeirantes begin their dramatic explorations and slave raids which ultimately won tremendous areas for Portugal. Urban life was less important in Brazil; economic and political power was concentrated largely in the hands of the great plantation owners.

Everything in Brazil was on a simpler basis. The imperial organization that made Spanish America a paradise for bureaucrats did not exist in Brazil; the Church was poor and could not indulge in the ostentation practiced in Spanish America, where half of the land and other property was Church-held. The Holy Office of the Inquisition was not formally established in Brazil, and Jews played a significant role in commercial life. No printing press was set up, no university founded, and a quiet, almost vegetative provincial society grew up. At the end of the colonial period when Napoleon's invasion of Portugal sent the royal family scurrying across the Atlantic for safety, the women of Rio de Janeiro were so unacquainted with the ways of the world that when they saw the Portuguese court ladies debarking with shaved heads they hastened to cut off their own hair, not knowing that shipboard vermin, not Portuguese fashion, had decreed this drastic measure.

Another contrast between the Iberian empires in America lay in their relations with the native populations. In Brazil Indians played only a minor role, but in Spanish America the thorny question of their proper treatment was a dominant problem. In their effort to govern the natives, Spaniards adapted some institutions from their own medieval experience of fighting against the Muslims and created others to meet the needs of New World conditions. The determination of the Crown and the Church to Christianize the Indians, the need for labor to exploit the new lands, and the attempts of some Spaniards to protect the Indians resulted in a very remarkable complex of customs, laws, and institutions which even today leads historians to contradictory conclusions about Spanish rule in America. The encomienda system, by which groups of Indians were assigned to Spaniards, a device to provide labor and goods to the Spaniard and protection and religious instruction for the Indians, was both stoutly defended and bitterly attacked throughout the sixteenth century by Spaniards themselves. The imperial policy of attempting to "civilize" the Indians by urbanizing them produced many curious results, and in the end destroyed large numbers of natives. Academic disputes flourish on this debatable and in a sense insoluble question, but there is no doubt that cruelty, overwork, and disease resulted in an appalling depopulation. There were, according to recent estimates, about 25 million Indians in Mexico in 1519, slightly more than 1 million in 1605.

Spain made efforts to mitigate the travail of the Indians by appointing official "Protectors" and by setting up special courts to try cases involving

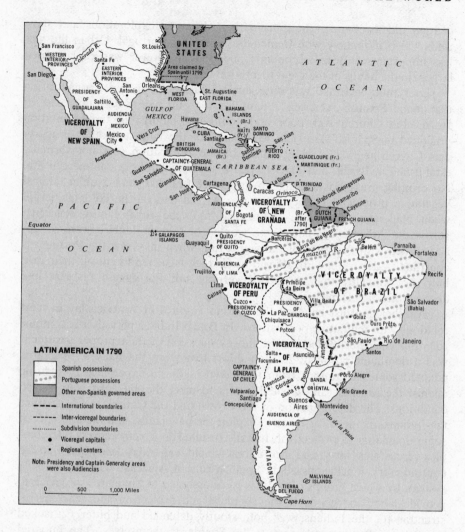

LATIN AMERICA IN 1790

Spanish possessions
Portuguese possessions
Other non-Spanish governed areas
International boundaries
Inter-viceregal boundaries
Subdivision boundaries
● Viceregal capitals
• Regional centers

Note: Presidency and Captain-Generalcy areas were also Audiencias

0   500   1,000 Miles

natives. The Crown dispatched numerous investigating groups and tried many stratagems, in the sixteenth century particularly, to ensure that Indians would be brought under Spanish rule by peaceful means alone, and be persuaded to accept Christianity by reason instead of by force. To achieve this end Bartolomé de Las Casas and his brother Dominicans preached the faith without the backing of the sword in Chiapas, and Vasco de Quiroga established his utopian communities in Michoacán. In many places a system of Indian segregation was worked out by friars and royal officials to protect them from Spaniards bent on exploiting them. This device, employed throughout the colonial period, culminated in the famous Jesuit missions of eighteenth-century Paraguay. Throughout the more than three centuries of Spanish rule in America, the difficult, indeed, impossible, double purpose of the Crown—to secure revenue and also to Christianize the Indians—inevitably led to angry disputes and evil compromises, along with some glorious episodes.

Looking back on the total encounter of Spaniards and Indians from the vantage point of the modern world with its multiplicity of cultures, two aspects of this confrontation hold special interest. For the first time in history one people—the Spaniards—paid serious attention to the culture of the peoples they met, because they felt a burning desire to establish a new Jerusalem in America. Protestantism had shattered the unity of Christendom in Europe, but many Spanish ecclesiastics saw in the New World a bright and shining opportunity for spiritual conquest. Many writers then and later pointed out that Luther and Cortés had been born about the same time: one to destroy Christian unity in Europe and the other to create a new community free from religious dissensions which were splitting the Old World asunder. To achieve this dream the souls of Indians must be won, and this could be done, the Spaniards believed, because the Indians were like soft wax, capable of being molded into true Christians. To accomplish this task the zealous friars learned the Indians' languages, familiarized themselves with their culture, and sought to make Christian doctrine intelligible to the Indian mentality.

The second, even more striking aspect of the Spanish-Indian relationship was the controversy which developed in the sixteenth century over the just method of treating the Indians. This issue led Spaniards to grapple with the ultimate problem—the nature of man himself. Of all the ideas churned up during the early years, none had more dramatic implications than the attempts some Spaniards made to apply to the natives the Aristotelian doctrine of natural slavery: the idea that one part of mankind is set aside by nature to be slaves in the service of masters born for a life of virtue. The scholar Juan Ginés de Sepúlveda sustained this view with great tenacity and erudition and concluded, without having visited America, that the Indians were in fact such rude and brutal beings that their forcible Christianization was both expedient and moral. But many ecclesiastics, most notably Bartolomé de Las Casas, opposed this idea scornfully, drawing upon divine and natural law as well as their own experiences in America. The controversy became so heated and the king's conscience so troubled over the question that in 1550 Charles V ordered the suspension of all expeditions to America while a junta of theologians, jurists, and officials, gathered at the royal capital of Valladolid, listened to the arguments of Las Casas and Sepúlveda. The Crown supported neither contestant fully, for Charles preferred to avoid clear-cut decisions whenever possible. But the basic law of 1573, designed to cover all future expeditions, required that future conversions be peaceful; "conquests" were henceforth to be called "pacifications."

In both Iberian empires, as in the colonial settlements of North America, there developed an "American" spirit which created a sense of alienation from the European powers and eventually led to a desire for independence. In both Brazil and Spanish America a mixed society grew up, unique in some respects because of the variety of the cultural and racial combinations that it produced. As the Liberator Simón Bolívar declared at the Congress of Angostura in 1819:

It is impossible to say to which human family we belong. The larger part of the native population has disappeared. Europeans have mixed with the Indians and the Negroes, and Negroes have mixed with Indians. We were all born of one mother America, though our fathers had different origins, and we all have differently colored skins. This dissimilarity is of the greatest significance.

One final contrast between the two Iberian empires remains to be discussed. Fearing enemy attacks, Portugal discouraged writing about Brazil and suppressed publications concerning it, but in the Spanish empire an extraordinary wealth of documentation was produced. Columbus started the practice of writing about the New World, and many Spaniards followed his example. The conquest so excited the imagination of Spaniards that they came to look upon it as the greatest event since the coming of Christ. As the conquistadors roamed over vast areas and the missionaries attempted to Christianize millions of Indians, they collected historical materials and wrote histories on a monumental scale. This concern that the record of their deeds be known and the nature of the overseas lands be described led the Council of the Indies to establish the office of a Cosmographer and Cronista Mayor whose function was to write the history of the Indies on a continuous basis.

Both empires prospered more in the eighteenth century than ever before. Iberian paternalism and exclusivism continued in both economic and political affairs, but a certain Enlightenment influence mitigated its rigors. The monarchs improved the efficiency of their imperial machinery, and economically at least, as the century ended, their immense empires were enjoying a kind of Indian summer.

Particularly in Spanish America, the cities manifested all the outward signs of opulence. Imposing public buildings and churches had been built. The arts flourished. Centers of learning abounded on a scale unknown in the English, French, or Portuguese colonies. There was a school of mines, for example, in Mexico City, an astronomical observatory in Bogotá.

Colonial literary culture proliferated: men of letters, scientists, historians, and priests kept many a New World printer busy. Even viceroys "were often men of education and personal distinction, some of whom dabbled in arts and letters and held literary salons in the viceregal palace."

This luxury and refinement was something of a façade, for as that perspicacious traveler Alexander von Humboldt noted about 1800, a fearful gulf separated the elite from the masses: "The architecture of the public and private edifices, the finery of the ladies, the tone of society, all announce a refinement with which the nakedness, the ignorance, and vulgarity of the lower people form the most striking contrast."

Revolutions convulsed these colonial societies in the years following 1810, heralding a generation of turbulence and confusion. These years of liberation—following the events of 1776 in the United States and the French Revolution—led to the overthrow of the Iberian empires in America and the beginnings of a new kind of civilization.

For Further Reading

Boxer, Charles R., *The Golden Age of Brazil, 1695–1750.*
Freyre, Gilberto, *The Masters and the Slaves.*
Gibson, Charles, *Spain in America.*
Haring, Clarence H., *The Spanish Empire in America.*

58   The Settlement of North America

Almost a century elapsed between Columbus' discovery of the New World and the beginning of settlement in the temperate parts of North America. During that time Spain spread northward into Mexico and Florida from its Caribbean bases, but the lands farther north remained largely ignored. They appeared to house no gold, no fabulous cities, no advanced civilizations. Explorations along the eastern shore of the northern continent were often frustrating. Every river seemed to lead endlessly inland; the fabled Northwest Passage proved as elusive as the Seven Cities of Cíbola.

Instead of quick wealth and easy access to the Orient, those who probed North America encountered a vast expanse of dense forest, sparsely occupied by primitive natives. Unlike their ethnic relatives in the Mexican highlands, Central America, and the Andes, the peoples north of the Rio Grande were living in the Stone Age. Without metal tools (except for an

CHRONOLOGY

A.D.

1497	John Cabot reaches North America
1513	Ponce de León establishes Spanish claim to Florida
1524	Giovanni Verrazano explores coast of North America
1534	Jacques Cartier explores St. Lawrence River
1560's	French attempts to settle in Florida thwarted by Spain
1565	Spanish found first permanent settlement north of Mexico at St. Augustine, Florida
1607	First permanent English outpost established at Jamestown, Virginia
1608	First permanent French outpost established at Quebec
1609	Henry Hudson claims part of North America for the United Provinces
1619	First Negroes brought to British America as forced labor; Virginia begins representative assembly
1620	Separatists found Plymouth Colony
1630	Great Migration to America begins; Massachusetts founded
1630's	Connecticut, Rhode Island, and New Haven colonies founded
1633	Colonization of Maryland begun
1636	Harvard College opened
1638	A Swedish settlement founded on the Delaware River
1640's	Civil wars in England cause shift in migration patterns
1655	Dutch from New Netherland conquer New Sweden
1660	Stuart monarchy restored
1660's	Legal definition of Negro slavery begun in Virginia and Maryland

1663   Charles II grants Carolinas to eight proprietors

1664   British seize New Netherland

1675–1676   Bacon's Rebellion in Virginia; King Philip's War in New England

1682   William Penn founds Pennsylvania

1684–1689   Dominion of New England places several colonies under royal authority

1685   Revocation of the Edict of Nantes in France spurs Protestant migration to America

1689–1713   King William's War

1691   New Massachusetts charter puts colony under royal authority; Plymouth Colony and Maine included in new Massachusetts boundaries

1693   College of William and Mary founded

1696   Parliamentary Act establishes vice-admiralty courts to try violators; Board of Trade created by the Crown

1702–1713   Queen Anne's War

1704   *Boston News-Letter* begins publication

1729   North and South Carolina become separate, royal colonies

1733   Colony of Georgia founded

1739   George Whitefield first visits America

1740–1748   King George's War

1749–1752   Benjamin Franklin experiments with electricity

1751   Philadelphia Academy (later University of Pennsylvania) founded

1754   George Washington's clash with French soldiers signals start of French and Indian War

1763   Treaty of Paris; French Canada and Spanish Florida ceded to Great Britain

occasional item of copper), domesticated animals, or a written language, the Amerinds—or "savages" as the English chroniclers usually called them—lived in simple agricultural and hunting societies. With little contact and even less cohesion between the scores of identifiable tribal units, the American aborigines could offer no effective resistance to European attempts to settle along the eastern seaboard. Actually, the Indians at first saw no need to resist; the white man could give them valuable tools, weapons, ornaments, and information. Furthermore, land was incredibly plentiful. To both European and native it seemed inconceivable that enough colonists would ever arrive to make the million Indians north of the Rio Grande feel cramped for space. Early contacts were for the most part peaceful except where marred by explorers who blatantly carried off a few Indians to show as oddities in the courts of Europe. Eventually, however, many tribes came to fear and hate the white man, perhaps as much for his arrogant assumption of superiority as for his hunger for land.

During the sixteenth century Europeans accumulated information about North America and debated rival territorial claims. Spain, busy plundering the Indian civilizations south of the Rio Grande, rested its case on the explorations of Juan Ponce de León (1513), and Pánfilo de Narváez (1528) in Florida, Hernando de Soto and Vásquez de Coronado in the lower Mississippi Valley and New Mexico (1539–1542), and Juan Cabrillo and Bartolomé Ferrelo along the west coast of the continent. The papal bulls of 1493, which allotted all the New World west of Brazil to Ferdinand and Isabella, provided ecclesiastical endorsement. But Spain's claims meant little to her European rivals. Some found new reason to embarrass His Most Catholic Majesty after the Protestant Reformation added religious conflict to Europe's problems. England, relying on the discoveries of John Cabot in 1497, developed enthusiasm for New World possessions under Elizabeth I; at the same time the French and Dutch began to take notice of the huge land mass to the west. The North American continent slowly gained appeal as a source of raw materials, an area to settle surplus population, and a place to build outposts against Spanish power.

France seized an early lead in the contest for possession of the temperate zones of North America. In 1524 Giovanni Verrazano investigated almost the entire coast from Spanish Florida to Nova Scotia; ten years later Jacques Cartier explored the St. Lawrence River and planted a small colony on the site of present-day Quebec. Within less than a year, finding no immediate wealth and unnerved by the climate, these colonists sailed home. But French Basque fishermen made increasingly frequent voyages to northern waters, often camping for months on the shores of New England and Newfoundland. Finally, in 1608 the French, following up earlier explorations by Samuel de Champlain, secured a permanent foothold at Quebec.

The next year a Dutch expedition under Henry Hudson laid claim to the river that bears his name. Actual Dutch settlement began there in 1624 and soon expanded into the Delaware and Connecticut river valleys. By 1638 Sweden also had footholds on the Atlantic coast, principally on the Delaware.

Despite an almost complete absence from the American scene between the voyages of the Cabots in the 1490's and Martin Frobisher in 1576, England's commercial and political growth soon thrust her into the forefront of the colonial race. Prodded by propagandists such as the two Richard Hakluyts, seadogs of the mettle of Francis Drake, Humphrey Gilbert, and Walter Raleigh began to make a mockery of Spanish claims to North America. They explored the region at will and set up colonies at several locations along the coast, some within a few hundred miles of Spanish garrisons. In 1578 and 1583 Gilbert tried to settle Newfoundland, but the climate proved too formidable. Raleigh's attempts in the 1580's at Roanoke Island off the North Carolina coast failed for reasons still mysterious. England, it seemed, could not extend its power into the New World until the troubles with Spain subsided and stronger inducements for colonization appeared. Smashing the Spanish Armada in 1588 was but the first step.

It is ironic that the unimaginative Stuart monarch James I rather than the visionary Elizabeth succeeded in finally planting the British flag on American shores. The reasons lie not so much with the efficiency or generosity of the Stuarts as with the disruptions in English life that accompanied their erratic rule, and the civil and religious disturbances that plagued seventeenth-century England. The disruptive effects of the enclosure movement and the rapid growth of an urban proletariat caused thousands of Englishmen to despair of earning a decent livelihood at home. The growing Puritan effort to reform the Church of England created equally profound discontent, as did, later in the century, the political fragmentation accompanying the Civil War. England, it seemed to contemporaries, was overpopulated. America beckoned. In the first half of the seventeenth century, more than 60,000 Englishmen sought refuge in the New World.

Although England rapidly gained ascendancy over most of North America, her early attempts at settlement came close to failure. The first permanent success occurred in 1607 at Jamestown, not far from the earlier site of Roanoke. Three shiploads sent out in late 1606 by the London Company of Virginia—which had a royal charter to settle between the 34th and 41st parallels—barely survived the first winter: only 32 of the

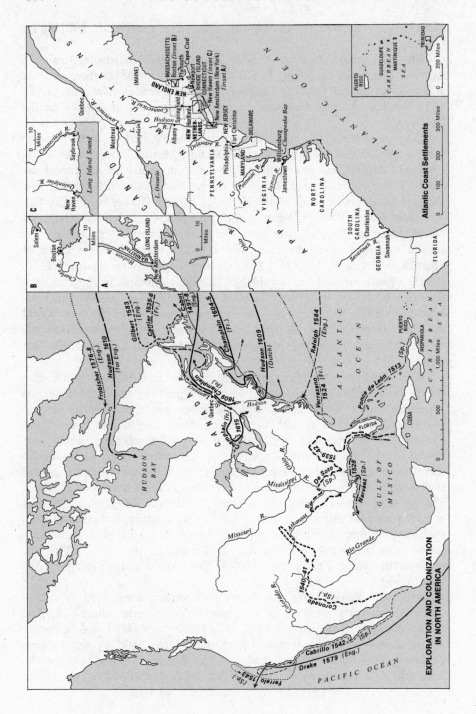

Atlantic Coast Settlements

EXPLORATION AND COLONIZATION IN NORTH AMERICA

original 105 members of the all-male expedition were alive seven months later. The colonists suffered from disease, hostile natives, and their own incompetence; only when Captain John Smith, a member of the governing council but of relatively low social status among the gentlemen leaders, imposed near-dictatorial authority on the survivors did Jamestown's prospects improve. After Smith left Virginia in 1609 the colonists again faced possible extermination. Starvation in the winter of 1609–1610 drove one man to cannibalism, and by spring the majority were ready to forsake the experiment—especially since they had discovered neither gold nor a northwest passage. But the arrival of new settlers and supplies in 1610, the exportation of tobacco after 1612, and some major administrative changes soon ensured stability and prosperity. Significant too were the introduction in 1619 of representative government—important to Englishmen who contemplated migration to the New World—and the beginnings of Negro servitude—important, despite its inhumanity, to the economic future of North America.

Although Jamestown survived, the London Company did not. The costs of ships and supplies and manpower were high, returns on investment disappointingly low. Factional rifts within the London Company, and a frightful combination of Indian massacres and epidemics propelled the company into bankruptcy. In 1624 the crown revoked its charter. Henceforth Virginia was administered by a royal governor under the supervision of the imperial bureaucracy.

Despite the failure of private enterprise in Virginia, British colonization of North America continued to be largely a private affair. The role of the crown was essentially legal, issuing charters which granted to one or more individuals the right to settle and govern specified portions of the New World.* Included in each charter were a few limitations on the patentees' powers—customarily a reservation that their laws not conflict with the laws of England and that legislation be passed only with the consent of the freemen. Not specified was the definition of freeman or the extent to which local laws must conform to the spirit as well as the letter of English law.

These matters became important in the second major plantation in British America. The same charter that permitted the settlement in Jamestown had also created a Plymouth Company of Virginia with authority to settle in the area between the 38th and 45th parallels. The Plymouth Company's initial attempt was short-lived, and by the time settlement was again attempted in New England—as Europeans after 1614 began to call the northern part of British America—it was less as a commercial venture than as a religious hegira. At this point the issues of the rights of colonists

* Of course these charters did not bind either the aborigines or England's European rivals.

and their authority to restrict membership in their own communities became paramount.

Since the accession of James VI of Scotland to the throne of England in 1603, the Puritan movement for reform of the Church of England had made remarkable headway. Inspired by such men as William Ames, William Perkins, and John Preston, a growing number of Englishmen sought to "purify" the Anglican Church in the light of reforms carried out by John Calvin in Geneva and other Protestants on the Continent. But the times seemed to conspire against them. The accession in 1629 of William Laud to the See of London signaled increasing determination by orthodox Anglicans to ignore Puritan protests; depressions in 1619–1624 and 1629–1631 coincided too closely with widespread epidemics in 1624–1625 and 1631–1632; and the crown under James I and Charles I appeared increasingly arbitrary and callous. "This lande," observed John Winthrop in 1629, "growes wearye of her Inhabitants." For Winthrop and many other Puritans salvation lay in America: there they could set up a model church and state which by its very perfection would serve as example and inspiration to those who remained in England. The Bible would regain its divinely intended role, and an orderly society would observe God's will—both in the structure and spirit of its religious services and in the organization and behavior of its citizens.

Two practical considerations had to be met first: the acquisition of a desirable piece of land and the establishment of a political authority that would free the experiment from the baneful intrusion of Bishop Laud and other officials at home. Both conditions were fulfilled in 1629. In March of that year the Crown issued to a group of ninety noblemen and gentry, most of them Puritans, title to an extensive strip of land between the Merrimac and Charles rivers, previously controlled by the now defunct Plymouth Company. In August, twelve of the most prominent patentees agreed at Cambridge to move themselves and their families to the New World provided they could take their charter along and thus ensure control by resident directors—an opportunity made possible by the omission from the document of the usual stipulation that the annual meeting of the company's General Court must be in England. Armed with the charter, the company's stockholders and officers would be free to govern as they saw fit, protected by 3,000 miles of ocean from the prying eyes of William Laud and King Charles.

The Puritan leaders had good reason to believe that America would provide both isolation and a free rein. A decade earlier a radical sect of English Protestants, descriptively labeled Separatists, had taken up land immediately south of their own, at New Plymouth. These Pilgrims, as their historian and ofttime governor William Bradford called them, had moved earlier in the century from southeastern England to Leyden. There the Dutch had treated them well, but the Pilgrims' urge to remain English and their fear of a bleak economic future in Holland combined with the imminent resumption of war between the Netherlands and Spain to convince them that America offered a better haven.

From the time of their arrival at Cape Cod in the fall of 1620 the Pilgrims demonstrated that dissenters from the Church of England could live in America much as they pleased—although not without hardships and danger. The Pilgrims in their first year suffered almost as severely as had the settlers of Jamestown, for they encountered similar problems with disease, neighboring Indians, and an unfamiliar climate. The Plymouth settlers did not, however, risk defeating themselves through poor leadership or internal dissension. An agreement (the Mayflower Compact) signed by all heads of households and all free single men, vested authority in elected leaders. And more important, most of the substantial settlers were carrying out a mission on behalf of their brethren who remained for the time being in Holland. Two-thirds of the expedition who boarded their ship, the *Mayflower,* in London, may not have shared the religious convictions of the Separatists, but at least the "strangers" understood and accepted the purpose of the expedition. Under the benign leadership of William Bradford and William Brewster, the little colony at Plymouth slowly recovered from the losses of the first year and by 1630 boasted a population of about 400 fairly prosperous and contented souls. Their example boded well for the nonseparating Puritans of Massachusetts.

In the summer and fall of 1630 a score of ships carried more than 1,000 settlers to Massachusetts Bay. Within a few years English settlement—predominantly Puritan—had spread into the surrounding river valleys and the population had more than quadrupled. Before emigration was curtailed in the early 1640's by the outbreak of civil war in England, more than 20,000 Englishmen made the pilgrimage to New England. For the most part they came in families so that New England, unlike Virginia, rapidly acquired the demographic characteristics of the mother country. In many respects, however, New England was unique. Its relatively high level of education, its religious consensus on major issues if not on particulars, and its widespread prosperity marked the Puritan migration as the most successful effort in the first half of the seventeenth century to colonize the North American mainland.

Before England's civil war, the Interregnum, and the Restoration caused profound changes in the pattern of colonization, Massachusetts had evolved stable forms of civil and religious society. A two-house legislature had emerged by 1644, with a governor and deputy governor elected annually by the freemen. The freemen, in turn, had to be full members of the church, which admitted them in the belief that they were chosen by God for everlasting salvation. Thus the Bay Colony represented—outwardly at least—a true Bible Commonwealth, governed by men who tried to live in accordance with holy injunctions and to make sure that the ungodly did not undermine the experiment. During most of the 1630's and 1640's the governor was John Winthrop, a former attorney and lord of the Manor of Groton, who combined brilliantly the religious fervor of the Puritan movement with administrative talent and common sense. Largely as a result of his moderate leadership, Massachusetts survived internal dissensions and external threats, the former taking its most serious forms in the religious heterodoxies of Roger Williams and Anne Hutchinson, the latter appearing most critically in the efforts of some Englishmen to revoke the Bay Colony's charter.

In order to prevent what they feared would be the subversion of their "errand in the Wilderness," the Puritans banished Williams and Mrs. Hutchinson. They and their followers settled in lands to the south, where in 1637 a separate colony emerged under the awkward name of "Rhode Island and Providence Plantations." In one sense the colony was an offshoot of Massachusetts, for most of its European inhabitants had originally migrated from England to the Bay Colony. They were, however, a dissident element, and their creation of a new colony was more a protest against the Puritan stronghold than an extension of it.

Not so Connecticut, which took root at about the same time as Rhode Island. Most of the early settlers in the Connecticut River valley were staunch Puritans, attracted by the fertile soil of the watershed and the network of streams that probed the interior and led to rich forests. During the mid-1630's several whole communities moved into Connecticut from Massachusetts; later migrants usually moved on to Connecticut after a brief sojourn in the Bay Colony, or sailed directly to Saybrook at the mouth of the river. A few years later, still another colony sprang up to the west of the Connecticut at the mouth of the Quinnipiac River. Under the leadership of Theophilus Eaton and the Reverend John Davenport, New Haven reflected Puritanism in its strictest form. However, New Haven never acquired a clear legal title, and by 1665 it had been absorbed into Connecticut.

Despite their loyalty to England, by the time of the civil war in the 1640's most Puritans who had settled in America were deeply rooted in their new homes. With the possible exception of Rhode Island, then plagued by dissension over political organization and land titles, the New England colonies were remarkably stable and prosperous. Connecticut, New Haven, and Plymouth all had representative governments, broad franchises (compared to England's), bustling trade with Europe and especially with the West Indies. More important, at least to the Puritan spokesmen, was the "New England Way" that had emerged. At bottom, the New England Way was English Independency. In its New World application, however, it evolved more rigid requirements for church membership and a more pervasive influence by the "visible saints," as the members of the New England churches called themselves. Throughout most of the seventeenth century they held a monopoly on the political franchise and on positions of prestige in New England.

One other major effort at settlement in British America succeeded before civil and religious strife descended on the home country. Roman Catholics, no less than Puritans, were unhappy with the Church of England and sought a means of promoting their faith without losing their freedom. In 1632, the Catholic George Calvert, a former secretary of state, received from Charles I a grant of land north of Virginia. George did not live to see his colony of Maryland established, but under the aegis of his eldest son Cecilius and the resident governorship of another son, Leonard, a settlement was established in 1633 at St. Mary's. In addition to the usual problems of creating a new society in the wilderness, from the beginning the colony at Maryland faced boundary disputes with neighboring Virginia and religious conflict between its Roman Catholic settlers and the more numerous Protestants. An Act of Toleration, passed in 1649 by the Maryland legislature at the suggestion of the proprietor, failed to ameliorate the antagonism, and by 1654 the act had been repealed and proscriptions again placed on papists. Partly as a side effect of the turmoil in England, Maryland after 1650 experienced friction between colonists and the proprietor. In addition the colonists suffered from continuing conflicts with Virginia and with Indians, and among themselves over theology and politics.

By 1650 the English wing of the Puritan movement had risen to power at home, decapitated Archbishop Laud and the king, and established a Puritan government under Oliver Cromwell. To some New Englanders it now seemed senseless to remain in the wilderness: the righteous now ruled in mother England and a man could be both patriotic and godly without self-exile. The result was intermittent migration from New England back to the homeland, a brief and curious break in the long history of the settlement of North America. In the end, the restoration of the Stuarts convinced many of the repatriots that New England had not been such a bad place after all, and they again took ship for the New World. But others, such as clergymen Hugh Peter, Thomas Welde, and Nathaniel Eaton, lived out their lives in the country of their birth. Meanwhile Virginians reacted very differently to the events in England. The rise of Puritan power at home appalled a colony that identified closely with the

Church of England and royal prerogative, and not until 1651, two years after the execution of the king, did Governor Berkeley submit to Cromwell's authority—then only in the face of a Parliamentary expedition. Most Virginians weathered the Commonwealth period in quiet anguish, covertly hoping for a revival of the Stuart monarchy. Neighboring Maryland, on the other hand, underwent a minor civil war of her own as Puritan, Catholic, and Anglican factions vied for supremacy.

The Restoration returned stability to most of British America and stirred new interest in settling the remaining unoccupied areas. Between Virginia and Spanish Florida lay several thousand square miles of territory, claimed by both Spain and England. In 1663 Charles II granted to eight proprietors all lands between the 31st and 38th parallels, from "sea to sea." Some settlement had already taken place in the scrub forests along the Virginia border, and the area soon became distinct, in social and ethnic composition as well as topographical features, from a second region of settlement farther south on the Ashley and Cooper rivers. The founding of Charleston in 1680 gave a cosmopolitan center to the latter section which quickly attracted large numbers of immigrants, especially from the West Indies. By the 1690's the area near Albemarle was known as North Carolina, although not until 1712 did it achieve a separate government. South Carolina in the meantime survived Indian wars and local rebellion. In neither region, however, could the proprietors, despite their legal ownership of the colony, resist the efforts of the settlers to break free from their paternalistic and exploitative hold. South Carolina ousted its last proprietary governor in 1719, and in 1729 both it and North Carolina became royal colonies.

A more successful effort to promote settlement under proprietary rule began north of Maryland in 1682. In that year William Penn gained title to a choice tract of land between New Jersey and Maryland, where he attempted a religious haven not unlike those of the Puritans and Catholics before him. Restoration England was more tolerant than Jacobean England, but there were limits, and the Quakers, who believed that God communicated with man through an "inner light" rather than through an established clergy, fell beyond them. By 1682 Penn had established Philadelphia as the nucleus of his "Holy Experiment" and had issued a Frame of Government which offered a tolerant and liberal administration. Quakers from both England and neighboring colonies made up the most influential groups of settlers, but Penn needed income and offered plots to all comers on attractive terms. Soon the fertile lands of the colony were filling with settlers of all faiths from England and the Continent, lured by promotional tracts and recruiting agents who made promises only slightly mixed with hyperbole.

The settlement of Pennsylvania under English auspices illustrates not only the ethnic mix that emerged in British America but as well the international rivalry that accompanied the European conquest of North America. Some of the land under Penn's jurisdiction had once belonged to the Dutch and even earlier to the Swedes. Indeed, Pennsylvania was the former Swedish outpost on the Delaware River, Fort Christina. For a time its settlers had been on friendly terms with the Dutch colony to the north, but in 1655 Governor Peter Stuyvesant of New Netherland took possession of New Sweden in the name of the States General. Although most of the settlers chose to remain where they were, they became politically subordinate to the Dutch colony on the Hudson.

The conquest of New Sweden marked the last act of expansion by the Dutch in North America. Their colonial enterprise had grown slowly from a few trading posts on the upper Hudson until it included footholds in present-day New Jersey, Delaware, and Connecticut. They suffered encroachments by the English on Long Island and the Connecticut Valley in the 1630's and 1640's, and less than ten years after taking over Fort Christina, Governor Stuyvesant had to surrender all the Dutch possessions to the English.

The conquest of New Netherland in 1664 brought England important but largely undeveloped territory. The Dutch had not conceived New Netherland as a haven for religious outcasts or the poor, for the home country had few of either. To enterprising Hollanders, an outpost in North America should serve as part of the Dutch commercial empire; it held vast deposits of fur, fish, timber products, and potentially, food crops. Settlers would be welcome but were not at first deemed essential. They proved scarce, in fact, for Englishmen were reluctant to migrate to New Netherland where they would have to accept Dutch rule, and the patroon system of land distribution offered little to the aspiring yeoman. During the Dutch period, settlement was mostly confined to eastern Long Island, Manhattan, the Hudson Valley, and Albany, for the powerful Iroquois Confederacy of Indian tribes controlled upper New York, thus closing it to colonization. Along the Hudson River a few large patroonships, farmed by tenants, were established but the great age of settlement in New York came late in the eighteenth century, under English rule.

In the process of reassessing their domestic situation after the Restoration of 1660, British leaders also took a long look at the organization of Britain's overseas outposts. For the first time since Englishmen sailed to the New World, a serious attempt was made to integrate and systematize the empire. During the remainder of the Stuart regime and in the years immediately following the Glorious Revolution, the imperial government made important and for the most part well-intentioned efforts to recast British America into a more efficient and governable polity.

Two basic priorities appear to have guided royal policy toward the colonies between 1660 and 1700. First, and most pressing, was the need to make sure that activities of both the colonies and the mother country were coordinated for the benefit of the whole empire. Accordingly, between 1660 and 1696 Parliament passed a series of Navigation Acts designed to keep the carrying trade of the empire in British bottoms. Cargo between England and the colonies had to be in British built, owned, and manned vessels; and an ever lengthening list of "enumerated goods" could be shipped only to another colony or to England, regardless of their ultimate destination. The Crown appointed customs collectors to levy duties in colonial ports and established a complex system of bonds and officials to ensure compliance. In the eighteenth century Parliament passed additional trade restrictions aimed at curbing colonial manufacturing and at tightening further the imperial economic system.

England's second priority after 1660 was the need to end the proliferation of small colonies and to place all of them under royal control or at least under more restrictive charters than those enjoyed by the early proprietors and corporations. In one of his last important acts, Charles II created the Dominion of New England, a federation of the New England colonies, New York, and New Jersey. Such drastic consolidation required the revocation of several royal charters, including the Bay Colony's charter of 1629, but in the interests of imperial efficiency and discipline, this was done. The Dominion was overthrown by the Glorious Revolution, but William and Mary seized the opportunity presented by the confusion to continue, though less drastically, the trend toward tightening royal political control. When Massachusetts, without a charter since 1684, applied for a new one, the colony was not permitted to return to its former condition of semi-independence. The charter of 1691 provided for a royally appointed governor, and at the same time added Maine and Plymouth to the Bay Colony's holdings, thus accomplishing both consolidation and centralization. The proprietary colonies of Pennsylvania and Maryland were also put under royal control, although both regained their original charters after protracted negotiations.

By the end of the seventeenth century, the colonies of North America had advanced dramatically since the first precarious settlements at Quebec and Jamestown. In 1700 there were perhaps 275,000 inhabitants of European and African stock. Many of them were American born, for large families proved an asset rather than a liability in the spacious farmlands of North America, but throughout the colonial period the flow of Europeans and Africans to American shores outnumbered the natural increase. Between 1607 and 1700 perhaps 200,000 Europeans and 25,000 Africans made the long passage to America, most of them to the British colonies. British America attracted mainly Englishmen, although a few Frenchmen,

Italians, Swiss, Germans, Welshmen, and Scots went too. Settlers in New France were almost exclusively French.

Patterns of migration changed dramatically in the eighteenth century. Between 1700 and 1763, Britishers from Scotland, Wales, and Ireland arrived in ever increasing numbers, seeking the peace and prosperity denied them at home. Settlement in North America had now become feasible for the masses, not merely the most hardy and discontent. At the same time, deep distress in several European lands encouraged continental migration. Lured by the propaganda pamphlets and speeches of "Newlanders" or "crimps" sent by American proprietors and land developers, Germans, Scandinavians, Swiss, Belgians, and Frenchmen by the thousands signed terms of indenture in return for passage to America. Some turned back before reaching a port town; others rapidly became disillusioned with the New World and returned to their homelands. Most stayed, however, and they gave to North America a peculiarly international character. Estimates are at best educated guesses, but fragments of evidence suggest that in 1763 about 50 per cent of the population was English, 18 per cent Scotch and Scot-Irish, 18 per cent African, 6 per cent German, 3 per cent Dutch, and the rest French, Spanish, Swedish, and other European stocks. But already intermarriage was making America somewhat of a "melting pot."

Religious variety represented as important a dimension of migration as did the variety of ethnic strains. From the British Isles came Scotch Presbyterians (both from Scotland and from Ulster, Ireland), Anglicans, Puritans (who by the eighteenth century were more frequently known by their organizational preferences as Presbyterians and Congregationalists), Quakers, and a few Baptists and Roman Catholics. From France came some Catholics and many Huguenots. German groups included Lutherans, Moravians, Dunkards, Schwenkfelders, Mennonites, and Amish. Sephardic Jews migrated from Spain and Portugal. Religious variety in turn generated pressure for toleration, a condition reached in most British colonies before 1763. It was an imperfect toleration, however, as the established churches in many areas imposed political limitations and social stigma on other denominations. Roman Catholics in particular continued to suffer from legal restrictions on voting and officeholding; and as late as the 1760's an Anglican missionary was roundly abused by Protestant dissenters in the Carolina backcountry.

Unlike British America, French Canada did not become a refuge for religious dissenters. Strict laws limited emigration from France to those who were theologically and politically orthodox. French Huguenots, most of whom undoubtedly would have remained loyal to their mother country had they been allowed to settle in her colony, were forced to expatriate themselves to the British colonies or remain at home. Furthermore, few

Frenchmen of any religious persuasion were keen on moving to the cold climate and rocky soil of New France. Some, of course, did go, but never enough to make the French part of North America a major place of settlement for the many thousands of Europeans who migrated to the New World. And throughout the colonial period, settlers in New France found a comparatively rigid society, heavy with feudal vestiges and dominated by church and government officials whose decisions were often dictated by the home country.

Population figures reflected the effectiveness of England's colonizing policies and her growing international power. In 1625 there were perhaps 500 settlers in Canada, 200 in New Netherland, and 2,000 in the English colonies of Virginia and Plymouth. By 1650 the figures were 2,000, 5,000, and 100,000 respectively. Fifty years later the Dutch settlements had been absorbed into the English sphere; the inhabitants of the English colonies then totaled about a quarter of a million while New France had perhaps 20,000. At the time of England's conquest of Canada in 1763, the population of British America numbered nearly two and a quarter million, that of New France less than 100,000.

Not all of the disparity in population can be attributed to differences in policy or systems of passage. More important were contrasts in climate and soil and in the verdict of arms. Yet the very fact that Sweden, the Netherlands, and France were unable to expand their original footholds into the choicest regions, and that they eventually lost everything to Great Britain, stems in large part from their failure to attract enough immigrants to offer effective resistance against the relentless British expansion. Throughout the seventeenth and eighteenth centuries larger neighbors swallowed smaller. The Dutch took New Sweden in 1655, England absorbed New Netherland in 1664, and finally took New France and Spanish Florida in 1763. By the eve of the American Revolution only two European powers held territory on the North American mainland, England controlling all lands east of the Mississippi, Spain all to the west; and Spain could hardly be said to have settled her territory. In all of the trans-Mississippi north of the Rio Grande there were only a few hundred residents of Spanish origin, most of them clustered in Catholic missions. Patterns of population would soon dictate the termination of Spanish control as the United States expanded westward in the nineteenth century.

In the century and a half before the American Revolution, the powers of Europe engaged in intermittent warfare on the new continent. Most of the conflicts were offshoots of European wars, but from time to time the colonies themselves initiated clashes. Thus settlement of North America gave rise to new international hostilities at the same time it served as a battle ground for nations already at odds. This proved especially true in the late seventeenth and early eighteenth centuries as settlers from England and Spain in the southern part of the continent and France and England in the northern segment vied for territory, trade, and the allegiance of Indian tribes.

The Indians played an integral part in most intercolonial conflicts, often merging their own feuds with those of their white neighbors. As early as 1608 Samuel de Champlain allied himself with Canadian tribes against the Iroquois of New York; settlers in Virginia, Plymouth, and Connecticut also took part in battles that had begun as intertribal hostilities. Occasionally too there were bloody conflicts within a European colony between its white settlers and one or more tribes (as in Virginia in 1622 and 1644, New Netherland in the 1640's and 1660's, New England in 1675), and there might have been more had not the native population been relatively small, materially unsophisticated, and rent by deep intertribal hostilities. Several tribes did attempt to prevent the intruders from gaining prized land and trade advantages, but for every tribe or faction that stood to lose, another stood to gain—in allies, new trade, or the booty of war. Almost invariably therefore, Indians fought on both sides of New World conflicts. And almost invariably, too, the Indians lost more heavily in numbers and land than did the Europeans whenever the races clashed. That proved true when the conflicts focused clearly on friction between the two ethnic groups—as in New England's King Philip's War of 1675–76—or when ethnic conflict entered the struggle only tangentially, as in Virginia's contemporaneous Bacon's Rebellion.

Not all relations between white men and red involved bloodshed, but too often they did. The efforts to promote peaceful cooperation between the races by men of good will such as the Puritan missionary and linguist John Eliot, the Pennsylvania proprietor William Penn, and Jesuit missionaries like Isaac Jogues in upper New York and Canada often went for naught. But the most lethal of all aspects of interracial contacts was the impact of European diseases, especially smallpox, which struck heavily among the native population. Most of the tribes encountered by white men during the first century and a half of colonization either succumbed to disease or retreated inland. One of the lasting tragedies of European colonization was the inability of diverse racial groups to exploit their mutual needs rather than their potential frictions. In the end the less numerous and less sophisticated society crumbled before the aggressive expansion of history's largest migration.

Throughout the seventeenth and early eighteenth centuries migrants to North America usually sought land along the bays and river valleys where access to the interior and communication with Europe were relatively easy. The sites of earliest settlement were the St. Lawrence, Chesapeake, Delaware, Hudson, Connecticut, and Charles; later Cape Fear and Savannah became secondary centers. It was on the Savannah that Georgia, England's final American colony, was founded in the 1730's. From the valleys colonists pushed relentlessly inland in search of cheaper land and more abundant game. By 1763 the frontier of British settlement had reached the foothills of the Appalachians. In the plantation areas of the south, rivers continued to dominate the pattern of settlement; smaller waterways became choice sites after the larger ones had been preempted. Farther north the colonists soon moved away from river valleys into the hill country, where roads replaced rivers as the main channels of internal communication. After 1763 in the trans-Appalachian region, rivers would again become the principal routes of settlement.

Partly because of the need for mutual protection and assistance, but mostly because of habits deeply ingrained by European experience, settlers in British America clustered in small villages centered on a church building and a common grazing field. Regional patterns varied widely, for the migrants brought different modes of life with them, but the principal concern throughout most of the colonies was to blend the social and political advantages of closely placed homesteads with the economic benefits of privately tilled fields stretching out from the village on all sides. Gradually larger villages emerged along the coast to serve as focal points of trade and communications. New Amsterdam by 1660 contained 2,400 inhabitants and provided a link between the Hudson Valley holdings of the Dutch West India Company and the home country. Boston performed a similar role for Puritan New England. Later in the seventeenth century Philadelphia and Charleston emerged as important centers of population. Farther inland towns like Albany, Springfield, Williamsburg, and Hartford achieved regional importance. Meanwhile Quebec and Montreal in French Canada tied the interior of the upper continent to the St. Lawrence River.

The cities of North America served not only as important centers of trade and communication but also as seedbeds for the emerging culture of the New World. During the seventeenth century American literature and art were imitative. During the eighteenth century, however, they began to show distinctively American characteristics. Whereas the writings of seventeenth-century authors had been largely didactic—histories, sermons, political pamphlets—in the eighteenth century there emerged the first tentative signs of uniquely American expression in belles-lettres, poetry, and even in portraiture. *The American Magazine,* despite its brief career, serves as a sign of native literary gropings, while Peter Harrison's design for Newport's Redwood Library and the portraits of colonial gentlemen by John Singleton Copley and Benjamin West reveal promising beginnings in architecture and art. Still, the civilization of North America before 1763 remained heavily dependent on England. Migrants continued to think of their colonies as outposts of the British Empire. Except for customs and skills brought as cultural baggage from their homelands, little thought was given to artistic expression. The dawn of a creative American culture would have to await the Revolutionary era.

In political, religious, and economic life, too, the settlers of North America leaned heavily on previous experience. Anachronistic ideas and forms were often discarded; new practices frequently emerged to herald the coming of a new society. But the Old World pattern clung tenaciously.

Because the bulk of migrants to British America in the seventeenth century came from England, the political structure of the colonies assumed a strongly English flavor. Each colony, in fact, became a miniature of the mother country: a governor and council represented the executive authority, a two-house legislature (the upper house serving also as council) became a miniature Parliament, while town and country governments closely resembled the local governments of England. Similarly, a sequence of local and colony-wide courts provided judicial systems. But in neither legislative nor judicial matters did the colony have final say; the Privy Council in England reserved the right to disallow acts and decisions of the colonial governments. New France, by contrast, had no representative assembly and no formal institutions of local government. A governor and council, both appointed by the crown, ruled the French territories, aided by an intendant, who had wide fiscal, judicial, and administrative authority, and a bishop, who had broad control over religious matters.

British America also differed from the mother country and from New France in the extent of its political franchise. In most of the English colonies, as in England, an adult free male could vote if he held property above a specified minimum—usually land earning 40 shillings per annum. In America that was not a difficult minimum to meet, and perhaps as many as 75 per cent of adult freemen were eligible to vote for colonial legislators and officials, in two of the colonies even for the governor. In some colonies the franchise was even broader on the local level. There were, however, religious as well as property restrictions in many colonies, discriminating in most cases against non-Protestants but occasionally against radical Protestant sects as well. In America, as in Europe, a clean line between politics and religion was seldom discernible. Disputes between rival sects formed a major part of the social turmoil of the times.

During the seventeenth century religious conflict usually took isolated episodic forms—as for example the persecution of Quakers in New England, discrimination against Puritans in Virginia, and anti-Catholic measures in all colonies. Important as these episodes were to the individuals involved, they were infrequent, for each major religious group had one or more colonies in its control where its devotees could enjoy freedom from persecution, and incidentally make life uncomfortable for other sects. By the eighteenth century, however, the ethnic and denominational exclusiveness of the previous century had largely disappeared; now Anglicans and Presbyterians, and even Jews, rubbed shoulders in the major cities. Much of the old hostility had died out. Some of it was replaced, however, by bitter rivalry within denominations during the Great Awakening of 1730–1760. First in the middle colonies, then in New England and eventually in the South, waves of religious enthusiasm rolled over areas in which the fervor of the seventeenth century had grown stagnant. Before it ended, America's first revival had contributed importantly to the growth of colleges, the spread of egalitarian ideas, and the lessening of clerical influence. At the same time it had fragmented most of the larger denominations—especially the Congregationalists, Presbyterians, Baptists, and Dutch Reformed—into Old and New factions, while the Anglicans saw many of their followers lean toward Methodism. Only the Quakers, centered in Pennsylvania, and the Roman Catholics, predominantly in Canada and Maryland, escaped the divisive effects of the revival.

The Great Awakening served notice that the settlement of North America was no longer simply a transit of civilization from the Old World to the New. To be sure, the revival and its opposite but parallel movement, the Enlightenment, drew heavily on European influences. But the American experience also fed ideas and attitudes back to Europe, where, for example, the writings of the Congregational clergyman Jonathan Edwards received serious attention. Furthermore, the revival had been initiated largely by native Americans—Gilbert Tennent, Samuel Davies, John Davenport, and Edwards; it was only after they had prepared the ground that the greatest preacher of the Awakening, George Whitefield, could journey from England to spellbind vast audiences from Massachusetts to Georgia. Finally, the Awakening, with an important assist from the liberal ideas of the Enlightenment, helped pave the way for the disestablishment of religion. At the beginning of the eighteenth century only Rhode Island, New Jersey, Pennsylvania, and Delaware did not support the dominant church out of public taxes. By the 1760's a move to discontinue such support was under way in most colonies.

Another indication that European colonies in North America were groping toward maturity and perhaps independence could be found in their remarkable economic growth. During the seventeenth century the infant colonies often had struggled with varying success to find feasible modes of production and trade, and the way was marked by frequent commercial failures. But each gradually found economic stability and a measure of prosperity. Canada, despite the meagerness of its population, made healthy profits in furs, fish, and lumber products. New England followed much the same pattern, though it added a lively trade in livestock and rum. The colonies of the middle area specialized in grains and livestock. Maryland and Virginia tied themselves to tobacco, for which the market in Europe was extensive, although chronically depressed. North Carolina excelled in lumber products and livestock, while South Carolina raised large quantities of rice and indigo. Exports from the colonies never exceeded imports in value, largely because the needs of a frontier society for manufactured goods and finished products were insatiable. The colonies' potential for manufacturing increased steadily, but the mercantile laws of England and France sought to prevent the growth of industries that would compete with their own, and investment capital was lacking in the frontier society.

Equally inhibiting to the growth of American industry was the persistent shortage of labor. High wages kept profits low. Paradoxically, the labor shortage also gave rise to two of the most distinctive features of the settlement of North America: indentured servitude and Negro slavery. During the seventeenth century most colonizing companies and their political successors, the provincial governments, lured settlers by granting fifty acres of land to anyone who paid the passage of indigent men, women, and children. The migrant, in return, signed an agreement to serve a stipulated number of years to the investor or his assignee. This system provided much of the manpower of British America's first century. In the eighteenth century the lures were increased by the promise of land to the laborer himself rather than to the investor who paid his passage; the latter made his profit by selling the worker's indenture to an assignee for more than the cost of passage. In addition, indentured servants received on expiration of their terms certain clothes, tools, and sometimes cattle.

Negro slaves made the passage to America under far less favorable conditions. Packed into cramped and unhealthy slave ships and sold on delivery to the highest bidder, the Negroes—some coming directly from Africa, others by way of the West Indies—were an important element in the economy of the southern states by the late seventeenth century. Some of the early blacks were freed after a period of service, and there were scattered attempts to end the forced importation of labor, but the practice persisted, and with it arose a system of permanent, inheritable servitude that would blight North America for generations. By 1763 Negroes, the vast majority of them bound for life, constituted about 15 per cent of the population north of the Rio Grande.

Despite the presence of Negro and Indian minorities isolated from the white culture of British America, there emerged by the mid-eighteenth century a society distinctively American—in fact the degraded role of black men and red men was a mark of that society. Other characteristics, as noted by European observers, were the high level of education, prosperity, widespread political participation, ethnic and religious variety, and the absence of rigid class divisions. All of these features were relative, not absolute, but when taken together and blended with the New World's spacious geography and varied climate, many contemporaries predicted that British America—and perhaps Canada—would one day become independent. But such prospects seemed unlikely so long as the colonies depended on their mother countries for protection from rival empires. Then, primarily as a result of the prolonged contest between European nations for control of North America, that necessity suddenly changed.

From its earliest exploration, North America had served as an international battle ground as well as a land of peaceful settlement. Englishman and Spaniard clashed frequently along the southern borders, while to the north, French and British colonists seemed forever at each other's throats. As early as 1613 an English squadron attacked French posts; in 1689 France and England began a protracted series of battles which developed, in most instances, as offshoots of larger conflicts in Europe. As a result of King William's War (War of the League of Augsburg) from 1689 to 1713, Queen Anne's War (War of the Spanish Succession) from 1702 to 1713, King George's War (War of the Austrian Succession) in the 1740's, and finally the French and Indian War (Seven Years' War), France lost her hold on the mainland of North America. Britain's victories and the Peace of Paris of 1763 relegated French control to two small islands in the mouth of the St. Lawrence River and the Caribbean islands of Guadeloupe and Martinique; Spain, at the same time, ceded Florida to the English. Thus almost two centuries after Sir Humphrey Gilbert's attempts to plant English colonies in the New World, His Britannic Majesty could claim control of the entire North American continent east of the Mississippi, with a population of almost 3 million persons representing nearly every ethnic and religious group in Europe. But the very size and diversity of the mainland colonies, together with the fall of New France, set the stage for the disintegration of England's vast American empire.

For Further Reading

Boorstin, Daniel J., *The Americans: The Colonial Experience.*

Craven, Wesley Frank, *The Colonies in Transition, 1660–1713.*

Morison, Samuel Eliot (ed.), *The Parkman Reader: From the Works of Francis Parkman.*

Pomfret, John, *Founding the American Colonies, 1583–1660.*

Thwaites, Reuben Gold, *France in America, 1497–1763.*

Ver Steeg, Clarence, *The Formative Years, 1607–1763.*

Wright, Louis B., *The Cultural Life of the American Colonies 1607–1763.*

The Enlightenment

59   The Scientific Revolution

Human skills for obtaining food and shelter are not inherited biologically. They are fruits of more or less reliable knowledge concerning how various things in the environment behave. And like the knowledge on which they are based, they are transmitted to succeeding generations through socially instituted processes. Some knowledge of this sort, however primitive it may be, is clearly indispensable for human survival, and no society could exist which lacked it completely. Were every item of such knowledge counted as a scientific achievement, science would be coeval with the human race.

But such an undiscriminating use of the word "science" would be incongruous with the historical meanings of the word, and would, in particular, fail to identify what is distinctive of modern science. Albert Einstein once characterized Western science as made up out of two basic ingredients: deductively organized theories formulating, often in mathematical terms, general relations of dependence between types of events; and systematic experimentation to suggest and test the theories. However, science so understood is a relatively recent achievement. Logical proof and demonstrative mathematics were invented by the ancient Greeks, who were also the first to construct mathematical theories for various classes of phenomena. Moreover, while a tradition of experimental study, especially in the arts and crafts, can be traced back to Greek antiquity and even beyond, the systematic use of controlled experiments to assess the worth of theories did not take place until the late Renaissance.

In any event, an experimentally controlled mathematical science of nature, resembling in essentials the science of our own day, did not become firmly established as a continuing institution in Western society until the seventeenth and eighteenth centuries. The new findings and habits of mind that resulted from scientific inquiry during those years and the century preceding them—especially in astronomy, physics, and biology—marked a major turning point in human history. They undermined the medieval view

CHRONOLOGY

B.C.	4th cent.	Establishment of the two major philosophical schools of Greek antiquity by Plato (427–347 B.C.) and Aristotle (384–322 B.C.)
	3d cent.	Outstanding developments in mathematics, astronomy and physics, among others by Euclid of Alexandria (330–260 B.C.), Aristarchus of Samos (310–230 B.C.), Archimedes of Syracuse (287–212 B.C.), and Apollonius of Perga (c. 220 B.C.)
A.D.	2d cent.	The synthesis of Greek astronomical thought, presented in his *Almagest,* by Claudius Ptolemy of Alexandria (A.D. 127–151)
	8th–12th cents.	Development and spread of Arabic science and philosophy; eventually the transmission of Aristotelian thought to the West by Islamic scholars, in particular by Averroes (1126–1198)
	13th cent.	Assimilation of Aristotelian philosophy into Christian doctrine in the epochal writings of St. Thomas Aquinas (1225–1274)
	1543	Publication of *De Revolutionibus Orbium Coelestium* by Nicholas Copernicus (1473–1543), also of *Concerning the Fabric of the Human Body* by Andrea Vesalius (1514–1564)
	1600	Publication of *Concerning the Magnet* by William Gilbert (1540–1603)
	1603	Founding of the Accademia dei Lincei in Rome
	1605	Publication of *Advancement of Learning* by Francis Bacon (1561–1626)
	1609	Publication of *Astronomia Nova* by Johannes Kepler (1571–1630), containing his statement of the first two laws of planetary motion
	1610	Publication of *Sidereal Messenger* by Galileo Galilei (1564–1642), describing his telescopic observations of the heavens
	1619	Publication of Kepler's *Harmonia Mundi,* an-

nouncing his discovery of the third law of
planetary motion

1628 Publication of *On the Motion of the Heart and
Blood in Animals* by William Harvey (1578–
1657)

1632 Publication of Galileo's *Two Chief Systems of
the World*

1637 Publication of the *Discourse on Method* by René
Descartes (1596–1650)

1638. Publication of Galileo's *Discourses and Demonstrations Concerning Two New Sciences*

1647 Revival of the ancient Epicurean atomic philosophy by Pierre Gassendi (1592–1655)

1657 Founding of the Accademia del Cimento in Florence

1660 Publication of *New Experiments Physico-Me-
chanical Touching the Spring of the Air* by
Robert Boyle (1627–1691)

1662 Founding of the Royal Society of London

1666 Founding of the French Academy of Science

1676 Determination of the finite velocity of light by
the Danish astronomer Olaus Roemer (1644–
1710)

1677 Discovery with the microscope of the existence
of male spermatozoa by Anton van Leeuwenhoek (1632–1723)

1678 A wave theory of light proposed by Christian
Huygens (1629–1695), subsequently developed
systematically in his *Treatise on Light* (1690)

1687 Publication of *Principia Mathematica Philosophiae Naturalis* by Isaac Newton (1642–1727)

1704 Publication of Newton's *Opticks,* some of whose
basic ideas had been communicated to the
Royal Society in 1672

1789 Publication of *Traité Elémentaire de Chimie* by
Antoine Lavoisier (1743–1794)

of the world and man's place in it by making untenable the Aristotelian physics and cosmology on which that view was in large measure based; they challenged entrenched conceptions of human reason and of how the investigation of nature must be conducted; and they produced tools of intellectual and physical analysis that eventually transformed the human scene almost beyond recognition.

These revolutionary changes did not take place suddenly or appear from nowhere. They owed much not only to the scientific achievements of Greek civilizations in antiquity, but also to the contributions of Arabic, late medieval, and early Renaissance thinkers. The great treatises of Greek science were lost to Western students for many centuries, and it seems unlikely that had they been lost permanently natural science anything like our current one would have come into being. However, those treatises did become available to the West gradually, in large measure from Islamic sources. In consequence, the centers of learning that were established in various parts of Europe during the twelfth and thirteenth centuries were heavily influenced by Greco-Arabic views in natural philosophy. But by the close of the fifteenth century the best scholars at these and other universities—men such as Robert Grossetest, John Buridan, and Nicolas Oreseme —were not mere expository commentators on ancient scientific texts, but creative thinkers who anticipated mathematical and physical ideas that came to be employed fruitfully only a century or two later.

The revolution in men's conception of their world occurred most dramatically in astronomy and mechanics. But science includes much more than these disciplines, and the scientific developments that transformed the medieval outlook took place on a broad front. But since it would be impossible in brief space to describe all these developments, which included such important discoveries as the circulation of the blood by William Harvey (1578–1657), the existence of microscopic organisms by Anton van Leeuwenhoek (1632–1723), and the nature of chemical combustion by Antoine Lavoisier (1743–1794), it is with the emergence of modern astronomy and mechanics that the present chapter is mainly concerned.

The expanding commercial economies of the Renaissance generated problems—such as the need for improved methods in navigation or in civil and military engineering—adequate answers to which required a sound theory of motion. Stimulated by these problems, and inspired by the writings of Archimedes that became generally available in the sixteenth century, a number of thinkers sought to construct such a theory. Although it is generally agreed that it was Galileo Galilei (1564–1642) who laid the foundations of the modern science of mechanics, there is also no doubt that he was heavily indebted to the work of these predecessors.

Ptolemy's geocentric theory of the heavens was a scientific achievement of the first magnitude. It illustrated the power of mathematical analysis to account systematically for the bewilderingly complex apparent motions of celestial bodies, though on the assumption that their actual motions must have uniform speeds on circular orbits. The apparent motions of the planets do not conform to this requirement. Relative to the fixed stars, at certain times they seem to move forward rapidly, at other times to stand still, and at still other times to have a retrograde motion. To account for such anomalous planetary motions, Ptolemy introduced a number of in-genious mathematical constructions, among others the notion of epicyclic motion. According to this idea, a planet moves with uniform speed in a circle, but the center of this circle (the epicycle) may in turn be moving uniformly on the circumference of another circle (the deferent circle); thus the apparent oscillatory motion of a planet could be shown to result from a combination of such uniform circular motions.

The central ideas of the Ptolemaic theory were simple enough. How-ever, agreement between those ideas and the known data on celestial motions could be obtained only by introducing many additional but arbi-trary assumptions. For example, the number of epicycles required to ac-count for the data had increased to 79 by the sixteenth century. Yet when Copernicus (1473–1543) developed his alternative theory, according to which the sun was at rest while the earth and the planets revolved around it, no new observations were available to him that challenged the Ptolemaic system but supported the heliocentric theory. Indeed, the observations at his disposal did not confirm some consequences implied by his theory, such as the conclusion that Venus ought to have phases or that there should be apparent shifts in the positions of the fixed stars. What Copernicus found unsatisfactory in the Ptolemaic system was the diversity of its supple-mentary assumptions, and the absence of any general principle which integrated them into a unified whole. He did not doubt that celestial motions must embody a simple, coherent order; and he believed his heliocentric theory to be true, because the logical structure of its ideas seemed to him to reflect that order.

De Revolutionibus Orbium Coelestium was published in 1543, when Copernicus was on his deathbed. For many years the book created little excitement, and was not felt to be a threat to the dominant scientific and religious conceptions of the world. Indeed, it was construed by many in consonance with the interpretation advanced in the preface, which was assumed to have been written by Copernicus though in fact it had been added by Osiander, his editor. On this interpretation, the heliocentric theory was not a new account of the actual physical organization of the heavens, but just a convenient device for simplifying astronomical calculations. Moreover, the Copernican hypothesis of a moving earth appeared to have consequences that were incompatible with what were generally regarded as the empirically well-supported principles of Aristotelian physics. Accordingly, until an alternative physical theory became available, and until fresh observational evidence was obtained confirming the heliocentric theory, men continued to accept the Ptolemaic conception of celestial motions. The Copernican notion that the earth is a moving planet was an important step in disproving the Aristotelian view that celestial and terrestrial objects and processes are utterly different in kind. But the successful undermining of this central thesis of medieval cosmology had to wait upon the work of Galileo, Kepler, and Newton.

The hold of this cosmology on men's minds was seriously weakened by Galileo's exploration of the skies, and by his vigorous defense of the Copernican theory. On learning that by combining two lenses a lensmaker in Holland was able to see remote objects more clearly, Galileo constructed a telescope with which he examined the heavens. His discoveries, published in his *Sidereal Messenger* in 1610, were astounding. He found that the moon's surface was not smooth but mountainous; that in agreement with Copernican theory Venus had phases; that the sun's face was blemished with moving dark spots, with the sun itself having a monthly axial rotation; and that Jupiter had four satellites revolving around it, thus providing a visible illustration of the Copernican conception of the solar system. These findings were a grave challenge to the established belief that unlike the earth celestial bodies suffer no alteration; and they made it difficult to construe the heliocentric theory as nothing more than a set of convenient rules for simplifying astronomical computations.

Moreover, Galileo also tried to construct a theory of mechanics that was fully compatible with, as Aristotelian physics was not, the assumption of a moving earth. In his great *Dialogue on the Two Chief Systems of the World, the Ptolemaic and the Copernican,* published in 1632, he showed that objections to this assumption, which were based on the supposed inconsistency between observed facts and consequences drawn from the assumption, were mistaken, since those consequences depended upon a false theory of motion. In developing the argument in the *Dialogue* Galileo complied formally with the injunction issued by the Church to discuss the heliocentric theory simply as a useful mathematical hypothesis. But his presentation of the issues was overwhelmingly favorable to the Copernican system as a physical theory of celestial motions, and no one was really in doubt about his convictions. He was compelled by the Inquisition to denounce the Copernican theory as heretical, and the *Dialogue* as well as the astronomical writings of Copernicus and Kepler were placed on the Index, where they remained until 1835.

A further major break with traditional assumptions about the constitution of the heavens was made by Johannes Kepler (1571–1630), who combined exceptional mathematical gifts and a meticulous respect for careful observations with a mystical Neoplatonic faith in the existence of a determinate mathematical order in nature. Kepler was an enthusiastic Copernican, in part because the heliocentric theory accorded with his own religious veneration of the sun. He found, however, that the positions of the planets, as observed with unprecedented precision by his one-time master Tycho Brahe (1546–1601), did not agree with their positions as calculated from the Copernican theory; and he devoted several decades of unflagging work to a search for the correct planetary orbits. After years of unsuccessful attempts to devise a combination of circular motions that would generate the observed planetary paths, the idea came to him that perhaps the planets move on ovals rather than on circles. Kepler had mastered the theory of conic sections which Apollonius developed in the third century B.C.; and he therefore tried to fit Brahe's data on the positions of the planet Mars to an elliptical orbit. This attempt eventually proved to be successful, and in 1609 he announced the great discovery known as Kepler's First Law, according to which the planets move on elliptic orbits with the sun at one focus. His Second Law of planetary motion, that the line from the sun to a planet sweeps out equal areas in equal times, was also discovered that year. His Third Law, on the relation between the time of one complete period of a planet and its average distance from the sun, was discovered ten years later.

Thus Kepler's Neoplatonic faith was confirmed. His three laws accounted for the apparent motions of the planets in a much simpler and more accurate manner than did the Copernican system, though at the cost of abandoning the assumption Copernicus (and indeed most of Kepler's own contemporaries) shared with ancient science that only uniform circular motion is appropriate for heavenly bodies. Kepler's labors thus helped forge a method of inquiry into nature that is characteristic of modern science—a method that combines the mathematical analysis of quantitatively specified properties with the scrupulous testing of the analysis by accurate observation.

However, as has already been noted, the conception of the earth as a rotating planet required the creation of a new dynamics (or theory of the conditions of motion) before that assumption could seem compatible with the supposed facts of common experience. The foundations of modern dynamical theory were laid by Galileo, though he built on the work of many previous thinkers, and are contained in his *Mathematical Discourses and Demonstrations Concerning Two New Sciences*—a book he completed after his banishment to a country estate by the Inquisition and published in

1638. The radical difference between Galileo's analysis of motion and Aristotle's is best seen in their accounts of bodies moving with uniform velocity (i.e., with constant speeds along straight lines). In Aristotle's view, a terrestrial body can remain in motion only if some force continues to act on it, but in Galileo's analysis, no force is needed to maintain the uniform velocity of a body. Accordingly, although in his discussion of such motion Galileo did not get the matter entirely right, he was in effect the discoverer of the principle of inertia, which Newton eventually stated as his first law of motion. More generally, Galileo's contributions to mechanics proved that terrestrial motions, and not only celestial ones, embody determinate orders of dependence which can be formulated quantitatively and explored mathematically.

Galileo supplied experimental support for some of his laws of mechanics. But experimental considerations played a subordinate role in his mechanical investigations. It would be an error to suppose that he thought scientific inquiry consists primarily in collecting observational and experimental data, or that laws of nature can be automatically extracted from them. He was convinced, as he once put it, that the characters of the language in which the book of nature is written are triangles, circles, and other mathematical figures; and he believed that to be scientifically significant "sensible experiments" must first be interpreted in terms of those characters. Moreover, he noted that laws hitherto not exemplified in experience may be discovered by deducing them from principles elicited in previous analyses of phenomena. Accordingly, while he apparently did not think that reason unaided by experience can certify the factual truth of a proposed law of nature, the function of experiment for him was to test such proposals or to persuade others of their truth.

Although Galileo envisaged the possibility of an all-embracing mathematical science of nature, the system of mechanics he actually constructed was only a partial realization of this possibility. Thus, his laws of mechanics did not account even for the planetary motions. Much more had to be done before the assumption that nature was to be understood as a mechanical order could completely replace the entrenched teleological accounts of events. One such task was the development of a philosophical basis for interpreting animate as well as inanimate processes in mechanical terms; another was the construction of a science of mechanics whose range of application included both terrestrial and celestial phenomena. The first task was in considerable measure the work of René Descartes (1596–1650), the second of Isaac Newton (1642–1727).

Descartes' philosophical views were closely related to his scientific work, especially to his important contributions to the development of analytic geometry, mechanics, and optics. He believed that fully certain knowledge is obtainable not only in arithmetic and geometry, but also in the study of nature, provided that we adopt in the latter the method of mathematics as he saw it. According to him, the certainty of mathematics flows from the certainty with which we can directly intuit the clear and distinct component ideas involved in those of number and figure, and then demonstrate further properties of extension that are not immediately evident. But he also maintained that the fundamental properties of bodies are their extensive ones, all others (such as weight, hardness, or color) being reducible to modes of extension, so that everything in the world, insofar as it is extended, is a proper subject for mathematical analysis. In consonance with this view, Descartes presented in outline a universal mechanics that attributed all changes in the motions of bodies to impacts between them. Except for God and the human soul, which he assumed to be unextended, all other existing things, whether animate or inanimate, were to be explained in such mechanical terms. For example, according to him the planets revolved around the sun because they were caught up in the vortex motions of a subtle matter pervading all space.

Descartes' formulation of the principle of inertia and his mechanical explanation of the refraction of light were direct sources of Newton's first two laws of motion. Moreover, his ideas on the foundations of science had a profound influence on the general climate of opinion during his own as well as later generations, and stimulated much research into the detailed mechanisms of nature. However, his proposed universal mechanics involved many speculative assumptions which turned out to be mistaken, nor did it provide adequate explanations for many phenomena of motion. It was the theory of mechanics developed with impressive mathematical rigor and detail by Newton in his *Principia Mathematica Philosophiae Naturalis* (published in 1687) that became the foundation and model for physical inquiry for more than two centuries. Newton's monumental achievement gave a unified explanation of the motions of bodies previously regarded as falling into disparate domains of existence; he presented an account of the system of the world so cogently reasoned that it replaced the traditional outlook on the nature of things.

The magnitude of Newton's accomplishments becomes evident from some examples. He completed Galileo's work on the construction of a science of motion by stating the general laws of dynamics; and he adopted the further assumption that every particle of matter attracts every other particle with a gravitational force whose intensity varies in a manner he specified. He then showed that from these assumptions it is possible to deduce improved versions of Galileo's laws concerning the acceleration of bodies falling toward the earth, as well as of Kepler's laws of planetary motion. He thereby produced compelling evidence for the universal scope of the principles of mechanics, and undermined once and for all the medieval belief that terrestrial and celestial motions conform to radically different laws. Those assumptions also enabled Newton to account for the behavior of the tides, the precession of the equinoxes, and much else. Moreover, in addition to the things he proved in the *Principia,* he made momentous contributions to physical optics and mathematics. To be sure, many questions about phenomena of motion were left unanswered, for the *Principia* deals mainly with the mechanics of systems of discrete particles; but the extension of Newtonian mechanics to the study of the behavior of fluids and other continuous media was successfully made in the eighteenth century. It is no wonder that Newton came to be widely regarded as the unequaled genius who discovered the ultimate principles of the world's invariable order.

Newton's views on how scientific inquiry should be conducted carried great weight, and influenced eighteenth-century investigations not only in physics but also in the psychological and social sciences. Like Descartes, he believed that the fundamental principles concerning the forces of nature must be formulated in mathematical terms, so that other laws about the phenomena of nature could then be systematically demonstrated. Unlike Descartes, however, he did not think that those principles can be asserted with self-evident certitude; he maintained that they are inductive conclusions drawn from properly analyzed experiments or observations. Newton articulated the complementary roles of mathematical reasoning and experiment in the study of nature, and so combined important components in the rationalist and empiricist philosophies of knowledge that went into the making of the new science.

As was noted earlier, the changes in astronomy and mechanics we have been recounting were only the most spectacular steps in the emergence of modern science; and during the three centuries we are considering, important advances were also made in other divisions of physics, in chemistry, and in the life sciences. Many of these inquiries were undertaken primarily to satisfy the desire to understand the nature of things, but many resulted in theoretical or experimental discoveries that contributed to the development of commerce, manufacture, and the military arts. Indeed, the chief value of the new science to some minds consisted in the greater control over nature it made possible, a view of the goal of scientific inquiry for which Francis Bacon (1561–1626) was an eloquent advocate long before the new science achieved its major triumphs. Although Bacon's ideas on how such inquiries ought to be conducted were quite inadequate, he saw the need for planned, cooperative effort if science was to yield increased human power over nature. The description in his *New Atlantis* of the House of Solomon, a projected center for experimental research, anticipated and influenced the institutionalization of scientific research as a profession.

It was not until the nineteenth century that the universities became the major centers of scientific research, and many contributors to the scientific revolution (such as Kepler and Descartes) had no university affiliations. On the other hand, by the end of the seventeenth century a number of societies for the experimental study of nature were formed in various countries. These societies provided opportunities for exchanging scientific ideas, engaging in experimental research, and witnessing experimental demonstrations, by making available to their members information and apparatus not generally obtainable otherwise. They frequently began as informal gatherings of experienced investigators of nature, amateurs of science, and even men whose concerns were primarily with the practical uses of scientific discoveries. Some societies had distinguished but relatively short careers, often terminating with the death of their financial patrons. This was the case with the Roman Accademia dei Lincei, which came into existence in 1603 and included Galileo as a member. Its energies declined after Galileo's Copernican views were condemned by the Church, and it came to an end in 1657. The Florentine Accademia del Cimento, founded in 1657 by disciples of Galileo, had an even briefer life, although in the ten years of its existence it made significant contributions to experimental knowledge of a variety of physical phenomena, and helped to improve a number of important instruments, such as the thermometer and barometer.

However, not all of these initially private scientific societies had such an ephemeral existence. Some of them were formally recognized by the state, though not always financially supported by it, and have continued to flourish. For example, the Royal Society of London for Promoting Natural Knowledge, incorporated by royal charter in 1662, grew out of weekly meetings of scientists and other interested persons that began to be held in 1645 in London. Its further growth brought innovations that reflected the increasingly professional and social character of the new science. Thus, although for many years there were no professional requirements for membership in the Society, even during its early years the experimental investigations in its own laboratory were the responsibility of the Curator of Experiments, a scientist of proved competence. Moreover, to keep the Society informed about scientific matters, its permanent secretary carried on a large correspondence with scholars at home and abroad. This task of disseminating scientific knowledge was made easier when the Society began in 1665 to publish its *Philosophical Transactions,* one of the earliest scientific journals. But the Baconian belief that scientific inquiry holds the promise of augmenting human power over nature was not confined to England. Officially approved scientific societies also appeared on the continent of Europe, although unlike the Royal Society they were created and financially supported entirely by the state. For example, professional qualifications for membership in the French Academy of Sciences, as well as the obligations and privileges of its members, were fully spelled out when it was established by Louis XIV in 1666. Many of the research centers that were eventually set up elsewhere in Europe resembled the French Academy in organization as well as in the regular publication of scientific periodicals.

This multiplication of scientific societies testified to a widely felt and growing need for institutional innovations essential for a flourishing science —for effective social mechanisms that would distribute the financial costs of experimental research; make possible the systematic exchange of ideas between investigators in different parts of the world or occupied with related problems; and develop common standards of workmanship in experimental as well as theoretical inquiry. Scientific societies provided such mechanisms, so that by the close of the eighteenth century scientific research as a recognized profession was firmly established.

For Further Reading

Burtt, E. A., *The Metaphysical Foundations of Modern Physical Science*.
Butterfield, Herbert, *The Origins of Modern Science*.
Kuhn, Thomas S., *The Copernican Revolution*.
Wolf, A., *A History of Science, Technology and Philosophy in the 16th and 17th Centuries*.

60   Society and Politics

It is from the new, radical opinions of the eighteenth century in western Europe—the so-called Enlightenment—that the two centuries following derived the notions of Individual Liberty, Political Rights, Equality, Democracy, and (to use the latest twentieth-century slogan) Participation. All these words point to large abstractions, and over the years they have been given varying embodiments in various national traditions and constitutions. To understand their meaning it is necessary to know how they emerged first as ideas, and then to trace their career, singly or in combination, to their present development.

On the continent of Europe, society in the eighteenth century can be

A.D. 1713–1715 Peace of Utrecht; death of Louis XIV; Vanbrugh's Blenheim Palace completed

1721 Bach's Brandenburg Concertos completed; Montesquieu's *Persian Letters*

1724 Fahrenheit's thermometer devised

1734 Voltaire's *Philosophical Letters on the English*

1748 Montesquieu's *Esprit des Lois*

1750 The *Encyclopédie* begun; the Diplomatic Revolution

1752 Franklin shows that lightning is electricity

1756–1763 Seven Years' War

1762 Rousseau's *Social Contract*

1764 Beccaria's *On Crimes and Punishments*

1765–1790 Enlightened despots in Austria, Germany, Spain, Portugal, and France

1776 Adam Smith's *Wealth of Nations;* American Declaration of Independence

1778 Beaumarchais' "private fleet" mustered in aid of rebelling Americans

1783 Beaumarchais' *Marriage of Figaro*

1787–1788 Assembly of Notables; censorship lifted; Sieyès' *What Is the Third Estate?*

1789 Outbreak of revolution in France

described as made up of classes that bore the marks of their medieval creation. But these classes were losing or had lost their functions; some had acquired new functions; others were without any; at the edges of contact there was blurring. In France, England, Italy, the Netherlands, and parts of Germany and Spain, the serfdom of the Middle Ages had largely disappeared and the tillers of the soil formed an actually "free" peasantry, though it was still burdened by old levies and duties, strong reminders of serfdom. Above them was the artisan class, hand workers who were also "free"—except that the old system of guilds retained enough control to be an annoyance and a barrier to self-help. The lower middle class, consisting of small shopkeepers and modest professional men, similarly felt capable but shackled.

And so did the higher bourgeoisie, which theoretically led all commoners, that is, the lowest of the three "estates" or recognized conditions of men. For the middle and upper bourgeoisie actually manned the civil service and often ran the government. The nobles or highest class had largely given up the responsibilities that had once justified their preeminence. Particularly in France, they lived as courtiers in Paris and Versailles; only a few of their number served in war, government, or diplomacy. As for the clergy or second estate, most of their upper ranks were filled as sinecures by aristocratic younger sons, who imitated the conduct of their secular relatives. The pastoral work of the church was done by the poor parish priests, who led the same life as the peasants and small bourgeois to whom they ministered.

Education was in the hands of the clergy, as had been true since Charlemagne, and more especially since the sixteenth century, when the Jesuit order had begun to organize first-rate schools. The university too was church-dominated, regardless of the country or the church established in it. Yet nowhere was the clergy distinguished for great religious fervor; indeed, "enthusiasm" was a common term of reproach akin to "fanaticism." The church was political and orthodox rather than religious.

In France, there was another group, forming neither an estate nor an economic class, but rather a closely held profession: the "nobility of the robe," that is, the judges whose prosperity rested on the fees, fines, and gifts that they were entitled to collect in dealing out justice. Akin to this group in feeling and type of income were the holders of purchasable offices under the crown. Many bourgeois, large or small, invested their fortune— painfully acquired through perhaps two or three generations—in some office that carried a known revenue and prestige and entailed no work: the use of a deputy was lawful and expected.

To picture English society at the same time—say, in the year 1715—it is necessary to modify some details. For example, the English aristocracy and bourgeoisie intermarried a good deal more readily than did the French; and England had a sturdy gentry that lived on the land and thus maintained personal bonds with its own peasantry. Squire Western in *Tom Jones* is a good example of the class; his tastes and manners show that though part of the local ruling class, he is still very close to the soil.

It is sometimes said that another characteristic of English society was the willingness of noble lords to engage in trade, as the French aristocrats would not. This is inexact. Astute French nobles engaged in trade by proxy and thereby kept up their fortunes when the land which they neglected failed them—or they profited from both trade and agriculture when they chose able stewards in each activity. It was not so much fear of degradation as the pleasures of idleness that kept the French nobles out of trade, coupled with the love of prestige, which could be satisfied only by assiduous attendance at court. The court of Versailles was the center of glory for the nation, just as its great "suburb" Paris was the hub of Western civilization for all Europeans of wealth, title, or talent.

What we see with the advantage of hindsight, then, is a society whose formal organization no longer corresponds to its actual functions, ambitions, and needs, while its consciousness dwells on the fact of having attained one of the high moments of perfection in European civilization. Writing of the Age of Louis XIV, who died in 1715, Voltaire a quarter-century later cites it as one of the four great eras of Europe, on a par with fifth-century Athens.

The comparison is apt in one way at least: in each case the high achievement immediately precedes the fall. Many thinkers of the eighteenth century had presentiments of revolution ahead; and it is now obvious that these thinkers themselves contributed to the upheaval, for the most part without desiring it or knowing how they were hastening the day. Their ideas, their hopes, their apprehensions fitted themselves to the unstable structure and helped bring it down. One can argue endlessly about the "causes" of great events and deny or affirm that ideas—"mere ideas"—are among the causes. It is more profitable to think of *conditions*—and among them are states of mind. For history is made by men, that is, more or less conscious beings, who in the mass continue to follow their habits and opinions in great circumstances as in small.

The eighteenth century strikes the observer as an age of opinion, of reasoning, *par excellence,* and it is not surprising that it should be so. The discrepancy between form and function that we have noted was an incitement to thought. The simplest form of critical thought is comparison: *This* does not match *That.* From one such observation by an alert mind a whole theory of society can grow, and the presence of the fact will seem to prove the theory.

Another circumstance helped: the Treaty of Utrecht in 1713 having put an end to half a century of exhausting wars, the public mind was open to new excitements. During this time of peace, flecked only by skirmishes, that mind became truly cosmopolitan. The educated class (now reaching through all three "estates") adopted French as the common language, traveled incessantly, read the same books, enjoyed the same neoclassic and baroque styles of art and dress and life, and adopted the same thought clichés as these fell from the worktables of the numerous and openly admired philosophes. Even in far-off central and eastern Europe, the "correspondence" of the Baron Grimm, stationed in Paris, carried week after week the news, gossip, and revelations of the great Thought-factory.

What is more, these publicists (which is the closest rendering of philosophes) by no means agreed among themselves, nor did the conservative, traditional opposition leave them a clear field for their debates. Important consequences followed from these two facts: first the debates, from vehement to acrimonious, accustomed the public to an incessant battle of ideas about political and social views. It was no longer a religious sect or the followers of a duke who formed a compact phalanx battling with another, but the articulate supporters of doctrines dealing with state and society. Nothing on that scale or of this degree of explicitness had been unleashed in Europe since the Protestant Reformation, which is to say another era of revolution. And now the reading public was larger and the subject matter more transparent. The harsh discord which we find on every page of our large metropolitan dailies and which is the essence of liberal democracy is first manifested in the intellectual politics of the eighteenth century.

The second effect of this debate was to stiffen the resistance of the old order. Diverse parties closed ranks against the new enemy, and since churchmen were the main and best spokesmen for what was old and established, the battle came to be drawn between the Church buttressing the Monarchy on one side and the philosophes on the other. That is why Voltaire, alluding to the Church, made the motto of his party *Ecrasez l'infâme*—tread down the loathsome thing!

What were these new ideas, this new "light," which has given to the eighteenth century and its galaxy of great writers the names Enlightenment, Age of Reason, philosophes, Rationalists? These ideas, in the first place, were *critical* ideas, ideas that did not so much propose goals as raise questions, point to absurd impediments to good sense, ridicule established beliefs and institutions. Pamphlets or treatises or encyclopedia articles were aimed at showing that the accepted beliefs were contrary to experience, that the institutions did not work. Thus in that brief series of two- or three-page articles which Voltaire called a *Portable Dictionary of Philosophy,* he says under the heading "Equality": "What does one dog owe to another or one horse to some other horse? Nothing. No animal depends on his fellow. But man, having received from God the light we call reason, has with it made himself—what? A slave nearly everywhere. . . All men would necessarily be equal if they were free from needs. It is want that subjects one man to another—not that inequality is in itself an evil, but dependency is. It does not matter if someone is called Your Highness and somebody else His Holiness, but it is grievous to slave for the one or the other."

The technique of the passage is characteristic not only of Voltaire's voluminous writings but also of his fellow critics'. First the innocent question that simplifies a whole tangled issue—dog and horse compared to man. Then a quick "solution" of the puzzle why some men are free and powerful, others slaves. Finally, the irony of accepting the status quo: "Highness" and "Holiness" stand for the king and the pope. They must not be attacked. Let us advocate keeping the titles—what does it matter if the names entail no servitude? But obviously, with the servitude removed the titles lose all meaning. Thus, without seeming to do so, you have abolished king and pope.

Voltaire does not really go as far as his words imply. He winds up justifying the present order, though he has implanted the germ of a new one. "Each man," he says, "can within his heart believe himself entirely equal to all other men. This does not mean that the cook of a cardinal should order his master to prepare dinner for him, but the cook can say: 'I am a man like everybody else, born like him in tears just as he will die like me in anguish and be given the same rites. We both perform the same animal functions. If the Turks capture Rome and I become cardinal and my master a cook, I shall take him into my employ.' " Every word of this monologue is reasonable, but while waiting for the Turks to take Rome, the cook must do his duty, or all human society is perverted.

"As for other men, who are not cooks or cardinals . . . but who are annoyed at being treated with contempt or condescension and who see that their lordships have no greater mind, knowledge, or virtue than themselves . . . what should they do? Simply go away."

In that last suggestion lies the grievance of the eighteenth-century intellectual and high bourgeois: he is misused and mistreated. He wants a state in which the inherited pretensions of superiority will be ignored in favor of ability and hard work. Voltaire consents to maintain the trappings (Highness, Holiness), but for two reasons only: first, he knows that equality is an inner feeling which, once aroused, will spread by itself. (One proof is that twenty years later, in *The Marriage of Figaro,* Beaumarchais demonstrated with the aid of comic situations that the nobleman was useless for all the serious business of life and his valet all-important.) And second, Voltaire pays ironic respect to the heads of church and state so that the censorship will let him alone.

Censorship in eighteenth-century France (and elsewhere) was a peculiar institution. It was fitful, inefficient, but always a threat. Voltaire built himself a house at Ferney on the Swiss-French border so that no matter whom he offended he could claim that he belonged to the other jurisdiction. Exile, imprisonment, the burning of condemned books, and other means of persecution and obloquy were always available. Still, there were loopholes, such as pseudonyms, false place names on title pages, and the like. In France, moreover, the censorship was in the hands of noblemen sympathetic to the new ideas. But these friends could not always resist pressures from the church or the court. That is how the great *Encyclopedia* came to be censored, behind the editor's back and with the connivance of his publisher. The *Encyclopedia* nonetheless became an institution in itself, and it is instructive to sketch its history.

A French man of letters, Denis Diderot, was invited in 1747 to bring out, purely as a piece of elevated hackwork, a French edition of the English encyclopedia of Ephraim Chambers. Mulling over the plan, Diderot conceived the idea of using the proposed work to carry the new doctrines, to spread the light. Starting from a plan he devised with the mathematician D'Alembert, and working with undiscourageable energy for years on end, Diderot produced between 1750 and 1772 the tremendous storehouse of fact and propaganda that swept Europe and taught it what "reason," "rights," "authority," "government," "liberty," "equality," and related social principles are or should be. The work was subversive in its tendency, not in its advocacy: *it took for granted* toleration, the march of mind exemplified by science, and the good of the whole people. It was a true encyclopedia, not a collection of pamphlets.

The full title of the work is: *Encyclopédie, ou Dictionnaire raisonné des arts, des sciences et des métiers.* The last of the three subjects is not the least important. Diderot, the son of a cutler, was concerned with artisanship and mechanics, and many of his hours of labor were spent in shops, studying the devices which his engravers illustrated for the encyclopedia. The eleven volumes of plates were in themselves a revolutionary force, for they made public what had previously been kept secret by the guilds, and thus supported the philosophe doctrine that the dissemination of knowledge was the high road to emancipation.

Another aspect of the *Encyclopédie* is worth noting: Diderot could not have written all the articles, even if his time had not been filled with editorial work and political skirmishing. He relied on several scores of contributors, scattered over French-speaking Europe, most of them confirmed adherents of the new ideas. In other words, by the middle decades of the century, the principles of the Enlightenment were already well diffused among the kind of people who think and write. The *Encyclopédie* did spread the attitudes and arguments still further among a population that was steadily becoming more literate, but those volumes so eagerly subscribed for despite their high price did not create the demand for reform, they fed it.

How is this situation to be explained? Through several circumstances. One is that the visible enlightenment of that century had hidden roots in the preceding one. Behind the *Encyclopedia* of 1750, behind Voltaire's guerrilla tactics, behind the incessant appeal to reason, stands Pierre Bayle's *Critical and Historical Dictionary,* written (for safety) in Holland in the 1690's. And Bayle was not alone. All through the seventeenth century we find in France, England, Holland, and Italy writers who in one domain or another of intellect and belief question, criticize, compare, and condemn. The so-called libertines in France include Protestant and Catholic thinkers who doubted orthodoxy. Their influence is paralleled or seconded by: statisticians and political economists like William Petty in England; sensationalist philosophers like Gassendi and Hobbes; English empiricists going back to Bacon: all these prepare the ground for the rational and naturalistic (soon "scientific") view of all human experience. And that view is the intellectual prerequisite to reform. For reform (and later revolution) is the application of systematic thought to society.

When, therefore, the Continental Enlighteners invoke as their heroes and torchbearers Newton and Locke, they are putting forward the great summarizers of a long movement. Newton is the culmination of a hundred years of discovery, as is Locke, whose three years in France and five in Holland made him, consciously or not, a disciple of at least three generations of intellectual "libertines" concentrated in those countries.

This historical reminder is not intended to redistribute credit for initiating the Enlightenment. Men and achievements maintain their old worth. But it is needful to look at origins when one wants to assess justly the different roles played by the first groping explorers and the later proclaimers of the gathered truth.

Nor is this all that needs to be said about origins. The politics and social ferment of the Age of Reason are sure to be misunderstood by anyone who clings to the cliché of "an upsurge of the bourgeoisie against the nobility" as the main explanation of the popularity of the philosophes. The "enlightened" in mid-century Europe numbered as many aristocrats and crowned heads as well-to-do commoners. The "enlightened despots" in Prussia, Austria, Russia, and Portugal are there to show that no "class war" is involved, since the efforts at reform in those countries came from the top—the monarch—and it was the peasantry and hinterland nobility who generally resisted change.

In Austria, for example, the Emperor Joseph was a headlong, "theoretical" man who entertained very "bourgeois" ideas of order and business-like regularity. He saw the need of them after the defeat of his empire at the hands of Frederick the Great, and he recognized that a "modern" people cannot be governed by amateurs chosen as favorites by the head of the state. Nations need a trained bureaucracy, organized in clear orbits like the universe of Newton. Joseph's attempts at reform failed in ten years, but the upheaval they caused was like a foretaste of revolution—everything made new—while the methods he used foreshadowed the police-state totalitarianism of a day even later than that of the French Revolution.

Even the generality about nobles and peasants needs modification. As everybody knows, when Revolution came, its leaders and encouragers numbered many aristocrats and members of the clergy. "Reason" had done its work upon their minds. On the strength of their example it can be said that revolutions are mostly made by their victims. How account for this seeming paradox? One important consideration here is that for more than a century the French aristocracy had been restless under the emasculating power of the monarchy. Deprived of their ancestral role as governors and warriors, the nobles discussed reform. They too were rebels, but what they rebelled for was a restoration of an intermediate power—theirs—between the exclusive and centralizing monarchy and the Third Estate.

They listened, therefore, when the jurist Montesquieu, using England in idealizing fashion, described in his *Spirit of Law* the mixed or balanced constitution, under which a parliament composed of lords and commons legislates, and other bodies divide the executive and the judicial functions. But France had no such institutions to reclaim and modernize for a reform of the monarchy. So the theorists of aristocratic power (seventeenth-century nobles such as Saint-Simon and Boulainvilliers) argued for a return to the Middle Ages, when the king was merely the first among peers.

We have, therefore, the political spectacle of certain eighteenth-century monarchs (Joseph, Frederick the Great) allying themselves with the commoners in an effort to modernize the state; of certain nobles, opposed to the monarchy, adopting bourgeois ideas of reform in hopes of restoring aristocratic power; and of the monarchy resisting them, because aware that centralized government depends not on abstract ideas but on habitual consent. Meanwhile the peasantry, most conservative of classes, begins to overhear remarks that suggest the possibility of emancipation—from ancient dues, from exclusive taxation, from inability to enrich themselves through buying the land engrossed by the Church. But so far the peasantry remains unenlightened, unwilling to change its habits and beliefs, suspicious of whatever comes from above, afraid of the confusion inherent in reform.

Yet orderly patterns were not wanting. In the second half of the eighteenth century, several of the French law courts (*parlements*), manned by an enlightened nobility of the robe, made attempts at systematic change. The famous *parlement Maupeou* in Paris tried to play the role of benevolent despot; the *parlement* of Provence in the 1760's sketched out most of the solid reforms achieved in the first years of the Revolution of 1789. Shortly before that revolution, men such as Turgot and groups such as the Assembly of Notables struggled with the mounting difficulties and with one another, in a fog of misunderstanding and futility. Group interest *does* come into play in these various abortive attempts, but the prospect is not that of an oncoming war between an oppressed majority and a frivolous ruling class drinking champagne while the people starve. That is but the Hollywood version of the complicated story. The reality is one of confusion about goals and suspicion about motives, in a society full of intelligent perceptions, yet divided between those who saw hopeless disorder in the present and those who saw endless disorder in the future if the edifice was tampered with. As in all tragedies, both sides were right.

At this point it should be clear why the reformers could unite under the intellectual leadership of the philosophes: their doctrine was abstract, even though illustrated by concrete examples. With the abstractions we are familiar today, since many of them have with much travail been turned into working devices. But it is necessary to rehearse these principles in order to appreciate how easy, natural, rational they seemed to those who first heard them expounded.

What they saw was this: monarchy, the class system, and the established church forming a conglomerate of institutions and laws held together only by the force of habit and the self-interest of groups. The "constitution" was a historical product of long growth and relatively infrequent revision. Although France and Prussia had rather recently invented and put into practice the essentials of modern bureaucracy, they could only apply these rules of efficiency to a society that was the very antithesis of order and system. It was like trying to run a large corporation from an old castle built at different times on different levels linked by meandering corridors.

The appeal of the Enlightenment was that it undercut this "absurd" clutter by proposing the great simplicities. Just as the philosophes mocked at the Ptolemaic scheme's trying to cope with celestial movements by hooking orbits upon orbits, and said, "Follow Newton instead and all is clear," so in human affairs they said: "Begin with Locke and all follows." Locke (they thought) begins with the human mind as a blank tablet. Experience in the form of sensations imprints whatever knowledge the mind acquires. Hence the teaching of superstitions, pious falsehoods, incredible myths, and social prejudices turns men into the wicked and suffering creatures that we see. Teach the simple truth as science has begun to disclose it and you will make men free, equal, and happy. That simple truth derives from axioms within the mental reach of anyone—just listen! And Voltaire would proceed with his little lesson on equality, the dog and the horse, the cardinal and the cook. Or Diderot or Helvétius or Condillac or D'Alembert or Quesnay—all preeminent in the art of enlightening—would take up a similar and supplementary demonstration. Altogether it amounted to a geometry of man and society.

From sensation furnishing the mind, one went on to a consideration of Man—born free, obviously, then giving up a part of his freedom for the advantage of mutual protection in society; therefore retaining a number of inalienable rights: security for life and property; entitled to a voice in government and to the tolerance of his beliefs; deserving of education; permitted to speak and print his opinions unhindered; subjected to laws, but guaranteed that they will be the same for all and administered without regard to persons. Reason, in short, dictated the Bill of Rights very much as we know it in the United States Constitution and based it on what seemed like a scientific study of the human condition. Such principles must inevitably bring about the release from that servitude which Voltaire noted as prevailing all over the earth. For like the propositions of geometry which they resembled, these principles could not be contradicted by anyone capable of reasoning at all.

To be sure, the practical steps toward making these relationships actual among men might be difficult. There was so much hardened prejudice in every institution, so many follies to eradicate, faith in omnipotent churches and kings being the chief ones. And then vested interests stood in the way: there were two hundred different sets of custom law in France, two kinds of provinces, and three or four layers of local government. Sinecures were bought and sold; nearly the whole weight of taxation bore on the peasant. Inevitably, those exempt or privileged thanks to such inequities clung to their private advantage. And the upshot of such a crazy-quilt constitution was that while the country was growing more prosperous, the government was going bankrupt, and while its bourgeois bureaucracy was perfecting its methods, old rights and powers hampered every action.

It is here that the bourgeois outlook, the tradesman's eye for profit and loss, his need of clear and simple accounting—in a word, his business sense—gave impetus to the rationalist theory of society. In one of its manifestations, this theory proposed the first form of free trade and the single tax. The school of thinkers known as Physiocrats and of which

Quesnay, Turgot, and Du Pont de Nemours were the chief members, argued very simply (as always) that only those who worked on the land, farmers and miners, produced wealth. Everybody else lived off their output. It was absurd, therefore, to tax the successive steps of manufacture and distribution, or to tamper with the natural flow of goods, especially within one country. To do so only raised prices and impoverished everybody. As for international trade, the old export bounties and import duties, like the list of articles prohibited from coming or going—all these rules known collectively as the mercantilist system—were an anachronism born of the needs of war and the selfishness of merchant groups. Free trade would mean peace as well as the return of economics to the wise governance of nature itself.

Here were practical proposals indeed, proposals which it took the studious amplifications and modifications of Adam Smith in *The Wealth of Nations* (1776) to make first palatable, then popular, in the early nineteenth century.

A similar evolution was needed for the reform of the law, particularly the criminal law, upon which obviously the liberty of the citizen as well as his equality and dignity depend. The rousing call to reform in this domain was the famous work of Beccaria *On Crimes and Punishments*. Everything about this essay (it covers fewer than 100 small pages) is symptomatic of the age that gave it birth. The author was a timid Italian nobleman of twenty-six, still under the thumb of an authoritarian father, whom he resented to the point of referring to this oppression in this very essay. In Milan, Beccaria formed with a few other young intellectuals an "academy of fists" devoted to waging war on economic and official misgovernment and religious bigotry. They published a periodical and discussed likely topics for articles. With these friends Beccaria was no longer timid but impassioned and articulate; he often worked himself into spasms of indignation when the subject of judicial torture came up. He knew in fact little or nothing about the law and its administration. But his friends (mainly Pietro Verri) coaxed and coached him until he had set down in continuous, and sometimes incoherent, fashion his eloquent protest against the ill adjustment of punishment to crime.

The work was published in 1764, anonymously to avoid censorship and its penalties. But the authorities seemed indifferent, and within two years the "treatise" had aroused all Europe. Beccaria was invited to Paris, but when there fled the tributes, from shyness and inability to converse. The book remained a force: it helped Blackstone in his Commentaries and spurred Jeremy Bentham to take up arms against the English penal code in the early nineteenth century.

That thorough reform of all penal codes was urgent appeared in the eloquent but fruitless appeals by Voltaire in the Calas and La Barre cases, both travesties of justice and memorials to an age of barbarous punishments. In the American colonies, John Adams, then defending the British soldiers accused in the Boston massacre, was inspired by Beccaria's words to see himself as also "defending the rights of man and unconquerable truth."

It was Beccaria's concluding maxim that struck the chord of reason in all these enlightened minds: "In order that punishment not be invariably an act of violence committed by one or many against a citizen, it must be essentially public, prompt, necessary, the least possible in the given circumstances, proportionate to the crime, and in accordance with the law." To the modern mind this seems a commonplace. But when new it had to be argued. What is the reason behind this reasonableness? Beccaria makes it explicit, and thereby puts into words the most powerful principle of modern times, the notion namely that the ultimate criterion of lawmaking must be "the greatest happiness to be shared by the greatest number." This idea of course governs not merely law reform; it underlies as well all the other abstractions of the Enlightenment. One might sum up its goal as *happiness spread wide*. Or, as the American Declaration of Independence says in its preamble, the guaranty to mankind of life, liberty, and the pursuit of happiness. It is easy to understand why, for this purpose, men must be considered equal, not to say identical; and why also the meanings of law, government, society, and happiness itself must become secular and practical, not to say materialistic. For what makes men equal is their common needs, practical and material.

From these roots the liberal tradition, now so widely and variously attacked, has grown and borne fruit. One complaint today is that it has not been able to transcend the utilitarianism just mentioned; its political arithmetic cannot rise, apparently, above this common denominator and its material base. Yet during that first "century of reason," there was one man, a member of the enlightened phalanx, who, because he saw man's needs as going beyond the utilities, came to occupy a third position, equidistant from the orthodox and the philosophes. That man was Jean Jacques Rousseau. His genius no one could dispute from the start, and despite many vicissitudes he wound up as the most influential thinker of his time, eclipsing Voltaire with the young generation that was to witness the upheaval of 1789.

What Rousseau provided for his contemporaries was the satisfaction which all the geometrical reasoning, all the appeals to practicality, denied or overlooked. Like their kind in all ages, the men and women of the eighteenth century did not live by reason alone—they had feelings, passions, fears, and prejudices. Not even the philosophes could exist as mere intellects stuffed with axioms. This is evident (if proof were needed) in the readiness with which the best minds of the period were moved to tears and tenderness by the simplest appeal to sentiment—to friendship, parenthood, self-sacrifice, heroism: these words sufficed by themselves to agitate their hearts. Whether the stimulus was found in the novels of Samuel Richardson or in the plays of Denis Diderot and other writers of "bourgeois drama," the rationalist responded like a virtuous, palpitating soul, regardless of his behavior or belief in other situations.

Rousseau's singular art and wisdom was to connect this fount of feeling, the inner reality of living man, with the critical doctrines of reason and reform. When he broke with the philosophes he gave up also the elegant life of the salons—he had never thought as highly of "civilization" as they did, and he sought a mode of life in which honesty, sincerity, hard work, and the absence of personal display would establish *in fact* that equality, that simplicity, that virtue advocated *in words* by his former companions in social philosophy.

As a poor and vagrant orphan from Geneva, Rousseau had observed European society from all levels and all sides. He had been a novice in a religious house and a footman waiting at the tables of the great; he had been the secretary of an ambassador in Venice; the kept protégé of a provincial bluestocking and the lover of titled Parisian ladies; a successful composer feted at the opera, the famed winner of a literary prize, the friend of the encyclopedists, and a common man living in a dingy quarter by copying music. He was a botanist, a musician, a mathematician, and a master of language; and by and large he prided himself on none of these roles and experiences. He was solely interested in finding out what this "Man" was whom the entire age kept defining in absolute propositions and trying to improve out of all recognition.

For his part, Rousseau began by representing Man as he might be imagined in his primitive simplicity, before the advent of property and of law, and again as he saw him in his sophisticated depravity, ornamented with the arts and sciences. Then Rousseau depicted man as fathered by the child, that is, man made or corrupted by his education. Next Rousseau provided the youth with a mate and subjected him to the storms and temptations of love. In the course of this narrative (*The New Héloïse,* a novel), Rousseau showed what a decent life might be: gambling and drunkenness replaced by outdoor sports, mothers nursing their own children and men wearing their own hair; work and modest sociability in place of finery, affectation, intrigue, and the competition over symbols of status.

After this, Rousseau dealt with the theory of government, both in the well-known *Social Contract* of 1762 and in the equally important practical works on the governments of Poland and of Corsica. Finally, that which sealed his reputation with the future revolutionists, Rousseau wrote his *Confessions,* in which he tried to show what the stuff of life is, how it feels, and how thought and emotion form but a single energy that eludes all abstract formulas. Though Rousseau frequently argued with the skill and the weapons of a geometrician, his whole work was an assault on the abstractions of the age, which he considered too facile and hence surely false.

To this day Rousseau's intention and philosophy are matters of debate. Because he gave his century the emotional outlet that it lacked and was himself taken up by diverse parties, the clichés about his views stand in the way of what he plainly said. For example, he did not say "Back to Nature!" nor did he want men to return to innocent (or noble) savagery. He thought "nature" was difficult to discover and was a goal to be attained by effort. It lay ahead, not in the past. Much of what we do today, how we dress and talk and act in our present democratic love of the simple and casual, is Rousseau in action. Likewise our feeling for nature, our appetite for greenery and holidays in the woods, our need of an antidote to the city—all are emotions prophetically given worth and form for the first time in Rousseau's work.

Much space and many examples would be required to expound the system of ideas that made Rousseau an original and far-reaching influence. Let it be said dogmatically here that his political conclusions led him to advocate representative democracy as the best device for ensuring at once individual rights and the sovereignty of the people. What is of equal importance, he saw that *Man* is a convenient fiction: the earth is populated by *men*—different, only partly rational, and moved by habit and history as much as by articulate ends. Moreover, man is inescapably religious and lives by the moral sense as much as by calculations of utility and material advantage.

It was these beliefs of Rousseau's that alienated the philosophes: they saw their handiwork being undone by a sophist of incredible popularity. He seemed to be the savior of the European soul against *their* pernicious aridity: the reversal was intolerable—and unjust. For Voltaire and Diderot and their friends were by no means unaware of human irrationality—look at *Candide,* look at Diderot's wonderful dialogues about sex and dreams and the mystery of life. But these perceptions, thought the philosophe party, must be kept out of the limelight for the good of the cause.

Unquestionably Rousseau's works and fame were confusing the great issues and even the battle lines. Some enemies of light, monarchist and clerical writers, were admitting that although a confessed heretic, Rousseau had in him the root of morality and faith. Others felt that he understood human beings and the historical nature of institutions better than the Voltairian cynics and atheists with whom he had once consorted. This acknowledgment on the part of *l'infâme* was enough to confirm the enlightened in feeling that they had been betrayed by their most gifted recruit.

The significance of this conflict goes far beyond any party quarrel. It is fundamental to an understanding of the whole modern age. The nineteenth and twentieth centuries were to witness the working out of the reformist ideas of the Enlightenment, from the birth of the liberal, parliamentary world of yesterday to the exacerbated populism of today, democratic or totalitarian. And during this same era the turmoil of that birth, the instability of those politics, tended to show that the abstract, regular, and utilitarian model of society does not suit the wayward moral being that man is, diverse and irrational as he evidently remains in his impulses, traditions, and faiths.

For Further Reading

Voltaire, *The Man with Forty Shillings*.
Fielding, *Joseph Andrews*.
Diderot, *Rameau's Nephew* (J. Barzun trans.).
Montesquieu, *Persian Letters*.
Rousseau, *On the Government of Poland*.
Beccaria, *On Crimes and Punishments*.

61   Science versus Theology

The history of Western thought since the eighteenth century has not borne out the familiar maxim that "a little science takes one away from God, but a great deal of science brings one back to Him." By the end of the nineteenth century, Friedrich Nietzsche felt entitled to state as a matter of observation that "God is dead"; and in the middle of the twentieth the same cry was repeated by many—characteristically—as if it were a new discovery. To retrace the decline and fall of theology and the rise of the secular outlook in which science and naturalistic presuppositions enjoy unbounded confidence is to explain the intellectual concerns and the moral anguish of ten generations. In this chapter the opening phase and main features of that decline will be retold.

Science and theology are rivals, because each professes to supply

CHRONOLOGY

A.D.

1687	Newton's *Principia Mathematica*
1690	John Locke's *Essay Concerning Human Understanding*
1697	Bayle's *Dictionnaire historique et critique*
1704	Death of John Locke
1713	The bull *Unigenitus* and the war against the Jesuits
1733–1734	Pope's *Essay on Man*
1736	Butler's *Analogy of Religion*
1741	Voltaire's *Mahomet* (on toleration) praised and rewarded by the pope
1747	La Mettrie's *Man a Machine*
1748	Hume's *Essay on Miracles;* Treaty of Aix-la-Chapelle; Montesquieu's *Esprit des Lois*
1750 ff.	Buffon's *Natural History* (evolutionary theory)
1750–1772	Diderot and D'Alembert's *Encyclopédie*
1751	Voltaire's *Age of Louis XIV*
1756	Voltaire's *Essay on the Customs and Manners of Nations*
1760 ff.	*Dictionnaire de Trévoux* (Jesuit response to *Encyclopédie*)
1762	Rousseau's "Confession of Faith of a Priest from Savoy"
1764–1765	Voltaire's *Candide* and *Dictionnaire philosophique portatif*
1778	Mesmer and mesmerism; death of Rousseau
1779	Hume's *Dialogues on Natural Religion* (posthumous)

mankind with a comprehensive account of the universe, including man and his deepest concerns. It is true that scientists often disclaim this large intention and assert that natural science (or, as it was called until about 1850, natural philosophy) deals only with inanimate things and is silent about the realm of consciousness which is man's. But this dividing line is not in fact respected. A science of living things and a science of man are goals actively pursued by the scientific mind from its earliest impulse toward universal knowledge; and so soon as "natural philosophy" boasts that its method holds a monopoly of tested, "objective" truth, it is inevitable that every great scientific advance should bring with it direct applications to man and society. At the least, "implications are drawn" in domains other than that of brute matter, which means supplanting the existing theological or philosophical teachings.

This is precisely what happened on a large scale under the impact of Newton's great synthesis of physics, optics, astronomy, and mathematics. As the fame of his *Principia Mathematica* (1687) spread throughout Europe and its leading ideas were popularized in numberless forms (there was even a French "Newton for Ladies"), the thoughtful, the curious, the ambitious, the anticlerical began to find in the new institution that we call modern science reasons for disputing or losing faith in Christendom's traditional and orthodox beliefs.

This is not to say that men of science and their admirers ceased to believe in God and the Bible. Newton himself was religious to the point of superstition; at the end of his days he spent more time studying and writing about the prophecies in the Book of Daniel than he did in charting the heavens. And to the present day it has been possible for some great scientists to retain a fervent faith in God and the Christian ethic. But that possibility depends on the willingness or the power to keep separate in the mind two sets of axioms and conclusions about reality.

What did Newton's scientific study of reality disclose to the men of the eighteenth century? It disclosed a machine. The system indeed is commonly known as "the Newtonian world machine." The meaning is obvious: by the law of gravitation every particle of matter attracts every other particle with a force proportional to the product of their masses and inversely proportional to the square of the distance between them. This force is the motor that keeps the machine going, for of itself matter is inert and motionless. The parts of the machine—and nothing exists outside it but space—consist of various aggregates of matter, from stones to stars. Their position, orbits, and destiny are determined inescapably by the nature of matter and the laws of motion, which in turn permit the mathematical expression of any given relationship. With the categories of matter, space, time, and motion anything perceptible to the senses as a body (or inferred, technically speaking, as "extension") can be fully "placed" and accounted for.

This full accounting obviously leaves no room for God or even mind. It is the distinguishing mark of early modern science that it excludes the observer—and of course the deity. For one thing the observer (or man's mind) is a variable, "subjective" element which cannot be taken as the cause of any event or brought into observation and calculation without rendering them uncertain. Since the world machine works by itself, the observer is necessarily outside. And so, for the same reason, is God. It may be that he has created matter and decreed its laws—indeed that would seem a likely explanation. But once his task has been accomplished, he by definition (and deference to Newton) stands outside his creation. Newton apparently believed that space was the *sensorium* of God, but the words have no imaginable meaning or much moral force. Unless God is inside the universe, steadily controlling its operation and using it as the theater of man's moral pilgrimage, there is no Providence. Revelation becomes an illusion, the law of the Prophets and the grace of the Gospels appear as man-made things. As for recorded miracles, they are but superstition. The very scheme of science, the logic of mathematics, rules out miracles from the outset.

Going through such reflections as these, the men of the late seventeenth and early eighteenth centuries arrived at two formulations to take care of their inherited beliefs at the same time as their glorious new science. The first came to be known by the suggestive name of "natural religion." Thinkers such as John Locke, Archbishop Tillotson, and Samuel Clarke took as their point of departure the unity of Reason and Truth. If reason leads to the truth of science, it leads to some matching truth of religion; there can be no different set of axioms and conclusions applicable to God and faith. Natural religion therefore denies and stands over against revealed religion. Far from being the fruit of an intuition or the outlet for an inborn emotion, religion in this new guise is a deductive science like mathematics. Natural religion forbids atheism and, just as compelling as natural science, commands the acceptance of every man able to use his reason. Its propositions are few and simple: since the universe is but a machine working according to law, it could not create itself. The beautifully made watch implies the watchmaker. So we infer a creator, who is God. His intellect must have been remarkably like Newton's, with the power of physical creation added. This is the point of Pope's intended epitaph for Newton:

> Nature and Nature's laws lay hid in night:
> God said, Let Newton be, and all was Light.

To which Warburton, Bishop of Gloucester and a man who considered himself devout, added the remark that "It had been better: 'and there was Light'—as more comfortable to the *fact* and to the *allusion*. . . ." By these words he was making Newton, Pope, and himself coauthors of a new Book of Genesis. The pride of the Age of Reason dismisses—most politely —the old Book of Genesis for its inadequate physics.

Natural religion, then, posits a God, not of love, wrath, or justice, but of supreme artisanship. He was in fact variously known to the enlightened minds of the eighteenth century as the "Great Architect," the "Divine Watchmaker" (or Artificer), the "Supreme Mechanic"—no longer *our* Maker, but the maker of the stuff dealt with in the *Principia*.

From this tremendous reduction of the complex, encrusted, mysterious Christian theology to a single, simple Entity with Technological Leanings, the believers in natural religion came to be called Deists, that is, God-ists, partisans of a streamlined God who was the first practitioner of automation.

At the same time, the rational mind of the age retained a conviction that morality was both natural and necessary. But lacking a God who could open his mind to Moses and Jesus, how could this morality be made solid and universal? The Deists replied: "Look within yourselves and you will find conscience, the moral sense, which tells you about right and wrong and which you disregard at the cost of remorse." This inner light is universal: by it all men are brothers. Civilized society, moreover, relies on this moral sense to sustain peace and fair dealing, which can never be ensured by force or threats alone. As in Newton, reason unites with utility and the result is beautiful to behold.

But how did conscience come to be rooted in man? The answer is, once again, God; the moral sense is another of his discreet creations. The argument here is not from any supposedly mechanical nature of right and wrong, for temptation does not attract the sinner with a force inversely proportional to the square of the distance; it is much less predictable. No: the argument is from universality, which is the very mark and proof of reason. Locke, Voltaire, and their fellow Deists were sure that all religions rest on a common, identical moral sense, and that the differences among creeds are merely superstitious and irrelevant accretions—the inventions of crafty priests to secure themselves power and riches by deceiving the people and keeping them ignorant.

A third and final proposition of the new theology is also self-evident. The moral conscience which is implanted by God works by approving or disapproving a man's acts, and so does God. He holds in reserve ultimate rewards and punishments. Men's souls must therefore survive death to receive their deserts. How this occurs is not amenable to observation and is therefore not explained. On earth morality is strengthened by the expectation of this deduced but unprovable judgment, and at this point the scheme begins somewhat to resemble a *moral* machine akin to Nature's material one.

A moment's thought will show that Deism amounts to a compromise position. It embraces science without abandoning God. But side by side with Deism in the eighteenth century stood, on the one hand, the ranks of the orthodox and, on the other, the growing numbers of materialists and atheists. What could the orthodox theologians argue against the powerful certainty of Newtonian physics and mathematics? In Catholic countries, the principal argument was drawn from the manifest authority of the Roman Church: so great, prosperous, and long-lived an institution could not have been founded on an imposture. Millions of believers strengthened the testimony of the wise and the saintly all the way back to the Gospels and the Old Testament. The continuity and coherence of the tradition, coupled with its power to convince and coerce, proved that Deism was but one of many frivolous heresies, the speculation of a few abstract minds, without true moral feeling or divine grace, and certainly without wide popular support. If universal experience was to be appealed to and serve as proof, it should be the universal fact that unsophisticated men everywhere believed in the direct governance of the world by God, in the ordained function of the church as mediator between man and God, and in the reality of miracles. The Jesuit order, founded in the sixteenth century, and in most countries the controlling force in education, was also the leader in the polemic which went on during most of the century with the Deists and other religious radicals. It was the Jesuit writers who denounced the works of Voltaire and the French *Encyclopedia* and who called down censorship or exile on others whom they suspected of atheism.

But entrenched as was the old orthodoxy, the spread of "light" was swift, and wherever the natural philosophers had well-placed partisans even kings were dazzled. Thanks to the influence of the ruling favorite Pombal, the Jesuits were expelled from Portugal and its colonies in 1759. (Did the catastrophic Lisbon earthquake of 1755 discredit Providence? Many said so throughout Europe. Voltaire wrote a poem about it.) In France and Spain the Jesuits were suppressed in 1767. Aranda in Spain also persuaded Charles III to abolish the Inquisition. Frederick the Great in Prussia and Joseph II in Austria decreed religious toleration; in England and elsewhere trials for witchcraft declined or disappeared; and finally in 1773, the enlightened pope whom even Voltaire loved and praised, Benedict XIV, abolished the Jesuit order altogether. To be sure, there were behind these moves political reasons added to the philosophical, but the tolerance that led to suppression marks all the same the progress of unbelief.

Meanwhile in Protestant England, Christian theology was defended on the same rational ground as that on which it was attacked. The appeal was to logic in the first place, not authority or ancientness. The boldest attempt along this high line was that made by Joseph Butler in *The Analogy of Religion, Natural and Revealed, to the Constitution and Course of Nature,* which he published in 1736 and which earned him the Bishopric of Bristol the following year. The phrase "Butler's *Analogy*" became by itself the magic formula by which for seventy-five years believers who never read the book invoked what they took to be a conclusive refutation of Deism. Later, orthodox faith was transferred to a more recent work, "Paley's *Evidences*" (*of Christianity*).

In the span between them the conservative position relied on the statement that it was just as difficult to ground the truth of natural religion in pure reason as it was to accept revealed religion without reason. How could reason alone bring man to believe in the immortality of the soul, rewards and punishments, and the sway of absolute moral law under God? To pretend to demonstrate these as true was only to borrow fragments of the Christian tradition and cut them off from their original source and warrant, revelation. Butler points out that far from natural reason being able to establish the universality of the moral law, history shows that the pagans "fared ill" in the light of nature alone; their minds struggled with a chaos of contradictory precepts. Further, if we examine the modern natural religion we find revealed religion to be a "republication of it in all its purity," but with divine guarantees and definite commandments added. In other words, the Christian tradition is a unity, to be taken or left as a whole.

To the arguments put forward by such writers as John Toland, a disciple of Locke's, or even by churchmen such as Tillotson, that only those parts of Christianity that passed the test of reason deserved belief, Bishop Butler answered that the course of nature, the scene of God's moral order (which the Deists accepted), was just as mysterious and hard to make out as anything in revelation; or (again in other words) that religion was the domain of faith, not demonstration. In either view, the universe remains beyond man's comprehension, which is why man has and needs a religion.

At this point a thinking man is in effect given the choice whether he will choose religion or Deism as a matter of taste, and it is evident that Butler's argument for religion may well push the resolute mind to abandon both revealed and natural religion, to find ultimate reason in atheism and materialism. This was the path followed by many eighteenth-century thinkers. They became materialists and atheists from logic, with or without the addition of lip service to Christian doctrine for the sake of avoiding trouble with the authorities.

Such was the position reached by the Scottish historian and philosopher David Hume a dozen years after Butler's *Analogy*. In his *Essay on Miracles* of 1748, Hume shows how the test of reason serves a consistent mind. Believing in the Newtonian system (for how can mathematics lie?), disbelieving, therefore, in the possibility of supernatural events, what Hume must meet head on is the testimony of the intelligent and honest minds on whose report miracles are believed. To do so, Hume turns the tables on these witnesses with the all-embracing formula that "no testimony is sufficient to establish a miracle, unless the testimony be of such a kind that its falsehood would be more miraculous than the fact which it endeavors to establish."

The catch lies in the phrase "more miraculous," for surely there can be no degrees in miraculousness. The slightest deviation from the order of nature is just as supernatural as the largest. What Hume means, then, is that any apparent deviation from the natural should at once be investigated by the method of science in order to be disproved—or else fitted into the system of science, instead of being taken as the miraculous support of a "subjective" belief. The test of reason boils down to this: the concurrence of trained minds when they use mathematics to control attentive observation. Newton had meant very much the same thing when in differentiating his work from others', he said: "I don't make up hypotheses" (*Hypotheses non fingo*). He was not referring to hypotheses in the usual sense, but to his conviction that science dealt with unquestionable evidences "out there." The realities themselves disclosed their order and system to a competent mind without the aid of intuition and imagination. Obviously, there could be no "evidences of Christianity" in the same sense.

The certainty felt by all the enlightened in this power of things "out there" to project themselves correctly on man's mind like a sharp beam of light on a screen is what gives the answer to the question: How is it that there is no argument about true science? What is it that produces the remarkable concurrence in observation and reasoning, now that we have found the true method? The theory of mind—it would be called today the psychology—that goes with eighteenth-century science is that known as "empirical" or "associationist." It was developed in England by a series of philosophers who are accordingly known as the British Empiricists. Their work established side by side with Newton's world machine its equivalent, the human mind machine.

The principle of this psychology is not a discovery of the Enlightenment. Philosophers here and there through the ages had flirted with the attractive but dangerous *nihil in intellectu quod non prius in sensu*—nothing is in the mind which is not first in the senses. The senses here mean what we feel, touch, hear, smell, and see. They are at once the channels through which experience imprints its multiple patterns on the plastic and receptive mind of man, and the contents of that natural operation. From the first minute of conscious life, the bombardment of sensations begins to "make" the mind. The pictures on it correspond to "reality" which exists "outside." It is these pictures which enable man not only to guide himself in his workaday affairs, but also, ultimately, permit Newton to recapture the mental operations of God when he was creating the heavens. For the sensations necessarily come in a sequence which by "association" generates true ideas.

From Hobbes to Locke and from Locke to Hume, Condillac, and Hartley, this "sensationalist" and "associationist" explanation of the workings of mind supplied the desired basis to a number of fundamental activities. If experience acting automatically on the mind reproduced reality there, this was sufficient validation for the experimental method of science. *Only* experience had authority, as Bacon had taught, and experiment was simply a bit of contrived experience. This was looping the loop: all normal minds receive the same impressions from the experiments of science because the source of these impressions is nothing but the consistent and unified order of nature. Science is thus true because it gives a summary of this natural order, and the summary is confirmed by the concurrence of these normal minds.

This mechanical model of the mind had other implications, for both the individual and society. It suggested first a far greater equality among minds than had ever seemed likely before, since in this new psychology all minds start equally blank. Upon these originally equal minds, accident and wicked imposture (by kings, priests, and others) had worked quite arbitrarily, had twisted or degraded them—which accounted for the diversity of customs and rituals, the wars of religion, the superstitious fears of primitive man, and indeed of "civilized" man too, when he was kept in ignorance as he was in contemporary Europe.

This being so, it should be possible by the right education to maintain the natural equality, or at least not utterly destroy it, and in time develop reasonable men. Let the common experience of the young be abundant, orderly, free from hobgoblins and old wives' tales, and the grown man will be a reasoning creature, fully capable of understanding Newton, and rational also in the sense of self-controlled and law-abiding. Right education supplementing a good environment will infallibly improve mankind. There was the key to progress, progress indefinitely extendable and depending only on the intelligent contriving of the right experiences, as in experimental science. Man's fate lay entirely in man's control.

Why, in these circumstances, was it said above that the root idea of the sensationalist psychology is dangerous? Its first proponents, of course, ran the risk of being burned as heretics who denied the existence of the soul. Later, as we have seen, the clumsy compromise of Deism took care of the theological objection, verbally at least, and fended off orthodox attacks. With the success of science as backing—almost as weapon—the empiricists of the eighteenth century need not fear the stake. But a far worse danger came from within rationalism itself. It took two forms—skepticism and thoroughgoing materialism—both of which led to the destruction not merely of the props supporting theology (as we have seen) but also of the props supporting science. Ultimately, rationalist analysis seemed to require giving up the vision of enlightened, progress-making man, and to replace it by the spectacle of a mindless universe in which automata (or at best animals) pursue mechanically a meaningless existence.

Both these outcomes of rationalist speculation were reached before the end of the Age of Reason, though their full impact over a wider public came only later. In the eighteenth century, skepticism and overt materialism created only ripples of disturbance; they did not dislodge the prevailing Deism of the advanced thinkers or the entrenched beliefs of the conservatives. The latter were learning to live at peace with the new doctrines, and toward the end of the century a placid, polished genius such as Edward Gibbon could, in his literary masterpiece on the decline and fall of Rome, devote two long ironic chapters to Christianity as the obscurantist creed that had helped to bring down the high civilization. To the author and his readers. one implication was: We, thank God, have just got over the effects of this protracted error and our rationalist civilization is secure.

But the inner corrosive was already at work. As early as 1747, the French writer La Mettrie gained the ear of the public (incidentally convincing the new king of Prussia, Frederick the Great) by the theory summed up in the title of his book *L'Homme-Machine* (Man a Machine). La Mettrie was a physician and a follower of the great seventeenth-century mathematician and philosopher Descartes. In Descartes' system there are only two entities—mind (or soul), which emanates from God, and matter, which is mindless "extension." The point at which the two substances meet, said Descartes, is the will of man, which presumably moves him in his actions and leads his mind to know and experiment with matter. But Descartes found it unnecessary to use soul and will in accounting for the behavior of animals. These he declared to be automata, pure machines. Likewise, he believed that there was no need to invoke the Creator's continuous action to explain the present state of the universe. It could have reached this state from any given beginning by a mechanical evolution.

With these two premises, it was tempting (and not difficult) for La

Mettrie to take the next step and to picture man as also a purely material arrangement of bones, nerves, and other fibers—a machine. All one has to suppose is that the interplay of these elements produces the phenomenon of consciousness—the *illusion* of a mind (or soul) independent of the body. The proof of materialism lay in the fact that drugs, fever, and other physical influences on the body are immediately translated into changes of sensation, feeling, and ideas.

La Mettrie, whose first essay had been entitled *The Natural History of the Soul* (1745), went on to write *L'Homme Plante* (Man a Plant), in which he drew other analogies not essentially different from his mechanical ones. He had inklings of the evolution of plants and animals, like several of his contemporaries, notably the great Buffon. This sharp observer and master stylist included in his vast *Natural History* an explicit theory of evolution, based on the similarity of structure between whole groups of animals, including man, and suggestive of far-reaching conclusions. But with the characteristic irony which was the safeguard of the advanced thinker, he added: "One would believe all this if one did not know by revelation that the animals were created as separate species by the creator."

Among the consequences of materialism was the disestablishment of morality. La Mettrie advocated complete hedonism, or the undeviating pursuit of pleasure. For all these heresies he had to flee France and even Holland and take refuge in Berlin with his convert Frederick, who practiced what his guests preached, as more and more of the enlightened came to do. Voltaire, a Deist to his last breath, called La Mettrie "the King's Atheist-in-Ordinary." But quips and flights into exile did not end the matter. Committed to science and to reasoning, the century could not stop where Voltaire arbitrarily and inconsistently chose to: he was all for Light, but he confessed that he would not teach his philosophy to his servants for fear that loss of belief would emancipate them so far that they would steal his spoons.

The post-Voltairian world pursued a more rigorous line of thought. For one thing it took in the reports of the many explorers whom a scientific generation kept sending out to the South Seas, in the course of which a new continent (Australasia) and innumerable primitive tribes were discovered. The simple or strange habits of these peoples taught Europe a complete moral relativism: right behavior was what society decreed to be such. Whatever the code, it had grown up by chance, or had been suggested by "benevolent nature," as in the easy and agreeable sexual morals of Tahiti. And if harmless and pleasant there, why not in Europe?

In short, though the total hedonism of La Mettrie and his pupils was an extreme position, it might still show the right direction. The richer and greater mind of Denis Diderot, the master encyclopedist, frequently played with this subject and veered toward a materialism coupled with a Deist morality. What kept Diderot from adopting the voluptuary's creed was his strong sense of obligation to others; his understanding of the *social* machine, which requires brakes and levers; and his vivid awareness of mind as an irreducible element. Diderot may not have believed in God and immortality, but neither could he accept consciousness as an illusion—for if matter alone has real existence, sensation itself and ideas and emotions are deceptive appearances.

Less questioning and introspective, the Baron d'Holbach, another French philosophe and encyclopedist, disposed both of God and of any proof of his existence drawn from the harmonious design of the cosmos by denying that special harmony. "Matter acts because it exists and it exists in order to act." We know this from ordinary experience and we can go no further. Why or by what means matter acts is beyond us. The reason for the existence of matter is locked up within matter itself, and we should rather inquire (d'Holbach was a physicist) *how* it acts than waste time looking for an external cause, a first cause, or a preordained purpose or end. Harmony is a fiction because the "fixed sequence of necessary motions" is at times favorable to us and at times disastrous. Order is only the unvarying effect of identical causes; in a word, it is regularity without point or purpose.

Even in man's man-made order, the uniformity of cause and effect determines acts and consequences, a determinism which disposes once and for all of the deist "morality" implanted by God in the heart of man. One has only to compare what the theologies pretend and what experience shows. Here d'Holbach quotes Epicurus, who two thousand years earlier had said: "Either God wants to prevent evil and cannot; or can and does not want to." The choice is between a God who is powerless and one who is lacking in love and justice. But evils we suffer are quite compatible with blind matter, which does not know that it is inflicting evil or serving good: the knife does not know that it is cutting meat or committing murder.

Thus does rationalist logic, starting from Cartesian and Newtonian science, end in a cold gray world, strictly determined and not likely to favor the hopes of Progress. But one must interpose here that such atheism does not necessarily lead to the hedonism of La Mettrie, who thought of death as the curtain rung down on the last act of a farce. D'Holbach was by contrast a stoical moralist with lofty notions of honor and humanity. But just as one can be sardonic or sad at the godless, mindless, universe, depending on one's temperament, so one can reach that same vision of the cosmos by other means than the study of matter. Simple skepticism will suffice. One can get there by following Locke instead of Newton, the "new" psychology instead of the "new" physics.

This second path is the one that Hume took to arrive at his distrust of science and theology alike. In an *Essay on Providence and a Future State* (1748) and a long dialogue *On Natural Religion* published after his death in 1779, Hume pursued his method of asking, first, what grounds there were in experience for believing that the imperfect world we see is matched by a perfect one hereafter. On earth we see men treated not according to their deserts; what evidence is there that a just ruler will later correct these injustices? It is all "mere possibility and hypothesis." But observe: we do not even know and cannot reasonably infer the existence of a creator. The analogy with a watch takes us nowhere, for we have seen a watch being made, but we have no good reason to think that a universe is also and similarly "made." Discarding d'Holbach's analysis of order as simple regularity, Hume suggests that the order we find may be accidental; chaos would be equally natural. Besides, there is every reason to suppose the world finite. Why then expect a finite product to have an infinite cause? For all we know, its maker may have been a limited, fallible being like ourselves, or he may be dead, or he may have worked with one or more other gods of either sex, each or none of them concerned with good and evil.

Hume's last word of doubt on religion carries with it such a doubt about the mind of man that the certainty of science goes down in shipwreck too. In its ultimate phase in Hume, the psychology of sensation turns upon and destroys itself. For Hume's last word is that there is no warrant for believing in the existence of anything but the sensations that we receive. To be sure, they follow in fairly usual order; our habits make them seem real and regular, but they are after all nothing more than impressions. Objects we can never know directly; still less do we know directly the relation of cause and effect. What we take to be such is our habitual expectation that the impact of one billiard ball on another will be followed by the motion of that other. This habit is good enough for the business of daily life, but it does not bestow certainty on the system of causal connections we proudly call science. The Lockean mind, in short, fails to support a rational belief in either the natural religion of the Deists or the natural science of the Newtonians, whether they be materialists or not.

Of course, the practicing scientists went on with their work regardless: Priestley, Lavoisier, Cavendish, Volta, and Laplace discovered elements, laid down chemical laws, developed electricity, predicted celestial events by mathematical deduction—quite as if Hume had never doubted. In psychology, the world was startled by the "immaterial" effects of hypnosis produced by Franz Anton Mesmer (mesmerism) and was taken in by the magnificent sleight of hand of the impudent adventurer Alessandro di Cagliostro; all this regardless of the "proofs" that only matter existed and that superstition could not survive reason. The "associationists" went on refining, and certain physicians among them (Pierre Cabanis, Destutt de Tracy) became interested in the abnormal mind. Under the name of Ideologues, they opened up inquiries of great moment for the future, not only of science but of art.

In short, man's mind is unconquerable in the sense that arguments found definitive by one generation sound either silly or irrelevant to the next. Arrived at the point where there seemed to be nothing more to say—Hume having uttered the last word—a new surge of energy and speculation kept philosophy going and began the restoration of theology. The German professor of logic and metaphysics at Königsberg in Prussia, Immanuel Kant, did not think Hume either silly or irrelevant: he found him a stimulus; the impasse was—so to speak—a springboard. Kant accepted the failure of speculative reason to establish the truth of theology or any part of it—God, free will, or immortality. All these truths belong not to pure reason but to practical reason. It was in *The Critique of Pure Reason,* published in 1781, that by this distinction Kant opened the way out of skepticism, renewed the possibility of religion and moralism, and slipped a fresh foundation under the work of science. The revival of the constructive energies in all realms marks the period known as Romanticism, which ushers in the nineteenth century.

But Kant's saving formula owes its existence to something else than reflection on the difficulties Hume had advanced. Seventeen years before Hume's death and the publication of his testament of skepticism, Rousseau had inserted in his *Émile* or treatise on education a remarkable chapter on religion, which he entitled "The Confession of Faith of a Priest from Savoy." In sixty short pages Rousseau shifted the ground of discussion entirely away from physics and psychology and made the knowledge of God rest on man's religious impulse. The inner consciousness of morality and love of God is first a feeling, later *aided* by reason; it is not a product of cogitation. *All* thought is of this character: need, impulse, will, precede intellect and argument. Being primary and instinctive, the feelings cannot be explained away: subtlety does not remove hunger.

Rousseau's "Confession of Faith" nevertheless takes up all the current arguments for skepticism, materialism, and orthodox dogmatism in the best eighteenth-century rationalist manner. It shows their futility by arguing both their inconsistency and their abstraction: they are not "practical." A man may *say* some of the things the philosophers write, but a man does not *live* them. They are debating points, not animating convictions. Belief is a living thing.

Brilliant and compact, the priest's discourse to his pupil Émile passes from the reasonings to the revelations, and there Rousseau again takes the "practical" view that three-quarters of the human race have never heard of European theology, so that if there is but one God and he a just one, he must expect and receive from men a worship of another kind than that preached as essential, eternal, and exclusive in Christendom. And since, as everybody knows, even Christendom is rent by virulent disputes based on differences of ritual and revelation, there can be no greater illusion than the belief in this exclusive truth about the one God.

Rousseau, in short, first puts himself inside man as he is, then takes all men in their concrete diversity and asks himself what religion can embrace the inner and the outer realities. It is still a *natural* religion, but not a rationalist one. It is a reasoned faith, but at many points reason declares itself powerless to know. It is a religion that sanctions and supports moral action, but in deciding what is moral it relies on feeling rather than casuistry. In its simplicity and humility it is what we should call a democratic religion, not a sophisticated or learned one—the priest from Savoy is only a vicar, which means that he has not even a parish. But his mind does embrace the whole world, and when he asks himself where he has learned to worship the one true and universal God, he answers that it is not in books of theology or of enlightened philosophy, for he is "unable to believe that God commanded him under pain of hell to be a scholar." From those treatises of sterility he turned to the open book of Nature, in which all may read and from which all can teach themselves to serve and adore the Creator. No one can be excused from going to it, for Nature "speaks to all men a language intelligible to all minds."

In saying this, Rousseau may have been anticipating. His contemporaries and disciples were just beginning to look at Nature as he did, and to discover there a divine presence that raised echoes in the human heart. When thirty years after him a whole generation spontaneously came to share such emotions, a new age was at hand. The quarrel of science and theology was in abeyance, displaced by the vivid synthesis of art, religion, and individual consciousness that we call Romanticism.

For Further Reading

Berkeley, *Commonplace Book.*
Voltaire, *Poem on the Lisbon Earthquake.*
Hume, *Dialogues on Natural Religion.*
Pope, *Essay on Man.*
Diderot, *Dialogue on Bougainville's Voyage.*
Kant, *Prolegomena to Every Future Metaphysics.*

IV

THE AGE OF REVOLUTION

Europe: The Great Powers

Revolution in the Western World

Reaction and Rebellion

The Industrial Revolution

New Forces, New Ideas

Europe: The Great Powers

62   Forming National States

It was a tribute to the effectiveness of their political institutions that in the 1640's France and Spain, despite the economic strains and the social unrest that their costly participation in the Thirty Years' War had produced, were still powerful nations, by far the most powerful in Europe. In France the Nu-Pied, or Barefoot, Revolt in Normandy (1639), in which thousands of peasants were joined by numbers of merchants and even by some local judges in resistance to high taxes in a period of poor harvest, could not shake the power of Richelieu. Spanish-controlled Portugal and Catalonia seethed with unrest, yet Prime Minister Olivares held them in check. Both powers sought by subversion to encourage rebellion among the other dissatisfied peoples, adding further to the internal unrest on both sides of the Pyrenees. At the same time they refused to invest any of their resources in measures that might ease the burden of their own unhappy subjects. To both victory in the war took precedence over all else. The common strategy was total offense—each would endure the risk of revolution rather than reduce the pressure on the enemy in any way. It was a policy of rule or ruin, and the fact that both monarchies survived this brutal policy explains why their governments were respected and admired by contemporary students of politics everywhere.

As early as 1463 the English legal theorist Sir John Fortescue had pointed to the French king's power to tax his people without their consent and to humble the proudest nobles of the realm as the hallmarks of absolute monarchy. At the end of the next century, after decades of debilitating war, the French crown under Henry IV and his minister Sully seemed by these standards more powerful than ever. This circumstance impressed every European politician enormously, which goes far to explain why the absolutist ideology flourished in the first half of the seventeenth century in almost every country of Europe. If only other rulers would copy the French

CHRONOLOGY

A.D.

1581	Proclamation of Dutch independence from Spain
1594	Henry of Navarre crowned as Henry IV of France
1603	Union of Scottish and English Crowns under the Stuart James I
1611–1614	Rebellion of the French princes
1624	Richelieu admitted to the Council of State
1625	Hugo Grotius publishes *De Jure Belli et Pacis* (international law)
1635	Founding of the French Academy, which establishes uniform grammar and usage for French language
1636–1637	Peasant revolts in southern and western France
1639	Nu-Pied, or Barefoot, Revolt in France
1640	Revolts of the Catalans, Portuguese, Irish and Neapolitans
1642	Outbreak of the civil war in England
1648	Peace of Westphalia; sovereignty granted to the Swiss and Dutch states
1648–1652	Civil war in France
1649	Repression of the Irish by Cromwell
1652	Anglo-Dutch War
1653	Defeat of Brandenburg Estates
1655–1660	Northern War; Brandenburg gains sovereignty of Prussia
1660	Charles II issues the Declaration of Breda
1661	Beginning of the "personal" reign of Louis XIV
1663	Louis XIV occupies the Papal State of Avignon (Comtat Venaissin)
1678	Elector of Brandenburg attempts to suppress Wendish speech
1680–1683	Chambers of Reunion
1685	Revocation of the Edict of Nantes

(and Spanish) model, they too could create powerful centralized states. In "mixed" monarchies where sovereigns depended upon representative bodies to raise money, the sovereign was, relatively speaking, poor and had little to offer those who served him. Thus, at least, it seemed to the ministers and bishops in the court of Charles I of England, to the courtiers and princes of Orange, and later to the noble followers of the Hohenzollerns in Prussia, of the Vasas in Sweden, and of the Romanovs of Russia. In all these countries the "ideal" of the absolute monarch was dangled temptingly before the noses of kings repeatedly over decades and centuries. Indeed the oppressive, blighting influence of the idea was not finally and totally eradicated from Europe until 1917.

Seventeenth- and eighteenth-century absolutism lacked, however, the cold, cruel power of twentieth-century totalitarianism. The ideology sanctioned the monarch's interference in every aspect of the national life. But most of the kings lacked both the temperament and the actual power to dominate their subjects totally or crush out racial and cultural minorities like a Hitler or a Mussolini or a Stalin. Haughty nobles posed a constant internal threat and formed the power center around which dissenters could rally. More basic, no absolute monarchy approached the modern totalitarian state in its degree of cultural and economic centralization. From southern Italy to Scandinavia, from Scotland to Auvergne, primitive semi-tribal social enclaves persisted unassimilated by the larger nations. Scottish kilts and the coifs of Brittany were superficial reflections of this insularity and diversity. Hundreds of dialects and equally numerous local semibarbaric religious cults sustained these pockets of the past in the midst of "modern" centralized states. Their existence seemed a constant threat to absolutism. This led, for example, statesmen as diverse as Cromwell and the Earl of Stratford to try to crush the Irish. Although most of these tribal-like subcultures were poor and primitive—inhabiting the poorest land and scraping a bare living from rocky soils or an unfriendly sea, ruled by feudal patriarchs—they somehow appeared to "civilized" European statesmen as ferocious beasts which must be subdued at all costs. Of course they stubbornly resisted surrendering their freedom or their ways of life, however mean. Bitter warfare resulted, warfare which the outlanders could never win. But rugged minorities could usually exact a terrible toll both physically and psychologically from their overlords. The screaming kilted Scotch highlanders terrified English troops. Well into the eighteenth century control of such tribal peoples sapped the resources of the powers, a drain similar to that exacted from the Roman Empire by the barbarians who ringed its perimeter in ancient times.

Moreover, even in France and Spain provincial loyalties remained strong even when unsustained by significant linguistic and cultural differences. Parish, village, county, and provincial council, diocesan and guild institutions, remained powerful centers of local life and government. Everywhere the landed gentry and the bourgeoisie drew upon economic power and local prestige to resist centralized authority. The great aristocratic families also employed these local loyalties in their larger struggles against absolute kings. Royal orders emanating from Paris, Madrid, London, or Vienna always met resistance, especially when they took the form of demands for money. When royal officials such as the intendants of France settled in the provinces, they tended soon to take on the ideological coloration of their surroundings and thus to defend the very local liberties they had been dispatched to destroy. This was especially true of ambitious officials drawn from the lower orders; they also proved particularly susceptible to the blandishments of the provincial ruling classes.

Everywhere in the provinces in rich Kent and Beauvais, as well as in poor Scotland and Brittany, subsistence agriculture was still the rule. Thus the poor classes lived under the constant threat of famine. After about 1620 the whole continent suffered from a food shortage as the population increased. Conditions were worse in some regions than in others, but the common result was political instability. During famines the upper classes tried to improve local controls to conserve scarce supplies; they dared not place their very survival in the hands of remote officials in the capitals. Inefficient and expensive means of transportation prevented the swift movement of food to stricken areas in any case. Therefore the most absolute kings met only frustration when they sought to break down regional economic barriers in the name of efficiency and centralization.

Coastal cities which profited from fishing and foreign trade opposed protective tariffs which interfered with their profit, whereas towns in the interior favored tariffs which were a source of income to officials and served to keep local food supplies in the area. Again local interests acted to hamper monarchical efforts to achieve uniformity and control. Even when the kings attempted to establish new manufactures in the towns, ostensibly to increase local resources as well as to make their kingdoms more independent of foreign supplies, the traditional guilds protested bitterly, arguing that the new businesses would stimulate competition and drive up wages. The mercantilistic dream of a self-sufficient, truly national economy dear to the hearts of the absolutists had no appeal to these local interests.

On the other hand, the nationalization of the culture of the upper classes proceeded swiftly. In France and Spain national courtly styles triumphed over the Italian fashions. Between about 1550 and 1680 provincials willingly aped the dress, speech, architecture, and diversions of the Escorial and Versailles. By way of contrast, however, the princes of Orange and the Stuart kings exercised no such dominance over the culture of the Netherlands or England. There national styles were chiefly fashioned by local institutions such as the universites and by the burghers of Amsterdam and the town oligarchs of London. Ambitious young men in these lands adopted the sober dress of scholars and merchants while the older generation clung to Elizabethan styles. In the Germanies the Viennese court styles were widely influential, but Protestant princes were oriented toward the Dutch, at least until the 1660's when the court manners and dress of the French "Sun King" Louis XIV slowly spread across the continent.

The printed word exerted an increasingly powerful impact. In states that succeeded in controlling the presses, most notably in Spain but also in eastern Europe, the monarchs maintained their grip on religious, social, and political thought. In most of northern Europe, however, the flood of printed matter prevented centralization and contributed to the breakdown of traditional values and institutions. Literacy was on the rise particularly in England, where groups that possessed power, the nobles, judges, and merchants, took a heated interest in books, pamphlets, and broadsides dealing with religious and political questions. But in Geneva as in Oxford, in Douai, Louvain, and in hundreds of Jesuit schools, young minds were taught to see Europe as divided by ideological and religious conflicts. Before the sixteenth century politics, foreign policy, and finance seemed beyond the scope of even educated nobles, merchants, and professional men; thereafter bewildered kings, cardinals, and their ministers of state found these classes clamoring for a voice in public affairs. The spread of printed matter aroused public opinion as parliaments ceased to be docile, and this explains why kings began to try to get along without them. One major aspect of absolute government was rule without estates.

The flood of printed matter seemed also to exacerbate the religious conflicts of the Thirty Years' War. Hundreds of pamphlets served to polarize opinions on theology, history, government, and morals, to say nothing of specific questions of foreign policy, taxation, and the like. How to deal with the resulting politicization of their subjects challenged the imagination of the monarchs. Although censorship had failed miserably against the Reformation, kings and bishops continued to try to stamp out ideas they considered subversive to the established order. But books could be easily transported across national boundaries, and secret presses were almost impossible to locate and destroy.

Some kings, James I of England for example, joined directly in this struggle to influence opinion by writing themselves; others hired propagandists to advance their cause and refute the arguments of their foes. Richelieu was a pioneer among the latter. From Paris poured a flood of print designed to influence French opinion. Théophraste Renaudot, editor

EUROPE IN 1660

Hapsburg possessions
Hohenzollern possessions
Holy Roman Empire boundary

of the influential *Gazette,* was in his pay, as were many intellectuals. Other national leaders, the Duke of Buckingham in England, Olivares in Spain, and Cardinal Mazarin in France, were less adept in the use of this tactic than the great Cardinal.

Nevertheless, by the 1640's rebellion was everywhere in the air. Heavy taxes and religious oppression lay at the root of the unrest along with famine and hard times. In the past such conditions had led the poor to focus their resentments upon local lords, but now the kings themselves stood in the path of the storm. Pamphlets and engravings of the period reveal the depth of popular resentment against royal tax collectors and other symbols of centralized authority.

The results of the upheavals of the 1640's varied from place to place, but in England and France, where absolute monarchs had suffered crushing defeats initially, stability could be restored only by reestablishing centralized royal power. The radicals, having broken the monarchical dominance, proved incapable of devising and maintaining responsible national governments without it. At the same time, European elites, the nobility, merchants, and gentry, did not really want to rule. Religious radicals had sought to legislate new Jerusalems or enforce the articles from the Council of Trent, while statesmen like Omer Talon in France, John Pym in England, or—somewhat later—the De Witt brothers in the Netherlands, could not create national policies that would transcend local interests, let alone establish a republic or mixed monarchy that could govern effectively. Their constitutionalist ideologies only led to more violence and social revolution. Thus even victory against absolute monarchy seemed to be to no avail. The Catalonian rebels chafed under the directives of their French liberators, until their contempt for the French soon equaled their contempt for the Castilians. Nor could the Anglo-Dutch wars of the 1650's, in which Protestants fought Protestants over trade and colonies, be explained by the dominant revolutionary ideologies of either country. Should not the Protestants be joined against Catholics? asked English and Dutch radicals. To his despair Cromwell was forced into a war with his religious allies.

Similarly, the Jesuits had never quite succeeded in portraying the Franco-Spanish war as a crusade against heresy, since both powers were Catholic. At every turn, as Cardinal Richelieu realized, these religious-political ideologies failed to explain either commercial rivalries or conflict between states. Thus the first ideologies to permeate European societies, dividing as they did Protestants from Catholics and constitutional monarchists from absolute monarchists, had to be rejected by statesmen. A new ideology would gradually replace them—it was political and economic in character and we call it mercantilism, or statism. From the mid-seventeenth century to the French Revolution late in the eighteenth, the idea that each state should seek its own economic independence by founding colonies and controlling large supplies of gold and silver shaped European politics and caused a series of imperial conflicts.

But if the revolutionary parties and programs were rejected, this in no way meant that powerful social groups wanted to return to the absolutism of the early seventeenth century. In his Declaration of Breda, Charles II of England made it clear that the restored Stuarts would rely on a "free Parliament" under the new order. When Mazarin returned to Paris after his expulsion during the Fronde, he accepted the fact that aristocratic privileges and the Parlement of Paris could no longer be ignored. The earlier type of absolutism survived only in a declining Spain, and there more in form than in substance. The revolutionary spirit of republican decentralization prevailed only in the Netherlands, long a haven of religious nonconformity and a monument to the commercial spirit. Spain and the Netherlands were in many ways the extremes of European social and political organization in the mid-seventeenth century. A prudish moral climate prevailed in both, despite their different political systems. Their differences but also their similarities survived in the work of the two great artistic geniuses of the era, Velázquez in Spain and Rembrandt in Holland—the royal decadence depicted by the one, the solid burgher substance of the other, and in both the mannered reality and humanity of the age.

For Further Reading

Aston, T., (ed.), *Crisis in Europe, 1560–1660*.
Clark, G. N., *The Seventeenth Century*.
Moote, A. L., *The Seventeenth Century*.

63   The Age of Louis XIV

To name an age after a man—any man—is, of course, to distort history. No human being, not even an Alexander or a Caesar, has ever shaped a whole society. Yet Louis XIV, who was certainly not an Alexander or a Caesar, during his incredibly long reign as king of France (1643–1715) affected the lives and thoughts of the peoples of Europe to such an extent that to name that time in his honor is only slightly an exaggeration. Because of what he did, peasants by the thousands exchanged their hoes and plows for the tools of war. To win his patronage, artists and writers adopted new styles and the children of noble families all over the continent bent with furrowed brow over grammar books to learn the new "universal" language. Like those who aped the great Sun King, those who most stubbornly resisted his influence—the English and Dutch for example—were themselves shaped by the mere act of resistance.

Louis, by establishing for France such a powerful political and cultural identity, awakened national feelings all over Europe. The totality of French achievements shook every other nation to the core. Where they were admired and adopted, as in Germany, they blended subtly with local tastes and habits; where they were hated and resisted the results, while different, were still profound and directly traceable to French influence. When Louis came to power European culture lacked a focus, a national center of

A.D.

1636	Corneille presents *Le Cid*
1637	Descartes publishes the *Discourse on Method*
1638	Birth of Louis XIV
1642	Death of Richelieu
1643	Death of Louis XIII; regency of Anne of Austria for Louis XIV; Battle of Rocroi
1648–1652	Civil Wars in France (the Frondes)
1656	Creation of the General Hospital, Paris
1660	Marriage of Louis XIV to Maria Theresa of Spain
1661	Death of Cardinal Mazarin, beginning of the "personal" reign of Louis XIV
1663	Le Nôtre designs the gardens of Versailles
1664	Molière presents *Tartuffe;* the play is banned
1664	Creation of the Compagnie des Indes
1665	Bernini visits Paris
1667	War of Devolution
1670	Promulgation of a reformed criminal code for France
1670	Treaty of Dover
1670	War with the Dutch; assassination of the De Witt brothers
1674	Invasion of the Franche Comté
1679	First fortress built by Vauban
1679	Bossuet publishes the *Politique tirée de l'Ecriture Sainte*
1679	La Fontaine publishes Books 7-11 of the *Fables*
1683	Death of Colbert
1685	Revocation of the Edict of Nantes
1688	War of the League of Augsburg; the Glorious Revolution in England; death of Frederick William the Great Elector
1691	Racine presents *Athalie*
1697	Bayle publishes *Dictionnaire historique et critque*
1700	Philip V proclaimed king of Spain
1702	Death of William III
1704	Battle of Blenheim
1713	Peace of Utrecht
1715	Death of Louis XIV

leadership. The decline of Spain, of the Holy Roman Empire, and of the papacy left the Catholic countries particularly without a focus. Italy was still rich and a center of culture and fine living, but politically unstable. Thus the monumental synthesis of military force and high culture that developed in France after about 1600 affected all Europe enormously.

France achieved political and social stability swiftly after the mid-seventeenth-century revolution, aided by a new professional army and a sound public administration guided by Cardinal Mazarin. In 1659 the long war with Spain was finally won and Spanish power pushed back once and for all behind the Pyrenees. Louis was the fortunate beneficiary of these developments; he had been only five when he inherited the crown in 1643. But from the very beginning of his reign his mother, Anne of Austria, along with Mazarin, taught him to believe that *he* ruled; he learned to act like a sovereign early, and by the time he actually could rule, he did so naturally, with total confidence. He was regal in every respect—in look and gesture as well as deed—the very epitome of the divine-right monarch. In addition, as the descendant of Clovis and Charlemagne, he even had a claim to the title of Holy Roman Emperor. When compared to the sorry Hapsburgs of his day—the ugly Leopold and the impotent Charles—or to a base-born pope, like Innocent XI, he seemed a true prince, one destined to conquer and to judge, to impose order on all Europe.

Louis in modern terms had charisma. But even if he had been a mediocre monarch like his father, France would have dominated Europe, partly because of the collapse of Spain, partly because of its effective government and army, and its culture and learning. This was the age of Descartes, Pascal, Corneille, Racine, Molière, La Fontaine, Bossuet, and many others whose work and thought shaped Western culture profoundly. At a time when convention demanded that artists and intellectuals, generals and statesmen, give praise to their monarch and credit him with their successes, the achievements of such men were bound to make even a third-rate ruler appear like a combination of Solomon and Marcus Aurelius.

Louis XIV first appeared on the European stage, after Mazarin's death in 1661, in the role of a militant bully—brash and offensive in his dealing with foreign heads of state. French diplomatic successes, however, resulted from the shrewd policies of Mazarin and then Lionne, who took advantage of the small German states which tried to use France against the Hapsburgs and found themselves French satellites. In Brandenburg-Prussia, however, the quiet but competent sovereign Frederick William the Great Elector, although beset by Swedish pressure from the north and the claims of Polish kings to the east, avoided commitments to France and concentrated on building up a small but sound professional army of 8,000 men, and on strengthening his internal control of his territory against the pretensions of the Junker families. The Austrian Hapsburg emperor Leopold would have liked to rekindle the religious wars but lacked both financial resources and freedom of action. The smoldering threat of revolution in Hungary and of Turkish invasion from the east held him back. Indeed, the possibility of a future war with France over the succession to the Spanish throne— Charles II of Spain had no heir—led Leopold to abandon all thought of another religious crusade. Later he would have to ally himself with the Protestant Dutch and English to stop the power of France.

In Spain, disorder and defeatism were the order of the day. Charles II was one of the most pathetic creatures ever to rule a great European state. Physically, mentally, and emotionally abnormal, he was impotent, plagued by superstitious fears, supernaturally devout. Spanish courtiers and states-men could look forward to little but the dismemberment of the empire, but like the Austrian Hapsburgs they continued to dream of past glories and to pretend that they possessed far more power than they really had.

In England the restoration of the Stuart king Charles II in 1660 brought no end to constitutional and religious conflicts. Popular fear of absolute royal power and of plots real or imagined to restore "popery" served to check Charles's freedom of action in foreign affairs. Although he was the cleverest monarch in his line by far, the London merchants, ac-customed since the English Revolution to influencing foreign policy, were less affected by the anti-Catholic hysteria; their interest in commerce had high priority. Charles dared not openly challenge the merchants, even going along with their desire for war with the Dutch. But eventually his fondness for Catholicism and absolutism and his need for money led him to a secret treaty (Dover, 1670) with Louis XIV and other devious tactics. He did not, however, dare to try to undo the result of the Puritan revolution.

Despite the backing of a Royalist Parliament, he could not keep the promises of the Declaration of Breda. Those Royalists who had lost their land in the 1640's could not be compensated without injury to those other Loyalists who had supported the restoration. Numbers of great families thus lost the economic basis of their social position and the Anglican Church suffered in a similar fashion.

Nor were the religious provisions of the Declaration fully honored. Parliament in a counterrevolutionary mood enacted the Clarendon Code, excluding non-Anglicans from public office. Although some Catholics and Dissenters made their peace with the established church, others went underground, adding to the conspiratorial climate of the times. Charles worked in various ways to control parliamentary elections, and this plus the pro-Catholic proclivities of his brother James, the heir to the throne, made Parliament increasingly refractory. On his deathbed Charles, keeping a promise made to Louis XIV, publicly declared himself Catholic. This contributed to the Sun King's illusion that he could restore unity to Western Christendom.

Only among the Dutch did republicanism and localism increase in strength in Europe after 1660. In the chaotic conditions that existed there in the seventeenth century, religious toleration had developed not out of conviction, but out of fear of violence and a passion for making money that had made the ruling oligarchs the richest merchants of Europe. Only when nationalist-oriented and protectionist groups in France and England won control of government policy in these powerful countries did Dutch economic power begin to decline. Despite their wealth, the Dutch were politically and religiously divided and militarily weak. Fearing that a large army would mean the rise of the House of Orange and therefore of monarchy, they ignored the dangers posed by English sea power and by the new armies of Louis XIV. While Mazarin lived, French policy was expressed in diplomacy rather than in war. But historic French territorial ambitions in the Netherlands and also in Italy did not die.

In 1666 Louis attacked the Spanish Netherlands, basing the invasion on his Hapsburg wife's claim to the area. The war quickly revealed the weakness of Spain and the strength of the new "model" French armies. The French war machine was closely controlled and well supplied. Instead of pillaging the countryside the armies were provisioned by bureaucrats called intendants who insisted that the generals follow orders from Paris and who commandeered supplies from local officials in an orderly manner. Louis himself accompanied his armies in the Netherlands, inspiring loyalty among the troops and the lesser officers but prudently leaving strategy and tactics to the professional soldiers. The era of the condottiere was over; no longer did generals as Wallenstein had in the Thirty Years' War pose a political threat to their governments. Condé and Turenne, generals famous throughout Europe, remained faithful servants to the Crown under the new system, and Louis, on the scene, could coordinate military and diplomatic policy efficiently. Thus the great problem of the Thirty Years' War was solved; war no longer served as a stepping stone to political power for generals and local aristocrats. Eventually the French system was imitated all over the continent. Armies were also growing larger; at the height of his power, Louis XIV had 400,000 men under arms, probably more than had ever been engaged at any one time by all the belligerents in the Thirty Years' War.

By the Treaty of Aix-la-Chapelle (1668) France gained part of the Netherlands from Spain. But this victory only inspired Louis and his ministers to play for larger stakes. Colbert had set high tariffs on imports into France, a direct blow at the commercial-minded Dutch. Louis, who

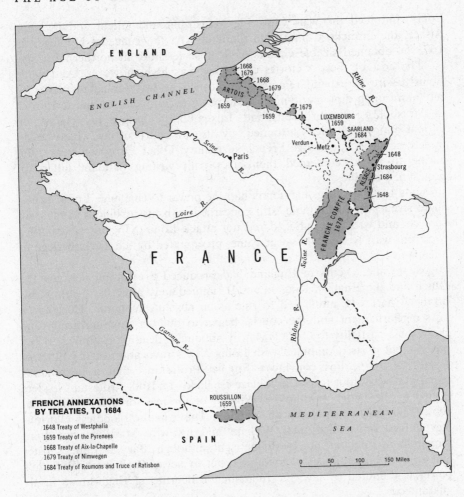

ENGLAND

ENGLISH CHANNEL

1668
1679
1668
1679
ARTOIS
1659
1659
1659
1679

LUXEMBOURG
1659
SAARLAND
1684
Verdun
Metz
1648
Strasbourg
1684
ALSACE
1648

Rhine R.

Seine R.

Paris

Loire R.

FRANCE

FRANCHE COMPTÉ 1679

Saône R.

Garonne R.

Rhône R.

FRENCH ANNEXATIONS
BY TREATIES, TO 1684

1648 Treaty of Westphalia
1659 Treaty of the Pyrenees
1668 Treaty of Aix-la-Chapelle
1679 Treaty of Nimwegen
1684 Treaty of Reumons and Truce of Ratisbon

ROUSSILLON
1659

SPAIN

MEDITERRANEAN
SEA

0   50   100   150 Miles

viewed the Protestant republican merchants who controlled the Netherlands with contempt, proceeded to spin a web of treaties to isolate them.
For example, the secret Treaty of Dover with Charles II brought a promise
that Charles would remain neutral in a Franco-Dutch war. Under Colbert's
direction a powerful navy was also constructed, and in 1672 French troops
launched a massive assault. At first the Dutch with their army in disorder
were routed. The oligarchy fell, the brilliant De Witt brothers who had run
the government were assassinated, and the youthful Prince of Orange,
William III, took over control of the country. Then with the French about
to envelop Amsterdam, the Dutch opened the dikes, flooding a huge area
occupied by French troops and thus avoiding a total disaster. Nevertheless,

Louis continued the war, capturing Maastricht and Ghent and invading Alsace, the Franche Comté, and Germany. At the Peace of Nijmegen in 1678 he obtained sizable chunks of Spanish territory in northern Europe.

The cost of these victories in money was high, however. And while Louis' desire to expand remained unsatisfied he was forced thereafter to rely more upon diplomatic means. He put great pressure on the territories of Strasbourg, Zweibrücken, and Luxembourg, basing his claims on various antiquated titles "sustained" by his own courts of law which forced these cities to acknowledge French suzerainty. Other European rulers, not daring to resist, contented themselves with writing petulant letters of protest to Versailles.

Only the Hapsburgs in Vienna had the power to challenge Louis' brutal aggressiveness, and Leopold, still concerned with his rebellious Hungarian subjects and with the Turks, dared not attack Louis XIV out of fear of a two-front war. Nevertheless war came, precipitated by the Turkish siege of Vienna in 1683.

Meanwhile, events in England had produced a coalition between the Dutch and the English. King James II, immediately after the death of his brother Charles II, attempted to rule as an absolute monarch. He ignored laws of Parliament and the courts, began to build a standing army, and showed his partiality to Catholicism by appointing leading Catholics to key government posts. Combined with Louis XIV's revocation of the Edict of Nantes in 1685, this convinced English Protestants that a horrendous papal plot was afoot to re-Catholicize England. In 1688 Protestant leaders turned to the Dutch stadtholder William of Orange for aid. William accepted the call and mounted an invasion. This was the bloodless Glorious Revolution. James fled, and William and his wife Mary became joint monarchs of England, not by divine right, although Mary as James's sister lent an aura of legitimacy to their rule, but by act of Parliament. William's power was limited by law, the fundamental liberties of Englishmen firmly guaranteed.

For his part, William gained the ships, soldiers, and money necessary to confront Louis. Swiftly putting down a French-supported Irish revolt, he turned to this task with a will. A Dutch English fleet smashed the French navy off La Hogue, and soon his combined army was masked behind the fortifications on the French border. Louis had foolishly assumed that William's invasion of England would produce a debilitating civil war. Now he miscalculated again, assuming he could crush the Protestant army easily. The war was, however, bloody, widespread, and long, lasting from 1688 to 1697. Once again the powers poured their wealth into sterile arms, crushing their subjects beneath heavy taxes. Crop failures heightened the suffering almost everywhere.

The Hapsburg Leopold joined the coalition against Louis, for after 1688 the Turkish pressure on his realm had lessened. Bitter, inconclusive fighting raged in the Rhineland. When the French failed to win a decisive victory, they resorted to a scorched-earth policy, seeking to insulate themselves against a counterattack by making the area so desolate that no army could cross it. But gradually the allies increased their pressure. By the late 1690's Louis' troops were everywhere on the defensive. King William, however, limited by his dependence upon Parliament for money, and willing to settle for containment rather than total victory, agreed to a peace in 1697, signed at Ryswick. The great Sun King surrendered some small bits of territory and, despite his monarchical and religious principles, officially recognized William as legitimate king of England. The threat of internal rebellion influenced his decision. "I sacrificed the advantages I had gained," he admitted, "[to] public tranquillity."

William had coolly abandoned his ally Leopold, who did not regain French-held imperial territory including the important city of Strasbourg. But although his armies continued to do well against the Turks, regaining (the Peace of Karlowitz, 1699) much of Hungary, Transylvania, and the Ukraine, he lacked the strength to fight France on his own. Nevertheless, the war had forced him to strengthen the administration of his ancient sprawling domain. Once again Hapsburg power in both eastern and western Europe was increasing.

In France, although half-surrounded by hostile powers, Louis ensconced in Versailles continued to rule with magnificent disregard of the changing times. For money he depended upon the sale of offices to the wealthy and the taille exacted from the peasantry. For policy he depended upon the game of dynastic politics and—he sincerely believed this—on God. To this amazing man, who had now ruled the most powerful nation in Europe for more than half a century, victory or defeat was God's reward or punishment. Other European rulers, and all but a few of their subjects, shared Louis' views. He sent thousands of men to their death and drove Protestant heretics from his realm to win the favor of the Lord, and it is an indication of the faith or the psychology of the age that the great majority of his subjects approved of his actions and of the motivation behind them. Indeed, in what is sometimes called the Age of Newton and Locke, it is likely that many English Tories also agreed with Louis. It was a time of change, of transition, in which old and new ideas existed side by side, sometimes in the same man. Newton, the discoverer of gravity, believed in miracles.

In such a time of change it is no wonder that the cultural monolith represented by the court of Versailles made an enormous impact on Europe. Love of elegant clothes, speech, and manners, along with a fondness for classical columns, formal gardens, and lofty sermons, united gentlemen and would-be gentlemen all over Europe in the admiration and envy of Versailles. Louis' personal charisma, sustained as it was by French culture, accounts for much of his political impact in Europe.

The patronage of the papal court had been the greatest in Europe until Louis enlarged both the Louvre and Versailles. The chief sculptor and architect of the age, Giovanni Bernini, was enticed to France to work for the Sun King. His visit marked a turning point in the cultural history of Europe, a shifting away from Italian dominance to French. With the help of the finest architects and designers of the age, the Sun King created a massive monument to himself and to the strength of the French monarchy, in the palace of Versailles, and with Italian help. At the court itself, with Molière and Racine furnishing the theatrical entertainment, Jean Baptiste Lully the music, with Nicolas Boileau, Jean de La Bruyère, and Jean de La Fontaine serving as satirists and critics, the French and the Europeans together witnessed a splendid spectacle. The spread of French among the educated nobles of Europe guaranteed a large and continuous international audience for the balls, hunts, and receptions of Versailles, with the principal actor himself serving as impresario.

But cultural influence alone did not decide the course of European power politics. Louis XIV had learned in the 1690's that he could not defeat all of Europe when every major power was allied against him. He therefore followed a more cautious policy. He compromised about the Spanish succession. He signed two treaties with the English which, had either gone into effect, would have partitioned the enormous Spanish empire to preserve the balance of power in Europe. But the Spanish grandees objected, and the superstitious Spanish king, Charles II, finally left his entire empire to Louis XIV's grandson. This put Louis in a difficult moral position. Should he profit from Charles's will or stand by his promise in the treaties? The fact that Spanish leaders were prepared to offer the whole empire to Leopold if Louis refused it helped him make up his mind. He accepted Charles's will and his grandson became king of Spain as Philip V. William III of England at first held his peace, for he had had enough of war and preferred to see a Bourbon on the Spanish throne to fighting still another world-wide war. But when Louis, sensing victory, boldly recognized the Stuart pretender as the legitimate heir to William III as king of England, Parliament and the English public cried out for war against France. This enabled William to win parliamentary support for raising the armies needed to fight France in the War of Spanish Succession, 1702–1714. Leopold, who did not have to concern himself much with public opinion and who was as convinced as Louis that God was on his side, in 1702 sent his best general, Eugene of Savoy, to attack French positions in

WAR OF THE SPANISH SUCCESSION

Grand Alliance
Franco-Spanish Coalition
× Battle

northern Italy. Eugene overran Spanish territories in Italy which the French could not defend, and then struck at France's satellites in Germany.

The war dragged on despite the deaths of both William (1702) and Leopold (1705). Eugene wielded great influence in the Hapsburg empire, and the great Marlborough backed by Parliament dominated English policy. When Louis organized an assault on Vienna, Marlborough and Eugene met his army at Blenheim in Bavaria. Although the French had taken a strong position, Marlborough launched a series of bloody frontal attacks, using his superior numbers recklessly until he had carried the day. What his critics called the "butcher's bill" was high, but Marlborough's victory was decisive. It was followed by further victories at Ramillies and

Oudenarde, after which the French armies ceased to be a threat to foreign nations.

This did not mean that France lay open to easy invasion. The great French military engineer, Marquis de Vauban, had fortified every strong point ingeniously; the war dragged on. Cost and casualties again mounted, with each side struggling to foment internal trouble in the other's domains.

During the bitter winter of 1708–1709, disastrous for harvests, France seemed on the brink of defeat, but Louis, truly by this time an institution in France, roused his people in defense of *la patrie*. A new army under General Villars met Marlborough at Malplaquet (1709). After a battle which left 40,000 dead or wounded, the allies held the field, but the French retreated in good order. The English public was now appalled by the heavy losses and tiny gains from the long war. Thus the result of more years of bloody destruction was another stalemate. Louis, publicly as haughty as ever, nevertheless made private overtures for peace. Marlborough fell from power, and new English leaders signed the Peace of Utrecht with France in 1713.

The treaty brought large colonial gains for England. The Dutch regained their fortifications along the French border, and the Austrian Hapsburgs got Naples, Sardinia, and Milan. Brandenburg-Prussia officially became a kingdom, and Savoy got control of Sicily. Louis XIV's grandson retained the throne and overseas empire of Spain. Although the Austrians were not a party to the Anglo-French negotiations, and bitterly opposed the placing of a Bourbon on the Spanish throne, they could make no military progress against the French armies and finally made peace. The balance of power had been restored, or better, the attempt to disrupt it had been tacitly abandoned. In effect, after Utrecht, the great powers gave up their attempts at continental expansion and thereafter for a long season, concentrated on building colonial empires and on expanding their commerce. In this sense, 1713 marked the end of the Age of Louis XIV. The sad and uncomprehending Sun King finally died in 1715.

For Further Reading

Ranum, O., *Paris in the Age of Absolutism*.
Rule, J. (ed.), *Louis XIV and the Craft of Kingship*.
Stoye, J., *Europe Unfolding, 1648–1688*.
Wolf, J. B., *Louis XIV*.

64 Europe in the Eighteenth Century

The philosophes of the eighteenth century were convinced that theirs was the age of enlightenment and progress *par excellence*. This view may seem naïve, even perverse, to one who knows the century well, but the philosophes, looking back on the disorders of the sixteenth and seventeenth centuries, were understandably impressed by the peace and political stability of their own times, by the slow but steady improvement of living conditions, and—at least in some of the countries of Europe—by significant increases in the personal liberties of individuals. Seventeenth-century thinkers had little reason to be optimistic, and their writings show that they were not. The writings of the philosophes of the eighteenth century reflect a new, hopeful world view. The philosophes, as Voltaire made so clear in *Candide*, were well aware that they were not living, despite Dr. Pangloss, in "the best of all possible worlds." They noted the injustices of European legal procedures, the poverty of the masses, the persistence of serfdom in eastern Europe and of slavery in the colonies of their own countries. They protested, sometimes despaired, over official censorship. They were worried by the sharp increase in Europe's population with its threat of famine. Nevertheless, and again Voltaire's view was typical, they believed that the Age of Louis XV, Frederick the Great, and Catherine the Great was a vast improvement over any period since the Renaissance, and in many respects they were right.

The eighteenth century, however, was also the time of the *ancien régime*, a time of bungling politicians, of nobles feeding off the labors of masses of peasants, of immorality and corruption among Europe's ruling elites. It is possible to see the French Revolution both as the final flowering of an age of liberal reform and as a cataclysm bringing just retribution to a century of stupidity, avarice, and corruption.

Progress or decline? The evidence points in both directions. After 1715 peace generally reigned and ideological and religious storms had subsided. Royal armies held rambunctious nobilities in check. Religious and political minorities were no longer subjected to mass persecution. Assassination ceased to be an acceptable device for settling political disagreements. Fewer witches and heretics were burned. Some leaders even began to think about improving the way government dealt with the poor, the sick, and the depraved, and even to see that the obtaining of abstract justice was a legitimate purpose of the state. In 1761 Jean Calas, a Huguenot merchant

CHRONOLOGY

A.D.

	1709	Battle of Poltava (defeat of the Swedes by Russians under Peter the Great)
	1714	George of Hanover becomes king of England
	1720	Collapse of Law's Mississippi Scheme in France, and English South Sea Bubble
	1721	Montesquieu publishes the *Persian Letters*
	1721–1742	Administration of Sir Robert Walpole
	1726	Cardinal Fleury becomes prime minister in France
	1734	Voltaire publishes *Philosophical Letters on the English*
	1736	John Wesley begins to establish Methodist Societies
	1740	Frederick II of Prussia invades Silesia
	1741	Empress Maria Theresa rallies Hungarian nobles to fight the Prussians
	1745	Battle of Fontenoy
	1747	Richardson publishes *Clarissa Harlowe*
	1748	Treaty of Aix-la-Chapelle
	1750	Death of Johann Sebastian Bach; Voltaire begins his visit at the court of Frederick the Great; Diderot and collaborators publish first volume of the *Encyclopédie*
	1756	Outbreak of the Seven Years' War
	1761	Resignation of William Pitt
	1762	Catherine II becomes ruler of Russia; Rousseau publishes the *Social Contract*
	1771	*Parlements* abolished in France by Louis XV
	1773	Diderot visits Catherine the Great in Russia
	1774	Louis XVI becomes king of France and recalls the *Parlements*
	1778	France intervenes in the War of American Independence
	1781	Joseph II promulgates the Edict of Tolerance
	1783	Russia annexes the Crimea; Beaumarchais presents *Marriage of Figaro*

in Toulouse, was accused of murdering his son in order to prevent him from becoming a Catholic. He was convicted, tortured, and executed, all on the flimsiest of evidence. (The young man probably had committed suicide.) In earlier times such an incident would have passed unnoticed. But Voltaire seized upon the case, and soon a wave of protest swept across France; prominent men expressed outrage at the way the religious authorities had interfered in the trial and at the brutal conduct of the judges. Fair play and proper procedure were becoming important.

Religious passions clearly had cooled; the diplomats at Utrecht in 1713 grappled with questions of national interest and the balance of power, not with religious issues such as had dominated their negotiations at Westphalia which ended the Thirty Years' War. After 1715 no monarch tried seriously to impose religious unity on Europe. At every royal court churchmen were less influential than in earlier times and a freer intellectual climate flourished. Despite the work of the Counter Reformation in stimulating religious feeling and rebuilding church institutions, church power did not increase in the eighteenth century even in Catholic states. The eighteenth was a century of weak popes, declining monasteries, lazy bishops.

The decline of the importance of religion in political affairs had profound effects on the general public. No longer were merchants and peasants and judges asked to pay such high taxes and make other sacrifices in the name of a particular faith. As early as 1709, Louis XIV made his dramatic appeal to save the nation, not the Church, even though the enemies were Protestants. Political stability enabled leaders to conduct diplomacy without constant appeal for public loyalty and support. Indeed, in a paradoxical way, eighteenth-century Europeans, while more cosmopolitan, were also more isolationist than those of the seventeenth. Both the lower classes and the educated elite "disengaged" themselves from politics. Frederick the Great of Prussia (and he was not very different in this respect from most absolute monarchs) fantasized that he could even fight a war without his subjects knowing about it.

No eighteenth-century king could realize this "ideal," but peace and the decline of ideological politics created a kind of isolationism which permitted both profitable colonial expansion and an increased concern for internal problems. Probably this isolationism also explains the increasing concern of the educated elite for justice and sound finance. Even in England, where bitter memories of the seventeenth-century revolution combined with problems resulting from the succession of the very Germanic George I to produce a period of plotting and rebellion, the trend was toward stability. Gradually the Whig Sir Robert Walpole built a system of control that extended from the king's cabinet to the lowest levels of the local bureaucracy. Whig supremacy, as Walpole well knew, depended on peace and economy in government; he constantly slapped down members of his own party, chiefly London merchants, who favored a more aggressive foreign policy.

Low taxes appealed to the rural gentry, and England was still primarily an agricultural country. The gentry families that Fielding described so well in *Tom Jones* owned most of the arable land, dominated local government, sat in Parliament, held the chief places in the Anglican Church and in the army and navy. Within this group, Tory contested with Whig for office, but on underlying social and economic issues all were united. The lower classes —the farmers and artisans—accepted political impotence in exchange for prosperity and lower taxes. Prosperity and commercial growth in the age of Walpole combined after about 1740 with a rising population to lay the groundwork for the Industrial Revolution.

Walpole was a master politician, personally familiar with officials high and low all over the kingdom. He was convinced that all Englishmen wanted what he wanted: peace and profit. These he could give them, thanks to the general European stability of his time. The decline of the Dutch merchants opened up vast opportunities, particularly in the Baltic. At the same time the growth of the American colonies provided both raw materials and markets, and gave bankers valuable new investment opportunities. A succession of good harvests kept food prices at reasonable levels. England, as the eighteenth century wore on, became richer, more sure of itself, and more tolerant. It was an age when the aristocracy built enormous and elegant country houses, often with money gained by accepting a merchant's daughter into the family. Andrea Palladio, the great Italian architect of the sixteenth century, inspired the Duke of Burlington in the building of Chiswick House. The monumental classical style which the English now favored harmonized with the splendidly designed plaster ceilings of Adam, the Chippendale furniture, and Gainsborough portraits of beautiful women and children. Alexander Pope, Samuel Johnson, and James Boswell, along with the novelists Samuel Richardson and Henry Fielding, gave England a kind of literary dominance in Europe similar to the scientific dominance established by John Locke and Isaac Newton.

Not even the religious revival of the Methodist zealot John Wesley could shake English society. Wesley made converts by the thousands, for the Anglican clergy of the time was, by and large, lazy and out of touch with the people. Religious enthusiasm seemed to many Anglican leaders positively dangerous, an invitation to revolution. But Wesley was not a social reformer—piety, not "progress," was his objective. In a society in which the ability to read was still considered an enormous accomplishment and in which prosperity bred complacency among the middle classes, most persons were content to remain "in their place."

When war broke out again on the Continent in 1740, Frederick of Prussia invading Silesia, this basic conservatism enabled the brilliant political tactician William Pitt to thrust Walpole and his system aside. The French became involved in aimless campaigning against Frederick, and Pitt saw this as a chance, by joining in the conflict, to strike at the rich French overseas possessions. Using their powerful navy effectively, the British by 1763 had swallowed up nearly all of the French colonies in America and in India. English arms were less successful in the European phases of the wars of this period, but maintaining the status quo on the Continent adequately suited British purposes. But even successful wars cost money. Country gentlemen began to balk at high taxes, and this combined with the death of George II and the succession of his politically ambitious grandson George III led to the ending of the imperial wars.

In France, too, conflicts were more political than social or economic in this era. Religious disputes inherited from the seventeenth century continued, but did not seriously threaten the peace of the realm. Old landed families and judicial nobles had common interests, most notably the desire not to pay taxes, while the lower orders, politically impotent to begin with, benefited from the lowering of taxes after the Peace of Utrecht and from commercial and agricultural prosperity. Louis XV's chief minister, the aging Cardinal Fleury, held together a coalition of nobles and merchants behind a policy of making the main function of the state the providing of offices and pensions.

But Frederick of Prussia's invasion of Silesia made Fleury as obsolete as Walpole, and France produced no William Pitt, who saw the significance of colonies in buttressing the state. Belle-Isle, who took over the role of chief royal minister in France, saw Frederick's attack on Silesia as an opportunity to resume the ancient war of Bourbon against Hapsburg. Without forethought or planning, France allied itself with Prussia and invaded Hapsburg Germany.

Frederick, however, made peace with the Hapsburg ruler, Maria Theresa, leaving the French, deep in Germany, to face the Hapsburg armies alone. The result was disaster, exacerbated by heavy losses to the British on the seas and in the colonies. The war had been undertaken mindlessly and the results should have been predictable.

Louis replaced Belle-Isle with the hard-working and honest Machault, who attempted to place new taxes on all classes of French society to get government finances on a sound basis. This produced grave protests, and Louis dismissed Machault rather than face the storm. Royal power was declining, that of the nobility on the rise, a fact Louis finally recognized in 1764 when his parliamentary enemies voted to dissolve the Jesuit order in the realm. The king then roused himself to the defense of his authority. He

CENTRAL EUROPE, 1740

- ⧸⧸⧸ Hapsburg possessions
- ▨ Hohenzollern possessions
- ⦀ Venetian possessions
- ▬ Holy Roman Empire boundary

NORTH
SEA

NORWAY
(to Denmark)

SWEDEN

Stockholm

FINLAND
(to Russia)

St. Petersburg

GULF OF FINLAND

RUSSIA

W. Dvina R.

Dnieper R.

BALTIC SEA

DENMARK

POMERANIA

EAST
PRUSSIA

Vistula R.

Warsaw

POLAND

HANOVER

Berlin

BRANDENBURG

HOLLAND

CLEVES

Elbe

Oder

SAXONY

SILESIA

Rhine
R.

Dniester R.

AUSTRIAN
NETHERLANDS

BOHEMIA

Paris

BAVARIA

Vienna

FRANCE

BREISGAU

AUSTRIA

Buda

Pest

HUNGARY

SWITZERLAND

TYROL

STYRIA

Danube

Rhône R.

SAVOY

VENETIA

Milan

Po R.

Venice

CROATIA

Sava R.

Genoa

ADRIATIC
SEA

DALMATIA

OTTOMAN

CORSICA
(to Genoa)

TUSCANY

PAPAL
STATES

Rome

EMPIRE

SARDINIA
(to Savoy)

Naples

KINGDOM

OF THE

TWO

SICILIES

MEDITERRANEAN SEA

0   100   200   300 Miles

tried to reduce the power of Parliament, to regain control of the judiciary, to make the nobles pay taxes. But he died in 1774, and his successor, the desultory Louis XVI, was incapable of carrying on the fight. Probably he could not have won it even if he had been able, courageous, and intelligent (he was none of these), for even the professional classes and the artisans were siding with the nobles in the struggle against what seemed to them royal despotism. A curious alliance of limited democracy and high privilege was in the making in France, one that would lead to the great revolution. Louis XV and Louis XVI were both ineffectual and unwilling to turn over the machinery of state to able ministers. A Colbert or a Richelieu might have saved the Crown, but a strong hand would have made open enemies, and both kings wished, above all, to be loved. They purchased this love by surrendering power, and paid for it, in the end, with their patrimony, the throne of France. Ironically the peace that came to France after 1763 had much to do with the inability of the rulers to strengthen the monarchy. Arbitrary royal power and the heavy taxation needed to institute social and fiscal reform were hard to justify when no foreign threat existed. The effort to revive the famous *capitation,* or head tax, for example, did not succeed because no pressing wartime expenses had to be made. In France, at least (although not in Germany or in eastern Europe), the consequences of peace for absolute monarchy were fatal.

As with France, Frederick the Great's invasion of Silesia had profound effects on the central European states. What was surprising about Frederick's decision was not his objective but his method. Instead of seeking to build an alliance against the Hapsburgs, whose potential enemies were legion—Turks, Russians, and French—he struck directly and alone in a bold bid to make Prussia a great power. His success, and the means of achieving it, shaped the later history of Prussia and of the other German states.

War, especially the Seven Years' War of 1756–1763, compelled the raising of taxes and increased royal power. In state after state in the Germanies representative assemblies declined in influence to the advantage of royal authority. Even tiny Denmark became an absolute monarchy. Frederick I and Frederick the Great dominated the Prussian nobility, built large, well-trained armies, the best in Europe, and reduced the proud aristocrats to the status of bureaucrats in the service of their war machine. Prussia in 1750 resembled France in 1675, the heyday of the great Sun King. Territorial expansion, governmental efficiency, and a mercantilistic economy were common to both. Frederick the Great, however, was a different man from Louis XIV. He stifled initiative among his ministers and generals and developed among the Prussian hierarchy a blind, total obedience that persisted long after his death. In seventeenth-century

France, courtiers were obsequious but independent-minded; in eighteenth-century Germany they were merely obsequious, and if they incurred the royal disfavor they could be dismissed or even imprisoned by royal fiat. The almost military discipline of the Prussian bureaucracy made for efficiency; thus monarchical absolutism weighed more heavily by far on Prussian society than Louis XIV's absolutism had ever weighed on French society. Hundreds of inspectors checked up on royal officials and submitted confidential reports to Berlin; junior bureaucrats were encouraged to report on the failings of their superiors to the king himself. Overlapping jurisdictions and wasteful rivalries, so common to the French bureaucracy, were virtually nonexistent. The price of such efficiency, of course, was the stifling of initiative and the imposition upon society of a militaristic, almost Spartan type of government. Frenchmen had surmounted absolutism by finding ways around it, especially where taxes and the judicial process were concerned. Prussians merely submitted. The rapidity of unification and the emasculation of the nobility left Prussian society without any group strong enough to resist the Crown. Frederick was his own foreign minister, treasurer, tax expert, chief justice, minister of the interior, and commander in chief. No earlier sovereign anywhere in Europe so thoroughly dominated the machinery of government. He was Europe's closest approximation to an Oriental despot.

By contrast, the Hapsburg monarchy, having survived the "reforms" of the Emperor Leopold, slumbered in feudal confusion. Each principality preserved many of its distinctive institutions and had its own army and laws and its own special relationship to the Crown in Vienna. Patronage, especially that connected with the Church, remained the principal instrument of royal authority, and it was often limited by local tradition and by the influence of the pope in Rome.

When Maria Theresa went to war with Prussia over Silesia, she and her ministers finally acted to strengthen control, but they did not succeed in developing a centralized system comparable to Frederick's, or even to that in France. Provincial opposition to Vienna was too strong and too well organized. Maria Theresa's son and heir, Joseph II, attacked the privileges of his nobles and of the Church even more vigorously. He has often been judged the most enlightened of all emperors, but he was as willing to use force against these powerful interests as any contemporary ruler. He closed down the monasteries and freed the serfs, thus delighting European philosophes, but he did so as much for reasons of realpolitik as for liberal and enlightened reasons. And he sought avidly to extend his sway over the new territories: in this sense he was a traditional Hapsburg.

In Russia, the death of Peter the Great in 1725 brought an end to his frenetic efforts to create a modern state. His passing was greeted with relief and pleasure by his troubled people. The kind of "Westernization" he favored was expensive, and destructive to Russian traditions, and imposed without regard for the primitive state of the Russian economy. The country remained agricultural; serfdom was as entrenched as ever after Peter's death. Peter did succeed, however, in increasing Russia's military power and thus in extending its territory. After he defeated the Swedes at the Battle of Poltava in 1709 he controlled most of the eastern Baltic and he also extended Russian power in the area of the Black Sea. His immediate successors were weak and plagued by court intrigues, but held the state together, thanks to the army Peter had created. And when the more forceful Elizabeth took the throne in 1741, she was able to exert considerable weight in international affairs, thanks to this army, especially during the Seven Years' War.

In Russia, however, a strong state was maintained by building a powerful landowning and military class. Peter had built that state without yielding to these interests, but his successors gave them new privileges and power to hold their allegiance. Their gains were paid for by the virtual enslavement of the peasants, whose taxes and obligations to their lords were sharply increased. Catherine II, known as the Great, was great only because she was the darling of these military and landed powers. Her domestic policies were determined by their needs and interests. Catherine admired Voltaire, Diderot, and other philosophes, but she ruled Russia like a reactionary absolutist, never hesitating, for example, to suppress peasant uprisings brutally. The difference between her pronounced objectives as queen and her actions was monumental, probably because the former were based on her wish to ape western European rulers, the latter on the social and political realities of eastern Europe.

Whether any of these monarchs were really "enlightened" is an interesting question. If we focus on how they admired the philosophes and talked of "reform" based on the enlightenment principles of these intellectuals, they do indeed seem like enlightened despots. Frederick, Catherine, Joseph II, Louis XVI, knew many of the philosophes, read their works, entertained some of them at their courts. But hard evidence that the philosophes influenced any royal policy is extremely scarce, as many of the philosophes themselves admitted. The eighteenth-century monarchs employed a rhetoric different from the sovereigns of the seventeenth century, but beneath and behind the rhetoric they were still sovereigns. Voltaire supposedly had the ear of Frederick the Great, but Frederick behaved very similarly to Frederick William, the great elector. Diderot was a confidant of Catherine the Great, but her policies resemble closely those of the tyrannical czar Peter. The philosophes condemned expansionism and war; Frederick and Catherine practiced both.

The eighteenth century, writes the German historian Fritz Hartung, was "the final phase in the history of hierarchical feudal society which descended from the Middle Ages. Already it had begun to doubt the rightness of the inherited division into classes determined by birth, and in having a privileged nobility which stood in contrast to a less free middle class and an unfree peasantry . . . as Pirenne pointed out enlightened absolutism was really nothing new, but rather a new version of an old idea of the prince as father of his country." Hartung prefers to speak of absolutism rather than despotism, and in the sense that these kings were reluctant to violate established principles of legitimacy, they were perhaps not despots. But when Frederick the Great called himself the "first servant of the state" and repudiated the divine right of kings, he was not thinking of abjuring power.

As for the elite elements in European society, the landed gentlemen, merchants, bishops, judges, and the like, in the late eighteenth century they were more relaxed and secure than their predecessors before 1715. They were less afraid of hell, smallpox, and revolution. But they were perhaps more concerned for the safety of their investments. Most European governments were in a dreadful financial state in the 1770's. Then the American Revolution weakened the fiscal structure of Britain and France still further. Moreover, that revolt engaged the elites of both these countries profoundly. Liberal ideas, long discussed, suddenly seemed possible of achievement. After the American victory in the revolution, while Louis XVI's ministers in Versailles were congratulating themselves on the humbling of the mighty British Empire, the cafés of Paris hummed with idealistic talk of political reform, tempered by anxiety about the powerless state of the French treasury. In 1784 Immanuel Kant wrote, "When we ask, are we now living in an enlightened age? the answer is, no, but we are living in an age of enlightenment." The question, sure to be answered, was: Has there been progress *enough*?

For Further Reading

Anderson, M. S., *Europe in the Eighteenth Century, 1713–1789.*
Dorn, W., *Competition for Empire, 1740–1763.*
Gay, P., *Voltaire's Politics: The Poet as Realist.*
Palmer, R. R., *The Age of Democratic Revolution: A Political History of Europe and America, 1760–1800.*

Revolution in the Western World

65   The American Revolution

Inaugurating an era of world revolutions, the American Revolution had points of similarity with the revolutions that followed. First of all, it was an anticolonial war waged by a colonial people for their independence; in that respect it was the seedbed for all later anticolonial movements in Latin America, Asia, or Africa. Second, it was a revolt against monarchy which supplanted the royal system by a republic. This was true of all the major revolutions down to the overthrow of the czarist regime in Russia in 1917. Third, it was a civil war fought not between great sections of the country, as the American Civil War, but rather in each state, county, and village. Fourth, it resulted in the creation in America of a nation different both in origins and in character from the nations of the Old World, thus touching off an era of revolutionary nationalism that has not yet run its course. Finally, it marked the formulation of new principles governing the relation of men to government, which might be put under the rubric of constitutionalism.

In other respects the American Revolution differed from those that followed in its wake. It was a civil war without being a clear-cut class war. The Patriot cause found recruits in all classes and economic groups, but members of the very same groups were numbered among the Loyalists. Even many poor tenant farmers and frontiersmen remained loyal to Great Britain. The American Revolution stands in notable contradiction to the French Revolution in that the former was accomplished without the seizure of power by extremists, without resort to dictatorship, and without that violent reaction that has come to be known as the Thermidor. However, if the American Revolution was not a clear-cut class war it did involve far-reaching democratic reforms. Self-government was inaugurated, but also relatively democratic government; egalitarian principles proved central to the American revolutionary ideology.

753

1763 Treaty of Paris ending Seven Years' War; Proclamation of 1763, restricting trans-Appalachian settlement; Patrick Henry's arguments in the Parson's Cause

1764 Passage of the Sugar Act and Currency Acts

1765 Passage of the Stamp Act; Resolves of Virginia House of Burgesses denouncing Stamp Act; Stamp Act Congress meets in New York and adopts Declaration of Rights and Grievances

1766 Repeal of the Stamp Act accompanied by passage of Declaratory Act

1767 Passage of Townshend Acts; revival of nonimportation agreements; publication of first of John Dickinson's *Farmer's Letters*

1768 Massachusetts House of Representatives adopts Circular Letter

1770 Townshend duties repealed in large part except for duties on tea

1772 Burning of the *Gaspee;* Committees of Correspondence organized by Samuel Adams

1773 Passage of the Tea Act; Boston Tea Party

1774 Passage of the "Intolerable Acts," including the Quebec Act; First Continental Congress convenes at Philadelphia, defeats Galloway's Plan of Union; adopts Declaration and Resolves and Continental Association

1775 Battles of Lexington and Concord; Second Continental Congress names Washington commander of the Continental forces; Battle of Bunker Hill

1776 Publication of *Common Sense* by Thomas Paine; Declaration of Independence; Battles of Long Island and Trenton

1777 Battles of Princeton and Germantown; Burgoyne's surrender, Saratoga; Congress adopts Articles of Confederation

1778 Franco-American treaties of amity and commerce and of alliance with the United States

1779 Formal entry of Spain into the war against England

1780 Siege of Charleston and fall to the British; treason of Arnold

1781 Ratification of the Articles of Confederation; surrender of the British at Yorktown to combined Franco-American forces

1782 Fall of Lord North's ministry; signing of Preliminary Articles of Peace in Paris

1783 Signing of Definitive Treaty of Peace with Great Britain; British evacuate New York City

While the American Revolution increased in complexity as the war progressed, it originated as a protest against the subordination by the mother country of colonies inhabited by people of the same nationality as the homeland, and grown to a degree of maturity that could no longer accept a status of total subordination within the British Empire.

That colonial discontent had long been smoldering is obvious in retrospect, but it is equally obvious that the beginning of the sharp cleavage between the colonies and Great Britain can be traced only to the closing years of the French and Indian War, the colonial phase of the last of the world wars fought between England and France in the period between 1689 and 1763. By that concluding war England acquired from France not only Canada but all land lying between the Appalachians and the Mississippi, along with East and West Florida, which were ceded by Spain.

The peace settlement posed innumerable administrative and fiscal problems for the victors while removing the threat of invasion by a hostile power which had long contributed to reconciling the English colonies in America to rule by the mother country. Indeed, the proposals to resolve these new and enlarged administrative and fiscal problems carried over at the peace triggered the crisis between the colonies and the mother country. For example, the effort to prevent smuggling and illicit trade with the enemy in wartime precipitated a confrontation in 1761 over the issuance of general search warrants ("Writs of Assistance"), which the Massachusetts lawyer James Otis exploited to the full. The exercise by the British home authority of the right to disallow colonial laws and hear cases on appeal from colonial courts precipitated a similar crisis when Virginia sought to pay its clergy in overvalued currency. In the so-called Parson's Cause, young Patrick Henry, arguing the colony's case, gained instant notoriety by his daring attack on the royal authority. To compound its difficulties, the British government antagonized a motley collection of land speculators by issuing the Proclamation of 1763, temporarily reserving land west of the Appalachians as Indian hunting grounds.

To meet the enormous new fiscal problems inherited from the war the Grenville ministry in 1764 proposed a tariff on sugar, molasses, and rum imported into America from the foreign West Indies. It did so not with the intent of stopping this trade, for the unenforceable Molasses Act of 1733 had shown that to be impossible, but rather to raise revenue in America. The enforcement of the Sugar Act involved overhauling the entire customs machinery and the relentless prosecution of smugglers. In addition, the Stamp Act of 1765 levied a tax within the colonies by requiring that stamps be affixed to newspapers, pamphlets, legal documents, and other items. While the Sugar Act was unpopular among merchants, the Stamp Act aroused even wider condemnation, touching off a violent three-pronged attack—an ideological assault on the nature of the British Constitution, an economic boycott of British goods, and civil disorder and disobedience. An extralegal Stamp Act Congress meeting in New York City denied the right of the British Parliament to tax the colonies without representation. The scale of the Americans' resistance, notably their ability to retaliate economically, astonished the home authorities. After fierce debate the Stamp Act was repealed. Deferring to the ill-omened advice of William Pitt, Parliament attached to its repeal a Declaratory Act explicitly asserting its unbounded right to legislate for the colonies.

A provocative element in these colonial disputes was the presence of the British army in America with its headquarters first in New York and then, after 1768, in Boston. The ostensible ground for maintaining troops in America after the French and Indian War was to secure peace on the frontiers, but as long as the colonies were torn by civil disorders it was obvious to everybody that the troops would be held in a state of readiness at strategic seaboard locations. A number of clashes between colonists and Redcoats occurred, culminating, on March 5, 1770, in the so-called Boston Massacre.

Meantime, the various British ministries, after backpedaling on the taxation issue, tried once again to raise revenue in America through the Townshend Acts of 1767, which imposed duties on a long list of imports. Once again the home government miscalculated: the American response repeated the pattern which had been set during the Stamp Act crisis. And once again the home government backed down, leaving merely a tax on tea, to uphold the principle of the Declaratory Act. That tax was still on the books in 1773 when the ministry of Lord North, seeking to rescue the East India Company from financial straits, secured the passage of the Tea Act by which the company acquired a monopoly of the tea trade with America. The colonial response was the Boston Tea Party of December 16, 1773, and it was this defiant action which confirmed George III in his resolve to use force to reduce Massachusetts to submission. Meanwhile, Parliament passed a series of punitive measures, the "Intolerable Acts." The Boston port was closed until that town had paid for the destroyed tea cargo, and in various ways the self-government of Massachusetts was severely restricted. In addition the Quebec Act, passed at the same time, turned over to the Province of Canada the lands north and west of the Ohio River which the colonies had long claimed by charter right.

The Intolerable Acts confirmed the Patriots in their conviction that Parliament had no constitutional right to tax or legislate for the colonies, a line which was forcefully advanced in the year 1774 by such noteworthy revolutionary political figures as James Wilson of Pennsylvania, Thomas Jefferson of Virginia, young Alexander Hamilton of New York, and John

Adams of Massachusetts. Indeed, the Intolerable Acts accomplished what a decade of laborious agitation had failed to bring about—union among the Thirteen Colonies. On September 1, 1774, a Congress convened at Philadelphia. Quickly routing a strong conservative element, the radicals secured the adoption of a drastic boycott of British goods and a Declaration and Resolves setting forth the colonists' right to "life, liberty and property." Congress took measures to put the colonies in a posture of self-defense, and before adjourning agreed to meet again on May 10, 1775, if by that date American wrongs had not been redressed.

With Redcoats vigilant and Minutemen organizing, drilling, marching, and stockpiling arms in various colonies, a confrontation seemed inevitable. It came on April 19, 1775, when some advance British units, rounding up subversives and searching for arms and munitions, clashed with seventy armed Minutemen on the town common of Lexington, Massachusetts. Marching on to Concord, the Redcoats destroyed such military stores as they could find, but their return march to the protection of the coast became a frantic retreat, with soldiers running a gauntlet of fire from the roadside and suffering surprisingly heavy casualties.

From that date until July 4, 1776, the Americans fought a fairly large-scale military action without avowedly seeking independence. The largest of these actions took place in June, 1775, when the British managed to drive a heavily entrenched American force from Bunker Hill in Boston. The British at Bunker Hill won only a Pyrrhic victory, however, for they suffered enormous casualties, while the Patriots demonstrated that their soldiers were no mere rabble in arms but the core of a disciplined army.

It was at this strategic time that Congress designated George Washington to be commander in chief of the Continental army. An affluent Virginia planter, Washington had gained seasoning by his experience commanding his colony's militia during the French and Indian War; a dedicated patriot, he possessed qualities that inspired confidence and commanded respect. Daringly stripping Fort Ticonderoga, on Lake Champlain, of its cannon, and transporting them 300 miles to Boston, Washington was able to fortify Dorchester Heights and place the British fleet in Boston Harbor in an untenable position. Deprived of naval support, on March 17, 1776, the British Army evacuated the city, ending an eight-month siege.

In other ways, however, the Patriots fared poorly in the north. A daring campaign to capture Quebec and make Canada the fourteenth state collapsed after a costly frontal attack was repulsed on the night of December 31, 1775. In turn, the British failed to exploit their adversary's weakness on the northern frontier.

For fifteen months American and British troops fought without a formal declaration of war, but various events conspired to work against reconciliation. King George III refused to receive a so-called Olive Branch Petition drawn for Congress by John Dickinson. Confronted with a poor enlistment rate for an unpopular war, the British Ministry bolstered its army with German mercenaries, loosely called "Hessians" because of the large number purchased from the Landgrave of Hesse-Cassel. Also contributing to the irreversible trend toward independence was Tom Paine's *Common Sense,* published in January, 1776. This pamphlet was a sensational and persuasive attack both on monarchy as an institution and on the monarch, George III, as a person. Town after town pressed for a public declaration of independence, and colonial leaders responded to the groundswell. Finally, on June 7, 1776, Richard Henry Lee of Virginia proposed a resolution in Congress that the United Colonies "are, and of right ought to be, free and independent states." Congress named a committee of five— John Adams, Benjamin Franklin, Thomas Jefferson, Robert Livingston, and Roger Sherman—to prepare a declaration. Jefferson, then only thirty-three, was chosen by the committee to give literary expression to the arguments justifying the colonies in dissolving their political bonds with the mother country. Congress endorsed the Declaration on July 4, 1776, at which time it was signed by John Hancock as president of the Congress. Subsequently the fifty-five signers attached their names to what has become the official proclamation of American sovereignty, of the principle of government by consent, and of the ideal of equality.

Although the British outnumbered the Americans both on sea and on land, and had incomparably superior financial resources, the Americans had the advantages of fighting from much shorter interior lines of communication and of conducting a war on familiar soil. They had, however, one serious disadvantage which the British expected to exploit: the presence in the colonies of a very substantial element of Loyalists or Tories, who opposed independence. In addition, the British counted upon the backing of their Indian allies on the frontiers, who could be expected to consider the king their protector against the aggression of colonial settlers. Unfortunately from the British point of view, neither Loyalists nor Indians proved crucial factors in the conduct of the war, nor were they effectively utilized to crush colonial resistance. To a large extent, however, the British military operation was inspired by the Loyalist presence. Having in effect abandoned New England, the British government decided to carry the war to the middle states and the south, areas which they were confident would rally to the support of the Redcoats. Except for an unsuccessful attempt in the year 1776 to capture the southern port of Charleston, the British for the next few years largely confined their efforts to the middle states. Thereafter, the main theater of operations was in the south.

In the battle for New York the British won all the opening engagements. Admiral Lord Richard Howe and General William Howe, conducting a successful amphibious operation on Long Island in August, 1776, quickly routed the American defenders at Brooklyn Heights, but allowed Washington to withdraw his main army across the East River to Manhattan. New York City quickly fell, forcing Washington to pull back his forces into Westchester and, after an inconclusive stand at White Plains, to retreat across New Jersey. As the year 1776 was coming to an end and enlistment time was running out, Washington decided in desperation to strike a blow while he still had an army. He surprised the Hessians at Trenton and defeated the British in a night march to Princeton. His nine-day campaign rid all but easternmost New Jersey of Redcoats and gave sinking American morale an incomparable boost.

The Patriot victories at Trenton and Princeton did not break the hold of the British on the middle states. Under a plan drawn up by General John Burgoyne in February, 1777, the British hoped to isolate New England by a three-pronged attack, a main army moving southward down Lake Champlain and the upper Hudson River, a second force operating through the Mohawk Valley from Oswego, both to be reinforced by a strong contingent dispatched up the Hudson from Howe's New York City base. A wonderful plan on paper, everything went wrong with it in execution. Howe decided to attack Philadelphia in the impractical belief that he could take the seat of the Congress and return in time to execute his role in the Burgoyne plan. Burgoyne himself suffered a series of setbacks. His auxiliary force from Fort Oswego was repulsed by the Americans, a raiding party into Vermont was trounced there by General John Stark, whereas the overcautious Sir Henry Clinton in command of the New York garrison moved too late and with far too little to reach Burgoyne at Saratoga. There, blocked by the army of General Horatio Gates, Burgoyne surrendered his entire force, bringing the war in the north to an end. While Burgoyne's grand scheme was collapsing, Howe managed to take Philadelphia, repulsing Washington's main army at Germantown but failing to capture or destroy it. In May, 1778, however, Philadelphia had to be evacuated on news that a French naval expedition was headed for America.

The disastrous middle-states campaign was followed by a new southern campaign which had as its initial objectives Georgia and then South Carolina. In 1780 Charleston capitulated to British besiegers, and the Redcoats soon brought the rest of the state to heel. However, here too the tide turned. The Patriots completely enveloped the Tory forces at King's Mountain, a short distance from the boundary line between North and South Carolina, thereby ridding North Carolina of Tory influence. This victory coincided with the appointment to the southern Patriot command of General Nathanael Greene. He dispatched General Dan Morgan to reduce the

British outpost in western South Carolina while he himself went to bolster the partisan forces led by Francis Marion and Thomas Sumter, then operating in the north-central part of the state. Morgan crushed the British at Cowpens in January, 1781, while in March of the same year Greene clashed at Guilford Courthouse with the forces of Lord Cornwallis. Cornwallis kept the field but at the expense of one-fourth of his army.

Disillusioned with his campaign in the lower south, Cornwallis moved his army into Virginia and, bowing to orders from Sir Henry Clinton, took his troops to Yorktown, which he heavily fortified. But reinforced by a French army under the Comte de Rochambeau, Washington eluded the British defenders of New York and moved down to Virginia, where he laid siege to Yorktown. When the British naval forces sailed to the Chesapeake to rescue Cornwallis they found French Admiral De Grasse, with a fleet he had brought up from the West Indies, barring the way. On October 19, 1781, Cornwallis' troops surrendered. Although a few scattered engagements took place thereafter, and the war continued at sea, to all intents and purposes the battle was transferred to the peace table.

The American Revolution posed novel issues in diplomacy. A cluster of colonies which had defied their monarch sought recognition as independent states from other nations which were ruled by monarchs and supported the principle of kingly authority. In addition to seeking recognition, the insurgent Americans counted on obtaining financial and military assistance from England's traditional enemies. In November, 1775, Congress had set up a five-man Committee of Secret Correspondence to make contact with "friends" abroad. The first prospective friend was France. Still nursing her wounds from the Seven Years' War, France had most at stake in the weakening of British power. In various underground operations, Silas Deane of Connecticut, joined shortly thereafter by Benjamin Franklin and Arthur Lee, secured French aid—military supplies and equipment, clothing, blankets, and above all cash. The kings of France and Spain secretly put up 2,000,000 livres to subsidize a private company to carry on these operations. In addition, the American commissioners recruited many French and European officers including the Marquis de Lafayette. Ultimately the triumvirate of quarreling commissioners was supplanted by a single man, the internationally renowned Benjamin Franklin. Franklin used his unique talents as a propagandist to win friends for America abroad.

The alliance with France, however, came not as a result of American pressure but as a consequence of the American victory at Saratoga. Fearful that the British government was about to come to terms with the Americans, the French entered into a treaty of amity and commerce and a treaty of alliance with the United States on February 6, 1778. The treaty bound both parties not to make a separate treaty with a common enemy without the consent of the other. In the spring of 1779 Spain came into the war on the side of France when England refused to cede Gibraltar. But Spain made it clear that she was not fighting for the independence of the United States. Finally the United Provinces (the Netherlands), which had provided the United States with an immense quantity of military stores, was dragged into the conflict late in 1780 when England declared war against the Dutch. By that date the American Revolution had become a world war, waged not only in continental North America but at Gibraltar, in the English Channel, in India, and off the African coast, and fought for national objectives quite different and distinct from American indepen-, dence.

Both sides were war-weary by 1780, and looked hopefully to foreign mediation. Austria and Russia proposed to force a truce upon all the parties and impose a settlement based on the military status quo. Had their diplomacy succeeded, Maine, New York City, and most of the Carolinas and Georgia would have remained part of the British Empire and a united nation might never have been achieved. However, the news of Yorktown put an end to these complicated backstairs intrigues and hardened the move in England for a quick peace. On March 4, 1782, the House of Commons resolved to consider as enemy of king and country all those who should further attempt to carry on the war. Two weeks later Lord North's ministry resigned. The new government was first headed by the Marquess of Rockingham and after his death, on July 1, by Lord Shelburne. Congress named as its peace commissioners Benjamin Franklin, who had been in France for the greater part of the war, John Jay of New York, who had attempted unsuccessfully to secure recognition of the United States from Spain, John Adams, who had negotiated a loan from the Dutch, and Henry Laurens of South Carolina, who had been captured by the British on the high seas and was released only in time to sign the preliminary treaty. By that treaty of November 30, 1782, confirmed by the definitive treaty of September 3, 1783, the United States secured recognition of its independence, its claims to the Mississippi as its western boundary, and fishing rights off Newfoundland and Nova Scotia.

As a war for independence or an anticolonial revolution, the American Revolution came officially to an end with the signing and ratification of the definitive peace. But as a movement of internal political and social reform the years of the Revolution marked merely the beginning of a long period of innovation. A new constitutional system was established based on the principle of consent of the governed. All the states with the exception of Connecticut and Rhode Island, which were satisfied with their liberal colonial charters, adopted constitutions which attested this principle. Indeed, Massachusetts went one step further when it submitted its constitutional draft to the people for ratification. Although they drew heavily on the colonial charters, the state constitutions reflected revolutionary experience in several of their aspects. The powers of the governor were diminished, the powers of the legislature enhanced. And the incorporation into the Virginia Constitution of 1776 of a Bill of Rights which also served as the model for most of the constitutions that followed, as well as the first Ten Amendments to the federal Constitution, proved to be pathbreaking.

The social and economic changes inspired by the American Revolution were less revolutionary but important. Thus, Tory estates were confiscated not to create a peasant freeholding class (a very broad class of freeholders already existed) but to punish Loyalists and to raise funds desperately needed for the war effort. Although much of the land eventually came into the hands of former tenants and small farmers, the initial purchases were often made by wealthy speculators. Some of the states canceled the debts owing to Tory and British merchants, and in Virginia, where the indebtedness of tobacco planters to British businessmen was massive, the struggle took on the character of a class conflict of creditor versus debtor.

One of the major areas of revolutionary reform was that of property law. Entail (in effect, an inheritable life estate) and primogeniture (exclusive inheritance of the first-born male heir) were abolished. It has been argued that the egalitarian effects of these reforms did not amount to much, since most southern planters made ample provisions for younger children in their wills, and legal devices already existed for breaking entail. Yet to a legal reformer like Thomas Jefferson the revision of the property laws was central to the reform of a society whose egalitarianism was based on land. In other areas such as the disestablishment of the Church of England, the extension of religious tolerance, and the reform of the criminal law, the Revolution can be shown to have created a climate which encouraged reform and innovation.

Slavery, on the other hand, was an institution that was substantially untouched in the great slave states by the Revolution. Though the war triggered a movement in the northern states to abolish slavery, none of the southern states, where most of the slaves were, acted against the institution. Some southerners, like Washington, George Mason, Jefferson, and Henry Laurens, explicitly avowed their opposition to the institution and their determination to bring it to an end, but the climate of opinion was not congenial to so radical a reform.

What gave to the American Revolution its durable qualities were the principles upon which it rested as enunciated in the Declaration of Independence. These served as a standard for defining a free society. Admittedly, the phrase "all men are created equal" did not accurately describe the America of 1776, where half a million persons lived in slavery. But as

Abraham Lincoln, speaking of Jefferson's generation in 1857, put it: "They meant to set up a standard maxim for free society, which should be . . . constantly looked to, constantly labored for, and even though never perfectly attained, constantly approximated, and thereby constantly spreading and deepening its influence and augmenting the happiness and value of life to all people of all colors everywhere."

For Further Reading

Becker, Carl L., *The Declaration of Independence.*
Jameson, J. F., *The American Revolution Considered as a Social Movement.*
Morgan, E. S. and H. M., *The Stamp Act Crisis.*
Morris, Richard B., *The American Revolution Reconsidered.*
————, *The Peacemakers: The Great Powers and American Independence.*
Peckham, Howard H., *The War for Independence.*

66 The French Revolution

Louis XVI began his momentous reign in 1774. The time was critical because France's enemy Britain was having serious difficulties with the American colonies. With a view to hurting the British and undoing some of the damage the French had suffered from their defeat in the Seven Years' War, Louis' government gave substantial financial assistance to the Americans. This French aid enabled the Americans to win their war of independence, but it complicated the already baffling difficulties of Louis' government. For although France was a rich country, the French government was repeatedly on the brink of bankruptcy because those with the capacity to pay taxes failed to bear their share of the burden. In addition, as scholars have emphasized recently, the growth rate of the French economy left much to be desired, and this further complicated the difficulties of the monarchy.

Year after year Louis sought advice from experts about the financial woes of his government, but to act on that advice invariably meant that some privileged group would lose some of its traditional exemptions. By 1787 the financial situation had become desperate, and so in the very year that the Philadelphia Convention met to draw up the American Constitution, Louis XVI summoned 140 leaders of the French aristocracy, both lay and ecclesiastical, to an Assembly of Notables, requesting that they con-

CHRONOLOGY

A.D.		
	1789	Meeting of the Estates General; conversion of Estates General into National Assembly; fall of the Bastille; Decrees Abolishing the Feudal System
	1790	Civil Constitution of the Clergy
	1791	King forgiven after attempt to flee from France; Legislative Assembly convenes
	1792	Beginning of war with Austria and Prussia; manifesto of the Duke of Brunswick; abolition of the Monarchy and establishment of the Republic
	1793	Execution of Louis XVI; arrest of the leaders of the Girondins
1793–1794		The Reign of Terror
	1794	Elimination of the Hébertists; elimination of the Dantonists; fall of the Robespierrists
1794–1795		The Thermidorian reaction
	1795	Constitution establishing the Directory; dissolution of the Convention
1795–1799		The Directory
1796–1797		Italian campaign of Napoleon Bonaparte
	1799	Overthrow of the Directory and establishment of the Napoleonic Consulate

---

sent to abandon some of their traditional fiscal privileges. Instead of cooperating with the monarchy to which they owed their special status, these notables hid behind a host of legalisms and insisted that they had no right to do what their king wished them to do. They urged the summoning of the old parliamentary assembly, the Estates General, last convened in 1614, arguing that it alone could legally deal with the fiscal crisis.

Thus the very aristocrats who benefited most from the old regime were the first to undermine it. They took advantage of the plight of their king to reassert their own authority and to reverse the whole trend of modern French history in the direction of strong centralized monarchy. Although aristocrats and their apologists everywhere like Edmund Burke and Friedrich von Gentz were soon eager to forget what they had done, the fact remains that they started resistance to the Crown—the Great French Revolution began as an aristocratic revolt. In 1787 French nobles were still fighting the memory of Richelieu, Mazarin, and Louis XIV. Dissatisfied with government of the people, by the king, for the aristocracy, they sought government of the people, by the aristocracy, for the aristocracy. The instrument of revolt would be the Estates General, they thought, for aristocrats, after all, controlled the first estate (the clergy) and the second estate (the nobility). Since voting, they expected, would take place by order, the two upper estates could always outvote the third, which represented the commoners.

After the dissolution of the Assembly of Notables, the king was subjected to enormous pressures to convene the Estates General. From almost everywhere in his realm and from all sections of society came petitions begging him to resurrect the old institution. Louis XVI, a good-natured, kind-hearted nonentity who wished to be the ruler of a happy people, at last consented. Once he did so, however, new pressures confronted him. For aristocrats, whether laymen or ecclesiastics, insisted that the old system of voting by order continue. Otherwise they would speedily lose control of the course of events. But articulate commoners, and some of their radical allies in the privileged estates, wanted the third estate to have what came to be called double representation—some 600 representatives for the third estate as opposed to about 300 representatives each for the clergy and the nobility. The king at last yielded, but he refused to act on the critical request of spokesmen for the third estate that voting be by head in an Estates General whose three orders sat and voted as a single body and which the third estate could therefore easily control.

When the Estates General met in May, 1789, the king insisted that it had one purpose: to solve the financial problems of the government. But few of his subjects shared his view. On the one hand, there were the nobles, still eager to carry through their aristocratic revolt. On the other hand, there were those members of the third estate who argued that their task was really to draw up a written constitution for a modern France. After weeks of delay, confusion, and frustration, three momentous events occurred. On June 17 the members of the third estate proclaimed themselves a National Constituent Assembly and urged the members of the other orders to sit with them—an unmistakable revolutionary step. Three days later, on June 20, came the Tennis Court Oath: members of the newly proclaimed Assembly swore that they would not disband until France had a written constitution "established and consolidated upon firm foundations." A week later, on June 27, Louis XVI ordered the members of the first and second estates to sit and vote with the third estate in a single body, in effect legalizing the extralegal actions of the third estate. Voting by head in the National Constituent Assembly meant the end of the aristocratic revolution and the beginning of the antiaristocratic revolution.

The best-known event in the history of the Revolution, the fall of the Bastille on July 14, 1789, was important in its own time not as an attack on a symbol of royal tyranny but as a step to save the National Constituent Assembly. Troop movements in the neighborhood of Paris as well as the dismissal of the popular minister Jacques Necker gave rise to suspicions that the king had changed his mind about the concessions he had made in June and that he would now use force to get rid of the Assembly. Parisian sans-culottes—mostly small shopkeepers and artisans—moved on the Bastille to find arms and ammunition with which to defend the Assembly against the king's evil designs. Taking the Bastille was no great military feat, but it was a critical event because it demonstrated that ordinary people in Paris were determined that the Assembly should not be disbanded until it had finished its work. The British ambassador did not exaggerate greatly when he noted that after the fall of the Bastille "we may consider France as a free Country, the King a very limited Monarch, and the Nobility as reduced to a level with the rest of the Nation."

Beginning in the summer of 1789, the National Assembly undertook some momentous changes in the interests of liberty, equality, and fraternity, changes that would have reverberations not only in France, but in the rest of Europe and the world. These changes were above all antiaristocratic—designed, in other words, to deprive the higher orders of the special privileges they had long enjoyed in French society. At the same time, these reforms reflected the needs of other social groups—notably the peasants and the urban middle classes.

The first important reform of the Assembly, passed early in August, 1789, was the series of "Decrees Abolishing the Feudal System," which entirely did away with certain kinds of manorial obligations that peasants owed to their landlords and guaranteed that other manorial obligations would also be abolished after suitable compensation had been made to landlords. In keeping, however, with the opening words of the Decrees —"The National Assembly abolishes the feudal regime entirely . . ."— peasants assumed that the abolition was total, immediate, and without compensation, and so they became in many cases loyal supporters of the Assembly. Although the Decrees were important for peasants above all, they also contained provisions that made them meaningful to middle-class, that is, business and professional, people as well. They wiped out special tax privileges and the privileges of geographical districts, and they opened all offices to all citizens "without distinction of birth."

The next important revolutionary change made by the Assembly—and the document by which French Revolutionary ideas were transmitted to other countries—was the Declaration of the Rights of Man and the Citizen (late August, 1789). It contained a moving preamble that attributed public misfortunes solely to ignorance, forgetfulness, and contempt for the rights of man. To prevent these hateful forces from operating in the future, the National Assembly spelled out the basic human rights and duties—freedom of speech, press, and assembly, freedom of religion, equality of all people before the law, the obligation of all people to pay taxes in keeping with their means, rights of private property, and rights to justice on the basis of due process of law.

The third key reform of the Assembly was the Constitution, completed in 1791. It provided for a limited monarchy run by property owners. It divided the French into active and passive citizens according to the tax burden they bore. Active citizens—about three-quarters of the adult males —could vote and hold office; passive citizens could not. The Constitution further provided for a one-house legislature, the Legislative Assembly, which for all practical purposes would rule France. The king would have a suspensive veto—he could delay but not thwart the enactment of laws.

The fourth major reform of the National Assembly was the Civil Constitution of the Clergy. This had nothing to do with doctrinal matters but concentrated on the reorganization of the episcopal structure and the status of clergymen as civilians. Since the National Assembly had taken over church lands and issued bonds, certificates, and paper money (*assignats*) with those lands as security, it now assumed the obligation of paying clergymen's salaries. In return, the Civil Constitution required that the clergy be elected and that they take an oath of loyalty "to be faithful to the nation, to the law, and to the King, and to maintain with all [their] power the Constitution decreed by the National Assembly and accepted by the King."

Not surprisingly, Pope Pius VI condemned the Civil Constitution of the Clergy, and not surprisingly Louis XVI, as a good Roman Catholic, was deeply moved by the papal action. In addition, Louis opposed the measures that limited his authority and left him only "a vain semblance of monarchy." In despair, he and the royal family tried to flee from France in June, 1791, but their flight was hopelessly mismanaged, and they were caught some 150 miles from Paris in Varennes, near the German border.

The embarrassment of the members of the National Constituent Assembly was immense. Having worked for many months to reshape French government and society in an antiaristocratic mold and having drawn up the measures that embodied their view of the right kind of limited monarchy, they were now faced with a king who would not serve. Thus the summer of 1791 saw a great debate in the Assembly between those who said that the king should be forgiven if he would promise to conduct himself as a proper constitutional monarch, and those who insisted that the king was untrustworthy and that the establishment of a republic was therefore necessary. It was the flight to Varennes that created the French republican movement as a significant political force.

Since most members of the Assembly thought republicanism both an alien and a dangerous doctrine, the group that favored the continuation of the monarchy won a temporary victory: so the Assembly finally put the Constitution of 1791 into effect. Elections were held, and the active citizens of France chose the members of what was to be known as the Legislative Assembly. Convened in October, 1791, this Assembly was faced with one problem that overshadowed all others. Within a few months of its meeting, war broke out between Austria and Prussia on one side and France on the other—a war that began as an attempt to take advantage of France's weakness but a war that became increasingly complicated as it dragged on for almost a quarter of a century. The Assembly, therefore, had one responsibility: to save France from the allies. The Prussians and Austrians considered the time to be ideal not merely to stop the Revolution but to reverse some of the defeats they had suffered at the hands of the French in previous wars. Within France itself two groups were especially eager for war: some republicans in the Legislative Assembly who were convinced that the king could not be trusted and who saw in the war a device by which to get rid of the monarchy and at the same time to bolster the French economy; and the king's court group, which worked on the assumption that the war could only benefit the Crown: if the king led France to victory, then his prestige would mount appreciably. If France lost, the allies would undoubtedly restore his authority.

In the early stages of the war, things went badly for the French. French troops broke and fled; inevitably rumors spread about treason in high places. Hence French aristocratic refugees, fearing for Louis' safety, prevailed on the Duke of Brunswick, the commander in chief of the Prussian and Austrian forces, to issue an incredible manifesto: he warned that if any harm was done to Louis and the royal family, Paris would be totally destroyed. The impact of this warning was profound. Within France itself the manifesto was speedily and understandably interpreted to mean that the king was really on the side of the enemy (which documents discovered later would prove him to be), and panic encouraged some ugly episodes of violence, including Louis' confinement. The experiment in limited constitutional monarchy had failed, a casualty above all of the war and the fears it inspired. New elections and a new constitution were necessary. The manifesto which was to protect Louis XVI served instead to undermine his position and usher in the democratic phase of the Revolution.

In the late summer of 1792, a new legislative and constitution-making body—the Convention—was chosen by universal manhood suffrage, though many of those eligible to vote did not do so. It met in September, and its first important act was to proclaim the formal end of the monarchy and the establishment of the French Republic. Hardly did it convene when word arrived of the Battle of Valmy, an engagement from which the Prussians withdrew because of a heavy fog and which the French claimed as a victory. It was an auspicious beginning. The Republic and victory, it seemed, went hand in hand. Yet in the whole history of politics it would be hard to find a government which faced so many difficulties simultaneously as the Convention. It had to cope with a foreign war, a civil war between republicans and royalists, and a virtual civil war among republican factions.

The foreign war became more menacing especially after the British joined the allies early in 1793, for the British brought into play both their navy and what was called, after the younger William Pitt, "Pitt's gold." To many well-informed contemporaries it was only a question of time before the French would be defeated, the Republic overthrown, and the monarchy restored. That this did not happen was due above all to the lack of unity among the allies. Indeed, Prussia and Austria were busy with the partitioning of Poland in 1793 and 1795 when they should have been concentrating on the defeat of France, and so it turned out that Poland helped to save the French Republic.

But it was not the suffering of Poland alone. The morale of French troops in the face of dangers to their country was high. The Republic's use of "propaganda decrees," which assured foreign peoples that France would support their attempts to overthrow their decadent monarchies, was ingenious. And the *levée en masse*—a universal conscription of people and resources—gave all sections of the population a sense of participation in their country and their war. In the words of one of the most famous Republican decrees: "The young men shall go to battle; the married men shall forge arms and transport provisions; the women shall make tents and clothes, and shall serve in the hospitals; the children shall turn old linen into lint; the old men shall repair to the public places, to stimulate the courage of the warriors and preach the unity of the Republic and hatred of kings." At all events, the fears that arose because of the foreign war throw much light on what happened to the French Republic in its early years. The Reign of Terror, with its guillotining of suspects and traitors, is unthinkable except in the context of the war.

At the same time that the republicans were fighting the Austrians, Prussians, and British, they also had to fight those of their countrymen who remained loyal to the monarchy. This struggle became more intense after the execution of Louis XVI in January, 1793, for "a multitude of crimes." The British in particular tried to work with and finance French royalists. Indeed, like the foreign war, the civil war between royalists and republicans helped to inspire the fear and panic that made for the Reign of Terror.

Foreign war and civil war were alarming enough, but to make matters worse the Convention was torn by a frightening factionalism. Between September, 1792, and June, 1793, the chief contending factions were the Montagnards and the Girondins. The Montagnards, or men of the mountain, derived their name from their seats in the highest part of the hall in which the Convention met. The Girondins derived their name from the Gironde, the region of France whose chief town was Bordeaux, since some of their leaders came from that area. They were also known as the Brissotins, after their leader Jacques Pierre Brissot de Warville. Both Girondins and Montagnards were not well organized and disciplined political parties, but loose coalitions of groups and individuals. Both were dedicated revolutionists and republicans, but the Girondins regarded the establishment of the Republic as the virtual end of the revolution, tended to be wary of government intervention in social and economic life, and stood for the rights of localities as against the power of the central government. The Montagnards, on the other hand, despite variations within their ranks, inclined to view the establishment of the Republic as the real beginning of the revolution. Lacking the Girondins' fear of state intervention in social and economic life, they saw further reforms as necessary. In fact, they looked at government as a positive force to protect the poor who could not otherwise hold their own in a competitive society. They sought to create an egalitarian society of small producers, both rural and urban, among whom democracy could thrive.

The victory of the Montagnards over the Girondins came in June, 1793, and it had much to do with the discrediting of two of the most important leaders of the Girondins, General Charles François Dumouriez and Brissot. Dumouriez's desertion to the side of the enemy and Brissot's involvement in financial scandal made it possible for the Montagnards to eliminate the Girondins from any significant role in the Convention. Nevertheless, this was not the end of republican infighting. During the Reign of Terror, the year of Montagnard ascendancy in the Convention (June, 1793–July, 1794), the Montagnards themselves broke up into warring factions: Hébertists, Dantonists, Robespierrists. The leaders of the Hébertists, or Ultrarevolutionaries, staunch advocates of popular radicalism and the de-Christianization of France, were executed in March, 1794, because their fellow Montagnards feared that they were doing untold damage to the Republic by their extremism and particularly their anti-Catholic outbursts —their attacks on nuns and priests and their burning of churches. The leaders of the Dantonists, or Citra-revolutionaries, were executed in April, 1794, in part for their involvement in some ugly bribery scandals—with Danton himself unable to explain how he came to be rich—in part for their power. And even the Thermidorians, who successfully conspired to overthrow Robespierre and his allies in July, 1794, had no intention of ending the terror. They simply wished to eliminate Robespierre and his cohorts before they were eliminated by them, for the Robespierrists set and demanded hopelessly high standards of morality and virtue, both public and private, and they tended to see betrayers of the Revolution everywhere.

Yet, despite all the difficulties the Convention had to deal with—factionalism, civil war with royalists, and foreign war—the republicans carried through important reforms. They committed themselves to a democratic regime in the Constitution of 1793, accepting universal manhood suffrage, the principle of representation in relation to population, and guarantees of civil liberties. They wiped out all remaining manorial obligations without compensation for landlords. They introduced compulsory rationing, passed "maximum laws" fixing prices and wages in a period of wartime shortages, and made profiteering a capital crime—all measures explicitly designed to help the poor to compete for goods with the rich. And while the republicans believed that in principle private property is sacred they also believed that this principle applied only to loyal citizens. Traitors, on the other hand, ceased to be citizens. They had no property rights, and their property should be distributed among the poor and the landless in their neighborhoods. In the words of the short-lived Ventôse decrees of 1794: "All the communes of the Republic shall draft statements of the indigent patriots within their confines, giving name, age, occupation, and the number and age of their children. . . . [The Government] shall make a report on the means of indemnifying all the unfortunates with the property of enemies of the Revolution. . . ."

Yet the most revealing measures enacted by the republicans were not so much political and economic as social and cultural. Believing in human dignity, equality, and fraternity, the republicans tried to make these beliefs part of the fabric of French life. In the eloquent words of one of their decrees:

The French nation, oppressed, degraded during many centuries by the most insolent despotism, has finally awakened to a consciousness of its rights and of the power to which its destinies summon it. . . . It wishes its regeneration to be complete, in order that its years of liberty and glory may betoken still more by their duration in the history of peoples than its years of slavery and humiliation in the history of kings.

In this spirit the republicans abolished slavery in the French colonies as well as imprisonment for debt. They proclaimed their faith in free public education. They discouraged the use of aristocratic words like Madame (my lady) and Monsieur (my sir) and replaced them with Citoyenne and Citoyen. They changed royalist names like Louis to good republican names like Benjamin (Franklin) and George (Washington). They reworked the calendar to get rid of its heritage of unreason, superstition, and tyranny. Thus November, the "ninth" month which was really the eleventh month, became Brumaire (the foggy month); and July (*juillet*) and August (*août*), named after those despots Julius and Augustus Caesar, no longer were permitted to disgrace the French calendar. Indeed, the republicans made clear their sense of their own importance in the sweep of human history by proclaiming the founding of the Republic on September 22, 1792, as the first day of the first month of the Year I. Ushering in a new age, they rid themselves of the old calendar that embodied so much inhumanity of man to man. And all this they did even as they fought a foreign war, even as they fought a civil war, and even as they fought among themselves.

The Montagnards, who overthrew Robespierre in Thermidor, 1794 (July, the hot month), did not intend to end the terror. Nonetheless, the aftermath of the fall of the Robespierrists saw an unanticipated revulsion against terrorism among members of the Convention. In part this was simply a moral outburst against some of the injustices done against some innocent, or relatively innocent, people in 1793–1794. Even more important, it was a reflection of the growing confidence that France could wage a successful war against its foreign enemies without recourse to terrorism at home. At all events, the period of the Thermidorian reaction (1794–1795) saw the decline of much of the panic and fervor of the previous year. It also saw the undoing of the most important reforms of the Montagnards, so that their permanent legacy became mainly ideological. The democratic Constitution of 1793 was replaced with the Constitution of 1795, which provided for a relatively conservative republic dominated by middle-class voters and officeholders. Furthermore, the Convention ended much of the Montagnards' interventionist legislation like rationing and price controls as well as the measures providing for the redistribution of land among the landless. On the other hand, the Thermidorians did important constructive work in the sphere of education. Indeed, some of the educational reforms for which Napoleon has been given credit were, in fact, the work of the Thermidorians, who sought to create an elite to meet their bureaucratic needs.

The Constitution of 1795 provided that France should be ruled by a two-house legislature and five executives known as Directors, and so this government (1795–1799) has been known in history as the Directory. It had some impressive achievements to its credit. Above all, it did magnificently from a military point of view, chalking up some momentous victories and carrying the war actively to foreign soil. And, despite efforts to dislodge it, the Directory survived year after year—longer than any previous revolutionary assembly. For all that, the Directory did not fare well in history, and has not fared well in history books. It was looked upon as a corrupt regime in its own time, and once General Napoleon Bonaparte overthrew it in 1799 his propaganda machine made it seem much more corrupt and immoral than it had really been. Otherwise, after all, he would have been hard pressed to justify overthrowing it. In part, too, however, the bad reputation of the Directory has been due to its unfortunate location in time. It ruled during the period of letdown between the two most dramatic periods of the Revolution—the age of the Montagnards and the age of Bonaparte. It was, in short, a fine period to precede but especially to follow. As Bonaparte bluntly put it, "On my return to Paris I found division among all authorities, and agreement upon only one point, namely, that the Constitution was half destroyed and was unable to save liberty."

For Further Reading

Cobban, Alfred, *A History of Modern France,* Vol. I.
Hampson, Norman, *A Social History of the French Revolution.*
Kaplow, Jeffry (ed.), *New Perspectives on the French Revolution.*
Rudé, George, *Revolutionary Europe, 1783–1815.*

Reaction and Rebellion

67 The Napoleonic Era

For two generations at least, in every European country, the memory of the French Revolution—still in some ways central to the French themselves—was a profound psychological fact. For most respectable, established, and propertied men and women, the main ingredient in that memory was fear, though they differed greatly over the means of exorcising the specter of revolution—whether by resistance, repression, or reform. But in their common anatomy of revolution, a cardinal assumption, preached in and out of season to those less fortunate souls who might imagine it a way out of their troubles, was that revolution inevitably ended in military despotism and the loss of the very liberties the revolutionaries had sought to gain. The historical text they had chiefly in mind was Napoleon Bonaparte, the man they had fought for so long at so much cost in blood and treasure. Despite their efforts, he was remembered by the dispossessed and ambitious as a deliverer, a guarantor not a destroyer of the Revolution. In time it became clear that he had also, unwittingly, stimulated still another profoundly creative force—the nation, as the nineteenth and twentieth centuries have understood it. If one had to choose a single man to stand at the turning point when we can begin to see the world as we know it—a man who summed up what was creative in eighteenth-century Europe and who prefigured (by design, accident, or reaction) the main impulses of the past 150 years, no one could qualify so well as Napoleon. It was surely Napoleon, more than Caesar, more than Luther, whom the German philosopher G. W. F. Hegel had in mind when he spoke of that rare but powerful phenomenon, the "world-historical individual." Hegel and Napoleon were after all, almost exact contemporaries.

Napoleon Bonaparte was born in Corsica in 1769 to a family of decayed but proud petty gentry. A year earlier, France had acquired Genoa's claims to that embattled and clan-ridden island. Born French by accident,

A.D.   1768   French take Corsica
            1769   Napoleon Bonaparte born at Ajaccio, Corsica
            1784   Napoleon enters the École Militaire
            1789   Meeting of the Estates General; beginning of the
                    French Revolution
            1790   Edmund Burke's *Reflections on the Revolution in
                    France* published
       1791–1792   Legislative Assembly
       1792–1795   Convention
            1793   Execution of Louis XVI; English evacuation of Tou-
                    lon; Napoleon becomes brigadier general
            1794   Fall of Robespierre
       1795–1799   Directory
            1796   Napoleon assumes command of the army of Italy
            1797   Treaty of Campo Formio
            1798   Napoleon sails from Toulon to begin Egyptian cam-
                    paign; Battle of the Nile
            1799   Napoleon returns to France; 18th Brumaire; Napo-
                    leon overthrows the Directory
       1799–1804   Consulate
            1800   Battle of Marengo; Battle of Hohenlinden
            1801   Treaty of Lunéville; Alexander I becomes czar of
                    Russia; French concordat with papacy
            1802   Treaty of Amiens; Napoleon becomes life consul
            1803   Bank of France founded
            1804   Napoleon proclaimed emperor; Napoleonic Code
                    promulgated
            1805   Battle of Trafalgar; Battle of Austerlitz; Treaty of
                    Pressburg
            1806   Death of William Pitt; Battle of Jena; Berlin Decree,
                    establishing the "Continental System"
            1807   Great Britain abolishes the slave trade; Napoleon
                    forces Ferdinand VII of Spain to abdicate and
                    installs his brother Joseph as king of Spain; Battle
                    of Friedland; Treaty of Tilsit; Milan Decree
       1807–1808   J. G. Fichte delivers his *Addresses to the German
                    Nation*
            1809   Battle of Wagram; Treaty of Schönbrunn

1810	Napoleon marries Marie Louise of Austria
1811–1813	Luddite risings in Great Britain
1812	Napoleonic invasion of Russia
1813	Battle of Leipzig (Battle of the Nations)
1814	Napoleon abdicates; Treaties of Chaumont, establishing the Quadruple Alliance; First Treaty of Paris
1815	The Hundred Days; Conclusion of the Congress of Vienna; Battle of Waterloo; abdication of Napoleon; the Holy Alliance; Second Treaty of Paris
1821	Napoleon dies at St. Helena

Napoleon was revolutionary by inheritance: his father was a close associate of General Pasquale di Paoli, the veteran Corsican patriot who had fought against Genoa and then against France until his defeat three months before Napoleon's birth. Napoleon's father chose to submit to the French rather than flee with Paoli to England; his noble status, however insubstantially based in wealth, was accordingly confirmed. Napoleon, the second of eight surviving children, benefited much from this decision. With the help of a benevolent patron, he got the best education that France could offer, first in one of the twelve recently founded royal schools for sons of nobles, at Brienne, then, after 1784, at the distinguished École Militaire in Paris, a training school for officers (like Sandhurst or West Point) founded in mid-century as one of the military reforms of the reign of Louis XV. Napoleon's small size and Corsican accent subjected him to taunts from the boys at Brienne, and his unimpressive lineage brought him up against the snobbish contempt of the cadets in Paris. But he was an ambitious, hard-working, and brilliantly successful student. Completing his course, astonishingly, in the space of a year, he was posted at an advanced rank to one of the best regiments in the army.

The Revolution found Napoleon in full sympathy, hardly surprising in view of his experience, his inheritance, or, perhaps more to the point, his thorough allegiance to the ideals of the Enlightenment and above all to Rousseau. With his brothers, he took the lead in implementing the Revolution in Corsica, but the influence this decision won for his family soon dissolved in defeat and exile: Corsica rebelled against France, and General

Paoli returned to deliver the island to the English. Forced to be wholly French, Napoleon managed to survive the kaleidoscopic changes of the early years of the Revolution. He was helped, of course, by the emigration of royalist officers, and he was able in one way or another to avoid postings that might have slowed his progress; but he also gave convenient and genuine support to successive Republican factions as they seized power.

In 1793, with Spanish assistance, the English had occupied the Mediterranean naval base at Toulon, situated in a region honeycombed with disaffection and torn by civil war. Sent to command the artillery in the place of a wounded officer, Napoleon so distinguished himself in the action that forced the English evacuation that he became a brigadier general at the age of twenty-four. Six months later occurred the Thermidorian reaction. Napoleon was then in service with the army of Italy, and though he was briefly imprisoned, the distance from Paris and some helpful connections protected him from the logical consequences of his close association with the Robespierrists. The next year, no doubt serving ambition and conviction as much as his professional obligations, he accepted command of the artillery that the Convention summoned to protect itself from popular protest against the new constitution of the Year III. Napoleon's famous "whiff of grapeshot" on 13 Vendémiaire (October 5) dispersed the insurgents, secured the Directory in power, and assured him of their gratitude. Reinforced by the patronage of Paul François Barras, one of the directors, and by his marriage to Josephine de Beauharnais, an able, flamboyant woman, somewhat older than himself (she had once been Barras' mistress), that gratitude brought the young general a further promotion and, at the age of twenty-six, command of the army of Italy. He now began to sign himself Bonaparte, rather than Buonaparte. It is a fitting sequel to this final commitment to France that his victories in Italy made his native Corsica, from which he had been driven three years before, untenable for its English conquerors.

Spain had quickly withdrawn from the First Coalition of 1793, leaving Austria standing alone with England against a revolutionary France victorious almost by default. To attack England—busy though she was picking up French overseas possessions—was not then practicable; but Austria could be fought on land most effectively in her valuable possessions in northern Italy; by 1797 Napoleon had brought a defeated Austria to the Treaty of Campo Formio and had made northern Italy a French possession.

Napoleon's military success did not lie in a revolutionary technology; even massed fire, his later contribution to the art of artillery warfare, depended on tactical insight, not technical innovation. Like his equipment, most of his tactical devices—the combination of line and column, for example—were well known earlier in the century to royalist officers who had had to plan almost continual wars against England. Revolutionary leaders had already evoked the nation in arms (less novel in theory than in practice), with its irresistible resource of numerous, enthusiastic citizens. What Napoleon brought to bear on this heritage was his skill at disposing and manipulating forces—which in the course of his wars grew to triple the size of mid-eighteenth-century armies—hurling them at the most decisive spot with startling speed and effect. The success of this maneuvering arose partly from his insistence on mobility: he preferred light to heavy cavalry, and his armies, independent of base stores, lived off the country—successfully in Italy, disastrously fifteen years later in Russia. But there was another explanation of his ability to move vast numbers of troops farther and faster than earlier generals: it lay in the steady appeal he made to the self-interest and loyalty of both officers and men. No one better exploited that potent corollary of the nation in arms—the career open to talents: fighting ability brought promotion, and privates could literally become field marshals. No one was better at the equally important task of maintaining or restoring morale by a timely appearance among tired troops to urge them on to the last ounce of effort. To the end Napoleon was a soldier's soldier, and (one is reminded of Erwin Rommel in the Second World War) he cast his spell over his opponents too.

Having beaten Austria in Italy, Napoleon turned to strike at the remaining enemy—not by direct assault but by invading Egypt, a romantic choice that was also rational, for Egypt was the key to control of the East and the route to India, where Britain was finally victorious over the French. But the only French victories in Egypt were those of the scholars and scientists whom Napoleon took along with him; they attained a new level of geographical knowledge, made striking reforms in public health, started the science of Egyptology, and indirectly inspired a new fashion in architecture and interior design. At the beginning of August, 1798, a British fleet, commanded by Horatio Nelson (soon to be Lord Nelson), sailed into the harbor at Aboukir Bay, east of Alexandria, and destroyed the French fleet in the Battle of the Nile, cutting off Napoleon's forces and leaving them to be mopped up slowly by a British army. Napoleon himself escaped to France, arriving on October 13, 1799; he was of course still celebrated for his performance in Italy.

He returned not merely to garner laurels, though they were his in plenty as he journeyed north to Paris. He went to Paris to secure himself in a political situation once more in rapid flux. The Directory was in trouble. Faced with a Second Coalition of Austria, Russia, and England, the French government was overextended in Italy and in financial difficulties, and its members were in disagreement among themselves. Emmanuel Joseph Sieyès, the former priest who had trumpeted the cause of the third estate in 1789 and had survived to become a director, intended to overthrow the system to his own advantage. For his coadjutor, he chose Napoleon, protected as he was by public acclaim from the suspicion rightly felt by the other directors of the young general's ambition. Napoleon's stated price was a central place in the new constitution. To get the constitution, the legislative councils were to be moved from Paris to St. Cloud, where, under Bonaparte's inevitable protection, they could deliberate with only the right pressures applied. But the Councils did not willingly take direction, and their openly expressed distrust of the "dictator" led Napoleon on November 9 (18th Brumaire), 1799, in the riskiest gamble of his career, to drive out the protestors, leaving a rump to agree to the new constitution.

In drafting the Constitution of the Year VIII, which followed the successful coup d'état, Sieyès ingeniously limited the ostensible grant of universal suffrage to the right of local electors to nominate "notabilities," who in turn would nominate a higher level of notabilities, and so on until from a final list the emasculated legislative bodies of the nation would be drawn. The executive power was conferred, as Napoleon wished, on three consuls; but, in the choosing, Napoleon outmaneuvered Sieyès, to emerge himself as first consul assisted by two henchmen. In 1802 he became consul for life, with power to nominate the other consuls and his successor. In some ways it was little more than a change in title when in 1804 Bonaparte became the Emperor Napoleon I. What was new, however, was reversion to the hereditary principle, necessary to the stability of the regime, faced as it was with a renewed war and internal dissension. A pretext was found in an abortive assassination plot early in 1804. The principal conspirators were quickly rounded up—one veteran antirevolutionary wryly remarked that they had set out to give France a king and had given her an emperor—but a grander victim was needed. The leader of the émigrés, the Comte d'Artois, eluded Napoleon's net; the Duc d'Enghien did not. Enghien, certainly not implicated in the plot, was reportedly about to lead an invasion; he was arrested illegally in the German state of Baden, kidnapped, brought to France, tried in secret, and executed. Napoleon thus put his opponents on notice and drove Ludwig van Beethoven, in a rage, to tear out from his *Eroica* symphony the dedication to Napoleon, who had shown himself, after all, a mortal who could turn tyrant. Most of Europe did not need reminding that the Napoleonic regime, still illegitimate, depended on force. To fulfill the hereditary principle, Napoleon needed an heir, and Josephine had been unable to bear him a child. Their marriage, damaged by Josephine's infidelity, had become an arrangement of mutual convenience, softened by a measure of respect and even affection. In 1809, the Emperor finally and reluctantly brought himself to divorce her; early the next year

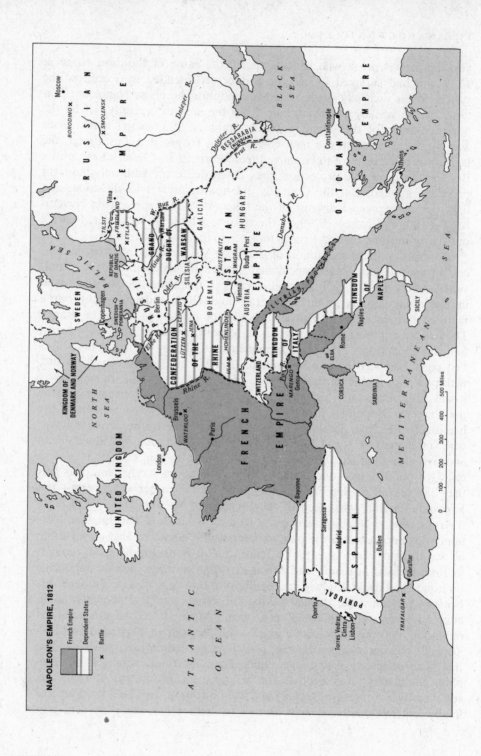

NAPOLEON'S EMPIRE, 1812

French Empire

Dependent States

Battle ✕

RUSSIAN EMPIRE

Moscow ✕

BORODINO ✕

✕ SMOLENSK

Dnieper R.

BLACK SEA

OTTOMAN EMPIRE

Constantinople

Athens

Dniester R.

BESSARABIA (RUSSIAN)

Prut R.

Vilna

W. Bug R.

GRAND DUCHY OF WARSAW

Warsaw ✕

GALICIA

✕ EYLAU

TILSIT

✕ FRIEDLAND

Vistula R.

Oder R.

SILESIA

BOHEMIA

HUNGARY

Buda ✕ Pest

✕ WAGRAM

✕ AUSTERLITZ

Vienna

AUSTRIA

AUSTRIAN EMPIRE

Danube R.

REPUBLIC OF DANZIG

SWEDISH POMERANIA

BALTIC SEA

SWEDEN

Copenhagen

Berlin ✕

PRUSSIA

LEIPZIG ✕

✕ LÜTZEN

Elbe R.

✕ JENA

CONFEDERATION OF THE RHINE

✕ HOHENLINDEN

✕ ULM

SWITZERLAND

Rhine R.

KINGDOM OF ITALY

ILLYRIAN PROVINCES

KINGDOM OF NAPLES

Naples

Rome ✕

ELBA

SICILY

SARDINIA

CORSICA

Genoa

✕ MARENGO

FRENCH EMPIRE

Brussels ✕

WATERLOO ✕

Paris ✕

Bayonne

KINGDOM OF DENMARK AND NORWAY

NORTH SEA

UNITED KINGDOM

London

ATLANTIC OCEAN

Saragossa

Madrid

Bailén

SPAIN

Gibraltar ✕

TRAFALGAR ✕

PORTUGAL

Oporto

Torres Vedras

Cintra

Lisbon

MEDITERRANEAN SEA

0 100 200 300 400 500 Miles

he married Marie Louise, a daughter of the Emperor of Austria. A son, known as the King of Rome, was born in 1811.

Meanwhile, Napoleon had carried French arms and influence to unimagined heights. At the end of 1799, while talking peace, he was preparing for a lightning descent, through the Alps, on Italy; there in June, 1800, he defeated the Austrians decisively in the hazardous Battle of Marengo. A further victory over the Austrians (won by General Jean Moreau, later to be exiled for his part in a plot against Napoleon) at Hohenlinden in Germany led Austria to sign a separate peace at Lunéville. Czar Paul I at once turned about face to form an "armed neutrality" of the Baltic powers against England, and it was only a matter of time until the Peace of Amiens was arranged with Great Britain in March, 1802.

Conflicting interests and the clash of Napoleonic ambition with British strategic imperatives brought the uneasy peace to an end a little more than a year after it was made. But the Third Coalition proved as unstable as the others. Austria, defeated at Austerlitz, signed the Treaty of Pressburg in 1805. Prussia, which had held aloof in the hope of getting the German state of Hanover, belonging to the English crown but occupied by Napoleon, came in only to be beaten at Jena in 1806. The Russians, also caught in the debacle at Austerlitz, were decisively defeated at Friedland in 1807. The result was the Treaty of Tilsit in that year, the high-water mark of Napoleonic success. Having defeated Prussia and Russia, Napoleon made them his allies. France held Italy completely, far surpassing the grasp of Charles VIII four hundred years before. On the Rhine, France had got not only the natural frontiers so dear to Louis XIV but a series of client states in southern Germany; even Holland, so long an unattainable goal of Bourbon ambition, had been reduced to a dependent kingdom.

Only Great Britain had eluded the Emperor, thanks to her navy. Nelson had followed his victory at the Nile by wrecking the Czar's Armed Neutrality in a raid on Copenhagen in 1801. Then, in 1805, as plans for an invasion of Britain were mounted and after a trans-Atlantic race resulting from a French attempt to lure the English fleet from the Channel to the West Indies, Nelson lay in wait off the Spanish coast until the French fleet decided to dash from their refuge in Cádiz for the safety of the Mediterranean. They were caught and decisively beaten in the Battle of Trafalgar on October 2, 1805; Nelson fell a victim, but only after the outcome was clear. The invasion plans were canceled; indeed many troops from Boulogne had already been dispatched to the east to face the Allies at Ulm and Austerlitz. For another ten years France and Britain confronted each other, the one supreme on land, the other at sea.

The Napoleonic era meant more, however, than the triumphant achievement of Valois and Bourbon dreams. Were the consuls right in declaring as they did in 1799 that the Revolution was complete? To say that would be to deny much of Napoleon's persistent appeal. It was in fact his greatest accomplishment that he consolidated and secured the creative impulses of the 1790's in viable form and, in actuality or by challenge, extended them to nearly the whole of the Continent. One could argue that Napoleon violated the basic Revolutionary principle of equality when he restored an aristocracy, or even when he instituted the Legion of Honor in 1802. But the Napoleonic aristocracy—in contrast to the aristocrats of the *ancien régime* for whom the Emperor retained a healthy contempt—was an aristocracy of service, even though tarnished by the corruption of some Napoleonic nobles by power or honor or money; while the Legion of Honor was the canonization of merit and the institutional warrant of the career open to talents. Napoleon's religious policy could also be used as an argument against a revolutionary interpretation of his career. The Concordat with the papacy in 1802 retreated from the advanced secularism of Revolutionary France and from Napoleon's own unreligious outlook; it created a host of problems for future statesmen by deeply embedding the Church (the clergy were paid directly by the state) in the fabric of national life. Yet it was a clear-eyed recognition of the social utility of religion, and it made a signal contribution to the pacification of the country. The majority of French citizens were not yet prepared for the heady laicism to which the Jacobins had called them and which republican politicians a century later were to echo.

Perhaps one could even condemn the Napoleonic Code, the great codification of law proclaimed in 1804, for its retreat to authoritarianism, particularly in the realm of family life. But the main legal victories of the Revolution—equality of men before the law, the rights of citizens, the abolition of manorial privileges—were retained and embodied in a form that has been France's most important cultural export. Indeed, the Code—in striking contrast to the chaotic, creaky, and often inequitable libertarianism of English law—points to the persuasiveness of the central legacy of the eighteenth century, rationality. Rationality was forced on every front. Administration was centralized with clear lines of responsibility running to the Council of State from new officials called prefects, each at the head of a department; with subprefects in the departmental subdivisions called arrondissements and a tight control over the selection of mayors, local government was established in the form it retains today. Taxation and national finances were recast, and in 1803 the Bank of France was founded to cap the nation's financial system as the Bank of England had done across the Channel for more than a century. Centralization was also rigorously applied, for good or ill, to the educational structure, culminating in the University of France. Here the regime built on foundations laid by the Convention and the Directory, but the Napoleonic period saw the effective beginning of those institutions—the lycées and the grandes écoles, above all the École Normale and the École Polytechnique—that have shaped the intellectual life of modern France. The Empire was a despotism still. The secret police, headed by the able Joseph Fouché, was new only in its efficiency; but in its contempt for opposition, increasingly stringent control of the press, and the systematic use of propaganda, the Napoleonic system points forward more than back. Still, this negation of rationality was itself rational: to the very end, Napoleonic France remained a state—a modern state—at war.

While the Revolution was consolidated at home, it was aggressively exported. Again, at first sight, one might be led to doubt that statement. Echoing the Corsican tradition of family loyalty, Napoleon put his relatives on the thrones of client states—he was himself king of Italy, with his stepson Eugene Beauharnais as viceroy, his brother Joseph was king of Naples and later of Spain, Louis was king of Holland, and Jerome king of Westphalia; only Lucien, having made a marriage of which his masterful brother disapproved, retired to private life. The client kingdoms paid tribute and (Italy especially) yielded up their art treasures. But French institutions were used to reduce the vast conquests to order and submission; above all, the Napoleonic Code was used to bring states, hampered by feudal survivals and administrative inefficiency, with a single lurch into the modern world. The example and philosophy of the Revolution went abroad as well. Ultimately the revolutionary parties, most evident in Italy, failed: they were tied too closely to France to survive the reaction of the victorious nation-states. But the legacy remained. The Neapolitan and Spanish constitutions of 1812, extreme and impracticable though they were, enshrined French principles and survived the reaction as spurs to generations of "liberals"; liberal principles informed new parties of the left and inspired recurring revolutions in one country after another.

The countries that escaped French occupation or reduction to the level of client states responded rather to the French challenge than to French principles. Here the best example is Prussia, where reform rested on the impressive Enlightenment that had flourished in the late eighteenth century, with borrowings from the British, notably Adam Smith and Edmund Burke. Indeed certain piecemeal reforms had been accomplished in Prussia before there was a French example, including some freeing of the serfs. But Prussia remained a congeries of scattered feudal segments. Its economy was overwhelmingly given over to agriculture, which became steadily more backward as one proceeded to the east. Its hardened military and bureaucratic tradition was less a viable system than a memorial to the Great Elector and Frederick the Great. But in the years after 1804, through the imagination and drive of a group of enlightened though far from radical administrators, Prussia was remade into a modern nation-state; chief among these legislators was the Freiherr vom Stein, an enlightened Anglophile descended from a family of Rhineland knights. The serfs were freed throughout Prussia, local and provincial governments were remodeled, commerce and industry were relieved of many of the old restrictions and controls, and the army (ultimately based on conscription) was made more efficient and humane. In education above all, the ideals of the Enlightenment were evident. The new *Gymnasien* (equivalent to English grammar schools or French lycées) were henceforth to mold Prussia's elite, and German universities leaped into the vanguard of European intellect. With education, Prussian reform touches most vitally the rapidly growing sense that Germany was a nation, its unity evoked in the potent *Addresses to the German Nation* by the philosopher J. G. Fichte, delivered in 1807–1808, and symbolized by the founding of the University of Berlin in 1810. Napoleon too had contributed to German unity by refusing in 1806 to recognize any longer the existence of the Holy Roman Empire; he thus turned the Hapsburg emperor back on his Austrian and east European domains, while the French consolidation of many petty German states laid the groundwork for still larger agglomerations and ultimately for unification. But the essential spirit, the capacity to think of Germany as something other than a geographical expression, sprang above all from the vision and passion of German philosophers and men of letters.

The three remaining Great Powers were much less touched by French-exported or French-inspired reform. Exhausted from defeat for much of the period, Austria had also reacted against the wholesale reforms of the enlightened emperor Joseph II; Joseph's nephew, Francis I, was far from a reformer. A brief flurry of reform after 1806, under Count Philipp Stadion, was a pale reflection of the Prussian marvel and a gesture at reclaiming German leadership. These reforms underlay, in their military aspect, one more effort against the French that ended disastrously at Wagram in 1809; the brief alliance that followed gave Napoleon his new empress. Thereafter, Francis fell under the influence of Count Metternich, who raised negative policy to the level of principle.

Russia showed no such consistency. More than any other European state, she took her character from her ruler. The early Revolutionary period had seen Russia ruled despotically, with relative efficiency and a decorative overlay of enlightenment, by Catherine the Great; she was succeeded in 1796 by Paul I, whose bitter opposition to Revolution was the only constant in an erratic policy that reflected his madness. His assassination in 1801 brought the young Alexander I to the throne. Himself unstable, and deeply affected by the horrible circumstances of his accession,

Alexander emerged from two mild but abortive reforming movements, one early in his reign, the other after Tilsit, into a conservative mysticism that was to leave its mark on the peace settlement and the postwar world.

In Great Britain, although the period of the Revolution is always counted (rightly) as a serious setback for the movement toward mild political, economic, and religious reform that had begun in the 1770's, a number of administrative and financial reforms were made under the aegis of the country's brilliant prime minister William Pitt. He was in office from 1783 until his death in 1806, except for three years after 1801, when he was forced to resign by the refusal of King George III to contemplate the quid pro quo that Pitt had promised the Irish for the loss of their parliament in the legislative union with Great Britain in 1800—the admission of Catholics to high office and to parliament.

French ideas had certainly infected some Englishmen, most evidently in the early 1790's, when radicalism took an enormous step, both forward and down in the social scale. But a country at war, increasingly impressed by Edmund Burke's arguments in his *Reflections on the Revolution in France,* could not tolerate that kind of dissent, and by 1800 a savage repression had brought open radical activity to an end. Though political and trade-union organizations were proscribed, admiration for French principles and even for Napoleon survived among workingmen and some of the more radical Dissenters from the Church of England, who had not entirely forgotten Cromwell. But throughout the period the invocation of French principles was rather a rhetorical addition to native radical ambitions, running back at least to the seventeenth century. These impulses barely touched a wide public opinion until the last years of the war, when signs of revolutionary ideas and organization reappear among the working classes in the Luddite risings—so called from their mythical leader King Ludd—of 1811–1813. But even among middle-class circles with grievances, the wars against Napoleon brought an upsurge of patriotic sentiment. Unlike Continental peoples, the English did not have to learn the lesson of nationalism; they had learned it at least as early as the sixteenth century and had so far assimilated it as to find newer manifestations of it incomprehensible. But whatever its discontents, the English nation benefited from the essential freedom of its institutions—the lesson that Bonaparte could never learn—and from a sudden, vast expansion of wealth resulting from economic revolution and war.

Robbed of his invasion, Napoleon determined to attack the "nation of shopkeepers" economically. Having got control of the Continent, he proclaimed "the Continental system" in the Berlin and Milan Decrees in 1806–1807, an attempt to exclude British goods to which the British replied with a blockade. The British navy enforced the blockade so efficiently that it became embroiled with neutral nations whose ships it insisted upon searching. This resulted in war with the United States in 1812. But even with his system of client rulers and subject peoples, Napoleon found it hard to enforce his ban on British trade. At times he frankly needed what the British could produce and had to license violation; there was a continual drain through smuggling. But in the two periods when enforcement was really tried, the impact on Britain was extremely harsh—in 1807–1808 and again in 1810–1812; the second of these crises underlay the Luddite risings.

The collapse of Napoleon's dominion began in its extremities, first in Spain. Determined to include Spain effectively in the Continental system, and appalled by the squalor and corruption of the Spanish king and queen and their favorite Godoy, Napoleon forced their abdication in favor of his brother Joseph. The Spanish people never agreed. They rose against the French, in regular and guerrilla military activity. Meanwhile, the flight of the Portuguese royal family to Brazil and the rejection of Joseph by Spanish colonies overseas gave the British two valuable footholds, the one strategic in Portugal, the other economic, on which a century of Latin American economic penetration was based. Although the British began the Peninsular War in 1808, as they were to begin their Continental campaigns in 1914 and 1939, with a brilliant retreat and evacuation, the forces sent to Portugal under Arthur Wellesley, later Duke of Wellington, paid careful attention to fortification, were willing to fall back on their bastions to wait, and finally wrecked the superbly mobile French forces by making them sit still. In 1811 the turning point came, and Wellington and his Spanish allies pushed slowly through Spain to enter southern France in 1814.

Meanwhile, to block the drain at the other end of the Continental system, Napoleon launched an invasion of Russia in 1812. At heavy cost, the Russians retreated to Moscow and beyond, drawing the French a thousand miles from home, where in time they were dealt with cruelly by cold and hunger. The long, tragic retreat from Moscow triggered revolts in other European nations. A Fourth Coalition was formed of Britain, Austria, Prussia, and Russia, and while Britain pushed up from the Peninsula (and provided, as always, endless subsidies) the other three allies massed their armies in Germany. At the Battle of Leipzig in October, 1813, they won a crushing victory, leaving France open before them. After futile negotiations, the allied march resumed, slowed but not stopped by Napoleon, for the numbers he could formerly command were shrinking away and the old spirit was gone. Behind the lines, one after another dignitary sought accommodation or peace, including Joseph Bonaparte and that inveterate schemer Talleyrand, who had already come to terms with Louis XVIII, commenting that treason was a matter of dates. Betrayed and deserted, Napoleon abdicated early in April, 1814. Louis XVIII was proclaimed as the allies entered Paris, and the victors sent the defeated emperor to his new kingdom, the island of Elba in the Mediterranean.

By the Treaty of Chaumont in March, 1814, the coalition was converted into an alliance, and in fairly short order the first Treaty of Paris was signed, providing generous terms for France, which, while losing her natural frontiers and her far-flung acquisitions, still kept more territory than she had had when Napoleon began his conquests; she was not to be occupied or forced to pay an indemnity. To deal with the vastly larger problem of remaking Europe, the powers adjourned to a congress that opened at Vienna in September, graced or overawed by the presence of the Czar, the Emperor of Austria, and the King of Prussia, by a number of lesser monarchs, and by a remarkable set of negotiators—Castlereagh and Wellington from England, Hardenberg from Prussia, Metternich from Austria, and the resilient Talleyrand.

Certain "principles" have been discerned in the settlement: the containment of France; the legitimacy of displaced dynasties; the compensation of states either for their sufferings or for lands they gave up in the general settlement; and, above all, the balance of power. Into the mill went those territories refashioned by Napoleon in southern Germany and the Low Countries; those kingdoms, like Saxony, that had collaborated with the French; and those regions so long subject to manipulation by the great powers, such as Italy or Poland, the latter three times partitioned already and temporarily rescued by Napoleon as the Grand Duchy of Warsaw. France was encircled by an enlarged kingdom of Holland, including the former Austrian Netherlands, by a strong frontier on the Rhine where Prussia was more firmly entrenched, by a revived and neutralized Switzerland, and by Austrian dominance in northern Italy, reinforced by the addition of Venetia (the republic had fallen to Napoleon in 1797) by way of compensation for the loss of her Belgian territories. Poland survived not at all, and Saxony only in truncated form. Denmark ceded Norway to Sweden, the Spanish and Portuguese royal houses were returned to their thrones to face two generations of intrafamily squabbling and civil war, and the Bourbons were restored to misgovern in Naples. Except perhaps for the declaration against the slave trade, inserted at the insistence of Great Britain, where that humanitarian reform had been accomplished in 1807–1810, the settlement was thoroughly obedient to the canons of eighteenth-century diplomacy; only the scale was different. Though in retrospect we can see nationalism as the most powerful solvent of Napoleon's conquests, it was something neither named nor appreciated. The statesmen at Vienna did not recognize it, and it counted only in the future by way of challenging or modifying the settlement.

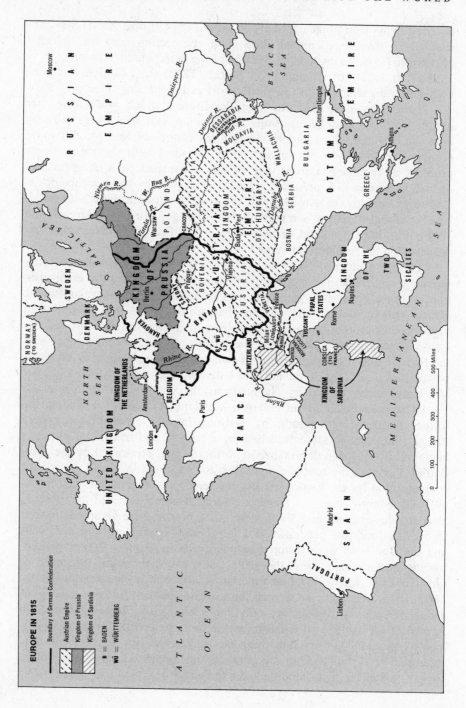

EUROPE IN 1815

Boundary of German Confederation

Austrian Empire

Kingdom of Prussia

Kingdom of Sardinia

B = BADEN
Wü = WÜRTTEMBERG

The splendor, gaiety, and sense of accomplishment in Vienna were crudely shattered in March, 1815, when Napoleon escaped from Elba. As he moved swiftly to Paris, joined by his old soldiers and heartened by an amazing outpouring of loyalty, the coalition was at once renewed, and Wellington and the Prussian general Blücher took up a stand in Germany. The end of the "Hundred Days" came on June 15–18 at Waterloo in Belgium, a battle that Napoleon came close to winning. Louis XVIII returned once more, and this time Napoleon was sent far away to the island of St. Helena in the South Atlantic, to spend the remaining six years of his life spinning reflections, self-justification, and a legend. The Allies had signed the final settlement at Vienna a few days before Waterloo; they went back to the conference table to fashion a second Treaty of Paris, reducing France's territory to the limits of 1790 and subjecting her to occupation and the payment of an indemnity; France was isolated but not ostracized. Other than the Treaty of Paris, the one new element in the settlement was the Czar's harebrained, mystical scheme for a Holy Alliance, by which the monarchs pledged themselves to a policy based on Christian precepts. The monarchs agreed to it as a gesture, except for the King of England, who kept aloof. It was the renewed Quadruple (and later, thanks to Talleyrand's skill, the Quintuple) Alliance on which the Concert of Europe rested in succeeding years. But the Holy Alliance, signed by three despots, became a new bogey to unite heated liberal imaginations that were only temporarily in eclipse.

For Further Reading

Connelly, Owen, *Napoleon's Satellite Kingdoms.*
Lefebvre, Georges, *Napoleon from 18 Brumaire to Tilsit, 1799–1807.*
Simon, Walter M., *The Failure of the Prussian Reform Movement, 1807–1819.*
Thompson, E. P., *The Making of the English Working Class.*
Thompson, J. M., *Napoleon Bonaparte.*
Webster, Sir Charles, *The Congress of Vienna, 1814–1815.*

68   The United States: 1789–1823

The men who made the American Revolution had hardly won independence when they turned to the task of making a nation. Most shared in some measure the mixed expectation of Alexander Hamilton when he wrote, "Happy America, if those to whom thou hast intrusted the guardianship of thy infancy know how to provide for thy future repose, but miserable and undone, if their negligence or ignorance permits the spirit of discord to erect her banner on the ruins of thy tranquillity." Few thought the task would be easy. Their newly independent domain encompassed a territory of imperial dimensions, and history seemed to militate against the success of republics, especially when expanded beyond the confines of a single city. Equally dangerous was the narrow parochialism that permeated the thinking of so many Americans. Only the smaller states, fearful of absorption by their larger neighbors, seemed committed to real cooperation.

But the severe economic and social dislocations that beset the country in the immediate post-Revolutionary years provoked a deepening uneasiness about the future and a growing readiness to consider closer ties. Efforts to resolve commercial difficulties at a meeting in Annapolis, Maryland, during the late summer of 1786 had attracted delegates from only five states, but this assemblage had called for an expanded convention of states to meet the following spring at Philadelphia. This call resulted in the drawing up between May and September of 1787 of the Federal Constitution, a document that defined the basic governmental structure of the new nation.

The liberal philosophy that informed the Constitution evolved from the Puritan and Glorious Revolutions. It expressed a profound concern for protecting the rights of the individual against the pretensions of authority. To assure a balance, it divided power through a system of checks and balances, a process which the Constitution's principal author, James Madison, explained as "giving to those who administer each department the necessary constitutional means and personal motives to resist encroachments of the others." Lest anyone misunderstand his intent, Madison added: "Ambition must be made to counteract ambition."

The founding fathers defined the dimensions of central authority broadly, but they retained also the already existing structure of state and local authority as a check on this central authority. Unlike the French, who

A.D.   1786   Annapolis Convention
      1787   Philadelphia Convention
      1789   George Washington inaugurated
      1791   First Bank of the United States established
      1795   Jay Treaty ratified
      1796   Washington's Farewell Address
      1797   John Adams inaugurated
      1798   Alien and Sedition Acts; first Kentucky and Virginia Resolutions
      1799   Second Kentucky Resolutions; undeclared naval war with France
      1801   Thomas Jefferson inaugurated
      1803   Louisiana Purchase
      1804   Alexander Hamilton killed
      1807   Embargo
      1808   African slave trade ends
      1809   Nonintercourse Act; James Madison inaugurated
      1811   First Bank of the United States expires
      1812   War of 1812
      1814   Hartford Convention; Treaty of Ghent ends War of 1812
      1816   Second Bank of the United States established
      1817   James Monroe inaugurated
      1820   Missouri Compromise
      1823   Monroe Doctrine

produced a Napoleon as an aftermath of their Revolution, Americans accepted a strong central government reluctantly, and only after most stringent efforts to restrict its activities. Ratification of the Constitution was assured only when it was agreed that it be amended to include a Bill of Rights, not the least of which was the right of the separate states to reserve to themselves all powers not "expressly delegated" by the Constitution to federal authority.

Once the great states of Virginia and New York ratified the Constitution in late June, 1788, the new government was launched, but it possessed only the barest administrative apparatus: a foreign office consisting of a secretary, two diplomats, and three clerks; a military establishment made up of one secretary and an 840-man army; and a bureaucracy of twelve (unpaid) clerks. The new government was burdened with a formidable if uncounted debt, and only the barest revenue and no credit with which to resolve its financial problems. Despite this somber inheritance, within less than a decade the new republic was a going concern.

Success in establishing the new government resulted from the unstinting efforts of men such as George Washington, Thomas Jefferson, Alexander Hamilton, James Madison, and John Adams. Washington's enormous prestige gave the Republic a legitimacy no one else could have bestowed, and when in 1797 he voluntarily surrendered the presidency, he set a precedent for the peaceful transfer of power that went far toward guaranteeing its stability. More immediately, as Alexander Hamilton acknowledged, Washington provided the "aegis" under which the Secretary of the Treasury could secure the national credit. He accepted without protest the large role assigned to him, aware that each of his acts converted the broad constitutional principles into the procedures which would guide his successors.

No less formidable, although more controversial, Hamilton persuaded the Congress to fund its inherited indebtedness. Overriding stubborn opposition, he also persuaded Congress to assume the outstanding state debts. The price he paid for this was minuscule: he surrendered the placing of the future federal capital to Jefferson, who located it in the present District of Columbia.

Hamilton was dubious about the prospects of the Constitution, a document which he feared conceded too much authority to the states, but he felt that an effective federal government must nonetheless be established. A weak central government would attach "to itself the disrespect incident to weakness and [be] unable to promote the public happiness." Subtly he set to work extending federal power at every opportunity. To secure the national finances, he maneuvered the First Bank of the United States through Congress. This agency assured the new government of a central bank through which its fiscal needs would be effectively managed. Over the opposition of Jefferson and Madison, he persuaded Washington that the "necessary and proper" clause of the Constitution allowed for the establishment of the Bank.

Hamilton's labors "to establish in this country principles more and more national" triggered deep-rooted fears of central authority and its concomitant threat to state sovereignty. Under the leadership of Madison and Jefferson, opposition arose that by the end of the first decade had become a political party. Unable to prevail within the Washington administration, Jefferson withdrew as Secretary of State to allow him free scope in speaking out for those interests he felt were slighted by the administration.

Central to the Jeffersonian appeal was his confidence in the people, and especially "those who labor in the earth," a group he designated "the chosen people of God." On more than one occasion, Jefferson challenged the idea that government should be "trusted to the rulers . . . alone." Instead he took the position that "the people themselves are its only safe depositories." Possessed of a supreme confidence "in the common sense of mankind in general," Jefferson expressed his "earnest wish . . . to see the republican element of popular control pushed to the maximum of its practical exercise." A government so controlled was bound to be "pure and perpetual." This attitude differed from that of Hamilton, who proclaimed: "Take mankind in general, they are vicious—their passions may be operated upon." Hamilton claimed to be "affectionately attached to the republican theory," but felt obliged to add that he was "far from being without doubts."

But it would be a mistake to identify Jefferson with modern equalitarian doctrine. "There is a natural aristocracy among men," he wrote John Adams. "The grounds of this are virtue and talents." Shaped in his youth by the deferential politics of Virginia, he anticipated that a knowledgeable public would choose to be ruled by the "natural aristoi." And he had no doubt that he was an "aristo" of the blood, a conviction confirmed by his frequent election to office. He also shared the attitudes that characterized the Virginia gentry. Although a staunch supporter of vigorous state government, at least while not himself in control of the federal apparatus, he firmly opposed development of a large federal establishment. "Let the general government be reduced to foreign concerns only," he wrote on the eve of his election to the presidency, "and our general government may be reduced to a very simple organization and a very unexpensive one: a few plain duties to be performed by a few servants."

The divergences between Hamilton and Jefferson were real, but as the first Treasury chief shrewdly observed, "while we were in the administration together, [Jefferson] was generally for a large construction of the Executive authority and not backward to act upon it in cases which coincided with his views. . . . To my mind a true estimate of Mr. Jefferson's character warrants the expectation of a temporizing rather than a violent system."

Hamilton was close to the mark. Both men started from political premises derived from seventeenth-century British revolutionary tradition; both made ready reference to Locke, Harrington, and other revolutionary apologists. Each at a different point in his career posed the great Leveller question, "Men begin to ask, everywhere: Who is this tyrant that dares to build his greatness on our misery and degradation?" Where they parted was in the tone of their expectations. Jefferson in the twilight of life asserted, "It is a good world on the whole. . . . I steer my bark with Hope in the head, leaving Fear astern." Hamilton shortly before his own tragic death said: "Every day proves to me more and more, that this American world was not made for me."

Hamilton's last remark had its ironic touch, for even as he made it, Jefferson, now President, confirmed the permanence of the administrative apparatus Hamilton had erected. Nonetheless, by 1804, Hamilton was an anachronism. In the late 1790's, unable to dominate the Federalist party, he had broken with his nominal chief, John Adams. As that stuffy but sturdy New Englander struggled to contain the undeclared naval warfare raging with France, Hamilton pressed for an open declaration of war. Made uneasy by the savagery of the Terror in France, Hamilton concluded: "None can deny that the cause of France has been stained by excesses and extravagances for which it is not easy, if possible, to find a parallel in the history of human affairs, and from which reason and humanity recoil." Adams did not dissent from that judgment, but he did not believe that the cause of France's enemy Great Britain was that of America. Instead, he insisted that the interests of America were best served by remaining neutral.

Such differences of opinion were significant only as they reflected more deeply rooted national sentiments. The future relations between the new nation and the outside world were at issue. The controversial nature of these differing views speeded the development of the new national parties, a situation many found alarming. "The situation of the public good, in the hands of two parties nearly poised as to numbers, must be extremely perilous," mused John Taylor of Caroline. "Truth is a thing, not of indivisibility into conflicting parts, but of unity. Hence both sides cannot be right." Despite such sentiments, the excitement generated by the signing of the Jay Treaty with Great Britain reached a climax with the emergence of two distinct political parties, the Federalists and the Democratic Republicans.

The Federalists had intended that the Jay Treaty would avoid the outbreak of war, but by failing to settle such issues as the impressment of seamen, ship seizures, and Indian depredations on the northwest frontier, it precipitated bitter protests from among Republicans. It also blighted relations with the French, who claimed that it violated the Franco-American treaty of 1778 and controverted current American sentiment. On the latter point at least, the French were correct. Washington hesitated to act on the treaty, well aware that his decision was bound to aggravate party divisions. "The peace of our Country stands almost committed in either event," the Federalist Noah Webster noted. "A rejection sacrifices Mr. Jay & perhaps many of his friends, a ratification threatens the popularity of the President, whose personal influence is now more essential than ever to our Union." After Washington approved it and obtained Senate ratification, the opposition tried to prevent the House of Representatives from appropriating the funds necessary to implement the treaty. This hurdle was overcome, but Washington sadly observed that public agitation was "higher . . . than it has been at any period since the Revolution."

Contemporary reactions to the Jay Treaty dispute ran the gamut of American fears. The prospect of foreign war, the threat of political dissolution, sectional antipathies, and hidden conspiracies conjured up a witches' brew that unnerved the victorious Federalists, even as it deepened the hostility of the defeated Republicans. Passion threatened to supersede reason. "What has been the conduct of government?" demanded one group of Virginians. "Under the corrupt influence of the [Hamiltonian] paper system, it has uniformly crouched to Britain." Within Congress, elemental decencies faded. Washington's Farewell Address was actually an effort to turn the tables upon those political opponents who were making his final presidential days miserable. With the collaboration of Hamilton, he set to work undermining what vestiges remained of the French Alliance. His famous "great rule of conduct" warned against a *political connection* with any foreign power. Alliances should be transitory, and only "for extraordinary emergencies." Washington recommended both neutrality and unilateralism, a combination he expected to be easily obtained, and he predicted that if the people remained united, national weakness would be succeeded by a strength which would make foreigners hesitant to challenge the country. The United States could then "choose peace or war, as our interest . . . shall counsel." The attainment of this objective became the central theme of American foreign policy.

Between the goal and its fulfillment stood the great European powers, battling for world supremacy. In their conflicts, the rights of neutrals fell by the wayside. Domestic tranquillity suffered further disruption as partisan politics intensified. Crusty and stubborn John Adams, ostensibly the head of the Federalist party, was undercut by Hamilton, even within his own cabinet. Yet he refused to engage in open warfare with France, settling instead for what has been called a quasi-war, while he worked to reconcile misunderstandings. (Adams, however, was no appeaser, while he worked to reconcile misunderstandings. "If infidelity, dishonor, or too much humiliation is demanded, France shall do as she pleases, and take her course," he said. "America is not SCARED.")

A further complication arose when, in response to Republican attacks, Adams reacted with a monumental blunder, the Alien and Sedition Acts. These laws were intended to silence "alien" agitation against the government and prosecute domestic "pests" and disturbers of order and tranquillity 'who write, print, utter, or publish false, scandalous, and malicious writings against the government of the United States.' " Jefferson denounced the Sedition Act as a "gag law," which prompted one Federalist editor to retort: "Nothing can so completely gag a Jeffersonian Democrat as to restrain him from lying. If you forbid his lying, you forbid his speaking."

Portentous with danger for the future was the response of Jefferson and Madison, who put their pens to resolutions, passed by the legislatures of Kentucky and Virginia, which defined federal authority in the narrowest of terms. If the federal government exceeded its constitutional powers, Madison contended, the states had the duty to interpose their authority against "the usurpations of Congress." Jefferson even advocated nullification, a demand that was included in the second set of Kentucky Resolutions of 1799. Although other state legislatures did not follow the lead of Kentucky and Virginia, the resolutions effectively rallied Republican opposition, thus contributing to Jefferson's triumph in the election of 1800.

But once in office, Jefferson, albeit reluctantly, left the Federalist administrative apparatus intact. The threatening tone of his language of the previous decade faded; he appealed for reconciliation and emulated his predecessors in seeking to detach the United States from European involvements. "We have a perfect horror," he declared at the inception of his administration, "at everything like connecting ourselves with the politics of Europe." The world struggle shaking Europe he interpreted as an opportunity to gain advantages in the New World. When Napoleon's plans for an American Empire went awry, Jefferson, uninhibited by his previous strict-constructionist arguments, purchased the vast Louisiana Territory.

But when confronted with renewed British and French attacks on American shipping, he could find no better response than an embargo on all foreign commerce. This boycott, designed to force the belligerents to relax their hostile orders and edicts, boomeranged. Federalist New England resorted to civil disobedience and, with fine irony, contemplated nullification. As Jefferson's second term drew to a close, Albert Gallatin, then Secretary of the Treasury, gloomily confessed: "A majority will not adhere to the embargo much longer. . . ." Congress shortly confirmed his prediction by repealing the act and replacing it with the less onerous Nonintercourse Act.

The Madison administration continued the search for a way to compel respect for American maritime rights. It was a task made doubly difficult by the unimpressive performance of Madison, who revealed a remarkable inability to control Congress or shape public opinion. Within Congress, discontent grew, allowing the more energetic members of the august body, dubbed "war hawks," to shape a policy committed to redeem national honor. Madison succumbed, calling for the expansion of federal arms. By the spring of 1812, Congress had taken so belligerent a stance that few members questioned the correctness of one Pennsylvanian who declared, "If we now recede we shall be a reproach to all nations." With the renewal of an embargo in early April, the drift toward war accelerated. On June 18, 1812, the United States went to war with Great Britain.

In short order, the ill-prepared American forces invaded Canada and were repulsed. Within a year, despite a few early naval successes, the American navy had been swept from the seas. The final indignity came in late August of 1814 when British forces seized and burned Washington. The obvious weakness of the federal government, more specifically its inability to protect the American coastline, excited renewed clamor in New England for an end either to the war or to the Union; a protest meeting at Hartford issued a vigorous defense of states' rights and contemplated secession. But the movement collapsed when peace was negotiated at Ghent in December, 1814. American spirits received an unexpected boost when news spread that Andrew Jackson had won a great battle over the Redcoats at New Orleans.

The war had ended with both belligerents about where they had started. Nonetheless, changes had occurred. Republicans could claim to have won "an honorable peace with a powerful and arrogant enemy." Federalists found it impossible to shake loose from the reputation of treason; the party disintegrated. With the accession of James Monroe to the presidency in 1817, the old divisions faded; seemingly a political consensus had been achieved.

In fact, a massive restructuring of political alignments moved along under a deceptive calm. The long preoccupation with European affairs ended as Americans turned their attention to domestic affairs. "The people have now more general objects of attachment with which their pride and political opinions are connected," Gallatin observed. "They are more American; they feel and act more like a nation; and I hope that the permanency of the Union is thereby better secured."

Events further conspired to ensure the United States greater security from foreign intervention. Napoleon's effort to establish French hegemony over Europe hastened the collapse of Spain's Latin American empire. The long rift between Britain and America was healed by the expectation of security and mutual profit at Spain's expense. When the other major European powers utilized the Holy Alliance to restore governments overthrown by revolutions, Americans moved to recognize the newly independent republics to the south. Any doubt about American views was stilled by the straightforward statements of the Monroe administration. "It may be observed," Secretary of State John Quincy Adams wrote, "that for the repose of Europe, as well as of America, the European and American political systems should be kept as separate and distinct from each other as possible." The government was, therefore, in a highly receptive mood when the British foreign secretary, George Canning, proposed a joint Anglo-American statement supporting Latin American independence. London acknowledged the United States as the dominant American power, a situation that made an understanding of the "great political and commercial interests which hung upon the destinies of the new continent" imperative.

When Britain backed away from implementing the proposal, Monroe and Adams decided to go it alone. The result appeared in Monroe's 1823 Annual Address. The United States unilaterally declared its decision "that the American Continents, by the free and independent condition which they have assumed and maintain, are henceforth not to be considered as subjects for future colonization by any European Power." No less emphatically, American policy renounced any intention of interfering in the internal concerns of Europe.

The long tutelage had ended. Whereas only a decade earlier, Americans had struggled to gain respect for their rights, Adams justified the new doctrine with a simple statement. "It would be more candid, as well as more dignified, to avow our principles explicitly to Russia and France than to come in as a cockboat in the wake of the British man-of-war." The experiment in independence had been completed triumphantly, at least as far as the outside world was concerned.

At home, one haunting doubt remained: the existence of slavery. Through 1819 and 1820, a legislative battle over the extension of slavery into Missouri had raged. It was settled by compromise, but as Jefferson anxiously exclaimed, a geographical line, coinciding with a marked principle, moral and political, had been exposed to angry passions, never to be stilled in the lifetime of man. More ominously, another observer wrote: "The impression produced upon my mind by the progress of this discussion is, that the bargain between freedom and slavery contained in the Constitution of the United States is morally and politically vicious, inconsistent with the principles upon which alone our Revolution can be justified." John

Quincy Adams would one day publicly air his views, and when he did the nation would be well on its way toward civil strife. The United States had avoided destruction from without. Could it avoid disruption from within?

For Further Reading

Dangerfield, George, *The Era of Good Feelings.*
Miller, John C., *The Federalist Era.*
Smelser, Marshall, *The Democratic Republic.*

69   Liberation Movements in Europe

In 1790 the citizens of Avignon declared their wish to be united with the rest of the French nation. They were French, but Avignon was papal territory. Their action nicely illustrated an issue that would become one of the most important sources of conflict and change during the nineteenth century: the principle of self-determination, the right of a people to choose its own allegiance, which ran counter to the generally accepted principle of the day, that a ruler's sovereignty ultimately rested on divine sanction.

The right of self-determination, like the democratic principle, was a vital part of the French Revolution. There was nothing peculiarly French about the idea; what had been done in France had equal validity anywhere. But it began in France: the course of events which resulted in war between revolutionary France and the rest of Europe saved the revolution in France, and the success of French arms spread the revolutionary principle abroad. Napoleon, for all that his regime was an empire and a dictatorship, worked to the same effect. Moreover, the Napoleonic conquests, being French, induced a strong anti-French reaction in which national feeling was crucial. This was particularly marked in Spain and in the Germanies. Modern nationalism, which contains the claim to the right of self-determination as an integral part, had its origin in the French Revolution and its Napoleonic sequel.

Napoleon and France were, of course, eventually defeated, and as we have seen, the Congress of Vienna attempted to restore the old order. But Europe could never be the same again; force can master force but is impotent in coercing ideas. Despite the "settlement" of 1815, the principles of the French Revolution remained the core of nineteenth-century liberalism. In post-Napoleonic Europe many people found themselves under alien

C H R O N O L O G Y

A.D.		
	1814–1815	Congress of Vienna
	1820–1821	Revolution in Naples; rising in Piedmont
	1821–1830	Greek War of Independence
	1823	The Monroe Doctrine proclaimed
	1830	Greece recognized by the Powers; Otto of Bavaria king; revolution in Paris; Louis Philippe "king of the French"; rising in Brussels; proclamation of Belgian independence
	1830–1831	Belgium recognized by the Powers; Leopold of Saxe-Coburg king
	1831	Revolution in Warsaw; risings in central Italy
	1819–1844	German Zollverein
	1836	Palacký's *History of Bohemia*
	1837	Rebellion in Upper and Lower Canada
	1839	Durham Report on the organization of Canada
	1840	Union of Canada
	1847–1848	Irish famine; *Young Ireland*
	1848	*Communist Manifesto;* revolution in Paris; Second French Republic; revolutions in central Europe; Austro-Sardinian War; Piedmontese *Statuto;* Frankfurt Parliament; counterrevolution in France and in central Europe; Louis Napoleon elected President of the Republic
	1849	Roman Republic; Austro-Sardinian War; Frankfurt constitution; Russian intervention in Hungary; the French in Rome
	1867	British North America Act creates Dominion of Canada

rule, and the course of the century saw their increasingly successful struggle to escape this domination. Save for the Scandinavian peninsula, the Atlantic states had long achieved national identity, but the area between the Rhine and the Alps and the Russian border was dominated by multinational empires. The struggle for national identity in mid-Europe took on two different aspects: in Germany and in Italy it sought to bring together separate political entities that "belonged" to a variety of "legitimate" rulers; elsewhere it attempted to disrupt existing political units.

This generalization calls for some qualification, both in the West and in the East. The Kingdom of the Netherlands, a creation of the Vienna settlement, compensated William of Holland for some Dutch colonial losses by giving him the Austrian Netherlands. Austria in turn was compensated with Lombardo-Venetia. The Netherlands had not been united since the days of Spanish rule in the sixteenth century; hence its northern and southern parts had developed quite differently. They were diverse in religion no less than in their economic life. While the Dutch Republic had become an imperial and maritime trading nation, manufacturing flourished in Belgium, the region which, after England, first felt the impact of the Industrial Revolution. In addition to these sources of tensions, the constitution of the new kingdom and the character of King William's rule created grievances among the Belgians who felt themselves treated as conquered subjects rather than equals.

These troubles might have come to a head even sooner than they did had it not been for conflicts within Belgium: Flemish-speaking Catholics stood against French-speaking Walloons, who were strongly influenced by the anticlerical French Enlightenment. The two groups eventually reconciled their differences, however, and the revolution of July, 1830, in Paris was the signal for a rising in Brussels in August. The intransigent attitude of King William led to a complete break and to the proclamation of Belgian independence in October.

Here was clearly a breach of the existing order of Europe which had been guaranteed by the powers at Vienna. William's appeal for support against the Belgians fell upon receptive ears in the conservative courts, the Russian most of all, but the powers had to reckon with the possibility that France might come to the rebels' assistance. But the new "king of the French," Louis Philippe, was a moderate, inclined to peace: he agreed not to intervene in Belgium provided others did not. The British attitude was crucial; when London became convinced that the French entertained no aggressive designs, the possibility of British intervention evaporated. Thus the Belgians were able to make good their independence. The powers, meeting in London, officially recognized it in December. The frontiers of

Belgium were drawn, its neutrality guaranteed, and Leopold of Saxe-Coburg was recognized as king. The Belgians went on to draft a liberal constitution later used as a model for many others. The Dutch king bowed to the inevitable, although he did not formally recognize the new nation for another nine years. The birth of an independent Belgium was a major achievement of liberalism and nationalism acting in unison.

It has been said that the independence of Belgium was won in Warsaw. Czar Nicholas I had assembled an army ready to march to the assistance of King William, but the Poles disliked Russian rule as much as the Belgians the Dutch. The proclamation of Polish independence in Warsaw in January, 1831, provided full employment for Czar Nicholas' army. Surrounded by unfriendly powers, and without the possibility of assistance from sympathetic western states, the Polish rebellion was doomed, though the Russians did not reenter Warsaw until September. The repression was harsh; Poland was virtually reduced to a Russian satrapy. But Polish nationalism did not die.

The events in Poland illustrate a much larger problem: outside of Russia proper the Slavic peoples of Europe were all under alien rule—Prussian, Austrian, or Ottoman. Most of them had lost their independence long before the Poles, but nationalism was everywhere on the rise. German philology and romanticism, searching for the identity of the *Volk,* stimulated it by reviving interest in languages—Czech, for example, which had no current literary status. A number of Czech scholars set about restoring their language to a more dignified position. František Palacký's *History of Bohemia,* written in German in 1836, became in 1848 the *History of the Czech People,* written in Czech. This work of erudition was duplicated elsewhere, among the South Slavs for example, and cultural revival became a characteristic preliminary to the assertion of political claims.

The progression from cultural to political nationalism had manifested itself in Greece as early as the eighteenth century. The Greeks could appeal to ancient glories that all Europe acknowledged. Together with the impact of French revolutionary ideas and Turkish maladministration, cultural nationalism produced revolution, and the proclamation of Greek independence in 1822. During the rest of the decade a struggle, often brutal, went on with alternating fortunes until British, Russian, and French intervention finally procured Greek independence.

The Greek problem was part of the larger "Eastern Question," the fate of the whole Ottoman domain. In Turkey's European possessions the Balkan peoples, Christians for the most part, all wanted independence. The continued decay of the empire, the possibility of the demise of "the Sick Man of Europe," and the question of how his corpse should be disposed of were the constant concern of the powers, ever jealous of each other yet reluctant to break the peace.

Russia, Britain, France, and to a lesser extent Austria had interests in the Mediterranean. The Czar was torn between sympathy for his coreligionists and respect for the legitimacy of the Sultan's rule over Greece; but he was ever alert to the possibility of Russian expansion southward toward the Straits. Britain and France were opposed to Russian expansion, and the result was a compromise of concerted action, the Treaty of London of 1827. The intervention of the three powers led, in 1830, to their recognition of the independence of a small part of the Greek-inhabited world; in 1832 Otto, the second son of the king of Bavaria, was named king of Greece. The Greeks' struggle for independence was far from over; it was to continue throughout the century.

The decades of the thirties and forties were generally quiet in Europe, but agitation went on. The flames of nationalism could not be extinguished by repression or partial concessions. Then, in 1848, revolutions broke out across Europe, some nationalist, some liberal, in inspiration. The first sign of general trouble came in February, 1848, in France.

King Louis Philippe abandoned all thought of resistance and took the road of exile. The triumphant rebels proclaimed the Second Republic. The regime at first reflected the more radical tendencies of the Parisian proletariat and proceeded to hold country-wide elections under universal manhood suffrage. But the country as a whole was less radical than Paris, and the new National Assembly balked at the ambitious program of social reforms proposed by the men of February. By June there was a counterrevolution, in which the workers were ruthlessly put down by the armed forces. By the time elections were held for the presidency, in December, an overwhelming majority endorsed Louis Napoleon, a nephew of the first Napoleon, who had presented himself as the candidate of "order" and had also skillfully capitalized on the magic of his name.

Though change took somewhat longer to effect and the course of events was more tortuous, a broadly similar pattern emerged in mid-Europe, where political liberalism was reinforced by demands for self-determination. This whole area had been under Metternichian direction since 1815, and to Metternich nationalistic aspirations were anathema. In March, 1848, a revolution in Vienna caused his downfall, and Metternich, like Louis Philippe, sought refuge in England. For the better part of two years turmoil prevailed. Taking advantage of the Austrian predicament, the Italians enthusiastically rose in rebellion. But the Austrian army remained loyal, and Marshal Radetzky, following some initial setbacks, retrieved the situation. Simultaneously, Prince Windishgrätz reestablished "order" in

Prague where the nationalistic Czechs had also revolted. The uprising in Vienna, led by liberal students and workers, was crushed as well. As in France, so in Austria, the months from June to December undid what the months of February and March had done.

In 1849 the Italians renewed the war with Austria, but the outcome was a repetition of the preceding year. In Italy as in the Austrian empire, the old order successfully regained the upper hand. All that remained was a constitution in the Kingdom of Sardinia, plus the ironic fact that the pope was restored in Rome through the intervention of French force. It took a little longer to subdue the Hungarians, who were not finally put down until a Russian army intervened.

In Germany, too, the tide of revolution rose and fell, and with the same rhythm. In May a parliament was convened in Frankfurt to frame a constitution and to answer the question: What is Germany?—the old Holy Roman Empire, with its variegated populations, or only German-speaking territories? The high intellectual caliber of the Frankfurt assembly proved on the whole an impediment to the making of decisions, and the national question was a fatal stumbling block. The German Confederation was tied to the Hapsburg domain proper, and by the time the delegates decided to exclude Austria itself and Bohemia from Germany it was too late. Frederick William IV, the Prussian king, had recovered from his initial fright and withdrawn the concessions he had originally granted. In 1849, though tempted, he turned down the offer of a crown made by the Frankfurt Parliament; in 1850, he proposed a scheme of his own for German unity. But confronted with an Austrian ultimatum he yielded. The Frankfurt Parliament exhausted itself in high-sounding but irrelevant talk and expired.

The revolutions of 1848 and 1849 did not affect Britain or Russia. The Irish famine of the mid-forties, terrible as it was, produced no clear movement for independence, and the Poles remained subdued. Britain was not unsympathetic to the liberal agitation across Europe but feared above all the extension of the revolutions into an international conflagration. What interventions there were—the Russian in Hungary, the French in Rome, and a brief German one in the Danish Duchies—thus remained localized. Most important, France, to which central European liberals looked for leadership and assistance, early proclaimed a policy of nonintervention. She saved the peace at the cost of killing the revolution.

The revolutions of 1848 failed; their promoters were too inexperienced and lacked a sufficiently broad base of popular support. The opposite ends of the social scale (the peasantry and the large landowners) resisted the penetration of liberal ideas, while the new industrial working class was still too small to have much influence. Thus the characterization "revolution of the intellectuals" is, especially in central Europe, largely justified. The residue of the upheavals was very small. There were constitutional changes in some small states, but fundamentally control remained everywhere in the same hands, even in France, now again a republic. One notable legacy of the revolutions, especially in the Austrian empire, was the setting of the forces of liberalism and of nationalism against each other.

The disturbances took on, nevertheless, considerable significance as a warning to the defenders of the old order. The forces of change, of liberalism, democracy, and nationalism, though momentarily defeated, were making progress. One relevant development was the altered tone of the social thinking of the revolutionaries. In France the socialism of Louis Blanc was no longer of the utopian kind. And Karl Marx's *Communist Manifesto* was published in 1848. Even though it had no effect on the course of contemporary events, it was a landmark in the evolving social and economic outlook.

Inevitably the passion for self-determination that redrew the map of Europe in the nineteenth century spilled over into European settlements overseas. England's largest collection of overseas settlers in America had of course won independence late in the eighteenth century, but there were settlements to the north of the young United States that remained within the British Empire. They too clamored for some sort of autonomy. The situation was complicated by the ethnic composition of the Canadian settlements. The French had come to the St. Lawrence valley in the sixteenth century, and through times of prosperity and defeat, they had resisted all attempts at assimilation into the dominant English culture. They were French and remained French.

From the beginning, the British recognized the delicacy of the situation, though not, in French eyes, sensitively enough. The Peace Treaty of 1763 had put all of Canada into British hands; in 1774, with the Quebec Act, the British government guaranteed the French settlers the free exercise of their religion (which was Catholic), their language (which was, of course, French), and their law (which was the old French civil law). But after the American colonies had won their independence, thousands of American Loyalists—Protestant, English-speaking, English-oriented—streamed into Canada, obtained land, and agitated to make Canada more clearly British than the Quebec Act had made it. The usual consequences of a moderate policy emerged in Canada, as they often emerged elsewhere: neither nationality was satisfied with the concessions made to the other.

Considering the difficulties, the British government acted wisely. In June, 1791, Parliament passed the Canada Act which divided the region into Upper Canada and Lower Canada, thus dividing (though not with perfect neatness) the British, who dominated the first, from the French, who dominated the second. The government of the two provinces was precisely alike: each had its governor, its appointed legislative council, and its elective assembly. And both were part of the British Empire: London was empowered to disallow colonial legislation. Moreover, the Canada Act undertook to respect the religious sensibilities of both sides: it set aside land for the maintenance of the Protestant clergy and guaranteed the traditional rights of the Catholic Church.

For a quarter-century there was peace in Canada; this was the time of westward expansion and exploration. The Canadian Pacific coast had been sailed as early as the 1780's; in 1792 Captain George Vancouver, an intrepid sailor, carefully explored and surveyed the region that bears his name. In the following year, Alexander Mackenzie reached the Pacific coast overland. The inland remained mostly barren, but by 1800 trappers and traders had crisscrossed the continent many times. Canada was becoming an economic reality, one the mind could grasp. The British-American War of 1812, in which Canadians fought loyally and well, even produced a temporary coalescence of sentiments between English and French Canadians—a convergence of feeling and action that did not long survive the settlement of the war in 1814.

In fact, however, discontent with the Canada Act of 1791 sprang less from national rivalries than from the desire for self-government. Both in Upper and in Lower Canada, new immigrants—mainly Scotch and Irish —complained of the old self-serving plutocracies which monopolized the governments of both provinces. In 1837 and 1838 rebellions broke out; they articulated the demands for a democratization of the government that had been voiced, with increasing irritability, since 1815. The British, heady with reforming fervor after the great Reform Act of 1832, responded with moderation and constructive statesmanship. In May, 1838, the Earl of Durham reached Quebec as the new governor-in-chief of both provinces. "Radical Jack" proved tactless and even more conciliatory to the rebels than the British government had instructed him to be. He resigned under pressure in October, but early the following year, in February, 1839, he issued a celebrated document, the *Report on the Affairs of British North America,* which outlined the policy an enlightened Britain should follow in Canada. The Durham Report, as it came to be known after its author, looked to the creation of Canadian self-awareness through political and economic means. It called for the gradual extinction of French separatism through the creation of a sense of Canadian citizenship, for intensive economic development supervised by the Crown, the reunification of the two provinces, and responsible self-government that would leave mainly the conduct of foreign affairs in British hands.

Much of what Durham asked for was granted with uncommon speed:

in 1840, Parliament enacted the Durham Report into law, although the Canadians did not enjoy fully responsible government until the governorship of Lord Elgin (1847–1854). This was vast progress in a short time. Nor was it all: in these years, Canada regulated its relations with its powerful neighbor to the south. In 1842, with the Webster-Ashburton Treaty, and in 1846, with the Oregon Boundary Treaty, Canada and the United States drew their frontiers to mutual satisfaction. Progress in self-government continued: in 1856, the legislative council was turned from an appointed into an elected body.

But progress in one area created discord in another. Durham's United Canada could not in the long run satisfy the French Canadians, especially since immigration from France was negligible and from Britain sizable. In this atmosphere, replete with tension but still open to reason, a solution emerged: a confederation. That solution was embodied in law in March, 1867, with the British North America Act. It was a piece of legislation of vital importance, for Canada to be sure, but for the rest of the British Empire as well; it was a model for other British colonies. The act provided for a Dominion of Canada, which included the provinces of Nova Scotia, New Brunswick, Quebec, and Ontario. The Dominion had a federal parliament with representatives from each of the provinces, and each of these, in turn, had its provincial government. What Britain had failed to do with its thirteen rebellious colonies, it did in Canada, illustrating that rarest of lessons: that men can learn from experience.

For Further Reading

Marriott, J. A. R., *The Eastern Question.*
Namier, L. B., *The Revolution of the Intellectuals.*
Rath, J. R., *The Viennese Revolution of 1848.*
Robertson, P., *Revolutions of 1848: A Social History.*

70   Liberation Movements in Latin America

The dissolution of the great European empires created by Portugal and Spain in the sixteenth century has long been considered the central event of the first half of nineteenth-century Latin American history. Historians have minutely examined the origins of the revolutions of 1808–1826 that resulted in political independence for thirteen nations. Among the explana-

CHRONOLOGY

A.D.   1804   Haiti declares its independence
       1808   Portuguese Court flees to Brazil
       1810   Autonomous governments set up in Argentina, Chile, Colombia, and Venezuela
       1815   Brazil declared a kingdom
       1816   Bolívar issues a decree against slavery
       1817   José de San Martín crosses the Andes to defeat Spaniards at Battle of Chacabuco
       1821   Victory of Bolívar at Carabobo, last major engagement of war in Venezuela; Mexico wins its independence, followed by short-lived (1822–1823) rule of Emperor Agustín Iturbide
       1822   Brazilian Empire declared independent under Pedro I
       1824   Battle of Ayacucho, last major engagement in South America
       1826   Congress of Panama, convoked by Bolívar
       1830   Death of Bolívar

---

tions they have found for these fundamental changes are the administrative ineptitude of Spain and Portugal, the influence of Britain, France, and the United States, the growing economic and political maturity of the colonies, and the impact of the European Enlightenment upon traditional values in the New World. But it was Napoleon's invasion of the Iberian peninsula which precipitated the events that led to the violent disruption of the Spanish empire in America and the peaceful entrance of Brazil into the society of independent nations.

The martial exploits of such figures as the Mexican priest-patriot Miguel Hidalgo, the dashing liberator Simón Bolívar, and the respected José de San Martín have until recently dominated the story of the revolts against Spain. Diplomatic maneuverings in European chancelleries and Washington have also been emphasized. Little attention has been paid to cultural, economic, and social developments. We have it on the authority of Bolívar himself that the revolutionary years brought no basic changes to the structure of Latin American societies. On his deathbed the Liberator declared that he had "plowed the sea," so far as changing the character of South American life was concerned.

More recently Marxist-oriented Latin American historians and others have made detailed studies and sophisticated analyses of the nonmilitary aspects of these turbulent decades. In certain respects independence marked no sharp break with the past, for despite the clash of arms and the multitude of pronunciamentos, many economic and political institutions persisted throughout the revolutionary era. But there were some decisive changes. Foreign trade increased when the old mercantilistic monopolies collapsed. Already strong movements for the suppression of the slave traffic and the abolition of Negro slavery grew still more powerful. During the revolutionary wars, although Negroes and Indians served chiefly as cannon fodder on both sides of the struggle, persons of mixed blood rose more easily in the social scale and mestizo army officers became more numerous. On the other hand, the colonial protective laws generally vanished with independence, and the missions which had protected many Indians were ruined. In the new competitive society the ill-prepared Indians suffered greatly.

The most marked social change, however, was the rift that developed between the urban elite who dominated the seaports and the capitals and the rural, provincial societies of the interior. Historian Charles C. Griffin explains it this way:

At the seats of government and in the ports upper and middle classes began to be affected by the streams of foreigners (diplomats, visiting scholars, pedagogues, merchants, soldiers and sailors). . . . Fashions began to ape the styles of London and Paris; new sports and pastimes replaced colonial recreations; even habits of food and drink changed. Provincial cities were but little affected by these newfangled notions and the countryside was largely unconscious of them. Thus, the wider, European outlook of the elite in almost every country began to show itself in minor ways long before it was enshrined in law, educational institutions, and in the arts.

Brazil's independence was accomplished far differently. The Prince Regent Dom João fled from Napoleon's army across the Atlantic, protected by the British fleet, and landed with some 15,000 courtiers in Rio de Janeiro in 1808. Thus, Rio became the temporary capital of an empire which included, besides Brazil, the islands of Cape Verde, Madeira, and the Azores, the vast unexplored territories of Angola and Mozambique in Africa, and scattered establishments in China, India, and Oceania. This momentous event both enhanced the pride of Brazilians and brought solid economic advantages. The old Portuguese mercantile monopolies were abolished and Brazilian ports opened to the trade of all friendly nations. The manufacture of iron and textiles was undertaken; a bank, a naval college, a medical faculty, a botanical garden, a public library, and a printing press were established. Agriculture improved as coffee production expanded under royal protection, and the Botanical Garden introduced the cultivation of Oriental tea.

To the capital came many distinguished foreigners, often under royal patronage. A mission of French artists in 1816—architects, musicians, painters, sculptors—became the nucleus later for an Academy of Fine Arts. European scientists arrived and prepared learned reports which greatly increased the world's knowledge about Brazil. But the presence of the Portuguese court brought some problems. Taxation increased, and arrogant courtiers, officials, generals, and hangers-on monopolized the offices of government, much to the chagrin of the Brazilians whom they displaced.

Even after Dom João granted the colony equality with the mother country in 1815, serious economic and political differences divided Brazilians and Portuguese. Dom João returned to Portugal in 1821, accompanied by some 3,000 courtiers and most of the cash in the Bank of Brazil. He left his son Crown Prince Pedro to govern Brazil. Aware of the growing Brazilian desire for independence and strengthened by the advice of the most distinguished Brazilian of the age, José Bonifácio de Andrada, Pedro led Brazil into independence with his famous "Cry of Ipiranga" (September 7, 1822): "Independence or death! We have separated from Portugal." Pedro was proclaimed emperor. But in 1831 he too departed, having proved almost as autocratic as the Portuguese parliament. He left behind his infant son, Pedro II, who was crowned emperor in 1841 at the age of fifteen, the only monarch in the Americas. Thereafter for almost forty years Pedro gave Brazil a degree of peace and stability unique in Latin American history. (Another unique phenomenon was that Negro slavery lingered on until 1888; Brazil was the last country in the Americas to abolish the peculiar institution.)

A deep cleavage between port and hinterland society also developed in Brazil, evidenced by the generational gap between the younger landed gentry who became urban leaders trained largely in the law and their patriarchal families who remained in the provinces: "In their material environment and, to a certain extent, in their social life," Gilberto Freyre has written, "the majority of the Brazilians of the fifties were in the Middle Ages: the elite only was living in the eighteenth century. Only a few men, such as the emperor himself, and a few women . . . were conscious of the Europe of John Stuart Mill, hoop-skirts . . . four-wheeled English carriages, and Pius IX."

Elsewhere in Latin America confusion and dictatorship often reigned. Mexico during these decades was bitterly divided between Federalists and Centralists, the latter group led by the colorful demagogue Antonio López de Santa Anna. This sorry period in Mexican history reached its nadir in

LATIN AMERICA AFTER
THE WARS FOR INDEPENDENCE

European possessions

• Capitals of independent countries

0   500   1,000 Miles

the war with the United States, 1845–1847, when internal politics as much
as the American army resulted in the fall of Mexico City. In Central
America the second quarter of the nineteenth century was so chaotic that
one American diplomat traveled over the length and breadth of the Central
American federation in vain search for a government to present his cre-
dentials to. Elsewhere confusion, sometimes chaos, prevailed. The Argentine revolutionary movement of 1810 gave the liberals an opportunity to
organize the country politically and to reform it socially and economically.
Despite the efforts of such able men as Mariano Belgrano, Manuel

Moreno, and Bernardino de Rivadavia, they failed, and Argentina fell under the dictatorship of the bloody tyrant Juan Manuel de Rosas (1835–1852). Defenders of Rosas (and they still flourish in Argentina) point to his maintenance of independence against attacks by France and Britain, which was indeed no mean achievement. But he also began the distribution of land to army veterans, which led to the growth of the enormous ranches which have so notably influenced Argentine economic and political life. In nearby Paraguay José Gaspar Rodríguez de Francia, an even more despotic dictator, kept his nation sealed off from effective contact with the outside world for most of the period 1814–1840.

Chile's revolutionary experience illustrates the difficulties confronting the friends of real reform. Bernardo O'Higgins possessed great power during his rule (1818–1823), but he could neither change the popular addiction to religious processions, cockfighting, and gambling nor take away from the aristocracy their privileged positions and great entailed estates. The principal result of the Chilean revolution was the transfer of economic and social control from a Spanish-led society to one dominated by conservative Creoles.

The monopoly of the Latin American Catholic Church was only slightly shaken in the post-revolutionary years. The British insisted in their 1810 treaty with Brazil on permission to hold Anglican services, but even this modest toleration found no favor in Spanish America. Despite the beginning of anticlerical movements, priests had an important voice in fashioning the basic policies of the new nations. In Peru, surprisingly, some religious leaders proposed to make the Church more relevant to the life of the people. They proposed to celebrate Mass in the vernacular, make church services less ornate, reduce the influence of Rome, do away with the Inquisition, and even relax the rule of celibacy for at least some of the clergy. But the priests who advocated these remarkable reforms were ahead of the times; the hierarchy condemned them and they were silenced.

The dreams of Bolívar for one Great Colombia were also dashed: Ecuador, Colombia, and Venezuela went their separate ways. Thus, nearly everywhere the immediate aftermath of the revolutionary wars was often frustration. Even in Brazil, regional rivalries and discontent led to disturbances that were not quelled before the middle of the century.

But did Bolívar and the other liberators really "plow the sea"? In large measure the answer to this question, unfortunately, is yes. The new nations were not stable enough or advanced enough to confront their fundamental problems—education, land reform, transportation, agricultural and industrial development—with any marked success. Yet the economic devastation and social changes that the wars caused permitted some new developments as traditional ways weakened. The political liberation of the Iberian empires in America made possible choices that would not have been open had Latin America remained in colonial bondage. The liberated nations, now open to world influences, aroused keen interest among European investors. Visions of El Dorado danced before the eyes of merchants, manufacturers, entrepreneurs.

British enterprises were particularly imaginative: Cornish miners were to bring new techniques, the Pacific and the Atlantic were to be joined by a canal, milkmaids were to be sent to Buenos Aires to improve butter production. Capital was available to launch a joint stock company for almost any project: to navigate the rivers of South America by steamboats, to fish for pearls in Colombia, to establish the unemployed poor of Great Britain and Ireland as agricultural colonists in the United Provinces of the Río de la Plata. Many of these schemes resulted in severe losses to European investors, but others helped to bring Latin America into the modern age. Ideas as well as techniques, capital, and manufactured goods flowed across the ocean. Although for many years her role remained passive, Latin America was becoming a part of the larger world.

For Further Reading

Bushnell, David (ed.), *The Liberator, Simón Bolívar: Man and Image.*
Humphreys, R. A., and Lynch, John (eds.), *The Origins of the Latin American Revolutions, 1808–1826.*
Masur, Gerhard, *Simón Bolívar.*
Robertson, William S., *The Rise of the Spanish American Republics as Told in the Lives of Their Liberators.*

71   The Near East

The eighteenth century marks one of the lowest points in the long history of the Middle East. Various causes, from the twelfth century onward, had contributed to the decline: the Crusades, the Mongol invasions, the breakdown of some of the major irrigation systems and the salination of the soil, the infiltration of nomadic tribes and the diversion of trade routes. In the fifteenth to sixteenth centuries the Ottoman Empire, and in the sixteenth to seventeenth Iran under the Safavids, had enjoyed a temporary revival, marked by strong government, economic recovery, and a high level of artistic creation—without, however, any accompanying technological or

CHRONOLOGY

A.D.

1774	Russo-Ottoman Treaty of Kuchuk Kainarji
1792–1793	Nizam-i Jedid; New Regulations reorganizing Ottoman military and civilian institutions
1794	Founding of Qajar dynasty in Iran
1804	Serbian revolt against Ottoman rule
1804–1812	Russo-Persian war, ended by Treaty of Gulistan in 1813
1805	Muhammad Ali becomes governor of Egypt and founds dynasty
1807–1808	Revolt of Janissaries, murder of Selim III, succeeded by Mahmud II as Ottoman Sultan
1811	Muhammad Ali massacres Mamelukes and consolidates his rule
1820–1822	Muhammad Ali conquers Sudan
1821–1830	Greek war of independence
1825–1828	Russo-Persian war, ended by Treaty of Turkmanchai, 1828
1826	Mahmud II massacres Janissaries and reorganizes Ottoman army
1832–1833, 1839–1840	Ottoman-Egyptian wars
1837–1838	Persian-Afghan war
1839	Hatt-i Sherif of Gulhane: reforms guaranteeing liberties of Ottoman subjects; British occupy Aden
1854–1856	Crimean War
1856	Hatt-i Humayun: extending of rights granted by Hatt-i Sherif; Anglo-Persian War
1860–1861	Communal conflicts in Lebanon and Syria
1868–1876	Ottoman Civil Code
1869	Opening of Suez Canal
1875–1878	Balkan and Russo-Turkish wars
1876	Proclamation of Ottoman Constitution, accession of Abdul Hamid II

1881–1882	Arab revolt in Egypt, followed by British occupation
1883–1885	Mahdist revolt in Sudan ending Egyptian rule
1896	Assassination of Nasiruddin Shah of Iran
1896–1898	Anglo-Egyptian reconquest of Sudan
1901	Oil concession granted to W. K. D'Arcy in Iran
1905–1909	Constitutional Revolution in Iran
1908–1909	Young Turk revolt restores constitution in Turkey; deposition of Abdul Hamid in 1909
1912–1913	Balkan wars
1914	Turkey enters war on side of Central Powers; Egypt becomes British protectorate
1916	Arab revolt against Turkey
1917	Balfour Declaration, promising Jewish national home in Palestine
1919–1922	Turkish war of liberation against Greek and Allied forces
1923	Treaty of Lausanne between Turkey and Allied Powers; deposition of sultan; Turkey proclaimed republic
1920	League of Nations assigns mandates to France over Lebanon and Syria and to Britain over Iraq, Palestine, and Transjordan
1921–1925	Riza Khan establishes control over Iran, deposes Ahmed Shah and founds Pahlavi dynasty
1922	Britain declares Egypt independent
1924	Ibn Saud conquers Hijaz and establishes rule over most of Arabian Peninsula
1932	Iraq granted independence

intellectual progress. But from 1514 until the middle of the eighteenth century these two empires were engaged in almost uninterrupted and inconclusive wars, which exhausted their strength and devastated the borderlands, especially Iraq and Azerbaijan. From the end of the seventeenth century, in both states, the central government's hold on the provinces gradually weakened. Revolts and tribal raids proliferated, order broke down, communications crumbled, and economic activity declined. In the course of the eighteenth century European commerce with Iran, Syria, and Egypt dwindled and cultural contacts diminished, increasing still further the already great isolation of the region. However, in Constantinople and the Balkans, both trade and cultural exchanges increased rapidly, setting in motion economic, social, and political forces that were to transform that region.

The Middle East was pulled out of its isolation by international political and economic rivalries. At first the main clash was between Britain and France, then between Britain and Russia, and finally, toward the end of the nineteenth century, between Britain and Germany.

From the time of Peter the Great, Russia had been encroaching on both the Ottoman Empire and Iran, while Britain's expanding empire in India made it increasingly anxious to secure the land and sea routes leading to the subcontinent. But it was Napoleon's conquest of Egypt in 1798, and his dispatch of a military mission to Iran in 1807, that drew attention to the strategic importance of the Middle East and made it a center of Great Power struggle.

Between 1804 and 1827 Russia defeated Iran in three wars, annexing Georgia and Azerbaijan. But no significant Russian conquests were achieved at the expense of Turkey because the British, and sometimes the French, resisted Russian expansion. Their opposition expressed itself most dramatically in the Crimean War. Russia's efforts did help to liberate the Balkan peoples, but did not lead to the domination of the area that the czars desired.

After the expulsion of Napoleon's troops from Egypt—owing to Nelson's victories—France lost all direct power in the Middle East; every French attempt to regain control of the area was frustrated by the other Great Powers. But France retained much influence in the region, thanks to its investments in the Suez Canal and various railways, its trade, its numerous cultural and religious contacts, and its acknowledged position as protector of Catholics in the Ottoman Empire. Britain became the dominant power in the Middle East after 1815. By its steady support of the Ottoman government it exerted much influence until the end of the century. Its naval supremacy was unchallenged, and its economic strength far exceeded that of its rivals. Except for the brief war with Turkey in 1807 and the expedition of 1840 against Muhammad Ali—undertaken at the request of the Porte—the short Persian War of 1856 was Britain's only direct clash with a major Middle Eastern state. In 1820–1853 treaties suppressing piracy and the slave trade ensured its predominance in the Persian Gulf. In 1839 it annexed Aden—for use as a coaling station and to guard the entrance to the Red Sea—and in 1878 Cyprus; in 1882 it occupied Egypt; and in 1896–1898 an Anglo-Egyptian force conquered the Sudan.

The rise of German power, and the increasing economic and military cooperation between Turkey and Germany, which culminated in the, alliance of 1914, forced a realignment of the rival forces. Britain settled claims with France in Africa in 1904—relinquishing Morocco in return for Egypt—and in 1907 came to an understanding with Russia about Iran, dividing the country into spheres of influence. Starting in 1915, Britain, France, Russia, Italy, and Greece began partitioning the Ottoman Empire. The Bolshevik Revolution and Turkey's victorious struggle against the Allied forces in 1918–1922 rendered many of the provisions of these treaties inoperative, but France emerged with control over Syria and Lebanon, thus fulfilling an ancient dream, and Britain was granted mandates over Iraq, Palestine, and Transjordan. Thereafter, with France as a junior partner, Britain dominated the Middle East until after the Second World War.

Repeated defeats by Austria and Russia and the successful Balkan national uprisings persuaded the Ottoman rulers to take radical steps in hopes of saving their empire. Selim III (1789–1807) and Mahmud II (1808–1839) broke the power of the Janissary army—once the finest and most disciplined infantry in the world, but by now an unruly, destructive mob—and cleared the way for the Tanzimat reforms. The army and the bureaucracy were reorganized; control of the central government over the provinces was greatly strengthened. In 1908 the Young Turk movement destroyed the absolutism of Abdul-Hamid II, ushering in a brief constitutional period that lasted until Turkey's entry into World War I. Underlying these political changes was steady, if very slow, modernization of the legal and judicial systems and some progress in economic, social, and intellectual activity.

Until shortly before the First World War, the official ideology continued to be "Ottomanism." All subjects of the Sultan were encouraged to think of themselves as equal. In 1839 even Christians and Jews were granted formal equality with Muslims. But the successful encroachments of the Balkan states, which by 1912 had absorbed practically the whole of European Turkey, along with Armenian national aspirations—which were ruthlessly repressed—and the rising tide of Arab nationalism, brought

THE MIDDLE EAST, 1880-1914

Maximum extent of the
Ottoman Empire,
1880-1914

0   100   200   300   400   500 Miles

about a sharp change in policy. Recognizing that the strength of the empire
lay in its Turkish component, the government tried to "Turkify" the other
peoples. This only exacerbated national feelings still further and led to the
Arab Revolt of 1916. In 1918 the empire was shorn of many of its Asian
provinces and occupied by Greek, British, French, and other troops. The
ensuing war of liberation revivified Turkish nationalism. It was led by
Mustafa Kemal Atatürk, a general who had won fame and popularity by
his brilliant defense of Gallipoli in 1915 and his dogged resistance to the
British advance in Syria in 1918. The ramshackle, multinational, archaic
Turkish empire emerged as a compact, homogeneous republic which, in the

course of the 1920's and 1930's, rapidly modernized its economic, social, and cultural institutions. The power of the Muslim clerical establishment was broken, the Arabic script was replaced by one based on Latin, the veil and polygamy were abolished, and education was expanded.

In the Arab provinces four separate forces eroded Ottoman rule. In Egypt Muhammad Ali, a tobacco merchant of Turkish origin, born in Albania in 1769, with no education but endowed with ability amounting to genius, landed as a soldier of fortune in the Ottoman army. By 1805 he had become pasha, or governor, and soon secured virtual independence and founded a dynasty that ruled the country until 1952. With the help of French and other foreign advisers, he established a modern army and navy and the most efficient government in the region and started a process of rapid economic and social development. In Arabia a puritanical religious revival, Wahhabism, enabled the house of Saud, after many vicissitudes, to extend its rule over the greater part of the peninsula under the leadership of Adul-Aziz ibn-Saud (1880–1953), the founder of modern Saudi Arabia. National movements in Lebanon, Syria, and Iraq took the form of secret societies which inspired the Arab Revolt during the First World War, under the leadership of the Sherif of Mecca. Lastly, Britain, France, and Italy occupied various countries in the Middle East and North Africa.

The postwar settlement caused great disappointments. Egypt, after much agitation, secured a limited measure of independence in 1922, which broadened in 1936 but still fell short of nationalist demands. The Fertile Crescent was placed under British and French mandates, and Palestine was declared a national Jewish home, to which more than 300,000 Jewish immigrants came by 1939. The interwar years witnessed continual agitation and revolts against the British and French but except in Iraq, which became independent in 1932, the results achieved were slight. And the nationalist struggle led to the frequent disruption of the constitutional processes introduced in these countries in the 1920's.

In Iran, which was less exposed to Western influences than the Ottoman Empire, the absolute rule of the Qajar dynasty (1794–1925) was not seriously challenged until the Constitutionalist Revolution of 1905–1909. After an initial success constitutionalism was, however, crushed with the help of Russian troops and the Russian-led Cossack Brigade. During the First World War Iran, notwithstanding its official neutrality, became a battle ground for Turkish, Russian, and British troops. The collapse of the Ottoman Empire and Russia left Britain as the predominant power, but a nationalist uprising and diplomatic pressures forced British withdrawal. One of the leaders of the uprising, Riza Pahlavi, an army officer of humble birth and little education but great ability, proclaimed himself shah in 1925, and started rapidly to modernize the country.

Western interest in both raw materials and swift connections with India led to the establishment, as early as the 1830's, of regular steamship services between Europe and the eastern Mediterranean and between India and Suez. Then the opening of the Suez Canal, in 1869, channeled a huge amount of traffic through the Middle East. Ports and internal transport were developed: the first Egyptian railway was opened in 1854, and others soon followed in Anatolia, Lebanon, Syria, the Sudan, and Iraq. Steamboats cruised the Nile, the Tigris-Euphrates, and the Karun. After the First World War road building was greatly accelerated.

All this, together with the inflow of European capital (nearly $2 billion by 1914) and the development of banking and other financial services, made it possible to integrate the Middle East in the international economy. Cash crops grown for export, such as cotton and tobacco, began to dominate the economy. The area under cultivation was greatly extended and large irrigation works were built, notably in Egypt.

The value of the foreign trade of the Middle Eastern countries multiplied manyfold in 1815–1914. And although population was growing everywhere, thanks mainly to improved hygiene, total output seems to have increased faster, with a consequent rise in the level of living. However, transport also opened the way for European factory products, which soon overpowered the Middle Eastern handmade goods, causing great hardships to the ancient handicraft centers—and to certain segments of the population.

In the 1920's, and still more in the 1930's, exports suffered greatly, because of the sharp decline in world agricultural prices. This brought home the need for industrial development, and by 1939 a start had been made in Turkey, Egypt, Iran, and Palestine. Foreign oil companies began drilling in the region before World War I, in Iran and Egypt, and by the beginning of World War II the Middle East accounted for some 6 per cent of world output.

Increased trade and the reorientation of trade and communications through the Middle East helped to spark an intellectual renaissance. Missionary schools were established in Lebanon in the eighteenth century and in the other countries in the nineteenth. All the main Christian sects participated in this movement, but the most active countries were France and the United States. In addition to elementary and secondary schools, foreign missions provided the Middle East with its first liberal arts colleges, notably the American University in Beirut (1866) and Robert College in Istanbul, and military schools, with technical branches, were founded in Istanbul, Cairo, and Tehran. But full-fledged national universities did not come into being until the decade of World War I. The Egyptian, Ottoman, and Iranian governments began sending students, mainly prospective technicians, to European centers early in the nineteenth century, and the number has expanded steadily down to the present time.* Soon Western books were being translated into Turkish, Arabic, and Persian, and were brought out, in large numbers, by the newly established printing presses. For although a printing press had been set up in Istanbul in the eighteenth century—and there had been even earlier ones among the Christian sects of Lebanon and Syria—it was not until the nineteenth century that printing attained significance. Almost simultaneously, newspapers began to appear in Egypt, Lebanon, Turkey, and Iran, spreading new ideas among a broad circle of readers. This was accompanied by a literary revival, marked by greater simplicity and clarity of style, enrichment of vocabulary to cope with modern needs, and the introduction of hitherto unknown forms such as novels and plays. And although by 1939 the Middle East had made no significant technical, scientific, intellectual, or artistic contribution, it had carried out a far-reaching and irreversible internal transformation. Writers of distinction, some of whose works were translated into various foreign languages, had appeared: for example, Peyami Safa and Zia Gök Alp in Turkey, Taha Husain and Tawfiq al-Hakim in Egypt, Muhammad Ali Jamal-Zadeh and Sadiq Hedayat in Iran. For the first time in centuries, women began participating in intellectual activity, notably the Turkish novelist Halide Edip and the Lebanese Mayy Ziadeh. Some sculptors and painters began to attract international attention. Scientists were grappling with local problems. Altogether, the intellectual and artistic horizons of the Middle East were being immeasurably broadened.

For Further Reading

Avery, Peter, *Modern Iran.*
The Cambridge History of Islam. (2 vols.)
Fisher, Sydney N., *The Middle East: A History.*
Hourani, A. H., *Arabic Thought in the Liberal Age.*
Hurewitz, J. C., *Diplomacy in the Near and Middle East.*
Issawi, Charles, *The Economic History of the Middle East.*
Lewis, Bernard, *The Emergence of Modern Turkey.*
Vatikiotis, P. J., *The Modern History of Egypt.*

* The only previous mission had been the sending of Iranian painters to study in Rome, in the 1640's. A few members of minority groups—Greeks, Armenians, Jews, and Catholic Lebanese—did, however, pursue theological or medical studies in Italy and other European countries.

The Industrial Revolution

72   The Industrial Revolution in England

The Industrial Revolution was essentially a rapid change in methods of producing goods other than crops, a change that involved a transition from making things by hand with the aid of simple tools to their production by increasingly complicated machines and chemical processes. In this great transformation, which quickened dramatically in the second half of the eighteenth century and continues to this day, mechanical contrivances performed more and more human tasks; machines were moved by energy derived from inanimate rather than animal, including human, sources; and goods increasingly came to be made out of inanimate materials. Not only did the Revolution put millions of mechanical slaves at the disposition of man, but it also permitted him greatly to increase the supply of raw materials at his disposal. It allowed him to tap the riches in the earth's crust that had been stored up over eons. Man was no longer restricted for the satisfaction of his needs and wants mainly to the current output of plants and animals—he could turn to his own purposes a wealth that would have made Midas seem like a pauper.

The advances which gave this great economic change the name Industrial Revolution occurred in Great Britain, yet it would be contrary to the facts to regard the mechanization of industrial processes as strictly an English experience. More in accordance with the evidence would be the view that this great transformation of industry and subsequently of society itself was a product of Western civilization, which in turn had borrowed widely from many civilizations. Indeed, one should remember that spinning and weaving, the making of pottery on the potter's wheel, the grinding of grain by composite mechanisms, the moving of machines by windmills and water wheels, the transmission of power by shafts and gears, the operation of atmospheric pumps like the water pump, and the fundamental processes of metallurgy were transmitted from the ancient past to modern man and

A.D.

1694	Founding of the Bank of England
1733	James Kay invents the flying shuttle
1769	Josiah Wedgwood opens pottery factory at Etruria, near Stoke-upon-Trent; James Watt patents the steam engine after years of experimentation; Richard Arkwright invents the water-powered spinning frame
1770	James Hargreaves patents the spinning jenny
1776	Adam Smith publishes *The Wealth of Nations,* the classic of classical political economy
1784	James Watt patents a locomotive, two years after Oliver Evans patents a similar device
1785	Edmund Cartwright patents the power loom
1793	Eli Whitney invents the cotton gin
1798	Eli Whitney builds a factory for the mass production of firearms near New Haven
1811	Pittsburgh's first rolling mill opens
1821	Great Britain adopts the gold standard
1822	First textile mills in Lowell, Massachusetts
1824–1825	Repeal of the Combination Acts in Britain, permitting trade unions to burgeon
1829	George Stephenson perfects the steam locomotive
1830	Railroad is put to its first serious uses in the United States
1846	Great Britain repeals the Corn Laws
1849	Great Britain repeals the Navigation Acts
1858	Henry Bessemer (later Sir Henry) builds Bessemer Steel Works at Sheffield, using a new process that makes large-scale production possible
1869	Transcontinental railway across the United States is completed

were developed and refined by Continental Europe. England, more than any other state between 1750 and 1850, had a number of advantages which joined in felicitous proportions and with proper timing to effect rapid industrial change. In this case, as in so many great movements in the past, the doctrine of *necessary concomitants* provides a framework for the most rational and most complete analysis of what took place.

England achieved its breakthroughs primarily, as we shall see, in the manufacture of textiles, especially cottons, in iron metallurgy, and in the development of the steam engine as a prime mover. Yet changes in spinning and weaving and in smelting were accompanied by a host of improvements in production—the invention of the circular saw and the rotary plane in the lumber industry, the slide rest on the lathe, the boring mill which allowed the making of more accurate guns and cylinders for engines, better glazes in making chinaware, breechloading and percussion guns, the cylindrical press for printing cloth, and new methods of making the basic industrial chemicals, sulfuric acid and soda. It seemed that "Necessity" had mothered a great brood of inventions in one mammoth birth.

England was the leading innovator of methods for rendering raw materials more useful to man, but it by no means had a monopoly of inventions. A Frenchman, Antoine Lavoisier, discovered the chemical nature of combustion; another Frenchman, Claude Louis Berthollet, developed prussic acid (hydrocyanic acid) and used chlorine for bleaching; still another, Nicholas Leblanc, discovered a way of making soda from sea water; and a fourth, Louis Robert, invented the process of making paper in continuous strips. An American, Eli Whitney, invented the cotton gin. And a German, Justus von Liebig, determined the chief chemical components of plants and thus laid the basis for a chemical fertilizer industry.

England had, however, a clear head start in the mechanization of industrial production, which gave her enormous economic advantages down to at least World War I. In the cotton textile industry England long held an overpowering position. In 1821, it took over 70 per cent of American exports of raw cotton. In 1840, Great Britain mined 31 million tons of coal, as against 4 million tons produced by Belgium, and 3 million by Prussia. Ten years later, Great Britain owned more net tons of commercial shipping than France, the United States, and the German states together, and in 1870 it produced more steel than France and Germany combined. In that year the United Kingdom produced 31.8 per cent of all the world's manufactured goods, and accounted for as much of the world's trade as France, Germany, and the United States put together.

The extraordinary jump that Great Britain got on other powers of Western civilization in the hundred years from 1750 to 1850 also gave that country important noneconomic advantages. It attained a position of military, especially naval, dominance that in turn gave it great "diplomatic" power. This meant that Britain's role in the affairs of Europe was greater than it had been in the seventeenth century and enabled it to capture the lion's share of the colonial areas that were being divided, especially in Africa, in the New Imperialism. Furthermore, industrialization and trade so elevated Britain's per capita national income that by the middle of the nineteenth century it was about twice that of France or Germany. Thus it became apparent to all other nations that if they were to play an important role in international affairs and if they were to enjoy a higher standard of living they must industrialize. Indeed, the history of the last century and a half has been characterized by a struggle to industrialize—and no end to that effort is in sight.

However, awareness of an "industrial revolution" as a great divide between an old world and our world was hardly paralleled by a similar awareness on the part of the people who lived through it. In the eighteenth century many well-informed Englishmen were barely conscious of factories, so often tucked away in inaccessible parts of the country, knew little of the men who ran or worked in them, and had little time or understanding to spare for the economic and social problems that are so likely to engage our attention. Nor did entrepreneurs or the hard-pressed if narrow-sighted local government officials who had to cope directly with those problems think in terms of a revolution; most of the problems—child labor, for example—and the remedies found by the state or by philanthropic individuals were commonplaces in preindustrial England, and the changes seemed only of degree, not kind. The new processes that appear to us so revolutionary were seen by their initiators rather as pragmatic solutions to immediate practical problems, and devoid of wide social significance. There were, moreover, many earlier innovations in both technology and organization, while in parts of the economy old methods persisted until the present century. Still, at some point in time, probably in the late eighteenth century, a crucial corner was turned, or, to borrow W. W. Rostow's phrase, there occurred a "take-off into sustained growth." To understand how it happened, we must reckon with economic developments that—like the optimism that suffused men's minds or the demand for political change that swelled toward the century's end—were deeply rooted in preindustrial circumstances.

In agriculture, the predominant industry in which the wealth and interests of England's social and political leadership lay, the eighteenth century saw the maturing of a series of important changes. From about the time of the Restoration, the owners of large landed estates began to consolidate and to add to them, frequently at the expense of small owner-occupiers (often called yeomen) handicapped by lack of capital, heavy taxation, and inefficiency. The most capable of small owners might in fact better their lot by becoming tenant farmers, and some managed to survive on their own lands into the nineteenth century. Others sold out and went into trade; many more no doubt declined into the ranks of laborers. Thus emerged the typical Victorian rural pattern of landlord—living primarily on his rents—farmer, and landless laborer.

The need to administer large estates profitably gave rise to changed methods. The most important and famous was enclosure, replacing the old system of open fields containing the scattered strips of individual holdings by the walled or hedged fields of compact, separately held farms. Parts of the country had been enclosed for hundreds of years, and in many places enclosure had gone on regularly by agreement among owners. But elsewhere the old system survived until the eighteenth century; then, helped in part by lower rates of interest, the process went on rapidly to create more or less the modern look of the English countryside by the early nineteenth century. Enclosure made possible new crop rotations and improved stock-breeding, and many proposals were made for the application of machines to agriculture. But machinery could not come into general use until there was industry to produce it, and much bad farming continued alongside the improved farming that attracted so much attention from contemporaries. Crop yields seem not to have increased markedly during the eighteenth century, and the growing population had to be fed more and more from imported grain.

Rooted in England's natural and political advantages, a striking prosperity came to English towns, reflected in improved standards of living, a flourishing provincial culture, and a growing pride and confidence. Early in the century what passed for public opinion found expression largely in a jingoistic hatred of the French or in sporadic outbreaks of hostility against town oligarchies or the central government; by the end of the century it had grown into a demand for political participation and reforms. But the forms of trade and industry that underlay these developments were not fixed, and, as in agriculture, the century saw important changes. In some industries—shipbuilding, for example, or brewing—the size of firms steadily increased. In others traditional organization was beginning to approach the limits of practicability; such was the "domestic system" of the textile industry in which outworkers in small villages or the countryside round about a large town were employed by a clothier who supplied them with raw materials and marketed the goods. In foreign trade, where the largest profits and the greatest risks had lain, England's markets were shifting. England's principal trade had always been with the Continent, but because she wanted more Continental wines, steel, naval stores, raw wool, and luxury goods than the Continental demand for English woolen cloth could pay for, the difference had had to be made up by reexporting tropical products from Africa, the Americas, and the Indies. The gradual shrinkage of the European market in the eighteenth century was, however, more than compensated for by a rising demand for English goods in the tropical areas and, above all, in the flourishing North American colonies. The growth of England's foreign trade provided a surplus of capital for investment and strengthened her commercial machinery.

The most fundamental change was probably the rapid growth in population that began in the 1740's. There was no census before 1801, but Malthus' essay on the principle of population, published three years earlier, gave powerful form to an awareness pressing in on all sides. The causes of this increase are obscure. In recent years historians have shifted their attention from a declining death rate to social and environmental factors raising the birth rate—the decline in apprenticeship, say, or lowered age of marriage. Whatever the causes, between about 1750 and 1820 the English population doubled. The growing population had to be fed, clothed, and housed. Towns, growing much more by natural increase than by immigration from the countryside, spawned problems far beyond the capacities of old medieval urban institutions.

The upward surge in population forced English industry to find ways of meeting the demand. But the hard-headed men who took the decisions did not all follow one particular course or turn at once to the use of machines and bringing together large numbers of workers in factories. Indeed, the more natural and profitable way in many industries lay in the increasing subdivision and specialization made possible by an expanding market. At one level the process led to a growing differentiation among those individuals or firms vaguely called merchants. In the early eighteenth century, a large merchant might buy and sell a wide variety of goods, own or hire ships, and function as an insurer or banker; by the latter part of the century these functions had generally split apart, and even those who bought and sold specialized increasingly in particular commodities. A similar course was followed in some of the metal trades—hardware among them—and thus some cities, like Birmingham, remained towns of small workshops until the late nineteenth century.

In other industries more obviously revolutionary means were employed. One such industry was iron. Steel was used only for fine work like cutlery; its widespread use had to wait until after the middle of the nineteenth century when ways were found to produce high-quality steel in quantity. So the first century of the Industrial Revolution was an age of iron, though the demand for it tended rather to follow the spread of industrialization than to anticipate it. The ancient English iron industry, based on small, migratory, charcoal-fired furnaces and forges, could not meet the challenge even after the discovery of the coking process early in the eighteenth century enabled manufacturers to substitute coal for vanishing supplies of English charcoal. It was not until the steam engine in the 1770's made possible the hot blast, and the Cort process the production of high-quality wrought iron, that the industry could move forward. Its rapid progress thereafter and the large, permanent installations of the new technology required larger units and huge investments. The iron industry also helped to revolutionize the mining industry; although the nature of the coal seams precluded much mechanization until fairly recent times, mines went deeper and required more expensive and sophisticated equipment for hauling, lifting, and pumping.

The textile industry did not require such high-cost and impressive equipment, but a seemingly insatiable world demand called for vastly greater productivity of both labor and capital. Wool, long England's major industry, was no longer in the vanguard: technical difficulties delayed the invention of machinery, and the complex structure of the industry, shot through with vested interests and stubborn traditions, was another powerful brake on progress, at least in the traditional textile centers in the west of England and East Anglia, which lost the initiative and ultimately succumbed to the more progressive ways of the new, less tradition-bound woolen manufacturers of the West Riding of Yorkshire. What the world wanted was cotton cloth. A new commodity in world trade, first introduced from India in the seventeenth century, cotton progressed slowly in early eighteenth-century England. But, unhampered by inherited organization and able to draw on a rapidly growing supply of raw material, English cotton manufacturers took advantage of a series of important inventions that first speeded up handwork (e.g., the flying shuttle) and that then, through the application of mechanical power, superseded handwork in one after another operation, improving quality at the same time. Mechanization came first to the spinning side of the industry; the expanded supply of yarn was made into cloth by handloom weavers who flocked into that easily learned and highly respectable trade to face a terrible future when it in turn was mechanized early in the nineteenth century. Prices fell dramatically, and it was soon possible for English calicoes, spun, woven, and printed by machine, to undersell handmade calicoes in India itself. Until well into the nineteenth century, the prosperity of England's export trade rested above all on cotton cloth.

The cotton industry was the first to turn to full-scale factory production. The reliance of cotton mills on water power imposed limitations on the industry as to location and, in dry seasons, even operation. In 1769, James Watt, a Scottish instrument maker, had found a way to bring new speed and efficiency to the cumbersome steam engines used since the late seventeenth century to pump out mines. Watt's steam engine was quickly applied to the iron industry to provide the hot blast and to power steam hammers. Then, in the eighties, Watt found a way to convert his engine's lateral stroke to circular motion; this made it possible to bring factories into towns, close to the supply of labor.

But what probably made most men aware for the first time of the extent of the industrial change that had come over the country was the use of the steam engine for still another purpose. The railway, fully launched with the opening of a line between Liverpool and Manchester in 1830, had grown out of the earlier use of railed ways over which stationary engines hauled heavy loads, coal particularly. The locomotive steam engine effected a major revolution. Intended at first as supplementary to the network of turnpikes and canals that had spread throughout England in the late eighteenth century, this new triumph of industrial organization ended by sweeping the field of transportation. Supported by local interests and by a remarkable outpouring of the nation's capital, but built without a national plan, English railways lurched through a succession of speculative booms, some spectacular failures, much trial and error, and far too many horrible accidents into approximately the modern system by the 1870's. Nearly all of English life was affected: the movement of passengers, mail, and goods was speeded up; bulky raw materials and manufactured goods were made available throughout the country; the look of the country was dramatically altered by viaducts, cuts, and tunnels; and men's imaginations were deeply stirred.

The Industrial Revolution was the work of thousands of men with an eye to profit, as much efficiency as they could afford, and survival, of men willing to work hard and to take sometimes disastrous risks. These entrepreneurs were drawn from a wide spectrum: merchants, yeomen, landed gentlemen (who were not prevented by social custom, as on the Continent, from open participation in trade), even dissenting clergymen. Their social and political attitudes varied as much as their origins. Some were narrow, bigoted, self-serving, and harsh; perhaps not far removed themselves from being workmen, they had to pinch every penny and exploit their workers as ruthlessly as they dared. Others were educated, enlightened men who did their best to provide as good working and living conditions for their workers as could be managed, took the lead in the religious and cultural life of their communities, held local office, and aspired to a role in national politics. More, in between the two extremes, moved toward the latter pole in the second or third generation or even escaped into the ranks of the landed gentry.

By law and inherited prejudice, they were denied the advantages of the modern joint-stock company: not until 1844 did it become easy and relatively inexpensive to incorporate, and not until 1855, and then against strong resistance, was limited liability allowed. But the family firms or partnership provided sufficient resources for all except the most extensive, capital-devouring enterprises like the railways. The railways performed an important service, however, in accustoming wealthy men and women to invest in industry rather than in land or government securities. By the 1870's and 1880's more and more firms were outgrowing limited resources, even when fed by plowing back profits, and the limited liability corporation began to come into its own.

England was fortunate in having a well-developed banking system that could make loans to investors or to firms and that moved funds from areas where money was plentiful to those where it was in short supply. At the head of the system was the Bank of England, founded in 1694, a privately owned joint-stock bank dealing primarily in government business. Beyond the well-established and generally solid London private bankers were the rapidly growing numbers of country bankers. But the system was remarkably freewheeling and betrayed a degree of ignorance of sound banking practice that seems appalling to modern eyes. The Bank of England did its best to avoid becoming a true central bank, a role it did not exercise fully until toward the end of the nineteenth century. With often the dimmest notions of liquidity, and with little experience to guide them in such important questions as the proper proportion of loans to deposits or the extent of reserves needed to support the issue of paper money, English bankers helped to feed the inflation of the period of the Napoleonic wars and often to worsen the cyclical fluctuations of the economy that came with such terrifying regularity in the early nineteenth century. Usually triggered by a crop failure or by some adverse development in international trade, these periodic crises were heightened by the lack of knowledge as to how to deal with them and by panic. Even the best firms could suffer, and those with the fewest resources or the most incompetent managements simply disappeared, and with them the livelihoods of their workers and the capital, and often the reputations, of the owners.

The men, women, and children who supplied the sinew and skill for English industry present a similarly complicated picture. In the eighteenth century English labor consisted of a mass of skilled and unskilled workers who fell into a complex hierarchy of income and social position. Industrialism increased this complexity by opening a new range of skills and responsibilities to the most able and ambitious and, at the other end of the social scale, by isolating workers in old, decaying industries from which the only escape was likely to be death or the workhouse. Moreover, industrialism gave new opportunities for the employment of women and children, often indeed in greater demand in some industries than men. Not only the economic but also the social and psychological effects of this development were enormous. Workingmen were well aware of the distinctions conferred by training, skill, and education; at the same time, they came increasingly to think of themselves as forming a class, with common interests to be defended against their masters.

It would be dangerous to take this essentially political self-evaluation at its face value, but English labor did have a few common characteristics. Workingmen were far better disciplined in the middle of the nineteenth century than they were at the beginning. To a considerable degree, this was the result of their having been broken to or having grown into an industrial discipline unlike the life of an agricultural or domestic-industrial community. The organization of a factory, the incessant demands of a single, tireless source of power, meant living by the clock, keeping the pace, and obeying orders, a hard set of lessons enforced by fines, discharge, the blacklist, and (on children) by beatings. The foreman, or overlooker, represented immediate authority, and a gulf opened between the owner and his workers that could not exist in a workshop. The most generous and foresighted provision by an employer for education or the improvement of his workers could seem condescending or self-serving at a distance. So too employers, fearful of any compromise of their authority, sometimes sought out the most docile labor—women and children where possible—and set themselves resolutely against trade unions. Trade unions had been outlawed in 1799 and 1800, but were again permitted, for dealing with wages and hours of labor, in 1824; after a succession of false starts, trade unionism took deep root among the skilled trades in the 1840's and 1850's, and within a generation they were strong and confident enough to seek for new economic and political conquests.

It is impossible to speak categorically about the effect of the Industrial Revolution on standards of living. Probably most workingmen who thought about such things would have said that their condition had deteriorated: the myth of a golden age in a rural past was strong. It was also largely untrue, if one considers the quality of the life of the poor in the eighteenth century. Certainly for most nineteenth-century workingmen and their families the expectation of life was increasing (save for the stubbornly high rate of infant mortality), and the disappearance of traditional, often brutal pastimes was matched by the appearance of others, among them by mid-century the music hall and organized sport. But to try to argue the case for either improvement or deterioration from statistics is a nearly hopeless task. Not until the middle of the century can one speak confidently about the pattern of wages and purchasing power: from then until nearly the end of the century, there was fairly steady improvement in standards of life throughout the working class, except in the worst of the so-called sweated trades, the remnants in tailoring, dressmaking, cigar making, and some other examples of a domestic system that had all but disappeared from the industrialized trades. Earlier in the century, however, such survivals created widespread social problems and provided the main mass support for radical movements like Chartism. Still, whatever improvement can be pointed to, nothing can gainsay the awful threat that lurked throughout the century in sickness, being orphaned or widowed, or being thrown out of work in a depression. Despite the enthusiastic and sometimes misguided work of private charities, such calamities more likely than not meant resort to the Poor Law, and that for many of its "beneficiaries" meant the hated workhouse. Leaving aside the small numbers of highly skilled "aristocrats of labor" who could limit entry into their trades and for whom trade unions or friendly societies provided insurance against illness or unemployment, the most constant and appalling characteristic of working-class life was a terrible sense of insecurity.

The most impressive and to some attractive guide to understanding the working of this complex and changing economy was the system of economic thought that has come to be known as classical political economy. To a large degree its categories were preindustrial. Adam Smith's seminal *Inquiry into the Causes of the Wealth of Nations* was published in 1776, and even David Ricardo's systematization of economic thought forty years later was obsessively concerned with problems drawn from agricultural experience, such as the interrelations of landlord, capitalist, and laborer, and the nature of rent. Still, classical economics could lead to highly relevant analyses of industrial society, and in time even to socialism, by way of the labor theory of value, as central to Ricardian as to Marxian economics. The essentially optimistic outlook of Adam Smith was given a gloomy turn by the engrafting of the Malthusian principle of population, and much Victorian economic and social thought was dominated by the notion of a wages fund, a fixed and not easily alterable supply of capital that had to be parceled out among available workers: the greater their numbers, the smaller the share of each. Despite the enlightened attitude toward labor of many of the leading economists, the popular version of the system often supported a fatalistic view of the possibilities of improvement and an ideological justification of the arbitrary power of the capitalist.

Many other currents of the age, however, led to a softening of this harshness and a blurring of the lines of the class struggle that men in all segments of opinion were not slow to discern. The stream of voluntary charitable activity had broadened to a flood by the end of the eighteenth century; much of it was foolish, but some was magnificent, finding expression in the founding of hospitals, schools, and other institutions to better the quality of human life. To its most devoted practitioners, such voluntary work seemed a far more certain and rewarding means of alleviating suffering than appealing to a state that had, in everyone's experience, proved to be lamentably inefficient and corrupt. It was even possible to imagine the creation or evolution of a perfect society through the generalization of education, discipline, and humanity. The notion of a creative individualism —so idealistic in its own time, so harsh in both appearance and reality in retrospect—was made more tolerable by the persistence and strengthening of certain social arrangements that men then took for granted—a newly humane but still stern administration of law, made the more efficient by the new police forces of which London's, founded in 1829, was the prototype; the social discipline of the family; the tradition of a hierarchical order in which, while men could rise and fall, they generally knew their place and kept to it. Above all, perhaps, a moral revolution spread rapidly beginning in the late eighteenth century. It rose partly from the demands of a more populous and interdependent society that could not tolerate the old laxity, partly in response to the imperatives of a revived and Evangelical religion. Attitudes toward work, sex, and private and public behavior were humanized, and the goal of "respectability," though peculiarly prized by a rapidly growing middle class, exerted an appeal throughout society. As with factory discipline, much was lost through the imposition of this new moral discipline—color, freedom, amusement, and possibly some important psychological outlets. Yet surely more was gained, for it helped to create a society that, for all its faults, was increasingly safe, comfortable, and peaceful.

The most enthusiastic advocates of laissez-faire could not, however, refrain from demanding that the state clear away mercantilist obstacles to free enterprise, revise the tax system in the interest of free trade, and ease the movement of labor and capital. Increasingly the state was called upon to deal with the consequences of urban and industrial civilization, consequences beyond the capabilities of the best-motivated and best-supported voluntary charity. Thus in 1802 factory legislation had begun with a pious injunction to cotton manufacturers to look to the welfare of children in their employ; by the sixties there was a broad regulatory code, enforced by government inspectors. Education long remained the province of private religious societies, but the state intervened in 1833 to provide building grants, to which inspection was soon attached, followed by ever more detailed regulation of curriculums and by state encouragement of a new profession of primary school teachers. Finally after 1870, public primary schools were founded to supplement the voluntary system, and secondary education followed in 1902. Railways, the formation of companies, banking, and communications all came to greater or lesser degree under state regulation, and in the case of railways the notion of state ownership was openly discussed as early as the 1840's, though it was not to come for another century.

Above all, the state had to cope with poverty. It did so harshly, if with a certain crude efficiency, through the hated New Poor Law of 1834. It also attacked problems of housing and public health in the rapidly growing towns. By mid-century the towns themselves, their governments reformed in 1835, were playing a larger and larger role of self-improvement, extending in some cases even to "municipal socialism," the ownership of gas and water works. Nearly inconceivable as an instrument of reform at the end of the eighteenth century, by the middle decades of the nineteenth century the state had become the major engine for controlling and guiding the lives of Englishmen. It made that transition because it had itself been reformed and had provided, in a new professional civil service, a means for analyzing its problems and working out solutions.

By the 1860's industrialization had stretched its original assumptions to the limit. The railway network was substantially completed, traditional English farming had reached its peak with the costly drainage and heavily capitalized methods of "high farming," and classical political economy had not yet attracted the critics who were soon to undermine it from within. Free trade had been firmly established as British policy (following a steady liberalization from the 1820's) with the repeal of the Corn Laws in 1846 and of the Navigation Laws in 1849; in 1860, the Cobden Treaty with France had brought a major competitor to look at trade in much the same way. In trade as in foreign policy, Britain was the unchallenged leader of the world, free trade, of course, being most likely to benefit the nation with a long industrial and commercial lead over other nations.

But, profitable though it is to be first, the lead can be lost to competitors who are keener, less set in their ways, and determined to beat the nation to which they have so long been tributary. From the 1870's, England had to face a new, more complex, less fortunate revolution—agricultural disaster overwhelmed the growers of wheat and meat, the mainstays of high farming, and more intense industrial competition appeared from new industrial countries. Britain did not lose her ability to innovate or adapt: in the late Victorian age, large-scale industry became the rule; new industries and technologies like steel, chemicals, and electricity were absorbed; the distributive trades were revolutionized by the coming of department stores and chain stores; and even in depression many parts of the economy prospered. But the industries on which the Agricultural and Industrial Revolutions had been built were in decline as other nations, often doing their jobs better, needed them less. England gradually lost her supremacy, to face a new century with a host of nearly insoluble problems and the cold comfort that she had once been an example to the world.

Further reading suggestions follow chapter 73.

73   The Spread of Industrialization

To a large extent the story of the industrialization of Western Europe, of America, and then of various other parts of the world is a study of diffusion. In general, whether they be inventors of spinning jennies, of flying shuttles, of steam engines, or creators of new styles in dress or painting, or new forms of business organizations, compared to the imitators or borrowers of what is new, originators are few in number. In the spread of the Industrial Revolution, the process of diffusion began with the realization by other nations that the British had certain industrial processes which gave them price and style advantages. In fact, so valuable did the new industrial secrets appear to be that the English enacted many laws, consolidated in 1795, intended to prevent the new machines, or their designs, or even workmen who could reproduce them, from leaving England. These laws were not abolished until 1843. The French, aware of the advantages which the new processes gave the English, sent industrial spies to England and offered large payments to English workers who could bring their techniques to France. As one result of this effort, William Wilkinson, an ironmonger and metalworker, went to France and aided in setting up the metallurgical center at Le Creusot. In a similar way William Cockerill and his son, John, brought plans for textile machines to what is now Belgium. The textile machine and metallurgy industry which they founded at Seraing, near Liège, still exists today. And Samuel Slater, a maker of textile machines, left his native Derbyshire for Rhode Island and in company with Moses Brown created a successful spinning business there.

In the first diffusion of industry, the new techniques went to areas which were in close communication with England, where economic conditions were very similar to those in which the breakthroughs of new methods of production had been made. Also, the industries which moved first and got the best foundations were those which were very close to processes in handicraft production and thus were relatively familiar to workers. Furthermore, except for blast furnaces, the industries which spread early in the nineteenth century did not require great initial investments. Capital could be built up gradually out of profits. And lastly, the new industries went to areas where markets already existed or where some local advantage like water power, iron ore, fuel, or an abundant labor supply seemed to assure low-cost production. In this way the cotton textile industry spread to such places as Mülhausen in Alsace, where water power

A.D.   1793   Alexander Hamilton, "Report on Manufactures"
        1859   Value added by manufacturing exceeds value of agri-
                cultural products sold
        1901   U.S. Steel Corporation, first business capitalized at more
                than a billion dollars, formed

----

from the streams coming out of the Vosges mountains was available, to New England, where there was also water power, and to Alpine regions. Soon it went to places like Ghent in Belgium and Chemnitz in Germany, where fuel to generate steam power was cheap.

By the middle of the nineteenth century the first period of the diffusion of mechanization had come to an end and the spread of industry entered a new phase that was to continue until World War I. Government efforts to retain the secrets of technological advance had broken down and were used thereafter only in rare instances, like that of nuclear fission, in which problems of national defense were involved. To be sure, individual firms continued to guard jealously their techniques and methods of production in order that their rivals could not compete with them so readily. Inventors won the legal right to a monopoly of their findings for a specified number of years. But in spite of such restrictions, indeed in part because of them, technical information became available to nearly everyone capable of understanding it almost as soon as it was discovered. Patents made known general conceptions of what was new and thus allowed experts to figure out what had been achieved. Firms that established branches abroad to tap new markets unavoidably exported their capital and their knowledge of production to other areas, and trained foreign workers in necessary new skills. Technical books had to be written, and these were sold everywhere. And trade associations published journals that revealed both what was being developed in their industries and what productive equipment was available in the market. Indeed, the second wave of diffusion was aided throughout by the older industrialized areas. As had happened so many times in the past, economically advanced regions were exporting the very things which had made them the most advanced and had given them positions of military and political superiority.

In this second period, industry moved first to peripheries of the earlier industrialized sections and then to places where raw materials could be assembled cheaply for processing. Inasmuch as coal had become "king" of all these materials because it provided power and heat energy for smelting iron, heavy industry tended to locate where coal could be had at low cost. Therefore regions like the Ruhr Valley and Silesia in Germany, the north of France, the Walloon part of Belgium, and cities or towns on the sea, on canals, and on rivers became favorable sites for industrial plants. To be sure, water power remained important for textiles and light industries generally; and some industries, like the needle trades, sought cheap labor. Still others, like baking, had to be near their markets and thus contributed to the self-industrialization of urban centers.

In this way the period from 1850 to 1914 saw the extension of mechanized industry to most of France, to more of Belgium, to all of Germany west of the Elbe, especially along the Rhine, in Hanover, and in Saxony, to Bohemia, the central part of Austria, and to the northern part of Italy, particularly Piedmont and Lombardy. Accordingly it was possible by 1914 to regard Europe as divided into two main regions, one industrial or "black" and the other agricultural or "green." The frontier between them ran roughly from the Elbe River to Budapest and thence to Rome. Indeed, in 1870 the United Kingdom, France, Belgium, Germany, Italy, and Sweden accounted for 83 per cent of all European manufacturing and even in 1913 for 74 per cent of it.

France progressed rapidly in its efforts to catch up with England until the Franco-Prussian War of 1870, but thereafter Germany made the most phenomenal economic strides forward. The reasons for the decline in the rapid rate of growth of both the United Kingdom and then of France are multitudinous, but some are particularly striking. Perhaps the most important was the fact that Germany acquired from England and France both capital and technology for its own industrialization. In addition, however, Germany seemed more determinedly bent on industrialization than did France, which put much of its resources into colonialism, invested its capital abroad, and refused to give up its style of gracious living. Then, too, Germany, with its coal and chemical resources, had advantages in raw material which France could not match. And lastly, Germany developed its scientific educational system and its research facilities far beyond those of its competitors. By its industrialization, it upset the previously existing balance of military power and became the center of a political alliance which was in a position to challenge the former leaders. And challenge them it did in two world wars.

Still another aspect of the second period of industrialization in Europe was the sizable contributions to the technology of mechanization made on the Continent. In the development of methods for making cheap steel, a product which was essential to large-scale and high-speed industrial production, important inventions were made by William Siemens, an Englishman of German birth, and by two French brothers, Émile and Pierre Martin, who patented their findings in 1866. Portland cement was invented by an Englishman, but methods of producing it were improved by both French and Germans. Aluminum was discovered by a German; the internal combustion engine was developed to the point of practicality by a German, Gottlieb Daimler; the electrolytic process for producing soda from common salt was developed by a Belgian, Ernest Solvay; Alfred Nobel, of Sweden, invented a cheap explosive in the form of dynamite; and an Italian, Guglielmo Marconi, invented radio.

Transportation developed along with the growth of industrial production in western Europe. Europe was crisscrossed with railways which tapped new markets and made available for processing raw materials located in remote places. Concurrently, ocean shipping grew rapidly, with steamships finally taking over from sail in the last quarter of the nineteenth century, and with interocean or sea canals like the Suez, the Panama, and the Kiel greatly shortening the distance between important shipping centers. In 1914 the world tonnage of ocean shipping was about 20.5 million tons, and 96 per cent of this tonnage was accounted for by Europe and the United States.

The great improvement of transportation permitted the exchange of goods over long distances and allowed areas with competitive advantages to specialize in producing particular goods. In a very general way, Europe may be said to have become the "workshop" of the world, selling to the rest its industrial surpluses and importing in exchange raw materials and foodstuffs. A system of multilateral commerce came into being which maintained a general and intricate balance of trade and payments. In the exchange of goods, the industrial states had a distinct edge, for at the going prices manufacturers required fewer "inputs" of capital and labor than did agricultural products.

In spite of the enormous increase in industrial output, the advance was not uninterrupted; the ascent was marked by declines as well as rises. Fluctuations in the progress of mechanized industry came to be known as business cycles or, to avoid the impression of extreme regularity, as business fluctuations. These waves went from crest to trough between two to four years and seemed to be generated by the operation of the economic system itself. The upward swing was characterized by optimism on the part of businessmen, by plant expansion, fuller employment, and rising prices. When a point was reached at which entrepreneurs believed that they could not sell more goods at existing prices, they stopped expanding plants, laid off workers, and began to cut prices to move inventories. The deepest of all the depressions was that of the 1930's, but before that catastrophe the

Western world had experienced a "long depression in prices" (which is to be distinguished from the business cycle phenomenon) that lasted from 1873 to 1896. Between these years prices fell so low and so far that many economists thought that the possibility of further economic expansion was dependent upon Europe's geographical expansion of its sphere of operation —an opinion that contributed much to the new wave of European imperialism which characterized the period from 1870 to World War I.

Another aspect of industrialization causing concern pertained to the labor force. Workers no longer owned the means of production and were dependent on their wages, which in turn were dependent upon the employer and his success. Many philosophers in accordance with their interests or sentiments endeavored to rationalize the situation of workers under capitalism. Capitalist economists usually took a laissez-faire attitude and thought that everything would work out under a scheme of "survival of the fittest." Economists who sided with the workers criticized the capitalist system and wanted either to supplant it with some utopian scheme or to overthrow it entirely. The solutions most widely adopted were, first, a great improvement in the condition of labor effected by employers on their own initiative or under pressure from trade unions; second, the gradual devolution to workers of many of the products of their labor; and, third, the growth of the "welfare state" idea—the notion that the state is responsible for the welfare of all and must, either by providing jobs or by social insurance schemes, protect the individual all the way from "the womb" (maternity insurance) to "the tomb" (death insurance).

The same industrializing forces that were transforming Great Britain and the Continent were also affecting the United States. The pattern of American development was somewhat different from that of the Old World; indeed an economic historian looking at the United States in the early twentieth century might well contend that the country had experienced no "industrial revolution" comparable to that which shook England and western Europe in the eighteenth and nineteenth centuries. Compared to conditions in 1815, American economic life in 1907 was incredibly more diverse, more productive, more highly capitalized, more technological, but the process of becoming a "developed" economy did not involve America in a dramatic revolution from an old economic order. Instead, there was simply a steadily accelerating evolution from a colonial economy which was production-oriented in spirit, capitalistic in character, and technological insofar as possible. Because there never was an *ancien régime,* there could be no real revolution. And because there was no real economic revolution, nineteenth-century America was largely spared the traumatic political, social, and intellectual repercussions produced by the

Industrial Revolution in other lands. The change, in other words, was gradual.

In a similar vein, John Adams once argued that the military conflict between the American colonies and Great Britain lasting from 1775 to 1783 was an anticlimax. The real revolution, he thought, had taken place much earlier, when the colonials began to think of themselves not as Englishmen living in the provinces, but as Americans. Later historians have extended Adams' argument to suggest that the revolution had begun with the act of emigration, which, consciously or not, constituted a declaration of independence from Old World politics, society, and culture.

At no time in the seventeenth or eighteenth century did the United States have a stable, settled agricultural economy. Despite the myth of the self-sufficient frontiersman entirely dependent on his own resources, as soon as a new area was opened for settlement, the pioneer, subsistence farmer quickly succumbed to commercial agriculture. He regarded land as a commodity to be exploited, not a place on which one "settled." Rural Americans never envisioned themselves as part of a timeless scheme of things, in which the climate, the seasons, and the configuration of the landscape established norms and disciplines for men. If the land "wore out," or if there was a prospect of better land over the next ridge, they simply "moved on." The symbols of the American countryside have not been the hearth, the barn, and the old oaken bucket, but the ax that felled the forest, the plow that broke the plains, the Conestoga wagon that carried the farmer to his next opportunity, and, eventually, the Model T Ford that took him to the main chance in the big city.

America never sustained a genuine "country interest," comparable to the squirarchy of England, the peasant proprietor parties in France, or the Junkers in Prussia. Not that there have not been, on occasion, wistful voices. Thomas Jefferson, for example, hoped that with the acquisition of the huge Louisiana Territory in 1803, America might remain (what in fact it had never been) a country of contented yeomen. But Jefferson lived long enough to see that the farmer in the Mississippi Valley, like his progenitors in the East, was neither yeoman nor contented. Take the Lincoln family. Thomas Lincoln moved frequently in the early nineteenth century, from Kentucky to Indiana to Illinois, always in search of better land; he never established an "old homestead" to blur young Abraham's recognition of the desirability of escaping from the country to such urban careers as storekeeping and the practice of the law.

Meanwhile, in the South, the development of large-scale plantations producing tobacco, rice, sugar, and cotton, along with the existence there of several million Negro slaves, led politicians, priests, and poets to proclaim that at least in this region a stable country interest had evolved. They were right in the limited sense that for a long period of time the region competed successfully in world markets with these staple crops. But there was nothing traditional or precapitalistic about these plantations. Analogies drawn between plantation owners and landed European nobility, and between Negro slaves and serfs or peasants, were spurious. Plantation owners, like other American farmers, ruthlessly exhausted the fertility of their lands and then sought out new ones. The "old mansions" which then and later seemed to symbolize the stability of Southern rural life flourished no longer than the farmhouses of other regions. Harriet Beecher Stowe's *Uncle Tom's Cabin* catches the precarious nature of plantation life far better than any song Stephen Foster ever wrote. When profits declined, slaves were "sold down the river," in the same matter-of-fact way a capitalist would get rid of any unproductive asset. In every important respect, southern agriculture was far closer to modern capitalistic enterprise than to the traditional rural order with which romanticists compared it.

Toward the end of the nineteenth century, a congeries of rural-based organizations appeared—Granges, Farmers' Alliances, Agricultural Wheels —to articulate the conviction of many farmers that national political life was increasingly oblivious to the aspirations and needs of rural America. Though on occasion almost all borrowed from the rhetoric of a pastoral, preindustrial society, the only desire held in common by a southern white sharecropper, a bonanza wheat farmer from the Red River Valley of North Dakota, and a Missouri corn-and-hog producer was for political-economic changes that would bring each greater profit. So William Jennings Bryan of Nebraska may be taken as representative of late-nineteenth-century agrarianism when, speaking to the Democratic national convention in 1896, he moved easily from an assertion of the moral primacy of tillers of the soil to the claim that farmers were, after all, just as much businessmen as the speculators who inhabited the Chicago Board of Trade.

In short, America did not experience, and did not need to experience, the kind of agricultural revolution that everywhere in Europe was the precondition to the development of modern industrialism. It was not necessary to shake people loose from the soil, destroy hereditary tenures, subvert a politically potent country interest, or replace a pastoral ethos with a capitalist one. The marked changes in American agriculture that took place in the nineteenth century—the disappearance of subsistence agriculture from all but scattered areas of America, the growth in the size of farms, mechanization, the sharp upturn in the amount of capital required for land and equipment, and the development of national and international markets —all these simply continued trends that had been apparent since the first settlements.

But if industrial development in America was not retarded by stubbornly entrenched agrarians, it was to some extent hampered—and to some extent aided—by a shortage of labor. No other country except Russia began industrialization with a surplus both of land and of economic opportunity, available to the man in search of work. Of course, it was romantic, even in America, to imagine that a young man from a worn-out Vermont or North Carolina farm could easily strike out for the rich virgin lands of Dakota Territory or Oregon. Yet publicists and historians who have described "the frontier" as a safety valve have been right in principle, if not always in their description of the precise mechanism by which men bettered themselves. Wages in the East, if usually lower than in the West, remained throughout the nineteenth century consistently higher than wages for comparable work in Europe.

At about the time the Englishman Thomas Malthus was making his dire predictions about the effect of the rapid growth of population on human well-being, in America Alexander Hamilton was explaining to Congress how the new nation might go about developing the manufacturing sector of the economy. One of the great benefits of industrialization, he argued, was that factories made women and children, often of only marginal benefit in farming, important productive assets. Given the labor shortage, this was an especially potent consideration.

Though Congress refused to take any of the steps Hamilton recommended to promote manufactures, his words were prophetic of the exigencies confronting industrialists. One of the wonders of the Western world in the 1830's was the textile mills of Lowell, Massachusetts, where girls from respectable farm families labored in a kind of paternalist Arcadia with their company-sponsored literary societies and their prim, chaperoned boardinghouses. A later generation would dismiss such enterprises as "company towns" designed to exploit the workers as efficiently as possible; but this was a misconception. The Lowell girls were not wage-slaves; most returned to the farm after a few years of work had earned them a competence, or at least a trousseau.

The Lowell experiment did not provide a long-range solution to the shortage of labor. More fundamental assistance came from the massive influx into America between 1830 and 1924 of some 35 million immigrants, the large majority of them men and women in their twenties and thirties, attracted by the greater opportunities and higher wages America offered. A few of these immigrants brought with them skills and technological knowledge acquired in the mines and manufacturing enterprises in western Europe; they played a very important role in speeding the development in America of efficient coal mines, canals and railroads, and of the textile and iron-and-steel industries. Dramatic as their contribution was, however, these skilled workers probably contributed less to American economic growth than the mass of newcomers who arrived with no industrial skills at all. Constituting a large mass of virtually unconditioned labor, they were available for any kind of task in any part of the country. The needs of the New England textile manufacturers were effectively met by the middle of the nineteenth century by Irish and German immigrant families (and later in the century by newcomers from French Canada and Italy). The canals and railroads of the Mississippi Valley and the Great West were constructed by Irish and Chinese, the timber of the north exploited by Scandinavians, the subways of New York dug by Italians, the steel mills and meat-packing plants of the Middle West manned by immigrants from eastern Europe, the clothing industry of New York by Jews. Because most of these immigrants brought no ingrained craft tradition with them, entrepreneurs encountered little resistance in introducing technological change. When, for example, it became technically possible to mechanize much of the production of boots and shoes, the old artisans were easily replaced (actually most of them became supervisors) by willing hands, as new to the trade as to the country. Conversely, immigrants—especially of the first generation—were by and large uninterested in unionization. For one thing, most of them could find more valued fraternity in associations of fellow immigrants in their neighborhood or church than with fellow workers, often of different ethnic origin, in the mines or factories. Even more important, they usually received wages that were recognizably better than those paid in the home country. And even those who were warned by American workers or alerted by socialist theory to the inclination of employers to reduce wages to subsistence levels had to cope with the fact that real wages in the United States rose every decade in the nineteenth century.

Like all industrializing countries, America needed large amounts of capital, for economic growth and for the "social overhead" of an urban, technological society. Immigration played some part in meeting this need. Willy-nilly, European countries had to pay the costs of nurturing immigrants who, when ready to become productive members of society, left for America. In the nineteenth century, the subsidy this practice bestowed on the American economy amounted to at least $1,000 for each new settler.

At the same time, European—and especially English—investors were attracted by the growth potential of the country. Much of the capital invested in canals and cattle ranches, in banks and commercial ventures, in textile factories and steel mills, and even in state and municipal bonds came from Europe. Until early in the twentieth century there continued to be a net flow of capital into the United States; the country benefited enormously from undergoing industrialization in that period in history when the flow of private capital was least hindered by governmental controls.

It would be a mistake, of course, to conclude that most investment capital was generated abroad, just as it would be a mistake to argue that the absence of an entrenched agrarian interest, or the influx of immigrants, was primarily responsible for the pace and relatively painless character of American economic development. The key factor, almost certainly, was the American ethos which gave unreserved sanction to all behavior conducive to rapid growth. Opinion in the United States stigmatized sloth and self-indulgence, and saw little virtue in humility or contemplation. It also firmly insisted that work was good in itself, and, besides, would lead to success. And success, it was agreed, was best measured by the capacity it bestowed to perform more work. Preoccupied with the duties and opportunities of the individual, it took pretty much for granted that the well-being of society would result automatically from the achieved well-being of individuals. Though each detail of this ethos had its origin or parallel in European attitudes, it enjoyed a singular power in America. Informing the expectations of most of those leaving Europe for America, it was reinforced by the spectacular "progress" and "success" it helped engender in this favored land.

Certainly it encountered no sustained, substantial criticism from religious leaders, those to whom Americans characteristically looked for intellectual guidance. The majority of churchgoing Americans adhered to evangelical Protestant denominations, which not only acknowledged one another's legitimacy but also agreed on the essential harmony of the "gospel of work" and the Sermon on the Mount. When Andrew Carnegie in 1889 combined the traditional doctrines of Christian stewardship with strictures against the least public interference with individualism, private property, competition, and the process of accumulation, most Protestants agreed that he had articulated a "gospel of wealth" that was both true and also characteristically American. A few Protestant ministers were beginning to call for a more "social Christianity," but they did not seriously threaten the commitment of Protestantism to a rugged individualism.

The same bourgeois ethic characterized the outlook of most Catholic, Lutheran, and Jewish leaders. Though obligations to orthodoxy made them somewhat tentative in endorsing a "Protestant ethic," they were powerfully attracted by its emphasis on work in the world. John Ireland, Roman Catholic Archbishop of St. Paul, was a prime exponent of this ethic. Affected no doubt by his own spectacular rise from humble immigrant antecedents, and by the success of many laymen in his diocese, he was able to declare to a stock-market group in the 1890's that "it is energy and enterprise that win everywhere; they win in the Church, they win in the State, and they win in business." Few orthodox churchmen were quite so confident. Yet it is hard to imagine a culture so formally committed to religions of otherworldliness so wholeheartedly endorsing a gospel of individual worldly enterprise.

Americans generally agreed that one of the most fundamental responsibilities of the political order was to foster economic growth; the best government was that which least inhibited the enterprise of the private individual, and—by so doing—created conditions favorable to progress. Education, it was believed, ought to be available to every young American, and by the middle of the nineteenth century most states had some kind of law requiring cities and villages to offer a free elementary education to all. By the end of the century, most states had taken the considerably more radical step of compelling each child to attend some school. Though the education was the responsibility primarily of the states, the federal government in the 1860's provided land grants to support state universities, and in the early twentieth century began to provide funds for specially deserving groups, like farm children.

So striking was the American commitment to public education that it is tempting to describe American political philosophy as faith in anarchy plus a schoolmaster. But most Americans wanted government to provide more than teachers. Towns and villages vied with one another in offering tax benefits to builders of canals, railroads, and factories. State legislatures offered bonuses to nascent enterprises, and state courts redefined ancient common law principles to permit railroads to use eminent domain powers which had not been allowed simpler kinds of transportation companies. The courts also strictly limited the railroads' liability to either passengers or employees, acknowledging that a new enterprise needed elbow room to thrive. By the middle of the nineteenth century, most states had passed "general" incorporation laws which extended to whole classes of would-be entrepreneurs the benefits of corporate organization.

The federal government was neither indifferent nor inactive to the needs of enterprisers. In defining the "American system," Henry Clay, like Hamilton before him, thought it essential to impose a tariff that would protect American industry from foreign competition, and to maintain a federally chartered bank that would perform for American businessmen services analogous to those provided by the Bank of England. He also favored federal transportation and communication projects. Between 1830 and 1860 the Congress was too riven by sectional conflicts to sustain coherent programs in any of these areas, but the Supreme Court proved able, then and throughout the rest of the century, to guarantee that capitalistic enterprise would not be *inhibited* by capricious state action. First by interpreting the prohibition in the federal Constitution against impairing the obligation of contracts, and—after the Civil War—by a strained construction of the Fourteenth Amendment denying to the states the right to deprive citizens of life, liberty, or property without due process of law, the Court zealously protected "the enterprise of a free people." It also jealously guarded the rights of corporations chartered in one state to do business in other states. American federalism, with its overlapping and at times competing jurisdictions, instead of retarding the development of a national economy, in practice maximized the possibility of innovation by the individual.

It goes without saying that rapid industrialization was not the only spectacular development in nineteenth-century America. Expansion across the continent was largely independent of the Industrial Revolution; efforts of Marxist scholars to see American expansion as the last stage of industrial capitalism are unpersuasive. The slow but steady growth of democratic political institutions, which, superimposed upon America's republicanism, made the country unique among nations, was not immediately dependent upon the Industrial Revolution, though it certainly gained strength from the prosperity industrialism fostered.

Furthermore, even if industrialization was the central theme of nineteenth-century American history, it is clear that the course of that development was not linear or uniform; three periods of markedly different character can readily be discerned. By 1859, the progress of industrialization was such that the value added by manufacturing surpassed the value of agricultural products sold, but the great majority of Americans still lived on farms, or in small towns in rural communities, and very little of the manufactured product was exported. In other words, in 1859 American manufacturing was still directed almost exclusively at a domestic market, expanding rapidly because of the construction of canals and railroads, and the widespread use of the steamboat.

During the second stage, which lasted until the turn of the century, industrialization broadened its base and extended its range enormously. By the late nineties steel manufactured in Pittsburgh undersold English steel in Liverpool, and American capital exports exceeded the infusions of capital from abroad. Even the agricultural sector became more broadly international: American wheat was being sold in ports as distant as Stockholm, Stettin, and Odessa.

In these last years of the nineteenth century, both factories and corporations grew dramatically in size; when the United States Steel Corporation was founded in 1901, it was capitalized at more than a billion dollars. Such corporations, enjoying broad legal privileges, engendered hostility among smaller businesses directly threatened by their economic power, fear among laborers whose unions proved quite incapable of coping with management, and unease among middle-class Americans startled by this emanation of "private enterprise." But hostility, fear, and unease did not produce in the nineteenth century any pronounced reaction against the prevailing government policies.

Then early in the twentieth century, the pace of economic development quickened still more. Consumer goods that were to be the hallmark, and the cherished vindication, of the twentieth-century American capitalism—the automobile, the household appliances, the suburban home itself—assumed a steadily increasing importance. New industrial and commercial processes accompanied this revolution. The larger corporations established research and development divisions charged with discovering new products. The factory assembly line appeared, producing identical items in profusion at high speed. Massive advertising campaigns stimulated demand. National distributing systems—chain stores and licensed dealerships, for example—satisfied customers wanting products with nationally known names.

These years also saw the welling up of the idea that the state had a moral obligation to act positively and firmly to promote the general welfare. The idea took a somewhat different form than it did in Europe. Its advocates called themselves "progressives." Convinced that government had largely failed in its task because of "corruption," these progressives saw a remedy in making public officials more responsive to "the people." If city bosses could be eliminated, senators elected directly rather than by state legislators, the legislators themselves made subject to recall by the citizenry, even judges deprived of their immunity from public control, the progressives believed that government would become pure in character, democratic in procedure, and scientific in the regulation of business. Most reform energies were invested in crusades for these essentially political goals; as a result, there was in America no such extensive regulation of business enterprise as occurred in industrialized countries of western Europe in these years. Nevertheless, American progressives played an indispensable role; by insisting that the government had the right and duty to shape the course of economic development, they readied their countrymen to accept the drastic regulation of industry which took place first during World War I, and later during the Great Depression.

For Further Reading

Cipolla, Carlo M., *The Economic History of World Population.*

Clough, Shepard B., *European Economic History: The Economic Development of Western Civilization.*

Cochran, Thomas, and William Miller, *The Age of Enterprise.*

Deane, Phyllis, *The First Industrial Revolution.*

Henderson, H. O., *Britain and Industrial Europe, 1750–1850.*

League of Nations, *Industrialization and World Trade.*

Svennilson, Ingvar, *Growth and Stagnation in the European Economy.*

74   A World Economy

Although industrialization was, in the nineteenth century, chiefly centered in western Europe and the United States, its *effects* were world-wide. Indeed, as early as the late eighteenth century, the outlines of a world economy were clearly discernible. Centered in western Europe, it included Russia, India, the East Indies, the Middle East, northern and western Africa, and the Americas. Trade had increased manyfold in the course of the century, shipping had grown in volume and speed, and strong financial links had been forged. The result was to connect the markets of the world more closely than ever before. Within three weeks after the signing of the treaty in 1814 ending the war between Great Britain and the United States, coffee prices in Jidda, on the Red Sea, had dropped 30 per cent. The expansion of Europe was also well advanced. In the Americas, an area equal to that of western Europe had been settled by a European population of somewhat less than 10 million, and more than half a million Russians lived in Siberia. Trade, migration, and settlement led to the diffusion not only of ideas, techniques, and products but also of basic crops—thus Old World plants like sugar, coffee, and cotton were grown on a large scale in the Americas while such New World crops as corn, potatoes, and tobacco were becoming the mainstay of many farmers in Europe, Asia, and Africa.

The world market, however, was confined to the coasts; except along rivers, its effects were rarely felt a hundred miles inland. The outline of a world economy remained sketchy and had not yet been filled in. The expansion of the rimland economy into the hinterlands, and its spread throughout China, Japan, Oceania, and Africa, was the task of the nineteenth century. It was accomplished through the transport revolution; the migration of huge numbers and the settlement of vast areas; the development of European industry, which required hitherto unknown quantities of raw materials; the investment of immense amounts of European capital overseas; and the manifold expansion of trade.

From the fifteenth century on, the sailing ship had been the main instrument of European economic and political expansion. Constantly growing in carrying capacity and speed because of improvements in design, built of cheap and easily available materials and needing no fueling stations, sailing ships continued to carry the greater part of international trade until the 1870's. American clipper ships represented the supreme achievement of the age of sail. Capable of speeds of up to 15 knots, a clipper could carry 5,000 tons across the Atlantic in less than two weeks.

A.D. 1807   Robert Fulton sails from New York to Albany in steamboat *Clermont*

1816   Regular transatlantic service, in sailing ships, between Liverpool and New York

1819   *Savannah* crosses Atlantic, mostly under steam

1821   Adoption of gold standard in England

1825   Opening of Stockton and Darlington railroad, in England

1844   Electric telegraph opens between Washington and Baltimore

1846   Repeal of Corn Laws

1866   Laying of first transatlantic cable

1869   Opening of the Union and Central Pacific's transcontinental railway; opening of Suez Canal

1876   Invention of telephone

1884   Invention of compound turbine in steam navigation

1887   Daimler's internal combustion engine automobile

1901   Marconi's first transatlantic radiotelegraphy message

1902   First transpacific cable

1903   Completion of trans-Siberian railway; airplane flight by Wright brothers

1909   First cross-Channel flight, by Louis Blériot

1914   Opening of Panama Canal

1919   First transatlantic flight by John Alcock and Arthur Brown

1924   First flight around the world by United States Army planes

1936   First television broadcast

No corresponding progress had been made in land transport; the bulk of internal trade continued to be carried by water. In western Europe attempts had been made for several centuries to supplement the excellent river network with canals, but it was the exigencies of the Industrial Revolution, and more particularly the need to move huge quantities of coal, that led to large-scale canal building in the years 1760–1850, first in Britain and then in western Europe and the United States. The introduction of steamboats gave a further impetus to river navigation and canal construction. In spite of some improvements, however, road transport continued to be slow, uncertain, and expensive. When, during the Cabinet crisis of 1834, Sir Robert Peel rushed back from Italy to London, his journey took as long as it would have in Roman times.

The obstacle to economic development presented by inadequate land transportation was overcome by the railroads. Following George Stephenson's success with the *Rocket* in 1829, railways began to spread rapidly; by the 1840's they had superseded roads in the more advanced countries, and canals could hardly stand their competition. By 1850, the United States had 9,000 miles of track, Britain almost 7,000, Germany nearly 4,000, France nearly 2,000, and small stretches were to be found in most other European countries, including Russia. In the 1850's railways began to be built in India, Egypt, Turkey, Algeria, South Africa, Argentina, and elsewhere—but not in Japan and China until the 1870's. By that decade the era of the transcontinental railways had begun: the United States in 1869, India (Bombay–Calcutta) in 1870, Canada in 1885, Europe (Calais–Constantinople) in 1888, Russia (Trans-Siberian) in 1903, South America (Argentina–Chile) in 1910. By 1913 the world's railway mileage was close to 700,000, of which 257,000 were in the United States, 49,000 in Russia, 40,000 in Germany, and 35,000 in India. Freight rates were sharply reduced, falling by a half or more in the last quarter of the nineteenth century. After World War I, however, railway building slowed down greatly, owing to the competition first of the automobile and then of the airplane; indeed, in several advanced countries many lines were abandoned. Today there is considerably less track in the world than in 1914.

Railway construction, which required enormous amounts of capital, was financed in very diverse ways. In England and America private companies built hundreds of uncoordinated projects, but on the Continent the state provided not only overall control but a large, and often predominant, share of capital. British capital also financed the greater part of the railways built in India, Canada, and Latin America, generally with financial guarantees by the national or state government concerned. French capital was active in building southern and southeastern European lines.

Steamboats proved their worth on American rivers in the 1810's, spread to Europe and Russia soon thereafter, and by the 1850's were navigating the Ganges, Nile, Amazon and La Plata, and other rivers. By the 1830's regular services were also operating in the Mediterranean, connecting with other steamship lines to India and England. Over the next few decades several innovations—the use of iron instead of wood, the replacement of paddlewheels by screw propellers, and the introduction of the compound engine—enabled steamships to compete with sailing ships on the oceans. Further boons to steam navigation were the opening of the Panama railway in 1855 and the Suez Canal in 1869. By the late 1880's maximum tonnage had risen to 11,000 and speed to 21 knots, and the Atlantic run had been reduced to six days. All this greatly raised the cost of ships, and led to the formation of large shipping companies. Competition, however, continued to be intense, and the economies achieved were such that freight rates, which had shown a downward trend since the end of the Napoleonic wars, dropped by a half to two-thirds between the 1870's and about 1900, when they began to be stabilized by the formation of "rings" and "pools" between the leading lines.

The shift from sail to steam was also one from American to British predominance, which lasted until World War II. Around 1890, Britain owned three-quarters of the world's tonnage and was launching two-thirds of all new ships, but thereafter both figures were steadily reduced by competition from Germany, the United States, Norway, Japan, and other countries. In 1914, total gross registered tonnage was 49 million, of which 21 million was under British flag, 5.4 under German, and 5.4 under American.

By World War I, the oil-burning internal combustion engine was widely used on ships, but the automobile was still an expensive luxury and the airplane in the experimental stage. The subsequent development of the car and plane not only greatly reduced travel time but also opened up large areas of the world hitherto unreached by modern transport. The concurrent rise of petroleum as the leading fuel necessitated new forms of transportation, notably tankers, which now account for one-third of all world shipping, and pipelines, many of which cross international frontiers.

Modern transport both facilitated and required the development of better communications. The fact that the declaration of war by Spain on England in 1779 was not known in Madras for nearly twelve months shows how slowly news then traveled, and even in the 1840's the swiftest steamship mails between London and Bombay took a month. However, the telegraph, first used in 1844, spread rapidly; in the United States it reached the Pacific coast by 1861. By the 1850's, European telegraph wires and underwater cables stretched as far south as Sicily and Malta, and long lines were in operation in India, the Middle East, and other parts of the world.

The growing needs of commerce and finance spurred the laying of deep sea cables, and in the 1860's India was linked with Europe, and Britain with the United States. By 1902 the Pacific had been spanned and a network of more than 300,000 miles of submarine cables, mostly owned by Great Britain, crossed the oceans and seas. The previous year the first radio message had been sent across the Atlantic, inaugurating a new era in communications.

It has been estimated that, in the course of the nineteenth century, some 8 or 9 million square miles of land were settled in North and South America and Oceania, an eightfold or ninefold increase over the area occupied in those regions in 1800. To this should be added a vast stretch of land in Siberia. This was made possible by the decline in transport costs, which greatly extended the area from which bulky crops, notably grains, and minerals could be marketed. Especially noteworthy was the introduction of refrigeration on railways and steamers in the 1870's, which opened huge markets for meat, dairy products, and fruit in the eastern United States and Europe. Other important factors were the rapid growth in capital accumulation, which financed much settlement, the free land and various facilities offered to immigrants, and the lowering or removal of duties on imports of agricultural products into western Europe. Spurred by such incentives, population, both immigrant and native-born, spread westward in the United States and Canada and northwestward in Australia, at an accelerating pace, so that by 1914 the process of settlement had been substantially accomplished in these countries. A similar movement in Argentina and Brazil started later and made relatively less headway, while in Africa—except for its Mediterranean and southern coasts—even the beginning of settlement had to await the establishment of European rule in the last quarter of the nineteenth century and the control of tropical diseases.

The migrations that accompanied this settlement were on a far larger scale than any previously known, and have since been matched only by the displacement of populations during and after World War II. Five main streams of intercontinental migration may be distinguished: from Europe, and elsewhere, to the Americas, Oceania, and South and East Africa, a total of about 60 million between 1815 and 1914; from Russia to Siberia and Central Asia; from southern Europe to North Africa; from China and Japan to eastern and southern Asia; and from India to southeastern Asia and South and East Africa. All five drew mainly from the lower strata of society, all were primarily motivated by the prospect of economic betterment, and all were greatly facilitated by the new cheap and swift means of transportation. Their effects on the countries from which the migrants came were diverse. Only in Europe, for example, did emigration significantly reduce population pressure. And their impact on the receiving countries also differed greatly.

Immigrants and their descendants accounted for more than half the population growth of Argentina and Siberia, two-fifths of that of the United States and Brazil, and less than one-fifth of that of Canada, from which emigration to the United States was always heavy.

Since the vast majority of immigrants were unskilled workers their main contributions were the raw labor they supplied, the external economies they created by raising the density of settlement, and the added inducement they provided for foreign investors.

The other streams of migration were very different in their character and effects. Starting around 1830, hundreds of thousands of southern Europeans (French, Spanish, Italian, and Greek) settled in North Africa, from Egypt to Morocco. At their peak, in the 1930's, they numbered more than 2 million. They controlled practically all industry, trade, and finance, and a large segment of agriculture. They formed the bulk of the entrepreneurial and professional classes and in some countries even provided most of the skilled workers. But since, for religious and cultural reasons, there was practically no intermarriage or social fusion between them and the local population, they remained a sharply distinct group whose privileges aroused increasing animosity in a region where national self-consciousness was rapidly growing. Hence, with the decline of European power during and after the Second World War, nationalist pressures forced a mass exodus which practically eliminated European settlement in North Africa.

The same has been generally true of Asian migration. The Japanese sent settlers to their overseas empire, providing it with capital, skills, organization, and enterprise. But following the loss of the empire in 1945, 6 million returned to the homeland—2 million from China alone. Similarly, Indians and Chinese spread along the shores of the Indian Ocean, in the wake of the colonial powers; at their peak Indian settlers in these areas numbered more than 3 million, Chinese some 12 million. Occupying an intermediate position between the Europeans who controlled the large enterprises and the local population, they worked as petty traders, moneylenders, clerks, and, where local labor supply was inadequate, as coolies. But they too did not fuse with the local population, and the financial success of many of their members made them an object of suspicion and resentment. With the achievement of independence they have come under heavy pressure in several countries. Thus, for example, large numbers of Indians in Burma and of Chinese in Indonesia have been forced to return to their original homelands.

"In the fifty or so years before 1914," the distinguished British economist R. C. O. Mathews writes, "the different parts of the world were linked together by trade and lending in a relationship closer, perhaps, than any that has existed before or since." The links were provided by convertible currencies based on gold; by a rapidly spreading network of international banking; by massive capital flows; and by the liberalization of trade, which led to a large increase in its value. The relative stability of prices prevailing in this period greatly helped this linkage and integration. In all these processes, the leading role was played by Great Britain, which continued to dominate the commercial and financial scene until the outbreak of the First World War, but France, Germany, and the United States were increasingly important.

As regards currency, until 1870 bimetallism was common, but after that the gold standard spread swiftly. Gold had begun replacing silver in England and France in the eighteenth century. The world trend was accelerated by the adoption of the gold standard in England in 1821 and by the liberal policy pursued throughout the century by the Bank of England. The successive increases in gold supplies from Siberia, California, Australia, and South Africa made it possible to expand the reserves of the central banks and to meet the rapidly growing needs of world production and trade. A further important source of finance was provided by the banking system, which was consolidated in the leading countries in the first half of the century and thereafter began to branch abroad. British, French, German, and other banks greatly facilitated the overseas trade of their homelands, and some of them served as channels for foreign investment.

Viewed as a whole, the period of the British gold standard, 1821–1914, was one of relative price stability. However, prices fluctuated quite sharply during the business cycles that succeeded each other in swift succession. The close relation between the levels of prices and business activity in all the highly developed countries shows the increasing interconnection of the world's leading trading and financial centers.

Still another link was provided by capital flows. Immediately after Waterloo, Britain began lending abroad on an unprecedented scale and, helped by a consistent surplus in its current accounts, rapidly raised its foreign holdings. By 1866 these had passed the £500 million mark, by 1874 £1,000 million, and by 1891 £2,000 million. At the outbreak of the war they stood at £4,000 million; by then nearly half the annual flow of British savings was being channeled abroad. French foreign investment became significant in the 1850's, accelerated in the 1880's, and soon absorbed about one-third of domestic savings. Germany gained importance in the 1890's but rarely invested more than a tenth of its savings abroad. A United Nations estimate put total long-term foreign investment in 1914 at $44 billion, of which Britain accounted for 18, France for 9, Germany for 5.8, and Belgium, the Netherlands, and Switzerland for 5.5. The United

States was still, on balance, a debtor, owing $6.8 billion and holding foreign investments worth $3.5 billion.

The bulk of this capital had flowed to areas of new settlement: the United States, Canada, Argentina, Brazil, Australia, New Zealand, South Africa, and Russia. Much of it was invested in railways and other "social overhead capital," either directly by the investor or by the local government. Hence it is not surprising that capital investment tended to proceed in spurts, being attracted by a wave of railway building associated with higher prices of primary products, and by accelerated migration and intensified settlement in new areas. Similarly much of the investment in India and Egypt was connected with cotton booms, particularly the sharp one provoked by the diminution of American exports during the Civil War. Most of this capital investment contributed significantly to the economy of the borrowing countries, but a substantial amount was put to unproductive use and left a heavy burden of debt, particularly in the Middle East and some Latin American countries. As for the lenders, experience varied, the generally good record of British overseas investment contrasting with the heavy losses sustained by France and Germany as a result of the First World War.

By developing transport and increasing the output of primary commodities, foreign investment helped to expand international trade. The value of all imports and exports skyrocketed from about £340 million in 1820 to £8,360 million in 1913, and in real terms the increase was even greater. Such a rate of growth was unprecedented, and has since been matched only in the years following the Second World War.

Here again Britain set the pace, by removing restrictions on foreign shipping and on commerce with the colonies, by abolishing prohibitions on the export of gold and machinery, and, above all, by reducing tariff barriers. The latter process, begun in 1824, was substantially completed by 1860, when almost all goods were admitted free of duty. Britain's example was followed by Germany, France, and other states, and the 1850's to 1870's were a period of virtually free trade between the major countries. The Great Depression of the 1870's, and other factors such as intensified national and imperial rivalries, set in motion a new wave of protectionism in most countries, but nevertheless trade in 1914 was far less restricted than it had been a hundred years earlier or than it was to be for nearly fifty years after that date. What made Britain's liberal policy still more important was the fact that it constituted by far the largest market in international trade, accounting for one-third of the total in the 1840's, a quarter in the 1870's and a sixth in 1913. Furthermore, both its total imports and its import surplus rose steadily, thus providing its suppliers with rapidly growing export proceeds. The buying power of these proceeds was further increased by the fall in the cost of textiles and other manufactured goods caused by the improvement in production methods.

In other words, British industrial development, capital exports, and commercial policy greatly stimulated the development of primary production overseas, a process from which Britain and western Europe benefited, both as importers of raw materials and as exporters of finished goods and equipment. When, after 1860, the terms of trade turned against primary products, importers of these goods derived a further benefit while exporters, such as the United States, Canada, Italy, Sweden, Russia, and Japan, gained an added incentive for industrialization. The wide diffusion of industry created new streams of trade. Alongside the exchange of manufactured products for raw materials, which had dominated the nineteenth century, there developed a swiftly expanding trade in manufactured products between industrial countries—a trade that has continued to grow in both absolute and relative importance and now exceeds the traditional exchange between advanced and backward countries.

By the turn of the century a clear pattern of world trade and payments between the main regions of the world had emerged, which can be schematically presented:

A. *Tropics* (agricultural and mineral producing tropical countries of Asia, Africa, and Latin America)—large export surplus, particularly in trade with the United States and western Europe.
B. *United States*—large export surplus except with Tropics.
C. *Regions of Recent Settlement* (Canada, Oceania, South Africa, Russia, and temperate zone of South America)—large export surplus with western Europe and Britain, partly offset by import surplus with United States and Tropics.
D. *Western Europe*—large import surplus except with Britain.
E. *Britain*—large import surplus except with Tropics.

Thus the two capital exporting areas, Britain and western Europe, had a huge import surplus in their merchandise trade with the rest of the world. This was, however, more than covered by their earnings from shipping, insurance, and various financial services, as well as by interest payments on their investments; hence their overall current account showed a surplus, enabling them to continue making foreign investments overseas. Conversely the debtor regions had a large overall export surplus, which enabled them to service their debt and, in the case of the United States, to redeem it. Within this broad division there were complex multilateral patterns, such as the triangular trade between the Tropics, the United States, and Britain.

The firmness of the ties that bound together the economies of the various parts of the world was dramatically demonstrated by the dislocations caused by the First World War. The advanced countries had become deeply dependent on the rest of the world for their food, raw materials, and certain essential producer goods like fertilizers. The backward countries were no less dependent for manufactured goods and equipment.

The war, however, shattered the international financial system and disrupted the flow of capital. It also created powerful pressures to reduce dependence on foreign trade and to develop domestic production through autarchy and national planning. The result was to accelerate the growth of nationalism all over the world; each "people," the theory dictated, must be both politically independent and industrialized in order to be strong.

The diffusion of industry, therefore, went on apace and along previous lines, but now the areas chiefly affected were eastern and southeastern Europe, the United States and Canada, and Asia. The proportionate share of western Europe in world manufacturing declined and with it the place in the sun of that part of the world. However, western Europe recovered its industrial capacities in some five or six years after the catastrophe, an eloquent testimony to the recuperative powers of the system. Indeed, even World War II did not destroy it. Germany, France, and Italy experienced economic recovery and expansion after 1949 which was universally recognized as "miraculous."

This most recent phase of industrialization has witnessed the development of machines that revolutionized transportation and communications. The motor truck gave a flexibility to carrying that allowed light industry, particularly, to leave urban centers; high-tension electrical lines gave greater mobility to power and to light; and radio and television changed very drastically the entertainment industry and the spreading of information. The automobile made it possible for man to live at a considerable distance from his work, to explore new regions, and to have a new form of recreation. Furthermore, automatic, computer-controlled machinery made technological unemployment a more pressing problem than it had been in the past and instilled a new sense of urgency in the need for men to determine the wisest and richest uses of their expanding leisure.

In these changes the sciences played a strikingly important role. The next "revolution" seemed destined to come from chemistry and physics, for from these disciplines must come new materials and sources of power to replace the natural resources that industrial societies were so rapidly exhausting. Chemistry had already performed wonders, and it continued to do so with the development of such things as artificial fibers and plastics, which brought important changes to the textile and packaging industries. Undoubtedly the most dramatic achievement of the sciences was the creation of a new source of power from nuclear fission. Here was an advance that showed promise of changing the power pattern of the world and of allowing the industrialization of areas devoid of conventional sources of power.

By the middle of the twentieth century, the most developed nations began to realize that it would be to their benefit to have the economically backward areas of the world industrialized; that they themselves would profit from a greater division of labor, an increase in international trade, and a general improvement in the world's standard of living. The United States undertook the greatest "foreign aid" program in history, and many of the other industrial states adopted similar programs, although of lesser magnitude. This turn of events, a far cry from the restrictive policies of England at the beginning of the Industrial Revolution, was strengthened by the fact that political colonialism was coming to an end and that the new form of "imperialism" was economic in nature.

As one comes to the conclusion of the study of any great change like that of industrialization, one cannot escape the question: Did the change redound to the benefit of mankind? To answer such a question is very difficult. But at least the analyst may point out that the new system did extend man's control over his physical environment—it allowed him to live better and with less fear of want. Indeed, the expectation of life at birth in western Europe rose from some thirty years in 1750 to some seventy years in 1965. Industrialization allowed the population of Europe to increase by nearly four times within this same span of years, despite the fact that more than 50 million emigrants left its shores between 1846 and 1930. Beneficial as such results appear to have been, industrialization has pushed people off the land into cities (only some 10 per cent of the occupied population in the more advanced economies are engaged in agriculture), where conditions of life leave much to be desired. In short, industrialization has helped to solve many of man's physical problems but has contributed to social problems of enormous gravity and complexity.

For Further Reading

The Cambridge Economic History of Europe, Vol. VI.

Feis, Herbert, Europe, The World's Banker.

Ferenczi, Imre, International Migrations, Vol. I, Statistics.

Hawtrey, R. G., The Gold Standard in Theory and Practice.

Imlah, Albert M., Economic Elements in the Pax Britannica.

Jenks, Leland H., The Migration of British Capital to 1875.

League of Nations, Economic Intelligence Service, The Network of World Trade.

Rostow, W. W., The Economics of Take-Off into Sustained Growth.

Thomas, Brinley (ed.), Economics of International Migrations.

Willcox, Walter F., International Migrations, Vol. II, Interpretations.

New Forces, New Ideas

75   Romanticism and After

If it is appropriate to speak of the machine as the symbol of Rationalist thought during the Enlightenment, then the proper symbol for Romanticist thought is the living organism. The favorite mode of the Age of Reason was analysis and simplification: the system of Newton and the model of the good society alike consisted of a few intelligible parts that worked smoothly together and could be readily understood by any unprejudiced observer. But analysis led to abstraction, which led to skepticism. In the end it seemed as if the love of simplicity and generality had simplified nearly everything out of existence. In Hume, as we know, the real world and its objects are reduced to a set of habitual impressions; the universe is no longer ruled by cause and effect; hence there is no science and certainly no God.

Besides these losses, which the mind of the post-Enlightened generation could grasp, the deeper self suffered a starvation of the feelings. The dwelling among abstractions, the business and duty of being Enlightened, is dry work. Any experience of life suggests that advising the soul to be lofty and the heart to keep calm while the intellect works out all the geometries needed by man and society is *too* simple. Rousseau had been the first to point this out. He had reminded Europe of the existence of emotion, not in order to have it substituted for reason, but in order to warn against an exclusive attachment to either. Speaking of religion and philosophy, he said categorically: "General and abstract ideas are the source of the greatest human errors; never has the jargon of metaphysics led to a single discovery, and it has filled philosophy with absurdities that make one ashamed as soon as one has stripped off the big words."

The Romantic generations, which span the half-century from one European crisis to the next—1789 to 1848—knew better than to confuse life with abstraction, or human salvation with comfortable reasoning. They

CHRONOLOGY

A.D. 1761–1762　Rousseau's *Émile* and *Nouvelle Héloïse*
1767–1769　Lessing's *Hamburgische Dramaturgie*
　　　1774　Goethe's *Sorrows of Young Werther*
　　　1790　Goethe's *Faust: A fragment*
　　　1796　Erasmus Darwin's *Zoonomia* (evolutionary theory)
　　　1798　Wordsworth's and Coleridge's *Lyrical Ballads*
　　　1803　Death of Herder; birth of Berlioz
　　　1804　Beethoven's *Eroica* Symphony
　　　1807　Hegel's *Phenomenology of Mind*
　　　1814　George Stephenson's first locomotive
1820–1830　Rediscovery of Diderot's *Rameau's Nephew, The Memoirs of Benvenuto Cellini,* the poems of François Villon, and the philosophy of Spinoza
　　　1822　Stendhal's *Racine et Shakespeare*
　　　1824　Death of Byron in Greece; Delacroix's first modern painting
　　　1827　Victor Hugo's Preface to his play *Cromwell;* death of Beethoven
　　　1830　Berlioz's *Symphonie Fantastique;* Revolution in Paris, Belgium, Italy, and the German Rhineland
1830–1842　Comte's Positivist philosophy
1833–1839　Invention of photography
　　　1835　David Strauss's *Life of Jesus;* Tocqueville's *Democracy in America*
　　　1837　Pugin's *Contrasts;* deaths of Leopardi and Pushkin
　　　1839　Turner's painting *The Fighting Téméraire*
　　　1845　Alexander von Humboldt's *Cosmos*
　　　1848　Revolutions on the Continent; Chartism threatening in England
　　　1850　Death of Wordsworth

had been marked by the tremendous experience of the revolution followed by Napoleon—twenty-five years of wars and overturns, of heroism and passion, of destinies made and unmade with dramatic suddenness—and they could tell at sight that the ironic anecdotes of Voltaire, the prose of Gibbon, or the bland indifference of Hume did not correspond with reality as the later comers knew it. Romanticism, before it was a movement or even a name, was a radically changed sensibility.

The first truth about Romanticism, then, is that its so-called reaction against the previous age was not born of mere impatience with outworn forms of art and inadequate social philosophies; rather, it sprang from the immediate awareness of a new world. That this awareness expressed itself in forms and concerns that sometimes seem remote from that new world is an appearance readily explained when we consider how the Romanticists undertook to revise rationalism, that is, to include reason in a larger view of experience; or putting it still another way, to transform the machine into an organism.

At the outset, almost any cultural change occurs by simply taking in neglected opposites. To find a new basis for reason one goes back to experience. When weary of established forms and admired models, one hunts out older forms and remote models. Instead of tired abstractions, one looks for the concrete instance. Whereas Sir Joshua Reynolds, say, had taught his academy students to paint the most general forms they could imagine, Blake says that all art consists of particulars. The particular is individual, unique, vivid. Fresh and original, it arouses strong feelings— possibly feelings of repulsion in some, but it banishes indifference. Accordingly, the Romantic thinkers and artists stop dealing with Man, a capital-letter abstraction. They seek out men—as Rousseau already had done when he passed from the theory of the social contract to the needs of the Polish nation and Corsican society.

Trusting experience and the individual, the particular, the Romanticist looks within himself and reports on his findings; that is why he is often an egotist, or seems so. Introspection of course makes him liable to error, fantasy, silliness. His dreams or illusions are part of reality, to be sure, but they need verification. Hence the Romantic passion for history, the storehouse of innumerable particulars, of countless individuals. Walter Scott, as a modern scholar has said, "taught Europe history," by showing in his novels how varied Man actually was, and (a subtler point) how irrelevant to men's lives were the rationalist statements that could be made about them. For example, the eighteenth-century conviction that "at bottom" all religions and moralities are one is quite useless for describing the Middle Ages or understanding a particular saint. To a genuinely religious age or being, all religions are *not* one. The saint and the crusader testify to the truth of *their* religion, not to the syllogisms of a Deist.

Other discoveries followed for the Romantics from an imaginative reading of history. They learned that the past is not a contemptible confusion best forgotten; it is a moving spectacle, a still-potent fragment of humanity. To dismiss the centuries since Rome as barbarian, to scorn Gothic architecture, to believe that human reason began with Newton, as the Enlightenment had done, was to ignore the depths of one's own life and to deny the spirit of one's own people. The people, who had made history in the revolutionary and Napoleonic wars, were now after a long neglect to be recognized as the reservoir of all genius, the agent of social continuity, the great democratic basis of western civilization.

As with the past, so with the remote or exotic parts of experience. Rousseau had shown the philosophes and the orthodox that they had no conception of the size of the world, a provincial outlook persuading them that the Christian God was *the* God, unknown though he was to three-quarters of the human race. The Romantics had the same intuition about the scenery, customs, and art of peoples lying beyond the comfortable cosmopolis of Europe. Chateaubriand drew wild word-pictures of the wild New World, Delacroix went to Morocco to paint, dozens of poets sought the Near East for its intimations of Asia. The realms of the exotic, like the Middle Ages or the hidden inner self, were not places into which to escape from contemporary reality; they were places with which to enlarge one's understanding of it.

Such feelings as these did not burst forth, in common life or in art, without the usual preparation and transition. To mention Rousseau is of course to name the great link between the earlier age and its successor. Rousseau stands out because his writings set Kant on the track of the "practical reason," which gave encouragement to resurgent piety; because he influenced Goethe's feeling for nature and shaped some of his attitudes toward science, love, and prose literature; and because his sway over the Western mind was lasting: sixty years after Rousseau wrote *The New Hé-loïse,* Shelley could still study it with a sense of revelation. And in his famous *Confessions* Rousseau furnished a guidebook to self-searching for all the lyricists and psychologists of the next century. If Wordsworth and the "nature philosophers" did not have to consult the credo of the priest from Savoy, it was only because the worship of nature had become a widespread cult. It aided in the rediscovery of Spinoza (freshly interpreted as a pantheist), and it gave body to the religious revivals, both Catholic and Protestant, whose common quality was now the aesthetic emotion— the *beauty* of the Christian ethic and architecture, of God's handiwork, of belief itself.

But Rousseau was not the only forerunner. The eighteenth century had felt and recorded many "Romantic" sentiments even while subduing them to physics and mathematics. The taste for Gothic architecture and wild gardens came in the 1760's, first as a fad, then as genuine feeling. Repressed emotion found a vent in sentiment and pathos (the "tearful comedy" as well as the folk ballads) or in manufactured fears and mysteries (the Gothic tale of ghosts and horrors, so unlike Reason and so close to superstition).

In Germany, moreover, a revolt had begun against the domination of French taste and the writings of M. de Voltaire. The scholar, critic, and playwright Lessing was the leader of this culural uprising, in which Shakespeare played the role of a hidden god, whose natural virtues would help the insurgents conquer the French. And as Herder, another critic, pointed out, those virtues—naturalness, depth of knowledge, and emotion—were also to be found in the ancient German literature hitherto neglected, the sagas and ballads and fairy tales that spoke of a world at once less artificial than the present and nearer the permanent human verities.

Deeper still ran the stream of old pietism which burst out in the late eighteenth century in Methodism and kindred movements marked by evangelical fervor, poetry, and humility. Finally, the French Revolution itself, though it cast patriotism in the classical roles of ancient Rome, was a school of modern heroism and a drama of contemporary life. All these elements merged in the Romanticist philosophy, which may be summed up as: the prevalence of drama in a world of animated beings.

Drama means conflict, which presupposes differences, individuality, unexpectedness, mystery. The human mind can grasp and mold reality, especially the passionate mind, but it can never exhaust reality or reproduce its richness. Recalling Pascal, whom the philosophes had derided, the Romantics saw man as simultaneously great and wretched, hero and slave. Goethe's Faust, exhibiting these "two souls in one breast," served as exemplar to the age and established its new morality by asserting that true living is striving rather than achieving.

Romantic art naturally matched the Romantic sensibility. Its preferred forms were "open," dramatic, dynamic rather than static or seeking perfection. Blake's love of concrete particulars was shared by poets, painters, and musicians alike, and "local color" became a leading virtue. The particular—minute, significant, true—consorted well with Scott's historical novels or with Balzac's studies of society in the *Comédie Humaine,* or with Stendhal's soundings of the psychological depths. Wordsworth's *Lyrical Ballads* were imitations of the street ballads retelling strange incidents of low life. Byron's early stories in verse mixed introspection with travel in the strange Near East. Goethe and Victor Hugo, Pushkin and Mickiewicz, Heinrich Heine, Alfred de Vigny, and Leopardi, Keats and Shelley, fed the vast desire to hear an individual voice, vibrant with passion and bringing to consciousness emotions and sensations that were new.

The element of drama was so diffused throughout these artistic revelations that little or none was left for drama itself: the stage was barren. But the canvases of Turner, Bonington, Géricault, and Delacroix made up for the lack, and so did the music of Beethoven, Weber, and Berlioz, of Mendelssohn, Glinka, and Schubert, of Donizetti, Bellini, and Chopin. It was, all over Europe, an explosion of genius, as if the very idea of genius defined what Romanticism as a whole had to contribute. For genius is individuality, the dredging of the depths, the mystery of mind and of its wayward power oscillating between grandeur and misery. To those observers of the time who could not understand the necessity of all the striving and who would not read *Faust,* Stendhal would cite the nearer prototype: Napoleon. And lest the point be missed, he patiently explained that Napoleon's genius lay in vastness of plan, mastery of detail, and rapidity of execution.

The Romantics, then, were realists in the plainest sense of the word, reality-seekers. But to make a cult of experience in this way, to try to embrace so much of the given diversity, must surely lead to confusion: "mastery of detail" is a great virtue, but it ends in chaos without "vastness of plan." How to organize the teeming facts of the living universe was the Romanticists' problem. Abstractions are more manageable. They are fewer and deductive logic connects them, as the philosophes had shown.

What then was the organizing principle of all this heaving, heedless life? The Romanticists were fortunate in having at hand the pattern they needed, the "plan" which their fellow seekers, the biologists, were beginning to employ. In truth, it was no accident that biology, whose realm is Life, should have served Romanticist thought. For the desire to replace the abstract and machine-like by a richer model of experience is equivalent to replacing physics and mathematics by biology, leaving the heavens and its circlings of dead matter for the earth peopled by organic forms. This parallel motion of the artistic, scientific, and philosophic spirit led, in the Romanticist period, to the triumph of the idea of evolution.

Buffon, as we know, was an evolutionist by 1750, when his descriptive work on animals drew attention to striking analogies. His collaborator and disciple, Daubenton, extended men's knowledge of comparative anatomy; Buffon's protégé and assistant, Lamarck, made an exhaustive study of species and devised the first tenable scheme of natural evolution. The use and disuse of organs, argued Lamarck, would modify the form of individuals and by "descent with modification" would in time make species evolve. Simultaneously with him, Erasmus Darwin, botanist, physician, and poet (and subsequently the grandfather of Charles Darwin), was setting down astute speculations on the same theme as Lamarck's. With systematic insight, Darwin anticipated his grandson's subdivision of subjects as well as some of his arguments, but he posited that the need and will of the creature to achieve its ends led to the variations of form, which then descended and produced the results we call evolution.

Soon the idea was in the air. Goethe was a convinced evolutionist before 1830, and in that year of political revolution the matter was openly debated by Cuvier and Geoffroy Saint-Hilaire in the French Academy of Science. Three years later, Charles Lyell published his *Geology,* based on evolutionary theory, in which a chapter is devoted to summarizing Lamarck. At that point the biological revolution may be said to be an accepted fact in European culture, whatever remained to be proved or argued in the technical domain of biological science.

The distinction just drawn should make it clear that evolution as a *form of thought* dates from the era of Romanticism and is one of its great contributions. It is still with us, as we know from our reliance on particular "histories"—of a medical case, of corporate profits, of an art form. It is our habitual method of understanding the present and of guiding life.

None of this insistence on living and evolving means that during the half-century under review physicists and mathematicians went into hibernation. On the contrary, they pursued their work, establishing (for example) the principle of the conservation of energy and enabling chemistry to attain the status of a separate science. But the scientists of that time were still "natural philosophers," most of them still unspecialized, and therefore under the influence of the new current of vitalism: it is characteristic that in the new chemistry, the combining properties of elements were called "elective affinities," and that this technical term could serve Goethe as the title of a novel.

Outside science, evolutionary thought found its readiest application and utility in social philosophy. Readmitting so large a slice of the past as the Middle Ages called for some account of institutional change. A nobleman at Versailles was a different creature from his ancestor at the court of Charlemagne. How did the change—in manners, dress, language, beliefs, economic condition, rights and privileges, attitudes toward women and children—come about? By evolution; by gradual changes, chiefly small and invisible but relentless. Such was the pattern and principle of the new history and the new philosophy. Earlier authors had written books about the "revolutions" of states, meaning the changes of dynasty or religion— the events at the top of the social pyramid. Now the only acceptable histories were those that traced the broader evolution—of law or kingship; occasional closer studies might be called "physiologies" (of marriage, of crime)—always the organismic analogy.

This mode of understanding past and present had immediate relevance to existing fears and hopes. The fear of revolution was in part allayed by the evidence of evolution, which showed that progress was as much hindered as aided by great upheavals. Across the chasm of the violent French revolution a line of development could be traced: how much wiser, then, was the English revolution of 1688, which was such only in name and which merely took a natural evolutionary step! These were arguments that also fed reformers' hopes; for, looking back, it seemed as if mankind never did stop in its forward march. In the worst of times something was stirring, evolving, along the line of progress, which entitled each political or social advocate to expect that by aiding the natural course through a demonstration of its inevitability the evolution might be quicker and the desired Utopia nearer.

This line of reasoning is familiar to all who have ever heard its loud echo in twentieth-century Marxism. Marx inherited the faith in it from Romantic evolutionism. In his formative years it was a commonplace; and so were a number of systems designed (like his later socialism) to explain how man had reached his present state, social and intellectual. The first of these systems in point of time was that of Comte Henri de Saint-Simon, who compared the earliest times known to him (ancient Egypt) to infancy; and Greco-Roman times to youth. After a protracted adolescence, modern times expressed maturity. This "law of the three stages" prepared the mind for accepting the ultimate form of maturity, the last phase of evolution, which was to be a highly organized technocracy. Industrialists and bankers were to assure prosperity, peace, and a just distribution of technological plenty. The Saint-Simonian movement was widely influential throughout Europe in the 1820's and 1830's, both among the idealistic young and among speculative thinkers.

The magic force of three stages also inspired the great Hegel to a philosophy of history in which he sought, among other things, to explain post-Napoleonic Europe. His compass was wider than Saint-Simon's; his analysis went deeper into the confusions of the past and the impenetrability of the Eternal. An apostle of freedom, he divided the evolution of man into three steps by means of the degree to which the idea of freedom found embodiment. In the ancient or Oriental world, only one was free—the tyrant. In the medieval world, a few were free—the nobility, a class. In the modern world, all were free—the whole nation.

All men, that is, were *to be* free: there was work yet to do, and Hegel had views on the process of historical evolution. The recent past had shown unmistakably that the idea of freedom realized itself in mankind through conflict. A force or thesis (which could be an idea-bearing group as well as an embattled institution or people) claimed or held power—only to be met by an antithesis or opposition, equally determined to prevail. The outcome of the struggle was that regardless of any victory neither idea conquered; rather a synthesis resulted, which fused elements from each set purpose into a higher expression of mankind's unconscious brooding will.

Besides explaining history, Hegel's "dialectical" movement of opposites supplied, in his estimation, a new logic to replace the traditional one, which falsifies the world by showing it static: his was dynamic, able to deal with life, which is a perpetual Becoming. Hegelism in this most general sense has been one of the lasting contributions of Romanticist thought. From the New England Transcendentalists of Emerson's generation to the Chinese Marxists of today, the form (not the doctrine) of the philosophy of becoming has molded the minds of even the least philosophical.

The third evolutionary scheme contemporary with Hegel's is Auguste Comte's, in which the crowning stage is what its creator called Positivism. In the infancy of the race, says Comte, man is religious—he endows every object with indwelling gods. Later (again in those conveniently placèd Middle Ages) man is metaphysical: he frames abstractions out of things and attributes the power of the thing to the abstraction. That is a great step forward, for it finally permits modern man, by dropping the abstraction, to reach the positive stage of thought: studying objects and their relationships simply as they are given by nature. To do so is to furnish positive knowledge or science. Positivism made many adherents, whose sense of historical evolution led them in various reformist directions. Proving a point while seeming only to unfold truth was the common feature of all the evolutionary histories that explained the present and forecast the future; in a word, it was the *genetic method,* fruitful, convenient, easy to misuse, but obviously the only fitting one for an age peculiarly sensitive to the energies of life.

Much has been written about the politics of Romanticism as distinguished from the speculative philosophies that spanned all of recorded time and offered a stopping place for human history where conflict was to cease and freedom without effort was to ensue. On the more mundane ground of politics, we ask: Were the less sibylline minds of the Romantic period liberal or reactionary? Did their work promote or retard the great evolution toward the parliamentary, democratic nation-state? The actual struggle of parties belongs to another chapter. At this point only beliefs concern us, and even more than beliefs, their relation to the main course of Romanticist art and opinion.

That relation, apparently, offers difficulties to some cultural historians, because they find undoubted Romanticists on both sides of the great divide. Scott was a confirmed Tory; Byron and Hazlitt were radicals. Victor Hugo and Lamennais ran the gamut from reaction through liberalism to socialism. The young revolutionists Wordsworth and Coleridge turned more and more conservative with advancing age. In Germany the confusion seems even greater. There are proponents of the self-contained nation and corporate state, like Fichte; cosmopolitan liberals like Heine; anarchists of every complexion; and converts to Catholicism who work back from liberal to reactionary positions. Obviously, statistics about thinkers mean nothing; each individual career must be studied and understood in the light of temperament and circumstance. Is it then possible at all to speak of the politics of Romanticism? Diffident observers are ready to deny unity to the movement because in its leaders practical goals shifted and diverged.

The unity is there, but these observers look for it in the wrong place. What unites a movement such as Romanticism, which virtually embraces the whole age, is not the many solutions brought forward by individuals and groups, but the concentration of all on a few issues. A unity of temper has already been shown, together with the method of discovery it applied. In politics the temper is the same, but the methods are many. The Romantics wanted for themselves and their peoples the freedom, diversity, self-reliance, and opportunity for self-development which they praised and used in their works of art and historiography. But they differed as to the means of achieving them. Yet nearly all agreed that revolution must not go on ad infinitum, for the very sake of the liberties sought.

But what was the true bulwark of those liberties? Some said monarchy and mother church—and among them were Balzac, Bonald, Joseph de Maistre, and John Henry Newman. Others said nothing short of universal suffrage and a republic: Victor Hugo was one of those. The many who turned nationalist, especially in Germany and Italy (and we may count Fichte, Hegel, Mazzini, and Manzoni in this group) were convinced that without a strong unified political state coextensive with the historic culture no freedoms could survive. Past experience lent color to their view: they had been invaded, cut up, trampled on for centuries. Some were now willing to accept tyranny rather than helpless disunity.

Finally there were the partisans of a neomedievalism (the kinship here is with Burke's and Scott's Toryism) who saw that in large aggregates men are rootless and unhappy. To avoid social atomism, men must work and be ruled by traditions rather than bureaucracies, live on a familiar spot of ground rather than in anonymous cities. Carlyle, the introducer of German Romanticism to England, became the tireless expounder of this view.

If one adds the individual variations on these large themes, the politics of Romanticism present the usual cacophony of any political period. But it is instructive to regard this grand debate as uncommonly consistent under its surface confusion. For a glance ahead shows us that from the French Revolution to the Russian, the search for freedom that inspired all Romantics led Western man to each of the solutions proposed in that earlier time. First, the complete laissez-faire of liberalism was won and found wanting. Then followed "Tory democracy" to protect the underdog from the rugged and ruthless liberal. That proved insufficient, and socialisms and communisms of every kind flooded Europe. The corporate state, totalitarian state, welfare state have by now tried in myriad ways to combine elements of all the hoped-for freedoms, including the utopian. The only plan that has not been gone back to is that of Church and King in close alliance. It is the only one, for by the 1960's there were signs that anarchism was once more a tempting hypothesis, especially to the young. Meanwhile it is clear that raging-blind nationalism still seems to many dissenters, even within the old unified countries, the key to all earthly blessings.

It is curious but true, therefore, that side by side with the abstract ideal of liberty which we draw from the legacy of the Enlightenment, the realized or imagined embodiments of that ideal that we still battle about or die for go back to the exuberant period that followed the French Revolution.

In one other realm likewise, the realm of art, Romanticism first brought about changes that we still take for granted as the normal order of things. There is much about Romantic art that we decry or despise and many assumptions underlying it that we wish to see discarded, but we have not yet gone beyond them. To take the most striking, it is from the time of Romanticism that art and artists have been regarded as of enormous social and spiritual importance. Gibbon would have smiled at the idea. Today art is commonly taken as the sign of true greatness in the life of a nation; art is the measure of "a healthy society"; also a precious, eternal possession of mankind; the artist (rivaled only by the great scientist) is an extraordinary being, divinely inspired and accordingly privileged. The genius, in short, is the first superman, and his deliverances have the force of revelation. The religion of art, art the twin of religion, are phrases that occur early in the Romantic century. Hegel and Walter Scott, sober men both, were not ashamed to make avowals of such feelings. Their first full-blown, widespread manifestation was Shakespeare-worship.

Nor was this Romanticist fervor what a later age would call aestheticism. The genius was worshiped for what he could create, which even in that age of renewal and exploration seemed miraculous. In technical innovations alone the Romanticists must be credited with an astonishing performance. What Goethe, Wordsworth, Hugo, and Pushkin did with language; Constable, Géricault, Bonington, and Delacroix with color and line; Beethoven, Weber, Berlioz, Chopin with rhythm and sound; Scott, Balzac, Stendhal, and Gogol with social and psychological observation— all this seems hardly believable even after 125 years.

So rich indeed was their output that they accustomed the Western world to another novelty, another aspect of the evolutionary view of the world: they created the Cult of the New and forced the public to accept pluralism in style. After the Romanticists it became a settled expectation that every succeeding wave of art should be new and that every individual artist should be original. Whatever the actuality of art in earlier ages, the professed aim was one style at a time, coupled with "perfection," which meant approaching the single ideal for the genre, not diversity but unity. Romanticism turned all these roles inside out, and in so doing helped create a rift between the bulk of polite society (the "philistines") and those who by taste or snobbery support the artistic avant-garde in its ever more startling innovations.

That split is of course reproduced in the difference between the bohemian life of the artist and those "bourgeois values" which by the end of the nineteenth century very few dared to defend openly. In the Art for Art's Sake movement, which should really be named Art for Life's Sake— art the redeemer of life—the bourgeois, ridiculed and condemned for the previous seventy-five years, could fittingly cry out, like the pagan emperor, "Thou hast conquered, O Esthetician!" So far as culture in the main is concerned, the central tendency of Romanticism in art is unbroken from its inception in 1790 to the First World War; and indeed to the present day.

What does modify it in detail about the midpoint of the last century is that all of Europe undergoes the great disillusionment and loss of hope after the failure of the revolutions of 1848. What this failure betokened is told in another chapter. Here the point is that the universal fear and despair—in both victors and vanquished—engendered in the artistic consciousness of Europe a revulsion against the enthusiasms, the energies of the period just preceding.

The need was felt for a shrinking of consciousness, a return to what was plain and possible; and as this more assured ground could only be the tangible and material, the name Realism was given to the new movement in literature and painting. It concentrated on the commonplace in order to transmute it into art, just as the new politics concentrated on things rather than principles. Realpolitik was the politics of material advantage, divorced as far as might be from loyalties and beliefs. "Look," said everyone to himself, "where faith and hope, liberalism and dreams of progress, have led us—to catastrophe. Give it up. Swallow your pride; forget your visions." That is the lesson of *Madame Bovary* and all aggressive Realism.

Yet in the works of the spirit, that mood was temporary. To it succeeded a stoical Neo-Classicism, also of short duration, and a Neo-Romanticism variously called Symbolism, Impressionism, Aestheticism. In literature, the "naturalistic" novel itself partook of the earlier exploratory zest of Romanticism, and in point of technique the later work in all genres and arts clearly owed its genesis to this or that element (sometimes a passing thought) in the earlier, inclusive, Romantic movement: evolution, descent with modification, could thereby be demonstrated again. Only now, after still more revolutions and world wars, does its force seem to be close to spent.

For Further Reading

Rousseau, *Confession of Faith of a Savoyard Priest.*
Scott, *Rob Roy.*
Delacroix, *Journals* (W. Pach trans.)
Goethe, *Faust* (Alice Raphael trans.)
Berlioz, *Memoirs* (David Cairns trans.)
Hegel, *Lectures on the Philosophy of History.*

76   From Liberalism to Democracy

The Congress of Vienna worked hard to make a settlement that should bring lasting peace to Europe after a quarter-century of war. Its twin principles of legitimacy and compensation were meant to pacify as many peoples and rulers as possible. Yet the new era that began after Waterloo in June, 1815, witnessed from the start a struggle among at least five overlapping groups, not counting the divergent interests of the great powers. Generally speaking, everybody approached the new age as the opportunity to carry on and settle Unfinished Business.

To the extent that the aristocracy, in France and elsewhere, could feel that it had won the long battle with the Revolution and Napoleon, they argued: We are the victors, we must work to restore the old regime. The liberals thought: We have had to make concessions, but the last word has not been said; we must work to complete the design sketched by the enlightened thinkers of the last century. The radical wing of the liberal party was sure that only political democracy—not just the parliamentarism of the upper bourgeoisie—would satisfy the needs of the people. And among the people and the democrats were some who denied the validity of mere political change. The system must be recast, by reform or revolution, so as to abolish poverty and inaugurate *economic* freedom through socialism.

Add to these demands the nationalist passions aroused by both the new romanticist temper and the cumulative hostility to the Napoleonic invasions, and it becomes clear why the first half of the nineteenth century in Europe was a time of uneasy equilibrium punctuated by armed revolts and repressions. Nationalism naturally found an enemy in the old dynastic

interests, which viewed territorial concerns in other than national terms. As for the other four parties, each viewed the other three as irreconcilable. Despite the great fatigue that follows long wars, despite a general desire to "cope with revolution" and substitute other means of social change, it was apparent that a showdown would come sooner or later, because in truth the legitimacy invoked by the powers at Vienna did not exist. Its former possessors had lost it irrevocably, and the new claimants (liberals, democrats, socialists) had not yet made good their claims.

No alliances were possible among the upstarts; their creeds were too divergent. And what is worse, the warring groups were shortly to fall under the hidden sway of a material force that had nothing to do with creeds, passions, memories, or hopes—the Industrial Revolution. Out of these disparate movements a one-to-one opposition gradually emerged: the emotion of nationalism came to be pitted against the desire for political liberalism. This crystallization of feeling around one or another goal occurred at different times in different countries, but the history of regimes and revolutions between Metternich's Congress at Vienna in 1815 and his flight from the same city in 1848 can be read as the triumph of nationalist feeling over liberalism.

Even the distant Americas, North and South, went through the same collective emotion, which testified to the belief—perhaps it was nothing more than an instinct—that man could better win his freedom through nationhood than through political machinery. The sensation of being kin, of being numerous, strong, and self-determining, seemed to offer a surer hope of social bliss than the complex, laborious effort of working a parliamentary system. These generalities—or rather, clues to a broad understanding not only of the period under review but also of the travail through which the wider world is now going—must now be tested by the recital of events in the principal countries of Europe until 1848.

The practical device attached to the Vienna peace in hopes of making it permanent was the Quadruple Alliance, a banding together of Austria, Russia, Prussia, and Great Britain for maintaining stability. The powers were to meet in periodic congresses and decide on armed intervention, if it seemed appropriate to preserve the terms of the treaty. In the event, those congresses only stimulated resistance against what came to be called "Metternich's system." The system was his chiefly in the sense that it was central Europe and Italy that kept trying to shake off repression. In the Hapsburg empire, Hungarians, Croatians (Yugoslavs), Czechs, Poles, and Germans had caught the nationalist fever. It expressed itself in journalism and plays, in student societies and professional groups. Censorship and police control were imposed to uproot doctrine and prevent the exchange of ideas with other countries. By an ill-judged policy, troops from one nationality were sent to garrison another, both groups of course being strengthened in their hostility by these enforced contacts.

Outside Austria, Metternich sought to control the similar patchwork of "the Germanies" to the north and Italy to the south. On this axis, there was not a self-contained nation between the Baltic and the Mediterranean; Austrians and Spaniards governed pieces of Italy, and to the east Russia played the same role of unwanted guardian over her border states, Finland, Latvia, Lithuania, and part of Poland. Against the liberalism at work within this conglomerate, Metternich secured from a congress at Carlsbad in 1819 a set of decrees muzzling the universities and the press, providing for a spy system, and forbidding the grant of any constitution "at variance with the monarchical principle." This was a rejoinder to student demonstrations in honor of Luther and to the assassination of the playwright Kotzebue, who had been a spy in the Russian service.

Germany was held down for a time, but Italy uprose. A rebellion in Naples in 1820 forced the Spanish Bourbon King Ferdinand IV to grant a constitution. Behind this overturn was the massed force of Carbonari or pretended charcoal burners. They were in fact young liberals and nationalists, who met in the woods and plotted resistance. The Congress of Troppau declared for intervention, and the next year at Laibach, the king of Naples "invited" the Austrian army into his realm to "restore order." This was done, with the usual sequel of fierce persecution. Comparison with modern methods of conducting international affairs shows that though the means have multiplied and the time lag has shortened, the scheme remains unimproved.

Other revolts followed in northern Italy (where the enemy was Austrian Hapsburg, not Spanish Bourbon); in Russia (where the once liberal czar, taught in youth by French rationalists, had turned reactionary); in Great Britain (where industrial unrest was harnessed to liberalism); in Spain (where the army mutinied and thus set off a full-scale uprising that forced a second constitution down a Spanish Bourbon throat); and in Portuguese America (where Brazil shook off the tutelage of the mother country and made itself into an independent empire).

Within a decade of the "permanent" Peace of Vienna, revolution had become endemic. Beyond the scope of Metternich's system, the Serbs won the first skirmishes toward national liberation from the Turks and within a few years more the Greeks did likewise. This time, however, popular opinion throughout western Europe was on the side of the Greeks. Lord Byron was in the peninsula supplying money and working for unity, and three years after his death at Missolonghi the great powers not only guaranteed an independent kingdom of Greece, but also gave virtual autonomy to Serbia and the Rumanian provinces of Moldavia and Wallachia.

Freedom was obviously easier to bear at a distance and when it was freedom from another power. This exception to Metternich's system was especially clear when Great Britain broke away from the Quadruple Alliance of 1823 and supported President Monroe in his declaration supporting the independence of the South American colonies from Spain: these new nations might be easier to trade with if they were not Spanish but free. And though Britain was neither giving up colonialism nor dealing liberally with her own dissidents at home, her nineteenth-century tradition of supporting national self-determination abroad had begun.

Yet by 1829 the meaning of so much independence won and condoned was still far from clear. Was the political and emotional response of European rulers and ruled based on a growing love of *free nations,* or was it inspired by the love of *free citizens?* It took two events of wider scope to suggest a likely answer. And to come to the first of these one must ask what had been happening since 1815 to the chief culprit and warmonger, which it had been the object of the Peace of Vienna to neutralize and contain, namely France.

At the outset it was in France that the sharpest conflict occurred between the victorious, "legitimate" aristocrats and the defeated liberals. Though the restored Bourbon king, Louis XVIII, wanted to pursue a middle-of-the-road policy, he was not allowed to. The charter he had promulgated in 1814 (before the return of Napoleon for a hundred days) guaranteed representative government, religious freedom, and civil rights. But after Waterloo, the reactionary wing of the King's party, known as "ultras," demanded a return to the *ancien régime.* Without waiting for the King, they took matters into their own hands and conducted a nation-wide persecution of liberals—a "White Terror" to match the red of Robespierre's time. During this purge, elections were held under the charter and, in the absence of liberal leaders (most of them in hiding), the chamber that was returned was manned by ultras. There followed a year's worth of repressive legislation: the press was controlled, divorce disallowed, and an ad hoc judicial system set up to protract the political purge. So extreme were these measures that in order to keep his hold on the mass of the people the King had to dissolve the Chamber. The new majority proved to be moderate, which left ultras and liberals as ineffectual minorities.

Since one naturally associates liberalism with representative government, it is necessary to understand at this precise juncture what made the French Charter of 1814 ephemeral and useless as a dike against the tide of liberalism. Ultimately, of course, later and more liberal constitutions suffered the same fate under the pressures of democracy and socialism. What is true of that first charter is true of all other instruments that limit or seem to limit the sway of popular sovereignty. For popular sovereignty is the great ideal legacy of the French Revolution of 1789, confirmed in his special way by Napoleon, and productive of the series of revolutions with which Europe and the world have had to deal ever since—the democratic evolutions based on universal manhood suffrage, and the dictatorial kind, by plebiscite, by the proletariat or by any other mode of populism. The latest is the revolution by direct action for continuous, total participation, in which the sovereign people exercises its rights in the manner that these descriptive words imply.

Back in 1815, the French Charter, like those extorted by force from this or that Metternichian satellite, restricted popular sovereignty by property qualifications. Only those who paid 1,000 francs a year in direct taxes were entitled to vote. What this meant can be measured by the fact that when under the moderate royalists, the sum was reduced to 500 francs, it shifted the majority from the aristocrats to the upper bourgeoisie. Extending the franchise by lowering property qualifications was thus the first step as well as the perennial demand of liberals in France, England, and elsewhere down to the day of universal suffrage.

The second liberal requirement is a free press, for the essence of liberal politics is to drum new ideas into the popular mind. European liberalism is inherently a concern of the articulate—students, journalists, university and professional men; in short, persons who live by ideas more than by custom, to whom change, reform, progress, are vivid realities, and who invent the political machinery that progress demands. The moderate royalists in France were so far in tune with the times as to liberalize the press laws and to institute national conscription for the army, a measure tending toward recognition of the principle of social equality which Napoleon had made so potent a political force.

An integral part of the liberal and egalitarian program is the removal of disabilities once imposed on special groups. In 1815 the Congress of Vienna had been liberal to the extent of decreeing the abolition of the slave trade. The liberal constitutions of the ensuing years variously freed Dissenters, Jews, or one-time political exiles from various restrictions. The conviction grew that any citizen had both civil and political rights. The only question was whether a regime of free-for-all such as liberal theory envisaged could show any stability. Soon after the mild relaxation of controls legislated by the moderate royalists in France, the Duc de Berri, the King's nephew, was assassinated. An immediate revulsion followed the outrage, and new laws reversed the previous trend. The election procedure was complicated by a provision that gave a double vote to the thousand-franc taxpayers, and the term of the legislature was lengthened to seven years. The Church was given a stranglehold on education, and the rudiments of a police state, equipped with internal espionage, were set up. To clinch the reaction, France was assigned the task of military intervention in Spain. A year later, in 1824, Louis XVIII died, leaving the throne to his brother, Charles X, long the leader of the ultras.

These typical details of the seesaw between liberty and repression in post-revolutionary Europe suffice to show how and why Europe in the first half of the nineteenth century lived either in fear or in hopes of further revolution. The example of the United States, where the election of Andrew Jackson as President in 1828 appeared as a step toward democracy, could not serve countries in which the very principle of representative government was disputed by half the population. England, as we shall see, barely avoided a revolution like the one that was becoming inevitable in France.

The decisive overthrow of the Bourbons, symbols of legitimacy, took place in France because of several converging reasons: France had a century of liberal ideas behind her; France was the initiator of revolutions; France had not one but half a dozen doctrines of reform; France had a bourgeoisie with a powerful motive of self-interest inciting to revolution. That motive was simple: the aristocrats led by Charles X had voted themselves a large indemnity for the loss of their estates suffered in the 1790's. To pay the indemnity, the state lowered the interest rate on the national debt, that is, took the money out of the pocket of the bondholders, mostly well-to-do bourgeois. The elections of 1827 brought into the Chamber a bourgeois majority, which the King disregarded. He appointed as minister an émigré of the old days, as stubborn as the King; and when the conflict between Chamber and minister grew tense, Charles issued ordinances against the press and the chamber and called for new elections.

The ordinances did not last a day: journalists and publicists at once called for a general insurrection in the name of popular sovereignty, and in three days' fighting forced the abdication of Charles. Workingmen fought side by side with students, lawyers, and soldiers, and disposed forever of divine-right monarchy in France. The next king was not *of France* but *of the French*. Louis-Philippe, a cousin of the former reigning line, owed his position, if not to an election, at least to an invitation. The republican party was still too urban and intellectual to prevail. The "country," which is to say the peasantry, was still wedded to the old forms, and the liberal leaders from the upper bourgeoisie were content with a king provided he was constitutional, as in England. In these characteristics, the French revolution of 1830, quickly imitated throughout the Continent, is as it were the diagram of the first effective advance of liberalism to catch up with the unfinished business of 1789.

The events that paralleled in England the forward march apparent in western and central Europe betoken a different kind of arrears. To be sure, England had for forty years contended with domestic adherents of the original French Revolution; indeed among the educated there were men (such as Hazlitt and Byron) who saw even in Napoleon the principle of liberty at work. But the great popular feeling that brought England to the verge of revolution between 1830 and 1832 was due to intrinsic factors as well as to imported ideas. The chief cause was a shift in population and wealth which made the English Parliament visibly unrepresentative. While the new factory towns of Manchester, Birmingham, Leeds, and Sheffield grew in size and the factory owners in influence, the "rotten boroughs" (whose voters were for sale) and "pocket boroughs" (sometimes uninhabited) returned Tory landowners to the House of Commons.

There were, moreover, whole classes that had long been exasperated by Tory complacency: the disfranchised Catholics, the nonconformist Dissenters (disabled on religious technicalities), the intellectual classes (philosophical radicals such as William Cobbett, liberal economists such as James Mill, law reformers such as Jeremy Bentham, theoretical democrats such as Francis Place the "philosophical tailor")—none of them, under the unreformed parliament, stood any chance to exercise a fraction of power.

Finally, the new business interests, typified in such a man as Richard Cobden, the cotton manufacturer, knew that the state had long been inefficiently run by the squires, the bishops, and the lords. "Economic reform" had been called for—and defeated—as far back as the 1780's. It was time for England, on the threshold of the greatest productive expansion in history, to set its house in order, beginning with the political representation of its most energetic leaders, the new industrialists.

These were aided, on one side by the equally new working class, whose lot in the cities was dismal and precarious, and on the other by the Whig party, which having long been out of office saw in the current agitation an opportunity to reenter. As early as 1819, an influential Whig, Lord John Russell, proposed giving the vote to the manufacturing class, but it was only ten years later that Earl Grey, the party leader, made reform a stated Whig policy. The Tories in power did not respond in the approved way of stealing the opposition's thunder. Their liberalism was for export only, as in the support of President Monroe and the rebellious Latin American colonies. It was with great difficulty that a few concessions were made in the late 1820's, notably that of relieving the Dissenters and Catholics of their political disabilities. For the rest, as the Duke of Wellington, the Prime Minister, maintained in 1830, the English Constitution was perfect as it stood.

But the July Days of that year in Paris threw a new light on the situation. The country rang with noisy demonstrations, at first spontaneous, soon well led and sustained. Tories in the Commons became nervous and lost confidence in Wellington. Earl Grey formed a new ministry and introduced the first Reform Bill. It was defeated in 1831, but in fresh elections Grey was returned, bringing with him a second Reform Bill.

It passed the Commons and failed in the Lords. When King William IV refused to create enough new peers to override that opposition, Grey resigned and Wellington attempted a comeback.

It was then that the English liberal "revolution" took place. Intellectuals of the radical school joined with the manufacturers in stumping the country and organizing protest meetings. Francis Place advocated a run on the banks; other speakers urged the nonpayment of taxes. In the crowded midlands, the workers were persuaded that their interest, from the price of bread to the continuity of employment, depended on sending their bosses to Parliament—which must be reformed before that desirable goal could be reached.

With the sound of mass meetings in their ears the Tories gave up. Earl Grey and his Whigs took power once more and won from the King a grudging assent to the creation of new (Whig) peers to neutralize the Lords' expected veto of a third Reform Bill. The threat sufficed, the Tory Lords choosing to be reformed rather than swamped. By becoming law, the Reform Bill of 1832, like the Paris revolution of 1830, reset in motion the liberal transformation of Europe which the Vienna settlement had sought to halt. Once past dead center, one reform bill begot another; each stimulated fresh demands on the part of groups deeming themselves neglected; democracy, equality, socialism became logical necessities. No obstacles of mind or matter could impede their forward march, though the path lay across rivers of blood.

The provisions of the great bill of 1832 did not of course foreshadow such consequences. The reform got rid of rotten boroughs, roughly readjusting representation to population. The big new cities were given seats, and at the same time the franchise was extended and simplified. In the towns a voter had to pay a rent of £10 a year; in the country he had to own land of the same rental value or be a tenant of land worth £50 a year. It is estimated that these changes increased the electorate by 1½ per cent. Voting continued to be by open ballot, so convenient for bribery and coercion; but at least the polling period was reduced from two weeks to two days, which both lessened the opportunity for traffic in votes and made elections more sober occasions.

Besides dislodging with a minimum of violence the old English oligarchy, the chief by-products of Reform were: the liberation of the municipalities from the control of self-perpetuating cliques; the steady reform of the criminal law; and the emancipation of the Jews on the same terms as the Catholics and the Dissenters.

On the Continent, the one firm result of the wave of 1830 revolutions was the separation of Belgium from Holland, a victory of nationalism rather than of liberalism: from the start the union imposed at Vienna had been unworkable. After some days' fighting in Brussels, in 1830, France and England joined forces to compel the Dutch king to let go his vassal state. Belgium became a liberal kingdom in its turn, but pledged to neutrality under the guarantee of all the great powers. It was the violation of that agreement in 1914 which symbolizes the breakdown of the supremacy of Europe.

Elsewhere after 1830, conservatism apparently recovered the upper hand and annulled all the concessions it had hastily made to the revolutionists. In the Germanies, particularly the Rhineland, liberals had extorted constitutions like the one France had enjoyed fifteen years earlier and had just replaced by a better one. This relationship is significant: the revolutions of Central Europe correspond in character to the advances made ten or fifteen years earlier in the westernmost countries, and down to the present this gap in time has not been closed.

In Italy, 1830 liberalism failed in the same way, thanks to the cooperation of the Hapsburgs and the pope. Russia suppressed the Poles' uprising of 1831 and seized the chance to make an end of Polish independence by annexing the kingdom, thus laying up for Europe an inexhaustible source of misery. As for the minorities ruled by Austria, their mutterings were still too indistinct to show anything more than the presence of a nationalist discontent which has in fact never yet been appeased.

One concludes that what sanguine liberals saw as political progress—the irresistible advance of enlightened mind against the forces of darkness and oppressive reaction—was in truth a double confusion and misunderstanding. On the one hand, the passion of nationalism innocently assumed the guise of love of liberty; on the other, the constitutions sought as the instrument of liberation were rarely matched by the necessary political maturity of the populations. Events proved that when national groups won freedom they did not scruple to oppress other minorities. Written constitutions did not of themselves guarantee order, justice, and civil rights. Throughout this tragicomedy the fraud was largely unconscious. Kings deceived their peoples "for their own good"; popular leaders adopted liberal slogans "as a first step" toward national selfhood; and the bourgeois who won the full franchise (as in England and France) mistook *their* coming to power as the final achievement of freedom for mankind.

On this last point the contrary demonstration was not slow in coming. Since the 1820's workmen in Paris, Manchester, Berlin, Rome, Warsaw, Naples, and Turin had fought side by side with students and journalists against the troops of the embattled monarchies. Indeed, ever since the original upheaval of 1789, the common people had been the great anonymous force behind every attempt to change the existing order. But by the

1830's the working class, whether industrialized as in England and Belgium, or still partly an artisan class, began to recognize that its lavishing of blood on the barricades did not much advance its prospects. Aristocrat or bourgeois, the men on top remained more intent on their own interests than on the workers'. In fact, the bourgeois was in several respects the less likely to favor the workers. His views (and his legislation) on economic matters were the so-called liberal ones, which regarded labor as a commodity and advocated laissez-faire as the healthiest state. This meant leaving the worker to shift for himself—out of work in bad times, starving when ill or old, dependent on the toil of his wife and small children to earn a bare subsistence. Compared with this rugged freedom of the manufacturing town, life on the land under a resident squire or lord was likely to be more bearable and secure.

These things being so, leaders and theorists of working-class liberty soon came to the fore. Their agitation followed two divergent lines. One set of reformers, divided among groups using various names, wanted to remake society from the ground up. They planned—and carried out—utopian schemes of community life, in which everyone had a function and a reward. Prosperity and happiness were ensured by obedience to the rule *and* the ruler of the utopia. Such schemes, fathered by Saint-Simon or Fourier or Cabet or (most successfully) by Robert Owen in Scotland, might be described as benevolent despotism adapting itself to socialist ideals. The Saint-Simonian propagandists enjoyed a great vogue throughout Europe down to the 1840's. The Owenites and others inaugurated a remarkable number of communities in the United States. And their writings as well as those of purely theoretical socialists, communists, and anarchists such as Sismondi, Bell, Gray, Moses Hess, and Proudhon were the first to attack the free-for-all doctrine of liberal economics. In so doing they determined the course of the later socialist theory which leads to Russian communism and the welfare state.

These early reformers were disposed to act directly on their beliefs, but without violence: simply show the world how to reorganize itself by giving it a model. The second and much larger working-class movement had faith in representative institutions; the object of its struggle was to make them completely democratic. In England, this doctrine was known as Chartism, from the "People's Charter" of liberties which was to establish the true Parliament and open the way to all needed reforms. In substance, Chartism boiled down to six demands, all but the first of which have become commonplaces of political democracy: (1) annual elections for parliament, (2) universal manhood suffrage, (3) the secret ballot, (4) salaries for members of parliament, (5) equal electoral districts, and (6) the removal of property qualifications for members of parliament.

To achieve these goals the Chartists were ready to petition the Queen and demonstrate in public. They felt no gratitude to the men who had pushed through the reform of 1832. Lord John Russell, who thought Parliament sufficiently reformed for decades to come, was derided as "Finality Jack." By the mid-1840's mere *liberalism* was already out of date, inadequate to the swamping needs. The railroad mania proved the frivolity of parliament and capitalism combined; the Irish famine showed that political problems were grounded in economic organization. Only the rock-bottom principle of one man, one vote, could ever give to the most numerous, most indispensable class in every country the leverage necessary to bring about a decent society. That society must be democratic, and some said republican as well.

The main objection to democracy was that it would put the state at the mercy of the ignorant and the illiterate. From antiquity it was well known that the mob was the ruin of civilizations. The rejoinder was: remove the mob's ignorance, make the masses literate, "educate your masters." But the time was not ripe. Too many thought it still possible to fend off the tide. The liberal manufacturing class, having arduously made its way to the top, felt that others should do the same. When during these same "Hungry Forties," the French lower middle and working classes were grumbling about the restricted franchise, about the feeble (non-nationalist) foreign policy, about the dullness of daily life, the liberal prime minister Guizot, despite his integrity, intelligence, and willingness to extend the free educational system, could only advise the dissidents to get rich and thus qualify for a seat in the Chamber.

In England or in France, the formula did not meet the case. Nobody needed to be told to get rich and nobody believed that everybody could. What is more, the clash of interest and outlook between the old aristocracy and the industrial bourgeoisie (quite different from the great merchant families) was driving the aristocrats to side with the people against the middle layer. Protecting the factory worker through legislation became a Tory aim, at once charitable to the worker and annoying to the entrepreneur. Hence the precarious internal situation of the two countries that led the Western world. Both the ideas they broached and the tremors they felt agitated the rest of Europe. From Scandinavia to Spain and from Prussia to Italy, men, books, parties, plots, demands, outbreaks, and defeats produced a harsh orchestration whose crescendo was reached in the quasi-universal revolutions of 1848.

England, as usual, escaped the worst of the upheaval and was in fact the exiles' sanctuary as the Continental uprisings were successively crushed. English Chartism failed quietly: the great parade and petition to the Queen was doused in torrential rain. Ten thousand special constables (including Louis Napoleon, future emperor of the French) ensured order in the London streets. In France the Republic established manhood suffrage but, rent by dissension and unemployment, succumbed to the coup d'état of Louis Napoleon. In central Europe, nationalist rivalries were played off against one another to their common destruction. And the hopeful yet divided Frankfort Assembly seemed to prove that men of ideas were incapable of transacting parliamentary business, let alone run a modern nation. To the south, Mazzini's Young Italy movement had inspired multiple outbreaks with which both the new Pope Pius IX and the king of Sardinia, Charles Albert, appeared to sympathize. But soon reaction set in. The pope changed his mind and Charles Albert was defeated by an Austrian army. Count Metternich, it is true, had fled Vienna forever, and Louis Philippe abdicated, but the system of Europe appeared unshaken. Under that appearance the reality was that Western culture had come to one of its periodic turning points.

Needless to say, these revolutions, protracted through nearly four years, did not mean the same thing for all the nations affected. The common turning involved only two facts that were clear. One was that henceforth nationalism proved a more unifying and hence a more potent ideal than liberty. A second was that idealism itself suffered a permanent loss of momentum. Among men of thought there was after 1848 a failure of nerve. The appeal to "practicality," to force and numbers, to the "politics of things" (realpolitik), to cynicism and the mass mind, replaced the earlier faith in the perfectibility of man, itself premised on his essential goodness. Liberalism, democracy, universal education and welfare did become features of Western civilization after 1870, but there is a sense in which the Enlightenment and the "principles of 1789" come to an end in 1848.

For Further Reading

G. L. Dickinson, *Revolution and Reaction in Modern France.*
Tocqueville, *Democracy in America.*
Sydney Smith, *Peter Plymley Letters.*
J. S. Mill, *Autobiography.*
Louis Blanc, *History of Ten Years.*
Karl Marx, *Communist Manifesto.*

77   The Rise of Socialism

Throughout the history of the Western world, men had from time to time imagined a golden age. Usually it was placed in the past, but sometimes it was a vision of the future—a utopia in which perfection was realized and which, by indirection, was a criticism of the shortcomings or iniquities of the world in which the critics had to live. Christianity could be a powerful stimulus to this kind of thinking, through its call to love and moral perfection and, more concretely, on the basis of hints in the Bible and practice among early Christians, through the ideal of property held communally not individually; this ideal was attained in some respects by medieval monasticism and was advocated, with terrible repercussions, by some more radical reformers in the sixteenth century and by such millennarian groups as the Diggers in seventeenth-century England.

In the early nineteenth century there appeared the first advocates of a new tradition that offered both a criticism of present-day society and a blueprint for a perfect future society; by the 1830's the name socialism had been coined for it. It was, however, sharply differentiated from earlier forms of utopian thought. For one thing, although there were specifically Christian forms of it, socialism was as a rule aggressively secular; for another, it held out for the first time the possibility of realization. The sources of this new confidence can be found, no longer in Christianity, but in the thought of the eighteenth century—in its humanity and secularism, in its confidence in the possibility of human and social engineering, and, among a few Enlightenment writers, in its faith in perfectibility—and in the French Revolution. Although the French Revolution was a liberal, not a socialist, revolution, a few aspects of it provided later socialists with inspiration and heroes: the Jacobins had stringently regulated the economy in the interests of both justice and equality, and in 1795–1796 François Noel Babeuf (who, characteristically, called himself Caius Gracchus Babeuf) led a rising, the Conspiracy of Equals, that was frankly communist and that, through a lieutenant, Filippo Michele Buonarotti, transmitted a conspiratorial tradition within which nineteenth-century socialism could, indeed often had to, flourish. But these examples did not exhaust the socialist significance of the French Revolution; far more important was the fact of the Revolution itself, proof that society could be altered and altered suddenly, if not by merely applying psychological and social theory, then by violence.

A.D.   1795–1796   Babeuf leads the proto-communist "Conspiracy of
                   Equals" in France
          1813   Robert Owen publishes *A New View of Society*
          1817   Ricardo's *Principles of Political Economy and Taxa-
                   tion* published, the definitive statement of classical
                   political economy
          1818   Karl Marx born at Trier in the Rhineland
          1832   Death of G. W. F. Hegel
          1840   Proudhon publishes *What Is Property?*
          1843   Marx expelled from Germany
          1844   Marx meets Friedrich Engels
          1845   Engels publishes *The Condition of the Working Class
                   in England in 1844*
          1848   Marx and Engels publish the *Communist Manifesto;*
                   European revolutions
          1849   Marx settles in England
          1864   Ferdinand Lassalle killed in a duel; International
                   Working Men's Association (First International)
                   founded in London
          1867   Marx publishes first volume of *Capital*
          1871   Commune established in Paris following French de-
                   feat in Franco-Prussian War
       1872–1876   Torn by internal divisions, the First International
                   gradually disintegrates
          1875   Social Democratic Party founded in Germany
          1883   Fabian Society founded in London; Marx dies
          1889   Second International founded; Eduard Bernstein
                   proposes his "revisionist" departure from ortho-
                   dox Marxism
          1893   Independent Labour party founded in England
          1900   Labour Representation Committee founded in Eng-
                   land, leading to formation of the Labour party in
                   1906
          1905   Russian Revolution
          1908   Georges Sorel publishes *Reflections on Violence*
          1914   Divisions in socialist parties on the question of the
                   war result in general support of the war and col-
                   lapse of Second International

The French Revolution belongs, however, to the prehistory of socialism; its real history takes its rise in the new economic circumstances of Europe. It will not do to invoke the Industrial Revolution and to let it go at that; although Owen in England and Saint-Simon in France were prophets of a new industrial order, in neither country was industrialism far enough advanced to allow it to be put forward as a sufficient explanation of their fertile imaginations. What was more at issue was the expansion of the preindustrial economy—the growth of manufacturing, trade, and accumulated wealth; the explosion of population; and the consequent problems of greater extremes of wealth and poverty. The problems of an expanding, incipiently industrial society, problems that for the first time could seem remediable, socialists proposed to cure.

In England, socialism began with Robert Owen, himself an enlightened and progressive factory owner and manager, and his disciples; in France, it began with a remarkable cluster of unusual, even eccentric thinkers, less rooted in economic reality but quite as prophetic in some respects of the future. In both countries, these originators of socialism drew on current psychological speculation: Owen, for example, was a firm believer in the doctrine stemming from Claude Adrien Helvétius and David Hartley that man was a creature of his environment and could be changed in his very nature by changing that environment. They could draw too on another magnificent creation of the eighteenth-century mind, the developing doctrines of classical political economy; these doctrines analyzed and prescribed for the economy with remarkable perception and relevance, but in their glorification of capital, commerce, and laissez-faire they came dangerously close to rationalizing the evident maldistribution of wealth, underconsumption, and poverty. This apparent rationalization became more striking early in the nineteenth century when the gloomy conclusions of T. R. Malthus about the threat of overpopulation were grafted onto the optimism of Adam Smith and Jean Baptiste Say to produce a theory of inevitable conflict among economic classes, found in the abstract analyses of the English economist David Ricardo; curiously, some of Owen's disciples (Thomas Hodgskin being the most famous) and later Karl Marx himself were to take much of Ricardo's teaching—his insistence on the Lockean notion of the origin of value in human labor, for instance, and his view of class conflict—and turn it back on classical economics to construct a theoretical justification for socialism.

The early French socialists were at once more original than the English and more fantastical. Charles-Edmond Fourier, for example, advanced a psychology that was a remarkable mixture of humane insight and patent silliness and urged a reconstruction of society with all the realism one might expect of a man who appeared promptly at his house at a fixed hour every day to await the arrival of some unknown philanthropist who would endow his schemes for social regeneration. Étienne Cabet went further than any other early socialist to advocate a true communism. It is perhaps to be expected that these early and transitional figures thought less in terms of reconstruction through large-scale social engineering than they did in terms of regeneration by example; they advocated the formation of communities, which would live by socialist rules and principles and would point the way to what Owen called "the new moral world"; it was this characteristic that led Marx and Engels in time to dismiss them scornfully (and not altogether wrongly) as "utopian" socialists.

To find a true advocate of social engineering, one must turn to Count Henri de Saint-Simon, a down-at-heels aristocratic intellectual, who by way of a temporary enthusiasm for economic liberalism ended in a remarkable anticipation of modern technological society, in which bankers and entrepreneurs would replace the old aristocracies of landowners and lawyers and in which remuneration would be decided in accordance with the social input of each individual. Saint-Simon's influence was far-ranging; it affected both Thomas Carlyle and John Stuart Mill in England, and, by way of disciples who avoided the neoreligious and sexual crankiness of some of the French Saint-Simonians, helped to shape the structure of the French economy: by mid-century the Saint-Simonians had produced a number of bankers, industrialists, and engineers, the most famous being Ferdinand de Lesseps, whose imagination and entrepreneurial skill brought about the digging of the Suez Canal. But the Saint-Simonians also point to a strand in the socialist tradition that particularly concerned the great French liberal historian Élie Halévy: while socialism sought to carry further the liberating impulses of the French Revolution, it proposed to do so by means of a more stringent organization of society, thus giving new economic and administrative form to the apparent paradox of freedom and organization in the political theory of Jean-Jacques Rousseau.

These varied and fertile currents of socialist doctrine were brought together with certain even more basic elements in contemporary thought in one of the most remarkable and original syntheses in the history of the human intellect, the work of Karl Marx. Marx was born in Trier, in the Rhineland, in 1818, the son of an enlightened liberal Jewish lawyer, who had converted, for convenience and without conviction, to Lutheranism. Warmly encouraged at home, Karl Marx studied law at the University of Bonn and went on to the University of Berlin, where he became a philosopher or, more properly, an enthusiastic intellectual. In these years immediately following the death of G. W. F. Hegel, the great philosopher who had dominated the university, his thought was subject either to the unimaginative form-filling of epigones or to the raking criticism of rebellious disciples who still could not escape the forms that Hegel had imposed on German philosophy. Since the conservative implications of Hegel's thought were intolerable to his activist mind, Marx fell in with the latter group, but in turn saw most of their remedies as pretentious and unreal. The work of Ludwig Feuerbach, a relatively unoriginal materialist philosopher, suggested to Marx a way in which greater specificity could be brought to Hegelianism, as well as a justification for political action: the solution lay in rejecting Spirit as the motive force of evolution and replacing it with material circumstances, in short with economics, of which the spiritual realm was an inevitable product and reflection. The final amalgam was "historical materialism," a view and interpretation of history that received no definitive statement from Marx's own hand but that underlay his entire enterprise and that, to a historically minded century, lent a special conviction to the Marxian analysis and program.

The full development of Marx's system had to wait on his absorption of still other currents of thought. Supported at first by his family, then by his journalistic efforts, Marx soon earned a reputation as a violent radical and in 1843 was forced to leave Germany. Already fascinated by the French socialists, Marx went to Paris, where he plunged into the socialist ferment, not only in the realm of ideas (where he was severely critical) but in the realm of organization and action (where he was a great admirer). In 1844 he met Friedrich Engels, the prosperous son of a German merchant who represented his father's firm in England and who the next year was to make something of a reputation by publishing an analysis of the situation of the working classes in industrial England. Engels, a Hegelian radical, an admirable popularizer, and for the rest of his life the devoted friend of Marx and the expounder of his philosophy, focused Marx's attention more clearly on the analysis of the regnant economic system by the English economists, notably David Ricardo; and when Marx's activities made him an unwelcome guest, first in France, then in Belgium, he took refuge (like so many Continental revolutionaries) in London.

During his stay in Paris, Marx had moved to the extreme wing of radicalism, to communism, a term that at the time was used to distinguish the more radically democratic socialists from the moderates. As was inevitable in the later years of Louis Philippe's reign, he was deeply impressed by the potential for success that seemed to lie in violent insurrection, an insurrection carried out by a band of perceptive and determined men who would act on behalf of the proletariat. Marx had come to see the proletariat, in Hegelian terms, as the ultimate negation of bourgeois society, just as the bourgeoisie had been the negation of feudal society, but until the proletariat was fully prepared to live in the final communist society, the leaders would exercise a dictatorship, a "permanent revolution."

In time, when the last remnants of the bourgeoisie and bourgeois property had been eliminated, the coercive power would disappear—the state would wither away—and free association, true communism, would take its place.

These ideas were summed up in one of the most brilliant documents ever written, the *Communist Manifesto;* issued jointly by Marx and Engels, but primarily the work of Marx, the *Manifesto* appeared on the very eve of the French Revolution that broke out in February, 1848: it is a sketch of the historical dynamics that led to the triumph of bourgeois civilization, a celebration of the accomplishments of that civilization, a scathing denunciation of its cruelties and vices, and a call to action on the part of the proletariat to speed on the historical process: "The proletarians have nothing to lose but their chains. They have a world to win. Workingmen of all countries, unite!"

Notorious now throughout Europe, Marx arrived in England in August, 1849; thereafter, along with deep involvement in the sectarian politics of working-class radicalism, some pamphleteering, and some journalism, Marx's major activity was the construction of his vast economic treatise, *Capital,* the first volume of which appeared in 1867; the two remaining volumes, less well worked out, appeared only after his death. Again, Marx produced an astonishing synthesis, though the conviction it has carried and still carries must rest on the schematic brilliance of its historical insights rather than on the economics itself, for Marx projected the categories of the classical economists forward at precisely the time that other, bourgeois economists were exploding the very foundations of that economics. What is perhaps more to the point is that in his years in London Marx turned away from the insurrectionary emphasis of the *Manifesto* to demand the thorough preparation of the working class for its historic role, temporary cooperation with the bourgeoisie, the encouragement of trade-union activity, and the passage of social legislation: he became in short the prophet of democratic as well as of insurrectionary socialism, though he never doubted that one day revolution would provide the means of overturning the present system. Therefore, just as Marx had brought together a wide variety of social, economic, and philosophical reflection and prescription, so there descended from him an almost equal variety of socialisms. He was the prophet of social democracy as well as of insurrectionary communism —and he was also the principal inspirer of the new discipline of economic history and (through his class analysis) of equally fruitful work in the field of sociology.

Although in time the varieties of Marxism would come to claim the mantle of orthodoxy, in Marx's own lifetime his doctrines, both theoretical and tactical, were sharply contested. Three other socialist thinkers may stand for the main countercurrents.

Pierre Joseph Proudhon, the son of working people and largely self-taught, burst on the shocked awareness of Europe in 1840 with a tract that asked in its title *What Is Property?* and answered, "It is theft." Proudhon was a superb maker of phrases and paradoxes, as well as a scorching controversialist, and in effect this appalling assertion argued only that profit constituted exploitation; in fact, never able to escape his peasant background and certainly never able to think consistently and logically about economics, Proudhon was a defender of individual property and opposed the bourgeois system only because it was unjust and exploitative. The essential victory of the proletariat, which would inaugurate a just order of mutuality and cooperation, was to be brought about, not necessarily by revolution (a question on which he blew hot and cold), but gradually through the establishment of a system of free credit, to liberate producers from the tyranny of lenders and to allow them to meet each other's needs freely: it was a plan fundamentally opposed to the then fashionable democratic state socialism of the reformer Louis Blanc as well as to the communism of Étienne Cabet or, indeed, of the early Marx. Now Marx, who had praised Proudhon at first but could not get on with him, had little trouble in exposing his ignorant analysis of the classical economists (Marx devastatingly replied to Proudhon's treatise called *The Philosophy of Poverty* with a tract called *The Poverty of Philosophy*) or in ridiculing the Hegelian veneer that Proudhon gave to his work, a borrowing of the dialectic in which the contradictions were seen not as motive power but as descriptive oppositions of good and evil. But Proudhon's profoundly felt though illogical moralizing, his individualism, and his hostility to the state, as well as his deep involvement in French working-class organization, were vital legacies to the syndicalist and anarchistic variants of socialism in the later nineteenth and twentieth century, particularly in France, Italy, and Spain.

If in Proudhon the cosmopolitan Marx was fighting an ingrained French tradition, in Mikhail Bakunin he was fighting a romantic revolutionism that was profoundly Russian. Again, the two men were entirely antithetical as personalities, but they disagreed as well on the question of ultimate goals and tactics. The theoretical opposition was not complete: Bakunin acknowledged Marx's centrality as a socialist theorist, translated the *Communist Manifesto* into Russian, and contracted to translate *Capital* as well. But he opposed the centralization advocated by Marx, preferring small units to be given freedom to revolt in their own interests, and true to his conspiratorial and flamboyant nature, he stuck by the notion of the violent revolution that Marx had tacitly abandoned in favor of political action. Bakunin made a vital contribution to anarchistic movements and was a source of the special characteristic that came to mark some of them, terrorism.

The third member of the trinity of Marx's great opponents, Ferdinand Lassalle, presents the most fascinating ambiguities. Not on the personal level, to be sure: here there could be nothing but hostility, after a brief initial collaboration, between the sober, respectable, scholarly Marx, and Lassalle, the intense, slapdash, self-dramatizing romantic who made himself famous in the 1840's defending the Countess von Hatzfeld against her husband and who got himself killed in 1864 at the age of thirty-nine in a duel over the beautiful Helene von Dönniges. Lassalle's unoriginal economics—he was famous for a reformulation of the English wages fund theory as the "iron law of wages"—hardly needed Marx's contempt; where the crucial opposition came was over Lassalle's intense German nationalism and over the question of political tactics. Lassalle was a believer in state socialism and in the last years of his life was in steady correspondence with Bismarck; he may, indeed, have indirectly inspired the state socialism to which that superb politician committed Germany in the 1880's. Marx, on the other hand, believed that the state must disappear. Lassalle was, moreover, the founder in 1863 of the first German socialist party, an ancestor of the great Social Democratic party that played so vital a part in German history until its extinction at the hands of Hitler in 1933. Although he had come to approve of political action as opposed to insurrectionism, Marx could not accept, as Lassalle did, political action that lay completely within the framework of the existing system or that gloried in patriotic nationalism. In 1869 a rival party, more orthodox, was founded; the two, finally unified in 1875, were subject to a steady stream of criticism from Marx and Engels.

The quarrels with the Proudhonians and Bakuninists were fought out in the stormy history of the International Working Men's Association (the First International), which was founded in London in 1864 and which ended, amid mutual recrimination, in the aftermath of the Franco-Prussian War and the Paris Commune of 1870–1871. The Second International, founded in 1889, was not so much an association of individuals and small groups as it was of great national parties, a confirmation of Élie Halévy's striking dictum that the ideological history of socialism came to an end with the publication of *Capital;* thereafter, he said, there was only the political history of socialism.

The founding of the great socialist parties occupied the last third of the century, beginning with Germany and ending with the formation of the Labour party in Great Britain in 1900–1906, although it did not become an avowedly socialist party until 1918. This politicization of socialism had profound effects on the social policy of European countries and on socialism itself. In country after country broad programs of social welfare legislation—factory laws; workmen's compensation; health, old age, and unemployment insurance—were adopted, in some instances at the promptings of conscience or broadened liberal theory (as in England), in others in response to the threat of labor and socialist organization or (as in Germany) as a Machiavellian device for undercutting it. But the spread of welfare and prosperity placed at further and further remove the possibility of imminent revolution and set some socialists at least, in the manner of millennarians in all times and places, to recalculating the prophecies. Of these recalculations, by far the most influential and attractive was the "revisionism" associated with the one-time orthodox Marxist Eduard Bernstein. It is possible to defend the paradox that Marx himself was the first revisionist in his turning away from revolutionary to political tactics; but Bernstein and his followers openly abandoned the goal of revolution in favor of a gradualist, political approach to social democracy, a heresy for which they were subjected to the most bitter attacks from those Marxists who fancied themselves the carriers of the true Marxist revolutionary heritage. But theoretical consistency was the last line of defense for orthodoxy against the manifest course of history, at least as it appeared in the late nineteenth century, and the self-evident spread of social equality and justice. And, European politics being what they were, the problem of political accommodation came to be presented in a particularly poignant form when the question arose, as it did for the French socialist politician Alexandre Millerand in 1904, of socialist participation with bourgeois parties in inevitable coalition governments.

Great Britain was spared most of these difficulties, in part because the theoretical constructions of Marxism held little appeal in the home of so many empirical and liberal philosophies, in part because the British trade-union movement was well established before any of the systematic social-isms were devised. Insofar as workingmen entered politics after 1870, it was largely as defenders of the pragmatic interests of labor, not as advocates of socialist reconstruction. Still, among some workingmen but more among middle-class intellectuals, certain idiosyncratic forms of socialism appeared. A variant Marxism was advanced in the Social Democratic Federation headed by the aristocratic and dictatorial stockjobber H. M. Hyndman, but in contrast stood the anarchism of the Socialist League, distinguished by the presence of the poet and designer William Morris, and the basically moral and religious socialism represented in the Independent Labour party, founded in 1893 by the working-class politician Keir Hardie. But the most famous of the English socialisms was that of the Fabians, headed by the remarkable partnership in historical scholarship and social engineering of Sidney and Beatrice Webb, and graced by the presence of the playwright Bernard Shaw and a host of distinguished intellectuals. Subject to intellectual schism, and undoubtedly elitist and paternalistic, the Fabians avowed a nonrevolutionary, gradualist policy to attain a highly organized democratic state socialism by way of scholarly demonstration, brilliant propaganda, and the permeation of established political organizations. Perhaps because the Fabians were so adept at self-advertisement, historians still argue about their exact role and about the success of the strategy of permeation; but the crucial role of the Webbs as inspirers (directly or by reaction) of two or three generations of English socialists and as architects of the socialism adopted by the Labour party in 1918 is not open to serious question.

Gradualism, an emphasis on legislation, and integration into established political processes inevitably provoked a reaction, particularly among trade-unionists who were experiencing greater and greater successes in organization and who, in the years immediately before the outbreak of the First World War, found more and more occasion to resort to direct economic action to gain their quite concrete ends. In France and throughout southern Europe a new heresy arose. Syndicalism, proceeding from Proudhonian theory and trade-union experience, emphasized an economy and state that would be organized on the basis of economic interests, following a revolution brought on by means of a general strike; a similar, antiparliamentary, but less extreme movement appeared in England in Guild Socialism, whose most distinguished representative was the dissident Fabian social philosopher G. D. H. Cole. The syndicalist movement, however, survived the war only as a legacy, as in the economic organization prescribed by the Fascists in Italy or in the British General Strike of 1926; it was replaced as a leftward force in the trade-union movement by communism. It would have been hard to see, however, from the vantage point of 1914 where a socialist victory would come from. The established socialist parties had in fact become respectable, and their ultimate bankruptcy was proved when, at the price of some defections, they each supported the war effort of their respective countries—the victory of nationalism over the class solidarity and cosmopolitanism for which Marx had stood.

Most believers saw Marxism as a doctrine suited to more advanced economies. Backward European countries spawned their own small socialist movements, chief among them the Russian socialist movement that grew up in opposition to reactionary agrarian populism, with excursions into anarchism and terrorism; the abortive revolution of 1905 against the deadly and inefficient czarist tyranny was in part socialist. It would have been difficult for most socialists, however—though Marx and Engels had anticipated the possibility at the very end of Marx's life—to predict that an overwhelmingly agrarian country with little industry and virtually no bourgeoisie would be the country to experience the first communist revolution and to present the principal socialist example to the twentieth century.

For Further Reading

Halévy, Élie, *The Era of Tyrannies: Essays on Socialism and War.*
Harrison, J. F. C., *Quest for the New Moral World: Robert Owen and the Owenites in Britain and America.*
Hobsbawm, Eric, *Primitive Rebels.*
Joll, James, *The Anarchists.*
Landauer, Carl, *European Socialism: A History of Ideas and Movements.*
Lichtheim, George, *Marxism: A Historical and Critical Study.*
———, *The Origins of Socialism.*
———, *A Short History of Socialism.*
Manuel, Frank, *The Prophets of Paris.*
Pelling, Henry, *A Short History of the Labour Party.*
Tucker, Robert C., *The Marxian Revolutionary Idea.*

78   The Antislavery Impulse in America

Few foreigners who visited the United States in the 1830's failed to note the inherent contradiction of a people who prided themselves in their equalitarian democracy, but who simultaneously kept subjugated the black sixth of their population. But the visitor had the advantage of detachment; he did not have to live with the consequences of their "peculiar institution." He could return home to muse upon a people who proclaimed themselves the vanguard of the modern world, even as they assented to the most ancient of man's systems of exploitation—slavery. For Americans who sustained the hypocrisy of preaching liberty and accepting slavery, the experience was often agonizing. "It is hardly fair for you to assume," wrote Lincoln to a southern friend, "that I have no interest in a thing which has, and continually exercises, the power of making me miserable." Trapped by a Constitution that legitimated slavery, many Americans struggled to reconcile their obligations as citizens with the maintenance of a labor system that crucified their consciences. Indeed, to be loyal to a nation that tolerated and in influential quarters even glorified slavery demanded a treason to conscience that was beyond the power of many.

Out of such conflicting emotions there gradually emerged a comprehensive antislavery movement. It was rooted in the intellectual currents of the eighteenth century, which by fusing the doctrine of man's natural rights and the law of God proclaimed slavery a monstrous injustice. Even before

A.D. 1777 Vermont ends slavery
     1804 New Jersey ends slavery
     1808 Slave trade ends
     1817 American Colonization Society established
     1820 Missouri Compromise
     1822 Denmark Vesey Conspiracy
     1829 David Walker *Appeal* published
     1831 *The Liberator* begins publication; Nat Turner rebellion
     1833 Britain ends slavery
     1836 Gag Rule
     1840 Liberty party formed
     1843 Repeal of Gag Rule
     1845 Texas annexed; Methodist Church splits along sectional
          lines
     1846 Mexican War; Wilmot Proviso
     1848 Mexican War ends; Free Soil party organized
     1850 Compromise of 1850
     1854 Kansas-Nebraska Act
     1857 Dred Scott decision
     1860 Abraham Lincoln elected; South Carolina secedes
     1861 Civil War begins
     1863 Emancipation Proclamation
     1865 End of Civil War, 13th Amendment ratified

independence had been achieved by the United States, a small but persistent group of Quakers denounced the "traffick of mens-body." Their opposition resulted from their interpretation of the New Testament. "Christ died for all," declaimed George Fox, "for the tawnies and for the blacks as for you that are called whites." The Quakers cataloged the moral and social consequences of slavery in words that were repeated with increasing frequency as the antislavery movement grew. The separation of families, the theft of the enslaved labor, the corruption of human values, all were inherent in slavery. It was a theme that Alexis de Tocqueville compressed into a single sentence: "It is easy to perceive that the lot of these unhappy beings inspires their masters with but little compassion, and that they look upon slavery, not only as an institution which is profitable to them, but as an evil which does not affect them."

What provokes assault invites defense. If the Bible legitimated an attack, so also it underwrote the justification of slavery. When the Missouri Compromise debate reached fever pitch in 1820, South Carolina's Senator Smith rumbled, "It is said that slavery is against the spirit of the Christian religion. Christ himself gave sanction to slavery. He admonished them to be obedient to their masters. . . ." To argue that the Bible restricted ownership of slaves to Israelites alone, as some abolitionists contended, led one Pennsylvanian to declare, "It would be pure heathenism to say, that ever God granted any thing as a privilege that was unjust in itself." Divine assent had universal implications.

The appeal to the Bible had subtle and explosive consequences. In a profoundly Protestant land like the United States, both supporter and opponent of slavery could eliminate moral doubt with an appropriate Biblical reference. If God is usually on the side of the largest army, in this debate, at least, he seemed to declare his neutrality.

The early criticisms of slavery were directed against a condition that had barely existed in North America in 1660. Introduced into the New World more than a century and a half earlier, it had arisen out of an elementary need for labor. The availability of free land lured away any workingman who could exercise a free choice. Anyone who wished to exploit the land on a large scale needed forced labor. As an Anglican priest explained, "to live in Virginia without slaves is . . . impossible." Thus the black slid into permanent subservience because economic necessity seemed to dictate it, and once slavery was established, a process of legitimation set in. A whole complex of laws codified the blacks' servile condition.

Although white masters preferred to believe their bondsmen relished, or at least tolerated, their condition, outbreaks of black violence, mainly sporadic, left them seemingly no choice but to build an effective police control. When colonial New York established special slave courts to try black infractions of the law, the governor attempted to explain the harsh procedures to London with the plea, "After the late barbarous attempt of some of their slaves nothing less would please the people." South Carolina accounted for its repressive code with the explanation that its slaves "are of barbarous, wild, savage natures, and such as renders them wholly unqualified to be governed by the laws, customs, and practices of this province." Black rebellion justified repression, and the need for repression proved black savagery. The white had built a self-legitimating system within which the black was hopelessly confined.

When independence was achieved in 1781, slavery was part of the American system, but so also was the soaring assertion of the Declaration of Independence that "all men are created equal." Thomas Jefferson, author of this hallowed phrase, harbored doubts on whether the principle applied to blacks. In his *Notes on Virginia,* he concluded: "This unfortunate difference of colour, and perhaps of faculty, is a powerful obstacle to the emancipation of these people." Abstractly committed to emancipation, he boggled at the prospect if the blacks were to remain within the body politic. "Among the Romans emancipation required but one effort," he wrote. "The slave, when made free, might mix with, without staining the blood of his master. But with us a second is necessary, unknown to history. When freed he is to be removed beyond the reach of mixture." The "stain" of racism marred the usually elevated tone of the great Virginian, but he was not alone, as the debates on the formation of the Constitution revealed.

When the call for an immediate end to the slave trade had been sounded at the Convention, Charles Cotesworth Pinckney, a South Carolinian aristocrat, stated flatly: "While there remained one acre of swampland uncleared in South Carolina, I would raise my voice against restricting the importation of negroes." With no less emphasis, he defended the permanence of slavery. "I am . . . thoroughly convinced . . . that the nature of our climate, and the flat, swampy situation of our country, obliges us to cultivate our lands with negroes, and that without them South Carolina would soon be a desert waste." In the resulting compromise, the importation of slaves was guaranteed until 1808, southern states were allowed to count three-fifths of their slaves in determining their congressional representation, and a fugitive slave law was promised. But the debate revealed the widely held conviction "that the States were divided . . . principally from . . . their having or not having slaves." The proudly conservative Pennsylvanian Gouverneur Morris spoke for a powerful strand of northern opinion. Slavery, he said, was "a nefarious institution . . . the curse of heaven on the States where it prevailed." The three-fifths compromise, he went on, "comes to this: that the inhabitant of Georgia and S.C. who goes to the Coast of Africa, and in defiance of the most sacred laws of humanity tears away his fellow creatures from their dearest connections & damns them to the most cruel bondages, shall have more votes in a Govt. instituted for protection of the rights of mankind, than the Citizen of Pa. or N. Jersey who views with . . . horror, so nefarious a practice."

Even as the federal Constitution was ratified, the antislavery agitation was achieving its first victories. Beginning with 1777, when Vermont, soon to become the fourteenth state, explicitly forbade slavery in its constitution, one northern state after another abolished slavery, a process which was completed in 1804 when New Jersey promulgated gradual emancipation. The revolutionary ferment, stirred by its espousal of the Rights of Man, had, at least north of the Mason and Dixon Line, adhered to principle. Colonial no longer, the new American sensed that to "persevere in this wicked practice," as one antislavery agitator argued, would lead "the world [to] call us liars and hypocrites." To redeem the revolutionary promise, slavery had to end.

From this starting point the agitation against southern slavery began, but the issue did not become critical until 1819 when the Missouri Compromise dispute arose. The fight to determine whether Missouri would enter the Union slave or free was won by the proponents of slavery, but in the compromise all the rest of the Mississippi Valley north of latitude 36° 30′ was closed to the peculiar institution. And whatever the settlement, the debate touched a raw nerve. Ex-President Thomas Jefferson proclaimed it "a firebell in the night," temporarily stilled but certain to ring again. Though President James Monroe thought the issue could be winked away by a compromise, John Quincy Adams, his Secretary of State, shared Jefferson's sentiments. "Much am I mistaken if it is not destined to survive his political and individual life and mine," he somberly commented. And he added dourly, "If the Union must be dissolved, slavery is precisely the question upon which it ought to break."

Powerful forces were gathering which would reopen the issue and sharpen its intensity until it swallowed up all other questions. Antislavery agitators who had placed their hopes in the moderate American Colonization Society suffered increasing doubts. The insistence upon making emancipation conditional upon expatriation to Africa, a point that commanded Jefferson's constant support, ran up against an insurmountable obstacle: few blacks evidenced a desire to retrace the journey from Africa, and sheer numbers made the enterprise implausible if not impossible. Outright abolitionists gradually increased their strength. In New England they published a *Black List* of northern congressmen who had had the temerity to support the Missouri Compromise and tried to wreak vengeance at the polls. Antislavery concealed a political potential that a quarter-century later would smash traditional alignments.

Outside the United States, British abolitionists under the militant leadership of William Wilberforce also attacked slavery. In 1833 the institution was finally abolished within the British Empire. Once Parliament had confirmed emancipation, the victorious antislavery leaders appealed to their American counterparts to emulate the British example. They gained a ready audience. "Let us imitate our British brethren," one abolitionist journal demanded, "and open the flood gates of light on this dark subject." Ralph Waldo Emerson spoke for many when he proclaimed the event "a day of reason; of the clear light. . . ." The transcendentalist philosopher, convinced of the efficacy of human progress, left no doubt of his expectations. "The Power that built this fabric of things," he said confidently, "has made a sign to the ages, of his will." Within the South, response to the British action was fearful, a harbinger of trouble. "It is not the fanatics at the North that the South fear," one South Carolinian admitted. "It is this abstract love for liberty, it is that the moral power of all Europe is against us." This fear was compounded guilt and the suspicion that their silent black gangs might someday rise in hideous rebellion.

Southern unease grew as the drum taps of abolitionist criticisms increased in tempo. Benjamin Lundy, Quaker born, had since 1821 used his journal, *The Genius of Universal Emancipation,* to lash out at the curse of slavery. In 1829, the free Negro David Walker published his chilling *Appeal . . . to the Colored Citizens . . . of the United States,* bluntly warning whites, "Some of you . . . will yet curse the day that you ever were born. . . . My [people] will yet root some of you out of the very face of the earth!" When, in 1831, a year after Walker's mysterious death, the Nat Turner rebellion brought savage and sudden death to sixty-two Virginia whites, Southerners had their worst fears confirmed. Although Nat Turner was caught and hanged, his memory lingered on, reminding slaveholders that behind black impassivity lurked hidden passions, awaiting only the chance to strike. One Virginian, after interviewing Turner in his death cell, commented, "I looked on him and my blood curdled in my veins."

The fears that permeated southern life were further reinforced when William Lloyd Garrison launched his antislavery paper, *The Liberator,* and rejected "moderation." Though he condemned the Turner uprising, he left no doubt of his own position. "Of all men living," he charged, "our slaves have the best reason to assert their rights by violent measures." It hardly mattered to southerners that Garrison's journal, two years after its first appearance, had fewer than 400 white subscribers, or that the bulk of his

funds came from free blacks, or that, in 1837, Elijah P. Lovejoy, an abolitionist editor, was murdered in Alton, Illinois, while defending his press
from a white mob. The fevered imagination of the South granted to all
abolitionists a clarion voice. They read of Garrison's intemperate attacks
and accepted as confirmed that his views held sway throughout the North.

Within the South, a handful of idealists, dismayed at the tightening
repression of slaves, fled into northern exile. The Grimké sisters, Angelina
and Sarah, embraced abolitionism. Angelina, soon to marry Theodore
Weld, the spokesman for political abolitionism, in a plea to southern
women to work against slavery remarked, *"God never made a slave, he
made man upright, his back was not made to carry burdens, nor his neck to
wear a yoke, and the man must be crushed within him, before his back can
be fitted to the burden of perpetual slavery."* For her temerity, Angelina
earned from the mayor of Charleston permanent expulsion from her native
city. No less instructive was the experience of James G. Birney, a former
slaveholder who emancipated his slaves and became an abolitionist. When
he attempted to publish an antislavery journal, he quickly learned that in
the South there existed freedom neither of the press nor of speech if either
was directed at the sacrosanct institution of slavery. His reception in
Cincinnati was no better. With the mayor looking on, a proslavery mob
destroyed his press. As the administration of Andrew Jackson entered its
final two years, the American scene revealed a profound inhospitality to
antislavery sentiment.

On December 7, 1835, in his annual message, Andrew Jackson called
upon Congress to prohibit the circulation through southern mails of
"incendiary publications intended to instigate the slaves to insurrection."
The postmaster of New York City had already refused to forward abolitionist tracts southward. John C. Calhoun, defender of southern minority
rights, although preferring state action to federal censorship of the mails,
recognized in the abolitionist movement an opportunity to unify southern
opinion. By exaggerating the importance of abolitionists, Calhoun hoped to
hold the South firm in support of slavery. Congress never complied with
Jackson's request, but until the outbreak of the Civil War no southern
postmaster delivered abolitionist mail. Northerners in general remained
quiescent, their calm to be broken only with the adoption of the "Gag
Rule" in 1836, which provided that petitions to Congress on the subject of
slavery be automatically tabled. This brought into the antislavery camp ex-
President John Quincy Adams, now a member of the House of Representatives. Outraged by this restriction of a fundamental liberty, he arose, time
and again, to challenge the gag rule, and as frequently, he was silenced by
his fellow members. But Adams, his long hostility to slavery now in the
open, pushed endlessly "for agitation, agitation, agitation, until slavery in

the States was shaken from its base." When, in 1843, the gag rule was finally repealed, the antislavery forces had scored a singular victory.

Whereas Garrison relied on "moral suasion," a new breed of anti-slavery agitators committed to the overthrow of slavery through political action had, in 1840, entered the struggle. With James G. Birney as their standard-bearer, they formed the Liberty party. But their bare 7,000 votes seemed piddling when compared to the millions who had rallied to the Whig and Democratic banners. The election convinced many abolitionists that only by working through the established parties could they achieve their objectives. Already within the Whig party a small but devout band, self-constituted as the Select Committee on Slavery and led by the gentle Joshua R. Giddings of Ohio, laid the foundations for the emergence of the Conscience Whigs. The Liberty party, broadened to include the whole spectrum of reform, increased its vote ninefold in 1844. Abolitionism in the mid-1840's was becoming increasingly pragmatic.

The issue of antislavery was steadily undermining established religious and political institutions. In 1844 the Methodist Church convened its annual conference at New York, and almost immediately bogged down in debate over slavery. When the weary delegates finally adjourned, Method-ism stood on the verge of a sectional split, and within the year the Methodist Episcopal Church South had broken away from the parent body. Similar agitation split the Baptist and then the Presbyterian Church. From the pulpits of the nation increasingly came defense and denunciation of the peculiar institution. The tone of the preachments was increasingly harsh, as indicated by one northern Methodist preacher who declared: "Southerners tell us that slavery 'is a political, domestic, and religious blessing;' if so, why not enter into the slave-trade, wholesale and retail? go with armed ships, kidnap human beings by the thousand, bring them to America, sell them into perpetual bondage? . . . Tell them . . . that it is to make Christians of them that you buy and transport them to 'the land of the free and the home of the brave.' "

Within the two major parties, the future of slavery was inextricably intertwined with the issue of territorial expansion. The long agitation for the annexation of Texas, following the Texas Revolt against Mexico in 1835, culminated in the election of 1844. Neither Henry Clay, the Whig presidential candidate, nor Martin Van Buren, the leading Democratic contender, supported annexation, a situation which convinced proannexa-tion Democrats that they had to block Van Buren. Skillfully they maneu-vered to control the Democratic convention at Baltimore, first eliminating Van Buren and then nominating the dark horse James K. Polk. Polk won the election on a platform calling for expansion in Texas and Oregon. Texas entered the Union by joint resolution of Congress before his inauguration. His appointment of a cabinet of men who had pushed Texas annexation together with Polk's vigorous support of expansion into both Oregon and southwestwardly into Mexican territory precipitated a split with the Van Buren faction. Democratic unity was further fractured when after agreeing to a compromise settlement in Oregon, the President precipitated a war with Mexico over the issue of expansion in the Southwest. The antislavery charge that the South meant to expand its peculiar institution by any means at its disposal took on added plausibility.

Northern Democrats who supported the Mexican War disassociated themselves from the charge that they intended to extend the domain of slavery. When in 1846 Congressman David Wilmot, a Pennsylvania Democrat, moved in a proviso that slavery be outlawed in any territories obtained from Mexico, they flocked to support the proviso. Only a negative response in the Senate kept it from becoming law. Those who opposed the war denounced it in unbridled terms. It was, the Massachusetts General Court declared, "a war against freedom, against humanity, against justice, against the Union, against the Constitution, and against the *Free States.*" In a tongue-lashing speech, Congressman Abraham Lincoln accused Polk of aggression. "He is deeply conscious of being in the wrong," Lincoln said. "The blood of this war, like the blood of Abel, is crying to Heaven against him."

Final victory over Mexico in 1848, and the vast Mexican Cession, only deepened the sectional rift. Within the North a coalition of dissident Democrats and agitated Conscience Whigs, unwilling to accept the major party candidates, formed the Free Soil party and ran Martin Van Buren for President, with Charles Francis Adams, son of John Quincy, as his running mate. The Free Soilers polled 291,000 votes, enough to defeat the Democrat, Lewis Cass, and deny either party control of Congress.

A hard, bitter struggle shook Congress when it convened after the election. Whether to extend or confine slavery was the central question, and as Senator Thomas Hart Benton of Missouri gloomily complained, the capital was "almost in a state of disorganization—legislation paralyzed—distant territories left without government—insult, violence, outrage on the floors of Congress." The impasse was broken only upon the unexpected death of President Zachary Taylor, whose threatened veto of any concession to southern slaveholders had obstructed compromise. In the settlement that followed, Clay lent his prestige to a wide-ranging compromise largely contrived by Stephen A. Douglas of Illinois. California came into the Union free, but the future of slavery in the territories of Utah and New Mexico was left to local settlers. This system, called "popular sovereignty," had been introduced as a response to free soil. The slave state of Texas gave up its claim to part of New Mexico Territory in return for federal assumption of its bonded indebtedness. As a concession to the North, the slave trade was terminated within the District of Columbia, but in exchange a strengthened fugitive slave act was passed. This last measure quickly became a dead letter as one northern state after another passed personal liberty laws that made it almost impossible to implement the act, an ironic twist by which northern antislavery elements resorted to the southern strategy of nullification to frustrate federal action in defense of slavery.

Increasingly, northern members of Congress expressed antislavery views. Growing numbers of them espoused the doctrine of the "higher law," the argument that when the Constitution was at variance with the inherent rights of mankind, no man was obliged to uphold it. As southerners insisted that their slave property was entitled to protection in all federal territory, these northerners adopted Salmon P. Chase's reasoning that "the law of the Creator, which invests every human being with an inalienable title to freedom, cannot be repealed by any inferior law, which asserts that man is property."

The divisive impact of the Compromise of 1850 proved lethal to the Whig party. The bulk of the Democratic supporters of the Free Soil party returned to their traditional allegiance, with the result that the Democrats won a thunderous victory in the 1852 presidential election. Briefly the antislavery agitation was muted. However, this momentary lull ended abruptly in 1854 when Stephen A. Douglas introduced the Kansas-Nebraska Act, a plan to divide the region west of Missouri and Iowa into two territories and allow popular sovereignty to determine whether or not slavery should be introduced.

Foes of slavery denounced this as an "enormous crime." Free Soil had come thunderously alive. Within months meetings were held throughout the North setting into motion the organization of the Republican party, dedicated to the restriction of slavery to the states where it already existed. This Republican policy was energetically expounded by speakers like Senator Charles Sumner of Massachusetts, who called for "the overthrow of Slave Power" and the ultimate goal of opening "the gates of Emancipation" in the slave states.

The struggle over slavery now approached its climax. At stake was nothing less than the control of the federal government. The issue was joined in Kansas, where antislavery and proslavery partisans fought bloody battles in their efforts to control the territory. Attempts by the Democratic administration to remove Kansas from the political arena by admitting it to the Union with slave property protected resulted in a party rupture, when Senator Douglas, well aware of the potency of the Free Soil issue in the North, insisted upon the maintenance of popular sovereignty. He understood that to abandon this policy would terminate any chance of winning northern support for his presidential aspirations. When the Supreme Court, seeking to take the issue out of politics, announced in the Dred Scott case (1857), "Congress has no rightful power to prohibit Slavery in the Territories," antislavery elements were outraged.

As the voters went to the polls in 1860, the long agitation over slavery had brought the nation to the brink of civil war. Everyone understood that the Republican candidate, Abraham Lincoln, was unalterably opposed to the expansion of slavery into the territories. To the plea of Alexander H. Stephens of Georgia for a word of reassurance to the South, Lincoln replied that his administration had no intention of interfering with slavery where it already existed. "I suppose," he added soberly, "this does not meet the case. You think slavery is *right* and ought to be extended; while we think it *wrong* and ought to be restricted. That I suppose is the rub." And so it was. To accept the Republican position was to admit that slavery was wrong, a concession which, once made, would have led to an assault upon slavery where it already existed, not merely where it might exist in the future. Rather than accept such a prospect, the South seceded, went to war, and lost.

When peace finally was restored in 1865, slavery was gone, its demise soon confirmed by constitutional amendment. Black Americans were also assured by the Fourteenth and Fifteenth Amendments of their civil rights. But the black American was soon to learn the sad truth that constitutional guarantees are frail reeds upon which to rely when such guarantees go contrary to popular prejudice. With slavery abolished, a new issue arose. The black abolitionist Frederick Douglass posed it eloquently when he asked, "Do you mean to make good to us the promises in your constitution?" More than a century later, no American knew for certain what the final answer would be.

For Further Reading

Barnes, Gilbert Hobbes, *The Antislavery Impulse, 1830–1844.*
Duberman, Martin (ed.), *The Antislavery Vanguard: New Essays on Abolitionists.*
Filler, Louis, *The Crusade Against Slavery, 1830–1860.*
Quarles, Benjamin, *Black Abolitionists.*
Zilversmit, Arthus, *The First Emancipation: The Abolition of Slavery in the North.*

79   Unification Movements

Until the middle of the nineteenth century, nationalism, though an active force in Europe, had achieved very limited successes. Especially in mid-Europe, the Metternichian order continued to prevail; to contemporaries, the revolutions of 1848 appeared to have been utter failures. The map of central Europe in 1850 was not appreciably different from the map drawn at Vienna in 1815.

This map, however, was radically revised in the course of the next two decades, most significantly with the emergence of two states, Italy and Germany—perfect examples of the success of nationalism. This great transformation took place during the period of the Second French Empire. The President of the Second Republic, Prince Louis Napoleon, soon Napoleon III, Emperor of the French, was sympathetic to nationalism everywhere. This sympathy, however, came into conflict with French national interest, which had traditionally fostered the political fragmentation of mid-Europe. Thus Napoleon III's policy was, not surprisingly, tortuous, and would prove a failure for himself and for France. He could not control events in Italy or in Germany.

The legacy of ancient Rome is one of the main strands of European civilization, but from the fall of the Roman Empire to the nineteenth century Italy was little more than a geographical expression. The long medieval period, and Italian association with the Holy Roman Empire, had created another legacy, that of divisiveness and of local strength; if the feeling of Italian unity and the desire for its political renewal persisted through the centuries, as the works of Dante and Machiavelli attest, they did so largely at the cultural and literary levels. When modern national monarchies began to emerge, rival Italian states became their political pawns; Italy was the battleground of French and Spanish armies and diplomats, and later, especially during the period of the French Revolution and Napoleon, of the Austrian Hapsburgs.

The impact of Napoleon I on Italy was considerable; it is to him that the origin of a conscious and active Italian nationalism can be traced, whether by imitation of or reaction to French rule. In 1815, in Italy as elsewhere, the Congress of Vienna restored the old order, and the Hapsburg acquisition of the Kingdom of Lombardo-Venetia confirmed Austrian predominance in the entire peninsula. Metternich was the willing guardian of these arrangements, which he identified with the Hapsburg interest.

A.D.	
1792–1815	The French Revolution and Napoleon; political rearrangements in central Europe; wars of liberation
1815	Settlement of Vienna
1815–1848	Italian Risorgimento; Metternichian system
1819–1844	German Zollverein
1846	Pius IX pope
1848	Piedmontese Statuto
1848–1849	Failure of revolutions in central Europe; Austro-Sardinian wars
1852	The Danish Duchies; London Protocol; Cavour prime minister of Sardinia
1854–1856	Crimean War; Sardinia joins in 1855
1856	Congress of Paris
1858	Plombières agreement between Napoleon III and Cavour; Franco-Sardinian alliance
1859	War between Austria and France and Sardinia; Armistice of Villafranca
1860	Collapse of the Italian structure; Garibaldi's expedition
1860–1861	Insurrection in Syria; French expedition; Statute of the Lebanon
1861	Proclamation of the Kingdom of Italy
1862	Bismarck minister president of Prussia; union of Moldavia and Wallachia under Alexander Cuza
1863	Polish insurrection; Alvensleben Convention
1864	War of Prussia and Austria against Denmark; cession of Schleswig and Holstein by Denmark
1865	Gastein Convention between Austria and Prussia; Biarritz meeting of Napoleon III and Bismarck
1866	Austro-Prussian War; Treaty of Prague; Italy acquires Venetia
1866–1868	Cretan revolt
1867	North German Confederation; Austro-Hungarian *Ausgleich*
1868–1870	Hohenzollern candidacy to the Spanish throne
1870–1871	Ems dispatch; Franco-Prussian War
1871	Proclamation of the German Empire at Versailles; Treaty of Frankfurt; annexation of Alsace-Lorraine

Italy faced added difficulties. Rome was the seat of the papacy and around it had grown the States of the Church, a state among Italian states. Yet it was endowed with a unique character. The papal argument—not an illogical one—was that the pope needed territorial sovereignty for the proper, unfettered discharge of his spiritual role. In any case the fate of the papacy was of international importance since, when threatened, the pope could seek the support of Catholic opinion everywhere.

Italians were overwhelmingly Catholic, and some of them thought they had found a way of reconciling their national aspirations with their religious allegiance: let the Italian states form a federation headed by the pope. In his *On the Moral and Civil Primacy of the Italians,* published in 1843, the priest Vincenzo Gioberti (1801–1852) clearly expounded the hopes of Italian liberal nationalists of this persuasion.

Others held more radical views. Giuseppe Mazzini (1805–1872) was a universal nationalist, a believer in free association of free peoples, among whom Italy would furnish leadership by example. Mazzini would have made a tabula rasa of all existing Italian regimes and set up a republic in their place. An ineffectual plotter and an exile during most of his life, he was yet a great influence on the future of Italy. The hopes and writings of such men set the climate of the Risorgimento, an effort to secure the "rebirth" of Italy. This movement was in large measure confined to the educated segment of society; the masses, most of them illiterate peasants, were passive bystanders. They justified the later quip: "We have made Italy; all that remains to do is to make Italians."

Italian hopes for unity had still another root—power politics. Among Italian states, only the Kingdom of Sardinia—also known as Piedmont— could claim real independence. There were many who thought that its unique position endowed Sardinia with the mission of leading the rest of Italy to freedom and unity. It was certainly clear that the making of Italy could only be an anti-Austrian operation; from his point of view, Metternich was quite right to detest and fear Mazzini.

It is in the context of these forces that the events of 1848–1849 operated. When Pius IX became pope in 1846, some of his measures gave rise to hopes for a liberal leadership on his part. But the revolutions of 1848, particularly the short-lived Roman Republic of which Mazzini was one of the leaders, made liberalism anathema to him. Thereafter he consistently denounced and opposed the ways of the modern world as the road to perdition. The Roman Republic was actually destroyed by French intervention, and France became the mainstay of the pope's position, somewhat reducing Austrian influence in Italy.

By late 1848 it was clear that the approaches of Gioberti and Mazzini had failed. There remained the third possibility: Sardinian-Piedmontese leadership. The initial surge of nationalist enthusiasm that swept the whole peninsula had resulted in war against Austria, under the leadership of the Piedmontese. The latter scored some successes at first, since the Austrians faced difficulties elsewhere, but Austria retrieved the situation and re-established control in Italy after the defeat of Piedmont in July, 1848. A renewed attempt in 1849 led to the same result—another Piedmontese rout.

Only British and French diplomatic intervention saved Piedmont from the consequences of this defeat. It suffered no punishment, and was even able to resist Austrian pressure and retain its constitution, the Statuto, of 1848.

The events of 1848 had yet another and decisive result: the emergence of Cavour as prime minister of the Kingdom of Sardinia. Camillo Benso di Cavour (1810–1861) belonged to the generation, and shared the ideals, of the Risorgimento. In contrast to Mazzini, Cavour was a practical man, aware of the active forces of his time and keenly interested in technological innovation; his general outlook was that of contemporary English liberals. After the political reorganization of Piedmont in 1848, he entered the government, and soon rose to its head, to remain there virtually without interruption until his death in June, 1861.

Cavour ranks as one of the outstanding European statesmen of the nineteenth century, the equal of Bismarck. Different from Bismarck in personality and in his liberal predilections, he resembles him in his manipulative skill. His objective was the modernization of the state: the encouragement of industry and the improvement of finances, administration, and the army. In addition, Cavour believed in "a free church in a free state," and had little confidence in the slogan *Italia farà da sè*—Italy will manage alone.

There was sympathy for Italian national aspirations in France and in England. But the British would not supply the necessary bayonets, and Cavour therefore procured them from France by reconciling Italian and French interests. While he was assisted by Napoleon III's natural sympathies, his success is a measure of his diplomatic skill.

Cavour brought Sardinia into the Crimean War, a seemingly far-fetched policy, which gave him an opportunity to air the Italian situation before the European powers at the Congress of Paris in 1856. While few listened to his claim that the need for reform in Italy was a European question and that reforms were the best way to forestall revolution, he now set about cultivating the French in earnest. His first success was the agreement, or plot, he contrived with the French emperor in July, 1858, at Plombières: France and Sardinia would maneuver Austria into war; the hoped-for victory would result in a rearrangement of the Italian structure.

Austria would be evicted from Italy, her holdings joined to Sardinia to constitute a Kingdom of Northern Italy. The Kingdom of Naples and the Papal States would be left unmolested; the rest of the peninsula would be merged into a central unit, possibly with a French prince at its head. Then the four units would federate under the pope's presidency. What made this scheme acceptable to France was the prospective enhancement of her influence at the expense of Austria's, the safeguarding of the pope's position —French Catholic opinion could not be ignored—and France's acquisition of Savoy and Nice.

After Plombières, Napoleon III had second thoughts and hesitated, for war with Austria might raise international complications. But Cavour managed to overcome his doubts, and the Plombières agreement was formalized into a defensive alliance in December. It remained only for Cavour to maneuver Austria into the position of agressor. Austria obligingly walked into his trap, in April, 1859, declaring war over a relatively minor dispute. Franco-Sardinian forces were victorious, though not without hard fighting. However, fearing larger European complications— Prussia had mobilized—Napoleon accepted an armistice at Villafranca, a compromise by which Austria would yield Lombardy alone. Sardinia had little choice but to accept the *fait accompli,* and its results were registered in the Treaty of Zurich the following November.

Cavour might be disappointed, even incensed, but it was too late to limit the effects of the war to the cession of a province. The time was ripe for the whole Italian structure to topple. While north central Italy was in ferment, clamoring for annexation to Sardinia, Giuseppe Garibaldi, the romantic knight of liberty, launched from Genoa the picturesque adventure of his Thousand Red Shirts; he landed in Sicily in May, 1860. His filibustering expedition may fairly be described as a joyous war. Sicily overrun, Garibaldi crossed the straits to the mainland; he entered Naples in September. Garibaldi was a colorful, romantic enthusiast, an appropriate symbol of Italian nationalist feeling, but he was no diplomat. The complications that would have resulted from his proceeding to Rome, as he would cheerfully have done, were obvious enough; there were French bayonets in Rome.

Cavour, who had resigned after the compromise of Villafranca, was back in office by this time, and fully understood the situation. A new treaty with France in March, 1860, superseding the alliance of the preceding December, had sanctioned the union of the north central states, the Duchies, and the Papal Legations with Piedmont; Napoleon, embarrassed by the awkwardness of Villafranca, was anxious above all for a termination of the Italian uncertainties. But he insisted on an independent pope, even if in a much reduced domain. Cavour proceeded with alacrity and determination. To forestall complications in Rome, a Sardinian army marched into the Papal States from the north; bypassing Rome, it met the forces of Garibaldi, who, as a good patriot, turned over his conquests to the King of Sardinia. This, in effect, was the making of Italy; formal proclamation of the Kingdom took place on March 17, 1861. Cavour lived just long enough to see the final crowning of his work. The new Italy joined the ranks of the powers, not quite certain whether she was the smallest among the great or the greatest among the small.

Yet Italy was incomplete; Venetia was still in Austrian hands and the pope still reigned in Rome. There was irony in the fact that the making of Italy at this particular point was the result of the war with Austria, a war which could not have been waged successfully without French arms. But in Italian eyes Villafranca had been a betrayal, and now it was French arms again which alone prevented the incorporation into Italy of the most Italian of cities.

It was less than a decade before these anomalies were redressed. In 1866 Italy joined Prussia in war against Austria. Though she herself did poorly in the war, she created a useful diversion of Austrian forces and was able to share in the fruits of Austria's final defeat: she acquired Venetia, leaving but a small irredenta (described by the subsequent cry for *Trento e Trieste*) which was finally obtained after the First World War.

As for Rome, a renewed Garibaldine attempt on the city in 1867 brought a French force again to protect the pope, but when France found herself at war with Prussia in 1870, she withdrew her forces. On September 20, against only token resistance, the Italian army entered Rome, which became the capital of Italy. Yet these triumphs were marred by a sense of uneasiness. The manner in which Italy acquired Venice and Rome, riding the coattails of Prussian success in both instances, left a legacy of inferiority feelings which repeatedly influenced the behavior of Italy as a national state.

The Germans, like the Italians, were a distinct people. Like them, too, they desired national unity for cultural reasons, and their nationalism drew inspiration from the romantic movement of which Germany was one of the original centers. The German equivalent of Italy's ancient Rome was the past glories of the Germanic people. In both cases, the impact of the Napoleonic era triggered the beginnings of active political consciousness.

There was no pope in Germany who might appeal to universal opinion for personal assistance. But the Germanies had long been a part of the Holy Roman Empire, itself the assertion of a universal idea. That empire was never so substantial as the Roman Church; even its name was finally abolished by Napoleon I. But though its successor, the German Confederation, created in 1815, could hardly claim universality, it rested on more than merely national foundations. Its head was the Austrian emperor, whose Germanic and Bohemian domains were included in the Confederation. This led to awkward conflicts, and it was inevitable that the Hapsburgs (and Metternich while he lasted) should be staunchly opposed to the assertion of the principle of nationality which could mean no less than the destruction of the Hapsburg empire.

Among the German states, Prussia alone had achieved the status of great power. The rivalry between Hapsburgs and Hohenzollerns was well established; but the intrusion of nationalism gave it a new turn, which, given the ethnic composition of the Hapsburg state, could only work to Prussia's advantage. History had produced particularism within the purely Germanic world, but it was less acute than the particularism engendered by the enormous diversity of the peoples under Hapsburg rule. Munich and Vienna may have felt no special love for Berlin, but they shared the same culture, whereas the Czechs and Hungarians were trying to revive distinct cultures of their own.

The revolutions of 1848 were deeply felt in the Germanic world, but, as we know, the old order triumphed, and the dilemma of definition, the choice between Grossdeutschland and Kleindeutschland, which beset the Frankfurt Assembly, remained unresolved. The Germans did not produce a Cavour in 1848, but the Italian success had an impact on Germany. Prussian mobilization during the war of 1859 had hastened its end, and the continuing uncertainties of the international situation made Prussia pay increased attention to military matters. Army reform and reorganization led to a demand for credits which the Prussian Diet would not grant, in part because the proposed reorganization of the army had political implications. The deadlock continued for a time until King William was persuaded by Albrecht von Roon, his minister of war, to make Bismarck his chief minister. The year was 1862.

Otto von Bismarck, Cavour's junior by five years, came, like Cavour, from the landed gentry. He had entered the diplomatic service and gained valuable experience in Frankfurt (where he observed the events of 1848), in St. Petersburg, and in Paris. His judgment of 1848, characteristic of his consistent outlook, was expressed in one of his most famous statements, made before the budget commission on September 30, 1862: "Not through speeches and majority resolutions are the great questions of the day decided—that was the great mistake of 1848 and 1849—but through blood and iron."

Bismarck's way out of the impasse of 1862 was of the simplest: if the Diet would not appropriate credits, he would dispense with legality. The interesting thing is that he succeeded so easily. In any event, what mattered more to him than the limited financial issue was the larger political one.

The first step in Bismarck's program was to settle matters with Austria; after that, like Cavour, he would observe events, and seize, or possibly create, further opportunities. Settling matters with Austria meant not its destruction but its reduction to the Hapsburg domain proper. This would mean the end of the German Confederation, a result not likely to be achieved without war. Bismarck's aims dictated his means: in order to wage a successful war with Austria two things were necessary—an adequate military force and the isolation of the conflict.

Favored though he was by circumstances, Bismarck's diplomatic maneuvering can only be described as masterful. Above all, he had to secure the good will of Russia and France. Czar Nicholas I had entertained friendly feelings toward Austria—witness his intervention in Hungary in 1849—but his successor, Alexander II, resented Austria's hostility at the time of the Crimean War. Then, in 1863, the Poles rose in rebellion. As thirty years before, no one came to their assistance, but while Britain, France and Austria sent the czar advice (which only irritated him) Bismarck offered cooperation. The episode gave Bismarck the opportunity of replacing a Franco-Russian with a Prusso-Russian amity.

Dealing with France was a more delicate operation. Nevertheless, at his meeting with Napoleon III at Biarritz in October, 1865, Bismarck dangled before the French emperor vague prospects of compensations, and came away with a reasonable assurance of at least initial French neutrality. Napoleon made the erroneous though not unreasonable calculation that a conflict between Austria and Prussia would be a protracted affair which would place him in the position of arbiter. Finally, in April, 1866, Bismarck concluded an alliance with Italy. Bismarck was now ready for the showdown. The Duchies of Schleswig and Holstein, the latter wholly German, the former partly Danish, were ruled by the King of Denmark, although Holstein also belonged to the German Confederation. Attempts by the Danish king to integrate the Duchies more closely into his other possessions, and complications growing out of the question of succession, had already produced a minor flare-up in 1848. That had been adjusted through the intervention of the powers in the London Protocol of 1852. But the question revived ten years later. Although it was in part a clash between Danish and German nationalism, Bismarck chose to pose as the defender of existing international arrangements in order to enlist Austrian support.

The result was a joint Austro-Prussian war against Denmark, whose outcome could only be the defeat of the Danes left unassisted. The Duchies were jointly ceded to Austria and Prussia. As with Cavour in 1859, Austria walked into Bismarck's trap: the Gastein Convention of 1865 for the administration of the Duchies was contrived by Bismarck with a view to fostering dissension between Prussia and Austria.

This dissension flared up into open war in June, 1866. The efficient Prussian military machine performed in accord with Bismarck's expectations. Other German states played no significant part in the conflict owing to the rapidity of operations, and the Battle of Sadowa, on July 3, while a close engagement, ended in a Prussian victory which settled the conflict. In the Treaty of Prague in August Bismarck demanded only one thing of Austria, but that was highly important: acceptance of the dissolution of the German Confederation. The empire of Austria would henceforth be confined to the Hapsburg domain.

Prussia's rapid victory led to a drastic reorganization of mid-Europe in 1867. The Austrian Empire became Austria-Hungary, the very name an acknowledgment of Hungarian parity with Austria—a success of Hungarian nationalism. The German states south of the Main were left to proceed as they wished without interference, while a North German Confederation was created. This new entity, dominated by Prussia, constituted a simplification of the earlier political structure. In Prussia proper Bismarck ironically indulged in the luxury of securing a bill of indemnity which legalized his unconstitutional rule. In view of his triumphs, even most of his former opponents endorsed this bill. Who would insist on doctrinaire objections in view of the outcome? Thus the curtain fell on the first act of the story of German unification: whatever one might think of the methods of the stage director, the performance had been without a doubt masterful.

The outbreak of the Austro-Prussian War had come as no surprise; its brevity had. As early as May, during the course of a debate in the French Corps Legislatif, Louis Adolphe Thiers had given a highly pessimistic, but as it turned out wholly correct, forecast of the future course of events. In a sense Sadowa was a French as much as an Austrian defeat, for that battle destroyed the calculations of Napoleonic policy: French attempts to secure from Bismarck some compensation after his victory were pathetic.

Yet Napoleon persisted. He was increasingly under attack at home for the failures of his foreign policy; his ill-contrived attempt to establish a puppet regime in Mexico under the rule of the luckless Maximilian had ended in ignominious failure. He felt he must achieve some compensatory success; almost anything would do. He suggested the Bavarian Palatinate, a part of Belgium, an alliance with Bismarck in turn. Bismarck never flatly rejected these proposals, but instead collected from the French ambassador incriminating memoranda that could be put to good future use. In 1867, negotiations for the purchase by France of Luxembourg from the Dutch king appeared promising until a storm was raised in the North German Reichstag. Bismarck, no stranger to the negotiations, pleaded helplessness in the face of aroused German national feeling, and the proposed deal fell through.

Nor were the prospects very promising that an intra-German equilibrium—North German, South German, plus an Austrian unit—within the larger European equilibrium would prove durable. Bismarck had no desire for war with France for its own sake, but he came to the correct conclusion that the completion of German unity would constitute so far-reaching an alteration of European power relationships that France would not let it take place passively. If there was to be war with France, Bismarck would adopt the same strategy as against Austria: effective use of the splendid Prussian military machine combined with isolation of the conflict.

The opportunity arose from an unexpected quarter, revolution in Spain, one of the consequences of which was a search for a new ruler. One candidate was a Hohenzollern prince, and his candidacy produced a very strong reaction in France. It was abandoned, but, not content with this minor diplomatic success, France sought to push her advantage. Instead, Bismarck turned the situation to Prussia's advantage with a crude but effective trick. Benedetti, the French ambassador, had discussed the Hohenzollern candidacy with William I, the Prussian king, at the bathing resort of Ems. The discussions had been entirely courteous, but Bismarck took his king's telegraphic report of the interviews and so doctored and condensed it as to make them appear a hostile and mutually insulting encounter. This fed the bellicose demands of the war parties in both countries, and in July, 1870, the French declared war. This made France technically the aggressor and gave Bismarck what he wanted: France stood alone.

At the same time, Bismarck held the Russians and the British in line. He enticed the Russians with prospects of support of their demand that parts of the Treaty of Paris (1856) demilitarizing the Black Sea be abrogated; he fed British suspicions of French designs by leaking details of French approaches concerning Belgium. The Austrians and Italians were soon pacified—by Prussian military successes. Within six weeks of the outbreak of war, in September, 1870, at Sedan, the Prussians compelled a French army to surrender. Paris held out for some months longer, and it was not until May, 1871, that the belligerents officially made peace at Frankfurt. The settlement imposed an enormous indemnity on France, and gave the new German Empire Alsace and part of Lorraine.

The new German Empire came into existence several months before the Peace of Frankfurt. On January 18, 1871, in the palace of the French kings at Versailles, King William was proclaimed German emperor; the locale of the ceremony, perhaps unwisely chosen, was nonetheless symbolic, expressing simultaneously the unification of Germany and its rise to first place among the Continental powers.

Unlike Italy, still claimant to an irredenta, Germany contained a number of non-German people: some Danes, a considerable larger number of Poles, and, most significant for the future, many Frenchmen in Alsace and Lorraine. Germany's annexation of these provinces introduced a festering sore in European relations, for it was regarded in France, and elsewhere, as a moral wrong. True, the people of Alsace were Germanic, and it had not become the property of Louis XIV until the seventeenth century. Yet by 1870 the overwhelming majority of Alsatians considered themselves French. The historian Heinrich von Treitschke's contention that they were really German, and that they should be made to understand this, if necessary by force, illustrates the degree to which nineteenth-century nationalistic aberrations could go.

Treitschke's view also illustrates the difference between two antithetical interpretations of nationality. Treitschke himself saw nationality as a fundamental, unchangeable fact, ultimately rooted in biological origins. Against this was the French and American, or democratic, view: nationality is essentially a matter of personal allegiance; a man is a Frenchman, a German, an American, or anything else, if he chooses to consider himself such. In this view nationality is not a fixed condition but a cultural phenomenon. Needless to say, long membership in a group or locale, common language and traditions, crystallize certain cultural characteristics: that is the basis of the ethnic variety of Europe. Yet, as American nationalism shows, nationality can rise from a synthesis of various ethnic strains.

The time lag in the emergence of nation-states in central Europe as compared with western Europe was an important historical fact, fraught with various consequences. For Italy and Germany, nationalism had been a unifying factor, bringing together scattered fragments. Considering the evolving technology of the day, the formation of larger political units seemed, certainly from the economic standpoint, a desirable development. At the same time, nationalism obviously had a disintegrating effect on multinational empires. The Austro-Hungarian *Ausgleich* of 1867 pointed in two opposite directions. On the one hand, what Hungarians had done might be emulated by others, opening up the possibility of a multinational state and justifying the observation that if Austria had not existed it should have been invented, for the Hapsburgs had played a useful role in Europe. Similarly, Switzerland was a living example of the harmonious and effective integration of various ethnic groups. But there was the opposite possibility: attempted suppression, as when the Hungarians breached the Croat constitution of 1868. Beginning with the *Ausgleich,* and for the remaining half-century of its existence, the Dual Monarchy grappled with the problem of subject nationalities, which, collectively, constituted a majority of the empire. Solving this fundamental issue was basic for Austria's survival.

Ottoman decadence, which the passage of time did not mitigate, was another source of strain. The theocratic foundations of the Ottoman state, in which law was based on religious affiliation, were ill suited to modern conditions, which call for territorial civil law, applicable to the confines of a state. In the Balkan dependencies, mainly Christian, the nationalist virus was making steady inroads, and the Crimean War further loosened the Turkish hold on the Balkans. Despite this, the Ottoman state was formally admitted to the Concert of Europe; the great European powers guaranteed its integrity and placed it under an implicit collective European protectorate.

The effects of this policy were soon felt in the Principalities of Moldavia and Wallachia, where the powers substituted their collective right of supervision for the exclusive right hitherto held by Russia. The Principalities desired to unite, and Europe allowed them identical, though still formally separate, administrations. The simultaneous choice of Alexander Cuza as ruler in both provinces in 1859 was the prelude to what happened three years later, when the Sultan agreed to the fusion of their two legislatures: Rumania had in effect been born, though still for a time subject to certain obligations to the Porte.

Nationalism thus was a unifying force for the Principalities; at the same time, from the Turkish point of view, their growing independence meant the loosening of Ottoman control. The same applies to Greece, which persistently strove to extend its domain to the Greek-speaking areas of the Balkans, to the Aegean islands, and in particular to Crete, which was in a state of endemic revolt against Turkish rule. Like the Hapsburg state, the Ottoman state was destined to ultimate disintegration into its distinctive ethnic parts.

The Russian situation was different: the Russians, with the Ukrainians, constituted the overwhelming majority of Russia's component peoples. But in the process of westward expansion initiated by Peter the Great, Russia had come to absorb Finns, Letts, Latvians, and Lithuanians along with a much larger Polish contingent. Among these people only Polish nationalism was vigorous—the final extinction of the Polish state was little more than half a century old. Czar Alexander II managed to split the Polish movement: his restoration of pre-1830 conditions was acceptable to moderates. But when in January, 1863, he attempted to deal with irreconcilables by drafting them into the army, an insurrection broke out in Warsaw. The rebels were subdued, but Polish nationalism, although rendered impotent for a time, was not destroyed.

Without a doubt the most significant achievement of nationalism during the nineteenth century was the redrawing of the map of central Europe, where it produced two large powers, Italy and Germany. These two new states adopted different internal organizations: the Italians wiped out all preexisting units, extended the Piedmontese constitution to the whole country, and made Italy a centralized entity on the French model.

The Germans adopted a less radical federal constitution, but the sheer dimensions, power, and population of Prussia inevitably gave her a dominant position in the whole. Besides, Germany had been made through Bismarck's blood-and-iron methods. In 1871 Bismarck's prestige stood high, though the legacy of his methods would weigh heavily on the future course of his creation. While he sincerely strove to keep the peace of Europe after 1871, the significant fact that Germany increasingly became the foremost power of the continent meant that first through Bismarck's active leadership, later through the more flamboyant policy of William II, Germany would determine the course of Europe's destiny.

Thus 1871 was a landmark. Apart from the emergence of Germany as a united country, a fact fraught with such heavy consequences for the future, there was a change in the effects and the tone of nationalism in the latter part of the century. In southeastern Europe, and to a lesser degree in Russia, nationalism became a disintegrating force, powerfully contributing to the outbreak of the First World War. But also, especially in the areas where it had been successful, it was increasingly appropriated by conservative elements, given to manifestations of intolerance and aggressiveness. Overflowing its original European confines, it even became associated with that characteristic activity of the latter part of the nineteenth century, an unprecedentedly vigorous imperial expansion.

For Further Reading

Darmstaedter, F., *Bismarck and the Creation of the Second Reich.*
Marriott, J. A. R., *The Eastern Question.*
Smith, D. Mack, *Cavour and Garibaldi, 1860.*
Taylor, A. J. P., *The Hapsburg Monarchy, 1809–1918.*

V

THE MODERN WORLD

Toward Disintegration

The Great World War: 1914–1945

The Brooding Present

Toward Disintegration

80   Imperialism in Africa

At the beginning of the nineteenth century the interior of Africa was still almost wholly isolated from the rest of the world. The slave trade, by its nature, discouraged penetration by foreigners, since the slaves were brought to the coast for sale, and potential buyers did not need to go into the interior. No diamond or gold strikes, such as occurred later in the century, lured prospectors inland, African kings and chiefs looked askance at white men entering their lands, and missionaries trying to proselytize mostly died, since no cures had yet been found for diseases like malaria, yellow fever, and sleeping sickness. On those parts of the coast where slave forts and trading posts existed, the resident Europeans lived precariously and by local African permission.

Along the wide belt of the Sudan running from Cape Verde to the Horn lay a series of states, many of them of great antiquity. In the middle Senegal valley and in the mountains of northern Guinea were the Fulbe-dominated theocracies of Futa Toro and Futa Jallon. In the Niger Bend, the great empires of medieval times had given place to numerous successor states, of which the chief were Segu, Ka'arta, and Masina. East of Masina lay the city-states of Hausaland. In the Lake Chad region the kingdom of Bornu controlled the area west of the lake and the sultanate of Bagirmi the lands to the east. Between Chad and the Nile ruled the sultans of Wadai and Darfur, and on the Nile itself the Funj sultanate of Sennar was the leading political authority, though its ruler had recently been compelled to give up his northern province of Nubia to nomad invaders. All these states except Segu and Ka'arta had Muslim rulers. The only Christian state in the northern half of Africa at that time, Ethiopia, had lost the unity it possessed in the Middle Ages, and an emperor without power was the nominal head of a country rent by rivalries among provincial warlords and subject to repeated attacks by Galla nomads to the south. In the forest zone of

CHRONOLOGY

A.D.

1805	Accession of Muhammad Ali, pasha of Egypt
1820	Egyptian conquest of the Sudan
1830	French occupation of Algiers
1833	Abolition of slavery in the British Empire
1836–1837	Great Trek in South Africa
1859–1860	Spanish-Moroccan war
1861	British annexation of Lagos
1869	Opening of Suez Canal
1872	Internal self-government in South Africa
1873–1874	Anglo-Ashanti war
1876	Founding of International African Association; European control assumed over Egyptian finances
1882	British occupation of Egypt; Makoko Treaty (Congo)
1884–1885	Declaration of German African protectorates; Berlin West Africa Conference
1885	Founding of the Congo Independent State; fall of Khartoum and death of General Charles Gordon
1886	Discovery of gold on the Witwatersrand; Anglo-German East African boundary agreement; grant of charter to Royal Niger Company
1889	Italo-Ethiopian Treaty of Wichale; grant of charter to British South Africa Company
1890	Anglo-German African boundaries agreement; British protectorate over Zanzibar and Pemba; "Pioneer Column" to Rhodesia
1893 ff.	French conquest of Dahomey
1894	British protectorate over Uganda; French occupation of Timbuktu
1894 ff.	French conquest of Madagascar
1895	Jameson Raid in the Transvaal; British protectorate over East Africa (Kenya)
1896	Battle of Aduwa; British occupation of Ashanti
1896–1897	Revolts in Matabeleland and Mashonaland
1898	French defeat of Samori Touré; Battle of Omdurman and "Fashoda Incident"
1899–1902	South African (Boer) War
1900–1903	British occupation of Northern Nigeria
1905–1907	Maji-Maji Rising (German East Africa)
1912	French protectorate over Morocco

West Africa the chief states were Ashanti (in modern Ghana), Dahomey, and Oyo and Benin (in modern Nigeria). A cluster of strong kingdoms, Bunyoro, Buganda, Ankole, Karagwe, Rwanda, and Burundi, had grown up in the area of the Great Lakes of East Africa. In the savanna country south of the Congo basin were the states of the Luba-Lunda peoples, ruled by the Mwata Yamvo and the Mwata Kazembe, while the kingdom of the Mwene Mtapa (in modern Rhodesia), first encountered by the Portuguese in the sixteenth century, still retained some of its former power, though hard pressed by the rival Rozwi state of the Changamires.

The rulers of these states were for the most part unconcerned with the wider world around them, yet they were not unfamiliar with that world's products. On the West Coast goods exchanged for slaves had for centuries included a wide variety of European manufactures, guns, gunpowder, cloth, and iron bars. The Sudanic states conducted an extensive trade across the Sahara with North Africa and Egypt, bartering slaves, leather goods, and kola nuts for weapons, horses, foodstuffs, and holy books. Merchants like the Dyula and Hausa of West Africa and the Nyamwezi and Yao of East Africa moved from marketplace to marketplace along trade routes many hundreds of miles long. Thus, when penetration by Europeans began, the intruders encountered well-organized kingdoms and chieftaincies, which were militarily strong, often highly centralized, with complex bureaucracies and established commercial and diplomatic procedures.

The banning of the Atlantic slave trade, agreed to by all but a few European states during the first two decades of the nineteenth century, signaled a new approach to tropical Africa. The trade in slaves could not be halted at once, but the abolitionists hoped it would gradually be replaced by "legitimate" trade. Naval patrols, mainly British, harassed illegal slavers, Christian missionary activity increased, the hinterland began to be systematically explored, and coastal chiefs were persuaded to accept protection and, in some cases, financial compensation in return for abandoning the slave trade and ceding small stretches of territory to one or other of the European powers. Palm oil, produced in many parts of Africa but particularly in the Niger delta, became an important export, and attempts were made to encourage the growing of cotton and groundnuts. Missionaries and traders found that they functioned more effectively when European consuls and gunboats were within call, and European influence gradually increased along the coasts.

These developments did not mean that much more of tropical Africa was being ruled by Europeans in 1880 than had been the case in 1800. A basis for later imperial competition, however, had been laid. This was especially true in West Africa, where commercial spheres of influence and areas of "informal empire" were coming into existence. The British were

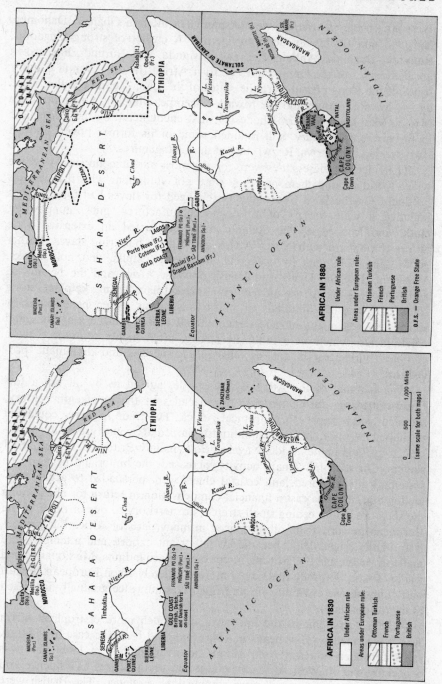

beginning to regard the lower Niger basin as their own—Lagos had been annexed as a British crown colony in 1861—and the French had begun a drive up the Senegal valley in an effort to make that region profitable through control of the gum trade.

In two parts of the continent actual European colonization took place. Following the French conquest of Algiers in 1830, undertaken more for reasons of prestige than to gain territory, a long war ensued between the French army and the indigenous Berbers. When the French eventually won this war, they turned Algeria into a colony of settlement, closely tied to metropolitan France. French influence also increased in Morocco, Tunis, and Egypt. In South Africa, dissatisfaction with British rule led large numbers of Boer farmers to break out of Cape Colony in 1836–1837 and establish their own independent republics, the Orange Free State and Transvaal. These changes in the far north and far south of the continent did not directly affect the situation in the tropical areas, but they heightened economic rivalries generally and raised many new problems of strategy and security for the European powers involved.

Nevertheless, it is doubtful that Britain, France, and Portugal, the states with the greatest holdings in Africa in the early 1880's, would have wished seriously to extend them if other powers had not intervened. It was the entry on the scene of two entirely new participants, Leopold II of the Belgians and Germany, that precipitated what has become known as the "Scramble for Africa." In 1882, moreover, the British occupied Egypt. This action was undertaken to safeguard the Suez Canal and the route to India, but it angered and alarmed the French, who regarded Egypt as belonging to their sphere of influence. Within three decades from 1884, when the competition for territory began in earnest, the entire African continent except for Ethiopia and Liberia was brought under one form or another of European rule.

The precise reasons why Europe rushed into Africa after having neglected it for so long have been much debated. The industrial nations, it has been said, needed new lands in which to invest their surplus capital, and knew that this capital would flow only into territory that Europeans controlled. On the other hand, only a small amount of capital was actually invested in Africa, even after the colonial regimes had been established, because speculators found Canada, Australia, Latin America, and other non-African areas more attractive. The attitude of the imperialists at the time, however, was clear. They may have been mistaken about Africa's overall economic potential, but in the 1880's and 1890's they unquestionably regarded the continent as a prize worth contending for—"ce magnifique gâteau africain," as Leopold II once called it—and took steps accordingly. Many imperialists were convinced that only by overseas expansion could their country's future place in the world be secured; some Frenchmen, for example, hoped to recoup in Africa in the nineteenth century what their ancestors had lost in India in the eighteenth. The ambitions of career-minded soldiers also played their part; the conquest of the French Sudan and Sahara was masterminded not in Paris but by French army officers on the spot. Finally, all the imperial powers were influenced by what has been called the "turbulent frontier." Empires have a way of extending themselves; to the imperial or colonial official it often seemed that the occupation of an area adjacent to his own was all that was needed to ensure prosperity for traders, security for missionaries, and peace of mind for himself. The resulting annexations and extensions of spheres of influence were often authorized by the official's home government after the event. Frequently this was done not as a sign of approval of the official's conduct, but because the alternative, to disavow his actions and recall him, might cause loss of prestige and diplomatic embarrassment.

When Henry Morton Stanley returned from his journey down the Congo in 1877, he offered his discoveries to Britain. The British declined, and King Leopold, who had long sought an outlet for his imperial ambitions, saw a unique opportunity. He took Stanley into his service and employed him to build a road from Stanley Pool on the Congo to the sea. (Without proper communications the interior could not be exploited because of impassable rapids on the lower river.) Stanley's activities alerted the French, on whose behalf another explorer, Savorgnan de Brazza, proceeded to sign treaties with the ruler of the Bateke kingdom on the north bank of the Congo, adjacent to the territory Leopold was hoping to control. Leopold then instructed Stanley to sign up as many chiefs as possible on the south bank to offset the advantages Brazza had won for the French. These actions stimulated a flurry of treaty making along the West African coast as far as Nigeria and Dahomey. In the lower Niger, too, relations between the British and French were deteriorating because of monopoly policies being pursued by Sir George Goldie's United African Company (later the Royal Niger Company) against competing French firms.

The second newcomer to the African scene was Germany. Pressure from commercial interests and colonial enthusiasts at home and a desire to drive a diplomatic wedge between France and Britain in Europe persuaded Bismarck to abandon his earlier opposition to overseas expansion. During 1884 and 1885 German protectorates were declared over four sections of the African coast not yet claimed by other powers. Southwest Africa, the East African coast between Mozambique and the future Kenya, and Togo and Cameroun in West Africa all became German.

Portugal, as a relatively weak colonial power with most to lose if the competition for Africa became serious, now proposed the calling of an international conference to discuss the principles which should guide the recognition or rejection of claims to African territory. The idea was taken up by Bismarck, and a conference on West Africa met at Berlin from November, 1884, to February, 1885. It was attended by all European states with interests in the continent and also by the United States and the Ottoman Empire. Its decisions, formalized by the Berlin Act of 1885, recognized Leopold's authority in the Congo, which became the Congo Independent State, declared the basins of both the Congo and the Niger rivers free trade areas, and asserted the intention of all signatories to suppress slavery and promote civilization. Of greatest importance, however, were two provisions of the act which laid down the procedures to be followed by imperial and would-be imperial powers. From now on, acquisitions of terriory would have to be formally announced, and would not be recognized internationally unless the claiming power could demonstrate that the regions were being effectively occupied. Thus, although the Berlin West Africa Conference was not summoned to carve up Africa, it did in fact give the signal for partition. The doctrine of effective occupation introduced a new element of urgency. No longer was it sufficient for an imperial power to point to long-standing claims to possession; such claims, if they were to be acknowledged by others, had to be supported by the placing of men actually on the ground.

The first phase of the partition of Africa was characterized by the deployment of relatively small European forces and, with some exceptions, by equally minor African resistance. Many kings and chiefs ceded lands and granted mineral rights without fully comprehending the significance of their actions. Some certainly hoped that, once the mysterious piece of paper on which their unwelcome visitors set so much store had been signed and handed over, the white men would go away. Of course the result was a rapid increase in the area of the continent subject, if only nominally for the time being, to Europe. In West Africa, the French increased their influence in Guinea, the Ivory Coast, Dahomey, and Gabon, and continued the drive they had begun in the 1860's up the Senegal valley into the Sudan. The British engaged in extensive treaty making in the lower Niger basin, secured control of the coast from Cameroun to Lagos, occupied Ashanti, took over the Northern Territories of the Gold Coast, and extended protection to the interior of Sierra Leone. In East Africa, agreements between Britain and Germany in 1886 and 1890 recognized Zanzibar, Uganda, and Kenya as belonging to the British sphere, and Tanganyika (then including Rwanda and Burundi) as German. In Central Africa, following the declaration of the Bechuanaland Protectorate in 1885, Cecil Rhodes's British South Africa Company dispatched a column to take over Southern Rhodesia in 1890, and this action was soon followed by the establishment of

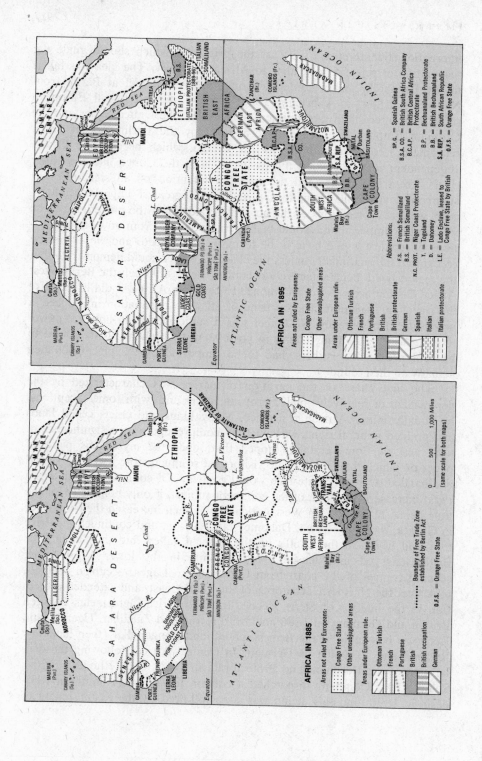

AFRICA IN 1895

Areas not ruled by Europeans:
- Congo Free State
- Other unsubjugated areas

Areas under European rule:
- Ottoman Turkish
- French
- Portuguese
- British
- British protectorate
- German
- Spanish
- Italian
- Italian protectorate

Abbreviations:
F.S. = French Somaliland
B.S. = British Somaliland
N.C. PROT. = Niger Coast Protectorate
T. = Togoland
D. = Dahomey
L.E. = Lado Enclave, leased to Congo Free State by British

SP. G. = Spanish Guinea
B.S.A. CO. = British South Africa Company
B.C.A.P. = British Central Africa Protectorate
B.P. = Bechuanaland Protectorate
B.B. = British Bechuanaland
S.A. REP. = South African Republic
O.F.S. = Orange Free State

AFRICA IN 1885

Areas not ruled by Europeans:
- Congo Free State
- Other unsubjugated areas

Areas under European rule:
- Ottoman Turkish
- French
- Portuguese
- British
- British occupation
- German

•••••• Boundary of Free Trade Zone established by Berlin Act

O.F.S. = Orange Free State

0   500   1,000 Miles

(same scale for both maps)

British protectorates over Nyasaland and Northern Rhodesia. In the Congo, the authority of the Independent State was extended inland. The Italians, belatedly infected by the imperialist spirit, installed themselves in Eritrea on the Red Sea.

However, during the second phase of the partition, which began about 1895, the extension of European control met increasingly bitter African resistance. Many Africans, realizing for the first time that the imperialists intended to stay, wanted to get rid of them. Some chiefs, learning by the experience of their neighbors, fought against annexation more violently than they would probably have done if their turn had come first. Yet the most important cause of growing hostility between African and European was the behavior of the imperialists themselves.

The setting up of colonial administrations, the payment of the salaries of colonial officials, soldiers, and police, the building of roads, railroads, bridges, and harbors, the financing of boundary commissions to survey frontiers decided on in Europe without proper geographical knowledge of Africa—all these activities cost a great deal of money and the necessary funds had to be provided. Home governments were willing, for a time, to make "grants-in-aid," but imperialism was not a form of philanthropy; all new colonies were expected to pay for themselves as soon as possible. Before the "Scramble" small coastal forts and settlements had struggled along financially on revenues derived from customs and excise duties. Now this source of funds, always meager because of the smallness of African purchasing power, had to be rapidly and drastically augmented. The colonial governments therefore turned to raising money by direct taxation. Hut and poll taxes forced many Africans to work for wages or grow cash crops to earn tax money, and when a man had no money, he could be made to give his labor instead. Corvée or forced labor systems became widespread in early colonial Africa. The obligation to work without pay, provided the tasks assigned were light and did not take a man away from his own district, did not necessarily provoke resentment. If, for example, a district officer instructed a chief to turn out the village young men to cut a path through the bush, the order did not go against established custom and was usually accepted. But when labor was recruited on a large scale, and when the conscripted workers were employed (sometimes in conditions of virtual slavery, as in the Congo) to build railroads, work plantations, and collect jungle products, resentment against the system became intense. Probably the two gravest injustices of early imperialism in Africa, and those which aroused the most anger among Africans, were this type of forced labor and the permanent expropriation of land by white settlers, such as occurred before the "Scramble" in South Africa and Algeria and in Southern Rhodesia and Kenya after it.

In the last years of the nineteenth century, therefore, and in the early years of the twentieth, wars in Africa became longer, more destructive, and more bitter. The French had to struggle hard to master Dahomey and Madagascar, and met strong resistance in the Western Sudan from the Tukolor Empire and from powerful warlords like Samori Touré and Rabeh. The Germans fought savage wars against the Herero in Southwest Africa and against the Maji-Maji rebels in Tanganyika. The British had to contend with Matabele and Mashona uprisings in Rhodesia, with the Hut Tax War in Sierra Leone, and with the Ashanti Revolt of 1900. Although they conquered the Sokoto Empire of Northern Nigeria without great difficulty, they encountered much stiffer resistance from the Ibos of Eastern Nigeria. All these and other contests the imperialists won, helped mainly by their superior weapons, in particular the machine gun, and by their better organization and resources. In one case, however, African resistance triumphed. The Italian attempt to enforce a protectorate over a newly unified Ethiopia collapsed after the defeat of an Italian army by the forces of the emperor Menelik II at the Battle of Aduwa in 1896.

In the eastern Sudan a special situation developed. The revolt of Muhammad Ahmad (the Mahdi) against Egyptian rule which led to the capture of Khartoum and the death of the Egyptian-appointed governor general of the Sudan, Charles Gordon, in 1885, endangered the security of the Upper Nile. A British army under General Horatio Kitchener accordingly invaded the Sudan, and in 1898 defeated the army of the Mahdi's successor, the Khalifa, at the Battle of Omdurman. Soon afterward a French force, led by Commandant Marchand, which had marched across Africa from the West Coast, confronted Kitchener at Fashoda. For several months the issue of peace or war between British and French in Africa hung in the balance, but in the end the French backed down, and the Sudan became an Anglo-Egyptian condominium.

The African war that caused the heaviest casualties, however, and in many ways marked the climax of imperialism in the continent was not fought by whites against blacks but among the whites themselves. This was the Anglo-Boer War in South Africa. In the last quarter of the nineteenth century the independence of the Boer republics began to be threatened by an influx of immigrants. These uitlanders, as the Boers called them, most of whom were British, were attracted to the northeastern part of South Africa by the discovery of diamonds at Kimberley in 1869 and of gold on the Witwatersrand in 1886. Cecil Rhodes, as prime minister of the Cape and a heavy investor in South African mining, favored the annexation by the Cape government of the Boer republics. The Jameson Raid, an attempt by Rhodes in 1895 to prod the uitlanders of the Transvaal into taking over its government by force, was a fiasco, and Rhodes fell from power. But the

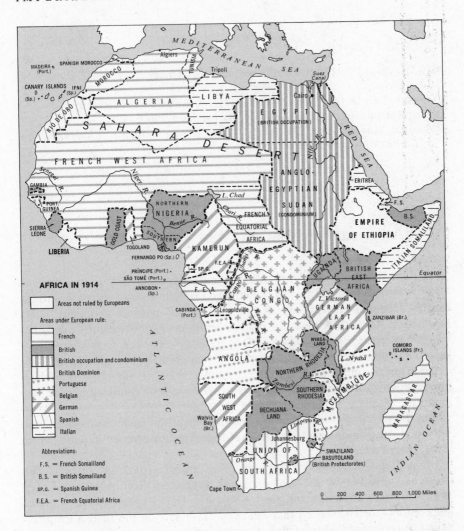

AFRICA IN 1914

Areas not ruled by Europeans

Areas under European rule:

French

British

British occupation and condominium

British Dominion

Portuguese

Belgian

German

Spanish

Italian

Abbreviations:

F.S. = French Somaliland

B.S. = British Somaliland

SP.G. = Spanish Guinea

F.E.A. = French Equatorial Africa

British imperial cause was sustained by the high commissioner to South Africa, Sir Alfred Milner, supported by some members of the British home government. Milner deliberately provoked war with the Transvaal, and hostilities began in 1899. The Boers of the Orange Free State fought alongside the Transvaalers, and the war dragged on until 1902, leaving behind it a legacy of mistrust and bitterness between Boer and Briton that the passage of time has only partially removed. Following the Peace of Vereeniging, which brought the war to an end, the whole of South Africa became part of the British Empire.

For Further Reading

Betts, Raymond F. (ed.), *The "Scramble" for Africa: Causes and Dimensions of Empire.*
Collins, Robert O. (ed.), *The Partition of Africa: Illusion or Necessity.*
Oliver, Roland, and Atmore, Anthony, *Africa Since 1800.*
Robinson, Ronald, and Gallagher, John, *Africa and the Victorians: The Climax of Imperialism.*

81   American Imperialism

The American venture into political imperialism in the late nineteenth century was the central fact in the changed relationship of the nation to the world. Imperialism—as old as the history of nations—contains many meanings, but as the economist Joseph Schumpeter once pointed out, it has always carried the implication of aggressiveness, "the true reasons for which do not lie in the aims which are temporarily being pursued." For Americans the aim was never clearly stated, although the rhetoric of high purpose which included such phrases as "the work of civilization" and "the uplifting of alien peoples" intrigued the general public. This sense of national mission and pride, obviously of deep psychological origin, may have been the most important single cause of nineteenth-century imperialism in the Western world.

The impelling sense of duty and the powerful national energies that were tied together by the zeal for colonies shaped the foreign policies of many Western nations from the 1860's on. Englishmen—the undisputed pacesetters—often boasted that "the sun never sets on the British Empire." Rival Europeans tried to explain that this phenomenon owed something to the fact that "the Lord wouldn't trust the British in the dark"; but when other nations expanded their horizons, the British Empire inevitably was the standard and the model.

Unquestionably many Americans were influenced by the arguments for acquiring colonies that drifted out of Europe in the late nineteenth century. These arguments, whatever their true character, were geared to the interests of industrial men—factory owners and factory workers alike. The appeal to national prestige permeating the seductive phrases of the publicists for imperialism ideally suited the outlook of enterprisers reaching for

C H R O N O L O G Y

----

raw materials to supply their industrial plants and for markets in which to sell their manufactured goods.

The economic arguments for acquiring colonies offered in the insistent propaganda were not so much justifications as rationalizations for action. The direct beneficiary of imperialism was not the business community as a whole, but only a fortuitously placed coterie that included shipbuilders, shipping magnates, the manufacturers of cheap alcoholic beverages, and the importers of tropical products like copra, rubber, cocoa, and coffee. This is not to suggest that no other groups profited: for example, the uniform and flag makers and the manufacturers of equipment for railroads and other heavy construction often made money out of colonies. But the benefits accruing to these capitalists were only marginally important to them.

The activities of Christian missionaries were as influential as those of the publicists in the making of modern imperialism. The "opening up" of inaccessible regions, a product of the increasing range of European mercantile activity and scientific curiosity, as well as of improved technology, created unexpected opportunities for Christian endeavor. The rapid urbanization of the industrial countries found church leaders unprepared and ill equipped to deal with new social problems of vast magnitude. Thus, the work of saving souls in distant places, besides appealing to the passion for adventure always alive in the population, supplied a substitute for religious energies frustrated or paralyzed at home.

The notions of "civilization" and "savagery" which were catchwords used by Christian missionaries had not yet been blurred by anthropologists

GROWTH OF THE UNITED STATES
★ National capital   Year of statehood thus: MICH. 1837

Territories acquired beyond the area of this map:

ALASKA purchased from Russia, 1867
    admitted as State, 1959

HAWAII annexed, 1898
    admitted as State, 1959

PHILIPPINE ISLANDS ceded by Spain, 1899;
    granted independence, 1946

PUERTO RICO ceded by Spain, 1898
    self-governing Commonwealth, 1949

PACIFIC ISLANDS (former Japanese Mandate)
    administered under United Nations Trusteeship after World War II

GUAM ceded by Spain, 1898

SAMOA acquired, 1899

PANAMA CANAL ZONE leased
    from Panama, 1908

VIRGIN ISLANDS purchased
    from Denmark, 1917

whose rise, incidentally, was in part an unintended by-product of imperialism. Armed with modern weapons as well as with the Bible and missal, missionaries found that their somewhat unwilling "hosts" lacked the capacity to defend their beliefs any better than they could defend their lands. And what passed for success in proselytizing the faith was often, in fact, for the colored populations involved, a way of gaining access to a superior technology.

Ancient and flourishing cultures, pursuing goals other than material gain, some of them incomprehensible to Western men, were shattered under the hammer of modern imperialism. In the process, peruked judges, ladies in white frocks sipping scotch-and-soda on the irrigated lawns of "white men's" clubs, the extravagant pomposities of nationalism, and rigid crop-production quotas imposed upon "natives" baffled and infuriated conquered peoples around the world.

The American drive for colonies matured with sudden force in the 1890's, after a desultory build-up in the generation following the Civil War. The first interest in owning faraway lands was, in some respects, the contribution of William Henry Seward. As Secretary of State under Lincoln and Johnson, Seward dreamed of the American eagle spreading its protective shadow alike over the warm waters of the Caribbean and the frozen wastes of the north. Like John Quincy Adams, the formulator of the Monroe Doctrine, whom he regarded as his mentor, Seward envisioned American expansion also in the Pacific—to those places, as Adams once put it, "where the strange roads go down." Still, most Americans of Seward's day did not share his enthusiasm for colonies; they had too much under way on their own soil: the physical and political reconstruction of the nation, the completion of the transcontinental railroads, the search for solutions to the problems of social disorganization produced by rapid industrialization. Aside from the acquisition of Alaska in 1867, Secretary Seward enjoyed no imperial triumphs. But as Europe's advocates of imperialism gained plausibility and stature, like-minded Americans began to find an enthusiastic reception. To engage in colony seeking could give a nation goals and ideals loftier and more inspiriting than the selfish, sordid purposes of spoilsmen and businessmen.

The American voices that responded to these arguments had many characteristics in common. Some had studied in Europe and absorbed the new "liberalism" on its native soil. Many were well-born and ostentatiously "gentlemen" who felt themselves congenial with aristocratic English society—a feeling not shared by the general population—and they respected Germany, a newcomer in the family of nations (though predominant in nineteenth-century scholarship). Above all, this rising group of Americans accepted as axiomatic the moral and intellectual superiority of white Anglo-Saxon Protestants over every other human type, and they allowed this view to inform their social and political attitudes. At home, the idea of racial superiority gave them political leverage on the urban immigrant masses. Abroad, it gave direction and focus to their longings for an American empire. Self-assured and full of energy, these striving men found leaders in politicians like Henry Cabot Lodge and Theodore Roosevelt, the poet-politician John Hay, and the clergyman Josiah Strong. The movement toward imperialism produced a "philosopher" too: Alfred Thayer Mahan, a naval officer with a gifted pen, who formulated a doctrine for naval expansion that appealed to steel manufacturers and diplomats as well as to the young idealists.

To the mass of Americans the last years of the nineteenth century presented many frustrations, including periodic economic depressions, a loss of a feeling of community in the large cities, the appearance of an industrial proletariat, and the rise of great monopolistic corporations seemingly immune to governmental control. Men and women feeling trapped by these powerful forces could find emotional compensation in overseas triumphs for their country. The conquest of "primitive" peoples might offer such perplexed Americans a basis for rebuilding their morale by resuscitating their faith in their power to shape the world. And if one kind of response to fear is to become a bully, an imperialist policy could restore the courage of millions.

The United States entered the ranks of the imperial nations in the early 1890's. A revolution against Spain was ravaging the island of Cuba. Supporting the *insurrectos* with money and advice, Americans did not at first envision official United States involvement. Yet the course of the Cuban struggle gradually enlarged the public sympathy in the United States for the beleaguered rebels, who seemed to millions of Americans comparable to the patriots of 1776. As emotions and concern rose in the United States, the idea of helping to expel Spain at last from the hemisphere gained converts rapidly.

The United States had not fought a foreign war in more than half a century; the memory of the Civil War was fading, and a new generation of young men felt ready for trial by battle. The "New Navy" constructed in the 1880's and 1890's was spoiling for action. President McKinley, who as a soldier in the Union army had seen the terror and horror of war, struggled manfully to keep the peace. By the spring of 1898, though, Congress stood on the verge of declaring war on Spain without a formal request from the White House, and the President capitulated to the pressure on him.

When, in April of 1898, war finally came, the outcome seemed by no means a preordained conclusion. Many feared a Spanish attack on the big eastern cities. But strident, jingoistic newspapers, particularly those published on the Atlantic coast, made the war generally popular. The "official" heralds of expansion, including many Senators, gave it a noble purpose: it would fulfill the nation's "destiny." Although some Americans recognized that Spain was not a very powerful foe ("If only Germany could be persuaded to come in," Commodore George Dewey had yearned privately), some astonishing military and naval luck protected the United States forces from a protracted encounter, if not from defeat itself.

Dewey's fleet in Pacific waters subdued the Spanish squadron in the Philippine Islands in a day, and other military and naval units demolished Spanish power in the Caribbean only slightly less swiftly. By the late summer, Spain had been crushed. The United States had become an imperial power with interests, proudly called "overseas possessions," including, besides the Philippines, the islands of Guam and Puerto Rico. New national heroes like Dewey (shortly to be an admiral) and Theodore Roosevelt (shortly to be President) proclaimed the new day.

Yet despite its enthusiasm for war, the nation was not of one mind about imperialism. Taking seriously the announced principles of the Republic, that "all men are created equal," and that governments exist at the "consent of the governed," many leading Americans took their stand against acquiring colonies and demanded that the nation turn off from the imperialist path. Some of these people, to be sure, were motivated chiefly by hostility to dark-skinned "alien races," but others, the morality of the issue aside, feared the pride of power that had been the ruin of so many strong nations in the past.

These anti-imperialists could not prevent the seizure of Spain's colonies, and many were angry as well as disappointed. Within a few years, however, the mood of the 1890's began to change. Except for the Canal Zone in Panama and the tiny Virgin Islands, the United States took no other lands. Cuba, in fulfillment of a pledge by Congress, was allowed to run its own affairs almost immediately—although the United States retained Guantanamo as a naval base on a long lease and exerted a powerful influence on the Cuban economy. Filipino patriots, believing that the Americans had come to the Philippines only to help them fight the Spanish, took up arms against their erstwhile "ally," precipitating a bloody insurrection not put down until 1902. When peace returned, a civil government was established, with the object of eventually granting full independence to the islands. This promise, reaffirmed by a succession of Presidents, was finally redeemed in 1946. Puerto Rico moved by comparable steps toward greater self-government; in 1952 it was granted commonwealth status, a political position poised uneasily between independence and statehood. Of the other important colonies, Hawaii, annexed in July, 1898, became the fiftieth state during the Eisenhower administration, and Guam, a poorhouse of the Pacific, remains under the administration of the Department of the Interior.

The United States never developed a coordinated colonial policy, and the public never acquired a taste for the pomp of empire. Perhaps Americans espoused imperialism too late, after the trappings of imperial power were already frayed even for the British in India. Perhaps, too, the cherished Revolutionary War traditions of Americans quickly reasserted themselves after the aberration of the 1890's. In Latin America especially, the enormous economic pressures generated by an expanding American capitalism kept the nations of the region in a state approaching vassalage and roused deep local resentments; according to their own lights, though, Americans did the best they could by their conquered peoples and by their neighbors, undertaking to inculcate American political principles in them, and to lead them on the road to economic development. Still, the sanitary engineering the United States introduced in its possessions may have been the most significant accomplishment. This immense labor, moreover, was profoundly symbolic: like Lady Macbeth, Americans seemed to cry, "Out, damned spot!" as if by a Herculean effort they could wash out the stain of having transgressed the unalienable rights of other peoples.

For Further Reading

Beisner, Robert L., *Twelve Against Empire: The Anti-Imperialists, 1898–1900.*
Freidel, Frank, *The Splendid Little War.*
LaFeber, Walter, *The New Empire.*
May, Ernest R., *Imperial Democracy.*
Pratt, Julius W., *The Expansionists of 1898.*
Wolff, Leon, *Little Brown Brother: America's Forgotten Bid for Empire Which Cost 250,000 Lives.*

82   China Under the Impact of the West

The history of China from the Opium War of 1839–1842 to the Revolution of 1911 is the story of the disintegration of a great and proud civilization. In the face of unrelenting pressures from the Western powers and devastating rebellions in the interior, the Chinese political and intellectual elite and the Manchu rulers clung tenaciously to the ideals and institutions that had preserved China for 2,000 years. But the failure of these ideals and institutions to meet the unprecedented threat from abroad eventually had to be conceded. It was a long and agonizing process, and in the end the slowness of the Chinese response determined the drastic nature of the final reaction—impossible to imagine in 1839: the end of dynastic rule and the repudiation of the whole Confucian social and intellectual tradition.

The first clash between China and the West, the Opium War, was a minor affair compared with what was to come, but it exemplified the fundamental conflict between two vastly different civilizations which was to last for more than a century. The immediate issue was trade. To the Chinese official, merchants were parasites, men motivated solely by material gain who exploited the labors of others and produced nothing of value. Foreigners were barbarians, ignorant of the ethical precepts that were the foundation of the civilization of the Middle Kingdom. It followed that foreign traders were particularly despicable, and that foreign trade should be closely supervised. By 1757, foreign sea trade was confined to Canton. The foreign merchants in Canton were frequently exasperated by the restrictions on trade and the aloofness of Chinese officials, who dis-

C H R O N O L O G Y

----

dained to deal with them directly. But high profits made the conditions tolerable.

In the last half of the eighteenth century, as tea became the national drink of England, the British came to dominate the Canton trade. To balance the import of tea, large quantities of opium, shipped from India, were eventually required. In the 1820's the Ch'ing government became alarmed, both because of the debilitating effects of the drug on the populace and because of an exaggerated estimate of the silver leaving China to pay for it. In 1838 Peking decided to crack down: the death penalty was prescribed for anyone dealing with opium in any way. A high official, Lin Tse-hsu, was dispatched to Canton to enforce the prohibition and to ensure that trade was conducted within the confines of existing regulations.

The English merchants and the British superintendent of trade in Canton saw the situation quite differently. For them, the issue was not the opium; it was that loftiest of civilized principles, freedom of trade. The "unreasonable" restrictions on trade and the haughty attitude of Chinese officialdom were intolerable, especially to Englishmen, and would have to be changed.

Since neither side was inclined to compromise on fundamental issues, and both sides were determined to use force if necessary, friction was inevitable. When Lin Tse-hsu stopped trade, confiscated and destroyed the opium held by foreign firms and refused to pay compensation, tension became acute. In November, 1839, a Chinese fleet exchanged volleys with British men-of-war near Canton. Thus began the Opium War, and a century of defeat and humiliation for China.

In the sporadic engagements that followed, British ships and guns demonstrated their superiority again and again, but the Ch'ing court refused to concede that the Celestial Kingdom was at the mercy of barbarian fleets, and so the war dragged on until 1842. Finally, with great reluctance, the Manchu government was forced to sign treaties that ceded Hong Kong to Great Britain, opened five coastal ports to trade, established a low, fixed tariff rate, and granted extraterritorial rights to foreigners in China. Through the most-favored-nation clause, the benefits of these and later treaties were extended to any nation that signed a treaty with China.

These were the first of many treaties—"unequal treaties," as they came to be called—imposed on China by foreign powers. For a time, the government evaded implementation of the Opium War treaties, but after defeat in another war (1856–1860), China was forced to comply with the provisions of these treaties, and in addition to legalize the opium traffic, to open other ports and the Yangtze River to trade, to permit the propagation of Christianity in the interior, to grant diplomatic recognition to foreign states on the basis of equality, and to permit foreign states to station resident ministers in Peking. China was thus forced to conduct her foreign relations according to European standards.

But there were far greater immediate problems facing the government than the foreign warships at China's gates. In the years from 1850 to 1873, China was convulsed by the most devastating rebellions of her long history. The largest of these, the Taiping Rebellion, resulted from a combination of tensions that had previously engendered rebellions and new ideological and economic forces from abroad. The leader of the Taiping, or Heavenly Kingdom of Great Peace, Hung Hsiu-ch'üan (1812–1864), came from a poor family of a minority group in south China. The emotional strain of repeated failures in the civil service examinations caused Hung to have visions, which were influenced by ideas from Protestant missionary tracts he had picked up in Canton. Hung came to believe that he was the younger brother of Jesus Christ, whose mission on earth was to rid China of evil demons—Manchus, Taoists, Buddhists, and Confucians. He went forth preaching a doctrine that combined traditional Chinese ideas with half-digested notions from the Bible.

Hung's teachings and his iconoclastic crusades against Confucian temples brought him into conflict with the local gentry. By 1851 he and his followers were in open rebellion. The small band was swollen by transport hands who had become unemployed owing to the shift in internal trade routes after the Opium War had opened new ports to foreign trade. And as Taiping expeditions roamed over large areas of southern and central China, they were joined by large numbers of peasants. Nanking was captured and made the capital of the Heavenly Kingdom, and for a decade much of the Yangtze valley was under Taiping control.

Although Taiping political and military organization and leadership were poor, imperial armies were generally ineffective against the rebels. But from the earliest stages of the rebellion gentry-led local militia demonstrated their ability to withstand Taiping forces. The Manchu government, always apprehensive of the latent strength of regionalism, was reluctant to surrender authority to the provinces, but eventually it had no other choice than to permit the formation of regional armies, led by prominent local gentry, as the only means of subduing the rebels. Furthermore, in order to finance the new armies, provincial officials were permitted to tax internal trade, and to use the receipts within their province.

Thus, the rebellions were vanquished not by the Manchu central government, but by the Chinese gentry, who saw the Taipings as a threat to the Confucian tradition and the existing social structure. The gentry leaders who emerged and rose to high office as a result of the rebellion were conservatives. The most prominent, Tseng Kuo-fan, was a top graduate of the civil service examinations, who exemplified the best in the gentry tradition. Tseng led the suppression of the Taipings, and in the following years he and similar regional leaders quelled the Muslim and other rebellions in northwestern and southwestern China.

The rebellions caused great death and destruction. Even before peace was restored, the immense task of reconstruction was begun. In the 1860's and 1870's the new leaders undertook a program not only of rural rehabilitation but also of "Self-Strengthening" to counter the foreign threat. Intelligent men, they saw that the West knew how to build excellent weapons, ships, and railroads; good Confucians, they believed that the ancient Chinese ideals of social harmony and the institutions that embodied these ideals were superior to European civilization. Western technology was to be used to strengthen China in order to preserve the traditional social order. To implement this program, arsenals and shipyards were built in several ports, and Western language schools and translation bureaus were established to enable Chinese to study Western science and technology. Although Self-Strengthening was essentially a conservative program, many among the scholar-official class viewed even these moderate innovations with hostility.

The limited achievements of the Self-Strengthening movement were insufficient to brace China against renewed foreign encroachment, which was climaxed by disastrous defeat in the Sino-Japanese War of 1894–1895. Despite diplomatic intervention on China's behalf by Germany, France, and Russia, the Japanese terms were harsh: a huge indemnity (three times the annual revenue of the Chinese government), the right to build industries in treaty ports, cession of Taiwan to Japan, and recognition of the independence of Korea, which was annexed by Japan in 1910.

The defeat by Japan was followed by new demands from the European powers for special privileges. Fear that China would be partitioned impelled some Chinese to insist on far-reaching reforms. The most prominent of these reformers, K'ang Yu-wei, argued that if China was to be strengthened and saved, government institutions had to be altered. To many this was profoundly immoral, for it would be unfilial for the emperor to modify the institutions established by his ancestors. But according to K'ang, even Confucius had been a reformer who had advocated the creation of new institutions to suit the changed circumstances of his own times. If Confucius could reform institutions, then so could K'ang. In 1895 K'ang led more than 600 examination candidates, in Peking for the metropolitan examinations, in submitting to the throne a lengthy memorial urging radical reforms. The memorial disappeared somewhere in the conservative bureaucracy and never reached the emperor. But by 1898, the emperor had been impressed by K'ang's ideas and summoned him to the capital. Edicts announcing sweeping reforms were promulgated: the government bureaucracy was to be revamped, sinecures abolished, modern industry encouraged, the army reorganized, and Western subjects given more attention in the schools.

The edicts were not implemented. Conservative Confucians and refractory bureaucrats dominated the government apparatus. To some, K'ang's theories were heresy; others saw their careers threatened. Moreover, real power lay in the hands not of the young emperor, but of his wily and bigoted aunt, the xenophobic Empress Dowager, who had been the power behind the throne for a generation. With ease, she forced the emperor into retirement, and the "Hundred Days of Reform" came to an end. K'ang and some of his supporters fled into exile, while others insisted on remaining to die as martyrs. The attempt to adapt Confucianism to the modern world and to modernize China under the auspices of the monarchy had failed.

Two years later, with the connivance of the Empress Dowager and a few reactionary officials, one last attempt to exorcise the foreigners was made, this time by a disorganized mass of superstitious peasants, known as the Boxers. The rabble entered Peking and besieged the foreign quarter. But peasants who thought they possessed magical powers were no match for the well-armed foreign troops who marched to Peking and lifted the siege. Meanwhile, Russian units occupied Manchuria to protect "public order" and Russian interests. They did not leave when the disorders had been quieted. In a few years, Japanese influence began to replace the Russians in Manchuria, and for a half-century after the Boxer Rebellion, Manchuria lay beyond the control of the government of China.

Even the Empress Dowager learned the lesson of the Boxer Rebellion: China had to modernize. Under the direction of Yüan Shih-k'ai, an able military commander, the army was enlarged and strengthened with Western weapons and organization. Railroads were built. A constitution and a cabinet were promised in an attempt to gain confidence in the government. More Western subjects were introduced into the educational system, and in 1905 the civil service examinations were abolished, sundering the institutionalized tie between the Confucian classics and the imperial system that had endured for more than 1,000 years. A Confucian education was no longer the prerequisite for a government career; this signified the imminent extinction of the Confucian-educated gentry elite.

The reforms were too late to save the dynasty. In 1908 the emperor and the Empress Dowager died, and a two-year-old boy succeeded to the throne under a regency. Yüan Shih-k'ai, now almost surely the most powerful man in China, and a potential threat to the dynasty, was forced into retirement. Concessions were made to stem growing provincial dissatisfaction with the central government and the Manchu house. But reform was no longer enough. Revolution was on the agenda.

Since the turn of the century, small bands of anti-Manchu revolutionaries had been fomenting uprisings, especially in south China. Outbreak after outbreak failed to gain support and was suppressed, but the revolutionaries persisted. Their most prominent leader was Sun Yat-sen, a Christian who had been educated in Western schools in Hawaii and Hong Kong; his rather crude political theories, which envisioned a new China founded on what he termed the Three People's Principles—Nationalism, Democracy, and People's Livelihood—were largely derived from Western political and social thinkers.

Sun was in America on a fund-raising tour when, on October 10, 1911, a revolt of the army garrison in the city of Wuchang set off the revolution that toppled the Ch'ing. The city fell to the revolutionaries, and in the next two months most southern and central provinces declared their independence of the central government. The Ch'ing court recalled Yüan Shih-k'ai from retirement. Yüan agreed to return to office—on his own terms. He was made prime minister and given command of the crack northern army. There was no real coordination between the newly independent provinces, and the revolutionaries were poorly organized. But the loyalty of some governmental units was doubtful, and although by late November the revolutionaries were on the defensive, Yüan did not commit his forces to a final test of strength. He had other plans. When Sun Yat-sen returned to China and was proclaimed president of the Republic by the revolutionaries, Yüan entered into negotiations with him. Sun agreed to resign the presidency in Yüan's favor if Yüan would arrange the abdication of the Manchu monarch and declare his support of republicanism. The Manchus had no choice. In February, 1912, the infant emperor was dethroned and given a comfortable pension to live within the Imperial

Palace. The Ch'ing had lost the Mandate of Heaven, and China embarked on a half-century of turmoil.

For Further Reading

Fairbank, John K., *The United States and China.*
McAleavy, Henry, *The Modern History of China.*
Schwartz, Benjamin I., *In Search of Wealth and Power: Yen Fu and the West.*
Wright, Mary C., *The Last Stand of Chinese Conservatism: The T'ung-chih Restoration, 1862–1874.*
———, ed., *China in Revolution: The First Phase, 1900–1913.*

83   India Under British Rule

The political unification of India in the first half of the nineteenth century and the rise of nationalism in the second half were linked in a multitude of ways with the new forces and ideas that were reshaping the Western world. Warren Hastings saw the conquest of territory in India in the 1780's as balancing British losses in the New World, and during the French revolutionary wars the danger of the spread of Jacobin ideas was seriously debated in Calcutta. France's European preoccupation during the Napoleonic wars made possible the spread of British power in India without a challenge from any European rivals. The impact of the new inventions for the manufacture of textiles was felt in India within a decade of their introduction in England. Jenner's method of smallpox vaccination was widely used in India during the first years of the century, and an experimental telegraph line was constructed in 1839. Indians petitioned for freedom of the press in 1823, arguing that they were "secured in the enjoyment of the same civil and religious privileges that every Briton is entitled to in England." Later, the writings of Giuseppe Mazzini were translated into Bengali, and the nationalist movements of Europe, particularly the unification of Germany and Italy, provided examples and illustrations for Indian writers.

Neither expansion nor the spread of Western ideas had been looked upon with favor in the early period of British rule. East India Company officials in London and the British Parliament had opposed the wars that added to the Company's territories, and the Indian Act of 1784, the first important constitutional document of modern India, had declared that conquests in India were "repugnant to the wish, the honor, and the policy of

A.D.

	1757	Battle of Plassey; sack of Delhi by Afghans
	1761	Marathas defeated at Panipat by Afghans and Mughals
	1765	Grant of *diwani* to East India Company by Mughal emperor
	1784	Pitt's India Act
1786–1793		Lord Cornwallis governor general
	1792	Ranjit Singh comes to power
	1793	Permanent Settlement in Bengal
1798–1805		Lord Wellesley governor general
	1799	Defeat of Tipu Sultan of Mysore
1817–1819		Final war against the Marathas
1828–1835		Lord William Bentinck governor general
	1835	Resolution on use of English for higher education
	1839	Death of Ranjit Singh
1839–1842		First Afghan War
	1843	Annexation of Sind
	1849	Annexation of Punjab
	1853	First railway line opened
1857–1858		Rebellions and army mutinies
	1858	Power transferred from East India Company to Crown
1880–1884		Lord Ripon governor general
	1885	Organization of Indian National Congress
	1892	India Councils Act
1899–1905		Lord Curzon governor general

the British nation." As for Western ideas and values, Company officials were convinced that the only possibility of maintaining British power in India, as well as the most moral course of action, was to maintain, with a minimum of interference, the existing laws and customs of the Indians.

The injunction against territorial conquests was never very seriously observed, however, and during the governor-generalship of Lord Wellesley (1798–1805) a series of wars brought most of the coastal regions and the Gangetic plain up to Delhi under direct British control. Wellesley's defense of his policy, used in one form or another throughout the century to justify conquest, was based upon his reading of the Indian and international situation. If Britain did not control India, France or Russia would; peaceful relations were impossible with Indian rulers, since "a restless spirit of ambition was characteristic of every Asiatic government"; the replacement of the misgovernment of the native rulers by the good government of the British carried its own moral justification; and finally, once the country was reduced to order, trade and commerce would prosper. Perhaps the basic cause of expansion was simply the political situation in India and the challenge this presented to restless, imaginative men like Wellesley. The point has already been made that one of the stress lines of Indian history is the tendency of a strong government, especially one based in the Gangetic plain, to expand, and the Bengal government was following this pattern. Some territories were annexed outright, becoming part of what was known as British India. Others were brought under control through a system of subsidiary alliances which left local rulers with considerable internal control in their territories, at the price of abandoning all claims to carry on relations with other Indian states. A second burst of expansion took place in the period from 1815 to 1825, when the Marathas were finally defeated and much of Burma was annexed. Then, after a pause to consolidate these gains, a new forward movement began, leading to a war against Afghanistan in 1839 which ended in a disastrous defeat for the British. But the Sind, the lower valley of the Indus, was annexed in 1843, and the Punjab, the last important Indian territory outside British control, was conquered in 1849.

The policy of not interfering with Indian laws and customs was challenged by representatives of two of the most potent intellectual and social forces of early nineteenth-century England, the Evangelicals and the Utilitarians. For the Evangelicals, the duty of the British government to bring about change in social customs was clear: Christians should actively seek to introduce Western light and learning into the darkness and ignorance of Hinduism. For the Utilitarians, India offered scope for social change through legal reform and the construction of a rational system of administration and jurisprudence. These pressures were greatly strengthened by

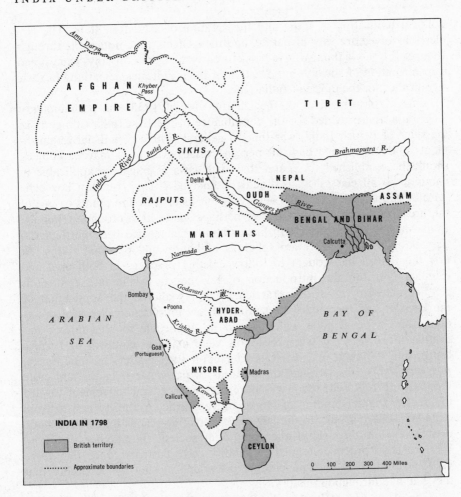

the enthusiastic response shown to Western ideas of change and improvement by a small but very influential group of Indians in Bengal. Ram Mohan Roy, the most notable of these men, pleaded with great eloquence for the introduction of Western science and technology and for the ending of what he regarded as social evils born of superstition, such as caste, child marriage, and suttee, the practice of widows immolating themselves on their husbands' funeral pyres.

Out of these divergent pressures came thirty years of effort, from about 1825 to 1855, to achieve what was known as "material and moral progress" through legislation, administrative reforms, and the introduction of the fruits of Western technology. The result, in general terms, was the political unification of India and the creation of a modern state. The elements involved are very disparate, and their effects were noticeable through changes in the administrative structures rather than in any widespread transformation of society, but a listing of them indicates something of their significance for the fabric of Indian life.

One of the directives of the Charter Act of 1833, the parliamentary legislation that provided for the continuance of the East India Company as the ruler of British India, was that "a general system of judicial establishments and police, to which all persons whatsoever . . . may be subject, should be established . . . and that such laws as might be applicable in common to all classes . . . should be enacted." This common law code for all citizens was never fully achieved, but its articulation points to one of the areas in which Western power perhaps made its profoundest impact. Indian law, whether under Muslim or Hindu rulers, had been particularistic, taking into consideration religious affiliation and personal status. At first the British had sought to follow existing practices in both civil and criminal law, but the introduction of law courts in the late eighteenth century modeled on British practice inevitably altered the application of the laws. It was recognized that criminal law must follow Western precedents, and a penal code which would be applicable to all subjects was drafted in 1837. Civil law procedures were made to conform to English usage, and although in cases touching upon such matters as inheritance, property rights, or marriage, the customs of particular religious and caste groups were followed, there was nevertheless a general movement toward the Western understanding of law as universalistic. Authority moved from caste and village groups to the law courts, creating strains that slowly made themselves felt throughout the traditional society. In another direction, Western legal practices tended to solidify caste customs: once they were used in court, they became binding precedents, losing the flexibility that they had had throughout history.

One of the first tasks that the British confronted was the establishment of a system of land revenue collection. Lacking detailed knowledge of the Mughal system, and without sufficient experienced personnel, they decided in 1793 to recognize the old Mughal tax farmers and district revenue officers as the actual owners of the soil in Bengal and to fix their taxes in perpetuity. The Permanent Settlement thus created a class of landlords, or zamindars, who, it was hoped, would provide stability in the countryside by supporting the government to whom they owed their existence. On the whole, the Permanent Settlement fulfilled this expectation, but it was not applied in the new areas that came under British control, for it had a number of major weaknesses. In fixing the landlords' taxes in perpetuity, the government had deprived itself of the right to profit from the increasing value of land, yet it had not provided any protection for the peasants, whose rents could be raised at will. Nor did the Bengal zamindars improve their properties on the model of their eighteenth-century English counterparts; many were unable to adjust their habits to the inexorable demands of the new government that taxes be paid in full and on time, and as a consequence were forced to sell their lands. Elsewhere the government either made arrangements to collect the land tax directly from the cultivator-owner, as in Madras, or from village communities, as in the Punjab. The actual tax demands were probably less than under previous governments, but collection was more regular, and there was less chance of using stratagems to avoid payments, which had to be made in cash. It is difficult to sense the quality of life in rural India at this time, but one gets the impression that while more secure than in the previous century, it was also pervaded by a vague disquiet as the new power reached down to the village level.

The use of legislation to institute social change began during the governor-generalship of Lord William Bentinck (1828–1835). The most dramatic example of this was the law passed in 1829 forbidding suttee. The frequency of this practice had been much exaggerated, but the question of its abolition assumed great importance because it constituted a clear invasion by government of an area guarded by religious sanction. Bentinck recognized this, but argued that in making moral decisions the rulers must consult their own consciences, not those of their subjects. This provided a guideline for other legislation. Action was taken to suppress female infanticide, slavery, and human sacrifice, which was common among the primitive people of Orissa.

Of a different order, but of great social significance, was the decision made by Bentinck's administration in 1835 to support higher educational institutions that used English, rather than an Indian language, as the medium of instruction. This move was opposed by the older generation of British officials who saw in it one more attempt to transform Indian society by interfering in its deepest intellectual and religious concerns, but it received eager support from other powerful interests. Many officials argued that the language of government must be the language of the rulers; the Evangelicals saw English as the medium for introducing a true understanding of the world; and, above all, Indians like Ram Mohan Roy saw English as the key that would open the door of the future of India.

These changes in administrative and social patterns were helped, as was the whole process of political unification, by the improvement of internal communications. Much of this took place during the energetic, modernizing administration of Lord Dalhousie (1848–1856). Twenty-five hundred miles of telegraph lines were completed by 1855; the Grand

Trunk Road linked Calcutta with northern India; and railway construction was begun. The impact of the new technology had been felt at an even earlier period in external communications: the first steam vessel arrived in India from England in 1826, and a steam-powered vessel was launched at Calcutta in 1828.

One of the most controversial aspects of nineteenth-century Indian history is the economic impact of Western rule, but a number of generalizations can be safely made. One is that trade and commerce responded to new conditions more extensively than industry. Another is that the creation of a market economy was an important factor in political unification. Calcutta, Bombay, and Madras were essentially nineteenth-century cities, which were linked to each other and their hinterlands through banking, insurance, and government.

Throughout the century India had a favorable balance of payments, brought about by a world demand for such products as jute, hides, oilseeds, and wheat, and a lack of internal demand for foreign goods. Both foreign and domestic capital investment throughout most of the century was in commercial enterprises relating to these basic agricultural products, not in industries based on the new technology. As part of the free trade economy of Great Britain, India had no tariffs to protect new industries, and this, combined with the lack of internal markets, was probably the major barrier to industrial growth. The result was that throughout the nineteenth century the rapidly increasing population pressed more and more heavily on the land instead of finding outlets in urban areas.

Two formal institutions channeled the innovative forces that were producing political unification and social change: the army and the bureaucracy. The East India Company administered India until 1858, but long before, its power had passed to the British Parliament, which in effect reigned through a governor general. In theory, the governor general was a despot, but in fact his power was circumscribed by Parliament, the system of laws under which he operated, and above all, by that unique bureaucracy, the Indian Civil Service, which consisted of approximately 1,000 British officials who were appointed from England, at first through patronage and after 1854 through competitive examinations, and who held all the senior posts in the Indian government. The exclusion of Indians from executive posts had been one of the results of the administrative reforms carried out in the 1790's by Lord Cornwallis, and the first Indian member of the civil service was not appointed until 1869. Below the top level, almost all the thousands of posts in the bureaucracy were held by Indians, but none of these positions had either the glamour or the prestige of the civil service, entrance into which became the symbol of Indian political aspirations. British India was divided up for administrative purposes into

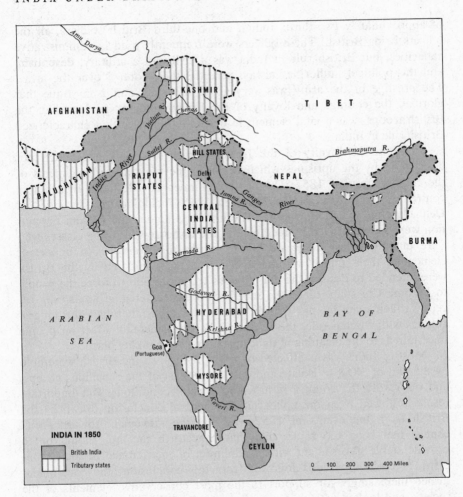

INDIA IN 1850
British India
Tributary states

0   100   200   300   400 Miles

districts, each with a population of about a million, and the district officer, who was almost always a civil servant, had a large degree of autonomy. Even a very energetic governor general could not make much headway in instituting measures that were not popular with the district officers, who prided themselves on knowing India, in contrast to the governor general, who seldom had any knowledge of conditions before coming to India and who generally remained in office for only five or six years.

Of the role of the army in creating a modern state in India surprisingly little is known, but the contrast between the functions and nature of the small, disciplined British military force and that of the Mughals is great. It was a professional army of never many more than 200,000 men, made up of approximately two-thirds Indian and one-third British soldiers, all the officers being British. These officers were frequently used in administrative capacities, but British rule in India was a civil, not a military, despotism, and the political authorities always asserted their control over the army. The prestige of the army was very great, however, and a mystique that glorified the courage and loyalty of the Indian soldiers, no less than the British troops, was a vital element in the self-confidence that characterized British rule in India.

Faith in the loyalty of the Indian soldier was shaken (though not destroyed) by the uprisings which began in the most trusted regiments of the Indian army in 1857. During the summer of 1857 the British lost control of large areas of the Gangetic plain, including the key cities of Delhi, Lucknow, and Cawnpore. The uprisings among the civilian population were frequently led by members of the dispossessed ruling classes who were making a last desperate bid to regain their power. An important element of their appeal was that the new changes initiated by the British were intended to destroy the old religious traditions and to force the people to become Christian. Since the rebellions were centered in areas only recently taken over by the British, not in the areas that had the longest contact with foreign rule, this argument had considerable effect on people uncertain as to the meaning of the changes that were taking place.

Most of India was unaffected by the uprisings, so the British were able by the end of 1858 to isolate and destroy the last of the rebellious groups, and outwardly the country returned to normal conditions. But important results followed from the upheaval. The general conclusion drawn by the British from the events of 1857 was that the movement toward social change had been too rapid, and that henceforth the aim should be to provide stable government with a minimum of interference in social concerns. A curious paradox followed from this conclusion: the government turned increasingly for support to the most conservative elements of the society, and looked with suspicion upon the English-educated groups in the great port cities that had most enthusiastically identified themselves with the British during the uprisings.

The result was estrangement in the last decades of the century between the intellectuals and the government. In Bengal especially there was a growing demand that those Indians who were, in Macaulay's famous phrase, "Indian in blood and color, but English in taste, in opinions, in morals and in intellect," should be allowed to participate in the administration the British had created. To men like Surendranath Banerjea, who became in the 1870's perhaps the best-known Indian of his time, the right to such participation had been earned not only through their acquiring Western knowledge but by their ready acknowledgment that British rule had been beneficial for India. A response to this demand came during the administration of Lord Ripon, the governor general appointed by Gladstone in 1880. A greater measure of freedom for the press and the creation of corporations for local self-government indicated the direction in which the British Liberals wanted to move, but the attempt to remove existing restrictions on the trial of Europeans by Indian judges provoked a storm of opposition from many officials as well as from the British business community in India. The legislation was withdrawn, and after Ripon's departure in 1884 the government moved away from his policy.

The widespread resentment caused by the British community's ardent defense of discriminatory laws, along with the expectations fostered by Gladstonian liberalism, led to the formation of various organizations intended to provide forums for the expression of Indian opinion. Most of these were local and short-lived, but the leaders of a number of them combined in 1885 to form what became known as the Indian National Congress. From the beginning the Congress spoke for an influential section of the new professional classes created by British rule—college teachers, lawyers, journalists, doctors—as well as for the students who were beginning to crowd into the colleges. It was this remarkable organization, perhaps unique among nationalist movements for its longevity as well as for its identification with the aspirations of the people, that dominated Indian political and social thinking during the twentieth century.

For Further Reading

de Bary, William T., et al. (eds.), *Sources of Indian Tradition*, Vol. II.

Seal, Anil, *The Emergence of Indian Nationalism*.

Spear, Percival, *India, Pakistan, and the West*.

Woodruff, Philip, *The Men Who Ruled India*.

84   Darwin and Freud

What Newtonianism had been to the eighteenth century Darwinism was to be to the nineteenth: the pivotal point in a crisis of faith and in a whole series of profound revaluations in philosophy and social thought. It animated scientists seeking truth and imperialists seeking colonies. It is, of course, always possible to overstate the novelty of Darwin's ideas; for at least a century and a half before the publication of his *The Origin of*

	A.D.		
CHRONOLOGY		1798	T. R. Malthus publishes *An Essay on the Principles of Population*
		1801	Lamarck publishes *Système des animaux sans vertèbres*
		1809	Charles Darwin is born
		1820	Herbert Spencer is born
	1830–1833		Charles Lyell publishes *Principles of Geology*
		1848	Darwin's theories are fully developed in unpublished papers
		1856	Sigmund Freud is born
		1859	Darwin publishes *The Origin of Species*
		1862	Spencer publishes *First Principles*
		1871	Darwin publishes *Descent of Man*
		1882	Darwin dies
		1897	Freud discovers essential principles of psychoanalysis; undertakes his self-analysis
		1899	Freud publishes *The Interpretation of Dreams*
		1905	Freud publishes *Three Essays on the Theory of Sexuality*
		1909	Freud, in the company of Jung, visits the United States to lecture at Clark University
		1910	Founding of the International Psychoanalytical Association; Jung president
	1911–1913		Falling out of Freud with Jung and Adler, mainly on issue of infantile sexuality
	1923 ff.		Freud publishes *The Ego and the Id;* period of the last works, including *The Future of an Illusion,* and *Civilization and Its Discontents*
		1939	Freud dies

Species in 1859, rationalist criticism had struck hard and wounding blows at Christianity, undermining not only its teaching of revelation and the miraculous but also the idea that its morality provided the only sound basis. for human conduct. A belief in changing species and in evolutionary development had been made familiar to educated men by a long line of speculative thinkers dating back to the previous century, whose tradition is evoked by the names of Buffon, Lamarck, and Charles Darwin's own grandfather, Erasmus Darwin. Geology, the most popular of the sciences in the first half of the nineteenth century, had prepared many people to understand that the world was much older than it appeared in Biblical chronology.

It is true that most geologists confined themselves to descriptive accounts of physiography and fossils, but in 1830 the first volume of Charles Lyell's *Principles of Geology* set forth in fresh and impressive terms an old theory, known as Uniformitarianism. According to Lyell, the geologic history of the earth had been a slow, uniform, orderly development brought about by the accumulation of constant small changes. This was, of course, profoundly at odds not only with the prevailing view among scientists but with the Biblical version of the creation and the flood. Cautious as Lyell was about the theological implications of his own findings, his authority weighed heavily toward a new view of the antiquity and history of the earth that was consistent with the evolutionary idea. Finally, religion was shaken from another quarter, the development of Biblical criticism, which flourished particularly in Germany. With their critical examination of Biblical texts, the new scholars threw into doubt the received version of the origins of the Bible, dwelled on its many inconsistencies, and encouraged the impious eighteenth-century view that it was not the product of divine inspiration but the work of many fallible human beings. By the middle of the nineteenth century it was quite possible, even for a pious man, to think about the natural world in a fashion uninhibited by the ancient Biblical cosmology; and indeed in some areas of science serious work was possible only after the scientist had discarded what we would today call the tenets of fundamentalist religion.

Still, Darwin himself was stunned by the implications of his own work, as they gradually became clear to him. Let us remind ourselves of the basic elements of his theory of natural selection, which was first drawn up in an unpublished paper of 1848—eleven years before *The Origin of Species*. First, as Malthus and Spencer had done before him, Darwin observed that within each species more organisms are constantly generated than can be nourished and supported by the environment. Second, the rapid rate at which living forms increase produces a constant struggle for existence, a competition for food and other means of survival. Third, some variation of physical type always occurs within a species. Thus not all organisms are equally equipped for survival: those whose variations are better adapted to the environment in which they must live are the ones that survive and reproduce themselves. Fourth, the offspring of these survivors inherit their favorable variations. Finally, the accumulation of these small favorable variations over a very long period of time introduces such changes of type that a new species emerges. On the strength of this theory, and of a study of the distribution of animal forms on the face of the earth, one could draw up a hypothetical picture of the development of complex forms from simple ones, a picture of evolutionary change beginning with rudimentary forms and ending with man. In 1871, with *The Descent of Man,* Darwin made it painfully clear that his theory embraced human origins as well as others, and disturbed many people who had been able to consider the idea of changes in all the other species.

It is hardly surprising that many religious people should see Darwinism not primarily as a scientific hypothesis but as a formidable challenge to revealed religion. Such challenges had been experienced before: as we have seen, the skepticism of the Enlightenment had left its mark; and the philosophes' favorite theology, the natural religion of Deism, had been set up as a competitor to the revealed religion of traditional believers. Darwinism, of course, went beyond natural religion in its own disturbing implications; it undermined the old view of nature as a stable framework of structures contrived as a rational and unchanging unity by God. And after Darwin the implications of this threat were to be pushed still further, as men argued that natural science could be applied to all the affairs of man and society as well as to nature, and indeed that the methods of natural science were the *only* methods by which anything could be learned about man and society.

It is important to recognize that men and women reacted to the threat of Darwinism in various ways. Some were panicked at the thought of a complete loss of religious faith to be followed, it was assumed, by a complete loss of morality. Others believed that a new and enlarged, and in many ways more imposing and more consoling, view of God and nature would finally emerge (like the clergyman who, reading Darwin's account of the devices by which orchids survived, exclaimed, "O Lord, how manifold are Thy works"). Some scientists, like Darwin himself, refrained from attacking the Bible. Others, like his friend Thomas Huxley, the primary publicist and promoter of evolutionism, believed that the victory of science depended upon vigorous combat. "Extinguished theologians," he wrote, "lie about the cradle of every science as the strangled snakes beside that of Hercules." It would be too much to say, as some nineteenth-century rationalists did, that there was a "war between religion and science." There was much conflict, to be sure, but there were too many effective diplomats on both sides to permit the tension between faith and inquiry to break out in general war; there were too many scientists who agreed that no matter what they learned about the universe it would always be possible to find God behind it, too many liberal clergymen and theologians who conceded that in this enlightened age the lines of the traditional, literal-minded Biblical faith had to be reformed and to give way to that even grander and more complex conception of God and nature that they thought they saw emerging from the new science.

That there was a net loss of faith one can hardly doubt. Others must have followed a course similar to that Darwin reported:

. . . I had gradually come, by this time, to see that the Old Testament from its manifestly false history of the world and from its attributing to God the feelings of a revengeful tyrant, was no more to be trusted than the sacred books of the Hindoos, or the beliefs of any barbarian. The question then continually rose before my mind and would not be banished,—is it credible that if God were now to make a revelation to the Hindoos, would he permit it to be connected with the belief in Vishnu, Siva, etc., as Christianity is connected with the Old Testament. This appeared to me utterly incredible.

By further reflecting that the clearest evidence would be requisite to make any sane man believe in the miracles by which Christianity is supported,—that the more we know of the fixed laws of nature the more incredible do miracles become,—that the men at that time were ignorant and credulous to a degree almost incomprehensible to us,—that the Gospels cannot be proved to have been written simultaneously with the events,—that they differ in many important details, far too important as it seemed to me to be admitted as the usual inaccuracies of eye-witnesses;—by such reflections as these, which I give not as having the least novelty or value, but as they influenced me, I gradually came to disbelieve in Christianity as a divine revelation. . . . This disbelief crept over me at a very slow rate, but was at last complete. The rate was so slow that I felt no distress, and have never since doubted even for a single second that my conclusion was correct.

Whereas Darwin looked upon the loss of faith as a possible anguish which he had happily been spared, Huxley saw the loss of faith as a necessary part of the combat. "I am very glad," he wrote to another biologist, "that you see the importance of doing battle with the clericals. . . . I desire that the next generation may be less fettered by the gross and stupid superstitions of orthodoxy than mine has been. And I shall be well satisfied if I can succeed to however small an extent in bringing about that result."

Over the perspective of a longer span of time, however, much of the trial and torment aroused by the challenge of Darwinism to religion appears to be one version of a recurring and never resolved struggle. In the seventeenth century—to go back no further—a struggle between traditional faith and the avant-garde criticism of miracles had been vigorously waged; this battle was repeated, in new variations, during the height of the eighteenth-century Enlightenment; and again in the Darwinian era. Each time, one may believe, there was a net loss of faith. But each time too, the lines reformed, with differing religious responses. In our own time, a modernist Christianity, fully at home with Darwinism, has survived; and it coexists with what we have come to call fundamentalist Christianity, which is still based upon Biblical literalism. For many enlightened men of the nineteenth century the faith in Christianity was replaced, or at least supplemented, by a new and stronger faith in progress—for evolution was all too simply construed to imply progress. Darwinism became a doctrine, for many an optimistic one, of social advancement.

The effect of Darwinism on social thought was almost as profound as its effect on religion. Darwin's thought won its sway over science at a time when conservatives were looking for new and more authoritative answers to democracy and liberalism, when spokesmen of private capitalism were trying to resist the encroachments of the national state, when the prophets of nationalism were seeking justifications for national self-assertion, and when imperialists were justifying the work of extending their dominance over less favored races. Hence the ideas of evolution and natural selection were absorbed into Western thought in the midst of arguments over competition and collectivism, laissez-faire and state control, democracy and liberty, nationalism and imperialism.

Social thinkers found it easy to translate Darwin's main hypotheses into social categories. The struggle for existence became economic competition or war; survival became economic or military predominance; the idea of inheritance of variations was further evidence of necessary human inequality; adaptation to environment was elevated to a social as well as a biological value. Many thinkers took the whole scheme of development to be a promising analogue of social progress; some writers indeed concluded that the mechanisms of natural selection were the chief means, perhaps the only means, of securing that progress. Even the conception of geological periods of time came to serve as a model for society: long periods of time would be necessary to bring about any social change, conservative theorists argued, just as it had taken eons to produce the highest forms of animal life. Therefore, all schemes for rapid reform fly in the face of nature.

Soon, however, opponents of these thinkers were able to point out that the Social Darwinists had got themselves into serious difficulties. It had proved to be all too easy to construct analogies between society and nature, but these pointed in all different directions. It was easy to look upon the life of men in society as a constant struggle, but not so easy to interpret the meaning of the struggle. Which, in fact, were the struggling units? Individual men, groups, business firms, tribes, races, nation-states? It made a great deal of practical difference how this question was answered. A social theory built upon the struggle of individuals would require one response, a social theory built upon the struggle of groups, another. The struggle of individuals seemed analogous to economic competition, that of tribes or races analogous to war. But, many writers argued, if war is the true equivalent of the struggle for existence in nature, then solidarity among the individuals in the warring tribes is necessary for the survival of the group. And, if so, how could one tolerate the competitive struggle among individuals which would be certain to destroy such solidarity?

Understandably, a whole generation was thrown into confusion by such problems. Some thinkers, notably Herbert Spencer, compounded the confusion by trying to have it both ways. As an individualist, Spencer was all for severe competition, and let the devil take the loser. But as an advocate of an organismic theory of the state, he seemed to give away most of his individualism—the parts of an organism can hardly be said to engage in a competitive struggle with one another. Karl Marx and his followers complicated matters by trying to take Darwinism away from both the individualists and the nationalists. The real natural struggle, they insisted, was between classes. Marx thought, as he put it, that Darwinism gave him a basis in natural science for the class struggle in history. Later social scientists concluded that the important struggle to consider was not among individuals, nations, or classes, but among institutions, habits, and types of character. But this took them a long way from Darwin.

At bottom, Darwinism was put to two basic and mutually antagonistic uses: first, it was placed into the service of conservatism, industrial capitalism, and laissez-faire by men like Herbert Spencer in England and William Graham Sumner in the United States. When Sumner said in the 1880's that "the millionaires are a product of natural selection, acting on the whole body of men to pick out those who can meet the requirement of certain work to be done," he laid down the essential tenet of this point of view. In due course the spokesmen of reform had little difficulty in demonstrating the pseudoscientific character, as well as the smugness, of such statements. Spencer himself, near the close of his lifetime, sadly admitted that the hopes of the Social Darwinian philosophers had not been justified. In 1893 he wrote: "The doctrine of evolution has not furnished guidance to the extent I had hoped. Most of the conclusions, drawn empirically, are such as right feelings, enlightened by cultivated intelligence, have already sufficed to establish."

The second phase of Social Darwinism was the racist-militarist phase, particularly influential on the Continent, though visible also in the Anglo-American world. As early as 1872 Walter Bagehot, the English economist, concluded in his *Physics and Politics* that those nations which are strongest tend to prevail and that in certain marked peculiarities the strongest are the best. Other writers, particularly in central Europe, raised the Social Darwinian tenets to a much more strident militarist creed. "War," wrote the German Marshal Helmuth von Moltke, combining evolutionary science with religion, "is an element of the order of the world established by God. Without war the world would stagnate and lose itself in materialism." This view of the matter was repudiated by most thinkers even before the terrible bloodletting of the First World War; and after the war it had no support among serious thinkers anywhere. There was, however, a reawakening of Social Darwinism in the ideologies of the Fascists, expressed both by Mussolini and by Hitler. "The stronger has to rule," Hitler proclaimed. "Only the born weakling can consider this as cruel. The fight for daily bread makes all those succumb who are weak, sickly, and less determined." With its harsh militarism and its genocidal mania, twentieth-century totalitarianism seemed like a ghastly caricature of the relatively innocent ideas of the nineteenth-century Social Darwinians, and its history suggests that this form of Social Darwinism could recur as a serious strain in human thought only with a grave lapse of humankind into barbarism.

The writings of Charles Darwin, well or ill understood, had a profoundly unsettling effect on men's perception of themselves. Some decades after him another scientist, Sigmund Freud, developed a psychology that would be even more unsettling. As Darwin had expelled man from his privileged place in nature, Freud expelled reason from its privileged place in human nature. Today, more than thirty years after Freud's death, the world is still assimilating (often distorting and vulgarizing, but always invoking) the revolutionary ideas he first articulated in 1899–1900 in *The Interpretation of Dreams*.

Freud was born in 1856, in the Moravian town of Freiberg, the son of a Jewish merchant. As a small boy he moved with his family to Vienna, a city he loved and hated; he was to live and work there down to 1938, the year before his death, when the Nazi seizure of Austria compelled him to seek refuge in London. Freud early displayed a sturdy talent for science and an inordinate ambition for greatness. "I am not really a man of science," he later said of himself, "not an observer, not an experimenter, and not a thinker. I am nothing but by temperament a *conquistador*—an adventurer, if you want to translate the word—with the curiosity, the boldness and the tenacity that belong to that type of being." The remark, though instructive, is rather unjust: curiosity, boldness, and tenacity Freud had in abundance, and needed for his radical, unpopular, shocking theories, but he disciplined these qualities with an iron will and a superb technical competence to enlist them in his search for a science of man.

It was a slow, time-consuming, often disheartening search: Freud did not discover the central principles of psychoanalysis until the late 1890's, when he was in his early forties. After he completed his medical training he began to specialize in neurology and wrote some meritorious papers on the physiological origins of nervous diseases: his first book, published in 1891, was on aphasia. But his ambitions were wider than this. Studying with pioneers in psychopathology—with physicians like Josef Breuer in Vienna and Jean Martin Charcot in Paris—Freud began to develop, in the early 1890's, remarkable hypotheses about the origins of hysteria and related nervous disorders. It is a heroic story: his most cherished guesses turned out to be untenable, but then, in 1897, the *annus mirabilis* of psychoanalysis, Freud turned defeat into victory, and used the very hypotheses he could no longer defend as the foundations for the theory he *could* defend. He had been impressed by the tales his female patients were telling him with remarkable consistency: all these hysterics, it seemed, had been sexually assaulted by their fathers. For some time Freud had already been conjecturing that anxiety neuroses must be traced back to some sexual experience, and now his patients were providing him with specific evidence of such an experience: incestuous seduction. But by mid-1897 his confident assumption collapsed under the weight of contradictory evidence. For a time, as he remembered it later, he felt "helpless bewilderment." He thought that his technique of inquiry was correct, and he continued to think that sex must have a decisive part in the origins of hysteria. Besides, as a strict scientific materialist, Freud could not doubt that every effect must have a cause. There was a moment, he confessed, when he "would gladly have given up the whole thing," but he persevered, sustained by the reflection, which came at last, "that, after all, one has no right to despair because one has been deceived in one's expectations; one must revise them. If hysterics trace back their symptoms to fictitious traumas, this new fact signifies that they create such scenes in phantasy, and psychical reality requires to be taken into account alongside actual reality." This was one quality that made Freud into the great scientist he was: his willingness to permit reality to impose itself on him.

All of Freud's central discoveries were contained in his reflections of these months in 1897, if often in still rudimentary form: the powerful role of the sexual drive in man's psychic economy, infantile sexuality, the distorting work of memory and fantasy, the need for interpretation, and the existence within every human being of a large subterranean realm: the unconscious. Later that year, in the summer, Freud took another step that would serve to confirm his guesses and supply him with a technique at once of interpretation and of therapy: he began his self-analysis.

This courageous act has often been praised, and justly so. "It is hard for us nowadays to imagine how momentous this achievement was," Ernest Jones, Freud's one-time associate and later biographer, has written, "that difficulty being the fate of most pioneering exploits. Yet the uniqueness of the feat remains. Once done it is done forever. For no one again can be the first to explore these depths." It was the act of a conquistador, glorying in the absence of a map. Since this was the first psychoanalysis ever conducted, Freud had to develop his own techniques as he went along. The discoveries that other, earlier searchers into the self had made were interesting and important, but they had been fitful, occasional; they did not build on one another. Freud now worked systematically, exploring every avenue that opened before him, always on the scientific assumption that there are no accidents in mental life. He investigated his dreams, and traced his feelings to their source; indeed, the very obstacles in the way of self-understanding—the resistance, as he came to call it—became meaningful material open to study, to be incorporated in Freud's emerging portrait of the human mind.

Freud was taking great risks with his self-analysis: the erotic and hostile wishes he uncovered within himself were terrifying, and he could not know just what kind of person he might become as he delved into himself, deeper and deeper. But the results of three or four years of analysis were enormously gratifying and doubly so: Freud found it possible to arrive at psychological laws; to generalize, on the basis of his own discovered feelings—especially his jealousy of his father and desire for his mother, the celebrated Oedipus complex—and then, as a personal bonus, he discovered that his neurotic symptoms had gradually disappeared. Understanding of a very profound kind, it seemed, was the way to psychological health.

The first public result of Freud's self-analysis—though not the last, since he faithfully continued that analysis for the rest of his life—was *The Interpretation of Dreams.* It was this book, more than any of his others, that exhibited Freud's daring. He was, after all, a physician, and the notion he was here espousing, that dreams yield meanings, had been for ages the property of the uneducated and the semiliterate, of peasant women and servant girls who studied dream books to discover what kind of husband they might catch or children they might have. Freud, of course, had no such concerns. For him, dreams were part of mental life, of particular value because they gave a kind of privileged access to the unconscious. In sleep, resistance to one's most deeply hidden desires is relatively weak, and they will emerge, as dreams. But even in sleep, censorship is at work, distorting and recomposing these wishes into bizarre shapes. Hence interpretation becomes necessary.

The Interpretation of Dreams is a milestone on the long road to the science of man, but for years the world passed it by without a glance: it took a decade, after the scanty first printing of 600 copies had been sold out, before a second edition appeared. Freud continued his work undeterred, certain that he was on the right track, and sustained by his own theories which taught him *why* the world resisted his insights: they were unwelcome, psychologically easier to deny than to face. For about twenty years, Freud elaborated his central views with only minor amendments; he published case histories notable for their lucidity; he delivered and published introductory lectures on psychoanalysis, quite as lucid; he applied his theories to ordinary experiences, like forgetting, or slips of the tongue, in a relatively popular book, *The Psychopathology of Everyday Life;* and he summed up his ideas on infantile sexuality in *Three Essays on the Theory of Sexuality,* which appeared only to confirm the already widespread impression that Freud was a dirty man with a dirty mind. Who else could attribute lustful desires to innocent babies—and for their parents at that! Freud's denigrators did not realize that he had been anything but pleased by his discovery of infantile sexuality. He was, in this as in so much else, a man of his age; his scientific probity alone had compelled him to affirm and to publish what had at first repelled him.

While the official world of Austrian and German psychology continued to treat Freud with studied contempt and elaborate silence, Freud's sense of isolation gradually diminished, as he found supporters and disciples. A small society, devoted to the discussion of Freud's discoveries, was formed in Vienna; from abroad, enthusiastic admirers like C. G. Jung, Ernest Jones, Sandor Ferenczi, and others began to correspond with Freud, and then to work with him. In 1909 Freud made a memorable visit to the United States—which, despite receptive audiences, he cordially disliked. And the following year, after much preparation, an International Psychoanalytical Association finally came into being.

Inevitably with a discipline as new, as unusual, as close to speculation and sheer eccentricity as psychoanalysis, dissension soon emerged. Those who had occasion to know Freud well found him ready to discuss and happy to acknowledge the contribution of others, but he was, naturally enough, inflexible about his major theories, especially about infantile sexuality, which, it seemed, other psychologists found particularly obnoxious. The first of several important defectors was Alfred Adler, who developed a version of "depth" psychology that practically dispensed with the unconscious and substituted what he called "masculine protest"—aggressiveness—for infantile sexuality. The second, and in the long run more important, defector was the Swiss psychiatrist Jung, a brilliant, highly intuitive, but erratic theorist, for whom Freud had developed a strong affection and on whom he had pinned high hopes. Jung turned away from the scientific materialism of Freud toward mysticism and mythology, and formed an influential school of his own. His evolution—or so it seemed to Freud—was mainly designed to avoid the harsh truths on which Freud had insisted. "Anyone who promises to mankind liberation from the hardship of sex," he wrote to Jones, "will be hailed a hero, let him talk whatever nonsense he chooses." Reluctantly, Freud entered the battlefield of polemics: in 1914, free from false modesty, he published a "History of the Psychoanalytic Movement" in which he reiterated his claim to being the founder and most authoritative interpreter of psychoanalyis. The specter of rival sects, each claiming equal authority, distressed him, and he used all the resources of his vigorous style to exorcise it.

Despite these factional struggles, despite the hardships that World War I and its hungry aftermath imposed on Freud and his followers, Freud himself continued to construct and reconstruct his psychology. In the 1920's, when he was in his late sixties, he clarified his theories of anxiety and developed his topography of the mind—the id, ego, and superego—specifying their respective functions in man's mental geography. In addition, he wrote a series of brief but brilliant essays that applied his radical ideas to social psychology, prehistory, and social theory. These were explorations, frankly labeled, but securely grounded in Freud's theories; they offered psychoanalytical views of culture and of history. Perhaps the most wide-ranging of these explorations was *Civilization and Its Discontents* (1930), an essay in which clear-eyed pessimism struggled with a modest confidence in the future. For Freud civilization is an arena of inescapable conflict between the wishes of individuals and the requirements of society. Individuals want to gratify their desires—to act out their aggressions, satisfy their erotic urges, or achieve tranquillity. Since society must frustrate many of these desires for the sake of order, men in civilization must learn to postpone or to relinquish much of what they most want. Civilization compels men to conform to social norms by imposing on them both external restraints and the equally effective internal restraint, the conscience. Civilization means limitation, total freedom means barbarism, and the two are forever in conflict. It follows that civilization must make men unhappy and that civilization is always precarious, always threatened by the impulses it represses: "The price of progress in civilization is paid by forfeiting happiness through the heightening of the sense of guilt." Which would win in the end—love or death? Freud did not claim to know, but he was not without hope. "Men have brought their powers of subduing the forces of nature to such a pitch that by using them they could now very easily exterminate one another to the last man. They know this—hence arises a great part of their current unrest, their dejection, their mood of apprehension. And now it may be expected that the other of the two 'heavenly forces,' eternal Eros, will put forth his strength so as to maintain himself alongside of his equally immortal adversary." In the light of events that Freud witnessed in his last years—the rise of Fascism, the triumph of Nazism, the purges in the Soviet Union—his tentative optimism seemed, if anything, not tentative enough.

By the 1920's and even more the 1930's, Freud's ideas and, often, his vocabulary, had entered the mainstream of Western civilization. The number of patients undergoing psychoanalysis grew considerably, though it remained small, for the treatment—a single person meeting the analyst several times a week for years to recount his dreams and explore his free associations—was both expensive and by its very nature restricted to the few. But many influential and articulate persons—novelists, journalists, professors—subjected themselves to it and began to use its ideas in their own work. Gradually, too, psychoanalytical ideas invaded academic disciplines like sociology, anthropology, and political science, and gained measurable influence over educational theory, over art and literature. In addition, and much to the dismay of responsible psychoanalysts, the notions of analysis—repression, complexes, Oedipal feelings—lent themselves admirably to parlor games. While the profession of psychiatry, most philosophers, and much of the general public remained hostile, and while many continued to treat psychoanalysis as a fad, a fraud, or a new religion, the movement made distinct progress in the public consciousness. In some respects, perhaps, it suffered quite as much at the hands of its friends as at those of its enemies: rival schools carried on their debates in public, and the "revisionist Freudians," notably Erich Fromm and Karen Horney, greatly reduced the Freudian emphasis on infantile sexuality and the inevitable paradoxes of culture to stress social determinants of neuroses and seek a possible alliance with reformist or revolutionary social theories like Marxism. Worse than that, rash interpreters hastily applied notions borrowed from Freud to offer explanations of art or of historical personages— areas into which Freud and his most faithful followers had ventured only on occasion and with great caution—and even to construct a new philosophy. Freud himself strenuously denied that psychoanalysis was a *Weltanschauung:* it was, he insisted, part of the general scientific view of the world, nothing more. He considered it wholly incompatible with mysticism, with supernatural explanations of the world—with all authoritarian systems of explanation. Referring to science generally, he once wrote: "Science is no illusion. But it would be an illusion to suppose that we could get anywhere else what it cannot give us." This statement applies splendidly to psychoanalysis—the branch of science that Freud literally created.

The present state and probable future of psychoanalysis are hard to assess. Since Freud's death, his daughter Anna Freud, Heinz Hartmann, and such theorists as David Rapaport have developed and clarified, but only slightly modified, his theories. Without doubt, the Freudian revolution was one of the greatest upheavals that Western man has experienced. Freud dethroned reason for the sake of reason—he laid bare the subterranean powers of the passions so that men might understand and master them. While his teachings incidentally contributed to the sexual revolution that seems to have swept the West since World War I, his doctrine was never directed at the elimination of all repression, but at the reduction of crippling pressures on man. Necessary pressures were to be retained. "Where id was," he said, "there shall ego be." Whatever may become of individual ideas that Freud advanced, his general achievement will last as long as rational civilization.

For Further Reading

DARWIN

De Beer, Sir Gavin R., *Charles Darwin.*
Eiseley, Loren C., *Darwin's Century.*
Hofstadter, Richard, *Social Darwinism in American Thought, 1816–1915.*
Moorehead, Alan, *Darwin and the Beagle.*

FREUD

Costigan, Giovanni, *Sigmund Freud: A Short Biography.*
Jones, Ernest, *Sigmund Freud: Life and Work.*
Rieff, Philip, *Freud: The Mind of the Moralist.*
Sachs, Hanns, *Freud: Master and Friend.*

85   The Great Powers to the Verge of War

The Pax Britannica of mid-century was undoubtedly British but far from peaceful, either in Europe or outside it. Between the Paris Commune of 1871 and the Balkan Wars of 1912–1913, though fighting was endemic in the rest of the world, Europe experienced only one small war and two revolutions, all confined to its margin in the reactionary empires of Russia and Turkey. Yet no one talks of a Pax Germanica. Perhaps the very horror of the catastrophe of 1914, following a decade of mounting tension, makes us too ready to submerge earlier diplomatic crises and war scares in a

A.D.   1867 Second Reform Act in Great Britain

            1871 Proclamation of William I as Emperor of Germany; Russia denounces the Black Sea clauses of the the Treaty of Paris (1856)

  1871–1875 Gradual emergence of Third Republic in France

            1873 Onset of agricultural depression in western Europe

            1876 "Bulgarian atrocities" committed by Turks in suppressing a revolt

            1877 Russo-Turkish War begins

            1878 Treaty of San Stefano; Congress of Berlin

            1879 Alliance of Germany and Austria

            1881 Czar Alexander II assassinated

            1882 Germany, Austria, and Italy form Triple Alliance; British invade and occupy Egypt

            1884 Third Reform Act in Great Britain

  1884–1885 Berlin Conference (on Africa)

            1886 Introduction of First Home Rule Bill in British Parliament; its defeat followed by splitting of Liberal party

            1887 Reinsurance Treaty between Germany and Russia

            1888 Death of William I; accession of Frederick III; death of Frederick III; accession of William II

            1890 Bismarck dismissed

  1893–1894 Franco-Russian Alliance

            1898 Fashoda Crisis; first Germany Navy Law begins naval race with Great Britain

            1899 First Hague Peace Conference; Boer War between Great Britain and Transvaal begins

            1902 Anglo-Japanese Alliance; Treaty of Vereeniging ends Boer War

            1904 Anglo-French Entente concluded

  1904–1905 Russo-Japanese War

            1905 First Moroccan Crisis

  1905–1906 Russian Revolution

            1906 Algeciras Conference

            1907 Second Hague Peace Conference; conclusion of Anglo-Russian Entente

            1908 Austrian annexation of Bosnia and Herzegovina

CHRONOLOGY

---

vague impending sense of doom. But to do so is to lose perspective and to miss what may have been most important in the life of late nineteenth-century Europe. In those years more and more western Europeans came to know prosperity and security. Despite the intensification of nationalistic feelings and the competition implied by increasingly protectionist national economies, Europe built up a practical internationalism. The gold standard was universal. It was possible to travel from one end of Europe to the other without a passport. And the industrial diplomacy of the giant firms that came to dominate the national economies evolved a system of agreements—it is tempting to say treaties—as conducive to peace as any creation of the foreign offices. The Hague Conferences of 1899 and 1907 successfully codified the laws of war and gave birth to the idea of an international court. That they failed to secure the peaceful settlement of all international disputes should not reduce them to aberrations in a world bent on war: they grew out of an experience of peace unparalleled in the history of Europe and from a desire to prolong and improve it.

Contemporaries were not aware that the years around 1870 were the watershed that they have come to appear to historians. The balance of power was unshaken as the ruling concept of diplomacy. The League of the Three Emperors, descended from the old Holy Alliance of 1815, was dutifully resurrected and then re-resurrected, surviving almost to the end of the eighties. That nobler creation of 1815, the Concert of Europe, survived as well. Gladstone invoked it in 1871 to ratify Russia's unilateral denunciation of the neutralization of the Black Sea, imposed on her in the Treaty of

EUROPE IN 1914

European Allied countries in World War I
The Central Powers in World War I
Neutral countries

Paris of 1856. The powers met again in 1876 and 1878 to try to settle the Eastern Question; another conference in 1884 imposed rules on the partition of Africa; and a faint echo of the Concert could be heard as late as 1906 when the powers met at Algeciras to sort out the Moroccan imbroglio.

It took time to appreciate the international implications even of such obvious changes as the emergence of Italy and Germany as unified states or the crushing defeat of France, no longer the threat to peace she had been under the two Napoleons. In the years immediately after Sedan some right-wing French leaders dreamed of reconquering the lost provinces of Alsace and Lorraine, and in the eighties and nineties the French displayed more initiative than any other European nation in the colonial game. But that was by way of compensating for a formidable decline: Bismarck encouraged the French in Africa to keep them in good temper on the northeastern frontier. And whereas the French menace had been the cornerstone of Bismarck's defensive diplomacy in the seventies, by the eighties it was more likely to be pulled out to serve his tactical needs: when that insubstantial demagogue General Boulanger stirred French political waters in 1886–1889, Bismarck used the reminiscence of Bonapartism to secure the election of a complaisant Reichstag that would pass an army law he was finding it difficult to carry. But not everyone was so perceptive as the Chancellor.

If any Englishman saw the years around 1870 as a turning point, it was probably because Gladstone was pursuing a foreign policy whose stated grounds lay not only in a novel estimate of the national interest but in that high moral sense that so moved or outraged English voters, depending on their party. But in fact realistic assumptions governed most essentials of Gladstone's policy, and when Disraeli returned to office in 1874, even the old gestures were revived. Sending the fleet to Besika Bay in 1877 to overawe the Russians, or the special train made ready to carry Disraeli away when the Congress of Berlin, the next year, showed signs of going against his wishes, were both splendid instances of Palmerstonian bravado. Again, change can be discerned in the eighties. Under Lord Salisbury after 1886, British foreign policy became a technically brilliant rear-guard action, and Salisbury is said to have been delighted with the Chinese ambassador who addressed him as the representative of one declining empire to another. In the nineties, Britain's old self-imposed isolation was reinforced by the determined hostility of the whole Continent; by the time of the Boer War, the dimmest minister could not be unaware of that. In the same decade the British public developed the alarming conviction that the country was being flooded with German goods—the high level of imports natural to a prosperous country had just been made evident by an indirectly protectionist measure requiring that imported goods be labeled with country of origin. In another ten years, the armaments race had made it clear to everyone that the real threat lay in Berlin.

Immediate sweeping changes were to be found about 1870 in internal, not foreign, policies. All the west European powers had to cope, for example, with pressing problems of industrial change. Here France fared least well. She was short of coal in any event, and losing Alsace and Lorraine deprived her of rich deposits of iron ore that could at last be exploited thanks to the discovery of a process for neutralizing the phosphorus they contained. French industrial output increased little, despite some brilliant inventions. Even more alarming, the country that had once been the most populous in Europe remained virtually stationary in population; its birth rate remained stubbornly low. In Britain the industrial situation was ambiguous, combining notable progress in some sectors of the economy with a sharp relative decline in world position and profitability among the basic manufactures of the Industrial Revolution; notwithstanding a fairly steady, if modest, rise in output and a marked rise in well-being among the working classes, men talked of a "great depression." Industrial Germany, on the other hand, moved ahead in great leaps, a performance owing much to a superb ability to turn science to productive ends.

All three nations, moreover, faced an agricultural crisis. Railways, steamships, and refrigeration made it possible for the vast new productive areas in Russia, North America, and Australia to sell grain and meat in the European market for lower prices than those needed to sustain the high-cost agriculture of western Europe. French farmers had to bear the added burden of the phylloxera, a disease that came near to destroying France's wine industry in the 1870's. Both Germany and France responded with tariff protection; smaller nations like Denmark even improved their position by specialization. But Britain, tied emotionally and institutionally to the free trade so advantageous to her in mid-century, could not accept protection. So, though some sectors of British agriculture (dairying and market gardening among them) prospered, the fall of wheat and meat prices speeded the breakup of rural society and undermined the economic foundations of the landed oligarchy, which at about the same time had to face the first fundamental political challenge to the continuance of its old supremacy.

The Western nations had, similarly, to absorb major constitutional changes. In default of a viable monarchical alternative, the French had backed into the Third Republic in the mid-seventies, an outcome to which the French right, firmly entrenched among the peasantry as well as in key national institutions like the Church and the army, was never reconciled. Politically, a multiplicity of parties made parliamentary government highly uncertain; policy appeared to be in a state of constant flux. But these tendencies to instability were counteracted by the strength of a centralized bureaucratic administration, and the dominance of cabinet making by various shades of radicals meant that politics oscillated, not violently from left to right and back, but less dramatically about the center. In the end policy changes were not so much matters of irreconcilable principles as of emphasis and personal style. This stability was reinforced by a strengthening of the republican spirit. The crucial question was education, for eradicating the power of the Church there would eliminate a major citadel of right-wing influence. The so-called laic laws of 1882 were aimed at securing a secular system of primary and secondary education; the late eighties and nineties even saw a "Ralliement," an attempt (encouraged by the new liberally inclined Pope Leo XIII) to bring the Church to support the Republic and to heal the breach in French opinion. Then, at the end of the nineties, the country was again split apart by the Dreyfus case: a Jewish bourgeois army officer had been convicted on trumped-up charges of espionage; defended by the left and execrated by the right, Dreyfus became the touchstone of political loyalty—and of nearly everything else—for a generation. There was a resurgence of the old republican anticlericalism. In 1904 religious orders were forbidden to teach, and secular education became obligatory; in the following year a new concordat with the Vatican brought about the definitive separation of church and state.

A similar pattern was to be found in Italy. The temporal power of the papacy was destroyed when Rome was at last occupied in 1870, at the very time that the pope's infallibility in questions of faith and morals was being proclaimed by the first Vatican Council. The papacy's steadfast refusal to exchange recognition of the new Italian state for recognition of its own privileged status within the Vatican worsened social divisions. The flux of parties, owing less to ideas and more to men, was far more unsettling than its analogue in France, while administrative centralization was prevented from attaining the French level of success by a stubborn regionalism, reinforced by the economic backwardness of much of the country. Least successful of the Western nations in solving her constitutional problems, Italy remained of little account in European affairs.

In Germany, Bismarck also faced—or created—a struggle with the Roman Catholic Church. The Liberals, with whom he was in uneasy alliance in the seventies, called it the Kulturkampf. But Bismarck was not motivated by Liberal ideology. Rather he was fighting the intrusion into politics of the Center party, a specifically Catholic party with sympathetic ties to Catholics in Austria, Poland, and France. But the Kulturkampf was less important as a weapon against encirclement than as a phase of Bismarck's war on his political enemies: as the Center party had succeeded the Liberals, whom he had pursued so implacably in the 1860's, so it was in turn succeeded by the Social Democrats; in 1877 Bismarck abandoned the Kulturkampf, leaving the Center party strengthened and political Catholicism as a political fact that has survived in German life to the present day. This political jousting suggests that Bismarck's basic problem was not the preservation of a constitution, as in France, but the preservation of his own power: the complicated federal structure on which his power rested was useful as long as it worked. But for all its success in neutralizing his enemies and competitors at home and abroad, Bismarck's system contained a fatal flaw: responsible only to the emperor, he could be dismissed by the emperor. It happened when Bismarck's willing if sometimes restive accomplice William I was succeeded in 1888—leaving out of account the three-month reign of Frederick III—by the young William II, who was determined to assert himself, and forced Bismarck to resign in 1890. The highly artificial machine could not be worked so well by the lesser men who were heirs to Bismarck's power.

The English constitution easily absorbed a succession of fundamental alterations—the enfranchisement of urban workingmen in 1867, the secret ballot in 1872, nearly universal male suffrage in 1884, and a drastic re-working of parliamentary representation the next year. The civil service was effectively reformed, and Parliament was brought under tighter execu-tive control, made necessary by the imperatives of increased legislation and consistent, programmatic appeals to the electorate. But Britain came close to political paralysis over Ireland. A short-lived ration of autonomy given to that agrarian, Catholic nation in the late eighteenth century had been extinguished by the Act of Union of 1800. Once Daniel O'Connell had won the battle for "Catholic Emancipation"—the right of Catholics to sit in Parliament and to hold office—in 1829, he began to agitate for repeal of the Union. The apathy that followed the terrible famine of 1845–1846—which killed nearly a million and drove another million abroad—led some Englishmen in the 1850's to think that the Irish problem had been solved by a cruel providence. But the famine lent a new dimension to Irish bitter-ness, and in the sixties and seventies the old land agitation was revived and a new drive to independence was launched by the Fenians, both move-ments secret and violent. The moderate answer to this extremism was Home Rule—not separation but autonomy in internal matters—fought for in Parliament in the eighties by an Irish party, superbly disciplined and led by Charles Stewart Parnell. It had proved hard enough for English opinion to accept the land reforms carried by Gladstone to provide some security for the hard-pressed Irish tenants; to accept even a partial severing of the political tie was unthinkable. Indeed when the Conservatives at the end of the century turned to a different kind of land reform and by subsidized land purchase created an Irish peasant economy entirely unlike the capitalist agriculture of England, their avowed intention was "to kill Home Rule by kindness." Gladstone's attempt to carry Home Rule in 1886 split the Liberal party, a second attempt failed in the Lords in 1893, and the third, successful attempt in 1914 was carried by the Liberals only after the powers of the House of Lords had been reduced and at the risk of civil war between the Catholics and the Protestant minority in the northern Irish province of Ulster, fully backed by much of English Conservatism.

Finally, the western European nations had increasingly to reckon with the growth of public opinion. Statesmen had once been able to act without constantly looking over their shoulders, except to the known or usually predictable pressures of a king, a court, or a small aristocratic class. The French Revolution, emerging working-class movements, and liberal nation-alism had helped to break up this old dispensation; after 1870, with the spread of education and literacy, the multiplication of newspapers, and the new complexity of social and economic life, all was in confusion. Even an authoritarian ruler like Bismarck was not untouched by the problem of public opinion, as he showed in his efforts to neutralize Pan-Germanism or in his reluctant concessions to the new German taste for colonies. In Great Britain, public opinion plunged from one emotional orgy to another—now protesting the massacre of Bulgarians by Turks, now cheering the heroic stand of the same Turks against the Russians, crying for vengeance for General Gordon's death at Khartoum, or rioting in rather ugly joy over the relief of Mafeking during the South African War. Great Britain was not unique, only advanced. In time, this uncertain force would be better understood and controlled, even used by demagogues with technical resources far beyond those of their pale ancestors. In the years between Sedan and Sarajevo, public opinion lends a fitful appearance to the age.

Below this troubled surface there were, of course, important basic shifts in attitude, among them a growth of racial thinking and of anti-Semitism in particular, a tendency to regard irrationalism and violence as norms, a flight from politics. For the most broadly symptomatic of these changes, one would probably turn to the gradual eclipse of mid-century liberalism by a resurgent conservatism on the one hand and an emergent socialism on the other. It was encapsulated in the confrontation of the Bismarckian state and German social democracy, both so alien to the liberalism of 1848; with the growth of syndicalist doctrines, it added a new dimension to the endemic split in French society. In Great Britain, the home of classical liberalism, the middle classes, their major ambitions gained, retreated from their old radicalism to the Conservatives; the Liberal party, though out of power for most of the twenty years after 1886, was to some extent freed by this desertion to become more radical, but after the brilliant Indian summer of social reforms enacted between 1906 and 1911, it fell victim to the war and to the very English socialism of the Labour party after 1918. In every country in western Europe to some degree, this polarization seemed to threaten dissolution in the years just before 1914, and men on both sides thought that when war came socialism might cut across national lines and lead soldiers to lay down their arms rather than fight in a capitalist war. But the mercurial nature of public opinion asserted itself again, and nationalism triumphed after all.

However greedy their colonial ambitions or intricate their diplomacy, the Western powers were committed to peace. England was isolated, France too weak to fight, and Germany "satiated." Beyond that, as beneficiaries of industrialism and the machinery of the nation-state, they stood to lose most from war. Ironically, the initiative lay with three powers surviving from an older imperial, preindustrial world. One of those powers, Turkey, an empire in name only, had long been transmuted into the "Eastern Question": what would happen to his holdings when "the Sick Man of Europe" died at last? In Austria-Hungary, tension between the

German and Magyar parts of the Dual Monarchy was compounded by the bitter quarrel of each of them with important minorities, Czechs or Croats. But while Austria-Hungary was making the transition from empire to question, she, like Turkey, was propped up because the Western powers knew of nothing better to take her place. Only the Russian autocracy showed signs of moving into the modern industrial world, with the help of massive infusions of Western capital, more and more of it French. Yet after the assassination of Czar Alexander II in 1881, the autocracy grew worse under his incompetent successors and their reactionary advisers. Russia's rulers could not be unaware of the movement of public opinion. But they would yield nothing to the desire for reform growing among the increasingly frustrated intelligentsia or to the idiosyncratic Russian socialism; they learned little even from their resounding defeat by Japan in 1904 or the abortive revolution of 1905. They responded only to old traditions like anti-Semitism or to the newer, though uneven, enthusiasm for Pan-Slavism. Russia did not make the transition from empire to question: war and revolution destroyed her.

These three empires ringed the Balkans. There Turkey was in retreat: her European provinces had broken away or were doing so by reproducing Western nationalism. Only occasionally would she try, violently, to reassert her suzerainty. In the Balkans Austria-Hungary could find an outlet for her commerce and capital. A forward movement, moreover, might bring her compensation for her loss of German leadership at Sadowa and prevent the formation of a large southern Slav state, a particularly threatening prospect, given Austro-Hungarian troubles with Slav minorities at home. In the Balkans Russia had two steady concerns—to erect a barrier against Austrian aggression and to assure that the Straits at Constantinople, commanding entry to the Black Sea, remained in control of a power that, if not friendly, was at least weak. But when she was seized with Pan-Slavic enthusiasm, Russia could go further and assume her old role as patron of her fellow Slavs and of the Orthodox Church. If the Balkans were, as the old saw has it, the powder keg of Europe, the danger of explosion lay not so much in the conscious, criminal wielding of a firebrand as in the flickers of spontaneous combustion arising from decay.

Rebellions in the Turkish provinces in 1875 provoked terrible massacres in Bulgaria. A European conference called in 1876 to impose reforms on Turkey got nowhere, and the following year Russia declared war. Turkish power proved far more resilient, and Russian armies far less efficient than expected; still, having staggered through to a victory of sorts by 1878, Russia demanded the creation of a "Big Bulgaria"—partly to bolster her sagging prestige, partly to provide a viable alternative to Turkish misrule—that she had agreed not to support the year before. Russian ministers were divided about the Pan-Slav implications of the Treaty of San Stefano; this provided an opportunity for Disraeli to reassert his pro-Turkish policy, now that Gladstone's anti-Turkish campaign had been momentarily neutralized by the Turks' heroic stand at Plevna. The main result of the ensuing Congress of Berlin was the partition of Big Bulgaria: one part, called Macedonia, was returned to Turkish misrule and more atrocities in the nineties; the remainder was broken into Bulgaria proper and Eastern Rumelia, though the two were reunited without serious protest seven years later. The British initiative, taken so dramatically at Berlin, was not maintained. In 1879, Gladstone's novel "Midlothian Campaign"— a minister had never before carried his case to the country—once more roused British voters against Disraeli's forward policy; but Gladstone's own government after 1880 was so divided that no clear line could come from the Liberals, and thus the way was opened for Salisbury's greater realism after 1886.

The nation that emerged from Berlin with its prestige most enhanced was Germany, although Bismarck had gained nothing but a reputation as an "honest broker." In 1879, to provide a firmer basis for the security he had gained opportunistically, Bismarck launched the first of the alliances that were to be the forms determining official and popular thinking about European alignments for a whole generation. His explicit alliance with Austria-Hungary was mildly reinforced in 1882 by the addition of Italy to create the Triple Alliance: Italy got some badly needed prestige, and there was a not very impressive exchange of promises of Italian neutrality in case of an Austro-Russian war and of German help for Italy in a French war. But Bismarck had no intention of alienating Russia, though the Alliance was clearly directed eastward. In 1881 he secretly revived the League of the Three Emperors, and when it expired in 1887 concluded a bilateral "Reinsurance Treaty" with Russia. When Bismarck fell in 1890, his successors at once refused to renew the unpopular Russian agreement; only then did Austria's strong confidence in German support begin to have some foundation in fact.

Bismarck's system for German security gained not only from his own skill but from the rupture of whatever tacit understanding existed between Britain and France when Britain unilaterally occupied Egypt in 1882. Bismarck neatly capped this estrangement by covertly encouraging the French to pursue an active colonial policy. With his own reluctant colonial enterprises, he thus helped to force Britain into the un-Palmerstonian necessity of adding more and more responsibilities to secure her traditional goals, protecting the route to India and isolating the Boer Republics in South Africa. But the occupation of Egypt had two further consequences for Europe. As the French could not allow themselves to be isolated, they edged, with whatever degree of republican discomfort, into an alliance with Russia, concluded in 1892–1894 and firmly sustained by rapidly growing French investment; the Triple Alliance was thus confronted with the beginnings of an opposing bloc. And now that Britain was firmly entrenched in Egypt, her superintendence of the Eastern Mediterranean could be conducted from there (and from Cyprus, which she occupied in 1877). The old need to prop up Turkey fell away, leaving Turkey open to German penetration.

Although in the 1890's the western European powers were primarily concerned with Africa and the Far East, the decade was a watershed in European diplomacy. Bismarck's fall in 1890 gave the working of German foreign policy to men without his percipience or skill. The British, to escape their isolation, began to look less than ever across the Channel and more across the ocean—to the growing Commonwealth of her self-governing colonies; to Japan, with whom she concluded an alliance in 1902; and, of most importance in the long run, to the United States, with whom a tacit alliance began to emerge as the two countries settled the last of the disputes that had kept them at loggerheads throughout the nineteenth century. Britain remained a European power, of course, but her new relationships with France and Russia, worked out from 1904 to 1907, were approached gingerly by settling outstanding conflicts (for example, delimiting Russian and British spheres of influence in Persia) and by military conversations. There was thus the risk that the Triple Entente, based on largely secret, certainly informal understandings, was likely to be seen as weaker than in fact it was.

Yet another element transforming European diplomacy was military. The wars of mid-century and the stunning German example brought home to Europe's statesmen the possibilities of modern warfare. Except in England, European nations relied increasingly on universal military service to provide manpower for their armies. This widening of the military net was paralleled by a growing professionalization among officers, particularly in the high commands, where the crucial invention was the general staff of the Germans; copied elsewhere (the British again resisting until the new century), it made possible long-range planning for mobilization and strategy against all eventualities. Supported in writings of military and naval theorists and by the work of publicists and historians caught up in the new enthusiasm, the professional soldiers became a powerful pressure group, far more regularly influential in government than military men had usually been before. Basic to this new military thinking was a revolutionary technology resting on rapid scientific development (in chemistry in particular) and on the growth of the heavy industry required to produce armaments and that in turn required them for its own perpetuation and profitability.

Although there was steady improvement in small arms and artillery, and although European armies broke through to new ideas in training, military engineering, and logistics (especially in the use of railways), the most striking technological changes affected the world's navies. The mine, the torpedo, and the submarine were all developed in these years and were to become major weapons in the future. But between 1890 and 1914 men's imaginations were captured far more fully by warships. The old wooden ships of the line, little changed for centuries, had given way in mid-century to ironclads; now there appeared a whole range of specialized ships—destroyers, cruisers, and battleships—protected by steel armorplate, propelled by triple-expansion steam engines and later by steam turbines, and equipped with fire power unimaginable a generation before. In 1898 William II and his chief naval adviser, Admiral Alfred von Tirpitz, launched, against considerable domestic resistance, a naval building program designed to bring the German navy into approximate equality with the British, who replied in turn. Reformed and expanded armies, the naval race, and the novel problem of an unceasing technological obsolescence sharply distorted traditional government policies, not only in strategic and diplomatic planning, but in finance. The need to meet vast expenditures, added to the demands of increasing social services, dictated levels of taxation unthinkable in the nineteenth century. That barrier broken, the resources of the modern leviathan state were there for the asking.

From about 1905 tension rose steadily in Europe, partly a result of the arms race, partly a consequence of an increasingly frenetic insistence by Germany on her claims as a world power. Once in 1905 and again in 1911, the Germans asserted their "rights" in the somewhat surprising locale of Morocco, a French sphere of influence under the terms of the Anglo-French entente; the earlier confrontation raised the prospect of Franco-German hostilities for the first time in thirty years, and the threat of war in the second was taken most seriously in Great Britain. But it was in the Balkans that the fuse was laid. In 1907, a revolution took place in Turkey, though the Young Turks proved immediately that they could do little more to solve Turkish problems than the deposed sultan. The revolution gave Austria-Hungary the chance formally to annex Bosnia and Herzegovina, which she had occupied since the Congress of Berlin as a hedge against the expected expansion of Serbia into the possibility of a southern Slav state that so troubled imaginations in Vienna. In 1912, when Turkey was further embroiled in a war with Italy over Italian designs on Libya, the Balkan states of Serbia, Greece, Bulgaria, and Montenegro united against Turkey, in the end limiting her to a tiny European foothold about Constantinople. But the victorious allies fell out, and in 1913, following a Bulgarian attack, Serbia and Greece were joined by Rumania to defeat Bulgaria and to make territorial gains for themselves.

The two Balkan wars provide a new context for the competing ambitions of Russia and Austria-Hungary, the latter perhaps especially dangerous from the blow to her prestige by the victories of the Balkan states. Bismarck had often said that the Balkans were not worth the bones of a single Pomeranian grenadier; now his successors, mesmerized for years by the prospects of a Berlin-to-Baghdad railway, found them well worth the living presence of Liman von Sanders, a general at the head of a military mission to Turkey, which was rapidly becoming a German protectorate. The Russians had been content to have the Straits controlled by a weak sultan; they could not be indifferent to their domination by Germany. Moreover, the Russians were forced into supporting Serbia in order to maintain a neutral buffer against any possible Austrian expansion. For their part, the Austrians continued their harassment of the Serbs. Not content with their Bosnian coup of 1908, in 1913, they conjured up an independent Albania to block Serbia's outlet to the Adriatic. The pretext they wanted for still further action arose on June 28, 1914, when the Archduke Francis Ferdinand, heir to the Austro-Hungarian throne, was assassinated at Sarajevo by a member of a secret society of Serbian nationalists.

Austria-Hungary at once consulted her principal ally. Germany, apparently willing to satisfy Austrian ambition and to see the Serbian problem solved by running the risk that the war could be contained, gave her ally a free hand. Although Serbia's reply to the Austrian ultimatum was an almost complete surrender, the Austrians deemed it insufficient. Their declaration of war on Serbia forced the Russians to reply, in an attempt to force Austria to back down, with a partial mobilization, made general on July 30. This triggered German mobilization the next day. Then, having failed to get guarantees of neutrality from Russia's ally France, Germany declared war on her on August 3. Germany's long-established western strategy committed her to strike at France through Belgium; her refusal to respect that neutrality, demanded in a British ultimatum, brought Britain into the war on August 4. Only Italy, whose ties to the Central Powers had progressively weakened, kept neutral, to enter the war (well rewarded) on the side of Britain and France in 1915. Since 1879 the developing alliance system had worked to keep the peace. Now, with that one exception, it continued to work perfectly. Once the switches were pulled in Vienna and Berlin, mobilizations followed in sequence, like an expertly engineered set of electrical relays, and the lights went out all over Europe.

For Further Reading

Albertini, Luigi, *The Origins of the War of 1914.*
Brogan, D. W., *France under the Republic (1870–1939).*

Ensor, R. C. K., *England, 1870–1914*.

Fischer, Fritz, *Germany's Aims in World War I*.

Lafore, Laurence, *The Long Fuse: An Interpretation of the Origins of World War I*.

Langer, William L., *The Diplomacy of Imperialism*.

Taylor, A. J. P., *Bismarck: The Man and Statesman*.

——, *The Struggle for Mastery in Europe, 1848–1918*.

The Great World War: 1914-1945

86 World War I

With what innocence, with what enthusiasm, did the Europeans of 1914 respond to the tocsin! No one foresaw even the contours of the disaster ahead, and most people welcomed the war as a great patriotic adventure. After a decade of worsening crises and a spiraling arms race, they had come to expect a final showdown, but after decades of peace, they had forgotten what war was like and few had an inkling that a modern war would multiply the terrors of earlier conflicts. Europeans marched off to battle with something close to exultation, proud in their patriotism and certain of their cause, confident of a victorious end in a short time. It was the last time in our civilization that war could be greeted in this fashion.

Patriotic exultation had been preceded by the solicitous efforts of all governments to save the appearances of peacefulness, to make it seem as if the enemy were also the unprovoked aggressor. None had pursued this policy of deception with more cunning or under greater difficulties than the German government, and nowhere was the appearance of fighting a defensive war more important than in Germany, where the Social Democratic party, with its avowed pacifism, represented a third of the electorate. Indeed, international socialism, pledged to oppose all imperialist wars, became the first victim of the war. Its most attractive leader, the French Socialist Jean Jaurès, was assassinated at the end of July, and socialists everywhere felt their national allegiance far more strongly than their commitment to international class solidarity. Socialist backing of the war made possible that instantaneous closing of national ranks—epitomized by the formation in France of the *union sacré*—that promised the adjournment of political conflicts for the duration of the war. In the passion of the moment, all parties and all classes pledged their full support to the nation, in what everybody expected would be a short, decisive test.

At the beginning of the war, the sides were fairly evenly balanced. In a

CHRONOLOGY

A.D. 1914   German declaration of war on Russia; German declaration of war on France; British declaration of war on Germany; Battle of the Marne

1915   *Lusitania* sunk by German submarine, 139 Americans lost; Italy enters war on Allied side; Dardanelles operation

1916   British Parliament passes conscription; Battle of Verdun; Hindenburg appointed chief of staff with Ludendorff as quartermaster general; Lloyd George becomes prime minister of Great Britain

1917   Germany notifies U.S. that unrestricted submarine warfare will begin the next day; provisional Russian government established under Prince Lvov; Nicholas II abdicates; U.S. declares war on Germany; mutinies in French army; beginning of ill-fated Brusilov offensive; German Chancellor Bethmann Hollweg forced to resign and succeeded by Dr. Michaelis; real power in hands of Hindenburg and Ludendorff; beginning of Italian disaster at Caporetto; Bolshevik Revolution; Clemenceau becomes prime minister in France; Bolshevik Russia concludes armistice with Central Powers

1918   Russia signs Brest Litovsk Treaty, ceding Poland, Lithuania, Ukraine, etc.; Germans begin great spring offensive in the west; Foch named commander in chief of Allied forces in France; first major, successful American engagement at Château-Thierry; Second Battle of the Marne; successful Allied counteroffensive in the west; Bulgaria receives armistice; new German government of Prince Max von Baden asks President Wilson for armistice based on Fourteen Points; armistice with Turkey; Allies sign armistice with Austria-Hungary; Germany accepts armistice and hostilities cease everywhere

short war, the Central Powers, with the German army as the backbone of their strength, would enjoy certain advantages. They were poised for action, and their interior lines of communication allowed for the quick transport of troops and equipment. The Allies held potential advantages in a long war: the vast manpower of Russia and the great naval superiority of England that guaranteed free access to foreign, especially American, supplies. In such intangible matters as leadership and morale, the great contestants—Germany, France, and England—were evenly matched, at least at the beginning.

German strategists had long hatched meticulous plans for a lightning war and for nothing else. In August, they set them in motion. By attacking France through Belgium, they expected to capture Paris from the west and to break French resistance in a matter of weeks. The Russian front, meanwhile, was to remain virtually undefended, until, after France's defeat, the bulk of the German army could be sent eastward, to crush the czarist armies. For four weeks, the German advance proceeded like clockwork, as Belgian defenses crumbled and French armies retreated.

In early September, German troops were within sight of Paris; the Germans, however, had weakened their right flank. They had changed their minds about Russia, and sent troops to the eastern front, while the French rallied for the defense of their capital. With magnificent, if costly, gallantry, they counterattacked, and the miracle of the Marne, as it came to be called, threw German troops back and ended the threat to Paris. Fighting then shifted to the northwest, with each side aiming to outflank the other; the Germans also hoped in the process to capture the channel ports, thus depriving the British army of its vital supply routes. The British bore the brunt of this savage "race to the sea," and denied the Germans this strategic prize as well.

Even after the Marne, the German people could comfort themselves; on the eastern front, they had won gigantic victories, notably at Tannenberg, victories they wrongly credited to the genius of Hindenburg, and which had weakened, but not destroyed, the Russian army. Everywhere German troops stood triumphant on enemy soil. But the decisive victory had eluded them, and would elude them forever. Six weeks after the outbreak of the war, most German leaders realized that their chances for winning a clear-cut victory had virtually vanished. The Allies, injured but intact and resolute, faced a Germany that had won enough in those early weeks to reject a peace that did not bring them large gains but not enough to impose its own terms on a world of enemies. The tragedy was that neither side could win.

The losses in those early weeks of fighting had been monstrous, especially to the British and French, whose casualties then and for the rest of the war consistently outran those of the Germans. The young elite of each army had been decimated, and the great blood bath which was to destroy so many talented Europeans had begun in earnest. The cost of a long war should have been clear to all, but war enhances man's capacity for self-delusion.

By the end of 1914, the western front had become stabilized, and the vast armies stretching from the Channel to the Alps dug themselves in, built trenches behind barbed wire, with a narrow gap between lines, known as no man's land. In trenches that were wet and crawling with rats, millions of soldiers huddled together, battling alternately monotony and death. Never before had so many soldiers faced each other in such futility, terrorized by the all-powerful machine gun which made every offensive action, every patrol, a death trap.

There were apparently no alternatives, no ways of escaping this bloody stalemate. Yet strategists devised many ingenious ideas and clever projects. The Germans, for example, sought to attack their enemies from behind, by fomenting revolution in the Near East or India or even Ireland. New weapons were invented; the Germans introduced zeppelins for bombing raids and poison gas for land attacks, forgetting that prevailing westerly winds would vitiate all but initial successes. Lloyd George championed armored vehicles, later known as tanks, and pushed their construction, despite Kitchener's sneer: "A pretty mechanical toy; the war will never be won by such machines." How was it to be won?

Two traditional means remained to be tried: the winning of new allies and the opening of new fronts. Diplomats on both sides worked on remaining neutrals. In September, 1914, Turkey joined Germany and Austria, not unexpectedly, thus blocking Allied access to Russian ports in the Black Sea. A few months later, the Allies persuaded—or bribed—Italy to enter on their side, in violation of her treaty obligations but in pursuit of her *"sacro egoismo,"* her immense annexationist appetite. The greatest neutral, the United States, admonished by its President to remain neutral in thought as well as deed, became an ever more important supplier of food, weapons, and credit to France and Britain, who controlled the sea. Germany's efforts to use her few submarines to cut off English supplies proved risky because, as the sinking of the *Lusitania* in 1915 showed, effective submarine action entailed the loss of neutral lives and evoked the threat of American retaliation. The English blockade of Germany also violated neutral rights—and humanitarian scruples—but took no American lives and hence aroused less opposition. Still, the submarine proved an enticing new weapon to the Germans, and her military leaders ceaselessly urged its unrestricted use.

There were some leaders in England, notably Winston Churchill, who

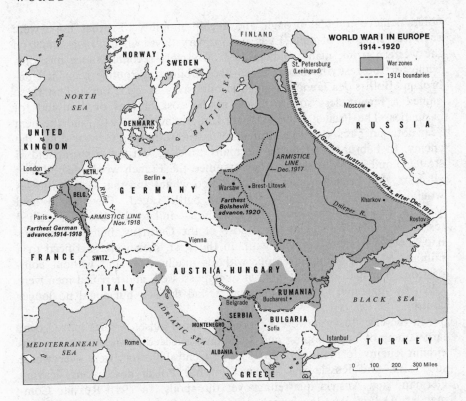

agitated for the opening of a new front that would break the western stalemate. After months of wrangling, an expedition for the capture of the Dardanelles Straits was launched; if it had been successful, it would have separated Turkey from the Central Powers and provided much-needed help for Russia. But staggering incompetence ruined the enterprise, and very nearly eclipsed Churchill's fortunes. Years later, he still viewed it as the decisive turn to disaster: "Thereafter events passed very largely outside the scope of conscious choice. Governments and individuals conformed to the rhythm of the tragedy, and swayed and staggered forward in helpless violence, slaughtering and squandering on ever-increasing scales, till injuries were wrought to the structure of human society which a century will not efface, and which may conceivably prove fatal to the present civilization."

The main reason for the failure of Gallipoli had been the unwillingness of Anglo-French military leaders to do anything that might weaken the western front. They—and their German opponents—were mesmerized by that front, certain that the next time around, "with one more push," they could achieve a breakthrough and regain mobility. To that hope were sacrificed millions of men. Even on ordinary days, when all was quiet on the western front, many soldiers died on useless reconnaissance missions, while for the rest, the monotonous and debilitating routine remained unbroken. Both sides launched gigantic offensives as well, but at best these gained a few useless square miles, at the cost of tens of thousands of casualties. The French launched such futile attacks in 1915, and the next year both sides resorted to a strategy of attrition, hoping to wear down the enemy. In February, 1916, the Germans attacked Verdun, a stronghold of strategic and symbolic value. They assumed the French would defend it at all costs, that French armies would be bled white, and that German losses would be lower. For four months the battle raged. The French held Verdun, at an immense price to themselves—and to the Germans. Allied losses were always heavier than those of the Germans, but the Germans had another front to contend with. In the west, men were sacrificed to a military Moloch without reason, without intelligence, and without compassion. War had lost what glory it once possessed, and terrified men were killed by machinery that human reason had devised but could no longer control.

In the east, the war wore a more traditional guise. Armies moved over large tracts of land, hoping and sometimes succeeding in trapping or encircling enemy formations. In 1915, the Central Powers were everywhere successful, and Russia was deprived of her Polish possessions, leaving Germany and Austria quarreling over the spoils. In 1916 Russian Commander Aleksei Brusilov launched a counteroffensive which attested and strained Russian resiliency and by its failure hastened the final collapse of czardom. The eastern front never acquired the horrid glamour of the western front; the territory was unfamiliar and the fighting less gruesomely novel. But it determined the shape of things to come for more than half a century; the Russian revolutions would have been unthinkable without the prior breakdown of Russian life owing to the war.

In fact, the war imposed a tremendous burden on all belligerent societies, and the universal response to this new burden was a degree of social regimentation undreamed of in earlier decades and centuries. The anticipated short war had become protracted and total—the first war in history that deserved the epithet. Since there was no precedent, there was no master plan of regimentation—only step-by-step innovation and improvisation in order to mobilize, clothe, feed, and equip millions of combatants, to maintain production when manpower was short and raw materials scant, to feed the civilian population and keep up their morale. Problems were innumerable, and bewildering in their intricacy and unexpected interrelatedness. In the early months of the war, the British carried on under the motto "Business as usual," while the German High Command was stunned when a great industrialist, Walther Rathenau, asked what provisions had been made for the stockpiling of raw material. War as usual, war as it had been taught at Sandhurst or St. Cyr or the Kadettenschule, was dead. The Great War, to paraphrase Georges Clemenceau, France's fiery premier, was too complicated to be left to the soldiers.

Under the duress of war, the modern Leviathan was born. The State— so exquisitely circumscribed by decades of liberal theory and practice— suddenly assumed new powers over realms hitherto deemed immune from its control. The State as night watchman, as the English myth had it, now became the mobilizer of men and property, the commander of economic life, the censor of men's expressions, and the manipulator of men's minds. All this took place while traditional politics were adjourned, and while dissent was often denounced as unpatriotic, so that governments could assume these new powers with a minimum of struggle or opposition. Indeed, as governments began not only to conscript their male citizenry— this was novel only in England, where conscription was adopted in 1916—but to impose rationing, to control prices, to allocate labor and resources, their own powers over against parliament greatly increased. War socialism, as the Germans called the new statist regimentation, went hand in hand with war dictatorships, and even in democratic countries like England and France, parliaments lost much power. Lloyd George entered office in December, 1916, and Clemenceau in November, 1917; in July, 1917, the seemingly moderate German chancellor, Bethmann Hollweg, had to surrender power to a thinly disguised military dictatorship under Ludendorff and Hindenburg. In Russia, on the other hand, where autocracy had been the rule of centuries, the government's gross inefficiency stimulated demands for some measure of parliamentary control. In all countries, however, the freedom of individuals contracted. This was assumed to be temporary, but the prewar balance between individual liberty and public authority would never be restored.

Civilians everywhere sacrificed comforts and suffered deprivations; soldiers suffered incomparably more, but at least the common terror at the front bred a kind of camaraderie that sustained their spirits. Soldiers and civilians alike lived under the shadow of sudden death, lived with the fear that their lives or the lives of those close to them might suddenly be snuffed out in one of those futile battles in what gradually appeared to be an endless war. By winter, 1916, the enthusiasm of August, 1914, had long since turned into a grim, sullen mood, relieved by bursts of mordant cynicism.

Governments did their best to whip up ever fresh enthusiasm for the killing, and in the process received ample help from the established classes.

The chauvinistic cant that poured from press and pulpit was meant to rouse flagging spirits to new sacrifices. The techniques of propaganda, borrowed from prewar modes of advertising, became so important in the hands of governments that one English wit spoke of "propagandocracy" as the new type of rule. Wartime propaganda became ever cruder and uglier: it started with the theme "love your country and defend it" and gradually turned to "hate your enemy and kill him."

Allied minds were poisoned by atrocity stories about the Huns mutilating bodies of Belgian children, and German minds by horror tales about English greed and hypocrisy that were responsible for the war and the starving of innocent women and children. Truth was devalued along with life, and hardly a voice was raised in protest. The guardians of God's word led the martial chorus. Total war came to mean total hatred, though perhaps least of all among soldiers, because they knew that the enemies across the trenches were fellow pawns.

The systematic poisoning of men's minds by paroxysms of nationalism —which at the time Corporal Adolf Hitler found most impressive and worthy of emulation—further obstructed the search for peace. As the war dragged on, as the vilifications of the enemy mounted, appetites increased and war aims became more grandiose in order to justify past and future sacrifices. "They shall not have died in vain" became the monstrous slogan by which the war was escalated, and the still living were led to ever greater slaughter—to justify the already dead. Could those who had died, thinking they were defending their country, be justified by others dying for some new annexation? Thus the war fed on itself, and governments became prisoners of their own propaganda.

The definition of war aims proved divisive among and within nations. The French demands were deceptively reasonable: they wanted the restoration of Alsace-Lorraine—which only a defeated Germany would yield; the English vowed to destroy Prussian militarism and terminate the German threat to the European balance of power. Colonial gains would be incidental rewards. Germany harbored the most ambitious war aims which would in fact have established her as the hegemonial power in Europe— hence a world power in England's place. The heart of Germany's programs—different groups embraced different varieties of avarice—was the establishment of a Central European Confederation, dominated by a victorious Reich. Many Germans thought of this new order as establishing in the twentieth century a Pax Germanica to replace the Pax Britannica. Whether flamboyant or seemingly reasonable, the war aims of the belligerents ruled out a compromise peace such as the pope or President Wilson hoped to mediate. The appetite grew with the eating—or, this time, with the dying.

The escalation of war aims had political origins and consequences. By and large, the traditional right in Europe propounded harsh war aims, hoping that visible, national gains would redound to the prestige and profit of the upper classes. German industrialists were vehement exemplars of this combined greed and fear. The European left was far more diffident, and a steadily growing minority of socialist militants demanded a peace without annexation or indemnity that would put an end to "the imperialist war." The suspicion that the war was being continued to serve class ends began to spread among radicals and working-class groups, particularly in Russia and Germany—in the very countries where the lower classes had to bear the brunt of mounting hardships, such as inflation, with wages lagging far behind the rise in prices, malnutrition, and the worst form of class warfare—the fight for bread. This suspicion and the daily experience of inequality fostered a new socialist militancy, which in Germany, for example, led to a schism among socialists and the founding of the Independent Socialists, a radical antiwar party. In neutral Switzerland, Russian exiles led by Lenin and radical socialists from other countries vowed to turn the imperialist war into a revolutionary struggle, to end the war by first ending capitalist oppression, as they called it. By 1916 the national unity that had swept across Europe in August, 1914, was shaken; in 1917 that unity collapsed in one country and was severely tried in all others.

In retrospect, 1917 looms as one of the decisive years in the history of European civilization. For in that year, the old system collapsed as America's entry into the war signaled the end of the more or less autonomous European states-system and the Bolshevik Revolution signaled the beginning of a new revolutionary challenge to Europe's social order. In 1917 Wilson and Lenin appeared simultaneously on the scene and faced each other across a prostrate Europe. In a sense both had been called forth by the challenge of German power; neither would disappear with its destruction. The implications of America's entry and Russia's revolutionary secession were not evident at first; they became clear gradually, as for half a century of disaster Europe fitfully suffered from the constellation that dominated 1917: German power, Bolshevism, and the intermittent need for an America that was by unpredictable turns too remote and too close.

These three elements were strangely intertwined from the beginning. Without the direct challenge of German power, embodied in her declaration of unrestricted submarine warfare, the United States would not have entered the war. Gratuitously, Germany's ruling classes, made arrogant by their victories and frantic by the elusiveness of victory, provoked their own nemesis: the Allies would never have been able to defeat Germany without American help. German power also paved the way for Bolshevism: indirectly, by precipitating the collapse of czardom and of its immediate, liberal successors, and directly, by transporting Lenin from Switzerland to the Finland Station, and by supplying Bolshevism with subsidies. Ludendorff's hope to use Lenin, and Lenin's to use Ludendorff, was but an early example of that collaboration between right and left extremists which was to prove so debilitating to political stability in the ensuing half-century. In 1917, Germany drew short-term advantages both from unrestricted submarine warfare and from her support of Bolshevism. The long-term advantages accrued to her enemies. The Germans, however, were not the only ones to stumble onto tactics that would defeat the very ends they were to serve: the politics of Europe had become so obscure, so filled with blinding hatreds and uncertainties, that clarity in political thought and action was virtually unattainable. The very pace of events suddenly outstripped the power of comprehension.

The beginning of 1917 saw a great intensification of hardships for all belligerents. Food shortages in England, Germany, and Russia worsened perceptibly, and people were alarmed that chronic malnutrition might turn into famine. In Russia, the workers first struck because of the breakdown of supplies; once out on the street, they demanded the end of czarism itself, and no group, not even the army, thought that Nicholas was savable. A provisional, bourgeois government was organized and vowed to fight on, but radical pressure forced it against its will to promise to seek a "peace without annexations and indemnities." War weariness spread in the East as in the West, where the stalemate continued bloody and unbroken. The much-heralded spring offensive of the French ended in failure and widespread mutinies. For the first time anywhere, the military's principal virtues, discipline and obedience, were flouted by exhausted and disillusioned men who, having lost their faith in their officers, refused to return to the trenches. Their new commander, Henri Philippe Pétain, went on the defensive: "I will wait for the Americans and for tanks." In Germany, there were wildcat strikes and some naval mutinies. War weariness—and the suspicion that the war was continued only for reasons of national greed—inspired an upsurge of left-wing militancy.

The greatest socialist victory came in Russia, where the Provisional Government's offensive ended in total disarray. Lenin's Bolsheviks seized power and demanded an immediate peace. France and England, close to collapse themselves, recognized that the Bolsheviks intended to desert them militarily and subvert them politically. The socialist agitation everywhere for an immediate revolutionary peace was most stimulated by the Bolshevik victory; it was only Wilson's promise of a liberal peace, based on national self-determination, that enabled the moderate left in the other belligerent countries to continue to support the war.

From the fall of 1917 to the following spring, the Germans had it all their own way, and they imparted some of their new energy to their lagging ally, Austria. In October, the Austro-German armies inflicted a monumental defeat on the Italians at Caporetto—a defeat that years later Mussolini's aggressive antics still sought to exorcise. At Brest Litovsk the Germans dictated a Carthaginian peace to the stunned Bolsheviks who had expected succor from their German comrades and instead saw most of industrial Russia torn from their hands. In March, 1918, Ludendorff, having shifted all but a million men from the east, threw the German armies into a series of offensives in the west that repeatedly broke through Allied lines. So precarious was their position that the Allies, who for three years had fought under separate and often poorly coordinated commands, finally appointed a French general, Ferdinand Foch, as supreme commander. By July, the Germans were once again across the Marne and within 35 miles of Paris. But this time, they quickly succumbed to Allied, including American, counterattacks. Weary, without reserves of men or supplies, they began a retreat which—if the Allies had had more strength or self-confidence—could easily have been turned into a rout.

Defeat threatened Germany's allies as well. Anglo-French offensives in the Near East and the Balkans—offensives that were not unrelated to imperialist aims—brought the Ottoman Empire and Bulgaria close to disaster. The tremors were felt farther north, and as Allied troops advanced in southeast Europe, the Austro-Hungarian monarchy, long plagued by internal strife, finally disintegrated into its national components. The Czechs and Slovaks, the Poles, the Hungarians, and the Yugoslavs proclaimed their independence. The venerable empire which, as Trotsky put it maliciously, "had long before hung out a sign for an undertaker, not demanding any high qualifications of him," ceased to exist. The Central Powers were crumbling at last—faster indeed than the Allies had thought possible.

In late September, Ludendorff precipitously demanded the creation of a democratic government that should immediately appeal to President Wilson for an armistice. The choice of Wilson was deliberate and cunning. His moral ascendancy in Europe was such that the Germans could hope that he would break Allied vindictiveness and insist on a "soft peace." For the moment, American power was the arbiter of Europe; Wilson told the Germans that they must first rid themselves of the imperial dynasty and told the Allies that they must grant Germany an armistice on the basis of his Fourteen Points. Weeks passed, until Foch finally presented the Germans with the terms of a harsh armistice. They had no choice but to accept, and on November 11, 1918, at eleven in the morning, the fighting stopped. Europe experienced its last day of universal rejoicing. The agony was over.

But life could never be the same. The very fact that the peace conference in Paris was dominated by a non-European, Woodrow Wilson, who had won the hearts of Europeans as no leader of their own ever had, symbolized the tremendous changes that the war had wrought in Europe. The physiognomy of Europe had been decisively altered, and historians have been debating ever since whether the war created or merely accelerated these changes. It certainly created the conditions for change—witness the Bolshevik Revolution: Bolshevism, long nurtured in prewar thoughts and antagonisms, could never have triumphed without the war.

The war had brought immense changes and taken an incalculable toll of European life. It is relatively easy to measure the material cost: the homes and factories destroyed, national economies exhausted, existing assets wasted, currencies ruined by inflation, and national debts acquired that a few years before would have been unimaginable. The total cost of the war has been estimated at $350 billion—the dollar reckoned at 1918 value. Europe's place in the world economy was impaired beyond recovery; two new giants, America and Japan, had been making colossal strides, while Europe bled.

The human cost is harder to assess. More than 10 million Europeans had died in battle—as well as 115,000 Americans. At least twice that number had been wounded, many of them left to live out their lives as cripples. Thereafter, millions of mutilated men walked the streets of Europe as reminders of the ravages of war. France lost half its men between the ages of twenty and thirty-two—and others suffered almost as much. But numbers fail to tell the full story. Among the dead was the promise and flower of Europe's youth. The potential leaders of the 1920's and 1930's had been decimated, as thousands of men of recognized talent died alongside others whose talents and genius would remain undiscovered forever. In those futile charges across no man's land, junior officers and young volunteers were mowed down first: nearly 20 per cent of all Oxford University men who served in the war were killed. Of 346 students of the École Normale Supérieure mobilized, 143 never returned. Even Europe, with its historic abundance of talent, could not suffer such losses without greatly impoverishing its future.

And what of the millions that finally returned from the trenches—to families that had been living in dread of their not returning? Their collective outlook, their moral expectations, had changed radically. The war, as one veteran turned historian put it, had scorched the minds and character of a generation. To many the war had been a discovery of violence, a lust for violence even in their own selves, that nothing in the genteel, repressed world of before 1914 had prepared them for. "Most men, I suppose, have a paleolithic savage somewhere in them. . . . I have, anyway," wrote a gentle English scholar about his experience in the trenches. In other ways, too, that earlier world had been thoroughly discredited. It had been discredited by the bloody bungling of incompetence, by the failure of leadership, by the greed of war aims, and by the hollow claims of church and state. The rough "deference" for church, fatherland, and social superiors that still existed in 1914 was hopelessly compromised four years later. Superiors had been proven inferior, and the old notion that there was a rough equivalent between performance and reward, that there was a social order that made sense, this too had broken down. What was to take its place? What faith would claim the disillusioned? The immediate reaction of many was a hunger above all for peace and "normalcy," though not a few, particularly among the defeated peoples, thirsted for the renewed glories of military companionship. The war left a legacy of cynicism and skepticism as the dominant mood, and a spiritual thirst for action among others.

Yet, even Europe's worst catastrophe brought hope and betterment to some. The war hastened the development of egalitarian democracy and brought new benefits to long-suffering minorities. By the end of the war, nationalities long oppressed attained their independence. During the war, women's rights had been more generally acknowledged, as it became clear that women's capabilities were fully as necessary to society as were men's. Religious minorities were further assimilated into national societies, and cherished prejudices were suspended, at least for the duration. In central Europe, for example, Jews, needed in wartime, were rewarded with greater privileges. The full integration of trade unions into national life greatly advanced the rights and expectations of labor. "A country fit for heroes" was Lloyd George's promise to the English, and the drabness of postwar performance contrasted ill with the new deal that had everywhere been expected.

Europe had suffered too much to honor its pledges, to satisfy the aroused expectations of millions of its citizens. Victor and vanquished alike were too enfeebled to build material conditions that would protect and promote the precarious stirrings of a new democracy. The war had not only immeasurably weakened the old order; it weakened the forces that could have built a new order as well. Despite the resiliency of man, despite brave beginnings, Europe proved incapable of dealing with this tangled legacy of war and revolution. Everywhere, in Europe and elsewhere, in Russia, the United States, the great Asian powers, the end of war did not bring peace.

For Further Reading

Churchill, Winston, *The World Crisis.*
Cruttwell, C. R. M. F., *A History of the Great War.*
Marwick, Arthur, *The Deluge.*
Mayer, Arno J., *Political Origins of the New Diplomacy, 1917–1918.*

87   The Russian Revolution and the Stalin Era

At a distance of more than half a century the Russian Revolution of 1917 appears as an enigmatic Janus: one face looking back to the classic revolutions of modern European history; the other looking to the future, to the turbulences and upheavals of the non-European world that so marked the second third of the twentieth century. Like its revolution, Russian history, too, seems to live in two worlds. In much it has followed general European patterns of development, though at its own tempo and with its own accent. But Russia has always stood on the borders of Europe; more than half its vast territory lies in Asia. Mongols, Turks, and Chinese as well as Poles, Swedes, and Germans have been its neighbors. Therein lies much of the fascination of Russian history and of the Russian Revolution: for good or ill they have spanned the European and non-European worlds.

This dualism lies at the root of much of the controversy about Russia in its age of revolution, an age extending roughly from the revolt of 1905, which shook the czar's throne but did not topple it, through the years of Stalin, who converted revolutionary Russia into a world power, the Soviet Union. From the European perspective a twentieth-century Russia ruled by an autocrat—Nicholas II, a man bearing many resemblances to such ill-fated earlier monarchs as Charles I of England and Louis XVI of France—was an evident anachronism bound to undergo vast change if it was to survive. At the same time, the example of Bismarck's Germany suggested that Russia, too, could warp its way into an age of industrialization, mass politics, and rational administration without necessarily undergoing the throes of violent political and social turmoil. From the non-European perspective this very challenge, confronting a sprawling, still poor, still largely agrarian country, was precisely a foreshadowing of the strains and dislocations that were to disrupt nearly every non-European society forced to cope with the problems of modernization and industrialization.

Although these contrasting perspectives must enter into any assessment of the Russian Revolution's place in general history, the actual course and outcome of the revolution itself were decisively influenced by two specific, and seemingly contingent, events: the outbreak of the First World War in the summer of 1914 and the arrival of Lenin (real name Vladimir Ilich Ulyanov) in Russia in April, 1917. The foreign policy of Imperial Russia undoubtedly played an important part in determining that the war

A.D.   1904 Outbreak of Russo-Japanese War

          1905 "Bloody Sunday," beginning of 1905 Revolution

          1914 Outbreak of First World War

          1916 Murder of Rasputin

          1917 March 8–15, "February Revolution"; April 16, Lenin returns to Russia; July 16–17, "July Days"; Sept. 9–14, Kornilov Affair; Nov. 7, Bolshevik seizure of power: "October Revolution"

          1918 Treaty of Brest-Litovsk with Germany

1918–1920 Civil war and foreign intervention

          1921 Kronstadt mutiny; beginning of New Economic Policy

          1922 Stalin named Secretary General of Communist Party

          1924 Death of Lenin

          1926 Zinoviev, Trotsky, and Kamenev removed from Politburo

          1928 Adoption of First Five-Year Plan

          1929 Bukharin ousted from Politburo

          1934 Assassination of Kirov; beginning of Great Purges

          1936 Stalin Constitution approved

          1939 Ribbentrop-Molotov Pact

          1941 German invasion of U.S.S.R.

          1953 Death of Stalin

should come about when it did and how it did, but in respect to domestic Russian affairs the war was a calamity from without. It seems likely that the old order was approaching a serious, possibly mortal, social and political crisis, but a revolutionary denouement was perhaps not inevitable. In a country belatedly groping its way to new forms of government and social organization—with a new parliament, the Duma, which had yet to prove itself, with a discontented peasantry in uncertain transition from old communal structures, with a satisfactory formula for the treatment of the numerous non-Russian nationalities still to be devised, with the rapidly expanding industrial centers trying to accommodate the influx of raw workers from the countryside—the fearful strain of sustaining a war against the most powerful army in the world led to disaster. Initially, the war caused the Russian people to rally in defense of the fatherland, and their military record was by no means one of unrelieved disaster. They fought a full-scale war for nearly three years. Still, the circumstances surrounding the astonishingly rapid and total collapse of the czarist regime in a single week of mounting disturbance in Petrograd (from March 7 to March 15, 1917) are virtually all related to the war, whatever the deeper sources may have been: open disaffection in the upper ranks of Russian society over what was deemed wretched, even treasonous, mismanagement of the war; the disruption in the bread supply to the capital, owing in part to an overtaxed transportation system; war-inflated industries with vast masses of unseasoned workers; and, perhaps most decisively, a capital glutted with ill-trained and undisciplined troops in replacement regiments, less than anxious to be sent to the front. The czar fell in March, 1917, not through palace coup or revolutionary plot or peasant uprising, but because the impingement of the war on Russian society, at top and bottom, had created a highly explosive situation in the center of the empire.

The war not only occasioned the fall of the czar, it also destroyed the short-lived Provisional Government of Aleksandr Kerenski, which sought to play the caretaker until such time as a constituent assembly should determine the future form of the Russian state. The role of "moderates" in a period of deepening revolution is always difficult, and one may wonder whether any government could have dealt adequately with the host of domestic issues created by the disappearance of the old order. But certainly Russia's continued involvement in the war exacerbated the sequence of crises the Provisional Government faced, and contributed mightily to the harsh polarization of political life in the summer of 1917 and to the eventual isolation of that government, assailed from both left and right. It was hard for the Provisional Government to withdraw from the war. The implications of such a step—the fair likelihood of a general German victory with a consequent hegemony over Europe—were daunting. Still, the Provisional Government might have defended its own front and resisted the temptation to demonstrate its vitality in the summer of 1917 by mounting an attack which failed and simply worsened matters. Whatever the alternative, the war, partly by its direct effect, partly by diverting energy and attention from other urgent problems, served to extend the chaos and push Russia to the social and political disintegration so poignantly depicted in Boris Pasternak's *Dr. Zhivago*.

Thus, the breakdown in 1917 was intimately associated with the vicissitudes of the Great War. And while this external calamity upset Russia's domestic equilibrium, there was at least a symbolic connection between this last of the classic European revolutions and the general catastrophe that overtook European power politics. A whole historical epoch reached tragic climax in these two experiences.

The contingency associated with the next phase of the Russian Revolution was, however, of a quite different kind. If Lenin had been unable to make his way from exile in Switzerland to Russia in April, 1917 (and it required the cooperation of the Germans, who were understandably eager to promote disorder in Russia), it seems unlikely that the Bolsheviks would have been able to seize power on November 7, 1917, and if the Bolsheviks had not done so at that time and in the way they did, the course of Russian history could well have been quite different.

The Provisional Government was probably fatally weak by the late summer of 1917, but what was to succeed it was problematic: possibly pure anarchy might ensue, perhaps Russia would break up into small units, perhaps (what most Russians either feared or hoped for), a military dictatorship might emerge. Or perhaps a left-wing coalition including the Bolsheviks (an eventuality Lenin fought desperately to avoid) might have resulted. Unlike the breakdown of an established order, the appearance of a new system or structure in the midst of chaos is by its nature a highly contingent matter; accidents of timing and personality can play a decisive role. Lenin ranks among those rare individuals in history who achieved a result that would not have come about through the "normal" play of politics, or through unilateral group action, or through the efforts of any other identifiable character on the scene. (Even Trotsky was of the opinion that Lenin was the indispensable man.)

Lenin's role is not easy to define precisely. Born in 1870 in a small town on the Volga to parents of comfortable circumstances, Lenin received a good education and, in the tradition of the time, moved into the ranks of the radical intelligentsia. Early in his career, however, there appeared a steely, uncompromising quality to his revolutionism that was to mark him off from most Russian radicals. His own synthesis of German Marxism and the Russian revolutionary tradition consistently aimed at forging the most effective revolutionary instruments. He fought against liberalism, revisionism, compromise, anything that might dampen the revolutionary impulse. The party he created (named the Bolsheviks after the split with the Menshevik faction of the Russian Social Democratic movement in 1903, and renamed the Communist party immediately after the 1917 revolution) was designed to serve as a vanguard of disciplined professional revolutionaries operating within a tightly controlled organization.

The instrumentalities Lenin had worked so hard to create before 1914 served him well, but perhaps better after the 1917 revolution than during it. During the critical months between March and November, 1917, the Bolsheviks were not particularly well organized—perhaps more so than the other parties, but still subject to the confusions and uncertainties of that frenetic year. Lenin and his followers played no significant role in the fall of the czar, for most of them were in prison or in exile. Joseph Stalin and Lev Kamenev were initially inclined to offer guarded support to the Provisional Government, and when Lenin, in the late summer of 1917, announced to his comrades from his hiding place in Finland that the time had come for armed insurrection, he alarmed them by his rashness. Two of his closest associates, Kamenev and Grigori Zinoviev, openly broke with him. Organizational genius does not seem to be the clue to Lenin's success at this particular point.

Rather it would appear that Lenin's great achievement in 1917 lay at the level of political instinct. First, immediately upon his return to Russia he strongly opposed any expression of confidence in the Provisional Government. By this unqualified stand he put himself in a unique position to profit when sentiments began to polarize with the deteriorating situation. Second, he immediately sensed the vulnerability of the Provisional Government when it came into conflict with General Lavr Kornilov, who was trying to reestablish order and discipline. Lenin recognized that growing peasant disturbances made it impossible for counterrevolution to assemble the countryside against the unruly cities.

These insights provided the key to Lenin's victory in November, 1917. The course by which this victory was achieved, however, was remarkably circuitous and included many forces over which he had no control; these were times of flux and accident. Two myths must be dispelled. Lenin did not ride to power on a mighty revolutionary upsurge channeled and directed by the Bolshevik party. Russia in the autumn of 1917 was breaking apart; a strange sense of emptiness, almost of vacuum, permeated the atmosphere. Not that the Bolsheviks were an insignificant minority; while they received only one-quarter of the vote in the elections to the Constituent Assembly held shortly after their access to power, their areas of strength were strategically located in the cities. It should also be noted that the vote in this unique free expression of Russian political sentiments was overwhelmingly for "radical" parties. Moreover, the Bolsheviks by October, 1917, dominated the workers' and soldiers' (though not the peasants') soviets, the somewhat irregularly elected representative bodies that sprang up throughout Russia in the wake of the March Revolution. Still, the myth of a massive revolutionary tidal wave is only a myth. The counterimage of a carefully planned, skillfully executed Bolshevik coup d'état is also false. As Bolshevik documents of the time make only too clear, the overthrow of the Provisional Government was neither well planned nor well executed. On the very eve of the seizure Lenin was frantically uncertain about the intentions and actions of his own Central Committee.

Yet, through a combination of governmental weakness, Bolshevik strength among the workers and troops in Petrograd, and the force of Lenin's demonic will to revolution, the Bolsheviks came to power and, as was apparent from the outset, not as the instrument of the soviets but as their masters, and not in coalition with the other radical parties, the Mensheviks and the Social Revolutionaries. The Bolsheviks took over the throne of the czars as autocrats.

Such was Lenin's tour de force of November, 1917. The term tour de force carries overtones of sleight of hand, of something not quite real. Much of Russia's subsequent history has been a playing out of the implications of that extraordinary event, successive stages in a continuing effort to bring Lenin's singular achievement into a reasonably harmonious relationship with the realities of Russia and the world. First, the seizure of power in Petrograd had to be extended into effective sovereignty over all Russia. This occupied the remainder of Lenin's lifetime. Second, this new revolutionary entity had to face the tough demands of life, economics, and power politics. It was Stalin's role to hammer out solutions of a sort to these demands. Third, there was the need to reconcile the internal contradictions produced by Lenin's revolution and Stalin's creation. This seems to have been the basic task of Stalin's successors.

Although the Bolsheviks quickly won control of the most important cities, it took them three years of bitter civil war to subdue the broad reaches of Russia. Casualties in the 1917 revolution had been relatively light, but the civil war exacted a fearful toll: battles without prisoners, organized terror and unorganized marauding, Red against White, village against city, nationality against nationality. Entire towns were depopulated. Inevitably, widespread famine followed.

Though they were on the brink of defeat in 1918 and again in 1919, the Bolsheviks enjoyed several advantages and profited from several bits of good luck. By moving the capital to Moscow early in 1918 they could defend interior lines in the heart of old Muscovy, whereas their opponents had to operate on Russia's vast periphery. The major threats came in sequence; the Bolsheviks never had to meet all opponents at once. The German threat evaporated in November, 1918. Thereafter French, British, Japanese, and American forces were in remote areas, and their efforts were generally half-hearted, ill-coordinated, and frequently at cross purposes. Moreover, the numerous domestic enemies of the Bolsheviks were never united and were frequently in open conflict. The military mistrusted the socialists; the Volunteer Army in the south was at odds with the Ukrainian nationalists, who had their own troubles with the Poles and with local peasant partisans. While the peasants resisted Bolshevik squads seeking grain, they also feared that the victory of the Whites would mean the return of the landlords. An effective and durable coalition of any of several sets of opponents could have crushed the Bolsheviks. But of course these antagonisms were an integral part of the confusion that had descended on Russia.

In addition, the Bolsheviks enjoyed a quality of leadership, most notably in the persons of Lenin and Trotsky, that their enemies could not match. It was a broken-backed struggle, often a sordid and horrible one, but it did prove the temper of the new rulers of Russia, who demonstrated that when survival was at stake they were more than visionaries, agitators, or theoreticians of revolution. Many of the grimmer features of the Soviet system emerged in those years, most notably the terror and xenophobia; implicit perhaps in Lenin's will to bring socialism to Russia by main force, they became manifest in the rigors of the civil war and foreign intervention.

These early years also witnessed a rash of extreme economic and social experiments, usually lumped under the term "war communism": the nationalization of industry, state control over labor, centralized management of the economy, state distribution of goods, and an effort to get away from a money economy. Although these steps were later rationalized as measures imposed upon the Bolsheviks in prosecuting the civil war, they certainly reflected some of the more utopian visions entertained by Lenin and his associates.

The Bolsheviks won the civil war, but they ruled a land bled white, facing famine and the prospect of a peasant convulsion. One of Lenin's important gifts, unusual in a revolutionary, was his ability to stop for a breathing space, and even to retreat. He forced through the bitter treaty of Brest Litovsk with Germany in early 1918 against the violent opposition of more sanguine comrades who thought Russia capable of leading a revolutionary war. He inaugurated the New Economc Policy (NEP)—a major retreat involving a partial return to a market and monetary economy—again with opposition from comrades who considered this the Thermidor of the revolution. But Robespierre had been executed in the French

Thermidor; Lenin and the Bolsheviks remained in power. The revolution had been neither defeated nor discredited; its ideology had not been called in question. The revolution was in this sense still open-ended.

In his last two years of active life, before the strokes that left him helpless until his death in January, 1924, Lenin wrestled with the problem of stabilizing and healing an exhausted nation without backsliding into old habits. As his powers faded he voiced his anguish at the retrograde trends he saw: the faltering élan, the reappearance of the old spirit of bureaucratic Russia, the ugly revival of chauvinism. At the end these fears tended to focus on the figure of Stalin, now coming rapidly to the fore.

Josif Vissarionovich Dzhugashvili, who took on the revolutionary name of Stalin, was born in Georgia in 1879. An early follower of Lenin, he played an important though not decisive role in 1917 and in the civil war. Viewed by his colleagues as a man of action rather than a theorist, he was at home in organizational and operational matters. He became general secretary of the Central Committee of the Communist party in 1922. From this strategic position he outmaneuvered his rivals and became undisputed master of Russia by the late 1920's.

Although Stalin came to the top through adroit manipulation of the party machinery and continued to use manipulation, laced with terror, throughout his long rule, he could not have become or remained master of Russia had he been nothing but an organization man or an executioner. He also had a policy, somewhat primitively and ambiguously expressed in the phrase "Socialism in one country." By the time of Lenin's death Russia seemed to be faced by two unacceptable alternatives. The prospects of an immediate world revolution were fading. To press forward on this front, as Trotsky advocated, promised only to destroy what was left of an exhausted Russia. On the other hand, the retreat to NEP seemed to threaten a return to old ways. Stalin cut through this quandary by proclaiming that, whatever happened in the outside world, Russia could proceed toward socialism on its own, through its own efforts and will.

This determination, which flew in the face not only of the Marxian view of history and economics but also of common sense, carried important implications. It required a massive and concerted assault on reality; any normal play of political and social forces would not suffice. And while Stalin has been described as a great realist there was undoubtedly a dark corner of his mind—the same dark corner that created the horrors of Stalinism—which saw reality as something to be created by his own will.

The abrupt and violent turning point came in 1928–1929, with the wholesale collectivization of agriculture and the inauguration of the first Five-Year Plan. While it is a debated point, it does not appear that the NEP had exhausted its potentialities, although it had run into some difficulties.

However, to continue the program threatened to undermine the role of the Communist party as the unique guiding force in Russia. There is an intimate connection between the twists and turns by which Stalin gained control over the party and the shift in economic policy that precipitated the forcible collectivization of the peasantry.

This shift has been termed a "revolution from above." It was certainly a revolution in that it rapidly, and permanently, altered the face of Russia. Millions of peasants were forced into collective farms; vast and incredibly ambitious plans were applied to the entire economy. The initial efforts had disastrous effects: agricultural production declined, livestock were killed off, an unnecessary famine hit several regions. Nevertheless, despite some brief pauses and retreats, the drive went on, guided and impelled by Stalin. The Communist party was by now merely his personal instrument.

The totalitarian regime that emerged in the 1930's has been interpreted by some as a necessary if highly unpleasant means to achieve rapid industrialization. Agriculture, the argument runs, had to be made to provide a collectable surplus, whatever the cost to the peasants; the workers had to labor more intensely than they would normally; the political system, and especially the coercive apparatus of police and courts, had to enforce these measures; and the party had to be an unfaltering executor of Stalin's commanding impulse. But this interpretation reverses cause and effect. The decision to mount an economic offensive in such circumstances was itself totalitarian.

Probably the most bizarre and baffling episode of the Stalin years was the period of the Great Purges, extending from 1934 to 1938. Triggered by the assassination of a leading Communist (in which Stalin himself may have had a hand), it soon extended to a settling of Stalin's accounts with former opponents, a virtual wiping out of Old Bolsheviks, and ultimately to a murderous purge even within the Stalinist ranks. Millions of people, Communists and non-Communists, were caught up in this nightmare of arrest, torture, slave labor camp, and execution. Stalin killed more Communists than any right-wing or fascist dictator ever did. He had more at hand.

Although amenable to rational analysis, the purges displayed neither objective nor subjective rationality. The liquidation of party factionalism, the prophylactic extirpation of real or potential traitors, the clearing of avenues of advance for a new party elite—all these explanations are at best marginally relevant. Even the picture of a terror apparatus out of control, devouring everything in sight including its own agents, while doubtless true at some levels, is not satisfactory. Stalin was able to call a halt rather abruptly before the fabric of Soviet society disintegrated. The ultimate explanation lies in the brooding, paranoid personality of Stalin. He saw enemies everywhere, and doom descended on any person, group, or even nationality which came under his suspicion.

Yet Stalin's actions occurred in a social setting. Purely maniacal actors are normally strait-jacketed. Stalin's distorted reality was after all a reality, partially inherited from the Russian past, significantly derived from Lenin's revolution, and partly brought into being by Stalin himself.

That Stalinism, for all the insanity of the purges, was still in touch with the real world, domestic and foreign, was demonstrated by Russia's ability to withstand the Nazi invasion of 1941. The "excessive excesses" of Stalinism exacted their cost in the war with Hitler. The purges did not strengthen the Red Army (its general staff was decimated in 1938), any more than collectivization heightened the patriotism of the Russian peasantry, or enforced Soviet nationalism led to loyalty among the Ukrainians. On the other hand, the savagery of the Nazi invasion and occupation of the Soviet Union in 1941–1943 does not explain the extraordinary powers of resistance and endurance displayed by the Russian people. Stalin had taken up Lenin's revolutionary tour de force and created a social mechanism capable of meeting the severe test of war.

While the Soviet Union was still dedicated to the ideals of the revolution, in many respects it was their antithesis: the inegalitarianism of Russian life (demonstrated, for example by increasing wage differentials), the appearance of a new Russian nationalism (marked by the resurrection of such figures as Ivan the Terrible and Peter the Great), the vast expansion of the bureaucracy (not a hint that the state would "wither away"), and the permanent institutionalization of terror (a quite different thing from revolutionary violence)—in all these respects the Soviet Union showed little resemblance to the goals of Marxism.

Perhaps these deformations were a necessary stage; perhaps the way to a freer society was open once the test of war had been survived. So many Russians thought. But Stalin was not willing, or not able, to entertain such thoughts. To some extent he was a victim of his own system, which certainly developed its own powers of self-perpetuation. The breakdown of the Big Three alliance and the onset of the Cold War provided a rationale for continued austerity and repression, but it is doubtful that this was really the cause. In some measure age played a part; in his last years Stalin was notably unreceptive to innovation. But basically, Stalin simply did not believe that there was any other way to run Soviet society, to advance toward Communism, and, ultimately, to see it victorious on a world scale.

Consequently, postwar Russia was forced to undergo new rigors. The Communist ideology, which had been overshadowed by nationalist themes during the war, came back in full force. There was renewed emphasis on the party, although it never really recovered from the bloodletting of the late 1930's. The command economy continued to give highest priority to industrial production, especially to areas of greatest military relevance. The consumer and the peasant stayed on short rations; indeed, at the time of Stalin's death the level of agricultural production still lagged behind that of 1913. Writers, artists, and musicians were brought under ideological constraint in the name of "socialist realism." The forced labor camps continued to receive their quotas, and important sectors of the economy were manned by unfree labor. Within the Communist party itself the pervading fear, never fully dissipated since the Great Purges, became more pronounced. In 1949 a number of prominent officials were liquidated—the so-called Leningrad Affair. As Stalin's health declined, his morbid suspicions increased, and on the eve of his death in March, 1953, a replay of the Great Purges seemed imminent.

But Stalin died. He had achieved much, at hideous cost, but he died. He was one of the most fearsome rulers of all time. It has been observed that the fate of newly created states or political systems often hinges on the presence of an able successor to the founder; without someone to translate his triumph into an ongoing system all may collapse. Surely the Lenin-Stalin sequence was one of the most formidable in recorded history. Just as the Communist victory in the Russian Revolution could scarcely have occurred without Lenin, so the conversion of this victory into a reality that would neither deny the victory (though it might pervert it) nor succumb to the drift of events was Stalin's singular achievement.

Yet for all its awesome massiveness, its effort to achieve a monolithic, totally integrated society, Stalinism did not, and could not, arrive at a stable equilibrium. By main force Stalin beat down domestic and foreign opponents; he was able, to a degree hitherto thought not possible, to shape whole economies, whole peoples, to his will. He institutionalized the precepts and principles of Marxism-Leninism-Stalinism, rendering them free of individual vagary to an astonishing degree. But Stalin could not reproduce himself, and his principal lieutenants, fighting among themselves, were in mortal terror lest they become victims. The immediate response to the death of Stalin was the search by the elite of the system for some assurance that they, their careers and lives, would not be in constant jeopardy. The problem was not so much operating the Stalinist system without Stalin as rendering the system less perilous to those close to the center of power. This search inevitably opened the way to much broader issues which have constituted the central challenge to post-Stalin Russia. Khrushchev contended with these and failed; they are still before the present rulers of the Soviet Union, men who rose to the top through the tough and unattractive Stalin school of advancement, men with an acute instinct for personal and political survival but without a notable sense of imagination.

Thus, out of Lenin's ambiguous achievement, a "socialist" revolution imposed by the Communist party on ill-prepared Russian soil, Stalin forced into being a political, economic, and social system capable of surviving the harsh atmosphere of this century (while contributing singularly to its harshness) and even of presenting itself as a plausible model for other societies. But how, in the long run, was this system to come to terms with its own internal, self-generating contradictions and conflicts? Old Russia was dead; there could be no Restoration. By the time of Stalin's death Russia could admit its past, even glorify selected parts. Could it build creatively from it? The industrial Western world had been the enemy for half a century; Soviet history and Soviet pride would not permit any simple acceptance of the virtues of "capitalist-imperialist" ways. Post-Stalin speculation in the West about prospects for "convergence" of the two systems offered little of relevance to Russia's problems. In the last third of the twentieth century the great challenge for the Soviet regime must be to seek a resolution of its revolutionary inheritance that would do less violence to the individual, who has problems enough adapting to the promises and perils of the contemporary world.

For Further Reading

Chamberlin, W. H., *The Russian Revolution.*
Deutscher, Isaac, *Stalin.*
Rauch, Georg von, *A History of Soviet Russia.*
Ulam, Adam B., *The Bolsheviks.*

88   The United States: Prosperity and Depression

The factory whistles and church bells that sounded the news of the armistice on November 11, 1918, signaled the end of a remarkable interlude in American history. The participation of the United States in World War I lasted but nineteen months; yet in that short period, the country underwent a number of "Europeanizing" experiences. For the first time, the national government, acquiring some of the character which European theorists gave to "the State," intervened directly in the American economy. It allocated resources, regulated prices, supervised cartels, ran the railroads, even commandeered factories. For the first time, too, American troops crossed the Atlantic to take part in an Old World conflict. Three weeks after the war ended, the American President, Woodrow Wilson, broke still another

A.D.		
	1918	End of World War I
	1919	U.S. Senate rejects League of Nations treaty; Red Scare; 18th Amendment (Prohibition) ratified
	1920	19th Amendment (Women's Suffrage) ratified; Republicans returned to power; census reveals U.S. predominantly urban
	1922	Nine-Power Treaty
	1928	The Big Bull Market; Kellogg-Briand Pact
	1929	Wall Street crash
	1932	Election of Franklin D. Roosevelt: Democrats new majority party
	1933	Bank crisis; beginning of New Deal; the Hundred Days; recognition of U.S.S.R.
	1935	Second Hundred Days; Social Security Act and welfare state; first neutrality legislation
	1937	Sitdown strikes; Constitutional crisis; recession
	1938	End of New Deal reforms
	1939	Outbreak of World War II in Europe

---

precedent by traveling to Paris to traffic with diplomats from foreign chancelleries on the shape of the postwar world.

But the war experience proved short-lived. For too many Americans it had been a wrenching upheaval. The war did not really head the nation in new directions; instead, the administration lost little time in dismantling the machinery of the mobilization. And when Wilson returned from Versailles with a treaty that included a League of Nations, the Senate rejected it. Disillusioned with the fruits of war, frightened by the spread of Bolshevism in Europe, the United States in 1919 turned in on itself. In the frenzy of the Red Scare it sought to exorcise all European ideas; in doing so, it released the psychic frustrations built up by the war through assaults on radicals and unionists.

The presidential election of 1920 confirmed the rising mood of isolationism and conservatism. The undistinguished Republican nominee, Senator Warren Harding of Ohio, insisted that the country needed "not nostrums but normalcy." He denounced revolution, agitation, experiment, and internationalism, calling instead for "serenity," "equipoise," and old-fashioned nationalism. Woodrow Wilson, seriously ill, wanted the election to be a "great and solemn referendum" on the League, but both parties muddled the question, and in the campaign Harding made full use of his exceptional talent for taking a simple matter and rendering it obscure. With the electorate swollen by millions of new women voters (the Nineteenth Amendment was ratified that summer), Warren Harding won a landslide victory.

Two days after the election, Harding announced that the League was "now deceased." The United States had come out of the war as the preeminent world power, but for the next two decades the country, with rare exceptions, followed a policy of withdrawal. Blithely ignoring the economic dislocations wrought by the war, the government insisted that its European allies pay their debts to the last penny. It raised mountainous tariff barriers, thus further hampering international trade. In 1922 at a conference in Washington, the United States negotiated a naval disarmament pact with the great powers and a Nine-Power Treaty guaranteeing the integrity of China and maintaining the Open Door, but these agreements set up no machinery for enforcement. Even more meaningless was the Kellogg-Briand Pact of 1928 in which nations renounced war as an instrument of national policy. By its failure to assume a more creative role in foreign affairs, the United States helped ensure that the two decades following the war would be nothing more than a "long armistice."

The 1920 election marked an end, too, to an era of progressive government. The Republican leaders of the decade were committed to minimal interference with business and to the Whig doctrine of the weak president. No one looked more a great statesman than Warren Harding, who, it was said, "needed only a toga to complete the illusion that he had come out of the ancient world." Yet few men less equipped for the task ever held so high an office. Harding's speeches were so devoid of ideas and so graceless in form that they reduced his critics to despair. The poet e. e. cummings alleged that "beautiful Warren Gamaliel Harding" was

> the only man or child who wrote
> a simple declarative sentence with seven grammatical
> errors. . . .

Harding is remembered chiefly for the scandals that disgraced his brief tenure. When as a consequence of his role in the Teapot Dome oil scandal, Secretary of the Interior Albert Fall was sentenced to the penitentiary, it marked the first time that such a fate had ever befallen a cabinet officer.

When Harding died in 1923, he was succeeded by Calvin Coolidge, a man with the instinctive resistance to change of a Vermonter who never went west. Coolidge reduced the role of his office to one almost of insignificance. "The kind of government that he offered the country," wrote the satirical essayist H. L. Mencken, "was government stripped to the buff." Coolidge's subordination of the government to business reflected the national admiration for corporation leaders like Henry Ford and the conviction that such men were wiser and infinitely more valuable to society than public officials. "Our business intelligence has so far outgrown our political intelligence that it looms like a white lily on a stagnant pool," commented one writer. "Are we approaching a millennium," asked an editorial in *Life,* "in which visible government will not be necessary and in which the job of running the world will slip away from obstructive politicians and be taken over by men trained in the shop?"

Yet even in the 1920's the state continued to grow relentlessly. A host of new government agencies sprang up: the Bureau of the Budget, the Grain Futures Administration, the Federal Radio Commission. In large part, this expansion resulted from demands by business groups which paid homage to laissez-faire but insisted on government favors to advance their own interests. The president of the National Association of Manufacturers remarked: "It is unthinkable that a government which thrives chiefly upon its industries will withhold from them for a single unnecessary moment the protection which they so sorely need and deserve."

"Never before, here or anywhere else," wrote the *Wall Street Journal,* "has a government been so completely fused with business." Federal regulatory agencies fell under corporation control. Secretary of the Treasury Andrew Mellon, under whom, it was said, three Presidents served, pushed a tax policy which benefited the rich. Both the Attorney General's office and the Supreme Court dealt heavy blows against the labor movement, which in these years declined markedly in strength. The Court invalidated two child labor acts, sanctioned yellow dog contracts, and struck down an anti-injunction law and a minimum wage statute for women.

The public's admiration of business rested on the stunning performance of the economy in these years. Between 1921 and 1929, as mechanization accelerated economic growth, industrial output nearly doubled. The pace-setting automobile industry (the number of cars in use almost tripled in a decade) was responsible for a number of subsidiary developments, including the building of a vast highway network which knitted the nation together and the burgeoning of suburbs from Shaker Heights to Beverly Hills. Reflecting the contagious optimism of these years, stock prices went up, up, and then up again; during the Great Bull Market in the summer of 1928, industrials climbed 110 points. Yet the structure of prosperity had weak underpinnings. Five per cent of the population received one-third of the income, and 25 million families—more than 87 per cent of the nation —lived on less than $2,500 a year.

Most Americans were impressed less by the frailty of the economy than by the marvelous new products it spewed forth. It was about 1920 that mechanization took possession of the American home. Countless new electrical appliances caught the public fancy: first, toasters and irons; then vacuum cleaners; then stoves; then refrigerators. At the same time, mass entertainment, especially radio and the Hollywood dream factory, became a major American industry. In 1920 the first radio station opened in Pittsburgh; ten years later there were nearly 13 million radios in American homes, by 1940, 52 million. Businessmen created a vast home market by developing new consumer products and by whetting the consumer's appetite through novel techniques of advertising, salesmanship, and installment buying.

In these years the New Middle Class, from the advertising man to the office machine clerk, moved to the center of the stage. The white-collar worker found himself in growing demand in an economy increasingly concerned with merchandising and distribution. This produced subtle alterations in the national character. The country was fast moving toward a Veblenian society in which styles of leisure and consumption determined status. Thrifty Poor Richard ceased to be the nation's culture hero. "The credit mechanism has made the Ant a fool and the Grasshopper a hero," one commentator observed.

The census of 1920 revealed that for the first time in the nation's history a majority of the population lived in urban areas, and the society of the twenties showed the increasing impact of metropolitan influence. Much of the attention of the decade concentrated on the world of the city: the jazz of New Orleans and Chicago, the soaring skyscraper, the brassy flapper. The literature of the period, too, focused on the experience of young men from "Gopher Prairie" or "Winesburg, Ohio," who had come to the big city; the novelist F. Scott Fitzgerald arrived in New York, he wrote, "like Dick Whittington up from the country." City-bred writers, far removed from the villages of Whittier and Twain, explored the asphalt world of Langston Hughes's Harlem and James T. Farrell's Chicago.

The antics of loose-living Hollywood stars projected on village screens distressed rural Americans, and so did the "revolution in morals" loosely associated with the name of Sigmund Freud. The swiftly rising divorce rate was cause for further alarm: the Democratic presidential nominee in 1920 had been divorced in 1911 and had remarried in 1917; he had children by both wives; nonetheless he won the nomination. Yet rural attitudes toward the metropolis were ambivalent; the city was viewed both as a den of evil and as an alluring bazaar of pleasure. By punishing urban institutions, the rural American could also suppress his own sinful fantasies.

The countryside scored an early victory in its war with the city through the ratification in 1919 of the Eighteenth Amendment, which prohibited the manufacture, sale, or transport of alcoholic beverages. The rural, Protestant, old-stock culture found in prohibition a way to impose its abstemious, work-minded style of life on the leisure-loving, loose-living city. One prohibitionist claimed: "Our nation can only be saved by turning the pure stream of country sentiment and township morals to flush out the cesspools of cities and so save civilization from pollution." Prohibition was deeply resented by city dwellers; Mencken complained that it had caused suffering comparable only to the Black Death and the Thirty Years' War. In the cities, the illegal liquor traffic often fell into the hands of gangsters; in Al Capone's Chicago, more men died violent deaths each year than in all of Great Britain.

The rural white Protestants, who for so long had been the unchallenged leaders of the nation, chalked up a number of other triumphs. Congress drastically restricted immigration and imposed a quota system to preserve America as an outpost of Anglo-Saxony. In the South, fundamentalists secured state laws banning the teaching of Darwinian evolution. More extreme elements organized the Ku Klux Klan, another vehicle of rural values, which waged war against Catholics, Jews, Negroes, foreigners, and all the forces of "metropolitan morality" which were creating "modern Sodom and Gomorrahs."

The politics of the 1920's centered less on liberal-conservative disputes over economic policy than on the resistance of rural and small-town America to the growing influence of the metropolis, as witness the division in the 1924 Democratic convention between the forces of the urban Northeast and the rural South and West that made possible Calvin Coolidge's landslide triumph over his disrupted opponents.

In 1928 Al Smith became the first Roman Catholic and the first spokesman of the Newer Americans to win the presidential nomination of a major party. Rural Protestant America perceived Smith's candidacy as a threat to national traditions. A leading Republican dry declared: "The stability and continuation of our democratic form of government depends on keeping in the political saddle what we used to call the frontier and what today we call Main Street; the virile, clean-minded, middle class mentality." Smith was soundly defeated, largely because the Republican candidate, Herbert Hoover, was the nominee of the majority party in a time of prosperity. But the cultural issues raised by Smith's candidacy also shaped the vote, as Hoover broke the Democratic hold on the Solid South.

When Hoover took office in March, 1929, the Republican party was at its zenith. Not once since the election of Franklin Pierce in 1852 had a Democrat entered the White House with a majority of the vote. Hoover spoke for the Old Order of individualism and Protestant morality but also for the New Era of corporation leadership and modern technology. Men had come to believe that they had achieved "a permanent plateau of prosperity." In his inaugural address, the new President claimed: "In no nation are the fruits of accomplishment more secure."

Just seven months later, the crash of the stock market shattered these illusions. In the next three years, the bottom dropped out of the economy. By 1932, American industry was turning out less than half its 1929 volume, and new investments had fallen from $10 billion to $1 billion. Blue chip stocks tumbled, General Motors from 73 to 8. As crop prices plunged downward, the farmer was driven to the wall. On a single day in April, 1932, one-fourth of the state of Mississippi fell under the auctioneer's hammer. One observer commented: "We seem to have stepped Alice-like through an economic looking-glass into a world where everything shrivels. Bond prices, stock prices, commodity prices, employment—they all dwindle."

In three years, national income was cut in half, and the number of unemployed soared to some 15 million. Thomas Wolfe wrote of the winter of 1930–1931 in New York: "I saw half naked wretches sitting on park benches at three in the morning in a freezing rain and sleet: often I saw a man and a woman huddled together with their arms around each other for warmth, and with sodden newspapers, rags, or anything they could find over their shoulders." At the end of 1931, a Philadelphia relief authority announced: "We have unemployment in every third house. It is almost like the visitation of death to the households of the Egyptians at the time of the escape of the Jews from Egypt."

The longer the depression persisted, the more it threatened to engulf everyone. "Anybody sinks after a while," commented one jobless man. "Even you would have if God hadn't preserved, without apparent rhyme or reason, your job and your income." Detroit's relief rolls, Mayor Frank Murphy told a Senate subcommittee, embraced doctors, lawyers, ministers, and "two families after whom streets are named."

Hoover attempted to meet this disaster with the ideas of the Old Order: faith in business leadership, trust in voluntary endeavor, and emphasis on action by local governments. To be sure, he assumed responsibilities that no President had undertaken before. But he placed his main reliance on budget-balancing and the staples of classical economics. When his Federal Farm Board boldly intervened in the economy to shore up farm prices, the program proved a dismal failure, because no restrictions were placed on production. Despite mounting evidence of privation, Hoover refused to sanction federal aid to the unemployed. A man hitherto known as a Great Humanitarian for his relief efforts in World War I, a leader identified with government intervention in the economy in wartime and with public works planning, Hoover during the depression displayed a rigidity which made him appear callous. Perhaps never in our history has a President entered office with such high expectations and left in such ill repute.

By the spring of 1932, the country faced a relief crisis. New York City, with payrolls down more than $80 million a month, was spending only $4 million a month on relief and had 25,000 emergency cases on its relief waiting list. Chicago separated families and sent husbands and wives to different shelters. Houston announced: "Applications are not taken from unemployed Mexican or colored families. They are being asked to shift for themselves." The vice-chairman of the Mayor's Unemployment Commission of Detroit saw "no possibility of preventing widespread hunger and slow starvation . . . through its own unaided resources."

As the depression deepened, the country came to question both the claims of business leaders and the worth of the capitalist system. Nothing seemed so severe an indictment of capitalism as the phenomenon of want in the midst of plenty. At a time when many lived on the edge of starvation, Montana wheat was left standing uncut in the fields, bushels of apples lay rotting in Oregon orchards. The breakdown of the market system and the social irresponsibility of business leaders produced a loud chorus of disapproval. The Methodists condemned the American industrial order as "unchristian, unethical, and antisocial"; the Episcopal *Churchman* pronounced capitalism "rotten to the core"; and the editor of the *Catholic World* denounced capital's treatment of labor as "worse than that accorded an animal."

This sorry state of affairs placed Hoover and the Republicans in an extremely vulnerable position. The Democratic party made the most of its opportunity by naming as its presidential candidate in 1932 the popular governor of New York, Franklin Delano Roosevelt. Although Roosevelt offered few specifics, he scored an emphatic victory in the November election, capturing 42 of the 48 states. The Democrats also won their biggest margin in the House since 1890, their largest majority in the Senate since before the Civil War. The election displaced the Republican party as the nation's majority party, and made possible a marked change of emphasis in American policies. As Hoover himself asserted: "This election is not a mere shift from the ins to the outs. It means deciding the direction our nation will take over a century to come."

During the four-month interregnum between Roosevelt's election in November, 1932, and his assumption of office on March 4, 1933, the economy plunged downward, and in the last three weeks of Hoover's term, the financial illness that had plagued the country took a critical turn. In the previous three years, more than 5,000 banks had collapsed, burying 9 million savings accounts in the debris. Now banks in every part of the country folded. On the morning of Roosevelt's inauguration, the president of the New York Stock Exchange mounted the rostrum to make a momentous announcement: the Stock Exchange was closing down. The decision symbolized both the disintegration of the nation's financial system and the surrender of initiative from Wall Street to Washington. By the morning of Roosevelt's inauguration, every state in the Union had closed its banks or permitted them to operate only on a restricted basis.

Moving swiftly to deal with the financial crisis, the President summoned Congress into special session, halted transactions in gold, and proclaimed a national bank holiday. When Congress convened on March 9, in an atmosphere tense as wartime, the administration submitted a bill validating a wide range of presidential powers over banking, and arranging for the reopening of banks with liquid assets and the reorganization of the rest. At 8:36 P.M., less than eight hours after the bill had been introduced, President Roosevelt, at a room in the White House littered with piles of books and pictures of the new tenants, signed the first measure of the New Deal. Three days later, FDR delivered the first of his "fireside chats" over the radio to reassure the nation about the safety of savings accounts. When the banks opened the next day in the twelve Federal Reserve cities, deposits far outnumbered withdrawals. The crisis was over. Roosevelt had vastly extended the sphere of government action, and yet he had left the financial institutions of the country essentially intact.

Thus began the historic "Hundred Days." Between March 9 and June 16, when Congress adjourned, a period of precisely one hundred days, President Roosevelt sent fifteen separate messages up to the Hill, and Congress enacted all fifteen proposals. No Congress in history had ever adopted such a panoply of legislation. During the Hundred Days, Roosevelt functioned under a kind of constitutional dictatorship which resembled such World War I governments as the Sacred Union in France, the Lloyd George coalition in Britain, and the Burgfrieden in Germany. Unlike such administrations, it was not a coalition government but a Democratic party operation. Nor was opposition ever stifled, nor did Congress ever become a rubber stamp. Yet the sense of crisis blunted partisanship and made it possible for FDR to have his way in almost every instance.

Few of the institutions of the 1920's could survive the test of hard times. Prohibition, which gave to the twenties much of its distinctive character, was doomed by the victory of the Democrats, with their big-city support. Before the year was out, the thirty-sixth state had ratified the Twenty-first Amendment, which repealed the Eighteenth Amendment.

The jovial reception accorded to the end of prohibition symbolized one of the most important contributions made by Roosevelt: the return of a sense of national confidence and the end of the gloom and torpor of the

Hoover years. Two weeks after the decisive new President took office, the spirit of the country seemed changed beyond recognition. "The people aren't sure . . . just where they are going," noted one business journal, "but anywhere seems better than where they have been. In the homes, on the streets, in the offices, there is a feeling of hope reborn."

The bank crisis resolved, prohibition repeal under way, a new spirit of confidence in government achieved, Roosevelt felt free to undertake the more difficult tasks of recovery and reform. The spearhead of his recovery program was the National Industrial Recovery Act, an omnibus law which made concessions to a number of different groups. Businessmen were authorized to draft industry-wide agreements, called "codes," which would be exempt from the antitrust laws but supervised by the government. Section 7(a) of the act guaranteed workers the right to collective bargaining and stipulated that the codes should set minimum wages and maximum hours. In addition, the law provided for $3.3 billion in public works. One Congressman charged that the measure was the product of Roosevelt's intellectual advisers, "fresh from the academic cloisters of Columbia University, and with the added inspiration of all they have learned in Moscow." Yet the act represented less a triumph of government planning than a willingness to permit business, free of the threat of antitrust prosecution, to negotiate industry-wide pacts controlling price and output.

To meet the farm crisis, Congress approved the Agricultural Adjustment Act, authorizing a project which one New Dealer called "the greatest single experiment in economic planning under capitalist conditions ever attempted by a democracy in times of peace." The law levied a tax on processors of agricultural commodities, and paid the farmer who agreed to restrict production a subsidy based on "parity," which would give him the same level of purchasing power he had had before the war. A companion Farm Credit Act made possible the refinancing of farm mortgages. Yet not until Roosevelt's second term did the government do anything, however modest, to aid the most depressed members of the farm community—sharecroppers, tenant farmers, and migrant laborers (vividly portrayed in John Steinbeck's *The Grapes of Wrath*). Roosevelt's farm program resulted in an unprecedented involvement of the government with the American farmer. William Faulkner later wrote: "Our economy is not agricultural any longer. Our economy is the federal government. We no longer farm in Mississippi cotton fields. We farm now in Washington corridors and Congressional committee rooms."

Roosevelt also heeded the ancient cry of the farmer for cheap money. Although his first steps, notably an Economy Act which slashed government salaries and soldiers' pensions, had been severely deflationary, he recognized the need for early action to boost prices. The President wanted to develop a carefully controlled inflation, but soft-money men from the South and West compelled him to go further. He took the nation off the gold standard; experimented with gold-buying, to raise prices; and, reluctantly, also undertook silver purchases. But by 1934 he had lost most of his interest in money manipulation, which had succeeded in halting deflation but had otherwise yielded little, and thereafter he fought a rear-guard action against the strong inflationist wing in Congress.

The NIRA, AAA, and managed currency constituted the New Deal's main recovery efforts, but even in his first weeks in office, the President was working toward a different aim: reform of the nation's financial system. In May, 1933, Congress approved Roosevelt's recommendation for federal regulation of securities. The following year, it brought the stock exchange under national control and created the Securities and Exchange Commission to administer the new regulations. The Glass-Steagall Act of 1933 separated investment from commercial banking and provided for a controversial innovation, government insurance of bank deposits, which turned out to be a brilliant success. In 1935, the Congress of the Second Hundred Days enacted a banking law, which centralized control of the Federal Reserve System, and the Public Utilities Holding Company Act, which leveled holding company pyramids. Well before the end of Roosevelt's first term, the country, which had once regarded Wall Street as the power center of the nation, had shifted its attention to Washington. As one writer noted, the front page of the newspaper had become "more important to the businessman than the market page, and the White House Press conference of vaster import than the closing prices of the New York Stock Exchange."

The Holding Company Act climaxed a 29-month campaign by the federal government to expand its influence in the electric power field and to initiate new conservation programs. The Tennessee Valley Authority, created in 1933, plunged the government into the generation of hydroelectric power and a series of experiments in planning for a region the size of England and Scotland. The Public Works Administration (PWA) helped construct such mammoth dams as Grand Coulee and Bonneville in the Pacific Northwest and Fort Peck in Montana. Even more dramatic was the work of the Rural Electrification Administration, set up in 1935. When Roosevelt took office, nine out of ten American farms had no electricity. Under the stimulus of the REA, by 1950 nine out of ten farms enjoyed the benefits of electric power. The New Deal also accomplished an enormous amount in the physical rehabilitation of the country, especially in soil conservation, and in coping with the prolonged drought which turned a large section of the Great Plains into a dust bowl. The Civilian Conservation Corps (CCC), another product of the Hundred Days, put thousands of young men into the forests to feed wildlife, count game, clear camping grounds, and above all, to plant trees.

Both the CCC and the PWA helped meet one of the most demanding problems Roosevelt faced—relief for the unemployed—but neither proved as important as the Federal Emergency Relief Administration created in 1933 to channel federal money to the jobless through state and local agencies. To head the FERA, the President named the dynamic New York social worker Harry Hopkins. A half hour after he left the White House, Hopkins set up a desk in the hallway of a government building, and in the next two hours "spent" $5 million. By the end of 1934, more than 20 million persons—one out of every six in the nation—were receiving public assistance.

In 1935, Congress voted nearly $5 billion for work relief. Hopkins directed the spending of most of this money for public works such as hospitals, schools, and airports under the aegis of a new agency, the Works Progress Administration. Determined to make use of the special skills of white-collar workers, and especially men and women of artistic talent, Hopkins created under the WPA a Federal Theatre, a Federal Writers' Project, a Federal Music Project, and a Federal Art Project; these agencies found employment for painters like Stuart Davis and writers such as Ralph Ellison. The National Youth Administration gave part-time jobs in the next eight years to over 600,000 college students and more than 1.5 million high school pupils.

In part as a consequence of these relief activities, the New Deal also took unprecedented steps in housing. The Home Owners' Loan Act of 1933 made it possible to save tens of thousands of homes from foreclosure. The following year, Congress set up a Federal Housing Administration which, by guaranteeing mortgages, enabled Americans to borrow money on reasonable terms to buy a new home or repair an old one. In the next three years, the FHA gave home-improvement loans to a million and a quarter people. The government sponsored more than a hundred model communities, some of them subsistence homesteads, and created "green-belt" towns which sought to combine the best in urban and rural living. Most important, especially after the establishment of the United States Housing Authority in 1937, the administration assumed responsibility for clearing slums and erecting projects to house the poor.

Although Roosevelt and his Secretary of Labor, Frances Perkins, the first woman cabinet member, did not intend to use government to foster unionization, organized labor benefited from the humanitarian emphases of the New Deal. Under the leadership of John L. Lewis, United Mine Workers' organizers told coal miners: "The President wants you to join." When the American Federation of Labor proved unsympathetic to the attempt to enroll workers in the mass industries, Lewis led a number of unions out of the A. F. of L. and created what would be known as the Congress of Industrial Organizations (CIO). The CIO's campaign received a boost when in 1935 Congress enacted the National Labor Relations Act; the Wagner Act, as it was called after its sponsor, Senator Robert Wagner of New York, forbade employers to interfere with union efforts at organization and empowered a National Labor Relations Board to enforce these prohibitions and to conduct plant elections. Yet labor learned that, even with a friendly government, it had to take the initiative if it was to break the resistance to unionism in the big industries. In 1937, it found an effective weapon in the sitdown strike; by March of that year, almost 200,000 workers—opticians, milliners, clerks, farm hands, even wet-nurses—were sitting down at their jobs somewhere in the country. Before the year was out, such titans as U.S. Steel, General Motors, and General Electric had capitulated, and the attempt to organize workers in the factories, frustrated for so many years, had scored a stunning success.

Of all the welfare measures of the New Deal, the most significant was the Social Security Act of 1935, which created a national system of old age insurance, set up a federal-state program of unemployment insurance, and authorized federal aid to the states, on a matching basis, for care of dependent mothers and children, the crippled, and the blind and for public health services. Republican Senator Daniel Hastings typified conservative response to Roosevelt's proposal when he stated: "I fear it may end the progress of a great country and bring its people to the level of the average European." But most Congressmen believed that such action had been too long postponed; decades earlier, European countries had provided for security against the perils of old age and joblessness in an industrial society.

The New Deal came a long way toward creating a welfare state. It accepted responsibility for aiding millions of unemployed; took at least preliminary steps to deal with the problem of rural poverty; engaged the government directly in clearing slums; focused national attention on the impoverished "one-third of a nation"; set federal standards of minimum wages and maximum hours; wiped out sweatshops and child labor; and set up a system of social security. The First Lady, Eleanor Roosevelt, whose career reflected the growing importance of women in politics, played an important role in nurturing the government's humanitarian concerns. "Government has a final responsibility for the well-being of its citizenship," Roosevelt declared. "If private co-operative endeavor fails to provide work for willing hands and relief for the unfortunate, those suffering hardship from no fault of their own have a right to call upon the Government for aid; and a government worthy of its name must make fitting response."

By 1936 the sorts of issues that had concerned the country in 1932 seemed as far removed from contemporary reality as the tariff debates of Calhoun and Webster a century earlier. Under Roosevelt, the government was engaged in a spectrum of activities—documentary films, Indian art, shelterbelts—that was different not merely in degree but also in kind from almost anything Washington had ever undertaken before. Just four years earlier no one could have anticipated that the government would be running its own circus, supporting Jackson Pollock's painting, paying farmers not to raise peanuts, attempting to regulate the brassiere industry, sending bookmobiles through the Tennessee Valley, patronizing the ballet, and teaching the Pine Ridge Sioux how to milk goats.

Before the New Deal, most Americans did not conceive of the national government as an agency that acted directly on them. By the end of Roosevelt's second term, it was affecting the everyday life of people in countless ways. Millions survived wholly because of relief payments. Others cashed Social Security checks or drew unemployment insurance benefits financed in part by the federal government. Millions of farmers cast ballots in AAA referendums, and factory workers voted in NLRB elections. Suburbanites lived in FHA-financed homes, and city dwellers in mammoth U.S. housing projects. Schoolchildren ate hot lunches provided by the federal government, college students received monthly NYA checks from Washington, and the WPA taught more than a million illiterates to read and write. At the beginning of the decade, the nation's primary loyalties were still to local and state governments. But local units of government proved unable to cope with the crisis, and by the end of the decade, it seemed natural to center one's attention on Washington.

To staff the new federal agencies, Roosevelt turned to university-trained experts. Save for a brief moment of glory in the wartime agencies in 1917, this new class of administrators did not make its appearance in the national arena in large numbers until the 1930's. Roosevelt made use of a "brain trust" in the 1932 campaign, and when he took office he combed the campuses for professors and authorized them to decide a range of economic questions. "On a routine administration matter you go to a Cabinet member," observed a reporter, "but on matters of policy and the higher statesmanship you consult the professoriat."

Roosevelt also succeeded in legitimizing this expansion of governmental power, although only after a fierce struggle. In the spring of 1935, the Supreme Court invalidated the National Industrial Recovery Act. Early in 1936 it held the AAA's processing tax to be unconstitutional. By a series of further decisions, the tribunal wiped other New Deal and state laws off the statute books. In retaliation, the President in 1937 sought to "pack" the Court with six additional justices. Congress balked, but in the course of the battle, the Court reversed itself, and sustained such New Deal laws as the Social Security Act and the Wagner Act. After the "revolution of 1937," there was almost no act of Congress in the area of economic regulation that the Court would not sanction.

Roosevelt and his political chieftains exploited the opportunity offered by the depression to establish the Democrats as the country's new majority party. The foundation of the new coalition was the support of the urban masses. In 1936, Roosevelt captured 104 of the 106 cities in the United States with 100,000 or more residents. Especially significant in this urban alliance were ethnic voters and organized labor. In 1932, most Negroes, still wedded to the party of Lincoln, had backed Hoover; in 1936, they switched emphatically to FDR. Although no civil rights legislation was adopted under the New Deal, unemployed Negroes received a large share of relief payments and other benefits and Roosevelt appointed men such as Robert Weaver and women like Mary McLeod Bethune to his "black cabinet." Labor in 1932 made almost no contribution to the Democratic cause; in 1936, the Mine Workers gave the party nearly half a million dollars, the largest donation from any source.

With 523 electoral votes to Alf Landon's 8, Roosevelt won reelection in 1936 by the largest margin in more than a century. The President swept so many Democratic Congressmen into office with him that a number of the newcomers had to sit on the Republican side of the aisle. A Chicago Democrat later reflected: "Franklin Roosevelt was the greatest precinct captain we ever had. He elected everybody—governors, senators, mayors, sheriffs, aldermen." Roosevelt would win two more terms in the White House, and even after he was gone, the Great Depression and the New Deal would leave its mark on the political alignments of the postwar world.

Yet for all the achievements of the New Deal, it failed to make much headway in its most important assignment: ending the depression. To be sure, this was a most formidable task. By the time Roosevelt took over, the economic structure had been so badly damaged and the morale of investors so shattered that even at best slow progress could be expected. New Deal policies resulted in a quick spurt in the spring of 1933, but for the next two years, little advance was made. Encouraging gains began in mid-1935. By the spring of 1937, the nation had finally risen above 1929 levels of production. But in August, 1937, a sharp recession struck, from which the country only painfully recovered. As late as 1939, ten years after the Wall Street crash, some 10 million were unemployed.

Although critics denounced Roosevelt as a profligate spender, the economy behaved so sluggishly chiefly because the New Dealers failed to appreciate the importance of deficit spending in bad times. Roosevelt felt almost as strongly as Hoover that an unbalanced budget was sinful. Not until 1938, and then only to a limited extent, did the President adopt the recommendation of British economist John Maynard Keynes to employ fiscal policy to achieve recovery. Moreover, for all the social measures of the New Deal, the basic pattern of distribution of income remained virtually unchanged. In May, 1940, Secretary of the Interior Harold Ickes noted in his diary: "This is our weakness. The New Deal has done a great deal during the last seven years, but we have not been able to force from those who own and control the preponderant part of our wealth the social and economic security that people are entitled to." Only with the coming of World War II, which sharply accelerated government spending, did the country once more enjoy full employment and effect a modest redistribution of income. Since the Roosevelt era, the severity of recessions has been mitigated by the stabilizers created by the New Deal, but the economy has never achieved full employment without the stimulus of military spending.

By the end of 1938, the New Deal had lost its impetus as a force for social reform, and Roosevelt was compelled to direct much of his attention to problems of foreign policy. Even before he took office, the post-Versailles world was disintegrating. When, in September, 1931, Japan invaded Manchuria, it demonstrated that neither the League of Nations Covenant, the Nine-Power Treaty, upholding the territorial integrity of China, nor the Kellogg-Briand Pact, outlawing war as an instrument of national policy, would suffice to contain a power bent on conquest. Hoover, when called on to enforce the Kellogg and the Nine-Power pacts, replied that they were "solely moral instruments." In Roosevelt's first week as President, the Reichstag granted absolute power to Adolf Hitler, and for the rest of his life FDR had to cope with the menace of totalitarianism. During Roosevelt's first term, Mussolini's forces would invade Ethiopia, Germany would march into the Rhineland, and both powers would convert Spain's civil war into a testing ground for the greater war that was to come.

Although by instinct and experience a Wilsonian internationalist, Roosevelt believed that he had to concentrate on pulling America through the crisis, and his first actions veered in an economic nationalist direction. When he began to consider a different course, isolationist and pacifist opinion left him little room to maneuver. Congressional isolationists insisted on an embargo on the sale of war material to belligerents, and they refused to grant the President the discretionary power he requested to decide whether an embargo should be applied, and, if so, to which nation. A series of neutrality laws, designed, as critics noted, to keep the United States out of World War I, tied Roosevelt's hands, and he was reduced through most of his first two terms to futile moralizing. By the summer of 1936, the President seemed to have surrendered altogether to the isolationists and pacifists. "We shun political commitments which might entangle us in foreign wars; we avoid connection with the political activities of the League of Nations," he asserted. Both the President and Congress were conforming to public opinion; in March, 1937, a Gallup poll (another innovation of the 1930's) reported that 94 per cent of Americans favored a policy of staying out of all wars instead of preventing these wars from erupting.

In other parts of the world Roosevelt had more maneuverability than he did with respect to western Europe. He implemented a "Good Neighbor" policy toward Latin America, "recognized" the Soviet Union, and negotiated reciprocity agreements which modified the high Hawley-Smoot tariff of 1930. In the Far East, where he also had a freer hand, he was more sympathetic than Hoover had been to the ideas of Henry Stimson, who sought to restrain the Japanese; yet, like Hoover, he and his associates opposed strong measures against Tokyo. "Then if moral ostracism is ineffective, how can we implement the Kellogg Pact?" asked Joseph Grew, ambassador to Japan. "Certainly not by force of arms, which would be contrary to the very principle for which the Kellogg Pact stands," Grew replied.

But by 1939 Roosevelt and many of the men around him had come to feel that the United States must make some contribution to halting fascist expansion, and they began to extend limited kinds of help to Britain and France. In September, 1939, the German invasion of Poland would set off a chain of explosions that would involve the United States ever more deeply in the spreading war. Little more than two years later, the United States would be fighting the war it had vowed never to fight. It would enter that war a vastly different nation from the country that engaged in World War I—more industrialized, more committed to the ways of the city, more cosmopolitan, less deferential to business leadership, more aware of the possibilities of the welfare state, more responsive to the demands of labor and of various ethnic groups, and, as its role in the creation of the United Nations would shortly demonstrate, much more willing to assume a role in world affairs commensurate with its power.

For Further Reading

Bernstein, Irving, *The Lean Years.*
Leighton, Isabel (ed.), *The Aspirin Age.*
Leuchtenburg, William E., *Franklin D. Roosevelt and the New Deal, 1932–1940.*
————, *The Perils of Prosperity, 1914–32.*
Schlesinger, Arthur M., Jr., *The Age of Roosevelt.*

89   Modern China

The fall of the Ch'ing was a real revolution, perhaps the first in Chinese history. Dynasties had been overthrown before, but no emperor had ever been succeeded by a president. With the Ch'ing traditional concepts of legitimacy, above all the hereditary principle, disappeared. Henceforth, China was to be a republic.

This was not immediately apparent. President Yüan Shih-k'ai's idea of what was best for China was far from revolutionary. In Yüan's view, China needed a strong executive, and this led him to the conclusion that he should establish a constitutional monarchy. One after another, possible rivals—the cabinet, the young political parties, and the parliament—were subdued by Yüan in the first years of his rule.

Yüan's acceptance in 1915 of the Japanese Twenty-one Demands, which granted far-reaching economic privileges to Japan in China, damaged his reputation as China's strong man, but did not deter him from his intention to establish a monarchy. But when Yüan launched his campaign to become emperor, he found little support. Opposition from the provinces and, more important, from military leaders, including some of Yüan's own subordinates, caused the monarchical movement to collapse, and in 1916 Yüan died a broken man.

For the next decade Chinese political life was dominated by Yüan's former subordinates and other militarists who had acquired power in the provinces after the revolution. The regionalism that had begun with the Taiping Rebellion now reached its final stage. China became a kaleidoscope of satrapies at the mercy of the warlords, each strong enough to control and exploit a few districts or a province or two, none powerful enough to eliminate his rivals. There was a central government in Peking, recognized by the powers, but its authority did not extend beyond the territories held by the armies of the warlords who formed it, and its composition changed with the frequent shifts in the balance of military power in north China.

With few exceptions, the warlords stood above all else for their own self-interest. In this they were symptomatic of the time, for, as the Confucian ethic, the traditional social fabric, and central political authority continued to disintegrate, there remained no higher principles compelling loyalty, no cohesive force to hold society together. In the words of Sun Yat-sen, China resembled "a sheet of loose sand." For a time it seemed that

A.D. 1912–1916 Yüan Shih-k'ai first president of the Republic of China
1919 May Fourth Movement
1924 Reorganization of the Kuomintang
1926–1928 Northern Expedition, and reunification of China under the Kuomintang
1934–1935 Chinese Communists' Long March
1937–1945 Second Sino-Japanese War

---

military power alone was strong enough to maintain order. But order was impossible in a country divided among contending mercenary armies, and so the warlords were eventually superseded by new political parties inspired by constructive programs and possessing disciplined armies—the Nationalists, then the Communists.

First, new ideological foundations had to be discovered. As during the late Chou and the Six dynasties, intellectual life was stimulated by the disintegration of political authority. The abolition of the examination system and the expansion of Western education spurred the search for new values to replace the discredited intellectual tradition. Adam Smith, John Stuart Mill, Dickens, Darwin, Spencer, Ibsen, and Tolstoy were translated and discussed. Several thousand students went to Europe, America, and Japan to get a closer view of the modern world. Most became convinced that the West had much to offer China. One of these, Hu Shih, who took a Ph.D. at Columbia in 1917, urged that colloquial Chinese replace the archaic classical style as the national literary language to facilitate the spread of literacy and Westernization. Others extolled individualism, women's rights, democracy, and science, and denounced Confucianism and the traditional family system. When these new ideas combined with nationalism, a new and powerful historical force was born.

This happened in 1919. In early May of that year it was learned in Peking that the Versailles Peace Conference had awarded former German rights in the Shantung peninsula to Japan. Indignation—at the powers, at Japan, and at pro-Japanese "traitors" within the Peking government—led to a demonstration of some 3,000 Peking students on May 4. The arrest of hundreds of the students only inspired more to join the protest. Within days the fever had spread to other cities. Students organized and demonstrated, workers struck, and merchants closed their shops as gestures of solidarity with the patriots. A nation-wide boycott of Japanese goods began. The government was helpless, and for a brief time it became evident that armed force was not the ultimate source of political authority. The cabinet fell. Nationalism had made a triumphant entry onto the political stage.

The students and professors who had participated in the events of May emerged as the intellectual leaders of the nation and used their new-found eminence to propagate their ideas. Within a few years more than 400 new periodicals appeared, filled with articles in the colloquial style about the Western world and the regeneration of China. No aspect of tradition was sacred, from Confucius and the most venerated legends of antiquity to arranged marriages and footbinding. Anarchism, Liberalism, Materialism, Pragmatism, German Idealism, Art of Art's Sake, Socialism, and the newest of all, Bolshevism, all found advocates. Some ideas took organizational form, in labor unions, literary societies, and political parties, including a small Chinese Communist party founded by Westernized intellectuals in 1921. The periodical press carried lengthy polemics about the ability or inability of science to solve all problems of human existence, and over the relative merits of Chinese and Western civilizations. One general conclusion soon became apparent: most educated Chinese now looked to the West, not to China's past, for their ideals.

The new ideas were invigorating, but they were also a source of frustration, for foreign privilege and warlord rapacity remained, and the gap between the imported ideals and Chinese realities was all too obvious. The ironies of this situation were a common theme in the fiction of the twenties, most especially in the trenchant satire of China's greatest modern writer, Lu Hsun. To the perspicacious it was clear that ideals alone could not save China; only force could root out the warlords and compel the foreigners to relinquish their privileges.

It was Sun Yat-sen who found a way to give the new nationalism military power. Over the years, Sun's requests for aid had been rejected by Japan, Great Britain, and the United States, but in 1923 Soviet Russia agreed to support him. Under the guidance of Soviet advisers, Sun's political party, the Kuomintang (Nationalist party), was reorganized along the lines of Bolshevik "democratic centralism." Military assistance, in the form of advisers and matériel, was also supplied by the Russians. A party military academy was founded at Whampoa, in the outskirts of Canton. There, under Commandant Chiang Kai-shek, officer candidates were trained in military science and indoctrinated in party ideology, which under Russian influence now included anti-imperialism and nationalization of major industries. The new party constitution and program and a united front with

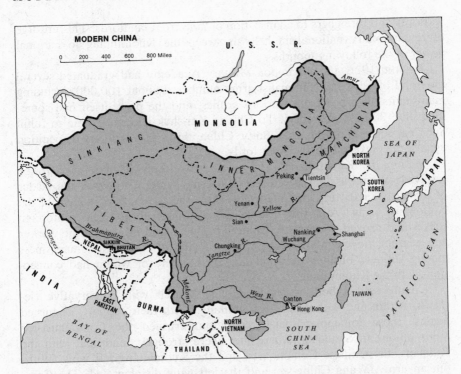

MODERN CHINA

0   200   400   600   800 Miles

U. S. S. R.

MONGOLIA

SINKIANG

INNER MONGOLIA

MANCHURIA

TIBET

NORTH KOREA

SOUTH KOREA

SEA OF JAPAN

JAPAN

Peking   Tientsin

Yenan

Sian

Nanking   Shanghai

Wuchang

Chungking

Yellow R.

Yangtze

Mekong R.

West R.   Canton

Hong Kong

TAIWAN

PACIFIC OCEAN

SOUTH CHINA SEA

NORTH VIETNAM

LAOS

THAILAND

BURMA

EAST PAKISTAN

BAY OF BENGAL

INDIA

NEPAL   SIKKIM   BHUTAN

Ganges R.

Brahmaputra R.

Indus R.

Amur R.

the infant Chinese Communist party were approved at the First National Congress of the reorganized Kuomintang in January, 1924, in spite of opposition from the party's right wing. Although the Kuomintang never became as efficiently regimented as its Leninist model, for many years it was superior in numbers, organization, discipline, and zeal to any other political group in China. By the time of Sun's sudden death in March, 1925, the Kuomintang controlled Canton, and had extended its influence into surrounding Kwangtung province.

Soon after Sun's death came another outburst of indignation at China's humiliating condition. In May and June, foreign police in Shanghai and Canton fired on student and worker demonstrations protesting the treatment of Chinese workers in foreign-owned factories. A number of the demonstrators were killed, and antiforeign feeling soared. Organized and led by the left wing of the Kuomintang and the Communists, and supported by Chinese businessmen, workers struck in Shanghai, Canton, Hong Kong, and other cities. The Hong Kong strike, which lasted well over a year, and a widespread boycott of British goods damaged British trade. Under similar leadership, in a number of southern provinces the peasant movement gathered momentum, and in some areas progressed from hostility against warlords and foreigners to confiscation of land from landlords. This upsurge of revolutionary nationalism help to sweep the Kuomintang to national power in the following months.

By mid-1926, the Whampoa Military Academy had graduated several thousand officers, the Nationalist army numbered about 100,000, including many units absorbed from warlord armies, and the party itself had something like 200,000 members. To Chiang Kai-shek it seemed time to fulfill Sun Yat-sen's ambition to reunify China through a military expedition against the powerful northern warlords.

Within the Kuomintang there were two closely related issues to be resolved: Who was to succeed Sun Yat-sen—Wang Ching-wei, the leader of the party's left wing, or Chiang Kai-shek, the commander in chief of the Nationalist army? And how far was the revolution to go? The antiforeign strikes had proved injurious to Chinese business, and in general the worker and peasant movements were becoming a cause of considerable uneasiness among Chinese businessmen and landlords, many of whom had connections with the Kuomintang.

Chiang settled both issues by allying himself with conservative elements, within and without the Kuomintang. With their support, he turned against those fomenting social revolution, crushed the Communist-led labor unions in Shanghai, where they were strongest, and split with the Russians, the Chinese Communists, and the Kuomintang left wing. Without an army, Wang Ching-wei and the left wing disintegrated. The Communists instigated several uprisings, all futile. The Russians quietly returned home. The power struggle temporarily retarded the progress of Chiang's "Northern Expedition," but it soon continued triumphantly northward through one province after another, culminating in the capture of Peking in June, 1928, and the formal submission of the northern warlords. Chiang was now paramount within the Kuomintang, and head of the newly proclaimed Nationalist government in Nanking. By the end of 1928, the new government had been granted diplomatic recognition by most of the foreign powers, with the United States in the lead.

The Nationalist government was formally the government of all China, but its direct influence was largely confined to the central and lower Yangtze provinces, which, along with the coastal ports, especially the great metropolis of Shanghai, provided its main sources of support. The land tax, the most important source of revenue, remained in the hands of provincial officials, many of whom were warlords who had nominally submitted to the new government, but who in reality were virtually autonomous within their territories. During the decade from 1928 to the outbreak of the Sino-Japanese War in 1937, such militarists occasionally joined and rose against the Nanking government, but they were no serious threat, and in the process of suppressing these revolts the central government extended its authority into new areas.

After Chiang's split with the Communists, the government cracked down on the party, driving many members from the cities to the country-side, where the party was to gain the understanding of rural China crucial to its eventual victory. In 1931 a "Soviet Republic" was established in Kiangsi province, but by 1934 the attacks of government armies forced the Communists to abandon Kiangsi, and they embarked on the epic Long March to the northwest, through 6,000 miles of the most difficult terrain in China. Only 30,000 of the original 90,000 reached their destination a year later. During the march a new group of tough and resourceful leaders emerged, headed by Mao Tse-tung.

Meanwhile, the Nanking government was slowly modernizing China. A provisional constitution and a modern law code were promulgated, and although both remained paper legislation in many respects, they were steps forward. The army was strengthened. Progress was made in public health, industry, transportation, irrigation, and flood control. Education continued to develop rapidly, particularly on the higher levels, although the infusion of Confucian precepts into the Kuomintang ideology taught in the schools was a sign of the regime's growing conservatism, and alienated many students and Westernized intellectuals. The currency reform of 1935 resulted in financial stability for a few years, before wartime inflation set in. In foreign affairs, tariff autonomy, lost in the Opium War treaties, was regained, providing the government with a valuable means of increasing revenue. Other onerous provisions of the "unequal treaties" were not abolished until 1943.

The threat of Japanese aggression was never absent. Nationalist troops had clashed with Japanese units as early as 1928. In 1931, the Japanese army took over Manchuria, in the next year the puppet Manchukuo regime was inaugurated at Mukden, and in the following years Japanese pressure on north China steadily increased.

In spite of growing popular demand to resist Japan, Chiang adhered to a policy of eliminating internal enemies, primarily the Communists, before confronting China's powerful external foe. But in December, 1936, when Chiang flew to the northwest to compel enforcement of this policy on recalcitrant subordinates, he was held captive by them until an agreement to halt the civil strife was reached. The hard-pressed Communists wel-comed this change, and so when the war with Japan began in July, 1937, there was some semblance of national unity.

The war had two important internal political consequences. The Japa-nese assault drove the Nationalist government inland from Nanking to Chungking in the southwest, severing it from its former sources of support in the coastal cities and Yangtze provinces. Although Chiang gained in personal prestige as the leader of the national resistance, the eight years of warfare left the Kuomintang and the Nationalist government considerably weakened and widespread corruption, which continued after the war, alienated many earlier supporters of the regime. The Communists, on the other hand, exploited the opportunity to extend their influence into rural areas over large parts of central China, which Nationalists had been forced to abandon, but which the Japanese were unequipped to administer. Through mobilization of the peasantry around a program of resistance to the foreign invader and moderate agrarian reform, designed to appeal to a broad stratum of the rural population, the Red army grew from about 90,000 in 1937 to almost 900,000 at the end of the Second World War, while in the same period the membership of the Communist party increased roughly from 40,000 to 1,200,000. Thus in 1945, although the Nationalists were still vastly superior in numbers and equipment, Mao Tse-tung had sufficient strength to challenge Chiang Kai-shek. The stage was set for the final and decisive contest for the mastery of China.

For Further Reading

Chow, Tse-tsung, *The May Fourth Movement: Intellectual Revolution in Modern China*.
Grieder, Jerome B., *Ha Shik and the Chinese Renaissance*.
Sharman, Lyon, *Sun Yat-sen, His Life and Its Meaning: A Critical Biography*.

90   Modernizing Japan

The Meiji Restoration of 1868* is a convenient event from which to date the beginning of Japan's rapid transition to a modern society. To be sure, some aspects of modernization had earlier origins. Recent historians have pointed out that late Tokugawa society provided a better base for modernization than was previously supposed, more affluent, less rigid in social stratification, and with a higher level of popular education. The shogunate had made an initial commitment to technological modernization in the

---

* Meiji was the name of the calendrical era proclaimed in that year. Later it became the posthumous name of the reigning emperor (1867–1912). The implication of the word "restoration" was not primarily the return of the imperial dynasty to power, but rather the return of the country to some earlier moral condition from which rule by military families had presumably been a deviation.

CHRONOLOGY

A.D. 1868 New imperial government established at Edo, re-named Tokyo

1871–1876 Basic policies of centralization and liquidation of caste privilege

1873 Universal military conscription; dispute over Korean invasion resolved in favor of peace faction

1877 Satsuma Rebellion

1881 Date set on constitution and parliament

1889 Promulgation of Meiji Constitution

1890 First session of Imperial Diet

1894–1895 Sino-Japanese War

1904–1905 Russo-Japanese War

1915 Japanese attempt to assert political and economic dominance over China (Twenty-one Demands)

1918 Cabinet of Prime Minister Hara, first to be headed by a member of the House of Representatives

1930 World depression reaches Japan

1931 Mukden Incident, leading to Japanese conquest of Manchuria

1932 Abandonment of party cabinets

1936 Abortive "February Mutiny"

1937 Incident at Marco Polo Bridge brings all-out war with China

1941–1945 Japan at war with Western allies

fields which it recognized as essential for national defense, though the actual accomplishments in industrialization and military preparations up to 1868 were very slender. The significance of the Restoration was that it brought to positions of leadership a new group with sufficient youth and vision to try new ways of action. Specifically, some of the group perceived the particular impediments in society that would have to be removed if modernization was to be accelerated. Two of these were among the most persistent and characteristic features of traditional Japanese society: political decentralization and caste privilege.

The political system immediately after the Restoration was not unlike that under the shogunate. The emperor and his government fell heir to the holdings of the Tokugawa shoguns, but much of the country continued to be semiautonomous domains of the daimyos. The imperial government lacked the power to tax these lands, or even, in the absence of a true national army, to exercise normal police and administrative powers over them. Centralization took the form of a voluntary return of domain land registers by the great western han, followed by a not quite so voluntary program of the same kind for all of the other domains. All of the territory of the country was then reorganized into prefectures, units of provincial administration strictly accountable to the central government.

The initial acts of the Restoration had left the ancient condition of class privilege little impaired. The daimyos were still daimyos; the samurai were still samurai; the peasants and urban commoners were still legally bound to their occupations and localities. Government leaders came to realize that national strength required the broad participation in public life by all classes on a merit basis, and this led them to their most revolutionary reform: the abolition of class qualifications for political or military office, with the concomitant abolition of the pensions and all other caste marks of the samurai. Social rationalization—or at least the firm national commitment to it—was furthered by a reform of agricultural policy: agricultural land was reappraised in terms of cash value instead of estimated annual yield, enabling the government to levy taxes on it that were constant in terms of money. A peasant's real property had been legally inalienable, but was now "freed" (i.e., made subject to sale or foreclosure) in the interests of economic rationalization.

Simultaneously other modernization policies were initiated. The government began to build telegraph lines and a railway system (100 miles of track being laid before 1880), supported by a loan from Great Britain of one million pounds. The central government fell heir to the factories and mines that had belonged to the shogunate and added to them. Industrialization was rigorously planned from the start, strategic industries taking first priority, followed by industries such as textiles that could be used as capital accumulators in foreign trade, and only last by industries specifically for domestic consumption. A modern army and navy were created, with universal military conscription (1873) and a general staff system modeled on that of Prussia (1878).

One major aim of the new government was the recovery of diplomatic equality, that is, revision of the unequal treaties that Japan had been forced to conclude with the Powers before the Restoration. Westerners based their extraterritorial rights on the contention that the Japanese legal system was inefficient and cruel. The Japanese commenced a program of wholesale legal reform, using foreign advisers.

The revolution of early Meiji attests to forthright, able leadership. In law the head of the new government was Emperor Meiji, but he was an adolescent at the time of his accession, and the traditional seclusion of his office made him at most a ratifying, rather than a deciding, figure in the politics of his time. The group actually in control was an oligarchy of men who had proven their mettle in the struggle against the shogunate. Most were from the great western domains that had overthrown the Tokugawa, and the remainder were mostly political activists among the imperial court caste (*kuge*). Despite desertions from the original group by dissenters and the addition to it of younger protégés, the oligarchy had remarkable cohesion and continued to dominate the administration until well into the twentieth century. An internal policy dispute of 1873 (over a quixotic scheme to invade Korea) left as survivors in the central government a group united on goals of international cooperation and internal improvements. That group was almost wholly comprised of former retainers of the Chōshū and Satsuma domains.

The Satsuma Rebellion of 1877 was the most serious of several uprisings by regional samurai bands protesting the abolition of the domains and dispossession of the samurai. The victory of the central government was decisive, demonstrating the superiority of its new citizen army and further strengthening the control of the oligarchy. But opposition to the oligarchy did not cease; in fact it became broader in extent, though less violent in means. The most characteristic form of that opposition from the late 1870's on was the movement for parliamentary institutions, and its first great accomplishment was the establishment of an elected national assembly in 1890.

The belief that Japan should eventually have representative institutions of some kind was widespread. It was in fact part of the craze for all kinds of Western traits, and even members of the oligarchy shared it to some degree. Their consistent position in the 1870's, however, was that the people lacked experience in politics, and that the necessity of rapid modernization would continue to demand authoritarian control for the foreseeable future. Against that view, a group of dissidents organized political action associations—the first political parties—whose aim was to break oligarchic control and inaugurate parliamentary government. The founders of the democratic movement were for the most part former Restorationists who had become disaffected with the government. Their initial objective was not mass egalitarian democracy, but the better representation of the samurai and of local interests. Only gradually did Japanese liberalism become a truly popular cause.

In 1881 the liberal campaign embarrassed the government into making the promise that a constitution would be promulgated eight years hence. The actual drafting of the document was secret and undertaken entirely by the conservatives in the oligarchy. It is not surprising, therefore, that the text which emerged was at best a compromise between liberal and authoritarian principles. It established a bicameral legislature, the Imperial Diet, to meet for the first time in 1890, but the powers of the lower house, elected by limited suffrage, were balanced by those of a House of Peers. Parliamentary power did not extend to certain matters (e.g., the governance of the army and navy) deemed imperial prerogatives, and was severely restricted even over budgetary appropriations.

In form the 1889 Constitution was described as a gift from the emperor, who was therefore regarded as beyond its control. The practical implication of that doctrine was that ultimate state power would continue to rest with any group, such as the existing oligarchy, which enjoyed imperial confidence or which could plausibly claim to speak for the emperor. The chief administrative organ under the throne was a cabinet without responsibility to the parliament, and it tended, with other major civil and military offices, to be manned by the oligarchs or their appointees.

No description of the authoritarian features of the Meiji government or of the opposition to it from outsiders should disguise the fact that the dominant popular mood of late-nineteenth-century Japan was one of ebullient, hopeful self-congratulation for the new paths on which the leaders had set the nation's course. Though some samurai resented the loss of privilege, many others welcomed the opportunities that a rapidly modernizing society gave them. Opposition to the government was sometimes directed against slowness of change. This is nowhere clearer than in the case of popular attitudes to foreign relations. The most important issue in early Meiji was revision of the unequal treaties, and here the almost universal public sentiment was that the government was insufficiently forthright in obtaining it from the Powers. Where relations with other Asian countries were concerned, the public consistently supported a more expansionist, nationalistic policy than the government was willing or able to pursue. Each of the three victorious wars that Japan fought between 1894 and 1918 was popular; each succeeding peace was unpopular because it failed to secure the territory, indemnification, or other gain that the public thought the country was entitled to.

Korea was the main issue in the Sino-Japanese War of 1894–1895 and the Russo-Japanese War of 1904–1905. In the first Japan acquired Formosa and the Pescadores, and made China relinquish her claim to suzerainty over Korea's foreign relations. In the second she won Southern Sakhalin and a concession on the Manchurian coast (including Dairen and Port Arthur), and as a by-product also gained a protectorate over Korea that was extended to outright possession in 1910. In the First World War Japan participated on the side of the Allies. She took advantage of the Powers' involvement in the war by attempting, in the famous Twenty-one Demands (1915), to establish a position of economic and political dominance on the mainland, and was rewarded in the Versailles Treaty with the former German colonial possessions in the North Pacific and on the China coast that she had taken in the fighting.

The generation between the opening of the Diet and the First World War saw internal maturation of several kinds. From this period on, Japan was an industrial power, though the population continued until after the Second World War to be predominantly rural. Education spread, and so did popular concern with national affairs. An incipient social movement created the first labor unions and the first socialist parties. Of far greater immediate importance was a change in the character of the older, main-line party movement. Having gained their rudimentary objectives of a constitution and parliament, liberals next turned to a campaign for broader participation in government by means of responsible party cabinets on the British model. For a decade or so after 1890 the Diet and political parties were dominated by men of such sentiments, but the executive of the government was just as securely dominated by the oligarchs and their protégés, who were opposed to party government. Bit by bit the two factions reached a compromise. Liberal leaders like Ōkuma Shigenobu and Itagaki Taisuke accepted invitations to sit with the oligarchs in the cabinet; oligarchs like Itō Hirobumi accepted leadership in political parties. All agreed that the future should bring a closer relationship between the executive and legislative branches. From about the turn of the century the aging first-generation oligarchs retired from titular executive positions, but retained considerable power behind the scenes in a semiofficial body known as Genro (Elder Statesmen). It was this group who determined the choice of a prime minister and other executive officers, and they turned with increasing frequency to party leaders.

In most of the years from 1918 to 1932 there were party governments—cabinets whose prime ministers and most other members belonged to the majority party in the House of Representatives, even though this had not yet been accepted as a regular constitutional procedure. During these years there was considerable hope from Japanese liberals that Japan was about to become democratic in its domestic institutions as well as peace-loving and cooperative abroad. That a disastrous career of authoritarianism and expansionism, war and defeat, intervened before that dream became possible was a great tragedy for Japan, for which a complex interaction of internal and external causes is responsible.

Public disenchantment with liberalism and party government was one contributing factor. Many associated the parties with opportunism and corruption. Some of the policies adopted by party governments were inept or unpopular. In 1930, for example, the cabinet of Prime Minister Hamaguchi Yūkō was blamed for economic disaster when the deflationary fiscal policy it had adopted to stabilize the international value of the yen coincided with the general world depression and priced Japanese goods entirely out of the world market. The same cabinet was also castigated by chauvinists for concluding the London Naval Disarmament Treaty.

If liberal institutions seemed doomed to frustrating failure, the tactics of rightists and militarists seemed all too often to get things done. The Mukden Incident of September, 1931, an instance of military direct action without the prior knowledge of the civilian government, led to an easy conquest of all of Manchuria. Not only did the army gain glory from this incident. An army-controlled state in Manchuria (ostensibly the independent Empire of Manchukuo) also provided a testing ground for military rule and controlled economy.

Extremist agitation sometimes took the form of assassinations of civilian leaders in politics or business, and in one incident, the attempted coup of February 26, 1936, a wide spectrum of moderate and conservative figures, including advisers to the emperor and antimilitarists in the armed services, were marked for liquidation. The army itself restored discipline, but exacted from frightened moderates a greater share in the government than before. Party cabinets had been abandoned in 1932; succeeding cabinets were made up of a variety of bureaucratic elements, with the army in increasing control.

Japanese foreign policy through the decade had the primary aim of protecting and extending Japan's economic and political interests in the Far East. In 1933 the frontiers of Manchukuo were extended through military means, and in 1935 further areas of northeast China were placed under Japanese surveillance. In July, 1937, a skirmish between Chinese and Japanese troops at the Marco Polo Bridge near Peking at last brought the two countries to war. Japan quickly took the coastal areas and leading cities, but the Chinese held the hinterland, where they stood off the Japanese for eight years.

The Western democracies opposed each new step in Japan's expansion.

Growing friction with them caused the Far Eastern crisis to become part of a world confrontation between fascism and its enemies. Japan joined the Rome-Berlin Axis in 1940 more from the perception that she shared common foes with the European fascists than from any fundamental community of positive goals. The pact further deepened American hostility, yet the United States still permitted the export of strategic materials to Japan until the following summer, fearing that to embargo them would only trigger Japanese seizure of new sources of supply in Southeast Asia. When Japan did occupy Indochina, in prelude to further thrusts southward, America responded with a general embargo. In ensuing negotiations aimed at reducing the tension the two sides made mutually incompatible demands: Japan, that the United States recognize her position in China; and the United States, that Japan withdraw from China. The Pearl Harbor attack of December 7, 1941, was a preemptive strike, based on the premise that the United States was already irrevocably committed to resist those actions of Japan's in East Asia that had by then become the unalterable conditions of her national policy.

For Further Reading

Beasley, W. G., *The Modern History of Japan.*
Fairbank, John K., Edwin O. Reischauer, and Albert M. Craig, *East Asia: The Modern Transformation.*
Reischauer, Edwin O., *Japan: The Story of a Nation.*
Tsunoda, Ryusaku, William Theodore de Bary, and Donald Keene, *Sources of Japanese Tradition.*

91   Nationalism in India

In a carefully phrased announcement to the British Parliament in August, 1917, the Secretary of State for India declared that the policy of the British government was to work for "the increasing association of Indians in every branch of the administration, and the gradual development of self-governing institutions, with a view to the progressive realization of responsible government in India as an integral part of the Empire." This emphasis on gradualism is a reminder that the roots of Indian nationalism were in nineteenth-century constitutionalism and liberalism, and that the cataclysmic forces released by the First World War and the Russian Revolution

CHRONOLOGY

A.D.		
	1905	Partition of Bengal
	1906	Founding of Muslim League
	1909	Morley-Minto Reforms
	1912	Delhi made capital of India
	1917	Announcement by British Parliament of responsible government as goal for India
	1919	Montagu-Chelmsford Reforms
	1920	M. K. Gandhi becomes leader of Indian National Congress
	1921	First Noncooperation Movement
	1927	Simon Commission
	1930	Civil Disobedience Movement
	1935	Government of India Act
	1937	Inauguration of provincial autonomy
	1939	Congress ministries resign on war issue
	1942	Last civil disobedience movement; August uprisings
	1946	Negotiations for transfer of power
	1947	Lord Mountbatten governor general; partition and independence

worked upon a nationalism whose course was already largely determined. The preoccupation of Indian nationalism was always with political, not social, solutions, and the common description of its culmination in 1947 as a "transfer of power" is exact. A social transformation had been neither promised nor expected; such social change as was necessary would follow, it was widely believed, from the transfer of political power from an alien to an indigenous elite.

Such a belief was consonant with the demands of the early nationalist leaders. As was noted previously, the men who organized the Indian National Congress had as their aim participation in the existing administrative structure that the British had created, not control of the mechanism of government, and certainly not its destruction. Almost without exception they were men who had made careers through social structures that were products of the modernizing impact of the west. Dadabhai Naoroji (1825–1917) was a businessman who became a member of the House of Commons; Surendranath Banerjea (1848–1925) founded a newspaper and a college; G. K. Gokhale (1866–1915) was a teacher of English. The early resolutions of the Indian National Congress define the concerns of both the leadership and their following: easier entrance into the Indian Civil Service, the tiny, all-powerful pinnacle of the bureaucracy; expanded membership in legislative councils; protective tariffs; and a decrease in military expenditure. Change would come about as the Indian intelligentsia made known both the needs of India and their own ability to share in the task of rule with the British, since, as Naoroji put it, "the genius of the British people is fair play and justice."

Almost from the very beginning of the nationalist movement there were those who challenged this faith in the British, arguing that no imperial power would act generously, and insisting that the Indian people should not be mendicants for power in their own homeland. The most influential exponent of this view was B. G. Tilak (1856–1920), who in his Marathi and English newspapers eloquently reminded his readers that in leaders like Shivaji, the Marathi chieftain who had defied the might of the Mughal empire, and in the ancient glories of Hinduism, the people of India had traditions of greatness upon which they could draw for strength.

This appeal to the Hindu past made explicit the tensions that had always been latent in the nationalist movement. The advocates of Western education, social reform, and constitutional gradualism, who styled themselves moderates, were dependent upon the examples and the ideals of the British; the forces of reaction were represented for them by India's own traditions. Over against the moderates were men like Tilak, whose whole-hearted acceptance of the Hindu heritage freed them from this ambiguity about their past, permitting them to make a self-confident appeal that gave their nationalism a Hindu vocabulary and Hindu symbols. They proudly accepted the title of "extremists" the moderates bestowed on them.

This emphasis created, or perhaps more accurately, brought to the surface, another tension: an overt hostility between Muslims and Hindus. Sir Syed Ahmed Khan (1817–1898), the leader of modernizing forces in Indian Islam, had argued that the democratic, representative institutions sought by the Indian National Congress would make Indian Muslims a permanent minority, and Tilak's appeal to a Hindu past as the basis of nationalist sentiment sharpened such fears.

Another element of tension came with the increasing emphasis by Tilak and others that violence, not constitutional gradualism, might be necessary for achieving India's freedom. In Bengal, Aurobindo Ghose (1872–1950) preached a passionate identification of the sacrifice required by the nation with the blood offerings made to Kali, the Mother Goddess. Tilak's revivalism and Ghose's mysticism were strengthened in 1905 by the Japanese victory over Russia. By using the West's own weapons, Japan, it was argued, had triumphed over the power Britain had feared for a century.

For the first time since 1857, the British were confronted with the politics of violence, expressed in sabotage and political assassinations.

The working out of the tensions within the nationalist movement emerged in a number of developments. In a struggle for control of the Indian National Congress, the Moderates won an uneasy victory in 1907, but at the price of losing the dynamism imparted to the movement by the passionate logic of the extremists. A group of Muslims responded to the growing concern with India's political future by founding the Muslim League in 1906 for the protection of Muslim interests. The British response to the violent expressions of nationalism was a campaign against the extremist leaders which included the jailing of Tilak, the suppression of newspapers, and the execution of a number of young men found guilty of sabotage and political assassinations. But at the same time an attempt was made to satisfy what were regarded as justified political aspirations through the constitutional act of 1909, known as the Morley-Minto Reforms, which gave the right to vote for members of the legislative councils to an electorate defined by a property franchise. But even the most moderate leaders of the Indian National Congress denounced the 1909 act for one of its provisions: the creation of special constituencies for Muslims. For Indian nationalists, this recognition of religion as a criterion of citizenship was a deliberate attempt by the British to create dissension between the two religious communities. On the other hand, the leaders of the Muslim League regarded it as minimal protection for Muslims from the dangers inherent in the electoral process, and they saw the Congress attack on the act as anti-Muslim in its motivation.

While the First World War was on the whole remote from Indian concerns, it led to a considerable realignment and readjustment of political forces. India's entrance into the war was taken as a matter of course in 1914, and the general acquiescence of the population is suggested by the reduction of British troops in India to 15,000 and the raising of a volunteer Indian army of 1,300,000 men. Economically, the war led to a rise in agricultural prices because of the increased demand for Indian goods, and the shortage of imports gave Indian manufacturers an opportunity to compete with foreign goods for the first time. In politics, the moderates in the Indian National Congress supported the war effort, but other groups began to question the identification of British and Indian interests that had for so long been the basis of political discussion. Indian Muslims had been inclined to regard British rule as the necessary countervailing force to Hindu nationalism represented by the Congress, but events in the Middle East, especially the war against Turkey, raised doubts in the minds of many Muslim leaders about the soundness of this alliance. A small but highly articulate group of Muslims began to argue that Muslim interests could best be safeguarded by Muslim participation in the Indian National

Congress. Among these leaders, known as "nationalist Muslims," were Maulana Azad, Zakir Husain, later President of India, and, for a brief period, M. A. Jinnah, founder of Pakistan. Within the Congress itself, Tilak and the other leaders who had been regarded as extremists in the early years of the century were assuming the position of elder statesmen, and their place as proponents of radical solutions was taken by groups who advocated, and plotted, the violent overthrow of British rule. Many of the revolutionary leaders had fled to exile in the United States, and from there they attempted, with limited success, to get help from Germany for armed insurrections in India.

The declaration in Parliament in 1917 was the British response to these varied political changes, and it was followed by constitutional changes in 1919 known, from the secretary of state and the governor general, as the Montagu-Chelmsford Reforms. The fundamental element of the new constitution was the creation in the provinces of what became known as dyarchy: responsibility for certain aspects of government was handed over to popularly elected ministers, while an appointed governor maintained final authority. No basic changes were made in the central government, but a greatly enlarged franchise gave some form of political representation to 8 million people.

The promulgation of the new constitution, with its provision for political parties to form provincial ministries, faced the leaders of the Indian National Congress with a momentous choice. While there was almost universal denunciation of what seemed to be the niggardly installment of responsible government, the Congress leaders were deeply divided over the question of participation in the elections to be held in 1920. The moderate leadership argued for full acceptance of the reforms; the old extremists, who now occupied a far less radical position in the political spectrum, wanted to use the elections as an occasion to attack the government; the new revolutionaries were calling for violence. The government, frustrated by the reception of the reforms and fearing an outbreak of violence, matched the movement toward responsible government with the passage of legislation, the Rowlatt Acts, that provided for the arrest and imprisonment of political agitators without trial. In this atmosphere of mutual resentment and distrust in April, 1919, an army officer in Amritsar, in the Punjab, opened fire on a political gathering which had been called in defiance of a government order, killing at least 400 and wounding more than 1,000. It was this incident which set the stage for the emergence of Mohandas K. Gandhi as the dominant figure in the nationalist movement.

Gandhi was already a famous man, highly respected by the British as well as the Indians for his work in South Africa on behalf of Indian immigrants in their struggles against discriminatory laws. He had given his full support to the British during the war and at first had been inclined to urge acceptance of the new constitution, but he abandoned this position in 1920. The failure of the British to punish the officials responsible for the Amritsar Massacre, combined with his assessment of the weakness of the divided and fragmented Indian National Congress, had convinced him that a radical departure in nationalist aims and strategy was needed, and in 1920 he persuaded the Congress to adopt a resolution urging noncooperation with the government.

In addition to withdrawing the Congress from participation in the elections, the noncooperation resolution of September, 1920, called for a boycott on foreign goods, the renunciation of all British titles, a refusal to attend government schools, and, ultimately, a refusal to pay taxes. All of these activities were to be carried on without violence, for the heart of Gandhi's campaign was that change in the political order would be produced through the withholding of cooperation, rather than through negotiation, compromise, or coercion. This point is worth special emphasis, since Gandhi's aims were never very clear. The British complained that each time the government made a concession Gandhi would shift his ground, but Gandhi's actions were intelligible from his strategy of noncooperation and his metaphysics, which held that truth could not be embodied in any formula but needed continual restatement in action. The title of his autobiography, *My Experiments with Truth,* is thus a clue to both his methods and his aims. Insofar as Gandhi's intentions can be summed up, he seems to have pursued two general ends: the withdrawal of the British on India's terms, not theirs; and the fostering of a spirit of nationhood defined by self-respect.

To assign to Gandhi the role of creator of Indian independence is to misread the events of modern Indian history; the main thrust of nationalism had already made itself felt, and Gandhi's work probably did not either greatly hasten—or delay—the actual date of the transfer of power. His real achievements were of another order: on one level, the reorganization of the Indian National Congress to make it responsive to central control while reaching down into the life of the nation; on another, the maintenance of a considerable degree of unity between the moderate constitutionalists and the revolutionaries; and, above all, the identification of the nationalist movement with the concerns of the masses. Through the use of symbols— homespun cloth, the spinning wheel, his own renunciation of the modes of Western living he had once followed—he dramatized his cause with a success perhaps without parallel in modern politics. The fasts to the death, the boycotts, the appeals for nonviolent action, all helped to create a national self-awareness among a people in whom it had been notably lacking.

In addition to the Gandhian theme, two other lines of development characterize Indian political life between the wars. One is the growing separatism among the Muslims; the other is the modification of the constitutional reforms of the 1919 Act. The rapprochement between the Indian National Congress and the Muslim League, which had begun in 1917 when the leaders had reached a rather tentative agreement on such matters as special representation for Muslims, was strengthened by Gandhi's enthusiastic support of the Khilafat movement. This was based on the resentment many Indian Muslims felt at the dismemberment of the Ottoman Empire under British auspices at the end of the World War, but the abolition of the Caliph by the Turks themselves undercut this emotional appeal, and by the mid-twenties the Muslim League moved into definite opposition to the Congress. The Hindu religious vocabulary in which Gandhi articulated his positions added to the growing estrangement. The Indian National Congress protested that it was an all-inclusive secular organization, but inevitably its definition of Indian culture and history, by emphasizing Hindu values, aroused fears among the Muslims, who constituted a quarter of the population. The position taken by genuine secularists like Jawaharlal Nehru, that religion is not a basis for nationality, was a denial of much that was fundamental to the Islamic understanding of the nature of the state and the community. Insofar as the British fostered, as Indian nationalists claim they did, the antagonism between the two religious communities, it was by sharing the Muslims' predilection for the primacy of religion as a determining factor in national identity. Given that assumption, many officials undoubtedly used the antagonism to rationalize the need for British rule. But probably the fundamental cause of the divergences between the aims of the Indian National Congress and the Muslim League was, in simplest terms, the possibility open to Jinnah and the other Muslim leaders of creating an alternative nationalist movement and, ultimately, although not through long-range planning, of a separate state. Every nationalist movement is marked by internal tensions and struggles for control; India's historical experience pointed almost irresistibly to the creation of rival movements by extremely able and ambitious men.

The constitutional modifications and revisions of the twenties and thirties were partly responses to nationalist pressures, but they were not the result of negotiations and compromises. The Simon Commission, appointed in 1927 by the British government to report on the working of the dual system of responsibility initiated in 1921, was fiercely criticized by the leaders of the Indian National Congress on the grounds that it did not have any Indian members. This occasioned a new noncooperation movement, but in the end, with the help of moderate Indian liberals, many of whom had broken with the Congress, a new constitution was introduced in 1935. Dyarchy was abolished, and the provincial ministries were given enlarged powers and a very real measure of autonomy. Less change took place in the central government, for the governor general retained most of his powers.

At first the Congress stated that it would refuse to cooperate with the new constitution, but the attraction of office for men of ability and ambition, combined with a realization that a policy of unbending refusal to accept partial solutions was leading the Congress into sterility, forced a change in policy. The Congress was elected to office in eight of the eleven provinces, showing that it was in fact what it had long claimed to be: the representative of the majority of the Indian people. The Muslim League won no comparable victories, but by this time M. A. Jinnah had assumed its leadership, and it became in effect the parliamentary opposition as well as the spokesman for Muslim nationalism.

The outbreak of the Second World War brought an end to the cooperation in the political process by the Indian National Congress. When the British government refused to grant India a larger measure of independence immediately in return for support of the war, the Congress ministries resigned in the provinces where they had formed governments, and in August, 1942, Gandhi announced that a new campaign of civil disobedience would begin with the purpose of making Britain leave India. The government responded by jailing all of the Congress leaders. Most of them remained in jail until the end of the war, but by 1945 British political circles generally recognized that a devolution of power in India was inevitable.

The urgent problem was to find a constitutional formula which would be acceptable to both the Indian National Congress and the Muslim League. The Congress party demanded a strong central state and emphasized its commitment to a parliamentary system with universal suffrage. The Muslim League, as an opposition party, did not have to state its aims so precisely; Jinnah, who by this time was its unquestioned spokesman, insisted that such a unitary state was utterly unacceptable to India's 100 million Muslims. Negotiations centered, therefore, on defining a form of government that would permit enough provincial autonomy to satisfy the League's insistence on areas which would be controlled by the Muslims while maintaining the unitary national authority the Congress wanted. The resolution of the impasse was the decision to partition India, granting the Muslims a homeland and the Indian National Congress a strong central state where citizenship would be without religious reference.

Until the summer of 1947 perhaps none of the leaders on either side, including Jinnah, really believed that partition was inevitable, and for the Congress the decision was a defeat for its long struggle to become the successor to the undivided British inheritance in India. Indian nationalism

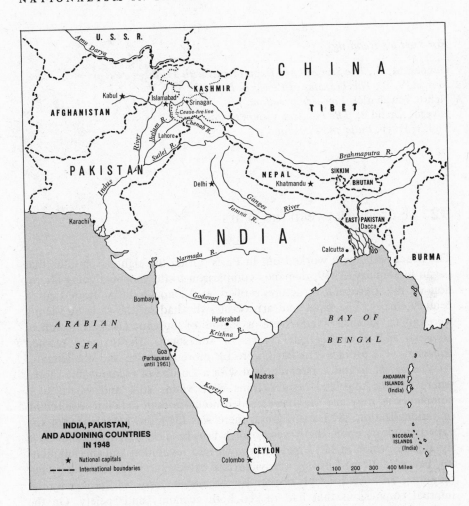

had predicated a unity which was rooted in the soil of India, and its most eloquent spokesman had insisted that Indian nationality transcended the diversities of regions, races, and religions which were so conspicuous a feature of Indian history. Partition was so complete a denial of this passionately held belief that Pakistan was long regarded as *India irredenta* by important political elements in Indian politics. The Pakistan response to this attitude was a sense of unease at not being accepted as a state that had a right to existence, thus adding to the many problems that necessarily exacerbated relations between the two nations carved out of a single political and economic unit.

For·Further Reading

Gandhi, M. K., *The Story of My Experiments with Truth.*
Menon, V. P., *The Transfer of Power in India.*
Nehru, Jawaharlal, *Towards Freedom.*
Sayeed, Khalid B., *The Political System of Pakistan.*
Tinker, Hugh, *India and Pakistan.*

92   Europe Between the Wars

The peace settlement worked out in Paris during the eighteen months that
began in January, 1919, demands comparison to the thoroughgoing alteration of the European structure ratified at Vienna a little more than a
century earlier. The kings and aristocrats who had set the style at Vienna
were gone; in their place were a legion of bureaucrats and technical
advisers and a largely new breed of statesmen. The experts seemed
necessary: the problems at Paris were far more extensive and challenging.
At Vienna the negotiators could deal with a Europe of recognizable shape,
where nations that had been nations were viable still, and where such
complexes as Italy and Germany needed no more than judicious reshuffling
or rationalization. At Paris, though there was far more knowledge for the
experts to draw upon, there was no such firm base on which to build. Save
for Russia, which in 1917 had withdrawn into revolution and the humiliating Peace of Brest Litovsk, the victorious Allies survived as nations, but
they were exhausted, deeply shaken by the terrible losses of life and by the
internal convulsions that had racked both economy and society. On the
losing side, there was only flux—revolution in Germany, disintegration in
the Hapsburg and Ottoman empires and on the borders of Russia. The
peacemakers had not so much to redraw the map of Europe as to create it
anew.

It proved necessary in Paris, as at Vienna, to cut through the irreconcilable interests and the hangers-on by confining decisions to a small group;
in time even the Council of Ten gave way to the Council of Four. Of those
four, Vittorio Orlando of Italy (who did not speak English) had the least
impact; the main outlines of the settlement were determined by Georges
Clemenceau of France, David Lloyd George of England, and Woodrow
Wilson of the United States. Only Clemenceau would have been compre-

A.D.   1919   Treaty of Versailles signed; Treaty of St. Germain
                      with Austria; Treaty of Neuilly with Bulgaria
              1920   U.S. Senate rejects League of Nations; Treaty of
                      Trianon with Hungary; Treaty of Sèvres with Tur-
                      key
              1921   New Economic Policy inaugurated in U.S.S.R.
              1922   Mussolini's March on Rome; Fascists take power
        1922–1923   Washington Naval Conference
              1923   French occupation of the Ruhr; Treaty of Lausanne
                      with Turkey; Adolf Hitler stages Beer Hall Putsch
                      in Munich
              1924   Lenin's death
              1925   Locarno Treaties
              1926   General strike in Great Britain; Stalin establishes
                      control in U.S.S.R.; Imperial Conference defines
                      nature of British Commonwealth of Nations
              1928   Pact of Paris, Kellogg-Briand Pact, "outlawing war"
              1929   Lateran Treaties between Italy and the papacy; stock
                      market collapses in New York, ushering in world-
                      wide depression
              1930   Reichstag election marks emergence of Nazis as
                      major party
              1931   Incident at Mukden provides pretext for beginning
                      of Japanese occupation of Manchuria; defeat of
                      Labour party in general election, followed by
                      formation of a National Government (a coalition)
                      in Great Britain
              1932   Japanese occupation of Shanghai; Reichstag elec-
                      tions, from which Nazis emerge as largest party
                      but without a majority
              1933   Hitler becomes chancellor in Germany
              1934   Purge of Nazi party
              1935   Italy invades Ethiopia
              1936   Germany reoccupies the Rhineland; Spanish Civil
                      War begins
              1938   Germany takes over Austria; Munich Conference
              1939   End of Civil War in Spain; nonaggression pact be-
                      tween Russia and Germany; Germany invades
                      Poland; Great Britain and France declare war on
                      Germany

CHRONOLOGY

EUROPE
AFTER WORLD WAR I

German Republic

TERRITORIES LOST

by Germany

by Austria-Hungary

by Russia

by Bulgaria

E = Eupen-Malmédy   R = Ruhr District   S = Saar Region

ICELAND
(Den.)

ATLANTIC OCEAN

NORTHERN
IRELAND

UNITED
KINGDOM

EIRE
Dublin

NORTH
SEA

London

NORWAY   SWEDEN

Oslo

Stockholm

FINLAND

AALAND
(Fin.)

Helsinki

Reval
ESTONIA

LATVIA
Riga

Murmansk

Leningrad
(St. Petersburg)

UNION OF

Moscow

SOVIET

SOCIALIST

REPUBLICS

Kiev

Dnieper R.

Odessa

BLACK SEA

DENMARK   Copenhagen

NORTH
SCHLESWIG

POLISH
CORRIDOR

Memel

LITHUANIA

Kaunas   Vilna

EAST
PRUSSIA

Brest-Litovsk

W. Dvina R.

Amsterdam

Brussels

NETH.

BELG.

RHINELAND

LUX.

ALSACE-
LORRAINE

Versailles   Paris

Seine R.

FRANCE

Bordeaux

GERMANY

Berlin

Elbe R.   Oder R.

Weimar

Danzig

Vistula R.

Warsaw

POLAND

UPPER
SILESIA

Lwow

GALICIA

Dniester R.

BESSARABIA

Prut R.

Prague

CZECHOSLOVAKIA

Munich

Vienna

SWITZ.

Geneva

Rhine R.

Rhône R.

Marseille

SPAIN

Barcelona

CORSICA
(Fr.)

AUSTRIA

SOUTH
TYROL

Trieste

ISTRIA

Budapest

HUNGARY

Danube R.

Drava R.

YUGOSLAVIA

Belgrade

Tisza R.

Morava R.

TRANSYLVANIA

RUMANIA

Bucharest

Danube R.

ITALY

Rome

SARDINIA
(It.)

MEDITERRANEAN

Algiers

ALGERIA
(Fr.)

Tunis

TUNISIA
(Fr.)

MALTA
(Br.)

Tripoli

TRIPOLITANIA
(It.)

BULGARIA

Sofia

Vardar R.

ALBANIA

to Greece

GREECE

Athens

CRETE (Gr.)

SEA

Istanbul

Izmir

Ankara

TURKEY

RHODES

CYPRUS
(Br.)

Cairo

EGYPT

Archangel

BALTIC SEA

0   100   200   300   400   500 Miles

hensible to the men of Vienna: tough-minded and even cynical, he was utterly devoted to the interests of France and equally determined to protect her against a recurrence of the devastation that the German war had brought. Wilson was at the other extreme: highly moral and rigid, determined to sweep away the old diplomacy, he was a political scientist increasingly isolated from the public opinion at home on which his success had ultimately to depend. Lloyd George, unlike Wilson a consummate politician, had just emerged from a general election, overwhelmingly victorious but ultimately compromised by his heavy reliance on Conservative support. He had played his part in a viciously anti-German campaign that suited the mood of the country; at the conference, however, he was all suppleness and the most responsive of all the leaders to Germany's claims as a great power. Perhaps Talleyrand would have understood him, but Talleyrand had spoken in 1815 for the defeated power: there was no one to speak for Germany in 1919.

The treaties with Germany and Poland were signed on June 28, 1919: there followed, over the next year, the treaties of St. Germain with Austria, Neuilly with Bulgaria, Sèvres with Turkey, Trianon with Hungary, and other treaties with lesser states. But the treaty with Germany, the Treaty of Versailles, fixed the main lines of the settlement; when it was completed, the Council of Four could abandon its work to other hands. Disarmed and stripped of her colonies, Germany had to return Alsace and Lorraine (which she had got in 1871) to France; she also gave up other bits and pieces of territory to Belgium and Poland, including the Polish Corridor which thereafter split East Prussia from the rest of Germany; and she faced the prospect (not confirmed by events) of losing still more through the vote of the inhabitants in plebiscites; the Rhineland was to be occupied by the Allies for fifteen years. Beyond paying the costs of the occupation, Germany had to make substantial restorations and compensations and was saddled with an enormous bill for reparations which her weakened economy had little chance of meeting. Added to the many potential grievances that were, understandably enough, built into the treaty, Germany was made to confess her responsibility for the war; this unfortunate clause, now given some diplomatic if not moral authority by historians, helped to compromise the treaty not only in German eyes but in those of many Allied citizens as well.

Any peacemaking tries to prevent the defeated powers from starting another war. But in 1919 a new device was put forward to check war and settle disputes, an institution far more positive and sophisticated than the periodic congresses of the old Concert of Europe or the vague and suspect Holy Alliance of Czar Alexander I. This was the League of Nations, set up on a model largely worked out during the war in Great Britain. The League was ultimately to fail in its grandest ambitions, in part because of the quick withdrawal of the United States into isolation, symbolized by the Senate's refusal to accept the Covenant of the League as a provision of the Treaty of Versailles. But the League was not hopeless from the start—some small disputes were effectively settled, and the Secretariat and its ancillary organizations opened a new era in international administration.

The statesmen at Vienna had not recognized and so did not need to cope with the problem of nationality, a problem that became the leitmotif of the history of the nineteenth century. At Paris the principle was fully recognized, and the negotiators seized the unparalleled opportunity to carry it through by creating "succession states" from the wreckage of the Austro-Hungarian Empire, by careful redrawing of national boundaries, and by resort to decisions as to national allegiance through plebiscites. But the two greatest geographical inventions of the settlement—Czechoslovakia and Yugoslavia—were themselves multinational states, ridden with tension and under constant threat of disintegration, like the empire from which they had sprung. A boundary line or a majority vote cannot disentangle mixed populations, and in some instances the need for compensation or insurance against new aggression left populations of clear nationality detached from their homeland, a problem particularly severe among the Germans. Still other countries saw portions of their territory taken away in the interests of minorities now seen as nationalities. So the peace settlement not only created minority problems in every country in central and eastern Europe but left a powerful irredentist spirit that threatened the peace from the moment of its completion.

Outside of Europe, three principal concerns deserve attention. Turkey, of course, lay in both Europe and the Near East. Greece and Italy had enforced claims against Turkey by occupying portions of her territory, and in Turkey a revolutionary movement led by Mustafa Kemal, ultimately fatal to the traditional forms of Ottoman rule, arose to drive out the invaders and to convert Turkey into a modern state on the European model. The Turkish pursuit of the Greeks, stopped at Chanak in 1921 by British forces, made it perfectly clear that the Turkish settlement foreseen in the still unratified Treaty of Sèvres had to be redone. In 1923 the Treaty of Lausanne confirmed the sovereignty of Turkey over the Straits and gave her a foothold in Thrace on the European continent. But she abandoned any claims to the Arab states that had been taken from her in the war and that had been carved up into spheres of influence by secret agreements between the English and the French. Some of these essentially artificial states were erected as independent kingdoms; others were given as "mandates" to the two European powers as, so to speak, temporary colonies. But dynastic ambitions were supplemented by only an incipient nationalism. Ironically, in the Balfour Declaration of 1917, Great Britain promised to create a national home for the Jews in the very heart of the Arab world, in what was to become the British mandate of Palestine; thus Britain, the principal patron of Arab independence, provided the major stimulus to the emergence of Arab nationalism as a real and explosive force.

The device of the mandate was also used to bring the former German colonies in Africa and Asia under the government of the victorious Allies, with Britain and Japan as the principal administering powers; in these areas of the world, too, nationalism was barely discernible and would not for thirty years begin to undermine this temporary European rule. But in a third, highly advanced non-European sector—Japan, the United States, and the British dominions, whose increasing autonomy was recognized by separate representation at the Peace Conference and in the League—there lay an immediate challenge, economic, political, and cultural, to the dominance of Europe. The United States retreated into its shell, to be sure, but Japan emerged from Paris unsatisfied, and the dominions, with one exception refusing to back the British stand at Chanak, went forward to establish themselves gradually as independent nations, tied at last by little but sentiment to the mother country, an arrangement defined and sanctified as the Commonwealth of Nations in 1926 and 1931. Ireland, the most rebellious and hostile of Britain's former colonies, won dominion status in 1922 and seized every opportunity to reduce even the appearance of a connection, although independence was not formally attained until 1949. For twenty years the victorious European nations could continue to fancy themselves the great powers they had once been. But the next world war would not be concluded by a primarily European settlement.

Even in Europe the Versailles settlement failed to work. Morally compromised among the defeated by its real or imagined injustices, and among the victorious by subtle and sophisticated criticism of some of its provisions, it was never given sufficient time. The new European nations were not always viable politically or economically, and, in the immediate aftermath of the war, some of the great powers were shaken by discontents that manifested themselves in new forms of government, as in Italy, or in abortive coups, as in Germany in 1919 and 1920. France had failed to get the guarantee she had wanted in the Treaty of Versailles against German resurgence; she had also been denied the collective security arrangements promised by the United States and Britain. Determined to get the reparations that Germany could not pay, France occupied the heavily industrial Ruhr Valley in 1923. The occupation provoked passive resistance from the German workers and inevitable clashes; moreover, a runaway inflation almost overnight destroyed the value of German money and threatened other currencies as well. Both sides drew back; the change was signaled by the succession to power in France and Germany of the pacific Aristide Briand and Gustav Stresemann. In 1924, under the so-called Dawes Plan, a scaled-down scheme of reparations payments was worked out, and the United States began to promote investment in Germany to make possible the production that had to underlie fulfillment of the plan, although investment was not as intelligently directed as it might have been. An effort in that year to promote collective security through arbitration procedures in the League, the so-called Geneva Protocol, came to nothing, but in 1925 a series of treaties signed at Locarno by the various European powers brought partial German acceptance of the Versailles terms, the reintegration of Germany into the European system, German membership in the League, and a general exchange of guarantees. In the glow of the "Locarno spirit," many of the postwar tensions dissolved; the new spirit reached its apogee in 1928 when the Kellogg-Briand Pact "outlawed war." Retrospectively, the gesture seems as ill-founded as the Holy Alliance, though its purposes were more beneficent; yet the ambition bespoke the weariness of Europe and its determination to escape from tragedy. No one could then quite imagine the collapse that would shatter the European system again and create new tensions that would end in another war.

In the twenties at least, men could be pardoned for not reading correctly the signs of approaching disaster. It is true that the economy of Europe was in a parlous state. All the combatant nations emerged from the war with their industrial plant and transportation facilities seriously run down, their capital resources depleted, and the relations between labor and management subject to new and puzzling strains, not least because of the rapid growth of Communist sympathies in some European trade-union movements; to these problems, France and Belgium, in particular, had to add the rebuilding made necessary by the physical destruction of the war. Currencies had been dislocated, and the entire machinery as well as the traditional channels of international trade were disrupted: a preoccupied Europe saw some of its best prewar markets lost to the United States and Japan, and European businessmen showed less determination than they might have done to recapture their primacy. Pent-up civilian demand fed a brief postwar boom, which quickly evaporated; it led men to think for a time, however, that the prewar economy might be restored, and it stimulated both the destruction of wartime controls, which might have helped moderate the unfortunate effects, and capital investment in traditional but no longer highly profitable sectors of industry. The collapse in turn led businessmen and governments to excessive caution and promoted the raising of tariff walls that further cut down the possibilities of international trade on which the health of the economy (not to mention reparations) depended. The state of economic knowledge had simply not advanced to a comprehension of or solutions for an economy, international or domestic, that could no longer depend on the self-regulating mechanisms of the nineteenth century. Still, despite the disaster of the inflation of 1923, there was gradual recovery. By the mid-twenties, currencies were largely stabilized, and the gold standard—that sacred cow of old economic thinking—resumed its sway. Much of the wartime wastage and destruction had been made up, and the prosperity of the newer industries—automobiles, aircraft, electricity, radio communications, chemicals—not only pushed forward a general recovery of the economy but, in increasing degree, changed the quality of life in the more advanced nations. Synchronized with the relaxation of international tensions in the Locarno period, this diffusing prosperity created a sense of confidence that proved, in the event, dangerously misplaced.

The international monetary system of the twenties no longer rested on the extensive reserves of gold and securities that had characterized the prewar system; rather, it was supported by a fabric of loans, with the United States as the principal lender. When in 1928 the unhealthy boom in the United States showed signs of faltering, followed by a decline in domestic demand and the psychologically destructive stock market collapse in October, 1929, American investments were recalled and then disappeared, and one after another national economy fell in the wake of the American disaster. By the early 1930's, every major advanced economy— except that of Russia—was in deep trouble, marked by a drastic fall in production and by widespread unemployment. The gold standard was nearly universally abandoned, the state intervened in the economy in ways unthinkable only a few years before, and industry itself undertook some long-overdue rethinking of its structure and priorities, although, given the psychologically demoralizing circumstances, that rethinking looked more toward contraction and sharing a limited market than toward the restoration of intelligent and healthy growth. The recovery of the late thirties was sparked, ominously, by the growing business of rearmament.

To hindsight the twenties show a similar undermining of the political arrangements of Europe. The war, in Wilsonian rhetoric, had been fought to make the world safe for democracy, and the forms of government in the new states, and above all in the Weimar Republic in Germany, suggested that that noble purpose had in fact been accomplished. But German democracy, handicapped by the apolitical attitude that had almost always characterized German intellectuals and by a steady barrage of destructive criticism from its enemies, was compromised for many more of its citizens by its origin in defeat, while in other countries, notably Poland and Hungary, the immediate postwar instability led ultimately to the establishment of regimes that might be in form democratic but that were in essence highly authoritarian.

The sharpest turn in this rightward direction was taken in Italy, where economic chaos, wounded nationalism, and frustrated ambition led to rapidly growing support for the Fascist movement headed by Benito Mussolini, a former socialist journalist. After some political successes, in 1922 Mussolini led the "March on Rome," to claim and be given political power. His regime had two faces. It relied in part on naked force, expressed in the organized ruffianism of the "Black Shirts," the destruction of trade unions, censorship of the press, the repression of dissent, and a growing tendency to regiment all of society. At the same time, much in the new regime was welcome to powerful parts of Italian society. The longstanding hostility between the Roman Catholic Church and the Kingdom of Italy was brought to an end in the Concordat of 1929. Mussolini's early liberalism in economic matters gave way after the abrogation of the old constitution in 1925 to the "corporative state" that took form over the next several years; this industry-by-industry organization of the economy— owing something to early twentieth-century syndicalist ideas—could be seen both as a means of gaining national efficiency and as a way of avoiding the destructive conflicts of labor-management relations under a freer system. Although the workers and, above all, the peasants gained least from the Fascist system, some effort was made, paternalistically enough, to confer social benefits, and it was possible for observers from more securely democratic countries to look benevolently on the Fascist experiment.

That this favorable judgment was possible for Frenchmen and Englishmen suggests a decline in the democratic impulse in the two countries that had given democracy its modern forms. In both nations, but particularly in France, the twenties were marked by a turning away from political commitment or interest. To some extent, the rejection of politics grew out of disgust with the war the politicians had made, but that disgust had simply exacerbated a current of political disillusion clearly evident before the war. The greater personal freedom that had burst on the Western world during and after the war—a breaking down of old conventions, sexual liberation, a frank hedonism—despite its enormous benefits to the quality of some individual lives and, above all, to the arts, could be read as indicating a loss of national or public purpose, a purpose that had been still recoverable when the nations went to war with near-unanimity in 1914 but that seemed now beyond recapture. Growing freedom and prosperity could mean, moreover, that many of the problems that had commanded political attention before the war had been solved and that the postwar problems were too complex and remote to bring ordinary men into political action, the more so when it was easy to assume cynically that they were beyond solution. It is not hard to understand, in such a situation, how forms of government (to borrow Alexander Pope's phrase) might be something for which only fools would contest. But forms revealed substance, and the

substance, once made manifest, could be utterly subversive of the prosperity and the way of life that had been won at such cost and with so little
promise of permanence.

Nothing reflects the ambiguities of the western European attitude
toward politics more clearly than the strange role played throughout the
twenties and thirties by the Soviet Union. During the civil war that followed the Revolution in 1919 and 1920, small Allied forces were in action
around the edges of Russia, at first to prevent the Germans from taking the
utmost advantage of the swift and complete Russian surrender, then in ill-
judged and futile support of some of the anti-Bolshevik forces. At the same
time, the victorious Bolsheviks eagerly set about fomenting the revolution
many of them expected momentarily in more advanced countries; the Third
International was founded to promote international communism and,
incidentally, created in the West a standing fear of subversion. Despite
these tensions, the early twenties saw a relaxation in relations with Russia,
paralleling the adoption of the New Economic Policy in Russia itself and
the calculated "liberalism" of Lenin's last years. Although there was much
criticism of the policy, the Western powers were disinclined to go to war to
save the eastern frontiers arranged in the peace settlement and that stood
as perhaps the worst grievance of the Germans. Into this chink in the wall
was built a strange cooperation between Russia and Germany, old enemies
who thus bought time and release from pressure to forward their own
internal development; the collaboration was made official in the Treaty of
Rapallo in 1922. Other nations in the West soon recognized the Soviet
government, although in Britain, for example, diplomatic relations were
broken off again for a time. But after Lenin's death in 1924, and with the
emergence of Stalin as the victor in the struggle with Trotsky for supreme
power, Russia turned inward once more.

The course of Stalin's Russia posed a challenge difficult to comprehend. The forced drive to industrialization and collectivization in agriculture, the grisly and dramatic purge trials in the 1930's, and the ruthless
elimination not only of political or military leaders who had fallen foul of
Stalin's plans or megalomania but of hundreds of thousands of lesser
people—notably the kulaks, rich peasants who had done well under the
NEP but who were an obstacle to collectivization—brought home to European minds and consciences the full impact of totalitarian rule. When the
response was not incomprehension or numbness, it was almost certain to
be ideological. Men of the left, inspired by the Revolution and enamored of
the seemingly rapid and certain Russian path to economic and social
progress, obediently followed the twists and turns of Soviet policy, which
had long since subordinated international communism (and the Communist parties in other countries) to Russian national ends; to men on the

right, there was the bogey of Bolshevism, as pervasive as the fear of Jacobinism after 1815. On the one side the cry was "no enemies to the left"; on the other, only a plea of anti-communism was needed to forgive any authoritarian regime, however dreary or despicable.

The thirties were punctuated by crises, played out against a background of economic disaster, that even now, in their very appearance of inevitability, recall the sense of doom that lay over that troubled decade. In 1931 Japan marched into Manchuria and began her long, systematic effort to turn China into a client state; the League of Nations protested but had no force to bring to bear, and Japan showed her contempt for censure by simply resigning from the League and going on with her conquests. Meanwhile, in Germany, the Weimar Republic was tottering to its fall. With Gustav Stresemann's death in 1929 began a new era of political instability, heightened by the economic collapse that was worse in Germany than in any other European country. Seeking both security and scapegoats, German voters turned away from the mistrusted, even hated, republic, some to the extreme of communism, many more to the National Socialist (Nazi) party, which promised a Germany purged and regenerated.

The leader of the Nazis was a former Austrian house painter, Adolf Hitler, whose wartime experiences (he was a corporal) had turned him into a bitter and fervent nationalist. Like the Fascists in Italy, he exploited the growing taste for violence through the organization of his "storm troopers," and increasingly he found his major scapegoats in the Jews, a prosperous minority more fully assimilated into German society than perhaps any other society in Europe, though anti-Semitism was an old strain in German life and thought. Beyond this, Hitler's progress could be summed up in the main as anti-Versailles and anti-Communist. In 1923 he attempted a putsch in Munich, a miserable failure that seemed to doom his tiny party as Hitler himself went to prison. After his release, however, he slowly and systematically built up his political strength, depending on his effective mob oratory and on a simplistic analysis of causes and remedies for Germany's troubles, an analysis that became suddenly more persuasive after 1929. In 1930, the Nazis got more than 6 million votes and 107 seats in the Reichstag; in July, 1932, with 230 seats, they became the largest party in the legislature. The successive elections were part of a series of complicated parliamentary maneuvers aimed at keeping Hitler out of power. But the Social Democrats, the party that had given the strongest support to Weimar but which had precipitated the political crisis by withdrawing from the "Great Coalition" in 1930, were unimaginatively led and offered no visible alternative. The Papen government, in office from July to December, 1932, attempted to conciliate and use the Nazis only to be denied Hitler's cooperation; the next chancellor, General Kurt von

Schleicher, considered strong measures to break the Nazi movement but could not carry with him the aged president, Field Marshal von Hindenburg. Although—and perhaps because—the Nazis' representation in the Reichstag had dropped in the November elections to 196, Hindenburg installed Hitler as chancellor on January 30, 1933. Hitler asked for and got new elections that, under systematic terrorization, gave him (with some minor allies) a bare majority; he used it to suspend the constitution, and for the remainder of the Nazi era, the country was ruled by decree. All parties but the Nazi party and all trade unions were eliminated, censorship and propaganda were used intensively to mobilize opinion, and violence continued (visited even upon the Nazis themselves in the purge of 1934), compounded by the outright rejection of most of the rational, civilized, and intellectual values of which nineteenth-century Germany had in many ways been so remarkable an exemplar: in their place were put mystical evocations of a barbaric German past and idealization of the intuitional leader. The drive for "racial purity" was taken up in earnest in decrees of 1935 and 1938; and the S.S.—Hitler's elite corps within the army—and the Gestapo, the secret police, were used to bring the entire country under subjection. The Nazis' social program was at best piecemeal; the success the regime needed was to be found in adventure abroad.

Throughout the Weimar period, both government and army had connived at evasion of the limitations imposed on German militarism by the Treaty of Versailles. Shortly after coming into power, Hitler withdrew from the League and announced that he would undertake rearmament openly in defiance of the Versailles restrictions, for which no one in the West was willing or able to fight. Although it was four or five years before the German army was fully ready for war, Hitler was able to get his way in Europe by improvisation and bluff, certain that England and France would not fight.

In 1935, however, attention was distracted from Germany by Mussolini, who had managed until then to hold back his ambition to create a new Roman Empire dominating the Mediterranean. On the pretext of a border incident he launched from Eritrea and Italian Somaliland an invasion of Ethiopia. Although the Ethiopians had beaten the Italians at Aduwa in 1896—a stain Mussolini was eager to wipe out—they were no match for this new invasion. Nor was the League of Nations, which condemned the Italian action and launched its first and last venture with sanctions. The vital sanction on oil was withheld, however; Italy had declared that the oil sanction would mean war, and, again, the British and French were not prepared to take the risk. To be sure, a shift in public opinion in favor of collective security and even willingness to fight for the League had taken place in England; but France was crucially preoccupied with the German threat and troubled by grave domestic instability; her wily foreign minister Pierre Laval was dedicated to maintaining the "Stresa front," a flaccid agreement of 1934 by which the British and French hoped to secure Mussolini as a benevolent neutral, if not as an ally, in their posture toward Hitler. An agreement, secretly made in 1935 between Laval and the British foreign minister Sir Samuel Hoare, called for the handing over of much Ethiopian territory to appease Mussolini; when the news of the agreement leaked out, whatever good intentions the League had were undercut, and it was only a matter of time until Ethiopia was reduced to colonial status.

In 1936 a civil war broke out in Spain between the defenders of the recently established republic, supported by left-wing sentiment around the world and to some extent materially by Russia, and the nationalist forces under General Francisco Franco, supported by both Italy and Germany. For three years the war ground on, with terrible cruelties on both sides, again presenting an issue of conscience to the world. Although the Spanish Civil War had no central importance in the diplomatic history of Europe, it was of the first moral and psychological importance and convinced a number of pacifists on the left that some causes might be worth fighting for, thus helping to build the acceptability of war against Hitler.

In 1936 Hitler made perhaps his boldest gamble, against the advice of his generals, when he occupied the demilitarized Rhineland; there were protests but nothing more, even from the French, caught up at the time by domestic politics. Early in 1938 he seized Austria, after having systematically paralyzed the Austrian government through the activities of indigenous Nazis and by extraordinary personal abuse of Kurt von Schuschnigg, the Austrian chancellor. The independence of Austria had been of some concern to Italy, but the "Axis" concluded in 1936 between the German and Italian dictators proved strong enough and the task of watching over Austria tiresome enough to allow Mussolini to give Hitler free rein, and to put an end to any English and French hopes for Italy. There was little enough objection elsewhere: the Austrian regime had not been popular, and the Anschluss seemed yet another affirmation of nationality.

Hitler's next gamble was made by invoking the same principle, this time in support of the Sudeten Germans, who had been incorporated into Czechoslovakia at its creation. But beyond nationality, Hitler foresaw the elimination of Czechoslovakia, the most stable and liberal state in central and eastern Europe, by playing on the jealousies of her neighbors to the east and her discontented universities. Czechoslovakia's stability and liberalism had made her of particular interest to the Western powers, and her defense was guaranteed by the Russians, provided the French also would join. The principal response to this new threat, however, came from Neville Chamberlain, prime minister of England since 1937. A man of great administrative ability and of high though narrow rectitude, Chamberlain abhorred war and continued to believe that Hitler could be dealt with rationally and traditionally by agreement. In this case Czech concessions were to be the price of a general revision of the settlement of 1919. After his first visit to Hitler in September, 1938, Chamberlain persuaded the Czechs to give up the Sudeten frontier, territory that included besides the militant and discontented Germans the bulk of the country's defensive fortifications. When Chamberlain returned a week later with the Czech concessions, he was astonished to find that they were no longer acceptable, that Hitler had speeded up his timetable and had escalated his demands to include other Czech territories where there were Germans and the satisfaction of other minority claims as well. Chamberlain returned to London in a temper, and after the new terms were rejected by the Czechs, the British began moves toward mobilization. But Chamberlain made one more effort, at a four-power agreement between Italy, Germany, France, and Britain. Concluded in Munich on September 29, the agreement conceded the harshest of Hitler's terms, and the Czechs were given no choice but to accept or be abandoned. Chamberlain returned to London with what he most prized, an agreement that Britain and Germany would settle all their problems by consultation and never go to war again: it meant, he said on his return, "peace in our time."

Early in 1939 Germany eliminated what was left of Czechoslovakia; the Western powers were relieved of their military commitment by the apparent internal collapse of their ally. But, despite some diplomats who kept seeking terms for the final appeasement, most British subjects and statesmen, including even Chamberlain, had come to realize that Hitler was not to be trusted; Britain therefore scattered guarantees across eastern Europe. It was to one of those nations that Hitler next turned his attention: pressure on Poland not only aimed at redressing the German grievance about the eastern frontiers but gave expression to Hitler's bitter racial hatred against Slavs. Dramatically, Germany's design on her eastern neighbor turned into a new partition of Poland. Negotiations had been going on in a desultory and perhaps not wholly serious way between Russia and the Western powers; now aware of Russian military weakness, fearful of the German eastward movement and perhaps with aggressive designs of his own, Stalin entered on a nonaggression treaty with Hitler, signed on August 23, to the astonishment and confusion of Western ideologues who had believed fervently either that Hitler's Germany was a bastion of anti-communism or that Russia could have no truck with evil. But the two powers gained from the pact a temporary security for their own designs, and two days later Hitler ordered the attack on Poland, which began on September 1. After a last offer of negotiation, the British sent an ultimatum to Germany on September 3; there was no response and by late afternoon Britain and France were at war with Germany.

For Further Reading

Brogan, D. W., *France under the Republic (1870–1939)*.
Bullock, Alan, *Hitler: A Study in Tyranny*.
Holborn, Hajo, *The Political Collapse of Europe*.
Kirkpatrick, Ivone, *Mussolini: A Study in Power*.
Mowat, C. L., *Britain Between the Wars, 1918–1940*.
Seton-Watson, Christopher, *Italy from Liberalism to Fascism, 1870–1925*.
Thomson, David, *Democracy in France since 1870*.
Thorne, Christopher, *The Approach of War, 1938–1939*.

93   World War II

The First World War had ended on a note of high expectations, but disillusionment was not long in coming. The Peace of Versailles left all dissatisfied, although there is little warrant for attributing to it all the subsequent ills of the world. The hopes centering on the League of Nations proved illusory. The nineteenth-century liberal wave of which it was, in a sense, the culmination soon began to recede. The United States endeavored to pretend that it was not part of the world; victorious France, beset by fear and weakness, and seeking to organize Europe for her safety, pursued an incoherent policy, allowing the Nazi revival in Germany; Britain made appalling misjudgments and became the chief advocate of appeasement. European leadership, in the second half of the thirties, passed from the hands of the victors to the vengeful Germans. Thus, after twenty years of truce, came a renewal of hostilities, a recurrence of the key issue that the earlier conflict had failed to resolve: Germany's bid for world power.

In keeping with their disregard for the niceties of legal procedure, German forces invaded Poland on September 1, 1939. The Western powers, Britain and France, honoring their obligation to Poland, after a brief hesitation, formally declared war on Germany two days later. As in 1914, Germany enjoyed the advantage of better preparation while the Western allies possessed greater potential. Speed was Germany's need, time the allies' asset. As in the First World War, the German military perfor-

A.D.   1939   Nazi-Soviet Pact; Germany invades Poland; Britain
                     and France declare war on Germany; partition of
                     Poland between Germany and Russia
         1939–1940   The "phony war"; first Russo-Finnish War
              1940   Denmark and Norway overrun by Germany; Germany
                     launches attack in the west; Churchill succeeds
                     Chamberlain as prime minister; Battle and col-
                     lapse of France; Dunkirk evacuation; French ar-
                     mistice; Vichy regime; De Gaulle launches Free
                     French movement; Italy enters the war; Battle of
                     Britain; destroyer-bases deal between U.S. and
                     Britain; FDR reelected for third term
              1941   Central and eastern European rearrangements;
                     Lend-Lease legislation; Yugoslavia and Greece
                     overrun; Hitler attacks Russia; Atlantic Charter;
                     Japanese attack on Pearl Harbor
         1941–1942   Germans reach Caucasus; Japanese spread over
                     Southeast Asia, Indonesia, and the Pacific
              1942   Battle of the Coral Sea; Battle of Stalingrad; El
                     Alamein; all France occupied; North African land-
                     ings
              1943   Russia withdraws recognition from Polish govern-
                     ment in exile; French Committee of National
                     Liberation in Algiers; invasion of Sicily; Italian
                     armistice; collapse of Fascist regime, meeting of
                     Allied foreign ministers in Moscow; Teheran Con-
                     ference of the Big Three; Cairo declaration re
                     China
              1944   Normandy landings; FCNL becomes provisional
                     French government; Rome entered; Warsaw rising;
                     liberation of Paris; Battle of the Bulge
              1945   Yalta Conference of the Big Three; death of FDR;
                     Harry S. Truman President; Germany surrenders;
                     Hitler commits suicide; Potsdam Conference;
                     first atomic bomb dropped, on Hiroshima; Japan
                     surrenders

mance was impressive, but prompt victory eluded her and in the end she succumbed to the weight of incomparably greater resources.

Germany easily crushed Poland in three weeks, the mechanized Blitzkrieg demonstrating German military capabilities. In accordance with the secret terms of the Nazi-Soviet Pact, Russian forces moved in from the east, and the fourth partition of Poland took place, with a thoroughly dependent state, the *gouvernement général,* being set up in the section occupied but not annexed by Germany.

Then ensued a curious six-month pause, the "phony war." In keeping with the Maginot Line mentality, the French, instead of launching an offensive, waited passively behind that supposedly impregnable barrier. And the Germans did not attack. The war of words continued, during which attempts of neutral powers—the Low Countries, the Vatican— failed to move the belligerents. There had been little enthusiasm for war in Germany at first, but understandable elation at the easy victory in Poland; Hitler's intuition was proved right again and his prestige stood high. Conversely, the allies, especially the French, were still suffering from the prewar confusion of their irresolute policies and divided opinions.

The Soviet Union, coolly pressing its advantage, extended its influence through nonaggression pacts and the acquisition of naval bases in the three small Baltic countries. Then, in November, Russia attacked the recalcitrant Finns; this furnished the grounds for the expulsion of the Soviet Union from the League of Nations in December. Russia's performance was inglorious, but in March, 1940, Finland was forced to yield.

Since no accommodation could be found on the basis of the *fait accompli* Germany moved to further initiatives. In April, 1940, Denmark was overrun in the course of one day, and a skillfully managed operation swiftly gave the Germans control of Norway. There was little the Norwegians could do, though they fought hard, and the attempted allied assistance had to be abandoned by June.

The real war could now begin. Adopting a modified version of the 1914 plan designed to bypass French border fortifications, the Germans attacked both Holland and Belgium in May, to the accompaniment of the bombing of neutral, undefended Rotterdam, a demonstration of Nazi frightfulness. The German tactics were a demonstration of the validity of the prescient analysis of the future war which had been offered by a young French officer, Charles De Gaulle, a prophet without honor in his country. The major part of Holland was quickly overrun, but the breach of the Belgian fortifications, and most of all the breakthrough at Sedan, was a more serious matter. The massive use of tanks and air power brought the Germans to the Channel coast, trapping a portion of the French army and the relatively small, but well-armed and efficient British Expeditionary Force that had moved into Belgium.

These troops, along with the Belgian army, were caught in a narrowing ring of steel and fire, and driven to the sea. The Belgians withdrew from the struggle; then came the evacuation of allied forces from the Dunkirk beaches. A large proportion of the men reached England, but the British land force had been destroyed as an instrument of war.

Having regrouped their forces, the Germans and the French faced each other along the Somme at the beginning of June. The fate of battle was not long in doubt; the campaign of France turned into a complete rout. The Germans entered Paris on June 13. France was reduced to a state of chaotic confusion, much of the population seeking the elusive safety of disorderly flight southward. The German booty in prisoners of war and matériel was enormous. France had collapsed.

The French army had been the chief allied instrument of war; it now lay irretrievably broken. A major decision faced the French government: what hopes were there, behind the shield of the British navy, that adequate power might be rebuilt? Might not Britain seek accommodation with Hitler, possibly even at France's expense? French counsels were divided, but following the resignation of Premier Paul Reynaud, who favored continued resistance, and the advent of Marshal Henri Pétain in his place, the defeatist view prevailed. The aged hero of Verdun considered the war lost; he would not abandon the country but would use his prestige to shield his people and secure terms from the Germans. Hostilities ceased with the conclusion of an armistice on June 22, a ceremony that reenacted in locale and details the 1918 armistice, the ignominy of which it was symbolically meant to erase.

Italy had remained neutral at the outset of the war despite her pact with Germany, offering her unpreparedness as a pretext. Many efforts were made—by the allies, the United States, and the pope—to keep her neutral, but the unfolding of events in France convinced Mussolini that he must be present at the kill, if for no other reason than to be in a better position to assert his future claims. On June 10 he declared war on both Britain and France. Italy played an insignificant military role, and her poor performance in Greece, which she had attacked the preceding October, was calculated to confirm the view of those who held Italian military competence in low esteem.

Not all Frenchmen surrendered. Charles De Gaulle, now a two-star general and holding a minor ministerial post in Reynaud's cabinet, escaped to England at the last moment. On June 18, proclaiming that a battle had been lost but not the war, he called upon all Frenchmen to join him in continued resistance. This was the birth of the Free French movement. He found little response at first, for the French people, thoroughly demoralized, thought the war lost. At this point they put their trust in Pétain.

The terms of the French armistice were harsh, yet they could have been

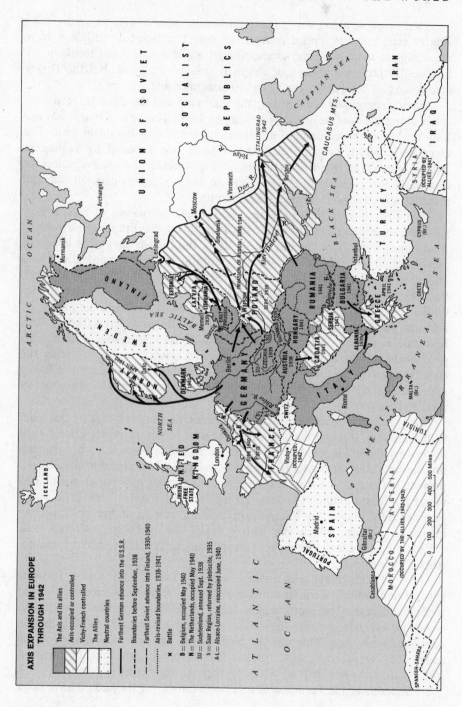

AXIS EXPANSION IN EUROPE
THROUGH 1942

- The Axis and its allies
- Axis-occupied or controlled
- Vichy-French controlled
- The Allies
- Neutral countries
- Farthest German advance into the U.S.S.R.
- Boundaries before September, 1938
- Farthest Soviet advance into Finland, 1939–1940
- Axis-revised boundaries, 1938–1941
- × Battle

B = Belgium, occupied May 1940
N = The Netherlands, occupied May 1940
SU = Sudetenland, annexed Sept. 1938
S = Saar Region, returned by plebiscite, 1935
A-L = Alsace-Lorraine, reoccupied June, 1940

harsher. Hitler restrained himself because, defeated though she undoubtedly was, France still held important assets: her fleet and her overseas empire. To press her unduly might have thrown these assets into British hands. Conversely, Britain was deeply concerned lest these fall to the Germans; she too would not press France too hard. For a time the fleet and the empire were merely neutralized.

Though she would not make formal peace with the Germans, France was in effect out of the war. Her influence on its course could only be minimal. What little remained of the French army overwhelmingly gave its allegiance to the Vichy regime. Only some fragments of the empire in equatorial Africa and some scattered island possessions rallied to the Free French movement. Although that movement received some form of recognition from the British, on whom it was totally dependent, Vichy was undoubtedly the legal government of France. De Gaulle's initial gesture, quixotic as it may have seemed at the time, was important nevertheless, for in it lay the seed of the future reconstruction of France.

But in June, 1940, there was no question that Britain stood alone against the Nazis. The emergency brought out the staunchest qualities of the British people. The vacillating policy of the Chamberlain administration had come to an end at the time of the Norwegian invasion; in May, 1940, Winston Churchill, long an isolated and unheeded voice, succeeded Chamberlain as prime minister. Churchill infused his unquenchable energy and resolution into the prosecution of the war; for the moment he could offer little more than words, but these, magnificently eloquent, were an effective tool; the channel moat, for the last time perhaps, still made it possible for England to prepare her defenses.

In the summer of 1940 there was an epic battle in the British skies as the German Luftwaffe sought to crush the people's will to resist. It was a close call, but the combination of faulty German strategy and British technical skill turned the tide in September. This "Battle of Britain" had the same effect as the Battle of the Marne in 1914; Germany was not defeated, but compelled to engage in a struggle of indefinite duration and doubtful outcome.

The British accomplishment could not, however, prevent the organization of Europe by the Nazis and their allies. Spain's dictator, Franco, skillfully resisted Hitler's blandishments and adhered to his neutral status, but in effect collaborated with Germany. Vichy France's collaboration was not very satisfactory from the German point of view, but French resources could be and were commandeered. In September, 1940, Italy launched an offensive from Libya into Egypt, but it was checked and turned back, bringing German forces under the brilliant General Erwin Rommel into the North African theater.

Greece and her Balkan neighbors were the hinge where the southern and eastern theaters joined. In view of unchallenged German power on the continent outside of Russia, these small states of central and southeastern Europe endeavored to accommodate themselves to German demands as best they could. Hungary and Bulgaria, both of whom had territorial grievances stemming from the First World War, won benefits by cooperating with Hitler; conversely, Rumania suffered, losing some territory to Hungary and to the Soviet Union.

In Bulgaria German and Russian influences were in competition. Refusing a Russian guarantee, Bulgaria adhered to the Rome-Berlin-Tokyo combination in March, 1941, and allowed German forces into the country. Nazi negotiations with Yugoslavia seemed to be leading to a similar result until an unexpected coup ousted the regent. The Yugoslavs then opted for resistance to the Axis demands. Another demonstration of German efficiency and frightfulness (the bombing of Belgrade) was followed by an all-out invasion. Having disposed of Yugoslavia, the Germans went on to overrun Greece, incidentally rescuing the incompetent Italian operation in that country. The governments of both Yugoslavia and Greece went into exile, a fact pregnant with consequence, for at the end of the war they would appear as allies of the victors, in contrast with Hungary, Bulgaria, and Rumania.*

From mainland Greece the Germans went on to capture Crete, giving another impressive demonstration of the possibilities of air power. The British, who had diverted some forces from North Africa to the assistance of Greece, proved incapable of preventing this German success, and their depleted North African forces were also evicted from Libya. Pushing into the Middle East, the Germans gave assistance to an anti-British coup in Iraq, partly with the connivance of the Vichy regime. British troops rescued the situation, and one of the incidental consequences of the abortive coup was the virtual ouster of French influence from France's Middle Eastern mandates.

The continent, apart from Russia and some neutrals, was now under effective German control. Russia had lived up to the terms of the Nazi-Soviet Pact and even used her influence among continental Communists on Germany's behalf, but distrust persisted between the two partners. Hitler decided to dispose of the potential threat to his rear; on June 22, 1941, his forces crossed the Soviet border.

Surprisingly, and despite various warnings, the Russians' preparations were inadequate, and initially the Nazi war machine repeated its earlier successes. By the close of 1941 Moscow and Leningrad were under siege

---

* Rumania eventually threw in her lot with the Axis.

and the Germans had reached the Crimea. But Russia is a huge country, and her two classic assets, Generals Winter and Space, again saved the day. Despite frightful losses, the Russians managed to hold out. The stupid application of Nazi racial policy to Slavs turned what might have been a war of liberation from Communist tyranny into a struggle for national existence for the Russian people. They fought desperately and stopped the Nazi advance.

The third member of the Rome-Berlin-Tokyo triangle, Japan, had followed European events closely, taking advantage of the war to promote the organization of what was euphemistically called the "Greater East Asia Co-Prosperity Sphere." Pursuing her undeclared war with China, Japan also moved into Indochina after the French collapse. Britain and Holland were not in a position to resist a further Japanese advance southward, and Russia was neutralized by the signing of a nonaggression pact in April, 1941.

One country alone was in a position to offer possible resistance, the United States, which had clearly registered its hostility to Japanese aggression. But the United States was still laboring under the illusions born of the First World War; its first concern was to avoid involvement in the second. Indeed, the outbreak of war in 1939 had confirmed America's tendency toward isolation, though American sympathies were undoubtedly with the allied cause. The collapse of France was a shock, but the presidential election of 1940 was reminiscent of that of 1916, which Wilson had won behind the slogan, "He kept us out of war." President Roosevelt, while pursuing a somewhat ambiguous policy of assisting the allies within the bonds of the American neutrality legislation, was reelected for an unprecedented third term while promising not to involve American boys in a "foreign" war.

Britain was hard pressed at sea. German submarines were taking a heavy toll of her shipping, while her naval establishment had been relatively neglected. Roosevelt's destroyers-for-bases deal in September, 1940, transferred to Britain fifty overage American destroyers in exchange for 99-year leases on British bases in the western Atlantic that would be useful in the defense of the American continent, hence presumably enhancing its isolation. The extension of the zone of forbidden hostilities to 300 miles from the American shores and the Atlantic Charter in August, 1941, pointed in the same direction. Meanwhile the imaginative Lend-Lease Act had become law: the President was given wide discretion in assisting any country, even the Soviet Union, whose defense was deemed vital to the United States. American neutrality was stretching thin; it consisted of "all assistance short of war."

Yet the domestic debate went on in the United States, and it was

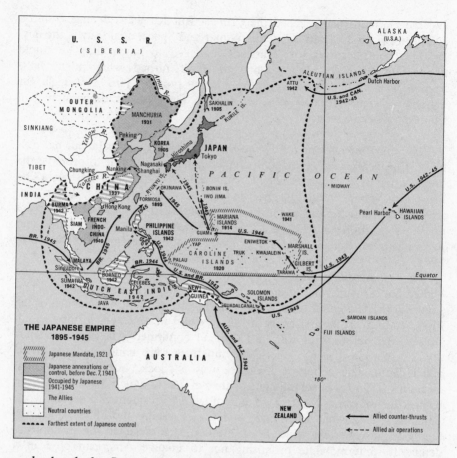

THE JAPANESE EMPIRE
1895-1945

Japanese Mandate, 1921

Japanese annexations or control, before Dec. 7, 1941

Occupied by Japanese 1941-1945

The Allies

Neutral countries

Farthest extent of Japanese control

Allied counter-thrusts

Allied air operations

resolved only by Japan. Taking a leaf from an earlier performance—the sneak attack on Russian Port Arthur in February, 1904—on December 7, 1941, Japanese aircraft struck the naval base of Pearl Harbor with telling results. The American reaction was an immediate declaration of war on Japan. This was followed by declarations of war by Germany and Italy against the United States, catapulting the country into the midst of the global conflict.

Americans never had doubts about the final result, and the war never came to America in the way that it did to much of the rest of the world. Behind the shelter of two oceans the American economy set about mobilizing its resources. Ultimately, these resources were the decisive factor in the outcome of the war, but in December, 1941, they were still largely potential. It took time to translate them into effective instruments of war.

As a consequence, the year 1942 marked the nadir of allied fortunes. The Germans reached the Caucasus while the Japanese overran much of the western Pacific and reached the gates of India. Axis forces in Africa were not far from Alexandria, and the prospects of a truly global strategy seemed open: a pincer movement from the Nile and the Caucasus that would engulf the Near East, and then turn toward India and effect a junction with the Japanese.

Since the British and the Russians were in desperate straits, the correct American decision was to give priority to the European and Mediterranean theaters, confining itself to a holding operation in the Pacific. Within a year of Pearl Harbor, sufficient resources had been accumulated to enable the allies to assume the offensive. Three almost simultaneous events turned the tide. The successful Russian stand at Stalingrad destroyed a whole German army and compelled a German retreat that would not stop until Berlin was reached. An Anglo-American force landed in Morocco and Algeria.* And a British offensive from Egypt was launched at El Alamein. Both African operations were successful; pushed from the west and the east, Rommel's Afrika Korps was finally smashed in Tunisia in May, 1943.

The writing on the wall was now clear, but German leadership lacked the element of rationality which had enabled Ludendorff to call a halt in 1918 when he became convinced that victory was no longer possible. Furthermore, the allies had adopted a policy of unconditional surrender: the war must go on until *Festung Europa* was completely reduced.

To achieve this result took another two years. In July, 1943, the allies overran Sicily; the collapse of Mussolini's Fascist regime followed. Seeking to escape further punishment, Italy sued for an armistice. However, announcement of the armistice led to the German occupation of most of the country, and the allies were compelled to inch their way at heavy cost over the length of the peninsula during the next two years. They reached Rome on June 4, 1944. Two days later the allied landings on the Normandy beaches began the reconquest of France. By the end of the year the fronts, both east and west, were nearing Germany. Nevertheless Hitler preferred Götterdämmerung to surrender. The Battle of the Bulge in the Ardennes Forest of Belgium in December stayed the allied advance only momentarily. Germany was overrun, Hitler committed suicide in his Berlin bunker, and on May 7, 1945, at Reims in France, the European phase of the war ended.

At the same time, the Japanese had been retreating in the Pacific. The air-sea battles of the Coral Sea and Midway in the middle of 1942 were the turning point. During the next two years the Japanese were gradually evicted from their island conquests, and by 1945 they were retreating in

---

* The North African landings resulted in a complete German occupation of France, though the French fleet was scuttled in Toulon harbor to keep it from the Germans.

Southeast Asia as well. The allies invaded the Philippines in October, 1944, the naval battle of Leyte Gulf marking the final crushing of the Japanese navy and air force.

The allies pushed relentlessly toward the Japanese home islands. The end came abruptly as a consequence of a revolutionary technical development: the atomic bomb. The first of these lethal weapons, exploded over Hiroshima on August 6, resulted in some 100,000 casualties. The second, dropped three days later on Nagasaki, induced the Japanese to surrender. The end came on September 2, 1945.

The war had resulted in the destruction of the power of all three members of the Rome-Berlin-Tokyo triangle; their future lay in allied hands, as did that of much of the rest of the world. The damage wrought during the long conflict was far greater than that of the First World War. Reconstruction at the most elemental level—the prevention of starvation, the repatriation of prisoners—was the most pressing concern, but important as it was it was overshadowed by the long-term problem of political and economic reconstruction. The impact of the Nazis' dreadful racial fantasies further exacerbated the situation. Some 6 million Jews and countless other innocents had been exterminated. The horrors of the concentration camps and gas chambers left memories that it would take a long time to erase. These profoundly affected the climate of the postwar world.

In 1919 many had looked upon the war as an interruption of the normality of peace, and thought it possible to return to the good old days of before 1914. No one in 1945 clamored for a return to the conditions of 1939. The Second World War was in many respects a continuation of the first, and it liquidated much of that war's incomplete business, but it left in its train another legacy of problems. Nevertheless, whatever the new world would be like, it was expected to be new.

The Nazi conquest had destroyed the structure of Europe. In certain cases, with Belgium and Holland, Denmark and Norway for example, whether their governments had gone into exile or stayed at home, there was little difficulty in restoration. The French situation, however, was different. The Vichy government of Marshal Pétain, hedging between collaboration and caution, had sought to create new institutions for France. But after recovery from the initial shock of defeat, under the stress of Nazi exactions, and especially after November, 1942, and as the tide of war turned, opposition to Vichy and to the Nazis began to increase. General De Gaulle's initial appeal had met with little response, and the allies showed considerable hesitancy in cooperating with his Free French. But after the North African landings nearly the whole of the French empire supported De Gaulle. A provisional government was organized in Algiers with De

Gaulle eventually in control. By 1944 the allies had little choice but to grant him recognition, although, especially in American quarters, it was grudgingly given. France thus managed to achieve representation among the victors in both the German and the Japanese armistices.

In France the Resistance had grown strong during the occupation. The Communists had played a large and honorable part in this movement— Russia after all was an ally. They commanded about one-quarter of the popular vote in French elections. Might the time be ripe for revolution? Whatever the answer, the war had laid the ground for appreciable changes in the social, no less than in the political, structure of France.

The Italian case presents some similarities with the French. There had been little enthusiasm for the war among the Italian people, one reason for the country's poor military performance. No sooner had the allies landed in Sicily than Fascism collapsed. The king dismissed Mussolini, who was imprisoned, and appointed Marshal Badoglio in his place in July, 1943. But Italy could not escape from the war so early. While she sought to enlist herself in the allied camp most of the country remained in German hands. Moreover, the Germans rescued Mussolini and set him up in the north as head of a puppet regime. It was a sad and sordid episode; Italy was beset by near civil war in addition to being a battle ground in the main struggle. The Italian Resistance, much of it, as in France, Communist, was both anti-German and anti-Fascist. As in France, the Communists commanded between a quarter and a third of the popular vote.

Both France and Italy, however, had been liberated by nations that eyed the rise of Communist influence in Europe with suspicion. In eastern Europe, where the liberating armies had been Russian, the situation was quite different. The Russians adopted a relatively simple stance, insisting that the liberated countries have governments friendly to them. This would have been reasonable, had not "friendly" and "subservient" been synonymous in their lexicon. The ironic truth was that authentic Communist sentiments were much stronger in France and Italy than in eastern Europe.

This led to all manner of complications, not least in the relations between the Russians and the Western powers. Differences between the Americans and the British pale into insignificance by comparison. Fighting a common enemy was a powerful binder of the alliance, but ideological differences between the Soviet Union and the West had only momentarily been put aside by the necessities of the war. Reciprocal distrust remained deep; Russian memories of Franco-British performance at Munich and Western memories of the Nazi-Soviet Pact could not be easily eradicated.

Once the danger of defeat was over and the prospects of victory began to brighten, increased emphasis on the political aspects of the war and on the implications of military decision was inevitable. In this respect Churchill and Stalin had a better understanding of the facts of power than President Roosevelt. That is why, for example, the British favored invading the Balkans; realizing that possession is nine points of the law, they hoped to occupy that area before Russia. But they were unable to convince the Americans, and the Red army controlled the region when the fighting stopped.

The effort to maintain the unity of the alliance found expression in several wartime meetings of the Big Three, Roosevelt, Churchill, and Stalin. The central and east European region was the sharpest focus of difference. As for Poland, there was little prospect that the Russians would relinquish the fruits of the Nazi-Soviet Pact; yet they agreed that there must be a separate Poland after the war. This raised the question of boundaries and the nature of the new Polish government. The Polish government in exile had been recognized during the war as the legitimate spokesman of the Polish people, but the Russians withdrew that recognition in April, 1943, granting it instead to a Polish Committee of National Liberation, essentially a Communist puppet. When the Poles rose against the Nazis in Warsaw in June, 1944, the failure of Russian assistance resulted in their being crushed, and as the Russians finally advanced through Poland the prospects of any authentically independent Polish regime became very dim.

Yugoslavia was another case in point. Exploiting internal tensions, most of all between Serbs and Croats, the Axis had broken up the country into its component elements. There arose in Yugoslavia two rival resistance movements: the Chetniks, adherents of the government in exile; and a Communist group led by Josip Broz (Tito). Thus, in addition to troubles with native collaborators, mainly Croatians, Yugoslavia faced virtual civil war. As time passed, the effectiveness of the Communists increased until they gained recognition from all the allies. When the country was liberated, it also asserted territorial claims against Italy. In 1945 there was a sharp confrontation in Istria and Julian Venetia between the western forces and the native Yugoslavian, largely backed by the Russians, until an uneasy truce was achieved and a temporary line of demarcation agreed upon between the two.

Czechoslovakia was by common consent restored in her pre-Munich borders, but although President Eduard Beneš, leader of the government in exile, persistently strove to maintain good relations with all the allies and accepted Russia's "amputation" of the extreme Ruthenian segment of his country, the effectiveness of Russian control over the whole of Czechoslovakia was not weakened. Hungary and Rumania had both waged war against Russia, and Finland had reentered the war on the German side. These nations were treated as defeated enemies. Bulgaria had been at war only with the Western allies. In order to exert her influence in her affairs, Russia now declared war on her. Greece, on the other hand, another point of conflict among the victors, and torn by virtual civil war, was liberated and occupied by Western forces. All these difficulties, of course, dwindled into insignificance compared to the problem of what to do with Germany.

These political issues, inseparable from the course of military operations, were discussed by the Big Three at Teheran in November, 1943,* and at Yalta in February, 1945. The latter meeting, held when the end of the war was in sight, was of crucial importance. While Japan and a future world organization were on the agenda, Germany was the chief subject under consideration, and its dismemberment was accepted in principle. The British insisted that France be given an equal voice in the discussion of German affairs, but France was not represented at Yalta—this had unfortunate consequences. No agreement could be reached on the troublesome Polish question; the promise to assist in the establishment of a democratic government there was in effect an evasion.

President Roosevelt was a very sick man at Yalta. Two months after his return, on April 12, 1945, he died. In the same month, following careful preparations, there met in San Francisco the conference from which the United Nations was born. In order to avoid a repetition of the awkwardness of 1919—the disowning of its child by the United States— the future world organization was deliberately divorced from the treaties of peace. The charter which emerged after two months of sometimes difficult discussions was little different in its essentials from the Covenant of the League: in deference to the facts of power, yet also glossing over some enormous differences, five permanent members of the Security Council —the United States, the Soviet Union, the United Kingdom, France, and China—were endowed with the power of veto.

On July 17, following the termination of hostilities in Europe, the Big Three met again in Potsdam, outside Berlin. Recriminations over Russian high-handedness in the east—the brutal assertion of power in Bucharest for example—countered by Russian ones on the score of Greece, led to no change in anyone's behavior or position. Germany was to remain under occupation, divided into several zones, deprived of a central government, disarmed, demilitarized, and de-Nazified. Berlin, within the Russian zone, was to be under quadripartite administration. By putting territory east of the Oder-Neisse line under Polish administration, the powers placed a heavy mortgage on the future. The division of East Prussia between Poland and Russia had the same effect. It was also decided that peace treaties would be drafted first with the other enemy powers, and a Council of Foreign Ministers was entrusted with the task. Undoing Hitler's notorious An-

* Immediately after this meeting came the meeting in Cairo between Roosevelt, Churchill and Chang Kai-shek; the conferees agreed that Japan must be reduced to her pre-1894 position, and Formosa was wrested from her.

schluss, the allies decided to deal with Austria as a separate entity. Like Germany she was divided into zones of occupation with Vienna under joint occupation and administration.

Much of Germany was rubble; its people were stunned, the general chaos compounded by the influx of Germans expelled from other parts of Europe. (Thus the German people were united, though hardly in the manner Hitler had intended.) But the pressing problems of economic reconstruction did not affect Germany alone. In many countries production had fallen to a fraction of the prewar level; indeed, the very structure of European society had been shaken, a fact which helped the Russians to capitalize on the situation. Great Britain, though bled white by the war, remained stable. There was no Communist threat in England, but the election that took place in July, 1945, resulted in victory of the reformist-socialist Labour party. Churchill, the architect of victory, was compelled to yield his place at Potsdam to Clement Attlee. Thus, as the postwar era began, the future of Europe remained unsettled; no one could say whether a true peace had been achieved or only, as in 1919, a truce.

Perhaps even more foreboding and uncertain was the situation created by the dropping of the atom bombs on Japan. No more striking manifestation of war as an instrument of change could be cited than this event. New weapons have been a familiar experience in the story of mankind, but what happened at Hiroshima sent a shudder of apprehension throughout the world. Primitive as it was, the first atom bomb raised the possibility of total destruction. How politics would deal with this problem was a question; the new development pointed with unusual sharpness to the urgency of an issue that has been in the making since the launching of modern science and technology. Could modern society, beset by the problem of its proliferating numbers, depending on highly complex economic relationships, and possessed of such lethal weapons, preserve freedom and individualism, even the human race itself? In this question lay perhaps the supreme irony of the struggle against the totalitarian regimes. Unlocking of the power of the atom raised the possibility of an age of unprecedented ease for mankind, but it plainly required the revision of certain modes of thought, and the adjusting of power relationships. This was the great issue that confronted the world at the end of World War II.

For Further Reading

Falls, C., *The Second World War: A Short History*.
Liddell Hart, B. H., *The Other Side of the Hill*.
Ryan, C., *The Longest Day*.
Trevor-Roper, H. R., *The Last Days of Hitler*.

The Brooding Present

94 Europe Since World War II

In 1940, after the collapse of France, Marshal Jan Smuts of South Africa delivered himself of the judgment that "France is gone in our day and perhaps for many a day." In 1945 it might seem that "Europe" could be substituted for "France" in that verdict, allowing for the exception of two peripheral entities, Britain and Russia. The Continental countries lay prostrate and powerless.

The first need was to restore social services and political order; the second was to draft formal treaties of peace. The Council of Foreign Ministers of the great powers set about this second task, and by 1947 treaties were made with Italy, Hungary, Bulgaria, Rumania, and Finland, though not with Germany and Austria. With two exceptions, the new map of Europe was not very different from that of 1937: the Soviet Union recovered much of Russia's loss from the First World War, and Poland was bodily shifted westward. The rest were minor changes. Broadly speaking, the application of self-determination remained the guiding principle, as it had been after the First World War.

The nature of domestic regimes was a different matter. In France Vichy disappeared and a new constitution established the Fourth Republic, largely a replica of the Third. In 1946 Italy became a republic. In both countries the structure of politics reflected a return to parliamentary democracy under a multiparty system, though the Communists greatly increased their strength. Catholic parties also grew in influence: in Italy the Catholics were strong enough to obtain a majority for some years. In France General De Gaulle "withdrew" in 1946 because he considered the new constitutional arrangements unsatisfactory; thereafter the country reverted to the pattern of ministerial instability so characteristic of the prewar period.

Both in France and in Italy the Communists were maneuvered out of

CHRONOLOGY

A.D.		
	1945	Surrender of Germany; San Francisco Conference; The United Nations; Potsdam Conference; Labour in office in Britain; surrender of Japan
	1946	Fourth French Republic; Italy becomes a republic; Churchill's "iron curtain" speech in Fulton, Missouri; De Gaulle "withdraws"
	1947	Communists out of government in France and in Italy; Truman Doctrine; beginning of the Cold War; India and Pakistan emerge to independence; UN establishes State of Israel
	1948	Communist coup in Prague; Marshall Plan and OEEC; Yugoslav-Soviet break
1948–1949		The Berlin blockade
	1949	Signature of NATO Treaty; emergence of the West German Federal Republic; the German Democratic Republic
	1950	The Korean War; Indonesian independence
	1952	Elizabeth II queen of the United Kingdom
	1953	Death of Stalin; Eisenhower President of the U.S.; East Berlin rising; ECSC launched
	1954	Geneva conference and agreement re French Indochina; EDC proposal defeated in French parliament
	1955	Bandung meeting; Treaty of Peace with Austria; Warsaw Pact; emergence of Nikita Khrushchev in control

---

participation in the government in 1947. Yet in both, as in Britain and elsewhere, the nationalized sector of the economy was markedly expanded. Divided Germany offered initially a contrast between ruthless Russian exploitation in the east and in the west assistance given with a view to restoring the economy. The result was large-scale migration westward: western Germany had soon absorbed some 11 million refugees from Russian-controlled areas.

In countries under Russian occupation matters were relatively simple. It did not take very long before dependable Communist regimes were established everywhere; Czechoslovakia, the last holdout, was brought into

1956   Twentieth Party Congress of U.S.S.R.; independence
        of Tunisia and Morocco; Hungarian rising crushed
        by Soviet intervention; Israeli attack on Egypt;
        Anglo-French intervention at Suez
1957   *Sputnik*
1958   Treaty of Rome launches the Common Market (EEC);
        De Gaulle called back to power; the Fifth French
        Republic; the Eisenhower Doctrine re the Middle
        East
1960   Abortive summit meeting in Paris; independence
        of the Belgian Congo; independence of French
        Black Africa; beginning of Sino-Soviet conflict
1962   Independence of Algeria; Cuban missile crisis
1963   France vetoes British application to Common Market
1964   Ouster of Khrushchev
1967   The Six-Day War between Israel and the Arab coun-
        tries
1968   Student agitation and strikes in France; Warsaw pact
        countries occupy Czechoslovakia
1969   De Gaulle quits office; Pompidou president, Ameri-
        can moon landing
1970–1971 Issue of Britain's adherence to the Common Market;
        Sino-American relations; problems of the Amer-
        ican and world economies

---

line by a coup in February, 1948. There was one exception, and that a portentous one: in the summer of 1948, Marshal Tito, though still proclaiming himself a Communist, rejected Russian dictation. This first successful assertion of heresy within the Communist fold initiated a highly important line of future development.

Impotent Europe could not escape the impact of the Cold War, the larger contest between the two superpowers which had emerged from the hot war. The division became very sharp in 1947, with the proclamation of the Truman Doctrine—the American decision to take up the burden of assistance to Greece and Turkey that Britain felt unable to carry any longer—providing a convenient landmark of the change. Henceforth the United States would use its power to help those seeking to "contain" Communist expansion. The highly imaginative Marshall Plan for the economic rehabilitation of Europe which came into effect in 1948, apart from its very real humanitarian motivation, was a most successful instance of enlightened self-interest on the part of the United States; it did much to check Communism in the West.

It was a natural next step to reorganize military power in western Europe. The creation of the North Atlantic Treaty Organization (NATO) in 1949, an alliance of fifteen nations, subsequently extended to include both Greece and Turkey, accomplished this goal by announcing that they would consider an attack against any one of them an attack against all the NATO powers. But NATO raised some difficult questions to which the outbreak of the Korean War in 1950 gave added point. After the defeat of Japan, Korea had been divided into Communist and American zones. Following the successful Communist takeover of mainland China, an attack by the North Koreans against the south resulted in the intervention of the United Nations. But the United States carried by far the main burden of the war; in the Far East it was performing the same task of containing Communism as in the West. Thus it was all the more eager to organize Europe's military potential.

This brought the German question to the fore. The three sectors under western control were united into the Federal Republic of West Germany under the guidance of Konrad Adenauer, leader of the Christian Democratic party. A drastic currency reform in 1950 led to an outstanding economic recovery; one soon began to hear about *Wirtschaftswunder,* the German "economic miracle." But American interest in the rebuilding of military power in Europe led to the question of German rearmament, an alarming prospect to all who remembered the ruthlessness and brutality of Germany during the war. The so-called European Defense Community was long debated, and finally rejected by the French in 1954. However, subsequent negotiations led to Germany's rearmament and her participation in NATO.

The Communist world, allowing for the Yugoslav heresy, still presented a monolithic structure under the guidance of the Muscovite mother church. The death of Stalin in January, 1953, produced a contest for the succession finally resolved with the emergence of Nikita Khrushchev to a position of leadership. This raised new possibilities; Khrushchev's surprising attack on Stalin at the Twentieth Party Congress in 1956 induced hopes of change. Open opposition to Russian domination developed in some of the satellite countries. Poland managed to steer a middle course and thus staved off Russian intervention, but violence broke out in Hungary, where

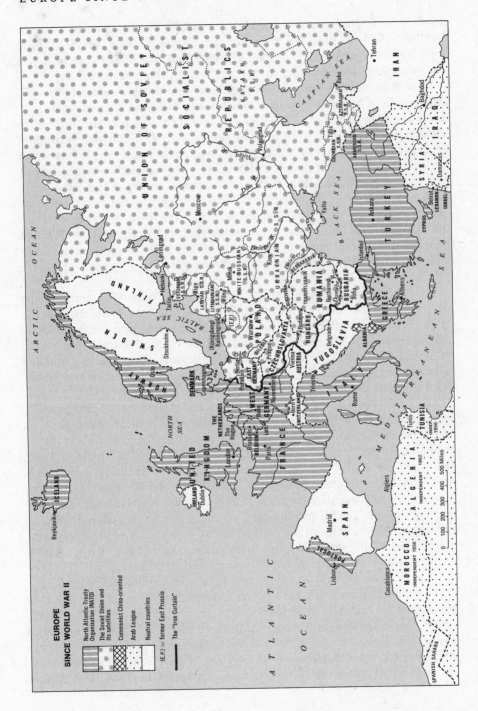

EUROPE
SINCE WORLD WAR II

North Atlantic Treaty
Organization (NATO)
The Soviet Union and
its satellites
Communist China-oriented
Arab League
Neutral countries
(E.P.) = former East Prussia
The "Iron Curtain"

a rebellion in Budapest was ruthlessly crushed by the Russian army in October, 1956. Neither the West nor the United Nations would help the frustrated Hungarians. Yet despite this assertion of Russian control it was clear that there were growing strains within the Communist structure.

But there were not merely strains; there were notable successes as well, especially in a field in which the United States had long claimed primacy—technology. In October, 1957, Russia launched *Sputnik,* the first earth satellite, a severe jolt to American pride, and a world-wide sensation. Despite this illustration of Soviet power, and even despite the failure of an attempted summit meeting in Paris in 1955, there seemed to be indications of a changing climate within the Soviet Union. Changes in leadership were no longer followed by executions. While the government continued its efforts to keep up with American armaments, which put a severe strain on the Russian economy, there were signs that the desire of the Russian people for a greater share of the goods of this earth might lead to a less bellicose Soviet stance in international affairs.

At the end of the war European nations still controlled much of the planet; the French empire, for example, had been a very useful asset to the allies. But the war intensified the desire for independence among colonial peoples, while the setbacks inflicted for a time by the Japanese also served to debase the prestige of white-skinned Westerners. Thus the war initiated a movement which in the course of two decades resulted in the virtual liquidation of all the European empires save the Russian.

By 1950 the Dutch, after some unsuccessful attempts at compromise, were evicted from their East Indian possessions, which emerged as an independent Republic of Indonesia. The British tried to adhere to an evolutionary policy for their huge empire. They relinquished India in 1947, but what the British had held together fell apart once independence was won: rivalries and bloody disputes resulted in the division of the vast subcontinent between India proper, largely Hindu, and Pakistan, predominantly Muslim. The British adopted a similar course of action elsewhere, notably in Africa. Most of the former British possessions retained membership in the Commonwealth, but British hopes of keeping the Commonwealth a unit of international importance proved an illusion.

The French attempt to reorganize their empire into a French Union was equally unsuccessful. France was evicted from the Levant and soon found herself mired in a desperate war in Indochina. In 1954, finally, under the leadership of Premier Mendès-France, the French disengaged themselves from Indochina, leaving the region as a problem, and later a dilemma, for other powers, particularly the United States. French protectorates over Tunisia and Morocco were abrogated in 1956, but Algeria

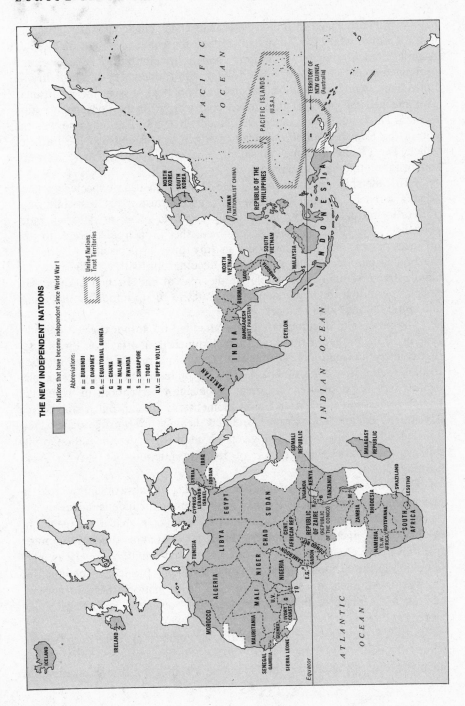

THE NEW INDEPENDENT NATIONS

Nations that have become independent since World War I

United Nations
Trust Territories

Abbreviations:

B = BURUNDI
D = DAHOMEY
E.G. = EQUATORIAL GUINEA
G = GHANA
M = MALAWI
R = RWANDA
S = SINGAPORE
T = TOGO
U.V. = UPPER VOLTA

had been incorporated into metropolitan France. This constitutional device did not work: while the European settlers, the colons, insisted on keeping Algeria French, the native majority sought to cut loose. A savage and prolonged conflict followed, a war fought with ruthlessness and brutality on both sides, while it produced increasing political dissension in France. This reached the point of threatened civil war, with the consequence that General De Gaulle came out of retirement in 1958. The outcome was the end of the Fourth Republic, instead of which was established the Fifth, of which De Gaulle became president, endowed with extensive powers, somewhat on the American model.

His leadership was paradoxical. De Gaulle had been expected to keep Algeria French; moving circumspectly, and arousing his erstwhile supporters to murderous fury, he gradually began to speak of Algerian independence. By 1962 he had accustomed the French electorate to the prospect of such independence, and in July, after a plebiscite, Algeria left the French empire. At the same time, decolonizing with a vengeance, De Gaulle freed virtually the whole of the rest of the French empire. His policies permitted the new independent states to retain important economic and cultural bonds with France.

The process of decolonization was attended by an unexpected episode. Late in 1956, France, Britain, and Israel launched an attack on Egypt after that country had nationalized the Suez Canal and proclaimed its intention to destroy the new state of Israel. The Egyptians fared poorly, especially against Israeli troops, but the threat of outside intervention, in which the United States and the Soviet Union momentarily joined, put a stop to the adventure. Britain and France suffered heavily in prestige from their bungled efforts, but Israel had given an impressive demonstration of its military capabilities, and notice of its firm intention to survive Arab hostility.

The United States played a complex and not always happy role in decolonization. Sympathetic a priori to the clamor for independence everywhere, it was insufficiently aware of the problems that the freeing of colonies must inevitably produce. In 1960, Belgium suddenly granted freedom to the Congo. Chaos was the result, and tentative American participation in the turmoil proved an embarrassment. Ironically, for much of the world, America, once the friend of aspiring nationalities everywhere, has taken the place of the former imperialist powers as the villain of the piece.

Most of the newly emerged states, a number of them very small, achieved membership in the United Nations. The unforeseen proliferation of members did not facilitate the operation of the world organization, in which Communist members cheerfully endorsed all anti-imperialist claims, seemingly oblivious to the persistent imperialism of the Russians.

The demise of empire might be taken as evidence of the decline of the former European great powers. Demoted from that rank indeed they were, but an unmitigated picture of decline would be highly misleading.

During the fifties, the German economic miracle had its counterpart elsewhere, especially in France and in Italy. After a long period of stagnation, France's population began to grow, with the important consequence of changing the age composition of the country. Everywhere the state interfered in the economy in behalf of recovery; extensive nationalization and planning became commonplace.

Another important and novel development also occurred in Europe: the havoc of two wars and the common loss of world power began to convince numbers of Europeans of the futility of internecine quarrels. The idea of European unity has a long background which nationalistic passions have never succeeded in destroying. Out of the 1950 proposal of French foreign minister Robert Schuman—the name of Jean Monnet deserves equal mention—the Coal and Steel Community was born (1953). These two basic industries were to be integrated, or "scrambled," in six countries, France, West Germany, Italy, Belgium, the Netherlands, and Luxembourg. The scheme, designed with a view to economic advantage as well as to decrease the possibility of war, prospered, and on January 1, 1958, the Treaty of Rome brought into existence the European Economic Community, usually referred to as the Common Market. The same six countries launched upon the ambitious undertaking of creating a free trade area among themselves and of integrating their entire economies. The Common Market was a resounding success—industrial tariffs, supposed to disappear by 1970, were reduced ahead of schedule—and the whole region boomed.

In the eyes of many of its advocates the Common Market was but a prelude to political integration, which offered, among other things, a possible solution of the German problem. The Europe of the Six is but a part of Europe, roughly coterminous with Charlemagne's empire, but it holds a vital core of some 235 million people. The Franco-German relationship, so different from what it was forty years ago, is of crucial importance, for Europe cannot "unite" without including both France and Germany in the merger.

There remains the question of Britain. That country, fallen upon hard times, faces troubles reminiscent in some respects of those of France after the First World War, when the cost of victory came too high. Unlike the rest of western Europe Britain did not enjoy the advantage of defeat. Attempts to continue to play a major world role, reliance on the Commonwealth or on the special link with the United States, have led only to disillusionment. Britain initially took an unfavorable view of the efforts toward European integration, of which she might have been the leader. EFTA (European Free Trade Association) has been no adequate answer to the Common Market, and Britain has been evolving toward the view that her future lies in Europe. Here is perhaps the most important issue for the Europe of the future: will the legacy of superseded quarrels result in continued division, or can Europe, returning to the legacy of both pagan and Christian Rome, become a major unit, comparable to the United States, the Soviet Union, and China, in the world tomorrow?

The changing face of the Vietnam war, the persistence of Sino-Russian differences, the divergences which have broken the unity of the Communist world, the possibility of change in the relationship between the United States and China, and many other issues, are problems which are not primarily European. Their importance bespeaks the passing of the European Age, yet a Europe united even in part would remain one of the major factors in the affairs of the world.

For Further Reading

Aron, R., *A Century of Total War.*
Brzezinski, Z. K., *The Soviet Bloc: Unity and Conflict.*
Djilas, M., *The New Class: An Analysis of the Communist System.*
Fontaine, A., *A History of the Cold War.*
Lichtheim, G., *The New Europe Today—and Tomorrow.*
Seton-Watson, H., *Neither War Nor Peace: The Struggle for Power in the Postwar World.*

95   The Cold War

The term "The Cold War" came into popular use in 1947: it was the title of a pamphlet by Walter Lippmann critical of certain views expressed by George F. Kennan (writing as Mr. X) in a widely read and discussed article, "The Sources of Soviet Conduct." Yet, as Mr. Kennan later observed in his memoirs, he had already set down these views in government memoranda two years before, in early 1945. Indeed, one may date the beginning of the Cold War, in its more restricted sense, from about that time—in the last year of the Second World War, with the emergence of

A.D. 1939 German-Soviet nonaggression treaty

1941 Germany invades Soviet Union; Pearl Harbor

1943 Discovery of Katyn massacre; U.S.S.R. rupture with Polish government in exile; Teheran Conference

1944 Normandy landing; pro-Soviet Polish National Committee created; Warsaw uprising; Churchill-Stalin agreement in Moscow; civil conflict in Greece

1945 Yalta Conference; pro-Soviet Groza government formed in Rumania; Potsdam Conference; first atomic bomb dropped, on Hiroshima; Moscow Conference

1946 Churchill's "iron curtain" speech in Fulton, Missouri

1947 Announcement of "Truman Doctrine" for aid to Greece and Turkey; Marshall Plan launched; creation of Cominform

1948 Communist coup in Prague; Tito's Yugoslavia expelled from Cominform; beginning of Berlin blockade

1949 North Atlantic Treaty signed; Chinese People's Republic proclaimed

1950 North Korean invasion of South Korea; Atlantic Council agrees on measures of West German rearmament

1953 Death of Stalin

1956 Khrushchev denunciation of Stalin; Gomulka becomes First Secretary of Polish Communist party; abortive Hungarian uprising

1957 Khrushchev defeats "anti-Party group"; launching of first Soviet *Sputnik*

1959 Fidel Castro victory in Cuba

1960 Revelation of Sino-Soviet rift

1961 Abortive Bay of Pigs invasion in Cuba; erection of Berlin wall

1962 Cuban missile crisis

issues (and the search for methods of dealing with them) that were to disrupt the wartime alliance of the United States, the Soviet Union, and Great Britain against the Axis powers.

The Cold War can, of course, be given broader meanings that encompass the breakup of the Big Three Alliance and the onset of the postwar Soviet-American antagonism. One could say that a state of cold war has marked the relations of the Soviet Union with the other leading powers ever since the cessation of open conflict between the new Bolshevik regime and the "imperialists" in the early 1920's. The hostility between "Communism" and "capitalism," or between "totalitarianism" and "democracy," sometimes enlarged to signify a cultural, almost ethnic, conflict between "East" and "West"—all very unsatisfactory but misleadingly handy terms—has been a major feature of the international scene for half a century. Cold war can be defined, too, as a form of conflict taking place below the level of hot war in a thermonuclear age, that is, as a means of pursuing antagonistic aims at a time when the full use of material power appears unbearably costly and destructive for all concerned. Although there were numerous limited hot wars and skirmishes in the decades after 1945, the threatening mushroom cloud in the background influenced profoundly the international climate in those years. Both of these definitions of "cold war" are extremely general, however, and concern virtually the entire range of recent international affairs. The present chapter limits itself to the narrower conflict.

In retrospect it is apparent that the Big Three Alliance, called into being by World War II, was never a closely knit coalition of mutual trust. In addition to the twenty years of enmity that lay behind it, both the Western powers and the Soviet Union harbored suspicions that the other might conclude a separate peace with the Axis if it seemed advantageous to do so. Stalin's role in partitioning eastern Europe with Germany during the period of the Nazi-Soviet Pact (1939–1941) and the Anglo-American delays in launching a second front in Europe in 1942 and 1943 contributed importantly to these mutual suspicions. A revealing indication of this mood on the Russian side is Stalin's remark in 1944, reported by the Yugoslav Communist Milovan Djilas: "Perhaps you think that just because we are the allies of the English that we have forgotten who they are and who Churchill is. They find nothing sweeter than to trick their allies. . . . And Churchill? Churchill is the kind who, if you don't watch him, will slip a kopeck out of your pocket."

This persistent mutual suspicion was accompanied by the bickering over relative contributions and sacrifices that seems to be a part of all "grand alliances." The Cold War as such, however, was precipitated and took form in eastern Europe, initially in disputes concerning the postwar status of Poland and Rumania. The discord first surfaced in Poland, but the Cold War actually started in Rumania. It is worth looking into these two disputes briefly, since they illustrate many of the problems and ambiguities associated with the Cold War as it later expanded. Even in the afterlight of a quarter-century it is difficult to determine the extent to which the crisis concerning these two countries was a consequence of Soviet intentions, present from the outset, to dominate these two states and remodel them in its own image, the unhappy but possibly avoidable crossing of wires in the mutual reading of intentions, or simply that Poland and Rumania happened to be the loci of an essentially unavoidable rupture of a wartime alliance that had lost its function with the anticipated defeat of the common menace, Nazi Germany.

From the summer of 1941 on, the Polish question was confused by the interplay of two related but distinct issues: (1) whether Poland was to regain the eastern territories lost under the unsavory circumstances of the Nazi-Soviet Pact, and (2) whether the Poles would be free to determine their own domestic political and social order. Most Poles naturally connected the two, seeing the restoration of the eastern territories as a legitimate restitution and as a sign of good faith that the tradition of partition and dismemberment was at an end. Great Britain and the United States were less than enthusiastic about the restoration of the 1939 frontier, which contained large numbers of non-Poles, and they proved to be unwilling to make this the occasion for a break with the Soviet Union. On the contrary, they were inclined to argue that chances for decent Soviet-Polish relations and the preservation of Polish independence depended upon Poland's willingness to acquiesce in the permanent loss of the lands beyond the so-called Curzon Line. As for the Soviet Union, it was clear from the beginning that it intended to reclaim all territories gained and incorporated in the years 1939–1941. Whether, if these demands had been acceded to gracefully at the beginning (in all likelihood a political impossibility for any representative Polish regime), the Russians would have been content to let the Poles create a regime of their own choosing remains an open question. We have no real knowledge of Soviet plans and intentions in those years.

Given these incompatible interests and intentions a clash of some sort was probably inevitable despite the continuing common need to fight Hitler. The Polish government in exile in London and the Soviet regime came to an open breach in 1943 as a consequence of the German discovery of mass graves of Polish officers in the Katyn forest—a massacre almost certainly perpetrated by the Russians, though for reasons that remain obscure. Shortly thereafter Stalin threw his weight behind a Polish Communist group as the nucleus for the future government of Poland. The abortive Warsaw uprising of August, 1944, which Stalin icily refused to assist, or permit to be assisted, produced a real, though not publicized, crisis of confidence in the Big Three Alliance. Still, at the Yalta Conference in February, 1945, the Allies did arrive at formulas regarding the frontiers of Poland and the composition of its government, which, while stacked in the Soviet Union's favor, seemed to give promise of an agreed-upon solution. Indeed, a fully Communist-controlled government did not emerge until 1947, by which time the situation throughout eastern Europe had deteriorated beyond hope of Soviet-Western agreement. The Polish question, then, had seriously darkened allied relations but did not lead to an explicit breach.

In the case of Rumania, in contrast, overt disagreement among the allies developed in a relatively short span of time; the forcible installation of the Communist-dominated Groza government in March, 1945, a government which the United States and Great Britain refused to recognize, may be said to mark the beginning of the Cold War, before the final defeat of Germany or the first explosion of an atomic bomb. Although a territorial issue—Bessarabia and northern Bukovina—also divided Rumania and the Soviet Union, it was not central. Rather, the ouster under Soviet insistence of a post-armistice coalition government and the installation of a regime effectively controlled by the Communists directly and flatly affected the domestic structure and independence of Rumania. This was no native revolution; the Rumanian Communists came to power through the will and the presence of the Soviet Union. Occurring a few weeks after the Yalta Conference, it was clearly not in accord with the Declaration on Liberated Areas, which provided for broadly representative interim governments as well as for the holding of early free elections. It did correspond, however, to the terms of the Churchill-Stalin agreement of October, 1944 (Roosevelt did not participate in this agreement but knew of it), which had in effect assigned spheres of influence in southeastern Europe (ostensibly only for a period of military occupation following the expulsion of the Germans), with Greece falling to Great Britain, but Rumania to the Soviet Union. It is evident that Stalin regarded this agreement, rather than the more general provisions of the Yalta agreement, as operative. Throughout 1945 the United States and Great Britain rejected the Groza government as being in contravention to the Yalta agreement; the Soviet Union strongly supported it. There was a fleeting possibility, arrived at in the Moscow Conference of December, 1945, of a mutually acceptable formula involving token representation of non-Communists in the government and the holding of free elections. This quickly broke down: the Soviet Union would not accept elections that would assuredly return an anti-Soviet majority in a country on its frontiers. Although the Western powers did in fact recognize the Groza government and did sign a peace treaty with it, and although King Michael was not forced to abdicate until 1947, the Rumanian impasse was never really resolved, and it hung over all the post-Yalta conferences of the Great Powers until the conferences themselves eventually broke down.

The Polish and Rumanian crises point up two prominent problems and quandaries in the Cold War. First, was the major Soviet concern territorial and defensive, did it want only to strengthen its western approaches and have regimes on its periphery that were "friendly" enough to accept the necessary measures, or was it intent upon imposing its own form of social and political organization on all states within its effective reach (perhaps as the only way it could conceive to assure a "friendly" regime)? Second, was the way to deal with the power vacuum resulting from the destruction of Hitler's empire the classic one of agreed-upon spheres of influence (certainly Stalin's preference, at least for the short run) or was it the Wilsonian principle of self-determination, through the holding of free elections? Unfortunately, the United States and Great Britain did not see eye to eye on this matter, with the result that in the critical year 1945 the policies of the Western allies were not always in consonance. The confusions resulting from this difficulty in reading intentions and from conflicting strategies for resolving the problem of power and influence in eastern Europe contributed greatly to the escalation and extension of the Cold War.

In the three years after the end of the Second World War the Cold War expanded and deepened—in Bulgaria, Yugoslavia, Albania, Hungary, and, most dangerously, in a divided and occupied Germany, with its capital, Berlin, deep inside the Soviet zone of occupation. The February, 1948, Communist coup in Prague ended the independence of the last non-Communist regime in east central Europe (with the interesting but precarious exception of Finland at the north, and Greece, in the throes of a civil war, at the south). The Cold War spilled into the Middle East, with the revival of the perennial Straits question and the sharp dispute over the continued Soviet occupation of northwestern Iran. In February, 1946, Stalin reintroduced the theme, muted during the war, of the inevitability of conflicts under "imperialism." Winston Churchill, in his speech at Fulton, Missouri, the next month, referred to the "iron curtain" that was dividing Europe.

Increasingly the Cold War colored other international problems, not only the peace treaties with the defeated Axis powers, Germany and Japan, but also the civil war that was to rage in China until the victory of the Chinese Communists in 1949. The announcement in March, 1947, of the Truman Doctrine—American aid and support for Greece and Turkey on the fringes of the Soviet imperium—has been taken by some as inaugurating the Cold War. Quite clearly the conflict was well in progress by that time, but the Truman Doctrine did indicate that the United States was moving beyond diplomacy and verbal protest to throw its own power and resources into the conflict. While the creation of the Communist Information Bureau (Cominform) in October, 1947, was a somewhat pale and limited resurrection of the old Comintern, it showed that for the Soviet side, too, the world was now divided into hostile Communist and "imperialist" camps.

The year 1948 witnessed both a climax and a testing point in the Cold War, but also a foreshadowing of things to come. The Communist coup in Czechoslovakia, destroying a democratic regime that had sought desperately to maintain good relations with the Soviet Union and to serve as a bridge between the two worlds, seemed to mark the end of any hope for accommodation. Four months later the Soviet Union imposed a blockade on Berlin. The blockade, and the airlift which was successfully mounted to counter it, gave some definition to the nature and precarious limits of a Cold War at the advent of the age of atomic and thermonuclear weaponry. The crisis was passed without a violent confrontation, but the margin of tolerance between a Western abandonment of its position in Berlin and an open test of strength between predominant Soviet land power (still mauled from the war, but massive and on the scene) and predominant American air power (with a growing atomic arsenal) was extremely narrow.

In the same month, June, 1948, occurred the first of a set of events that in the subsequent two decades was significantly to alter one of the major premises of the Cold War. The Tito regime in Yugoslavia was expelled from the bloc of Communist states. This rift within the newly created Soviet cosmos, while not immediately destructive of its unity—indeed, Draconic steps to impose conformity were the immediate consequence— did display the uncertain foundations of a system that attempted to be at once monolithic and multinational.

Perhaps the single most salient feature in the evolution of the Cold War from its origins in the concluding phase of the Second World War to its establishment as an international fact of life and a label for the times by 1948 is that while the mounting conflict between the Soviet Union and the Western powers was reciprocal it was not symmetrical. This is of some importance for understanding the dynamics of the Cold War and the debates and historical controversies that accompanied it. Soviet-Western relations were reciprocal in that the actions of one side profoundly affected those of the other. In this respect the Cold War is intelligible only as a sequential, escalating contest. In many of its twists and turns it provides classical examples of the mutually produced exacerbations that mark great power politics. At the same time, the relationship was not a symmetrical one despite much talk about the rivalry of superpowers and the creation of mirror images. Several obvious points of "asymmetry" in the antagonism may be offered. Thus, Soviet insistence upon having "friendly regimes" on its western frontiers meant in effect the imposition of Communist regimes; Western insistence upon free elections meant in effect regimes unfriendly to the Soviet Union. Hence, the controversy was not one that could be resolved by the outcome of elections, but involved the acceptability of self-determination itself. Second, once the options of mutual agreement or accommodation seemed closed the choices open to American policy were framed in the debate "containment versus liberation"—holding the line against further Soviet expansion or undertaking to "roll back" the extension of Soviet control in Europe. While these formulations were ambiguous and did not adequately define the range of choices open to the United States, they were, nonetheless, the alternatives for popular and passionate debate in this country in the 1950's. It is reasonable to suppose that debates of some type were also going on in the Soviet Union during these years, when the unpleasant consequences of the collapse of the alliance were making themselves felt. Yet quite obviously the terms of the debate were not, and could not have been, the same in the Soviet Union. Third, the strategic implications of control over eastern Europe were quite different for the Soviet Union and for the United States and Great Britain. A Continental power occupying much of the great Eurasian heartland, Russia clearly looked upon its western approaches (whether its intentions were defensive, offensive, or a mixture of both) in a quite different light from that of the United States or Great Britain, both offshore powers as far as Europe was concerned and both acutely concerned over an irreversible tilting of a traditional European balance of power, the fulcrum of which was somewhere in central Europe. Fourth, and related to this, in the immediate postwar years there was a vast lack of symmetry between the land-based Soviet Union with its armies-in-being and close to the scene and the more remote if fearfully destructive aerial-atomic potential of the United States. Finally, at the level of ideology there was a profound lack of symmetry between the perceptions, goals, and expectations of the Communist leaders and those of the Western leaders. Even granting, as seems quite likely, that in his later years Stalin was hardly a revolutionary and indeed had a real mistrust of any spontaneous revolutionary impulse that would not be firmly under his control, still, his view of the international scene and of the relations between states was not that of a Churchill, a Roosevelt, a Truman, or an Attlee.

Exclusive emphasis upon the reciprocal features of the Cold War can too easily lead to a kind of Olympian neutralism about the conflict and its sources, just as too exclusive emphasis upon one or another feature of asymmetry can lead to a "good guys—bad guys" view of this dangerous and disheartening period of history. Much of the rather fruitless debate about the origins and causes of the Cold War stems from such selective oversimplification.

In the years after 1948 the term Cold War came to describe a whole complex of international tensions seen as deriving from the bipolar antagonism of the two superpowers, the Soviet Union and the United States. Certain things happened to the meaning of the Cold War in consequence. The North Korean invasion of South Korea in June, 1950, was read as a part of this pattern of conflict, but with the war now becoming hot. The Asian conflict in turn increased fears of a military attack in Europe and led to a certain shift in emphasis from efforts to bolster European economic recovery, as through the Marshall Plan, to defending Europe militarily by strengthening NATO and moving toward West German rearmament. The vast anticolonial movement in Asia and Africa, an impulse that had its own roots and was bound to make its appearance in one form or another in the aftermath of the Second World War, was also warped, by both sides, into the Cold War polarization—with eventually unfortunate consequences for all concerned.

By the time of Stalin's death in March, 1953, the atmosphere of the Cold War had also penetrated into the domestic climate of both sides. From 1948 on, the Communist party line in Russia and in the satellites became tougher and tougher, partly to achieve an impregnable front against the imperialist enemy, partly to guard against the Titoist heresy, though partly, no doubt, for reasons of purely domestic infighting. In the United States the Cold War, combined with the separate but apparently related challenges in the Far East, produced the phenomenon that has been loosely labeled McCarthyism, although a temper of frustration and suspicion had been mounting for some time before the Senator cometed across the scene.

Stalin's death did not end the Cold War, but it did lead to a series of changes within the Soviet Union and the Soviet bloc that significantly modified the setting. The struggle for succession within the Kremlin, the gingerly efforts to move away from some of the excesses and rigidities of Stalinism, the growing restiveness in the east European satellites, the appearance of "thaws" and "new courses"—all pointed to some shift in the foundations of that vast imperium Stalin had created and the creation of which had been the central occasion for the Cold War. A climax was reached in 1956, with Khrushchev's denunciation of Stalin at the Twentieth Congress of the Soviet Communist party, with the successful Polish move to a more independent status, and with the violent spasm of the Hungarian Revolution.

The events of 1956, however, while demonstrating that important changes had taken place, also demonstrated the persistence of certain decisive features of the Cold War. For if 1956 served to demolish the Stalin myth as well as the pretension that Soviet Communism was a freely accepted and popular way of life, it also showed that when the chips were down, as in Hungary, the Soviet Union had the power and the will to maintain its position in eastern Europe. The failure—and, it should be said, the inability, except at fearful cost—of the United States to exercise its will in the Hungarian crisis rather effectively ended the theme of "liberation" or "rollback" which had been one of the planks in the domestic debate about the Cold War since the onset of the conflict. From this time on, there was relatively little talk—there had never been much action—about freeing the nations of eastern Europe.

Following on the heels of the crisis in eastern Europe, and in part a consequence of it, was the tremendously important schism between the two major Communist powers, the Soviet Union and China, which festered and then erupted between 1957 and 1960. The impact on the Communist world of this rift and of the appearance of two rival centers of Communist ideology and influence lies beyond the scope of this chapter, but it was bound to affect the nature of the Cold War. More than the Titoist heresy, more than other departures, defections, or attempted defections, the Sino-Soviet break was instrumental in destroying the image of the Communist bloc as having a single will and purpose.

Nikita Khrushchev's emergence from the post-Stalin interregnum as the new leader in 1957 did not effectively counter this drift toward divisiveness within the Communist bloc. Indeed, his rather erratic policies and style of behavior contributed to sharpening the Sino-Soviet conflict. The seven years of Khrushchev's leadership, from 1957 to 1964, did, however, lead to some modifications in the content of the Cold War. Soviet-American relations alternated between efforts at some type of détente and, after *Sputnik,* an intensified race in the missile and space programs. The "third world" became increasingly the object of international attention and competition. A critical intersection of these two trends occurred with the Cuban missile crisis in October, 1962. Like earlier major Soviet-American confrontations in the Cold War—notably the Berlin blockade in 1948 and the Hungarian Revolution in 1956—the resolution of the crisis seemed to carry a dual message: the United States was forced to face the unwelcome fact of a hostile, virtually Communist regime close at hand in the Western Hemisphere; the Soviet Union failed dramatically in its effort to exploit this fact by playing thermonuclear brinkmanship.

In the 1960's there was throughout the world a growing sense that times were changing, if not necessarily for the better. The term Cold War, which had become a blanket description to cover most postwar antagonisms, came to seem less and less appropriate, and the phrase itself fell out of usage, except in historical studies, which now attempted to put the Cold War "in perspective" or to describe its rise and fall. No statesman now liked to have the epithet Cold Warrior hurled at him. Somehow the equally ambiguous term "peaceful coexistence" had crept in.

Several reasons, apart from the mere passage of time and boredom with a turn of speech, may account for this fading of the image of the Cold War. For one thing, the characterization of the world as bipolarized seemed an increasingly inapplicable and inaccurate way of describing the international scene in the 1960's. Despite the tremendous resources and military destructiveness at their disposal, the Soviet Union and the United States did not dominate the globe as they appeared to in the two preceding decades. China was contending with Russia for at least the moral and ideological leadership of the Communist world. In the West, France, under De Gaulle, had moved off on a course of its own determination. The Vietnamese conflict had come to absorb a high percentage of American attention and energies. The lines of cleavage in Africa and the Middle East were following their own logic and no longer fell into the force field of two superpowers.

In central and eastern Europe, the place of origin of the Cold War, further change was taking place. True, the problem of a divided Germany remained, and as the periodic alarms and crises involving Berlin demonstrated (notably the building of the Berlin wall in 1961), it was still a most refractory and dangerous one, capable of bringing the Cold War back into very sharp focus and even of leading to a disaster of incalculable proportions.

Among the Communist states of eastern Europe, one after another came to mark out its own course. Albania had broken with Khrushchev by 1960 and held to neo-Stalinist orthodoxy in fear of Yugoslavia. Later Rumania and then Czechoslovakia, previously exceptionally docile regimes, asserted their freedom of action, the one primarily in the area of foreign economic and defense policy, the other in domestic liberalization.

The apprehensive and at times forceful response of the Soviet Union reflected the alarm with which its leadership witnessed these changes, especially as they corresponded in part to moods within its own population. But on the whole these changes and crises caused far less reaction in the United States than had the events of the 1940's and 1950's. Clearly something had happened to the Cold War even in eastern Europe.

In sum, it appeared that while the Soviet Union and the United States would continue to have a relationship not inappropriately described as Cold War—recent history and habits by now ingrained would probably

assure that for some time—by the end of the 1960's this particular relationship was only one among a number in the world at large. Cold War no
longer seemed fitting as a general description of a new age which was at
once hotter and less controllable and yet displayed increasing revulsion to
the idea of war as such, hot or cold. After a quarter of a century under the
sign of the Cold War the world was groping its way toward different
configurations and different styles.

For Further Reading

Fontaine, Andre, *History of the Cold War.*
Halle, Louis J., *The Cold War as History.*
Hammond, Paul Y., *The Cold War Years: American Foreign Policy Since
    1945.*
McNeill, William H., *America, Britain and Russia: Their Cooperation and
    Conflict, 1941–1946.*

96 Latin America in Ferment

From the mid-nineteenth century to the Spanish-American War in 1898
the world at large was little aware of Latin America. The brief rule in
Mexico of the French Emperor Maximilian caused a flurry of interest, but
his death in 1867 before the firing squad of Benito Juárez was soon followed by the seemingly perpetual dictatorship of Porfirio Díaz (1876–
1911). Giant Brazil was held together for almost half a century by the
paternalistic Emperor Pedro II until the Republic dismissed him in 1889.
The one nation that steadily progressed economically and politically
was Argentina, whose beef and wheat were consumed by the more industrialized nations. Throughout most of Latin America the economies of the
nineteen nations that had won their independence became increasingly
dependent on a few products exported to Europe and the United States.
Most emigrants from Europe seeking homes in the New World considered
the United States more attractive, and the foreign travelers who had earlier
found the newly liberated nations exotic places to visit and report on had
few successors. Cultural, economic, or political developments in Latin
America rarely held the attention of any foreign nation for long.

The nations south of the Rio Grande began to come of age internationally after 1900, but the pace was slow until Fidel Castro won Cuba in

CHRONOLOGY

A.D.

1898	Spanish-American War
1910	Revolution begins in Mexico
1912	Universal compulsory male suffrage law passed in Argentina
1916	First popularly elected president in Argentina, Hipólito Irigoyen
1918	Student movement begins in Córdoba, Argentina
1930	Getúlio Vargas begins 15-year rule in Brazil; the depression comes to Latin America
1934–1940	Lázaro Cárdenas stabilizes Mexico, implements the revolution, expropriates foreign oil properties (1938)
1943–1955	Perón dominates Argentina
1952	Bolivian Revolution
1959	Fidel Castro triumphs in Cuba
1961	Bay of Pigs invasion of Cuba fails; Trujillo assassinated, ending 31-year dictatorship in the Dominican Republic
1962	Missile crisis between Russia and the United States
1965	First Pan-American Assembly on Population meets in Colombia; President Lyndon Johnson sends Marines to the Dominican Republic
1970	Salvador Allende elected president of Chile

1959. The Mexican Revolution beginning in 1910 wrought great changes in Mexico, but nowhere else, and until World War II Latin America was little seen and not much heard on the international scene. The Good Neighbor Policy of Franklin D. Roosevelt turned some attention and aid southward, but his successors in the White House showed little interest because they were engaged in the enormous United States effort during World War II and the Cold War era which followed. Events like the Bolivian Revolution of 1952 or the stirring of the masses in the other tradition-bound republics roused little interest in the United States. However, Castro's triumph set in motion events that dramatized the explosive nature of Latin America's problems and their significance to the world at large, and the Cuban missile crisis between Soviet Russia and the United States in October, 1962, was the shock that put Cuba and Latin America on the map as never before.

Western Europeans and others realized that a dispute between the nuclear giants over a Caribbean island could put all civilization in mortal peril. Governments and universities hastened to examine the political, cultural, and economic conditions of this relatively unknown continent. Research institutes devoted to Latin American affairs sprang up throughout the United States; millions of dollars were made available by Washington and private foundations. Similar institutes were established in Great Britain, France, East and West Germany, and Japan. Soviet writings on Latin America grew from 3 titles in 1918 to 4,200 during 1960–1964. One result of this activity was that in a decade more serious studies of Latin America appeared than in the entire previous century.

The facts revealed in these studies are somber and puzzling. The economic position of a few countries has improved, but the leaders and people of this vast region are more disturbed and dissatisfied than ever before. They have entered the world scene, but are distinctly unhappy with their position, and a spirit of disenchantment is pervasive.

Clearly Latin America is in ferment, but no one pattern of distress may be found in this vast area, and the enormous variety of peoples, economies, and prospects makes generalization difficult. Mexico survived the fires of the revolution of 1910–1920, although the country's population declined by a million people. Large landowners, newspapers, banks, professors, and much of the government bureaucracy disappeared in the holocaust. Confusion followed for twenty years, but beginning with General Lázaro Cárdenas' presidency (1934–1940) there was progress. The Revolution slowed down; some claim that it has stopped altogether because one political party (Partido Revolucionario Institucional) dominates the country and thus far has won all elections. But the country has passed beyond its profound social revolution to achieve a special kind of stability which gives it a unique position in Latin America.

In sharp contrast to Mexico, proud of its Indian past and determined to achieve an independent position in the world even against its powerful neighbor to the north, is Argentina, which has been in the political doldrums since the fall of Juan Domingo Perón, who, with his charismatic wife Eva, revolutionized this wealthy country between 1943 and 1955. Perón continued some traditional policies—opposition to the United States and determination to be the leader in Latin America—and adopted a program of economic nationalism long advocated by important groups. But however much Perón resembled the typical Argentine caudillo, he brought one new and powerful element, the workers, into the mainstream of national life. His political power rested solidly on the army and the workers. Perón gave industrialization a forward thrust and assured an improvement of the workers' living conditions, but at the expense of the agricultural and pastoral sector of the economy. On balance when the armed forces rose in 1955 and the dictator fled, many Argentines, particularly the middle and upper classes, felt profound relief, for the corruption and pillaging of the Perón regime had brought Argentina close to economic and moral disaster.

The smoke of the fires Perón lighted still hangs over Argentina, and Peronism is still a dominant issue in Argentine political life. The uncertainty left in his wake affected all groups: labor unions, landowners, army, church, industry, and political parties. Both elected presidents, Arturo Frondizi (1956–1962) and Arturo Illía (1963–1966), were removed by the army before their terms ended. The wounds Perón inflicted on the body politic have not yet healed, nor has the economic balance between agriculture and industry been worked out. The Peronistas remain as an important political force, but in typical Argentine fashion they too are divided; the country has not yet created a true community. Perón gave the workers for the first time in Argentine history significant material benefits and a new sense of personal dignity, but Peronistas are not yet fully accepted by other powerful political elements. The army, therefore, has stepped in and shows little disposition to relinquish its control.

Portuguese-speaking Brazil is the country in Latin America with the most of everything—the most inflation, the most voters, the most workers, the most consumers, the most illiterates, and the greatest economic potential. Its population of about 100 million increases by more than 2 million every year, an increase larger than the total population of many other Latin American countries. Brazilians have been proud that in a hemisphere of sharply divisive racial strains they alone have evolved a culture marked by the fusion of European, Indian, and Negro stocks, and that, situated among countries where violence has often occurred, they have rarely used force to settle their disputes.

The immense size and diversity of Brazil are the overriding facts of its existence. This large tropical world, 3,294,000 square miles in area, would hold the entire continental United States with room for an extra Texas; it has the largest river in the world, the Amazon; two of its waterfalls, Iguassú and Paulo Afonso, are higher than Niagara; the island of Marajó at the mouth of the Amazon is as big as New England. Brazil produces much of the world's coffee (despite Africa's increasing competition), grows more bananas than any other country, possesses in Itabira an iron deposit estimated at more than a billion tons, and is so rich in plants that some 50,000—one-fourth of all known species—are found within its borders.

Yet Brazil has developed slowly and erratically. The abolition of Negro slavery in 1888 and the fall of the Empire in 1889 led to a series of uncertain Republican years; Brazil entered the modern world only in 1930, when Getúlio Vargas began his largely benevolent rule. A master politician who well understood the needs and aspirations of his people, he shrewdly played off the army, big business, and labor against one another and used regional rivalries to hold power until his suicide in 1954. During unprecedented social and economic ferment, which he encouraged by his support for economic nationalism and by laws protecting workers, Vargas was sufficiently flexible and skillful to hold Brazil together like a twentieth-century Emperor Pedro II.

No president after Vargas has demonstrated his ability in political maneuver; each has faced mounting economic and social problems. Juscelino Kubitschek (1956–1960) built the new capital Brasília but impoverished the country thereby. Jânio Quadros, elected president in 1960 by the largest popular vote in Brazilian history, proved an unpredictable leader. When he unexpectedly resigned in August, 1961, he plunged Brazil into a prolonged political crisis.

Since 1945 the army has been the decisive force in Brazilian politics. Traditionally disposed to uphold the established government and to guarantee constitutional and civilian rule, it has intervened whenever it considers Brazil threatened from any direction. It removed Vice-President João Goulart, who had succeeded Quadros, because it did not trust him, and replaced his left-leaning regime in 1964 with a military-dominated, middle-class supported government under Marshal Humberto Castelo Branco, who in November, 1965, by decree abolished existing political parties and substituted one "official" party and one "loyal opposition." The election of Marshal Artur da Costa e Silva by Congress in October, 1966, introduced another uncertain element in the country's confused situation.

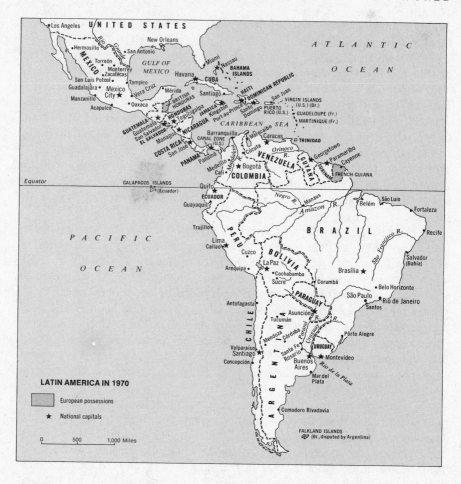

LATIN AMERICA IN 1970

European possessions

★ National capitals

0   500   1,000 Miles

When the marshal assumed the presidency in March, 1967, he promised to "humanize" the revolution. Instead he and the other stern army figures who succeeded him in power have apparently decided that Brazil's many problems can only be solved in a harsh military spirit. The relatively peaceful period of Brazilian history apparently has now ended.

At the turn of the century, in his classic *Revolt in the Backlands,* Euclydes da Cunha described the poor, ignorant fanatics of the northeast led by António Conselheiro. The shock inspired by this book was forgotten once the army had destroyed these rebels. But the poor and dispossessed in Brazil cannot be ignored today. No matter who holds political power in Brazil, or indeed in most Latin American countries, one persistent, inescapable problem remains: extremely rapid population growth. Before the year 2000, some 600 million Latin Americans will probably share the hemisphere with 300 million North Americans. This problem is connected with all the great questions at issue today.

Will Latin America, assisted by the United States, be able, in John F. Kennedy's words, "to satisfy the basic needs of the American peoples for home, work and land, health and schools" without major convulsions of governments and societies? Will the policy of "armed conflict" which Castro proclaimed in August, 1967, at the first meeting of the Latin American Solidarity Organization, achieve its radical aim to rouse the masses to overthrow the present power structures by force? Will reforming groups in Latin America, such as the Christian Democratic parties in several countries and Chile's socialist government led by Marxist Salvador Allende, elected in 1970 to a six-year term as president, be able to find a way to achieve economic and social justice by evolution rather than revolution? Many thoughtful and intelligent groups in Latin America do not accept guidance from either Washington or Havana, and are determined to change their societies by their own methods for their own national purposes.

At this point in history, Latin America is struggling to enter the society of developed nations and to play a larger role in the world. The struggle sometimes becomes bitter, the range of problems is comprehensive: "What is under debate," says Luiz Auguiar Costa Pinto, "is the whole heritage of the archaic society—the economic, political, and intellectual heritage—as well as the archaic society itself—its structures, its values, its prospects." One controversial but inescapable element in the discussion is the widespread opposition expressed inside and outside Latin America to United States intervention—cultural, economic, political, and military. While this debate goes on, the forces representing entrenched tradition, liberalizing evolution, and open revolt confront one another with increasing hostility. No one can predict the outcome with certainty, but fundamental and unexpected changes are possible. For in Latin America there has long existed, as Robin Humphreys has emphasized, both a revolt against tradition and a tradition of revolt.

For Further Reading

Adams, Richard, et al. (eds.), *Social Change in Latin America Today.*
Graham, Richard (ed.), *A Century of Brazilian History Since 1865.*
Hanke, Lewis, *Contemporary Latin America.*
Lambert, Jacques, *Latin America: Social Structures and Political Institutions.*

97   The Middle East Since 1940

During the Second World War, major campaigns were fought along the borders of the Middle East—in the Caucasus, Greece, Crete, the Western Desert of Egypt, and in Ethiopia—but the region itself escaped unscathed. However, a cataclysm of such magnitude could not but have deep repercussions, and in fact the war shattered the social and political order which had been established through European influence. In addition to the revolutionary ideas let loose in the region, there was the presence of several hundred thousand allied troops, whose upkeep added hundreds of millions of dollars to the foreign exchange reserves of the various countries, but also created shortages and raised prices sharply, exacerbating social tensions. The allied powers—especially the British—understandably subordinating local considerations to overall strategy, made the Middle Eastern governments take unpopular measures and, where necessary, as in Iraq and Iran in 1941, and in Egypt in 1942, coerced or overthrew such governments. And, more generally, the war interrupted or reversed the process of imperial disengagement in the region. The result was to intensify the already great political ferment and to increase nationalist resentment of the occupying powers.

The end of the war was, therefore, the signal for repeated attempts to end foreign control. These were generally successful, since the local forces could usually enlist the support of the United States, and sometimes that of Britain and the Soviet Union as well. Thus France, which had formally granted independence to Lebanon and Syria in 1943, was forced by Britain and the United States to withdraw its troops from those countries by 1946. In Iran withdrawal of American, British, and under strong American pressure, Soviet forces early in 1946 was followed by the collapse of a Soviet-sponsored separatist government in Azerbaijan. Anglo-Egyptian negotiations were fruitless until 1954 when, thanks to United States efforts, an agreement was reached. Two years later, British troops were withdrawn from the Suez Canal zone, paving the way for the granting of independence to the Anglo-Egyptian Sudan. In Iraq, repeated attempts to amend the 1930 treaty with Great Britain were unsuccessful, but British forces were withdrawn following the conclusion of the Baghdad Pact in 1955. As regards the smaller countries, Jordan received independence in 1946, Cyprus in 1960 (after prolonged guerrilla fighting), Kuwait in 1961, and Southern Yemen in 1968.

A.D.   1941   Anglo-Soviet troops occupy Iran; Riza Shah deposed
                      and replaced by son
              1945   Formation of Arab League
         1945–1947   Azerbaijan crisis
              1946   French troops evacuate Lebanon and Syria; Britain
                      recognizes independence of Transjordan (Jordan)
              1947   Truman Doctrine promising support to Greece and
                      Turkey; United Nations partition of Palestine,
                      evacuation of British troops
              1948   Proclamation of State of Israel
         1948–1949   Arab-Israeli war
              1949   First of series of military revolts in Syria
              1951   Nationalization of oil industry in Iran
              1952   Military revolution in Egypt overthrows monarchy
                      and establishes republic
              1954   Anglo-Egyptian Treaty providing for evacuation of
                      British troops
              1955   Baghdad Pact
              1956   Granting of independence to Sudan; nationalization
                      of Suez Canal; Anglo-French-Israeli invasion of
                      Egypt
              1958   Military revolt in Iraq ends monarchy
              1962   Civil war in Yemen, overthrow of monarchy
              1967   Arab-Israeli war
              1968   Independence of Southern Yemen

In Palestine reconciliation of Arab and Zionist aspirations proved impossible. A United Nations resolution in 1947, partitioning the country, was followed by the withdrawal of British troops and fighting first between Zionists and Palestine Arabs and then, after the proclamation of the State of Israel in 1948, between it and the neighboring Arab countries. Hostilities erupted repeatedly, as in the "Six-Day War" of 1967, an overwhelming Israeli triumph that resulted in the occupation of important parts of Egypt, Jordan, and Syria. Diplomatic and commercial relations remain broken; no solution has been found for repatriating the 750,000 Arab refugees who fled Palestine after the creation of Israel, and the danger that Arab-Israeli conflict may trigger a third world war remains grave.

The unity imposed on the greater part of the Middle East by the Ottoman Empire broke down after the First World War, and that provided by Britain's predominance disappeared after the Second. Since then various attempts, both internal and external, to unite the Middle Eastern countries have met with little success, and the region has been the scene of conflicts between the Great Powers. American and British efforts to bring Middle Eastern countries into a defense pact or alliance have also generally failed. A Middle East Defense Pact proposal of 1951 foundered on Egyptian opposition. The Baghdad Pact, concluded in 1955, linked Iran, Pakistan, and Turkey with Britain, but the only Arab country to join was Iraq, which withdrew in 1959.

The main internal attempt at integration was that of the Arab League, founded in 1945, to promote political and economic cooperation among its members. This too has had little success because of the clash of rival dynastic and national ambitions and divergent interests. The various Fertile Crescent schemes, aiming at uniting Syria, Lebanon, Palestine, Jordan, and Iraq under the Hashimi royal house—one of whose branches ruled Iraq and another Jordan—were thwarted by Egypt and Saudi Arabia, while Egyptian leadership has been opposed by Iraq, Jordan, and Saudi Arabia. Two unions formed in 1958, the United Arab Republic between Egypt and Syria and the Arab Union between Iraq and Jordan, soon broke down. In addition to these conflicts between the Arab states, and between them and Israel, there have been tensions between Turkey and Syria, Iran and Iraq, Iran and the United Arab Republic (Egypt), and Iraq and Kuwait.

Local quarrels have both invited, and been aggravated by, Great Power intervention. A series of crises centered on Syria in 1955–1957 led to an American-Soviet confrontation. Egypt's nationalization of the Suez Canal in 1956, and the subsequent attack on that country by Britain, France, and Israel, led to United Nations action and to American and Soviet pressures, compelling withdrawal of the invading forces. The civil war in Lebanon in 1958, and the support given to the rebels by the United Arab Republic

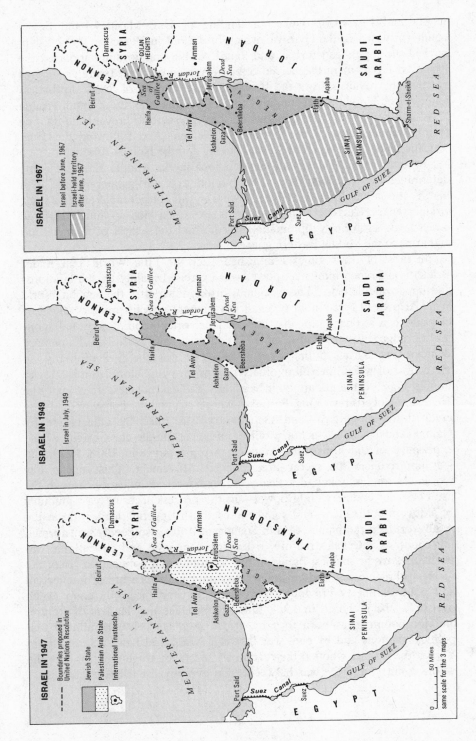

ISRAEL IN 1967

Israel before June, 1967

Israeli-held territory after June, 1967

ISRAEL IN 1949

Israel in July, 1949

ISRAEL IN 1947

Boundaries proposed in United Nations Resolution

Jewish State

Palestinian Arab State

International Trusteeship

0   50 Miles

same scale for the 3 maps

(Syria and Egypt), provoked a landing of U.S. Marines—and Soviet counterprotests. In the civil war which broke out in Yemen in 1962 Egypt backed the republican forces, and Saudi Arabia and Jordan supported the royalists. Egypt in turn received Soviet arms and aid, and similar support reached the royalists from the British-ruled territories of South Arabia; in addition the United States, anxious to preserve the stability of Saudi Arabia and the other oil-producing countries, used pressure to prevent the fighting from extending beyond the borders of Yemen. And following the 1967 war, the Arabs have received Soviet backing and the Israelis American.

In sum, although international relations in the Middle East are being determined by the countries of the region to a far greater degree than before, the influence of the Great Powers is still considerable and, in some circumstances, decisive. This power is exercised not so much through direct force as through diplomatic pressure and the supply of financial aid and arms to the Middle Eastern governments.

In most of the regimes established after the First World War under British and French influence, power was exercised mainly by the landlords and upper middle class. These regimes broke down after the Second World War. At present three main types of government prevail: military dictatorships with a strong nationalist and socialist orientation; traditional monarchies engaged in modernizing their countries; and liberal parliamentary democracies. Syria's military revolt of 1949 was the first of many, in the course of which the ruling officer groups, drawn mainly from the lower middle class, came to apply increasingly radical policies. In Egypt the 1952 coup overthrew King Farouk—whose scandalous behavior had discredited the monarchy—and the country was ruled by officers led by Gamal Abdel Nasser—a burly officer of lower-middle-class origin whose experience of the disastrous campaign against Israel in 1948–1949 had led him to start the secret Free Officers Movement. This regime has reoriented foreign policy, drastically reduced Western influence through the use of Soviet countervailing power—in the process securing vast amounts of aid from both sides—and sought to establish Egyptian leadership in the Arab world. In the name of Arab Socialism, it has also deeply transformed the country's internal structure, extending economic and educational opportunities to the masses, breaking the economic and political power of the former ruling classes, and curtailing the appreciable measure of intellectual and political liberty previously prevailing. In Iraq the army coup which overthrew the monarch in 1958 failed to produce any leaders of stature, and the country has been torn by armed conflicts between military and political factions and by civil war between Arabs and Kurds. Similarly, in Yemen the officers who led the revolt of 1962 failed to get control over the whole country, and the war between them and royalist tribes continues.

The surviving monarchies in Iran, Jordan, Kuwait, and Saudi Arabia have so far succeeded, thanks to the loyalty of their armies, in the twofold task of staving off internal onslaughts, often supported by more radical neighbors, and rapidly modernizing the economic and social structure of their countries. This has necessitated some far-reaching changes, such as the Iranian land reform of 1963, which greatly reduced the power of the landlords, and the political and administrative reorganization in Saudi Arabia. Their task has been facilitated by oil revenues in Iran, Kuwait, and Saudi Arabia and American and British aid in Jordan.

In Turkey the one-party rule established by Mustafa Kemal Atatürk continued under his successor and faithful lieutenant İsmet İnönü, who in spite of his advanced age had retained much intellectual vigor, realized that Turkey was ripe for a multiparty system, and commanded the widespread respect required to make the transition possible. The 1945 elections were contested by the Democrat party, which in 1950 took office. The following decade saw much economic and social progress, but this was accompanied by rising prices, imbalances, repressions, and growing tensions which exploded in the army coup of 1960. In contrast with other Middle Eastern countries, however, the more radical army officers failed to gain control of the movement, and power was gradually handed back to civilians.

Lebanon's constitutional system has also endured, surviving a bloodless revolution in 1952 and a short but devastating civil war in 1958. Here the main tensions have been between Christians and Muslims, aggravated by struggles between rival ideologies and power groups in the other Arab states. Similarly, Israel's broad-based democracy has not been threatened by fairly frequent changes in party alignments. Thanks to the high educational and social level of its people and to considerable, some would say lavish, foreign aid, the country has overcome the difficulties posed by isolation from its Arab neighbors and the task of absorbing well over a million immigrants, most of them Oriental Jews with cultural values different from those of the predominant Western-born or native Israelis.

After 1945 Middle Eastern oil resources—which at present amount to 60 per cent of world reserves—were rapidly developed and the producing countries bordering the Persian Gulf now account for more than 25 per cent of world output and more than 50 per cent of exports. Oil revenues, which are running at over $3 billion a year, play a dominant part in their budgets and serve to finance a large part of the region's expenditure on defense and development.

Industrialization is also proceeding at an accelerating pace, and in several countries manufacturing and mining now account for a fifth or more of the gross national product. Transport and communications have developed rapidly; railways and ports have been built, roads have been vastly extended and improved, and a network of airlines covers the region. However, as in other underdeveloped regions, agricultural output has generally lagged behind the rapid population growth (3 per cent per annum in several countries), and the Middle East, formerly a net exporter, has become increasingly dependent on imports of grain, mainly from the United States. The Middle East has also had heavy deficits in its balance of payments which have been met by very large amounts of aid from the United States, the Soviet Union, Western Germany, Britain, and other countries. Thanks to oil and foreign aid, the rate of economic growth in most Middle Eastern countries has been distinctly above that of other underdeveloped regions, and the level of living is higher than ever before.

The progress achieved has, in the main, taken place within the framework of private enterprise. But in all countries the government has played a leading part, contributing heavily to investment, extending social services, and seeking to secure greater social justice through taxation and, in several countries, land reform. In Egypt since 1961, and later in Syria and Iraq, the bulk of industry, finance, and transport has been nationalized and a socialist system is well under way. And in the whole region socialist ideas, drawn from west European, Russian, and Chinese sources, are capturing the allegiance of the intelligentsia, along with nationalism. Generally, the two beliefs amalgamate to form the same kind of socialist nationalism which is widespread in other underdeveloped regions.

The size of the intelligentsia is growing rapidly, because of the expansion of education and the increase of the urban population. For the first time in history more than half the boys and nearly half the girls in the Middle East are attending school and hundreds of thousands of students of both sexes are receiving higher education. Particularly noteworthy has been the expansion of technical and scientific education and research. Middle Eastern scientists are making an appreciable contribution to the progress of their countries, and a few are doing work which has wider significance. Similarly, the literature being produced in the region has reached a high level, and works written in Arabic, Hebrew, Persian, and Turkish have been translated into various Western languages. Among the most distinguished are the novelists Samuel Agnon, the Nobel Prize winner, and Haim Hazzaz in Israel, the novelists and short story writers Nagib Mahfuz and Yusif Idris in Egypt, Mahmut Makal and Kemal Yashar in Turkey, and Sadiq Chubak and Jalal Ali Ahmad in Iran.

Except in Israel and Lebanon, illiteracy is widespread but may be expected to fall sharply in the next decade or two. In the meantime other media are reaching the masses: transistor radios have opened the remotest villages to the outside world, and movies and television are now available in the smaller towns. Rural electrification and the spread of social services are transforming still further the outlook of the peasants who still constitute the bulk of the population. Thus the Middle East, so long left behind by history, torn by tensions, perplexed by conflicting ideologies, facing grave economic and social difficulties, but with renewed vitality and hope, is making its way into the modern world.

For Further Reading

Berger, Morroe, *The Arab World Today.*
Fein, Leonard, *Israel.*
Hurewitz, J. C., *Middle East Politics: The Military Dimension.*
───── (ed.), *Soviet American Rivalry in the Middle East.*
Karpat, Kemal (ed.), *Political and Social Thought in the Contemporary Middle East.*
Shwadran, Benjamin, *The Middle East, Oil and the Great Powers.*

98   Africa Since 1945

In 1945, independence for African states in the reasonably near future seemed an absurdity to the colonial powers. Nor were there many African political leaders who thought it plausible to demand it. The French government had made its view very clear at the Brazzaville Conference of 1944, stating: "The establishment one day of self-governments in the colonies, even a day far off, is to be eliminated from any consideration." The British Report of the Commission on Higher Education in West Africa in June, 1945, was less negative but equally complacent: "Somewhere, in West Africa within a century—and what is that in the life of a people—a new African State will be born."

In East and Central Africa, it is not clear that anyone expected that there would ever be an *African* state. Rather, a significant segment of those in positions of authority looked forward to the gradual devolution of power primarily to the white settler community, a modified version of the Union of South Africa, albeit one more devoted, it was hoped, to the Crown.

Indeed, with one or two possible exceptions, it is doubtful that there existed in 1945 a genuine African nationalist movement anywhere on the continent. Such political organizations as did exist demanded changes that would end various discriminations of the colonial governments, but usually within the context of pledges of loyalty to the imperial system. There was,

CHRONOLOGY

A.D.

1944	Brazzaville Conference of French Union
1945	Fifth Pan-African Congress, Manchester
1948	Nationalist Party comes to power in Union of South Africa
1952	Overthrow of King Farouk in Egypt; Mau Mau emergency proclaimed in Kenya
1954	Algerian war of independence begins
1955	Bandung Conference
1956	Independence of Sudan, Tunisia, Morocco
1957	Independence of Ghana
1958	Referendum in French Africa; conference of Independent African States, Accra; All-African People's Conference, Accra; independence of Guinea
1960	Year of Africa (independence of 17 states); Congo crisis breaks out; Katanga secession
1961	Creation of Casablanca and Monrovia groups; Angola rebellion begins (first in Portuguese Africa)
1962	Algeria gains independence; end of Katanga secession
1963	Creation of Organization of African Unity
1965	Unilateral Declaration of Independence by Southern Rhodesia
1966	Coups in Nigeria (death of Balewa) and Ghana (fall of Nkrumah)
1967	Secession of Biafra
1970	End of Biafra secession

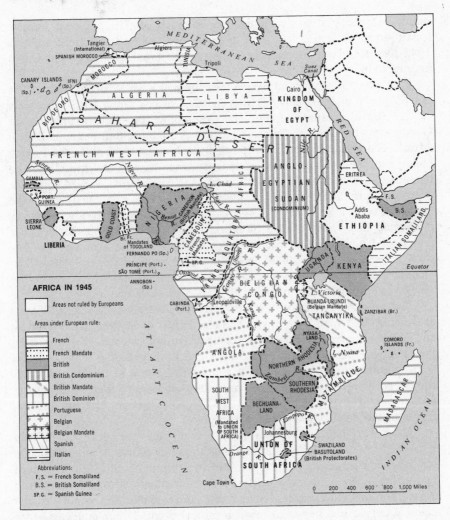

AFRICA IN 1945

☐ Areas not ruled by Europeans

Areas under European rule:

French
French Mandate
British
British Condominium
British Mandate
British Dominion
Portuguese
Belgian
Belgian Mandate
Spanish
Italian

Abbreviations:
F.S. = French Somaliland
B.S. = British Somaliland
SP.G. = Spanish Guinea

to be sure, an avant-garde: those who met in Manchester in October, 1945, at the Fifth Pan-African Congress and bluntly demanded independence. This group included not only such great figures of the pan-African movement as W. E. B. DuBois and George Padmore but many who would later become leading nationalists: Kwame Nkrumah (Ghana), Jomo Kenyatta (Kenya), Hastings Kamuzu Banda (Malawi), and Obafemi Awolowo (Nigeria).

Yet despite the attitude of the colonial powers and the timidity of African political organizations, the years after 1945 saw the continuous, rapid, and accelerating decolonization of much of Africa. There were at least four major factors that most of those involved on the African scene in 1945 had not taken into consideration, two external to the continent, two internal to it.

One was the impact of Asian developments on African affairs. The independence of India and Pakistan in 1947 placed Great Britain squarely on the path of creating a multiracial Commonwealth, and the influence of Gandhi and the Indian Congress party was to be felt throughout British Africa. The abortive decolonization of Indochina in 1946 made the French Union face squarely the issue of independence as an option, and had an immediate effect on political sentiment in North Africa and Madagascar which in turn affected French black Africa. The proclamation of the Chinese People's Republic in 1949 had a clear bearing, partially insofar as it affected the world balance of power, but more directly as it led to a period of Chinese-Indian friendship culminating in the Bandung Conference of 1955. The consequent emergence of the concept of the Afro-Asian bloc, in the United Nations and elsewhere, was of critical importance to the success of decolonization in Africa.

The second factor was the world struggle between the United States and the Soviet Union. As the struggle terminated its acute Cold War phase and became an armed truce (or "competitive coexistence"), dating from the Geneva Conference of 1954, the U.S.S.R. began actively to support African nationalist movements. The eventual response of the United States was to give limited and tacit but important support to these same movements and to put pressure on its NATO allies (Great Britain, France, Belgium, and Portugal) to decolonize rapidly.

These two external factors greatly facilitated the work of African nationalist movements, but internal conditions in Africa account basically for their emergence and the response of the colonial authorities. The third factor that escaped attention in 1945 was the ripeness of most territories in Africa for the emergence of nationalist movements. The strains of the colonial period had begun to reach a critical point. Urban-educated elites were beginning to butt hard against the limitations to their advancement inherent in the colonial situation. On all the fronts they pushed—in the civil service and other bureaucracies, in local political structures, in commercial enterprises—they found barriers or obstacles to their hopes and ambitions.

The rural peasants were no happier with their situation. Peasant turbulence and rebellion had been a constant of the colonial scene. The declining authority of most traditional chiefs (because of the ambiguous role they were called upon to play by colonial authorities) combined with the increasing usurpation of land for cash-crop production (by those of traditionally high status and, in some areas, by white settlers) was leading to acute discontent. The link between the discontent of the educated elite and the peasants was provided by "lower-middle-class" elements (junior clerical personnel, artisans, schoolteachers, health personnel, skilled workers) whose numbers grew significantly during World War II. The economic recession of the early postwar years, combined with a decline in real wages, made this stratum willing to join a mass nationalist movement that would canalize the various discontents into a demand for political independence.

The fourth factor to account for the misperceptions of 1945 was the failure to anticipate the nature of the response of the colonial administrations. Both colonizers and colonized thought administrations would respond to nationalism by repression. This was indeed the initial response everywhere. Repression, however, has its costs, and in most of Africa after 1945 the costs turned out to be too high. In areas where there were few white settlers and not much mineral wealth, pure repression seemed very expensive indeed for the metropolitan power. Almost immediately, Britain and France decided to mix repression with political and economic concession. As the pressure continued, the investment in education and health burgeoned, and the cost of resisting nationalism mounted steadily. There came a point at which the costs of maintaining the territory became greater than those of letting it go. This was reinforced by the following consideration: if in the late nineteenth century one of the motives of establishing colonial rule was the establishment by European powers of preemptive monopolies (a game which, if one plays, all must play), so it was in the later period that if one goes (decolonizes), others are pressured to go (and also are more willing to go). The various European powers began to discover the economics of neocolonialism and slowly became aware that, under certain conditions, it made economic sense to pull out. These conditions involved an accord with the urban educated elite of a transfer of power to them in return for a continued involvement in the ex-colonial international economic network. When they realized this fact (a realization which occurred at different moments for different powers), they shifted their policy.

Great Britain took the lead. Independence of the Indian subcontinent and the gradual withdrawal from the Middle East was matched by early moves to decolonize the Anglo-Egyptian Sudan and British West Africa. Successive constitutional reforms culminated in independence for the Sudan in 1956, and for the Gold Coast in 1957. The constitutional path was slower in Nigeria because of the split in the nationalist movement, reinforced by the establishment of a federal system in 1951. However, regional self-government was achieved in 1956 and independence in 1960.

In British East and Central Africa, constitutional reform was complicated by the presence of white settlers. Particularly in Kenya and Southern Rhodesia the settlers intended that whatever devolution of powers might occur should go to them as a group rather than to the black majority. Indeed, to ensure that this was so, white settlers sought to achieve federations of the strong settler territory with its immediate neighbors, among other reasons lest power be turned over to black Africans in the neighbors and thus affect by example the settler territories. In East Africa, the federation was to bring together settler-dominated Kenya with Uganda and Tanganyika. In Central Africa, it was to bring together settler-dominated Southern Rhodesia with Northern Rhodesia and Nyasaland. The federation idea ran aground in East Africa because of spirited resistance in Uganda (leading to the exile of the Kabaka of Buganda, an important traditional ruler, from 1953 to 1955) and the outbreak of Mau Mau insurrection in Kenya in 1952. However, Central Africa was more fertile ground, and in 1953 the British established the Federation of the Rhodesias and Nyasaland. As a result, African nationalists in Nyasaland and Northern Rhodesia had to seek withdrawal from and dissolution of the Federation as a prerequisite to their own independence (such dissolution being accomplished only in 1963).

The French government at first was deeply resistant to the idea of independence or self-government in any form. Algeria had known violent repression in 1945. Madagascar was the scene of a bloody rebellion in 1947. The Ivory Coast had its famous "incidents" in 1949. Tunisia had *fellaghas* (guerrillas) beginning in 1953. The Sultan of Morocco was deported because of his nationalist sympathies in 1953. It was only in 1954, the year of the Geneva Accords on Indochina, that the French government, then led by Pierre Mendès-France, granted internal autonomy to Tunisia. This led to independence for both Tunisia and Morocco in 1956. Part of the reason for the rapidity, however, was the desire to resist decolonization in Algeria, where the war for independence had begun in late 1954. The combination of the Algerian war and the imminent independence of the Gold Coast (Ghana) helped to push the French to a willingness to grant limited self-government to French black Africa and Madagascar under the Loi-Cadre of 1956 which became full autonomy under the De Gaulle referendum of 1958 (except Guinea, which opted for independence) and then to independence for 14 separate states in 1960.

The accelerating pace affected other colonial powers as well. Italy, as a defeated Axis power in World War II, had little choice. The United Nations had already decided in 1949 that Libya would become independent in 1951 and Somalia in 1960. Belgium was directly affected by the French developments. It was only in 1956 that the political future of the Congo became a matter for public discussion and only in January, 1959, following the granting of autonomy to neighboring French Congo, that the first serious political troubles occurred in the Congo. The haunting example of Algeria led the Belgians to concede rapidly and grant independence on June 30, 1960.

Thus when Harold Macmillan, then prime minister of the United Kingdom, told the Houses of Parliament of the Union of South Africa on February 3, 1960, that a "wind of change" was sweeping Africa, his hearers were shocked at the unwelcome statement but not unaware of what he was talking about. At the United Nations, 1960 was called the Year of Africa because 14 former French colonies, the Belgian Congo, Somalia, and Nigeria all achieved independence (and admission to the UN) that year. Independence had taken the form of a downward sweep of the continent: Libya in 1951; Tunisia, Morocco, and the Sudan in 1956; Ghana in 1957; Guinea in 1958; virtually the whole of the northern half of the continent by 1960 (with the notable exception of Algeria).

Furthermore, in the course of this downward sweep, pan-Africanism had gained much ground. In April of 1958 the first Conference of Independent African States was convened at Accra, in Ghana. The eight then-independent states committed themselves to joint international activity, in the United Nations and elsewhere, on behalf of African liberation movements. And what is striking is that this grouping bridged black and Arab Africa for the first time in a significant way. This conference was followed in December, 1958, by a nongovernmental All-African People's Conference, also in Accra, which brought together political leaders and trade unions from all over the continent, from both independent and colonized states, even including the Union of South Africa.

Thus, 1960 was a highpoint of achievement and optimism for African nationalism. Yet it is also a turning point away from optimism, for it saw the outbreak of the Congo troubles, the first internal crisis of major proportions in an independent African state and one which had direct consequences for the liberation of southern Africa, for African unity, and for the role of outside powers on the African continent.

Within the first month of the Congo's independence, its army rebelled, Katanga province seceded, the Belgians invaded, and the Congo appealed for UN assistance, which it got in the form of contingents of troops from a large number of countries, including many African states. By September the governing alliance in the Congo had split, two rival groups claiming to be the legitimate government. By November, each group controlled substantial territory of the Congo (and Katanga still was governed by the secessionist regime). It was not until mid-1961 that the two claimants to central power were fused, and only in December, 1962, was the Katangese secession definitively put down. In the meantime, and in many ways because of the Congo crisis, the African world changed.

The whites of southern Africa took heart and decided to halt the downward sweep of African liberation. Its thrust was still strong enough to bring about the independence of six more countries in East and Central Africa from 1961 to 1964, but the movement rapidly decelerated. An alliance came to be forced in the so-called white redoubt of southern Africa between South Africa (since 1961 a republic and not a member of the Commonwealth), the white regime in Southern Rhodesia, and Portugal (concerned for Angola and Mozambique).

The Congolese crisis affected the United States, drawing the nation into African affairs with a new intensity. Until 1960 the United States played the role of the benign, mildly anticolonial outsider. After 1960 it was to become the most influential outside power on the African continent and one whose benignity many Africans would contest.

The independent states of Africa, faced with the two-way split in the central governments of the Congo, were forced to take sides. They grouped themselves into two blocs, each supporting one faction in the Congo but proceeding from there to positions on other issues, such as Algeria and the Cold War. The "radical" bloc was known as the Casablanca group, the more "moderate" as the Monrovia group. This split among African independent states broke the African unity which had been created between 1958 and 1960. Once the Congolese split was temporarily healed in 1961 and Algeria received its independence in 1962 it was possible for the Casablanca and Monrovia groups to merge into the Organization of African Unity (OAU) at Addis Ababa in May, 1963, but the basis of compromise was fragile.

The Congo merely crystallized this split among Africans; it did not create it. The independence of a large number of African states meant that the nationalist movements, now in power, had to make decisions, opt for solutions, make both internal political choices and international alliances. In the majority of cases, the leadership of the nationalist movement represented an urban educated elite who saw the end of colonial rule as a removal of the barriers they had felt to their own advancement in terms of political power and economic rewards. They were quite content to reap the rewards of their struggle, rewards which were likely to be far more ample in the immediate future if good economic relations were maintained with ex-colonial powers and the developed world in general.

For some nationalists this attitude was a betrayal of previous ideals and promises: it would replace colonialism with neocolonialism. This postindependence split was made more acute by the fact that those with the more radical vision retained power in some independent states. Thus the split was not only within independent states but between states. Furthermore, similar groups in neighboring countries were in contact one with the other. The links of radical groups, in power in one country and out of power in another, led quickly to charges by some of the Monrovia states of "subversion." In the polarization initiated by the Congo issue, these charges became a major bone of contention between certain African independent states.

A second source of contention was support for independence movements in nonindependent African states. The Casablanca states gave high priority to political and military aid to liberation movements, and resented the more limited and often only verbal support such movements found in many of the Monrovia states.

The compromise of the OAU was essentially that the Casablanca powers renounced their "subversive" support of opposition movements in Monrovia states in return for a more active commitment by Monrovia powers to African liberation movements in southern Africa. A special African Liberation Committee (ALC) was established under the OAU to coordinate financial and military assistance to liberation movements. This compromise, however, soon became obsolete. The independent states began to run into more serious internal difficulties than "subversion," and it took more than the ALC to liberate southern Africa.

The internal political difficulties of contemporary independent African states derived from two aspects of their situation which became increasingly evident as the first euphoria of achieving sovereignty wore off. One was the fragility of the state machinery. Armed with brief histories as nation-states and consequently thin national solidarities, and faced with severe economic problems, many citizens—*especially* the educated ones—fell back on ethnic (so-called tribal) solidarities to assure their protection and advancement as individuals. This led to nepotism, ethnic riots, and secessionist movements. It has made these states susceptible to outside political pressure. No African nation was exempt from this phenomenon.

Second, there was the uncertainty of state revenues. Demands for state expenditures for education, job creation, infrastructure, and welfare grew steadily while revenue did not keep pace, partly because of a relative decline in world commodity prices and partly because a reduction of East-West tension resulted in cuts in foreign aid, loans, and subsidized purchase prices. As a result the state budgets suffered an increasing gap which led to internal squeezes.

Neither conservative nor radical regimes were able to cope with these dilemmas adequately. The result was a series of coups, yet the new regimes coped with the problems no better than their predecessors. The successor regimes tended, however, not to be radical ones.

Thus, the period beginning in 1963 has seen coups, attempted coups, mutinies, and plots in almost every African nation—French-speaking or English-speaking, North, West, Central, and East. In the process, there

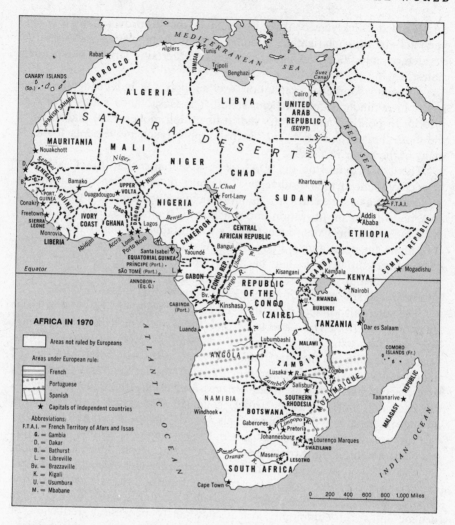

occurred the second Congo crisis from late 1963 through early 1965 which threatened the existence of the OAU; the downfall of "radical" regimes in Ghana and Mali; and the series of tragedies that have plagued Nigeria, Africa's most populous state (two military coups, riots, the secession of Biafra, civil war). As crisis piled on crisis, it became very difficult for the African states to devote much attention to liberating southern Africa.

Meanwhile, the plans of the OAU's African Liberation Committee were repeatedly frustrated. They had hoped that Portugal would give up its colonies with the application of a little force. They had hoped that Great Britain would bring Southern Rhodesia to independence under majority rule. They had hoped that the World Court would rule that South Africa had violated its mandate in Southwest Africa. They had hoped that, eventually, the collapse of these "buffer" units would permit a successful revolution in South Africa. Instead, Portugal resisted strongly the armed revolts in Angola, Portuguese Guinea, and Mozambique. The white settlers of Rhodesia made a "unilateral declaration of independence" in 1965 and the British failed to use force to stop them. (A UN economic boycott has proved ineffectual.) The World Court threw out the Southwest Africa case on a technicality in 1966. South Africa not only severely repressed its underground movements; it even began to acquire black client states in independent Africa. Liberation movements in southern Africa had to retrench for the long haul.

Thus, Africa saw a moment of very swift change, particularly around 1960. Many states came to independence. This rapid change of the political map was made possible by a particular conjuncture of a favorable international climate (East-West competition) and accumulated African frustration, which had ripened into revolutionary zeal.

Independence released and appeased those frustrations. It has, to be sure, created new, even worse ones, but these have not yet ripened. And the international climate has become less permissive for Africa since 1960. The continent has entered into a phase of internal difficulties which are largely cordoned off and ignored by the rest of the world. This phase will probably last until the internal strains become more intolerable and the world system becomes less able to contain African eruptions.

For Further Reading

Davidson, Basil, *Which Way Africa?*
Green, Reginald, and Ann Seidman, *Unity or Poverty? The Economics of Pan-Africanism.*
Wallerstein, Immanuel, *Africa: The Politics of Unity.*

99   The New Asia

Since World War II, Asia* has undergone profound changes. The war itself resulted in a drastic restructuring of power relations in the region. It also released forces which have subsequently changed the face of Asia and fundamentally altered its role in world affairs.

' * For the purposes of this discussion, "Asia" is understood to mean the countries stretching from Korea to Pakistan.

A.D. 1945 Dropping of first atomic bombs; Soviet entry in the Pacific war; Japanese surrender and the end of World War II in Asia

1946 Unsuccessful U.S. attempt to mediate Nationalist-Communist conflict in China and renewal of Chinese civil war; independence of the Philippines

1947 Independence of India and Pakistan

1948 Independence of Burma; outbreak of Communist-led rebellions in Burma and several other Southeast Asian areas; assassination of Gandhi in India

1949 Communist victory over Chiang Kai-shek's regime in China and establishment of the People's Republic of China under Mao Tse-tung; independence of Indonesia under Sukarno

1950 Sino-Soviet alliance; outbreak of Korean War

1951 Japanese peace treaty and U.S.–Japan security treaty; start of Korean peace negotiations at Panmunjom; India's first Five-Year Plan

1953 Truce in Korea; China's first Five-Year Plan; election of Magsaysay as president of the Philippines

1954 Geneva Conference and French withdrawal from Indochina; establishment of SEATO (Southeast Asia Treaty Organization)

1955 Bandung Conference of Asian-African leaders; start of U.S.–China Geneva-Warsaw talks

1957 Malayan independence; Sukarno's introduction of "guided democracy" in Indonesia; revolt in Sumatra and outer islands of Indonesia

----

In the years since 1945, Asia has been swept by political and social revolutions. The colonial and traditional regimes that existed before the war have been replaced by a wide variety of new states. And powerful new forces—nationalism, Communism, the drive for self-determination, and demands for social change—have shaped the development of the region.

Processes of modernization and economic growth have also accelerated. Most of the new leaders in Asia are dedicated to social change, rather than to the preservation of tradition-rooted values. The drag of tradition

1958   "Great Leap Forward" in China; "offshore islands" crisis on China coast
1959   Tibetan revolt; Chinese-Indian border incidents
1960   Open debate in Sino-Soviet relations; renewed conflict in Vietnam; revision of the U.S.–Japan security treaty
1962   China-India border conflict; Geneva Conference on Laos; Ne Win coup d'état in Burma
1964   China's first nuclear test; death of Nehru; Indonesian "confrontation" with Malaysia
1965   Attempted Communist coup in Indonesia, resulting in military control under Suharto; major U.S. intervention in Vietnam; India-Pakistan conflict over Kashmir
1966   "Great Proletarian Cultural Revolution" and purge of Liu Shao-chi in China; opening of Asian Development Bank; founding of ASPAC (Asian and Pacific Council)
1967   Founding of ASEAN (Association of Southeast Asian Nations)
1968   Cessation of U.S. bombing of North Vietnam and start of Paris negotiations on Vietnam
1969   Sino-Soviet border conflict; Nixon's "Guam Doctrine"; U.S. agreement with Sato government on the return of Okinawa to Japan; death of Ho Chi Minh in North Vietnam; growth of Japanese gross national product makes Japan third-largest economy in the world
1970   Overthrow of Sihanouk and U.S. military intervention in Cambodia
1971   Announcement of planned Nixon trip to Peking

----

has been strong, however, and the gap between aspirations and accomplishments has in many places created frustration, instability, and conflict.

Despite the instability of the region, and the enormous internal problems facing Asian countries, most of the new nations have been incorporated into the Western-created international system. (Communist China, however, has been only partially absorbed into the system. The United States and a sizable number of other non-Communist nations have not yet recognized the Peking regime, and the regime has only recently gained

United Nations membership. It has, though, established diplomatic relations with approximately fifty Communist and non-Communist states.) In a variety of ways, the new nations are increasingly active participants in world politics.

In the power balance in Asia itself, two countries, one Asian and one Western, emerged into dominant roles in the postwar period. The hostile confrontation between these two—Communist China and the United States —has, for most of the period, been the most important single influence shaping the configuration of power relations in the region. Mainland China, genuinely unified for the first time in a half-century, and ruled by a Communist regime, has attempted to assert its regional primacy and has called for world-wide Communist revolution. The United States, victorious in World War II, and directly involved in Asia as never before, has attempted to maintain the power balance in Asia, "contain" China, and combat the spread of Communism. In the latter 1960's, however, the power balance became increasingly complex. Japan began to reemerge as a potent economic power, and the Soviet Union, partly as a result of its disputes with China, increased its diplomatic activity in the region. As a result, a multipolar four-power balance seemed to be emerging.

The extent of revolutionary changes in Asia can be grasped only if one compares the situation of today with that which prevailed prior to World War II. Before the war, most of Asia was dominated by external powers, first by Western nations, and then by Japan, which rose to challenge the West and attempted to conquer much of Asia in the process.

European colonial nations, most notably Britain, France, and the Netherlands, controlled almost all of South and Southeast Asia. (Only Thailand was able to preserve its independence by playing the French and British against each other.) While embryonic nationalist movements had begun to grow in the region, they were still weak and ineffective. The United States had projected its power into part of the area, as a result of the Spanish-American War, and it ruled the Philippine Islands; however, it had promised to grant independence to the Philippines—although this promise was yet to be fulfilled.

Russia, which had expanded steadily eastward throughout the nineteenth century, had encroached on all of China's borderlands and established firm control in eastern Siberia and the Maritime Provinces. Its expansionist drive in northeast Asia had been blocked by Japan, but after the Bolshevik revolution its Communist government still exerted pressures at many points on China's periphery. It also attempted to stimulate Communist revolutions in many Asian countries; except in China, however, Communist movements had achieved little success prior to World War II.

China had been able to maintain a precarious independence, despite internal decay and external pressure, but it was already undergoing a process of revolutionary change. The impact of the West in the nineteenth century had helped to undermine the 2,000-year-old Chinese imperial system, and following the collapse of the Manchu dynasty in 1911, the country was weak and divided. Both the Western powers and Japan competed for influence in China and severely compromised its sovereignty. However, the nationalist movement led by the Kuomintang, which came to power in the late 1920's, had begun to unify and modernize the country, even though it faced a serious internal challenge from the Communists and from 1937 on was engaged in a fight for survival against Japanese aggression.

Japan was the only Asian nation which, in response to the nineteenth-century impact of the West, had been able not only to preserve its independence but also to carry out a program of rapid modernization. As it built up its industrial and military strength, it first joined the Western powers in their imperialist encroachments on the Asian mainland (in the process defeating China and Russia, in wars fought, respectively, in 1894–1895 and 1904–1905), then embarked on a major war against China in 1937, and finally, in 1941, decided to challenge both the United States in the Pacific and the European powers in Southeast Asia.

Both Japan's initial successes against the Western powers in the war, and then its ultimate defeat, fundamentally altered the character of Asia as it had existed before 1941. It is no exaggeration, in fact, to say that out of the war there emerged a new Asia.

For a brief period Japan expelled the Western powers from Asia and controlled a large part of the region from Korea to Burma, but by 1945 Japan itself was devastated and prostrate. Occupied by American troops, it was forced to give up its imperial pretensions, disarm, and draw into its home islands.

China, although a victorious power, emerged from the war gravely weakened and internally divided. Even though the Nationalist government was initially able, with American support, to reassert control over China's major cities, it faced a major challenge from the Chinese Communists, who during the war had built a powerful peasant-based revolutionary army and controlled most of the countryside in north China. Despite American efforts to mediate the Kuomintang-Communist conflict, China was plunged into open civil war in 1946.

The United States, whose military forces had been primarily responsible for Japan's defeat in the Pacific, found itself in the immediate postwar situation as the only real power in most of the region. As the occupier of Japan and South Korea, and the unsuccessful mediator of civil conflict in

China, it was drawn deeply into Asian political affairs. Except where American power was exerted, the region was in many respects a power vacuum.

The Soviet Union, which had entered the Pacific war in its closing days, was able, however, to reinject itself into the power equation in Asia, at least to a degree. It temporarily occupied China's Manchurian provinces and North Korea, and while promising to support the Chinese Nationalist government, it proceeded to give indirect support to the Communists in their struggle against the Nationalists.

In Southeast Asia, although the United States fulfilled its pledge to grant independence to the Philippines, the European powers at first attempted to reestablish prewar patterns of colonial rule. They soon discovered, however, that they were incapable of doing so. The strong anticolonial, nationalist movements which had sprung up throughout the region during the war were led by men who demanded immediate independence.

Similar nationalist movements had developed in South Asia, and by 1947 Britain, acquiescing in the face of the new forces, began granting independence, to India, Pakistan, Burma, and Ceylon. In Southeast Asia, however, the Dutch and French were less willing to recognize the revolutionary changes that had taken place, and it was not until they had fought bitter, unsuccessful, colonial conflicts that they agreed to withdraw from Indonesia, in 1949, and Indochina, in 1954. (The Geneva Conference which ended the French-Vietnamese struggle left Indochina divided; Laos and Cambodia were separated from Vietnam, and Vietnam was divided at the 17th parallel between Communist and non-Communist regimes.)

The struggles between the Dutch and Indonesians, and between French and Vietnamese, were by no means, however, the only conflicts which kept much of Asia in turmoil in the immediate postwar years. Many conflicts occurred between competing Asian leaders and groups. While nationalism was clearly the predominant new social-political force in the emerging nations, Communism was a strong competitor, and in the late 1940's Communist parties attempted to seize power through violent struggles in many Asian countries.

In China, after full-scale civil war erupted in 1946, the Communists—who already controlled large areas of the country and constituted, in effect, a state within a state—soon achieved major military successes in Manchuria and north China. Weakened by disintegrative processes that had sapped its vitality during World War II, the Nationalist regime deteriorated rapidly. By 1948, the balance of military power in the struggle shifted in the Communists' favor, and by the fall of 1949 they had achieved control over most of the country. The Nationalists under Chiang Kai-shek retreated to Taiwan (Formosa), where they continued to maintain a competitive regime which still exists today—a de facto separate regime which claims to be the government of China but has no prospect of regaining control of the China mainland.

In October, 1949, the Communists set up a new regime in Peking, the People's Republic of China headed by Mao Tse-tung. It immediately established relations with the other Communist states (except Yugoslavia) and in February, 1950, signed a thirty-year Treaty of Friendship, Alliance, and Mutual Assistance with the Soviet Union. As Mao put it, China "leaned to one side." The basic realignment of China's entire international position which this involved had a great and immediate impact not only on Asia but on the entire world balance.

During this same period, Communist parties in many other parts of Asia challenged the new non-Communist nationalist leaders and made their own bids for power. In fact, during 1948, with Soviet encouragement, Communist rebellions broke out or were intensified throughout much of South and Southeast Asia—in Indonesia, Malaya, Burma, the Philippines, and India, as well as in Indochina. The Chinese Communist regime, after it was established, gave strong moral support to these insurrections.

For a period of time, the Communists threatened to topple many of the new non-Communist regimes. But eventually it became clear that most Communist parties did not have sufficient support to succeed. Only in Indochina, in fact, were the Communists able to capture a significant part of the nationalist movement. Elsewhere, the insurrectionary struggles ultimately failed, and by 1950–1951 many Asian Communist parties started shifting toward less violent tactics.

Communal strife, based on religious and other cultural differences, also created turmoil in many parts of Asia. Establishment of independent states did not automatically create consensus within the new nations, solve the problems of nation building, or eliminate deep-rooted conflicts within and among them. The most serious of the communal conflicts was the one that broke out between Hindus and Muslims in India and Pakistan at the time of independence in 1947. It left a residue of bitterness which has caused tensions in that area ever since.

In the context of both the instability which characterized the new Asia in the early postwar years and the Cold War between the Communist and non-Communist nations that had already started in Europe, the establishment in 1949 of a strong, dynamic, and militant Communist regime in China, allied with the Soviet Union and openly proclaiming its belief in world-wide revolution, had a disruptive impact. The new sense of threat in Asia felt by many non-Communist nations was then magnified when, in mid-1950, Communist North Korea, with Soviet backing, launched an attack on South Korea.

The Korean War was a major turning point in the postwar history of

Asia. During 1949 and early 1950, the United States appeared to be disengaging its power from any involvement in the affairs of the Asian mainland. It had dissociated itself from the defense of the Chinese Nationalist regime on Taiwan and was "letting the dust settle," apparently in preparation for ultimate recognition of the new Chinese Communist regime.

The Korean War fundamentally changed the situation. Not only did the United States and other United Nations forces go to the defense of South Korea; Washington also announced its intention to "neutralize" the Taiwan Strait, thereby preventing Communist takeover of Taiwan and reengaging American forces in the Chinese conflict. Then, after Chinese Communist troops crossed the Yalu River in late 1950, the major fighting in Korea was between Chinese and American forces.

The Korean War stimulated the United States to rearm and to start building a network of military alliances in Asia, designed to "contain" China and check any further expansion of Communist control or influence. Between 1951 and 1954 military pacts were signed between the United States and Japan (a peace treaty, without Chinese participation, was also concluded with Japan in 1951), the Philippines, South Korea, and Nationalist China, and in 1954 the multilateral Southeast Asia Treaty Organization (SEATO) was formed, including Thailand, the Philippines, Pakistan, the United Kingdom, Australia, New Zealand, and France, as well as the United States.

The war also left a heritage of mutual suspicion and enmity in both the United States and Communist China. The United States evolved a policy of "pressure and diplomatic isolation" directed against Peking, and the main elements of this policy—nonrecognition of the Chinese Communist regime, opposition to its seating in the United Nations, an embargo on all American trade with mainland China, and opposition to other contacts with it—were all to persist long after a truce had brought the fighting in Korea to a halt in 1953.

Only a minority of the new Asian nations were predisposed, however, to join the United States in anti-Communist military alliances or in its efforts to isolate Communist China. Influenced in part by residual anti-colonial feelings which created suspicion of American motives, in part by sympathy for China as an Asian and "socialist" state, and in part by preoccupation with their own internal problems, a majority of Asian states, especially in South and Southeast Asia, chose to adopt a posture of neutralism or nonalignment.

International crises in Asia did not end when the Korean truce was signed in 1953. Almost immediately, attention shifted to Indochina, where the war between the French and the Communist-led Viet Minh (under Ho

Chi Minh) intensified. Both the United States and the Chinese Communists increased their support of the combatants. However, when the fighting reached a high pitch in 1954, the major participants agreed to negotiate. The Geneva Conference held that year resulted in a temporary settlement which, like the one in Korea, halted the fighting but failed to produce a viable political agreement or unification of the country.

In late 1954 and early 1955, Communist China precipitated still another crisis by launching an intense bombardment of the Nationalist-held offshore islands lying near the China coast. When the United States responded by increasing its defensive support of the Nationalists, the crisis gradually abated.

The atmosphere in Asia changed substantially in 1955 when the historic Bandung Conference that met in Indonesia heralded a period of reduced tension, greater moderation in Chinese Communist policies, and increased attempts at collaboration among the Asian and other non-Western countries. The principal leaders of 29 Asian and African nations attended this meeting, where Peking's Premier Chou En-lai, together with Nehru of India, played a leading role. The conference was a dramatic symbol of the rising importance of the new nations in world affairs, but it did not lead to real unity among them. In fact, when a decade later an attempt was made to convene a second such meeting, the effort failed.

The almost uninterrupted series of international crises which kept Asia in a state of high tension during the early 1950's tended to determine the world's image of the region, but many of the most significant developments of the period were actually taking place within the Asian states themselves, rather than in their external relations. Major political, economic, and social transformations were under way, as great efforts were made, in both the non-Communist and the Communist nations, to modernize and spur economic growth.

In their initial years in power, the Communist leaders in China were able, with impressive speed, to unify most of the country and build a totalitarian apparatus of power. They also carried out domestic programs of social revolution and rehabilitated the economy they had inherited. Then, in 1953 they launched China's first Five-Year Plan, modeled on Stalin's plans in the Soviet Union. Under the slogans of "socialization" and "industrialization" they collectivized agriculture, as well as socializing industry and commerce, and initiated a fairly rapid process of growth. On balance this was a period of significant economic achievement in China, during which the economy grew at an average rate of 6 to 8 per cent a year (in GNP), and industrial output more than doubled.

Serious problems remained unsolved, however, as agricultural output lagged and population soared, and in 1958 the Chinese Communists turned to radical new policies—establishment of communes in the countryside and total mobilization of labor for a "great leap forward" in both agriculture and industry. The failure of these policies created a serious economic crisis during 1959–1961, set China's development program back by several years, and tarnished the Chinese Communist "model" of development, which prior to the "great leap forward" had had a significant impact on many Asian leaders. In contrast with the 1950's, China made little progress economically in the 1960's.

Throughout the 1950's, Communist China was also convulsed by numerous "mass campaigns" designed to reindoctrinate the population and restructure society. These slackened during the post-"leap" crisis, but after 1962 new campaigns were launched, leading to a massive "great proletarian cultural revolution" in 1966. Party chairman Mao Tse-tung, with the backing of some of China's military leaders, including Lin Piao, Peking's minister of defense, mobilized the youth of the country into Red Guards units, to combat "erosion" of the revolution, and to attack the party and government bureaucracies. As it developed, the campaign shattered the unity of the regime's leadership and developed into a major power struggle. Mao purged a large proportion of the regime's top party and government leaders, and the army had to step in to run the country. After the Ninth Party Congress was held in early 1969, efforts were made to reunify the badly disrupted society and rebuild the party, but progress was slow.

Despite Communist China's growing military establishment and international influence, from the late 1950's on, Communist China experienced major setbacks in its foreign as well as domestic policies. At the end of 1957 it abandoned the moderation of the "Bandung period" and put renewed emphasis on revolutionary militancy, precipitating the second offshore islands crisis in 1958, as well as border conflicts with India in 1959 and 1962, and exerting pressure again on many Asian countries on its periphery.

Sino-Soviet relations seriously deteriorated during the late 1950's. This was a result not only of ideological problems and basic differences regarding world strategy (including policy toward the United States) but also of serious clashes of national interests. Moscow, in Chinese eyes, failed to give adequate backing to Peking in both the second offshore islands crisis and the border conflicts with India, and it reneged, the Chinese claimed, on promises to support Peking in its program to develop nuclear weapons. Bitter Sino-Soviet debates broke out in 1960, and by 1963—after the Soviet Union had signed a limited nuclear test ban treaty with the United States—the Chinese and Russians, instead of collaborating, were engaged in intense competition throughout the world Communist movement and the underdeveloped world. The deterioration of Sino-Soviet relations had a great impact on the entire world balance, just as the signing of the Sino-Soviet alliance also had a little more than a decade earlier. By 1969 tension between the two countries was such that border incidents brought them close to war.

In the early 1960's, Peking's interest turned increasingly toward the underdeveloped nations, in Africa and Latin America as well as Asia, but during 1965–1966 China experienced serious setbacks in these regions too, and found itself increasingly isolated internationally. Its loss of prestige from these developments was only partially offset by its success in exploding its first nuclear device in 1964. During the "cultural revolution," in the latter 1960's, China retreated into fairly extreme isolation. In 1969, however, it began to look outward again and renew its diplomatic activity abroad. Then, in early 1971, Peking adopted a dramatically new and more flexible policy toward the United States and invited President Nixon to visit Peking.

Japan, during most of these years, was largely insulated from the violence and conflict that afflicted so much of the rest of Asia, but it too underwent internal transformations which, though peaceful, were in many respects no less significant. During the American occupation, many reforms were introduced, with the aim of democratizing as well as demilitarizing Japanese society. Equally important, as the Cold War developed, and the United States began treating the Japanese as allies rather than defeated enemies, Japan was able to repair the wartime damage to its economy, and then it rapidly rebuilt Japan into a modern, industrialized nation of the first rank.

In the mid-1950's, despite some American pressure on Japan to rearm, strong pacifist tendencies and constitutional barriers to rearmament led successive Japanese governments to rely primarily on American power for their national security. Left-wing groups strongly opposed Japan's security treaty with the United States, and some Japanese groups favored moves toward neutralism, but the conservative governments in power argued for continued reliance on American forces for protection; this enabled Japan to limit its defense expenditures to a minimum and greatly facilitated the growth of its civilian economy. In the latter 1960's, however, Japanese defense forces did grow somewhat, and debate on security policies increased. Nevertheless, the Liberal Democratic government in power signed the treaty barring nuclear proliferation, and opposition in Japan to major rearmament remained strong.

The economic growth rate in Japan in the latter 1950's and 1960's, which was one of the highest in the world, was nothing short of phenomenal. The Japanese themselves referred to it as an "economic miracle." As a consequence, living standards rose significantly, and Japan enjoyed a high degree of domestic political tranquillity. Despite the existence of a strong socialist opposition to the government and considerable disaffection among intellectuals, Communism remained a relatively weak force.

Abroad, the expansion of Japan's foreign trade and aid paralleled the growth of its domestic economy, and Japan became a major force in the world economy. In the 1950's and early 1960's, the Japanese were slow to try to reassert any major political role in international affairs. Closely tied to the United States, both by the Japanese-American security treaty and by trade, Tokyo generally followed Washington's lead on foreign policy issues. Like the United States, for example, it pursued a nonrecognition policy toward Peking, although it did promote trade and nonofficial contacts with Communist China. It was cautious about trying to assert any role of political leadership in Asia. In the latter 1960's, however, Japanese leaders were groping toward a more independent foreign policy, and it seemed likely that even without major remilitarization they would gradually assume, because of their great economic power and growing political influence, a role of greater leadership in non-Communist Asia. The return of Okinawa by the United States to Japan in 1969 symbolized Japan's search for a more independent posture.

In contrast with China, India after independence created a Western-type constitutional regime and adopted moderate democratic, socialist methods to pursue its goals of modernization and economic growth. Like China, and unlike Japan, however, it had to struggle with enormous domestic problems created by extreme poverty, agricultural backwardness, and a population lacking many of the skills essential for modern development. Under the leadership of Jawaharlal Nehru and the Congress party, it made some impressive gains, but accomplishments clearly lagged behind aspirations.

The heritage of British legal and administrative skills was a great asset to independent India, but this fact alone did not provide easy answers or automatic solutions to the country's enormous difficulties, political as well as economic. Huge refugee problems and Hindu-Muslim communal strife plagued the government right after independence, and the tasks of creating a unified nation, coping with linguistic regionalism and other divisive forces, and finding a viable balance between political centralization and decentralization posed continuing challenges.

In 1951, nevertheless, the Indian government was able to launch the first in a series of five-year development plans. Compared with the Chinese development program, India's plans placed greater stress on voluntarism and democratic methods, improvement of consumer welfare, and a balance between agriculture and industry as well as between state and private enterprise. While the pace of development in India was slower than that in

China in the 1950's, it avoided the kind of social upheaval that Chinese policies produced and did not encounter major setbacks comparable to those which resulted in China from the failure of the Communists' most radical policies, such as the "great leap forward." Even though progress in India took place at a relatively moderate rate, it nevertheless was impressive in many respects. It did not, however, produce immediate solutions to such basic problems as the nation's insufficiency of food and the necessity to rely on large-scale foreign economic assistance.

In foreign affairs, India's most immediate and pressing problem following independence was its dispute with Pakistan over control of Kashmir, which periodically erupted into open conflict, in both the 1950's and the 1960's. (When Pakistan, which had received large-scale American military assistance in the 1950's, concluded that the United States would not help it assert its claims to Kashmir, it turned in the 1960's increasingly toward Communist China for support.) Civil conflict erupted in East Pakistan in 1971 and the resulting flow of refugees to India created severe new strains in Indian-Pakistan relations, posing the danger of war.

On the broader world stage, India pursued a policy of nonalignment, dissociated itself from the Cold War, and attempted to promote "peaceful coexistence." It was particularly insistent, until 1959, on the need to establish friendly relations with Communist China. Under Nehru, who emerged as perhaps the most influential world-wide spokesman for the neutralist nations, India was able to play a far larger role in international affairs than its actual economic and military strength warranted.

India's hopes for friendship with Communist China, and for Sino-Indian collaboration in promoting world-wide "peaceful coexistence," were rudely shattered, however, when serious clashes took place on the Sino-Indian border in 1959 and 1962, and Peking adopted an openly hostile attitude toward the New Delhi government. The Chinese Communists simultaneously took steps to try to improve relations with all of India's neighbors—Pakistan, Afghanistan, Nepal, Burma, and Ceylon—in an effort to isolate India politically and reduce its international influence. These developments, and the death of Nehru, caused a significant decline in India's international prestige. Within India, hostility toward China grew, and apprehension about a potential threat from the north took its place, alongside the problem of relations with Pakistan, as a major continuing preoccupation of Indian policymakers. In response to the new situation, the Indian government, while still proclaiming its faith in nonalignment, fostered closer relations with both the Soviet Union and the United States, and looked to both for greater economic and military support. In 1971 relations between India and the U.S. deteriorated but India and the Soviet Union signed a 20-year friendship pact.

The most volatile and unstable region in Asia during most of the postwar period was neither Northeast Asia nor South Asia, but Southeast Asia. During the first two decades after the war, insurrections, coups d'état, and wars were endemic in the region and affected almost every Southeast Asian state.

Vietnam (formerly part of Indochina) was the prime focus of major military conflict which involved the great powers as well as local contestants for power. The uneasy truce between the Communist north and non-Communist south that resulted from the Geneva Conference of 1954 lasted for only a brief period. In the late 1950's and early 1960's the Communist-led Vietcong and National Liberation Front renewed the struggle in the south, with substantial and growing support from North Vietnam in the form of men and supplies. Before long the conflict posed a real threat to the continued existence of the non-Communist regime in the south, and in response to this situation the United States greatly increased its level of intervention, especially from 1965 on, pouring large numbers of American troops into South Vietnam and initiating bombing raids on the north to reduce its flow of aid. Both Communist China and the Soviet Union countered with increased material assistance to North Vietnam, although they were unable to cooperate effectively in doing so and both refrained from open intervention with their own forces. Over time the intensity of the conflict mounted. Many attempts were made to find a basis for a negotiated settlement, and after the United States halted its bombing of North Vietnam in October, 1968, negotiations were initiated in Paris, but as of mid-1971 no substantial progress had been made. Mounting casualties in Vietnam and growing antiwar sentiment at home led President Lyndon Johnson to decide in 1968 not to run for reelection. After Richard Nixon assumed the presidency, he began a gradual withdrawal of U.S. troops under a policy of "Vietnamization." He also put forward his "Guam Doctrine," or "Nixon Doctrine," calling for reduced American military responsibilities in Asia. Partly as a result, the Vietnam War became a less intense political issue in 1969. When, after a coup in Cambodia overthrew Prince Norodom Sihanouk, Nixon ordered United States troops into Cambodia, antiwar sentiment broke out again with even greater intensity, and Cambodia became more deeply involved in the war. However, as the withdrawal of American forces proceeded in 1970–71, fighting declined to a low level. But the prospects for a political settlement remained uncertain as of mid-1971.

In Laos, a similar conflict between Communist and non-Communist forces destroyed the tranquillity of this small, isolated nation; it too involved the major powers. In the early 1950's the Communist-led Pathet Lao, with North Vietnamese support, seized control of two northern provinces in Laos and initiated an insurrectionary struggle against the existing non-Communist government. A temporary settlement that would have incorporated the Pathet Lao into the government was agreed upon in 1957, but by 1959 the conflict was renewed, with the Russians and Chinese giving assistance to one side and the Americans providing support on the other. To deal with the crisis a new Geneva Conference was convened in 1962; its participants signed agreements calling for guarantees of Laos' independence and neutrality, and the major Laotian factions agreed to the formation of a coalition government. Despite these agreements, the struggle for power soon broke out again, and the Pathet Lao seized sizable portions of the country. The government was able to prevent a Communist takeover, however, and the struggle continued, although at a relatively low level of violence by comparison with the war in Vietnam. By 1971, however, the future of Laos seemed dependent mainly on the outcome of the Vietnam War, and the direction of future American policy.

Elsewhere in Southeast Asia, the Communist insurrections which had taken place in the late 1940's and early 1950's in Burma, Malaya, and the Philippines were effectively brought under control by the mid-1950's, but almost every small country in the area faced recurring threats to its stability. However, faced by the twin dangers of potential subversion at home and increased influence exerted by a powerful and militant Communist China to the north, they responded in a variety of ways.

Thailand decided to abandon its traditional neutrality and aligned openly with the United States. It joined SEATO—the only mainland Southeast Asian nation to do so—and when the United States intervened in Vietnam on a large scale, Thailand cooperated by providing air bases to the American forces. By 1970, however, when it appeared that an eventual reduction of the United States military role in Asia was likely, the Thais began to show increased interest in broadening relations with the other major powers. At home, ruled by a conservative monarchy and military dictatorship, Thailand escaped much of the social upheaval characteristic of the region, although it was troubled by localized Communist-led guerrilla activity—in the north and northeast of the country, and in the south on the Malayan border. In the latter 1960's Peking gave strong moral support to these guerrillas, but Chinese material support remained limited.

Cambodia, also led by a conservative government under Prince Sihanouk, resisted internal change and was successful in maintaining a fairly high level of domestic stability. But, fearful of pressures from its immediate neighbors—South Vietnam and Thailand—it sought security by proclaiming its neutralism and at the same time establishing closer ties with Communist China. For many years Sihanouk succeeded in surviving politically, preserving Cambodia's independence, and insulating most of Cambodia from the conflicts in neighboring Vietnam and Laos, but to do so he allowed the North Vietnamese to create military sanctuaries in Cambodia. In 1970 he was overthrown by a coup. United States and South Vietnamese forces then intervened in Cambodia to attack North Vietnamese positions, while Sihanouk, with Chinese political support, set up an exile government. By mid-1971 Cambodia had become increasingly involved in the Vietnam War.

The government of Burma was harassed throughout the 1950's by many internal challenges, from a variety of separatist as well as Communist groups, and from Chinese pressures on its border as well. Frustrated by the ineffectiveness of civilian-led democratic institutions, General Ne Win staged a coup d'état in 1962 and established a military government. Thereafter, Burma not only reaffirmed its long-standing neutralism but retreated into extreme isolation, attempting to minimize its contacts with both the Communist and the non-Communist powers. Domestically, it attempted to implement its own brand of "socialism" under a strict military dictatorship.

Malaya, for most of the decade prior to achieving independence in 1957, was preoccupied with the task of defeating a major Communist insurrection. Thereafter, under Tunku Abdul Rahman, it achieved considerable success in creating a functioning democratic political system and fostering economic growth. It still faced major problems at home, however, most notably the problem of improving relations between the Malays and Chinese, the two major ethnic groups in its population, and in the late 1960's renewed Malay-Chinese conflict resulted in a major crisis which led to a temporary suspension of the constitution. (In almost every Southeast Asian country, unassimilated overseas Chinese minorities have exercised economic power out of proportion to their numbers. Southeast Asian governments have imposed many controls on them, and over time pressures for acculturation or assimilation have increased.) In its foreign policy, Malaya—after independence—while avoiding formal membership in any Western-led alliance, continued to rely on British and Commonwealth forces for its protection, particularly against threats from Indonesia, which militantly opposed a plan to create a greater Malaysia incorporating Singapore and part of Borneo. Even after the British decided to withdraw their forces, Kuala Lumpur was able to convince Australia and New Zealand to continue military support. Continuing tensions and problems complicated relations between Malaysia and Singapore, but in the latter 1960's relations between Malaysia and Indonesia greatly improved.

The Philippines, under President Ramon Magsaysay, successfully suppressed the Communist-led Hukbalahap rebellion in the early 1950's, and, like Thailand, it joined SEATO and clearly aligned itself with the United

States. However, despite the fact that its democratic institutions, modeled on those of the United States, introduced democratic processes of government, the government was slow to attack the nation's basic social problems or to mobilize its resources effectively for economic development. In the latter 1960's, in fact, deteriorating conditions were accompanied by renewed insurrectionary activity, which raised basic questions about the future stability of the country.

Indonesia, the largest and potentially the richest nation in Southeast Asia, encountered some of the greatest difficulties in creating a viable state after independence. Under Sukarno, the republic started its existence with high hopes, but ineffective government soon resulted not in progress but in political and economic deterioration. In 1957 Sukarno ended parliamentary democracy and introduced what he called "guided democracy." A major revolt then broke out against the government, in Sumatra and the eastern islands, and it was suppressed only with great difficulty. Thereafter, Sukarno moved increasingly toward personal rule, based on a delicate balance of forces between non-Communist army officers and local Communist leaders (who led a party that was not only the largest organized political group in Indonesia but the largest Communist party in Asia, outside of China).

In his foreign policy, although Sukarno proclaimed a neutralist position, in the late 1950's he became increasingly strident in his denunciations of the United States and other Western "imperialist" powers and greatly strengthened his ties with both Communist China and the Soviet Union. In Southeast Asia he aggressively opposed the plan to create Malaysia, and through his policy of "confrontation" exerted strong pressure against it.

External adventures did not halt the process of deterioration within Indonesia, however. In the fall of 1965 there was an attempted coup d'état in which the Communists tried to seize power. Indonesia's anti-Communist military leaders took over instead, and bloody reprisals throughout the country decimated the Communist party. The new leaders under General Suharto then proceeded to end the "confrontation" policy directed against Malaysia, and slowly eased Sukarno out of power. They also reduced their ties with the Communist countries and restored friendlier relations with the United States. At home they took steps to halt the process of economic decline, and with multilateral foreign economic assistance they were able to make some progress.

In short, two decades after World War II, Asia was still unstable and was still undergoing great changes. Most of Asia now consisted of independent countries, rather than colonial domains, but the new nations varied greatly in their interests, problems, and course of development, and the problems of nation building were enormous.

Not only was Asia divided between Communist and non-Communist countries; among both the Communists and the non-Communists there were tremendous differences. The tendencies toward bipolarity which characterized the 1950's were followed by increasing multipolarity in the 1960's.

New elite groups and political leaders had emerged in every Asian state, and they were all dedicated to political, economic, and social change. However, they looked in many different directions for "models" and inspiration, and each nation was trying to reshape its policy, economy, and society in its own way, drawing on many ideas from both the non-Communist and the Communist nations as well as from their own Asian traditions.

Apart from the leaders in Communist China and its small Asian Communist neighbors, a majority of the new leaders in Asia professed belief in some form of parliamentary democracy comparable to that in the West. But it proved no easy task in many of the tradition-rooted agrarian societies of Asia to transplant Western political forms into settings where some of the most basic prerequisites for effective, stable democracy were lacking. As a result, even though democratic institutions and processes appeared to be taking root in some Asian countries—such as Japan, the Philippines, and Malaya—in others—such as Burma, Indonesia, Thailand, and Korea—when democratic institutions faltered, military coups occurred. Throughout Asia, however—even in the countries ruled by Communist parties or military dictatorships—there was a notable increase in mass political participation.

Throughout Asia, also, modern science and technology were spreading fairly rapidly (in part as a result of vastly expanded mass education), and all the new states, whatever their political system, were attempting to promote processes of economic growth. Industrialization was increasing in many areas, and new seeds and agricultural methods held forth the promise of a "green revolution" that might greatly increase food output. Here again, however, there was great variety in the approaches to development adopted in different countries (even though some form of planning by government authorities became almost universal), and in the degree of success achieved. Not only in Japan, but in a number of other countries as well—including Nationalist China, South Korea, and Malaya—impressive growth rates and rising living standards were actually realized, but in some others—for example, Burma—there was little real success. The two most populous Asian nations—Communist China and India—using very different methods, both initiated significant planned programs of development, but both faced enormous continuing problems in implementing them.

"Asian solidarity"—a powerful slogan in the 1950's—proved to be a will-o'-the-wisp, at least in the short run, as conflicting interests of many sorts continued to divide the states in the region. Some forms of limited regional collaboration among the non-Communist nations of Asia did slowly evolve, however, and in the mid-1960's it appeared as if this trend might become increasingly important.

The most serious unresolved active conflicts in the region were those in the three Indochinese states, Vietnam, Laos, and, as of 1970, Cambodia as well. The future peace and stability of the region depended in considerable part on whether, and how, these conflicts could be resolved.

Relationships between the major powers involved in Asia were undergoing considerable change at the start of the 1970's. Whereas in the 1950's and part of the 1960's the balance was essentially a bipolar one, involving hostile confrontation between Communist China and the United States, as a result of the Sino-Soviet split the balance became increasingly a triangular one in the 1960's, and then, with American talk of partial disengagement and the rapid reemergence of Japan's influence, it seemed destined to become a four-power balance in the 1970's.

By the latter 1960's, war between China and the Soviet Union appeared to be, in some respects, a greater danger than any major U.S.-Chinese conflict. Gradually, there were some signs of reduced tension between the United States and China. Both President Johnson and President Nixon called for greater contacts with the Peking regime. In 1969 the United States reduced its restrictions on China travel and trade. Finally in 1971 Peking and Washington startled the world with the announcement that President Nixon would meet with Chinese leaders in Peking before May 1972. The results of this meeting will have a profound effect on the entire pattern of big power relations in Asia.

In Asia as a whole, the processes of modernization and social change seemed destined to continue, and Asian nations could be expected steadily to emerge into roles of increased international importance. What the trend of events in the period immediately ahead would be seemed to depend on the answers which history would give to a variety of key questions. When and how would the conflicts in the Indochina area end? Would any rapprochement between the United States and China be possible? Could war between China and the Soviet Union be avoided? What role would the Japanese play in the region? Would a four-power balance be stable? Would peaceful cooperation among Asian nations grow? None of these questions can presently be answered with certainty.

For Further Reading

Butwell, Richard, *Southeast Asia Today and Tomorrow—Problems of Political Development.*

Clubb, O. Edmund, *Twentieth Century China.*
Fairbank, John K., *The United States and China.*
Gordon, Bernard K., *The Dimensions of Conflict in Southeast Asia.*
Ho, Ping-ti, and Tsou, Tang (eds.), *China in Crisis.*
Jan, George P. (ed.), *International Politics of Asia: Readings.*
Kahin, George McT. (ed.), *Governments and Politics of Southeast Asia.*
Langer, Paul F., *Japan, Yesterday and Today.*
Mason, Philip (ed.), *India and Ceylon: Unity and Diversity.*
Morris-Jones, Wyndraeth H., *Government and Politics of India.*
Reischauer, Edwin O., *The United States and Japan.*
Schurmann, Franz, and Schell, Orville (eds.), *The China Reader,* Vol. 3: Communist China.
Sen Gupta, Bhabani, *The Fulcrum of Asia.*
Tilman, Robert (ed.), *Man, State and Society in Contemporary Southeast Asia.*
Ward, Robert E. (ed.), *Political Development in Modern Japan.*

100   The United States Since World War II

Alone among the great powers, the United States emerged from World War II practically unscathed; except for the bombing of Pearl Harbor and damage to installations on islands in the Pacific, no American territory was ever attacked, and while nearly 300,000 American soldiers and sailors died in battle, these losses, too, were insignificant when compared to the 7.5 million Russians, the 2.2 million Chinese, the 3.5 million Germans, the 1.2 million Japanese, who were killed, or to the lesser but proportionately heavy casualties suffered by Britain, France, and the other belligerents. Nevertheless, few nations were more changed by the war than the United States.

To begin with, the war destroyed American isolationism. The nation had never really been isolated from affairs in the rest of the world, but as late as the 1930's large elements in the population turned their backs psychologically on most of the rest of humanity. Isolation had been produced by a strange combination of insularity and idealism. Separated from Asia and Europe by great oceans and intent upon the development of a continent, Americans had little reason to devote their energies to foreign affairs, or so it seemed. Their sense of their own uniqueness and virtue, products of their democratic system and the rich natural resources of their land, made them look on other peoples as either (in the case of Europeans) evil and corrupt or (in the case of most others) benighted. Al-

A.D.   1946   Employment Act creates Council of Economic Advisors
           1947   Truman Doctrine and the Marshall Plan
           1949   North Atlantic Treaty Organization approved
           1950   Outbreak of the Korean War
      1950–1960   Sale of television sets averages over 7 million a year; by 1960, 88 per cent of all households have television
           1954   Supreme Court declares racially segregated schools unconstitutional
           1956   Martin Luther King, Jr., organizes Montgomery, Alabama, bus boycott
           1958   First commercial jet airplanes in service
           1962   Cuban missile crisis
           1963   Assassination of President John F. Kennedy
           1964   Student riots at the University of California, Berkeley
           1965   President Lyndon B. Johnson "escalates" the Vietnamese War; Education Act provides first comprehensive federal aid to education; race riot in Watts district, Los Angeles, California
           1968   Assassination of Martin Luther King, Jr.
           1969   Astronauts land on the moon

though many persons had always regretted this isolationism, recognizing that events in the rest of the world vitally affected American interests and believing that the nation had an obligation to spread and share its political and economic advantages, it took the war to convince the great majority that this was the proper way to look at the question. By 1945 technology had caused the protecting oceans, so to speak, to evaporate, the excesses of the totalitarians had reaffirmed Americans' faith in their own values, and the desperate condition of so much of the rest of humanity had touched them deeply and made them willing, even eager, to share some of their wealth with those less fortunate.

But the postwar internationalism contained also a strong illiberal element—it was in part a new imperialism, a reflection of American power. The military and industrial might generated in order to defeat the Axis powers, capped by the enormous force of the atom bomb, still an American monopoly, made the United States seem like a colossus among pygmies when the war ended. Although Russia quickly demonstrated that it, too, possessed tremendous strength, this merely stimulated American competitiveness, and combined with genuine dislike of Communist repression of individual self-expression and fear of Soviet expansionism to produce the Cold War. That conflict aside, however, American internationalism had its aggressive side. Huge sums were spent to rehabilitate Europe and help underdeveloped regions to improve themselves, but the nation collectively and American businessmen individually also poured billions into foreign nations for purely material purposes, often without regard for the welfare of the people who were affected by this investment. And when conflicts developed between the desire to help others and the supposed national and personal interests of Americans, these were usually resolved in a narrowly selfish way. Thus the United States, while committed to aiding poverty-stricken Latin American countries, repeatedly supported reactionary and undemocratic regimes in the hemisphere either because they were anti-Communist or because they were willing to make favorable economic arrangements with Americans, often at the expense of their own people.

The war also affected American foreign policy in another unfortunate manner: its "lessons," like most of the lessons of history, were applied too literally by the postwar generation to its own problems. First of all, the idea of appeasement was almost totally rejected. Failure to move soon enough to check the Nazis had undoubtedly cost the United States and Europe heavily, but the refusal to "appease" nondemocratic governments, especially Russia, was often carried to unreasonable and self-defeating extremes after 1945. The idea that the United States must intervene to thwart aggression *anywhere* if it was not itself to be overrun, put into effect most disastrously in Vietnam during the administration of Lyndon

Johnson, but more or less accepted by every postwar President, resulted in a severe straining of American resources and also in the undermining of the faith of many nations in America's good intentions. It was probably inevitable, given the wealth and power of the United States, that many small and poor nations would resent and envy America, but the policy of intervening diplomatically and even militarily in every corner of the globe at the first sign of trouble and often without the invitation of the local populace was bound to exacerbate these feelings. More important, the growth of nationalism in the underdeveloped countries and the fragmentation of the unity of the Communist powers made the fear that a Russian Hitler might soon seek world domination progressively more unrealistic, and in any case, events repeatedly demonstrated that the United States simply could not, through its own determination, control the course of history all over the world. The result was a great loss in American prestige abroad and an enormous waste of American resources that had serious domestic repercussions.

At home the chief effect of the war was to confirm the American commitment to the basic principles of the welfare state and a managed, as distinct from a laissez-faire, economy. Wartime demand had finally ended unemployment and restored full prosperity, and experience had demonstrated the soundness of the major New Deal reforms. The Employment Act of 1946, establishing a Council of Economic Advisors to plan policies aimed at promoting employment, production, and purchasing power, gave the force of law to an attitude toward the role of the government in managing the economy that only a generation earlier had seemed to millions the antithesis of free-enterprise capitalism. Even when the Republicans regained control of the White House under Dwight D. Eisenhower, the new point of view remained in force. Eisenhower neglected many problems related to social welfare, and his stress on budget balancing caused a series of minor depressions (euphemistically called "recessions"), but he did not even suggest the repeal of New Deal laws, and his talk about the virtues of individualism and free enterprise, if not mere talk, never went much beyond suggestion.

Nevertheless, and despite Eisenhower's enormous personal popularity, his less than forceful application of the new tools for managing the economy caused widespread public dissatisfaction, and when John F. Kennedy succeeded to the presidency in 1961 after having campaigned on the promise to "get the country moving again," the time was ripe for more positive action. Instead of seeking to stimulate the economy by increasing government spending, which would either drain off funds from the private sector or, if not paid for by increased taxation, trigger an inflationary spiral, Kennedy suggested a sharp reduction in taxes, which would free private capital for new investment and stimulate consumption, and thus demand. This policy of deliberately unbalancing the budget ran into considerable opposition, but in the brief period of national chagrin after Kennedy's assassination in November, 1963, President Johnson persuaded Congress to act. The result fully bore out the hopes of the plan's sponsors; the gross national product increased at a swift pace, unemployment declined sharply. Reversing the process to slow down the boom and check inflation, equally important in the view of economists, proved much more difficult to achieve for political reasons. Despite a rapid upward movement of prices, Congress hesitated to raise taxes, delaying until 1968 when a 10 per cent "surcharge" was added to the federal income tax. Inflation seemed at the end of the sixties a perennial problem. Nevertheless, the argument had become one of means, not of principle—that the economy could and must be managed by the government was no longer challenged.

General prosperity, freedom from fear of a major depression, rapid economic expansion, a sharp increase both in the standard of living of the people and in the kinds of goods and services available to them, made the immediate postwar era a time of complacency for most Americans. For the middle-class majority, conditions had never been so good, and they were improving at a spectacular rate. Antibiotics almost eliminated the dangers of contagious diseases. Television brought the world into everyone's living room while the jet airplane enabled millions to see the world at first hand with remarkable ease and at relatively low cost. Every form of leisure activity—from golf, skiing, and boating, to the spectator sports, to concert and theater going, reading, and a dozen others—experienced an unprecedented boom. A style of life that had once been the exclusive privilege of the upper levels of society was suddenly opened up not merely to white-collar workers but also to factory laborers and other wage earners. Educational opportunities proliferated, the population of American colleges rising in the 1950's and 1960's from well under 3 million students to well over 6 million. Home ownership soared, as millions of wage-earning city dwellers found themselves able to afford houses in the burgeoning suburbs. Electronic computers, performing in seconds calculations that human brains could not manage in years, speeded the flow of business, freed countless thousands from drudgery, and made possible enormous scientific advances in a variety of fields that promised still greater material rewards. Space itself was conquered, as Americans, responding to the challenge posed by *Sputnik,* the first Russian earth satellite, in 1957, swiftly developed a series of extraterrestrial vehicles, culminating in the first landing of men on the moon in July, 1969.

Yet despite, and to a degree because of, the new progress, grave social problems soon began to surface. One involved the downtrodden condition of American Negroes. For two centuries a dreadful race prejudice had survived in the United States for a variety of reasons. Its origin lay in slavery—the age-old monument to human selfishness and unreason. It was reinforced by the effects of slavery on the slaves; the belief that black "savages" were so inferior that they might rightfully be kept in bondage like horses and cattle was a self-fulfilling prophecy, for the system crushed many of the slaves psychologically and by preventing their education kept them ignorant and undeveloped and thus by practical standards actually inferior to their masters. Unsophisticated observers, seeing the behavior of the *average* bondsman—the exceptions were conveniently ignored—could easily conclude that as a race Negroes lacked potential for the higher human achievements, and that even from their own point of view they were better off as slaves than as free men. Most white men who advocated reform of the system did so on humanitarian or paternalistic grounds, and sought not true equality for blacks but merely the amelioration of their wretched condition.

The Civil War destroyed slavery but it did not produce equality. The experiment of Reconstruction was a flat failure, and by the early twentieth century the Negro tenth of the population was mired in what at best could be called second-class citizenship. World War I brought some economic improvement, World War II still more. The reaction to Hitler's nonsense about race and his slaughter of 6 million Jews because of their supposed racial inferiority could not help stirring the consciences of many white Americans. The performance of Negro troops in the war inspired a new respect for their courage and patriotism, and the shortage of labor produced by the wartime boom enabled many blacks both to improve themselves economically and to develop new self-respect. Less immediately obvious but in the long run probably more important, social research in the 1920's and 1930's had proved that Negroes were not physiologically or mentally inferior to whites, but that their low estate was the result of the very repression that white prejudice had imposed upon them.

By the early 1950's the true nature of this prejudice was clear to the majority of educated Americans. The Supreme Court decision in *Brown* v. *Board of Education* (1954) outlawing segregation in the public schools was based on this awareness that their environment, not their genes, made Negroes "inferior." The entire civil rights movement followed logically, but not, alas, smoothly, from the same premise. Two forces checked the movement. Once the injustice of repression was admitted by the oppressors, Negroes naturally began to *demand,* not merely to plead for, full equality. (They too, perhaps, had unconsciously believed themselves inferior to whites.) Their demands offended the really deep prejudices of many whites who, if allowed to preserve the comfortable paternalism of the past, would have willingly "improved" the Negroes' position. More significantly, the mass of lower-middle-class whites had never really grasped the relationship between the behavior of Negroes and their environment. They saw results as causes—black poverty, black crime, black "shiftlessness" still seemed to indicate congenital flaws in the Negro character. Such white men also felt strongly the pressure of the new black competition—for jobs, for places in already crowded schools, for housing, for all the other advantages of modern life. Thus, while it was obvious that equal treatment would benefit everyone, achieving equality was no easy matter. Black aggressiveness took the form of riots, demands for "compensation" for past injustices, even talk of a new black-inspired segregation and a separate black nation. A white "backlash," although mostly bluster, further rent the fabric of society. By the end of the sixties Negroes had improved themselves enormously, but this improvement was merely a measure of how depressed their condition had been. The nation was still paying a heavy price for having so long held its black citizens in bondage.

Poverty was in large measure a by-product of the race problem, but it was also paradoxically related to the character of prosperity. The marvelously efficient American system of production was based on a complex technology that required highly skilled labor to make it function. Automation eliminated many jobs, of course, but also created new ones; the difficulty lay in the fact that the demand for unskilled labor declined while that for skilled labor rose. The need for well-educated workers expanded, too, so that many posts existed that were beyond the capacity of a large percentage of the population. While high-paying jobs for engineers and technicians went begging, thousands of willing workers could not find decent employment. The poverty problem was also related to urbanization and the emergence of an impersonal civilization that destroyed men's sense of individual accomplishment and weakened both their will to work hard and their sense of being necessary parts of a social organism. In turn this led to a breakdown of community loyalty, the casting off of moral restraints, and a retreat into passivity and self-indulgence. The welfare state, conceived of as a humane way to deal with misfortune, a kind of social insurance, was thus to a degree corrupted and corrupting.

Young people were particularly hard hit by the complexities of modern life. The poor and the dull tended to give up or strike out resentfully at a world they did not make and could not change. The affluent and intelligent, in increasing numbers, tended to "drop out." Reared in comfortable circumstances by indulgent parents, they did not seem capable of enduring frustrations of any sort. Trained by well-meaning but complacent teachers to be idealists, they looked at the irrationalities and injustices around them and (failing to recognize that these were inevitable aspects of the human condition that men of good will must seek to ameliorate but must learn to live with) concluded that they were living in a uniquely rotten society. Many became revolutionaries of the spirit; others were overwhelmed by their contempt and turned to drugs and other deviant forms of behavior.

The senseless and apparently unending war in Vietnam was only one of the causes of youth's discontent. The two great wars of their century seemed to prove that patriotism was a force for viciousness and destruction alone, while the revolution in communications and the general decline of provincialism made nationalism appear an anachronistic form of political organization. The nuclear bomb, they correctly understood, made war not merely horrible but absurd. Yet while millions suffered from actual deprivation and millions more from exasperating, spirit-crushing social inconveniences, the nation was spending billions on its gigantic military machine.

Materialism, racism, the "rat race" of modern life, further offended the young idealists and strengthened their natural tendency to rebel against the values of their fathers. The very complexities of the social problems of the age which made their elders gravitate toward moderation, compromise, and "consensus" made young people insist on one or another absolute. But perhaps most of all, they suffered from the general sense of individual powerlessness that was psychologically frustrating to all men in a world of gigantic, impersonal institutions. Old and young, rich and poor, found it ever more difficult to make an identifiable impact on society. Egos demanded expression. Labor, thought, and feeling commonly produced everything but this sense of purpose—unless directed toward some destructive goal. The greatest statesmen could not achieve true world peace, but a single demented zealot could start a war. Martin Luther King and a host of dedicated followers could not eliminate racial prejudice, but a sordid drifter, shooting King down from ambush, could cause a dozen cities to burn. In an important way, the violence and disorder that plagued the nation was produced not so much by social injustice as by the desperate need of confused individuals to express themselves.

Of course, none of these terrible and terrifying conditions has yet destroyed American society; all are under attack from a hundred directions. What the outcome will be is for the future, not for the historian, to determine.

For Further Reading

Carmichael, S., and Hamilton, C. V., *Black Power*.
Congressional Quarterly Service, *Congress and the Nation: 1945–68*.
Galbraith, J. K., *The New Industrial State*.

Goldman, E. F., *The Crucial Decade—and After.*
Halle, L. J., *The Cold War as History.*
Harrington, Michael, *The Other America.*
Malcolm X, *Autobiography.*
Riesman, David, et al., *The Lonely Crowd.*

101   The State of Culture Today

In present-day discussions of the contemporary scene the main topic is: Are we seeing the breakdown of our civilization?

Sooner or later, the sophisticated person who reads or hears such discussions reminds himself that to the living "the times" always seem bad; in most eras many voices cry out against the visible decadence; in every generation—and especially to the aging—the world has always been going to the dogs. By showing that life continues and new energies arise, the study of history cannot help inspiring skepticism about the recurrent belief in decline.

But sophistication—and skepticism—should perhaps go a step further and ask why that same phenomenon recurs; in other words, the historical-minded should look into the meaning and cause of the undying conviction of decadence. One cause, one meaning, is surely that in every era some things are in fact dying out and the elderly are good witness to this demise. Manners, styles of art and politics, assumptions about the aim of life or the nature of man and of the universe change as inevitably as fashions in dress; and just as no one could deny that men's stiff collars two inches high have vanished into the attic of history, so no one should deny that less tangible entities—say, the idea of "a man of honor"—have vanished too. The very words look quaint and evoke no answering emotion. What is involved here is of course the vivid faith and the cultural form, not the underlying reality that there are always honest and dishonest men. If, then, such faiths and forms are considered good by a generation that grew up to value them, that generation will experience at their passing a legitimate feeling of loss.

The very notion of change, of which the twentieth century makes such a weapon in the advocacy of every scheme, implies the notion of loss; for in society as in individual life many desirable things are incompatible—to say nothing of the fact that the heedlessness or violence with which change takes place brings about the incidental destruction of other useful attitudes and institutions. In 1971, for example, one can ask whether all over the world the idea of a university has not been damaged, without hope of

A.D.   1870   Education Acts passed in most countries of western Europe: free compulsory education; beginnings of industrial literacy

              1871   End of Franco-Prussian War; beginning of armed diplomacy leading to 1914

              1889   Paris World's Fair: the Eiffel Tower and the triumph of machinery; London dockers' strike

        1890–1905   The new Romanticism: Symbolism; Art for Art's Sake; Decadence; Post-Impressionism

        1890–1910   Invention or discovery of: the automobile; serum therapy; Diesel engine; Kodak roll film; motion pictures; heavier-than-air flying machine; fingerprinting; striptease; tuberculin; appendectomy; plastic surgery; color photography; wireless; artificial diamonds; spinal anesthesia; psychoanalysis; Mendelian genetics; histidine; radioactivity; vacuum tube; artificial insemination; organ transplant; quantum theory; relativity; Salvarsan for syphilis; anaphylaxis; artificial materials from resins and cellulose

        1894–1906   The Dreyfus Affair: the intellectuals a new political force

        1895–1917   The emergence of Marxism and Syndicalism; *Reflections on Violence* (1908); the suffragettes; the coming "century of the child"

              1900   "The Yellow Peril"; Western envoys besieged in Peking and relieved by a European army under a German general

        1900–1911   The century turns; Art Nouveau and the new democratic life—penny press, peace crusades, Balkan Wars, international crises

        1905–1915   The Cubist Decade—innovation in all the arts, notably architecture

        1914–1918   The Four Years' War, ultimately the First World War, shatters European power

        1919–1939   "Between Wars"—unrest and indifference under the sway of diminished intelligence; culture imitative, regressive, and derisive of itself; second youth movement and yearning for peace

1929–1939 World-wide economic depression
1939–1945 The Second World War; military application of scientific power, culminating in atomic explosion at Hiroshima
1945 ff. The Age of Anxiety; the Cold War in a divided world; local wars linked with decolonization and universal shrinkage of power; the race to reach the moon: ostentation and propaganda
1964 The cellular revolution: internal and external disorder, the third youth movement, and the second women's liberation; decay and stasis of institutions; art against society; anti-art against the culture and the self; the absurd and the obscene in the effort at destruction or recovery; the drug experience and the experience of dissolution

---

recovery for a very long time. This conclusion, if correct, has nothing to do with the merits of the cause that produced the onslaught: the historian notes results in the way an insurance assessor notes a broken shopfront.

Before one can go on to assess with the same detachment the extent to which the hitherto dominant Western civilization is damaged or dying, one must be reminded of still another historical datum, which is that entire civilizations do perish. The tremendous endings of Greece or Rome are not a myth. Life somehow continues after the fall, to be sure, but it is that very "somehow" which tells us that something above mere existence has disappeared. That something is what we call civilization. It is an expression of collective life cast in determinate ways, an expression which includes power, "growth," a joyous or grim self-confidence, and other obvious signs of a going concern. But it consists also of tacit individual faith in certain ideals and ways of life, seconded by a general faith in the rightness of the whole. It follows that widespread disbelief in those intangibles and the habits they produce in day-to-day existence brings on the dissolution of the whole.

The only question then is: How deep goes the disbelief? For history shows both big and little decadences. Decadence means "falling off," and it is possible for a civilization to experience a lesser fall from trust in its own ways without wrecking the entire fabric. The passage from what we call the High Middle Ages to the Renaissance and Reformation is one such falling away and new beginning. The era of the French Revolution is another. At both these moments—roughly the end of the fourteenth century and the end of the eighteenth century—Europe saw old institutions crumble, long-accepted thoughts dissolve, feelings fade away, and new ones take their place.

Those times were "epochs," which strictly speaking means *turnings*. The old system comes to what looks like a halt, during which all the familiar things seem empty or wrong. Despair, indifference, the obsession with cruelty and death, the Samson-complex of wanting to bring down the whole stupid edifice on one's head and the heads of its retarded upholders —these passions seize the souls of the young generations and turn them into violent agents of change, or else into what we now call dropouts from society. From both the activists and the negators come the new ideas and ideals which permit the march of civilization to continue. But it can also happen that not enough new ideas, no energizing hopes, emerge, and civilization falls apart in growing disorder, mounting frustration, and brainless destruction.

The judgment as to which took place at a given moment in the past is naturally easier to make than the judgment as to which is happening now. But it is again possible to draw guidance from history and take an inventory of significant activities and institutions so as to gauge the degree to which fruitful novelty is keeping pace with obvious destruction. The state in which we find government, religion, morality, social intercourse, language, the arts, and that ultimate basis of civilized life, public hope, permits us to form at least a tentative conclusion about the magnitude of the present *epoch*.

Government is first in the list and first in importance. Many would disagree, but that is in itself a symptom of the contemporary condition. For sixty years or more, advanced opinion in the West has regarded politics and politicians as beneath contempt and the State as an imposition and an imposture. The law and its enforcers are increasingly held in opprobrium as mere tools of "the power group," variously defined but deemed to have won its position largely by fraud and force.

Meanwhile crime stalks the capitals of the world, and its suppression is neither feasible nor in keeping with enlightened thought. The value of the State can stand no higher than the utility of its laws, which in turn must command public support and approval. Though the Western system of justice is perhaps the most solicitous ever devised to protect the rights of the accused, its administration has bogged down, and the march of mind has substituted the idea of illness and treatment for that of evil intent and penalty. Doctrines on the subject are, however, confused, with resulting disparities in pleading, sentencing, and paroling which can only wind up as manifest injustice.

Overcrowded and antiquated prisons provoke justifiable riots, and while some prisoners linger awaiting trial, others escape or revolt or come to the end of their sentence after a much abridged term. Nine years is the usual length of the "life" sentence that replaces the "cruelty" of capital punishment. But recidivism is high, robbery with violence is common and enjoys a large immunity, and the criminally insane when released repeat their senseless horrors—the fit counterpart of what is practiced upon them during their periods of confinement. As in so many realms of social existence, Western man has all the right ideas except that which would turn them into actualities. The net result is contempt for law, for the State that enforces it, and for the governors that still believe in both.

If we ask whether this marks a decadence, we need only observe that the present outlook contrasts sharply with that of a century ago, when the citizen took pride and satisfaction in being an amateur lawyer and parliamentarian. The constitution, the electoral campaign, the jury, and the vote ruled the imaginations of men. The courts and other public authorities earned the respect of the vast majority; they were regarded as the creations of the sovereign people, and such respect and origins helped them to function. Today these same ideas and words evoke only derision. Law-abiding, law-and-order, are terms of contempt meaning hypocrisy or cynicism. The police are considered a kind of malignant growth on the body politic, and among some that body itself is felt to be a usurpation of evil forces over simple human nature. These changes mark the end of the liberal ideal, which saw in universal suffrage for self-government and in the rule of law the keys to a good society. So far is this ideal sunk that the rightness of any minority has become an axiom, and more and more people feel themselves to be not sovereign, but shamefully oppressed—a desperate minority.

In the place of the former attitude toward the State stands what might be called for short the Marxist analysis. It does not of course stem from Marxist propaganda alone; but its spirit is that which informs the literature of Marx and his disciples; it is the spirit of exposure and revelation, the animus of the war against appearances, in search of a reality made up of conspiracies and their victims. It does not so much examine as classify and denounce.

It is a democratic spirit insofar as the passion for equality naturally stimulates envy and suspicion; but it is also a racist spirit in that it attributes virtues and violated rights to one group, wickedness and wrongful supremacy to another. In this sense, visibly, women are a race oppressed by the race of men; the old and the "square" are races unjustly dominant over the race of the "under thirty"—and so on. *La guerre des races* is fought in every public place and public print.

Its aim is still tinged with traditional liberalism to the extent that it takes thought of the "forgotten man" (and woman); while in its indignation it also shows the puritanical spirit of inquisition which belongs to the vigilant free press and which works on the premise that every person and event has its inside (and dirty) story. But with or without cause, the net effect cannot but be lowering, whether the target be a man or an institution, a regime or a "race." This is true even when nothing discreditable is revealed: the act of digging-to-uncover tells its own accusatory tale and reduces public faith in what is.

From the point of view, not of what is thus tarnished, but of the art of governing taken in the abstract, it is clear that the incessant eroding of faith and trust must in the end nullify all public authority and with it the general will. When the general will does not habitually prevail over particular wills, nothing is left but the arbitrary acts of improvised centers of power.

The evidence for this conclusion is seen today in the myriad demonstrations occurring all over the world, sometimes against dire oppression, more often against perfectly legal but unpopular measures, and sometimes again from habit, with no defined object in mind, save expressing hostility to whatever is established. The word Establishment, torn from its precise meaning, now denotes any institution, even benevolent (such as the fire department), which is tainted with having existed prior to the mood of protest.

Another name for that mood is Civil Disobedience, also a term divorced from its true meaning, which was: defiance of a bad law to show that it was bad, by accepting the consequences of breaking it. Now Civil Disobedience is the breaking of any law so as to show that existing society commits injustices at large, and on this ground the lawbreaking asks to be excused. The riots, protests, sit-ins, and strikes have this in common that they substitute the pressure of group blackmail for the force of law and put both the law and the officers of government on the defensive as usurpers.

In countries that have traditions and charters of popular sovereignty, these outbreaks are protected by the guaranteed rights of assembly and petition, though the physical destruction, obscene libel, and disruption of ordinary life which now mark "protest" go far beyond the right of assembly and petition as originally defined, and could not be envisaged as a right by any sane instrument of government. The interpretation of a violent act as "a statement" is correct only in the context of revolution. The falling away here is from the idea of systematic government itself.

In countries where liberalism never won a firm seat—generally those of eastern Europe, Asia, and Latin America—these extreme ways of political action may seem to be indigenous and familiar: coups d'état, street riots, and assassinations apparently continue their long history. They have provided in the past a rough substitute for general elections and a fitful tempering of despotism. But nowadays these uses of force have taken on a new aspect. Formerly, an uprising was an act of civil war; force was met with force, men died, and no one was astonished. Now uprisings large and small, kidnappings and killings of hostages, and highjackings of planes are expected to be acknowledged as legitimate means of communication between the people and their governors. Vandalism and riot having become channels of free opinion, authority must be patient, must withhold force and enter into negotiations, often on the simple terms of "Accept all our demands, or we shall do worse."

What Western civilization is witnessing, in short, is the last phase of the great emancipation promoted in the eighteenth century, and that last phase resembles the first, when all enlightened men agreed that authority and the State were always and a priori in the wrong. Whenever this feeling holds, any retaliation is necessarily "against the people" and thus a crime. What was then theory is now practice backed by the same theory: *écrasez l'infâme* now serves against any agency of restraint. Intellectual opinion leans automatically toward the objector, supports local animus against any central authority, and protests against all sanctions. In other words, power has ceased to be legitimate except when the people take it into their hands. If, as is only fair, we entertain the possibility that this conclusion is justified by enormous, incurable evils on the part of those who rule, then the decadence is from both sides, and the structure of civilization no longer has either faith or power to sustain itself with.

Under the populism now become universal—since even the totalitarian regimes profess to embody it: the "People's Republic," the People's Party, or whatnot—a perpetual referendum or plebiscite would be required to bring into being a new kind of sovereignty. But "total consultation" is hardly workable for the day-to-day conduct of government, if indeed continuous participation in public affairs is compatible with the other demands of civilized existence. At the present time, in nations not ruled by a dictatorship, the verdict on many issues is more and more often rendered by groups which are or which imitate professional revolutionary cells. To the degree that students all over the world have taken a hand in politics, that is the pattern they have successfully adopted for quick results.

The original model of rule by collective resistance and organized menace has of course been legalized and at work in the West almost since the start of the period under review: the trade unions, wielding the strike, the closed shop, and various other devices for coercing their own members have taught the public the power not only of disruption but even of mere interruption. To sum up, rule by direct-action groups is gradually replacing rule by individuals supposedly free, who delegate their unit of power to a legitimate authority.

In this political transformation, the only difficulty is to fashion a group coherent enough to coerce by these means. The trade unions took eighty years to win their privilege. But with the rising interdependence of industrial needs and services, smaller and smaller groups can disrupt the common life and bring about partial or total surrender. Success televised inspires imitation, just as local grievances, real or fancied, inspire revolt. A decision by a zoning board or a school superintendent, or again, the appointment of an unpopular person, even to a private institution, suffices to set off the indignation needed to create ad hoc parties of protest. "Regular channels" being both slow and suspect, "confrontation" ensues. Thanks to the floating feelings of aggression generated by other factors within industrial society—feelings kept fresh by report and example—the natural tendency is toward "action," a slogan which ensures that today in many parts of the world forces are ready at a word to storm city hall, break up a public hearing, ravage a university, or detonate an embassy.

The international scene has of course displayed this kind of behavior for a long while. Profit-by-outrage is an old game. The twentieth century has only added its peculiar tone of vulgar arrogance and boastfulness, aimed at impressing the home front. But the kidnapping and ransoming of envoys, the storming of embassies and the hatred of foreigners on grounds of "policy" take us back to the primitive times, the Venetian days, of diplomacy. All in all, the growing resemblance between the traditional anarchy of the great powers and the anarchy within each nation marks the decline of the very idea of nation.

And yet, when a principle happens to be invoked as the reason or occasion for modern outbreaks against the state, the principle generally belongs to the established liberal-socialist collection: it is "Down with imperialism"—or racism, or capitalism. Outbursts of hostility directed at another country usually spring from one or more of these same principles. No new ones, no practical or utopian schemes of society or plans of life, have yet emerged. This has significance for the observer assessing Western civilization's chances of survival. What strikes such an observer is that besides being unoriginal, these old-new ideals and doctrines are also undisputed. The evil which the doctrine attacks may still exist, but it exists without support from any principle widely held. Just as all regimes are "for the people," so all responsible groups and classes are "for equality and justice" and "against poverty and discrimination." Imperialism (colonialism) has no proponents left; racism as an overt policy is restricted to the southern tip of Africa; and capitalism has been so modified that it is at many points indistinguishable from communism, itself also hybridized. Nobody supports the view that the poor are necessary to society or that "inferiors" exist or have a role to play in some hierarchical order. Egalitarianism is affirmed as universally as pauperism is condemned.

Indeed, the only political ism surviving in full strength from the past is nationalism. This was partly to be expected from the liberation of so many colonies simultaneously, beginning in the 1920's. But this nationalism differs from the old in two remarkable ways: it is not patriotic and it does not want to absorb and assimilate. On the contrary, it wants to shrink and to limit its control to its own small group of like-minded we-ourselves-alone. It is in that sense racist, particularist, sectarian, minority-inspired. In truth, it flourishes as an expression of the antinomian passion which is the deepest drive of the age. In Asia and Africa the fission of kingdoms and regions into smaller states, and of these states again into smaller ones, shows an impatient mistrust of all central authority, regardless of its source or form. In Europe, nearly every "old" nation has one or more "subnations" demanding independence—Scotland and Wales from England; Brittany from France; Catalonia from Spain. The rage for absolute freedom is virulent. Ireland is in civil war. Little Belgium is rent by strife between two linguistic groups, and her great university has had to be split into two. Germany is a gerrymander. To the east and south, Balkanization has been overlaid but not extinguished by Soviet domination. Cyprus is a battlefield. In the Far East unity, never great, is less and less. No sooner is Pakistan free of that imperial monster India than East Pakistan cries out for liberation from the imperial monster West Pakistan.

In the United States the struggle to enforce the Constitution upon the South is still going on as if the federal union were trying to interfere in a foreign country, while a black nationalism demands (and in small ways obtains) total segregation. In Canada, French nationalism has likewise turned from sullen resistance to armed violence. And everywhere, regardless of doctrine or regime, the same ferment works inside common institutions under the name of decentralization. When sex adds its explosive force, the movement is called Women's Liberation.

In short, the one political and social ideal, the one motive power of the time is Separatism, no matter what other rags of older philosophy it masquerades under. If this is not yet Breakdown, it is undeniably Breakup.

Further evidence comes to us from the churches in the form of ecumenism (counterpart of populism), and of "the Underground" (counterpart of revolution). That the Catholic Church, long the model of hierarchical organization, should revise its doctrines with the aid of a large representative assembly is nothing new. What is new is that the rather impolitic decrees subsequent to the Second Vatican Council should be flouted by groups of priests who maintain that they are "not attacking" the authority they defy. The same contention is made by individuals in every church. Ministers take a stand against their governing synods on this or that article of faith, on ritual or private conduct, and call the public to witness whether their autonomy is not in truth justified by the act of challenge itself.

As in the rest of society, the one new idea is that authority exists to ratify the decisions of its declared enemies. Time has not yet shown whether such an arrangement can continue beyond phase one, that is, its first application by the first dissidents. At the moment, the assumption is warranted. Responsible and "wise" authorities hesitate to find heresy, to unfrock or disqualify, not so much afraid as ashamed of wielding any power at all, imbued as they are with the principle of whatever is is wrong.

A frequent characteristic of dissolving times is—almost by definition —their tendency to blur distinctions of purpose and of function. Men and institutions find themselves desiring to fuse aims, activities, and moods formerly held separate. This urge is in keeping with the main drive, which is to *undo,* to remove barriers and recover a primal unity of being with other men. It is the will to mix, merge, and forget. The business conglomerate is a conspicuous example. It owes its being not alone to diversification for commercial safety, but to a sort of reckless and derisive pleasure in flouting industrial specialization: the new corporation produces bathroom fixtures with the right hand and art books with the left. The supermarket and shopping center similarly bring the consecrated chapel for the weary next to the concourse of groceries which has made them so. Students have sought and won the right to eat in libraries and make love in dormitories. The church succeeds in attracting new young worshipers by combining the service with their favorite combo; while a rebellious priest thinks he has made an important religious point by marrying a couple in a subway station.

It is not so far-fetched as it may seem at first to find in the Cold War itself a conglomerate of acts and attitudes which matches this general liking for the mixed and indeterminate. The Cold War is a potpourri of diplomacy, verbal aggression, secret violence, assassination, and open fighting on shifting fronts. Peace is seldom signed, armistices are not kept, partitioned countries stay dismembered, and everybody talks peace and disarmament simultaneously with world revolution and armed intervention for abused nationhood. If either side—or indeed any human group—did believe in the rightness of its system, the spectacle would surely be different. We may think ourselves fortunate that the crusading spirit is dead, or that the fear of atomic war does govern the imagination of peoples; nevertheless, a genuine conviction against the Cold War, a strong skepticism about all ideology, would also achieve a different outcome—a different diplomacy, less childish provocations, and more sober efforts at peacemaking. An observer's tenable conclusion on looking at the Cold War is not that other times and nations have secured peace and good will by simply wanting it, but that those tougher, clearer, less sentimental periods did not bear the mark of the hybrid in all things as we inescapably do. What makes it inescapable is our preference for it.

The arts, of course, have been our instructors. They are always tempted by mélange and ambiguity, and now many practitioners prove by example that machinery and sculpture and painting are one, as life is one. The theater in the round means to refute the error that theater means show, and kindred dramatic groups try to rub out the distinction between player and audience by circulating, sometimes in the nude ("the way we are all born"), among the spectators. Hundreds of other examples of the alloyed arts will suggest themselves.

And perhaps one can go further and infer that the forces at work to eliminate differences between the sexes also aim at an ultimate unity. The former division of labor in the family—home and job—has largely disappeared. The young dress and grow hair alike, or nearly. The appeal of pornography and promiscuity, the publicity desired for the sexual act, and the charm exerted by the commune as domestic unit—all imply the partly conscious intent to get rid of the individual, with his rigid contours, in favor of a more homogeneous human material. To this end the taking of drugs contributes its share of abolition by removing the no doubt arbitrary limits of the real. Partakers maintain that drugs afford an expansion of consciousness, hence a liberation from the narrow and sterile life of reason. It might be more accurate to say that by drowning consciousness in sensation, drugs bring the user back to the starting point of his development, when he had to organize experience and draw the lines he now wishes to erase. The modern artist has done little else for eighty years than use sensation and purposeful confusion to restore (not expand) aboriginal consciousness.

The link between this important emotion and the quasi-religious feeling among the young is easy to trace. The dropout, the communard, the flower people are preaching or practicing a kind of primitive Christianity, though so far without a messiah. Like the early Christians they say no to the Empire and spurn its tolerant advances. They prefer a life without possessions, fixed abode, or clear relationships. The Essenes, too, we are told, picked up a clean garment at the next port of call, leaving behind the one just worn. Likewise—it is well known—primitive churches are always accused of sexual looseness. The charge is probably true. But its meaning of course differs for the practitioner and his critic. The religious neophyte bases his life on the law of love, in which there are no dividing lines. Stranger, acquaintance, friend, lover, relative are all one. Chance and impulse replace system and convention. Only by being simple and poor, natural and good, can the world be saved from Caesar and his legions (read: General Motors and the Pentagon).

Such a life is at first deliberately marginal. It is only because others tolerate and feed the dropouts and first Christians that they survive; but the force of their example is not to be measured by their numbers or their visible influence. For their appeal is to an emotion buried in every member of the high civilization, buried indeed in every human being: the impulse to knock down the building blocks so painfully erected; the longing to start afresh; the Crusoe fantasy and Walden instinct. Strictly speaking, these feelings are delusive. Crusoe had a shipful of civilized products or he would have perished, just as Thoreau brought with him an ax, a bag of nails, some beans, and other forms of capital. But feelings are stronger than facts when it is a question of bringing a civilization to its close; for the particular feelings that demand renewal at any cost have behind them the tremendous force of unreasoning hate against what must seem to a passionate man an endless series of cages. "I feel something within me," said the Chieftain from the North, "that compels me to burn Rome."

The attitude in our churchmen and churchgoers which responds kindly to such feelings argues a lack of faith not simply in the government of the church but in the government of God. Reports of high church attendance alternate with reports of widespread religious indifference. These statistics are probably equally correct. They do not impinge on the plain fact that religious fervor is rare and commands no intellectual support. Nietzsche's observation of eighty years ago that "God is dead" was taken up again recently as a liberating idea. But all it records is the upshot of the long secularization of life since the seventeenth century. What it states is that the citizens of the modern industrial world do not habitually reckon with Providence or appeal to a deity. They reckon with and appeal to machinery, medicine, money, the enemy on the other side of various curtains, and the forces of the unconscious. These are not gods. Even when feared or trusted too far, these forceful entities of the modern world are neither worshiped nor selflessly served. Science has been called a religion, and the analogy has meaning as regards its revelations of nature, but no one sings "O Science, our help in ages past"—the relation of grateful intimacy, of mutual love, is wanting.

Men in Western civilization have thus been thrown back wholly on themselves, and they find themselves wanting. They see more and more clearly that they are not in control of their individual lives or collective destiny, and that their simplest practical goals elude their reach. Because of increasing populations, because of the dread momentum of things—machines and their products—it appears harder and harder for anyone to accomplish any purpose, even one that commands general agreement. To get pollution out of the air or provide housing or realize the theoretical possibilities of communication and transportation become mighty "problems" whose solutions recede further and further away. It is doubtless from this growing feeling of impotence in the midst of technique that the heirs of 2,500 years of Western culture develop the anger of frustration leading to vandal revolt. Technique and reason, being shown powerless, are called unnatural.

Liberal thinkers down to very recent days had been confident that education would be the civilizing force sustaining orderly government in a good society. The experiment of democratic education was tried with enthusiasm and at great cost, relative to what any earlier civilization had done. And the effort still continues, though with growing dismay. For it now appears that education too has its limits. Literacy cannot be spread indefinitely but turns back on itself; teachers cannot be mass-produced at will like cars; and worst blow of all, the beneficiaries of free schooling resist or scorn the benefit. Accordingly, the latest "solution" offered the once-hopeful world is: "de-schooling society." It sounds like a new-found freedom.

When closely examined, the problem turns out to be not an educational one, not the removal of ignorance, but the need for the school to effect a magical reconciliation of the pupil with society, perhaps with life itself. Seeing the poor, the rich, and the middling all contributing their quota of vandals and dropouts of school age, seeing "the young" as a new class or race in open warfare with the world, the liberal imagination of educators and social philosophers concludes that here is one more witness to the bankruptcy of "bourgeois values." Like representative government, like capitalism, like traditional religion, the culture that the West has been painstakingly fashioning since Renaissance and Reformation has ceased to serve.

This verdict which condemns the bourgeoisie or middle class as responsible for the individual and collective evils of the age is not being uttered today for the first time. Nor was it first pronounced by the Marxians or their predecessors and successors in socialism. As we shall see in a moment, it is not a purely economic indictment in any case. When the anti-bourgeois commonplaces, which are now nearly two hundred years old, are repeated today in newspapers or in liberal households, they imply something more—and other—than the need to rescue the poor from the "tyranny of the powerful." They imply, to begin with, confusion of thought and self-disgust. After all, our conception of the general welfare springs from liberal thought itself, and liberal thought is a bourgeois creation. In the same way, "the rights of the people" are not in opposition to the "materialism" which is imputed to the bourgeois as a sin, for surely the rights of the people and the welfare of the people include their material prosperity.

And topping these paradoxes is the supreme one that the present spiritual distress and revolutionary surge come at a time of general affluence and high productivity; a time, moreover, when thanks to industry Western civilization has reversed the age-old proportions of rich and poor. It is certainly our shame that 15 to 20 per cent of our most advanced populations are in want, yet it is not by accident that the ratio is no longer what it ever used to be—20 per cent in comfort and 80 per cent in want. But nothing is harder to bear than the contrast between what is and what might be. Machine civilization's power to create wealth has given mankind a glimpse of universal plenty, and when we find ourselves far from abundance on a global scale, our impatience turns into fury.

And if we look deeper still than these matters of common anguish and revolutionary propaganda, we come upon signs that even a much nearer approach to planetary prosperity would not in fact relieve our pain. Just as when John Stuart Mill, then a young liberal reformer, fell into a deep depression and asked himself whether the instant realization of all his hopes would make him happy, and he answered no, so today the realization of the Western world's practical concerns would not reconcile and make happy its chief denouncers. It might make the poor and disfranchised happier, but one may wonder for how long, since those already free from want, tyranny, ignorance, and superstition declare themselves the most oppressed and miserable of men and willingly risk all they have in order to smash the system.

This abolitionist outlook, as was said a moment ago, is not new and not radical in the political sense. It is moral and aesthetic, and it was first given form by the artists who came to maturity during or shortly after the French Revolution. It was then that art took over the role that religion had formerly played in holding up to the impure world the divine promise and reproach of a pure one. With the Romanticists, the city of God became the vision of art. It was then also that the bourgeois citizen became an object of hatred and contempt, because he believed in the world—in trade, in politics, in regular hours, a steady life, a safe marriage, sound investments, and a paunchy old age. His moral complacency and artistic philistinism made him appear the enemy of all generous emotion, the antithesis of everything spiritual and selfless in man.

The great popular and national disillusionment after the failure of revolution in 1848 intensified this antagonism. With the onset of industrialization, the uglification of cities, the degradation of the poor, the demagogy and sensationalism of the penny press, the cheapening of taste through the early crude mass production, the raucousness of advertising, the emotional disturbances connected with the change from manual to mechanical work that makes man a cipher—with all these and a dozen other consequences of man's entry into the industrial age, the moral and aesthetic conscience of the West, manifesting itself through its artists, began to repudiate society as a whole. This manifold denunciation is what Flaubert and Ruskin, Baudelaire and William Morris, are all about—and not only they, but hundreds of others in every language of Europe. Their despair is universal and the depicted evil remarkably uniform. In American literature its recording goes from Melville to Mark Twain and Henry Adams and then to Dreiser and Scott Fitzgerald.

After 1870 in Europe, two movements prepare the present embattled or alienated stance of the arts. One movement takes the path of withdrawal, self-enclosure in the "genuine" world of spirit and sensation. Its present-day continuation may be seen in all the groups, hippie or other, which take every means to secede from society and the common self, including the chemical means called drugs. The results, thanks to the despised technology that manufactures heroin and LSD, are extreme, but the tradition is, as it were, respectable. Bohemia was the first form of Hippieland, and it is more than a hundred years since Baudelaire justified the "artificial paradise" of drug taking as a necessary antidote to urban life.

The other movement was from the start activist and used art to shock the bourgeois into a realization of his own turpitude. The line from the Naturalists and satirists of the eighties (Zola, Jarry) through the Futurists, Surrealists, Dadaists, and Expressionists to the Existentialists and others of our contemporaries is perfectly clear. Indeed, the explosive substance and devices change remarkably little. The poets since Laforgue are virtually one (minor) poet. The dose of shock is merely increased to keep up with the inevitable inflation of all effects. When Genêt becomes an artistic hero and civic model on the strength of being a gifted thief and homosexual, or when novelists and playwrights depict torture, madness, rape, and coprophilia in parables meant to shine upon the paying public the light of self-reformation, then surely the entire bourgeois class aimed at has been fully convinced of its abominableness. For all the while the less violent writers and dramatists have preached from the same book. Joyce and Gide and Proust and D. H. Lawrence and E. M. Forster "show up" the bourgeois and "his" society, dig down into the murk of motive, and prove that not a word can be said for things as they are.

The arts of storytelling being almost wholly devoted to this propaganda, it was left to music and the plastic arts to satisfy the inarticulate emotions of a hard-driven society. And it is certainly true that since the first decade of this century the appeal of line, color, and sound has outstripped that of words. But even if many of the compositions in concrete or pigment or tone have furnished the aesthetic pleasure that strengthens the soul, many more have had the effect—intended or not—of once again "facing" the beholder with the despair and disharmonies of his own life. The cult of originality, the growing need of artists to singularize themselves within the growing mass of the talented, has encouraged the strong and arrogant to administer ever more brutal shock treatments to the public. This has meant more than merely abandoning representation or simple one-step abstraction from objects. First "the work" has been reduced to mere sensation; then the beholder has been excluded by saying that painting is only an act of the painter's, preferably a random act, as in dripping or throwing paint on canvas; finally the artist has eliminated himself, either by repudiating the making of objects or by preferring to collect and assemble and exhibit oddments from the junkheap of civilization.

In music a parallel development has occurred, though more difficult to make clear because of apparent exceptions. Still, the insistence of some experimenters that silence is more important than sound, or the great efforts made to impress concertgoers with the "elemental" by tapping on the frame of a piano with mallets—all these reductions and innovations betoken a desire common to many artists to achieve at least two ends in one: to exert some form of violence on the public and to disinfect art from any suggestion of past humanity. Dehumanization both condemns present man as vile and concentrates his gaze on the raw materials—noise, color, line, words as words, all to be taken with forced innocence.

There is, besides, the necessity of the modern artist to avoid comparison with the crushing legacy of earlier art, the masterpieces produced since the Renaissance that have exhausted all possible forms and genres and left to present performers only the choice of sterile imitation or total abstention.

All this taken together supplies the meaning of the label "anti-art," which has significantly united different kinds of avant-garde. "Anti-" is the effective bond. It corresponds precisely to the political, religious, and emotional need to be rid of whatever lingers on from yesterday. And it stimulates that emotion as well. The hunger is for a completely purged existence, an environment like a blank slate. Considering the radical hatred, the unforgiving thoroughness behind all these separate moves toward the perfect emancipation, the student of contemporary culture hazards a guess that the relaxing of manners and morals is rather a consequence than a cause of the social disarray.

The blank slate anticipated from razing everything to the ground is wanted for the purpose of writing upon it the mark and merit of a new man. The new man must therefore prepare himself to be new. He has to be young. With the aid of prophetic elders, he widens and deepens the gap separating him from his progenitors. He has in this way persuaded the civilized world that "the young" exist as an absolute. The abandonment of civility, soap, the mother tongue, and other features of inherited manners makes vivid the distance. The feeling that honesty need no longer control dealings with "those others" is logical as well—it is at any rate common to revolutionists and other killers. Still more radical is the transformation of sex into something indeterminate, depersonalized, and therefore weakened in emotional associations—perhaps weakened also in sensual pleasure through the absence of the usual barriers.

Communal living in conditions of Asiatic indifference goes with this reduction of consciousness of the self and within the self to the mood. The individual is thus made ready for the political struggle. From the immediacy of frustration, which makes the industrial state and its "bourgeois values" hateful, to the immediacy of the will, which aims at settling something by violence if need be, is a straight path that can be traveled in either direction. Whether the act succeeds or helplessness prevails, another stroke has helped bring down the city of the world which the vision of art has made so intolerable.

Nor is the world intolerable because it lacks "reasonable" or humane intentions. Such elements are not unknown among us, but ignored; and they are ignored because the difficulty of turning a good and approved plan into a reality has become monumental. There stands in the way all that democracy has decreed shall be respected—the right of individuals and groups to be consulted and conciliated. In that abstract form, no one can or would want to object to this right of resistance. But in actuality the resistance includes both sensible and ignorant criticism, both legitimate and dishonest interests, both wise and stupid apprehension; which is why in the once excellent New England town meeting it may now take eight years to settle the site of a new high school after the decision to build it has been taken. Such examples also tell us why everybody is starved of the pleasures of accomplishment, why everybody talks like a lunatic about Creativity, why there are myths about national goals and planning ahead.

The combination of these objective facts with the insistent propaganda against "the system" is what produces the state of mind in which total decadence—falling away, dissolution—is possible and, indeed, likely. The artists and intellectuals of the century have done their work so well that most bourgeois themselves, for all their advanced years and their innate philistinism, feel strong stirrings of sympathy with the young who want to devour them and with the minorities that want to replace them. Guilt is as strong a bourgeois tradition as complacency, and in every great revolution of mankind the victims (or a good segment of them) can be counted on to help. Today one finds throughout Western civilization men in high places who freely confide their self-hatred and openly envy their antagonists—and sometimes subsidize them in secret.

But the inchoate movement for renovation is not so simple as even this double twist would suggest. Among the young there are, as always, manipulators of others' ideals; they have set plans and sure techniques, but their goal is indistinct. Among the idealists (and sometimes within the rebel himself) there is a split in the method of making all things new. The cry of Participation heard in Europe and America points to this uncertainty. Participation means sharing the power, but this in turn means entering the Establishment, joining the bourgeois and working with them. Is this practicable, even if conceivable? The young and the dispossessed are no more sure of the answer than are the factory workers who also want Participation in management: independence and responsibility tug opposite ways. The only settled point is that the new man, the new Left, the new wave, the new cry in art, films, dress, lingo, or morals, toil together to hasten the work of time and oblivion.

If it were not for the striking convergence of these forces in our own day, there would be no point in discussing the nature of the so-called crisis in Western civilization, the character of the turning point which we are said to have reached or passed or sighted ahead. And the books of Spengler, Toynbee, Riencourt, Pickman, and others would not furnish (via their reviewers) catchwords and arguments for general conversation. The frame of mind of a high civilization is always self-conscious, but perhaps none before ours has attained such an extreme of self-consciousness. We owe this sensitivity to the length of our memory, that is, to our historical studies; to the speed of our communications, which give us no respite wherein to take the world as it is; to the peculiarity of our literature and our psychology, both introspective and ruthless in dissecting and imputing motives, suspicious of the slightest self-satisfaction; to the bleakness of our science, which shows us a purposeless universe of not even rational design; and finally to the fears which our great cleverness has raised up for us— fear of atomic destruction, fear of overpopulation, fear of our massed enemies; and in daily life, fear of all the diseases, mishaps, and dangers that our technology advertises in warning. It seems very apposite and not wholly accidental that one of the most popular genres of casual literature is the spy story: in it everyone sees himself as the lonely soul hiding among enemies, guilty actor and frightened fugitive, and at the same time freed from the usual restraints of honor; ready to kill for the cause, while frequently uncertain what the cause is and whether the enemy spy is not one's closest fellow, all others being the Establishment—order, system, police—the Kafkaesque bureaucracy.

These speculations, like the appeal of this pseudocharacter, the spy, fall within the realm of sensibility. They constitute no positive evidence of our historical condition, for the sensibility and its taste in popular literature can change overnight without leaving a trace. Yet the circumstances and events embraced in this ultimate chapter do permit us to say that Western civilization does not appear to contain in any class, in any nation, a healthy reserve of animal faith. Rather, faith is on the list of shortages, like all other natural resources. But much more than they, faith is needed for action, innovation, risk-taking, heroism. The spy who wants to come in from the cold obviously lacks this warming fire within. He carries on from duty, and when he talks of "the cold" he is only projecting his inner lack of natural heat.

It may be hazarded as a historical generality that the periods of creation, and even the effectiveness of single movements, occur when the vision of Possibility is vivid to many minds, when it is obvious that the ground can be made level and ready to be built on. Then the presence of obstacles and opposition is only another incentive to struggle. The uphill fight is going to be rewarded by an incomparable view from the summit won. This was the feeling widespread among the gifted at the height of the eighteenth century, and again in the great flowering of Romanticism. It sprang up once more after the *fin de siècle* lassitude, as our own century began. The Cubist Decade was a great producer of models. Then came the great catastrophe of the Four Years' War of 1914–1918, which not only swept from the earth innumerable young geniuses, but showed the Western world that it could not protect civilization from its own stupidity or evil impulse.

The spirit of the West has never really recovered from that shattering. Lately, scholarship has come to see that for half a century we have been living on the ideas generated during the two decades before that war, 1895 to 1914. In science, art, technology, philosophy, social and political thought, all the new principles were set forth with finality, from aviation, wireless, and motion pictures to abstract art, city planning, aesthetic simultaneity, quantum physics and genetics, relativity and psychoanalysis. We have only elaborated those teachings, or tried, when we could, to evade them by jumping back to earlier models, quite in vain. The question now is whether the events we are witnessing are preparing another open and level ground for a reawakened animal faith and the creation of undreamed-of new things, or whether on the contrary our sullen doings have reached repetition in futility.

While "awaiting confirmation or adversity," as the poet put it, we can recapitulate and take stock each for ourselves. There is no doubt that regarding the outer shell or container of civilization, which is the State, all our efforts tend against aggregation and toward disintegration. Yearning and action alike are moving us toward the small, self-contained unit which can be "free." Maybe it is a wise unconscious preparation for the time when atomic war has pulverized all large-scale existence and the survivors must be content with the isolated "villa" (= settlement) of late Roman times. In that case the deliberate pigsty mode of communal life which many of the young cultivate is a sign of remarkable prescience.

But it is also possible that the centrifugal force that drives us all to flee the octopus organization and the remote control of unseen hands, so that we may huddle with a few friends, bemoan our lot or demonstrate against it, will suffer a check. Anarchy, whether permissive or fostered by intemperate leaders, goes so far; then it generates repression. The present assumption that protest warrants every license may well end in a blood bath; or even without it, in a tyranny more relentless than any of recent date, and vindictive in proportion to the arrogance of those who provoked it into being. With such a repression would come necessarily a puritanism of the most searching kind. Artists, free thinkers, and free lovers who currently denounce the Western nations as police states would from their future labor camps long for the good old days.

In either event, the present failure of authority is a prime symptom. It tells us that on the all-important question of how to live together, the contemporary world has not a single new idea to offer, not one.

The next diagnostic point is the question of morals and religion. Morality, like religion, has the double aspect of satisfying an emotional need and serving a social purpose. Without morality—some inner restraint —society must assign two policemen to watch every citizen day and night. And without a religion which sustains conduct or at least organizes the facts of life and the cosmos, men seek in vain for the meaning of their existence. Not all can find in art or science a substitute justification, and even private ambition or calculated hedonism demands special gifts. Great populations without a goal outside themselves will turn to nationalistic war or race hatred to find the call to transcendence that the human spirit requires. On these points too, at the present time, the Western mind is mute. Popular revivalist religion captures only a few more souls than does subtle philosophic or aesthetic religiosity, leaving a void for the seven devils of partisan hatred to disport in. As for the embodiment of the fundamental decencies through manners and conduct, we have not as a civilization even begun to think about—let alone discuss—what would be desirable for an overcrowded industrial world. We have only drifted into the casual style, of which the extremes incite to a dangerous disgust with one's fellowman.

Art and science, just mentioned, look like better grounds for self-congratulation. Within our period both have gained enormously in prestige and support. Their practitioners are in fact the only admired leaders of the civilization. Ostensibly, then, art and science are flourishing, which argues a "healthy society." But are they healthy in themselves and in their relation to mankind? The metaphor of health is misleading in all such questions—a healthy malignancy kills the patient. The arts are not malignant, but as was shown above they are hostile, dehumanized, unnaturally self-conscious. They mean to awaken the complacent to their condition of sin and they succeed. But how long must the lesson last? And what does perpetually teaching it do to the propagandist himself? The imagination of disaster is a great gift, but after the disaster what? Cassandra's employment ends with her success. One congenial conclusion about the contemporary arts is that they are performing the great task of detaching us from all old models of feeling, seeing, and thinking, in preparation for the indescribable new.

Science, too, has little to say *comprehensively* to this civilization. It is none too well integrated within itself. One thinks not merely of the thirty to forty particles that have been found "basic" to matter-energy (not a simple plan, surely); one thinks also of the proliferating specialties, each with its private language and its stream of discoveries that do not somehow cohere and settle any large subject. It has become a matter of pride that science is never done: her name is Penelope. But if that is so, then science is not what its founders expected, a source of knowledge; rather, it is an absorbing activity, whose results can never give its patron civilization any conception of the world, much less of that other fugitive, man.

There is not even, for the educated, the prop of an all-embracing speculative philosophy. Ethics and metaphysics are no longer subjects for self-respecting philosophers to think about. For half a century or more, professional thinkers have preferred to analyze language, to attempt the quantification of the intuitive, or to uncover the rational bases of science. The next-door neighbors of philosophy—psychology and theology—leave the intelligent layman equally uncared for amid a plethora of myths and metaphors, of "personal statements" and "scientific" studies: there is no mediation or reconcilation between Ouspensky and Dr. Kinsey. As for the common man, he has been left more than ever at the mercy of his penchant for superstition. Technology as advertised supplies the miraculous, aided by science talking of inhabited planets, while astrology enlivens the newspapers and unidentified flying objects the heavens.

To be sure, science is now wedded to technology and faithful in its service. Many who are close to the work retain their enthusiasm for the future of civilization, precisely because technology can create abundance and replenish or eke out the supply of natural goods. But there are two obstacles on the road to material welfare. One is how to distribute it. Western nations have never found the way—the pitiful Common Market is the furthest they have attained in mellowing international trade. Internally they are stumped by political facts; in the United States at least, abundance rots in silos while our own poor and others starve. None of this proceeds from ill will, blindness, or indolence—except insofar as these vices afflict every inhabitant of the globe and preclude paradise.

The second and worse barrier to technological blessedness is that it has created conditions of life that more and more people find unendurable. There is no need to rehearse the cries of pain. They form the daily chorus of anguish—in common talk, in the newspapers, in plays and novels, in the grave studies of sociologists and psychiatrists. Against this sort of testimony no argument and no promise will avail. When the sweetness of life, such as it is at the best of times, vanishes altogether, the weak go under and the strong go elsewhere.

So as the last third of the century opens we find both the social and the political impulses at one in urging flight or destruction; from science and the arts, little or no solace; from religion hardly a clear pointer to duty or justification. The observer feels himself carried back among the prophets and thaumaturgists of St. Augustine's day, with no better guide than dumb instinct to find the way out. If these are not the signs of an emphatic ending, they look uncommonly like it.

Remains one question: if the description is correct, if it is an ending, a thoroughfare leading into the desert, of what magnitude is the predictable pause and turn? To answer this is to push the observer beyond his limits. He can safely say that we are seeing something of greater moment than the close of neoclassicism at the end of the eighteenth century. What is dying out now is the individualism and high art of the Renaissance, the fervor of the Reformation, the hopes of liberalism, the zest of the free and patriotic nation-state. But is it more than the close of a brilliant half-millennium? Is it akin to the fall of Rome, the death of paganism, and the turmoil of barbarian clusters under a primitive and precarious Christianity?

Or is it some third phenomenon—for where are now the vigorous, untroubled barbarians and the heroic bishops and missionaries bearing the Word? Meditation is the best answer, and from it at least one assurance will emerge, which is that as long as man exists, civilization, art, society, and science also exist in germ. Man's civilization is not identical with *our* civilization, and the building or rebuilding of states and cultures, now or at any time, is more becoming to our nature than longings and lamentations.

For Further Reading

Barzun, Jacques, *Science: The Glorious Entertainment.*
Brown, Norman O., *Life Against Death.*
Gilbert, Felix, *The End of the European Era.*

Gray, Francine, *Divine Disobedience*.
Linder, Staffan B., *The Harried Leisure Class*.
Lukacs, John, *The Passing of the Modern Age*.
Ortega y Gasset, *The Revolt of the Masses*.
Trilling, Lionel, *The Opposing Self*.
Wilson, Colin, *The Outsider*.

Notes on Contributors

RENÉ ALBRECHT-CARRIÉ (Ph.D., Columbia, 1938) is Professor Emeritus of History at Barnard College and the School of International Affairs of Columbia University. His specialty is the diplomatic history of Europe in the nineteenth and twentieth centuries. He has written *A Diplomatic History of Europe Since the Congress of Vienna; Italy at the Paris Peace Conference; Italy from Napoleon to Mussolini; France, Europe and the Two World Wars; Britain and France;* and a number of other books. (Chapters 69, 79, 92, 93, 94.)

HERMAN AUSUBEL (Ph.D., Columbia, 1948) is Professor of History at Columbia University, where he teaches modern British and European history. He has written *Historians and Their Craft; The Late Victorians; In Hard Times: Reformers Among the Late Victorians;* and *John Bright, Victorian Reformer.* He has edited *The Making of Modern Europe; Some Modern Historians of Britain* (with J. B. Brebner and E. M. Hunt); and *The Making of English History* (with R. L. Schuyler). (Chapter 66.)

A. DOAK BARNETT (M.A., Yale University, 1942; LLD, Franklin and Marshall College, 1967) was a professor of government at Columbia University from 1961 to 1969. He is now a Senior Fellow in the Foreign Policy Studies Division of the Brookings Institution. He specializes in Chinese politics and foreign policy and U.S. Far Eastern policy. He has written and edited more than a dozen books, including *Communist China and Asia: Challenge to American Policy; Cadres, Bureaucracy, and Political Power in Communist China; China on the Eve of Communist Takeover; China After Mao;* and *A New U.S. Policy Towards China.* (Chapter 99.)

JACQUES BARZUN (Ph.D., Columbia, 1932) is University Professor at Columbia University, where he specializes in the cultural history of the period 1750 to the present. He has written topical studies that span those centuries: *The French Race: Theories of Its Origins; Classic, Romantic, and Modern; Darwin, Marx, Wagner; Berlioz and the Romantic Century;* as well as contributed essays on historiography, notably (with Henry F. Graff) *The Modern Researcher.* (Chapters 60, 61, 75, 76, 101.)

ELIAS J. BICKERMAN (Ph.D., Petrograd, 1918; Berlin, 1926) is Professor Emeritus of History at Columbia University, and Professor of Jewish History at the Jewish Theological Seminary. Internationally known for his work on ancient history, especially that of the Hellenistic world and of Graeco-Roman Judaism, he has written *Der Gott der Makkabäer* (1937); *Institutions des Séleucides* (1938); *From Ezra to the Last of the Maccabees* (1962); *Chronology of the Ancient World* (1968); and a number of other books. His collected papers will be published by Brill of Leiden in 1972. (Chapters 5, 6, 7, 8, 12, 13, 14, 15, 16, 17, 18, 19, 20, 21.)

HANS H. A. BIELENSTEIN (Ph.D., Royal University of Stockholm, 1954) is Professor of Chinese History at Columbia University and specializes in the Han Dynasty (206 B.C.–A.D. 220). He has written several volumes on the history of that period. (Chapters 10, 11, 27, 28.)

SHEPARD B. CLOUGH (Ph.D., Columbia, 1930) became in 1970, after 42 years of teaching at Columbia University, Professor Emeritus of European History. He specialized in the economic history of Western Europe and of the United States. His principal works include *A History of the Flemish Movement in Belgium; France 1890–1939, A Study in National Economics; The Rise and Fall of Civilization,* an economic history of modern Italy; *European Economic History;* and *History of American Life Insurance.* (Chapters 72, 73, 74.)

GERSON D. COHEN (Ph.D., Columbia, 1958) is Jacob H. Schiff Professor of Jewish History at The Jewish Theological Seminary of America, where he specializes in Talmudic and medieval Jewish history. He has edited and translated Abraham Ibn Daud's *Book of Tradition* and written the section on the Talmudic age in Schwarz's *Great Ages and Ideas of the Jewish People.* (Chapters 25, 35.)

ROBERT D. CROSS (Ph.D., Harvard, 1955) is President of Swarthmore College, where he also teaches part-time in American social history. He published *The Emergence of Liberal Catholicism in America* (1958), a study of conflict and change within the Roman Catholic Church in the United States in the late nineteenth century, and edited *The Churches and the City* (1965). He has published a variety of articles on men and movements in social and cultural history of the United States. Previous to his present post, he taught at Harvard, Swarthmore, and Columbia, and was for two years President and Professor of History at Hunter College, City University of New York. (Chapter 73.)

AINSLEE T. EMBREE (Ph.D., Columbia, 1960) who taught at Columbia from 1958 to 1969, is Professor of History at Duke University. He is the author of *Charles Grant and British Rule in India* and *India's Search for National Identity.* He is the co-author, with Fredrick Wilhelm, of *Indien,* and with S. M. Ikram of *Muslim Civilization in India.* He has edited a number of books, including *The Hindu Tradition.* (Chapters 30, 54, 83, 91.)

RHODES W. FAIRBRIDGE (B.A., Queen's U., Canada; B.Sc., Oxford, England; D.Sc. U. of W. Australia, 1944) is Professor of Geology at Columbia University, with interests in general earth sciences, geomorphology, stratigraphy, sedimentology, geotectonics, astrogeology, oceanography, and environmental problems. He has been on expeditions to the South Pacific,

Australia, New Guinea, Southeast Asia, Arabia, North Africa, and Brazil. Author of about 400 scientific papers, he has edited some 30 professional books, notably the *Encyclopedia of Earth Sciences* (8 vols.). (Chapter 2.)

JOHN A. GARRATY (Ph.D., Columbia, 1948) is Professor of History at Columbia University, where he specializes in late nineteenth- and early twentieth-century American History. He has written biographies of Silas Wright, Henry Cabot Lodge, Woodrow Wilson, and George W. Perkins, and also *The Nature of Biography; The New Commonwealth: 1877–1890;* and *The American Nation,* a college textbook. He has edited *Interpreting American History: Conversations with Historians,* and a number of other books. (Chapter 100.)

NINA G. GARSOÏAN (Ph.D., Columbia, 1958) is Professor of Armenian Studies and Professor of History at Columbia University, where she specializes in the relations of the Byzantine Empire with the Near East. She has written *The Paulician Heresy: A Study of the Origin and Development of Paulicianism in Armenia and the Eastern Provinces of the Byzantine Empire,* the Ancient and Early Medieval sections of *A History of the Western World,* S. B. Clough, general editor, and several studies in early Armenian history. She has also edited and translated N. Adontz, *Armenia in the Period of Justinian* and a number of other books. (Chapters 36, 37, 38, 52.)

PETER GAY (Ph.D., Columbia, 1951) is Professor of History at Yale University, where he specializes in European intellectual history. He has written a two-volume study of the Enlightenment, Volume One of which won a National Book Award, and a number of other books, including *Voltaire's Politics; The Bridge of Criticism; Weimar Culture;* and *A Loss of Mastery,* an analysis of Puritan historians in colonial America. (Chapters 50, 84.)

J. MASON GENTZLER (Ph.D., Columbia, 1966), is Professor of History at Sarah Lawrence College, where he specializes in modern Chinese history. He is the author of *A Syllabus of Chinese Civilization.* (Chapters 55, 82, 89.)

HENRY F. GRAFF (Ph.D., Columbia, 1949), is Professor of History at Columbia University. His field of special competence and interest is the history of the foreign relations of the United States. His books include *Bluejackets with Perry in Japan; American Imperialism and the Philippine Insurrection;* and *The Tuesday Cabinet: Deliberation and Decision on Peace and War under Lyndon B. Johnson.* He is co-author with Jacques Barzun of *The Modern Researcher.* He holds a Presidential appointment to the National Historical Publications Commission. (Chapter 81.)

LEWIS HANKE (Ph.D., Harvard, 1936) is Clarence and Helen Haring Professor of History at the University of Massachusetts, Amherst. He has published a number of books on Bartolomé de Las Casas; the *Villa Imperial de Potosí;* and *Contemporary Latin America.* His present research focuses on the Spanish Viceroys in America under the Habsburgs. (Chapters 57, 70, 96.)

RICHARD HOFSTADTER (1916–1970) was De Witt Clinton Professor of American History at Columbia University, where he taught from 1946 until his death. The wide scope of his work resists conventional categories. He wrote on a variety of subjects in American intellectual, political, educational, and social history, including *Social Darwinism in American Thought* (1944); *The American Political Tradition* (1948); *The Age of Reform* (1955); *Anti-Intellectualism in American Life* (1963); and posthumously published *America at 1750: A Social Portrait* (1971). (Chapter 84.)

GRAHAM W. IRWIN (Ph.D., Cambridge, 1953) teaches African History at Columbia, having taught previously at universities in Ghana, Singapore, and Australia. He is the author of *Nineteenth-Century Borneo: A Study in Diplomatic Rivalry,* and the co-editor (with Richard B. Morris) of the *Harper Encyclopedia of the Modern World.* (Chapters 26, 31, 53, 80.)

CHARLES ISSAWI (M.A., Oxford) is Ragnar Nurkse Professor of Economics at Columbia University, specializing in the Middle East. His books include: *The Economic History of the Middle East; The Economic History of Iran; Egypt in Revolution* and *An Arab Philosophy of History;* and he is co-author of *The Economics of Middle Eastern Oil.* (Chapters 71, 74, 97.)

EDWARD P. LANNING (Ph.D., University of California at Berkeley, 1960) is Professor of Anthropology at Columbia University. His specialty is South American archaeology. He has written *Peru Before the Incas; A Ceramic Sequence for the Piura and Chira Coast;* and a number of other works. (Chapters 4, 56.)

WILLIAM E. LEUCHTENBURG (Ph.D., Columbia, 1951) is De Witt Clinton Professor of History at Columbia University, where he specializes in twentieth-century American history. His book, *Franklin D. Roosevelt and the New Deal, 1932–40,* won the Bancroft and Parkman prizes. His other works include *The Perils of Prosperity, 1914–32,* two volumes in *The Life History of the United States,* and, with Samuel Eliot Morison and Henry Steele Commager, the two-volume *The Growth of the American Republic.* (Chapter 88.)

MAAN Z. MADINA (Ph.D., University of Chicago, 1957) is Associate Professor of Arabic at Columbia University, where he teaches Arabic language and literature and courses in modern Islamic movements. He is author of *A Concise Arabic-English Dictionary of the Modern Literary Language* and is currently working on a study of consensus in Islamic society. (Chapters 22, 23, 24.)

JOHN A. MOORE (Ph.D., Columbia, 1940) is Professor of Biology at the University of California (Riverside), where he specializes in evolution and embryology. He has been active in various national curriculum projects such as the Biological Sciences Curriculum Study and he is currently chairman of the Commission on Science Education. He is the author, co-author, or editor of *Interaction of Man and the Biosphere; Biological Science: An Inquiry into Life; Principles of Zoology; Heredity and Development; Readings in Heredity and Development; Ideas in Modern Biology; Ideas in*

Evolution and Behavior; The Frogs of Eastern New South Wales; Physiology of the Amphibia; and *A Guide Book to Washington.* (Chapter 3.)

RICHARD B. MORRIS (Ph.D., Columbia, 1930) is Gouverneur Morris Professor of History at Columbia University where he teaches American colonial history. He is the author of *The Peacemakers: The Great Powers and American Independence; The American Revolution Reconsidered;* and *The Emerging Nations and the American Revolution.* Co-editor with Henry Steele Commager of *The New American Nation Series,* he also co-edited, with Graham W. Irwin, the *Harper Encyclopedia of the Modern World,* and is editor of the *Encyclopedia of American History* and the multivolume *Documentary History of the United States.* He has lectured at universities both here and abroad. (Chapter 65.)

JOHN H. MUNDY (Ph.D., Columbia, 1950) teaches medieval European history at Columbia University. He has written studies on the history of the town and region of Toulouse, essays on the medieval town and society, and a general history of Latin Europe from 1150 to 1300 in Longman's *History of Europe* series. (Chapters 32, 33, 34.)

ERNEST NAGEL (Ph.D., Columbia, 1930) is University Professor Emeritus at Columbia University, where (as Special Lecturer in Philosophy) he continues to offer courses and seminars in the philosophy of science and the philosophy of law. His publications include *An Introduction to Logic and Scientific Method* (with the late Morris R. Cohen as co-author); *Principles of the Theory of Probability; Sovereign Reason; Logic Without Metaphysics;* and *The Structure of Science.* (Chapter 59.)

PETER A. PARDUE (Ph.D., Harvard, 1965) is Associate Professor of Religion at Indiana University (Bloomington), where he specializes in the history and sociology of Asian religions and cultures. In addition to numerous articles on Hinduism and Buddhism, he is author of *Buddhism: A History of Doctrine, Social and Political Teachings.* (Chapter 9.)

OREST RANUM (Ph.D., Minnesota, 1960) is Professor of History at the Johns Hopkins University, where he specializes in early modern European history. He has written *Richelieu and the Councillors of Louis XIII* and *Paris in the Age of Absolutism.* In addition, he has edited *Searching for Modern Times, 1500–1789* and *The Age of Louis XIV.* (Chapters 44, 45, 47, 49, 62, 63, 64.)

EUGENE F. RICE, JR. (Ph.D., Harvard, 1953) is Professor of History at Columbia University, where he specializes in fifteenth- and sixteenth-century European history. He is the author of *The Renaissance Idea of Wisdom; The Foundations of Early Modern Europe;* and *The Prefatory Epistles of Jacques Lefevre d'Étaples and Related Texts.* (Chapters 39, 40, 41, 42, 43.)

HENRY L. ROBERTS (D. Phil., Oxford, 1948) is Professor of History at Dartmouth College; his specialty is twentieth-century Russian and Eastern European history. He has written, among other works, *Russia and America: Dangers and Prospects; Rumania: Political Problems of an Agrarian State;*

and *Eastern Europe: Politics, Revolution, and Diplomacy.* (Chapters 87, 95.)

JAMES P. SHENTON (Ph.D. Columbia, 1955) is Professor of History at Columbia University. A specialist in the Civil War and Reconstruction periods, he has written and edited a number of books, including a biography of Robert J. Walker. (Chapters 68, 78.)

J. W. SMIT (Ph.D., Utrecht, The Netherlands, 1958) is Queen Wilhelmina Professor of History at Columbia University; his field is early modern European history. His earlier work (in Dutch) is concerned with nineteenth-century Dutch historiography. He has written a number of articles in English about the revolt of the Netherlands. (Chapters 46, 51.)

MORTON SMITH (Ph.D., the Hebrew University, 1948; Th.D., Harvard, 1957) is Professor of History at Columbia University. His field is the religious history of ancient Greece and of the Graeco-Roman Near East. He has written a college textbook, *The Ancient Greeks,* and a number of specialized studies: *Palestinian Parties and Politics That Shaped the Old Testament; Tannaitic Parallels to the Gospels;* and, with Moses Hadas, *Heroes and Gods.* (Chapters 12, 13, 14, 15, 16, 17, 18, 19, 20, 21.)

FRITZ STERN (Ph.D., Columbia, 1953) is Seth Low Professor of History at Columbia University and permanent Visiting Professor at the University of Konstanz in Germany. He specializes in the cultural and political history of modern Europe since the French Revolution, with particular emphasis on modern Germany. He has written *The Politics of Cultural Despair* and *The Failure of Illiberalism.* He edited *The Varieties of History* and co-edited *The Responsibility of Power.* (Chapter 86.)

ALDEN T. VAUGHAN (Ph.D., Columbia, 1964) is Professor of History at Columbia University, where he specializes in American colonial history. Among his publications are *New England Frontier: Puritans and Indians, 1620–1675; America Before the Revolution 1725–1775; Chronicles of the American Revolution;* and *The Puritan Tradition in America, 1620–1730.* He has completed an extensive bibliography on *The American Colonies in the Seventeenth Century.* (Chapter 58.)

IMMANUEL WALLERSTEIN (Ph.D., Columbia, 1959) is Professor of Sociology at McGill University, where he specializes in the sociology of African and other underdeveloped nations. He has written, among other works, *The Road to Independence: Ghana and the Ivory Coast; Africa: The Politics of Unity;* and *Social Change: The Colonial Situation.* (Chapter 98.)

HERSHEL WEBB (Ph.D., Columbia, 1958) is Associate Professor of Japanese History at Columbia University, where he teaches modern Japanese history and Japanese bibliography. He is the author of *The Japanese Imperial Institution in the Tokugawa Period* and *Research in Japanese Sources: A Guide.* (Chapters 29, 55, 90.)

R. K. WEBB (Ph.D., Columbia, 1951), managing editor of the *American Historical Review,* was a member of the Columbia department from 1953 to 1970. He works primarily in the social and intellectual history of Great

Britain in the period since 1760. In addition to a biography of the Victorian radical Harriet Martineau he has written *The British Working-Class Reader, 1790–1848: Literacy and Social Tension* and *Modern England, from the Eighteenth Century to the Present.* He has also translated *The Era of Tyrannies: Essays on Socialism and War* by the French social historian Élie Halevy. With Peter Gay he is co-author of a forthcoming college textbook on modern European history. (Chapters 48, 67, 77, 85.)

LODEWIJK WOLTJER (Ph.D., University of Leiden, 1957) is Rutherfurd Professor of Astronomy at Columbia University and editor of the *Astronomical Journal.* He specializes in the structure and dynamics of galaxies and in radio and X-ray studies. In addition to editing *Interstellar Matter in Galaxies* and *Galaxies and the Universe,* he has published several dozen articles in scientific journals on various aspects of astronomy. (Chapter 1.)

Index